BARRON'S

HOW TO PREPARE FOR THE

COOP/HSPT

CATHOLIC HIGH SCHOOL ENTRANCE EXAMINATIONS

3RD EDITION

Jerome Shostack
Former District Supervisor of Guidance
New York City Schools

Max Peters
Former Chairman, Mathematics Department
George W. Wingate High School, New York

BARRON'S

Some material previously published in *Barron's How to Prepare for the SSAT/COOP,* © copyright 1988, 1985, 1983, 1980, 1973, 1966, and 1961 by Barron's Educational Series, Inc. New material in this edition contributed by George Ehrenhaft and Allan Mundsack.

All inquiries should be addressed to:
Barron's Educational Series, Inc.
250 Wireless Boulevard
Hauppauge, New York 11788
http://www.barronseduc.com

Library of Congress Catalog Card No. 00-067449

International Standard Book No. 0-7641-1377-1

Library of Congress Cataloging-in-Publication Data

Shostak, Jerome.
How to prepare for the COOP HSPT, Catholic high school entrance examinations / by Jerome Shostak, Max Peters.— 3rd ed.
         p. cm.
     Peters's name appears first on the earlier edition.
     ISBN 0-7641-1377-1
     1. Catholic high schools—United States—Entrance examinations—Study guides—Juvenile literature. [1. Catholic high schools—Entrance examinations—Study guides.] I. Title: COOP HSPT.   II. Title: How to prepare for the Catholic high school entrance examinations.   III. Peters, Max, 1906– IV. Title.
LB3060.24.P45 2001   00-067449
373.126'2—dc21

PRINTED IN THE UNITED STATES OF AMERICA
9 8

Contents

DIGEST OF MATHEMATICAL SKILLS 321

Test Taker's Checklist on the Day of the Test

1. Check and recheck the date, time, and place of the exam. Avoid last-minute haste and anxiety.

2. Plan to arrive at the test center between 8:30 and 8:45 A.M. You will not be admitted if you arrive after the test has begun.

3. When you choose your clothing, remember that the temperature in the test room may be lower or higher than you are accustomed to working in. Be sure to dress accordingly. Layers of clothing, which can be retained or removed as needed, will enable you to adjust to the room temperature.

4. Be sure to have with you
   - your admission ticket or other authorization to take the test
   - 3 or 4 soft-leaded pencils (equivalent of U.S. No. 2)
   - a good eraser
   - a working pen if required

5. Do not plan to take any books, papers, notes, calculators, calculator watches, snacks, or beverages into the test room.

6. Before you start to answer any questions, clear your head. Don't clutter your mind with unrelated thoughts. You can cross only one bridge at a time!

7. Pace yourself. Work without haste, but as rapidly as you can without sacrificing accuracy.

8. Bear in mind that you don't have to answer every question. Many test takers leave some questions unanswered.

Ten Test-Taking Tips

1. The best preparation for any test such as these is to study well in your classes at school. But even the best students need to brush up on some things. Memory fades and skills diminish over time. This book is designed to give you ample opportunity to review and practice the skills needed to do well on these tests. You should allow yourself adequate time to make full use of this book—at least a month. Establish a schedule that enables you to spend some time each day on the material in this book but not feel hurried or panicky.

2. Be well rested on test day. Get a good night's sleep, and eat a good breakfast; do not stray too far from your regular schedule. Try not to let other things intrude on your concentration. Don't plan any other activities following the test. You will probably want to rest.

3. Be sure you understand what materials you may have with you during the test. Take advantage of every opportunity, but do no more than what is permitted. An adequate supply of pencils of the appropriate type, an eraser, and your wits are the minimum to have with you.

4. Follow the directions of the people giving the test. Be sure you understand the bathroom rules. Plan to use the full time allotted.

5. All answers must be recorded accurately and clearly on the answer sheet. Be sure that you fill in the circle for each answer fully and darkly. If you can change an answer, be sure that your eraser will erase cleanly. If you temporarily skip a question, be doubly sure that later answers are recorded in the correct space. Don't make any stray marks or notes on the answer sheet. The scoring machine may read them as answers.

6. Do not spend too much time on any one question. Skip questions that you know will take you a long time to do; come back to them later.

7. In some math questions it might be a more efficient use of time to plug in possible anwers to determine the correct response. Usually performing the indicated operations is more efficient, but if the math is too difficult, you can eliminate some answers as being impossible

and plug in the others until you find one that works.

8. DO NOT leave any answer blank. The machine that scores your test does not know whether you guessed or not. If at the end of the test you find some questions that you just cannot answer, try to eliminate some responses as being impossible or unlikely, and GUESS. Keep an eye on the clock toward the end of the test, and use the last few minutes to be sure that every question has a response.

9. When time is called, stop immediately, and follow the directions given for handing in the test.

10. Celebrate having done the very best you can do.

Answer Sheet Strategies

1. All of your answers must be recorded directly on the Answer Sheet, not in the Test Booklet.

2. Using the soft-lead pencil, fill in the circle completely:

Ⓐ Ⓑ Ⓒ Ⓓ ●

The answer machine will not credit any of the following:

Ⓐ Ⓑ Ⓒ Ⓓ Ⓔ
Ⓐ Ⓑ Ⓒ Ⓓ Ⓔ
Ⓐ Ⓑ Ⓒ Ⓓ Ⓔ
Ⓐ Ⓑ Ⓒ Ⓓ Ⓔ
Ⓐ Ⓑ Ⓒ Ⓓ Ⓔ

3. As you answer each question, check that the number of the exam item and the number of the answer are the same. Don't skip an answer space and put the answer for Question 3 in the space for Question 4.

4. If you make a mistake or change your mind, erase completely. You will receive no credit for a partially blackened space.

5. Make certain that you blacken only one choice for each question. If you mark more than one choice, you will receive no credit even if one of your choices is correct.

What You Need to Know About Catholic High School Entrance Examinations

The majority of students entering junior or senior high school are not required to take entrance examinations, because they will be attending general public high schools. However, each year thousands of students—and the numbers increase every year—are asked to take comprehensive entrance examinations when they apply to private secondary schools, to secondary schools affiliated with various religious faiths, and to specialized public junior and senior high schools (such as Hunter College High School and the science high schools of New York City). Examinations for admission to these schools are becoming as rigorous at their level as the college entrance examinations are at the college level.

Which High School Entrance Examination Should You Take?

The high school applied to, not the candidate or his or her parents, determines which local or nationwide examination is to be part of the candidate's admission record. After consultation with the principal or guidance counselor in the school now being attended, the student and parents usually begin the process by sending requests for applications for admission to the schools selected. Letter forms and school addresses can be supplied by the guidance office.

When the high school being applied to sends the forms to be filled out and the list of its application requirements, it may include a bulletin of information and an application for the specific examination required, or it will tell the candidate how to obtain this material. It is the student's responsibility to send the applications and fees to the proper testing authorities. The student must also advise the testing company of the schools that should receive test scores. Here, too, the school counselor can be of assistance in explaining procedures.

How Are Successful Candidates Selected?

Most counselors and admission officers review a number of criteria in evaluating the appropriateness of their school for a student. Among the factors likely to be considered are the following:

curriculum followed
grades
teachers' recommendations
personal recommendations
extracurricular activities
standardized test results
writing sample
interview

Most of these items give a picture of the candidate in relation to the other students currently attending the school. Only the standard test results—and the entrance examination scores are included among these—compare the student's record with the records of all the other candidates for admission. Entrance examination results, therefore, can play an important part in the selection process.

An Overview of the Most Popular Tests

GROUP ONE: STANDARDIZED TESTS

The tests in this group take, with time-outs included, approximately 2½ to 4 hours to administer. The basic areas that they all cover are reading comprehension, computational skills, other mathematical skills, and vocabulary. Many also include the language arts (grammar, usage, sentence sense, etc.). A few tests require the writing of an essay; otherwise, the questions are of the multiple-choice variety.

The scores on these tests as they are sent to the schools and to the candidates do not represent the number of questions answered correctly. Rather, the results are given in the form of a ranking. In other words, the results indicate how the present candidates compare with all of the other students who have taken any form of the same test. A significant aspect of this type of scoring is that a school can compare the scores of present candidates with those of all of the students who have been successful or unsuccessful in that school. From the scores, the school can judge what a particular student's chances of success will be if he or she is admitted.

Of course, admissions officers rarely rely on only one aspect of the admissions process. The final decision is usually based on a weighting of all of the components of the student's school record: curriculum, grades, extracurricular activities, and teachers' recommendations. However, you can readily see how important standardized test results can be in a school's final decision about admitting a particular candidate.

Cooperative (COOP) Admissions Examination

The Cooperative Admissions Examination is available only to eighth graders applying for admission to specific Catholic high schools in New York City, Buffalo, and parts of Westchester, Nassau, and Suffolk counties. Candidates may take the examination, which is given on a designated day in November, once and once only. Students may send their test results to three high schools.

In order to evaluate both academic potential and achievement, the Coop test contains ten units. The items measuring potential resemble those found on IQ tests. The achievement items range from mathematical problems and conventional reading comprehension, spelling, and vocabulary questions to units on grammatical terms.

High School Placement Test (HSPT)

The HSPT, administered by the Scholastic Testing Service, is one of the most widely used high school tests; it is given in approximately 50% of Catholic high schools in various regions of the country. Used nationwide for both admission and placement, it is scored separately for cognitive skills (potential) and achievement in basic skills.

This test has a flexible schedule. It is administered at times set by the individual school, school district, or diocese.

The cognitive skills questions tend to resemble those found in IQ tests, while the achievement questions are in the traditional format.

The school may also administer three optional test sections: Science, Mechanical Aptitude, and Catholic Religion. The results on these sections are not included in the standardized score used for admission and placement.

Secondary School Admission Test (SSAT)

The SSAT, administered by the Educational Testing Bureau, has been used since 1957 by nonpublic schools to aid in the selection of students. Today more than 500 schools rely upon this five-part test to help them choose the best candidates from among the nearly 30,000 students who take the test annually.

Although the SSAT can be taken during any month, most candidates take the test in a local school test center on one of seven Saturday administrations planned during the school year. Special arrangements can be made to accommodate Sabbath observers, students living abroad, and, in special cases, walk-in applicants.

The SSAT has four sections, plus an experimental section, and all questions are multiple choice. Since each part has a 25-minute time limit, the test booklet scrambles the units. One candidate may be answering math questions while the person sitting in front or beside her is doing the verbal ability section.

The SSAT has two additional unusual aspects:

1. A right answer is given one credit. For each wrong answer $\frac{1}{4}$ point is subtracted from the total in order to discourage wild guessing.

2. The results on only four of the sections are included in the rating. The other section is considered as experimental. Since, however, the candidates do not know which is the experimental section, they have to do their best on all five!

The companion book to this one—*Barron's How to Prepare for High School Entrance Examinations: SSAT/ISEE*—contains a fuller discussion of the SSAT, as well as a diagnostic and two practice tests following the format of the actual SSAT.

Independent School Entrance Examination (ISEE)

The ISEE is a relatively new entrant into the field. The Educational Records Bureau (ERB) administers the test, which was developed for the ERB by the Educational Testing Bureau.

The ISEE has become the test of choice for the member schools of the Independent Schools Association of New York City. Many other schools now accept ISEE scores as an alternative to SSAT scores. If you are applying to a school that accepts either the ISEE or the SSAT, you and your parents should consult with your present guidance counselor or principal to find out which examination you should take. If you still find yourself in doubt, take the practice examinations in this book to find out which test will show your abilities to better advantage.

The ISEE consists of four multiple-choice sections and an essay section. The essay is sent unmarked, along with your score on the rest of the test, to the schools of your choice. The essay enables the admissions officers to make a comparative

evaluation of your theme-writing ability and general language mastery.

The companion book to this one—*Barron's How to Prepare for High School Entrance Examinations: SSAT/ISEE*—contains a fuller discussion of the ISEE, as well as a diagnostic and two practice tests following the format of the actual ISEE.

National Educational Development Test (NEDT)

The NEDT, published by CTB/Macmillan/ McGraw-Hill, was designed primarily to assess the skills levels of ninth- and tenth-grade students. It is also used as a high school entrance exam.

The test is given twice a year during a two-week period in October and February. Each school or district selects its own date (within the two-week period) and its own time and place. Make-up testing for absentees is at the discretion of the school or district.

The test consists of five parts: English usage, mathematics usage (problems), natural science reading, social studies reading, and a fifth unit that covers verbal, numerical, reasoning, and spatial abilities. While taking any one part of the exam, a student is not permitted to look ahead or back at any other section of the test booklet.

Comprehensive Testing Program (CTP II)

The CTP II was planned cooperatively by the Educational Records Bureau (ERB) and the schools that administer it, primarily to compare the performances of students in similar schools. Level 4, which is designed to be used with students from the spring of sixth grade through the fall of the ninth year, has become an instrument for evaluating candidates for admission to the high schools enrolled in the ERB program. Because of the length of the examination (six hours), it is usually given in two sessions. See Outline of High School Entrance Exams for the subjects covered.

3R Placement and Counseling Test

The 3R Placement and Counseling Test, published by CTB/Macmillan/ McGraw-Hill, is part of an entire program designed for students in the fourth through the tenth grades. The testing program has forms for three levels of difficulty based on given age ranges. The entire program is used to evaluate student progress through the grades and to provide long-range career counseling.

The entire program involves a full day of testing annually. Most schools using the test for admission purposes require that the students take only the appropriate 3R portion of the test, which lasts about two hours.

The 3R Placement and Counseling Test is given on a flexible schedule set by the school or district to which the candidate applies for admission.

GROUP TWO: SPECIALIZED TESTS

In addition to the schools that require that candidates for admission take nationwide standardized tests, there are many high schools that have their own entrance examinations developed by the faculty to help in student selection. Too few students take any one of these tests for it to be standardized. As a result, the score achieved is based on the number of correct answers, and the highest rank is that of the student with the greatest number of right answers. For this reason, the abilities of current classes cannot be compared with those of previous ones on the basis of these test scores.

Catholic High School Entrance Examination

The Catholic High School Entrance Examination is administered to graduating eighth-grade students applying for admission to the ninth grade in any one of the 13 high schools located within the Diocese of Rockville Centre in New York State. The examination is administred in each of these schools on the same day in November. (There is a make-up test held in December in two of the schools.)

The test, lasting for approximately three hours, measures both ability and achievement. All of the items, except writing, consist of multiple-choice questions.

The first section, which tests ability, resembles an intelligence test. The achievement sections consist of items in reading, mathematics, language and a writing exercise.

The reading items consist of questions based on given paragraphs. The math items are mainly of the problem-solving type. The language items include spelling, vocabulary, capitalization, and punctuation. The writing section consists of straight copying and a brief composition on a given topic.

Because this test most closely resembles the Coop Examination, the diagnostic and two practice tests for the Coop Examination presented in this book will reveal your weaknesses, and the study guide in Chapter 2 will help you overcome them.

Hunter College High School Examination

Hunter College High School is one of the oldest schools established in our country for the intellectually gifted. Enrolled students must be residents of New York City from the seventh through the twelfth grade.

The entrance examination for Hunter College High School is usually given to sixth-grade New York City students, whose applications are processed through the principals of their schools. Approximately 3,000 students take the entrance examination in January of their sixth-grade year. Of these, 280 are admitted.

The examination consists of multiple-choice items in mathematics and English, and an essay question. The math items are of the problem-solving type. The English items include vocabulary, reading comprehension, and language usage. The English and mathematics parts are given equal weight. In addition, candidates are asked to write a short essay as evidence of their ability to express themselves effectively in standard written English.

New York City's Science High Schools

These three schools are Bronx High School of Science, Brooklyn Technical High School, and Stuyvesant High School. Only residents of New York City may apply for admission to these prestigious schools. Eighth- and ninth-grade students residing in the five boroughs of the city are eligible to take the two-hour test consisting of 115 multiple-choice questions.

The same examination is given for all three high schools, and students who qualify may attend whichever school they choose. Candidates take the exam at the schools of their choice. To be accepted, students must score above the established cut-off score, which may vary from school to school. Since the offerings and specializations of the three schools differ, it is imperative that student and parents discuss the choice of school before the exam is taken; a student who is accepted must attend the school that he or she has designated.

LOOKING AHEAD

See the Outline of High School Entrance Exams that follows for important information about the various tests: description/purpose, format, time allowed, and subtests. Also included, in the first column, is the address to which you should direct questions regarding each test. If any unanswered question remains, see your guidance counselor.

OUTLINE OF HIGH SCHOOL ENTRANCE EXAMS

Exam Title/Administering Organization	Description/Purpose	Format of Exam	Total Time Allowed	Subtests (Subject, Number of Questions, Time)	Corresponding Section of This Book
COOPERATIVE ADMISSIONS EXAMINATION (COOP) Admissions Examination Office CTB 20 Ryan Ranch Road Monterey, CA 93940	Widely used by Catholic, parochial high schools, both parish and diocesan.	Multiple-choice questions; machine-scored answer sheet.	About 4 hours	**Sequences** (20 questions, 12 minutes) **Analogies** (20 questions, 7 minutes) **Memory** (20 questions, 20 minutes) **Verbal Reasoning** (20 questions, 12 minutes) **Reading Vocabulary** (40 questions, 18 minutes) **Reading Comprehension** (34 questions, 32 minutes) **Mathematics Computation** (30 questions, 25 minutes) **Mathematics Concepts and Applications** (35 questions, 27 minutes) **Language Mechanics** (20 questions, 10 minutes) **Language Expression** (32 questions, 25 minutes)	Chapter 13 Chapter 13 Chapter 13 Chapter 4 Chapter 5 Chapters 7–12 Chapters 7–12 Chapter 6 Chapter 6
HIGH SCHOOL PLACEMENT TEST (HSPT) Scholastic Testing Service 480 Meyer Road Bensenville, IL 60106-1617	Used for high school admissions, grade placement, and scholarship awards, predominantly by Catholic high schools.	Multiple-choice questions; machine-scored answer sheet.	About 2½ hours	**Verbal Skills** (60 questions, 16 minutes) Synonyms (15 questions) Antonyms (9 questions) Analogies (10 questions) Logic (10 questions) Verbal classifications (16 questions) **Quantitative Skills** (52 questions, 30 minutes) Numbers in series (18 questions) Geometric comparisons (9 questions) Nongeometric comparisons (8 questions) Number manipulations (17 questions) **Reading** (62 questions, 25 minutes) Comprehension (40 questions) Vocabulary (22 questions) **Mathematics** (64 questions, 45 minutes) Mathematical concepts (24 questions) Problem solving (40 questions) **Language** (60 questions, 25 minutes) Capitalization, punctuation, and usage (40 questions) Spelling (10 questions) Composition (10 questions)	Chapter 4 Chapters 12–13 Chapter 5 Chapters 7–12 Chapter 6
CATHOLIC HIGH SCHOOL ENTRANCE EXAMINATION Catholic Secondary School Administrators P.O. Box 361 Mineola, NY 11501	To evaluate candidates for admission to 13 high schools located in the Diocese of Rockville Centre, New York.	Multiple-choice questions; machine-scored answer sheet; essay and copying section.	About 3 hours	**Ability Test** about 80 questions, 45 minutes on four of the following: verbal analogies, diagrammed reasoning, number relations, reasoning, number relationships, comparisons **Achievement Test:** Part I **Reading** (40 questions) 6 reading passages (40 minutes)	Chapter 13 Chapter 5

Test	Description	Time	Format	Content	Reference
				Part II **Word Study** (25 minutes) Spelling (30 questions)	Chapter 6
				Vocabulary (20 questions)	Chapter 4
				Part III **Language** (50 questions, 30 minutes) Capitalization, punctuation, usage, sentence sense	Chapter 6
				Part IV **Mathematical Problems** (40 items, 35 minutes)	Chapters 7–13
				Part V **Writing** (15 minutes) Straight copy of a short passage Brief written reaction to a statement	Chapter 6
SECONDARY SCHOOL ADMISSIONS TEST (SSAT) Educational Testing Service CN 6450 Princeton, NJ 08541-6450	The most popular of all the high school entrance and scholarship tests. Required by over 500 private, tuition-charging academies and prep schools. Two forms of the test—Lower Level and Upper Level—are given.	About 2½ hours	Multiple-choice questions; machine-scored answer sheet.	**Quantitative Ability** Mathematics (25 questions, 25 minutes) Additional mathematics section (25 questions, 25 minutes) **Verbal Ability** (25 questions total) Vocabulary—synonyms (30 questions) Vocabulary—analogies (30 questions) **Reading Comprehension** (40 questions, 25 minutes) **Experimental Section** (25 minutes)	*
INDEPENDENT SCHOOL ENTRANCE EXAMINATION (ISEE) ISEE Operations Office 423 Morris Street Durham, NC 27701	To evaluate candidates for admission to high schools. Two forms of the test—Middle Level and Upper Level—are given.	About 3 hours	Multiple-choice questions; machine-scored answer sheet; essay section.	**Verbal Ability** (40 questions, 20 minutes) Synonyms Sentence completion **Quantitative Ability** (40 questions, 35 minutes) Concepts/Understanding Application **Reading Comprehension** (40 questions 35 minutes) Science passages Social Studies passages **Mathematics Achievement** (50 questions, 40 minutes) Computation } Middle Level Applications Arithmetic concepts Algebraic concepts } Upper Level Geometric concepts **Essay** (30 minutes)	*

*Refer to *How to Prepare for High School Entrance Examinations (SSAT/ISEE)*, also published by Barron's.

OUTLINE OF HIGH SCHOOL ENTRANCE EXAMS

Exam Title/Administering Organization	Description/Purpose	Format of Exam	Total Time Allowed	Subtests (Subject, Number of Questions, Time)	Corresponding Section of This Book
NATIONAL EDUCATIONAL TEST DEVELOPMENT (NEDT) Admissions Examination Office CTB/Macmillan/McGraw-Hill 2500 Garden Road Monterey, CA 93940	To test developed skill levels; to select students for admission.	Multiple-choice questions; machine-scored answer sheet.	About 3 hours	**English Usage** (50 questions, 30 minutes) General usage (30 questions) Sentence reconstruction (20 questions)	Chapters 4–6
				Mathematics Usage (56 questions, 40 minutes) Number problems (40 questions) Verbal problems (16 questions)	Chapters 7–12
				Natural Science Reading (32 questions, 30 minutes)	Chapter 5
				Social Studies Reading (32 questions, 30 minutes)	Chapter 5
				Educational Abilities Part I (40 questions, 10 minutes) Word groupings (10 questions) Vocabulary (30 questions) Part II (25 questions, 10 minutes) Number series (4 questions) Letter series (6 questions) Spatial relations (15 questions)	
COMPREHENSIVE TESTING PROGRAM (CTP II) Educational Records Bureau 3 East 80th Street New York, NY 10021	To evaluate candidates for admission to high schools enrolled in the ERB program.	Multiple-choice questions; machine-scored answer sheet.	About 6 hours	**Analogies** (50 questions, 20 minutes)	Chapter 4
				Quantitative (50 questions, 20 minutes)	Chapter 4
				Vocabulary (35 questions, 20 minutes)	Chapter 5
				Reading Comprehension (45 questions, 45 minutes)	Chapter 6
				Spelling (20 questions, 10 minutes)	Chapter 6
				Capitalization (25 questions, 15 minutes)	Chapter 6
				Punctuation (35 questions, 20 minutes)	Chapter 6
				Grammar and Usage (50 questions, 40 minutes)	Chapter 7
				Mathematics Basic Concepts (50 questions, 40 minutes)	Chapter 7
				Mathematics Computation (60 questions, 40 minutes)	
3R PLACEMENT AND COUNSELING TEST CTB/Macmillan/McGraw-Hill 250 Garden Road Monterey, CA 93940	To evaluate candidates for admission to high schools.	Multiple-choice questions; machine-scored answer sheet.	About 2 hours	**Reading** Words in context (20 questions, 8 minutes) Comprehension (28 questions, 22 minutes)	Chapter 5
				Mathematics Arithmetic computation (22 questions, 18 minutes) Concepts and problem solving (32 questions, 30 minutes)	Chapters 7–12

Test	Purpose	Format	Time	Content	Chapter
SCIENCE HIGH SCHOOLS ADMISSIONS TEST Brooklyn Technical High School 29 Fort Greene Place Brooklyn, NY 11217 Bronx High School of Science 75 West 205th Street Bronx, NY 10468 Stuyvesant High School 345 Chambers Street New York, NY 10280	To select students for the New York City public high schools for academically gifted students.	Multiple-choice questions; machine-scored answer sheet.	About 2½ hours	**Language Arts** Sentence sense (16 questions, 8 minutes)	Chapter 6
				Usage (21 questions, 10 minutes) Spelling (16 questions, 8 minutes)	Chapter 4
				Verbal Ability (55 questions, 70 minutes) Word Meaning (10 questions) Sentence Completion (10 questions) Logical Reasoning (10 questions) Reading Comprehension (25 questions on 5 passages) **Mathematics** (50 questions, 70 minutes) Greater of two quantities Word problems Computation	Chapter 7
HUNTER COLLEGE HIGH SCHOOL ENTRANCE TEST Hunter College High School 71 East 94th Street New York, NY 10028	To select students for admission to Hunter College High School, a school for intellectually gifted students in grades 7–12. (The school is administered by the City University of New York, and students must be New York City residents.)	Multiple-choice questions; (machine-scored answer sheet); essay.	About 3 hours	**Language** (75 questions) Vocabulary Sentence Completion Grammar Reading Comprehension Spelling Punctuation	Chapters 4–6
				Mathematics (25 questions) **Essay**	Chapter 7

Planning a Study Strategy

The book includes many features that will enable you to prepare thoroughly for virtually any academic high school entrance examination. It has been designed with a particular study strategy in mind, one that involves several distinct steps and can be used regardless of how much time you have to prepare for an exam. The six steps follow:

➤ Begin by looking at the Outline of High School Entrance Exams in this chapter to determine exactly what subject areas are covered in the test you plan to take. The Outline of High School Entrance Exams includes the most popular tests; however, if you are taking a test not listed, you will have to consult the literature on that particular test.

➤ Once you have determined what general subject areas will be covered, turn to Chapters 2 and 3 and take the corresponding Diagnostic Tests.

➤ Having taken the appropriate Diagnostic Tests, turn to the answer key and, based on the "Rating Your Results" charts, see how you have done on each test or each test subsection. Now you can make lists of tests or test subsections on which you rated (1) superior, (2) average, and (3) below average. Include on these lists the page references indicated in the rating charts.

➤ Next, set up a study schedule. The amount of time you spend preparing obviously will depend on how many days you have before the exam and how many hours each day you can devote to this purpose. You will benefit more by studying every day rather than trying to cram just before the exam. Also, plan to devote two thirds of your study time to the subject matter on your "below average" list.

➤ Once your study schedule is established, turn to the pages of this book that correspond to one of the subject areas on your "below average" list. Review the material and do the exercises, practice tests, and/or Mastery Exams. By the time you have finished working on a certain subject area, you should have a strong command of it. At that point, go on to another subject on your "below average" list. Continue in this manner, covering "below average" subjects, then "average" subjects, and finally "superior" subjects.

➤ If you plan to take the Coop or the HSPT, do one final thing the day before the actual exam: take one or both of the appropriate practice exams in the final section of this book.

If you follow these steps, you will use your study time most efficiently and will gain confidence in your knowledge of the subjects you will be tested on.

If You Are Taking the Cooperative Admissions Examination

CHAPTER 2

Students in the eighth grade applying for admission to specific Catholic high schools in the Greater New York area, Rockville Centre, Buffalo, and Paterson, New Jersey, are required to take the Cooperative Admissions Examination in November. An applicant must preregister for this examination either through his or her own parochial elementary school or, if enrolled in a public school, by obtaining an application at a local parochial school.

The Coop test is a multiple-choice examination that measures two important aspects of the applicant's preparation for high school:

1. It evaluates what you have achieved so far in developing reading skills, and in the mastery of fundamental concepts in mathematics and language.
2. It evaluates your academic aptitude, the extent to which you have the ability to profit from high school academic studies.

Because it measures both what you have learned and how well you learn, the Coop is different from any other test that you have taken. For this reason it is important that you work with a practice book such as this so that you become acquainted with the types of questions asked. Without such practice, you could lose valuable time just in learning how to handle the test questions.

The Coop test is divided into ten sections:

Test 1 Sequences
Test 2 Analogies
Test 3 Memory
Test 4 Verbal Reasoning
Test 5 Reading Vocabulary
Test 6 Reading Comprehension
Test 7 Mathematics Computation
Test 8 Mathematics Concepts and Applications
Test 9 Language Mechanics
Test 10 Language Expression

This chapter has been organized in parts that parallel the specific tests of the Coop Examination. In each part, through sample questions, you will become acquainted with the same types of questions you will meet in the examination. Strategies for success in handling question type will help you avoid many of the pitfalls that lead to lowered marks. The Diagnostic Tests will enable you to discover your strengths and weaknesses. For further help in improving your score, the study plans will direct you to reviews and practice exercises in the sections that follow.

Frequently Asked Questions About the Coop Examination

To how many parochial high schools may I apply?

You are permitted to list three high schools on your application.

Which parochial high schools should I list on my application?

The guidance counselor or principal in your present school is best qualified to help you and your parents make this important decision.

How many times may I take this test?

This test may be taken only once.

How important are the code and identification numbers on the application?

Since your application will be analyzed by a computer, any error in code or identification number can cause serious complications. The correct high school code number must be entered on your admission card and on your answer sheet as well. The identification number that appears on your admission card must be copied correctly onto your answer sheet. If the numbers are wrong, the results may go to the wrong school or be credited to another candidate. The correct code number is particularly important in the case of schools with the same name.

How long does the test take?

The examination session lasts approximately 4 hours with time out between sections.

Is there any penalty for guessing?

On this examination there is no penalty for guessing. Therefore it is better to try than to leave the answer blank. Answer as many questions as you can in the time available.

Where can I do scratch work?

Your answer sheet is for answers only. All computations must be done in the question booklet.

How can I correct a wrong entry on the answer sheet?

Make certain that you use a clean eraser and remove all marks that the computer could pick up. Only one letter should be blackened out for any one question. If two items are blackened out, the answer is scored as incorrect.

Before you complete a section, make certain that you have one and only one blackened letter for each answer group.

In what order are the questions arranged?

Generally, the questions in each section are arranged in order of difficulty, with easier ones first. However, what one applicant may find puzzling, another may find rather simple. Therefore, go through as many questions as time allows. Avoid spending too much time on any one question. Circle the number of a tricky one, and go on. After you have finished, come back to it if you have time. Very often, your own mental computer will sort things out, and the question will seem much more understandable the second time!

Test 1 Sequences

The Sequences Test consists of some 20 questions in which sets of figures, numbers, or letters are given. You are asked to select the figure, number, or letter that will continue the pattern or sequence.

Sample Questions

Examples of the various types of questions are given below.

EXAMPLE 1:

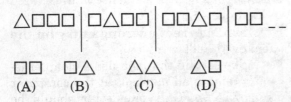

EXPLANATION: Each section consists of one triangle ($\triangle$) and three squares ($\square$). In the first section the triangle appears in the first place; in the second section, in the second place; and in the third section, in the third place. To continue the pattern the triangle should appear in the fourth place.

The correct choice is **B**.

EXAMPLE 2:

5 15 11	6 18 14	7 21 __

18	15	16	17
(F)	(G)	(H)	(J)

EXPLANATION: In each of the first two sections, the second number is equal to three times the first number and the third number is 4 less than the second number. To continue the pattern the third section should be 7 21 17.

The correct choice is **J**.

EXAMPLE 3:

$A_1B_2C_1$ $A_2B_3C_2$ $A_3B_4C_3$ ___ $A_5B_6C_5$

$A_3B_4C_5$	$A_4B_5C_3$	$A_4B_5C_4$	$A_5B_4C_5$
(A)	(B)	(C)	(D)

EXPLANATION: In each of the first three sections, the A and C subscripts are identical and the B subscript is greater than the other two. This is confirmed in the fifth section.

The correct choice is **C**.

EXAMPLE 4:

JKL KLM LMN __ NOP

NPO	MPO	MNO	MOP
(F)	(G)	(H)	(J)

EXPLANATION: The letters form a sequence in alphabetical order. In each case, the first two letters are identical with the last two letters of the preceding section.

The correct choice is **H**.

STRATEGIES FOR SUCCESS

The sequences on this test appear to be of four types. Strategies for handling each type are described below.

➤ Patterns are formed by geometric figures. In this type, study the difference between the second and first panels of figures with special emphasis upon the changes made in the first panel to reach the second panel. See if this change between the first and second panels is repeated in going from the second to the third panel. Now, apply this change in going from the third to the fourth panel to select the correct answer. This type of sequence is illustrated in Example 1.

➤ Patterns are formed by groups of three numbers. In this type, study the relationships among the three numbers in each panel. For example, consider the panel

| 3 15 11 |

Notice that the second number (15) is five times the first number (3). And the third number (11) is 4 less than the second number (15). If these number relationships hold in the second panel, you have discovered the pattern. Now, apply this pattern in the third panel to obtain the answer. This type of sequence is illustrated in Example 2.

➤ Patterns are formed by subscripts of letters. In this type, study the subscripts of letters to find a pattern. For example, consider the letters $A_5B_6C_4$. In this case, the subscript of B is 1 greater than the subscript of A and the subscript of C is 2 less than the subscript of B. If this pattern holds for the next grouping of letters and also for the third grouping, it may be applied to the fourth grouping to obtain the correct answer. This type of sequence is illustrated in Example 3.

➤ Patterns are formed by groups of letters. In this type, concentrate on the first two groupings to detect a pattern. This pattern should hold throughout the other groupings. For example, consider the groupings:

FGH GHI

Notice that the letters are arranged in alphabetical order and the second grouping begins with the last two letters of the first grouping. Therefore, the third grouping should be HIJ. If this is true then apply the pattern to the fourth grouping to obtain the answer. This type of sequence is illustrated in Example 4.

Diagnostic Test 1   Sequences

DIRECTIONS: For numbers 1 through 20, make the choice that will continue the pattern or sequence.

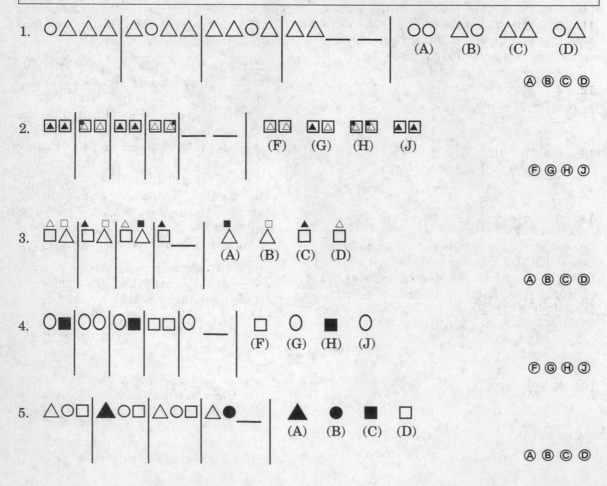

6. ⊡△|▣▲|⊙▲|▣ ___ | ⊡ ▣ △ ▲
                       (F) (G) (H) (J)

Ⓕ Ⓖ Ⓗ Ⓙ

7. 2   4   8 | 6   12   24 | 9   18   ___ | 24   28   36   40
                                                (A)   (B)   (C)   (D)

Ⓐ Ⓑ Ⓒ Ⓓ

8. 3   14   5 | 7   18   9 | 14   ___   16 | 11   25   9   7
                                                (F)   (G)   (H)   (J)

Ⓕ Ⓖ Ⓗ Ⓙ

9. 3   9   27 | 5   15   45 | 7   21   ___ | 24   59   63   147
                                                (A)   (B)   (C)   (D)

Ⓐ Ⓑ Ⓒ Ⓓ

10. 3   22   2 | 7   26   6 | 12   ___   11 | 31   21   41   19
                                                (F)   (G)   (H)   (J)

Ⓕ Ⓖ Ⓗ Ⓙ

11. 6   3   7 | 10   5   9 | 12   6   ___ | 8   10   11   12
                                                (A)   (B)   (C)   (D)

Ⓐ Ⓑ Ⓒ Ⓓ

12. 4   8   7 | 6   12   11 | 9   18   ___ | 16   17   19   20
                                                (F)   (G)   (H)   (J)

Ⓕ Ⓖ Ⓗ Ⓙ

13. 5   7   10 | 6   8   11 | 7   9   ___ | 10   11   12   15
                                                (A)   (B)   (C)   (D)

Ⓐ Ⓑ Ⓒ Ⓓ

14. 9   4   8 | 12   7   14 | 15   10   ___ | 20   21   22   24
                                                (F)   (G)   (H)   (J)

Ⓕ Ⓖ Ⓗ Ⓙ

15. $A_5B_4C_4$ $A_4B_3C_3$ ___ $A_2B_1C_1$ | $A_4B_4C_4$ $A_4B_3C_2$ $A_3B_3C_2$ $A_3B_2C_2$
                                                            (A)   (B)   (C)   (D)

Ⓐ Ⓑ Ⓒ Ⓓ

16. $X_1Y_2Z_2$ $X_2Y_3Z_3$ ___ $X_4Y_5Z_5$ | $X_2Y_2Z_3$ $X_3Y_4Z_4$ $X_4Y_4Z_5$ $X_4Y_5Z_4$
                          (F)   (G) | (H)   (J)

Ⓕ Ⓖ Ⓗ Ⓙ

17. AEC ECB ___ BDF

    EBD   CBA   BDG   CBD
    (A)   (B)   (C)   (D)

                     Ⓐ Ⓑ Ⓒ Ⓓ

18. RST TSR XWV ___

    VWX   WVX   XVW   WXY
    (F)   (G)   (H)   (J)

                     Ⓕ Ⓖ Ⓗ Ⓙ

19. BDG GDA ___ CDE

    AGD   ADC   AGC   BCG
    (A)   (B)   (C)   (D)

                     Ⓐ Ⓑ Ⓒ Ⓓ

20. STV VTS ___ XYZ

    TSV   YZX   ZYX   XZY
    (F)   (G)   (H)   (J)

                     Ⓕ Ⓖ Ⓗ Ⓙ

Answers—Diagnostic Test 1 Sequences

1. **B**		6. **J**		11. **B**		16. **G**
2. **J**		7. **C**		12. **G**		17. **D**
3. **A**		8. **G**		13. **C**		18. **F**
4. **H**		9. **C**		14. **F**		19. **B**
5. **D**		10. **F**		15. **D**		20. **H**

Rating Your Results	
Superior	17–20 correct
Average	13–16 correct
Below Average	12 or fewer correct

Material to Review: Chapter 13

Explanations

1. **B** As we move from left to right, the circle changes position from first place to second place to third place. In the fourth segment the circle belongs in the fourth place.

2. **J** The pattern indicates that two shaded triangles appear in the first, third, and fifth segments.

3. **A** According to the pattern, each segment has a rectangle and a triangle topped by a small triangle and a small square, respectively. The top triangle and square follow this pattern—| hollow, hollow | shaded, hollow | hollow, shaded | shaded, shaded |.

4. **H** The pattern indicates that the first, third, and fifth sections consist of a hollow ellipse and a shaded square.

5. **D** According to the pattern, each section has a triangle, a circle, and a square. The second and fourth sections each have one shaded figure. Therefore, the square in the fourth section is unshaded.

6. **J** The pattern is as follows: | unshaded, unshaded | shaded, unshaded | unshaded, shaded | shaded, shaded |.

7. **C** In each section, each number after the first one is obtained by multiplying the preceding number by 2.

8. **G** In each section, the second number is obtained by adding 11 to the first number, and the third number by subtracting 9 from the second number.

9. **C** In each section, each number is obtained by multiplying the preceding number by 3.

10. **F** In each section, the second number is obtained by adding 19 to the first number, and the third number by subtracting 20 from the second number.

11. **B** In each section, the second number is obtained by taking one-half of the first number, and the third number by adding 4 to the second number.

12. **G**   In each section, the second number is obtained by doubling the first number, and the third number by subtracting 1 from the second number.

13. **C**   In each section, the second number is obtained by adding 2 to the first number, and the third member by adding 3 to the second number.

14. **F**   In each section, the second number is obtained by subtracting 5 from the first number, and the third number by doubling the second number.

15. **D**   According to the pattern, the subscripts follow this order: 544, 433, 322, 211.

16. **G**   According to the pattern, the subscripts follow this order: 122, 233, 344, 455.

17. **D**   According to the pattern, each section begins with the last two letters of the preceding section.

18. **F**   According to the pattern, each set of letters is obtained by reversing the order of the preceding set.

19. **B**   According to the pattern, each set of letters begins by reversing the last two letters of the preceding set.

20. **H**   In this pattern, the second set of letters is obtained by reversing the first set and the fourth set is obtained by reversing the third set. Thus, the missing third set is the reverse of the fourth set.

STUDY PLAN

The best way to do well on the Sequences Test is to obtain as much practice as possible. You will find practice on sequences in Chapter 13. The Practice Coop Examinations will provide further exposure to this type of question.

Test 2 Analogies

The Analogies Test consists of some 20 questions in which two pictures are given on the top line and a single picture and an empty box are given on the lower line. You are required to select a picture to fit the empty box so that the two pictures on the bottom will be related in the same way as the pictures on the top.

Sample Questions

Several examples of analogies are presented below.

EXAMPLE 1:

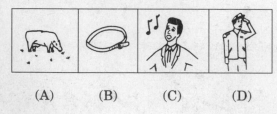

(A) (B) (C) (D)

EXPLANATION: A cowboy uses a lasso; a singer, a microphone.

The correct choice is **C**.

EXAMPLE 2:

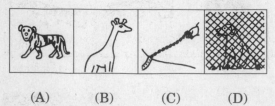

(A) (B) (C) (D)

EXPLANATION: A lion is confined in a cage; a dog, by a fence.

The correct choice is **J**.

EXAMPLE 3:

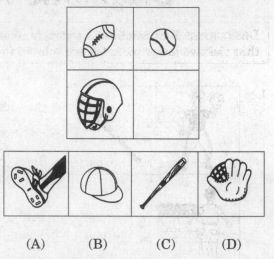

(A) (B) (C) (D)

EXPLANATION: The pictures on the top show two types of balls; the pictures on the bottom show the types of hats worn by players who use these balls.

The correct choice is **B**.

STRATEGIES FOR SUCCESS

Although each analogy question is slightly different, analysis of one example may suggest a procedure that can be followed for all analogies. Consider this example:

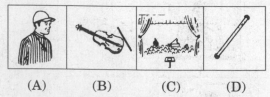

(A) (B) (C) (D)

You know that a coach leads and teaches a football team and a conductor leads and teaches an orchestra. The correct choice is **C**.

The following procedure is suggested:

➤ First identify the relationshp between the two pictures on the upper lines.

➤ Then select a fourth picture from among the answers so that the third and fourth pictures have the same relationship as that between the first and second pictures.

Diagnostic Test 2 Analogies

DIRECTIONS: For numbers 1 through 10 select the picture that will fit in the empty box so that the two lower pictures are related in the same way as the two upper pictures.

1.

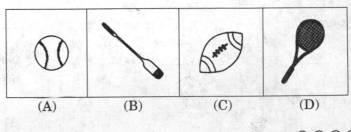

(A)   (B)   (C)   (D)

Ⓐ Ⓑ Ⓒ Ⓓ

2.

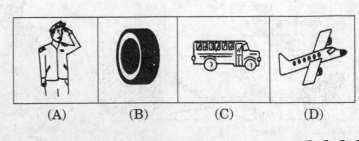

(F)   (G)   (H)   (J)

Ⓕ Ⓖ Ⓗ Ⓙ

3.

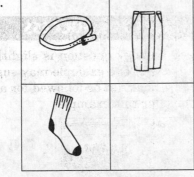
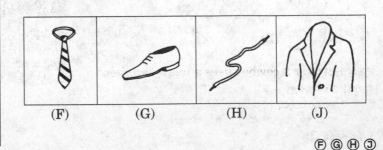

(A)   (B)   (C)   (D)

Ⓐ Ⓑ Ⓒ Ⓓ

4.

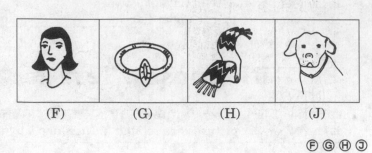

(F)   (G)   (H)   (J)

Ⓕ Ⓖ Ⓗ Ⓙ

5.

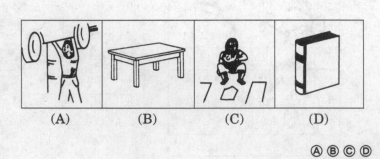

(A)   (B)   (C)   (D)

Ⓐ Ⓑ Ⓒ Ⓓ

6.

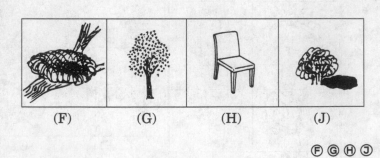

(F)   (G)   (H)   (J)

Ⓕ Ⓖ Ⓗ Ⓙ

7.

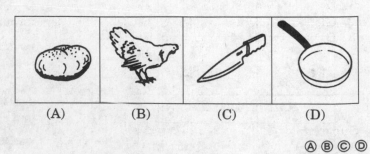

(A)   (B)   (C)   (D)

Ⓐ Ⓑ Ⓒ Ⓓ

8.

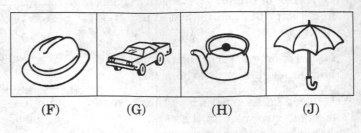

(F)   (G)   (H)   (J)

Ⓕ Ⓖ Ⓗ Ⓙ

9.

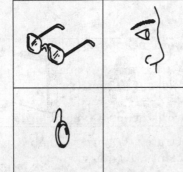

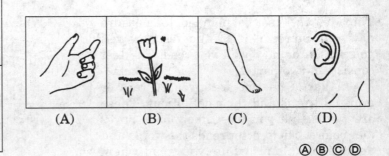

(A)   (B)   (C)   (D)

Ⓐ Ⓑ Ⓒ Ⓓ

10.

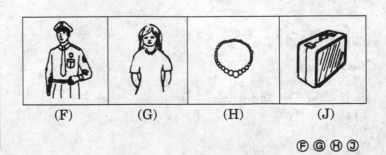

(F)   (G)   (H)   (J)

Ⓕ Ⓖ Ⓗ Ⓙ

Answers—Diagnostic Test 2 Analogies

1. **D**	4. **F**	7. **D**
2. **G**	5. **C**	8. **G**
3. **D**	6. **F**	9. **D**
		10. **G**

Rating Your Results

Superior	9–10 correct
Average	7–8 correct
Below Average	6 or fewer correct

Material to Review: Chapter 13

Explanations

1. **D** A baseball player uses a bat, and a tennis player uses a racket.

2. **G** A belt is worn with trousers, and socks are worn with shoes.

3. **D** A driver drives a car, and a pilot pilots an airplane.

4. **F** A man wears a shirt, and a woman wears a skirt.

5. **C** A policeman wears a badge, and a baseball catcher wears a mask.

6. **F** A kennel is a dog's home, and a nest is a bird's home.

7. **D** A slice of bread is heated in a toaster, and a slice of meat is heated in a frying pan.

8. **G** A reporter works on a newspaper, and a mechanic works on a car.

9. **D** Eyeglasses are worn on the nose, and earrings are worn in the ears.

10. **G** A boy will grow into a man, and a girl will grow into a woman.

STUDY PLAN

The best way to develop skill in analyzing analogies is to obtain as much practice as possible. You will find practice on analogies in Chapter 13. The Practice Coop Examinations will provide further exposure to this type of question.

Test 3 Memory

The Memory Test is planned to measure how well you recall. It does not test how well you reason or how well you read. The test consists of two parts.

In Part One you are given 20 rare or unusual words and their definitions. These are words that you most likely have never met before. The proctor reads the words and definitions aloud while you read them silently. In Part Two, taken 25 minutes later, you are asked to match the words and definitions.

Sample Questions

Part One
While someone reads aloud to you the following words and their definitions, read them silently to yourself.

Words and Definitions

1 An acolent is a neighbor.
2 Yirn means to whine.
3 An abra is a narrow mountain pass.
4 Capistrate means having a hood.
5 The quawk is a type of bird.

Part Two
After an interval of about 25 minutes, continue the Memory Test on a separate sheet of paper, away from the words and definitions given above.

Circle the letter of the word that means the same as the underlined phrase.

1. Which word means <u>hooded</u>?

   (A) abra (B) yirn (C) quawk
   (D) acolent (E) capistrate

2. Which word means <u>a type of bird</u>?

   (F) capistrate (G) yirn (H) abra
   (J) acolent (K) quawk

3. Which word means <u>to whine</u>?

   (A) abra (B) quawk (C) yirn
   (D) capistrate (E) acolent

4. Which word means <u>a narrow mountain pass</u>?

   (F) quawk (G) acolent (H) yirn
   (J) capistrate (K) abra

5. Which word means <u>a neighbor</u>?

   (A) quawk (B) capistrate (C) acolent
   (D) yirn (E) abra

ANSWERS:
1. **E**   2. **K**   3. **C**   4. **K**   5. **C**

STRATEGIES FOR SUCCESS

➤ Keep up with the proctor as the words are read so that you both see and hear the words.

➤ Write the word and the defining term as you read them.

➤ Underline the word and the definition.

➤ Try to develop an association between the word and its definition. For example:

abra—*abyss*   deep valley

acolent—*acquaintance*   neighbor

capistrate—*cap*   hooded

quawk—*squawk*   bird call

yirn—*sound of a whine*   whine

➤ Read each word and its definition silently to yourself as many times as the study period allows.

➤ Form a clear mental picture to associate with the word and its definition.

abra	Picture a deep mountain ravine with cowboys riding into an ambush.
acolent	Associate a mental picture of a neighbor whom you admire.
capistrate	Picture a red bird with a black cap or hood.
quawk	Bond the word with a mental picture of a large, noisy bird looking for fish.
yirn	Picture a turning, high-speed wheel that emits a whining sound, or a sick child whining in fear and pain.

Diagnostic Test 3   Memory

Part One

DIRECTIONS: For a period of 12 minutes, study the following 20 words and their definitions:

1 Buldering means hot and muggy.
2 A godwit is a kind of bird.
3 A kickshaw is a trinket.
4 Madefy means to dampen.
5 Riant means laughing.
6 A cushaw is a vegetable.
7 An anorak is a hooded jacket.
8 Ustulate means sunburned.
9 A pintado is a kind of fish.
10 A rabiator is a violent person.
11 A tupelo is a type of tree.
12 Nodose means having many knots.
13 Suggilate means to beat black and blue.
14 Procellous means stormy.
15 Yemelous means neglectful
16 A rebec is a musical instrument.
17 Remeant means to weaken.
18 Sacculate means to enclose.
19 Ramfeezled means exhausted.
20 Quinse means to carve.

At the end of 12 minutes, cover the words and their definitions. Spend the next 28 minutes doing Test 4 and Test 5, which follow on pages 26–35. At the end of the 28 minutes, return to Part Two of this Memory Test.

Part Two

DIRECTIONS: For numbers 1 through 20, select the word that means the same as the underlined phrase.

1. Which word means <u>a violent person</u>?
   (A) godwit (B) rebec (C) anorak
   (D) rabiator (E) kickshaw

   Ⓐ Ⓑ Ⓒ Ⓓ Ⓔ

2. Which word means <u>exhausted</u>?
   (F) nodose (G) buldering (H) yemelous
   (J) riant (K) ramfeezled

   Ⓕ Ⓖ Ⓗ Ⓙ Ⓚ

3. Which word means <u>a type of tree</u>?
   (A) tupelo (B) cushaw (C) pintado
   (D) anorak (E) rubiator

   Ⓐ Ⓑ Ⓒ Ⓓ Ⓔ

4. Which word means <u>to weaken</u>?
   (F) quinse (G) ustulate (H) madefy
   (J) remeant (K) suggilate

   Ⓕ Ⓖ Ⓗ Ⓙ Ⓚ

5. Which word means <u>stormy</u>?
   (A) ustulate (B) nodose (C) procellous
   (D) buldering (E) riant

   Ⓐ Ⓑ Ⓒ Ⓓ Ⓔ

6. Which word means <u>to enclose</u>?

    (F) madefy   (G) quinse   (H) suggilate
    (J) remeant   (K) sacculate

    Ⓕ Ⓖ Ⓗ Ⓙ Ⓚ

7. Which word means <u>hot and muggy</u>?

    (A) ramfezzled   (B) buldering
    (C) yemelous   (D) ustulate   (E) nodose

    Ⓐ Ⓑ Ⓒ Ⓓ Ⓔ

8. Which word means <u>a kind of fish</u>?

    (F) godwit   (G) rebec   (H) kickshaw
    (J) pintado   (K) tupelo

    Ⓕ Ⓖ Ⓗ Ⓙ Ⓚ

9. Which word means <u>to carve</u>?

    (A) madefy   (B) suggilate   (C) ustulate
    (D) remeant   (E) quinse

    Ⓐ Ⓑ Ⓒ Ⓓ Ⓔ

10. Which word means <u>a trinket</u>?

    (F) rebec   (G) godwit   (H) tupelo
    (J) kickshaw   (K) quinse

    Ⓕ Ⓖ Ⓗ Ⓙ Ⓚ

11. Which word means <u>neglectful</u>?

    (A) ramfezzled   (B) yemelous
    (C) nodose   (D) riant   (E) rabiator

    Ⓐ Ⓑ Ⓒ Ⓓ Ⓔ

12. Which word means <u>a vegetable</u>?

    (F) cushaw   (G) pintado   (H) anorak
    (J) tupelo   (K) sacculate

    Ⓕ Ⓖ Ⓗ Ⓙ Ⓚ

13. Which word means <u>having many knots</u>?

    (A) cushaw   (B) yemelous   (C) riant
    (D) nodose   (E) ramfeezled

    Ⓐ Ⓑ Ⓒ Ⓓ Ⓔ

14. Which word means <u>a kind of bird</u>?

    (F) anorak   (G) rebec   (H) tupelo
    (J) godwit   (K) sacculate

    Ⓕ Ⓖ Ⓗ Ⓙ Ⓚ

15. Which word means <u>to dampen</u>?

    (A) quinse   (B) madefy   (C) ustulate
    (D) remeant   (E) nodose

    Ⓐ Ⓑ Ⓒ Ⓓ Ⓔ

16. Which word means <u>to beat black and blue</u>?

    (F) quinse   (G) cushaw   (H) riant
    (J) rabiator   (K) suggilate

    Ⓕ Ⓖ Ⓗ Ⓙ Ⓚ

17. Which word means <u>a musical instrument</u>?

    (A) godwit   (B) kickshaw   (C) rebec
    (D) pintado   (E) cushaw

    Ⓐ Ⓑ Ⓒ Ⓓ Ⓔ

18. Which word means <u>sunburned</u>?

    (F) ustulate   (G) buldering
    (H) ramfeezled   (J) sacculate
    (K) procellous

    Ⓕ Ⓖ Ⓗ Ⓙ Ⓚ

19. Which word means <u>laughing</u>?

    (A) pintado   (B) riant   (C) buldering
    (D) nodose   (E) procellous

    Ⓐ Ⓑ Ⓒ Ⓓ Ⓔ

20. Which word means <u>a hooded jacket</u>?

    (F) remeant   (G) rabiator
    (H) kickshaw   (J) anorak
    (K) rebec

    Ⓕ Ⓖ Ⓗ Ⓙ Ⓚ

Answers—Diagnostic Test 3   Memory

1. **D**	6. **K**	11. **B**	16. **K**
2. **K**	7. **B**	12. **F**	17. **C**
3. **A**	8. **J**	13. **D**	18. **F**
4. **J**	9. **E**	14. **J**	19. **B**
5. **C**	10. **J**	15. **B**	20. **J**

Rating Your Results	
Superior	17–20 correct
Average	12–16 correct
Below Average	11 or fewer correct

Material to Review: Chapter 13

Associations

Word	Meaning	Association or Mental Picture
1. rabiator	violent person	rabid dog
2. ramfeezled	exhausted	fizzled out
3. tupelo	tree	tulip tree
4. remeant	weaken	older person growing meek and feeble
5. procellous	stormy	picture storm clouds
6. sacculate	enclose	place in a sack
7. buldering	hot and muggy	humidity building up
8. pintado	kind of fish	highly colored (painted) tropical fish
9. quinse	carve	picture marble and Michelangelo
10. kickshaw	trinket	rhymes with geegaw
11. yemelous	neglectful	picture a neglectful pet owner
12. cushaw	vegetable	picture a squash
13. nodose	knotted	picture a rope filled with knots

Word	Meaning	Association or Mental Picture
14. godwit	type of bird	bird with head of a god
15. madefy	to dampen	picture a dampened bundle of clothes
16. suggilate	beat black and blue	picture a gang beating
17. rebec	musical instrument	picture a violinlike instrument
18. ustulate	sun burned	red, blistered sun-bather
19. riant	smiling	picture a film star's famous smile
20. anorak	hooded jacket	picture an Inuit wearing an anorak

STUDY PLAN

The best way to do well on the Memory Test is to practice as much as possible. Learning a foreign language and systematic study of vocabulary lists are most helpful. You will find two practice tests on Memory in Chapter 13. The Practice Coop Examinations at the end of the book will provide further exposure to this type of question.

Test 4 Verbal Reasoning

The Verbal Reasoning Test has some 20 questions in which you are required to identify essential features of objects, to find logical relationships between sets of words, or to draw logical conclusions from facts presented.

Sample Questions

Examples of the various types of questions are given below.

EXAMPLE 1:

Select the word that names a necessary part of the word underlined.

kitchen

    (A) door (B) dishwasher (C) sink
     (D) microwave oven

EXPLANATION: Only a sink is essential in a kitchen.
    The correct choice is **C**.

EXAMPLE 2:

The three words on the top row are related in a certain way. Choose the word to complete the bottom row so that these three words will be related in the same way as the words in the top row.

paint   color   red

room   furniture   __

    (F) wall (G) tapestry (H) blanket
     (J) sofa

EXPLANATION: In the top row, paint has color and red is a color. In the bottom row, a room has furniture and a sofa is furniture.
    The correct choice is **J**.

EXAMPLE 3:

Select the sentence that is true according to the facts given in paragraph.

    Ed Faber has held a variety of jobs. As a young man Ed was an insurance agent and before that he was a clerk. In his more mature years Ed became a manager in a manufacturing plant.

    (A) Ed enjoyed his job as an insurance agent.
    (B) Ed was quite young when he worked as a clerk.
    (C) Ed earned a large salary as a manager.
    (D) Ed is planning to change his manager's job soon.

EXPLANATION: There is no evidence as to the truth of A, C, or D.
    The correct choice is **B**.

EXAMPLE 4:

The following words are translated from an artificial language:

derbil means highway

felbil means midway

felzam means midair

Which of the words below means airway?

    (F) derfel (G) zamder (H) zambil
     (J) felbiz

EXPLANATION: The words *highway* and *midway* have *way* as a common syllable. The words *derbil* and *felbil* have *bil* as a common syllable. Therefore, *bil* means way, *der* means high, and *fel* means mid. Since *felzam* means midair and *fel* means mid, then *zam* means air. Since *zam* means air and *bil* means way, the word for airway is *zambil*.
    The correct choice is **H**.

STRATEGIES FOR SUCCESS

There are many types of verbal reasoning questions. As you saw in the preceding examples, Test 4 includes four types. Strategies for handling these types can be suggested by analyzing an example of each.

➤ Select a word that names a necessary part of the underlined word.

table

(A) chairs (B) napkins (C) dishes
 (D) legs

If we examine the choices, we note that a table can exist without chairs. A table does not have to have either napkins or dishes on it. But a table must have legs, so the correct choice is **D**.

In this type of question, the word *necessary* is the key to your strategy. Some choices may be related to the underlined word but not to essential parts. You must learn to make this distinction and to select the one choice that names a necessary part.

➤ The three words on the top row are related in a certain way. Choose the word to complete the bottom row so that the three words will be related in the same way as the words in the top row.

<u>sound</u>   music   <u>jazz</u>

food   meat   __

   (F) butter (G) lamb (H) symphony
   (J) fish

In the top row, music is a kind of sound, and jazz is a kind of music. In the bottom row, meat is a kind of food and lamb is a kind of meat. The correct choice is **G**.

The relationship of the three words in the top row may differ from question to question. Sometimes all three words are the same class. In other cases, the second and third word may be subclasses of the first word. The three words may be related in many different ways. Your best strategy is to become familiar with varied types of word relationships.

➤ Select the sentence that is true according to the facts given in the following paragraph.

After working hard all week John Gordon enjoys the weekends. He plays tennis, attends the movies, goes dancing with his girl friend, and engages in a variety of other activities. John feels refreshed when he goes back to work on Monday morning.

   (A) John enjoys his job.
   (B) John spends most of his weekend with his girl friend.
   (C) John finds that his weekend activities refresh him for his job.
   (D) John either plays tennis or sees a movie every weekend.

The last sentence in the paragraph leads you to infer that weekend activities refresh John for his job, so the correct choice is **C**.

The strategy for this type of question involves the use of logic. Do not make incorrect inferences. Use only what is stated to come to the logical conclusion stated in the correct answer choice.

➤ The following are words translated from an artificial language.

<u>franol</u> means nighttime

<u>kenfra</u> means midnight

<u>kenhig</u> means midday

Which word means <u>daytime</u>?

   (F) kennol (G) fraken (H) hignol
   (J) higfra

The words *nighttime* and *midnight* have *night* as a common syllable. The corresponding words *franol* and *kenfra* have *fra* as a common syllable. Therefore, *fra* means night, *nol* means time, and *ken* means mid. Since *kenhig* means midday and *ken* means mid, then *hig* means day. Since *hig* means day and *nol* means time, the word corresponding to daytime is *hignol*. The correct choice is **H**.

The strategy here is to dissect each word given and find the meaning of each syllable. Then use logic to put the correct syllables together so that they produce the desired word translation.

Diagnostic Test 4 Verbal Reasoning

DIRECTIONS: For numbers 1–7 select the word that names a necessary part of the word underlined.

1. automobile

   (A) driver   (B) gasoline   (C) motor
   (D) radio

   Ⓐ Ⓑ Ⓒ Ⓓ

2. violin

   (F) music   (G) orchestra   (H) baton
   (J) strings

   Ⓕ Ⓖ Ⓗ Ⓙ

3. tire

   (A) steel   (B) rubber   (C) air
   (D) car

   Ⓐ Ⓑ Ⓒ Ⓓ

4. ship

   (F) passenger   (G) sails   (H) purser
   (J) deck

   Ⓕ Ⓖ Ⓗ Ⓙ

5. garden

   (A) roses   (B) trellis   (C) soil
   (D) hose

   Ⓐ Ⓑ Ⓒ Ⓓ

6. airplane

   (F) field   (G) pilot   (H) passengers
   (J) engine

   Ⓕ Ⓖ Ⓗ Ⓙ

7. restaurant

   (A) counter   (B) food   (C) customers
   (D) wine

   Ⓐ Ⓑ Ⓒ Ⓓ

DIRECTIONS: For numbers 8–12, the three words in the top row are related in a certain way. The words below the line are related in the same way. In each case, select the missing word so that the three words in the bottom row will be related in the same way as the words in the top row.

8. river   lake   ocean

   hat   coat   ____

   (F) cloth   (G) pin   (H) leather
   (J) jacket

   Ⓕ Ⓖ Ⓗ Ⓙ

9. building   bank   shop

   cheese   swiss   ____

   (A) teller   (B) cheddar   (C) milk
   (D) slice

   Ⓐ Ⓑ Ⓒ Ⓓ

10. art   painting   sculpture

    game   baseball   ____

    (F) tennis   (G) bat   (H) ball
    (J) umpire

    Ⓕ Ⓖ Ⓗ Ⓙ

11. sky   cloud   star

    ocean   shipwrecks   ____

    (A) planet   (B) man   (C) whale
    (D) sail

    Ⓐ Ⓑ Ⓒ Ⓓ

12. automobile   wheel   gas tank

    airplane   engine   ____

    (F) flight attendant   (G) passengers
    (H) galley   (J) landing gear

    Ⓕ Ⓖ Ⓗ Ⓙ

DIRECTIONS: For numbers 13–16, select the statement that is true according to facts given in the paragraph.

13. Kenneth Bates is the manager of the ABC Supermarket. Since Tuesday is usually a slow day, he has special sales with reduced prices on that day. On Thursday and Friday evenings he keeps the store open late to accommodate shoppers for weekend supplies. Kenneth also hires extra help for Thursdays and Fridays because he knows from experience that more people shop on those days.

    (A) Kenneth Bates is a successful store manager.
    (B) Kenneth Bates hires extra help for weekends.
    (C) Kenneth Bates cuts prices on all items early in the week.
    (D) The ABC Supermarket remains open later on Friday evening than on Monday evening.

    Ⓐ Ⓑ Ⓒ Ⓓ

14. Jose Fernandez is an engineer specializing in construction work. Jose and his wife, Maria, are required to move whenever he is assigned to a new project. As a result, Jose and Maria have friends in several parts of the United States. They attempt to keep their friendships alive by telephone and correspondence.

    (F) Jose and Maria Fernandez feel sad at losing friends when they have to move.
    (G) Jose and Maria Fernandez use the mail as one way to maintain friendships.
    (H) Jose Fernandez is kept busy because he is an expert engineer.
    (J) Maria Fernandez telephones each of her friends at least once a week.

    Ⓕ Ⓖ Ⓗ Ⓙ

15. Ruth Harvey likes to read books during her leisure time. Ruth especially enjoys novels and mystery stories, but she occasionally reads biography and history. She finds that her wide reading helps her in her school work.

    (A) Ruth Harvey's reading habit helps her to achieve higher grades in her school work.
    (B) Ruth Harvey dislikes reading science books.
    (C) Ruth Harvey neglects her home duties becuase she is busy reading.
    (D) Ruth Harvey reads biography only when she cannot find a novel to read.

    Ⓐ Ⓑ Ⓒ Ⓓ

16. The town of Springdale is located in summer resort country. Springdale is 4,000 feet above sea level, and a mountain stream flows past the edge of town. The town is busy during the summer catering to visitors who escape from the heat of large cities to enjoy the cool mountain air.

    (F) Everyone leaves Springdale during the winter when it gets very cold.
    (G) The altitude of Springdale is higher than the altitude of any other town in the state.
    (H) Springdale attracts large-city dwellers who enjoy cool mountain air.
    (J) People enjoy swimming in the stream at the edge of town.

    Ⓕ Ⓖ Ⓗ Ⓙ

DIRECTIONS: For numbers 17–20, select the correct answer.

17. The following words are translated from an artificial language:

    <u>bordac</u> means football

    <u>fildac</u> means baseball

    <u>filgre</u> means baseman

    Which of the words below means <u>footman</u>?

    (A) gredac (B) borgre (C) borfil
      (D) fiber

    Ⓐ Ⓑ Ⓒ Ⓓ

18. The following words are translated from an artificial language:

    <u>habcor</u> means telephone

    <u>habjil</u> means television

    <u>cormar</u> means phonograph

    Which of the words below means <u>telegraph</u>?

    (F) marcor (G) habmar (H) corfil
      (J) jilmar

    Ⓕ Ⓖ Ⓗ Ⓙ

19. The following words are translated from an artificial language:

    <u>pelbir</u> means output

    <u>peldut</u> means outside

    <u>fakbir</u> means input

    Which of the words below means inside?

    (A) dutbir (B) pelfak (C) bikfar
      (D) fakdut

    Ⓐ Ⓑ Ⓒ Ⓓ

20. The following words are translated from an artificial language:

    <u>balker</u> means footpath

    <u>balvel</u> means footman

    <u>numvel</u> means baseman

    Which of the words below means <u>basepath</u>?

    (F) numbal (G) numker (H) kervel
      (J) levbar

    Ⓕ Ⓖ Ⓗ Ⓙ

Answers—Diagnostic Test 4
Verbal Reasoning

1. **C**	6. **J**	11. **C**	16. **H**
2. **J**	7. **B**	12. **J**	17. **B**
3. **B**	8. **J**	13. **D**	18. **G**
4. **J**	9. **B**	14. **G**	19. **D**
5. **C**	10. **F**	15. **A**	20. **G**

Rating Your Results	
Superior	17–20 correct
Average	13–16 correct
Below Average	12 or fewer correct

Material to Review: Chapter 13

Explanations

1. **C** A motor is a necessary part of an automobile.

2. **J** Strings are a necessary part of a violin.

3. **B** Rubber is a necessary part of a tire.

4. **J** A deck is a necessary part of a ship.

5. **C** Soil is a necessary part of a garden.

6. **J** An engine is a necessary part of an airplane.

7. **B** Food is a necessity in a restaurant.

8. **J** The top line consists of bodies of water; the bottom line, of types of apparel.

9. **B** The top line consists of the word *building* and two types of buildings; the bottom line, of the word *cheese* and two types of cheese.

10. **F** The top line consists of the word *art* and two types of art; the bottom line, of the word *game* and two types of games.

11. **C** The top line consists of the word *sky* and two objects in the sky; the bottom line, of the word *ocean* and two objects found in the ocean.

12. **J** The top line consists of the automobile and two essential parts; the bottom line, of the airplane and two essential parts.

13. **D** The third sentence states that the store remains open late on Thursdays and Fridays.

14. **G**   The last sentence states that Jose and Maria keep their friendships alive by telephone and correspondence.

15. **A**   The last sentence states that Ruth's wide reading helps her in her school work.

16. **H**   The last sentence states that the town caters to visitors who leave large cities to enjoy the cool mountain air.

17. **B**   The word *bordac* means football, and *fildac* means baseball. Since *dac* is a common syllable, it must mean ball. Also, *bor* means foot and *fil* means base. Since *filgre* means baseman and *fil* means base, *gre* must mean man. Thus, *bor* (foot) + *gre* (man) = *borgre*, footman.

18. **G**   The word *habcor* means telephone, and *habjil* means television. Since *hab* is a common syllable, it must mean tele. Also, *cor* mean phone and *jil* means vision. Since *cormar* means phonograph and *cor* means phone, *mar* must mean graph. Thus, *hab* (tele) + *mar* (graph) = *habmar*, telegraph.

19. **D**   The word *pelbir* means output, and *peldut* means outside. Since *pel* is a common syllable, it must mean out. Also, *bir* means put and *dut* means side. Since *fakbir* means input and *bir* means put, *fak* must mean in. Thus, *fak* (in) + *dut* (side) = *fakdut*, inside.

20. **G**   The word *balker* means footpath and *balvel* means footman. Since *bal* is a common syllable, it must mean foot. Also, *ker* means path and *vel* means man. Since *numvel* means baseman and *vel* means man, *num* must mean base. Thus, *num* (base) + *ker* (path) = *numker*, basepath.

STUDY PLAN

The best way to prepare for the Verbal Reasoning Test is to study the explained examples and get as much practice as possible. Practice may be found in Chapter 13. The Practice Coop Examinations will provide further exposure to this type of question.

Test 5   Reading Vocabulary

High school success is closely bound to the student's ability to understand the vocabulary used in the textbooks and classroom discussions that are the primary sources for acquiring knowledge. Therefore, this examination evaluates your knowledge of words in formal written English rather than of words and terms used in everyday speech. The Reading Vocabulary Test consists of four types of questions, 40 questions in all.

Sample Questions

The four types of questions are described and exemplified below.

1. ***Words with the Same Meaning:*** An underlined word is given in a phrase. It is followed by four choices. You are required to choose the word that means the same or almost the same, as the underlined word.

EXAMPLE:
a fortunate <u>incident</u>

(F) remark   (G) choice   (H) happening
(J) result

The correct choice is **H**.

2. ***Words with Opposite Meanings:*** An underlined word is given in a phrase. It is followed by four choices. You are required to choose the word that means the opposite of the given word.

EXAMPLE:
a <u>permanent</u> home

(A) neat   (B) beautiful   (C) temporary
(D) renovated

The correct answer is **C**.

3. ***Words in Context:*** A sentence containing a blank is given and is followed

four choices for completion. You are required to choose the word that best fits the context.

EXAMPLE:

The label on the bottle definitely warned that taking too many sleeping pills could be
_____ .

   (A) annoying (B) stimulating
   (C) fatal (D) expensive

The key to meaning is in the word *too,* stressing that the result of overdosing would be destructive.

The correct choice is **C.**

4. *Words with Multiple Meanings:* Some words have two or more meanings.

Rose means *ascended:* The balloon *rose* to great heights.
Rose means a *flower:* She gave me the red *rose!*

This type of question requires you to choose the word that has the same meaning as *both* of two underlined words.

EXAMPLE:

stem and follow secretly

   (F) pursue (G) track (H) stalk
   (J) shadow

The correct choice is **H.**

STRATEGIES FOR SUCCESS

➤ If you have easy recognition of the underlined word, its synonym or antonym will stand out among the four choices. But, to prevent careless haste, eliminate the other choices before marking the Answer Sheet.

➤ For words that do not come easily, use the negative approach. Begin by eliminating the choices that you "know" are wrong. Of those that are left, choose the one that seems correct "always" or "most frequently." If you wind up with two (or three) possible answers, put a circle around the number of the question and leave it. Don't spend time agonizing. Plan to come back to the circled items if time permits. Very often the pause gives your mind time for reflection, and when you return for the second try, the answer becomes clear.

➤ Since there is no penalty on this test for guessing, select the most likely choice rather than giving up. In this case, unless you have made an obvious error, do *not* change your answer. Usually, the first guess is the better one

➤ Beware of discouragement. Remember that no one is expected to finish all the tests and have all the answers correct.

Diagnostic Test 5 Reading Vocabulary

> DIRECTIONS: For numbers 1–10, choose the word that means the same, or almost the same, as the word underlined.

1. adhere to the surface
   (A) add (B) cling (C) come
   (D) bring
         Ⓐ Ⓑ Ⓒ Ⓓ

2. cherish their friendship
   (F) seek (G) lose (H) hold dear
   (J) recall
         Ⓕ Ⓖ Ⓗ Ⓙ

3. make a compact
   (A) an agreement (B) a statement
   (C) an error (D) a duplicate
         Ⓐ Ⓑ Ⓒ Ⓓ

4. their cordial reception
   (F) usual (G) formal (H) friendly
   (J) noisy
         Ⓕ Ⓖ Ⓗ Ⓙ

5. in a haughty tone
   (A) loud (B) scornful (C) forceful
   (D) low
         Ⓐ Ⓑ Ⓒ Ⓓ

6. the <u>hostile</u> audience

   (F) scanty   (G) sophisticated
   (H) youthful   (J) unfriendly

   Ⓕ Ⓖ Ⓗ Ⓙ

7. prove to be <u>incompetent</u>

   (A) unskilled   (B) unfortunate
   (C) unknown   (D) invaluable

   Ⓐ Ⓑ Ⓒ Ⓓ

8. period of <u>recuperation</u>

   (F) recovery   (G) success
   (H) learning   (J) hard work

   Ⓕ Ⓖ Ⓗ Ⓙ

9. <u>curb</u> her curiosity

   (A) praise   (B) develop   (C) understand
   (D) control

   Ⓐ Ⓑ Ⓒ Ⓓ

10. <u>misplace</u> his old hat

    (F) repair   (G) replace   (H) lose
    (J) lend

    Ⓕ Ⓖ Ⓗ Ⓙ

DIRECTIONS: For numbers 11–20, select the word that means the opposite of the word underlined.

11. <u>diminish</u> the amount

    (F) lose   (G) increase   (H) total
    (J) notice

    Ⓕ Ⓖ Ⓗ Ⓙ

12. <u>eager</u> to go

    (A) expected   (B) unprepared
    (C) impatient   (D) unwilling

    Ⓐ Ⓑ Ⓒ Ⓓ

13. a <u>growing</u> business

    (F) successful   (G) famous   (H) local
    (J) declining

    Ⓕ Ⓖ Ⓗ Ⓙ

14. <u>nimble</u> dancers

    (A) clumsy   (B) experienced
    (C) youthful   (D) intelligent

    Ⓐ Ⓑ Ⓒ Ⓓ

15. <u>suspend</u> activities

    (F) enjoy   (G) continue   (H) table
    (J) postpone

    Ⓕ Ⓖ Ⓗ Ⓙ

16. an <u>experienced</u> bookkeeper

    (A) inconsiderate   (B) apprentice
    (C) unfriendly   (D) unidentified

    Ⓐ Ⓑ Ⓒ Ⓓ

17. a door left <u>ajar</u>

    (F) closed   (G) unpainted
    (H) unrepaired   (J) unhinged

    Ⓕ Ⓖ Ⓗ Ⓙ

18. the <u>grim</u> scene

    (A) quiet   (B) beautiful
    (C) forgotten   (D) cheerful

    Ⓐ Ⓑ Ⓒ Ⓓ

19. their <u>fitting</u> remarks

    (F) humorous   (G) incidental
    (H) inappropriate   (J) sharp

    Ⓕ Ⓖ Ⓗ Ⓙ

20. <u>impartial</u> witnesses

    (A) truthful   (B) prejudiced
    (C) unreliable   (D) unwilling

    Ⓐ Ⓑ Ⓒ Ⓓ

DIRECTIONS: For numbers 21–30, select the word that best fits into the blank.

21. Nations should not attempt to settle their differences by threatening armed _____.

    (A) discussions   (B) representatives
    (C) allies   (D) conflicts

    Ⓐ Ⓑ Ⓒ Ⓓ

22. The long-distance runner was _____ when he learned that he had set a new record.

    (F) exhausted   (G) elated
    (H) consulted   (J) dejected

    Ⓕ Ⓖ Ⓗ Ⓙ

23. In the darkened room, Paul had to _____ frantically for the light switch.

    (A) rush   (B) saunter   (C) fight
    (D) grope

    Ⓐ Ⓑ Ⓒ Ⓓ

24. Many normally pleasant people are _____ when they first wake up.

    (F) grouchy   (G) silent   (H) smiling
    (J) hungry

    Ⓕ Ⓖ

25. Because of the coming cold snap, the farmer spent the day in the woods _____ timber for the wood stove.

   (A) selecting (B) examining
    (C) labeling (D) hewing

            Ⓐ Ⓑ Ⓒ Ⓓ

26. Come _____ , my young lad, and let me get a good look at you.

   (F) away (G) tearfully (H) yonder
    (J) hither

            Ⓕ Ⓖ Ⓗ Ⓙ

27. A gust of wind _____ bits of paper and dust down the street.

   (A) uncovered (B) switched
    (C) whirled (D) contained

            Ⓐ Ⓑ Ⓒ Ⓓ

28. This story is a _____ on her otherwise perfect record.

   (F) blemish (G) decoration
    (H) commendation (J) splurge

            Ⓕ Ⓖ Ⓗ Ⓙ

29. With the throttle open all the way, the well-conditioned motorboat was going at its _____ speed.

   (A) safest (B) maximum (C) slowest
    (D) considerable

            Ⓐ Ⓑ Ⓒ Ⓓ

30. Despite all hardships, Ellen _____ in her efforts to complete her college education.

   (F) relaxed (G) faltered (H) failed
    (J) persisted

            Ⓕ Ⓖ Ⓗ Ⓙ

DIRECTIONS: For numbers 31–40, select the word whose meaning is the same as *both* of the words or phrases underlined.

---

31. press flat and vegetable

   (A) flat top (B) kale (C) compress
    (D) squash

            Ⓐ Ⓑ Ⓒ Ⓓ

32. struggle and fish

   (F) whale (G) shark (H) flounder
    (J) trout

            Ⓕ Ⓖ Ⓗ Ⓙ

33. hold back and container

   (A) jar (B) hamper (C) case
    (D) retreat

            Ⓐ Ⓑ Ⓒ Ⓓ

34. cut and fasten

   (F) snip (G) snap (H) clip
    (J) cleave

            Ⓕ Ⓖ Ⓗ Ⓙ

35. leave helpless and color

   (A) crimson (B) forsake (C) cringe
    (D) maroon

            Ⓐ Ⓑ Ⓒ Ⓓ

36. weaving frame and threaten

   (F) shuttle (G) glower (H) menace
    (J) loom

            Ⓕ Ⓖ Ⓗ Ⓙ

37. hold back and part repeated

   (A) withhold (B) chorus (C) refrain
    (D) curtail

            Ⓐ Ⓑ Ⓒ Ⓓ

38. fight and become ragged

   (F) ravel (G) skirmish (H) fray
    (J) feud

            Ⓕ Ⓖ Ⓗ Ⓙ

39. start out and type of boat

   (A) depart (B) inaugurate (C) contain
    (D) launch

            Ⓐ Ⓑ Ⓒ Ⓓ

40. shape and fungus

   (F) contour (G) mold (H) mushroom
    (J) outline

            Ⓕ Ⓖ Ⓗ Ⓙ

Answers—Diagnostic Test 5 Reading Vocabulary

1. **B**	11. **G**	21. **D**	31. **D**
2. **H**	12. **D**	22. **G**	32. **H**
3. **A**	13. **J**	23. **D**	33. **B**
4. **H**	14. **A**	24. **F**	34. **H**
5. **B**	15. **G**	25. **D**	35. **D**
6. **J**	16. **B**	26. **J**	36. **J**
7. **A**	17. **F**	27. **C**	37. **C**
8. **F**	18. **D**	28. **F**	38. **H**
9. **D**	19. **H**	29. **B**	39. **D**
10. **H**	20. **B**	30. **J**	40. **G**

Rating Your Results	
Superior	36–40 correct
Average	29–35 correct
Below Average	28 or fewer correct

Material to Review: Chapter 4

Explanations

1.–10. There is only one synonym for each given word.

11.–21. There is only one antonym for each given word.

21. **D** The word *armed* suggests conflicts.

22. **G** The runner was *elated* because he had set a new record.

23. **D** The key is the *darkened room*.

24. **F** *Normally pleasant* requires the contrast in *grouchy*.

25. **D** The clue is the *coming cold snap*.

26. **J** The lad had to come closer (*hither*) for the inspection.

27. **C** The sudden wind blew (*whirled*) the paper and dust.

28. **F** *Otherwise* requires the contrast between *blemish* and *perfect*.

29. **B** An open throttle means highest (*maximum*) speed.

30. **J** The clue is *Despite all hardships*.

31.–40. In each case there is only one word that means the same as the two given words or phrases.

STUDY PLAN

The key to improving your score in this area is the amount of time you can spend on the lists, practice tests, and mastery exams in Chapter 4, Vocabulary.

Long-Term Program

1. Review the lists in Chapter 4. Check the words you are unfamiliar with and review them four or five at a time. You will be pleasantly surprised at how quickly you will master them! A daily ten-minute session each day is the secret to success.

2. Do not skip the varied practice tests and mastery exams. They will reinforce your control of your growing vocabulary and increase your speed in handling the actual examination items.

3. Use the Practice Cooperative Admissions Examinations in the last section of this book as your final step in preparation.

Crash Program

1. Concentrate your study time on doing the practice tests and mastery exams in Chapter 4, Vocabulary.

2. Several short sessions are much more effective than one long one. The varied tests will help you gain speed and accuracy in handling vocabulary questions.

3. Use the Practice Cooperative Admissions Examinations in the last section of this book as your final step in preparation.

Test 6 Reading Comprehension

A basic key to academic success is skill in extracting information from the printed page. Because our schools are geared to using books as the primary communication medium, Test 6 evaluates your ability to handle the many types of reading materials you will meet in high school.

The test section consists of approximately eight reading passages selected from the varied reading matter in books, magazines, and newspapers. Each passage is followed by a series of questions, 34 in all. The questions test your ability to find details, analyze characters, identify main ideas, and interpret events. You must also be able to differentiate between writing techniques and between forms of writing.

Sample Questions

The following reading passage and questions will familarize you with the Test 6 format.

> DIRECTIONS: Read the selection below and answer the questions that follow it. Choose your answers based on the selection.

As regularly as I eat my three meals, brush my teeth, practice the piano—and I do enjoy practicing—I set aside a few minutes toward the end of the day for rating myself. The early evening, when the family is in the television den, and I am still at my desk with my homework completed, is the time that I find best for this necessary but unpleasant task. I suppose that if I were all goodness, the work could be called pleasant.

1. Which description most likely fits the writer?

    (A) seven-year-old
    (B) high-school student
    (C) teacher
    (D) young mother

2. How could the writer be characterized as a person?

    (F) as one who dislikes family obligations
    (G) as one who follows impulses
    (H) as one who avoids facing issues
    (J) as one who enjoys being well organized

3. Which daily activity does the writer *not* seem to engage in on a regular basis?

    (A) review the events of the day
    (B) do school assignments
    (C) develop musical skills
    (D) watch television programs

4. Which of the following statements is true of the writer?

    (F) The writer evaluates daily activities in order to prove what her capabilities are.
    (G) The writer daydreams while self-rating.
    (H) The writer readily admits making mistakes.
    (J) The writer's parents supervise the self-evaluation.

Explanations

1. With music lessons and self-direction in doing homework, the writer must be of high school age. Therefore, the correct choice is **B**.
2. Choice F is incorrect because there is no mention of disliking or liking the family; G is incorrect because the writer is too well organized to follow impulses; H is incorrect because, by going through a daily self-criticism, the writer must be facing the issues that come up. Therefore, the correct choice is **J**.
3. Choices A, B, and C are specifically mentioned as regular tasks. Therefore, the correct choice is **D**.
4. There is no mention of F, G, or J. Therefore, the correct choice must be **H**.

STRATEGIES FOR SUCCESS

➤ Zero in on the paragraphs to be read. Clear your mind of everything else.

➤ Since this is a test of your ability to read, do not rely on your own knowledge as the basis of your answer. Each passage contains all the information you will need to answer the questions.

➤ Read the passage quickly to decide what it is about.

➤ Before you turn to the questions, read the passage a second time, sentence by sentence.

➤ Take the questions in order. Read all the choices before you select the best answer.

➤ Do not hesitate to turn back to the paragraph to verify your choices.

➤ Passages about familiar subjects or areas of your interest take less time than others. However, if you find a passage that seems too difficult, go on to the next; come back to the troublesome one later if you have time. When you return to the passage, it may seem much easier to grasp.

➤ Often picking out the key sentence will organize your thinking about the selection.

Some people find that looking at the questions first can provide clues to the meaning of a difficult paragraph. Others find this approach very time-consuming; they prefer to identify the main ideas in the selection before looking at the questions. While taking the practice test in Chapter 5, try both methods to see which one works better for you.

Some people find underlining key phrases helpful, but this process may slow your reading down too much. It may be better to concentrate on the sentence-by-sentence reading approach to find principal ideas, facts, and the author's point of view.

There is no substitute for practice. The more varied your reading, the better your score. Set aside some time each day for recreational reading and reading for information. The editorial page of the daily newspaper is an ideal source. And so are your textbooks!

Diagnostic Test 6
Reading Comprehension

DIRECTIONS: For questions 1 through 34, read each selection below and answer the questions that follow it. Choose your answer based on the information in the selection.

Members of one of the finest detective forces in the world wear no badges and carry no revolvers. Their only weapons are their strength and courage and a diploma from an intensive school—The Police Service Dog Center near Ottawa, Canada. Yes, these tough, intelligent sleuths are *dogs*—German Shepherds and Dobermans—trained by the Royal Canadian Mounted Police to track down criminals and aid those in trouble.

From the time he enters school, each dog recruit is instilled with severe military discipline. First he is taught to heel, sit, and lie down. Next comes field training where he learns how to track down clues, guard prisoners, and rescue a drowning person or a victim pinned under a fallen tree. Another difficult lesson the dog detective must master is to accept food only once a day—and from no one but his trainer. This lesson is his best insurance against the jaws of a baited trap or a painful death from poisoned meat. In his final lessons the Police Service dog learns to jump through windows, to climb up and down ladders, to scramble across narrow logs, and to fell an armed thug without getting shot. Not only must the four-footed Mountie be tough—he must be gentle, too, because many of his missions involve retrieving lost children and snow-bound campers.

Trotting beside his Mountie master, the dog detective shares the blizzards and loneliness of Canada's bush country and knows no other code than the Mounted Police motto: "Maintain the Right."

1. Which quality besides strength and courage must the Police Service dogs possess to a high degree?

(A) curiosity
(B) intelligence
(C) unselfishness
(D) sympathy

Ⓐ Ⓑ Ⓒ Ⓓ

2. What is the first important lesson taught to these dogs?

(F) how to identify criminals
(G) to be obedient
(H) when to be gentle
(J) not to react to gunfire

Ⓕ Ⓖ Ⓗ Ⓙ

3. Which statement best expresses the main idea of this passage?

   (A) Some Police Service dogs are brighter than others.
   (B) Police Service dogs are both vicious and kind.
   (C) Training is discipline.
   (D) Police Service dogs are high in ability and sense of duty.

   Ⓐ Ⓑ Ⓒ Ⓓ

4. What does the writer of this passage believe about Police Service dogs?

   (F) They should be treated more kindly.
   (G) They should be insured against poisoning.
   (H) They have a code of their own.
   (J) They perform a valuable service.

   Ⓕ Ⓖ Ⓗ Ⓙ

One of the most important steps ever taken by primitive people in their unconscious efforts to escape from barbarism was the discovery of the wheel. It took humans a long time to discover that rolling produced less friction than sliding, and even then they had no idea of the mechanical principle involved. Nor was the discoverer urged on by visions of luxury and ease. He or she simply discovered that rounding the wood would make locomotion easier and increase the group's power over their surroundings. Here was a contrivance that made it easy to move huge weights and to cover great distances. There were neither patent laws nor factories for mass production. Yet, this fortunate discoverer, together with the person who first produced fire, was the forerunner of all the engineers and manufacturers, scientific discoverers and inventors of today.

5. Which one of the following was true when human beings invented the wheel?

   (A) They planned to live in luxury.
   (B) They did not understand the principles involved.
   (C) They lost their power over their surroundings.
   (D) They produced more friction.

   Ⓐ Ⓑ Ⓒ Ⓓ

6. Which of the following is the central idea of the passage?

   (F) The discovery of fire was more important than the discovery of the wheel.
   (G) People found it hard to escape from barbarism.
   (H) The discoverer of the wheel was a forerunner of the discoverer of fire.
   (J) The discovery of the wheel was a great forward step in human progress.

   Ⓕ Ⓖ Ⓗ Ⓙ

Cyrus McCormick invented the first American reaper in 1831 but did not secure the patent on it until three years later. Meanwhile, in 1833, a Baltimore seaman named Obed Hussey was granted a patent for a reaping machine which was not as successful as McCormick's.

McCormick's work was aided greatly by the experiments of earlier inventors. In 1822, Henry Ogle invented a reaper in England; however, farm laborers feared that they would be thrown out of work, and public opinion prevented him from manufacturing it. Then, in 1826, the Reverend Patrick Bell in Scotland combined the plans of earlier inventors and brought out a successful reaper. For this he was given a prize by the Scottish Agricultural Society. Some of the Bell reapers were brought to the United States, and it is quite probable that McCormick was acquainted with the machine. However, McCormick's invention was superior, and he deserves the credit he has received.

Others were working on models of reaping machines, and each one added new ideas. One of the first improvements was a device that raked the grain as the knives cut it. Another was a seat for the operator, and still another tied the grain into bundles. Throughout the 75 years which followed McCormick's invention, additional improvements made the reaping machine more efficient. Perhaps the most important was the gasoline tractor, which was attached to the reaper and propelled it, taking the place of the slower moving horses.

7. Who received the first American patent for a reaping machine?

  (A) Obed Hussey
  (B) Henry Ogle
  (C) Reverend Patrick Bell
  (D) Cyrus McCormick

  Ⓐ Ⓑ Ⓒ Ⓓ

8. What was the main reason that the reaper developed by Ogle was not manufactured?

  (F) People feared that it would cause unemployment
  (G) There was no seat for the operator.
  (H) McCormick's reaper was already on the market.
  (J) Ogle refused to join the Agricultural Society.

  Ⓕ Ⓖ Ⓗ Ⓙ

9. Which of the following was lacking in the reaper of 1831?

  (A) means of propelling it
  (B) cutting edges
  (C) means of gathering the cut grain
  (D) solid construction

  Ⓐ Ⓑ Ⓒ Ⓓ

10. Which statement is true according to this passage?

  (F) McCormick invented his first reaping machine while living in England.
  (G) McCormick's reaper was imitated by British inventors.
  (H) McCormick's reaper was better than those made by other inventors of his time.
  (J) No improvements were added to reaping machines for 75 years after McCormick's invention.

  Ⓕ Ⓖ Ⓗ Ⓙ

Greece, whose shores are washed by the warm waters of the Mediterranean Sea, lies midway between the tropics of the south and the cold country of the north. Her climate, especially in summer, is usually mild and sunny. Sometimes in the winter the chill winds, which the poet Hesiod said were "a great trouble to mortals" blow over the land. However, the ancient Greeks as a whole were very well pleased with their climate, for Herodotus wrote that it was "the lot of Hellas [the name which the Greeks gave their country] to have its seasons far more tempered than other lands." Since it was almost always like summer in Greece, the men of ancient Greece were outdoor people. Much of their business was transacted outside and their public meetings were usually held in the open.

Though the highest mountains were too rocky to support vegetation, laurel, oleander, and myrtle were found at lower altitudes. When the plentiful rains clothed the uplands with rich, green grass, the shepherds allowed their sheep and goats to roam over the hillsides. On the more fertile lowlands, wheat, olives, and grapes could be raised without cultivation. These products were changed into the three articles that were essential to the ancient Greeks—bread, wine, and oil. The oil was used as butter for their bread and for lighting and cleaning purposes. Bread and wine were served at nearly every meal.

11. Which condition sometimes made the Greeks uncomfortable?

(A) warm waters of the Mediterranean
(B) mild climate
(C) central position of the country
(D) cold winds

Ⓐ Ⓑ Ⓒ Ⓓ

12. What is the most likely source of this passage?

(F) a novel dealing with Greek heroes
(G) a social studies textbook
(H) a how-to book on dieting
(J) a modern travel guide

Ⓕ Ⓖ Ⓗ Ⓙ

13. Why did the people of ancient Greece live mainly outdoors?

(A) There was very little rain.
(B) They were easy-going people.
(C) They enjoyed public meetings.
(D) The weather was usually mild.

Ⓐ Ⓑ Ⓒ Ⓓ

14. Where were the best farms in ancient Greece?

(F) in the lowlands
(G) where the laurel grew
(H) in the areas along the shoreline
(J) in the uplands

Ⓕ Ⓖ Ⓗ Ⓙ

15. Which of the following statements is *not* true?

(A) The high mountains of ancient Greece were bare above the tree line.
(B) The essential foods in ancient Greece were grown within the country.
(C) Butter was an important commodity of ancient Greece.
(D) Wine took the place of coffee and tea in the diet of the ancient Greeks.

Ⓐ Ⓑ Ⓒ Ⓓ

The kangaroo is found nowhere in the world but in Australia. Ages ago, when that part of our earth was cut off from the Asian mainland, this fantastic animal from nature's long-ago was also isolated. There are about two dozen species distributed through Australia, southward to Tasmania and northward to New Guinea and neighboring islands. Some are no bigger than rabbits; some can climb trees. They are known by a variety of picturesque names: wallabies, wallaroos, potoroos, boongaries, and paddymelons. But *the* kangaroo—the one that is Australia's national symbol—is the great gray kangaroo of the plains, admiringly known throughout the island continent as the Old Man, and also as Boomer, Forester, and Man of the Woods. His smaller mate, in Australia talk, is a flyer. Their baby is known as a joey.

A full-grown male kangaroo stands taller than a man, and commonly weighs 200 pounds. Even when he sits in his favorite position, reposing on his haunches and tilting back on the propping support of his "third" leg"—his tail—his head is five feet or more above the ground. His huge hind legs, with steel-spring power, can send him sailing over a ten-foot fence with ease, or in a fight can beat off a dozen dogs. A twitch of his tail can break a man's leg like a matchstick.

Kangaroos provide an endless supply of tall tales to which wide-eyed visitors are treated in the Land Down Under. The beauty of tall tales about the kangaroo is that they can be almost as tall as the teller pleases and still be close to fact.

16. Which of the following is *not* true of kangaroos?

    (F) Both male and female kangaroos have approximately the same weight.
    (G) Most people associate the name of kangaroo with only one of the twenty-four species now alive.
    (H) Some kangaroos climb into the branches of trees for protection.
    (J) The kangaroo has been on earth for many centuries.

    Ⓕ Ⓖ Ⓗ Ⓙ

17. According to the author, the same forces that separated Australia from the major continents did which of the following?

    (A) created the variety among the kangaroos
    (B) increased the number of kangaroos
    (C) made the kangaroo a powerful killer
    (D) prevented the spread of the kangaroo

    Ⓐ Ⓑ Ⓒ Ⓓ

18. To what is the jumping power of the kangaroo chiefly due?

    (F) the power of its hind legs
    (G) its tilted sitting position
    (H) the support of its tail
    (J) the type of grass growing in Australia

    Ⓕ Ⓖ Ⓗ Ⓙ

19. What is a wallaby?

    (A) It is a young kangaroo.
    (B) It is another name for a Boomer.
    (C) It is a species of Australian kangaroo.
    (D) It is the name given to a tame kangaroo living in a zoo.

    Ⓐ Ⓑ Ⓒ Ⓓ

20. What does the author believe regarding the stories told about kangaroos?

    (F) They are usually harmful.
    (G) They are mostly true.
    (H) They are generally pure fabrication.
    (J) They are most frequently exaggerated.

    Ⓕ Ⓖ Ⓗ Ⓙ

The old frontier was real. There were Indians and the fear of foreign conquest. People in the older states had to stand together against actual danger that existed as close as the clump of trees across the narrow clearing. As the frontier was pushed westward, new dangers held the people together. Even those living in more settled areas could understand the experiences and tales told by the frontiersmen. Many had been on the frontier themselves or they could recall stories learned from parents or grandparents. The old frontier had a great effect on the character and hopes of Americans. Just exactly what this effect was is open to debate.

Some writers believe the frontier made the frontiersmen individualists. They suggest that each man and woman faced the dangers of the frontier alone. Each had to be prepared to fight, to farm, or to build. These pioneers learned to be rugged and to rely on themselves.

Other writers point out that many of the frontiersmen did things together. They built stockades where groups could defend themselves from attack. They had barn-raising parties where groups joined to erect a building no one man could build alone. They also joined in posses to enforce the laws.

Perhaps both views are true. Men and women were often alone, but at other times they joined forces. Perhaps the chief contribution of the frontier to the United States was to unite the nation in a common goal—the conquest of the West. In fact, perhaps it was this common experience that gave the United States her unity in the beginning. If this is true, then the emphasis upon frontier individualism or upon frontier togetherness is not very important. What does matter is that as a nation Americans shared the frontier experience.

21. Which of the following titles best expresses the main theme or subject of this passage?

    (A) Individualism and Togetherness
    (B) The Frontier and American Unity
    (C) The American Frontier
    (D) Frontier Individualism

    Ⓐ Ⓑ Ⓒ Ⓓ

22. What reason do some writers give to explain why the frontier produced individualists?

    (F) The pioneers had to fight to survive.
    (G) The pioneers had to build forts for protection.
    (H) The pioneers often had to face dangers alone.
    (J) The pioneers had to farm under very primitive conditions.

    Ⓕ Ⓖ Ⓗ Ⓙ

23. Why did the frontiersmen build stockades?

    (A) as a protected area during raids
    (B) as a safe place to store excess grain
    (C) as temporary quarters for others passing through
    (D) as a place for keeping their cattle

    Ⓐ Ⓑ Ⓒ Ⓓ

24. Why did the frontiersmen join together to form posses?

    (F) to help a neighbor complete a house or barn
    (G) to see that the laws were obeyed
    (H) to bring new settlers into the community
    (J) to teach self-reliance

    Ⓕ Ⓖ Ⓗ Ⓙ

25. With which statement would the author of the passage *not* agree?

    (A) Living on the frontier was harsh and filled with danger.
    (B) The entire nation was involved in the settling of the frontier.
    (C) People on the frontier had to learn to depend on themselves and not on others.
    (D) The frontier changed us into a nation.

    Ⓐ Ⓑ Ⓒ Ⓓ

26. What does the author believe to be the chief importance of the frontier to the United States?

    (F) Individualism was born there.
    (G) Dangers were encountered there.
    (H) It gave the experience of unity to the nation.
    (J) The romance of the frontier stories evolved.

    Ⓕ Ⓖ Ⓗ Ⓙ

Austria, in the very heartland of central Europe, was for centuries the center of a great empire ruled by the Hapsburg family. The empire ended with Austria's defeat by the Allied Powers in World War I. For a brief time Austria was a small, independent republic. Then Hitler made Austria part of Germany in 1938. After World War II Austria was occupied by the victorious powers, including Russia. In 1955 she again became an independent republic. In the treaty that was signed in 1955 Austria proclaimed her permanent neutrality. She maintains this position in her actions in the United Nations.

Austria has substantial natural resources and has developed a good industrial base using them. The supplies of lumber, iron ore, magnesite, and oil are particularly important. Austria's agriculture is productive, but the nation must import fruits and vegetables.

One of the most important sources of income for the nation is tourism. The country's ski slopes are famous, and many visitors come to enjoy the beautiful Alps. The alpine scenery is considered by many the most beautiful in the world. Tourists also enjoy the excellent spring festival in Vienna, Austria's capital. The summer music festival at Salzburg is world famous.

27. Which title below best expresses the main theme or subject of this selection?

   (A) Music in Austria
   (B) Austrian History
   (C) Austria—a Small but Successful Nation
   (D) The Wealth of Austria

   Ⓐ Ⓑ Ⓒ Ⓓ

28. Which of the following is one of Austria's major attractions to visitors?

   (F) mineral resources
   (G) natural surroundings
   (H) major industries
   (J) agriculture

   Ⓕ Ⓖ Ⓗ Ⓙ

29. Which one of the following is *not* discussed in this selection?

   (A) famous Austrians
   (B) Austria's present form of government
   (C) Austria's recent history
   (D) the sources of wealth in Austria

   Ⓐ Ⓑ Ⓒ Ⓓ

30. Which statement best expresses the author's attitude?

   (F) She thinks that Austria should grow its own fruits and vegetables.
   (G) She is more interested in presenting facts than in giving a definite point of view.
   (H) She favors Austria's becoming a monarchy once again.
   (J) She believes that Austria will never again be a major world power.

   Ⓕ Ⓖ Ⓗ Ⓙ

An "Atalanta race" is one in which the contest is won through a trick or ruse. In ancient Greece, Atalanta was a swift runner who refused to marry anyone unless he first defeated her in a race. Any suitor who failed was put to death.

Hippomenes fell in love with Atalanta and challenged her. The goddess of love, Aphrodite, came to his aid. She gave him the golden apples of the Hesperides, which he carried into the race. He dropped them one at a time at key moments, knowing that Atalanta would pause to pick them up. The strategy worked, and Atalanta married Hippomenes.

Many people claim that Atalanta and not Hippomenes was the one who made the ruse a success! Some feel that a marriage based on trickery and an obvious battle for supremacy cannot lead to mutual understanding and lasting happiness. Others wonder what the moral of this age-old tale could be.

31. Why were the other suitors put to death?

   (A) They failed to tell the truth.
   (B) They threatened Hippomenes.
   (C) They were too slow.
   (D) Aphrodite cast a spell on them.

   Ⓐ Ⓑ Ⓒ Ⓓ

32. Which of the following is *not* explained by the author?

   (F) why Aphrodite gave the apples to Hippomenes
   (G) how the unsuccessful suitors were killed
   (H) why Atalanta picked up the apples
   (J) why Hippomenes accepted the challenge

   Ⓕ Ⓖ Ⓗ Ⓙ

33. Which of the following is probably true of Atalanta?

    (A) She felt that she was too old to play games.
    (B) She disliked all men.
    (C) She had fallen in love with Hippomenes.
    (D) She regretted having the other young men killed.

    Ⓐ Ⓑ Ⓒ Ⓓ

34. Which of the following sayings is most appropriate as a moral for this story?

    (F) The early bird catches the worm.
    (G) There's always a calm before the storm.
    (H) There's more than one way to skin a cat.
    (J) There's more than one fish in the sea.

    Ⓕ Ⓖ Ⓗ Ⓙ

Answers—Diagnostic Test 6
Reading Comprehension

1. **B**	10. **H**	19. **C**	28. **G**
2. **G**	11. **D**	20. **G**	29. **A**
3. **D**	12. **G**	21. **B**	30. **G**
4. **J**	13. **D**	22. **H**	31. **C**
5. **B**	14. **F**	23. **A**	32. **G**
6. **J**	15. **C**	24. **G**	33. **C**
7. **A**	16. **F**	25. **C**	34. **H**
8. **F**	17. **D**	26. **H**	
9. **C**	18. **F**	27. **C**	

Rating Your Results	
Superior	32–34 correct
Average	27–31 correct
Below Average	26 or fewer correct

Material to Review: Chapter 5

Explanations

1. **B** "Yes, these tough, intelligent … dogs …"

2. **G** "Each dog recruit is instilled with severe military discipline. First he is taught to heel, sit, and lie down."

3. **D** None of the other three choices is mentioned.

4. **J** They "Maintain the Right."

5. **B** "They had no idea of the mechanical principle involved."

6. **J** "One of the most important steps … was the discovery of the wheel."

7. **A** "In 1833 … Obed Hussey was granted a patent.…"

8. **F** "… farm laborers feared that they would be thrown out of work."

9. **C** "One of the first improvements was a device that raked the grain."

10. **H** "McCormick's invention was superior."

11. **D** "Chill winds … blow over the land."

12. **G** Heroes, travel, and diets are not mentioned.

13. **D** "Since it was almost always like summer.…"

14. **F** "On the more fertile lowlands.…"

15. **C** "The oil was used as butter.…"

16. **F** "His smaller mate.…"

17. **D** "… this fantastic animal … was also isolated."

18. **F** "His huge hind legs … can send him … over a ten-foot fence."

19. **C** "They are known by a variety of names."

20. **G** "… and still be close to the fact."

21. **B** The passage deals with the effect of the frontier on American unity.

22. **H** "They [some writers] suggest that each man and woman faced the dangers of the frontier alone."

23. **A** "… where groups could defend themselves from attack."

24. **G** "They also joined in posses to enforce the laws."

25. **C** "Men and women were often alone, but at other times they joined forces."

26. **H** ". . . Americans shared the frontier experience."

27. **C** The passage deals with many aspects of Austria.

28. **G** "Visitors come to enjoy the beautiful Alps."

29. **A** No notables are discussed.

30. **G** The selection contains no opinions, only sets of facts.

31. **C** Atalanta outran them.

32. **G** The other three are explained.

33. **C** "Many people claim that Atalanta . . . made the ruse a success!"

34. **H** Only H supports the concept of trickery. Note the first sentence of the passage.

STUDY PLAN

The key to improving your score in this area is the amount of time you can spend on the exercises and practice tests in Chapter 5, Reading.

Long-Term Program

1. The pages on Work-Study Skills contain exercises and techniques to improve your speed and comprehension. Typical examination questions are analyzed in the sections that follow. The master exams will assure increased ability and speed.

   The lists of things to do and facts to master in this section are long—and rewarding! All you have to do is budget your time properly. Browse through Chapter 5 and decide where to begin. Spend no more than 25 minutes on each practice session. Do not skip the varied exercises and practice tests. They lead to confidence and speed in handling the actual examination.

2. Use the Practice Cooperative Admissions Examinations in the last section of this book as your final step in preparation.

Crash Program

1. Use the Diagnostic Test to discover which type of question requires the most study time.

2. Do as many of the exercises and practice tests as you can to gain speed and accuracy. Several short sessions are always more productive than one long one.

3. Use the Practice Cooperative Admissions Examinations in the last section of this book as your final step.

Test 7   Mathematics Computation

Of the ten sections that comprise the Cooperative Admissions Examination, Test 1—Sequences, Test 7—Mathematics Computations, and Test 8—Mathematics Concepts and Applications involve mathematical operations and mathematical reasoning. The test preparation for the mathematics tests involves coverage of the wide range of basic arithmetic, algebra, and geometry. The outline below lists the areas to be covered. All of these areas are developed in this book with a considerable amount of practice material. To provide for efficient self-study, you are given the answers to all exercises and tests.

Here is what you need to know in mathematics if you are taking the Coop Examination:

1. Basic mathematical operations with whole numbers, fractions, decimals, and percents.

2. Common units of measure and operations with these measures.

3. The metric system.

4. Ratio and proportion.

5. Mathematical applications and problem solving:

   A. Using basic operations.
   B. Percentage problems.
   C. Profit and loss.
   D. Taxation.

E. Commission.
F. Discount.
G. Interest.
H. Averages.

6. Basic algebra:

A. Algebraic representation.
B. Exponents and evaluation of algebraic expressions.
C. Evaluation of formulas.
D. Solving equations.
E. Solving problems by using equations.
F. Solving inequalities.

7. Numbers and number systems:

A. Sets.
B. Numeration.
C. Exponents and expanded form.

8. The set of natural numbers and the set of whole numbers:

A. Factors and primes.
B. Divisibility.
C. Symbols of inequality.
D. Order in the set of integers.

9. The set of rational numbers.

10. The set of real numbers.

11. Laws of operation for real numbers.

12. Interpreting tables, maps, and graphs.

13. Geometry:

A. The basics.
B. Perimeter, area, and volume.
C. Indirect measurements:
    1. Pythagorean Theorem and square root.
    2. Congruence and similarity.
    3. Coordinate geometry.

14. Mathematical reasoning.

15. Venn diagrams.

16. Sequences.

Sample Questions

Test 7 covers the fundamental operations of addition, subtraction, multiplication, and division with mixed numbers, decimals, fractions, percents, and integers.

EXAMPLE 1: $6 - 3\frac{2}{7} =$

(A) $3\frac{5}{7}$ (B) $2\frac{5}{7}$ (C) $3\frac{1}{7}$ (D) $2\frac{6}{7}$

(E) None of these

SOLUTION:

$$\begin{array}{r} 6 \\ -3\frac{2}{7} \\ \hline \end{array}$$ First, we write 6 as $5\frac{7}{7}$

$$\begin{array}{r} 5\frac{7}{7} \\ -3\frac{2}{7} \\ \hline \end{array}$$ Now we can subtract

The correct choice is **B**.

EXAMPLE 2: $(-3)(4)(-5) =$

(F) 15   (G) –15   (H) 17   (J) 23
(K) None of these

SOLUTION:
$(-3)(4) = -12$, $(-12)(-5) = 60$
The correct choice is **K**.

STRATEGIES FOR SUCCESS

This test consists of some 30 questions that involve straightforward computation with mixed numbers, fractions, decimals, percents, and integers. You are given 25 mintues to complete the 30 items. Each item has five answer choices, and the last choice is "None of these."

➤ *Tactic 1:* Do not get upset if you do not see an approach to the solution of a problem. You do not have to answer every question to get a good score. Leave the troublesome problem and return to it later if you have time.

➤ *Tactic 2:* In many computation problems you can avoid gross errors by estimating the answer in advance.

EXAMPLE 1: $0.95 \times 2.4 =$

(A) 228   (B) 22.8   (C) 0.228   (D) 2.28
(E) None of these

EXPLANATION: Since 0.95 is slightly less than 1, the answer should be slightly less than 2.4. This elminates A, B, and C.

The correct choice is **D**.

EXAMPLE 2: $7 - 2\frac{3}{4} =$

(F) $5\frac{1}{4}$ (G) $5\frac{3}{4}$ (H) $4\frac{1}{4}$ (J) $3\frac{1}{4}$

(K) None of these

EXPLANATION: Since $2\frac{3}{4}$ is slightly less than 3, the answer should be a bit more than 4. In other words, the answer should be between 4 and 5. This eliminates F, G, and J.

The correct choice is **H**.

EXAMPLE 3: 85% of 20 =
(A) 170   (B) 17   (C) 1.7   (D) 0.17

EXPLANATION: 85% = 0.85,
  $0.85 \times 20 = (8.5)2 = 17.$

The correct choice is **B**.

EXAMPLE 4: 24 is what percent of 60?
(F) 48%   (G) 60%   (H) 250%   (J) 40%

EXPLANATION: $\frac{24}{60} = \frac{4}{10} = 40\%$.

The correct choice is **J**.

➤ *Tactic 3:* Do not spend too much time on any one question. Since you have 25 minutes to answer 30 questions, you cannot afford to dwell on a troublesome problem.

➤ *Tactic 4:* If you have time, check your answers. The estimation process described in Tactic 2 can help you to detect illogical answers.

Diagnostic Test 7
Mathematics Computation

DIRECTIONS: In each case, select the correct answer.

1. 507 − 498 =

  (A) 19   (B) 29   (C) 9   (D) 99
  (E) None of these

  Ⓐ Ⓑ Ⓒ Ⓓ Ⓔ

2. 0.98 + 0.09 =

  (F) 10.7   (G) 107   (H) 0.107   (J) 1.07
  (K) None of these

  Ⓕ Ⓖ Ⓗ Ⓙ Ⓚ

3. $2\frac{2}{7}$
  $+ 4\frac{5}{7}$

  (A) $7\frac{1}{7}$ (B) 6   (C) $6\frac{1}{7}$ (D) $6\frac{6}{7}$

  (E) None of these

  Ⓐ Ⓑ Ⓒ Ⓓ Ⓔ

4. 5.14 − 0.8 =

  (F) 5.06   (G) 4.34   (H) 5.34   (J) 4.06
  (K) None of these

  Ⓕ Ⓖ Ⓗ Ⓙ Ⓚ

5. $7\frac{3}{4}$
  $- 2\frac{1}{8}$

  (A) $5\frac{5}{8}$ (B) $5\frac{3}{4}$ (C) $4\frac{5}{8}$ (D) 5

  (E) None of these

  Ⓐ Ⓑ Ⓒ Ⓓ Ⓔ

6. (−3)(−2)(5) =

  (F) 10   (G) −10   (H) −30   (J) 30
  (K) None of these

  Ⓕ Ⓖ Ⓗ Ⓙ Ⓚ

7. $4\frac{2}{3} + 3\frac{5}{6} =$

(A) $7\frac{7}{9}$ (B) $8\frac{5}{6}$ (C) $8\frac{1}{4}$ (D) $8\frac{1}{2}$

(E) None of these

ⒶⒷⒸⒹⒺ

8. $(-3) + (-2) + 5 =$

(F) 10 (G) 30 (H) 11 (J) –25
(K) None of these

ⒻⒼⒽⒿⓀ

9. 0.694
  $\times$ 7

(A) 48.58 (B) 0.4858 (C) 4.918
(D) 4.858 (E) None of these

ⒶⒷⒸⒹⒺ

10. $7 - 3\frac{2}{5} =$

(F) $4\frac{2}{3}$ (G) $4\frac{3}{5}$ (H) $3\frac{3}{5}$ (J) $3\frac{1}{5}$

(K) None of these

ⒻⒼⒽⒿⓀ

11. $0.6\overline{)0.204}$

(A) 3.4 (B) 0.34 (C) 0.304 (D) 340
(E) None of these

ⒶⒷⒸⒹⒺ

12. $(-6) + (-5) =$

(F) 11 (G) –1 (H) –11 (J) 30
(K) None of these

ⒻⒼⒽⒿⓀ

13. $9 - 3\frac{5}{8} =$

(A) $5\frac{3}{8}$ (B) $6\frac{3}{8}$ (C) $6\frac{1}{8}$ (D) $5\frac{1}{8}$

(E) None of these

ⒶⒷⒸⒹⒺ

14. $4\frac{1}{8} \div 3 =$

(F) $\frac{8}{11}$ (G) $\frac{11}{8}$ (H) $2\frac{3}{8}$ (J) $12\frac{3}{8}$

(K) None of these

ⒻⒼⒽⒿⓀ

15. $8\frac{1}{6} - 5\frac{1}{2}$

(A) $3\frac{2}{3}$ (B) $3\frac{1}{3}$ (C) $2\frac{5}{6}$ (D) $2\frac{2}{3}$

(E) None of these

ⒶⒷⒸⒹⒺ

16.   0.62
   $- 0.49$

(F) 0.13 (G) 2.11 (H) 0.0211 (J) 1.029
(K) None of these

ⒻⒼⒽⒿⓀ

17. $\frac{1}{2} + \frac{1}{3} + \frac{1}{6} =$

(A) $\frac{5}{6}$ (B) $1\frac{1}{6}$ (C) $\frac{11}{12}$ (D) 1

(E) None of these

ⒶⒷⒸⒹⒺ

18. $5\frac{1}{4} \div 2\frac{1}{3} =$

(F) $1\frac{2}{3}$ (G) $18\frac{3}{4}$ (H) $2\frac{1}{2}$ (J) $\frac{1}{4}$

(K) None of these

ⒻⒼⒽⒿⓀ

19. 15% of 18 =

(A) 27 (B) 2.7 (C) 33 (D) 270
(E) None of these

ⒶⒷⒸⒹⒺ

20. 45% =

(F) $\frac{9}{20}$ (G) 4.5 (H) $\frac{9}{25}$ (J) 45

(K) None of these

ⒻⒼⒽⒿⓀ

21. $3.9\overline{)41.34}$

(A) 106 (B) 1.06 (C) 10.6 (D) 0.106
(E) None of these

ⒶⒷⒸⒹⒺ

22. $7\frac{1}{2}\%$

(F) 75 (G) 7.5 (H) 0.75 (J) .075
(K) None of these

ⒻⒼⒽⒿⓀ

23. What percent of 45 is 18?

    (A) 5%   (B) 40%   (C) 52%   (D) 25%
    (E) None of these

    Ⓐ Ⓑ Ⓒ Ⓓ Ⓔ

24. 5 feet 6 inches × 3 =

    (F) 15 ft. 6 in.   (G) 19 ft. 3 in.
    (H) 16 ft. 6 in.   (J) 19 ft.
    (K) None of these

    Ⓕ Ⓖ Ⓗ Ⓙ Ⓚ

25. $\left(7 - \dfrac{1}{4}\right) \div 3 =$

    (A) $2\dfrac{1}{9}$ (B) $2\dfrac{1}{4}$ (C) $20\dfrac{1}{4}$ (D) $\dfrac{4}{9}$

    (E) None of these

    Ⓐ Ⓑ Ⓒ Ⓓ Ⓔ

26. $8\dfrac{1}{3} + 2\dfrac{3}{4} =$

    (F) $11\dfrac{1}{12}$ (G) $10\dfrac{1}{12}$ (H) $11\dfrac{5}{12}$

    (J) $10\dfrac{4}{7}$ (K) None of these

    Ⓕ Ⓖ Ⓗ Ⓙ Ⓚ

27. Which one of the following is correct?

    (A) $\dfrac{1}{2} > \dfrac{1}{4} > \dfrac{1}{3}$ (B) $\dfrac{1}{3} > \dfrac{1}{4} > \dfrac{1}{2}$

    (C) $\dfrac{1}{4} > \dfrac{1}{2} > \dfrac{1}{3}$ (D) $\dfrac{1}{2} > \dfrac{1}{3} > \dfrac{1}{4}$

    (E) None of these

    Ⓐ Ⓑ Ⓒ Ⓓ Ⓔ

28. 0.014 ÷ 0.7 =

    (F) 0.2   (G) 0.002   (H) 0.02   (J) 0.098
    (K) None of these

    Ⓕ Ⓖ Ⓗ Ⓙ Ⓚ

29. 6 pounds 3 ounces – 2 pound 10 ounces =

    (A) 2 pounds 9 ounces
    (B) 4 pounds 9 ounces
    (C) 3 pound 9 ounces
    (D) 8 pounds 13 ounces
    (E) None of these

    Ⓐ Ⓑ Ⓒ Ⓓ Ⓔ

30. 16 is 20% of what number?

    (F) 64   (G) $3\dfrac{1}{5}$ (H) 32   (J) 80

    (K) None of these

    Ⓕ Ⓖ Ⓗ Ⓙ Ⓚ

Answers—Diagnostic Test 7 Mathematics Computation

1. C	9. D	17. D	25. B
2. J	10. H	18. K	26. F
3. E	11. B	19. B	27. D
4. G	12. H	20. F	28. H
5. A	13. A	21. C	29. C
6. J	14. G	22. J	30. J
7. D	15. D	23. B	
8. K	16. F	24. H	

Rating Your Results

Superior	26–30 correct
Average	19–25 correct
Below Average	18 or fewer correct

Material to Review: Chapters 7–12

STUDY PLAN

The amount of time required for a thorough study program in preparation for Test 7 of the Coop Examination will vary greatly from individual to individual. Questions on Test 7 cover the four fundamental operations with mixed numbers, fractions, decimals, percents, and integers. The material in Chapter 7 on whole numbers, fractions, percents, and decimals is complete and thorough. Thorough coverage of operations with integers can be found in Chapter 10.

It is not necessary to work through all the detailed exercises given in the book. On any given topic it is suggested that you take one of the practice tests. If you can answer correctly at least 80% of the questions on the test, there is no need for you to linger; you may proceed to the next topic. Such a plan of procedure will enable you to concentrate on the areas in which you are weak.

Test 8 Mathematics Concepts and Applications

Sample Questions

This test covers mathematical theory and applications involved in such topics as numeration, number sentences, number theory, problem solving, measurements, and geometry.

EXAMPLE 1: What is another way to write $5 \times 5 \times 5 \times 5 \times 5 \times 5$?
(A) 5^2 (B) 25×25 (C) 6^5 (D) 5^6

EXPLANATION: Since 5 is a factor 6 times, the correct answer is 5^6.
The correct choice is **D**.

EXAMPLE 2: If $3 < \square < 5$ and $\square$ is an integer, then the value of $\square$ is
(F) 2 (G) 4 (H) 6 (J) 1

EXPLANATION: The sentence $3 < \square < 5$ tell us that 3 is less than $\square$ and that $\square$ is less than 5. Since 3 is less than $\square$ and $\square$ is an integer, then $\square$ may be 4, 5, 6, ... Since $\square$ is less than 5 and $\square$ is an integer, then $\square$ may be 4, 3, 2, 1, ... To satisfy all conditions, $\square$ must be 4.
The correct choice is **G**.

EXAMPLE 3: The Venn diagram below shows how many students are enrolled in the science classes at Lincoln High School. How many students are enrolled in both biology and chemistry classes?

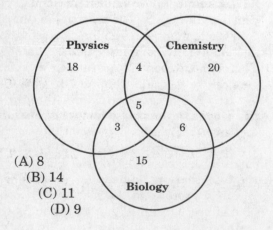

(A) 8
(B) 14
(C) 11
(D) 9

EXPLANATION: The numbers 5 and 6 lie in both the biology circle and the chemistry circle. Therefore, $5 + 6 = 11$ students take both biology and chemistry.

The correct choice is **C**.

EXAMPLE 4: The measure of $\angle AOB = 40°$, and the area of the circle is 72 square inches. What is the area of sector AOB in square inches?
(A) 10 (B) 9 (C) 8 (D) 12

EXPLANATION: The sum of the measures of the angles around a point in a plane is $360°$. Therefore, the area of sector OAB is equal to $\frac{40}{360}$ of the area of the circle

$$\frac{40}{360} = \frac{1}{9}, \text{ and } \frac{1}{9} \text{ of } 72 = 8 \text{ square inches.}$$

The correct choice is **C**.

EXAMPLE 5: In a triangle the measure of one angle is twice the measure of another angle, and the measure of the third angle is $48°$. What is the measure of the largest angle of the triangle?
(F) $48°$ (G) $64°$ (H) $80°$ (J) $88°$

EXPLANATION: Let $x =$ the measure of one angle of the triangle,
and $2x =$ the measure of the second angle of the triangle.

$x + 2x + 48 = 180$
$3x + 48 = 180$
$3x = 180 - 48$
$= 132$
$x = 44$
$2x = 2(44) = 88$

The measure of the three angles of the triangle are $44°$, $88°$, and $48°$.
The correct choice is **J**.

STRATEGIES FOR SUCCESS

Test 8 contains 35 items, each with four answer choices. This test measures your understanding of mathematical concepts and your ability to solve problems in arithmetic, simple algebra, and basic geometry. The suggestions below are designed to help you to attain your best score.

➤ *Tactic 1:* Read each question carefully. Every word in a mathematical statement is precise and is important.

➤ *Tactic 2:* Determine what information is given and exactly what must be found. This analysis will give you the gist of the problem.

➤ *Tactic 3:* Develop a plan for a solution. Such a plan will involve a link between the given information and what you must find.

➤ *Tactic 4:* Use your plan as a guide to complete the solution to the problem.

➤ *Tactic 5:* Check your answer. You may use the method of estimating the answer described in Tactic 2 in connection with Test 7.

➤ *Tactic 6:* Be sure that your answer is given in the units specified in the question.

➤ *Tactic 7:* Do not get upset if you cannot answer a question. You do not have to answer every question to get a good score. If you do not see an immediate approach to the solution of a problem, leave it and return to it later if time permits.

➤ *Tactic 8:* Do not spend too much time on any one question. Since you have 27 minutes to answer some 35 questions, you cannot afford to dwell on a troublesome problem.

Diagnostic Test 8   Mathematics Concepts and Applications

DIRECTIONS: In each case, read the problem and select the correct answer.

1. Which number sentence is true?

    (A) $-6 > 2$ (B) $5 < -3$ (C) $-3 > -7$
    (D) $-5 > -1$

    Ⓐ Ⓑ Ⓒ Ⓓ

2. A dealer placed an order for 144 suits. Of the suits ordered, $\frac{1}{2}$ were blue, $\frac{1}{3}$ were gray, and the rest were brown. How many brown suits were ordered?

    (F) 26   (G) 120   (H) 48   (J) 24

    Ⓕ Ⓖ Ⓗ Ⓙ

3. Mr. Kelly estimates that he pays out 30% of his gross annual income in taxes. What is his gross annual income if he pays $8,400 in taxes?

    (A) $30,000   (B) $28,000   (C) $32,000
    (D) $24,000

    Ⓐ Ⓑ Ⓒ Ⓓ

4. At a speed of 40 miles per hour, how many minutes does it take to cover 1 mile?

    (F) $\frac{2}{3}$ (G) $1\frac{1}{3}$ (H) 2   (J) $1\frac{1}{2}$

    Ⓕ Ⓖ Ⓗ Ⓙ

5. Which set of numbers in the box will make the following sentence true?

    $$7 > \square > 3$$

    (A) 7, 4   (B) 3, 5   (C) 4, 5, 6
    (D) 3, 4, 5, 6

    Ⓐ Ⓑ Ⓒ Ⓓ

6. What are the prime factors of the number 42?

    (F) 2, 7   (G) 6, 7   (H) 7, 21   (J) 2, 3, 7

    Ⓕ Ⓖ Ⓗ Ⓙ

7. On the number line what is the location of the point X?

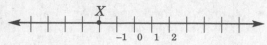

(A) 2   (B) –3   (C) –2   (D) –4

ⒶⒷⒸⒹ

8. Which of the following is equal to 7^5?

(F) 35   (G) $7 \times 7 \times 7 \times 7 \times 7$
(H) $5 \times 5 \times 5 \times 5 \times 5 \times 5 \times 5$ (J) $(7^3)^2$

ⒻⒼⒽⒿ

9. Of the 180 graduating students at Lincoln High School, $\frac{3}{4}$ are going on to college. How many students in the graduating class are going on to college?

(A) 135   (B) 125   (C) 120   (D) 140

ⒶⒷⒸⒹ

10. Which of the following is equal to 35%?

(F) 0.7   (G) 3.5   (H) $\frac{7}{20}$ (J) $\frac{5}{20}$

ⒻⒼⒽⒿ

11. If a motorist pays \$19.62 for 15 gallons of gasoline, how much does she have to pay for 20 gallons at the same rate?

(A) \$26.08   (B) \$28.16   (C) \$26.20
(D) \$26.16

ⒶⒷⒸⒹ

12. Which of the following numbers has 6 in the hundreds place and 4 in the tenths place?

(F) 9,362.48   (G) 8,675.49   (H) 2,653.74
(J) 8,641.95

ⒻⒼⒽⒿ

13. Which is the measure of an acute angle of a right isosceles triangle?

(A) 60°   (B) 40°   (C) 45°   (D) 75°

ⒶⒷⒸⒹ

14. A team has won 14 games and lost 10. If the team wins one-half of the next 16 games played, what percent of the games played will it have won?

(F) 55%   (G) 64%   (H) 60%   (J) 75%

ⒻⒼⒽⒿ

15. A ladder 10 feet in length leans against the side of a building. If the base of the ladder is 6 feet from the building, how high up the building does the ladder reach?

(A) 7 feet   (B) 9 feet   (C) 8 feet
(D) 10 feet

ⒶⒷⒸⒹ

16. Which number is a solution of the inequality $3x - 1 < 5$?

(F) 2   (G) 3   (H) 6   (J) 1

ⒻⒼⒽⒿ

17. The diagram shows the number of students enrolled in algebra, geometry, and physics at St. Mary's High School. How many students are enrolled in both geometry and physics?

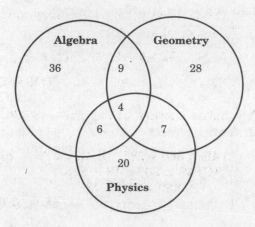

(A) 77   (B) 17   (C) 11   (D) 19

ⒶⒷⒸⒹ

18. At a party 2 gallons of fruit juice were served. If each serving contained 8 ounces of fruit juice, how many servings were there?

   (F) 30   (G) 24   (H) 28   (J) 32

   Ⓕ Ⓖ Ⓗ Ⓙ

19. If $2x + 5 = 19$, what is the value of x?

   (A) 5   (B) 7   (C) –7   (D) 6

   Ⓐ Ⓑ Ⓒ Ⓓ

20. If $A = 6s^2$, what is the value of A when $s = \frac{1}{3}$?

   (F) 54   (G) $\frac{2}{3}$ (H) 1   (J) 4

   Ⓕ Ⓖ Ⓗ Ⓙ

21. A recipe calls for 1 cup of milk and $2\frac{1}{4}$ cups of flour. If 3 cups of flour are used, how many cups of milk should be used?

   (A) $1\frac{1}{2}$ (B) $1\frac{1}{4}$ (C) 2   (D) $1\frac{1}{3}$

   Ⓐ Ⓑ Ⓒ Ⓓ

22. An oil tank contains 480 gallons of heating oil. During the month of November, $\frac{1}{3}$ of the oil is consumed. During December, $\frac{1}{3}$ what is left is consumed. How many gallons of oil are left?

   (F) 224   (G) 240   (H) 300   (J) 320

   Ⓕ Ⓖ Ⓗ Ⓙ

23. What is another way to write 48(360 + 295)?

   (A) $48 \times 360 + 295$ (B) $360 + 48 \times 295$
   (C) $48 \times 360 + 48 \times 295$
   (D) $360 + 295 \times 48$

   Ⓐ Ⓑ Ⓒ Ⓓ

24. A circle graph is used to represent the total annual expense budget of a city. What fractional part of the expense budget is represented by a sector whose central angle measures 80°?

   (F) $\frac{2}{9}$ (G) $\frac{4}{5}$ (H) $\frac{4}{9}$ (J) $\frac{1}{5}$

   Ⓕ Ⓖ Ⓗ Ⓙ

25. If a pen costs y cents, what is the cost, in cents, of a dozen pens?

   (A) $12 + y$ (B) $y \div 12$ (C) $12 - y$
   (D) $12y$

   Ⓐ Ⓑ Ⓒ Ⓓ

26. On a bar graph, a 1-inch bar represents a population of 12,000. What is the length, in inches, of the bar needed to represent a population of 32,000?

   (F) $2\frac{1}{3}$ (G) $2\frac{1}{4}$ (H) $2\frac{2}{3}$ (J) $2\frac{5}{6}$

   Ⓕ Ⓖ Ⓗ Ⓙ

27. A plane travels at a steady speed of 420 miles per hour. How many miles does the plane travel between 10:30 A.M. and 1:15 P.M.?

   (A) 1,655   (B) 1,155   (C) 1,575
   (D) 1,250

   Ⓐ Ⓑ Ⓒ Ⓓ

28. Which replacement for □ will make the equation $3 \times □ + 2 = 17$ true?

   (F) 3   (G) –5   (H) 4   (J) 5

   Ⓕ Ⓖ Ⓗ Ⓙ

29. There are 240 students in the freshman class at St. Barnabas High School. If this is 30% of the total enrollment of the school, how many students are enrolled at St. Barnabas High School?

   (A) 8,000   (B) 720   (C) 800   (D) 960

   Ⓐ Ⓑ Ⓒ Ⓓ

30. Which of the following is an example of two similar figures?

   (F) a triangle and a square
   (G) any two rectangles
   (H) a father and his son
   (J) a photograph of a girl and an enlargement of this photograph

   Ⓕ Ⓖ Ⓗ Ⓙ

31. A rectangular garden plot is $x + 5$ feet in length and x feet in width. What is the perimeter, in feet, of this garden plot?

   (A) $2x + 5$ (B) $4x + 5$ (C) $4x + 20$
   (D) $4x + 10$

   Ⓐ Ⓑ Ⓒ Ⓓ

32. If $a + 4 = b + 1$, which of the following is true?

    (F) $a > b$ (G) $a = b$ (H) $b > a$
    (J) $a - b = 3$

    Ⓕ Ⓖ Ⓗ Ⓙ

33. When a certain number is divided by 3, the quotient is 8 and the remainder is 2. What is the number?

    (A) 13   (B) 26   (C) 22   (D) 25

    Ⓐ Ⓑ Ⓒ Ⓓ

34. On a motor trip Mr. Marino covered $\frac{1}{4}$ of his planned mileage the first day and $\frac{1}{6}$ of his planned mileage the second day. If he still had 350 miles to go, what was the total mileage that Mr. Marino planned to cover?

    (F) 600   (G) 500   (H) 450   (J) 400

    Ⓕ Ⓖ Ⓗ Ⓙ

35. If $3.9 \times 0.79 = 39 \times \square$, what is the value of $\square$?

    (A) 79   (B) 7.9   (C) .079   (D) 790

    Ⓐ Ⓑ Ⓒ Ⓓ

Answers—Diagnostic Test 8
Mathematics Concepts and Applications

1. **C**	10. **H**	19. **B**	28. **J**
2. **J**	11. **D**	20. **G**	29. **C**
3. **B**	12. **G**	21. **D**	30. **J**
4. **J**	13. **C**	22. **G**	31. **D**
5. **C**	14. **F**	23. **C**	32. **H**
6. **J**	15. **C**	24. **F**	33. **B**
7. **C**	16. **J**	25. **D**	34. **F**
8. **G**	17. **C**	26. **H**	35. **C**
9. **A**	18. **J**	27. **B**	

Rating Your Results

Superior	32–35 correct
Average	24–31 correct
Below Average	23 or fewer correct

Material to Review: Chapters 7–12

Explanations

1. **C**

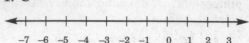

$$-7 \quad -6 \quad -5 \quad -4 \quad -3 \quad -2 \quad -1 \quad 0 \quad 1 \quad 2 \quad 3$$

If we examine the number line, we see that –7 is to the left of –3.
Therefore, $-3 > -7$.

2. **J** $\frac{1}{3} + \frac{1}{2} = \frac{2}{6} + \frac{3}{6} = \frac{5}{6}$ of the suits were blue or gray. Therefore, $\frac{1}{6}$ of the suits were brown.

$$\frac{1}{6} \times 144 = 24$$

3. **B**   Let x = gross income.
$0.30x = 8,400$
$$x = \frac{8,400}{0.30} = \frac{84,000}{3} = \$28,000$$

4. **J**   40 miles are covered in 1 hour, or 60 minutes.
Then 1 mile is covered in $\frac{60}{40}$ minutes.
$$\frac{60}{40} = \frac{3}{2} = 1\frac{1}{2}$$

5. **C**   The sentence $7 > \square > 3$ tells us that $\square$ is less than 7 and greater than 3. The numbers in the set 4, 5, 6 are less than 7 and greater than 3.

6. **J**   2 is the smallest prime number. If we divide 2 into 42, we have 21. 21 is not a prime number since $21 = 3 \times 7$. Since 3 and 7 are prime numbers, the prime factors of 42 are 2, 3, and 7.

7. **C**   Since X is located 2 units to the left of 0, X corresponds to the number –2.

8. **G** 7^5 means $7 \times 7 \times 7 \times 7 \times 7$. Also note that $(7^3)^2 = 7^6$, not 7^5.

9. **A** $180 \times \frac{3}{4} = 135$.

10. **H** $35\% = \frac{35}{100} = \frac{7}{20}$

11. **D**   Let x = cost of 20 gallons of gasoline. Then set up the proportion
$$\frac{19.62}{15} = \frac{x}{20}$$
$$15x = 20(19.62)$$
$$x = \frac{20(19.62)}{15} = \$26.16$$

12. **G** The number 8,675.49 has 6 in the hundreds place and 4 in the tenths place.

13. **C** In a right isosceles triangle the measures of the acute angles are equal. Since the measure of $\angle C$ is 90°, the measure of each acute angle is 45°.

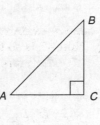

14. **F** The team wins 14 + 8 = 22 games. The total number of games played is 14 + 10 + 16 = 40.

$$40\overline{)22} = 0.55 = 55\%$$

15. **C** Let x = height ladder will reach. We use the Pythagorean theorem to obtain

$$x^2 + 6^2 = 10^2$$
$$x^2 + 36 = 100$$
$$x^2 = 100 - 36 = 64$$
$$x = \sqrt{64} = 8$$

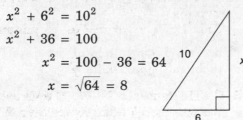

16. **J** If we replace x by 1, we have

$$3(1) - 1 < 5$$
$$3 - 1 < 5$$
$$2 < 5 \text{ true}$$

The replacement of x by any other choice will not yield a true sentence.

17. **C** The physics circle and the geometry circle intersect in the sectors marked 4 and 7.

$$4 + 7 = 11$$

18. **J** 4 quarts = 1 gallon
    1 quart = 32 fluid ounces
    2 gallons = 8 quarts = 8(32), or
    256 ounces
    $256 \div 8 = 32$

19. **B** $2x + 5 = 19$
    $2x = 19 - 5 = 14$
    $x = 14 \div 2 = 7$

20. **G** $A = 6s^2$

$$= 6\left(\frac{1}{3}\right)\left(\frac{1}{3}\right)$$
$$= \frac{6}{9}, \text{ or } \frac{2}{3}$$

21. **D** Let x = number of cups of milk to be used. Set up the proportion

$$\frac{3}{2\frac{1}{4}} = \frac{x}{1}$$
$$2\frac{1}{4}x = 3$$
$$\frac{9}{4}x = 3$$
$$x = 3 \div \frac{9}{4} = 3 \times \frac{4}{9} = 1\frac{1}{3}$$

22. **G** $480 \times \frac{1}{5} = 96$

$480 - 96 = 384$ gallons left after *November*

$384 \times \frac{1}{3} = 128$

$384 - 128 = 256$ gallons left after *December*

23. **C** According to the distributive property,
$$a(b + c) = a \times b + a \times c$$
Therefore,
$$48(360 + 295) = 48 \times 360 + 48 \times 295.$$

24. **F** The sum of the measures of the angles around a point in a plane is 360°. The fractional part of the expense budget that is represented by a sector whose central angle measures 80° is
$$\frac{80}{360} = \frac{2}{9}.$$

25. **D** A dozen pens cost 12 times as much as 1 pen. Since 1 pen costs y cents, 12 pens cost $12y$ cents.

26. **H** Let x = length of the bar needed. Set up the proportion
$$\frac{1}{x} = \frac{12}{32}$$
$$12x = 32$$
$$x = \frac{32}{12} = 2\frac{8}{12} = 2\frac{2}{3}$$

27. **B**   From 10:30 A.M. to noon is $1\frac{1}{2}$ hours. From noon to 1:15 P.M. is $1\frac{1}{4}$ hours. Thus, the plane flies

$$1\frac{1}{2} + 1\frac{1}{4} = 2\frac{3}{4} \text{ hours.}$$

$$2\frac{3}{4} = \frac{11}{4}, \quad \frac{11}{4} \times 420 = 1,155 \text{ miles}$$

28. **J**
$$3 \times \square + 2 = 17$$
$$3 \times \square = 17 - 2 = 15$$
$$\square = 15 \div 3 = 5$$

29. **C**   Let x = number of students enrolled at St. Barnabas High School

$$30\% = \frac{30}{100} = \frac{3}{10}$$

$$\frac{3}{10}x = 240$$

$$3x = 240(10) = 2400$$

$$x = 2400 \div 3 = 800$$

30. **J**   The photograph and its enlargement are similar because the two figures have corresponding angles of equal measure and sides whose lengths are in proportion.

31. **D**   To find the perimeter, we find the sum of the lengths of the sides:
$$x + x + 5 + x + x + 5 = 4x + 10$$

32. **H**   The given equation is $a + 4 = b + 1$. If we subtract 1 from both sides of this equation, we have
$$a + 3 = b$$
This result tells us that b is 3 more than a, or $b > a$.

33. **B**   Let x = unknown number.
$$\frac{x}{3} = 8 + \frac{2}{3}$$
$$x = 8(3) + 2 = 24 + 2 = 26$$

34. **F**   Let x = total mileage planned
$$\frac{1}{4} + \frac{1}{6} = \frac{3}{12} + \frac{2}{12} = \frac{5}{12}$$

Thus, Mr. Marino still had $\frac{7}{12}$ of his trip to cover.

$$\frac{7}{12}x = 350$$
$$7x = 12(350) = 4200$$
$$x = 4200 \div 7 = 600$$

35. **C** $39 \times \square = 3.9 \times 0.79$
We note that $39 = 10(3.9)$. If 3.9 is multiplied by 10 to equal 39, 0.79 must be divided by 10 to equal $\square$ if the equation is to be kept in balance. Thus, $\square = \frac{0.79}{10} = .079$.

STUDY PLAN

The amount of time required for a thorough study program in preparation for Test 8 will vary greatly from individual to individual. In general, there are three major areas to cover.

1. *Basic arithmetic*. This area will have been covered in preparation for Test 7. A knowledge of basic arithmetic is necessary in order to complete the solutions of problems on Tests 8. It is suggested that you cover Chapter 8, "Application of Basic Mathematical Skills," in some detail. The emphasis in this chapter on verbal problems and special topics will be found very helpful in developing problem solving skills.

2. *Algebra.* The algebra content on the Coop Examination is limited and is thoroughly covered in Chapters 9 and 10. In preparing for the test, you are advised to study these chapters carefully. The exercise material is especially useful preparation.

   The material in Chapter 12 on tables, maps, and graphs also anticipates likely test question.

3. *Geometry.* The geometry content required on the Coop Examination is also limited and is concisely covered in Chapter 12, which should be studied in detail.

Chapter 13, "Memory and Reasoning Skills," will help you develop resourcefulness in tackling a typical mathematical problem situation.

Test 9   Language Mechanics

Test 9 measures your ability to apply the rules of capitalization and punctuation in standard written English. The questions are not on the rules but, rather, on the application of the rules.

The Language Mechanics Test consists of three types of questions, 20 items in all.

Sample Questions

The three types of questions are described and exemplified below.

1. *Capitalization.* A sentence is divided into parts, each identified by a letter. You are required to tell which part of the sentence, if any, contains a word that should be capitalized. If no capital is required, the correct choice is "None."

EXAMPLE 1:

Of all the countries | in south america, |
      (A)   (B)
this is the one | she visits | most frequently.
  (C)   (D)
None
 (E)

EXPLANATION: The names of continents—in this case, South America—are capitalized. Therefore, the correct choice is **B**.

EXAMPLE 2:

Lucy says that | she is not impressed | by
  (F)   (G)
royal titles | or honorary degrees. None
 (H)   (J)   (K)

EXPLANATION: The first word of an indirect quotation is not capitalized, and no specific titles or degrees are mentioned. Therefore, the correct choice is **K**.

2. *Punctuation.* A sentence is followed by four punctuation marks, each identified by a letter. The fifth choice is "None." You are required to decide which punctuation mark, if any, is needed in the sentence.

EXAMPLE 1:

How often I have regretted the angry words I spoke

  (A) . (B) ? (C) ! (D) " " (E) None

EXPLANATION: A sentence that expresses strong emotion is followed by an exclamation point. Therefore, the correct choice is **C**.

EXAMPLE 2:

When the bear cub injured its paw on a rock the attendant called the vet.

  (F) . (G) , (H) ' (J) ; (K) None

EXPLANATION: An introductory adverbial clause—in this case, *When ... rock*—should be followed by a comma unless the clause is very short. Therefore, the correct choice is **G**. (The possessive pronoun *its* requires no apostrophe.)

3. *Capitalization and Punctuation.* A paragraph is presented, with certain parts underlined and numbered. For each such part five choices are given. You are required to read the paragraph and then choose the answer that shows the best capitalization and punctuation for each underlined, numbered part.

EXAMPLE:

The Hummingbird was so named, because
       1   2
its wings beat so rapidly that they make a

low humming sound. Because it is able to fly
   3
backward it can quickly—and safely remove
 4   5
it's long bill from the flowers. It spends the
 6
summer rushing from flower to flower to
 7
obtain nectar or tiny insects. It not only

helps to pollinate our Planet's plants but
           8
also rids them of insect pests.

1. (A) hummingbird, was
   (B) Hummingbird was,
   (C) Hummingbird was:
   (D) hummingbird was
   (E) Best as is

2. (F) named because
   (G) named. Because
   (H) named; Because
   (J) named; because
   (K) Best as is

3. (A) low, humming sound
   (B) low—humming sound
   (C) low—humming—sound
   (D) low humming, sound
   (E) Best as is

4. (F) backward. It
   (G) backward, it
   (H) backward; it
   (J) backward! it
   (K) Best as is

5. (A) quickly, and safely,
   (B) quickly, and safely
   (C) quickly and safely
   (D) quickly, and, safely
   (E) Best as is

6. (F) remove it's long, bill
   (G) remove its long bill
   (H) remove its' long bill
   (J) remove, its long bill
   (K) Best as is

7. (A) Summer, rushing
   (B) summer, rushing
   (C) Summer. Rushing
   (D) Summer rushing
   (E) Best as is

8. (F) Planet's plants
   (G) planets plant's
   (H) Planets' plants'
   (J) planet's plants
   (K) Best as is

Explanations

1. Common nouns are not capitalized; subjects and verbs are not separated by commas; there is no reason to place a comma or a colon after the verb. Therefore, the correct choice is **D**.

2. The verb and *because* should not be separated by a comma or other punctuation mark. Therefore, the correct choice is **F**.

3. Two adjectives (*low* and *humming*) should be separated by a comma. Therefore, the correct choice is **A**.

4. An introductory adverbial clause should be separated from the main clause by a comma. Therefore, the correct choice is **G**.

5. Compound modifiers (*quickly* and *safely*) joined by *and* do not require a comma or dash before the *and* or any punctuation after it. Therefore, the correct choice is **C**.

6. *It's* is a contraction of *it is*; here the possessive pronoun *its* is needed. There is no reason to place a comma after the adjective *long* or the verb *remove*. Therefore, the correct choice is **G**.

7. Names of the seasons are not capitalized, and no punctuation is needed after summer. Therefore, the correct choice is **E**.

8. The word *planet* is not capitalized, although the names of specific planets (Mars, Jupiter, Earth) are. Since planet is singular, the possessive is formed by adding an apostrophe and *s*: *planet's*. Therefore the correct choice is **J**.

STRATEGIES FOR SUCCESS

➤ For *capitalization,* follow these steps:

1. Read the sentence part by part, looking for an obvious error. Here are some examples:
   Omission of required capital

	Wrong	Right
name of person	helen smith	Helen Smith
name of place	new zealand	New Zealand
name of institution	notre dame university	Notre Dame University
title	professor Anderson	Professor Anderson
half of title	secretary of State	Secretary of State
half of name	mount St. Helens,	Mount St. Helens,
	New York city	New York City
	Mississippi river	Mississippi River

Incorrect addition of capital

	Wrong	Right
season	Autumn	autumn
relationship	my favorite Cousin	my favorite cousin
geographical area	nearby Mountains	nearby mountains
untitled institution	go to College	go to college

2. If nothing is obvious, go through the sentence again, checking each noun for an omitted or an unnecessary capital.

➤ For *punctuation,* follow these steps:

1. On first reading the sentence, look for an obvious error. Here are some examples:

Omission of required punctuation

	Wrong	Right
period	Dr Henderson	Dr. Henderson
apostrophe	peoples court	people's court
question mark	Who did it	Who did it?
comma in series	red white, and blue	red, white, and blue
exclamation point	What a night it was	What a night it was!

Incorrect addition of punctuation

	Wrong	Right
apostrophe	it's injured bark	its injured bark
comma	loud, and clear	loud and clear

2. If nothing is obvious, check each of the given choices for possible use in the sentence.

➤ For *combined capitalization and punctuation,* follow these steps.

1. Read the selection quickly to find out what it is about.

2. Locate the underlined section for each question in turn. Check all five choices as replacements in the sentence. Here, too, look for obvious errors first. Make certain that you check every choice before marking the answer sheet.

➤ For the *test as a whole,* remember these strategies:

1. If you wind up with two (or three) possibilities, put a circle around the number of the question and leave it.

2. Don't spend time agonizing. Plan to come back to the circled items if time permits. Very often the break gives your subconscious time to work, and when you return for the second try, the answer becomes clear.

3. Since there is no penalty on this test for guessing, select the most likely choice before finally abandoning an item. Then, unless you realize that you have made an obvious error, do not change your answer. Usually, the first guess is the better one!

Diagnostic Test 9   Language Mechanics

DIRECTIONS: For numbers 1–6, determine which part of the sentence, if any, has a word that requires a capital letter.

---

1. For how many months | of the year | does the sun | shine on Mars?   None
    (A)   (B)   (C)   (D)   (E)

Ⓐ Ⓑ Ⓒ Ⓓ Ⓔ

2. My mother | went to the reception | for the local celebrity | governor Elson.   None
    (F)   (G)   (H)   (J)   (K)

Ⓕ Ⓖ Ⓗ Ⓙ Ⓚ

3. Of all the holidays, | I enjoy the best of gifts, | christmas, | because of the weather.   None
    (A)   (B)   (C)   (D)   (E)

Ⓐ Ⓑ Ⓒ Ⓓ Ⓔ

4. The great depression | was one of | the outstanding events | of the twentieth century. None
   (F)   (G)   (H)   (J)   (K)

Ⓕ Ⓖ Ⓗ Ⓙ Ⓚ

5. We traveled westward | to reach the far east | in a giant | jet plane. None
   (A)   (B)   (C)   (D)   (E)

Ⓐ Ⓑ Ⓒ Ⓓ Ⓔ

6. "Don't leave now!" | Phyllis implored. | "the festivities | are about to commence." None
   (F)   (G)   (H)   (J)   (K)

Ⓕ Ⓖ Ⓗ Ⓙ Ⓚ

DIRECTIONS: For numbers 7–12, determine what punctuation, if any, is required in this sentence.

---

7. I cannot do the cooking set the table, and listen to you at the same time.

   (A) . (B) , (C) ; (D) ' (E) None

   Ⓐ Ⓑ Ⓒ Ⓓ Ⓔ

8. Our teacher, Sister Helen told us about the new system.

   (F) " " (G) , (H) ! (J) : (K) None

   Ⓕ Ⓖ Ⓗ Ⓙ Ⓚ

9. I admit the pie is a failure however, you can see from the mess that I made that I really tried.

   (A) : (B) . (C) ; (D) ? (E) None

   Ⓐ Ⓑ Ⓒ Ⓓ Ⓔ

10. Theres never a dull moment when Howard is around.

    (F) , (G) ; (H) ' (J) . (K) None

    Ⓕ Ⓖ Ⓗ Ⓙ Ⓚ

11. Alice threatened to go immediately to the dean and report the entire incident.

    (A) ; (B) , (C) ! (D) ? (E) None

    Ⓐ Ⓑ Ⓒ Ⓓ Ⓔ

12. He is all wrong, but how can I tell him so

    (F) : (G) ? (H) , (J) " " (K) None

    Ⓕ Ⓖ Ⓗ Ⓙ Ⓚ

DIRECTIONS: For numbers 13–20, read the passage and note the underlined, numbered parts. Select the answer that shows the best capitalization and punctuation for each part.

The American chestnut tree, earlier in this century, was almost wiped
                  13   14

out by parasite, a Fungus that invades the tree through an injury to the
               15   16

bark the same blight is now attacking certain oak trees in the south.
      17   18

Although no fungicide is available to kill the parasite there is hope for
                                 19

members of this family, these trees are doing a fine job of resisting the
                  20

killing organism.

13. (A) The american chestnut tree,
    (B) The american 'chestnut tree'
    (C) The American Chestnut Tree
    (D) The American, Chestnut tree
    (E) Best as is

    Ⓐ Ⓑ Ⓒ Ⓓ Ⓔ

14. (F) earlier in this century
    (G) earlier in This Century
    (H) earlier in this Century,
    (J) earlier in this Century
    (K) Best as is

    Ⓕ Ⓖ Ⓗ Ⓙ Ⓚ

15. (A) parasite. A fungus that
    (B) parasite, a fungus that
    (C) parasite a fungus that
    (D) parasite; a Fungus that
    (E) Best as is

    Ⓐ Ⓑ Ⓒ Ⓓ Ⓔ

16. (F) invade's the tree through
    (G) invades' the tree through
    (H) invades, the tree through
    (J) invades the tree, through
    (K) Best as is

    Ⓕ Ⓖ Ⓗ Ⓙ Ⓚ

17. (A) bark! the same blight
    (B) bark: the same blight
    (C) bark, the same blight
    (D) bark. The same blight
    (E) Best as is

    Ⓐ Ⓑ Ⓒ Ⓓ Ⓔ

18. (F) Oak trees in the South
    (G) Oak Trees in the south
    (H) oak trees in the South
    (J) Oak Trees in the South
    (K) Best as is

    Ⓕ Ⓖ Ⓗ Ⓙ Ⓚ

19. (A) parasite; there is
    (B) parasite. There is
    (C) parasite, there is
    (D) parasite: there is
    (E) Best as is

    Ⓐ Ⓑ Ⓒ Ⓓ Ⓔ

20. (F) family these trees
    (G) family, these trees'
    (H) family these tree's
    (J) family. These trees
    (K) Best as is

    Ⓕ Ⓖ Ⓗ Ⓙ Ⓚ

Answers—Diagnostic Test 9 Language Mechanics

1. E	6. H	11. E	16. K
2. J	7. B	12. G	17. D
3. C	8. G	13. E	18. H
4. F	9. C	14. K	19. C
5. B	10. H	15. B	20. J

Rating Your Results

Superior	17–20 correct
Average	13–16 correct
Below Average	12 or fewer correct

Material to Review: Chapter 6

Explanations

1. **E** The word *sun* is capitalized only in a scientific sense. The name of a specific planet (*Mars*) is correctly capitalized.

2. **J** A title preceding a name (*Governor Elson*) is capitalized.

3. **C** The name of a holiday (*Christmas*) is capitalized.

4. **F** Historical events (*Great Depression*) are capitalized; *twentieth century* is not.

5. **B** The name of specific geographical area (*Far East*) is capitalized. A word denoting direction (*westward*) is not.

6. **H** Each complete sentence in a long direct quotation begins with a capital letter (*The*).

7. **B** A comma takes the place of the missing *and* in a series (*do the cooking, set...*).

8. **G** Two commas are used with a term in apposition (*teacher, Sister Helen,*).

9. **C** When used to join two clauses, *however* is preceded by a semicolon (*... failure; however,...*).

10. **H** An apostrophe is used to designate a missing letter (*There's = There is*).

11. **E** Compound elements—in this case two infinitives, *to go* and (*to*) *report*— are not separated by a comma (*...dean and report...*).

12. **C** An interrogative sentence is followed by a question mark.

13. **E** An adjective derived from the name of a country is capitalized (*American*); names of trees are not.

14. **K** The word *century* is not capitalized; parenthetical elements inserted between the subject (*tree*) and the verb (*was wiped out*) are set off by commas.

15. **B** A period or semicolon after *parasite* would create a sentence fragment; *fungus* is not capitalized.

16. **K** The third person singular form of the verb (*invades*) requires no apostrophe; a preposition (*through*) is not normally preceded by a comma.

17. **D** A period and a capital letter (*bark. The*) separate two complete thoughts.

18. **H** There is no reason to capitalize *oak trees*. The noun *South* is capitalized because it designates a specific area of the country.

19. **C** The introductory adverbial clause, *Although...parasite* is properly set off by a comma.

20. **J** Since *These trees...organism* is a complete idea following a complete idea (*Although...family*), it must be preceded by a period (*family. These*), not a comma.

STUDY PLAN

The key to improving your score in this area is the amount of time you can spend on the rules and exercises for capitalization and punctuation in Chapter 6, Language Arts.

Long-Term Program

1. The *capitalization* area is highly limited. Within a relatively short time, you can master the most important rules. Two or three 15-minute sessions can lead to full control.

2. For *punctuation,* the major hurdle is mastery of the rules for the most frequently used symbols: period, comma, colon, semicolon, question mark, exclamation point, and quotation marks. Check the rules and examples for each, and master one punctuation mark before proceeding to the next. Here, too, short but frequent study sessions bring the best results.

3. Use all of the varied exercises and practice tests to increase and to test your control of the capitalization and punctuation rules.

4. As the final step in your preparation, take the Practice Cooperative Admissions Examinations, in the last section of this book.

Crash Program

1. Since the field is so limited, memorize the rules of *capitalization*. Two or three 15-minute sessions are all that most students require. Then do the practice test on capitalization to check your mastery of the rules.

2. For *punctuation,* concentrate your study time on the exercises and practice tests. Check your answers with the answer key to find out which rules you need to study.

3. Use the Practice Cooperative Admissions Examinations, in the last section of this book, as your final step in preparation.

Test 10 Language Expression

Test 10 is a measure of your competence in written language usage. All the items on the test are based on the rules of standard written English, the form of language used in the textbooks that you will study in high school.

The field is so wide that the variety of possible questions becomes immense. Below you will find examples of the types of questions included in recent tests. However, you should be prepared for variations from this sampling.

Recent Language Expression Tests consisted of 8 basic types of questions, 32 items in all.

Sample Questions

1. *Use of Connectives.* This type of item consists of one or two sentences that contain a blank. You are required to select from four choices the connective word that best completes the single sentence or joins the two sentences.

EXAMPLE 1:

Permission was not granted for the interview. _____ the reporter never gave up hope.

    (A) Therefore (B) Nevertheless
      (C) Because (D) Hence

EXPLANATION: *Because* would create a sentence fragment. *Therefore* and *Hence* do not make sense. *Nevertheless* shows the proper relationship between the thoughts in the two sentences. Therefore, the correct choice is **B**.

EXAMPLE 2:

The automobile dealer repossessed the car _____ the payments weren't made.

    (F) although (G) besides (H) also
      (J) because

EXPLANATION: The only answer that makes sense is *because*, which introduces a reason. Therefore, the correct choice is **J**.

2. *Identifying Correct Sentences.* This type of item evaluates your ability to distinguish among complete sentences—that is, those that are acceptable as standard written English—run-on sentences, and sentence fragments. You are asked to choose the correct sentence from a group of four.

EXAMPLE 3:

(A) At the end of the trial, when the truth was finally known.
(B) The trial ended the truth was finally known.
(C) When the trial ended and the truth was finally known.
(D) At the end of the trial, the truth was finally known.

EXPLANATION: Choices A and C are sentence fragments, and choice B is a run-on sentence. Choice **D** is correctly written and therefore is the right choice.

3. *Use of Various Parts of Speech.* This type of question tests your knowledge of the correct usage of nouns, pronouns, verbs, and other parts of speech.

- A sentence with a blank is presented, and you are required to select, from four choices, the answer that is acceptable usage in standard written English. You are not asked to give the grammatical reason why the form you choose is acceptable.

EXAMPLE 4:

He just _____ interest in hockey.

(F) hasn't no
(G) hasn't got no
(H) hasn't any
(J) hasn't gotten no

EXPLANATION: Choices F, G, and J contain double negatives and hence say the opposite of what is meant. Therefore, the correct choice is **H**.

EXAMPLE 5:

Of the two brothers Mario is by far the _____ .

(A) quicker
(B) more quicker
(C) quickest
(D) most quickest

EXPLANATION: Quicker is used for two; quickest is used for three or more. More and most are unnecessary because they repeat the sense of the suffixes -er and -est. Therefore, the correct choice is **A**.

- Four sentences are presented, and you are asked to choose the one in which the verbs are used correctly.

EXAMPLE 6:

(F) Every time it snowed, we have to clear the driveway.
(G) As the burly stranger strutted toward me, I realized that I will have trouble.

(H) They could have been most helpful if you had taken the time to explain the problem to them.

(J) The hour hand of the clock was approaching five, and they know that the time for fun was fast coming to a close.

EXPLANATION: In choice F, since *snowed* is past tense, *had* is required. In choice G, the past tenses *strutted* and *realized* require *would,* the past tense of *will.* In choice J, *was approaching* is past, and the past tense *knew* is required.

In choice **H**, the verb forms are correct: *could have been* is past, and the past perfect *had taken* is required for action that would have preceded it.

4. *Writing for Clarity—Dangling and Misplaced Elements.* This type of question tests your ability to deal with sentence faults that cause loss of clarity. Included are dangling and misplaced elements, lack of parallel structure, and ambiguous antecedents. You are required to select from four choices the one that is most clearly written. You are not asked to identify the fault.

EXAMPLE 7:

(A) When looking at the high cost, the trip is definitely not worth the expense involved.

(B) Looking at the high cost, the trip is definitely not worth the cost involved.

C) The trip is definitely not worth the expense involved, looking at the high cost.

(D) Looking at the high cost, I realize that the trip is definitely not worth the expense involved.

EXPLANATION: The participle *looking* must have a correct word to modify. Choice **D** is the only one that supplies that word; *I,* not *trip,* was *looking.*

EXAMPLE 8:

(F) She can now use for minor luxuries the money formerly spent for child care.

(G) For minor luxuries she can now use the money formerly spent for child care.

(H) She can for minor luxuries now use the money formerly spent for child care.

(J) For minor luxuries the money she formerly spent for child care she can now use.

EXPLANATION: *For minor luxuries* tells how she can now use the money and should be placed near the verb *can use.* Therefore, the correct choice is **F**.

EXAMPLE 9:

(A) The booklet clearly instructed us to write in ink and that we should use only one side of the paper.

(B) The booklet clearly instructed us that we must write in ink and to use only one side of the paper.

(C) The booklet clearly instructed us to write in ink and to use only one side of the paper.

(D) The booklet clearly instructed us that when writing in ink, we should use only one side of the paper.

EXPLANATION: For parallel structure the conjunction *and* should connect two elements of the same kind—for example, two infinitives (*to write, to use*) or two clauses (*that we must write in ink, that we should use*). Choice D is wrong because it contains a change in meaning. The correct choice is **C**.

EXAMPLE 10:

Nan told her mother <u>that if she did not give her money she could not go</u>.

(F) that if her mother did not give her the money she could not go

(G) that if she did not give her the money her mother could not go

(H) "If you do not give me the money, I cannot go."

(J) Best as is

EXPLANATION: The only way to express the meaning clearly without awkward repetition of *Nan* and *her mother* is to use a direct quotation. Therefore, the best choice is **H**.

5. *Combining Sentences.* Each of these questions consists of two underlined sentences and four choices in which the two sentences are combined. You are required to identify the sentence that is a clear and correct combination.

EXAMPLE 11:

<u>Sarah warned her friends not to call that night. Sarah needed all the time to study for the big test</u>.

(A) Sarah warned her friends not to call that night, and Sarah needed all the time to study for the big test.
(B) After warning her friends not to call that night, Sarah needed all the time to study for the big test.
(C) Sarah warned her friends not to call that night because she needed all the time to study for the big test.
(D) Warning her friends not to call that night, Sarah needed all the time to study for the big test.

EXPLANATION: C is correct because it shows the causal relationship between the warning and the need to study for the test.

EXAMPLE 12:

<u>The procession moved slowly down Main Street. Thousands of loyal fans lined both sides of Main Street</u>.

(F) When thousands of loyal fans lined both sides of Main Street, the procession moved slowly down Main Street.
(G) The procession having moved slowly down Main Street, the thousands of loyal fans lined the street.
(H) Moving slowly down Main Street, thousands of loyal fans watched the procession.
(J) The loyal fans who lined both sides of Main Street watched the procession move slowly by.

EXPLANATION: Choices F and G establish a time relationship that does not exist in the original sentences. In choice H the loyal fans are moving down the street. Choice **J** is the best combination.

6. ***Identifying the Topic Sentence.*** Each of these questions contains a brief paragraph. You are required to select, from the four choices that follow, the most suitable topic sentence for the paragraph.

EXAMPLE 13:

_____ It ran from San Antonio, Texas, to Abilene, Kansas. It was used for more than 20 years after the Civil War. In 1872 alone, almost 500,000 Texas longhorns used it as the trail leading to the slaughter houses. Today remnants still remain along the route of the Sante Fe Railroad.

(A) The Chisholm Trail was marked by both dull routines and unexpected danger.
(B) In the nineteenth century the best-known meat supply route was the Chisholm Trail.
(C) Many people believed that the Chisholm Trail helped to unify our country.
(D) Many a young cowhand learned the ropes on the Chisholm Trail.

EXPLANATION: Choice A mentions routines and dangers, C deals with unification, D tells of young cowhands—none of these topics is developed in the paragraph. The phrase meat supply route in choice B is the key to the content of the selection. **B** is therefore the correct answer.

7. ***Development of the Paragraph.*** In these questions you are given a topic sentence followed by four pairs of sentences. Three of the choices are related only partially or not at all to the topic sentence. You are required to identify the pair of sentences that best develops the topic sentence.

EXAMPLE 14:

"Big Ben" is the name of more than just a clock in the tower of the Houses of Parliament in London.

(F) The bell was named after Sir Benjamin Hall. He was an official in charge of public construction.
(G) Big Ben is one of the chief tourist attractions in London. Every year thousands of people from all over the world visit the tower to see and hear the famous clock.
(H) Actually, the largest clock in London is not Big Ben. That distinction belongs to the clock on top of Shell-Mex House, a commercial building.

(J) At first, "Big Ben" was the name of only the bell that rings the hours. Now it is also the name of the tower that houses both the clock and the bell.

EXPLANATION: Only the two sentences that explain why "Big Ben" is the *name of more than just a clock* are relevant. Therefore, the best choice is **J**.

8. *Identifying Unrelated Sentences.* In this type of question you are given a paragraph of four sentences and are required to identify the sentence that does not belong in the paragraph.

EXAMPLE 15:

1. In 1792, Congress adopted the bald eagle for the design of the Great Seal of the United States.
2. It was chosen as a symbol of strength and liberty.
3. Today the bald eagle is on the endangered species list.
4. Ben Franklin objected to the choice of a bird of prey to represent the new nation.

(A) Sentence 1
(B) Sentence 2
(C) Sentence 3
(D) Sentence 4

EXPLANATION: Sentence 3 describing the present status of the bald eagle is not related to the discussion of the Great Seal of the United States. The correct choice is **C**.

STRATEGIES FOR SUCCESS

➤ *Use of connectives*

This type of question contains the clues you need to spot the correct choice. The clues may lie in the content or in the punctuation.

1. Content clues. Test each choice by placing it mentally into the blank space. Often you can eliminate one or more possibilities because the result is a sentence that lacks meaning or is self-contradictory.
2. Punctuation clues. Look for internal punctuation before or after the blank. A conjunctive adverb such as *however, moreover,* or *consequently*

requires either a preceding period or a preceding semicolon, and a following comma: *For weeks she refused to see me. However, I never became discouraged.* Without such punctuation, these choices can be eliminated.

If, however, the blank is preceded by a comma, a conjunction such as *and, but, or,* or *so* is needed: They said the price was reasonable, but we disagree emphatically.

➤ *Identifying correct sentences*

The essential first step is to read the four choices word by word for units of thought. In most instances, this close reading will result in a tentative choice. To prevent carelessness, however, make certain that you recheck the other choices for units of thought before marking the answer sheet.

The following tests can help:

1. A *run-on sentence* contains two or more ideas that may or may not be separated by a comma: Don't try to fool me, you knew it all the time!
2. A *complete sentence* may contain (*a*) one main idea: Just let me show you the picture; (*b*) two main ideas connected by a conjunction such as *and, but, or,* or *so*: We will go to the party, or the party will come to us; or (*c*) a main idea and one or more dependent ideas introduced by a connecting word: I went to the meet because I care.
3. A sentence fragment does not make sense; it requires an addition: When I saw the accident in front of my house.

➤ *Use of various parts of speech*

1. Look first for the obvious, the glaring error. Below are some errors that fit this description:

Double negative:	I don't want nothing (*anything*).
Incorrect verb form:	He has broke (*broken*) my pen.
Incorrect pronoun:	Give it to Meg and I (*me*).

Lack of agreement of subject and verb:	One of the fires were (*was*) put out.
Confusion of adjective and adverb:	I did good (*well*) on that test.
Needless word:	This here (*This*) is the one I want.

You will find a more complete list of problem areas in the section entitled Standard American Usage in Chapter 6.

2. To avoid carelessly making the second best choice, eliminate the three other choices before writing on the answer sheet.
3. If in doubt, rely on the level of usage you find in books assigned in school.

➤ *Writing for clarity*

1. Since various errors are involved, the first thing to do is to read the four sentences word for word. A comparison of the sentences will often pinpoint the error.
2. Look for obvious errors first: dangling elements, misplaced sentence elements, ambiguous antecedents, lack of parallelism.
3. If the best choice is not obvious, use the process of elimination. Eliminate the obviously wrong answers. What remains usually provides the needed clue as to what the error is.
4. To avoid making a careless mistake, eliminate the other choice a second time before marking the answer sheet.

➤ *Combining sentences*

1. Read the two sentences word by word to learn what they are about.
2. Keep in mind that, if there is an area of repetition, it can involve the doers (subjects), the action (verbs), or the receivers of the action (objects). Before writing, try to eliminate the repetition. Be certain to make any needed grammatical adjustment to the rest of the sentence.

3. If there appears to be a time sequence, try to combine the two sentences by using a time word: *before, when, while, during, after, since.* Again, before picking up your pen, test to see that your combination does not change the meaning of the two sentences.
4. If there appears to be a causal relationship, try to combine the two sentences by using a causal word or phrase: *because, since, therefore, consequently, as a result.* Again, before indicating your answer, check to see that you have not changed the meaning of the sentences.
5. As a final check, make sure that your combination is a correct sentence and not a run-on sentence or sentence fragment.

➤ *Identifying the topic sentence*

1. Read the short paragraph carefully.
2. Ask yourself, "What is this paragraph about?"
3. If you are unsure what the topic is, reread the paragraph.
4. Now consider each answer choice. List it by asking, "Does this sentence deal directly with the topic? Does it lead naturally into the rest of the paragraph?"
5. Eliminate choices that do not pass the test.
6. Before marking the answer sheet, read the complete paragraph with your choice inserted as the topic sentence. Are you satisfied that you have selected the best answer?

➤ *Development of the paragraph*

To handle questions on paragraph unity, follow these steps:
1. Read the topic sentence word for word before looking at the choices. Try to pick out the key words: The *computer* has *revolutionized* the world of *youth.*
2. Read the four choices through once; then go over them a second time to eliminate the pair that is most obviously off the topic. If you can, decide next on a second irrelevant pair.

3. Now try to find the pair that definitely develops the topic sentence. Keep in mind the key words.

➤ *Identifying the unrelated sentence*

1. Read the entire paragraph sentence by sentence.
2. Find the topic sentence and underline the key words: The *computer* has *revolutionized* the world of *youth*. This sentence can now be eliminated as an incorrect choice.
3. Read the other three choices word by word to see how they develop or relate to the key words in the topic sentence. Use the process of elimination to decide on the one unrelated sentence.

➤ *For all types of questions, keep these recommendations in mind:*

1. Don't dawdle. If you can't decide on the correct choice in a reasonable time, circle the item number and return to the question later—if time permits.
2. Since no credit is deducted for wrong answers, when you return to an item, eliminate, if you can, any obviously wrong choices. Then, if no one answer seems clearly right, select the one that you consider most appropriate—and do not change it without good reason. Usually the first choice is the best one.
3. Take the Diagnostic Test.
4. Turn to the appropriate sections in Chapter 6, Language Arts, for a digest of rules and exercises and practice tests.
5. Take the Practice Cooperative Admissions Examinations in the final section of this book.

Diagnostic Test 10
Language Expression

When you take this Diagnostic Test, simulate examination conditions as closely as you can. Choose a quiet time of the day and a quiet room. Try to avoid interruptions. Concentrate on the test and give it your undivided attention.

DIRECTIONS: For numbers 1–9, select the word that best completes the sentence.

1. There was an extremely heavy rain Saturday night. _____ the storm was over, the streams were overflowing

   (A) Because
   (B) After
   (C) Anyway
   (D) Therefore

   Ⓐ Ⓑ Ⓒ Ⓓ

2. Helen did not like the movie at all; _____ , she was willing to leave before the first intermission.

   (F) meanwhile
   (G) however
   (H) because
   (J) consequently

   Ⓕ Ⓖ Ⓗ Ⓙ

3. Congress passed the bill only after long hours of debate _____ there were strong feelings on both sides.

   (A) nevertheless
   (B) since
   (C) also
   (D) so

   Ⓐ Ⓑ Ⓒ Ⓓ

4. The swimming pool was originally intended for the exclusive use of the members, _____ it is now open to visitors as well.

   (F) since
   (G) but
   (H) meanwhile
   (J) and

   Ⓕ Ⓖ Ⓗ Ⓙ

5. I could have lost the notebook when I _____ to run up the stairs.

   (A) begin
   (B) began
   (C) begun
   (D) beginned

   Ⓐ Ⓑ Ⓒ Ⓓ

6. Stan and _____ will be there on time.

   (F) myself
   (G) I
   (H) me
   (J) me myself

   Ⓕ Ⓖ Ⓗ Ⓙ

7. Of the three, Beth has always been the _____ sport.

   (A) better
   (B) more better
   (C) best
   (D) most best

   Ⓐ Ⓑ Ⓒ Ⓓ

8. _____ ready to leave now.

   (F) There
   (G) Their
   (H) They're
   (J) Theyre

   Ⓕ Ⓖ Ⓗ Ⓙ

9. Between _____ , she should have listened more carefully.

   (A) I and you
   (B) you and me
   (C) you and I
   (D) you and myself

   Ⓐ Ⓑ Ⓒ Ⓓ

DIRECTIONS: For numbers 10–12, choose the sentence that is correctly written.

10. (F) None of us spoke to him he was an outcast as far as we were concerned.

   (G) Because he was an outcast since none of us were speaking to him.
   (H) With none of us speaking to him because he was an outcast.
   (J) None of us spoke to him since he was an outcast as far as we were concerned.

   Ⓕ Ⓖ Ⓗ Ⓙ

11. (A) Depressed because he had not been invited to the meeting, Frank decided to take a long walk in the woods.

   (B) Frank decided to take a long walk in the woods, he was depressed because he had not been invited to the meeting.
   (C) When Frank was depressed because he had not been invited to the meeting and was therefore taking a long walk in the woods.
   (D) Because he had not been invited to the meeting, Frank was depressed he took a long walk in the woods.

   Ⓐ Ⓑ Ⓒ Ⓓ

12. (F) It all happened during the dress rehearsal, whatever could go wrong, did.

   (G) During the dress rehearsal, whatever could go wrong, did.
   (H) When we held the dress rehearsal, it was fantastic, everything seemed to go wrong.
   (J) As the dress rehearsal progressed and everything seemed to be going wrong.

   Ⓕ Ⓖ Ⓗ Ⓙ

DIRECTIONS: For numbers 13–16, choose the sentence that is most clearly written.

13. (A) After traveling widely throughout our country, the seacoast is still my favorite place.

   (B) The seacoast is still my favorite place after traveling widely throughout our country.
   (C) The seacoast is still my favorite place when traveling widely throughout our country.
   (D) After traveling widely throughout our country, I still enjoy the seacoast most.

   Ⓐ Ⓑ Ⓒ Ⓓ

14. (F) It is a miracle that old magicians can perform.
    (G) It is a miracle that can be performed by oldtime magicians.
    (H) It is a miracle that old magicians can work.
    (J) It is what I call a miracle that old magicians can perform.

    Ⓕ Ⓖ Ⓗ Ⓙ

15. (A) Brian told his father that his solution was more logical.
    (B) Brian told his father that his was the more logical solution.
    (C) Brian told his father, "Your solution is more logical."
    (D) Brian told his father that the solution he offered was more logical.

    Ⓐ Ⓑ Ⓒ Ⓓ

16. (F) She began to lose her desire to improve her typing skills after a time.
    (G) After a time she began to lose her desire to improve her typing skills.
    (H) Her typing skills she began to lose her desire to improve after a time.
    (J) Her desire to improve her typing skills she began to lose after a time.

    Ⓕ Ⓖ Ⓗ Ⓙ

DIRECTIONS: For numbers 17 and 18, choose the sentence that uses verbs correctly.

17. (A) The alarm bell rang and all of the workers run to their stations.
    (B) Even though she had been absent all last week because of illness, she achieved top grades on today's tests.
    (C) After things have quieted down, I began studying again.
    (D) A fight is in progress, and a crowd gathered around to watch the awkward spectacle.

    Ⓐ Ⓑ Ⓒ Ⓓ

18. (F) The teacher walked into the room, and the lesson starts immediately.
    (G) He has been standing in the doorway for hours and refuses to let us close the door.

(H) While the instructor lectures the class, the students took notes.
(J) Even though there was frost in the air, the children will refuse to wear their mittens.

    Ⓕ Ⓖ Ⓗ Ⓙ

DIRECTIONS: For numbers 19–22, read the underlined sentences. Choose the sentence that best combines the two sentences into one.

19. The current was very swift.
    Susanna was unable to swim to shore.

    (A) The current was very swift since Susanna was unable to swim to shore.
    (B) The current was very swift, but Susanna was unable to swim to shore.
    (C) The current being very swift and Susanna being unable to swim to shore.
    (D) Because the current was very swift, Susanna was unable to swim to shore.

    Ⓐ Ⓑ Ⓒ Ⓓ

20. You must preheat the oven.
    Then you can put the rolls in to bake.

    (F) You can put the rolls in to bake, and you must preheat the oven.
    (G) Preheat the oven before putting the rolls in to bake.
    (H) To put the rolls in to bake, you preheat the oven.
    (J) Preheating the oven, put the rolls in to bake.

    Ⓕ Ⓖ Ⓗ Ⓙ

21. The winters here are mild. I cannot say the same thing for the summers.

    (A) The winters here are mild, and I cannot say the same thing about the summers.
    (B) The winters here being mild, I cannot say the same thing about the summers.
    (C) Although the winters here are mild, I cannot say the same thing about the summers.

(D) When the winters here are mild, I cannot say the same thing about the summers.

Ⓐ Ⓑ Ⓒ Ⓓ

22. <u>There is a roadside stand just outside Lucerne. You can buy your fresh corn there</u>.

(F) There is a roadside stand just outside Lucerne where you can buy your fresh corn.

(G) There is a roadside stand just outside Lucerne, but you can buy your fresh corn there.

(H) Just outside Lucerne there is a roadside stand where you can buy your fresh corn.

(J) Being just outside Lucerne, you can buy your fresh corn at the roadside stand.

Ⓕ Ⓖ Ⓗ Ⓙ

DIRECTIONS: For numbers 23–25, choose the topic sentence that best fits the paragraph.

23. _____ Thousands of years ago, prehistoric people had no safety pins, snaps, or buttons. They used thorns to clasp together their animal-skin capes. Thorns definitely were not then the nuisance that they are to the gardeners of today.

(A) Living in unheated caves, our early ancestors used animal skins to protect them from the cold.

(B) Our early ancestors discovered early the advantage of garments made from skins of animals.

(C) Life is much more comfortable for us than it was for our early ancestors.

(D) Our early ancestors had a special need for thorns.

Ⓐ Ⓑ Ⓒ Ⓓ

24. _____ The store of oral literature has grown immensely since the beginning of African society. Notable are the countless proverbs that convey the accepted social code. The many myths and legends explain the origins and development of states.

(F) Early African storytellers entertained the tribal units around the campfires.

(G) Brilliant storytellers enriched the lives of early inhabitants of Africa.

(H) Today stories cannot only be told; they can be printed as well.

(J) Africa has a rich and varied literature that has been passed on by word of mouth.

Ⓕ Ⓖ Ⓗ Ⓙ

25. _____ Is it one of the towering, multifloored skyscrapers that have mushroomed in the big cities of the world? Or is it the Vatican Palace in Vatican City, the home of the Pope and his administrative leaders? It covers 13 acres, contains more than 11,000 rooms, and has more than 200 staircases.

(A) Which building would you call the most beautiful one in existence in the world of today?

(B) Can you name the building that is most admired today?

(C) Which building you consider the largest in the world depends on what you mean by largest.

(D) Which of all the buildings in existence today has the best chance of surviving into the thirtieth century?

Ⓐ Ⓑ Ⓒ Ⓓ

DIRECTIONS: For numbers 26–29, select the pair of sentences that best develops the topic sentence.

26. Birdwatchers seem to vary in the number of species they observe and can identify.

(F) Birdwatching is an absorbing and enjoyable hobby. Many people agree with Roger Tory Peterson, who wrote, "I, for one, would find the world quite desolate if the birds were eliminated."

(G) Any interested person can find birds to observe and study—even in big cities. In the spring and fall thousands of migrating birds pause to rest in Central Park in the shadow of New York City skyscrapers.

(H) Building a large life list is not in itself a major goal. Many people enjoy watching birds even if they cannot identify them.

(J) The average amateur logs and classifies in a lifetime about 300 species at the most. Some few serious birders, however, have seen more than 600 species north of the Mexican border.

Ⓕ Ⓖ Ⓗ Ⓙ

27. Some physicians intentionally place barriers between themselves and their patients.

(A) Such medical practitioners use terms like *hematoma* for a bruise and *alopecia* for baldness. Most medical doctors still write prescriptions with Latin abbreviations that are not understood by patients.

(B) Many doctors have assistants to help them maintain contact with their patients. The aids in a busy office can anticipate a misunderstanding of procedures and give simple explanations.

(C) Computerized equipment is invaluable to the modern doctor. It has greatly increased the diagnostic potential of the profession.

(D) So complicated is some of the medical equipment in use today that a new profession, medical engineering, has resulted. The medical engineer develops, operates, and maintains highly sophisticated devices and machines.

Ⓐ Ⓑ Ⓒ Ⓓ

28. Irving Berlin, who was born in 1888, wrote some of our best-loved songs.

(F) Irving Berlin's father was a rabbi. His parents emigrated to the United States from Russia.

(G) The family was very poor, and as a boy Irving began to contribute to its income. At age 14 he was working as a singing waiter.

(H) Perhaps his most popular song is "White Christmas," introduced by Bing Crosby in the motion picture *Holiday Inn.* Another favorite is "God Bless America," which Kate Smith made famous during World War II.

(J) Mr. Berlin did not participate in any of the nationwide celebrations of his hundredth birthday. He died in September 1989.

Ⓕ Ⓖ Ⓗ Ⓙ

29. Of all the national parks Mesa Verde Colorado has a unique distinction.

(A) The visitor to Mesa Verde can see at least one ruin of each type of habitation once occupied by prehistoric Indians. First came the pit house, then the pueblo, and finally the cliff dwelling.

(B) Before the ruins in Mesa Verde came under the protection of the National Park Service, some were badly damaged by careless people. Today no one can enter a cliff dwelling unless accompanied by a ranger.

(C) Vandalism is a major, ever-increasing problem in all the national parks. So is the trend toward commercialism and exploitation of the natural resources the various parks contain.

(D) Mesa Verde is the only park that was set aside for preservation primarily for its historical significance rather than its natural features. This park is regarded as the key to the puzzle of the now-vanished cultures once dominant in the Southwest.

Ⓐ Ⓑ Ⓒ Ⓓ

DIRECTIONS: For numbers 30–32, read the paragraph. Then choose the sentence that does *not* belong in the paragraph.

30. 1. Many precautions are taken to protect and preserve the original five pages of the Constitution and the single page of the Declaration of Independence. 2. Thousands of visitors view them daily. 3. The documents are sealed in bronze and glass cases filled with helium. 4. At a moment's notice they can be lowered into a large safe that is bombproof, shockproof, and fireproof.

(F) Sentence 1
(G) Sentence 2
(H) Sentence 3
(J) Sentence 4

Ⓕ Ⓖ Ⓗ Ⓙ

31. 1. The varying hare was so named because its color changes seasonally. 2. It changes from white to brown in spring, and from brown to white in the fall. 3. In-between times it is a mottled brown and white. 4. A native of the Northeast, it is also called the snowshoe hare and the white rabbit.

(A) Sentence 1
(B) Sentence 2
(C) Sentence 3
(D) Sentence 4

Ⓐ Ⓑ Ⓒ Ⓓ

32. 1. It never rains on the moon because there is no water there. 2. The surface of the moon is exposed to an endless bombardment. 3. Meteorites and debris are constantly landing on its surface. 4. There is no atmosphere to slow them down or cause them to self-destruct.

(F) Sentence 1
(G) Sentence 2
(H) Sentence 3
(J) Sentence 4

Ⓕ Ⓖ Ⓗ Ⓙ

Answers—Diagnostic Test 10 Language Expression

1. **B**	9. **B**	17. **B**	25. **C**
2. **J**	10. **J**	18. **G**	26. **J**
3. **B**	11. **A**	19. **D**	27. **A**
4. **G**	12. **G**	20. **G**	28. **H**
5. **B**	13. **D**	21. **C**	29. **D**
6. **G**	14. **G**	22. **H**	30. **G**
7. **C**	15. **C**	23. **D**	31. **D**
8. **H**	16. **G**	24. **J**	32. **F**

Rating Your Results	
Superior	30–32 correct
Average	26–29 correct
Below Average	25 or fewer correct

Material to Review: Chapter 6

Explanations

1. **B** *Because, Anyway,* and *Therefore* do not make sense. *After* shows the appropriate time sequence.

2. **J** *However* contracts the meaning of the sentence. *Meanwhile* and *because* do not make sense. *Consequently* conveys the correct sense of "as a result."

3. **B** *Nevertheless* and *also* would require different punctuation, a preceding semicolon. *Since* makes clear the causal relationship between the two ideas.

4. **G** Note the contrast between *originally* in the first main clause and *now* in the second. *Since* introduces a reason; *meanwhile* has a temporal sense; *and* introduces another, similar idea. Only *but* tells the reader that a new idea will follow.

5. **B** The past tense *began* is correct after *could have lost. Begin* is the present tense; *begun* requires a helping verb; *beginned* is incorrect English.

6. **G** The subject form *I* is required. *Myself* cannot be used alone as a subject. *Me* and *me myself* would be correct as objects.

7. **C** In a comparison of three or more, *best* is required. The forms *more better* and *most best* are substandard English.

8. **H** A subject and a verb are required. *They're* is the contraction of *they are.*

9. **B** The preposition *between* requires the objective form of the first-person pronoun: *you and me.*

10. **J** Choice F is a run-on sentence containing two main clauses without a linking conjunction. Choices G and H are sentence fragments lacking a main clause. Choice J, containing one main clause and two dependent clauses, is correct.

11. **A** Choices B and D are run-on sentences with two main clauses; C is a sentence fragment, lacking a main clause. Choice A, containing one main and one dependent clause, is correct.

12. **G** Choice F is a run-on sentence with two main clauses; H, also a run-on, has two main clauses and one dependent clause; J contains two dependent clauses and a sentence fragment. Choice G, with one main clause, is correct.

13. **D** This is the only sentence with a pronoun (*I*) to answer the question: Who traveled?

14. **G** This is the only sentence that answers the question: What is the miracle, the magician or the trick?

15. **C** This is the only sentence that answers the question: Was it the father or the son who had the more logical solution?

16. **G** In this sentence the phrase *after a time* is closest to the verb it modifies, *began.*

17. **B** Action that precedes another past action requires the past perfect; here, *had been* (absent) precedes *achieved.*

18. **G** Action begun in the past and continuing into the present requires the present perfect (*has been standing*).

19. **D** This sentence conveys the causal relationship between the two ideas that are combined.

20. **G** This sentence expresses the necessary time relationship. Choices F and H reverse the action; J ignores the relationship.

21. **C** *Although* in choice C shows the contrast relationship between the two sentences.

22. **H** Choices F and J change the meaning of the sentences. In G, *but* confuses, rather than clarifies the relationship. Choice H is correct because the *where* clause is close to *stand,* the word it modifies.

23. **D** Choice D is correct since it introduces the topic, thorns, which is discussed in the paragraph.

24. **J** Choice J prepares the reader, by the use of the phrases *rich and varied literature* and *word of mouth,* for the examples of oral literature mentioned in the paragraph.

25. **C** This is the only choice dealing with the concept of largeness developed in the other sentences of the paragraph.

26. **J** The key phrase in the topic sentence is *number of species.* Only J deals with numbers of birds observed.

27. **A** Choice A reinforces the idea of intentional barriers. Choice B deals with a contrasting idea, that is, physicians' attempts to maintain contact with patients. Choices C and D deal with the complexity of modern medical equipment.

28. **H** The main idea is *Irving Berlin... wrote some of our best-loved songs.* Choices F and G do not develop this topic, and choice J is relevant, in part, only to the subordinate idea *who was born in 1888.*

29. **D** Note *Mesa Verde . . . has a unique distinction* (topic sentence) and *Mesa Verde is the only park ...* (choice D).

30. **G** No words in this sentence relate the thousands of visitors to the precautionary measures taken to protect the documents.

31. **D** This sentence does not relate color change to the fact that the rabbit is a native of the Northeast or that it has other names.

32. **F** The lack of rain is not related to the type of bombardment reaching the surface of the moon.

STUDY PLAN

The key to raising your score in this area is the amount of time you can spend on the lists, exercises, and practice tests in Chapter 6, Language Arts.

Long-Term Program

1. Concentrate on one area at a time. The study material includes rules, examples, exercises, practice exercises, and Mastery Exams. The list of things to do and facts to master can be overwhelming unless you apply a familiar addage: Divide and conquer. Therefore, begin with the area that needs most attention. When you feel reasonably confident, move on to another topic.

2. Spend no more than 20 minutes on each practice session.

3. Do not skip any of the varied exercises and practice tests. They not only help you to remember rules but also promote confidence and speed in handling the items on the actual examination.

4. Use the Practice Cooperative Admissions Examinations, in the last section of this book, as your final step in preparation.

Crash Program

1. Use the Diagnostic Test to discover which areas require most of your study time. Then concentrate on the section of Chapter 6, Language Arts, that has the required rules and exercises. Remember that several short sessions are more productive than one long period of cramming.

2. Use the Practice Cooperative Admissions Examinations, in the last section of this book, as your final step.

If You Are Taking the High School Placement Test

The High School Placement Test (HSPT) measures two important factors that help to determine how successful you will be in high school.

1. It evaluates what you have achieved so far in developing reading skills and in the mastery of fundamental concepts in mathematics and language.

2. It evaluates your academic aptitude, that is, your ability to profit from high school academic studies.

Because the HSPT measures both what you have learned (comprehension) and how well you learn (cognitive skills), it is different from most other tests you have taken. For this reason, it is important that you work with a practice book like this type so that you will become acquainted with the types of questions asked. Without such prior experience, you could lose valuable exam minutes learning how to handle the test questions.

The HSPT is divided into five sections:

1. Verbal Skills: verbal analogies, synonyms, logic, verbal classification, antonyms

2. Quantitative Skills: number series, geometric comparison, nongeometric comparison, number manipulation

3. Reading: vocabulary and comprehension

4. Mathematics: concepts and problem solving

5. Language: punctuation, capitalization, usage, spelling, composition

This chapter has been organized in parts that parallel the specific subtests of the HSPT. In each part, through sample questions, you will become acquainted with the same types of questions you will meet in the examination. Strategies for Success will help you avoid many of the pitfalls that lead to lowered marks. The Diagnostic Tests will reveal to you your specific strengths and weaknesses. For further help in improving your score, the study plans will direct you to reviews, exercises, practice tests, and Mastery Exams in the sections that follow.

Frequently Asked Questions About the HSPT

When is the HSPT given?
There is great flexibility in scheduling the HSPT. Each school or district, after consultation with the publisher, the Scholastic Testing Service, may set its own time and place. Your guidance counselor or the high school admissions committee will give you the necessary information.

How long does the test take?
The actual testing time is 2 hours and 21 minutes with an additional 25 to 30 minutes for reading test instructions, distributing materials, and providing 5-minute breaks.

If I finish a section early, may I go back to a previous section?
You may not go back to a previous section, nor may you go forward to another section, if you finish early. You may, however, review your answers in the section on which you have been working.

Is there any penalty for guessing wrong?

On this examination, there is no penalty for guessing. Of course, you increase your chances of guessing correctly if you can eliminate one or more of the answer choices as obviously incorrect. Even if you can't, however, it is better to guess than to leave the answer blank.

Where can I do my scratch work, especially in math?

You may not write in the question booklet. The proctor will give you three blank sheets for scratch work. The answer sheet or folder should contain only the data you were told to fill in and your answers.

Do I have to take any of the optional sections?

You do not have the choice. The high school to which you will apply makes the decision. You will be told whether you have to take one or more of the optionals: Mechanical Aptitude, Science, Catholic Religion.

Are the optional sections included in my score?

No. Your score is based on your answers for the five required sections.

How much will my score on the HSPT count toward admission?

Each school sets its own standards. The admissions committee examines individually the qualifications of each candidate. The composite HSPT score is just one of the factors taken into consideration. However, this score is the only factor that makes it possible to compare one candidate with all the others, and therefore admission committees tend to weight it more heavily.

Subtest 1 Verbal Skills

The Verbal Skills Subtest consists of 60 questions, with a time limit of 16 minutes. There are five types of questions: Synonyms, Antonyms, Analogies, Logic, and Verbal Classification.

Sample Questions

Synonyms
EXAMPLE 1:
Ascend most nearly means

(A) climb.
(B) defeat.
(C) recover.
(D) die.

SOLUTION: Ascend means rise, go up. Therefore, **A** is correct.

Antonyms
EXAMPLE 2:
Grasp means the opposite of

(A) breathe.
(B) clutch.
(C) release.
(D) gulp.

SOLUTION: *Grasp* means to snatch, take. The opposite is to release. Therefore, **C** is correct.

Analogies
EXAMPLE 3:
Wolf is to pack as sheep is to

(A) mutton.
(B) lamb.
(C) meadow.
(D) flock.

SOLUTION: The basis of comparison is the name for a group of the animals in question. Wolves congregate in a pack; sheep, in a flock. Therefore, **D** is correct.

Logic
EXAMPLE 4:
Pies are more expensive than buns. Eclairs are more expensive than pies. Eclairs are less expensive than buns. If the first two statements are true, the third is

(A) true.
(B) false.
(C) uncertain.

SOLUTION: If the first two statements are true, then eclairs are more expensive than buns. Therefore, **B** is correct.

Verbal Classification
EXAMPLE 5:

Which word does <u>not</u> belong with the others?

(A) horn
(B) sound
(C) siren
(D) bell

SOLUTION: Choices A, C, and D produce sounds; a sound is what we hear from a horn, siren, or bell. Therefore, **B** is correct.

STRATEGIES FOR SUCCESS

➤ **Synonyms.** If you know the given word well, the answer will come quickly as you look through the choices. Make certain, however, to check all four choices before marking an answer. Sometimes the choices are very close in meanings and unless you check all four, you may miss the "most nearly" choice.

➤ **Antonyms.** First consider the meaning of the given word; then look among the choices for the *opposite.* In most instances, one choice will stand as correct. However, do not mark the answer sheet before you eliminate the other three possibilities; otherwise, you may be choosing a "near best" rather than the best. If you have difficulty with a particular item, don't dawdle over it. Check the question and plan to return to it if you have time at the end. Very often these trouble spots solve themselves on the second run.

➤ **Analogies.** The formula is as follows: A is to B as C is to D; that is, the words in the second pair must show the same relationship to each other as do the words in the first pair. The key is to substitute, in turn, each choice to find the correct second pair. Before marking your answer, check to see that your choice will establish a relationship with C that is the same as the one between A and B.

➤ **Logic.** Here, too, the problem involves relationships. Watch carefully for words like *some, none, all; must, may, could; sometimes, always.*

If only two items are involved, words like *all, some,* and *none* very often are the key to the solution.

All acids are corrosive. Therefore *some* corrosives are acids. (True)

If three or more items are involved, diagramming reveals the ladder of relationships.

Mel is taller than Adam. Jerry is shorter than Adam. Therefore Mel is shorter than Jerry. (False)

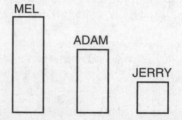

As you can see, the answer becomes clear when you diagram the relationship. For *larger, smaller, brighter, taller,* and similar comparisons, draw and label a rectangle for each person or item named. For *all* or *some,* where groups are included or excluded, use a circle for each group: separate circles or smaller circles within a larger circle. With practice you will learn to enjoy logic questions!

For a fuller explanation and practice exercises, see "Using Diagrams to Solve Verbal Problems," in Chapter 13.

➤ **Verbal Classification.** First, you must establish a relationship among three of the four items. Now ask yourself, "In what aspect is one different?" In difficult choices, sometimes between synonyms, look for the word that is least closely related to the others.

Diagnostic Subtest 1 Verbal Skills

DIRECTIONS: For each of the following, blacken the circle containing the letter that corresponds to the best answer.

1. Which word does <u>not</u> belong with the others'?

    (A) chair   (B) sofa   (C) table   (D) radio

    Ⓐ Ⓑ Ⓒ ⬤

2. Endure means most nearly

    (A) question   (B) err   (C) last
    (D) delay

    Ⓐ Ⓑ Ⓒ ⬤

3. Astronomer is to telescope as bird-watcher is to

    (A) meadow   (B) specimens
    (C) eagles   (D) binoculars

    Ⓐ Ⓑ Ⓒ ⬤

4. All blondhaired people have blue eyes. Adam has blue eyes. Adam must have blond hair. If the first two statements are true, the third is

    (A) true   (B) false   (C) uncertain

    Ⓐ Ⓑ Ⓒ

5. Which word does <u>not</u> belong with the others?

    (A) haze   (B) mist   (C) hurricane
    (D) fog

    Ⓐ Ⓑ ⬤ Ⓓ

6. Warm is to hot as cold is to

    (A) frigid   (B) miniscule   (C) chilly
    (D) temperate

    Ⓐ Ⓑ ⬤ Ⓓ

7. Which word does <u>not</u> belong with the others?

    (A) congenial   (B) agreeable   (C) aloof
    (D) friendly

    Ⓐ Ⓑ Ⓒ Ⓓ

8. Insinuate means most nearly

    (A) hint   (B) falsify   (C) attack
    (D) insulate

    ⬤ Ⓑ Ⓒ Ⓓ

9. Contempt means the <u>opposite</u> of

    (A) loyalty   (B) envy   (C) fear
    (D) admiration

    ⬤ Ⓑ Ⓒ Ⓓ

10. Penny is to dime as dime is to

    (A) nickel   (B) quarter   (C) half-dollar
    (D) dollar

    Ⓐ Ⓑ Ⓒ ⬤

11. Which word does <u>not</u> belong with the others?

    (A) steer   (B) zebra   (C) sheep
    (D) goat

    Ⓐ ⬤ Ⓒ Ⓓ

12. Adversary means most nearly

    (A) counselor   (B) teacher   (C) relative
    (D) enemy

    ⬤ Ⓑ Ⓒ Ⓓ

13. Which word does <u>not</u> belong with the others?

    (A) counterfeit   (B) duplicate   (C) fraud
    (D) sham

    Ⓐ Ⓑ Ⓒ ⬤

14. Bess has a larger vocabulary than Edna. Phyllis knows more words than Bess. Phyllis has a smaller vocabulary than Edna. If the first two statements are true, the third is

    (A) true   (B) false   (C) uncertain

    Ⓐ Ⓑ ⬤

15. Prune is to fruit tree as plow is to

    (A) soil   (B) furrow   (C) farmer
    (D) seed

    Ⓐ ⬤ Ⓒ Ⓓ

16. Which word does <u>not</u> belong with the others?

    (A) book   (B) movie   (C) magazine
       (D) pamphlet

       Ⓐ Ⓑ Ⓒ Ⓓ

17. Gladden means the <u>opposite</u> of

    (A) handicap   (B) depress   (C) tarnish
       (D) resist

       Ⓐ Ⓑ Ⓒ Ⓓ

18. Anonymous means most nearly

    (A) famous   (B) nameless   (C) modern
       (D) ancient

       Ⓐ Ⓑ Ⓒ Ⓓ

19. Alex has 25 cents more than Sylvia. Richie has 20 cents less than Alex. Sylvia has more money than Richie. If the first two statements are true, then the third is

    (A) true   (B) false   (C) uncertain

       Ⓐ Ⓑ Ⓒ

20. This pasture can support 3 sheep per acre. We have 500 acres. There is enough room for 800 sheep. If the first two statements are true, the third is

    (A) true   (B) false   (C) uncertain

       Ⓐ Ⓑ Ⓒ

21. Ample means most nearly

    (A) plentiful   (B) powerful   (C) tiring
       (D) lost

       Ⓐ Ⓑ Ⓒ Ⓓ

22. Plane is to woodworker as word processor is to

    (A) painter   (B) electrician
       (C) sculptor   (D) author

       Ⓐ Ⓑ Ⓒ Ⓓ

23. Which word does <u>not</u> belong with the others?

    (A) cheat   (B) scout   (C) liar
       (D) thief

       Ⓐ Ⓑ Ⓒ Ⓓ

24. Concur means most nearly

    (A) agree   (B) confine   (C) compromise
       (D) consider

       Ⓐ Ⓑ Ⓒ Ⓓ

25. Orderly means the <u>opposite</u> of

    (A) inexpensive   (B) healthy
       (C) disorganized   (D) relative

       Ⓐ Ⓑ Ⓒ Ⓓ

26. Building A has fewer stories than Building B. Building C has more stories than Building B. Building A has fewer stories than Building C. If the first two statements are true, the third is

    (A) true   (B) false   (C) uncertain

       Ⓐ Ⓑ Ⓒ

27. Enlarged means most nearly

    (A) sold   (B) built   (C) expanded
       (D) discontinued

       Ⓐ Ⓑ Ⓒ Ⓓ

28. Hammer is to nail as bat is to

    (A) mitt   (B) pitcher   (C) puck
       (D) baseball

       Ⓐ Ⓑ Ⓒ Ⓓ

29. Which word does <u>not</u> belong with the others?

    (A) spear   (B) lance   (C) harpoon
       (D) gun

       Ⓐ Ⓑ Ⓒ Ⓓ

30. Glorify means most nearly

    (A) criticize   (B) extol   (C) protect
       (D) shun

       Ⓐ Ⓑ Ⓒ Ⓓ

31. Luis is the youngest boy in his class. Luis is six months older than Sam. Luis and Sam are in the same class. If the first two statements are true, the third is

    (A) true   (B) false   (C) uncertain

       Ⓐ Ⓑ Ⓒ

32. Ruddy means the <u>opposite</u> of

    (A) pale   (B) shipshape
    (C) uncontrolled   (D) radical

    Ⓐ Ⓑ Ⓒ Ⓓ

33. Which word does <u>not</u> belong with the others?

    (A) hut   (B) lean-to   (C) cave   (D) cabin

    Ⓐ ⬤ Ⓒ Ⓓ

34. Juvenile means most nearly

    (A) mature   (B) young   (C) false
    (D) profound

    Ⓐ Ⓑ Ⓒ ⬤

35. Snarl is to roar as whisper is to

    (A) shout   (B) talk   (C) mumble
    (D) converse

    Ⓐ Ⓑ ⬤ Ⓓ

36. Hinder means the <u>opposite</u> of

    (A) promote   (B) forsee   (C) desist
    (D) defer

    Ⓐ ⬤ Ⓒ Ⓓ

37. Milton is a better player than Herb. Herb is a better player than Tom. Milton's rating is lower than Tom's. If the first two statements are true, the third is

    (A) true   (B) false   (C) uncertain

    Ⓐ ⬤ Ⓒ

38. Which word does <u>not</u> belong with the others?

    (A) molasses   (B) honey
    (C) horseradish   (D) sugar

    ⬤ Ⓑ Ⓒ Ⓓ

39. Novice means most nearly

    (A) veteran   (B) professional
    (C) amateur   (D) supervisor

    Ⓐ Ⓑ ⬤ Ⓓ

40. Alice types faster than Carrie, but slower than Sarah. Judith is faster than Sarah but slower than Ida. Carrie is the slowest typist in the group. If the first two statements are true, the third is

    (A) true   (B) false   (C) uncertain

    ⬤ Ⓑ Ⓒ

41. Obvious means the <u>opposite</u> of

    (A) controlled   (B) obscure
    (C) sensational   (D) consistent

    Ⓐ Ⓑ Ⓒ ⬤

42. Which word does <u>not</u> belong with the others?

    (A) sedan   (B) truck   (C) convertible
    (D) limosine

    ⬤ Ⓑ Ⓒ Ⓓ

43. Perpetual means most nearly

    (A) unceasing   (B) national
    (C) limited   (D) inexpensive

    ⬤ Ⓑ Ⓒ Ⓓ

44. Pedestrian means the <u>opposite</u> of

    (A) automaton   (B) official   (C) leader
    (D) rider

    ⬤ Ⓑ Ⓒ Ⓓ

45. Mount Marcy is north of Mount Potash. Mount Potash is north of Tongue Mountain. Tongue Mountain is south of Mount Marcy. If the first two statements are true, the third is

    (A) true   (B) false   (C) uncertain

    Ⓐ Ⓑ ⬤

46. Which word does <u>not</u> belong with the others?

    (A) golden   (B) maroon   (C) lemon
    (D) yellow

    Ⓐ Ⓑ ⬤ Ⓓ

47. Ruse means most nearly

    (A) pet   (B) idea   (C) trick
    (D) companion

    Ⓐ Ⓑ Ⓒ Ⓓ

48. Acrobat is to trapeze as scholar is to

    (A) study   (B) intelligent   (C) books
    (D) knowledge

    Ⓐ ⬤ Ⓒ Ⓓ

49. Vigorous means most nearly

    (A) attractive   (B) intelligent
    (C) energetic   (D) companionable

    Ⓐ Ⓑ ⬤ Ⓓ

50. Pallid is to rosy as sharp is to

    (A) peaceful (B) blurred
      (C) arduous (D) acute

    Ⓐ ⬤ Ⓒ Ⓓ

51. Quell means the opposite of

    (A) encourage (B) enjoy (C) entitle
      (D) riot

    ⬤ Ⓑ Ⓒ Ⓓ

52. Restrain means most nearly

    (A) teach (B) lecture (C) consider.
      (D) curb

    Ⓐ Ⓑ Ⓒ ⬤

53. Which word does not belong with the others?

    (A) supervisor (B) colleague
      (C) partner (D) teammate

    ⬤ Ⓑ Ⓒ Ⓓ

54. School is to fish as forest is to

    (A) hikers (B) woodsmen
      (C) teachers (D) trees

    Ⓐ Ⓑ Ⓒ ⬤

55. Which word does not belong with the others?

    (A) reveal (B) expose (C) conceal
      (D) exhibit

    Ⓐ Ⓑ ⬤ Ⓓ

56. Jenny has $3 less than Beth. Beth has $2 less than Angie. Angie has $5 more than Jenny. If the first two statements are true, the third is

    (A) true (B) false (C) uncertain

    ⬤ Ⓑ Ⓒ

57. Which word does not belong with the others?

    (A) telescope (B) spectacles
      (C) magnifying glass (D) microscope

    Ⓐ ⬤ Ⓒ Ⓓ

58. Robust means the opposite of

    (A) elderly (B) fragile (C) mature
      (D) colorless

    Ⓐ ⬤ Ⓒ Ⓓ

59. Which word does not belong with the others?

    (A) shorten (B) prolong
      (C) abbreviate (D) limit

    Ⓐ ⬤ Ⓒ Ⓓ

60. Annoyance is to frown as pain is to

    (A) grimace (B) stare (C) glance
      (D) smirk

    ⬤ Ⓑ Ⓒ Ⓓ

Answers—Diagnostic Subtest 1
Verbal Skills

1. **D**	16. **B**	31. **B**	46. **B**
2. **C**	17. **B**	32. **A**	47. **C**
3. **D**	18. **B**	33. **C**	48. **C**
4. **B**	19. **B**	34. **B**	49. **C**
5. **C**	20. **A**	35. **A**	50. **B**
6. **A**	21. **A**	36. **A**	51. **A**
7. **C**	22. **D**	37. **B**	52. **D**
8. **A**	23. **B**	38. **C**	53. **A**
9. **D**	24. **A**	39. **C**	54. **D**
10. **D**	25. **C**	40. **A**	55. **C**
11. **B**	26. **A**	41. **B**	56. **A**
12. **D**	27. **C**	42. **B**	57. **B**
13. **B**	28. **D**	43. **A**	58. **B**
14. **B**	29. **D**	44. **D**	59. **B**
15. **A**	30. **B**	45. **A**	60. **A**

Rating Your Results	
Superior	55–60 correct
Average	49–54 correct
Below Average	48 or fewer correct
Material to Review: Chapter 4	

Explanations

1. **D** The other choices are articles of furniture; a radio is merely a room accessory.

2. **C** To endure is to continue, to last.

3. **D** An astronomer uses a telescope to see the stars; a birdwatcher uses binoculars to sight the birds.

4. **B** There is no statement that all blue-eyed people are blond. Adam *may* or *may not,* not *must,* have blond hair.

5. **C** A hurricane features high winds and rain; the other three choices involve low visibility.

6. **A** Hot is a greater degree than warm; frigid is more than cold.

7. **C** The other three choices suggest sociability; aloof connotes remoteness.

8. **A** To insinuate is to communicate something indirectly; to suggest, to hint.

9. **D** Contempt looks down on some act or person; admiration looks up.

10. **D** There is a 1:10 ratio between a penny and a dime and between a dime and a dollar.

11. **B** Zebra is the only undomesticated animal among the choices.

12. **D** As adversary is an opponent, an enemy.

13. **B** A duplicate is a copy, good or bad. The other three choices all have negative implications of intent to deceive.

14. **B** If Phyllis knows more words than Bess, her vocabulary is also larger than Edna's.

15. **A** In cultivation, fruit trees are pruned and the soil is plowed.

16. **B** Movie is the only nonprinted matter.

17. **B** To gladden is to raise spirits; to depress is to lower them.

18. **B** To be anonymous is to be unknown, or nameless.

19. **B** Sylvia has 5 cents less than Richie.

20. **A** Since the pasture can support 1500 sheep (3 × 500), it can certainly support 800 sheep.

21. **A** To be ample is to be abundant, plentiful.

22. **D** Both relationships involve workers and their tools.

23. **B** The other choices describe people who behave in undesirable ways; a scout does not fit in this category.

24. **A** To concur is to go along with, to agree.

25. **C** A disorganized person is the opposite of an orderly one.

26. **A** From the first two statements we know that Building C has more stories than either A or B.

27. **C** Something that has been enlarged has been made greater, expanded.

28. **D** The relationship is between instruments that hit and the objects acted upon.

29. **D** The other three choices have a cutting or incising action; a gun does not.

30. **B** To glorify is to bestow praise or admiration, to extol.

31. **B** If Luis is six months older than Sam, Sam cannot be in a class in which Luis is the youngest boy.

32. **A** Pale (deficient in color) is the opposite of ruddy (reddish).

33. **C** The other three are manmade shelters; a cave is natural.

34. **B** Juvenile means immature, young.

35. **A** A roar is louder than a snarl; a shout is louder than a whisper.

36. **A** Promote aids advancement; hinder retards it.

37. **B** Milton is better than Herb, who is better than Tom.

38. **C** Horseradish is the only substance that is not sweet.

39. **C** A novice is a beginner, a tyro, an amateur.

40. **A** The progression, from fastest to slowest, is Ida, Judith, Sarah, Alice, Carrie.

41. **B** What is obvious is clear; what is obscure is dim, vague, unclear.

42. **B** The truck is the only vehicle in the group that is not intended for pleasure driving.

43. **A** To be perpetual is to be continual, unceasing.

44. **D** A pedestrian walks, unlike a rider on a horse or in a vehicle.

45. **A** Going from north to south, a traveler would first reach Mount Marcy, then Mount Potash, and finally Tongue Mountain.

46. **B**   The other three choices are all in the same color family; maroon is in a different (the red) family.

47. **C**   A ruse is a deception, a trick.

48. **C**   The relationship involves tools of the trade.

49. **C**   To be vigorous is to be forceful, energetic.

50. **B**   Pallid is the opposite of rosy; sharp is the opposite of blurred.

51. **A**   To quell is to stop; to encourage is to signal to go on.

52. **D**   To restrain is to hold back, to curb.

53. **A**   The other three choices imply equality of rank; a supervisor is a superior.

54. **D**   A school is a collection of fish; a forest, a collection of trees.

55. **C**   Conceal means to hide; the other three choices mean to show openly.

56. **A**   Angie has $2 more than Beth, who has $3 more than Jenny. $2 + $3 = $5.

57. **B**   Spectacles, unlike the other choices, need not magnify; they may be prescribed for some other purpose.

58. **B**   To be robust is to be strong and healthy; to be fragile is to be weak and delicate.

59. **B**   Prolong means to lengthen; the other choices mean to lessen or restrict.

60. **A**   A frown is an expression of annoyance; a grimace is an expression of pain.

STUDY PLAN FOR THE VERBAL SKILLS SUBTEST

The key to improving your score on the Verbal Skills Subtest is the amount of time you can spend on the lists, exercises, and practice tests in Chapter 4, Vocabulary.

Long-Term Program

1. Review the lists in Chapter 4. Check the words you are unfamiliar with, and review them four or five at a time. You will be pleasantly surprised at how quickly you will master them! A daily ten-minute session is the secret to success.

2. Do not skip the varied exercises and practice tests. They will reinforce your control of your growing vocabulary and will increase your speed in handling the actual examination items.

3. Use the Practice HSPTs in the last section of this book as your final step in preparation.

Crash Program

1. Concentrate your study time on the exercises and practice tests in Chapter 4, Vocabulary. Several short sessions are much more effective than one long one. The varied exercises will help you gain speed and accuracy in handling vocabulary questions.

2. Use the Practice HSPTs, in the last section of this book, as your final step.

Subtest 2   Quantitative Skills

As you read a daily newspaper, you will find reference to budget considerations, public expenditures, shopping prices, stock market quotations, and sports standings. These and other topics of general interest cannot be fully understood unless you can use your mathematical experience freely to solve problems related to a variety of situations. Also, your chance of success in high school will be enhanced if you can readily apply mathematical analysis when needed.

The Quantitative Skills Subtest consists of the following types of questions:

Number series: 18 questions
Geometric comparison: 9 questions
Nongeometric comparison: 8 questions
Number manipulation: 17 questions

You will be given 30 minutes to answer these 52 questions.

You will find that the solution to a number series question depends upon your ability to find the pattern that relates the numbers in the series to each other. Your ability to see these patterns in the time limit given will determine your score.

Geometric comparison questions involve your ability to compare the sizes of geometric figures or parts of geometric figures. If you understand the question precisely, you should have little difficulty in finding the correct answer. In other words, read each question carefully.

Nongeometric comparison questions involve your ability to simplify a set of numerical expressions and to draw conclusions from this set of simplified results. There is essentially nothing new here except the format of the problem.

Number manipulation involves your ability to read and interpret a number problem and then to use one or more indicated operations to achieve a result. You will find a wealth of practice material in Chapter 7 of this book.

Sample Questions

EXAMPLE 1:
Look at this series: 9, 5, 1, –3, __. What number should come next?

(A) –5   (B) –6   (C) –7 (D) –10

SOLUTION: We observe that each successive number in the series is 4 less than the preceding number: 4 less than –3 is $-3 - 4 = -7$.
The correct choice is **C**.

EXAMPLE 2:
The measure of $\angle B = 70°$, and the measure of $\angle C = 60°$. Which side of $\triangle ABC$ is the smallest?

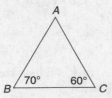

(A) AB (B) BC (C) AC
(D) The three sides are equal.

SOLUTION: Since the sum of the measures of the three angles of a triangle is 180°, the measure of $\angle A = 180 - (70 + 60) = 50°$. Thus,

$\angle A$ is the smallest angle of $\triangle ABC$. In a triangle, the smallest side lies opposite the smallest angle. Therefore, BC is the smallest side of $\triangle ABC$.
The correct choice is **B**.

EXAMPLE 3:
Examine (X), (Y), and (Z), and select the correct answer.
(X) $(9 \times 6) \div 3$
(Y) $7(5 + 1)$
(Z) $(3 \times 8) \times 1$

(A) $Z = X + Y$ (B) $Y = X + Z$
(C) $X = Y + Z$ (D) $Y = 2XZ$

SOLUTION: $X = (9 \times 6) \div 3 = 18$
$Y = 7(5 + 1) = 7 \times 6 = 42$
$Z = (3 \times 8) \times 1 = 24 \times 1 = 24$
$X + Z = 18 + 24 = 42$, and $Y = 42$

Thus, $Y = X + Z$
The correct choice is **B**.

EXAMPLE 4:
Which number sentence is true?

(A) $-4 > 3$ (B) $-2 > -5$ (C) $-7 > 0$
(D) $0 > 2$

SOLUTION: If we locate these numbers on the number line, we can compare them at a glance.

$$-7 \quad -6 \quad -5 \quad -4 \quad -3 \quad -2 \quad -1 \quad 0 \quad 1 \quad 2 \quad 3 \quad 4 \quad 5 \quad 6 \quad 7$$

Since –2 is to the right of –5 on the number line, $-2 > -5$.
The correct choice is **B**.

STRATEGIES FOR SUCCESS

The suggestions below are designed to help you attain your best score on the Quantitative Skills Subtest.

➤ *Tactic 1:* Read each question carefully. Every word in a mathematical statement is precise and is important in understanding the problem.

➤ *Tactic 2:* Determine what information is given and exactly what must be found. This analysis will give you the gist of the problem.

➤ *Tactic 3:* Develop a plan for a solution. Such a plan will involve a link between the information you are given and what you must find.

➤ *Tactic 4:* Use your plan as a guide to complete the solution to the problem.

➤ *Tactic 5:* Check your answer. You may use the method of estimating to save time.

➤ *Tactic 6:* Be sure that your answer is given in the units specified in the question.

➤ *Tactic 7:* If you do not see an immediate approach to the solution of a problem, leave it and return to it later if time permits.

➤ *Tactic 8:* Do not get upset if you cannot answer a question. If you can eliminate some choices, do so. Then, since there is no penalty for guessing, choose what seems the best answer. You do not have to answer every question correctly to get a good score.

➤ *Tactic 9:* Do not spend too much time on any one question. Since you have limited time, you cannot afford to dwell on a troublesome problem.

Diagnostic Subtest 2 Quantitative Skills

DIRECTIONS: For each of the following, blacken the circle containing the letter that corresponds to the best answer.

1. Select the number that should come next in the following series: 3, 9, 15, 21, __.

    (A) 25   (B) 27   (C) 29   (D) 30

    Ⓐ ● Ⓒ Ⓓ

2. If $\frac{5}{6}$ of a number is 20, then $37\frac{1}{2}$ % of the number is

    (A) 9   (B) 12   (C) 45   (D) 60

    ● Ⓑ Ⓒ Ⓓ

3. In a right triangle the measures of the acute angles are in the ratio 2:3. What is the measure of the smaller angle?

    (A) 45°   (B) 54°   (C) 40°   (D) 36°

    Ⓐ Ⓑ Ⓒ ●

4. Examine (X), (Y), and (Z), and select the correct answer.

    (X) $18 \div 3 - 6$
    (Y) $(9 - 5) - 2$
    (Z) $10 - 3 \times 4$

    (A) $Y + Z = X$ (B) $Y \cdot Z = X$
    (C) $X + Y = Z$ (D) $Y - Z = X$

    ● Ⓑ Ⓒ Ⓓ

5. If $3x - 2 = 16$, then $x^2 =$

    (A) 12   (B) 18   (C) 36   (D) 40

    Ⓐ Ⓑ ● Ⓓ

6. $2\frac{2}{5} \times 3\frac{1}{3} \times \frac{3}{4} =$

    (A) $\frac{3}{2}$ (B) $\frac{1}{6}$ (C) 6   (D) 4

    Ⓐ Ⓑ Ⓒ Ⓓ

7. Look at the following series, and determine which number should come next: 3, 5, 9, 17, 33, __.

    (A) 60   (B) 66   (C) 65   (D) 70

    Ⓐ Ⓑ ● Ⓓ

8. The prime factors of 165 are

    (A) 3, 11   (B) 3, 5   (C) 5, 11
    (D) 3, 5, 11

    Ⓐ Ⓑ Ⓒ ●

9. The number that is 8 less than 64 is the product of 7 and

    (A) 9   (B) 8   (C) 11   (D) 12

    Ⓐ ● Ⓒ Ⓓ

10. What is the next number in the following series:

$$\frac{1}{3}, \frac{1}{6}, \frac{1}{12}, \frac{1}{24}, -?$$

(A) $\frac{1}{4}$ (B) $\frac{1}{10}$ (C) $\frac{1}{30}$ (D) $\frac{1}{48}$

Ⓐ Ⓑ Ⓒ ●

11. The perimeter of a rectangle is 70 inches, and its width is 15 inches. Its area, in square inches, is

(A) 300 (B) 250 (C) 240 (D) 200

● Ⓑ Ⓒ Ⓓ

12. A notebook sells for *x* cents. What is the cost of 4 such notebooks?

(A) *x* + 4 cents (B) *x* ÷ 4 cents
(C) 4*x* cents (D) 4 − *x* cents

Ⓐ Ⓑ ● Ⓓ

13. In adding the fractions $\frac{1}{3}, \frac{5}{6},$ and $\frac{7}{12}$, the least common denominator is

(A) 24 (B) 72 (C) 12 (D) 18

Ⓐ Ⓑ ● Ⓓ

14. Which of the following is correct?

(A) $\frac{2}{3} > \frac{5}{8} > \frac{4}{7}$ (B) $\frac{5}{8} > \frac{2}{3} > \frac{4}{7}$

(C) $\frac{4}{7} > \frac{5}{8} > \frac{2}{3}$ (D) $\frac{2}{3} > \frac{4}{7} > \frac{5}{8}$

● Ⓑ Ⓒ Ⓓ

15. What is the next number in the following series: 8, 5, 2, −1, __?

(A) −3 (B) 4 (C) −5 (D) −4

Ⓐ Ⓑ Ⓒ ●

16. A woman has 4 blue dresses, 3 green dresses, and 5 tan dresses. If she selects a dress at random, what is the probability that it will be a tan dress?

(A) $\frac{5}{7}$ (B) $\frac{5}{12}$ (C) $\frac{12}{5}$ (D) $\frac{4}{9}$

Ⓐ ● Ⓒ Ⓓ

17. A student's marks on 5 tests are 65, 85, 90, 75, and 80. What is his average on the 5 tests?

(A) 80 (B) 74 (C) 79 (D) 82

Ⓐ Ⓑ ● Ⓓ

18. Examine (*X*), (*Y*), and (*Z*), and select the correct answer.

(*X*) $2 \cdot 2^3$
(*Y*) $3 + 8 \div 4$
(*Z*) $9 - (7 - 2)$

(A) $Z > Y$ (B) $X = Z^2$
(C) $Y + Z = X$ (D) $Y^2 = X + Z$

Ⓐ ● Ⓒ Ⓓ

19. What number should come next in the following series: −10, −7, −4, −1, __?

(A) −2 (B) 2 (C) 3 (D) 5

Ⓐ ● Ⓒ Ⓓ

20. *O* is the center of a circle inscribed in square *ABCD*. If *AB* = 10, find the area of the shaded portion.

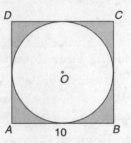

(A) $100 - 25\pi$ (B) $100 - 100\pi$
(C) $100 - 50\pi$ (D) $100 + 25\pi$

● Ⓑ Ⓒ Ⓓ

21. A merchant sold a chair for $280 at a profit of 40%. How much did the chair cost the merchant?

(A) $240 (B) $220 (C) $250 (D) $200

Ⓐ Ⓑ Ⓒ Ⓓ

22. The number $(4 \times 10^3) + (5 \times 10^2) + (9 \times 10) + (3 \times 1) =$

(A) 4,935 (B) 4,359 (C) 4,593
(D) 459.3

Ⓐ Ⓑ Ⓒ Ⓓ

23. Written as a base-10 number, the number $312_{(five)} =$

    (A) 62 (B) 82 (C) 22 (D) 42

    Ⓐ Ⓑ Ⓒ Ⓓ

24. Which of the following is true?

    (A) $-5 > 0$ (B) $-3 > -1$ (C) $-6 > 2$
    (D) $-2 > -7$

    Ⓐ Ⓑ Ⓒ Ⓓ

25. A shirt and a tie cost $22. If the shirt costs $8 more than the tie, what is the cost of the tie?

    (A) $7 (B) $8 (C) $15 (D) $10

    Ⓐ Ⓑ Ⓒ Ⓓ

Answers—Diagnostic Subtest 2 Quantitative Skills

1. **B**	7. **C**	13. **C**	19. **B**
2. **A**	8. **D**	14. **A**	20. **A**
3. **D**	9. **B**	15. **D**	21. **D**
4. **A**	10. **D**	16. **B**	22. **C**
5. **C**	11. **A**	17. **C**	23. **B**
6. **C**	12. **C**	18. **B**	24. **D**
			25. **A**

Rating Your Results

Superior	21–25 correct
Average	16–20 correct
Below Average	15 or fewer correct

Material to Review: Chapter 7–12

Explanations

1. **B**   As we move along from left to right, we note that each member of the series is 6 greater than the preceding member: $9 = 6 + 3$, $15 = 6 + 9$, $21 = 6 + 15$, and $27 = 6 + 21$. The correct choice is **B**.

2. **A**   Let x = the number.

   Then $\frac{5}{6}x = 20$

   $$x = 20 \div \frac{5}{6}$$

   $$x = 20 \times \frac{6}{5} = 24$$

   $$37\frac{1}{2}\% = \frac{3}{8}, \text{ and } \frac{3}{8} \times 24 = 9$$

   The correct choice is **A**.

3. **D**   Let $2x$ = the measure of the smaller acute angle.
   And $3x$ = the measure of the larger acute angle.
   Then $2x + 3x = 90$
   $$5x = 90$$
   $$x = 18$$
   $$2x = 2(18) = 36°$$
   The correct choice is **D**.

4. **A** (X) $18 \div 3 - 6 = 6 - 6 = 0$
   (Y) $(9 - 5) - 2 = 4 - 2 = 2$
   (Z) $10 - 3 \times 4 = 10 - 12 = -2$
   $Y + Z = X$ is $2 + (-2) = 0$
   The correct choice is $(\mathbf{A})$.

5. **C** $3x - 2 = 16$
   $$3x = 16 + 2 = 18$$
   $$x = 6$$
   $$x^2 = 6 \times 6 = 36$$
   The correct choice is $(\mathbf{C})$.

6. **C** $2\frac{2}{5} = \frac{12}{5}$
   $$3\frac{1}{3} = \frac{10}{3}$$
   $$\frac{3}{4} = \frac{3}{4}$$
   $$\frac{\overset{3}{\cancel{12}}}{5} \times \frac{\overset{2}{\cancel{10}}}{3} \times \frac{3}{4} = 6$$
   The correct choice is **C**.

7. **C**   As we move along the series from left to right we note that each term is obtained from the preceding term by adding a power of 2 to the preceding term: $5 = 3 + 2^1$, $9 = 5 + 2^2$, $17 = 9 + 2^3$, $33 = 17 + 2^4$, $65 = 33 + 2^5$
   Alternatively, as we move from left to right, each term can be obtained by multiplying by 2 and then subtracting 1: $3 \times 2 - 1 = 5$, $5 \times 2 - 1 = 9$, $9 \times 2 - 1 = 17$, $17 \times 2 - 1 = 33$, $33 \times 2 - 1 = 65$. The correct choice is **C**.

8. **D**   3, 5, and 11 are prime numbers.
   3, 5, and 11 are factors of 165.
   Also, $3 \times 5 \times 11 = 165$.
   Thus, 3, 5, and 11 are the prime factors of 165.
   The correct choice is **D**.

9. **B**   8 less than 64 = 64 − 8 = 56
The product of 7 and 8 = 56
The correct choice is **B**.

10. **D**   As we move along the series from left to right, we note that each term is obtained from the preceding term by multiplying the preceding term by $\frac{1}{2}$.

$$\frac{1}{6} = \frac{1}{3} \times \frac{1}{2}, \frac{1}{12} = \frac{1}{6} \times \frac{1}{2}, \frac{1}{24} = \frac{1}{12} \times \frac{1}{2},$$
$$\frac{1}{48} = \frac{1}{12} \times \frac{1}{2}.$$

The correct choice is **D**.

11. **A**   Since the perimeter of the rectangle is 70 inches, we have $x + 15 + x + 15 = 70$, where x is the length.

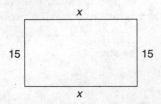

$2x + 30 = 70$
$\quad 2x = 70 − 30 = 40$
$\quad\ \ x = 20$
Area = 20 × 15 = 300 square inches.
The correct choice is **A**.

12. **C**   To obtain the cost of 4 notebooks, we must multiply the cost of 1 notebook (x) by 4. The result is $4x$.
The correct choice is **C**.

13. **C**   We find the L.C.D. for $\frac{1}{3}, \frac{5}{6}$, and $\frac{7}{12}$ by writing the multiples of the denominators. The first number that appears in all three sets of multiples is the L.C.D.
Multiples of 3: 3, 6, 9, 12, 15, 18,...
Multiples of 6: 6, 12, 18,...
Multiples of 12: 12
Since 12 is the first number that appears in all three sets of multiples, it is the L.C.D.
The correct choice is **C**.

14. **A**   To arrange the fractions in order of size with the largest one first, it is convenient to write the fractions as decimals:

$$\frac{2}{3} = 0.67, \quad \frac{5}{8} = 0.63, \quad \frac{4}{7} = 0.57$$

Thus, we have $\frac{2}{3} = \frac{5}{8} = \frac{4}{7}$.
The correct choice is **A**.

15. **D**   As we move from left to right in the series, we note that each term is obtained from the preceding term by subtracting 3 from the preceding term:
$5 = 8 − 3$, $2 = 5 − 3$, $−1 = 2 − 3$,
$−4 = −1 − 3$.
The correct choice is **D**.

16. **B**   The woman has a choice of 4 + 3 + 5 = 12 dresses. Of these 12 dresses, 5 are tan. Thus, the probability of selecting a tan dress is $\frac{5}{12}$.
The correct choice is **B**.

17. **C**   To obtain the average on the 5 tests, we add the 5 test marks and divide this sum by 5.
65 + 85 + 90 + 75 + 80 = 395
395 ÷ 5 = 79
The correct choice is **C**.

18. **B** $(X) = 2 \cdot 2^3 - 26 \cdot 8 = 16$
$(Y) = 3 + 8 \div 4 = 3 + 2 = 5$
$(Z) = 9 − (7 − 2) = 9 − 5 = 4$
$X = Z^2$ because $16 = 4^2$
The correct choice is **B**.

19. **B**   As we move from left to right in the series, we note that each term is obtained from the preceding term by adding 3 to the preceding term: $−7 = −10 + 3$, $−4 = −7 + 3$, $−1 = −4 + 3$, $2 = −1 + 3$.
The correct choice is **B**.

20. **A**   To find the area of the shaded portion, we first find the area of the square. Then we subtract the area of the circle from the area of the square.

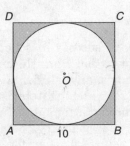

Area of square $ABCD$ = 10 × 10 = 100
Area of circle = $\pi r^2 = \pi \times 5 \times 5 = 25\pi$
Area of shaded portion = $100 − 25\pi$.
The correct choice is **A**.

21. **D** Let x = the cost of the chair to the merchant

Then $1.4x = 280$

$$x = \frac{280}{1.4} = \frac{2800}{14} = 200$$

The correct choice is **D**.

22. **C** $4 \times 10^3 = 4,000$

$5 \times 10^2 = 500$

$9 \times 10 = 90$

$3 \times 1 = 3$

The number is 4,593.

The correct choice is **C**.

23. **B** $312_{(five)} = 2 + (1 \times 5) + (3 \times 5^2)$

$\qquad\qquad = 2 + 5 + 75 = 82$

The correct choice is **B**.

24. **D** $-2 > -7$ since -2 is to the right of -7 on the number line, as shown below:

The correct choice is **D**.

25. **A** Let x = the cost of the tie

And $x + 8$ = the cost of the shirt

$x + x + 8 = 22$

$2x + 8 = 22$

$2x = 22 - 8 = 14$

$x = 7$

The tie costs $7.

The correct choice is **A**.

STUDY PLAN FOR THE QUANTITATIVE SKILLS SUBTEST

The best plan for study is to get plenty of practice in answering questions of the types you will encounter on this test. The following references will help you to find appropriate practice material.

Number series: Chapter 10

Geometric comparison: Review Chapter 12. This relatively short chapter contains all of the material on geometry that you will need.

Nongeometric comparison: Chapter 13, Memory and Reasoning Skills, has a wealth of helpful material.

Number manipulation: Chapter 8, Application of Basic Mathematical Skills, has a wide variety of practice problems.

Subtest 3 Reading—Comprehension and Vocabulary

A basic key to success in school is skill in getting information from the printed page. Even though many students now spend more time in watching television than in reading printed matter, our schools still use books as the primary communication resource. The HSPT, therefore, tests your ability to handle the many types of reading materials that you will meet in high school.

The Reading Subtest, which consists of 62 questions with a time limit of 25 minutes, has two parts:

A. Comprehension: 40 questions based on a variety of reading matter: books, magazines, newspapers.

B. Vocabulary (Words in Context): 22 questions that present words in short phrases (context) and require you to select, from four choices, a synonym for each underlined word.

READING—COMPREHENSION

Sample Questions

This section consists of several reading passages, followed by a series of questions that test your understanding of what you have read. These questions are of four basic types.

Knowledge of Word Meanings

EXAMPLE:
As used in this selection, _____ means most nearly

Literal Understanding of Content
Details

EXAMPLE:
The number of brothers is _____

Sequence of events
EXAMPLE:
Before leaving, Eileen _____

Cause and effect
EXAMPLE:
As a result of _____ , Joseph had to quit his job.

Inferential Understanding of Content
Main idea (or title)
EXAMPLE:
A suitable title for this passage is _____

Inferences and implications
EXAMPLE:
From these remarks, the reader can infer _____

Drawing conclusions
EXAMPLE:
When the crisis ends, John will probably not _____

Evaluation of Content
Author's purpose, message or theme
EXAMPLE:
The theme of this selection is _____

Author's qualifications
EXAMPLE:
How well qualified is the author to write on this topic?

Fact or fiction
EXAMPLE:
These events could never have happened because _____

Comparisons or contrasts (literary)
EXAMPLE:
The narrator resembles Scrooge because _____

The sample passage and questions that follow are similar to those you will meet on the Reading—Comprehension Test of the HSPT.

> DIRECTIONS: Read carefully the selection below. Then answer the questions that follow it. Choose your answers on the basis of the information in the selection.

In the years following the American Revolution, the cause of democracy was greatly aided by the breakup of the large estates established by the grants of the English monarchs. With the defeat of the British, many of the largest landowners fled to Canada, the West Indies, and England. Their estates were seized and sold to small farmers.

In memory of its founder, Pennsylvania gave the Penns £ 130,000. Hartford gave the Baltimore family £ 10,000. North Carolina seized the Granville holdings of millions of acres. Sir John Johnson's estate in upper New York was sold to more than 10,000 farm people. Throughout the 13 states small farmers joyfully moved on to rich lands that would once have accepted them only as tenants.

Shopkeepers, farmers, and artisans took control and were free to create a civilization based on equality and opportunity for all.

1. The founder referred to in the second paragraph was

   (A) George Washington.
   (B) William Penn.
   (C) Lord Baltimore.
   (D) King George III.

2. Which of the following titles best expresses the main idea or topic of this selection?

   (A) "Getting Rid of Tyrants"
   (B) "Revolutionary Revenge"
   (C) "Tenant Farmers No Longer"
   (D) "Democratizing the Land"

3. Most of these lands were seized because their owners

(A) refused to sell them.
(B) wanted too much money for them.
(C) had left the country.
(D) had been convicted of crimes.

4. What is the main purpose of this passage?

(A) to arouse the reader's anger toward the landowners
(B) to present facts objectively
(C) to convince the reader that the landowners were mistreated
(D) to appeal to the reader's patriotism

Explanations

1. **B** "In memory of its founder, Pennsylvania gave the Penns..."

2. **D** Note the first sentence: "... the cause of democracy was greatly aided by the breakup of the large estates..." and the last paragraph.

3. **C** "Many of the largest landowners fled..."

4. **B** The author does not take sides. Only facts, not opinions, are given in an objective way.

STRATEGIES FOR SUCCESS

➤ Zero in on the paragraphs to be read. Clear your mind of everything else.

➤ Since this is a test of your ability to read, do not rely on your own knowledge as the basis of your answer. Each passage contains all the information you will need to answer the questions.

➤ Read the passage quickly to decide what it is about.

➤ Before you turn to the questions, read the passage a second time, sentence by sentence.

➤ Take the questions in order. Read all the choices before you select the best answer.

➤ Do not hesitate to turn back to the paragraph to verify your choices.

➤ Passages about familiar subjects or areas of your interest take less time than others. However, if you find a passage that seems too difficult, go on to the next; come back to the troublesome one later if you have time. When you return to the passage, it may seem much easier to grasp.

➤ Often, picking out the key sentence will organize your thinking about the selection.

➤ Some students find that looking at the questions first can help them to understand a difficult paragraph. Others find this approach very time consuming; they prefer to identify the main ideas in the selection before looking at the questions. While taking the practice tests in Chapter 5, try both methods to see which one works best for you.

➤ Some people find underlining key phrases helpful. This process may, however, slow your reading down too much. It may be better to concentrate on the sentence-by-sentence reading approach to find principal ideas, facts, and author's point of view.

➤ There is no substitute for practice. The more varied your reading, the better your score. Set aside some time each day for recreational reading and reading for information. The editorial page of the daily newspaper is an ideal source. And so are your textbooks!

Diagnostic Subtest 3A
Reading—Comprehension

Directions: Read each selection below and answer the questions that follow it. Choose your answer based on the information in the selection. Then blacken the circle containing the letter that corresponds to your choice.

Students who are successful in high school have learned to make systematic use of their study time. They do this by first developing the necessary habit of concentration. To prevent their minds from wandering from the work before them, they do their homework regularly at a scheduled time in the same place. They know approximately how much time they can afford for each assignment and how to make the best use of this time. Because they concentrate on the work, these students do not have time to consider whether they find the material difficult or easy, interesting or dull. Their main <u>concern</u> is mastering the material to the best of their ability. The joy of doing satisfying work is soon theirs as they continue to do their homework assignments in this manner.

1. Which of the following would be the best title for this passage?

   (A) "Doing School Work"
   (B) "Proper Use of Leisure Time"
   (C) "The Study Habits of Successful High School Students"
   (D) "Mastery of Material"

   Ⓐ Ⓑ Ⓒ Ⓓ

2. Successful high school students

   (A) avoid boring work.
   (B) feel satisfied with what they do.
   (C) find school work easy.
   (D) put off doing their school work.

   Ⓐ Ⓑ Ⓒ Ⓓ

3. Ability to concentrate

   (A) is inborn.
   (B) can be taught by teachers.
   (C) is contagious.
   (D) can be increased.

   Ⓐ Ⓑ Ⓒ Ⓓ

4. The word <u>concern</u>, as underlined and used in this passage, most nearly means

   (A) disturbance.
   (B) consideration.
   (C) worry.
   (D) apprehension.

   Ⓐ Ⓑ Ⓒ Ⓓ

5. Students who want to cure themselves of daydreaming during homework time should

   (A) set a time limit for each assignment.
   (B) watch less television.
   (C) take easier courses.
   (D) listen to the radio as they work.

   Ⓐ Ⓑ Ⓒ Ⓓ

6. The key to success in high school, according to this author, is

   (A) studying hard.
   (B) hiring a sympathetic tutor.
   (C) studying with a group of serious students.
   (D) learning how to do your best.

   Ⓐ Ⓑ Ⓒ Ⓓ

A tropism is the simplest kind of <u>behavior</u>. The one-celled amoeba reacts to strong light by moving away from it. A plant reacts to light in a different way. The tomato plant, for example, moves (by growing) toward the light. Organisms that lack nervous systems, such as the amoeba and the tomato plant, react to stimuli with the type of behavior called tropism.

A tropism involves only motion toward or away from a stimulus. This behavior is <u>innate</u>; that is, the organism makes the response from the beginning of life without having to learn how to carry out the behavior. Most tropisms seem to be controlled by chemicals. For example, the chemicals called auxins control the growth of a plant toward light.

7. The word <u>behavior</u>, as underlined and used in this passage, most nearly means

   (A) aptitude.
   (B) attitude.
   (C) response.
   (D) act.

   Ⓐ Ⓑ Ⓒ Ⓓ

8. The best title for this passage is

   (A) "Adjusting to Change."
   (B) "Chemical Controls."
   (C) "Let There Be Light."
   (D) "Amoebas and Tomatoes."

   Ⓐ Ⓑ Ⓒ Ⓓ

9. The word <u>innate</u>, as underlined and used in this passage, most nearly means

   (A) learned.
   (B) acquired.
   (C) primitive.
   (D) inborn.

   Ⓐ Ⓑ Ⓒ Ⓓ

10. In order for tropism to occur, the organism requires

    (A) controls.
    (B) a stimulus.
    (C) a nervous sytem.
    (D) a will.

    Ⓐ Ⓑ Ⓒ Ⓓ

11. The amoeba's reaction to strong light, when compared to that of a plant,

    (A) is the opposite.
    (B) is more intense.
    (C) is slower.
    (D) is the same.

    Ⓐ Ⓑ Ⓒ Ⓓ

A <u>fuse</u> contains a small strip of metal that melts at a lower temperature than will the other wires in the <u>circuit</u>. A fuse is connected with each branch of a house circuit. Therefore the same amount of electricity that passes through the house circuit passes through the fuse. If an excess amount of electricity flows through the circuit, the heat produced may cause the fuse metal to melt. The circuit then breaks, and the electricity stops flowing, thus preventing the circuit from overheating. A fuse or other type of circuit breaker is a safety device that is essential in all electrical circuits.

12. The word <u>circuit</u>, as underlined and used in this passage, most nearly means

    (A) complete path.
    (B) enclosed space.
    (C) events.
    (D) diagram.

    Ⓐ Ⓑ Ⓒ Ⓓ

13. The main idea of this passage is that

    (A) electricity can be dangerous.
    (B) a fuse is an essential safety factor in an electrical circuit.
    (C) a fuse is just one type of circuit breaker.
    (D) everyone should know how to change a fuse.

    Ⓐ Ⓑ Ⓒ Ⓓ

14. If too much electricity flows through the circuit, the metal that melts is

 (A) as thick as the other wires in the circuit.
 (B) thinner than the other wires in the circuit.
 (C) different from the metal in the other wires.
 (D) thicker than the wire in the circuit.

 Ⓐ Ⓑ Ⓒ Ⓓ

15. The word <u>fuse</u>, as underlined and used in this passage, most nearly means

 (A) pulley.
 (B) an interrupter.
 (C) electrical fusion.
 (D) a wick.

 Ⓐ Ⓑ Ⓒ Ⓓ

16. A house circuit in working order need *not* contain

 (A) electricity.
 (B) branches.
 (C) circuit breakers.
 (D) wires.

 Ⓐ Ⓑ Ⓒ Ⓓ

17. This selection is most likely a passage from a

 (A) novel.
 (B) book of essays.
 (C) sports magazine.
 (D) science textbook.

 Ⓐ Ⓑ Ⓒ Ⓓ

Before the nineteenth century, language study was mainly a field of philosophy. It was believed that language arose <u>spontaneously</u> from the human spirit. Therefore, languages are different as human beings are different. Each national group with its distinct language supposedly had instincts and emotions different from those possessed by peoples of other countries.

The students of language today are called linguists. The belief that languages grow out of some mystical connection between sound and human emotions has been discarded. Language sounds are accepted as a series of linguistic signs chosen by chance. All languages have common elements, and no one language is more beautiful or more difficult than another. The languages are different because different environmental factors reacted on the same element—human beings.

18. The best title for this passage would be

 (A) "Languages Then and Now."
 (B) "Changing Concepts of Language."
 (C) "Linguistic Signs and Symbols."
 (D) "Human Beings and Language."

 Ⓐ Ⓑ Ⓒ Ⓓ

19. The word <u>spontaneous</u>, as underlined and used in this selection, most nearly means

 (A) completely.
 (B) instinctively.
 (C) accidentally.
 (D) partially.

 Ⓐ Ⓑ Ⓒ Ⓓ

20. Two hundred years ago, people believed that the French language differed from the Spanish because French and Spanish people

 (A) have different inherited traits and emotions.
 (B) are similar physically and mentally.
 (C) come from different environments.
 (D) are not of equal intelligence.

 Ⓐ Ⓑ Ⓒ Ⓓ

21. Today, students of language believe that

 (A) all languages follow the same general rules.
 (B) Spanish is easier to learn than Portuguese.
 (C) we do not have to be taught to speak a language.
 (D) who we are is more important than where we were when, as infants, we were learning to talk.

 Ⓐ Ⓑ Ⓒ Ⓓ

22. An example of "a series of linguistic signs" would be

    (A) the human spirit.
    (B) the words "Have a nice day!"
    (C) human emotions.
    (D) the field of philosophy.

23. The author of the passage

    (A) offers examples to disprove old theories.
    (B) believes that different nationalities have different instincts.
    (C) believes that some languages are more beautiful than others.
    (D) thinks that language differences are the result of natural causes.

    Ⓐ Ⓑ Ⓒ Ⓓ

Each generation has its own crop of best-sellers on the theme "How to Get Along with Others." High on the list for all times and all ages is the rule governing positive and negative values. Some word it, "If you cannot say something positive (good, complimentary), don't say anything." Others say, "Set an example instead of using words when you want to be critical." The more cynical write, "All that you accomplish by trying to correct others is to lose friends." Finally, those with a psychological <u>bent</u> summarize the rule as "You are really being critical of yourself when you criticize others!" What do you think is the best way to help others when they need unasked-for advice?

24. "A crop of best-sellers" consists of

    (A) ideas.
    (B) books.
    (C) magazine articles.
    (D) fresh fruit.

    Ⓐ Ⓑ Ⓒ Ⓓ

25. Which of the following would be the best title for this passage?

    (A) "A Patient Adviser"
    (B) "Advice to Social Beings"
    (C) "Modern Etiquette"
    (D) "Getting to Know You'"

    Ⓐ Ⓑ Ⓒ Ⓓ

26. The word <u>bent</u>, as underlined and used in this passage, most nearly means

    (A) adjustment.
    (B) experience.
    (C) education.
    (D) inclination.

    Ⓐ Ⓑ Ⓒ Ⓓ

27. Which of the following remarks is positive and helpful, rather than negative?

    (A) "If I've told you once, I've told you a thousand times . . . stay away from him!"

    (B) "Why can't you ever learn not to volunteer!"
    (C) "Never say 'No' in the first sentence!"
    (D) "I liked the polite way you let him know how you feel! I was proud of you!"

    Ⓐ Ⓑ Ⓒ Ⓓ

28. A person with a psychological bent will probably

    (A) analyze why you said rather than what you said.
    (B) disregard facts in order to win an argument.
    (C) have a short attention span.
    (D) never get into an argument.

    Ⓐ Ⓑ Ⓒ Ⓓ

29. In this selection the author fails to

    (A) stick to the topic.
    (B) give her own opinion.
    (C) involve the reader.
    (D) give examples of advice.

    Ⓐ Ⓑ Ⓒ Ⓓ

Most spiders are venomous, but usually their <u>fangs</u> are too short or fragile to penetrate human skin. The most dangerous spider known is the black widow. Its <u>venom</u> is 15 times more poisonous than that of the prairie rattlesnake. The black widow's venom is a nerve poison that can cause muscle pain, tightness in the chest, abdominal pain, convulsions, paralysis, and shock. Because the black widow has very little venom, however, only 1 in 100 untreated black widow bites is fatal, as against a 15 to 21 percent fatality rate for the rattler.

Insects are less venomous than spiders but cause more deaths because many people are sensitive to the stings of bees, wasps, and ants.

30. The word <u>venom</u>, as underlined in this passage, most nearly means

(A) toxin.
(B) bite.
(C) danger.
(D) fangs.

Ⓐ Ⓑ Ⓒ Ⓓ

31. The best title for this passage would be

(A) "Black Widows and Rattlers."
(B) "Desert Death-Dealers."
(C) "Queen of the Dangerous Biters."
(D) "Insects and Spiders."

Ⓐ Ⓑ Ⓒ Ⓓ

32. Based on the data in the selection, we can infer that the fangs of the black widow

(A) are shorter than those of most spiders.
(B) are stronger than those of most spiders.
(C) cannot penetrate deep into the skin.
(D) are fragile and easily broken.

Ⓐ Ⓑ Ⓒ Ⓓ

33. The statistics included in the passage indicate that

(A) black widow bites are more dangerous than those of killer bees.
(B) fewer people are killed by rattlers than by black widows.
(C) more people are killed by rattlers than by insects.
(D) a person has a better chance of surviving a bite from a black widow than from a rattler.

Ⓐ Ⓑ Ⓒ Ⓓ

34. The word <u>fangs</u>, as underlined and used in this passage, most nearly means

(A) sharp beaks.
(B) flexible tongues.
(C) nailed claws.
(D) elongated teeth.

Ⓐ Ⓑ Ⓒ Ⓓ

35. The black widow's venom attacks the cells in the

(A) bloodstream.
(B) brain.
(C) nerves.
(D) lymph glands.

Ⓐ Ⓑ Ⓒ Ⓓ

Water is an excellent <u>solvent</u>. It dissolves out many minerals from rocks and soil as it flows over them. Some of the minerals are compounds of magnesium and calcium. Water containing such dissolved minerals is called hard water. Hard water is undesirable for washing purposes because the dissolved magnesium and calcium compounds prevent the formation of soapsuds. In addition, hard water deposits minerals in boilers and water pipes. As the minerals accumulate in a pipe, the inner diameter becomes narrower. As the pipe becomes clogged, the passage of water from the boiler slows down and eventually stops. Boiler explosions are sometimes caused by this stoppage.

36. The word <u>solvent</u>, as underlined and used in this selection, most nearly means

    (A) purifier.
    (B) dissolver.
    (C) cleanser.
    (D) liquid.

    Ⓐ Ⓑ Ⓒ Ⓓ

37. The best title for this passage would be

    (A) "Boiler Explosions."
    (B) "Dangerous Waters."
    (C) "Mineral Water."
    (D) "Watery Compounds."

    Ⓐ Ⓑ Ⓒ Ⓓ

38. Boilers may explode because

    (A) the water becomes too hot.
    (B) the pipes weaken.
    (C) the minerals become too concentrated.
    (D) the steam cannot escape.

    Ⓐ Ⓑ Ⓒ Ⓓ

39. How can we tell whether water is hard or soft?

    (A) by observing its color
    (B) by determining its temperature
    (C) by stirring a bar of soap in it
    (D) by smelling it

    Ⓐ Ⓑ Ⓒ Ⓓ

40. In order for water to be hard it must contain

    (A) soap.
    (B) sediment.
    (C) bacteria.
    (D) minerals.

    Ⓐ Ⓑ Ⓒ Ⓓ

Answers—Diagnostic Subtest 3A Reading—Comprehension

1. C	11. A	21. A	31. C
2. B	12. A	22. B	32. B
3. D	13. B	23. D	33. D
4. B	14. C	24. B	34. D
5. A	15. B	25. B	35. C
6. D	16. B	26. D	36. B
7. C	17. D	27. D	37. C
8. A	18. B	28. A	38. D
9. D	19. B	29. B	39. C
10. B	20. A	30. A	40. D

+---------------------------------------+
| **Rating Your Results** |
| |
| Superior   36–40 correct |
| Average   29–35 correct |
| Below Average   28 or fewer correct |
| |
| **Material to Review:** Chapter 5 |
+---------------------------------------+

Explanations

1. **C** The first sentence, the topic sentence, points clearly toward choice (C). Choices (A) and (D) are too general, and leisure time (choice (B) is not mentioned in the selection.

2. **B** "The joy of doing satisfying work is soon theirs…"

3. **D** This can be inferred from the entire selection, particularly sentence 2.

4. **B** A concern is a matter of interest, a consideration. The other choices do not fit the context.

5. **A** "They know…how much time they can afford for each assignment."

6. **D** "Their main concern is mastering the material to the best of their ability."

7. **C** Behavior is a response to stimulation or to the environment.

8. **A** Although general, this is the only title that includes the idea of adjustment. Choice (B) is wrong because the selection deals with behavior, not chemical controls. Choice (C) is unrelated to tropism, and choice (D) is based on examples, not the main idea.

9. **D** Innate behavior is present at birth, is unlearned or inborn.

10. **B** This is inferred from the fact that the amoeba's or tomato plant's change in behavior results from a change in the environment.

11. **A** The amoeba withdraws from the light; the plant goes toward it.

12. **A** A circuit is the complete path that electricity travels.

13. **B** The last sentence summarizes the main idea: "A fuse…is a safety device that is essential in all electrical circuits." Choices (A) and (C) express minor points, and choice (D) is not mentioned.

14. **C**   This can be inferred, since the metal in the fuse melts at a lower temperature.

15. **B**   A fuse melts and interrupts the circuit. Note "The circuit then breaks."

16. **B**   From the passage it is clear that electricity, circuit breakers (or fuses), and wires are essential in a house circuit. Therefore it can be inferred that branches are not necessary.

17. **D**   The passage clearly describes and explains an electrical device. The selection does not tell a story (A), deal with opinions (B), or discuss reports (C).

18. **B**   The first paragraph describes the early attitude; the second, the modern view.

19. **B**   What is spontaneous arises from natural feeling, that is, instinctively.

20. **A**   "Each national group with its distinct language supposedly had instincts and emotions different from those possessed by peoples of other countries."

21. **A**   "All languages have common elements."

22. **B**   "Language sounds [words] are accepted as a series of linguistic signs . . ."

23. **D**   By inference, we can conclude that, since language differences are not inborn, the environment must bring them about. This idea is stated in the last sentence.

24. **B**   Of the choices listed, "best-sellers," is associated with only one—books.

25. **B**   "Advice to Social Beings" means the same as "How to Get Along with Others."

26. **D**   A bent is a special inclination or aptitude.

27. **D**   This remark tells through praise what to do, rather than what not to do.

28. **A**   A person with a psychological bent is interested in understanding the causes of human behavior. Note "You are really being critical of yourself [criticizing yourself] when you criticize others!"

29. **B**   The author describes the behaviors others criticize or suggest. She does not give her own opinion; in fact, she ends with a question.

30. **A**   The definition "poison" can be reached by eliminating the other choices as the passage is read.

31. **C**   The main topic is the black widow spider. The rattler does not deserve equal billing (A), and (B) and (D) are too general.

32. **B**   Although the fangs of most spiders are "too short or fragile to penetrate human skin," we can infer that the black widow, which does bite people, has stronger fangs.

33. **D**   Compare "1 in 100" to "15 to 20" percent.

34. **D**   Fangs are long, hollow or grooved teeth.

35. **C**   The black widow's venom is a nerve poison . . .

36. **B**   "Water . . . solvent. It dissolves . . ."

37. **C**   This title is an appropriate play on words. Boiler explosions (A) are mentioned only briefly. The water is dangerous (B) only after a period of mineral accumulation. In choice (D), "Watery" suggests dilution, an aspect not dealt with.

38. **D**   We know that a boiler boils water, thus producing steam. By inference we can conclude that, if the pipes are clogged, the steam cannot escape and pressure builds up, causing pipes to burst.

39. **C**   Note ". . . the dissolved magnesium and calcium compounds prevent the formation of soapsuds."

40. **D**   "Water containing such dissolved minerals is called hard water."

READING—VOCABULARY (WORDS-IN-CONTEXT)

Sample Questions

This section tests your mastery of words and is therefore similar to part of the Verbal Skills unit in Chapter 3, where many of the questions had you pair a word with a synonym.

On the Vocabulary Test you have to select the synonym of a word in a given phrase. It is important to remember that some words have several meanings.

EXAMPLE:

serve a sentence   serve the meal
serve the ball   serve as a substitute

The synonym that you choose must be the one that is appropriate to the underlined word in the given phrase. In *peer into the future, peer* means "look." In *judged by his peers, peers* means "equal." In *pitted prunes, pitted* means "pits out." In a *pitted road,* the pits are in.

STRATEGIES FOR SUCCESS

➤ If you have easy recognition of the underlined word, its synonym will stand out among the four choices. To prevent careless errors, however, eliminate the other choices before marking the answer sheet.

➤ For words that do not come easily, use the negative approach. Begin by eliminating the choices that you know are wrong. Of those that are left, try to choose the one that fits the context. If you still wind up with two (or three) possible answers, put a circle around the number of the question and leave it. Don't spend time agonizing. Plan to come back to the circled items if time permits. Very often, when you return for that second try, the answer becomes clear.

➤ Since there is no penalty on this test for guessing, select the most likely choice before you finally leave the question. Then, unless you have made an obvious error, do not change your answer. Usually, the first guess is the better one!

➤ Beware of discouragement. Remember that no one is expected to finish all the sections and have all the answers correct.

Diagnostic Subtest 3B
Reading—Vocabulary

DIRECTIONS: Choose the word that means the same, or most nearly the same, as the underlined word, and blacken the circle containing the letter that corresponds to your choice.

41. an <u>incompetent</u> driver

(A) beginning   (B) unskilled
(C) overtrained   (D) careless

Ⓐ Ⓑ Ⓒ Ⓓ

42. the <u>biased</u> referee

(A) prejudiced   (B) capable   (C) placid
(D) experienced

Ⓐ Ⓑ Ⓒ Ⓓ

43. <u>churning</u> the ocean

(A) navigating   (B) mapping
(C) agitating   (D) cursing

Ⓐ Ⓑ Ⓒ Ⓓ

44. to <u>contend</u> for the prize

(A) fight   (B) wish   (C) rush
(D) nominate

Ⓐ Ⓑ Ⓒ Ⓓ

45. <u>impaired</u> vision

(A) incredible   (B) damaged
(C) destroyed   (D) acute

Ⓐ Ⓑ Ⓒ Ⓓ

46. <u>morose</u> followers

(A) disappointed   (B) faithful
(C) rebellious   (D) sullen

Ⓐ Ⓑ Ⓒ Ⓓ

47. <u>perplexed</u> by her remarks

(A) puzzled   (B) pleased
(C) angered   (D) fooled

Ⓐ Ⓑ Ⓒ Ⓓ

48. to <u>acquit</u> the accused

(A) fine   (B) clear   (C) sentence
(D) charge

Ⓐ Ⓑ Ⓒ Ⓓ

49. offer <u>solace</u>

(A) advice   (B) strength   (C) comfort
(D) recompense

Ⓐ Ⓑ Ⓒ Ⓓ

50. in a <u>pugnacious</u> mood

(A) contemplative   (B) talkative
(C) quarrelsome   (D) happy

Ⓐ Ⓑ Ⓒ Ⓓ

51. to <u>laud</u> the students

(A) praise   (B) instruct   (C) lecture
(D) confuse

Ⓐ Ⓑ Ⓒ Ⓓ

52. <u>grimy</u> hands

(A) strong   (B) delicate   (C) skilled
(D) dirty

Ⓐ Ⓑ Ⓒ Ⓓ

53. to <u>doff</u> her hat

(A) decorate   (B) remove   (C) wear
(D) misplace

Ⓐ Ⓑ Ⓒ Ⓓ

54. <u>dogged</u> determination

(A) persistent   (B) misguided
(C) youthful   (D) quiet

Ⓐ Ⓑ Ⓒ Ⓓ

55. to <u>chastise</u> the child

(A) amuse   (B) tend   (C) praise
(D) punish

Ⓐ Ⓑ Ⓒ Ⓓ

56. to <u>annihilate</u> the enemy

(A) trap   (B) destroy   (C) detect
(D) appease

Ⓐ Ⓑ Ⓒ Ⓓ

57. a <u>brazen</u> beggar

(A) shameless   (B) shy
(C) professional   (D) ragged

Ⓐ Ⓑ Ⓒ Ⓓ

58. to <u>berate</u> the children

    (A) comfort   (B) restrict
      (C) accompany   (D) scold
                                          Ⓐ Ⓑ Ⓒ Ⓓ

59. to <u>deplete</u> the bank account

    (A) examine   (B) empty   (C) control
      (D) establish
                                          Ⓐ Ⓑ Ⓒ Ⓓ

60. involved in a <u>fracas</u>

    (A) brawl   (B) scandal   (C) compromise
      (D) deal
                                          Ⓐ Ⓑ Ⓒ Ⓓ

61. <u>marital</u> problems

    (A) mathematical   (B) health
      (C) marriage   (D) money
                                          Ⓐ Ⓑ Ⓒ Ⓓ

62. a <u>scrupulous</u> shopkeeper

    (A) haphazard   (B) shrewd
      (C) cheerful   (D) honest
                                          Ⓐ Ⓑ Ⓒ Ⓓ

Answers—Diagnostic Subtest 3B
Reading—Vocabulary (Words-in-Context)

41. **B**	47. **A**	53. **B**	59. **B**
42. **A**	48. **B**	54. **A**	60. **A**
43. **C**	49. **C**	55. **D**	61. **C**
44. **A**	50. **C**	56. **B**	62. **D**
45. **B**	51. **A**	57. **A**	
46. **D**	52. **D**	58. **D**	

Rating Your Results

Superior	20–22 correct
Average	17–19 correct
Below Average	16 or fewer correct

Material to Review: Chapter 5

STUDY PLAN FOR THE READING SUBTEST

The key to raising your score in this area is the amount of time you can spend on the exercises and practice tests in Chapter 5, Reading.

Long-Term Program

1. The pages on Work-Study Skills consists of exercises and techniques to improve your speed and comprehension. Typical examination questions are analyzed in the sections that follow. The Mastery Exams will assure increased ability and speed.

2. The lists of things to do and facts to master in Chapter 5 are long—and rewarding! All you have to do is to budget your time properly. Browse through the Reading chapter and decide where to begin. Spend no more than 25 minutes on each practice session. Do not skip the varied exercises and practice tests. They lead to confidencc and speed in handling the actual HSPT.

3. Use the Practice HSPTs in the last section of this book as your final step in preparation.

Crash Program

1. Turn to Chapter 5, Reading. Do as many of the exercises and practice tests as you can to gain speed and accuracy. Several short sessions are always more productive than one long haul.

2. Use the Practice HSPTs in the last section of this book as your final step.

Subtest 4 Mathematics—Concepts and Problem Solving

The Mathematics Subtest consists of two types of questions:

> Concepts: 24 questions
> Problem Solving: 40 questions

You will be given 45 minutes to answer these 64 questions.

Progress in our society is often achieved by discoveries and inventions in science and technology. We are thrilled by the wonders of space exploration, atomic power, computer versatility, and disease control by the use of newly discovered drugs. Much of this scientific advance is made possible by the application of mathematical concepts and problem-solving techniques. The variety of fields that depend upon these concepts and techniques is astounding. Here are a few examples:

> All branches of engineering
> Architecture
> Space and space exploration
> Computer applications
> Environmental design

As you would expect, mathematical concepts are involved in scientific and industrial applications. It is important that students have a precise understanding of the basic mathematical concepts; a fuzzy understanding will produce fuzzy results. The 24 questions on concepts on the HSPT are designed to test such precise understanding.

Probably the most important goal of a student's concentration on mathematics is to develop problem-solving ability. The 40 questions on problem solving on the HSPT evaluate progress along these lines.

Sample Questions

EXAMPLE 1:
On a map, 1 inch represents 400 miles. The distance between the towns of Benson and Herlow is $3\frac{1}{2}$ inches on the map. How many miles apart are the two towns?

(A) 1,200   (B) 1,500   (C) 900   (D) 1,400

SOLUTION: To find the number of miles between the two towns, we must multiply 400 by $3\frac{1}{2}$.

$$400 \times 3\frac{1}{2} = 400 \times \frac{7}{2} = 1,400$$

The correct choice is **D**.

EXAMPLE 2:
On a cold day, the temperature at noon was 7° above zero. By midnight, the temperature had fallen 15°. What was the temperature at midnight?

(A) 15° below zero   (B) 8° above zero
(C) 8° below zero   (D) 7° below zero

SOLUTION: To solve the problem, we must subtract 15° from 7°.

$7° - 15° = -8°$, or 8 degrees below zero

The correct choice is **C**.

EXAMPLE 3:
If $3x - 2 = 4$, then the value of $6x^2$ is

(A) 10   (B) 24   (C) 144   (D) 72

SOLUTION:
$$3x - 2 = 4$$
$$3x = 4 + 2 = 6$$
$$x = \frac{6}{3} = 2$$
$$6x^2 = 6 \cdot 2 \cdot 2 = 24$$

The correct choice is **B**.

EXAMPLE 4:
The sum of $\frac{1}{2}$ of a number and $\frac{1}{5}$ of the same number is 7. Find the number.

(A) 7   (B) 9   (C) 49   (D) 10

SOLUTION: Let x = the number.

$$\frac{x}{2} + \frac{x}{5} = 7$$

If we multiply both sides of the equation by 10, we have

$$5x + 2x = 70$$
$$7x = 70$$
$$x = \frac{70}{7} = 10$$

The correct choice is **D**.

EXAMPLE 5:
The width of a rectangle is 6 inches, and the length of its diagonal is 10 inches. The perimeter of the rectangle is

   (A) 32 inches (B) 28 inches
    (C) 24 inches (D) 36 inches

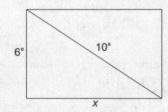

SOLUTION: Let x = the length of the rectangle.
$$x^2 + 6x^2 = 10^2$$
$$x^2 + 36 = 100$$
$$x^2 = 100 - 36 = 64$$
$$x = \sqrt{64} = 8 \text{ inches}$$

Perimeter = 6 + 8 + 6 + 8 = 28 inches.

The correct choice is **B**.

STRATEGIES FOR SUCCESS

The Mathematics Subtest measures your ability to answer two basic types of questions.

Concepts: You must understand the meanings and applications of the main ideas in basic mathematics.

Problem Solving: You must be able to solve a wide variety of problems such as the following:

Number problems
Simple algebra problems
Simple geometry problems
Problems based on applications of mathematics in real-life situations

The suggestions below are designed to help you attain your best score.

➤ *Tactic 1:* Read each question carefully. Every word in a mathematical statement has a precise meaning.

➤ *Tactic 2:* Determine what information is given and what must be found. This analysis will give you the essence of the problem.

➤ *Tactic 3:* Develop a plan for a solution. Such a plan will involve a link between the information you have been given and what you must find.

➤ *Tactic 4:* Use your plan as a guide to the solution of the problem.

➤ *Tactic 5:* Check your answer. To save time, you may use the method of estimating the answers.

➤ *Tactic 6:* Be sure that your answer is given in the units specified in the question.

➤ *Tactic 7:* Do not get upset if you cannot answer a question. If you can eliminate some choices, do so. Then, since there is no penalty for guessing, choose what seems the best answer. You do not have to answer every question correctly to get a good score.

➤ *Tactic 8:* If you do not see an immediate approach to the solution of a problem, leave it and return to it later if time permits.

➤ *Tactic 9:* Do not spend too much time on any one question. Since you must answer 64 questions in 45 minutes, you cannot afford to dwell on a troublesome problem.

Diagnostic Subtest 4 Mathematics— Concepts and Problem Solving

1. Expressed as a percent, 0.49 =

    (A) 0.049%   (B) 0.49%   (C) 4.9%
    (D) 49%

2. If $\frac{2}{3}$ of a number is 8, what is 40% of that number?

    (A) 12   (B) 4.8   (C) 6   (D) 8

3. If O is the center of the circle and the measure of $\angle AOB = 80°$, what fractional part of the circle is sector OAB?

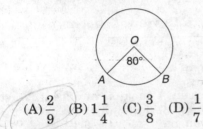

    (A) $\frac{2}{9}$ (B) $1\frac{1}{4}$ (C) $\frac{3}{8}$ (D) $\frac{1}{7}$

4. Solve: $2^4 - 9$.

    (A) –1   (B) 1   (C) –7   (D) 7

5. What number should replace n to make $\frac{5}{8} = \frac{35}{n}$ a true proportion?

    (A) 23   (B) 64   (C) 56   (D) 72

6. A dealer bought a table for $120 and sold it at a profit of 40%. What was the selling price of the table?

    (A) $168   (B) $180   (C) $150   (D) $170

7. If $2x + 5 = 11$, find the value of $x^2 + 6x$.

    (A) 72   (B) 54   (C) 27   (D) 36

8. In the figure shown, $ABCD$ is a rectangle. $AB = 6$ inches, $AD = 8$ inches, and $EC = 5$ inches. Find the area of the figure.

    (A) 60 square inches
    (B) 65 square inches
    (C) 70 square inches
    (D) 63 square inches

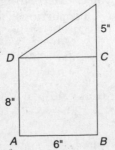

9. After driving 120 miles, a motorist found that he had covered 40% of his trip. How many more miles did he have to travel to complete his journey?

    (A) 150   (B) 300   (C) 180   (D) 20

10. The sum of two numbers is x, and one of the numbers is 10. What is 5 times the other number?

    (A) $5x$ (B) $5x - 10$ (C) $5(x - 10)$
    (D) $10 - 5x$

11. Find half the difference between $5\frac{1}{8}$ and $2\frac{3}{4}$.

    (A) $4\frac{1}{2}$ (B) $4\frac{3}{4}$ (C) $2\frac{3}{8}$ (D) $1\frac{3}{16}$

12. In $\triangle ABC$, the measure of $\angle B = 60°$ and the measure of $\angle C = 50°$. Which side of $\triangle ABC$ is the largest?

    (A) AB (B) AC
    (C) BC
        (D) the three sides are equal

13. What percent of 72 is 27?

    (A) $37\frac{1}{2}$%   (B) $3.7\frac{1}{2}$%   (C) $0.37\frac{1}{2}$%
    (D) 4.19%

14. Solve: $\frac{7}{9} + \frac{5}{12}$.

    (A) $\frac{12}{21}$ (B) $1\frac{3}{12}$ (C) $\frac{84}{72}$ (D) $1\frac{7}{36}$

15. When a number is increased by 25% of itself, the result is 95. What is the number?

    (A) 80   (B) 76   (C) 75   (D) 85

16. In a right triangle, the measure of one acute angle is 4 times as great as the measure of the other acute angle. What is the measure of the larger acute angle?

    (A) 18°   (B) 60°   (C) 72°   (D) 64°

17. A chicken weighs 3 pounds 12 ounces. What is the cost of the chicken at $0.60 per pound?

    (A) $2.00   (B) $2.50   (C) $2.25
    (D) $2.75

18. Which of the following is a solution of the sentence $2 > x > -1$?

    (A) 3   (B) –3   (C) 0   (D) 4

19. Solve: $\frac{7}{8} - \frac{5}{6}$.

    (A) $\frac{1}{24}$ (B) $\frac{3}{48}$ (C) $\frac{2}{8}$ (D) $1\frac{1}{24}$

20. Ms. Martinez bought a new car. She made a down payment of $6,300. If this down payment was 35% of the price of the car, what was the total price?

    (A) $15,000   (B) $18,000   (C) $16,500
    (D) $19,000

21. The exact number of hundreds in 5,780 is

    (A) 578   (B) 780   (C) 57.8   (D) 5.78

22. $(-4)^3 + (-3)^2 =$
    (A) 21   (B) –55   (C) –73   (D) 73

23. Solve: $\frac{4}{9} \times \frac{3}{7} \times \frac{5}{8}$.

    (A) $\frac{60}{63}$ (B) $\frac{5}{42}$ (C) $\frac{17}{24}$ (D) $\frac{47}{56}$

24. Solve: $-8 - (-3)$.

    (A) –11   (B) –5   (C) 5   (D) 11

25. A sofa and a chair cost $680. If the sofa costs $440 more than the chair, what is the cost of the sofa?

    (A) $120   (B) $240   (C) $560   (D) $580

Answers—Diagnostic Subest 4 Mathematics—Concepts and Problem Solving

1. **D**	7. **C**	13. **A**	19. **A**
2. **B**	8. **D**	14. **D**	20. **B**
3. **A**	9. **C**	15. **B**	21. **C**
4. **D**	10. **C**	16. **C**	22. **B**
5. **C**	11. **D**	17. **C**	23. **B**
6. **A**	12. **C**	18. **C**	24. **B**
			25. **C**

Rating Your Results	
Superior	21–25 correct
Average	16–20 correct
Below Average	15 or fewer correct

Material to Review: Chapters 7–12

Explanations

1. **D** "Percent" means hundredths, so 49% = 0.49, or 49 hundredths.

2. **B** Let x = the number.

    $$\frac{2}{3}x = 8$$
    $$x = 8 \div \frac{2}{3}$$
    $$x = 8 \times \frac{3}{2} = 12$$

    40% of 12 = 0.4 × 12 = 4.8

3. **A** The sum of the measures of the angles around a point in a plane is 360°.

    $$\frac{80}{360} = \frac{2}{9}$$

    Thus, sector AOB is $\frac{2}{9}$ of the circle.

4. **D** $2^4 = 2 \times 2 \times 2 \times 2 = 16$

    16 – 9 = 7

5. **C** According to the Principle of Proportions,

    $$5 \times n = 8 \times 35$$
    $$5n = 280$$
    $$n = 56$$

6. **A** 40% of 120 = 0.4 × 120 = 48.0
    120 + 48 = $168

7. **C** $2x + 5 = 11$
$$2x = 11 - 5 = 6$$
$$x = 3$$
$$x^2 + 6x = (3)^2 + 6(3) = 9 + 18 = 27$$

8. **D**   Area of rectangle

$ABCD = 8 \times 6 = 48$ square inches.

Area of $\triangle DCE$
$= \frac{1}{2}(DC)(EC)$
$= \frac{1}{2}(6)(5) = 15$
   square inches
$48 + 15 = 63$ square
   inches

9. **C**   Let x = the total distance to be covered.

Then, $0.4x = 120$
$$4x = 1,200$$
$$x = 300$$

Since the motorist had already covered 120 miles, he had $300 - 120 = 180$ miles to go.

10. **C**   If the sum of the two numbers is x and one of the numbers is 10, the other number is $x - 10$.
   Five times the other number is $5(x - 10)$.

11. **D** $5\frac{1}{8} - 2\frac{3}{4} = \frac{41}{8} - \frac{11}{4}$

$$\frac{41}{8} - \frac{11}{4} = \frac{41}{8} - \frac{22}{8} = \frac{19}{8}$$

$\frac{19}{8}$ = time difference between the two numbers.
One-half of the difference =

$$\frac{1}{2}\left(\frac{19}{8}\right) = \frac{19}{16}, \text{ or } 1\frac{3}{16}.$$

12. **C**   Since the measure of $\angle B = 60°$ and the measure of $\angle C = 50°$, the measure of $\angle A =$ $180 - (60 + 50)$.

The measure of $\angle A =$ $180 - 110 = 70°$.
   Thus, $\angle A$ is the largest angle of $\triangle ABC$. Therefore, BC is the largest side of $\triangle ABC$, since the largest side is

opposite the largest angle in a triangle.

13. **A**   Write the fraction: $\frac{27}{72} = \frac{3}{8}$

Change the fraction to a decimal:

$$\begin{array}{r} 0.375 \\ 8\overline{)3.000} \\ \underline{2\,4} \\ 60 \\ \underline{56} \\ 40 \end{array}$$

Write the decimal as a percent:
$$0.375 = 37\frac{1}{2}\%$$

14. **D**   Write the two fractions with the L.C.D.:

$$\frac{7}{9} = \frac{28}{36}, \frac{5}{12} = \frac{15}{36}$$

$$\frac{28}{36} = \frac{15}{36} > \frac{43}{36} = 1\frac{7}{36}$$

15. **B**   Let x = the number.
$$x = \frac{1}{4x} = 95.$$
If we multiply both sides of the equation by 4, we have
$$4x + x = 380$$
$$5x = 380$$
$$x = 380 \div 5 = 76$$

16. **C**   Let x = the measure of the smaller acute angle, and
   $4x$ = the measure of the larger acute angle.
$$x + 4x = 90$$
$$5x = 90$$
$$x = 90 \div 5 = 18$$
$$4x = 4(18) = 72$$

17. **C**   12 ounces = $\frac{12}{16}$, or $\frac{3}{4}$, of a pound.

The chicken weighs $3\frac{3}{4}$ or $\frac{15}{4}$, pounds.
$\frac{15}{4}(0.60) = \$2.25.$

18. **C**   In the given inequality, x is less than 2 but greater than -1.
We consider the choices in turn until we reach a solution:
a): 3 is not less than 2.
b): -3 is less than 2 but is not greater than -1.
c): 0 is less than 2 and greater than -1.

19. **A** Write the two fractions with the lowest common denominator:

$$\frac{7}{8} = \frac{21}{24}, \frac{5}{6} = \frac{20}{24}$$

$$\frac{21}{24} - \frac{20}{24} = \frac{1}{24}$$

20. **B** Let x = the price of the car.
Then $35x = 6{,}300$
$x = 6{,}300$
$0.35 = \$18{,}000$

21. **C** $5{,}780 \div 100 = 57.80$, or 57.8.

22. **B** $(-4)^3 = (-4)(-4)(-4) = -64$
$(-3)^2 = (-3)(-3) = 9$
$-64 + 9 = -55$

23. **B** Before multiplying, divide and cancel:

$$\frac{\overset{}{4}}{\underset{3}{9}} \times \frac{3}{7} \times \frac{5}{\underset{2}{8}} = \frac{5}{42}$$

24. **B** $-8 - (-3) = -8 + 3 = -5$

25. **C** Let x = the cost of the chair, and $x + 440$ = the cost of the sofa.
$x + x + 440 = 680$
$2x + 440 = 680$
$2x = 680 - 440 = 240$
$x = 120$
$x + 440 = 120 + 440 = \$560$

STUDY PLAN FOR THE MATHEMATICS SUBTEST

The best preparation for this test is to get plenty of practice in interpreting and solving problems. The references below identify sections in the book that are especially rich in challenging problems.

Arithmetic: "One Hundred Verbal Problems," Chapter 8
Mastery Exams
Chapter 13, Memory and Reasoning Skills
Algebra: Practice Tests 1–10, Chapter 9
Geometry: Practice Tests 1–10, Chapter 12

Subtest 5 Language

In this test you are given 25 minutes to answer 60 questions on the mechanics of composition: capitalization, punctuation, usage, spelling, thought expression, and sentence order. The questions are not on rules or principles but, rather, on their application. You are required only to identify the errors, not to correct them.

Overview of Content

The questions are based on a limited area, which includes most of the errors committed by high school students. The specific items that are covered are listed below, with examples for clarification. This list does not, however, represent all of the information you should have at your command. For a broader treatment turn to Chapter 6, Language Arts.

Punctuation

1. Period

   a. As end stop: I did not go there.

   b. After an abbreviation: Mr. Smith

2. Comma

   a. In a series: science, mathematics, and English.

   b. With an appositive: Mr. Blesser, our new coach, . . .

   c. In a direct quotation: I said, "I will do it."

   d. In direct address: Edna, please come here.

3. Question mark as end stop: Where shall I go?

4. Apostrophe

   a. To show omission: can't, I'll, O'Reilly.

   b. To show possession: Lucy's book, ladies' coats

5. Quotation marks

   a. In the title of a short work: the poem "Subways to Safety."

   b. In a direct quotation: He shouted, "Now is the time!"

6. Colon

    a. After the salutation in a business letter: Dear Mr. Dobren:
    b. To separate chapter and verse when referring to a Biblical quotation: Matthew 3:21.
    c. After an introductory clause that precedes a list: He included four books: . . .
    d. Between the hour and minutes in a numerical expression of time: 6:15.

Capitalization

1. For the first word in a quotation: She asked, "Shall I leave now?"
2. For an adjective or proper noun: American, Paul, Oregon, St. Louis, Colorado River.

Usage

1. The seven parts of speech: verbs, nouns, pronouns, adjectives, adverbs, prepositions, conjunctions.
2. Homophones (words that sound alike but are spelled differently and have different meanings): _loan-lone, would-wood, sight-cite, altar-alter._
3. Double negatives: I don't want (_any, no_) more.

Recognition of Correct Forms

1. Correct verb with indefinite pronoun: Every one of the books (_is, are_) accounted for.
2. Correct case of subject pronouns: (_They, them_) are the ones I want.
3. Correct case of pronouns that are objects of prepositions: Between you and (_I, me_), he is wrong!
4. Correct use of adjectives and adverbs: I did (_good, well_) on that test.
5. Correct use of collective nouns: The committee (_is, are_) in agreement on this issue.
6. Correct tenses in a sentence: He left early and (_goes, went_) home.
7. Subject-verb agreement: Every nail in the two boxes (_was, were_) defective.
8. Correct punctuation of an exclamatory sentence in a quotation: "Never, never, never! I never said that!"

Spelling

Perennial demons: _separate, similar, all right._

Composition: Handling Sentences and Paragraphs

1. Proper use of connectives: I have a big test tomorrow; (_however, and, therefore_) I can't go to the movies tonight.
2. Clear thought expression: Given four sentences, choose the one that expresses the thought most clearly.
3. Unity (adherence to topic)

    a. Given the assigned topic and a choice of four sentences, determine which sentence is most clearly related to the topic.
    b. Determine which of four topics is best for a one-paragraph theme.
    c. Given a short paragraph, determine which sentence does not belong in the paragraph.
    d. Determine where, in a given paragraph, a given sentence should be placed.

Sample Questions

There are three groups of questions, each with a defined area and its own set or sets of directions.

1. _Capitalization, Punctuation,_ and _Usage._ You are required to identify the sentence, if there is one, that contains an error. You are not required to correct the error.

EXAMPLE:
(A) I plan to take Biology in high school.
(B) Every student knows exactly what he or she should expect in class.
(C) I exclaimed, "No! That isn't fair."
(D) No mistakes.

EXPLANATION: Only the names of school subjects derived from names of languages are capitalized. Therefore, **A** is the correct choice.

2. *Spelling.* You are required to identify the sentence, if there is one, that contains a misspelled word.

EXAMPLE:
(A) Between you and me, how wrong can he be?
(B) Coming into the room, we saw the flames.
(C) Hardly any of the plants survived the frost.
(D) Is their a doctor in the house?

EXPLANATION: The introductory word *there,* not the possessive *their,* is required. Therefore, **D** is the correct choice.

3. *Composition*

a. Conjunctive phrases. You are required to choose the most appropriate word or phrase to join the thoughts in a sentence.

EXAMPLE:
The machinery in the entire factory came to an abrupt halt _____ the supply of oil was exhausted.

(A) but   (B) although   (C) and
(D) because

EXPLANATION: Since there is a causal relationship, *because* is most appropriate. Therefore **D** is the correct choice.

b. Thought expression. You are required to choose the sentence that expresses the idea most clearly.

EXAMPLE:
(A) She froze in fear every time she almost heard the siren.
(B) She almost froze in fear every time she heard the siren.
(C) She froze in fear almost every time she heard the siren.
(D) She froze almost in fear every time she heard the siren.

EXPLANATION: *Almost* must be placed close to *every time,* the phrase it modifies. Therefore, **C** is the correct choice.

c. Adherence to topic. You are required to identify the sentence that best fits a given topic, the topic best suited for a one paragraph theme, the sentence that does not belong in a given paragraph, and the proper position in a given paragraph for a particular sentence.

EXAMPLE:
Which sentence does not belong in the following paragraph?

(1) I had not had time to complete the homework. (2) The teacher called on me to read my answers. (3) He was seated at his desk. (4) Before 1 could rise from my seat, the period ended.

(A) sentence 1   (B) sentence 2
(C) sentence 3   (D) sentence 4

EXPLANATION: The fact that the teacher was seated at his desk is irrelevant. Therefore, **C** is the correct choice.

STRATEGIES FOR SUCCESS

➤ For *capitalization,* follow these steps:

1. Read the sentence part by part, looking for an obvious error. Here are some examples: Omission of required capital

	Wrong	Right
name of person	helen smith	Helen Smith
name of place	new zealand	New Zealand
name of institution	notre dame university	Notre Dame University
title	professor Anderson	Professor Anderson
half of title	secretary of State	Secretary of State
half of name	mount St. Helens,	Mount St. Helens,
	New York city,	New York City,
	Mississippi river	Mississippi River

Incorrect addition of capital

	Wrong	Right
season	Autumn	autumn
relationship	my favorite Cousin	my favorite cousin
geographical area	nearby Mountains	nearby mountains

2. If nothing is obvious, go through the sentence again, checking each noun for an omitted or an unnecessary capital.

➤ For *punctuation,* proceed as follows: Read the sentence carefully, looking for an obvious error. Here are some examples: Omission of required punctuation

	Wrong	Right
period	Dr Henderson	Dr. Henderson
apostrophe	peoples court	people's court
question mark	Who did it	Who did it?
comma in series	red white, and blue	red, white, and blue
exclamation point	What a night it was	What a night it was!

Incorrect addition of punctuation

	Wrong	Right
apostrophe	it's injured bark	its injured bark
comma	loud, and clear	loud and clear

For *usage,* follow these steps:

1. Look for the obvious, the glaring error. Below are some errors that fit this description:

Double negative: I don't want nothing (*anything*).

Incorrect verb form: He has broke (*broken*) my pen.

Incorrect pronoun: Give it to Meg and I (*me*).

Lack of agreement of subject and verb: One of the fires were (*was*) put out.

Confusion of adjective and adverb: I did good (*well*) on that test.

You will find a more complete list of problem areas in the section titled Standard English Usage in Chapter 6.

2. To avoid carelessly making the second best choice, eliminate the three other choices before marking the answer sheet.

3. If in doubt, rely on the level of usage you find in books assigned in school.

➤ For *composition,* proceed as outlined below.

1. To handle questions on choosing proper connectives, follow these steps.
   a. Read the sentence or sentences to find out what the thought connection is between the two parts. The usual connection can involve:

   time sequence (*first, after*)

   explanatory (*for example, that is*)

   result (*thus, therefore, hence, consequently*)

   contrast (*instead, however, on the other hand, nevertheless*)

   additional fact (*moreover, besides, also, furthermore*)

   b. Check the choices by placing them one at a time into the blank space. Don't skip any one of them. The correct choice will reveal a clear relationship.

2. To handle questions on expressing an idea most clearly, follow these steps.
   a. Read each of the four choices, looking for one of the following errors:

   Error resulting from omission of a necessary noun or pronoun: Meg's head ached and *so wouldn't* dance.

   Dangling participle: *Looking for a solution,* the problem seemed insurmountable.

   Dangling infinitive: *To reach a proper conclusion,* the facts must be clearly evaluated.

   Misplaced modifiers: He sat on the chair in the lobby *which was broken.*

   Misplaced adverb: I *only* had three pennies left.

   b. Before indicating your choice on the answer sheet, check the other three sentences to make certain that they are error free.

3. To handle questions on paragraph unity, follow these steps:
   a. Read the topic sentence word for word before looking at the choices. Try to pick out the key words: The *computer* has *revolutionized* the world of youth.

b. Read the four choices through once; then go over them a second time to eliminate the one that is most obviously off the topic. If you can, decide next on a second seemingly irrelevant possibility.

c. If you find it difficult to eliminate the second choice, try to find the choice that definitely develops the topic sentence. Keep in mind the key words.

d. Before marking the answer sheet, reread the topic sentence and then each of the choices. Make certain that you blacken the appropriate circle.

➤ For *all types* of questions, keep these recommendations in mind:

1. Don't dawdle. If you can't decide on the correct choice in a reasonable time, circle the item number and return to the question later if time permits.

2. Since no credit is deducted for wrong answers, when you return to an item, eliminate, if you can, any obviously wrong choices. Then, if no one answer seems clearly right, select the one that you consider most appropriate and do not change it without good reason. Usually the first choice is the best one.

Diagnostic Subtest 5   Language

DIRECTIONS: For questions 1–40, look in each group for a sentence containing an error in punctuation, capitalization, or usage, and blacken the circle with the letter that corresponds to your choice. If there is no error, blacken (D).

1. (A) "Ah, now you are on my side!"
   (B) After fifty kneebends, she could scarcely stand.
   (C) A group of strangers were seen walking toward the school yard.
   (D) No mistakes
   Ⓐ Ⓑ Ⓒ Ⓓ

2. (A) Ann told Edna that she could not go to the party.
   (B) "Alan, I'm in need of immediate assistance."
   (C) To solve the problem quickly, use algebra.
   (D) No mistakes
   Ⓐ Ⓑ Ⓒ Ⓓ

3. (A) At the age of nineteen, Geraldo was a piano virtuoso.
   (B) Sarah is a much better writer than him.
   (C) Peanut butter and jelly is my favorite sandwich mix.
   (D) No mistakes
   Ⓐ Ⓑ Ⓒ Ⓓ

4. (A) What were her principal arguments?
   (B) We couldn't hardly wait for the results.
   (C) Whose hat did I borrow?
   (D) No mistakes
   Ⓐ Ⓑ Ⓒ Ⓓ

5. (A) To be able to drive a car well is my present goal.
   (B) Barbara said to Muriel, "You passed the test!"
   (C) They just don't want anybody else to know.
   (D) No mistakes
   Ⓐ Ⓑ Ⓒ Ⓓ

6. (A) Did everyone of the students correct his or her own errors?
   (B) She has fewer friends now than ever before.
   (C) Helen wants neither the book or the pencil.
   (D) No mistakes
   Ⓐ Ⓑ Ⓒ Ⓓ

7. (A) Do you approve of his being chosen moderator?
   (B) Everybody, including the four visitors, knows the answer to that question.
   (C) Here lies the remnants of my fondest dreams.
   (D) No mistakes
   Ⓐ Ⓑ Ⓒ Ⓓ

8. (A) Her answers are different from ours.
   (B) Only I had seen the pictures before.
   (C) We can begin the test, when the bell rings.
   (D) No mistakes

   Ⓐ Ⓑ Ⓒ Ⓓ

9. (A) Philip yelled that he badly needed us to help him.
   (B) I started to scream when he comes toward me.
   (C) We voted that Mike and I would attend the meeting.
   (D) No mistakes

   Ⓐ Ⓑ Ⓒ Ⓓ

10. (A) They lived in that house for the past ten years.
    (B) The bell had already rung.
    (C) Put your money back in your pocket.
    (D) No mistakes

    Ⓐ Ⓑ Ⓒ Ⓓ

11. (A) "Tea for Two," a real old classic is my favorite.
    (B) They will take notes for Susanna and me.
    (C) Have you ever been in Washington, D.C.?
    (D) No mistakes

    Ⓐ Ⓑ Ⓒ Ⓓ

12. (A) I lay in bed all day with a frightful headache.
    (B) Nevertheless I shall not oppose you.
    (C) Neither the cookies nor the cake were there.
    (D) No mistakes

    Ⓐ Ⓑ Ⓒ Ⓓ

13. (A) You cannot both talk about a person and have her as a friend.
    (B) We had to borrow knives, forks, and spoons from the commissary.
    (C) These here bats are just what the coach ordered.
    (D) No mistakes

    Ⓐ Ⓑ Ⓒ Ⓓ

14. (A) What is the reason for the delay.
    (B) Drive slowly around the corner.
    (C) Between you and me, I think she has gone too far.
    (D) No mistakes

    Ⓐ Ⓑ Ⓒ Ⓓ

15. (A) She is the more intelligent of the two.
    (B) The winner, tired and content, listened quietly to the broadcast of the official results.
    (C) Place the girl's coat on the chair.
    (D) No mistakes

    Ⓐ Ⓑ Ⓒ Ⓓ

16. (A) My aunt lives near lake Michigan.
    (B) We could hardly wait for the coach to arrive.
    (C) What shall we have for dessert'?
    (D) No mistakes

    Ⓐ Ⓑ Ⓒ Ⓓ

17. (A) Remember to drive carefully through this congested area.
    (B) Long may his humor reign in our comic strips.
    (C) Amanda boasted that she could have did it by herself.
    (D) No mistakes

    Ⓐ Ⓑ Ⓒ Ⓓ

18. (A) The cat leaped off the chair and approached her and I.
    (B) The machine certainly runs smoothly now.
    (C) I was so angry I could have wrung her neck.
    (D) No mistakes

    Ⓐ Ⓑ Ⓒ Ⓓ

19. (A) Chris is somewhat shy most of the time.
    (B) Do you know where they put the men's jackets?
    (C) You will have to do more better if you expect to become a member of the team.
    (D) No mistakes

    Ⓐ Ⓑ Ⓒ Ⓓ

20. (A) You will have to decide between Charlie and us.
    (B) You ought not to listen to such rumors!
    (C) Terry turn down the volume on your stereo.
    (D) No mistakes

    Ⓐ Ⓑ Ⓒ Ⓓ

21. (A) The best scene in the story occurs when the bridge collapses.
    (B) He stayed in the cabin for two months this summer.
    (C) I have just read the life of Magic Johnson one of basketball's greats.
    (D) No mistakes

    Ⓐ Ⓑ Ⓒ Ⓓ

22. (A) It was, fortunately, a most minor accident.
    (B) He is by far a more skillful player than I.
    (C) The three ladies' entered the room.
    (D) No mistakes

    Ⓐ Ⓑ Ⓒ Ⓓ

23. (A) You will have to do it without our helping you.
    (B) Place it near that officer's documents.
    (C) He had spoke to me about it.
    (D) No mistakes

    Ⓐ Ⓑ Ⓒ Ⓓ

24. (A) They swam across the river this morning.
    (B) We seniors must plan a yearly reunion.
    (C) The time is exactly 4:11.
    (D) No mistakes

    Ⓐ Ⓑ Ⓒ Ⓓ

25. (A) They have tried to learn many of the popular American customs.
    (B) "I don't know the answer" said Charlotte honestly.
    (C) May I borrow the pen for a moment?
    (D) No mistakes

    Ⓐ Ⓑ Ⓒ Ⓓ

26. (A) Did you spend the summer in Albany?
    (B) Please sit quiet beside your sister.
    (C) There's no reason for your becoming so angry.
    (D) No mistakes

    Ⓐ Ⓑ Ⓒ Ⓓ

27. (A) Every one except Mel and me received an invitation.
    (B) The thief had sneaked in through the porch door.
    (C) When will you notify me of their arrival.
    (D) No mistakes

    Ⓐ Ⓑ Ⓒ Ⓓ

28. (A) Let us slay the dragon of tyranny.
    (B) There's three letters waiting for you.
    (C) Dear Sir:
    (D) No mistakes

    Ⓐ Ⓑ Ⓒ Ⓓ

29. (A) Neither Albert nor his sisters were planning to see the new play.
    (B) Did you see that woman's hat?
    (C) Edna enjoys reading those kind of books.
    (D) No mistakes

    Ⓐ Ⓑ Ⓒ Ⓓ

30. (A) John said, "I'll really try this time."
    (B) Think twice before you become annoyed.
    (C) I wondered whether Tom would come.
    (D) No mistakes

    Ⓐ Ⓑ Ⓒ Ⓓ

31. (A) She works much faster than he.
    (B) They wanted to know, "How old he was?"
    (C) It's a matter of his solving his own problems.
    (D) No mistakes

    Ⓐ Ⓑ Ⓒ Ⓓ

32. (A) Since it is late, we will have to leave now.
    (B) President Bush called a special session of Congress.
    (C) You must do like I tell you.
    (D) No mistakes

    Ⓐ Ⓑ Ⓒ Ⓓ

33. (A) Her name is always spelled with two *m's.*
    (B) When she broke her ankle, she stood in bed for a week.
    (C) Eric fell off the ladder.
    (D) No mistakes

    Ⓐ Ⓑ Ⓒ Ⓓ

34. (A) I can scarcely believe what I am hearing.
    (B) "I don't know the answer," Helen said, "but I'll find out."
    (C) Bring these articles with you, scissors, paste, and construction paper.
    (D) No mistakes

    Ⓐ Ⓑ Ⓒ Ⓓ

35. (A) Have you written to them lately?
    (B) The near east is rich in oil deposits.
    (C) The work having been completed, the plumber left.
    (D) No mistakes

    Ⓐ Ⓑ Ⓒ Ⓓ

36. (A) We have not done anything wrong.
    (B) I just cant do it.
    (C) Everybody except them agreed to arrive early.
    (D) No mistakes

    Ⓐ Ⓑ Ⓒ Ⓓ

37. (A) How can you let her do all that heavy work without offering to help her!
    (B) Tabby, our cat, is laying on the rug.
    (C) Is Election Day a legal holiday?
    (D) No mistakes

    Ⓐ Ⓑ Ⓒ Ⓓ

38. (A) They hadn't ought to have done it.
    (B) None of us is ready.
    (C) Philip sneered, "And who will stop me?"
    (D) No mistakes

    Ⓐ Ⓑ Ⓒ Ⓓ

39. (A) If it weren't for Jack, where would we be now?
    (B) Why do you like Frankie better than me?
    (C) I will never forget my first glimpse of the atlantic ocean.
    (D) No mistakes

    Ⓐ Ⓑ Ⓒ Ⓓ

40. (A) Whose is it?
    (B) She borrowed the money off me last night.
    (C) The torch of freedom burns brightly throughout the world.
    (D) No mistakes

    Ⓐ Ⓑ Ⓒ Ⓓ

DIRECTIONS: For questions 41–50, look in each group for a sentence containing a spelling error, and blacken the circle with the letter that corresponds to your choice. If there is no misspelling, blacken (D).

---

41. (A) She will be most disappointed.
    (B) I never suspected the existance of such a problem.
    (C) We sent for a copy of the Christmas catalog.
    (D) No mistakes

    Ⓐ Ⓑ Ⓒ Ⓓ

42. (A) We will have to plan for a new delivery date.
    (B) Begin at the begining, please.
    (C) Put sufficient postage on the package.
    (D) No mistakes

    Ⓐ Ⓑ Ⓒ Ⓓ

43. (A) Rest. Don't aggravate the condition.
    (B) The agreement was satisfactorily concluded.
    (C) Who will be the defense attorney?
    (D) No mistakes

    Ⓐ Ⓑ Ⓒ Ⓓ

44. (A) Please enter the appointment on the calender.
    (B) I do not know why they would want to deceive us.
    (C) They should be compelled to resign.
    (D) No mistakes

    Ⓐ Ⓑ Ⓒ Ⓓ

45. (A) When did you two become aquainted?
    (B) That is no reason to condemn all of them.
    (C) They were most sincerely sorry and apologized.
    (D) No mistakes

    Ⓐ Ⓑ Ⓒ Ⓓ

46. (A) I will give you a definate answer in an hour.
    (B) You will have to see the superintendent.
    (C) I spoke to two of her colleagues.
    (D) No mistakes

    Ⓐ Ⓑ Ⓒ Ⓓ

47. (A) It is a genuine antique.
    (B) When does the guarantee go into effect?
    (C) Tomorow is the day of the street fair.
    (D) No mistakes

    Ⓐ Ⓑ Ⓒ Ⓓ

48. (A) I tried desperately to please them.
    (B) I am not entirely disatisfied with the results.
    (C) They are at the peak of their efficiency.
    (D) No mistakes

    Ⓐ Ⓑ Ⓒ Ⓓ

49. (A) May I congratulate you on your excelent choice!
    (B) I was invited to join the new committee.
    (C) Where is the letter they addressed to me?
    (D) No mistakes

    Ⓐ Ⓑ Ⓒ Ⓓ

50. (A) Finally, who will evaluate the criticism?
    (B) Which brand will you recommend?
    (C) Nothing startling occured during the meeting.
    (D) No mistakes

    Ⓐ Ⓑ Ⓒ Ⓓ

DIRECTIONS: For questions 51–60, follow the directions for each question, select the correct answer, and blacken the circle with the letter that corresponds to your choice.

51. Choose the best word to join the thoughts.

    He greeted us with a cold stare; _____ we smiled warmly and put on a bold front.

    (A) therefore,
    (B) nevertheless,
    (C) moreover,
    (D) None of these

    Ⓐ Ⓑ Ⓒ Ⓓ

52. Choose the best word to join the thoughts.

    They are coming here today; _____ they are due right now!

    (A) on the other hand,
    (B) namely,
    (C) in fact,
    (D) that is,

    Ⓐ Ⓑ Ⓒ Ⓓ

53. Choose the words that best complete the sentence below.

    To finish the essay,

    (A) several books were needed from the library.
    (B) Meg needed several books from the library.
    (C) a trip to the library was needed to get several books.
    (D) Meg had to go to the library to get several books she needed for her essay.

    Ⓐ Ⓑ Ⓒ Ⓓ

54. Which of the following expresses the intended meaning most clearly?

    (A) While still a child, Mother read modern poetry to my sister and me.
    (B) When we were little, Mother read modern poetry to my sister and me.
    (C) While little children, Mother read modern poetry to my sister and me.
    (D) Mother read modern poetry to my sister and me while still a child.

    Ⓐ Ⓑ Ⓒ Ⓓ

55. Which of the following expresses the intended meaning most clearly?

    (A) Coming to the top of the hill, the town could be seen in the distance.
    (B) The town could be seen in the distance coming to the top of the hill.
    (C) Coming to the top of the hill, we saw the town in the distance.
    (D) When coming to the top of the hill, in the distance the town could be seen.

    Ⓐ Ⓑ Ⓒ Ⓓ

56. Which of the following sentences fits best under the topic "Recent Increases in Educational Opportunities Beyond High School"?

    (A) Basic college costs have greatly increased.
    (B) With increasingly flexible admission requirements, more students find that college doors are open to them.
    (C) Twenty-five years ago, nursing education began to shift from hospitals to junior and senior colleges.
    (D) None of these

    Ⓐ Ⓑ Ⓒ Ⓓ

57. Which of the following sentences fits best under the topic "Environmental Effects on the Sphinx"?

(A) The giant human head with a lion's body was dug out of the sand in 1926.
(B) Erosion, pollution, and sewage seepage into the surrounding water have had alarming effects on the porous limestone.
(C) The statute first underwent repair in 1401 B.C.
(D) None of these

Ⓐ Ⓑ Ⓒ Ⓓ

58. Which of the following topics is best for a one-paragraph theme?

(A) The Major Causes of Violence in Our Cities
(B) The First Thing to Do When a Fire Breaks Out at Home
(C) Why My Candidate Should be Elected President
(D) How to Survive a Divorce in the Family

Ⓐ Ⓑ Ⓒ Ⓓ

59. Which sentence does not belong in the paragraph below?

(1) In wartime, the helicopter serves as the eyes and ears of the troops. (2) The helicopter is steered by inclining its main rotor. (3) In peace, the helicopter has brought new dimensions to sea-air rescues. (4) As we can see, the helicopter can compete with the airplane as an airborne service unit for humanity.

(A) sentence 1   (B) sentence 2
(C) sentence 3   (D) sentence 4

Ⓐ Ⓑ Ⓒ Ⓓ

60. Where should the sentence "The major instrument of emotive language is not words but body movement, body language" be placed in the following paragraph?

(1) I. A. Richards claimed that there are two types of language. (2) One is the symbolic, in which sounds are used to convey ideas and information. (3) The other is the emotive, which expresses feelings and attitudes.

(A) before sentence 1
(B) before sentence 2
(C) before sentence 3
(D) after sentence 3

Ⓐ Ⓑ Ⓒ Ⓓ

Answers—Diagnostic Subtest 5 Language

1. C	16. A	31. B	46. A
2. A	17. C	32. C	47. D
3. B	18. A	33. B	48. B
4. B	19. C	34. C	49. A
5. D	20. C	35. B	50. C
6. C	21. C	36. B	51. B
7. C	22. C	37. B	52. C
8. C	23. C	38. A	53. B
9. B	24. D	39. C	54. B
10. A	25. B	40. B	55. C
11. A	26. B	41. B	56. B
12. C	27. C	42. B	57. B
13. C	28. B	43. D	58. B
14. A	29. C	44. A	59. B
15. D	30. D	45. A	60. D

Rating Your Results	
Superior	54–60 correct
Average	47–53 correct
Below Average	46 or fewer correct

Material to Review: Chapter 6

Explanations

1. **C** Singular subject requires a singular verb: *A group ... was*. Here the strangers are thought of collectively, rather than as individuals.

2. **A** Ambiguous pronoun: Who is *she*? Ann? Edna?

3. **B** Incorrect case of pronoun. Complete the sentence: *than he is ...*

4. **B** Double negative: *could hardly wait*.

5. **D** No mistakes.

6. **C** Paired connectives: *neither ... nor*.

7. **C** Lack of subject-verb agreement: *Here lie the remnants.*

8. **C** No comma precedes *when* if it introduces a subordinate clause.

9. **B** Wrong tense: *came* is needed to agree with *started.*

10. **A** Action begun in the past and continued into the present requires present progressive tense: *have lived.*

11. **A** Appositive within a sentence must be set off by two commas: *classic, ...*

12. **C** The second subject, not the first, determines verb form: *nor the cake was there.*

13. **C** *Here* is not required after *this* or *these.*

14. **A** A direct question requires a question mark.

15. **D** No mistakes.

16. **A** Proper name requires capitals: *Lake Michigan.*

17. **C** Incorrect verb form: *could have done it.*

18. **A** Incorrect case of pronoun. Leave out *her and: approached me.*

19. **C** Double comparative. *More* is not needed with comparative form *better: do better.*

20. **C** Noun in direct address is followed by a comma: *Terry,....*

21. **C** Appositive at the end of a sentence must be preceded by a comma: *Johnson, one....*

22. **C** A simple plural does not require an apostrophe: *three ladies.*

23. **C** Incorrect verb form: *had spoken.*

24. **D** No mistakes.

25. **B** A direct quotation is set off by a comma: *answer," said.*

26. **B** Adverb, not adjective, is needed to modify set: *sit quietly.*

27. **C** Direct question requires a terminal question mark.

28. **B** Lack of subject-verb agreement: *There are three letters.*

29. **C** Lack of adjective-noun agreement: *that kind.*

30. **D** No mistakes.

31. **B** Quotation marks and a comma are not used to set off an indirect question: *to know how old he was.*

32. **C** A conjunction, not a preposition, is needed to introduce a clause: *as I tell you.*

33. **B** Word confusion: *stayed* (remained) is needed, not *stood* (on one's feet).

34. **C** A colon is needed to introduce a list: *you: scissors.*

35. **B** Name of a specific area requires capitalization: *Near East.*

36. **B** Apostrophe is required for missing letter or letters: *can't = cannot.*

37. **B** Word confusion: *lying* (reclining) is needed, not *laying* (placing)

38. **A** Incorrect usage: *ought not.*

39. **C** Capitalization is required for proper nouns: *Atlantic Ocean.*

40. **B** Incorrect usage: *borrow from.*

41. **B** *existence*

42. **B** *beginning*

43. **D** No mistakes.

44. **A** *calendar*

45. **A** *acquainted*

46. **A** *definite*

47. **D** No mistakes.

48. **B** *dissatisfied*

49. **A** *excellent*

50. **C** *occurred*

51. **B** The element of contrast (*cold stare* vs. *smiled warmly*) requires *nevertheless.*

52. **C** The emphasis of *in fact* (*coming today, due right now*) is appropriate.

53. **B** To avoid a dangling participle, we must supply the proper subject. *Meg,* not *books* or a *trip,* is correct. Choice (D) has the correct subject but is wordy and repetitious.

54. **B** *While still a child* does not refer to *Mother* and must not be close to that word.

55. **C** *Coming to the top of the hill* requires the correct noun or pronoun to modify. *We,* not the *town,* is correct.

56. **B** Only this sentence mentions a recent increase in educational opportunities.

57. **B** Only this sentence develops the topic of environmental effects.

58. **B** Adequate development of choices (A), (C), and (D) would require more than one paragraph.

59. **B** The steering mechanism is not related to the topic of helicopter service in peace and war.

60. **D** This sentence explains *emotive,* which is introduced in sentence 3.

STUDY PLAN FOR THE LANGUAGE TEST

The key to raising your score in this area is the time you can spend on the lists, exercise, and practice tests in Chapter 6, Language Arts.

Long-Term Program

1. Concentrate on one area at a time. The study material includes rules, examples, exercises, practice exercises, and mastery exams. The list of things to do and facts to master can be overwhelming unless you apply a familiar adage: Divide and conquer. Therefore, begin with the area that the Diagnostic Test has revealed as needing most attention. When you feel reasonably confident, move on to another topic.

2. Spend no more than 20 minutes on each practice session.

3. Do not skip any of the varied exercises and practice tests. They not only help you to remember rules but also promote confidence and speed in handling the items on the actual examination.

4. Use the Practice HSPTs, in the last section of this book, as your final step in preparation.

Crash Program

1. Use the Diagnostic Test to discover which areas require most of your study time. Then concentrate on the sections of Chapter 6, Language Arts, that have the required rules and exercises. Remember that several short sessions are more productive than one long period of cramming.

2. Use the Practice HSPTs, in the last section of this book, as your final step.

DIGEST OF COMMUNICATION SKILLS

Vocabulary

The HSPT and the Coop ask four types of multiple-choice vocabulary questions:
1. Synonyms
2. Words in Context
3. Antonyms
4. Analogies

The HSPT also contains several Verbal Classification questions.

This section will review the question types and show you some useful strategies for answering each type. Practice tests and Mastery Exams will familiarize you with the questions, increase your speed in answering them, and help you evaluate the extent of your vocabulary. Use the Answer Keys at end of this chapter, pages 172–173.

Synonym Questions

A *synonym* is a word that has the same meaning, or almost the same meaning, as another word. Each synonym question asks you to identify the word that comes closest in meaning to the capitalized, or key, word.

> **EXAMPLE**
>
> BRAGGART: (A) support   (B) brigand
> (C) ignorant   (D) boaster   (E) veteran
> Ⓐ Ⓑ Ⓒ ● Ⓔ

ANALYSIS: Study the key word for clues to its meaning. Notice that it contains the word *brag*. Because *brag* means *boast*, choice D is a possible answer. Choice A, *support*, may have been listed because one of its synonyms, *bracket*, sounds a bit like *braggart*. Although choice B, *brigand* (an outlaw), contains many of the same letters as the key word, don't let similar spelling fool you into picking it. Notice that C is an adjective. Because the key word is a noun, and four of the five choices are also nouns, C is not a likely answer. The remaining choice is E, but *veteran* is not related to the key word. Because a *braggart* tends to boast quite a lot, D is the correct answer.

HOW TO HANDLE SYNONYM QUESTIONS

Before you look at the answers, read the key word carefully. If you know the word, find the answer among the choices. If the word is vaguely familiar, perhaps you have a general sense of its meaning. Think of a synonym, if possible. While you may not think of an exact synonym, you may come up with something close. If you have no idea of the word's definition, try the following:

➤ Look for word parts—prefixes, suffixes, roots. These may help you detect the meaning.

➤ Say the word silently to yourself. "Hearing" the word may open its meaning to you.

➤ As you read the choices, try to eliminate any that are definitely wrong. Be wary of words that sound the same or are spelled like the key word. They may have been put there to mislead you.

123

➤ If you know the word but cannot find a synonym among the choices, remember that many words have more than one meaning. Go back to the key word and think of other definitions for it. (The verb *sow*, for example, means to plant; the noun *sow* refers to a female pig.)

➤ Be sure your answer is the same part of speech as the key word. If the key word is a verb, for example, the answer will also be a verb, never a noun, adjective, or other part of speech.

It is better to guess than leave the item blank. You might get lucky and choose the right answer.

PRACTICE TEST 1

DIRECTIONS: For each of the following, choose the word or phrase that most nearly means the SAME as the capitalized word. Circle the letter of the correct answer.

EXAMPLE:

ENRAGED: (A) involved (B) furious
(C) troubling   (D) betrothed   (E) defeated

1. ACCOMPLISH: (A) redo (B) struggle
   (C) conspire (D) achieve (E) continue

2. APPAREL: (A) reality (B) garb
   (C) umbrella (D) style (E) appearance

3. BRAND: (A) trait (B) premium
   (C) trademark (D) relative (E) novelty

4. COLOSSAL: (A) immense (B) queer
   (C) frantic (D) superior (E) tasty

5. CLEAVE: (A) erupt (B) control
   (C) depart (D) grind (E) split

6. GHASTLY: (A) massively destructive
   (B) frighteningly terrible (C) primitive
   (D) royal (E) deeply offensive

7. MORTGAGE: (A) heavy fog
   (B) debt on a property (C) prospect
   (D) mortality (E) estate

8. TREACHEROUS: (A) traitor
   (B) betrayal   (C) danger
   (D) disloyal (E) terrorist

9. GRUDGING: (A) hateful (B) clumsy
   (C) anticipation (D) doubting
   (E) reluctant

10. COUNSEL: (A) cash register
    (B) advice (C) city governing body
    (D) pluck (E) comfort

11. VAIN: (A) beautiful (B) fun-loving
    (C) valiant (D) desperate
    (E) conceited

12. ORATORY: (A) dignity (B) eloquence
    (C) purity (D) musical solo (E) trickery

13. REALIZE: (A) bring (B) analyze
    (C) accomplish (D) conquer
    (E) consume

14. RELISH: (A) mutilate (B) refrain
    (C) enjoy (D) replenish (E) recite

15. EGRESS: (A) bird (B) exit (C) leak
    (D) departure (E) excuse

16. SHUN: (A) avoid (B) attend
    (C) pursue (D) shudder (E) wander

17. INFRACTION: (A) violation
    (B) portion   (C) command
    (D) design (E) denial

18. TERMINATE: (A) inflate
    (B) persecute (C) imitate (D) end
    (E) rule

19. SYNONYMOUS: (A) murmuring
    (B) meaning the same (C) persistent
    (D) inciting to sin (E) common

20. ULTIMATE: (A) next to last (B) petty
    (C) final (D) mimicking (E) essential

21. SUBMISSIVE: (A) obedient
    (B) marauding (C) mythical
    (D) pertaining to marine life
    (E) wintry

22. UNEMPLOYED: (A) insecure
    (B) unsure (C) without employees
    (D) jobless (E) wandering

23. VEHICLE: (A) spectacle
    (B) conveyance (C) flight (D) dexterity
    (E) cabin

24. VULGAR: (A) angry (B) coarse
    (C) vigorous (D) fervid (E) offhand

25. MALADY: (A) tune (B) flattery
    (C) sickness (D) reputation (E) mood

26. UNDISPUTED: (A) arguing (B) plain
    (C) unchallenged (D) wretched
       (E) victorious

27. MERE: (A) not more than (B) total
    (C) motherly (D) frantic
       (E) pertaining to horses

28. ACKNOWLEDGE: (A) write (B) admit
    (C) wisdom (D) advice (E) represent

29. UNCOMPROMISING: (A) pleading
    (B) meeting half-way (C) unyielding
       (D) tiresome (E) untruthful

30. LEGAL: (A) manufactured
    (B) pertaining to a limb (C) papal
       (D) lawful (E) expensive

31. TIMID: (A) faint-hearted
    (B) punctual (C) prompt (D) tasteless
       (E) controlled

32. OBLIGATORY: (A) pleasing
    (B) required (C) excessively polite
       (D) untiring (E) defective

33. GROUCH: (A) bungler (B) bag
    (C) optimist (D) grumbler (E) bully

34. ENVIOUS: (A) previous (B) jealous
    (C) joyful (D) inquisitive (E) unforgiving

35. ADMONISH: (A) befit (B) abandon
    (C) promote (D) rebuke
       (E) imprision unlawfully

36. BLEAK: (A) sleek (B) playful
    (C) desolate (D) wistful (E) noisy

37. CONSPIRACY: (A) circulation
    (B) secret plot (C) shaded terrace
       (D) fight to the death (E) treason

38. BOUNDLESS: (A) preceding
    (B) explicit (C) without limit
       (D) immense (E) energetic

39. BLUFF: (A) triumphant (B) trying
    (C) secretive (D) frank (E) timorous

40. ENRICH: (A) befall (B) arouse
    (C) adore (D) resolve (E) improve

41. ABRIDGE: (A) cross over (B) cover
    (C) elevate (D) straddle (E) shorten

42. ANALYZE: (A) disturb (B) paralyze
    (C) examine closely
       (D) praise insincerely (E) develop

43. ENDURE: (A) detour (B) last
    (C) occupy (D) exceed (E) harden

44. BRACKET: (A) nature
    (B) supporting piece (C) loud noise
       (D) tennis equipment (E) inclusion

45. EMBRACE: (A) love (B) resist
    (C) hug (D) recover (E) certify

46. SUPERB: (A) questionable
    (B) splendid (C) fairly good (D) scant
       (E) relevant

47. CRITICAL: (A) harmful
    (B) fault-finding (C) thoughtful
       (D) highly emotional (E) essential

48. REVITALIZE: (A) capture (B) trust
    (C) return (D) furnish (E) strengthen

49. SULLEN: (A) excessive (B) natural
    (C) rational (D) ill-tempered (E) soiled

50. INTERMINABLE: (A) powerful
    (B) endless (C) taut (D) tiresome
       (E) boastful

Words-in-Context Questions

Here your vocabulary is being tested in actual use. Therefore, these questions ask you to identify the word that comes closest in meaning to a word that appears in a phrase, a sentence, or a short paragraph.

> **EXAMPLE:**
>
> Choose the word that means the same as the word in boldface type in the following sentence:
>
> The waters were **ruffled** by the wind.
>
> (A) frozen (B) smoothed (C) disturbed
>   (D) driven (E) cooled
>
> Ⓐ Ⓑ ● Ⓓ Ⓔ

ANALYSIS: Since *ruffled* means upset or disturbed, the correct answer is *disturbed*.

PATTERNS TO WORDS-IN-CONTEXT QUESTIONS

1. The entire sentence or paragraph may be a definition of the word.

> **EXAMPLE:**
>
> *Anatomy* is the science that deals with the study of the physical structure of an organism.
>
> Anatomy
>
> (A) is a recent discovery
> (B) is based on physics
> (C) describes how to dissect animals
> (D) deals with the makeup of a body
>
> Ⓐ Ⓑ Ⓒ ●

ANALYSIS: The selection does not tell us how old anatomy is; therefore (A) is wrong. The selection does not describe where anatomy comes from; therefore (B) is not correct. Anatomy may involve dissections, but that aspect is not stressed in the sentence; therefore (C) is eliminated. (D) paraphrases "the study of the physical structure of an organism" and is the correct choice.

2. The key word may be followed by a synonym.

> **EXAMPLE:**
>
> *Manumission,* the liberation of slaves, was practiced by many people when the slave had served adequately for a definite period of time.
>
> *Manumission* means most nearly
>
> (A) purchase (B) freeing (C) capturing
>   (D) elevation
>
> Ⓐ ● Ⓒ Ⓓ

ANALYSIS: Liberation, manumission, and freeing are synonyms; therefore (B) is the correct choice.

3. The selection may contain an example or illustration that explains the key word.

> **EXAMPLE:**
>
> The reasoning that leads to the *traitorous* deeds of a Benedict Arnold is beyond my comprehension.
>
> *Traitorous* means
>
> (A) kindly (B) deadly (C) disloyal
>   (D) patriotic
>
> Ⓐ Ⓑ ● Ⓓ

ANALYSIS: The key to the answer—Benedict Arnold, who went over to the enemy—is in the given sentence. Therefore, *patriotic* is wrong. Arnold is not known for being *kindly* or *deadly*. The only possible answer is *disloyal*, as proved by Arnold's actions.

4. The action in the rest of the sentence serves as a clue to the meaning of the test word.

> **EXAMPLE:**
>
> Marjorie's skill in handling words made her speech most *stimulating.*
>
> *Stimulating* means
>
> (A) dull (B) wordy (C) intelligent
>   (D) exciting
>
> Ⓐ Ⓑ Ⓒ ●

ANALYSIS: The sentence is in praise; therefore *dull* and *wordy* can be eliminated. Intelligence is not under discussion; therefore, *intelligent* can be eliminated. *Exciting* is correct by the process of elimination, and because *exciting* fits in with *skill* and *speech.*

HOW TO HANDLE WORDS-IN-CONTEXT QUESTIONS

➤ Don't even think about answering the question without first reading the whole passage, sentence, or paragraph.

➤ Look for clues to the correct answer. Clues often lie hidden in definitions, in carefully placed synonyms, and in examples. Sometimes a description will contain a clue to the right answer.

➤ Once you've found a promising clue, read all four choices (A–D) before determining your answer.

➤ Use the process of elimination to prove the other choices wrong.

➤ Once you have chosen an answer, check it by substituting it in the phrase, sentence, or paragraph. If it doesn't make sense, pick another answer.

➤ If you are stumped, don't dawdle. Go on to the next question, but make a note to come back later and try again. If you still can't answer the question, give it a guess. You may get lucky. You have a 25 percent chance of guessing the correct answer.

PRACTICE TEST 2

DIRECTIONS: Each of the following sentences is followed by an incomplete statement. Circle the letter of the choice that best completes the statement.

1. Alison walked her bicycle across the *heath* because there were no trails to ride on.

   A *heath* is most like a

   (A) flat meadow (B) stream
      (C) road (D) small park

2. In recent years motorists have grown *accustomed* to additives which are said to increase the power of gasoline.

   Accustomed means most nearly

   (A) wise (B) hardened (C) used
      (D) similar

3. The storm *baffled* the weather forecaster, who couldn't figure out what caused the snow to fall nonstop for three days and nights.

   Baffled most nearly means

   (A) threatened (B) advised (C) puzzled
      (D) delighted

4. Habits are learned behavior which has become automatic because of repetition.

   Actions become habits when

   (A) they are taught
      (B) they are mastered
         (C) they are avoided
            (D) they are done often enough

5. The first method for producing an electric current involved batteries, but batteries are not practical as sources of current on a large and continuous scale.

   Batteries will not

   (A) store electricity
      (B) produce electricity
         (C) store an indefinite amount of electricity
            (D) store a sufficient amount of electricity

DIRECTIONS: Select the correct SYNONYM for the italicized word in each sentence.

6. The defenders tried in vain to *expel* the invaders

   (A) conquer (B) meet (C) force out
      (D) envelop

7. The successful sales person is always *punctual* for appointments.

   (A) on time (B) prepared (C) anxious
      (D) anticipating

8. The criminal and his *accomplice* were captured by the alert detectives.

   (A) lawyer (B) helper (C) driver
      (D) victim

9. The angry father *chastised* his disobedient son.

   (A) scolded (B) praised (C) discovered
      (D) beat

10. Because the students were *boisterous* during the assembly, the principal kept them after school.

    (A) unruly (B) unafraid
      (C) uninterested (D) lethargic

11. The coach *lauded* his assistant for planning the winning play.

    (A) rewarded (B) praised
      (C) publicized (D) ignored

12. Only a *dolt* would believe such a ridiculous story.

    (A) coward (B) friend (C) fool
      (D) small child

13. Do not be so *rash* that you feel compelled to climb the mountain with them.

    (A) reckless (B) insensitive
      (C) sensitive (D) foolish

14. A *titanic* wave battered the small boat and drove it toward the rocks.

    (A) tremendous
      (B) produced by a storm (C) sudden
        (D) unexpected

15. The president *rescinded* the order when he realized it would cause too much friction.

    (A) enforced (B) broke (C) repealed
      (D) issued

> DIRECTIONS: Select the correct SYNONYM for the italicized word in each phrase.

16. appear *unconcerned* when told the news

    (A) interested (B) fearful
      (C) uninterested (D) disturbed

17. arrange a *truce* between the two warring groups

    (A) treaty (B) temporary peace
      (C) lasting agreement (D) contest

18. *replenish* their arms supply

    (A) create (B) refill
      (C) purchase illegally (D) uncover

19. a *minute* defect

    (A) very small (B) serious
      (C) trivial (D) costly

20. *quell* their fears

    (A) analyze (B) quiet (C) show (D) hide

Antonym Questions

An *antonym* is a word that means the *opposite* of another word. An antonym question requires that you identify a word opposite in meaning to a given word.

> **EXAMPLE:**
>
> PRESERVE: (A) observe (B) destroy
> (C) enjoy (D) present (E) disregard
>   Ⓐ●ⒸⒹⒺ

ANALYSIS: To *preserve* liberty means to protect it. Therefore, *destroy* is the closest to the opposite of *preserve*. Let's look at the other choices: *enjoy* and *disregard* are unrelated to *preserve*. *Observe* contains many of the same letters. So does *present*. But neither word is related to the key word, *preserve*.

> ### HOW TO HANDLE ANTONYM QUESTIONS
>
> ➤ Read the instructions carefully. Are you required to find a word that is the same (synonym) or the opposite (antonym) in meaning?
>
> ➤ Eliminate the obviously wrong answers. Narrow down your choices. Then select the answer most nearly or most usually correct.

PRACTICE TEST 3

DIRECTIONS: This a test of your ability to find words that mean the OPPOSITE of other words. For each of the fifty words below, there are five choices. Circle the letter of the best choice.

EXAMPLE:

FLIGHTY: (A) soaring (B) whirling (C) level-headed (D) lucky (E) imaginative

1. GENUINE: (A) banished (B) average (C) insincere (D) economical (E) greedy

2. OUTSTANDING: (A) condensed (B) interior (C) commonplace (D) reckless (E) innocent

3. MOCK: (A) fling (B) startle (C) fail (D) mutilate (E) praise

4. TARDY: (A) smooth (B) bristly (C) strong (D) punctual (E) concealed

5. EXCLUDE: (A) admit (B) excuse (C) console (D) excel (E) separate

6. IMPAIR: (A) import (B) improve (C) console (D) deceive (E) separate

7. GRAVITY: (A) cemetery (B) thankfulness (C) attraction (D) indebtedness (E) unimportance

8. DRAB: (A) humid (B) exorbitant (C) vivid (D) rigid (E) restful

9. RESENT: (A) intrude (B) prefer (C) send again (D) misaddress (E) welcome

10. PRUDENT: (A) novel (B) considerate (C) careless (D) sane (E) insurable

11. FORMAL: (A) neat (B) casual (C) obscure (D) apprehensive (E) presentable

12. BOISTEROUS: (A) deplorable (B) fretful (C) bright (D) placid (E) childish

13. TENSE: (A) miserable (B) calm (C) adopted (D) partial (E) unnoticed

14. JOVIAL: (A) melancholy (B) curious (C) inert (D) subsequent (E) failing

15. RESPONSE: (A) notation (B) rest (C) stimulus (D) rally (E) stature

16. FRIGID: (A) in bondage (B) imprisoned (C) adapted (D) torrid (E) dreamy

17. ORIGIN: (A) conflict (B) universe (C) outcome (D) ordinance (E) resource

18. DON: (A) lead (B) yield (C) doff (D) yearn (E) molest

19. OBVIOUS: (A) dubious (B) certified (C) suspicious (D) apart (E) ardent

20. LAUNCH: (A) sail (B) conclude (C) explain (D) stumble (E) finance

21. MOURNFUL: (A) majestic (B) visual (C) cheerful (D) supreme (E) minor

22. RADIATE: (A) absorb (B) elate (C) denounce (D) restrict (E) examine

23. JUSTICE: (A) cheerfulness (B) blame (C) hysteria (D) partiality (E) recklessness

24. WANE: (A) please (B) wax (C) gauge (D) strive (E) conceal

25. PARTICIPATE: (A) hesitate (B) counsel (C) abstain (D) coach (E) employ

26. VACANT: (A) occupied (B) sanctified (C) decorated (D) desolate (E) surrounded

27. CLASSIFY: (A) commence (B) disarrange (C) discover (D) ratify (E) enumerate

28. GENERAL: (A) superlative (B) indifferent (C) chronic (D) specific (E) elegant

29. HAMPER: (A) hurdle (B) impress (C) encase (D) assist (E) enforce

30. PATIENT: (A) docile (B) restless (C) uncooperative (D) pliable (E) polite

31. OBEDIENCE: (A) observance (B) commencement (C) rebellion (D) extravagance (E) management

32. ENORMOUS: (A) minute
    (B) momentary (C) drab (D) pompous
       (E) selective

33. IDEAL: (A) improbable (B) craven
    (C) imperfect (D) critical
       (E) momentous

34. SLUGGISH: (A) insignificant
    (B) powerless (C) brisk (D) willing
       (E) particular

35. TERRIFY: (A) reassure (B) control
    (C) strengthen (D) restore
       (E) empower

36. UNIFORM: (A) varied
    (B) conventional (C) total (D) dyed
       (E) universal

37. CHECK: (A) release (B) retrain
    (C) hover (D) repay (E) diminish

38. QUELL: (A) extol (B) correspond
    (C) incite (D) whisper (E) defer

39. AFFILIATE: (A) confer (B) separate
    (C) deter (D) consign (E) arrest

40. LIBERATE: (A) lend (B) falsify
    (C) enslave (D) settle (E) continue

41. PURCHASER: (A) contender
    (B) seller (C) monopolizer (D) consumer
       (E) agent

42. HAGGARD: (A) young at heart
    (B) companionable (C) well-nourished
       (D) dependable (E) edible

43. REJECT: (A) resist (B) abound
    (C) accept (D) flit (E) finance

44. LADEN: (A) wound up (B) delighted
    (C) gladdened (D) unburdened
       (E) stooped

45. BARREN: (A) pleasant (B) brooding
    (C) productive (D) calm (E) sultry

46. SHREWD: (A) serene (B) hypocritical
    (C) considerate (D) stupid
       (E) insulting

47. INDENT: (A) bend (B) project
    (C) ignite (D) punch (E) purify

48. SPECIFIC: (A) calm (B) slavish
    (C) vague (D) concentrate
       (E) innocent

49. UNIMPRESSIVE: (A) invaluable
    (B) placid (C) outstanding
       (D) subversive (E) free

50. ACQUIRE: (A) lose (B) placate
    (C) gratify (D) inspire
       (E) refine

Word Analogy Questions

A *word analogy* is a relationship between two words. The word analogy question requires that you determine the relationship between a pair of words, then, given another word, you are to complete a second pair of words by finding a word that relates to the given word *in the same way* that the words in the first pair relate.

ANALYSIS: The symbol : means *is to* and the symbol :: means *as*. The words can be read as follows: NOSE *is to* SMELL *as* eye *is to* ….

The main function of the nose is to smell. Another way to put it is, a nose is a tool used for smelling. Similarly, the eye is used for sight. Therefore, *sight* is the correct answer.

EXAMPLE 1:
   NOSE:SMELL::eye:
   (A) people (B) animals
       (C) heart (D) sight (E) distance
                             Ⓐ Ⓑ Ⓒ ● Ⓔ

EXAMPLE 2:
   ROOSTER:HEN::ram:
   (A) cow (B) lamb (C) heifer (D) ewe
       (E) boar
                             Ⓐ Ⓑ Ⓒ ● Ⓔ

ANALYSIS: Read the analogy this way: "Rooster is to hen as ram is to _____ . *Rooster* is male, *hen* is female. Because *ram* is also male, the answer must be female. Choice A is female. So is choice D. Since both *ram* and *ewe* belong to the sheep family, however, *ewe* is a better choice than *cow*. D is the correct answer.

EXAMINATION FAVORITES

As you might imagine, there are more possibilities for word relationships than you can count. But there are favorites that show up over and over on exams like the HSPT. Among them are:

1. SYNONYMS:
   hate/despise   brave/couragous
   gale/storm

2. ANTONYMS:
   hot/cold   humble/proud   real/artificial

3. TOOL AND WORKER:
   wrench/plumber   brush/artist
   glove/shortstop

4. TOOL AND OBJECT WORKED ON:
   hammer/nail   mop/floor   pen/paper

5. WORKER AND FUNCTION:
   teacher/instruct   coach/train
   violinist/play

6. ACTION AND MEANING:
   wave/greeting   yawn/tired   fever/illness

7. SYMBOL AND MEANING
   wings/angel   ring/marriage
   wreath/Christmas

8. DEGREE OF SIZE OR INTENSITY:
   chilly/freezing   old/ancient
   damaged/destroyed

9. CLASS AND MEMBER:
   amphibian/frog   clergy/priest
   furniture/bed

10. DEFINING QUALITY:
    mouse/quiet   fire/hot   razor/sharp

11. PART AND WHOLE:
    keyboard/computer   finger/hand
    street/city

HOW TO HANDLE ANALOGY QUESTIONS

➤ Before looking at the answer choices, try to find the relationship between the words in the first pair. Put that relationship into words. Then find among the choices a pair that has the most similar or parallel relationship.

➤ Treat the choices as *pairs,* that is, consider *both* words. Do not try to find a relationship between the first word of a given pair and the first word of any of the choices.

➤ If the relationship between the words in a given pair seems difficult to find, proceed as follows:
  • Remember that a word can have several meanings. Often checking whether a key word has a second meaning can reveal the relationship.

➤ Stay alert to parts of speech. If both the given words are nouns, for example, then the answer must also be nouns. If the pair of given words is made up of an adjective and a noun, your answer must also be adjective and noun—and in the *same order* as the given pair.

➤ Sometimes two words spelled the same change meaning when pronounced differently. A *contract,* for example, is a type of legal document when the accent is on the first syllable. When the accent switches to the second syllable, the word becomes a verb that means to grow smaller.

➤ Watch for words that have more than one meaning. *Seal,* for example, can be that playful animal found in coastal waters or what you do after you lick an envelope. If you set your mind only on the first definition when the second is intended, you may not answer correctly

➤ If you have difficulty in selecting one of two choices, the criterion to use is clear: Select as the correct answer the choice that has most nearly the same relationship as the given pair.

EXAMPLE:

Tree is to Seed as
(A) gasoline is to automobile
(B) bear is to cave
(C) farmer is to livestock
(D) starling is to egg
(E) inventor is to device

 Ⓐ Ⓑ Ⓒ ● Ⓔ

ANALYSIS: The relationship seems to be between *tree,* a natural object, and *seed,* its origin or its offspring: a tree develops from a seed *(origin),* and its *offspring* (seed) develops from the tree.

Eliminating:
(A) *Gasoline* is not involved in the creation of an *automobile.*
(B) A *bear* may raise its cubs in a *cave,* but the cave is neither an offspring nor a parent.
(C) A *farmer* cares for his *livestock* but does not create it.

Making the choice: The choice is between (E), an inventor who originates a device, and (D) a starling that creates or originates an egg. However, the tree-seed process is biological and so is the starling-egg; the inventor-device is not. Also, as in the tree-seed case, there may be a twofold relationship between the starling and the egg: the starling develops from an egg, and a female starling produces eggs. Therefore, the correct answer is (D).

PRACTICE TEST 4

DIRECTIONS: In each item the first two words can be combined as a pair. Find the alternative that combines with the remaining word to form a similar pair, and circle the letter that corresponds to your choice.

EXAMPLE:

MAN:TORSO::tree:
(A) roots (B) trunk (C) leaves (D) leaf
(E) branch

1. COMB:TOOTH::fork:
   (A) knife (B) food (C) point (D) prong
   (E) tone

2. CIRCUMFERENCE:BALL::perimeter:
   (A) circle (B) arc (C) track (D) train
   (E) walker

3. ADOLESCENT:YOUTHFUL::adult:
   (A) teenager (B) childish (C) citizen
   (D) infantile (E) mature

4. ASTRONOMER:PLANET::botanist:
   (A) earth (B) tree (C) disease
   (D) plant (E) science

5. COW:BARN::bear:
   (A) cub (B) cube (C) prairie (D) cave
   (E) mountaintop

6. AXE:CHOP::scissors:
   (A) sew (B) tear (C) cut (D) repair
   (E) patch

7. LETTER:ENVELOPE::dollar:
   (A) store (B) wallet (C) pennies
   (D) coins (E) bank teller

8. COAL:MINE::marble:
   (A) farm (B) cave (C) plant (D) quarry
   (E) factory

9. SAME:OPPOSITE::timid:
   (A) shy (B) backward (C) bold
   (D) quick (E) reluctant

10. AUTOMOBILE:WHEEL::boat:
    (A) rudder (B) sail (C) portable
    (D) stern (E) steerage

11. DUCK:FLOCK::sheep:
    (A) ewe (B) lamb (C) crowd (D) bevy
    (E) flock

12. QUIET:NOISY::safe:
    (A) distant (B) dangerous (C) home
    (D) protected (E) lovely

13. NEAR:CLOSE::large:
    (A) small (B) minute (C) distant
    (D) oral (E) gigantic

14. SWITZERLAND:SWISS::Denmark:
    (A) Danish (B) Flemish (C) French
    (D) Dutch (E) Swedish

15. CLOTH:GARMENT::leather:
    (A) soul (B) shoe (C) hide (D) tan
    (E) animal

16. RULER:DISTANCE::gauge:
    (A) pressure (B) fire (C) press
    (D) number (E) direction

17. ACTOR:PLAY::musician:
    (A) music (B) score (C) baton
    (D) orchestra (E) pit

18. FUEL:HEAT::food:
    (A) delight (B) hunger (C) energy
    (D) money (E) digestion

19. FALLS:WATER::avalanche:
    (A) aviator (B) snow (C) height
    (D) winter (E) danger

20. CRANE:LIFT::bulldozer:
    (A) destroy (B) convert (C) move
    (D) build (E) recover

Verbal Classification Questions

Note: The verbal classification question is included in the Verbal Skills section of the HSPT. However, students preparing for the Coop or other examination may also find the exercises helpful in increasing mastery of examination-level words.

In the verbal classification question you are given a list of four words. Three of the words are related. You are to identify the fourth, unrelated word.

> **EXAMPLE:**
>
> Which word does not belong with the others?
> (A) comma (B) letter (C) semicolon
> (D) dash
>
>

ANALYSIS: Three of the words refer to marks of punctuation: *comma, semicolon, dash. Letter* is different, since it is not a mark of punctuation. Therefore, **B** is the correct answer.

EXAMINATION FAVORITES

Word relationships come in countless varieties. Some exam favorites include

1. Synonyms: *spot, speck, blot*
2. Parts of a whole: *spokes, rim, hub*
3. Function: *timer, barometer, thermometer*
4. Unfavorable qualities: *cowardly, unfaithful, boorish*
5. Favorable qualities: *honest, courageous, charitable*
6. Related types: *opera, symphony, cantata*
7. Homophones: *weigh, whey, way*
8. Texture: *coarse, smooth, nubby*
9. Parts of speech: *of, between, for*
10. Composition: *cotton, wool, silk*
11. Occupation: *salesperson, computer programmer, writer*

On your own you could probably think of many other word relationships within a few minutes.

HOW TO HANDLE VERBAL CLASSIFICATION QUESTIONS

➤ Concentrate on the group of four words. Look for the related three. Don't turn to the Answer Key until you have tested the fourth word to make certain that it does not bear a similar relationship to any one of the other three.

➤ Look for obvious relationships first: synonyms, parts of a whole, functions. Don't begin by looking for complicated connections.

➤ Spotlight one word at a time, and compare it with the other three. This approach can often point to the clue that will reveal the related groups of three. The unrelated word may be an antonym of the other three.

➤ Very often, if the meaning of the one word is not clear, you can find the answer by working with the other three only. If two of the words bond together and the third is clearly unrelated or is an antonym of the pair, then the logical guess is to assume that the unknown word is unrelated to the two that bond. The same logic works if three words clearly bond together and the fourth is the unknown word.

➤ If the relationship does not become evident quickly, look for a word that has several meanings. You may be hung up on just one of the possible meanings: *drone* as a sound, *drone* as a type of bee.

➤ If you have difficulty with one item, do not dawdle over it. Go on to the next, which may be easier. You can always go back if there is time.

➤ Do not place speed over accuracy in handling relationship questions. Work for accuracy first; speed will follow with practice.

PRACTICE TEST 5

DIRECTIONS: Circle the letter of the unrelated word in each of the following groups of four.

1. (A) chew (B) nibble (C) gulp (D) munch

2. (A) waterwheel (B) utensil (C) generator (D) windmill

3. (A) totality (B) entirety (C) wholeness (D) segment

4. (A) sheriff (B) desperado (C) brigand (D) swindler

5. (A) handcuffs (B) uniform (C) manacles (D) fetters

6. (A) old (B) aged (C) juvenile (D) venerable

7. (A) worsen (B) mend (C) recuperate (D) heal

8. (A) slovenly (B) neat (C) messy (D) grubby

9. (A) spinach (B) asparagus (C) cauliflower (D) apple

10. (A) sentence (B) theme (C) chapter (D) paragraph

11. (A) golf (B) football (C) baseball (D) basketball

12. (A) praise (B) extol (C) laud (D) criticize

13. (A) oculist (B) pharmacist (C) gardener (D) chiropractor

14. (A) cautiously (B) boldly (C) recklessly (D) imprudently

15. (A) announce (B) herald (C) proclaim (D) suppress

16. (A) shutter (B) microscope (C) lens (D) film

17. (A) nylon (B) orlon (C) cotton (D) polyester

18. (A) condominium (B) house (C) palace (D) pastures

19. (A) check (B) goad (C) prod (D) spur

20. (A) lily (B) spruce (C) aster (D) rose

Building Your Vocabulary

A big vocabulary will help you read better, speak better, and of course, do better on the exam. Vocabulary is like money. You can never have too much of it.

While no single technique for building vocabulary works for everyone, a tried-and-true method that helps just about everyone is studying word parts, namely *prefixes, suffixes, roots,* and *stems.* For example, the prefix of a word can often give you at least a general sense of the word. The very word *prefix* contains the common prefix *pre,* meaning before, as in *prewar* (before the war) and *predict*—to foretell something before it happens.

A prefix is the name of a group of letters at the beginning of some words that help convey the meaning of the word. You can't speak English without using words that contain prefixes, such as

re, meaning *again,* as in *repeat, reread,* and *revisit*

co meaning *together,* as in *cooperate* and *cocaptain*

mis meaning *bad* or *improper,* as in *mistake* and *misdemeanor*

Suffixes, like prefixes, also convey meaning, but suffixes are found at the ends of words such as:

> *oid*, meaning *resembling*, as in ov*oid* (like an egg) and human*oid* (like a human)
>
> *er* or *eer* or *or*, meaning *a person who*, as in mountain*eer* (a person who climbs mountains) and sail*or* (a person who sails)

A great many words contain roots or stems. Roots are word parts that originated in other languages, mostly Latin and Greek, that have been absorbed by English. Stems are a variety of roots that have evolved into new forms. Both stems and roots convey meaning, just as though they were prefixes or suffixes. For example:

> *tempor*, meaning *time,* as in temporary (for a short time) and contemporary (at the same time)
>
> *terr*, meaning *land,* as in terrestrial (of the earth) and subterranean (underground)

There are literally hundreds of prefixes, suffixes, roots, and stems. Knowing many of them can help you figure out the meaning of unfamiliar words. Not all of them can be listed in this book, but here is a basic list that could help you to improve your score on the exam.

PREFIX	DEFINITION	EXAMPLE
a, an	without, not	*amoral*, without morals *anarchy*, without government *anemia*, lack of blood
ab, abs	away, from	*absent*, not here *abduct*, take away
ambi	both	*ambiguous*, two meanings *ambidextrous*, both hands
ante	before	*anteroom*, entryway or foyer *antebellum*, before the war
anti	against	*antiwar*, opposed to war *antiseptic*, against germs or infection
arch	first, head	*archbishop*, head bishop *arch-rival*, main competitor
bi	two	*bicycle*, two-wheeler *bimonthly*, twice a month
circum	around	*circumnavigate*, sail around (the world) *circumspect*, careful, cautious
co, con, col	together, with	*confer*, talk with *combine*, join with *collaborate*, plan with
de	down, away	*depart*, go away *defer*, put off
di	two	*divide*, split in two *diverge*, spreading in two directions
dia	across	*diagonal*, from one side to another (at a slant) *diameter*, across a circle
dis	not, apart	*disappear*, to not appear, vanish *distant*, away from
e, ex	out of	*expel*, to throw out *emit*, to send out

PREFIX	DEFINITION	EXAMPLE
extra, extro	outside	*extraterrestrial*, out of the world *extraordinary*, beyond the ordinary
in, im	not	*invalid*, not valid *imperfect*, not perfect
inter	between	*interfere*, to come between *interscholastic*, between schools
intra, intro	within	*intramural*, within the walls *introspective*, looking within
micro	small	*microscopic*, tiny *microbe*, tiny organism
mis	not, bad	*misaligned*, not lined up properly *misjudge*, to judge badly
mono	one	*monarch*, single ruler *monopoly*, one owner or controller
multi	many	*multitude*, big crowd *multinational*, many nations
neo	new	*neophyte*, beginner *neonatal*, newborn
non	not	*nonsense*, no sense *nonhuman*, not human
ob, opp	against	*obstruct*, to stop or interfere with *oppose*, to be against
para	beyond	*paranormal*, beyond normal *paragon*, outstanding example
peri	around	*periphery*, outside edge *perimeter*, outside boundary
poly	many	*polygon*, many-sided figure *polyglot*, speaking many languages
post	after	*postwar*, after the war *posterior*, rear end
pre	before	*preface*, forword to a book, etc. *prejudice*, prejudgment
prim	first	*primary*, first or most important *prime*, first or best
pro	forward, in favor of	*propose*, to put forward an idea *promote*, to advance or support
re	backward, again	*repeat*, to do again *return*, to go back, bring back
se	away, aside	*secret*, hidden, concealed *seclude*, shut away
sub	under	*subway*, underground passage *subzero*, below zero
super	above	*supermarket*, store bigger than others *superior*, above or better than others

PREFIX	DEFINITION	EXAMPLE
trans	across	*transfer*, to go from one to the other *transport*, to take across
ultra	beyond, extreme	*ultramodern*, extremely modern *ultrasound*, beyond sound, unheard
un	not	*unknown*, not known *unaware*, not aware
uni	one	*uniform*, always the same *united*, together as one

SUFFIX	DEFINITION	EXAMPLE
able, ible	capable of being done	*washable*, able to be washed *drinkable*, able to be drunk
acious, icious	full of	*malicious*, full of malice (hatred) *delicious*, full of good taste
ate	to make	*penetrate*, to make a hole through *dilate*, to make larger
ation, ition	that which is	*conflagration*, that which is on fire *position*, that which is in a certain place
cy	state of being	*lunacy*, state of being crazy *accuracy*, state of being correct
fy	to make	*terrify*, to make scared *sanctify*, to make holy
ism	belief	*extremism*, belief in extremes *monotheism*, belief in one god
ist	one who does or believes	*artist*, one who does art *communist*, one who believes in communism
ity	state of being	*amiability*, state of being friendly *ability*, state of being able
ize, ise	make	*familiarize*, make familiar *realize*, make a reality
ous	full of	*ridiculous*, full of foolishness *porous*, full of holes

ROOTS/STEMS	DEFINITION	EXAMPLE
alt	high	*altitude*, height *exalted*, having high honor
alter	other	*alternating*, every other *altruistic*, considerate of others
am	love	*amity*, friendliness *amorous*, loving
ann, enn	year	*annual*, every year *perennial*, yearly
anthrop	man	*anthropology*, study of man *anthropomorphic*, in man's form
apt, ept	fit	*aptitude*, able *inept*, unfit

ROOTS/STEMS	DEFINITION	EXAMPLE
aqua	water	*aquatic*, of the water *aqueduct*, passage for water
aster	star	*astronomy*, study of stars *asteroid*, starlike object
aud	hear	*auditorium*, place to hear others *auditory*, related to hearing
auto	one	*autocrat*, one ruler *automatic*, unassisted or without help
belli	was	*antebellum*, before the war *belligerent*, inclined to fight
ben, bon	good	*benefit*, something good *bonus*, reward or extra pay
biblio	book	*bibliography*, list of books *bibliophile*, lover of books
bio	life	*biology*, study of life *biography*, story of a person's life
carn	meat	*carnal*, of the flesh *carnivorous*, meat-eating
ced, cess	give up, to go	*accede*, to agree, to give in *antecedent*, that which goes before
cent	one hundred	*cent* (1/100th) of a dollar *century*, one hundred years
chron	time	*chronicle*, history of events *anachronistic*, out of time's sequence
cide, cis	cut, kill	*suicide*, to kill oneself *excise*, to cut out
corp, corpor	body	*corpse*, dead body *corporation*, unified body of many parts
cred	believe	*incredible*, hard to believe *credible*, believable
curr, curs	run	*current*, ongoing at the present *cursive*, flowing (handwriting)
dem	people	*democracy*, government by the people *epidemic*, spread through the people
derm	skin	*dermatologist*, skin doctor *epidermis*, skin
dict	say	*diction*, speech *verdict*, statement by judge/jury
duc, duct	lead	*duct*, passage *conductor*, one who leads
eu	good, pleasant	*eulogy*, praise *euphemism*, pleasant way of saying something unpleasant
fid	truth, belief	*confidence*, belief in *fidelity*, truth

ROOTS/STEMS	DEFINITION	EXAMPLE
fin	end	*finish*, end *infinite*, having no end
flect	bend	*flexible*, able to bend *inflection*, change in speech
frag, fract	break	*fragile*, breakable *infraction*, violation
gen	classification	*gender*, classification by sex *general*, with no specific class
gress	go	*digress*, to depart from *regress*, to go backward
graph, gram	writing	*pictograph*, writing with pictures *autograph*, written signature
jec, jact	throw	*projectile*, missile *eject*, to throw out
loqu, locut	talk	*locquacious*, talkative *elocution*, speech
luc	light	*lucid*, clear *translucent*, letting light in
magn	large, great	*magnify*, to enlarge *magnificent*, great
mal	bad	*malodorous*, smelling bad *malicious*, nasty
mar	sea	*marine*, having to do with the sea *submarine*, under the sea
mater, matr	mother	*maternity*, related to mother *matricide*, to kill one's mother
mit, miss	send	*remit*, to send in *missionary*, one sent out
mor	die	*immortal*, never dying *morgue*, place for the dead
morph	shape	*amorphous*, shapeless *metamorphosis*, change of shape
nat	born	*nativity*, birth *neonatal*, newborn
nov	new	*novice*, beginner *novelty*, something new
omni	all, many	*omnivorous*, eating everything *omnicient*, all-knowing
pater, patr	father	*patriot*, one who loves his or her country *patricide*, killing one's father
path	feeling	*sympathy*, feeling for others *pathetic*, feeling of pity or sadness
ped, pod	foot	*pedestal*, base for a statue *podiatrist*, foot doctor

ROOTS/STEMS	DEFINITION	EXAMPLE
ped	child	*pediatrician*, children's doctor *pedagogue*, teacher of children
pel, puls	drive	*repel*, to withstand *repulse*, to drive back
phil	love	*bibliophile*, lover of books *philanthropist*, lover of humanity
port	carry	*transport*, to carry across *portable*, able to be carried
psych	mind	*psychologist*, one who studies minds and behavior *psyche*, workings of the mind
quer, quir	ask	*inquire*, to ask *inquisition*, investigation
reg, rect	rule	*regal*, pertaining to rulers *correct*, according to the rules
rupt	break	*interrupt*, to break into *corruption*, breaking of rules or law
sci	know	*conscious*, aware *science*, knowledge
scrib	write	*transcribe*, to write down *scribble*, to write aimlessly
sect	cut	*section*, piece cut from a whole *bisect*, to cut in two
sequi, secut	follow	*sequel*, something that follows *consequence*, result
soph	wisdom	*sophomoric*, without wisdom *sophisticated*, knowing or worldly
spec, spect	see, look	*spectator*, onlooker *spectacle*, something to see
tang, tact	touch	*tangent*, touching *tactile*, touchable
tempor	time	*temporary*, short time *contemporaneous*, same time
tort, tors	twist, turn	*distort*, to twist the truth *tortuous*, winding
tract	pull, drag	*tractor*, machine that drags a plow *distract*, to pull (attention) from
urb	city	*urban*, citylike *suburban*, outside the city
vac	empty	*vacuum*, empty of air *vacate*, to leave empty
vent	come	*advent*, arrival *convene*, to come together
ver	true	*veracity*, truthfulness *verify*, to check the truth of
viv, vit	alive	*revive*, to bring back to life *vitality*, liveliness

Words Commonly Confused

The following groups of pairs and triplets cause confusion of meaning and spelling. Do not run through the list in one sitting. Do study a column at a time. Check the items that cause you difficulty. Each time you turn to a new column, review the ones you checked previously. Use the Practice Test that follows to see how effectively your study time was spent.

accept *v.*   to receive
except *prep.*   leaving out
except *v.*   to leave out

access *n.*   approach
excess *n.*   more than enough

addition *n.*   increase, a term in arithmetic
edition *n.*   printing, a term in publishing

advice *n.*   counsel
advise *v.*   to notify

affect *v.*   to influence
effect *n.*   a result
effect *v.*   to bring about a result

aisle *n.*   a passage between rows of seats
isle *n.*   a small island
I'll *pron* and *v.*   contraction of "I shall"

allowed *v.*   gave permission
aloud *adv.*   loud enough to be heard

all ready *pro.* plus *adj.*   everybody prepared
already *adv.*   by now

allusion *n.*   reference
illusion *n.*   something that deceives the eye or mind

altar *n.*   an elevated structure for worship
alter *v.*   to change

arc *n.*   any part of a circle
ark *n.*   a ship

ascent *n.*   an upward slope
assent *v.*   to agree

assistance *n.*   aid, a helping hand
assistants *n.*   plural of "assistant"; people who help

band *n.*   a group of people; a narrow strip for holding things together
banned *v.*   forbidden

bare *adj.*   naked
bear *v.*   to carry, endure
bear *n.*   an animal

base *n.*   foundation; a sack or plate in baseball
bass *n.*   deepest voice in singing

beach *n.*   a sandy shore
beech *n.*   a tree with smooth gray bark

beau *n.*   an escort, a sweetheart, a steady boyfriend
bow *n.*   a knot; a weapon to propel an arrow; a wooden rod used in playing a musical instrument; a simple curve

berry *n.*   a small juicy fruit
bury *v.*   to cover up

berth *n.*   a bed
birth *n.*   beginning of life

blew *v.*   past tense of "to blow"
blue *adj.* or *n.*   a color

boar *n.*   a male pig or hog
bore *v.*   to pierce
bore *v.*   to be uninteresting to (people)

born *v.*   brought to life
borne *v.*   carried

bough *n.*   a branch
bow *v.*   to bend

brake *n.*   part of an automobile
break *v.*   to smash or injure

bread *n.*   food made of wheat
bred *v.*   raised, brought up

bridal *adj.*   relating to a bride or wedding
bridle *n.*   head harness for horse

canvas *n.*   cloth
canvass *v.*   to solicit

capital *n.*   the chief city
capitol *n.*   a building in which a state or national legislature meets

carat *n.* a unit of weight
caret *n.* a mark showing where something was omitted
carrot *n.* a vegetable

cede *v.* to give up
seed *n.* a part of a plant

cell *n.* a small room
sell *v.* to get money for (an object)

cellar *n.* a room under a building
seller *n.* one who sells

cent *n.* a coin
scent *n.* an odor
sent *v.* did send

cite *v.* to quote or refer to
sight *n.* a view
site *n.* a place

climb *v.* to ascend; mount
clime *n.* a climate

coarse *adj.* rough
course *n.* a route

colonel *n.* an army officer
kernel *n.* a grain of corn or wheat

core *n.* the central part
corps *n.* a body of troops

council *n.* a meeting
counsel *v.* to advise

councilor *n.* a member of a council
counselor *n.* an advisor; lawyer

creak *v.* to squeak
creek *n.* a small stream

dear *adj.* beloved; expensive
deer *n.* an animal

descent *n.* a downhill slope
dissent *n.* disagreement

desert *v.* to abandon
dessert *n.* last course, usually sweet, of a meal

dew *n.* moisture from air
due *adj.* owed

die *v.* to lose one's life
dye *v.* to change color

doe *n.* a female deer
dough *n.* a mixture of flour for baking bread or cake

dual *adj.* double
duel *n.* a fight between two combatants

earn *v.* to receive pay for work
urn *n.* a vase with a pedestal

faint *v.* to lose consciousness
feint *v.* to move in such a way as to trick the opponent

fair *adj.* just; honest
fare *n.* money paid for transportation

fate *n.* destiny
fete *n.* festival

find *v.* to come upon
fined *v.* penalized (past tense of "to fine")

fir *n.* an evergreen
fur *n.* soft hair covering skin of certain animals

flea *n.* a small insect
flee *v.* to run away

flew *v.* past tense of "to fly"
flue *n.* a chimney; an air-shaft

flour *n.* wheat that has been ground into powder
flower *n.* a blossom

for preposition
four *n.* or *adj.* 2 times 2 or 3 plus 1

formally *adv.* properly; ceremoniously
formerly *adv.* in the past

forth *adv.* forward
fourth *adj.* following the third and before the fifth

foul *adj.* nasty; outside the playing field
fowl *n.* a chicken

gait *n.* manner of walking or running
gate *n.* the moveable part of a fence

gamble _v._ to bet
gambol _v._ to dance

gilt _n._ gold paint
guilt _n._ the opposite of innocence

grate _n._ framework of iron to hold a fire
great _adj._ big; large

groan _n._ a short moan
grown _adj._ increased in size

guessed _v._ past tense of "to guess"
guest _n._ a visitor in the house

hail _v._ to greet
hale _adj._ strong and well

hair _n._ the threadlike outgrowths from the head
hare _n._ a rabbit

hall _n._ a passageway
haul _v._ to move by pulling

hart _n._ a male deer
heart _n._ the blood-pumping organ of the body

heal _v._ to become well
heel _n._ the back of the foot

hear _v._ to listen
here _adv._ in this place

heard _v._ past tense of "to hear"
herd _n._ a group of animals

higher _adj._ further up (comparative of "high")
hire _v._ to pay for the use of something; to use

him _pron._ objective case of "he"
hymn _n._ a religious song of praise

hoarse _adj._ harsh in sound
horse _n._ animal

hole _n._ a hollow place
whole _adj._ entire

holy _adj._ sacred
wholly _adv._ entirely

hour _n._ sixty minutes
our _pron._ belonging to us

idle _adj._ doing nothing
idol _n._ an image for worship

in _prep._ within; not outside
inn _n._ a tavern or hotel

instance _n._ an example
instants _n._ moments

its _pron._ belonging to it; possessive of "it"
it's _pron._ and _v._ contraction of "it is"

knight _n._ a man with the title of Sir; a man on horseback
night _n._ the time between evening and morning

know _v._ to be sure of; to have information
no _adv._ opposite of yes

lain _v._ rested (past participle of "to lie")
lane _n._ a narrow path

lead _n._ metal
led _v._ past tense of "to lead"

lessen _v._ to diminish; make smaller
lesson _n._ something to be learned or studied

lie _v._ to recline
lye _n._ a strong alkaline

load _v._ to pile on a truck
lode _n._ a vein of metallic ore

loan _n._ something lent
lone _adj._ by oneself; solitary

mail _n._ and _v._ letters; to post
male _adj._ and _n._ masculine; a man or boy

main _adj._ most important
mane _n._ long hair on the neck of animals

meat _n._ flesh
meet _v._ to come together

metal _n._ a substance such as iron or gold
mettle _n._ high spirit; courage

miner *n.*   one who digs coal
minor *n.*   one who is under 21 years of age

morn *n.*   morning
mourn *v.*   to grieve

one *adj.*   less than two
won *v.*   gained; past tence of "to win"

pail *n.*   a container for liquids
pale *adj.*   without much color

pain *n.*   feeling of being hurt
pane *n.*   a sheet of glass

pair *n.*   a set of two
pare *v.*   to trim off
pear *n.*   fruit

pour *v.*   to cause to flow
paw *n.*   the foot of an animal

peal *n.*   a loud sound
peel *n.*   the skin of fruit

peace *n.*   quietness; absence of strife
piece *n.*   a part

plain *adj.*   easy to understand
plane *n.*   flat or level surface; machine that flies

pray *v.*   to speak to God in worship
prey *n.*   victim

principal *adj. and n.*   chief
principle *n*   a truth; a rule of conduct

profit *n.*   gain
prophet *n.*   one who predicts the future

rain *n.*   shower
reign *v.*   to rule

rap *v.*   to knock
wrap *v.*   to fold a covering around

read *v.*   to understand written words
reed *n.*   a hollow stalk

read *v.*   past tence of "to read"
red *adj. or n.*   a color

real *adj.*   actual; true
reel *n.*   spool

right *adj.*   correct
rite *n.*   ceremony
write *v.*   to put words on paper

ring *n.*   a circle
wring *v.*   to twist

road *n.*   a highway
rode *v.*   past tense of "to ride"
rowed *v.*   past tense of "to row"

role *n.*   actor's part in play
roll *v.*   to revolve

root *n.*   source; the part of a plant in the ground
route *n.*   course

rote *n.*   fixed routine
wrote *n.*   past tense of "to write"

sail *v.*   to travel on a ship
sale *n.*   exchange of goods for money

scene *n.*   a part of a play
seen *v.*   past participle of "to see"

sea *n.*   a large body of salt water
see *v.*   to use the eyes

seam *n.*   line where edges join
seem *v.*   to appear

sew *v.*   to stitch
so *adv.*   in this way
sow *v.*   to scatter seed in the ground

slay *v.*   to kill
sleigh *n.*   a sled

soar *v.*   to fly upward
sore *adj.*   painful

sold *v.*   past tense of "to sell"
soled *adj.*   having a sole, like a shoe

sole *adj.*   one and only
soul *n.*   spirit

some *adj.*   few; not many
sum *n.*   total; amount

son *n.*   a male offspring
sun *n.*   the star that gives us daylight

stake *n.* a post driven into ground
steak *n.* a slice of choice meat

stare *v.* to gaze at
stair *n.* a step

stationary *adj.* standing still
stationery *n.* writing materials

steal *v.* to take
steel *n.* to metal made from iron

straight *adj.* without a bend or curve
strait *n.* narrow passage of water between two seas

suite *n.* a set of rooms; a musical composition
sweet *adj.* sugary

tail *n.* part of an animal's body
tale *n.* a story

team *n.* a group of players
teem *v.* to swarm

their *pron.* belonging to them
there *adv.* 1. not here; in that place 2. an expletive (introductory word)
they're *pron.* and *v.* contraction of "they are"

threw *v.* past tense of "to throw"
through *prep.* all the way in or past

throne *n.* a chair for a king or queen
thrown *v.* past participle of "to throw"

tide *n.* alternate rise and fall of the ocean
tied *v.* past tense of "to tie"

toe *n.* a digit of the foot
tow *v.* to pull by a rope or chain

told *v.* said; past tense of "to tell"
tolled *v.* rang; past tense of "to ring"

vain *adj.* conceited
vane *n.* blade of a windmill
vein *n.* blood vessel

vale *n.* a valley
veil *n.* a covering for the face

vial *n.* small glass bottle
vile *adj.* very bad

wade *v.* to walk through shallow water
weighed *v.* past tense of "to weigh"

wail *n.* lament or cry
whale *n.* a large sea animal

waist *n.* the middle part of the body
waste *v.* to make poor use of

wait *v.* to remain
weight *n.* heaviness

ware *n.* anything for sale
wear *v.* to use as clothing
where *adv.* at what place

weak *adj.* not strong
week *n.* seven days

weather *n.* the daily changes in climate
whether *conj.* if

which *pron.* this or that?
witch *n.* a supernatural woman with evil powers

whine *v.* to complain in a sniveling way
wine *n.* fermented grape juice

wood *n.* timber
would *v.* should

your *adj.* belonging to you
you're *pron.* and *v.* contraction of "you are"

PRACTICE TEST 6

DIRECTIONS: In the sentences below fill in the blank space with the appropriate word.

1. **accept, except**
   We shall _____ applications on Monday.
   This homework is correct _____ for two mistakes.

2. **access, excess**
   We have _____ to the Senator's record.
   The last person in the row will bring up any _____ papers.

3. **addition, edition**

This is the fourth _____ of this book.

John is a welcome _____ to this honor class.

4. **affect, effect - n., effect - v.**

The different shades of blue create a beautiful _____.

The failing mark will _____ your average.

With the mayor's help, the union and the employer will _____ a settlement of the dispute.

5. **aisle, isle, I'll**

The bride walked down the _____ in the church.

I should like to spend my vacation on a beautiful _____.

_____ see you at the theater.

6. **allowed, aloud**

Read that passage _____.

I am _____ to stay up every evening until 10 P.M.

7. **all ready, already**

We are _____ to join in the game.

Has the game _____ started?

8. **allusion, illusion**

We found an _____ to myths on page 230.

The green lights in the dark room created an eerie _____.

9. **altar, alter**

The _____ was decorated with flowers for the wedding.

We will _____ the dress to fit you.

10. **arc, ark**

A pop fly to the first baseman describes a short high _____.

Noah's _____ floated on the water for forty days.

11. **ascent, assent**

The _____ up the mountain side was very steep.

Mother has given her _____; I may have my ears pierced.

12. **assistance, assistants**

The surgeon will have two _____ in the operating room.

Will you need my _____ in order to finish the job?

13. **band, banned**

The _____ of rebels captured the city.

Smoking is _____ in public libraries.

14. **bare, bear, bear**

The big brown _____ was in the cage.

The _____ walls made the room look gloomy.

_____ these rules in mind when you take the test.

15. **base, bass**

The _____ of the lamp is made of brass.

Our quartet has one tenor, two baritones, and a _____.

16. **beach, beech**

We sat under the shade of the _____ tree.

In the summer we go to the _____ to keep cool.

17. **beat, beet**

The _____ of the drum was steady.

The _____ is a red root vegetable.

18. **beau, bow**

At sixteen I had a very handsome young _____.

Please tie a _____ in my shoelace.

19. **berry, bury**

    The dog will _____ his bone and eat it later.

    A _____ is good to eat only when ripe.

20. **berth, birth**

    The _____ of the child brought joy to the family.

    I reserved a _____ on the overnight train for Chicago.

21. **blew, blue**

    Tom _____ the candles out.

    The sky is _____.

22. **boar, bore, bore**

    The uninteresting story will _____ you.

    The carpenter will _____ a hole in the wood.

    In the hog family, the _____ is the father, the sow is the mother, the pigs are children.

23. **born, borne**

    George Washington was _____ on Feb. 22, 1732.

    A kite is _____ upward by the wind.

24. **bough, bow**

    A bird was standing on a _____ of the tree.

    The boys will _____ to the girls.

25. **brake, break**

    To stop the car, he applied his _____.

    Be careful not to _____ the dishes.

26. **bread, bred**

    Tom is a very well _____ young man.

    I like whole wheat _____.

27. **bridal, bridle**

    On her wedding day Linda looked beautiful in her _____ gown.

    The jockey put the _____ on the horse.

28. **canvas, canvass**

    We slept in a _____ tent.

    Salesmen _____ our neighborhood for new business.

29. **capital, capitol**

    Albany is the _____ of New York State.

    Each Congressman is given office space in the _____.

30. **carat, caret, carrot**

    May's ring had a two _____ diamond.

    The rabbit's favorite treat was a _____.

    He placed a _____ between the two words to note a missing word.

31. **cede, seed**

    At the end of World War I, Germany agreed to _____ Alsace-Lorraine to France.

    In the spring I will plant the _____.

32. **cellar, seller**

    The buyer and _____ drew up an agreement.

    The furnace is in the _____ of the house.

33. **cent, scent, sent**

    Gum costs one _____ a slice.

    The book was _____ to you by air mail.

    Perfume has a pleasant _____.

34. **cell, sell**

    The prisoner was asleep in his _____.

    We are going to _____ our house.

35. **cite, sight, site**

    The _____ for the new school has been selected.

    The view from the hill was a beautiful _____.

    The officer will _____ John for bravery.

36. **climb, clime**

    Ralph will _____ the mountain.

    In the winter the sunny _____ of Florida attracts many visitors.

37. **coarse, course**

    The scout master mapped out the _____ for our hike.

    _____ salt is used on slippery roads to melt ice.

38. **colonel, kernel**

    Mr. Hamilton is a _____ in the army.

    The _____ of the corn is a seed.

39. **council, counsel**

    My teacher offered me some wise _____.

    The city _____ voted against the sales tax.

40. **core, corps**

    Michael is an officer in the air _____.

    We eat most of the apple and throw the _____ away.

41. **councilor, counselor**

    Only one _____ voted against the bill to install traffic lights on Main Street.

    After graduation, he opened an office as _____ at law.

42. **creak, creek**

    The door will _____ when you open it.

    There weren't many fish in the _____.

43. **descent, dissent**

    _____ by one juror can hold up a verdict.

    There is a steep _____ down the mountain side.

44. **dear, deer**

    The _____ is a very graceful animal.

    Memories of my grandparents are very _____ to me.

45. **desert, dessert**

    Chocolate pudding is a popular _____.

    Mary did not _____ her friend in need.

46. **dew, due**

    Pay the salesman what is _____ him.

    The _____ on the ground in the morning makes the grass wet.

47. **die, dye**

    The plants will _____ without water.

    I am going to _____ my dress red.

48. **doe, dough**

    The _____ is ready to be baked into bread.

    The _____ is a female deer.

59. **dual, duel**

    He holds the _____ job of secretary-treasurer.

    Zorro never loses a _____.

50. **earn, urn**

    He will _____ his day's pay.

    This beautiful _____ was used for water.

51. **faint, feint**

    Linda thought she would _____ when she heard the bad news.

    The boxer will _____ a punch in order to fool his opponent.

52. **fair, fare**

    The referee made a _____ decision.

    We paid our _____ on the bus.

53. **fate, fete**

    Mary's _____ was already decided.

    The Mardi Gras is a gay _____ in New Orleans.

54. **find, fined**

    Jack was _____ ten dollars for speeding.

    It is hard to _____ your way in the dark.

55. **fir, fur**

    There were tall _____ trees in the forest.

    A _____ coat is very warm.

56. **flea, flee**

    We had to _____ from the burning house.

    There was a _____ on the dog.

57. **flew, flue**

    The parakeet _____ out of the cage.

    The smoke escapes through a _____.

58. **flour, flower**

    Bread is made of _____ .

    A rose is a beautiful _____.

59. **for, four**

    I will buy it _____ you.

    I have _____ minutes to leave the house.

60. **formally, formerly**

    Mary was _____ introduced to her future-in-laws.

    The house was _____ a one family house.

61. **forth, fourth**

    Bring _____ the gifts.

    I was _____ on line; you are fifth.

62. **foul, fowl**

    The _____ ball rolled outside the third-base line.

    Chickens and turkeys are _____.

63. **gait, gate**

    Close the _____ when you enter the yard.

    The pony trotted with a steady _____.

64. **gamble, gambol**

    It is unwise to _____.

    The lambs _____ in the pasture.

65. **gilt, guilt**

    The painter put _____ around the edge of the chair.

    The concrete evidence proved the man's _____.

66. **grate, great**

    We built an outdoor _____ to barbecue our steaks.

    There was a _____ celebration when we won.

67. **groan, grown**

    The sick man let out a _____.

    The boy has _____ two inches this year.

68. **guessed, guest**

    From this clue you might have _____ the answer.

    Frances is a _____ in our house.

69. **hail, hale**

    The doorman will _____ a cab for your.

    The old man appeared _____ and hearty.

70. **hair, hare**

    The _____ hopped away through the field.

    She wears her _____ in a bun.

71. **hall, haul**

    I walked through the _____ of the school.

    The sailor will _____ in the rope.

72. **hart, heart**

The _____ is a male deer.

The _____ pumps blood.

73. **heal, heel**

This new medicine will _____ the wound.

The shoe has a very high _____.

74. **hear, here**

I can _____ his voice above the others'.

Bring the man in _____.

75. **heard, herd**

I _____ the telephone ring.

The _____ of sheep was grazing in the hills.

76. **higher, hire**

Place the picture _____ on the wall.

The store will _____ more help for Christmas.

77. **him, hymn**

Give _____ the book.

Mahalia Jackson sang a beautiful _____.

78. **hoarse, horse**

I love to go _____ back riding.

She talked so much her voice was ____.

79. **hole, whole**

The men dug a big _____.

I want to hear the _____ story.

80. **holy, wholly**

Sandra visited the _____ shrines in Europe.

He does his work _____ and thoroughly.

81. **hour, our**

_____ car is being repaired.

We can park here for only one _____.

82. **idle, idol**

_____ hands get into mischief.

Before modern religion, _____ worship was common.

83. **in, inn**

We stopped at an _____ for dinner.

The keys are _____ my purse.

84. **instance, instants**

Several _____ passed before anyone spoke.

The _____ you cited in your report is important.

85. **its, it's**

_____ raining.

The wolf bared _____ fangs.

86. **knight, night**

Stories of long ago tell tales of many a brave _____.

It was late at _____.

87. **know, no**

I _____ you will do a good job.

There is _____ time to waste.

88. **lain, lane**

The beautiful _____ was lined with trees.

The newspaper has _____ on the doorstep all day.

89. **lead, led**

The pipe was made of _____.

The firemen _____ the family to safety.

90. **lessen, lesson**

Today we shall have a _____ on safety.

If you give me one package, it will _____ your burden.

91. **lie, lye**

The _____ burned a hole in the floor.

Let the book _____ on the desk.

92. **load, lode**

It is too heavy a _____ for one man.

A rich _____ of silver was discovered in the mine.

93. **loan, lone**

Mary will repay the _____ in six weeks.

He was the _____ survivor of the crash.

94. **mail, male**

Please _____ the letter.

We need a deep _____ voice to sing in the choir.

95. **main, mane**

The horse has a shiny, black _____.

The _____ role goes to the leading lady.

96. **meat, meet**

The children ate _____ and potatoes.

I will _____ you at two o'clock.

97. **metal, mettle**

The knives are made of _____.

A good team shows its _____ when it is losing.

98. **miner, minor**

A _____ works hard digging coal.

Florence is a _____ and therefore cannot sign legal papers.

99. **morn, mourn**

How pleasant to hear the chirping of birds on a summer _____.

We shall _____ the loss of our great leader.

100. **one, won**

I will carry _____ carton at a time.

Our bowling team _____ the game.

101. **pail, pale**

Lou carried a _____ of water to the horse.

Because Fred was ill, he looked rather _____.

102. **pain, pane**

The ball shattered the window _____.

The sprain caused a sharp _____ in his ankle.

103. **pair, pare, pear**

I bought a _____ of bookends.

I enjoy eating a juicy _____.

Sheila will _____ the apples for the applesauce.

104. **pour, paw**

Mrs. Johnson will _____ the tea.

The bear has a large _____.

105. **peal, peel**

He slipped on a banana _____.

The bells _____ loud and long.

106. **peace, piece**

When you do the right thing you have _____ of mind.

Please cut a _____ of cake for me.

107. **plain, plane**

It takes only four hours by _____ to reach Florida.

His reasons are quite _____.

108. **pray, prey**

We all _____ for peace on earth.

The eagle has as its _____ small birds and mammals.

109. **principal, principle**

We must adhere to the _____ of our constitution.

Mr. Smith is _____ of the new elementary school.

110. **profit, prophet**

Elijah was a great _____.

We _____ from our experiences.

111. **rain, reign**

The _____ of Queen Victoria was very long.

The _____ wet the clothes on the line.

112. **rap, wrap**

The _____ on the door disturbed the silence.

I will _____ a blanket around the shivering girl.

113. **read, reed**

I need a new _____ for my clarinet.

I want to _____ *Little Women*.

114. **read, red**

Hunters usually wear _____ hats.

I _____ two books last week.

115. **real, reel**

Tell of a _____ experience.

The fisherman let out his _____.

116. **right, rite, write**

Graduation is an important _____ of passage.

I cannot think of the _____ word.

_____ me a letter.

117. **ring, wring**

_____ out the wash before hanging it on the line.

_____ the bell.

118. **road, rode, rowed**

Joe and I _____ the boat.

The _____ was very bumpy.

We _____ for an hour in the car.

119. **role, roll**

The _____ of the lawyer was the biggest part in the play.

I _____ the ball to the child.

120. **root, route**

We chose the fastest _____ to Pittsburgh.

The _____ of the tree was buried deep in the earth.

121. **rote, wrote**

I _____ a letter to my friend.

We memorized the formulas by _____.

122. **sail, sale**

The dresses on _____ were very cheap.

I like to _____ a boat on the lake.

123. **scene, seen**

The first _____ of *Hamlet* occurs at midnight.

I have _____ Jimmy frequently.

124. **sea, see**

The _____ was very rough.

It is nice to _____ old friends.

125. **seam, seem**

It doesn't _____ to be a wise plan.

The tear in the _____ was easily sewed.

126. **sew, so, sow**

It was _____ easy I was surprised.

Please _____ a button on my shirt.

In March the farmer will _____ his seeds.

127. **slay, sleigh**

The _____ came down the snowy hill.

A merciful knight does not _____ his opponent.

128. **soar, sore**

The pilot loves to _____ above the clouds.

Our pitcher had a _____ arm.

129. **sold, soled**

The shoemaker _____ my shoes.

They _____ the cars at a profit.

130. **sole, soul**

He had the _____ of a saint.

The _____ reason for his coming was his concern for her welfare.

131. **some, sum**

I will buy _____ of your candy.

The _____ of two and four is six.

132. **son, sun**

Bob is Mrs. Jones's _____.

The _____ sets in the west.

133. **stake, steak**

The horse was tied to a _____.

I like a nice, juicy _____ for supper.

134. **stare, stair**

Do not jump down the _____ case.

I love to _____ at the beautiful countryside.

135. **stationary, stationery**

I am going to use my new _____ to write the letter.

The sink is _____ and cannot be moved.

136. **steal, steel**

Coal and iron ore are required to make _____.

Thou shalt not _____.

137. **straight, strait**

A narrow _____ separated the two islands.

He went _____ home from school.

138. **suite, sweet**

The king and queen occupied a _____ of rooms in the hotel.

Peaches taste _____.

139. **tail, tale**

A monkey has a _____.

This is a _____ of intrigue.

140. **team, teem**

Our football _____ lost every game.

Polluted waters _____ with germs.

141. **their, there, they're**

_____ are two new boys standing _____.

_____ house was newly decorated.

_____ the first tenants to live in the new house.

142. **threw, through**

He _____ the ball _____ the window.

143. **throne, thrown**

The halfback was _____ for a loss.

Prince Rainier sits on a _____.

144. **tide, tied**

The ocean is at low _____.

The boy scout _____ the knot.

145. **toe, tow**

The bat fell on his _____ .

We had to _____ the car to a garage.

146. **told, tolled**

The bell _____ for fifteen minutes.

The storyteller _____ an amusing tale.

147. **vain, vane, vein**

It was a _____ attempt to save the man's life.

A _____ carries blood to the heart.

We have a weather _____ on our roof.

148. **vale, veil**

We trudged down the hill and through the _____ .

The mother wore a dark _____ .

149. **vial, vile**

The small _____ held expensive medicine.

Rotten food has a _____ odor.

150. **wade, weighed**

I took off my shoes to _____ in the brook.

The grocer _____ the cheese.

151. **wail, whale**

The _____ of sick children kept us up at night.

The _____ is a huge mammal.

152. **waist, waste**

It is sinful to _____ food.

The belt was too tight around her _____ .

153. **wait, weight**

I will _____ for you on the corner.

Pat is gaining _____ .

154. **ware, wear, where**

I will _____ a new dress tonight.

We polished the silver _____ .

Show us _____ the new books are kept.

155. **weak, week**

John made a _____ effort to get up.

It will take a _____ for the watch to be repaired.

156. **weather, whether**

The game will be postponed if the _____ is bad.

Tell us _____ you will help us or not.

157. **which, witch**

_____ dress will you wear?

On Halloween, Maggie dressed up as a _____ .

158. **whine, wine**

The lonely dog's _____ was heard all night.

The men drank a glass of _____ at dinner.

159. **wood, would**

They brought _____ for the fireplace.

_____ you be interested in learning the guitar?

160. **your, you're**

_____ not leaving, are you?

_____ taxi is waiting.

Mastery Exams

FOR THE LOWER GRADES— EXAMS 1–15

EXAM 1

DIRECTIONS: For each word in capitals, select the word or phrase that means most nearly the SAME, then circle the letter of the correct answer.

EXAMPLE:

ABSENT: (A) present (B) soak in (C) not here (D) jumping (E) late

ANALYSIS: The correct meaning is "not here." Therefore the answer is (C).

1. BEVERAGE: (A) supper (B) lunch (C) food (D) animal (E) drink

2. ENERGY: (A) ability to do work (B) slowness (C) speed (D) unwillingness (E) ohm

3. ADMIRABLE: (A) naval officer (B) excellent (C) sunset (D) masterpiece (E) terrible

4. EMPLOYEE: (A) fiancee (B) worker (C) hire (D) slave (E) peasant

5. CARGO: (A) auto (B) ship (C) shipment (D) small bundle (E) envelope

6. ADULT: (A) dilute (B) voter (C) very old (D) grown-up (E) invalid

7. ENLARGE: (A) diminish (B) reduce (C) picture (D) expand (E) package

8. COLLIDE: (A) slide (B) hurting (C) glide (D) hunt (E) crash

9. DEPEND: (A) rely (B) protect (C) survival (D) help (E) request

10. CEMENT: (A) burial ground (B) rock (C) earth (D) sea (E) paving material

11. BLIZZARD: (A) bird of death (B) humming sound (C) drought (D) snowstorm (E) desert

12. CABARET: (A) nightclub (B) playboy (C) taxi (D) two-wheeled carriage (E) plow

13. DEBATE: (A) defeat (B) thwart (C) discussion (D) needle (E) obstruct

14. ADOLESCENT: (A) child (B) grown-up (C) perfume (D) adult (E) teenager

15. CANDIDATE: (A) elector (B) canned fruit (C) dandy (D) appointment (E) office-seeker

16. BALLET: (A) leap (B) spiral (C) vote (D) opera (E) dramatic dance

17. ENORMOUS: (A) fatness (B) very large (C) abnormal (D) glorious (E) preferring

18. CHICK: (A) duck (B) yearling (C) baby rooster (D) throw (E) watch out

19. DAZZLE: (A) fizzle (B) bewilder (C) flurry (D) bubble (E) ray

20. ADVISER: (A) voice (B) influence (C) speak (D) provider (E) counselor

EXAM 2

DIRECTIONS: For each word in capitals, select the word or phrase that means most nearly the SAME, then circle the letter of the correct answer.

1. BESEECH: (A) search (B) forgive (C) prove (D) beg (E) desert

2. BESIEGE: (A) beg (B) hinder (C) prove (D) surround (E) betray

3. BIAS: (A) cut in two (B) opinion
    (C) ribbon (D) persecute (E) sew

4. BLEAK: (A) desolate (B) beak
    (C) dispute (D) line (E) whiten

5. BLISS: (A) darkness (B) disposition
    (C) joy (D) humming (E) courage

6. BLUFF: (A) storm (B) outspoken
    (C) mountain (D) suave (E) cloud

7. BOISTEROUS: (A) noisy (B) frank
    (C) begging (D) rough
       (E) courageous

8. SOLEMN: (A) grave (B) holy
    (C) sunny (D) soft (E) peaceful

9. ABSURD: (A) leave out (B) eject
    (C) happy (D) foolish (E) critic

10. ABUSE: (A) injure (B) use
    (C) independence (D) poor
       (E) cubicle

11. CHAMPION: (A) runner-up
    (B) winner (C) brigadier
       (D) sparkling wine (E) breeding

12. EMERGENCY: (A) brilliant (B) crisis
    (C) brink (D) dilemma (E) escape

13. BANQUET: (A) formal dinner
    (B) speeches (C) tuxedo (D) deprive
       (E) forerunner

14. CHEF: (A) chief (B) chop
    (C) insert (D) choir (E) cook

15. BATCH: (A) spoil (B) rapture
    (C) bring out of shell (D) quantity
       (E) quality

16. ADMIRAL: (A) general (B) captain
    (C) commander (D) frightful
       (E) naval officer

17. EMBRACE: (A) ashes (B) strengthen
    (C) hug (D) love (E) hate

18. FLIMSY: (A) airborne (B) fragile
    (C) floating (D) aged (E) peaceful

19. COLT: (A) bravery (B) baby horse
    (C) protector (D) raccoon (E) mare

20. BARGAIN: (A) advantage (B) rally
    (C) low-priced purchase (D) gain
       (E) small, flat ship

EXAM 3

DIRECTIONS: For each word in capitals, select the word or phrase that means most nearly the OPPOSITE, then circle the letter of the correct answer.

EXAMPLE:

HIGH: (A) tall (B) low (C) way up
    (D) lofty

ANALYSIS: The opposite of "high" is "low"; therefore the answer is (B).

1. CAPTIVE: (A) inmate (B) persecuted
    (C) imprisoned (D) free

2. BID: (A) random (B) order (C) obey
    (D) refrain

3. DELAY: (A) accelerate (B) slow-down
    (C) cause (D) soften

4. ACCOMPLISH: (A) fail (B) solve
    (C) achieve (D) suicide

5. EAGER: (A) African bird
    (B) unwilling (C) slow (D) desirous

6. DEFINITE: (A) vague (B) exact
    (C) solemn (D) finished

7. BOLDNESS: (A) insolence
    (B) cowardliness (C) merciless
       (D) rashness

8. DECENT: (A) inexpensive
    (B) improper (C) ugly (D) rashness

9. ACCELERATE: (A) pedal
    (B) deceive (C) speed up (D) retard

10. EFFECT: (A) touch (B) result
    (C) physical law (D) cause

11. ELIMINATE: (A) dehydrate
    (B) include (C) elementary
       (D) get rid of

12. DECAY: (A) spoil (B) grow (C) boil
    (D) oxidized

13. DEMONSTRATE: (A) examine
(B) reveal (C) rally (D) conceal

14. CHAFE: (A) bake (B) irritate
(C) collect (D) soothe

15. DESERT: (A) course of a meal
(B) moisture (C) stay with (D) leave

16. ACQUIRE: (A) lose (B) obtain
(C) gain (D) prevent

17. DEFENDANT: (A) attorney (B) judge
(C) witness (D) plaintiff

18. BENEFIT: (A) infection (B) reward
(C) injury (D) help

19. ELIGIBLE (A) not serious enough
(B) unqualified (C) old enough
(D) able to serve

20. ABSORB: (A) take in (B) discharge
(C) retain (D) sponge

EXAM 4

DIRECTIONS: Circle the letter of the word or phrase that means most nearly the SAME as the phrase above.

EXAMPLE:

To keep from harm or change.
(A) repress (B) preserve (C) forbid
(D) unchanging (E) harmless

1. A story intended to teach a moral truth
(A) narrative poem (B) sonnet
(C) satire (D) fable (E) tall story

2. A solemn promise that God is called on to witness
(A) blood pledge (B) oath (C) reform
(D) testimony (E) evidence

3. One who pretends to have a skill that he does not possess
(A) expert (B) demon (C) authority
(D) legerdemain (E) quack

4. Something made by combining two different elements
(A) hybrid (B) fragment
(C) conspiracy (D) paradigm
(E) method

5. Careful and economical
(A) miser (B) frugal (C) rigid
(D) inexpensive (E) shoddy

6. To hold up to great admiration
(A) magnify (B) martyrize (C) glorify
(D) clarify (C) certify

7. The wormlike form in which insects hatch from the egg
(A) larva (C) chick (E) earthworm
(D) butterfly (E) eel

8. One who joins metals by melting and pressing
(A) hod-carrier (B) welder (C) mason
(D) alchemist (E) physicist

9. State of being adult or fully grown
(A) futurity (B) adolescence (C) old age
(D) maturity (E) minority

10. A record of proceedings
(A) newspaper report
(B) magazine article (C) journal
(D) ledger (E) notebook

11. One who goes on foot
(A) motorist (B) veterinarian
(C) vegetarian (D) footsore
(E) pedestrian

12. A firm belief serving as a rule of conduct
(A) principle (B) whim (C) impulse
(D) austerity (E) emotion

13. To give up in order to gain some other object
(A) save (B) sacrifice (C) exhaust
(D) dispair (E) revolt

14. Well-known in a bad sense
(A) famous (B) notorious
(C) celebrated (D) criminal
(E) foolhardy

15. One who builds with brick
(A) carpenter (B) contractor (C) mason
(D) machinist (E) artisan

16. An outbreak of wild emotionalism
(A) disorder (B) disobedience
(C) frantic (D) hysteria
(E) revolution

17. Proud and overbearing
    (A) haughty (B) prejudicial (C) selfish
        (D) pliable (E) docile

18. To approach with a request or plea
    (A) sell (B) purchase (C) bargain
        (D) suggest (E) solicit

19. Involving strong effort or exertion
    (A) invigorating (B) lackadaisical
        (C) painful (D) strenuous
            (E) disturbing

20. A graceful, privately owned pleasure ship
    (A) frigate (B) galleon (C) cruiser
        (D) yacht (E) motorboat

EXAM 5

DIRECTIONS: For each question determine which of the choices most nearly means the SAME as the word in **boldface** type. Circle the letter of your answer.

EXAMPLE:

The Willliams sisters became **proficient** in tennis at an early age.
(A) aggressive (B) wary (C) unimpressive
    (D) mediocre (E) skillful

1. Once again France has a **flourishing** tourist trade.
   (A) prospering (B) fluid (C) blazing
       (D) slumping (E) rigid

2. Weekend football games have become a **fixture** in American life.
   (A) frivolity (B) weakness (C) firm part
       (D) ideal (E) idleness

3. Humankind possesses only a **fragmentary** history of ancient times.
   (A) authoritative (B) indispensable
       (C) incomprehensible (D) incomplete
           (E) invaluable

4. Sending a human being into space is a **formidable** enterprise.
   (A) contemptible (B) frightening
       (C) simple (D) loathsome (E) alien

5. In his second year, the rookie went on to **fulfill** our highest expectations.
   (A) disappoint (B) splinter (C) stir up
       (D) revive (E) satisfy

6. In the last inning, our team made a **futile** attempt to win the game.
   (A) giddy (B) vain (C) successful
       (D) breathtaking (E) genuine

7. Many people were **gratified** when this style passed out of fashion.
   (A) pleased (B) in style
       (C) unconcerned (D) saddened
           (E) alarmed

8. Smoking is **habitual** with some teenagers.
   (A) taboo (B) unhealthy (C) necessary
       (D) customary (E) popular

9. Patrick Henry uttered the **immortal** words: "Give me liberty or give me death."
   (A) human (B) native (C) rebellious
       (D) never dying (E) famous

10. Alex Rodriquez wore a **jaunty** air as he came to bat.
    (A) taunting (B) irritable (C) placid
        (D) serious (E) cheerful

EXAM 6

DIRECTIONS: For each question determine which of the choices most nearly means the OPPOSITE of the word in **boldface** type. Circle the letter of your answer.

EXAMPLE:

UNTRUSTWORTHY: (A) sly
    (B) dependable (C) rash
        (D) confidence (E) savings bank

1. FLEECY: (A) silky (B) sulky
   (C) flighty (D) fiery (E) dense

2. GIDDY: (A) poised (B) flashing
   (C) vivacious (D) spherical
       (E) grateful

3. CORPULENT: (A) gaunt (B) hale
   (C) desecrated (D) hampered (E) shy

4. ILLUMINATE: (A) shave (B) darken
   (C) remove (D) imply (E) illegal

5. JEER: (A) sneer (B) taunt (C) mock
   (D) cheer (E) mimic

6. KINDRED: (A) kind (B) relative (C) neighborly (D) alien (E) laden

7. LEGITIMATE: (A) improper (B) impoverish (C) inflated (D) theatrical (E) fervent

8. LOATHE: (A) dote on (B) lofty (C) detest (D) protest (E) liberate

9. JOVIAL: (A) Jupiter (B) isolated (C) frugal (D) evil (E) stern

10. INTIMATE: (A) tolerate (B) hint (C) proclaim (D) close (E) variable

EXAM 7

DIRECTIONS: In each of the items below, decide which word or phrase has the SAME or nearly the same meaning as the underlined word. Circle the letter of your choice.

EXAMPLE:

a cheerful face   (A) sad (B) bashful (C) rough (D) happy

ANALYSIS: Letter D has been circled because a cheerful face is a happy face, rather than a sad, bashful, or rough face. The letter before "happy" is "D"; therefore, letter D is circled.

1. a massive structure   (A) trifling (B) tremendous (C) isolated (D) lovely

2. drawing nigh   (A) away (B) near (C) up (D) water

3. a startling observation (A) remark (B) view (C) service (D) claim

4. punctual arrival (A) late (B) early (C) on time (D) pointed

5. quelled the uprising (A) located (B) incited (C) approved (D) put down

6. radiated light (A) sent forth (B) obscured (C) rained (D) heated

7. replenish the supply   (A) use up (B) drain off (C) lose (D) replace

8. of the finest quality   (A) number (B) price (C) grade (D) worthlessness

9. pierce the skin (A) penetrate (B) hand from (C) burn (D) stretch

10. a deep resentment (A) kindness (B) animosity (C) obligation (D) corruption

11. a notable success   (A) outstanding (B) notice (C) taking notes (D) musical

12. for medicinal purposes (A) final (B) digestive (C) solving (D) curative

13. a minute detail (A) hourly (B) very small (C) timed (D) quick

14. necessary requirements (A) essential (B) plausible (C) partial (D) fulfilling

15. an obedient pupil   (A) rebellious (B) happy (C) dutiful (D) bright

16. a rugged pioneer   (A) colonist (B) conservative (C) radical (D) flower

17. a quaint restaurant   (A) dirty (B) unpleasant (C) a la carte (D) old-fashioned

18. the rehabilitated convict (A) remorseful (B) reformed (C) self-destructive (D) incorrigible

19. a respected doctor   (A) highy regarded (B) experienced (C) famous (D) engaged in research

20. quickened our interest   (A) explained (B) modified (C) deadened (D) aroused

EXAM 8

DIRECTIONS: Below are twenty pairs of words. The two words in a pair may be the same or nearly the same in meaning, or may be opposite or nearly opposite in meaning, or may be unrelated to each other. Circle S to the right of the question if the words in the pair have the same meaning; circle O if the words are opposite in meaning; and circle U if the two words are unrelated to each other.

EXAMPLES:

subside—sink	Ⓢ O U	
yonder—writhe	S O Ⓤ	
sentimental—unemotional	S Ⓞ U	

1. maim—wound	S O U
2. massive—light	S O U
3. mental—physical	S O U
4. melancholy—exhilarated	S O U
5. minute—huge	S O U
6. monotonous—ruinous	S O U
7. mutual—joint	S O U
8. observation—inspection	S O U
9. optimism—suspense	S O U
10. overseer—supervisor	S O U
11. pamphlet—booklet	S O U
12. panicky—cool	S O U
13. parliament—congress	S O U
14. patronage—support	S O U
15. perpetual—temporary	S O U
16. pious—indolent	S O U
17. preamble—preface	S O U
18. reward—penalty	S O U
19. prevalent—uncommon	S O U
20. prominent—obscure	S O U

EXAM 9

DIRECTIONS: Below are twenty pairs of words. The two words in a pair may be the same or nearly the same in meaning, or may be opposite or nearly opposite in meaning, or may be unrelated to each other. Circle S to the right of the question if the words in the pair have the same meaning; circle O if the words are opposite in meaning; and circle U if the two words are unrelated to each other.

1. prow—stern	S O U
2. qualify—fit	S O U
3. quicken—die	S O U
4. quaint—renovated	S O U
5. endless—limited	S O U
6. rapture—apathy	S O U
7. rare—raw	S O U
8. ration—allowance	S O U
9. recruit—veteran	S O U
10. recuperation—decline	S O U
11. rejoice—grieve	S O U
12. relative—absolute	S O U
13. replace—supplant	S O U
14. reply—answer	S O U
15. resident—inhabitant	S O U
16. resolution—firmness	S O U
17. respectful—courteous	S O U
18. route—defeat	S O U
19. rumor—evil	S O U
20. rural—cunning	S O U

EXAM 10

DIRECTIONS: In the exercises below, complete each sentence by selecting the one right answer from the five choices that follow. Circle the letter of the right answer, as in the example below.

EXAMPLE:

A *narrative* is a
(A) composition (B) musicale Ⓒ story
   (D) mystery (E) vehicle

1. A *manual* control would be operated
   (A) automatically (B) rapidly
   (C) quietly (D) by hand
   (E) electrically

2. An *objective* report by a committee
   would be
   (A) prejudiced (B) subjective
   (C) personal (D) offensive (E) fair

3. A colorful *pageant* is
   (A) a public entertainment (B) a party
   (C) a disorderly gathering
   (D) a client (E) a platter

4. To *account* for one's actions means to
   _____ them.
   (A) explain (B) prevent (C) plan
   (D) reject (E) add up

5. A man of *prowess* is
   (A) proud (B) excessively humble
   (C) extraordinarily able (D) cowardly
   (E) none of these

6. His *pugilistic* skill means _____
   skill.
   (A) athletic (B) musical
   (C) lack of (D) boxing
   (E) none of these

7. An *imposter* is a(an)
   (A) fraud (B) expert (C) model
   (D) specialist (E) none of these

8. A corrupt *regime* is
   (A) unheard of (B) for reform
   (C) a fine government
   (D) a democracy
   (E) none of these

9. To *resist* tyranny is to _____
   tyranny.
   (A) fight against (B) submit to
   (C) suffer (D) worship
   (E) none of these

10. A *robust* woodsman is
    (A) anemic (B) sturdy (C) pallid
    (D) frail (E) none of these

EXAM 11

> DIRECTIONS: For each item, determine
> whether the underlined word is used cor-
> rectly. If it is, circle T, if not, circle F.
>
> **EXAMPLE:**
>
> An <u>uninhabited</u> country is one
> that has a huge population.   T (F)

1. A <u>rapier</u> is a type of short, broad
   sword.   T F

2. <u>Rebellion</u> is a peaceful change
   of government.   T F

3. I can <u>recollect</u> events that
   happened when I was five
   years old.   T F

4. As security guard, you need a
   person of <u>reliability</u>.   T F

5. A repentant drunkard feels
   no <u>remorse</u> for his wasted life.   T F

6. Snakes and lizards are
   <u>reptiles</u>.   T F

7. *X* <u>represents</u> an unknown
   quantity in algebra.   T F

8. A scoundrel <u>resorts</u> to trickery.   T F

9. <u>Restraint</u> is required when
   criticizing our benefactors.   T F

10. <u>Plaid</u> is a colorless strip of
    material used as trimming.   T F

11. By using a <u>ruse</u>, he was able to
    gain his ends openly and fairly.   T F

12. The light snow <u>scorched</u> her
    face gently.   T F

13. <u>Sculpture</u> is one of the fine
    arts, the art of building
    beautiful structures.   T F

14. The knife was placed in a
    <u>sheath</u> to keep it away from
    the children.   T F

15. After a day in the desert, our
    food was <u>sodden</u>.   T F

16. A <u>spendthrift</u> saves money
    regularly.   T F

17. <u>Spontaneous</u> applause came
    all night from the paid
    applauders.   T F

18. The cattle remained calm
    during the <u>stampede</u>.   T F

19. There is no more <u>steadfast</u>
    friend than a fickle girl.   T F

20. His <u>boorish</u> manners were
    uncouth.   T F

EXAM 12

DIRECTIONS: For the underlined word in
each phrase, select the lettered word or
phrase that means most nearly the
SAME. Circle the letter of the correct
answer.

EXAMPLE:

an <u>overcast</u> sky
(A) brilliant (B) cloudy (C) windy
    (D) clear (E) starry

1. a noble <u>sacrifice</u>
   (A) impulse (B) act of truth (C) gaiety
       (D) response (E) act of unselfishness

2. with great <u>tact</u>
   (A) ability to say and do the right thing
       (B) inconvenience (C) exertion
           (D) facility at touching
               (E) piece of information

3. as a <u>consequence</u>
   (A) cause (B) arch (C) hook
       (D) agent (E) result

4. the bright <u>sash</u>
   (A) bloody wound (B) ribbon
       (C) dance step (D) battle
           (E) money

5. the <u>talented</u> singer
   (A) beautiful (B) boastful (C) gifted
       (D) scout (E) poor

6. <u>conventional</u> wisdom
   (A) common (B) unorthodox
       (C) unsuitable (D) disgusting
           (E) tardy

7. the <u>vague</u> answer
   (A) complete (B) stylish (C) stupid
       (D) unclear (E) scarlet

8. the <u>vacant</u> lot
   (A) parking (B) stupid (C) empty
       (D) whole (E) cultivated

9. the <u>unabridged</u> dictionary
   (A) incomplete (B) specialized
       (C) Webster's (D) unadulterated
           (E) unshortened

10. a <u>typical</u> teenager
    (A) rock 'n' roll (B) mature (C) happy
        (D) delinquent (E) average

11. the <u>significant</u> event
    (A) unhappy (B) wedding (C) following
        (D) important (E) last

12. a noble <u>sentiment</u>
    (A) feeling (B) sadness (C) cry
        (D) lament (E) silliness

13. the <u>turmoil</u> in the hills
    (A) quiet (B) confusion (C) girl
        (D) elephant (E) crowd

14. <u>unsound</u> reasoning
    (A) ringing (B) untested (C) intelligent
        (D) precocious (E) faulty

15. a hidden <u>hazard</u>
    (A) trail (B) peril (C) explosive
        (D) ice storm (E) disease

16. a <u>vision</u> of success
    (A) story (B) break (C) dream
        (D) fulfillment (E) example

17. with <u>uncommon</u> fervor
    (A) ordinary (B) dreamy (C) noisy
        (D) unrealistic (E) more than usual

18. the important <u>transaction</u>
    (A) business man (B) result
        (C) method of communication
            (D) piece of business
                (E) proceeding

19. the third <u>stanza</u>
 (A) song (B) repetition (C) lyric
  (D) portion of a poem (E) scale

20. the <u>subsequent</u> events
 (A) in place of (B) following
  (C) preceding (D) important
   (E) significant

EXAM 13

DIRECTIONS: For the underlined word in each phrase, select the lettered word or phrase that means most nearly the SAME. Circle the letter of the correct answer.

EXAMPLE:

an <u>ambitious</u> man
(A) lazy (B) energetic (C) purposeful
 (D) cruel (E) fine

1. the <u>customary</u> costume
 (A) young (B) ideal (C) tattered
  (D) traditional (E) colorful

2. <u>utilize</u> your talents
 (A) make use of (B) utilities (C) sing
  (D) modernize (E) undo

3. his <u>vigorous</u> objection
 (A) unhappy (B) strong (C) sunny
  (D) false (E) vivacious

4. the <u>vulgar</u> remark
 (A) coarse (B) poorly timed (C) vintage
  (D) wrong (E) tasteful

5. her <u>sullen</u> mood
 (A) happy (B) silly (C) brooding
  (D) sunny (E) distasteful

6. the <u>vast</u> garden
 (A) empty (B) outdoor (C) expansive
  (D) lovely (E) springy

7. <u>terminate</u> the business
 (A) start (B) remodel (C) refinance
  (D) exterminate (E) put an end to

8. a <u>cumbersome</u> package
 (A) erect (B) inverted (C) immovable
  (D) wrong (E) bulky

9. <u>veto</u> the bill
 (A) sign (B) withdraw (C) debate on
  (D) pass (E) refuse to sign

10. <u>variety</u> of acts
 (A) show (B) hall (C) sequence
  (D) assortment (E) poor quality

EXAM 14

DIRECTIONS: For each item choose the word or phrase that is closest in meaning to the capitalized word. Then circle the letter of the word or phrase you have selected.

EXAMPLE:

OBLIQUE: (A) blinking (B) scarce
 (C) level (D) criss-cross (E) diagonal

1. STUMP: (A) glide (B) walk noisily
 (C) imprint (D) strut (E) blast loose

2. PONDER: (A) sink (B) come after
 (C) drive a horse carriage
  (D) think (E) commute

3. SURGE: (A) swell (B) take a view of
 (C) influence (D) remove (E) excel

4. TAUNT: (A) placate (B) mimic
 (C) tangle (D) tease (E) tighten

5. TEMPO: (A) storm (B) largo
 (C) rhythm (D) tendency
  (E) symphony

6. THRIVE: (A) dishevel (B) push
 (C) bounce (D) confess (E) flourish

7. PLEAT: (A) beg (B) offer (C) crease
 (D) discuss (E) cry out

8. TUMULT: (A) wretchedness
 (B) noise and confusion
  (C) exciting anticipation
   (D) multiplication
    (E) deep and violent anger

9. TYRANT: (A) despot (B) ruler
 (C) sovereign (D) viceroy
  (E) premier

10. UNIQUE: (A) 100% (B) not basic
 (C) alone of its kind (D) changeable
  (E) extraordinarily large

EXAM 15

DIRECTIONS: Each of the following groups contains five pairs of words labeled (A), (B), (C), (D), and (E). For each group, select the pair of words that are OPPOSITE in meaning to each other. Circle the letter that corresponds to the pair of words you have chosen.

EXAMPLE:

  (A) nag—annoy
  (B) precaution—care
  (C) scent—odor
  (D) social—self-centered
  (E) subside—sink

1. (A) sadden—depress
  (B) sanitary—dirty
  (C) scarce—rare
  (D) sentinel—picket
  (E) serene—unclouded

2. (A) sequence—succession
  (B) sever—separate
  (C) shrill—dull
  (D) sift—separate
  (E) significant—meaningful

3. (A) solicit—entreat
  (B) solitary—joint
  (C) soothe—please
  (D) souvenir—keepsake
  (E) stature—standing

4. (A) stress—strain
  (B) sturdy—robust
  (C) submit—offer
  (D) supreme—utmost
  (E) tedious—stimulating

5. (A) tempest—storm
  (B) terminal—end
  (C) thrift—economy
  (D) tolerant—prejudiced
  (E) tributary—branch

6. (A) tropical—arctic
  (B) truancy—absence
  (C) trivial—unimportant
  (D) turmoil—confusion
  (E) unabridged—complete

7. (A) unaware—unconscious
  (B) undoubted—certain
  (C) unceasing—continuous
  (D) unruffled—disturbed
  (E) upright—honest

8. (A) urban—city
  (B) utility—usefulness
  (C) vagrant—tramp
  (D) van—front
  (E) violence—gentleness

9. (A) vision—dream
  (B) vital—living
  (C) vivacious—spiritless
  (D) wary—cautious
  (E) waver—hesitate

10. (A) wharf—dock
  (B) woeful—joyous
  (C) wrath—anger
  (D) yarn—wool
  (E) yield—produce

FOR THE UPPER GRADES— TESTS 16–22

EXAM 16

DIRECTIONS: Circle the letter of the best definition.

1. COARSE: (A) subject (B) track (C) rough (D) spotted (E) massive

2. ANTITHESIS: (A) grave (B) unfriendliness (C) part of flower (D) opposite (E) oration

3. ETHICAL: (A) causing sleep (B) racial (C) linguistic (D) moral (E) sensible

4. PREROGATIVE: (A) command (B) right (C) contradiction (D) early animal (E) haggard

5. INDEMNITY: (A) exemption (B) conviction (C) accusation (D) compensation (E) quell

6. CONCILIATORY: (A) winning over
(B) undoing (C) advisory
(D) defeating (E) subsequent

7. SALABLE: (A) marketable
(B) healthful (C) easily soiled
(D) old (E) preliminary

8. BOUNTEOUS: (A) beautiful
(B) elastic (C) liberal (D) heavenly
(E) mutinous

9. VANITY: (A) envy (B) saintliness
(C) humility (D) excessive pride
(E) urge

10. IMPERIAL: (A) royal
(B) like an empire (C) empirical
(D) principality (E) descendant

11. PORTLY: (A) from side to side
(B) oblong (C) fat
(D) perpendicular (E) vertical

12. JAUNTY: (A) subdued (B) retarded
(C) phlegmatic (D) unconcerned
(E) apathetic

13. VOID: (A) forested (B) unfilled
(C) colonial (D) chaotic
(E) substitute

14. ANTIDOTE: (A) against war
(B) against vivisection
(C) against poison
(D) against liquor
(E) against communism

15. PEEVISH: (A) frightened (B) amiable
(C) screaming (D) complaining
(E) juvenile

16. PLUMMET: (A) plunge (B) submerge
(C) walk through water
(D) tread water (E) hobble

17. WARRANT: (A) authorize (B) arrest
(C) guarantee (D) digest (E) dawdle

18. TAINT: (A) heir (B) spoil (C) tyranny
(D) poor taste (E) keen perception

19. VITAL: (A) propaganda
(B) acceleration (C) sudden pain
(D) essential (E) conscience

EXAM 17

DIRECTIONS: Circle the letter of the best definition.

1. DETER: (A) halt (B) steer (C) sting
(D) turn (E) hinder

2. DELVE: (A) halve (B) hide (C) dig
(D) divide (E) serve

3. NOMAD: (A) savage (B) fool
(C) cloak (D) wanderer (E) insect

4. EBB: (A) weave (B) flow (C) fill
(D) stretch (E) decrease

5. CARNAGE: (A) battle (B) war
(C) slaughter (D) theft (E) charge

6. CULPABLE: (A) innocent (B) able
(C) helpless (D) at fault (E) young

7. DISPENSE: (A) distribute (B) fling
(C) disgust (D) desert (E) scatter

8. FIASCO: (A) failure (B) plot
(C) carriage (D) comedy (E) loss

9. ERODE: (A) travel (B) wear down
(C) soothe (D) erupt (E) evoke

10. ALLUDE: (A) aid (B) plan
(C) deceive (D) escape (E) refer

11. GYRATE: (A) cheat (B) whirl
(C) sting (D) threaten (E) fly

12. MELEE: (A) mess (B) mix (C) mar
(D) mellow (E) fight

13. SEETHE: (A) storm (B) boil (C) stir
(D) placate (E) save

14. ENNUI: (A) entry (B) youth
(C) illness (D) boredom (E) energy

15. CELERITY: (A) speed (B) fame
(C) courtesy (D) health (E) purity

16. YIELD: (A) want (B) need
(C) subdue (D) give up (E) token

17. STATURE: (A) image (B) height
(C) sculpture (D) law
(E) radio interference

18. RELINQUISH:
    (A) abandon (B) vacant (C) profound
    (D) vast (E) triangular

19. SENTINEL: (A) middle (B) sentence
    (C) guard (D) tangle (E) legend

20. GENESIS: (A) tendency (B) ration
    (C) freight (D) insurance (E) beginning

EXAM 18

DIRECTIONS: For each word given, find
the CORRECT meaning among the
words or phrases labeled (A), (B), (C),
and (D).

EXAMPLE:

HEAVY: (A) sorry (B) interested
  (C) weighty (D) well

1. PAGAN: (A) sprightly (B) playful
   (C) worried (D) heathen

2. AFFECTATION: (A) illness
   (B) wordiness (C) oath (D) air

3. IMPLY: (A) suggest (B) furnish
   (C) deceive (D) oil

4. SUBMISSIVE: (A) obedient
   (B) angry (C) forlorn (D) total

5. DEFER: (A) second (B) postpone
   (C) give (D) propose

6. ADORN: (A) agree to (B) assist
   (C) decorate (D) communicate

7. TREAD: (A) help (B) swim
   (C) turn back (D) step

8. TESTIFY: (A) oath (B) legal trick
   (C) exam (D) report

9. IMMENSE: (A) object (B) huge
   (C) torn (D) decrepit

10. CONVERSE: (A) change (B) talk
    (C) fill (D) break into

11. SPLICE: (A) join (B) sell
    (C) give up (D) turn down

12. HAMPER: (A) notify (B) curse
    (C) find (D) obstruct

13. CONFUSE: (A) electrify (B) bewilder
    (C) make up (D) anger

14. DELUXE: (A) of note (B) temporary
    (C) selected (D) luxurious

15. REGAL: (A) royal (B) late
    (C) difficult (D) gold

16. PLEA: (A) command (B) note
    (C) barrier (D) request

17. SIFT: (A) alter (B) sort (C) thread
    (D) maneuver

18. GAUNT: (A) empty (B) vivid (C) thin
    (D) spiral

19. SUBSEQUENT: (A) in and out
    (B) in order (C) afterward
    (D) in reversed order

20. EXERT: (A) clamp (B) open (C) apply
    (D) create tone

21. INCARCERATE: (A) imprison
    (B) jailer (C) apply (D) captive

22. METROPOLITAN: (A) of note
    (B) with people (C) pertaining to order
    (D) pertaining to a large city

23. OBLIQUE: (A) compressed
    (B) scattered (C) overt (D) slanted

24. PATRON: (A) fool (B) store-keeper
    (C) braggart (D) supporter

25. METHODICAL: (A) frantic
    (B) careless (C) orderly (D) askew

26. ECSTATIC: (A) light-bearing
    (B) upright (C) being part of
    (D) supremely joyous

27. VISUAL: (A) round (B) partial
    (C) concerning time
    (D) dealing with sight

28. STATUTE: (A) order (B) candle
    (C) folder (D) law

29. REGIME: (A) bow shape (B) feathery coat (C) agreement (D) government

30. STAMPEDE: (A) make mild (B) force (C) run away (D) penetrate

31. CONFLICT: (A) will (B) battle (C) memory (D) convenant

32. DEFICIENCY: (A) excess (B) lack (C) quantity (D) falseness

33. PRECLUDE: (A) prevent (B) turn over (C) justify (D) convey

34. CHAPERON: (A) alien (B) student (C) learner (D) supervisor

35. TIMOROUS: (A) fearful (B) silly (C) generous (D) tenfold

36. TRANSFORM: (A) threaten (B) predict (C) convert (D) propose

37. PURLOIN: (A) withdraw (B) fulfill (C) pinpoint (D) steal

38. SCOWL: (A) frown (B) insist (C) dispel (D) picture

39. CONGENIAL: (A) baffling (B) loving (C) friendly (D) thoughtful

40. RAPTURE: (A) ecstasy (B) truth (C) worth (D) hostility

EXAM 19

DIRECTIONS: For each word given, find the CORRECT meaning among the words or phrases labeled (A), (B), (C), and (D). Circle the correct letter from choices given.

1. HEIR: (A) hither (B) successor (C) dam (D) predecessor

2. DETRIMENTAL: (A) perpetual (B) confident (C) harmful (D) idealistic

3. TAUNT: (A) be frivolous (B) tease cruelly (C) query (D) ply

4. RUGGED: (A) smooth (B) fertile (C) wavy (D) uneven

5. ABUNDANCE: (A) large amount (B) profundity (C) scarcity (D) country dance

6. INCLINATION: (A) mountain (B) prairie (C) preference (D) plane

7. GOBBLE: (A) talk a lot (B) eat greedily (C) rinse (D) mix up

8. REPOSE: (A) model (B) decline (C) hide (D) rest

9. PROHIBIT: (A) forestall (B) command (C) forbid (D) stain

10. TAINT: (A) pursue (B) infect (C) taunt (D) keep in step

11. BISECT: (A) go away (B) go in (C) divide in two (D) prescribe

12. COUNCIL: (A) lawyer (B) advice (C) governing body (D) will

13. BOLSTER: (A) rasher (B) support (C) rugged (D) persistent

14. TREPIDATION: (A) olden (B) fear (C) comical (D) trivial

15. STATURE: (A) standing (B) state (C) involvement (D) proclamation

16. PROMOTE: (A) backslide (B) support (C) reorganize (D) react

17. EMINENCE: (A) personality (B) decline (C) high position (D) sensation

18. PORTRAY: (A) settle (B) depict (C) take action (D) light up

19. ALLURING: (A) painted (B) attractive (C) sturdy (D) female

20. BAR: (A) fill (B) cohere (C) recede (D) prevent

21. CELESTIAL: (A) earthy (B) watery (C) heavenly (D) tempting

22. AGGRAVATE: (A) make worse (B) irritate (C) destroy (D) imitate

23. PLUCK: (A) adhere (B) entice (C) pull out (D) have good fortune

24. ADVOCATE: (A) lender of money (B) borrower of money (C) supporter (D) mortgage

25. PRELUDE: (A) preamble (B) loneliness (C) gaiety (D) aptitude

26. RETORT: (A) answer (B) garble (C) interfere (D) simulate

27. FACSIMILE: (A) imitate (B) copy (C) fabricate (D) send

28. BARD: (A) translator (B) religious leader (C) poet (D) gain

29. APPROXIMATE: (A) inexact (B) abridged (C) horizontal (D) suitable

30. CONSOLE: (A) adopt (B) comfort (C) disturb (D) grieve

31. CLANDESTINE: (A) outstanding (B) piddling (C) surreptitious (D) secret

32. TWINGE: (A) torture (B) sudden pain (C) extravagance (D) drive

33. SQUANDER: (A) support (B) bracket (C) purchase (D) waste

34. INTERCHANGEABLE: (A) luxurious (B) unreturnable (C) equal (D) familiar

35. GLOBAL: (A) conical (B) heavy (C) square (D) round

36. CRISIS: (A) trial (B) emergency (C) hurricane (D) sad effort

37. BRAWL: (A) fight (B) basement (C) bargain (D) saloon

38. APPARATUS: (A) personnel (B) reasoning (C) equipment (D) fantasy

39. BARBAROUS: (A) winsome (B) feminine (C) shrewd (D) savage

40. ALLEGE: (A) blackmail (B) claim (C) vow (D) deny

EXAM 20

DIRECTIONS: In each question below, one of the four words or phrases given as choices means almost the SAME as the italicized word in the preceding sentence. Circle the correct answer.

EXAMPLE:

Next to our house there is an *empty* lot.
(A) cluttered (B) full of flowers (C) vacant (D) dirty

1. A *diligent* student is well rewarded.
   (A) rich (B) skilled (C) punctual (D) conscientious

2. The mayor read his *proclamation* from the steps of city hall.
   (A) amnesty (B) freedom of slaves (C) denial (D) government announcement

3. The cheerleaders *strutted* at the head of the parade.
   (A) swindled (B) swaggered (C) waved batons (D) leaped high

4. My parents want me to *sever* ties with my friend Steve.
   (A) strengthen (B) trade (C) cut (D) imprive

5. Her *untimely* death robbed us of a great philosopher.
   (A) accidental (B) cruel (C) premature (D) merciful

6. *Vanity* keeps us from seeing our own faults.
   (A) success (B) excessive pride (C) friends (D) relatives

7. The May Day *pageant* was held on the lawn.
   (A) arena (B) exhibition (C) contest
   (D) race

8. Lucy finally succeeded in *unraveling* the wool thread.
   (A) untangling (B) knitting (C) selling
   (D) buying

9. We must learn to *stress* goodness above beauty.
   (A) emphasize (B) see (C) practice
   (D) foretell

10. Lila ate a *paltry* breakfast
    (A) enormous (B) nutritious
    (C) meager (D) hurried

11. It is time to *replenish* our supply of coal.
    (A) sell (B) buy (C) use up
    (D) make full again

12. You will not accomplish much with a *defiant* attitude.
    (A) friendly (B) discreet (C) placid
    (D) antagonistic

13. He wasted his time on *trivial* matters.
    (A) significant (B) metropolitan
    (C) unimportant (D) unsuccessful

14. Jerusalem is an *venerable* city.
    (A) holy (B) deserted (C) distinguished
    (D) old

15. Pioneers *thrust* westward across the mountains.
    (A) climbed (B) pushed (C) struggled
    (D) flew

16. We admired the graceful beauty of the *edifice*.
    (A) apartment house (B) large building
    (C) ranch (D) church

17. He was arrested as a *vagrant*.
    (A) homeless, unemployed person
    (B) traveler (C) immigrant
    (D) criminal

18. An *insolent* child is an unhappy one.
    (A) cooperative (B) hard-working
    (C) fresh (D) sickly

19. Once burned, twice *wary*.
    (A) nonchalant (B) careful
    (C) sunburned (D) warlike

20. His posture was erect and his *tread* firm.
    (A) confidence (B) rubber tire
    (C) stance (D) step

21. Civilians were trained as *combatants* in six months.
    (A) warriors (B) air-raid wardens
    (C) public officials
    (D) security guards

22. We are sending our *surplus* butter abroad.
    (A) rancid (B) excess (C) useless
    (D) spoiled

23. The newspaper received an *laudatory* letter.
    (A) complaining (B) full of praise
    (C) unsigned (D) critical

24. You cannot *withstand* progress.
    (A) gainsay (B) praise enough
    (C) fight off (D) compel

25. Proceed with *vigilance*.
    (A) business as usual (B) alterations
    (C) bidding contest (D) caution

26. *Pious* thoughts and generous actions characterize the good person.
    (A) pure (B) violent (C) faithless
    (D) patient

27. Hilary made a *brash* remark in class.
    (A) cheeky (B) boastful
    (C) irrelevant (D) funny

28. He used a *ruse* to gain admission.
    (A) ticket (B) free pass (C) trick (D) gun

29. *Valiant* efforts were exerted to elect our candidate.
    (A) vain (B) futile (C) courageous
    (D) foolish

30. This evidence will *vindicate* the defendant.
    (A) condemn (B) exonerate
    (C) implicate (D) reform

Answers to All Practice Tests and Mastery Exams

PRACTICE TESTS

TEST 1, p. 124

1. D	11. E	21. A	31. A	41. E
2. B	12. B	22. D	32. B	42. C
3. C	13. C	23. B	33. D	43. B
4. A	14. C	24. B	34. B	44. B
5. E	15. B	25. C	35. D	45. C
6. B	16. A	26. C	36. C	46. B
7. B	17. A	27. A	37. B	47. B
8. D	18. D	28. B	38. C	48. E
9. E	19. B	29. C	39. D	49. D
10. B	20. C	30. D	40. E	50. B

TEST 2, p. 127

1. A	5. C	9. D	13. A	17. B
2. C	6. C	10. A	14. A	18. B
3. C	7. A	11. B	15. C	19. A
4. D	8. B	12. C	16. C	20. B

TEST 3, p. 129

1. C	11. B	21. C	31. C	41. B
2. C	12. D	22. A	32. A	42. C
3. E	13. B	23. D	33. C	43. C
4. D	14. A	24. B	34. C	44. D
5. A	15. C	25. C	35. A	45. C
6. B	16. D	26. A	36. A	46. D
7. E	17. C	27. B	37. A	47. B
8. C	18. C	28. D	38. C	48. C
9. E	19. A	29. D	39. B	49. C
10. C	20. B	30. B	40. C	50. A

TEST 4, p. 132

1. D	5. D	9. C	13. E	17. D
2. A	6. C	10. A	14. A	18. C
3. E	7. B	11. E	15. B	19. B
4. D	8. D	12. B	16. A	20. C

TEST 5, p. 134

1. C	5. B	9. D	13. C	17. C
2. B	6. C	10. B	14. A	18. D
3. D	7. A	11. A	15. D	19. A
4. A	8. B	12. D	16. B	20. B

TEST 6, p. 145

1. accept
   except
2. access
   excess
3. edition
   addition
4. effect
   affect
   effect
5. aisle
   isle
   I'll
6. aloud
   allowed
7. all ready
   already
8. allusion
   illusion
9. altar
   alter
10. arc
    ark
11. ascent
    assent
12. assistants
    assistance
13. band
    banned
14. bear
    bare
    Bear
15. base
    bass
16. beech
    beach
17. beat
    beet
18. beau
    bow
19. bury
    berry
20. birth
    berth

21. blew
    blue
22. bore
    bore
    boar
23. born
    borne
24. bough
    bow
25. brake
    break
26. bred
    bread
27. bridal
    bridle
28. canvas
    canvass
29. capital
    capitol
30. carat
    carrot
    caret
31. cede
    seed
32. seller
    cellar
33. cent
    sent
    scent
34. cell
    sell
35. site
    sight
    cite
36. climb
    clime
37. course
    coarse
38. colonel
    kernel
39. counsel
    council
40. corps
    core

41. councilor
    counselor
42. creak
    creek
43. dissent
    descent
44. deer
    dear
45. dessert
    desert
46. due
    dew
47. die
    dye
48. dough
    doe
49. dual
    duel
50. earn
    urn
51. faint
    feint
52. fair
    fare
53. fate
    fete
54. fined
    find
55. fir
    fur
56. flee
    flea
57. flew
    flue
58. flour
    flower
59. for
    four
60. formally
    formerly
61. forth
    fourth

62. foul
    fowl
63. gate
    gait
64. gamble
    gambol
65. gilt
    guilt
66. grate
    great
67. groan
    grown
68. guessed
    guest
69. hail
    hale
70. hare
    hair
71. hall
    haul
72. hart
    heart
73. heal
    heel
74. hear
    here
75. heard
    herd
76. higher
    hire
77. him
    hymn
78. horse
    hoarse
79. hole
    whole
80. holy
    wholly
81. our
    hour
82. idle
    idol
83. inn
    in
84. instants
    instance
85. it's
    its

86. knight
    night
87. know
    no
88. lane
    lain
89. lead
    led
90. lesson
    lessen
91. lye
    lie
92. load
    lode
93. loan
    lone
94. mail
    male
95. mane
    main
96. meat
    meet
97. metal
    mettle
98. miner
    minor
99. morn
    mourn
100. one
    won
101. pail
    pale
102. pane
    pain
103. pair
    pear
    pare
104. pour
    paw
105. peel
    peal
106. peace
    piece
107. plane
    plain
108. pray
    prey

109. principle
    principal
110. prophet
    profit
111. reign
    rain
112. rap
    wrap
113. reed
    read
114. red
    read
115. real
    reel
116. rite
    right
    write
117. wring
    ring
118. rowed
    road
    rode
119. role
    roll
120. route
    root
121. wrote
    rote
122. sale
    sail
123. scene
    seen
124. sea
    see
125. seem
    seam
126. so
    sew
    sow
127. sleigh
    slay
128. soar
    sore
129. soled
    sold
130. soul
    sole

131. some
    sum
132. son
    sun
133. stake
    steak
134. stair
    stare
135. stationery
    stationary
136. steel
    steal
137. strait
    straight
138. suite
    sweet
139. tail
    tale
140. team
    teem
141. there
    there

their
they're
142. threw
    through
143. thrown
    throne
144. tide
    tied
145. toe
    tow
146. tolled
    told
147. vain
    vein
    vane
148. vale
    veil
149. vial
    vile
150. wade
    weighed

151. wail
    whale
152. waste
    waist
153. wait
    weight
154. wear
    ware
    where
155. weak
    week
156. weather
    whether
157. which
    witch
158. whine
    wine
159. wood
    would
160. you're
    your

MASTERY EXAMS

Rating Your Results

On exams with 10 questions:

Superior	9–10 correct
Average	7–8 correct
Below Average	6 or fewer correct

On exams with 20 questions:

Superior	18–20 correct
Average	14–17 correct
Below Average	13 or fewer correct

On exams with 30 questions:

Superior	27–30 correct
Average	21–26 correct
Below Average	20 or fewer correct

On exams with 40 questions:

Superior	36–40 correct
Average	28–35 correct
Below Average	27 or fewer correct

EXAM 1, p. 155

1. E	5. C	9. A	13. C	17. B
2. A	6. D	10. E	14. E	18. C
3. B	7. D	11. D	15. E	19. B
4. B	8. E	12. A	16. E	20. E

EXAM 2, p. 155

1. D	5. C	9. D	13. A	17. C
2. D	6. B	10. A	14. E	18. B
3. B	7. A	11. B	15. D	19. B
4. A	8. B	12. B	16. E	20. C

EXAM 3, p. 156

1. D	5. B	9. D	13. D	17. D
2. C	6. A	10. D	14. D	18. C
3. A	7. B	11. B	15. C	19. B
4. A	8. B	12. B	16. A	20. B

EXAM 4, p. 157

1. D	5. B	9. D	13. B	17. A
2. B	6. C	10. C	14. B	18. E
3. E	7. A	11. E	15. C	19. D
4. A	8. B	12. A	16. D	20. D

EXAM 5, p. 158

1. A	3. D	5. E	7. A	9. D
2. C	4. B	6. B	8. D	10. E

EXAM 6, p. 158

1. E	3. A	5. D	7. A	9. E
2. A	4. B	6. D	8. A	10. C

EXAM 7, p. 159

1. B	5. D	9. A	13. B	17. D
2. B	6. A	10. B	14. A	18. B
3. A	7. D	11. A	15. C	19. A
4. C	8. C	12. D	16. A	20. D

EXAM 8, p. 160

1. S	5. O	9. U	13. S	17. S
2. O	6. U	10. S	14. S	18. O
3. O	7. S	11. S	15. O	19. O
4. O	8. S	12. O	16. U	20. O

EXAM 9, p. 160

1. O	5. O	9. O	13. S	17. S
2. S	6. O	10. O	14. S	18. U
3. O	7. S	11. O	15. S	19. U
4. O	8. S	12. O	16. S	20. U

EXAM 10, p. 160

1. D	3. A	5. C	7. A	9. A
2. E	4. A	6. D	8. E	10. B

EXAM 11, p. 161

1. F	5. F	9. T	13. F	17. F
2. F	6. T	10. F	14. T	18. F
3. T	7. T	11. F	15. F	19. F
4. T	8. T	12. F	16. F	20. T

EXAM 12, p. 162

1. E	5. C	9. E	13. B	17. E
2. A	6. A	10. E	14. E	18. D
3. E	7. D	11. D	15. B	19. D
4. B	8. C	12. A	16. C	20. B

EXAM 13, p. 163

1. D	3. B	5. C	7. E	9. E
2. A	4. A	6. C	8. E	10. D

EXAM 14, p. 163

1. B	3. A	5. C	7. C	9. A
2. D	4. D	6. E	8. B	10. C

EXAM 15, p. 164

1. B	3. B	5. D	7. D	9. C
2. C	4. E	6. A	8. E	10. B

EXAM 16, p. 164

1. C	5. D	9. D	13. B	17. A
2. D	6. A	10. B	14. C	18. B
3. D	7. A	11. C	15. D	19. D
4. B	8. C	12. D	16. A	

EXAM 17, p. 165

1. E	5. C	9. B	13. B	17. B
2. C	6. D	10. E	14. D	18. A
3. D	7. A	11. B	15. A	19. C
4. E	8. A	12. E	16. D	20. E

EXAM 18, p. 166

1.	D	9.	B	17.	B	25.	C	33.	A
2.	D	10.	B	18.	C	26.	D	34.	D
3.	A	11.	A	19.	C	27.	D	35.	A
4.	A	12.	D	20.	C	28.	D	36.	C
5.	B	13.	B	21.	A	29.	D	37.	D
6.	C	14.	D	22.	D	30.	C	38.	A
7.	D	15.	A	23.	D	31.	B	39.	C
8.	D	16.	D	24.	D	32.	B	40.	A

EXAM 20, p. 168

1.	D	7.	B	13.	C	19.	B	25.	D
2.	D	8.	A	14.	D	20.	D	26.	A
3.	B	9.	A	15.	B	21.	A	27.	A
4.	D	10.	C	16.	B	22.	B	28.	C
5.	C	11.	D	17.	A	23.	B	29.	C
6.	B	12.	D	18.	C	24.	C	30.	B

EXAM 19, p. 167

1.	B	9.	C	17.	C	25.	A	33.	D
2.	C	10.	B	18.	B	26.	A	34.	C
3.	B	11.	C	19.	B	27.	B	35.	D
4.	D	12.	C	20.	D	28.	C	36.	B
5.	A	13.	B	21.	C	29.	A	37.	A
6.	C	14.	B	22.	A	30.	B	38.	C
7.	B	15.	A	23.	C	31.	C	39.	D
8.	D	16.	B	24.	C	32.	B	40.	B

Reading Comprehension

Reading Comprehension Questions

The HSPT usually includes six reading passages, each one the length of half a page in a regular book. You are given between five and eight questions about each passage.

The Coop usually includes four slightly longer passages, each accompanied by four questions.

On the HSPT, you must answer about 60 questions in 25 minutes. Since that includes reading the passage, you will have less than half a minute per question. The Coop asks about 34 questions in 32 minutes. Because the passages are longer, however, you have about the same amount of time to answer each question.

The passages are nonfiction and are meant to be understood by students who are soon to enter high school. They are not supposed to stump, trick, or confuse you. To grasp their meaning, however, you will have to read carefully and thoughtfully, staying alert to all the facts and ideas they contain. Everything you need to know to answer the questions is right in the passage.

TACTICS FOR ANSWERING READING QUESTIONS

Test-taking style varies from person to person. Not every tactic presented in this chapter will work equally well for every student. What works for you may not work for your best friend, and vice versa. That's why you should practice with this book. By experimenting with different methods, you'll find the one that produces the best results for you.

➤ *Option A. Read the passage carefully from start to finish before answering the questions.* Don't try to remember every detail, but ask yourself: What is this passage really about? When you are finished

reading, try to state the author's main point in your own words. Then start answering the questions, referring back to the passage as often as necessary.

➤ *Option B. Skim the passage rapidly for its general idea.* Read faster than you normally would, just intently enough to get an impression of its contents. Don't expect to remember every detail. Then start to answer the questions, referring back to the passage as often as necessary.

➤ *Option C. Skim the passage to get its general meaning, then go back and read it more thoroughly.* Two readings, one fast and one slow, will help you grasp the passage better than if you read it only once. Then proceed to the questions. Because you've read the passage twice, you may not find it necessary to refer to it as often as someone using Option A or B.

Try each of the options as you prepare for the exam. Gradually you will discover the one that helps you answer the most questions correctly.

Regardless of which option works best for you:

1. *Get psyched for success.* Be confident that you can answer the questions. You can go far by thinking positively. The test questions are straightforward. They are not meant to trick or confuse you. Don't look for hidden meanings where there are none to be found.

2. *Read each passage from start to finish.* It may be tempting to start answering questions as quickly as you can, but since the meaning of the passage can change as it goes on, be sure to read the whole thing in the order it was written before answering the questions.

3. *Pay close attention to what you are reading.* Even if the topic of the passage doesn't appeal to you, force yourself to concentrate. Don't let your mind wander. Think of the passage as something important that you must know about, almost as though your life depended on it.

4. *Concentrate on the opening and closing sentences of each paragraph.* That's where you are most likely to find the topic sentence, the sentence that contains the key to the overall purpose of the paragraph. Most of the time the topic sentence is located near the beginning. Sometimes, the final sentence states or suggests the main point of the passage. But remember, too, that some paragraphs do not have topic sentences, especially when the author's intent is clear without one.

5. *Use paragraph organization as a clue to comprehension.* Writers generally take pains to organize their material. They decide what goes first, second, third, and so forth. Usually the arrangement follows a logical order, usually from the most general statement to the most specific. The paragraph you are now reading follows that pattern. The first sentence is the most general. The sentences that follow become increasingly specific.

6. *Underline key ideas and phrases.* Since you have a pencil in your hand during the test, use it to highlight important points in the passage. When you come to an idea that sounds important, quickly draw a line under it or put a check mark next to it in the margin. Underlining should be selective. There's no point in underlining the whole paragraph.

   To illustrate how to underline key points in a passage, here is a sample passage about stuttering. The first sentence is the topic sentence. The remainder of the paragraph lists several theories of the cause of stuttering. Each theory is underlined.

While the symptoms of stuttering are easy to recognize, the <u>underlying cause remains a mystery</u>. Hippocrates thought that stuttering was due to <u>dryness of the tongue</u>, and he prescribed blistering substances to drain away the black bile responsible. A Roman physician recommended gargling and massages to strengthen a <u>weak tongue</u>. Seventeenth-century scientist Francis Bacon suggested hot wine to thaw a <u>"refrigerated" tongue</u>. <u>Too large a tongue</u> was the fault, according to a nineteenthth-century Prussian physician, so he snipped pieces of stutterers' tongues. Alexander Melville Bell, the father of the telephone inventor, insisted stuttering was simply <u>a bad habit</u> that could be cured by reeducation. Some theorists today attribute stuttering to problems in the control of the <u>muscles of speech</u>. Others think that stuttering arises from <u>deep-rooted personality problems</u> that may be lessened with drugs and therapy.

---

7. *Read all the questions at one time.* Some students find that reading all the questions before reading the passage gives them something to focus on as they read the passage. Sometimes they find answers to some questions right off the bat. Other students do better by reading all the questions right after finishing the passage. With the passage fresh in their minds, they might be able to answer a question or two immediately. In either case, reading the questions as a group instead of one by one may improve your score on the test. Try it.

8. *Forget what you already know about the topic in the passage.* The questions are derived from the passages. Answers are based on what the passage says, not on what you may know or think about the topic.

9. *Don't get bogged down on questions you find hard to answer.* This applies to all the questions on the test, but it's particularly easy to get stuck on reading questions. If you find yourself returning to the passage again and again in order to answer a question, you may be better off skipping it and making a note to try again later. Returning to the question with fresh eyes may help you answer it immediately.

TYPES OF READING QUESTIONS

The HSPT and the Coop contains four types of reading questions:

1. Main Idea
2. Words in Context
3. Fact
2. Inference

Each question type, along with some useful strategies for answering each type, is discussed below. The practice tests are highly recommended. By doing them, you'll become accustomed to dealing with the questions and increase your speed in answering them. Use the Answer Keys on, pages 240–243.

THE MAIN IDEA QUESTION

Now that you have been introduced to the types of questions on the exam, here are some ideas that will allow you to answer the questions correctly.

The exercises in this section are meant to help you become a better, more careful reader. With practice, you can become aware of pitfalls that often lead to reading errors. By doing the exercises you will see how the word choice contributes to the meaning of a reading passage. You will also learn how an understanding of the organization of a reading passage can help you to comprehend the contents of the passage.

This chapter will review the question types and show you some useful strategies for improving your reading comprehension and answering the questions.

You can recognize the main idea question because it is typically worded in one of the following ways:

1. The paragraph deals mainly with ...

2. The main idea of this selection may be best expressed as ...

3. The title that best expresses the ideas of this paragraph is ....

4. The writer's main purpose is apparently ...

5. The best name for this story is ...

6. The best title for this paragraph is ...

How successful are you in handling this type of question? Read the following paragraph and select, from the choices given, a suitable title for it. An analysis of the choices follows.

> **EXAMPLE:**
>
> One of the main traits desired in workers is dependability. The less supervision the employee needs, the more he or she is worth to the firm. Employees should be willing to do a full day's work even though they are not being watched. Supervisors will supply the necessary leadship and direction. Dependable employees will do their job well without complaining or trying to find unfair shortcuts.
>
> *The most suitable title for the paragraph is*
>
> (A) Supervisors on the Job
> (B) A Job Well Done
> (C) The Dependable Worker
> (D) Success on the Job

ANALYSIS: Let's analyze the choices to see how to arrive at the correct answer:

Choice A empasizes the supervisor, not the worker who is discussed in the paragraph.

Choice B refers to one task properly completed. The paragraph is devoted to general behavior in the workplace, not to a specific job.

Choices C and D are possibilities. However, there are many different ways to succeed on the job. Choice D is much more general than Choice C. Therefore, *The dependable worker* is the best title. Each sentence in the paragraph in some way or other explains the advantages of being dependable.

HOW TO HANDLE A MAIN IDEA QUESTION

➤ Choose Option A, B, or C on page 174.

➤ Locate the topic sentence, the sentence that summarizes the passage. It is usually at the beginning of the passage, but sometimes you'll find it at the end, or even in the middle. If you can't find it, it may be implied. In that case, ask yourself:

What is the main topic of the passage? What point is the author making about the topic?

➤ Watch out for choices that are more general than the material in the passage.

➤ Similarly, be alert for choices that are too narrow, choices that refer to specific examples or to material used only to support or develop the main idea of the passage.

SPEED AND ACCURACY

It is true that speed will be a factor in determining your score. However, the way to gain speed is through practice and not through rushing. The more of the exercises in this book you do, the faster you will complete them. Speed will come—after accuracy! Do not dawdle. Do not rush. Concentrate every minute of the time, and speed will come.

EXERCISE 1

Read each of the following paragraphs carefully. Then, from the choices given, circle the letter of the title that is most appropriate for each. Also, complete each sentence under "Analysis" by inserting the correct letter.

1. A new plastic bandage has been developed to help those suffering from burns. Antibiotic ointments are manufactured into the bandage. When the burns are covered with this material, the antibacterial action of the ointment develops slowly. The antibiotic action of the salve can be continued for two or more weeks. Used on extensive burns, this bandage eliminates frequent and painful changes of dressings. The dressing may also be used for skin infections such as poison ivy where one application would provide the full course of treatment.

   A suitable title for this paragraph is
   (A) Antibiotics
   (B) Treating Burns
   (C) Sure Cures
   (D) A New Germ-Killing Dressing

ANALYSIS:

The suggested title that is wrong because it refers to only one of the uses of the new bandage is _____.

The suggested title that is wrong because it refers to claims not made in the article is _____.

The title that is wrong because it refers to a large field of germ killers when only one of these is mentioned briefly is _____.

The title that is correct is _____ _____ because _____.

2. No one can claim to be a "pure American." Even the Indians whom Columbus found here have been traced to the tribes that invaded the lands now occupied by the Chinese. Our people have come from all nations and all races. They came here to establish a home that they could be proud of, a home for their children. Unfortunately the word *minority* creeps too often into the speech of some communities that claim to have a majority group. The majority group looks upon their minority neighbors with doubt or suspicion. We must ever remember that if we want our nation to be strong we cannot afford the luxury of having second-class citizens. A man or woman must be judged as an individual, as one of the many who make up our nation. There is no room in the heart of America for prejudice.

   A suitable title for this paragraph is
   (A) Pure Americans
   (B) Melting Pots
   (C) American Minorities
   (D) A Source of Prejudice

ANALYSIS:

The title that is wrong because the article proves such persons do not exist is _____.

The title that is wrong because no such expression is ever used is _____.

The title that is wrong because it is too general for the article is _____.

The title that is correct is _____ _____ because _____.

3. The development of the aluminum pram has given the American sportsman more mobility than he has ever had. This lightweight, sturdy boat usually weighs in the neighborhood of fifty pounds. It can easily be set securely on top of a car by one man. It can then be transported to any lake or stream within the reach of a road. Its draft is so shallow that it can be rowed through marshland and shallow inlets close to the waters inhabited by the largest of game fish. It is strong enough to be the basis for a blind built by the duckhunter who lies in wait for the unsuspecting wild mallards. With the coming of the new light weight outboard motors, it can even be propelled at slow speeds for the fisherman who prefers trolling. This boat is indeed the answer to the wishes of many sportsmen.

A suitable title for this paragraph is
(A) Drafting a Boat
(B) Traveling by Boat
(C) Hunting and Fishing
(D) An Ideal Boat for Sportsmen

ANALYSIS:

The title that is wrong because it includes many more types than mentioned in this selection is _____.

The title that is wrong because it is based on a misinterpretation of a word in the text is _____.

The title that is wrong because it stresses sports in general rather than an activity in sports is _____.

The title that is correct is _____ _____ because _____.

4. Total color-blindness is most uncommon among the people who are classified as color-blind. Actually, this disability covers three different types. Some color-blind people see all colors as we normally do—except for an inability to see green or red. These are the people who must memorize that the top light in a traffic signal is always the red one. Then there are others who are unable to distinguish yellows and blues. The person who is unable to see any colors at all sees the world in shades of light and dark grays. The world to him is much like a black and white movie.

A suitable title for this selection is
(A) Total Blindness
(B) Total Color-Blindness
(C) Distinguishing Colors
(D) Types of Color-Blindness

ANALYSIS:

The title that is wrong because it deals with a completely different type of eye difficulty is _____.

The title that is wrong because it deals with only one of the three classifications is _____.

The title that is wrong because it is much too general is _____.

The title that is correct is _____ _____ because _____.

5. In 1957 the United States Congress passed a highway construction program. At the time it seemed a wise and far-sighted measure. States did not have the funds to build enough good roads and traffic jams were an ever present headache. A national program of super-highway construction seemed a necessity and the only solution. What seemed wise in 1957 was called unwise and preposterous by many environmentalists in the early 1970s. Their argument was that the 1957 program was an unbalanced transport program. Superhighways

encourage the use of automobiles, and cars are one major source of pollution. Their use, especially by single operators, should not be encouraged. The environmentalists believe that the United States Congress in 1957 should have passed a comprehensive transportation program. Such a program, they maintain, should have included, in addition to highway construction, the development of mass transport facilities such as new interstate trains and commuter lines from suburbs to cities. They believe such a program would have reduced the use of the private car and that this would have substantially reduced air pollution. We will never know what might have happened if Congress had passed in 1957 the measure the environmentalists suggest.

A suitable title for this paragraph is
(A) Environmentalists
(B) Cars as Polluters
(C) Highway Act of 1957
(D) A Balanced Transportation Program

ANALYSIS:

A title that is wrong because it is too general is _____.

The title that is wrong because it deals with only one idea presented in the paragraph is _____.

The title that is wrong because it refers to only one type of transportation is _____.

The title that is correct is _____ because _____.

PRACTICE TEST 1

DIRECTIONS: Beneath each of the following paragraphs you will find five descriptive expressions. After reading each paragraph, select the expression that contains the main idea of the passage. Circle the corresponding letter.

1. Do you really believe that the ostrich buries its head in the sand so that it cannot see the trouble that it is in? Nobody knows just when this strange belief was started, but there are very few people who have not heard it. If the ostrich were silly enough to follow this procedure, it would suffocate, once its head was buried in the sand. The ostrich really has no need for such a defense. It can kick with the full power of a mule, and it can run faster than a horse. It would be foolish indeed for the bird to stand without protecting itself when in danger.
(A) Stranger than fiction
(B) False belief
(C) Heading into sand
(D) Ostrich power
(E) Mules and ostriches

2. When speaking to the governor of a state, a visitor addresses him as "Your Excellency." The proper address to use when before a judge is "Your Honor." However, the President of the United States is simply "Mr. President." One of the earliest debates in Congress was on the issue. A Senate Committee voted that the President be addressed as "His Highness, the President of the United States of America, and Protector of their Liberties." James Madison objected. He claimed that the Constitution limited the title to just "President of the United States." James Madison and his supporters won, and that is why when a letter is sent to our chief executive in Washington it is addressed to "The President, The White House."
(A) Titles of honor
(B) The President's title
(C) Paying respect
(D) Madison's revenge
(E) A quaint idea

3. As one of the safety measures taken in the house, a package of baking soda should be kept near the kitchen range. There is always the danger of grease catching fire during the cooking process. Water must not be used on the burning grease. The water will only scatter the fiery grease and spread the fire. Baking soda scattered on the flaming grease has a different effect, however. The soda absorbs the grease and releases carbon dioxide that smothers the fire. If the fire is confined to a

greasy pan, putting a tight lid on it will also smother the flames quickly.

(A) Fire fighting
(B) Baking soda to the rescue
(C) The cooking process
(D) Handling grease
(E) Handling grease fires on the stove

4. The variety of behaviors insects show toward their eggs after laying them is almost without number. Some insects just lay their eggs anywhere and forget all about them. Many others set their eggs near food material and then go off. Butterflies, for example, lay their eggs on a plant which the young, when hatched, will feed on. The ants and the bees, on the other hand, give their young the greatest protection. The young have nursemaids to feed them and soldiers to protect them while they are carefully tended in their individual cells in the beehive or antnest.

(A) Ants and bees
(B) Insect variety
(C) Protection of baby insects
(D) Egg laying
(E) Careful butterflies

5. When considered in the light of the needs of pupils both in their present lives and as adults, oral expression merits greater time and attention than written expression. But, for the sake of economy of instruction time, the initial process and the drill that leads to the eradication of errors can tend toward written exercises rather than oral drill. Written work guarantees more individual student participation when the average class size is large.

(A) Meeting pupil needs
(B) Oral and written class-work
(C) Economy of effort
(D) Eradication of errors
(E) Oral instruction

PRACTICE TEST 2

DIRECTIONS: Read each of the following paragraphs carefully. Then select from the choices given, the title that is most appropriate for each, and circle the corresponding letter.

1. Meat is an ideal food for humans—and for mold and bacteria as well. When it is fresh, it is one of the best culture mediums. It consists of 20 percent protein, fats, mineral matter, and organic compounds. The rest of it is water. This combination of moisture and solids makes it one of the most perishable of foods. The bacteria produces discoloration and bad odors. The mold fills the meat with black spots and other discolorations.

The most appropriate title is
(A) Spoilage of Meat
(B) Meat and Molds
(C) Ideal Food for Humans
(D) Fresh Meat

2. Georges Claude of France invented a process for extracting neon and other gases from the air at reasonable prices. In 1920 he began to make neon tubes for commercial purposes. Although the tubes are called neon, they may contain many different gases. Neon itself gives a brilliant red light while argon and mercury give a bright blue light. Krypton and mercury give a green light when in a yellow tube. Helium in a yellow tube gives a yellow light. The neon tubes can be made in enormous lengths.

The most appropriate title is
(A) Georges Claude
(B) Rare Gases at Work
(C) Neon Light
(D) Reasonable Tubes

3. There are many essentials of life that we are willing to take for granted. Our families and continuing good health are not questioned. Even food and shelter are rarely causes of troubling thoughts. However, if most teenagers were asked to list the one or two things most important to their happiness, high on the list would be friends or friendships. Life, so they seem to feel, would lose its sparkle and vitality if friends were not present. This intense need for being part of a group or being accepted by one's equals in age lessens with maturity.

The most appropriate title is
(A) Essential Life
(B) Troubling Thoughts
(C) Friendly Youths
(D) Need for Friends in Adolescence

4. Early in the sixteenth century the Spanish explorers reached a part of Mexico that they called Yucatan. There they found more than sixty cities that were no longer inhabited. The cities were all in ruin. They had been built by the Maya people. There were temples, palaces and great underground reservoirs. The Mayas had developed a civilization of which the people of Europe had known nothing. Mayan culture had grown and then decayed without ever having spread far afield. Will future explorers who travel into space have similar experiences? Will they too come upon cities in ruins on distant shores—of other planets?

The most appropriate title is
(A) Civilizations of the Future
(B) Spanish Explorers
(C) Unknown Civilizations
(D) Exploring the Future

5. The Renaissance was a movement away from medieval ideals. There were many ways in which this movement away from the medieval period manifested itself. It can be seen in the copying of antique Roman and Greek ideas in literature and philosophy, in the developing of new approaches in science, in the discovering of new trade routes and the New World, in the using of more luxuries and new inventions. Most important, however, it can be seen in the way humanity was regarded by the people of the Renaissance period. To them man was important as an individual. We see his individuality in the realism of art, in the new centralized government, in philosophy, in attitudes toward religion, and in the emphasis on personal talent.

The most appropriate title is
(A) Medieval Ideals
(B) Renaissance Philosophy
(C) Individualism in the Renaissance
(D) Rebirth of Greek and Roman Ideas

WORDS IN CONTEXT

Can you figure out the meaning of unfamiliar words when they are used in sentences? This is called obtaining the meaning of words it context. Read the following paragraph carefully, then complete the sentence below it.

EXAMPLE:

The trilobites, ancient relatives of the present-day lobster, ruled the seas millions of years ago. These sea-animals were usually just about three inches long. However, some of them grew to two feet long, weighing as much as fifteen pounds. They usually lived in shallow water near the shore. They walked over the floor of the sea on their jointed legs. Their multiple eyes and long feelers helped them to find their prey. The trilobites were in evidence in the seas for some three hundred million years. These sea-dwellers died out about two hundred million years ago. The fossils that we find in rocks tell their story.

The fossils are
(A) alive (B) remains (C) dangerous
  (D) photographs

ANALYSIS: Let's analyze this first one together. See if you agree with our reasons for selecting the answer we think is correct.

The key sentence is "The fossils that we find in rocks tell their story." Add to this the sentence "These sea-dwellers died out about two hundred million years ago."

(A) *alive* must be wrong because the trilobites died out years ago.

(B) *remains* is the only answer left and rocks could contain the remains of the skeletons of these animals.

(C) *dangerous* must be wrong since the trilobites are no longer living.

(D) *photographs* must be wrong because these fossils are found in rocks, which do not contain photographs.

HOW TO HANDLE A WORD-IN-CONTEXT QUESTION

➤ Read the entire paragraph before answering the question. The context in which the word appears may alter its usual meaning.

➤ Find the word. Sometimes the word is underlined or printed in boldface type.

➤ Look for clues to the meaning of the word by rereading the sentence in which the word appears. Look particularly for a synonym, a definition, or an example.

➤ If no clue is given, reread the sentences that come before and after that sentence, looking for synonyms, a definition, or an example.

SPEED AND ACCURACY

Once again, you cannot sacrifice accuracy for speed. It is useless to be able to boast that you were the first one to finish—and fail. Fight against carelessness. Train yourself to be accurate. Don't dawdle, and speed will come eventually.

EXERCISE 2

The following paragraphs will help you to increase your speed and accuracy. Read the directions. After you have answered the question, analyze your answer.

Read each of the following paragraphs carefully. Then complete each of the incomplete statements under "Analysis." Most of the statements can be completed by selecting the correct lettered choices.

1. Over fifty million years ago the ancestor of the modern horse, the eohippus, lived in the swampy woodlands of western North America and of Europe. The eohippus, no bigger than the modern fox, was well fitted for living in swamplands. Its feet with definite toes helped it walk across the soggy terrain. Its teeth were well adapted to eating the leaves on the bushes and on the lower branches of the trees. Its swiftness saved it from the enemy that lurked among the trees.

Soggy terrain is typical of
(A) life fifty million years ago
(B) the present day horse
(C) swamplands
(D) the eohippus

ANALYSIS:

When used to complete the sentence, three answers do not make sense. They are _____, _____, and _____.

The correct answer is _____ because the eohippus lived _____ and walked _____.

2. The employment of mercenaries was not unusual at the time of the American Revolution. Several small German states and Swiss cantons would let out all or part of their armed forces for hire. When George III of England was unable to recruit many Englishmen to fight the rebellious colonials, he made an agreement with Frederick II of Hesse-Kassel. The ruler of Hesse-Kassel received about 1,500,000 pounds for his 22,000 men. Of these an estimated 10,000 never returned to Germany. About 1,000 were killed in action. Almost 5,000 died from disease and accidents in the service. Approximately 4,000 settled in the United States when the hostilities were over. Since most of the mercenaries came from Hesse-Kassel, those that fought in America were called Hessians.

The hostilities were over when
(A) George III paid for the use of the soldiers
(B) the fighting ceased
(C) the mercenaries came to America
(D) the mercenaries were called Hessians

ANALYSIS:

The sentence that is the key to the answer is _____.

The three suggestions that are wrong because they are not connected with the key sentence are _____, _____, and _____.

The correct answer is _____ because the Hessians could never have _____ unless the end of hostilities meant that _____.

3. Naturalists may dispute about which trees are the largest in the world. One giant eucalyptus in Australia, measured after it had been felled, was more than 500 feet long. A giant sequoia of California, called the Father of the Forest, measured a mere 400 feet when it fell. However, scientists agree that the tallest plants are not among these trees. The seaweed of the ocean can tower over any of the trees so far measured. Seaweed over 600 feet tall has been found in the ocean at the Straits of Magellan, near the southern tip of South America. These plants are more than twice as tall as the Statue of Liberty!

People who dispute
(A) argue
(B) agree
(C) tell tales about trees
(D) measure carefully

ANALYSIS:

The sentence that is the key to the answer is _____.

The suggested answer that is an antonym of *dispute* is _____.

A suggested answer that is wrong because it is unrelated to the word *dispute* is _____.

The correct answer is _____ because the paragraph offers as a contrast to the fact that "Naturalists may dispute" the fact that _____.

4. We are never alone. We cannot claim that any of our actions involve only ourselves and no other people. At all times the frame of reference for our conduct must be the group most closely involved with the activity. Sometimes the team that we are part of is our family. At other times it is the group of friends that we have or even our school or community. When, in time of emergency, we fight as a member of the armed forces, we are part of a national unit. How right was the poet who said that no man is an island isolated from his fellow humans. Therefore, in all of our decisions, we must take into consideration the degree to which others are involved in our actions.

According to the author, a selfish person would be
(A) a frame of reference
(B) a national unit
(C) time of emergency
(D) an isolated island

ANALYSIS:

The suggested answer that is wrong because it confuses a person and war is _____.

The suggested answer that is wrong because it confuses a person with a philosophical term is _____.

The suggested answer that is wrong because it confuses a person with a group of many people is _____.

Since the author describes a person who is the opposite of _____, what this person is not would be correct; therefore, _____ is, correct.

5. Polyethylene was a war-time product first developed in England during World War II. It was first used to encase radar cables to protect them from being shattered by shells explod-

ing nearby. After the war, many additional uses for this synthetic were developed. At first it was used to insulate electric wires and cables. Then it was manufactured as bags for use in the deepfreeze. Because it is waterproof, millions of miles of tubes and pipes have been made from this product that has to be manufactured under thousands of pounds of pressure.

Polyethylene is a synthetic product because
(A) it is waterproof
(B) it is manufactured
(C) thousands of pounds of pressure are required
(D) it has so many uses

ANALYSIS:

The sentence that is the key to the answer is _____.

The suggested answer that is wrong because it gives only one of polyethylene's qualities is _____.

The suggested answer that is wrong because it involves an interesting but unimportant detail is _____.

The suggested answer that is wrong because it is not mentioned in the paragraph is _____.

The portion of the key sentence that explains *synthetic* is _____.

The correct answer is _____.

PRACTICE TEST 3

DIRECTIONS: Below each of the following paragraphs you will find an incomplete sentence and five descriptive expressions. After reading each paragraph, select the expression that best completes the sentence, and circle the corresponding letter.

1. In the 1600s the region between the lower Hudson and Connecticut rivers was inhabited by the Wappinger Confederacy, a small group of Algonquin tribes. The Manhattans, one of these nine tribes, had its main village in the vicinity of present day Yonkers. The Manhattans used Manhattan Island as a fishing and hunting preserve, and they built temporary huts there. The name Manhattan itself may have been derived from Algonquin words that mean "island of the hills."

Preserve as used in paragraph refers to
(A) conservation
(B) icing foods
(C) canning foods
(D) canned fruits
(E) none of the above

2. Marco Polo in his famous *Travels* makes no mention of the important invention of paper, a product first introduced by the Chinese. The Moors are credited with having brought paper into Europe by way of Samarkand, a remote land in central Asia. The Moors were taught by two Chinese paper makers captured during one of their raids. By the twelfth century Spain and then France knew the art of paper-making thanks to their Moorish invaders. However, at that time, most of the European printing continued to be done on parchment, since the paper was considered too fragile.

Early European printers avoided paper because
(A) it tore easily
(B) the Moors were invaders
(C) it had not as yet been invented
(D) it was too costly
(E) the Moors had made it

3. Early human beings had to concentrate all of their energies to secure food, shelter, and freedom from dangerous attackers. Human development from this state has been a slow and painful process. Today, man has advanced so far that he can control natural forces so immense that his power for good or evil is lightening. Today humans need have little fear of annihilation by the forces against which early man had to fight. Man no

longer fears greatly the violence of the elements or of creatures many times his own size or strength. The only cause of fear for the humans of today is man himself.

The annihilation of human beings would result in
(A) the disappearance of humans
(B) the victory of humans
(C) violence of the elements
(D) immense power for good or evil
(E) a painless process

4. One of the most astonishing tricks of the amateur magician involves a mixture of tincture of iodine and cornstarch dissolved in water. Before the very eyes of his onlookers, he writes boldy on a piece of paper a long message. Then a look of annoyance fills his countenance. He exclaims that he wished that he had not written the missive. He slowly looks for a cloth, in order to allow the ink to dry. When he is certain that it has dried, he finds his handkerchief and wipes the entire message clean off the paper. He does not, of course, tell his audience that the cornstarch has prevented the ink from penetrating the paper.

The missive is the
(A) magician
(B) ink
(C) paper
(D) letter
(E) book

5. The English language has achieved its richness and forcefulness as a result of its being a mixture of many tongues rather than the purified result of the endeavors of one people. The base of present-day English is a core of words used by the Angles, Jutes and Frisians, the basis of what is called Old English. To this were added direct borrowings from French and Latin. Once this amalgam had grown into a useful language, the English borrowed from all of the known word-patterns used throughout the world. Since English is made up of words from all languages, many scholars have urged that English be the universal language of the United Nations of the world.

An amalgam is a
(A) language
(B) mixture
(C) borrowing
(D) core
(E) people

PRACTICE TEST 4

DIRECTIONS: Read each of the following paragraphs carefully. Choose the most appropriate completion for the incomplete sentence that follows each, and circle the corresponding letter.

1. Near the edge of the water, snails crawled along the ground. Near the edges of the nearby swamplands were animals of a more important kind—amphibians. Most amphibians live a part of their lives in water and a part on land.

Amphibians are
(A) swamp snails
(B) types of land and water animals
(C) land and water dwellers
(D) types of snakes that crawl

2. Mediation is a means of maintaining peace between employers and employees. The agreement or settlement reached is made only by and between the members of each of these groups. The community or law enforcement agencies are not party to settlement other than as interested parties.

Mediation results when
(A) a strike is declared
(B) a strike is won
(C) both sides talk over their problems
(D) a strike is settled

3. The Russian intelligentsia had the advantage of wealth and education. They are often considered together as a group but there were many different attitudes held by the members. Some supported the Bolshevik revolutionar-

ies while others strongly supported conservative Tsarist policies. None were considered, however, merely members of the business or working class.

When a person is a member of the intelligentsia, he
(A) supports revolutionaries
(B) is a business man
(C) belongs to a wealthy and educated group
(D) likes conservatives

4. The Olympic Oath is repeated by all the contestants during the commencement exercises. "We swear that we will take part in the Olympic games in loyal competition, respecting the regulations which govern them and desirous of participating in them in the true spirit of sportsmanship for the honor of our country and for the glory of sport."

This oath is taken when
(A) the contests begin
(B) the contests are over
(C) the players prove their sportsmanship
(D) there is glory in the sport

5. Since 1871 smoking has been prohibited on the floor of the House of Representatives. Previously only a few legislators had smoked while listening to the debate among their fellow members. However it was generally felt that smoking during a legislative session was incompatible with the dignity of Congress.

Smoking has been prohibited among Representatives when the House is in session because the practice was thought to be
(A) undignified
(B) filled with dignity
(C) unsanitary
(D) unhealthful

THE FACT QUESTION

Students usually find the fact question the easiest to handle, since it is the most definite one in the group. The author makes a definite statement somewhere in the paragraph. The reader is asked to find the statement.

There are pitfalls, however. Students who try to gain speed by reading the questions first are too often trapped when the questioner skillfully repeats some phrases that can be found in the paragraph, but that do not lead to the correct answers.

To add difficulty to the level of the question, the examiner will often substitute synonyms for the words in the paragraph. The question then almost becomes a word-in-context question (see preceding section). The student must be alert and be ready to find such changes in the wording.

Because fact questions are often found in clusters, two or three of them to a paragraph, students are prone, through haste or carelessness, to skip some of them. A question not answered or omitted is the same as an incorrect answer. In your haste to make speed, do not overlook what you have to do!

HOW TO HANDLE A FACT QUESTION

➤ Read the entire paragraph before answering the question. By familiarizing yourself with the paragraph, you will know approximately where to seek your answer.

➤ Determine from the wording of the question that it is a fact question rather than another type.

➤ Search the paragraph to find the exact phrase or sentence or idea that contains the answer.

➤ After making your choice, review the other answers just in case you missed the point of the question.

EXERCISE 3

Read each of the following paragraphs carefully. Then complete the incomplete sentences below the paragraph.

There are many reasons that people can give for wanting to go to college. Some of those reasons are based on snobbishness. "Cousin John or Aunt Harriet went, and my parents would be embarrassed endlessly if I didn't go." "Everyone who is anybody goes to college, you know." Some people want to go to college out of fear, fear that when depressions come, they will lose out to college graduates. Some others go to college to choose a future mate or to avoid going to work. All these reasons are sincere and honest ones, but college is a miracle worker. Regardless of the reasons that moved people to attend college, the training given there teaches them to think better, to plan better, and to live better. A higher education is a must, then, for everyone who has the ability to gain from it.

1. The snob wants to go to college to
   (A) live better
   (B) earn more money
   (C) imitate his relatives
   (D) get married
   (E) plan better

   The sentence that answers this question is _____.

   Therefore, the correct answer is _____.

2. College teaches all who attend how to
   (A) be snobbish
   (B) be better human beings
   (C) choose a mate
   (D) earn money
   (E) think

   The sentence that answers this question is _____.

   Therefore, the correct answer is _____.

Each group in society develops a vocabulary, a group of words to describe the tools and operations involved in its trade or profession. These words are part of the daily lives of the group. Just listen to the waitress in the diner speak to the short-order cook or the shoe salesman talk to the manager. The words all sound familiar, but they just do not make sense to anyone who is not in the trade. This jargon, as it is called, is different from slang which is used by many groups in society. Jargon is usually limited to only one group of workers.

3. When two workers describe to each other an operation in their work, they use
   (A) slang
   (B) vocabulary
   (C) jargon
   (D) short-order
   (E) familiar sense

   The sentence that contains the answer is _____.

   The correct answer is _____.

4. Slang is different from jargon because
   (A) only workers use it
   (B) it is used by many groups
   (C) it is filled with trade terms
   (D) salesmen use it
   (E) it is unacceptable in polite society

   The sentence that contains the answer is _____.

   The correct answer is _____.

Amber began as resin that oozed from pine trees. Water, pressure, and time changed the gum into a clear, glasslike yellow substance. Human beings have long used amber to make varnish or ornamental jewelry. This lightest of all precious gems differs from the other jewels in that it has a plant origin rather than a mineral base. In ancient times amber was supposed to have worth as a medicine for treating diseases. The people of the Near East thought that amber prevented infections from spreading from person to person. That is the reason for its popularity as the material used in making cigarette holders.

5. Amber came originally from
   (A) water
   (B) trees
   (C) pressure
   (D) the Near East
   (E) precious gems

   The sentence that contains the answer is _____.

   The correct answer is _____.

6. Amber was used in the making of cigarette holders because
   (A) it kept the user from getting sick
   (B) it was light
   (C) it was pretty
   (D) it was worth much money
   (E) it was used in the making of varnish

The sentence that contains the answer is _____.

The correct answer, therefore, is _____.

The cold is the most common human ailment, yet it has stumped medical authorities. Many more dread diseases have come under control as the result of knowledge gained in research laboratories. Investigators have assumed that the cold is usually caused by a virus. However, no method of studying this virus has been devised. The chimpanzee is the only amimal to which the disease can be given experimentally. The use of this animal is limited by its cost and by the fact that so many of the animals die of pneumonia during the experiments. This leaves for all practical purposes only human volunteers to be used in research projects. Many inmates of prisons have aided in this work, but because of these limitations research into the cause and cure of colds has progressed very slowly.

7. Research into the cause and cure of colds has
   (A) gone ahead very slowly
   (B) gone ahead very rapidly
   (C) been filled with dread
   (D) been very common
   (E) been impossible

The sentence that contains the answer is _____.

The correct answer, therefore, is _____.

When out-of-state Americans think of Kentucky, they always imagine fleet, young thoroughbreds frisking in the blue grass fields under the watchful eyes of men well-trained in the art of winning on the racetracks of the world. They also imagine that they can see tobacco toasting in the sun. The farms are large, and the work is carried on under most pleasant circumstances. The workers go from task to task humming or singing aloud gentle sentimental tunes. Every once in a while, the entire staff will come together and harmonize—while the work waits. Kentucky has come to mean a happy way of country life filled with horses, sunshine, and tobacco leaf. These beliefs did not come about accidentally. The romantic writers of stories and of popular music deserve full credit for what Kentucky is supposed to be. Stephen Foster was only one of the many who idealized this eastern state.

8. The picture of life in Kentucky is
   (A) true
   (B) false
   (C) filled with hard work
   (D) the work of writers
   (E) a lazy one

The sentence that contains the answer is _____.

The correct answer, therefore, is _____.

9. This picture of life in Kentucky is in the minds of
   (A) all workers
   (B) many Americans
   (C) young thoroughbreds
   (D) Kentuckians
   (E) singers

The sentence that contains the answer is _____.

The correct answer is _____.

PRACTICE TEST 5

DIRECTIONS: After each of the following paragraphs, you will find three incomplete statements about the paragraph. Each statement is followed by five words or phrases lettered (A) to (E). After reading the paragraph, read the statements. Then select the word or phrase that most satisfactorily completes each statement, and circle the corresponding letter.

In 1910 Congress appropriated enough money to have the *Maine* raised. The sinking of the *Maine* in the harbor of Havana was one of the immediate causes of the Spanish-American War. No one ever determined what had caused the fatal explosion. The American newspapers blamed the Spanish commander in Cuba. The Spanish claimed that they had not put any mines into the harbor and denied any responsibility for the explosion. When the *Maine* was raised and examined by naval experts, they were unable to determine the cause of the explosion that had cost the lives of 229 Navy men. Since the wreck was a danger to ships sailing in and out of the harbor of Havana, what was left of the *Maine* was towed into the Gulf of Mexico, where it was sunk in 600 fathoms of water, while its flag fluttered in the breeze and American Navy vessels fired farewell salutes.

1. The *Maine* was a
   (A) state
   (B) Spanish Commando
   (C) Spanish boat
   (D) American Navy vessel
   (E) harbor

2. The ship was raised
   (A) to save the men
   (B) to make money
   (C) to punish the Spanish
   (D) to please the Spanish
   (E) to help determine causes

3. The Americans sank the ship
   (A) in deep water
   (B) in the Havana harbor
   (C) in Mexico
   (D) in Maine
   (E) after an explosion

The status quo antebellum was the basis of the peace settlement developed at the Congress of Vienna. The victorious nations had fought France and the new ideas of the French Revolution for twenty-five years. They were glad to be rid of their enemy leader of the last sixteen years, Napoleon, and they wanted peace based on the conditions of the old days. They really believed they could wipe out the new ideas and restore Europe to the conditions of 1789. Metternich, the Austrian leader and most important person at the Congress, presented plans for the peace settlement. The plans have been summed up in the terms legitimacy, restoration of former rulers to their legitimate throne, and compensation, donation of added territory to those nations bordering on France which suffered heavily during the war.

4. The restoration of former rulers to their thrones was referred to at the Congress of Vienna as
   (A) legitimacy
   (B) Metternich
   (C) compensation
   (D) status quo antebellum
   (E) the old days

5. The leader of the Congress of Vienna was
   (A) Napoleon
   (B) the victorious nations
   (C) France
   (D) Metternich
   (E) Austria

6. The nations that met at the Congress of Vienna had been
   (A) writing a peace treaty
   (B) supporting the French Revolution
   (C) fighting France for twenty-five years
   (D) fighting Napoleon
   (E) restoring Europe to the conditions of 1789

In his *Autobiography,* John Stuart Mill revealed the unusual method of education that his father had planned for him. By the time he was three, he was being taught Greek, arithmetic, and English grammar. He began the study of Latin when he was eight. Before he was twelve, he had read much Greek and Roman literature in the original. He was well-acquainted with the philosophers and writers of history. His recreation consisted chiefly of taking walks with his father and in reading works of history, fiction, and poetry, all selected for him. Since his health remained good during most of his life, this manner of living probably agreed with him. Could the child of today accept such a rigid training? Or are the temptations that radio, television, and theater place in our paths too great?

7. Mill learned his first foreign language when he
   (A) wrote his *Autobiography*
   (B) was three
   (C) was taking walks with his father
   (D) was eight
   (E) was twelve

8. For relaxation, he would
   (A) do more reading
   (B) take long walks by himself
   (C) play ball
   (D) listen to the radio
   (E) watch old movies

9. When Mill was growing up there were no
   (A) schools
   (B) teachers
   (C) writers
   (D) manners
   (E) radio sets

Modern philosophers differ greatly from those of earlier ages. The modern philosophers are usually scientific in their attitudes. The ancient ones were concerned with the pursuit of beauty while the thinkers of the Middle Ages were primarily interested in theology. Truth, beauty, and goodness were the centers of thought for the ancients. The man of the Middle Ages placed the doctrines of religion above concern about pure philosophy. Philosophy existed to clarify religious doctrines. Today, philosophy has freed itself from the search for truth in terms of beauty or goodness or theology. The main path of the modern philosopher pursues the need for interpreting the rapidly advancing sciences.

10. According to the author of this paragraph, modern philosophers study
    (A) beauty
    (B) religion
    (C) science
    (D) theology
    (E) goodness

11. The philosophers of Greece two thousand years ago were concerned with the study of
    (A) religion
    (B) the Middle Ages
    (C) science
    (D) beauty
    (E) doctrines

12. Philosophy existed in the Middle Ages to
    (A) strengthen religious beliefs
    (B) explore science
    (C) study the meaning of pure philosophy
    (D) reveal goodness wherever it may be
    (E) explain the terms of beauty

PRACTICE TEST 6

DIRECTIONS: Read each of the following paragraphs carefully. Then choose the letter of the word or phrase that best completes each of the incomplete sentences, and circle it.

The early English swimmers soon developed two strokes. The preferred stroke was the breast stroke which was alternated with the side stroke. These two for long remained the English style. They were used in all of the races among the competitors from the six swimming pools that developed in London in the early nineteenth century. This English style of swimming was far different from that of Native Americans, who thrashed the water violently with their arms and beat rapidly downward with their feet.

1. Most English swimmers used
   (A) the Native American stroke
   (B) freestyle
   (C) the breaststroke
   (D) the sidestroke
   (E) thrashing the water

2. The style of swimming of the Native American
   (A) resembled that of the English
   (B) resembled that of London in the early nineteenth century
   (C) was smooth and silent
   (D) was noisy and splashing
   (E) was unnecessary

The wagon cook had to carry two months' provisions for a crew of men through the heat of the western summer, without refrigeration. Therefore fresh vegetables and eggs were never present in the chuck wagon. The basic foods that the cook stored were dried varieties. The cowboys had to learn to survive on such starchy foods as beans, bread, corn, potatoes, rice. The cowboy rarely grew stout on such fare, however. The long hours of hard work in the saddle burned up all the energy the food gave him. Yet, something can be said in favor of the simplicity of the cowman's menu. The man in the saddle was not afflicted with stomach ailments and ulcers.

3. One of the main difficulties facing the wagon cook was
    (A) storage
    (B) quality of the food
    (C) dried varieties
    (D) menus
    (E) ulcers

4. The diet of the cowboy was
    (A) dried
    (B) unvaried
    (C) lacking in starch
    (D) refrigerated
    (E) fresh eggs and vegetables

Red tape is a term used today to refer to unusual amounts of complications filled with paper work, and procedures that seem to hinder rather than help when work must be done. The expression had its origin in England where official papers and packages of documents were tied in red tape. This cord was constantly being tied and untied. Thomas Carlyle and Charles Dickens used the phrase red tape so often in their writings that it is part of the common vocabulary of everyday people.

5. *Red tape* was really used in
    (A) Russia
    (B) America
    (C) England
    (D) Thomas Carlyle
    (E) complications

6. *Red tape* refers to
    (A) writers
    (B) Communists
    (C) Americans
    (D) helpful procedures
    (E) hindering complications

Bats are found throughout the world from the Arctic Circle almost into Antarctica. They are mammals with relatively large brains. They branched off the main stem of the mammalian family tree millions of years ago. They are the second largest order of mammals. Millions have been found sleeping in one cave. Almost all bats rest and sleep in the same position. They hang upside down, suspended by either one or both hind feet. Despite the reputation of the vampire bats that live exclusively on the blood of other animals, most bats feed on insects which they catch and eat while they are flying.

7. Bats are found
    (A) only in Africa
    (B) almost everywhere
    (C) in the Arctic Circle
    (D) in cold climates
    (E) in northern regions only

8. Most bats
    (A) are vampires
    (B) live on insects
    (C) live on flies
    (D) eat little
    (E) are large

For hundreds of years the madder plant was our sole source of yellow dye. The dye was extracted from the roots of the plant and sold all over the world. The great plantations in southern France were devoted to the cultivation of the madder plant until 1869. In that year German scientists discovered that the dye could be produced artificially. A chemical that was extracted from coal tar was their answer. Alizarine, as it is called, was cheaper to produce, easier to use and more permanent in coloring. The dyers of cloth turned to this new product, and the madder growers of France had to seek new crops to cultivate.

9. Our only source in former times for yellow dye was
   (A) chemicals
   (B) German plantations
   (C) dyers of cloth
   (D) coal tar
   (E) plant

10. The chemists discovered
    (A) a better dye
    (B) coal tar
    (C) the madder plant
    (D) French plantations
    (E) yellow dye

THE INFERENCE QUESTION

Inferring involves passing from one proposition, statement, or judgment to another whose truth follows from that of the former. In the inference question, you are asked to draw a conclusion based on what you have read in a passage.

The basic purpose of this type of question is to rate your ability to:
- detect a hidden meaning in a paragraph
- use the information conveyed in a reading selection
- extend the author's statements to other cases

HOW TO HANDLE AN INFERENCE QUESTION

➤ Read the entire paragraph before answering the question. Keep asking yourself, "What is the author's intent?" This is important to understand because inference questions ask you to "read between the lines."

➤ Once you've read the question, reread the section of the paragraph likely to contain the clues on which to base your judgment.

➤ Locate the words from which to draw your inference.

➤ Ask yourself whether your understanding of the author's intent is consistent with the answer you chose; that is, would the author be likely to agree with you?

➤ Avoid falling for an answer that simply restates material in the passage. Although the idea comes from the passage, it may not be the answer to the specific inference question.

➤ Eliminate the wrong answers. Have a logical reason for eliminating each one.

➤ Check the answer that is left. Test it against the facts in the paragraph.

SPEED AND ACCURACY

Do not fall into the trap of rushing through a judgment question. It is useless to be able to boast that you were the first to finish—and fail! Fight against the desire to pounce on the first likely answer. Concentrate on accuracy. Speed will come with practice.

EXERCISE 4

The following paragraphs will help you increase your speed and accuracy. Read the directions. After you have answered the question, analyze your answer.

Read each of the following paragraphs carefully. Circle the letter of the correct choice. Then complete each of the incomplete statements below.

Mars and Venus are the two planets that are the next door neighbors of Earth. Venus circles the Sun at an average distance of about 67 million miles. The average distance between the Earth and the Sun is 93 million miles. Mars, on the other hand, circles around the Sun in an ellipse that averages 141 million miles away from the Sun. At times the planets are on opposite sides of the Sun. Earth and Venus at such a time are 167 million miles apart. When they are closest, they are about 30 million miles away from each other. The nearest that Mars comes to Earth as they swing in their orbits that center around the Sun is about 35 million miles.

1. The closest neighbor to Earth among the planets is
   (A) the Moon
   (B) the Sun
   (C) Mars
   (D) Jupiter
   (E) Venus

ANALYSIS:

The two choices that are wrong because they are not planets are _____ and _____.

The choice that is wrong because it is a planet not mentioned in the article is _____.

The closest neighbor is _____ because it is _____ million miles closer than _____.

2. Closest to the Sun is
   (A) the Moon
   (B) the stars
   (C) Mars
   (D) Earth
   (E) Venus

ANALYSIS:

Since they are not mentioned in the article, I can eliminate _____ and _____.

The average distance away from the Sun for the Earth is _____ million miles, for the planet Mars is _____ million miles, and for Venus is _____ million miles. Therefore, the closest to the Sun is _____.

One of the tests that are basic to chemical analysis involves litmus paper. The name means *colored moss,* since it is obtained from certain primitive plants called lichens. If litmus paper comes into contact with an acid liquid, it turns reddish. The degree of reddishness depends on the concentration of the acid in the liquid. If litmus paper is dipped into an alkaline liquid, it turns various shades of blue. Many students remember the phrase "in a base, blue litmus" to associate the colors with the correct reactions.

3. Lichens are a type of
   (A) paper
   (B) litmus
   (C) moss
   (D) acid

ANALYSIS:

Since lichens are _____ which belong to the _____ family, the answer is _____.

4. If the litmus paper turns blue, it has been previously
   (A) wet
   (B) red
   (C) white
   (D) alkaline

ANALYSIS:

Since litmus paper is either _____ or _____ in color, _____ must be wrong.

Since both acid and base must be _____ for the litmus paper to react, _____ is wrong.

Since the color for acid is _____ and the color for base is _____ and another name for base is _____, therefore _____ is wrong.

Since the litmus paper turns from _____ to _____ in color, the answer must be _____.

An eternal weariness seemed to settle over his entire being. The strong, quick movements were replaced by the slow-motion of a tired old, old man. The glow was gone from his skin, and a pasty, sickly, whiteness colored its moistness. It was incredible that just a few minutes ago he had been so confident of the outcome of his encounter with his adversary. He had been positive that his youth and energy would be more than the age and experience of the other could overcome. How wrong he had been! Yet, all that he had done was to make one error, a slight one, but one that his crafty opponent had taken full advantage of. His guard had slipped for a brief second, the power-packed right had snaked through, and the end had come.

5. The main character in this incident had just
   (A) been knocked out
   (B) been injured badly in an accident
   (C) hurt another
   (D) found old age

ANALYSIS:

If he is facing a "crafty opponent," then _____ must be wrong.

Since he had "youth and energy" in facing an opponent, _____ must be wrong.

Since he is the one who is a sickly white, _____ must be wrong.

The description in the _____ sentences shows that he is a boxer who is about to lose _____; therefore _____ is right.

6. The cause of his condition was
   (A) his slow movements
   (B) lack of experience
   (C) inability to drive
   (D) trickery

ANALYSIS:

Since he had allowed_____, the correct answer must be _____.

Missouri was first explored by the French under Joliet and Marquette in 1673. It was part of the Louisiana Purchase Territory of 1803 and was included in the section then known as Upper Louisiana. Louisiana separated itself from the rest of the territory on April 8, 1812, when it became one of the states of the Union. For nearly two months, the territory, excluding Louisiana, continued to be called the Louisiana Territory. On June 4, 1812, its name was changed to Missouri. Part of this Missouri territory became the state of Missouri on August 10, 1821.

7. By 1732, Louisiana was known as
   (A) Upper Louisiana
   (B) French territory
   (C) Missouri
   (D) a state of the Union

ANALYSIS:

Since Louisiana became a state in _____, _____ is wrong.

The article does not give enough information to allow verification or denial of _____ and _____.

Since the Louisiana Purchase took place in _____ and it was purchased from the _____, the correct answer must be _____.

8. The territory of Missouri
   (A) became the state of Louisiana
   (B) became the state of Missouri
   (C) was too large to become one state
   (D) was too small to become a state

ANALYSIS:

The sentence that is the key to this answer is _____.

Since only _____ of the Missouri Territory became the _____, the correct answer must be _____.

The tourist suddenly brought his car to a stop, and just in time, too. He had heard the beginning hiss of the escaping air, and his foot had pressed hard on the brake. When the car stopped, he walked out of the car and stared at the tire that was going flat. Suddenly he realized that he had stopped close to a Utah rattlesnake den. A thirteen-footer was fast approaching the tire. The man retreated as he saw the rattler strike the flattened end. The poison in the venom of the snake was so strong that the solid rubber swelled back to normal size and the tourist was able to drive more than 200 miles to Salt Lake City and a repair station.

9. Stories of this type prove
   (A) the toughness of rubber
   (B) the deadliness of rattlesnakes
   (C) the imaginative powers of Americans
   (D) the stupidity of some people

ANALYSIS:

The reader must realize that this is a _____ story.

If the reader sees the _____ in the story, then _____ must be the correct answer.

PRACTICE TEST 7

DIRECTIONS: Below each of the following paragraphs, you will find two incomplete statements. Each statement is followed by five words or phrases lettered (A) to (E). After reading each paragraph, read the statements beneath it. Then select the word or phrase that most satisfactorily completes each statement, and circle the corresponding letter.

Corn in its original state had grown wild. Primitive human beings must have found a simple way to cultivate it while it was a wild grass. Although it still resembles two of the wild grasses found today, the origin of our corn plant is lost somewhere in the long-distant past. If the corn stalks are not harvested, the cobs will, in time, fall to the ground, and the kernels on the cob will start to grow. The closely packed young plants will soon smother and choke each other. For this reason corn is thought to have been cultivated longer than other farm products.

1. Corn must be hand-planted because
   (A) it will not grow wild
   (B) the seeds must be separated
   (C) the seeds must be put into the ground
   (D) the kernels are delicate
   (E) the kernels are young

2. Primitive corn did not have
   (A) a cob
   (B) kernels
   (C) so many kernels
   (D) a stalk
   (E) few kernels

Francois René de Chateaubriand was born in 1768, and died in 1848. He devoted his life to the writing of novels. He marked the change from the old classical to the modern romantic French literature. He helped to continue the naturalism of Rousseau in two of his significant novels, *Atala* and *Rene*. Like so many others in the history of literature, he is little read today. He is important historically because he influenced so many later French writers, but his stories have lost their appeal to the reading public. They are to be found only on the shelves of the universities and not in the bookstores.

3. Chateaubriand
   (A) lived before Rousseau
   (B) was influenced by Rousseau
   (C) influenced Rousseau
   (D) disliked Rousseau
   (E) was disregarded by Rousseau

4. Chateaubriand's stories are
   (A) old-fashioned
   (B) not true to life
   (C) illogical
   (D) without merit
   (E) unreadable

Shall is derived from the Anglo-Saxon word *sceal,* which means *I am compelled* or *obliged. Will,* on the other hand, comes from *willan,* another Anglo-Saxon word, which means *I intend* or *plan.* Over the years, tradition has established certain rules for the use of *shall* and *will. Will* used with *I* or *we* shows internal resolve, as does *shall* used with the second or third person. When the two words are reversed, however, they express simple futurity. In other words, simple futurity is intended when *shall* is used with *I* or *we* or when *will* is used with other persons. However, in present-day usage, these fine distinctions between *shall* and *will,* which are still found in some grammar books, are no longer observed. Thus, this is an area in which the careful student of language must learn to find new means of expressing fine shades of difference.

5. Many writers of today
   (A) follow the rules for *shall* and *will* as found in grammar books
   (B) do not follow any of the rules in grammar books
   (C) do not follow the rules for *shall* and *will*
   (D) make up their own rules for *shall* and *will*
   (E) are slow to change

6. *Will*
   (A) had only one meaning
   (B) has so many meanings that it has lost all meaning
   (C) can be used as a helping verb
   (D) cannot be used as a helping verb
   (E) can be used only with *shall*

The man who boasted that he grew pumpkins so large that his wife hollowed one out and used half as a cradle, met his master. When he told his story, the other man told of two full-grown policemen in his city being found asleep on one beat. The latter added that in one of the backyards, the cornstalks were cut after harvest and sold as telephone poles.

7. From this you can conclude that
   (A) both men are married
   (B) only one is married
   (C) neither one is married
   (D) both men may be married
   (E) none of these

8. The master was a
   (A) policeman
   (B) farmer
   (C) citizen-farmer
   (D) townsman
   (E) truthseeker

An allegory is a story in which the characters are symbols of ideas. The actions and the settings may also be symbolical. A fable, on the other hand, is a short tale meant to convey a useful lesson. The characters are usually birds or animals that speak and act like human beings. The most famous fables are those of the Greek slave, Aesop. A para-

ble, finally, is a short narrative designed to convey a useful lesson, a moral or spiritual truth. The characters and the actions are like those in our everyday surroundings. An example of a famous parable is that of the prodigal son in the *New Testament*.

9. The story of the Three Little Pigs, in this classification, would be
   (A) tale
   (B) allegory
   (C) fable
   (D) parable
   (E) narrative

10. A parable could be
    (A) an allegory but not a fable
    (B) a fable but not an allegory
    (C) a fable but not a story
    (D) an allegory and a fable
    (E) neither an allegory nor a fable

PRACTICE TEST 8

DIRECTIONS: Read each of the following paragraphs carefully. Then choose the phrase that best completes each of the statements below, and circle the corresponding letter.

The connection between the amount of cholesterol in the body and heart disease has not as yet been definitely proved. Much research is being conducted to determine whether this fat-hormone-like substance that floats around in the blood stream actually is a factor causing some forms of heart trouble and arterial disease. All that can be said now about this substance is that cholesterol can be made from food products already stored in the body.

1. Cholesterol is being investigated because
   (A) it causes heart disease
   (B) it is found in the blood stream
   (C) it is a fat-hormome-like substance
   (D) it can be stored in the body.

2. As a result of reading this paragraph doctors should tell their patients
(A) to avoid foods containing cholesterol
(B) to forget all about cholesterol
(C) to eat less fatty food
(D) nothing about cholesterol

The tourist was obviously one who was greatly amused by the countrified atmosphere of the lake district. He turned to one of the natives who was passing by. "I am most anxious," he said slowly, "to find accommodations for the night. Could you tell me which way the village lies?"

The man whom he had stopped looked at him unsmilingly. "It's likely to lie in almost any direction," he replied. "However, since this is the summer, it's usually about the size of the fish that we catch."

3. The villager replied to the visitor in this fashion
(A) to be polite
(B) to show off
(C) to teach him a lesson
(D) to sell him vegetables

4. As a result of the villager's reply, the tourist
(A) had to ask more questions
(B) became angry and left
(C) went to the tourist home
(D) was willing to buy the vegetables

The unbroken silence filled the vast plant that had been filled with the thunderous noises of modern machinery only a few hours ago. Time was when the giant wheels never ceased their grinding and shaping of cold metal under thousands of tons of pressure. The footsteps of trained mechanics had been muffled for years by the pounding conveyor-belt pulleys. But the mastermind of humanity had never left the plant during those busy productive years. However, now that the economy of the entire nation had slowed down, daily periods of silence filled the vast auditorium with uneasy emptiness. Occasional gusts of fresh night air eddied down the long corridors.

5. The time of this paragraph is
(A) late morning
(B) summertime
(C) late evening
(D) wintertime

6. The cause of the silence is
(A) strikes
(B) war
(C) death
(D) economic depression

Fear filled the eyes of the silent farmhand as he took a second glance skyward. He had not been mistaken. There it was growing larger and larger in all of its black ugliness. Like a giant funnel made of billowing cloth that could not hold its shape, it loomed larger and larger. The man no longer could control his panic as he rushed toward the house. If he could only have enough time to warn the others of the awful danger bearing down on them. His plan of action was clear. He would first awaken the others, and then he would rush to the barn and lead the animals to the comparative safety of the storm cellar. His breath was coming in sobs now as he bent down and grabbed a large stone that he hurled at the upper story window. He shouted, "Hurry! Get up!" as he stumbled against the door and pushed it open. "Hurry, if you want to live, hurry! A twister!"

7. The other people were most likely in
(A) the kitchen
(B) the barn
(C) the bedroom
(D) the cellar

8. The man was
(A) a coward because he cried
(B) a coward because he ran
(C) brave because he ran to the cellar
(D) brave because he tried to save others

As he left the room, he knew that he had been wrong. If he could only control his temper! He had let his anger flare up too quickly. His father did not let the remark go by. His mother as usual had sent the warning glance too late. She had kept her customary silence while the loud tones flew across the table. Then came the usual command. As he walked to his room, that familiar sense of unhappiness took the place of his spent anger. All this was so unnecessary. If only he could learn control! If only he could go beck into the room and tell them that it was all a mistake. He had let his tongue run away from him. He really did love his parents. They really were trying to do their best to help him grow up with self-respect.

9. The boy is most likely
   (A) four years old
   (B) eight years old
   (C) fourteen years old
   (D) twenty years old

10. The boy went to his room
    (A) to avoid continuing the fight
    (B) to get over his feeling of misery
    (C) because he had been told to
    (D) to receive his punishment

Improving Your Reading Skills

Here is a sound self-help plan for reading improvement.

1. Have a daily, varied reading program:
   browse through the encyclopedias,
   read sections of the daily newspaper
     (news stories, editorials, special
       columns),
   become interested in the lives of
     memorable people and read their
     biographies,
   read books dealing with hobbies,
   read and reread supplementary text-
     books.

2. Be word-conscious. Add daily to your store of worthwhile words.

3. Concentrate when you read. *Nothing* should be able to distract you!

4. Read as fast as you can comfortably— and no faster. Speed comes from practice; don't let your anxieties rush you into skimming or scanning.

Below are key work-study skills designed to bring you up to the level of competency required to do well on the reading comprehension sections of standard examinations. Following each work-study skill is an exercise that will help you master it. After you have completed this section of this chapter, you will be ready to tackle the reading comprehension section that follows. Go through the latter section step by step. Use the diagnostic test in the beginning of the book to pinpoint your particular weakness in reading comprehension, and focus on that weakness. Do not, however, skip any part of the reading comprehension section if you wish to achieve the best results on a standard examination. Use the answer key at the end of the chapter to check your performance on exercises, practice tests, and Mastery Exams.

COMPOUND WORDS

Compound words are words made by combining two or more words:

   haircut   watchman   nevertheless

While most compound words have a meaning derived from their parts, this is not true of all of them. Nevertheless, the skilled reader very often gains the meaning of an unfamiliar term by recognizing one or more of its elements.

LITERAL AND FIGURATIVE MEANINGS

Literal means true to the word-by-word meaning. The coach or the doctor may tell you to "go soak your head," meaning that you are to douse yourself with water.

Figurative denotes an implied meaning. When a friend angrily refuses your request and tells you to "go soak your head," he is telling you what he thinks of your request.

If the writer intends a figurative interpretation, readers will be out in left field if they take the statement literally. Let the next two sets of exercises help you to evaluate your ability in this area.

EXERCISE 5

If the italicized phrase in each of the following sentences is to be taken literally, then write literal *in the space provided; if it is meant to be understood figuratively, then write* figurative.

1. Within a few minutes, the skillful lecturer had his youthful audience *eating out of his hand.* _____

2. When I say *"Hands off!"* I mean just that! _____

3. I have to *hand it to you;* you certainly knew just what had to be said. _____

4. *All hands* on deck! _____

5. Give the new singer *a big hand!* _____

6. Keep your *big hands* out of the cookie jar! _____

7. The store on the corner *changed hands* four times in the past two years. _____

8. The fretful baby is *more than a handful* even for an experienced baby-sitter. _____

9. Please *hand me* a copy of the textbook. _____

10. Keep *the change!* _____

11. We arrived just when the train was *pulling out* of the station. _____

12. The pressure was so great on the fishing line that I felt that my arm was *being pulled out of its socket.* _____

13. You'll have to get up much earlier if you want to *pull the wool over her eyes!* _____

14. The storekeeper said that he *has enough pull* to have the police overlook the violation. _____

15. The car skidded and *turned turtle* before it smashed into the retaining wall. _____

16. *Turn into* Gelton Street and stop near the corner. _____

17. She has had a *splitting headache* all day. _____

18. How much did they pay you for *splitting the logs?* _____

19. If she ever *gets wind* of this, we will truly be in a *mess!* _____

20. How long does it take to *wind up* the clock? _____

21. I need two more hours *to wind up* my business with them. _____

22. I am not ready to *play second fiddle* to anyone! _____

23. Stop *playing with* your food! _____

24. To treat your friends that way is not my idea of *playing fair.* _____

25. He *has more heart* than any other player I know. _____

EXERCISE 6

Literal statements are usually easier to understand than ones requiring a figurative interpretation. The exercise that follows will help you sharpen your control of sentences that gain in meaning when taken figuratively.

Circle the letter of the word or phrase that most appropriately completes each of the following sentences.

1. Well done is better than well _____.
   (A) made (B) said (C) furnished
   (D) finished

2. They do not always _____ who put their boots on.
   (A) pay (B) sigh (C) shine (D) ride

3. They who feel the benefit should feel the _____.
   (A) time (B) cloth (C) burden (D) anger

4. The bell calls others but never minds the _____.
   (A) sermon (B) cost (C) danger
   (D) weather

5. The fuel removed, the fire will _____.
   (A) rise (B) begin (C) spread (D) die

6. The goodness of a thing is known when it is _____.
   (A) stored (B) lacking (C) described
   (D) totaled

7. Learning has no enemy but _____.
   (A) ignorance (B) time (C) waste
   (D) use

8. Promises and pie crusts are made to be _____.
   (A) seen (B) eaten (C) broken
   (D) well-baked

9. Drive the nail that will _____.
   (A) bend (B) loosen (C) rust (D) go

10. Suspicions are _____ the guilty.
    (A) natural to (B) unusual to
    (C) evidence to (D) wrong for

11. They that stay in the _____ will never get over the hill.
    (A) struggle (B) saddle (C) wagon
    (D) valley

12. It is impossible to _____ what never was good.
    (A) improve (B) spoil (C) destroy
    (D) discover

13. In crossing the ocean, we change the climate, not the _____.
    (A) cost (B) danger (C) person (D) joy

14. A grain of _____ is worth a pound of medicine.
    (A) sand (B) caution (C) food (D) gold

15. Do not _____ two rabbits with one dog.
    (A) hunt (B) house (C) compare
    (D) train

16. The coat does not make the _____.
    (A) cost (B) paint (C) brush (D) person

17. They must _____ who cannot sit upright.
    (A) argue (B) weep (C) stoop
    (D) explain

18. Wine has _____ more people than the sea ever did.
    (A) fancied (B) drowned (C) saved
    (D) enriched

19. The spider extracts _____ where the bee gathers honey.
    (A) poison (B) air (C) fear
    (D) goodness

20. Doing things by halves is _____; it may be the other half that counts.
    (A) sensible (B) valuable (C) poetic
    (D) worthless

21. If you have nothing to _____, you can try anything.
    (A) offer (B) say (C) lose (D) reveal

22. Don't _____ ideas; put them to work.
    (A) execute (B) entertain (C) interpret
    (D) request

23. The great _____ of life is not knowledge but action.
    (A) end (B) cause (C) person (D) loss

24. Real _____ is when you don't try to make the best of a bad bargain.
    (A) success (B) failure (C) worry (D) joy

25. _____ makes time fly swiftly.
    (A) Lectures (B) Happiness (C) Homework (D) Illness

SPECIFIC AND GENERAL MEANINGS

A *specific statement* is based on a given instance.

> At three o'clock, I went shopping.

A *general statement* (generalization) deals with a group or class of actions as a principle, a rule.

> I always go shopping at three o'clock.
> All the students go shopping at three o'clock.

Specific statements are usually easier to comprehend; they require less of the reader. The general statement demands an additional step; the alert reader must examine it for a possible range of exceptions that may weaken its validity. Use the exercises that follow to check your control of specific statements and generalizations.

EXERCISE 7

In the space provided, label each of the following statements as either specific (S) *or* general (G).

___ 1. Just when the TV play reached its most exciting moment, our set went out of order.

___ 2. I always have to do the dishes when my sister forgets.

___ 3. Every student should support our school teams.

___ 4. The coach praised the captain of the team for his wise decision.

___ 5. Our football coach never forgets to give credit where credit is due.

___ 6. I would no more keep an animal in a cage in a zoo than I would so imprison myself as a spectacle behind bars!

___ 7. The officers did not have time yesterday to react to our list of complaints.

___ 8. The sound of the TV program is so loud, I can't hear myself think!

___ 9. Why must you always play your radio so loud!

___ 10. The first of the disarmament conferences was the Washington Conference for the Limitation of Armaments in 1921.

___ 11. The great advances in medical science have produced one of our major problems—the population explosion.

___ 12. Every generation has felt that it was progressing too fast for its own benefit.

___ 13. The doctor checked my glasses when I told him I was having trouble reading.

___ 14. Teenagers tend to imitate their friends rather than their elders.

___ 15. My sister generously offered to help me when I told her that I couldn't do my math homework.

___ 16. You always become irritable when someone tries to help you!

___ 17. I can't do the problem!

___ 18. That type of problem always gives me trouble.

___ 19. The truth will out!

___ 20. The more you have the more you lose!

EXERCISE 8

General statements are usually more difficult to handle than specific statements. Try your hand at the following.

Following each of the given generalizations is a group of words or phrases. Circle the letter of the word or phrase that most satisfactorily completes each sentence.

1. Think like a person of action, act like a person of _____.
   (A) activity (B) wealth (C) thought
   (D) fear

2. When you see a snake, never _____ where it came from.
   (A) tell (B) mind (C) depict (D) gaze at

3. A hero is no braver than others; he is only _____ five minutes longer.
   (A) present (B) fearful (C) concerned
   (D) brave

4. I am always ready to learn, although I do not always like being _____.
   (A) taught (B) right (C) seen
   (D) lenient

5. There is no _____ in any job. The future lies in the person who holds the job.
   (A) greatness (B) future (C) promotion
   (D) wealth

6. The way to win a nuclear war is to make certain it never _____.
   (A) starts (B) ends (C) is encouraged
   (D) is negotiated

7. We have to live today by what truth we can get today, and be ready tomorrow to call it _____.
   (A) honestly (B) falsehood
   (C) everlasting (D) narrow

8. Most people like hard work, especially when they are _____ for it.
   (A) paid (B) paying (C) dressed
   (D) punished

9. Every age is _____ to those living in it.
   (A) stern (B) useless (C) humorous
   (D) modern

10. The chief cause of human errors is to be found in the _____ picked up in childhood.
    (A) prejudices (B) toys (C) friends
    (D) joys

11. People have one thing in common: they are _____.
    (A) generous (B) different
    (C) thoughtful (D) concerned

12. A proverb is a short sentence based on long _____.
    (A) words (B) days (C) ideals
    (D) experience

13. Words are the signs of our _____ only and are not things themselves.
    (A) times (B) ideas (C) property
    (D) concerns

14. Even if you are on the right track, you will get _____ if you just sit there.
    (A) run over (B) ahead (C) in trouble
    (D) tired

15. If you want the present to be different from the past, _____ the past.
    (A) reject (B) flee (C) study (D) live in

16. You get the chicken by _____ the egg, not smashing it.
    (A) eating (B) boiling (C) finding
    (D) hatching

17. Pride makes some people appear _____ but prevents others from becoming so.
    (A) clever (B) ridiculous (C) wealthy
    (D) sensible

18. A city on a hill cannot be _____.
    (A) hidden (B) bombed (C) developed
    (D) excavated

19. Books that are kept on a shelf and never read will help _____.
    (A) nobody (B) solve problems
    (C) prevent war (D) the poor student

20. The process of learning is neither _____ nor always pleasant.
    (A) inspired (B) easy (C) productive
      (D) constructive

21. _____ makes no distinction between good and evil.
    (A) Justice (B) Government
      (C) Nature (D) Punishment

22. It is possible to _____ too much. A person with one watch knows the time; a person with two watches is never quite sure.
    (A) know (B) own (C) develop (D) tell

23. Today the real test of power is not the capacity to make war but the capacity to _____ it.
    (A) analyze (B) foresee (C) encircle
      (D) prevent

24. _____ boats must keep near shore.
    (A) Sturdy (B) Big (C) Cargo (D) Little

25. The hen is the egg's way of producing another _____.
    (A) roast (B) error (C) egg (D) meal

EXERCISE 9

Examination items on figurative language often require the candidate to explain a generalization.

Following each of the proverbs presented below is a series of sentences. Circle the letter of the sentence that is the most appropriate application of the proverb.

1. Little boats should keep near shore.
    (A) Children should be seen and not heard.
    (B) The smaller you are, the more fearful you must be.
    (C) Never take chances.
    (D) Know your own limits and act accordingly.

2. We boil at different degrees.
    (A) Not everyone can be a good cook.
    (B) Some people are much more tolerant than others.
    (C) The sun affects different people differently.
    (D) We are all brothers under the skin.

3. When all else is lost, the future yet remains.
    (A) Tomorrow is always another day.
    (B) We learn too slowly where our fortunes lie.
    (C) Always hope for the best.
    (D) Always do your best.

4. When the blind carry the banner, woe to those that follow.
    (A) It is always better to be modest and not boastful.
    (B) The wise learn from the mistakes of others.
    (C) Success of a group effort depends on the skill of the leaders.
    (D) Prejudice can make the efforts of any group a failure.

5. They know the water best who have waded through it.
    (A) Perseverance is the secret of success.
    (B) Water should be tested before it is used for drinking purposes.
    (C) Even the best swimmers must be cautious.
    (D) Practice is the best teacher.

6. The dog that trots about finds the bone.
    (A) Hours of dreaming are hours of accomplishing.
    (B) Dogs make the best pets.
    (C) Nothing comes without toil.
    (D) Talking things over can lead to successful planning.

7. Old foxes want no tutors.
    (A) Animals learn through imitation how to do things.
    (B) It is not hard to teach an old dog new tricks.
    (C) Elderly people are set in their ways.
    (D) Senior citizens deserve special considerations.

8. The smallest worm will turn, being trodden on.
   (A) Even the most timid can be made to fight back.
   (B) Every worm has its turn.
   (C) One good turn deserves another.
   (D) Good things come in small packages.

9. The shell must break before the bird can fly.
   (A) We must do first things first.
   (B) The early bird catches the worm.
   (C) We must keep our houses in order.
   (D) Birds of a feather flock together.

10. It never troubles the wolf how many sheep there are.
    (A) The one who works alone does best.
    (B) Evil doers are not concerned about their victims.
    (C) There is comfort in numbers.
    (D) You can't tell a wolf by its clothing.

11. All sunshine makes the desert.
    (A) Water is essential to life.
    (B) Rome was not built in a day.
    (C) Too much of a good thing can be harmful.
    (D) Study thoroughly; work hard; enjoy much.

12. Small to great matters must give way.
    (A) In an emergency, you must set priorities.
    (B) Little children, little worries; big children, big worries.
    (C) It is the purpose, not the deed, that decides worth.
    (D) Success waits for no person.

13. They who seek truth should be of no country.
    (A) Patriotism must not be questioned.
    (B) There is no American chemistry, no Russian biology, no English physics.
    (C) Research contradicts the brotherhood of man.
    (D) Prejudice can injure us.

14. Vanity is the fruit of ignorance.
    (A) Those who are in love with themselves are on the way to lose themselves.
    (B) The more we know, the more we realize how insignificant we are.
    (C) The greater the task, the greater the person who must do it.
    (D) Pride leads to humility.

15. Wealth consists not in having great possessions but in having few wants.
    (A) The miser is always poor.
    (B) Count your good deeds as your true wealth.
    (C) Need not, want not.
    (D) He is rich who is in control of his desire.

SIGNAL WORDS

Signal words are words or phrases that do not contain the main ideas but show relationships.

Time: when, before, soon, during
Order: least, of most importance, next
Joining: and, in addition, also
Separating: but, on the other hand, yet
Summarizing: therefore, all-in-all, now

The list of signal words is endless, but the alert reader looks for these words and phrases because they group ideas and aid in anticipating the author's intent.

EXERCISE 10

Circle the letter of the word or phrase that best fits each of the following descriptions.

1. A word that introduces secondary rather than main ideas
   (A) the (B) a (C) while (D) however

2. A phrase that begins a qualifying or contradictory statement
   (A) on the other hand
   (B) in the meantime
   (C) whichever comes first
   (D) rising to the occasion

3. A word or phrase that does *not* usually introduce equal elements
   (A) and (B) either (C) or (D) since

4. A word that does *not* usually signal cause
   (A) since (B) consequently
   (C) altogether (D) because

5. A word that is *not* used to signal time
   (A) when (B) since (C) while (D) what

6. A word that is *not* used to point out
   (A) that (B) this (C) those (D) any

7. The word among the following that shows least frequency
   (A) seldom (B) customarily
   (C) usually (D) rarely

8. A word that shows both place and action at the same time
   (A) in (B) into (C) on (D) by

9. A word that can be used to signal either time or place
   (A) and (B) in (C) but (D) nor

10. A word used to refer mainly to people rather than to places or things
    (A) which (B) that (C) who (D) what

11. A word or phrase that signals a change in thought direction
    (A) however (B) of course
    (C) continuing (D) in addition

12. A word or phrase that does *not* show that the end is approaching
    (A) hence (B) lastly (C) in conclusion
    (D) in order that

13. A word that does *not* point toward a specific time of the day
    (A) sun-up (B) sunset (C) daily
    (D) twilight

14. A word *not* used to point out location
    (A) from (B) over (C) if (D) by

15. A word used to point out an exception
    (A) and (B) if (C) but (D) consequently

16. A word rarely used to point out cause or result
    (A) because (B) even (C) for (D) since

17. Two words or phrases *not* usually used as a pair
    (A) both...and (B) not only...but also
    (C) neither...together (D) either...or

18. A word that rarely introduces a question
    (A) who (B) which (C) what (D) there

FACTS AND OPINIONS

Facts are beliefs that are widely accepted as having been proved or capable of being proved for a given group. At one time, that the world was flat was an accepted fact!

Opinions are beliefs that are accepted by a limited portion of a group. Evidence must be presented to convince others. "*I think it is wrong (right) because . . .*" is always involved with opinions. Alert readers must always be ready to classify authors' statements as facts or opinions. Having our critical reasoning thus involved in what we read always increases our concentration and makes the material easier to understand.

EXERCISE 11

In the space provided, label each of the following statements as either fact (F) *or* opinion (O).

___ 1. Four ounces of cottage cheese contains fewer calories than four ounces of cheddar cheese.

___ 2. Cottage cheese is tastier than cheddar cheese.

___ 3. Beginning in July 1940, German aircraft bombarded England day and night.

___ 4. The British held out throughout 1940–41 despite all the destruction caused by the German round-the-clock bombing.

___ 5. The unconquered British showed more courage than did their Allies whom the Germans had conquered.

___ 6. The class that people belong to in South America is generally based on the amount of money they make.

___ 7. Few of the South American countries in 1979 had much industry or mechanization.

___ 8. People may someday conquer the Amazon the way they have gained control over the other major rivers of the world.

___ 9. Elementary school students wear uniforms in many South American countries.

___ 10. The University of San Marcos in Lima, Peru, began in 1551.

___ 11. Haiti won its independence in 1863, years before any of the other Latin American colonies.

___ 12. There should be no charge for parking in small-town business sections.

___ 13. People today spend too much of their spare time watching television programs.

___ 14. There are more suburbanites today than there are central city residents.

___ 15. People years ago were convinced that the sun revolved around the earth.

___ 16. We should think twice before contacting creatures living in outer space because they might come and conquer us as we have conquered the other creatures on earth.

___ 17. Anything that significantly changes the composition of the air around us can be a threat to our survival.

___ 18. All who are willing to work hard and do what they are told will get ahead and make it to the top.

___ 19. People cannot be hypnotized against their will.

___ 20. If others have survived experimenting with dangerous drugs, so will I!

PICKING THE SUBJECT

The *subject* is what the sentence or paragraph deals with. Usually the subject is a single noun or a noun phrase.

The *price* is much too high.
Scientific ingenuity has both simplified and complicated our lives.

The author does not always signal the subject by putting it at the beginning of the sentence or even in the first sentence.

On the floor next to the large carton was the missing *notebook*.

After long hours of bitter anxiety, it suddenly dawned on me! There was no longer any doubt where the *key* was hidden.

Often the grammatical subject of the sentence can be different from the logical subject of the sentence or sentences.

The *creation* of new weaponry has resulted in dynamic changes of army strategy.

In the above sentence, *creation* is the grammatical subject, but *new weaponry* is the logical subject of the thought content.

Your first task, as a reader, is to find the logical subject of a selection. Once you have located the key word or phrase, following the author's thoughts becomes much simpler. How skillful are you at unraveling sentences?

EXERCISE 12

Circle the word or phrase that is the logical (not necessarily the grammatical) subject of each of the following sentences.

1. Even at very early stages of development, human beings lived together in social groups.

2. When underground water comes in contact with lava, it will often emerge as a hot spring when it flows to the earth's surface.

3. Within the enlarged base of the flower are tiny white structures known as ovules.

4. In July 1945, on a remote desert spot in New Mexico, there occurred an event that will affect countless generations to come—the explosion of the first atomic bomb.

5. Not too many years ago, airplane travel was avoided by many people who considered it dangerous and uncertain.

6. In many local elections, the school budget becomes one of the major issues.

7. More than any other court in the United States, the Supreme Court creates precedents through its decisions and interpretations.

8. Finally in July 1953, shortly after the death of Stalin, a cease-fire agreement was reached in Korea.

9. One of the pressing problems of our times has been the alarming increase in crimes of violence.

10. A second industrial revolution is being brought about by automation, the use of machines to control other machines and to take the place of human effort, observation, and even judgment.

11. In most instances, inventions consist mainly of combining a number of already known ideas into something new.

12. Specifically, urban renewal consists of much more that just the construction of public housing for low-income families.

13. In the other countries of the world, too, there has been a startling and rapid development of mass communication.

14. In the foundation years of the United States, there was practically no free public education as we know it today.

15. That success in life does not necessarily bring happiness or a sense of security has long been shown by psychological and sociological investigations.

16. One of the remarkable political developments of our history is the way in which the powers of the president have increased.

17. In general, however, inorganic compounds have relatively simple chemical structures.

18. Although some types of bacteria cause human diseases, others assist us by causing the decay of dead plants and animals, thus returning organic matter and minerals to the soil.

19. Because Hinduism does not insist that all its adherents agree on what they believe or in how they worship, the chief ideas of Hinduism are difficult to describe.

20. Even though more than 15 major languages are recognized in India, the government has declared English and Hindi as the two official languages.

SENTENCE SENSE

The sentence is a unit of thought. It is the building block in the development of a paragraph. If the reader of a selection understands the thought content sentence by sentence, he or she soon grasps the meaning of the paragraph.

The following exercises will help you judge your control of sentence meanings.

EXERCISE 13

Circle the letter of the pair of words or phrases that most appropriately completes each of the following sentences.

1. In the early days of the factory system, people thought that the government had no right to _____ with business, and so no one forced the factory owners to treat their workers_____.
   (A) combine...poorly
   (B) interfere...fairly
   (C) deal...consistently
   (D) discuss...as partners

2. President Franklin D. Roosevelt _____ the Good Neighbor policy, which called for action by all the American governments, rather than by the United States alone, when _____ arose in any of the American nations.
   (A) condemned...dictators
   (B) praised...peace
   (C) ended...prosperity
   (D) established...difficulties

3. _____ of refuse and garbage at open dumps long remained a major _____ of air pollution in many of our cities.
   (A) Purchasing...result
   (B) Burning...cause
   (C) Consideration...concern
   (D) Collection...benefit

4. More than 2,000 years ago, the Chinese emperors _____ a postal system so that they could send official _____ throughout the empire.
   (A) imagined...programs
   (B) instituted...decrees
   (C) improved...judges
   (D) destroyed...agents

5. Thomas Jefferson _____ the role of the President as the party leader who _____ the legislative branch of the government.
   (A) rejected...joined
   (B) ridiculed...rejected
   (C) relied on...established
   (D) established...dominated

6. Children have to be _____ slowly and patiently the skills which are needed to deal with the _____ of living.
   (A) taught...problems
   (B) allowed...art
   (C) denied...cost
   (D) clarified...possibilities

7. The emphasis on violence and crime in so many TV programs has led young people to _____ violence as a means of _____ problems.
   (A) reject...causing
   (B) accept...solving
   (C) use...making
   (D) realize...dissolving

8. When India gained its _____, the organization and principles of the new nation _____ basic features of American, British, French, and other democratic governments.
   (A) reputation...formed
   (B) independence...reflected
   (C) wealth...rejected
   (D) power...desired

9. When a bar magnet is _____ at the center so that it may _____ freely, it always comes to rest pointing north and south.
   (A) fastened...not move
   (B) split...spin
   (C) painted...settle
   (D) suspended...swing

10. Because of political and military _____ the United States has always been eager to _____ stable, friendly, peace-loving governments throughout the Western Hemisphere.
    (A) considerations...see
    (B) dictators...vote for
    (C) dangers...reject
    (D) power...combine

11. The small force under Cortez was _____ to conquer the Aztec empire because Indian war clubs were so _____ to cannon and muskets.
    (A) foolish...incomparable
    (B) unwilling...superior
    (C) seen...comparable
    (D) able...inferior

12. When a stream of water flows in a _____ path, it tends to wear away the softer and looser material to _____ a ditch or gully.
    (A) slow...elevate
    (B) downward...form
    (C) swift...erect
    (D) steady...destroy

13. Customs tend to remain _____ once they become firmly _____ a group.
    (A) weak...developed
    (B) effective...rejected by
    (C) colorful...discussed by
    (D) unchanged...established in

14. As modern life becomes more complex, government _____ its functions and becomes more _____.
    (A) enforces...unacceptable
    (B) slows down...effective
    (C) multiplies...powerful
    (D) considers...considerate

15. The modern period of African history _____ in the fifteenth century with the _____ of Portuguese sailors, explorers, and settlers.
    (A) ended...loss
    (B) flourished...atrocities
    (C) lasted...destruction
    (D) began...coming

EXERCISE 14

From the list of words below each of the following sentences, select the two that most appropriately complete the sentence. Write them in the spaces provided.

1. What is needed in Alaska today is not the complete ___(A)___ of productive activities but a ___(B)___ of such activities to make sure that they do not destroy our last fontier.
    ownership   government   control
    source   banning
    (A) _____
    (B) _____

2. In Lamarck's theory, millions of years ago the giraffes were ___(A)___ animals that ate leaves from lower branches, and as they stretched their necks to reach the higher branches, their necks tended to grow longer; the ___(B)___ done by the parents gave their children longer necks before they were born.
    intelligent   thinking   stretching
    mischief   short-necked
    (A) _____
    (B) _____

3. When DDT was first used, there were very few flies which were immune to this poison. The only ones that survived were those few that spread rapidly without the ___(A)___ of the others. Soon DDT-resistant types ___(B)___ a large part of the total fly population.
    destroyed   competition   destruction
    made up   aid
    (A) _____
    (B) _____

4. In the past, most of the peoples of Africa grew their own food and made their own clothing. They had little use for ___(A)___. Whatever ___(B)___ was done was on the barter system. Products and crops were traded for foreign goods and bright clothing.
    travel   trading   agriculture
    money   wealth
    (A) _____
    (B) _____

5. A vaccine obtained from the blood of calves that have had cowpox is injected into people's arms. If the people are susceptible to the disease they develop a mild case of smallpox. Their bodies produce antitoxin to ___(A)___ the virus, and they soon recover. The antitoxin remains in their bloodstream for several years, thus protecting them from further ___(B)___ of smallpox.
    destroy   reproduce   injections
    protect   attacks
    (A) _____
    (B) _____

6. The Supreme Court by a unanimous vote in 1954 declared that racially segregated education can never be truly _____(A)_____ education. The Court further ordered local school boards to set up programs of _____(B)_____ with all deliberate speed.

> significance   integration   valuable
> equal   irrigation
>
> (A) _____
> (B) _____

7. Most of the year, the ports of the former Soviet Union that border on the Arctic Ocean are icebound and much of the coast is closed to _____(A)_____. Because it is adjacent to the North Atlantic Drift, a warm current which _____(B)_____ from the Gulf Stream, Murmansk is Russia's only northern-most harbor that is free from ice throughout the year.

> empties into   flows from   attack
> industry   navigation
>
> (A) _____
> (B) _____

8. Experimental study of animal behavior has shown that the behavior of animals can be _____(A)_____ when changes in the environment so dictate. Animals have shown amounts of intelligence beyond our expectations. The differences between human beings and other animals is a matter of degree, not in the kind of _____(B)_____.

> brutality   modified   causation
> behavior   sensed
>
> (A) _____
> (B) _____

9. Plastics are an increasingly _____(A)_____ element in solid wastes. Many of them cannot be reduced to simpler forms that then can be put back into the life cycle. In incinerators most plastics foul the grate because they melt rather than _____(B)_____.

> disappear   beneficial   dissolve
> troublesome   burn
>
> (A) _____
> (B) _____

10. The kerosene lamp works on the same principle as the candle. However, the fuel in the lamp starts as a liquid rather than a _____(A)_____. The kerosene is drawn up through the wick and is vaporized by the heat of the _____(B)_____.

> solid   flame   candle
> gas   draft
>
> (A) _____
> (B) _____

SENTENCE RELATIONSHIPS

Each sentence in the paragraph is related in thought content to the others. The reader must be trained to look for this relationship, which reveals the meaning of the entire selection. The exercises that follow will help you to review three of the more usual sentence connections.

EXERCISE 15

Main Ideas and Related Details
In the space provided, label each sentence in each of the following sets as main idea (M) *or* detail (D).

1. __ (A) More than 70% of the people of Japan live in big cities.
   __ (B) The islands of Japan contain more than 100 million people.

2. __ (A) Superiority based on arms is at best relative and temporary.
   __ (B) The advantage gained by a nation when it acquires a new weapon disappears when its rival acquires a similar weapon.

3. __ (A) Almost a century of campaigning was necessary before the women's liberation movement brought about significant changes.
   __ (B) Often a great deal of opposition must be overcome before changes are made in our society.

4. __ (A) To keep an idea alive, propagandists present it over and over, again and again.
   __ (B) One of the basic principles of propaganda is repetition.

5. __ (A) Dogs seem to suffer from the same types of air pollutants as human beings do.
   __ (B) Many of the air pollutants have proved to be highly poisonous to animals.

6. __ (A) The beneficial as well as the pest varieties of insects are killed.
   __ (B) When DDT is spread through an area, it kills all insects.

7. __ (A) Iron ore, coal, and oil are said to be found in great amounts.
   __ (B) Russia claims that it has mineral wealth beyond measure.

8. __ (A) A number of organisms are used in the study of heredity and genetics.
   __ (B) The fruit fly *Drosophila* has long been a major experimental animal.

9. __ (A) Radiation time-clock methods have been used to study the age of the older layers of rocks in the earth.
   __ (B) The uranium-lead ratio and the potassium-argon ratio have been most accurate.

10. __ (A) Under Genghis Khan, the Mongols were organized into one of the most dreaded war machines in human history.
    __ (B) The Mongols conquered or destroyed all that stood in their path.

11. __ (A) Peter the Great wanted to make Russia into a rich commercial country.
    __ (B) Peter the Great established many new industries.

12. __ (A) The greatest of all eroding forces is running water.
    __ (B) Waterfalls, rivers, and ocean waves have done more to alter the surface of the earth than any other factor.

13. __ (A) Corn, for example, is the most important cereal grown in the United States.
    __ (B) Cereals are grasses that yield a grain that is used for food.

14. __ (A) The dhoti is worn by men and the sari by women in the villages of India.
    __ (B) In the villages of India, custom has decreed a traditional dress.

15. __ (A) With one Representative and two Senators, Alaska has three electors in the Electoral College.
    __ (B) Each state is allowed the same number of electors in the Electoral College as it has members in Congress.

EXERCISE 16

Cause and Effect

In the space provided, label each sentence in each of the following pairs as cause (C) *or* effect (E) *(result).*

1. __ (A) The nomads in the Sahara in Africa spend their lives in search of waterholes and green grazing grass.
   __ (B) There is never enough plant life in the Sahara to feed the goats and cattle on which their lives depend.

2. __ (A) Parents could do almost anything to their children.
   __ (B) Children were regarded as property of their parents.

3. __ (A) Women had been taught that their major role was to do what their fathers and husbands told them to do.
   __ (B) For generations women destroyed their ability to think and act for themselves.

4. __ (A) At present levels of TV advertising, the typical 17-year-old will have been exposed to more than 350,000 commercials.
   __ (B) Young people watch more than 24 hours of TV a week.

5. __ (A) Until 1947, princes ruled about 40% of India.
   __ (B) The maharajahs had the power of life and death over their subjects.

6. __ (A) Nitrogen neither burns nor supports combustion.
   __ (B) Nitrogen is a rather inactive element.

7. __ (A) We may someday live in a world without the necessity of work.
   __ (B) As more and more industries become automated, machines are taking over the means of production.

8. __ (A) A true pacifist feeling appeared in wide evidence among the Japanese people.
   __ (B) It is unlikely that any large scale revival of military aggression against its neighbors would be considered.

9. __ (A) The general flow of air on the earth's surface is toward the equator away from both poles.
   __ (B) There are great differences in temperature between the polar regions and the equatorial zone.

10. __ (A) People who have experienced severe poverty in childhood may be haunted for the rest of their lives by a fear of being poor.
    __ (B) The fear of poverty may show up later on as a drive to be better than all the other workers in the factory.

11. __ (A) During his lifetime Buddha did not put his teachings in written form.
    __ (B) After Buddha's death, his faithful followers collected his beliefs in books called *Sutras*.

12. __ (A) French governors often removed African rulers and chiefs.
    __ (B) French policy showed little respect for the traditional way of life in their colonies.

13. __ (A) The tsar's greatest ambition was to make Russia like the nations of Western Europe.
    __ (B) Peter the Great developed many new industries.

14. __ (A) Islam regulates all aspects of life.
    __ (B) Islam is an all-embracing religion.

15. __ (A) Whenever the vice presidency becomes vacant, the President nominates a new Vice President.
    __ (B) The person nominated by the President takes office after being confirmed by a majority vote of both houses of Congress.

EXERCISE 17

Reaching Conclusions
From the lettered statements below each of the following sentences, choose the one that is the most logical conclusion that can be drawn from the sentence. Circle the letter of that conclusion.

1. The nation's industries use very large quantities of fresh water for cooling during many manufacturing processes.
   (A) Only purified water can be used in cooling processes.
   (B) The manufacturers can use the same water over and over.
   (C) Industry must develop systems for disposing of considerable amounts of hot water.
   (D) The water used by industry is polluted and cannot be used again.

2. Planet Earth is a closed system with limited space and limited resources.
   (A) Earth is continually shrinking.
   (B) There is no limit to the number of human beings Earth can support.
   (C) Life on Earth is doomed.
   (D) A point could be reached at which Earth could no longer support life.

3. In traditional Japanese ink drawings, the artist tries to paint a state of mind rather than an exact copy of some object.
   (A) Japanese ink drawings resemble camera snapshots.
   (B) Japanese ink drawings have vivid colors.
   (C) Most Japanese ink drawings are of people.
   (D) Japanese ink drawings give the feeling rather than the appearance of some living quality.

4. Very little of the Aztec goldwork remains because the Spaniards melted it down into bars.
   (A) The Aztec jewelry was all of gold.
   (B) The Spaniards felt that the Aztec gold designs were not beautiful.
   (C) The Aztec jewelry was in thin, leaflike designs.
   (D) Gold bars are easier to transport than gold jewelry.

5. Only about one in ten of the known microbes is harmful to human beings.
   (A) There are more beneficial than harmless microbes.
   (B) There are more harmful than harmless microbes.
   (C) There are more harmful than beneficial microbes.
   (D) None of the above statements can be inferred from the given sentence.

6. About one fourth of the workers in the United States belong to some kind of labor union.
   (A) Most older workers belong to unions.
   (B) Most workers do not belong to unions.
   (C) Unions have bettered the living conditions of workers.
   (D) Unions encourage young people to learn trades.

7. In Russia, parents are often blamed by the authorities if children misbehave.
   (A) Russian children are the wards of the state.
   (B) Russian children are given more freedom than are American children.
   (C) Russian parents can be fined if children cross against a traffic light.
   (D) Russian parents are better than are American parents.

8. The greater number of men than women working in such areas as business and government is due to social rather than biological factors.
   (A) Women are physically weaker than men.
   (B) Women are better workers than men.
   (C) Custom has kept women out of politics.
   (D) There is proof that women could not do as well as men do as mayors, governors, or President.

9. The machinery of the Industrial Revolution made the production of goods easier and quicker.
   (A) Machinery improved the appearance of the goods being sold.
   (B) Machinery speeded up the manufacturing process.
   (C) Machinery added to the cost of production.
   (D) Machinery lessened the cost of production.

10. There are many more divorces today than in the first half of the twentieth century.
    (A) People now are less happy than they were then.
    (B) Divorce as a solution is more acceptable today.
    (C) There are more people living today.
    (D) People are marrying at an earlier age today.

EXERCISE 18

Review of Sentence Relationships
In the spaces provided write the words that are missing in each of the following groups of sentences.

1. At the close of World War II, the Soviet Union created a belt of satellite states in Eastern Europe. The key purpose was to create a _____(A)_____ zone to absorb any possible ___(B)___ attack from the West.

    (A) _____
    (B) _____

2. Agriculture had long been the major occupation of Canada. Because of its vast expanses of __(A)__ soil, it is one of the world's __(B)__ exporters of wheat.

(A) _____

(B) _____

3. The very existence of nuclear weapons confonts humanity with the most fateful choice in its history on earth. Steps must be taken to __(A)__ their use by irresponsible governments to bring about the inevitable __(B)__ of life on earth.

(A) _____

(B) _____

4. Labor's efforts to bring more people into unions have not had marked success in recent years. The high wage scales for blue-collar workers __(A)__ workers' interest in joining unions; clerical workers usually are by and large __(B)__ to unionization.

(A) _____

(B) _____

5. In the fourth century, the people of Ghana created a vast empire because they were able to exploit their advantage over their neighbors. They alone knew the secret of making iron __(A)__ and __(B)__ .

(A) _____

(B) _____

6. While the League of Nations controlled the ambitions of smaller nations, it was not powerful enough to enforce obedience among the larger countries. It could not __(A)__ Japan from __(B)__ Manchuria from China or __(A)__ Italy from seizing Ethiopia.

(A) _____

(B) _____

7. The deep snow and ice of Russian winter stopped the tanks and motorized units of the Germans, but the Soviet soldiers, who were __(A)__ to these conditions, were able to __(B)__ and retake many important places.

(A) _____

(B) _____

8. We seek peace—enduring peace. More than an __(A)__ to war, we want an end to this brutal, inhuman method of __(B)__ the differences between governments.

(A) _____

(B) _____

9. The pictures that the ancient Egyptian artists drew in their temples and tombs are still considered beautiful and are greatly __(A)__ today. The colors they used were so good that in most cases they have not __(B)__ through all the centuries that have passed.

(A) _____

(B) _____

10. The family is the most important unit of society in Latin America. The father is the recognized __(A)__ of the family with the mother next in __(B)__ .

(A) _____

(B) _____

11. In Japan there was a heavy demand after World War II for wood products because the bombings had destroyed many structures. To save their forests from being wiped out, the Japanese __(A)__ the steel and concrete industries to aid in new __(B)__ .

(A) _____

(B) _____

12. All streams normally carry amounts of soil and rock particles. Only when the siltation becomes __(A)__ does a pollution __(B)__ exist.

(A) _____

(B) _____

13. The use of the energy of flowing or falling water to create electrical power is ideal from the ecological point of view. Power derived from water creates no __(A)__ and uses up no __(B)__ fuel resources.

(A) _____

(B) _____

14. The public expects the police and the law courts to enforce the law and punish lawbreakers. These agencies cannot do an _____(A)_____ job unless they have the full support of the ___(B)___.

(A) _____
(B) _____

15. An audience is different from a crowd. Audience refers to _____(A)_____ come together for the purpose of listening to or observing some proceedings in accordance with a _____(B)_____ set in advance.

(A) _____
(B) _____

PARAGRAPH UNITS

Effective readers rarely go through a paragraph word by word. Rather, they see the paragraph as a series of connected word groups. The smaller groups, phrases, flow together into a thought unit, a sentence. When readers come to the end of each sentence, they pause, if necessary, to make certain that they have followed the trend of thought. They thus continue from sentence to sentence through the paragraph.

Use the following exercise to evaluate your ability to recognize thought units in a paragraph.

EXERCISE 19

Place the missing periods and capital letters in each of the following paragraphs and then fill in the blanks in the sentences below.

Psychologists taught Washoe to communicate in a sign language used by deaf people it took five years for her to learn 160 words five years is a long period of time Washoe, however, was the first chimpanzee to use sign language.

1. The paragraph contains _____ sentences.

2. The second sentence begins with _____.

3. The last sentence begins with _____.

The Gypsies probably originated in India there are more than three million Gypsies throughout the world the word *Gypsy* derives from the false idea that the group came from Egypt Gypsies call themselves *Rom,* their word for man.

4. The paragraph contains _____ sentences.

5. The last word in the first sentence is _____.

6. The third sentence ends with the word _____.

There are 35 to 40 known varieties of electric fish capable of discharging electricity that they produce themselves all except two, the electric eel and the torpedo ray, are harmless the torpedo ray and the electric eel when full grown are capable of injuring large mammals the electric eel is probably the only one capable of killing a full-grown person in good health.

7. The number of sentences in the paragraph is _____.

8. The second sentence begins with _____.

9. _____ is a word below that does not begin a sentence.

    there   the   all   that

10. The last word of the third sentence is _____.

Uri Geller became known throughout the world for his claims as a person having psychic power he says that he bends spoons, pins, and other things through the power of his mind some scientists claim that he has shown his abilities under laboratory conditions others call him a clever trickster out for fame and fortune.

11. The number of sentences in this paragraph is _____.

12. _____ is a letter below that does not begin a sentence.

    S   H   O   A

13. The last word of the third sentence is
_____.

14. The first word of the second sentence is
_____.

Benito Juarez led the Mexicans to victory
over the French who tried to establish
Maximilian of Austria as Emperor of Mexico
Juarez has often been compared to Abraham
Lincoln Lincoln and Juarez had many of the
same liberal ideals Juarez tried to make land
ownership possible for wealthy farmers he
tried to spread the tax burden more evenly he
wanted the same justice for both rich and poor.

15. The number of sentences is _____.

16. No sentence begins with_____.
Benito   who   Juarez   Lincoln

17. The first sentence ends with _____.

18. The third sentence ends with _____.

19. The last sentence begins with _____.

20. The word below that seems to have
been used in error is _____.
Juarez   wealthy   Lincoln   ideals

EXERCISE 20

*Decide, from the lettered choices, the best order
in which to arrange the sentences in each of the
following groups to form a well-organized
paragraph. Circle the letter of your choice.*

1. A. To the astonishment of the nearby
farmers, the mountain began to
move down the valley.
   B. In 1972, a strange event occurred in
the Soviet Caucasus.
   C. The mountain slid over a mile in
eight days.
   D. Heavy rains had swelled the under-
ground river.
   E. As it often happens, there was a river
flowing below a large mountain.
   (A) ECDBA
   (B) EBCAD
   (C) BEDAC
   (D) BDAEC
   (E) ABDCE

2. A. That's how *tip* came into the
language.
   B. Printed on the box was *To Insure
Promptness.*
   C. It was to remind customers to leave
something for the waiter—if the
service was good.
   D. In no time at all the phrase was
abbreviated as *T.I.P.*
   E. Old-English inns kept a box near
the entrance door.
   (A) EADBC
   (B) BCAED
   (C) ABDCE
   (D) DACBE
   (E) ECBDA

3. A. At the river mouth, the soil spreads
out into a triangular shape.
   B. When a river flows through the
countryside, it picks up soil.
   C. The river loses speed as it approach-
es the sea, and it drops the soil.
   D. The triangular shape resembles the
fourth letter of the Greek alphabet,
delta.
   E. How did the land at the mouth of a
river get the name of delta?
   (A) AECBD
   (B) DBECA
   (C) BCADE
   (D) EBCAD
   (E) CABDE

4. A. One of the latter is the most famous
chair handed down to us from the
past.
   B. It is the one called *Chair of St.
Peter.*
   C. It is exhibited once every 100
years.
   D. Some are kept on exhibition while
others are stored in carefully guard-
ed vaults.
   E. The Vatican possesses many unusu-
al and rare treasures.
   (A) BECAD
   (B) EDABC
   (C) CEDAB
   (D) ACBDE
   (E) ECBAD

5. A. Knowing us, Susanna did not break down!
   B. She refused to show us what it was.
   C. We were all very curious and promised not to tell Adam her secret.
   D. To honor Adam's return, we all planned to give him presents.
   E. Susanna told us that she had made a gift for him.
   (A) EDBAC
   (B) BECDA
   (C) EABDC
   (D) DECBA
   (E) BCEAD

6. A. Our house was the only one for miles around.
   B. Our woodlands gradually were replaced by houses and paved streets.
   C. Then a big factory was built in the nearby town.
   D. Many of the workers wanted to live in the country
   E. When we moved into the neighborhood, woods surrounded our property.
   (A) EACDB
   (B) ACEDB
   (C) BDACE
   (D) CEDBA
   (E) AECBD

7. A. Others like Matt Dillon and Doc never really existed.
   B. According to the script writers, each of them polished off scores of bad men.
   C. Bat Masterson and Wyatt Earp were real lawmen.
   D. Some of the sheriffs made famous in western movies really existed.
   E. But according to fact, each of them was in only one fatal fight.
   (A) EDBAC
   (B) DCEAB
   (C) CBADE
   (D) DACBE
   (E) EDCAB

8. A. We knew that our lives, however, could never be the same.
   B. The sun rose as usual the next day.
   C. Only time will tell but we fervently hope so.
   D. Our neighbors continued to follow the routines of their daily lives.
   E. Relatives and friends told us that the ache would grow more bearable in the weeks ahead
   (A) BECAD
   (B) ABDCE
   (C) DCEBA
   (D) BDAEC
   (E) BACED

9. A. It is now west of the date line and thousands of miles west of San Francisco.
   B. The tip of the island of Hawaii, South Point, has the honor.
   C. For many years it was Key West, Florida.
   D. The title changed when our 49th state joined the Union.
   E. What is the southern most spot in the United States?
   (A) EBDCA
   (B) CABDE
   (C) ACEBD
   (D) DBECA
   (E) DCEBA

10. A. History proves that Rome did suffer from a devastating fire.
    B. The violin was invented a thousand years after Nero's death.
    C. It is also true that Nero had been Emperor of Rome.
    D. Legends and facts often differ considerably.
    E. However, he never could have fiddled on a violin during the fire.
    (A) BCADE
    (B) DACEB
    (C) ACDBE
    (D) DBAEC
    (E) ABECD

IRRELEVANT SENTENCES

Irrelevant sentences are sentences that are not related to the other sentences in a paragraph. This exercise will help you to evaluate your ability to see the logical building blocks in the construction of paragraphs and to recognize unrelated material.

EXERCISE 21

Each of the following groups of sentences contains one sentence that is not related to the others. Circle the letter of the unrelated sentence.

1. (A) Democracy came to Great Britain in gradual stages.
   (B) It came by means of laws.
   (C) The democratizing laws were called reform acts.
   (D) Parliament passed laws to reduce the working hours of children
   (E) The laws were passed in response to the demands of the people.

2. (A) The Incas were far advanced as farmers.
   (B) Agriculture has long been the backbone of the economy of South America.
   (C) They used nitrates for fertilizers.
   (D) They had planned irrigation to insure a proper amount of water for crops.
   (E) Despite their technology, the Incas' crops were not large enough to support their population.

3. (A) The village council in India is the local governing organization.
   (B) Called the panchayat, it is elected by the entire adult population of the village.
   (C) A villager who breaks a law can be fined or even expelled from the village.
   (D) It is responsible for the smooth functioning of the village.
   (E) It is in charge of the roads, water system, medical care, and child welfare.

4. (A) There are many Shinto shrines throughout Japan.
   (B) They are usually located in a lovely natural setting.
   (C) Shinto is based on people's response to the world around them.
   (D) The shrine is usually simple in design and without elaborate decorations.
   (E) Some of the shrines reflect Chinese rather than Japanese architecture.

5. (A) Growth goes on despite reverses or disappointments.
   (B) It is sometimes necessary to get angry and let others know it.
   (C) It always means giving up what is familiar and comfortable.
   (D) It is ever accompanied by difficulties and pains as well as by rewards.
   (E) Whether it will be distorted or proceed in a natural way depends on the strength of the individual.

6. (A) The craft guilds resembled the National Manufacturers Association rather than modern unions.
   (B) The guild membership consisted of the employers and not the workers.
   (C) The workers were called journeymen and apprentices.
   (D) The guilds controlled all phases of the industry.
   (E) Inspectors checked up on the members, who could be fined if they lowered the price or the quality of the goods produced.

7. (A) The total cost of air pollution in the United States amounts to many billions a year.
   (B) However, it cannot be calculated precisely.
   (C) Damage to buildings and agricultural crops is estimated at more than $900 million a year.
   (D) The time lost from work as the result of illness caused by air pollution is incalculable.
   (E) The cost of safety devices in motor vehicles cannot be calculated in dollars and cents.

8. (A) The physical features of Africa have kept the peoples of Africa apart.
   (B) The desert, rain forests, and mountains prevented the coastal groups from exploring the interior.
   (C) Africa's rivers have many spectacular falls, rapids, sandbars, and swamps, making them difficult to navigate.
   (D) The vast deserts contain no roads and a people who are not interested in building any.
   (E) The soil and irregular rainfall pose great obstacles to large-scale agricultural productivity.

9. (A) In ancient times China was ruled by a series of dynasties.
   (B) The dynasties consisted of a succession of rulers who were members of the same family.
   (C) The Hsia Dynasty, for example, ruled for over 500 years almost 3,500 years ago.
   (D) During this time there was a written language and most of the people were farmers.
   (E) The Hsia Dynasty consisted of a group of related princes, each of whom controlled specific areas.

10. (A) In Southeast Asia, titles and names of respect are given to individuals of great merit.
    (B) The title *U* is one of respect and is given only to those of outstanding accomplishment.
    (C) The Secretary General of the UN was named U Thant because of his role in keeping world peace.
    (D) In Moslem areas the title *Haji* is added to the names of those who have made the religious pilgrimage to Mecca.
    (E) Throughout Southeast Asia, people are still addressed formally by their first names.

TOPIC SENTENCES

The topic sentence is the sentence that contains the main idea in a paragraph. It is the sentence that the other sentences explain, prove, expand, develop, illustrate. Most frequently, the topic sentence is placed first in a selection. However, this is not always the case. It can be set anywhere in the selection. It can even be inferred— and not be stated in the paragraph. Use the exercise that follows to test your ability to locate the topic sentence.

EXERCISE 22

Each of the following groups of sentences belongs in a single paragraph, but the individual sentences are not presented in their logical order. Circle the letter of the topic sentence.

1. (A) The most common form is that of walking over a shallow trench filled with glowing coal.
   (B) In some areas the performer walks over a bed of hot stones.
   (C) Fire walking takes various forms.
   (D) Some fire walkers go through a log fire.

2. (A) The tsar relied on aristocratic advisers who were interested in mainly receiving bribes.
   (B) The soldiers went into battle without essential equipment.
   (C) When the people demanded food, they were ignored.
   (D) The government of Russia in 1914 was cruel, inefficient, and corrupt.

3. (A) Power from the atom will keep our wheels of industry going.
   (B) In the years ahead, nuclear energy may change our lives more profoundly than did the Industrial Revolution.
   (C) The atom is becoming even now increasingly important in diagnosis and treatment of diseases.
   (D) Controlled nuclear explosions can make possible stupendous engineering feats.

4. (A) Native Americans have witnessed the almost total obliteration of their cultures.
   (B) The victims of cruel injustice, most Native Americans have been torn away from their physical heritage.
   (C) Blundering federal policies led to the violation of solemn treaties.
   (D) The original American has been a tragic figure in American history.

5. (A) The League was formed to bring in to reality one of humanity's strongest hopes, peace among nations.
   (B) The League was doomed almost from the start when the United States failed to join.
   (C) The League was an idea whose time had almost arrived.
   (D) The League proved to be only a first attempt at the prevention of war.

6. (A) The land mass of the islands covers more than 700,000 square miles.
   (B) There are over 3,000 islands in the chain.
   (C) There are so many islands in the Republic of Indonesia that no textbook can do justice to all of them.
   (D) The Republic of Indonesia is one of the largest island chains in the world.

7. (A) It was a war on every front.
   (B) The Chinese declared war on "rats, flies, mosquitoes, and grain-eating sparrows."
   (C) The death rate of newborn infants and their mothers was drastically reduced.
   (D) Thousands of tons of precious grain were saved for human consumption.

8. (A) Knowledge, however, in Zen comes from within the individual.
   (B) Introduced by way of China, Zen had a profound effect on the Japanese.
   (C) The followers of Zen must lead a simple life close to nature.
   (D) Zen is a branch of Buddhism.

9. (A) City dwellers looked to his leadership because of his background of experience.
   (B) Gandhi won the support of large segments of the Indian population.
   (C) The Indian villagers gave him unquestioning loyalty because he crusaded to improve their lives.
   (D) Political leaders were impressed by his depth of understanding.

10. (A) The Aztecs believed that they had to offer human blood to their god Quetzalcoatl as repayment for his protection.
    (B) The supply of victims for their sacrifices came from the enemy captured.
    (C) When more victims were needed, the Aztecs went to war to get them.
    (D) The debt to Quetzalcoatl was great, and so the sacrifices had to be many.

11. (A) The patient is made to feel guilty and ashamed of his condition, thus retarding his path to recovery.
    (B) Families will often hide the fact that one of their members is suffering from such an ailment.
    (C) The attitude of the average family toward mental illness must be changed.
    (D) The chance of treating the patient at an early and easier stage is lost.

12. (A) Many of the pesticides that break down rapidly kill all insects where applied, whether the insects are beneficial or harmful.
    (B) These nonpersistent pesticides lead to the development of insect varieties that are not harmed by them.
    (C) Many of these poisons are extremely deadly.
    (D) Even the pesticides that last for just a few days have serious disadvantages.

Mastery Exams

Now that you have studied each type of question likely to appear in the Reading Comprehension Section of any standard examination, it is time to put everything together. The following are Mastery Examinations. Take each exam under conditions similar to those you will meet when you take the one that counts—no TV, no radio, no food, no cooperation! Let the score represent the best you can do now.

EXAM 1

> DIRECTIONS: Carefully read each passage below, and then answer the questions that follow. Select the choice that, on the basis of the passage, best answers the question. Then circle the letter that corresponds to the correct answer.

Hatting was one of the first domestic industries to develop in the colonies. As early as 1640, American hats were one of the homemade articles used for barter and exchange. By the beginning of the eighteenth century, hatting had become one of New England's important industries; in the 1730s hats were being exported from the colonies in sufficient numbers to arouse uneasiness among hatters in the mother country and to cause them to exert successful pressure on Parliament for a law prohibiting the export of hats from one colony to another, and from any colony to Great Britain or any other country.

Wool was the principal raw material, but a considerable proportion of the hats were made of fur felt, using beaver fur as the base. The average price of wool hats during the eighteenth century ranged from 40 to 80 cents, and beaver hats ranged fom $2.50 to $3.50.

1. The phrase that best expresses the main idea or subject of this selection is:
   (A) Raw materials for hats
   (B) Colonial exports
   (C) How hats were made
   (D) Kinds of hats in America
   (E) An early American industry

2. A law regarding the hat trade was enacted by Parliament in response to a complaint by
   (A) colonists
   (B) Indians
   (C) English noblemen
   (D) citizens of foreign countries
   (E) English hatmakers

3. This law made it illegal for
   (A) Great Britain to export hats
   (B) the colonies to import hats
   (C) the hatters to use beaver fur
   (D) the colonies to export hats
   (E) the colonies to change the price of hats

4. American hats
   (A) were made principally of wool
   (B) did not suit the customers in Great Britain
   (C) were an unimportant part of New England industry
   (D) were sent only to Great Britain
   (E) were not made until 1730

5. Beaver hats
   (A) were unpopular
   (B) were much cheaper than those of wool
   (C) were made mainly for barter with the Native Americans
   (D) cost more than wool hats
   (E) were not exported

The Republic of India is one of the largest nations in the world. It has a large population made up of many ethnic groups. Each of the major racial divisions, Negroid, Australoid, Mongoloid, and Caucasoid, can be found on the Indian subcontinent

The land mass of India is a peninsula that juts into the Indian Ocean from the Asian heartland. It is separated from the heartland by the Himalayas, the world's greatest mountain mass. These mountains plus the ocean provide the subcontinent with good natural borders. Unfortunately, the subcontinent contains another nation besides the Republic of India. The nation of Pakistan rules two sections in the northern part of the peninsula, making it the only nation in the world with two separated areas, East and West Pakistan, to be ruled as one nation.

The division of the subcontinent took place in 1947. The British granted independence to the subcontinent, but the inhabitants could not agree on one nation to rule them. The widely diversified ethnic groups were committed to only two religions— Hindu and Muslim. The adherents of each faith demanded their own nation. The natural borders and great ethnic variety were ignored and the borders of divided Pakistan were drawn to include most Muslims. The Republic of India is a predominantly Hindu nation.

The division satisfied neither the Muslims nor the Hindus. Warfare broke out and many lives were lost. Tensions still exist between the two nations which might have shared the natural borders and ethnic diversity of the region. Instead, time, effort, and money has been devoted to military actions. This has prevented the Republic of India from being as significant a world power as its size suggests it could be.

6. The title that best expresses the main idea or subject of this selection is:
   (A) India
   (B) Muslims and Hindus
   (C) Races of India
   (D) Division of the Subcontinent
   (E) Pakistan

7. The Himalayas are
   (A) mountains
   (B) hills
   (C) a plateau
   (D) India's border
   (E) Pakistan's border

8. A fact stated by the writer about Pakistan is that
   (A) it has no mountains
   (B) the nation is divided into two parts
   (C) it is one of the largest nations in the world
   (D) it juts into the sea
   (E) the people are Hindus

9. The Indian subcontinent
   (A) is hilly
   (B) is overcrowded
   (C) juts into the Indian Ocean
   (D) is attached to Africa
   (E) contains one nation

10. The Republic of India has
    (A) all Australoids
    (B) mainly Hindus
    (C) more Muslims than Hindus
    (D) mainly Muslims
    (E) equal numbers of Hindus and Muslims

11. Pakistan and India were
    (A) separated according to natural borders
    (B) ancient nations
    (C) separated by the British to keep them weak
    (D) divided on ethnic grounds
    (E) divided by themselves on religious lines

Freedom of the press is often taken for granted in our nation. It is hard for Americans to realize that in many countries, publishers and writers are not always allowed to criticize and comment upon the way the country is run. We are so used to reading different opinions and to hearing praise or criticism of our government quoted from newspapers we do not recall that it was not always this way.

In colonial days there were few newspapers. People read them with care as they were almost the only source of news. Colonial governors realized how important the newspapers were in forming opinions. They often wished to suppress or prevent stories from appearing. The governors did not like to be criticized but such criticism is essential to democracy.

One governor who tried to control the press was Governor Cosby in New York. John Peter Zenger published in his paper, the *Weekly Journal,* criticism of the Governor. Zenger was arrested. The Governor stated Zenger was printing lies. Zenger's lawyer, Alexander Hamilton, at the trial in 1735 proved to the jury's satisfaction that Zenger was speaking and writing the truth. The spectators at the trial cheered this decision which is the basic decision establishing freedom of the press in our country.

12. The title that best expresses the main idea or subject of this selection is:
    (A) Colonial Newspapers
    (B) Governor Cosby's Attack
    (C) Freedom of the Press
    (D) John Peter Zenger
    (E) The Trial

13. John Peter Zenger was arrested for
    (A) telling lies
    (B) writing stories about New York
    (C) criticizing Governor Cosby
    (D) printing the *Weekly Journal*
    (E) writing Alexander Hamilton

14. The author of the selection believes that
    (A) Zenger was wrong
    (B) many Americans take freedom of the press for granted
    (C) colonial newspapers were poor
    (D) Governor Cosby was right
    (E) many countries have freedom of the press

15. The trial of Zenger established the
    (A) basis of the freedom of the press in America
    (B) reputation of the *Weekly Journal*
    (C) reputation of Alexander Hamilton
    (D) importance of Governor Cosby
    (E) role of juries in trials

The regular unit of European life in the Middle Ages was not the city or the open farmstead. It was the feudal castle—a fortification situated if possible upon a lofty hill, and often with a little village of the crude huts of the lord's peasants clustered close beside it. During the earlier feudal period the castle in most cases would be simply a single huge tower, round or square, with merely a crude palisade and a ditch for outworks. The height would baffle any scaling-ladder. There would be no opening in its blank masonry until a considerable distance from the ground. Then the narrow door would be entered only by a flimsy wooden bridge, easy to demolish, or by a frail ladder, drawn up every night. Inside the tower there would be a series of dark, cavernous rooms, one above another, communicating by means of ladders. The sole purpose of such a comfortless castle was defense, and that defense by mere height and mass, not by any special skill in arranging the various parts.

Little by little this simple donjon became more complicated. The original tower was kept, but enclosed by other lines of defense. To force the outer barriers meant simply that you had a far stronger inner bulwark before you. The best kind of medieval castle needed only a very small number of soldiers. From behind its walls even an inferior baron could protect himself from a kingly army.

16. European life in medieval times centered around the
    (A) king's army
    (B) farm
    (C) city
    (D) castle
    (E) peasant village

17. The most important part of the fortifications was the
    (A) palisade
    (B) ditch
    (C) tower
    (D) drawbridge
    (E) hill

18. The chief value of the castle was
    (A) strategy in attack
    (B) a good view
    (C) simple defense
    (D) warmth
    (E) comfortable living

19. To defend a well-built castle the lord needed a
    (A) small group of soldiers
    (B) kingly arms
    (C) peasant family
    (D) great deal of skill
    (E) more complicated system

20. A true statement about the medieval castle is that
    (A) a hill was its ideal situation
    (B) the peasants lived in the tower
    (C) its innermost fortifications were its weakest parts
    (D) it was entered through a wide door
    (E) it was made completely of wood

EXAM 2

> DIRECTIONS: Carefully read each passage below, and then answer the questions that follow. Select the choice that, on the basis of the passage, best answers the question. Then circle the letter that corresponds to the correct answer.

Money has now become so important that we often lose sight of what lies behind it. The usual way to regain our focus is to ask a question like this: "If you were without food on a desert island with no chance of rescue for a long time and had to choose between a million dollars in gold or a fifty-pound Wisconsin cheese, which would you take?" I think it is extremely necessary to see clearly and simply what lies behind the dollars. I doubt if we can solve our financial problems unless we see the people, the land, the machines, the houses, the freight cars, the loaves of bread which alone give dollars any meaning. In the long run it is human labor, capital investment, raw materials, mechanical energy and scientific knowledge which form the chief parts of the economic machine.

1. The phrase that best expresses the main idea or subject of this selection is:
   (A) Solving our financial problems
   (B) The real meaning of dollars
   (C) Wisconsin cheese
   (D) Money and the machine
   (E) Living on a desert island

2. The author suggests that if one were away from civilization
   (A) money would be the most important possession
   (B) one would miss the economic machine
   (C) food would be of greater value than money
   (D) it would be necessary to solve financial problems
   (E) human labor would be unnecessary

You may think that totem poles were some sort of strange idol used in religious services. That is not true. Among the Pacific Coast Native Americans totem poles were like the coats-of-arms used by medieval knights in Europe. Each figure carved on the wooden pole had some meaning. It stood for a title held by the owner or for some family connection of the chief. The Native Americans raised their totem poles in front of their houses. To them they were very natural and did not seem strange at all. The totem pole was part of their life and everyone in the village understood what it meant.

3. Totem poles are similar to
   (A) coats-of-arms
   (B) religious symbols
   (C) idols
   (D) medieval knights
   (E) a title

4. The figures on the totem pole were
   (A) scratched
   (B) grotesque
   (C) carved
   (D) colored blue
   (E) Indians

5. The story assumes that things that are not familiar to us often appear
   (A) unappealing
   (B) strange
   (C) European
   (D) medieval
   (E) forbidding

Liberia, the tiny republic on the west coast of Africa, has long been of interest to the United States. This is partly because it was founded as a sovereign state by little bands of freed slaves from the United States and the West Indies who settled there over a century ago, and partly because of its fast-developing rubber plantations.

Only slightly larger than Ohio, Liberia is unique in that it is the only part of the African continent remaining in black hands and under black control. Its name refers to the new-found liberation of the former slaves who colonized its shores, and whose descendants today rule the little nation. Besides some 2,000,000 primitive natives who live in the tropical inland areas, there are about 70,000 civilized inhabitants with a standard of living patterned after that of the United States or Europe. Only blacks may be citizens of Liberia.

Although tiny, Liberia is of some military importance. It has no good ports, but its capital, Monrovia (named for President Monroe), is practically next door to the great British naval base at Freetown. Liberia exports some $3,000,000 worth of crude rubber annually.

6. The phrase that best expresses the main idea or subject of this selection is:
   (A) Rubber from Liberia
   (B) The west coast of Africa
   (C) Descendants of the slaves
   (D) A black republic
   (E) A colony of the United States

7. Liberia was settled
   (A) before the United States
   (B) twenty-five years ago
   (C) more than one hundred years ago
   (D) about eighty years ago
   (E) two hundred years ago

8. The name "Liberia" was chosen because
   (A) it described the small size of the country
   (B) the founders had recently been freed from slavery
   (C) the United States was interested in it
   (D) rubber was an important crop
   (E) President Monroe suggested it

9. The citizens of Liberia are
   (A) of many races
   (B) American slaves
   (C) all blacks
   (D) British subjects
   (E) mostly civilized inhabitants

10. From the selection we may conclude that
    (A) Liberia has no military importance
    (B) the Liberian landscape is similar to that of Ohio
    (C) the seaports of Liberia are exceptionally good
    (D) the United States has had no influence on Liberia
    (E) Liberia is important for its export of rubber

It was none too soon that a national forest should bear the name of Gifford Pinchot, and it was appropriate that the forest selected for this honor was the Columbia National Forest on the slopes of the Cascade Range in Washington. This national forest was originally established and named when Clifford Pinchot was Chief of the United States Forest Service, and its administration was begun under his direction. In June of 1949, President Truman signed a proclamation officially changing the name to Gifford Pinchot National Forest, and in October the million and one-quarter acres were officially dedicated when the Society of American Foresters held its annual meeting in Seattle. Mr. Pinchot was born in the greatest era of waste of national resources in our country's history. And he chose a profession then almost unknown in America—forestry. As the country's first "consulting forester" he discovered, however, that there were many who felt some concern for the future of our forest resources. In 1898 Mr. Pinchot became Chief of the Division of Forestry in the Department of Agriculture; in 1900 he helped organize the Society of American Foresters; in 1905 he became Chief of the new United States Forest Service and took over the administration of the forest reserves of the public domain. The rest of his life was devoted to public service, with conservation ever foremost in his mind. No memorial to his contribution could be more appropriate than a great forest of green and growing trees.

11. The phrase that best expresses the main idea or subject of this selection is:
    (A) The boyhood of Gifford Pinchot
    (B) A memorial to a great conservationist
    (C) The United States Forest Service
    (D) The importance of our national forests
    (E) The waste of natural resources

12. It was appropriate to name this forest after Mr. Pinchot because
    (A) it is more beautiful than any other forest in the country
    (B) it is the only national forest
    (C) it is the one Mr. Pinchot wanted
    (D) it is one of those forests he supervised when they first became national forests
    (E) it is in the state of Washington

13. Mr. Pinchot devoted his life to
    (A) satisfying his own selfish desires
    (B) serving the public in the field of forestry
    (C) withdrawing from public contact
    (D) choosing a suitable memorial
    (E) encouraging lumbermen

14. The author of the selection shows clearly that he
    (A) admires the work that Mr. Pinchot did
    (B) does not approve of changing the names of forests
    (C) thinks the need for conservation is overrated
    (D) is himself a "consulting forester"
    (E) was a close friend of Gifford Pinchot

EXAM 3

DIRECTIONS: Carefully read each passage below and then answer the questions that follow. Select the choice that, on the basis of the passage, best answers the question. Then circle the letter that corresponds to the correct answer.

The Gulf Stream, which runs like a friendly blue river across the cold, green Atlantic Ocean, is one of the mightiest powers in the world. By comparison, the Mississippi and the mighty Amazon are but small rivers. Two million tons of coal burned every minute would not equal the heat that the Stream gives forth in its Atlantic cross-ing. Without the Stream's warmth England's pleasant green countryside would be as cold as Labrador, which is no farther north than England. If this "river of blue" were cooled as much as 15 degrees, England, Scandinavia, northern France and Germany would probably become a region for the Eskimos.

The general course of the blue river has never been known to change. From Florida north the Stream follows the curve of the coast but stays well away from the shore. When the warm waters meet the icy Labrador currents, the Stream loses some speed and heat, but even with icebergs at its margin it stays warm enough for tropical sea life.

As the Stream nears Europe it divides north and south. The northern drift mixes with the Arctic Ocean. The southern drift comes again into the path of Africa's hot trade winds, and the waters hurry back to the Gulf of Mexico, gathering again their store of heat. The complete course of the Stream, therefore, is like a tremendous 12,000-mile whirlpool.

Scientists think that it takes three years for the Stream to make a complete trip. Their belief is based on the courses of bottles that have been thrown into the Stream to drift. These bottles contain papers, printed in many languages, requesting the finders to note the places and dates of finding and mail them back. Government experts on ocean currents have records of thousands of these "bottle papers."

Other oceans have such currents. In the North Pacific, for example, the Japanese Current makes the climate of coastal Alaska and our west coast moderate. Science is still not satisfied with what it knows about these currents. But for most of us it is enough to know that the Gulf Stream and similar currents give warmth to countries that would otherwise be very cold indeed.

1. The phrase that best expresses the main idea or subject of this selection is:
    (A) Interesting facts about the Gulf Stream
    (B) Currents similar to the Gulf Stream
    (C) What Florida owes to the Gulf Stream
    (D) Scientific experiments on the Gulf Stream
    (E) Tropical sea life in the Gulf Stream

2. The water in the Gulf Stream is
   (A) cold and green
   (B) coal-colored
   (C) icy and blue
   (D) warm and blue
   (E) pleasantly green

3. The effect of the Gulf Stream on England is to
   (A) cool the air pleasantly
   (B) make possible the green country-side
   (C) make necessary the burning of two million tons of coal
   (D) cool England's rivers 15 degrees
   (E) make England a region for Eskimos

4. The number of miles covered by the waters of the Gulf Stream is
   (A) considerably different each year
   (B) about 100 billion
   (C) about 12 thousand
   (D) undetermined
   (E) about 2 million

5. Scientists have used papers in bottles to determine the number of
   (A) languages spoken along the course of the Gulf Stream
   (B) people who are alert to such things
   (C) government experts on ocean currents
   (D) beliefs about the course of the bottles
   (E) years needed for the Gulf Stream to make a complete round trip

6. The author says that a person who finds one of the bottles is asked to tell
   (A) his name and birth date
   (B) where and when the bottle was found
   (C) how many languages he speaks
   (D) how many other bottles he has found
   (E) how far he was from home at the time

7. Many countries should be thankful to the Gulf Stream and similar currents for
   (A) cool summers
   (B) moderate climates
   (C) thousands of specific records
   (D) scientific progress
   (E) trade winds

8. Scientists believe that
   (A) their knowledge of these currents is complete
   (B) these currents are of little use
   (C) they need to know more about these currents
   (D) only one ocean has such a current as the Gulf Stream
   (E) their "bottle papers" have not been useful

Tom Sawyer said to himself that it was not such a hollow world after all. He had discovered a great law of human action without knowing it—namely, that in order to make a man or boy desire a thing it is only necessary to make the thing difficult to attain. If he had been a great and wise philosopher, he would now have understood that work consists of whatever a body is obliged to do, and that play consists of whatever a body is not obliged to do. And this would help him to understand why constructing artificial flowers or performing on a treadmill is work, while rolling tenpins or climbing Mont Blanc is only amusement. There are wealthy men in England who drive four-horse passenger coaches 20 or 30 miles on a daily line in the summer, because the privilege costs them considerable money; but if they were offered wages for the service, that would turn it into work, and then they would resign.

9. The "law of human action" discovered by Tom could be stated as follows: A man wants most that which
   (A) he already has
   (B) he is obliged to do
   (C) he cannot easily attain
   (D) no one else likes
   (E) he can get for nothing

10. According to the author, play consists of
    (A) the things a person does of his own free will
    (B) the things a person has to do
    (C) jobs such as working a treadmill
    (D) the things that make this a hollow world
    (E) tasks done for wages

11. A man who does such a thing as drive a coach for amusement would resign if offered wages for the activity because
    (A) he doesn't want to earn money
    (B) it is a dangerous activity
    (C) he would lose money
    (D) he doesn't have time
    (E) the activity would then become work

Many people know that Ben Franklin's kite experiment helped to prove that lightning is electricity. Kites have been used for scientific purposes since the middle 1700s—for testing weather conditions, taking aerial photographs, and so on. They have also been employed in many interesting ways during wartime. Centuries ago, a Korean general sent a kite, with a line attached, to the opposite bank of a river. A cable followed the line, forming the nucleus from which a bridge was built. The Japanese developed a man-carrying kite, invaluable in scouting the enemy's position. Many armies used to employ kites for signaling purposes. Now some airplane lifeboats are equipped with kites carrying radio antennas which automatically signal S.O.S.

12. The phrase below that best expresses the main idea or subject of this selection is:
    (A) Kite making as a hobby
    (B) Methods of signaling
    (C) Uses of kites through the years
    (D) Our debt to Ben Franklin
    (E) Wartime use of kites

13. The author tells us that the Japanese used kites for
    (A) photography
    (B) scouting
    (C) radio signaling
    (D) scientific studies
    (E) weather predicting

14. The most recent use of kites mentioned is carrying
    (A) bridge cables
    (B) soldiers
    (C) photographers
    (D) electricity
    (E) radio antennas

On the whole the Inuit are a coastal people. Their total number is not more than 35,000. Of these about 14,500 live along the coast of Greenland. Inuit settlements are scattered along the northern coast of North America from Labrador to Alaska's Panhandle. On Baffin Island and on other large islands there are Inuit villages. The Inuit spend most of their time near the sea and get much of their living from the sea. However, one tribe, the Caribou Inuit, live inland west of Hudson Bay. Some of them have never seen the sea.

Although life in one village is, in many ways, very much like life in another, there are some differences. The reason is that the Inuit must use what they find in the particular district where they live. The Copper Inuit who live beside Coronation Gulf build thick-walled winter houses of snow blocks. Alaskan Inuit do not use such houses and most of them have never even seen one. Their winter homes are made of turf and mud. The Inuit of southern Greenland are expert in handling a kayak, or Inuit canoe. They fish in the open water of the sea. The Inuit of northern Greenland have little chance to use kayaks because the water along the coast is frozen almost all the year. All tribes, however, have one thing in common. They are primarily fishermen and hunters.

15. The phrase below that best expresses the main idea or subject of this selection is:
    (A) The Caribou Inuit
    (B) The Inuit
    (C) Inuit fishing
    (D) Inuit homes
    (E) The Copper Inuit

16. Most Inuit live
    (A) near the water
    (B) on the plains
    (C) in the forests
    (D) inland
    (E) on islands

17. The Caribou Inuit are
    (A) from the coast of Greenland
    (B) not hunters and fishermen
    (C) scattered along the coast of North America
    (D) not coastal people
    (E) skilled at gaining their living from the sea

18. A comparison of different Inuit villages shows that the way of life in each
    (A) is quite similar to that in the others
    (B) is very unlike that in the others
    (C) has nothing to do with the location
    (D) is very civilized
    (E) is much like our own way of life

19. Alaskan Inuit make their winter homes of
    (A) snow blocks
    (B) skins and furs
    (C) wood
    (D) turf and mud
    (E) stones

20. A kayak is a kind of
    (A) sled
    (B) house
    (C) boat
    (D) animal
    (E) spear

21. All Inuit tribes
    (A) are skilled in the use of the kayak
    (B) hunt and fish for a living
    (C) make homes of snow blocks
    (D) live in Greenland
    (E) depend on the ocean for a living

EXAM 4

DIRECTIONS: Carefully read each passage below, and then answer the questions that follow. Select the choice that, on the basis of the passages, best answers the question. Then circle the letter that corresponds to the correct answer.

Education was free. That subject my father had written about repeatedly, as comprising his chief hope for us children, the essence of American opportunity, the treasure that no thief could touch, not even misfortune or poverty. It was the one thing he was able to promise us when he sent for us, more sure, safer than bread or shelter. On our second day I was thrilled with the realization of what this freedom of education meant. A little girl from across the alley came and offered to conduct us to school. My father was out, but we five among us had a few words of English by this time. We knew the word _school_. We understood. This child, who had never seen us till yesterday, who could not pronounce our names, who was not much better dressed that we, was able to offer us the freedom of the schools of Boston! The doors stood open for every one of us. The smallest child could show us the way. This incident impressed me more than anything I had heard in advance about the freedom of education in America. It was a concrete proof—almost the thing itself. One had to experience it to understand it.

1. The phrase below that best expresses the main idea or subject of this selection is:
   (A) My first day in America
   (B) The schools of Boston
   (C) My father's education
   (D) Our greatest opportunity in America
   (E) The little girl next door

2. When the father sent for his children, the only thing he could surely promise them was
   (A) bread
   (B) friends
   (C) shelter
   (D) schooling
   (E) wealth

3. The father believed that
   (A) he should have stayed in Europe
   (B) education was not worth while
   (C) the children could not learn English
   (D) he would always live in poverty
   (E) education was one possession that could not be stolen

4. The word *school*
   (A) was unknown to the children
   (B) frightened the children
   (C) was one of the first English words the children had learned
   (D) reminded the children of unhappy days in Europe
   (E) was difficult for the children to understand

5. The children fully realized the meaning of their father's words when they discovered that
   (A) the little girl across the way had better clothes than they did
   (B) they could not understand the little girl
   (C) the Boston schools didn't want them
   (D) in America even a little girl could take them to school
   (E) the little girl could not pronounce their names

High in the Swiss Alps long years ago, there lived a lonely shepherd boy who longed for a friend to share his vigils. One night, he beheld three wrinkled old men, each holding a glass. The first said: "Drink this liquid and you shall be victorious in battle."

The second said: "Drink this liquid and you shall have countless riches."

The last man said: "I offer you the happiness of music—the alphorn."

The boy chose the third glass. Next day, he came upon a great horn, ten feet in length. When he put his lips to it, a beautiful melody floated across the valley. He had found a friend.

So goes the legend of the alphorn's origin. Known in the ninth century, the alphorn was used by herdsmen to call cattle, for the deep tones echoed across the mountainsides. And even today, on, a quiet summer evening, its music can be heard floating among the peaks.

6. The story tells us that of the three old men, the one whose glass the boy chose was the
   (A) smallest in size
   (B) most wrinkled
   (C) first to speak
   (D) oldest
   (E) last to speak

7. One liquid offered to the boy would have brought him
   (A) defeat in battle
   (B) great wealth
   (C) lonely vigils
   (D) another boy to help him
   (E) three wishes

8. To the boy, the alphorn
   (A) seemed too heavy to play
   (B) seemed like a real friend
   (C) brought unhappiness
   (D) sounded unpleasant
   (E) brought great riches

9. The practical use of the alphorn is to
   (A) summon the three old men
   (B) make friends
   (C) call cattle
   (D) give summer concerts
   (E) tell the legends of the Alps

The region that lies between the Tigris and Euphrates Rivers was once a rich and flourishing land. The people built great cities such as Ur and Babylon. They established government and the world's first empires grew up in the region. They developed fine arts and some of the gold cups and jewelry from the area are as beautiful as any ever made. Agriculture was highly developed with extensive and complex irrigation systems. The reign of Hammurabi (often dated at around 1750 B.C. but historians differ on the exact date of his reign) was one of the high points of ancient civilization.

But all of this changed. The decline was gradual, and the reasons offered are many. Among them are climatic changes brought about by such geological events as the change in size of the ice cap at the North Pole. Another suggested reason is the way the people treated their environment. They cut down the forests outside the cities thus exposing the land to eroding rains at certain seasons, and to the rapid runoff of water which lowers the underground water level. They may also have overgrazed the grasslands. A third suggestion is the action or raids of enemy groups which wrecked or blocked the irrigation canals. These canals were the basis of survival for the society.

The food needed by the many city dwellers could only be supplied if the canals were working. If the farmers had to spend their time repairing the canals, they could not grow food and the city population starved or left the cities. Thus the level of civilization declined. The land was left without trees and open to erosion. With little demand for food from cities, farmers took little care of the land.

10. Agriculture in the age of Hammurabi was highly developed with
    (A) extensive irrigation
    (B) use of horses
    (C) steel plows
    (D) priests running the farms
    (E) control by the King

11. Historians differ about the exact date of Hammurabi's reign but the author suggests as a date
    (A) around 2000 B.C.
    (B) the second millennium
    (C) 1750
    (D) around 1750 B.C.
    (E) around 1750 A.D.

12. The region described lies between the Tigris and the
    (A) Nile
    (B) Euphrates
    (C) Danube
    (D) Congo
    (E) Euhate

13. When forests were cut down, the land in this region was exposed to
    (A) eroding rains
    (B) sunshine
    (C) irrigation
    (D) enemy raids
    (E) the plow

14. With the decline of the city population the author suggests the farmers took
    (A) advantage of the people
    (B) little care of the land
    (C) the chance to buy city homes
    (D) over the canals
    (E) the grazing areas

15. One possible geological explanation of the change in fertility of the region described is due to the
    (A) rainfall
    (B) level of the rivers
    (C) river flooding
    (D) ice cap size
    (E) erosion

The word *atom* has captured the human imagination. In addition to atomic bombs and atomic energy, we see signs advertising products with names such as "atomic-energized gasoline." Who invented the word *atom,* and what does it mean?

The inventor was a Greek philosopher named Democritus, who lived about 400 B.C. Even then, Greek physicists were wondering about the structure of matter. Democritus suggested that matter is not what it seems—a continuous mass of material. He thought that matter could be broken up into finer and finer parts until finally it could be broken no further. These basic particles he called atoms, something which could not be cut or divided.

We can see for ourselves that Democritus did have a good idea. When a teaspoonful of sugar is put into a cup of coffee, the sugar dissolves and disappears. If coffee—or water—were solid and continuous, there would be no room for the sugar. But since the sugar does disappear, we must conclude that the water and sugar are both made up of tiny particles with spaces between them. The sugar particles slip into the spaces between the water particles.

In one way, however, we have come to disagree with Democritus. Following his lead, for hundreds of years men thought of atoms as solid little bits of matter. Newton spoke of them as being "so very hard as never to wear or break into pieces." John Dalton, an English chemist, in 1807 called atoms "indivisible, eternal and indestructible."

Today we know that atoms are not solid and not indestructible. We now think of an atom as a miniature solar system, with a central nucleus or "sun" around which tiny particles revolve.

16. The word *atom* was first used by
    (A) an English chemist
    (B) a Greek philosopher
    (C) an American scientist
    (D) an advertising writer
    (E) a Greek physician

17. The author indicates that Democritus' theory of the atom was
    (A) partly right
    (B) completely wrong
    (C) never accepted by others
    (D) too imaginative
    (E) contradicted by Dalton's theory

18. Sugar is believed to dissolve in water because
    (A) the water is solid and continuous
    (B) the sugar is solid and continuous
    (C) they are both solid and continuous
    (D) only a teaspoonful is used
    (E) there is room for sugar particles between the water particles

19. For centuries men believed that atoms
    (A) were destructive
    (B) had revolving parts
    (C) were really unimportant
    (D) could not be divided
    (E) were like sugar particles

20. An atom can be compared to a solar system because an atom
    (A) is round
    (B) is unbreakable
    (C) has particles revolving around a center
    (D) is "indivisible, eternal and indestructible"
    (E) is a continuous mass of material

EXAM 5

DIRECTIONS: Carefully read each passage below, and then answer the questions that follow. Select the choice that, on the basis of the passage, best answers the question. Then circle the letter that corresponds to the correct answer.

One of the most fascinating questions of technology is how the great pyramids of Egypt were built. These great tombs of the Old Kingdom Pharaohs still stand as monuments to a civilization that many people think of as primitive. They were built without electricity, internal combustion engines, cranes, bulldozers, or any of the many machines used by men today. The builders did not attend engineering schools and not one of them knew calculus or modern mathematics. How could such huge monuments—for the pyramid of Pharaoh Cheops (also spelled in English, Khufu or Kheops) is twice as high as the capitol in Washington and covers thirteen acres—have been built?

For many years scholars believed that the pyramids were built by slaves working in the hot sun under harsh slave drivers. Plans were drawn showing how ramps of sand built around the pyramid would allow the slaves, using log rollers, to pull the two and a half ton stone blocks up to their location. Archaeologists have found the remains of dwellings around the pyramids where scholars suggested the slaves lived.

Recently, the slave theory has been questioned. The numbers that would be required, the amount of earth that would have to be moved to build ramps, and the difficulty of getting the top stone in place present problems. Also, the source of so many slaves is debated since there is little evidence of international warfare at the time.

A new theory suggests that the builders worked in the flood season when they could not farm. They worked voluntarily for the Pharaoh in return for food and shelter in the dwellings around the pyramids. Instead of ramps on which to pull the stones, it is now suggested the Egyptians used simple machines employing levers and weights. Such devices are still used in Egypt to raise water for irrigation from one level to the next. It is possible that with such simple technology and a small number of workers, the great pyramids of Egypt were built.

1. The pyramids were built as
   (A) training exercises in technology
   (B) tombs
   (C) capitols
   (D) slave quarters
   (E) monuments

2. Some scholars believed that the pyramids were built by slaves using
   (A) ramps of sand
   (B) bulldozers
   (C) floods
   (D) calculus
   (E) slave drivers

3. A new theory suggests the pyramids were built using
   (A) slaves
   (B) simple machines employing levers and weights
   (C) food and shelter
   (D) simple machines
   (E) the flood season

4. Compared with the capitol at Washington the pyramid of Pharaoh Cheops is
   (A) similar to the capitol
   (B) has more tourists
   (C) was built later
   (D) twice as high
   (E) built of larger stones

The famous Pony Express started at St. Joseph, Missouri, and followed the Oregon and California trail for the most part, with many short cuts because mountain-bred horses, sure-footed as goats, could travel where no stagecoach could go. It ended at Sacramento, California where a river steamer carried the mail on to San Francisco. Post stations were built along the trail at intervals of about 70 miles in open country, or 35 miles in the mountains. Each station was provided with food, shelter, a corral of horses, and two keepers. Between post stations, at intervals of about ten miles (which is as far as they wished their horses to run at high speed) were several relay stations, each with a keeper and a few extra horses, one of which was always saddled and ready to run.

Coming with a rush into the relay station, the post rider would swing down from his lathered mount, swing up on a fresh horse with his precious *mochila* (saddle bag), and be off without a moment's delay. He was expected to reach the next post station on time, and he did it or died trying. More than one rider came at dawn or dusk to find the post station burned, its keepers killed, its horses run off by Indians; and in that case he had to keep on to the next station without food or rest. The longest continuous run, 384 miles, was made by "Buffalo Bill," then a boy of 18; the fastest by Jim Moore, another youngster, who rode 280 miles in 22 hours.

Ninety riders were running the long trail at all hours of the day or night, often taking their lives in their hands to get the mail through within the time limit set for the run. Ten days was the time set, but the job was regularly done in eight. The average speed was eleven miles an hour, which was fast in a region where at one hour a horse might run his best and the next hour be swimming a river or cat-footing along a trail where a misstep meant death for horse and rider.

This daring Pony Express ran for less than two years; it ended in 1861, when a telegraph line offered a swifter means of communication.

5. The Pony Express ran between
   (A) St. Joseph and San Francisco
   (B) Oregon and California
   (C) St. Joseph and Sacramento
   (D) Sacramento and San Francisco
   (E) St. Joseph and Oregon

6. The greatest distance between post stations along the Pony Express run was about
   (A) 10 miles
   (B) 35 miles
   (C) 50 miles
   (D) 70 miles
   (E) 105 miles

7. The principal duty of a keeper of a relay station was to
   (A) guard the mail pouches
   (B) prepare meals
   (C) hunt Indians
   (D) plan short cuts for riders
   (E) have a horse ready for an incoming rider

8. The Pony Express riders waited at relay stations only long enough to
   (A) allow a stagecoach to pass
   (B) get a fresh mount
   (C) catch a few hours' sleep
   (D) escape thieving Indians
   (E) sort the mail

9. From this passage it would seem that most of the riders were
   (A) surefooted
   (B) faithful to duty
   (C) middle-aged
   (D) mountain-bred
   (E) carefree

10. A Californian sending mail by Pony Express could expect his mail to reach the eastern end of the run
    (A) within 22 hours
    (B) between dawn and dusk
    (C) within 10 days
    (D) in about a month
    (E) in about 90 days

11. The Pony Express ended in 1861 because
    (A) messages could be sent more quickly by wire
    (B) fast horses had become scarce
    (C) riders would not work under such conditions
    (D) river boats had come into wider use
    (E) so many stations had been attacked by Indians

One of America's famous and interesting shrines is the National Baseball Hall of Fame and Museum located in the village of Cooperstown, New York, also celebrated as the home of James Fenimore Cooper, the novelist. Dedicated in 1939, the building attracts thousands of visitors who come from far and wide each year to see the birthplace and mementos of "America's national pastime." Cooperstown was chosen as the site of this museum because baseball is said to have been originated there by General Abner Doubleday in 1839 when he was a student at a military academy.

The museum houses a collection of baseball relics that are the delight of all sports lovers. Here also can be found the names and pictures—as well as some of the equipment they used—of the "Immortals" who have been elected to the Baseball Hall of Fame by the nation's sportswriters. One of the interesting displays, the locker of former Yankee great, Lou Gehrig, holds his old uniform and some of the playing equipment used when he gained his fame as baseball's "iron man." Another popular attraction is an exhibit of duplicates of the diamond rings awarded annually to World Series participants.

The accomplishments of such classic heroes as Babe Ruth, Cy Young, Ty Cobb, Christy Matthewson, and Lou Gehrig will live on forever in this popular shrine, which is a sanctuary for thousands of budding young athletes.

12. Cooperstown was chosen as the site of a baseball museum because
    (A) sportswriters had selected it
    (B) baseball is said to have originated there
    (C) World Series trophies are on display there
    (D) James Fenimore Cooper had lived there
    (E) several baseball "Immortals" had been born there

13. The baseball museum was first opened to the public about
    (A) three years ago
    (B) twenty-five years ago
    (C) a half century ago
    (D) sixty years ago
    (E) over a hundred years ago

14. Baseball is said to have been originated by a
    (A) sportswriter
    (B) novelist
    (C) former Yankee player
    (D) military student
    (E) group of sportswriters

15. Baseball's "iron man" was
    (A) Babe Ruth
    (E) Ty Cobb
    (C) Abner Doubleday
    (D) Cy Young
    (E) Lou Gehrig

Milk is a suspension of nourishing materials in water, which constitutes about 86 percent of the total weight. The total 14 percent of nutrient solids consist of the following: milk sugar, 5 percent; fat, about 4 percent; protein just a fraction less than that; and finally minerals and vitamins. It can readily be seen that milk is a kind of natural combination containing most of the body's requirements for growth and health. What is unique about milk is its richness in minerals and vitamins. Fat, sugar, and protein can come from other sources, but the vitamin A and the minerals of milk cannot be easily obtained elsewhere. It is also rich in the vitamin B group so urgently needed for health. Calcium and phosphorus are two minerals contained in milk that are of primary importance. These minerals are essential for normal development and maintenance of bones and teeth. Not only is milk rich in bone-forming calcium and phosphorus but also it carries them in a form that is much more readily assimilated than the same minerals found in vegetables. Yet it is fortunate for us that we do not have to subsist on milk alone. Milk does not supply the body with the iron needed to prevent anemia. Milk also lacks vitamin D, although sunshine easily compensates for that shortage. Under our conditions of preparing milk, it also lacks vitamin C, which is the antiscurvy vitamin of many fruits and vegetables. Cream and butter contain the fat of the milk, while cheese contains its solidified protein plus some fat, its vitamin A, and some minerals. We also have, of course, the concentrated forms of milk, such as evaporated, condensed, and powdered. These are whole-milk equivalents minus some or all of the water.

16. The phrase that best expresses the main idea or subject of this selection is:
    (A) A history of milk
    (B) The sources of milk
    (C) Milk, a perfect food
    (D) Food values in milk
    (E) Popular milk products

17. The largest part of milk is composed of
    (A) fat
    (B) sugar
    (C) water
    (D) minerals
    (E) vitamins

18. Milk is an especially important food because
    (A) it is cheap
    (B) it is easily available
    (C) it contains so much protein
    (D) its fat content is so large
    (E) its minerals cannot be readily obtained otherwise

19. Milk is deficient in
    (A) phosphorus
    (B) iron
    (C) fat
    (D) protein
    (E) vitamin A

20. In order to have good teeth, a person should have plenty of
    (A) calcium
    (B) iron
    (C) protein
    (D) sugar
    (E) cheese

21. Sunshine is a good source of
    (A) vitamin A
    (B) vitamin C
    (C) vitamin D
    (D) phosphorus
    (E) calcium

EXAM 6

DIRECTIONS: Carefully read each passage below, and then answer the questions that follow. Select the choice that, on the basis of the passage, best answers the question. Then circle the letter that corresponds to the correct answer.

The Homestead Act was a great boon to western settlement. Two acts passed by Congress in the early 1860s were the keys to the rapid settlement of the West. The first was the Pacific Railway Act, which authorized the building of a transcontinental railroad. The route, completed in 1869, provided rapid and easy transportation westward for many settlers.

The second act, the Homestead Act, had to do with public lands; that is, land that belonged to the federal government. Before this act land was sold to settlers for as little as $1.25 per acre but each settler had to buy many acres. Thus many poor families could not afford to settle in the West. The new act stated that any head of a family could become the owner of a farm or homestead of 160 acres if he lived on it and worked the land for five years. The act made it possible for many Civil War veterans to move west and settle on their own land. Together with the Pacific Railway Act the act made it certain the West would be settled rapidly.

1. The phrase that best expresses the main idea or subject of this selection is:
   (A) Pacific Railway Act
   (B) Two acts
   (C) Homestead Act
   (D) The opening of the West
   (E) Land ownership

2. Before the Homestead Act, a settler could
   (A) not buy public land
   (B) take any homestead
   (C) not travel by railroad to the West
   (D) buy land at $1.25 an acre
   (E) own land by working it

3. The Pacific Railway Act provided for
   (A) rapid transportation
   (B) a transcontinental railroad
   (C) quick western settlement
   (D) public lands
   (E) unemployed Civil War veterans

4. Public lands are
   (A) lands owned by each state
   (B) lands used by the government
   (C) lands open to sale by the government
   (D) lands owned by the federal government
   (E) lands owned by a government

For the colonists of Portugal and Spanish America, self-government began during the period of the Napoleonic Wars. Brazil, the colony of Portugal, became a separate nation without any war of independence. The Portuguese king fled from Napoleon to Brazil. When he returned to Europe after the wars, the basis of Brazil's independent existence as a free nation was established.

The Spanish colonies had to fight for their independence in the same way the United States had done. Napoleon conquered Spain in 1808 and deposed the King, Ferdinand VII. Napoleon made his own brother King of Spain. When this happened, Spanish colonists in different areas of South America formed governing groups called juntas and declared they would rule in the name of King Ferdinand VII until he could get his throne back. In 1814 Ferdinand regained his throne in Spain but the juntas refused to give up the power they had originally seized in the name of the King. The colonists had found that their independence gave them advantages they did not wish to give up. They were able to trade freely with England and the United States. They were no longer under the rule of Spanish nobles sent out by the King as governors. These nobles often ruled badly and took advantage of the colonists. Finally, the non-Spanish inhabitants believed they would have more rights if they were not ruled by nobles from Spain.

King Ferdinand sent troops to help his appointed governors reestablish their authority. The result was a war for independence that lasted ten years. By 1824 the brilliant military leadership of Simón Bolívar and José de San Martín had freed all of the Spanish territory in South America from the rule of the Spanish King. Only three small areas in northeastern South America were not self-governing. These three areas, ruled by the English, French, and Dutch, finally gained their independence after World War II.

5. The phrase that best expresses the main idea or subject of this selection is:
   (A) Origin of self-government in South America
   (B) Bolívar and San Martín
   (C) King Ferdinand VII
   (D) Reasons for South American Wars of Independence
   (E) Spanish self-government

6. Napoleon deposed
(A) San Martín
(B) his brother
(C) King Frederick VI
(D) Frederick the Great
(E) the King of Spain

7. The Spanish colonists in South America began their war of independence in
(A) 1814
(B) 1824
(C) 1808
(D) 1945
(E) 1834

8. Simón Bolívar and José de San Martín were
(A) Spanish nobles
(B) advisers to the King
(C) outlaws
(D) military leaders
(E) Brazilians

9. A junta is
(A) a committee
(B) a group formed to govern
(C) a Spanish word
(D) a military group
(E) a Spanish nobleman

10. By 1824 all of South America was self-governing except for three small areas ruled by the
(A) French, English, Spanish
(B) Spanish, Brazilians, French
(C) English, French, Dutch
(D) Germans, French, Spanish
(E) English, French, Portuguese

Harriet Tubman was, perhaps, the most remarkable of many remarkable people who worked on the Underground Railroad. She was called the "Moses of her people" because she led so many slaves out of bondage just as Moses had done for his people. She had been born a slave and at 25 managed to escape. She then organized escape routes over which she led out her sisters and brothers and her parents. She led more than three hundred of her fellow slaves to freedom. Each trip was tightly organized and her word was law. The route was more important than any individual, since runaway slaves, if caught, would be tortured and they might reveal the escape patterns.

Slaveholders hated and feared Harriet Tubman. They offered $40,000 in reward money for her capture dead or alive but she was never caught. During the Civil War she served as a nurse. After the war she continually worked for rights for her people.

11. The phrase that best expresses the main idea or subject of this selection is:
(A) Harriet Tubman's escape
(B) The way to freedom
(C) Harriet Tubman and the Underground Railway
(D) The Underground Railway
(E) Moses of her people

12. Slave owners showed their feelings toward Harriet Tubman by
(A) freeing three hundred slaves
(B) offering a reward for her capture
(C) offering her a reward
(D) calling her "Moses of her people"
(E) torturing runaway slaves

13. The purpose of the Underground Railway was to
(A) give Harriet Tubman a job
(B) anger slave holders
(C) organize slaves
(D) free runaway slaves
(E) provide an escape route for slaves

From earliest times, eggs have been an important human food. The Eskimos gather the eggs of ducks that visit the Arctic in the spring. African Bushmen and Hottentots eat ostrich eggs. The eggs of sea birds are the chief and favorite native food of the Easter Islanders. Turtle eggs are eaten in South America. Eggs of fishes are considered a great delicacy. The eggs or roe of the sturgeon of the Caspian sea are salted and appear on our tables as caviar.

Since eggs must give rise to full-fledged organisms, it is not surprising that their yolks are extremely rich in minerals, such as phosphorus and particularly iron. Milk, perhaps the most valuable of protective foods, has a weak spot in its shortage of iron. Eggs have a far richer supply of iron, but they have less calcium proportionately than milk. Young chicks get their calcium from the eggshells. Eggs also have a good supply of phosphorus, which is as badly needed in the formation of bones and teeth as is calcium. So far as vitamins are concerned, eggs are about as rich and varied a source as can be found. They contain all the vitamins but C. There is an abundance of vitamin A in them and they also form an excellent source of the several components of the vitamin B group. Besides, eggs also contain the precious sunshine vitamin known as vitamin D. Their principal nutrient is protein. All of these nutrients—minerals, vitamins and proteins—make eggs an excellent protective food.

14. The phrase that best expresses the main idea or subject of this selection is:
    (A) A comparison of milk with eggs
    (B) The formation of an egg
    (C) Various kinds of eggs
    (D) Eggs as a food
    (E) Vitamins in eggs

15. Ostrich eggs form an article of diet among the
    (A) South Americans
    (B) Eskimos
    (C) Easter Islanders
    (D) Europeans
    (E) Hottentots

16. Milk as a food is deficient in
    (A) water
    (B) fat
    (C) iron
    (D) calcium
    (E) vitamins

17. The part of the egg that provides the young chicken with the needed calcium is the
    (A) white
    (B) yolk
    (C) shell
    (D) watery content
    (E) membrane lining the shell

18. Most of the food substance of the egg is composed of
    (A) proteins
    (B) fats
    (C) carbohydrates
    (D) calcium
    (E) phosphorus

19. Eggs lack vitamin
    (A) A
    (B) B_1
    (C) B_2
    (D) C
    (E) D

Were all mosquitoes males, the human race would doubtless pay them small attention, for the male mosquito's food is vegetable juice. It is only the female mosquito that has an appetite for animal blood and an apparatus for procuring it. The female mosquito's proboscis (feeding organ) is a flexible tube with a groove on the upper side. Within this groove are sheathed six needle-keen stylets with points like lancets. It is these with which the tapping of the blood streams is done. When the mosquito has discovered a good feeding-site, she presses her proboscis against it until the external sheath is bent back and the stylets are allowed to plunge into the flesh. Upon the uppermost of these piercing organs there is a tiny trough or channel through which the blood of the victim is drawn up. So tiny and quick is the mosquito's puncture that in itself it would cause no distress to human being or other animal. The distress is caused by a different operation. As she draws in the blood, she pours out also the secretion of her salivary glands—a fiercely irritant spittle which she injects deep into the wound. The purpose of this is to delay the coagulation of the blood until her feeding is completed.

20. The phrase that best expresses the central idea of this paragraph is:
    (A) The mosquito appetite
    (B) Male vs. female mosquitoes
    (C) The structure of a male mosquito
    (D) Why mosquitoes bite human beings
    (E) How a mosquito bites

21. The male mosquito lives on
    (A) dew
    (B) vegetable juice
    (C) blood
    (D) grass leaves
    (E) spittle

22. The female mosquito pierces the skin of her victim by means of her
    (A) lancets
    (B) stylets
    (C) groove
    (D) glands
    (E) sheath

23. The irritation resulting from a mosquito bite is due to
    (A) pressure of the proboscis
    (B) coagulation of the blood
    (C) puncture of the skin
    (D) sucking of the blood
    (E) injection of a liquid

Answers to All Exercises, Practice Tests, and Mastery Exams

EXERCISES

EXERCISE 1, p. 177

1. **B**; **C**; **A**; **D** ... each sentence helps to explain the germ-killing quality of the bandage.
2. **A**; **B**; **C**; **D** ... the article explains the meaning of minority and how prejudice gathers around it.
3. **B**; **A**; **C**; **D** ... the article shows the advantages of the boat to the sportsman.
4. **A**; **B**; **C**; **D** ... the article explains the three types of color blindness.
5. **A**; **B**; **D**; **C** ... the paragraph shows how the 1957 Act has affected U.S. transportation.

EXERCISE 2, p. 182

1. **A**, **B**, and **D**; **C** ...lived "in the swampy woodlands," ... walked "across the soggy terrain."
2. "Approximately 4,000 settled in the United States when the hostilities were over." **A**, **C**, and **D**; **B** ... have "settled in the United States" ... meant that fighting had ceased.
3. "Naturalists may dispute about which trees are the largest in the world." **B**; **C** or **D**; **A** ... "However, scientists agree ..."
4. **C**; **A**; **B**; selfish ... **D**.
5. "Polyethylene was a war-time product first developed in England during World War II." **A**; **C**; **D**; war-time product; **B**.

EXERCISE 3, p. 186

1. "Cousin John ... go." **C**.
2. Regardless of the reasons ... better." **B**.
3. "Jargon ... workers." **C**.
4. "This jargon ... society." **B**.
5. "Amber ... trees." **B**.
6. "The people ... person." **A**.
7. "Many inmates ... slowly." **A**.
8. "The romantic ... be." **D**.
9. "When out-of-state ... world." **B**.

EXERCISE 4, p. 192

1. **A** and **B**; **D**; **E** Venus... 5 ... Mars.
2. **A** and **B**; 93 (Earth), 141 (Mars), 67 (Venus). Closest is **E**.
3. plants ... moss ... **C**.
4. blue ... red ... **C**; wet ... **A**; red ... blue ... alkaline ... **D**; red to blue ... **B**.
5. **B**; **D**; **C**; first three sentences ... consciousness ... **A**.
6. his guard to slip for a brief second ... **B**.
7. 1812 ... **D**; (**A**) ... (**C**) 1803 ... French ... **B**.
8. Part of ... 1821; part ... state of Missouri ... (**C**).
9. tall (humorous)
10. Humor ... **C**.

PRACTICE TESTS

TEST 1, p. 179

1. **B**   2. **B**   3. **E**   4. **C**   5. **B**

TEST 2, p. 180

1. **A**   2. **B**   3. **D**   4. **C**   5. **C**

TEST 3, p. 184

1. **E**   2. **A**   3. **A**   4. **D**   5. **B**

TEST 4, p. 185

1. **C**   2. **C**   3. **C**   4. **A**   5. **A**

TEST 5, p. 188

1. **D**	2. **E**	3. **A**
4. **A**	5. **D**	6. **C**
7. **B**	8. **A**	9. **E**
10. **C**	11. **D**	12. **A**

TEST 6, p. 190

1. **C**	2. **D**
3. **A**	4. **B**
5. **C**	6. **E**
7. **B**	8. **B**
9. **E**	10. **A**

TEST 7, p. 195

1. **B**	2. **C**
3. **B**	4. **A**
5. **C**	6. **C**
7. **B**	8. **D**
9. **C**	10. **A**

TEST 8, p. 196

1. **B**	2. **D**
3. **C**	4. **A**
5. **C**	6. **D**
7. **C**	8. **D**
9. **C**	10. **C**

EXERCISE 5, p. 199

1. figurative	14. figurative
2. literal	15. figurative
3. figurative	16. literal
4. figurative	17. figurative
5. figurative	18. literal
6. literal	19. figurative
7. figurative	20. literal
8. figurative	21. figurative
9. literal	22. figurative
10. literal	23. literal
11. literal	24. figurative
12. literal	25. figurative
13. figurative	

EXERCISE 6, p. 200

1. **B**	6. **B**	11. **D**	16. **D**	21. **C**
2. **D**	7. **A**	12. **B**	17. **C**	22. **B**
3. **C**	8. **C**	13. **C**	18. **B**	23. **A**
4. **A**	9. **D**	14. **B**	19. **A**	24. **B**
5. **D**	10. **A**	15. **A**	20. **D**	25. **B**

EXERCISE 7, p. 201

1. S	11. G
2. G	12. G
3. G	13. S
4. S	14. G
5. G	15. S
6. G	16. G
7. S	17. S
8. S	18. G
9. G	19. G
10. S	20. G

EXERCISE 8, p. 202

1. **C**	6. **A**	11. **B**	16. **D**	21. **C**
2. **B**	7. **D**	12. **D**	17. **B**	22. **B**
3. **D**	8. **B**	13. **B**	18. **A**	23. **D**
4. **A**	9. **D**	14. **A**	19. **A**	24. **D**
5. **B**	10. **A**	15. **C**	20. **B**	25. **C**

EXERCISE 9, p. 203

1. **D**	4. **C**	7. **C**	10. **B**	13. **B**
2. **B**	5. **D**	8. **A**	11. **C**	14. **B**
3. **A**	6. **C**	9. **A**	12. **A**	15. **D**

EXERCISE 10, p. 204

1. **C**	5. **D**	9. **B**	13. **C**	17. **C**
2. **A**	6. **D**	10. **C**	14. **C**	18. **D**
3. **D**	7. **D**	11. **A**	15. **C**	
4. **C**	8. **B**	12. **D**	16. **B**	

EXERCISE 11, p. 205

1. F	11. F
2. O	12. O
3. F	13. O
4. F	14. F
5. O	15. F
6. F	16. O
7. F	17. O
8. O	18. O
9. F	19. F
10. F	20. O

EXERCISE 12, p. 207

1. human beings	12. urban renewal
2. underground water	13. mass communication
3. ovules	14. public education
4. first atomic bomb	15. success in life
5. airplane travel	16. powers of the President
6. school budget	
7. Supreme Court	17. inorganic compounds
8. cease-fire agreement	18. bacteria
9. crimes of violence	19. chief ideas of Hinduism
10. automation	20. official languages
11. inventions	

EXERCISE 13, p. 208

1. **B**	4. **B**	7. **B**	10. **A**	13. **D**
2. **D**	5. **D**	8. **B**	11. **D**	14. **C**
3. **B**	6. **A**	9. **D**	12. **B**	15. **D**

EXERCISE 14, p. 209

1. (A) banning
   (B) control
2. (A) short-necked
   (B) stretching
3. (A) competition
   (B) made up
4. (A) money
   (B) trading
5. (A) destroy
   (B) attacks
6. (A) equal
   (B) integration
7. (A) navigation
   (B) flows from
8. (A) modified
   (B) behavior
9. (A) troublesome
   (B) burn
10. (A) solid
    (B) flame

EXERCISE 15, p. 210

1. (A) D
   (B) M
2. (A) M
   (B) D
3. (A) D
   (B) M
4. (A) D
   (B) M
5. (A) D
   (B) M
6. (A) D
   (B) M
7. (A) D
   (B) M
8. (A) M
   (B) D
9. (A) M
   (B) D
10. (A) M
    (B) D
11. (A) M
    (B) D
12. (A) M
    (B) D
13. (A) D
    (B) M
14. (A) D
    (B) M
15. (A) D
    (B) M

EXERCISE 16, p. 211

1. (A) E
   (B) C
2. (A) E
   (B) C
3. (A) C
   (B) E
4. (A) E
   (B) C
5. (A) C
   (B) E
6. (A) E
   (B) C
7. (A) E
   (B) C
8. (A) C
   (B) E
9. (A) C
   (B) E
10. (A) C
    (B) E
11. (A) C
    (B) E
12. (A) E
    (B) C
13. (A) C
    (B) E
14. (A) C
    (B) E
15. (A) C
    (B) E

EXERCISE 17, p. 212

1. **C** 3. **D** 5. **D** 7. **C** 9. **B**
2. **D** 4. **D** 6. **B** 8. **C** 10. **B**

EXERCISE 18, p. 213

(In this exercise appropriate synonyms for the indicated answers can be acceptable for credit.)

1. (A) safety
   (B) future
2. (A) fertile
   (B) greatest
3. (A) prevent
   (B) destruction
4. (A) lessened
   (B) cool
5. (A) tools*
   (B) weapons*
6. (A) stop
   (B) seizing
7. (A) accustomed
   (B) advance
8. (A) end
   (B) settling
9. (A) admired
   (B) faded
10. (A) head
    (B) authority
11. (A) developed
    (B) construction
12. (A) excessive
    (B) problem
13. (A) pollution
    (B) irreplaceable
14. (A) effective
    (B) people
15. (A) people
    (B) program

(*reversible answers)

EXERCISE 19, p. 215

1. four
2. It
3. Washoe
4. four
5. India
6. Egypt
7. four
8. All
9. That
10. mammals
11. four
12. A
13. conditions
14. He
15. six
16. who
17. Mexico
18. ideals
19. He
20. wealthy

EXERCISE 20, p. 216

1. **C** 3. **D** 5. **D** 7. **D** 9. **A**
2. **E** 4. **B** 6. **A** 8. **D** 10. **B**

EXERCISE 21, p. 218

1. **D** 3. **C** 5. **B** 7. **E** 9. **D**
2. **B** 4. **C** 6. **C** 8. **E** 10. **E**

EXERCISE 22, p. 219

1. **C** 4. **D** 7. **B** 9. **B** 11. **C**
2. **D** 6. **C** 8. **D** 10. **A** 12. **D**
3. **B** 6. **D**

MASTERY EXAMS

Rating Your Results

On exams with 17 questions:

Superior	15–17 correct
Average	12–14 correct
Below Average	11 or fewer correct

On exams with 19–20 questions:

Superior	17–20 correct
Average	14–16 correct
Below Average	13 or fewer correct

On exams with 21–22 questions:

Superior	19–22 correct
Average	15–18 correct
Below Average	14 or fewer correct

EXAM 1, p. 221

1. E	5. D	9. C	13. C	17. C
2. E	6. D	10. B	14. B	18. C
3. D	7. A	11. E	15. A	19. A
4. A	8. B	12. C	16. D	20. A

EXAM 2, p. 224

1. B	4. C	7. C	10. E	13. B
2. C	5. B	8. B	11. B	14. A
3. A	C. D	9. C	12. D	

EXAM 3, p. 226

1. A	6. B	10. A	14. E	18. A
2. D	7. B	11. E	15. B	19. D
3. B	8. C	12. C	16. A	20. C
4. C	9. C	13. B	17. D	21. B
5. E				

EXAM 4, p. 229

1. D	5. D	9. C	13. A	17. A
2. D	6. E	10. A	14. B	18. E
3. E	7. B	11. D	15. D	19. D
4. C	8. B	12. B	16. B	20. C

EXAM 5, p. 232

1. B	6. D	10. C	14. D	18. E
2. A	7. E	11. A	15. E	19. B
3. B	8. B	12. B	16. D	20. A
4. D	9. B	13. D	17. C	21. C
5. C				

EXAM 6, p. 235

1. D	6. E	11. C	16. C	20. E
2. D	7. A	12. B	17. C	21. B
3. B	8. D	13. E	18. A	22. B
4. D	9. B	14. D	19. D	23. E
5. A	10. C	15. E		

CHAPTER 6

Language Arts

This chapter contains digests of what you should know about:
- Spelling
- Punctuation and Capitalization
- Standard English Usage

Each section includes exercises and practice tests that will not only familiarize you with typical examination questions but also give you maximum control of the subject matter.

However, the areas covered in this chapter are those that receive the most varied treatments on examinations. Before you spend time reviewing any particular area, therefore, you should make certain that it is included in the examination you plan to take.

Answer Keys for all exercises and tests, except for spelling, are given at the end of the chapter. In the spelling section, the answers follow immediately after each test.

Spelling Aids and Rules

This section contains a review of basic rules and aids to correct spelling. Probably there is much here that you already know. The various tests will help you to identify the areas that require continued attention.

HOW TO MASTER SPELLING

Write. Every time you write a word, you are taking a spelling test. The more you write (notes, letters, homework, compositions), the more you are practicing spelling.

Check. As you write, you will be in doubt about the spelling of some words. Check these immediately in your dictionary.

Carry. Carry a pocket dictionary with you whenever possible, so that you can look up the spelling of a word immediately.

List. On a special page in your notebook list every word you misspell.

*Rewrite. (the asterisk is for emphasis). Rewrite every misspelled word five times CAREFULLY and CORRECTLY. Cover the word each time; don't copy.

Memorize. Memorize the correct spellings of the words you have misspelled so that you never make the same mistake twice.

Study. Study lists of spelling demons, words that have given everybody trouble for a long time.

Analyze. Analyze each spelling demon and try to figure out a way to remember the difficult part. Invent a mnemonic (memory) device for each word. (See page 246.)

Learn. Learn the rules and their exceptions. One rule and ten exceptions may help you learn fifty to one hundred words.

Test. Test yourself frequently on those words that bother you most. Mother, Dad, Brother, Sister, or a friend will dictate to you. Since spelling is a writing technique, write the words from dictation. Do not spell aloud.

Spelling Diagnostic Test: The 100 Demons

DIRECTIONS: In each of the following groups of words, one word is misspelled. Find the word, and spell it correctly in the blank space.

1. finaly, original, criticism, expense, further

   _____

2. written, excelent, purchased, returning, decision

   _____

3. comittee, merely, secretary, interested, busy

   _____

4. awfuly, particularly, character, addressed, stating

   _____

5. usual, recommendation, possibly, due, alright

   _____

6. correspondence, customers, allowed, realy, representative

   _____

7. expect, accordingly, existance, suggest, experience

   _____

8. extremely, character, reciept, organization, material

   _____

9. cancel, considerably, useing, assume, bearing

   _____

10. definate, commission, decided, literature, entitled

    _____

11. imagine, balance, doubt, acquainted, refered

    _____

12. executive, preferrence, surprised, library, concerning

    _____

13. experiment, sincerly, disappoint, satisfactorily, course

    _____

14. sufficient, returning, different, truely, accepted

    _____

15. forward, guarantee, recomend, attaching, planning

    _____

16. similiarly, catalog, memorandum, approximately, association

    _____

17. accordingly, bulletin, mortgage, therefore, conection

    _____

18. delivery, begining, waste, inquiry, superintendent

    _____

19. business, remittance, extension, occured, actually

    _____

20. terrible, haveing, disposition, obliged, apparently

    _____

Answers—Diagnostic Test

1. finally	11. referred
2. excellent	12. preference
3. committee	13. sincerely
4. awfully	14. truly
5. all right	15. recommend
6. really	16. similarly
7. existence	17. connection
8. receipt	18. beginning
9. using	19. occurred
10. definite	20. having

Score

(number CORRECT multiplied by 5) ____

Plan for 100%! Begin your own list of words to study now.

Misspellings I overlooked: _____

Correct spellings I was mistaken about:

_____

Correct spellings I was not sure of:

_____

Practice the REWRITE rule now! On a separate sheet of paper:

1. Carefully and correctly write each word from your list five times.

2. Cover the word each time you write it.

3. Don't copy.

MNEMONIC DEVICES, OR TRICKY WAYS TO REMEMBER TRICKY WORDS

Here are just a few examples of some clever, original ways to remember the kind of spellings we call demons because they have a way of tripping you up, and they keep on doing it. You can make up your own mnemonic device for any word that gives you particular trouble.

piece — Everyone likes a piece of pie. Look for PIE in PIEce.

theirs — The heirs will get theirs. Look for HEIRS in tHEIRS.

believe — Would you believe a lie? How strange to find a LIE in beLIEve.

principal — (head of a school) The principal of the school is everybody's pal. Look for PAL in princiPAL.

principle — (a law of conduct or *rule*) Look for the *le* in ruLE and princiPLE.

there — (over there; not here; in that place) Look for HERE in tHERE.

there — (introductory word) There is no spelling difference between "there" (introductory word) and "there" meaning "in that place."

Memorize these trick sentences:

④   ③   ①
There is no room over *there* for *their* coats,
②
so *they're* going to wear them.

1. their   belonging to them
2. they're   they are
3. there   in that place
4. there   introductory

③   ②   ①
It's *too* bad that when you *two* boys came *to*
②
the party you didn't bring your *two* friends
④
too.

1. to   in the direction of
2. two   more than one
3. too   very
4. too   also

①   ②
It's too bad the cat caught *its* tail in the door.

1. it's   it is
2. its   belonging to it

stationery — PapER for a lettER is called stationERy.

stationary — Something that stAys in the sAme plAce is stationAry.

cemetery — There are three E's buried in cEmEtEry.

Now make up your own mnemonic devices for your own spelling demons, devils, and friends.

SPELLING RULES AND TESTS

RULE 1:

*Place **i** before **e** (except after **c**) when sounded like **e** as in **he, she,** and **me**.*

EXAMPLES: -ie-

field	believe	collie
brief	prairie	pier
shriek	movie	grief
fiend	fierce	frontier

-cei-

receive	deceive	ceiling
conceit	receipt	deceit

EXCEPTIONS: -ei-

either	weird	sheik
neither	seizure	protein
seize	leisure	

-cie-

financier	species

Memorize the rule plus these ten exceptions and you will be able to spell over fifty difficult words. See test on Rule 1 for other e-sounding words, below.

RULE 2:

*Place **e** before **i** when sounded like **a** as in **neighbor** and **weigh**.*

EXAMPLES:

beige	heinous	skein
deign	inveigle	sleigh
eight	lei	veil
feign	neigh	vein
feint	neighbor	weigh
freight	reign	weight
geisha	rein	weighty

Note: There are no exceptions to this rule.

Test on Rules 1 and 2

DIRECTIONS: In the space beneath each of the following groups, rewrite the misspelled word correctly. There is one misspelled word in each group.

EXAMPLE: believe deceive preist

ANSWER: priest

1. peice   relieve   either
   _____

2. thief   receipt   breif
   _____

3. shriek   financeir   neither
   _____

4. seizure   achieve   protien
   _____

5. movie   caddie   greif
   _____

6. deciet   relief   fierce
   _____

7. pier   fronteir   wield
   _____

8. receive   beleif   besiege
   _____

9. bier   perceive   wierd
   _____

10. sieze   siege   field
    _____

11. hygiene   cieling   masterpiece
    _____

12. peirce   fiend   leisure
    _____

13. brigadier   liege   concieve
    _____

14. conceit   prairie   repreive
    _____

15. neice   yield   inveigle
    _____

16. wieghty   heinous   sleigh
    _____

17. rien   vein   feint
    _____

18. skein   frieght   neighbor
    _____

19. geisha   collie   niegh

_____

20. eight   reign   decieve

_____

Answers—Rules 1 and 2

1. piece   8. belief   15. niece
2. brief   9. weird   16. weighty
3. financier   10. seize   17. rein
4. protein   11. ceiling   18. freight
5. grief   12. pierce   19. neigh
6. deceit   13. conceive   20. deceive
7. frontier   14. reprieve

Words I missed:

_____

RULE 3:

Adding a suffix to a word ending in a vowel and consonant

When a one-syllable word ends in a vowel and consonant, double the consonant when adding a suffix beginning with a vowel.

EXAMPLES: "beg" + "-ed" equals "beGGed."

bag	baggy	baggage
clan	clannish	
bid	bidding	
squat	squatted	
sad	sadder	saddest
drug	druggist	
war	warrior	

Note: There are no exceptions to this rule.

When a two-syllable word ends in a vowel and consonant, double the consonant if the suffix begins with a vowel and the accent remains on the second syllable.

refer   referring   rebut   rebuttal
occur   occurrence   rebel   rebellion
compel   compelled   concur   concurrent

Complicated as it sounds, the rule is simple to apply once it is understood.

Note: There are very few exceptions to this rule. Here they are:

inferable   (accent on second syllable, yet no doubling)
transferable   (accent on second syllable, yet no doubling)
cancellation   (accent on third syllable, yet the "l" is doubled)
excellent   (accent on first syllable, yet the "l" is doubled)

Other Advantages of Rule 3: If you learn Rule 3, it will help you in spelling dozens of other words. For example, take words like *cool, weep, chirp, happen, offer, repeat, extend, annex, allow,* and *display.* Do they ever double the final letter? NEVER, because they do not come under the rule for doubling.

cool   weep   repeat
cooling   weeping   repeater

No doubling, *because there are two vowels before the consonant.*

cost   chirp   extend
costing   chirping   extending

No doubling, *because these words end in two consonants.*

happen   offer
happened   offered

No doubling, *because the accent is always on the first syllable.*

annex   allow   display
annexed   allowed   displaying

No doubling of "**w**," "**x**," or "**y**" ever takes place ("**x**" is really two consonants, "**ks**"; "**w**" and "**y**" act like vowels at the end of words).

patrol   equip   defer
patrolman   equipment   deferment

No doubling, *because the suffix begins with a consonant.*

infer   inference

No doubling, *because the accent shifts from second to first syllable.*

refer   referee

No doubling, *because the accent shifts from second to third syllable.*

Test on Rule 3

DIRECTIONS: *Supply the missing letters where needed*

EXAMPLES: bag_age   equip_ ment

ANSWER: baggage (Supply "g" in the blank space.)
equipment (Supply nothing in the blank space.)

1. ship_ment
2. stun_ing
3. want_ing
4. bat_er
5. wrap_ing
6. drag_ed
7. wit_y
8. drug_ist
9. tan_ing
10. begin_ing
11. bid_er
12. commit_ee
13. blur_ed
14. happen_ed
15. war_ior
16. stand_ing
17. suffer_er
18. depend_ence
19. offer_ed
20. cool_ing
21. prefer_ence
22. occur_ing
23. omit_ing
24. infer_ing
25. occur_ence
26. prefer_ed
27. remit_ance
28. refer_ee
29. control_able
30. compel_ed

31. allot_ing
32. allot_ment
33. regret_ed
34. admit_ing
35. admit_ance
36. plan_ed (intended)
37. stop_ed
38. infer_ence
39. recur_ent
40. rebel_ion
41. get_ing
42. got_en
43. credit_or
44. edit_or
45. profit_ing
46. profit_eer
47. prefer_ential
48. mention_ed
49. succeed_ing
50. avail_able
51. appear_ance
52. await_ing
53. benefit_ed
54. exist_ence
55. allow_ance
56. annex_ed
57. dispel_ed
58. defer_ed
59. defer_ence
60. defer_ment

DIRECTIONS: *Fill in the blanks where necessary.*

61. commit_ee
62. equip_ing
63. defer_ence
64. concur_ent
65. refer_endum
66. begin_er
67. regret_ed
68. admis_ion
69. big_er
70. chop_ing
71. patrol_man
72. profit_ed
73. suffer_ance
74. chat_y
75. differ_ence

76. hot_est
77. repeat_er
78. extend_ing
79. acquit_al
80. impel_ed
81. rebel_ious
82. emis_ion
83. permis_ion
84. begot_en
85. rebut_al
86. beg_ar
87. transfer_ed
88. refer_ence
89. quit_er
90. deter_ent

Answers—Rule 3

2. stunning
4. batter
5. wrapping
6. dragged
7. witty
8. druggist
9. tanning
10. beginning
11. bidder
12. committee
13. blurred
15. warrior
22. occurring
23. omitting
24. inferring
25. occurrence
26. preferred

27. remittance
29. controllable
30. compelled
31. allotting
33. regretted
34. admitting
35. admittance
36. planned
37. stopped
39. recurrent
40. rebellion
41. getting
42. gotten
57. dispelled
58. deferred
59. deference
60. deferment

61. committee
62. equipping
64. concurrent
66. beginner
67. regretted
69. bigger
70. chopping
74. chatty
76. hottest
79. acquittal
80. impelled

81. rebellious
82. emission
83. permission
84. begotten
85. rebuttal
86. beggar
87. transferred
89. quitter
90. deterrent

Words I missed: _____

RULE 4:

Adding a suffix to a word ending in a silent e.

Add the suffix to the whole word if the suffix begins with a consonant.

EXAMPLES:

immediate	resource	whole
immediately	resourceful	wholesome
manage	cruel	noise
management	cruelly	noiseless

EXCEPTIONS:

abridge	awe	due
abridgment	awful	duly
acknowledge	argue	true
acknowledgment	argument	truly
judge	wise	whole
judgment	wisdom	wholly

Drop the e and add the suffix if the suffix begins with a vowel.

EXAMPLES:

dine	force	shine
dining	forcible	shiny
love	struggle	blue
lovable	struggling	bluish
continue	style	
continuous	stylish	

EXCEPTIONS:

agree	dye	singe
agreeable	dyeing	singeing

(to avoid confusion with dying and singing)
(Tests on Rules 4 to 10 follow Rule 10.)

RULE 5:

When a word ends in -le, change silent e to y to form the adverb.

EXAMPLES:

possible	audible	wile
possibly	audibly	wily
considerable	scale	
considerably	scaly	

EXCEPTIONS: whole wholly

RULE 6:

When a word ends in -ll, add y to the original word to form the adverb.

EXAMPLES:

dull	full	smell	chill
dully	fully	smelly	chilly

Note: There are no exceptions.

RULE 7:

When a word ends in -l, form the adverb as follows:

For adjectives ending in -l add -ly to the original word.

EXAMPLES:

cruel	natural	foul
cruelly	naturally	foully
actual	cool	beautiful
actually	coolly	beautifully

For nouns ending in -l, add y.

curl	oil	steel
curly	oily	steely
meal	pearl	wool
mealy	pearly	wooly or woolly

RULE 8:

Adding a suffix to a word ending in **-ce** *or* **-ge.**

Drop the **e** *before* **e, i,** *or* **y.**

EXAMPLES:

arrange	arranged	arranging
change	changing	
charge	charger	charging
encourage	encouraging	
manage	managing	
notice	noticing	
range	rangy	
service	servicing	
trace	tracing	

Keep the **e** *before (1)* **a** *or* **o** *and (2) before a* consonant.

(1) Before **a** or **o**	(2) Before a consonant
advantageous	
arrangeable	arrangement
changeable	changeling
chargeable	
courageous	
	encouragement
manageable	management
noticeable	
outrageous	
peaceable	
serviceable	
traceable	

PRONUNCIATION RULES THAT AFFECT SPELLING

To understand Rule 8 more fully, it is advisable to consider several pronunciation rules.

1. **C** is pronounced like *s* before *e, i,* and *y.*
    ceiling Cinderella Nancy

2. **C** is pronounced like *k* before *a, o,* and *u* and before consonants.
    cat comic cut lecture crease

3. **G** is pronounced like *j* before *e, i,* and *y.*
    George religion gyroscope

4. **G** is pronounced like the *g* in *go* before *a, o, u,* and any consonant.
    gave got gun egg segment recognize

5. The letters **dg**, when sounded as one, are always pronounced like *j.*
    judge ridge acknowledgment

Examine these pronunciation rules now for their effect on spelling. The word *manage* under Rule 8 ends in a *soft g* or *j* sound. It drops the final *e* before *-ing* because the *g* in both *manageing* and *managing* would retain the *j* sound of the original word. Therefore, the correct spelling (Rule 8) is *managing,* without the *e.* On the other hand, *manageable* must keep the *e* (Rule 8, 1) to have the soft *g* (*j*) sound of *manage.* If the word were spelled managable, it would have the hard *g* of gun. The same rule of pronunciation guides us in the spelling of management. *G* before *m* (a consonant) would be hard. We need a soft *j* sound and therefore the *e* must be kept in management (Rule 8, 2).

Test any other word under Rule 8 by these pronunciation rules.

RULE 9:

When a word ends in **-dge,** *drop the silent* **e** *before any suffix.*

abridgment   acknowledgment   judgment

In the past, these words were spelled with the silent *e* since the suffix started with a consonant *(m).* However, in view of Pronunciation Rule 5 above, the combination *dg* is pronounced like *j* anyway. Since the *e* is not needed, modern spelling experts have recommended that it be dropped before any suffix. Nevertheless, students will still see the old spellings (judgement, knowledgeable, lodgement) because the writers went to school before the changes were adopted. British writers usually retain the *e.*

RULE 10:

Adding a suffix to a word ending in **-c.**

Add **k** *before* **e, i** *or* **y.**

frolic	panic	picnic
frolicking	panicky	picnicked

Frolic + ing (without a *k*) would have had *c* before *i.* According to Pronunciation Rule 1, *c* before *i* is pronounced like an *s.* To keep the *k* sound of the *c* in frolic, a *k* must be added to the *c.* The same is true for *panic + y* and *picnic + ed.*

*Add nothing before **a, o,** or **u.***

critic	critical	critically
fantastic		fantastically
comic	comical	comically
basic		basically
organic		organically

Here again, pronunciation decides spelling: *c* keeps its *k* sound before *a o, u*—hence, needs no "support."

Test on Rules 4 to 10

DIRECTIONS: Circle the letter of one misspelled word in each of the following groups of five.

EXAMPLE:

(A) circling (B) refuseing (C) dully
(D) pearly (E) purely

ANSWER:

Letter (B) has been circled because *refuseing* is a misspelling of *refusing*.

1. (A) resourcful (B) wisdom
 (C) argument (D) cruelly
 (E) changeable

2. (A) curly (B) singeing (C) singing
 (D) politly (E) politically

3. (A) artistically (B) basically
 (C) professionally (D) pokeing
 (E) racing

4. (A) receding (B) arrangment
 (C) realizing (D) receiving (E) mealy

5. (A) grieving (B) rhetorically
 (C) retirement (D) rhythmically
 (E) rideing

6. (A) immediatly (B) shiny (C) shrilly
 (D) normally (E) dining

7. (A) pitifully (B) plentifully
 (C) judgment (D) useable
 (E) factually

8. (A) serviceable (B) believable
 (C) wholly (D) dodgeing (E) timing

9. (A) mercifully (B) duely (C) grateful
 (D) noticeably (E) masterfully

10. (A) agreeable (B) fuly (C) wholesome
 (D) rhyming (E) sensibly

11. (A) unruly (B) ably (C) possibly
 (D) decideing (E) forcible

12. (A) fancifully (B) peaceable
 (C) amusement (D) noiseless
 (E) achievment

13. (A) abridgment (B) actualy
 (C) dutifully (D) bereavement
 (E) struggling

14. (A) frilly (B) truly (C) naturally
 (D) hilly (E) considerably

15. (A) fantastically (B) capitally
 (C) cruelly (D) regionally
 (E) outragous

16. (A) advantageous (B) really (C) stylish
 (D) vaguly (E) lovable

17. (A) physically (B) managment
 (C) smelly (D) parallel (E) rebel

18. (A) dyeing (B) dying (C) audibly
 (D) continual (E) chargable

19. (A) aweful (B) careful (C) wonderfully
 (D) beautiful (E) trifle

20. (A) curlly (B) acknowledgment
 (C) radiating (D) wooly
 (E) enforceable

DIRECTIONS: Supply the missing letters where necessary.

EXAMPLE: picnic_ed

ANSWER: picknicked

21. rac_ing	30. su_ing
22. saf_ty	31. cano_ing
23. fat_ful	32. amus_ment
24. arriv_al	33. argu_ment
25. mov_ment	34. excit_ing
26. peac_ful	35. tru_ly
27. abridg_ing	36. mov_able
28. ach_ing	37. griev_ance
29. blu_ish	38. forc_ible

39. lov_able

40. argu_ing

41. tast_ful

42. creat_or

43. admir_able

44. manag_able

45. ting_ing

46. ho_ing

47. charg_able

48. du_ly

49. wis_dom

50. valu_able

51. notic_able

52. outrag_ous

53. arrang_able

54. picnic_ing

55. fantastic_ly

56. judg_ment

57. wool_y

58. chang_ing

59. critic_ly

60. mimic_ry

61. encourag_ing

62. abridg_ment

63. traffic_ed

64. peac_able

65. possibl_y

66. servic_able

67. unrul_y

68. aw_ful

69. grat_ful

70. cruel_y

71. full_y

72. considerabl_y

73. colic_y

74. basic_ly

75. continu_ous

76. shin_y

77. styl_ish

78. dull_y

79. undu_ly

80. chronic_ly

90. charged _____

91. panicked _____

92. changing _____

93. chronically _____

94. frolicking _____

95. frantically _____

96. arranging _____

97. artisticly _____

98. noticing _____

99. courageous _____

100. trafficing _____

101. changeably _____

102. tracable _____

103. basically _____

104. judging _____

105. acknowledgeing _____

106. encouragment _____

107. abridgment _____

108. outragous _____

109. acknowledgment _____

110. judgement _____

DIRECTIONS: Next to each word, write *c* if it is correctly spelled. Rewrite the word correctly if it is misspelled.

EXAMPLES:

mimicked	____c____
panicy	panicky

81. arrangable _____

82. fantasticly _____

83. encouraging _____

84. picnicking _____

85. peaceably _____

86. noticeable _____

87. colicky _____

88. shellaced _____

89. advantageous _____

Answers—Rules 4 to 10

1. **A**	5. **E**	9. **B**	13. **B**	17. **B**
2. **D**	6. **A**	10. **B**	14. **E**	18. **E**
3. **D**	7. **D**	11. **D**	15. **E**	19. **A**
4. **B**	8. **D**	12. **E**	16. **D**	20. **A**

22. safety   53. arrangeable

23. fateful   54. picnicking

25. movement   55. fantastically

26. peaceful   57. wooly or woolly

31. canoeing   59. critically

32. amusement   63. trafficked

41. tasteful   64. peaceable

44. manageable   65. possibly

45. tinging or tingeing 66. serviceable

46. hoeing   69. grateful

47. chargeable   70. cruelly

51. noticeable   73. colicky

52. outrageous   74. basically

                         80. chronically

(The other words on the test needed no letters added.)

81. arrangeable
82. fantastically
83. c
84. c
85. c
86. c
87. c
88. shellacked
89. c
90. c
91. c
92. c
93. c
94. c
95. c
96. c
97. artistically
98. c
99. c
100. trafficking
101. c
102. traceable
103. c
104. c
105. acknowledging
106. encouragement
107. c
108. outrageous
109. c
100. judgment

Words I missed:

1.–20. _____

21.–80. _____

_____

_____

81.–110. _____

RULE 11:

Adding suffixes to words ending in -y, and forming plurals and some verb forms.

If the y follows a consonant, as in

du*ty*   vic*tory*   magni*fy*   app*ly*
car*ry*   bu*sy*   la*zy*   i*cy*

change the y to i when you add a suffix, as in

du*tiful*   victor*ious*   magni*ficent*
app*licant*   carr*iage*   bus*iness*
laz*iness*   ic*iness*

Also, change y to i and add es for the plural of nouns, and for some verb forms, as in

lady   carry   reply   sky   supply
ladies   carries   replies   skies   supplies

EXCEPT: 1. *When the suffix begins with an i, the y is kept:*

hurry   bury   defy   copy
hurrying   burying   defying   copyist

EXCEPT: 2. *When the y keeps the i sound before a consonant, the y is kept.*

dry   shy   sly   spry
dryness   shyness   slyness   spryness

Do not change y to i when adding a suffix to a word ending in a vowel + y.

b*uy*   buyer   buying
joy   joys   joyful
day   days
mon*key*   monkeys
pay   payable
emp*loy*   employed   employable

EXCEPTIONS:

day   lay   pay   say   slay
daily   laid   paid   said   slain

Note: When the word ending in -y combines with another word, the y is kept.

anyone   drypoint   copywrite

(Test on Rule 11 follows Rule 12.)

RULE 12:

When a word ends in -ie, change ie to y when adding -ing.

lie   tie   belie   vie
lying   tying   belying   vying

Test on Rules 11 and 12

DIRECTIONS: Supply the missing letters.
EXAMPLE:
juicy juic_ness
ANSWER:
juiciness

any   1. an_thing

             2. an_where

birthday   3. birthda_s

beauty   4. beaut_s

             5. beaut_ful

carry	6. carr__ing	**library**	41. librar__s
	7. carr__ed		42. librar__ian
	8. carr__age	**marry**	43. marr__d
city	9. cit__s		44. marr__age
	10. cit__zen	**memory**	45. memor__s
die	11. d__ing		46. memor__al
	12. d__d	**necessary**	47. necessar__ly
donkey	13. donk__s	**necessity**	48. necessit__s
dye	14. d__ing	**obey**	49. ob__ing
	15. d__d		50. ob__ed
easy	16. eas__ly	**ordinary**	51. ordinar__ly
	17. eas__er	**pay**	52. pa__d
	18. eas__est	**plenty**	53. plent__ful
employ	19. emplo__ees	**pony**	54. pon__s
	20. emplo__er	**ready**	55. read__ness
	21. emplo__ment	**reply**	56. repl__d
emergency	22. emergenc__s		57. repl__ing
Friday	23. Frida__s	**responsibility**	58. responsibilit__s
funny	24. funn__er	**say**	59. sa__d
	25. funn__est		60. sa__s
gloomy	26. gloom__ness	**Saturday**	61. Saturda__s
	27. gloom__er	**stay**	62. sta__d
greedy	28. greed__ness		63. sta__ing
hobby	29. hobb__s	**strawberry**	64. strawberr__s
history	30. histor__an	**they**	65. the__r
	31. histor__cal	**try**	66. tr__ing
icy	32. ic__ness		67. tr__d
	33. ic__cle		68. tr__al
injury	34. injur__s	**university**	69. universit__s
	35. injur__ous	**unnecessary**	70. unnecessar__ly
key	36. k__s	**vary**	71. var__d
kindly	37. kindl__ness		72. var__ous
lay	38. la__d		73. var__ing
lie	39. l__d	**vie**	74. v__ing
	40. l__ing	**volley**	75. voll__s
			76. voll__ing

worry   77. worr__d

                 78. worr__ing

                 79. worr__s

worthy   80. worth__ness

DIRECTIONS: In each group of five words, one is misspelled. Pick out the incorrect word and write it correctly in the space below.

---

81. defied   layed   days   copying   lying

_____

82. iciness   spys   beautiful   carrying   joyful

_____

83. luckyly   curliness   colonies   readily   days

_____

84. playful   giddiness   business   birthdaies   applies

_____

85. loveliness   modifies   courtesies   countries   spriness

_____

86. swaying   supplies   buying   lieing   buried

_____

87. moneys   accompanies   dryness   armys   slain

_____

88. slyly   playing   colonies   difficulties   payed

_____

89. delaid   wryness   earliness   applying   easiest

_____

90. employed   buyers   defied   steadiness   familys

_____

Answers—Rules 11 and 12

1. anything	41. libraries
2. anywhere	42. librarian
3. birthdays	43. married
4. beauties	44. marriage
5. beautiful	45. memories
6. carrying	46. memorial
7. carried	47. necessarily
8. carriage	48. necessities
9. cities	49. obeying
10. citizen	50. obeyed
11. dying	51. ordinarily
12. died	52. paid
13. donkeys	53. plentiful
14. dyeing	54. ponies
15. dyed	55. readiness
16. easily	56. replied
17. easier	57. replying
18. easiest	58. responsibilities
19. employees	59. said
20. employer	60. says
21. employment	61. Saturdays
22. emergencies	62. stayed
23. Fridays	63. staying
24. funnier	64. strawberries
25. funniest	65. their
26. gloominess	66. trying
27. gloomier	67. tried
28. greediness	68. trial
29. hobbies	69. universities
30. historian	70. unnecessarily
31. historical	71. varied
32. iciness	72. various
33. icicle	73. varying
34. injuries	74. vying
35. injurious	75. volleys
36. keys	76. volleying
37. kindliness	77. worried
38. laid	78. worrying
39. lied	79. worries
40. lying	80. worthiness

81. laid
82. spies
83. luckily
84. birthdays
85. spryness

86. lying
87. armies
88. paid
89. delayed
90. families

Words I missed:

1.–80. _____

_____

_____

81.–90. _____

RULE 13:

*Distinguishing between **fore-** and **for**.*

*Spell the prefix **fore-** in words meaning* **before**.

To *foretell* the future means to *tell* about a future happening *before* it happens.

forebode	foreknowledge	foresight
forecast	foreman	forestall
foreclose	foremost	foretaste
forefather	forenoon	forethought
forefinger	forerunner	forewarn
forefront	foresee	forewoman
foreground	foreshadow	foreword
forehand	foreshorten	aforesaid
forehead		

*Spell the prefix **for-** in words meaning* **off**, **away**, *or* **without**.

To *forbid* means to *bid* some action *away*, that is, to bid some action not be done.

forbear	forget	forsake
forfeit	forlorn	forswear
forgive		

EXCEPTION: forward
This word has the meaning *before,* but it contains no *e.*

Be aware that two words are commonly spelled either way.

forgather   forgo
foregather forego

Forgo means *to go without; forego* means *to go before.*

Test on Rule 13

> **DIRECTIONS:** Supply the missing *e* in the words that require it.

1. afor__said
2. for__sake
3. for__bode
4. for__swear
5. for__get
6. for__cast
7. for__word
8. for__close
9. for__man
10. for__bear
11. for__hand
12. for__noon
13. for__head
14. for__feit
15. for__lorn
16. for__stall
17. for__see
18. for__sight
19. for__ground
20. for__most

Answers—Rule 13

1. aforesaid	12. forenoon
3. forebode	13. forehead
6. forecast	16. forestall
7. foreword	17. foresee
8. foreclose	18. foresight
9. foreman	19. foreground
11. forehand	20. foremost

(All the other words are spelled without the *e.*)

Words I missed:

_____

_____

RULE 14:

When adding the word **full** *as a suffix to another word, drop the final* **l**.

    cup + full = cupful
    spoon + full = spoonful

    awful   handful   masterful plentiful
    beautiful fanciful merciful   sorrowful
    dutiful   grateful pitiful   wonderful

(There are many other *full* compounds; they are all spelled -ful.)

STUDY HINTS:

1. The only word in the language ending in f-u-l-l is the word *full* itself.

2. Note the demons *awful* (without an *e*) and *grateful* (with an *e*).

3. Notice that *beauty, duty, fancy, mercy, pity,* and *plenty* drop *y* and add *i* before *-ful*. See Rule 11.

Test on Rule 14

DIRECTIONS: Add the word *full* as a suffix to each of the words below.

1. skill   _____
2. wonder   _____
3. hand   _____
4. ear   _____
5. beauty   _____
6. purpose   _____
7. forget   _____
8. barrel   _____
9. soul   _____
10. duty   _____
11. fancy   _____
12. grace   _____

13. shovel   _____
14. pity   _____
15. tear   _____
16. wake   _____
17. mourn   _____
18. care   _____
19. venge(ance)   _____
20. rest   _____

Answers—Rule 14

1. skillful   11. fanciful
2. wonderful   12. graceful
3 handful   13. shovelful
4. earful   14. pitiful
5. beautiful   15. tearful
6. purposeful   16. wakeful
7. forgetful   17. mournful
8. barrelful   18. careful
9. soulful   19. vengeful
10. dutiful   20. restful

Words I missed: _____

Spelling Mastery Test 1

DIRECTIONS: On the line provided, re-write correctly the misspelled word in each group.

EXAMPLE:
    breakfast thier children's neighbor
                       ANSWER: their

1. faucet, picnic, series, sieze

    _____

2. pastime, tomatoes, supprised, imaginary

    _____

3. devine, mischief, ridiculous, haven't

    _____

4. definate, machinery, descendant, contemptible

    _____

5. cathedral, discription, stationery, simile

_____

6. eight, marriage, reciept, choir

_____

7. consistent, genuine, muscle, Febuary

_____

8. glimpse, dairy, dissipline, creature

_____

9. transfered, successful, village, woman

_____

10. becoming, earnest, embarass, suite

_____

11. ninteenth, supersede, persuade, circular

_____

12. bureau, forehead, momentous, mischeivous

_____

13. missionary, suspicious, thoroughly, perserverance

_____

14. colleague, heros, minimizing, itemized

_____

15. humane, pitifully, garranty, eliminate

_____

16. harrass, monotonous, lightning, hymn

_____

17. compelled, mobilize, submitted, volenteer

_____

18. bycicle, monetary, reference, prestige

_____

19. courteous, neccesity, inadequate, unconsciously

_____

20. colonel, angle, antique, liesure

_____

Answers—Mastery Test 1

1. seize	11. nineteenth
2. surprised	12. mischievous
3. divine	13. perseverance
4. definite	14. heroes
5 description	15. guarantee
6. receipt	16. harass
7. February	17. volunteer
8. discipline	18. bicycle
9. transferred	19. necessity
10. embarrass	20. leisure

Words I missed: _____

Spelling Mastery Test 2

DIRECTIONS: In each of the following groups, 1 to 20, one word is misspelled. In each case spell correctly, on the line provided, the misspelled word.

1. attach, voucher, twins, assistence, cordial

_____

2. faculties, people's, indetedness, ignorant, resource

_____

3. wholly, apitite, twelfth, unauthorized, embroider

_____

4. certified, attorneys, foggy, potato, extravagent

_____

5. hysterics, simelar, intelligent, label, salaries

_____

6. apponants, we're, finely, herald, continuous

_____

7. cancellation, athletic, perminant, preference, utilize

_____

8. urns, zephir, tuition, incidentally, acquisition

_____

9. kinsman, bazaar, foliage, wretched, asassination

_____

10. insignia, bimonthly, typewriting, notariety, psychology

_____

11. lieutenant, abandoned, successor, phisycal, inquiries

_____

12. nuisance, coranation, voluntary, faculties, herald

_____

13. indipendance, notwithstanding, tariff, opportunity, accompanying

_____

14. statutes, rhubarb, corset, unauthorized, subsedy

_____

15. partisan, initiate, colonel, ilness, errand

_____

16. acquired, wrapped, propriater, screech, duly

_____

17. sufraige, countenance, fraternally, undo, fireman

_____

18. ladies', chef (cook), spirituel, Sabbath, itemized

_____

19. ere, interests, cheesecloth, paridoxical, assessment

_____

20. bulletin, everlasting, porttiere, discretion, inconvenienced

_____

Answers—Mastery Test 2

1. assistance
2. indebtedness
3. appetite
4 extravagant
5. similar
6. opponents
7. permanent
8. zephyr
9. assassination
10. notoriety
11. physical
12. coronation
13. independence
14. subsidy
15. illness
16. proprietor
17. suffrage
18. spiritual
19. paradoxical
20. portiere

Words I missed: _____

Spelling Mastery Test 3

DIRECTIONS: In each of the following groups, 1 to 20, one word is misspelled. In each case, rewrite the misspelled word correctly on the line provided.

1. advising, recognize, seize (grasp), supply, tradegy

_____

2. intensive, stationary (fixed), benifit, equipped, preferring

_____

3. predjudice, pervade, excel, capitol (building), chimneys

_____

4. all right, ninty, cronies, nervous, separate

_____

5. atheletic, queue (waiting line), furl, schedule, abusing

_____

6. skein, wholesome, witches, coherent, defenite

_____

7. aggravate, counsel (advice), deplorable, proficiancy, interested

_____

8. suppressed, lugubrious, pecuniary, boulevard, fourty-fourth

_____

9. militarism, pilot, crimnal, monotonous, tendency

_____

10. prevalent, berth (for sleeping), auxiliary, priveleges, women's

_____

11. acquired, mercury, stetistics, thought, vassal

_____

12. tempature, calendar, series, gout, alcohol

_____

13. important, foreigner, Australia, leggend, rhythm

_____

14. height, achevment, monarchial, axle, fertile

_____

15. falsity, prestige, conquer, arketecture, Jerusalem

_____

16. magniffecent, bacteria, holly, diseases, cellar

_____

17. medicine, grievous, beaker, benefits, attendents

_____

18. military, vacancy, weird, feudalism, hybird

_____

19. adopted, agrigate, Renaissance, tournament, colonies

_____

20. vivisection, penitentiary, candadacy, ere, Sabbath

_____

Answers—Mastery Test 3

1. tragedy
2. benefit
3. prejudice
4. ninety
5. athletic
6. definite
7. proficiency
8. forty-fourth
9. criminal
10. privileges
11. statistics
12. temperature
13. legend
14. achievement
15. architecture
16. magnificent
17. attendants
18. hybrid
19. aggregate
20. candidacy

Words I missed: _____

Punctuation and Capitalization

If you are using this book to prepare for a specific test, make certain that the material in this section is included in the test items before you begin to allot time to study sessions.

This section contains a review of basic rules of punctuation and capitalization.

There is much here that you already know. Use the exercises and practice tests to find the areas that require your continued attention.

Turn to pages 317–320 for Answer Keys to all exercises and practice tests in this section.

PUNCTUATION MARKS: REVIEW AND RULES

The Apostrophe (')

The apostrophe shows where sounds or letters have been left out.

> can't (cannot)
> *B'klyn* (Brooklyn)

The plurals of letters and numbers need an apostrophe.

> How many *6's* are there in your phone number?
> My name is spelled with two *l's.*

The possessive case of nouns and pronouns (except personal pronouns) needs the apostrophe.

> Harry's hat   the Joneses' house
> the cat's paw   the owls' nests
> someone's cry

Use no apostrophe with personal pronouns!

> his   yours   theirs
> hers   ours   its

To understand the use of the apostrophe with the possessive case more clearly, it is necessary to know a few rules. The following will explain what you must know:

Singular Possessive

If a singular word ends in a letter other than **s,** *add an apostrophe and* **s.**

> man   man's
> coat   coat's

When a name ends in the letter **s,** *add either just an apostrophe or an apostrophe and* **s.**

CORRECT: *Dickens'* books or *Dickens's* books.

If a word ends in *s,* sometimes you add only the apostrophe. It is usually the sound that determines the choice.

> *goodness'   cross's*

Compound or hypenated nouns have the apostrophe and **s** added to the last word in the group.

> John, Mary, and *Sal's* project
> My sister-in-*law's* cake

Plural Possessive

If the plural form of the word or name ends in the letter **s,** *just add an apostrophe after the* **s.**

> horses   *horses'*
> schools   *schools'*
> Murphys   *Murphys'*

If the plural form does not end in the letter **s,** *add an apostrophe and* **s.**

> men's
> mice's

EXERCISE 1

Read the following paragraph carefully. Look at the word preceding each number. Next to the same number below, write the letter C if an apostrophe has been correctly used, or if an apostrophe has been omitted where none belongs. If an apostrophe has been incorrectly omitted or used, write out the full word, placing the apostrophe where it belongs.

In many ways the ancient Greeks' (1) coins were different from our's (2). Their coins werent (3) made for utility only, but were also works (4) of art. Artists commissioned to fashion these coins drew their material from nature and mythology. An interesting coin from Agrigentum pictured eagles paired in 2s (5), while another had four dolphins surrounded by dots. Often a great mans (6) portrait was used, or that of a relative. One famous Syracusan coin bears the kings (7) mother-in-laws (8) likeness. The coins (9) edges were more uneven than they are on today's (10) coins, because money then was handmade.

1. _____ 6. _____
2. _____ 7. _____
3. _____ 8. _____
4. _____ 9. _____
5. _____ 10. _____

EXERCISE 2

On the line provided, rewrite correctly any word that requires an apostrophe or that contains an apostrophe incorrectly used. Write the letter C *if no correction is needed.*

1. Is that really the latest in mens' hats?

   _____

2. It was really theirs and not ours.

   _____

3. The policemens' lot can really be a happy one.

   _____

4. The lady's hats are over there.

   _____

5. Place it near that officers documents.

   _____

6. His work is as good as anyones.

   _____

7. My French teachers notes were left on the shelf.

   _____

8. The razors edge has been dulled by exposure to the dampness.

   _____

9. Phyllis answers are as good as yours.

   _____

10. Please learn to dot your is.

    _____

11. Did you see Paul and Harriets latest project?

    _____

12. Its an old story by this time.

    _____

13. Its fine finish is the result of James hard work.

    _____

14. Hes the best swimmer in camp.

    _____

15. Wont you please listen to my side of the story!

    _____

16. Youd have done the same yourself.

    _____

17. It was just the worms turn to turn.

    _____

18. The trees leaves are turning pale with the cold.

    _____

19. The hurt animals cry filled my dreams for many nights after that incident.

    _____

20. The boys father and mother told his friends the entire story.

    _____

The Semicolon (;)

The semicolon is used where a conjunction has been left out of a sentence.

Alexander Pope was a classical poet; he used the heroic couplet.

The semicolon is used before certain words, such as

moreover	consequently
however	nevertheless
hence	thus
subsequently	as a result

when they introduce an additional thought to an otherwise complete statement. Notice that a comma usually follows such an introductory word.

He told me it would be advisable to join; however, I used my own judgment and refused.

EXERCISE 3

One sentence in each group of four is incorrectly punctuated. Circle the answer choice of that sentence.

1. (A) Rocket ships will eventually explore new worlds. They will penetrate far into outer space.
   (B) A person who wishes to be an astronaut must be in perfect physical condition; however, more than physical stamina will be needed to qualify.
   (C) Imagine the feelings of the command pilot; when she guides her ship into sky roads never before traveled by human beings.
   (D) Space travelers will probably be fearful at first; then, when they gain experience, they will gain courage.

2. (A) The distance between Earth and Mars varies; consequently, any space flight to our sister planet will start when she is closest to us.
   (B) Scientists feel that some form of life may well exist on Mars; since they have detected what seem to be signs of water and vegetation.
   (C) Many people wonder if there are any strange, purple-hued beings on Mars; they forget that bug-eyed monsters are the creation of fiction and songwriters.
   (D) The hazards of a trip to Mars will be great; nevertheless, many will be eager to go.

3. (A) Scientists believe that there are millions of planets capable of supporting life; they feel that it is far from unlikely that animal life of some kind exists on many planets.
   (B) There are also many planets whose chemistry is vastly different from ours; it's possible that weird and fantastic forms of plant life exist on these.
   (C) Human beings know so little of the vast sea of space that surrounds them; however, one day they will certainly know much more!
   (D) Many people now are so thrilled by the possibility of exploring outer space that they cannot wait; until they soar off into the limitless sea of stars beyond us.

EXERCISE 4

For each of the following, write A *if the semicolon is used correctly. Write* B *if the semicolon is used incorrectly.*

___ 1. Don't come any closer; the shell can explode at any moment.

___ 2. I told him the facts; and he believed everything I said.

___ 3. Listen to him; then, follow his plan.

___ 4. The man almost lost his life; and his car as well.

___ 5. Mike knows the answer to our problem; and we should ask him to help us.

___ 6. Only one sentence is incorrect; the other contains no error.

___ 7. We will have to see her soon; because she left her notebook in our locker.

__ 8. Tell him to see me; or the custodian.

__ 9. Over on the shelf; you will find the missing cover.

__ 10. Play fair; let the others break the rules.

__ 11. I could have left early; since I had finished my work hours ago.

__ 12. The recorder supplied all of our music; but it was just a bit too low for my comfort.

__ 13. The price is reasonable; however, I shall have to think your proposition over for a day or so.

__ 14. The melody is a haunting one; I just cannot forget it.

__ 15. Watch me; and I'll show you how to operate the tape deck.

The Comma (,)

The comma is used to separate words, phrases, or clauses in a series of three or more.

Words: He decided to take French, elementary algebra, English, and science.

Phrases: The horse galloped furiously over the hill, across the valley, through the meadow, and into the lake.

Clauses: The brothers worked steadily. John sawed the wood, Harry planed it, and Fred stacked it.

A comma is used to separate adjectives modifying the same noun, or adverbs modifying the same verb.

The rambling, old, colonial house was charming.
He advanced slowly, stealthily.

A comma is used after an introductory word, phrase, or clause.

Word: Nevertheless, the view was beautiful.

Phrase: After long hours of waiting, we found the solution.

Clause: When I saw him enter the room, I realized that our troubles were over.

Clause: Although nothing was changed, the room somehow looked different.

A comma is used to set off words or phrases in apposition.

Mr. Edmonds, my teacher, speaks very effectively.
The Golden Leopard, largest and most luxurious liner of its class, makes a transatlantic crossing in record time.

A comma is used to set off a clause that could be dropped out of the sentence without damaging its meaning

Edwards, who has a great deal of wisdom, was elected president.

The clause "who has a great deal of wisdom" merely tells us a little more about Edwards; it is not absolutely necessary to the main statement, "Edwards was elected president." Compare this with the following:

The person whom we elect to the presidency must have widsom.

The clause "whom we elect to the presidency" is indispensable. To say "The person must have wisdom" would be incomplete and even meaningless; the reader would instantly say "What person?" Therefore, no commas should be used.

A comma is used after an interjection.

Ah, so you have decided to come!

A comma is used after the name of a person who is addressed directly.

John, will you please turn off your radio?

Commas are used to set off adjectives that are placed after words they modify.

The umbrella, torn and flimsy, was no protection against the sweeping rain.

EXERCISE 5

In each sentence you will find a word in italics. If you think that there should be a comma after the word in italics, write the letter C next to the number. If you feel there should be no comma write the letter N.

___ 1. It was a *very* difficult journey.

___ 2. The *cloud* dark and threatening, hovered over the town.

___ 3. "John," said the *teacher* "you are late."

___ 4. He preferred *fruit* and cheese for dessert.

___ 5. The *game* which I like best is basketball.

___ 6. *Eagerly* he volunteered to go.

___ 7. *Oh* you are much too kind to me.

___ 8. The Concorde, the latest advance in aeronatical *science* is twice as fast as a regular jet plane.

___ 9. *Tony* who is the youngest member of the class, is also the best baseball player.

___ 10. The team worked as a perfect unit. The fielding was *excellent* the batting was powerful, and the pitching was superb.

___ 11. Oh, puppy, *puppy* come here.

___ 12. The *college* that I choose to attend must have a first-rate science department.

___ 13. The *very* old book is a valuable antique.

___ 14. He was most interested in stamp collecting *and* photography.

___ 15. While the skipper watched the horizon for signs of storm *clouds* the passengers laughed, unaware of danger.

EXERCISE 6

For each of the following pairs, circle A if the first sentence needs a comma. Circle B if the second sentence needs a comma.

1. (A) I saw Helen and called to her.
   (B) I saw Helen and she spoke to me.

2. (A) Alexander the Great is one of my heroes.
   (B) Lincoln was a great president a man who truly loved his country.

3. (A) Yes I will definitely be there on time.
   (B) No is a word I use frequently.

4. (A) I love my cream cheese and olive sandwich.
   (B) I lived for two weeks on jelly cream cheese, and milk.

5. (A) Helen will please do as she was told.
   (B) Helen please do as you are told.

6. (A) Incidentally I could have told you that myself.
   (B) Next in line was the winner of the contest.

7. (A) Because he would not listen to me he found himself in difficulty.
   (B) He soon found himself in difficulty because he would not listen to me.

8. (A) Coming to my last reason I found that the facts are not in his favor.
   (B) Coming to my last reason was the most difficult thing for me to do.

9. (A) We told the story to my brother who had been in the next room.
   (B) We told the story to the officer who was in charge of the investigation.

10. (A) I can still see her standing there teary-eyed and smiling.
    (B) She was teary-eyed and smiling all during the interview.

The Colon (:)

A colon is used after the salutation in a formal letter.

> Dear Mr. Evans:

A colon is used to separate chapter and verse when referring to Biblical quotations.

> Matthew 2:3

A colon is used to separate hours and minutes when expressing the time of day in numbers.

> It is now 3:25.

A colon is used after an introductory clause that precedes a listing or enumeration of items.

> I believe in these truths: a person has freedom of will; a person is obligated to act in accord with one's own conscience; a person must respect others in order to respect oneself.

> The curriculum included the following subjects: accounting, bookkeeping, commercial law, computer usage, and record analysis.

EXERCISE 7

Each sentence in the paragraph below is numbered, and the number is repeated, with a line beside it, below the paragraph. Read each sentence. If you think that the sentence should have a colon, write in the proper numbered space the word or expression from the sentence that should be followed by a colon. If you think that the sentence needs no colon, write the letter N in the numbered space.

(1) It is now 11 43 of a moonless, cold night on the desert. (2) Having spent months and months of incessant and often useless toil exploring this region, I am reminded of Job's words, "So am I made to possess months of vanity, and wearisome nights appointed to me." Job 7 3. (3) In my painstaking researches, I have discovered much evidence that this desert was once a vast ocean bottom. (4) A list of the evidence would include the following shellfish deposits, many salt lakes, beds of rock salt, and large areas filled with saline clay. (5) It seems indisputable to me that this region was once wave covered. (6) I planned to write you a letter. (7) It would have begun with these words. (8) Dear Dr. Evans I am adrift in the Sea of the Sahara, seeking the ghosts of departed fish. (9) Yet, today, water is indeed the scarcest commodity for hundreds and hundreds of miles. (10) I have, however, seen the following a violet tinted fog, a furious, destructive hot wind, and endless clouds of hot dust.

1. _____   6. _____

2. _____   7. _____

3. _____   8. _____

4. _____   9. _____

5. _____   10. _____

End Punctuation—The Period (.)

The period puts a stop to a complete statement, or sentence.

> He is the oldest boy in the group. (A statement)

> Leave the room as quickly as possible. (A quiet order)

> They wished to know what his name was. (An indirect question)

> Kindly enclose a sample of the product. (A request)

End Punctuation—The Question Mark (?)

The question mark follows a direct question.

> When will you go?

End Punctuation— The Exclamation Mark (!)

The exclamation mark ends a statement that is either a strong command or an expression of strong feeling

> Keep still and mind your own business! (A command)

How dare you!
(Notice that this is not really a question, though it is phrased like one, but an expression of anger.)

Look, there's a man falling from the roof!
(An outcry)

EXERCISE 8

Some of the following sentences have the correct end punctuation, others have not. Next to the number, write the letter C if the end punctuation is correct; if it is not correct, write the correct punctuation mark on the line provided.

___ 1. Will you please leave the room quietly and immediately?

___ 2. They wanted to know how old he was.

___ 3. Leave this room at once.

___ 4. He is the smartest boy in the class!

___ 5. Where do you plan to go for your vacation?

___ 6. Are you, a private, telling your sergeant how this should be done!

___ 7. I want to know the simple facts.

___ 8. Please do as you are told!

___ 9. What are you planning to do at the end of this term?

___ 10. The general wanted to know how the enemy troops were disposed of.

EXERCISE 9

In each of the following sentences, on the line provided: Write A if a period should precede Margie. Write B if a question mark should precede Margie. Write C if an exclamation mark should precede Margie. Write D if no punctuation mark should precede Margie.

___ 1. You will have to tell that story to us again Margie was not listening.

___ 2. Leave now Margie will never wait for you!

___ 3. They plan to visit Margie when they arrive in San Francisco.

___ 4. How can I ever thank you Margie will be ever grateful to you for your kindness.

___ 5. Will you help me carry the package Margie plans to use as one of the items on the stage during the rehearsal.

___ 6. He will have to be the one who will help Margie to rewrite the entire second act.

___ 7. When is the report due Margie said that she would help me do the typing.

___ 8. They asked that we remind you to complete the assignment Margie was also absent today.

___ 9. Will you kindly come this way Margie is in charge of the next demonstration.

___ 10. What can I do now Margie left with the keys to the car!

___ 11. Listen to that racket Margie is practicing again.

___ 12. He will be able to help Margie if he is told just what work must be done.

___ 13. The music is hauntingly beautiful Margie must get us that record the next time she goes to the city.

___ 14. Which one is mine Margie had said that I would be given one.

___ 15. Copy the homework assignment quickly Margie will explain how to do the fourth problem.

Quotation Marks (" ")

A pair of quotation marks is used to set off a direct quotation.

John said, "I don't really have the qualifications for the job, but I'll try."

"I don't really have the qualifications," said John, "but I'll try." (broken quotation)

Single quotation marks are used for a quotation within a quotation.

John said, "Mother's exact words were, 'Dust the furniture carefully,' and I'll do just as she said."

The titles of books, magazines, newspapers, plays, movies, television series, and long (epic) poems should be italicized. Titles of chapters, articles, television shows, and works of art and music require quotation marks.

Did you read "On Language" in last Sunday's *New York Times*?

"Walnuts" was one of the funnier episodes on the old *Dick Van Dyke Show*.

"Mona Lisa" is a lovely work of art, as Nat King Cole sang in the 1950's song, "Mona Lisa."

Quotation marks are used to set off words used sarcastically or words of a technical nature, or to show the attitude of the author, usually ironical.

We call him "Skinny." He weighs 284 pounds.

Since he began studying chemistry, all he talks of is "isotopes" and "valences."

Quotation Patterns for Dialogues

1. He said, "We _____."

2. "We _____," he said.

3. He asked, "Are we _____?"

4. "Are we _____?" he asked.

5. "We _____," he said. "We _____. We _____. They _____." (four sentences)

6. He said, "We _____. They _____. Then _____." (three sentences)

7. "We _____." (one speaker)

"Are _____?" (a second speaker)

"Yes, we_____." (first speaker)

CHECK YOUR ABILITY TO USE QUOTATION MARKS CORRECTLY.

EXERCISE 10

In the following paragraph there are numbered, italicized word groups. If you think that quotation marks belong around the italicized group, then place the letter Q after the corresponding number at the end of the paragraph. If you think that there should be no quotation marks, write the letter N.

Did you ever read (1) *This Earth of Ours* by (2) *Jean Henri Fabre?* It is a fascinatng account of the earth's geography and (3) *physiography.* Reading it, you may wonder why Fabre calls the (4) *Sahara Desert* (5) *the Sahara Ocean.* You may be surprised to find that he said (6) *that volcanoes are really helpful to humanity.* In Fabre's words, (7) *they furnish a vent for confined gases.* He also informs us that (8) *many mountains began as masses of lava.* He wrote, (9) *these masses erupted from early volcanoes.*

1. _____   4. _____   7. _____

2. _____   5. _____   8. _____

3. _____   6. _____   9. _____

EXERCISE 11

For each of the following sentences, on the line provided: Write A if quotation marks are needed. Write B if a comma is needed. Write C if a period is needed. Write D if the sentence is punctuated correctly.

___ 1. He said that Paul would not be allowed to visit us.

___ 2. How could you ever do a thing like that! I said.

___ 3. I just finished reading *Tom Sawyer*.

— 4. Ever since I read the book, Tom Sawyer has been one of my best friends.

— 5. I shouted "Don't walk in that direction!"

— 6. The book was written by Mark Twain.

— 7. We subscribe to The New York Times.

— 8. "Why did you do that!" he demanded angrily.

— 9. He demanded to know why I had done it.

— 10. Rowena is one of the main characters in *Ivanhoe*.

— 11. Did you ever do the Funky Monkey? she demanded.

— 12. He told me that I could do all of the experiments by myself.

— 13. Do all of the work yourself, he told me quietly.

— 14. I said I could never leave them.

— 15. He is called the intellectual monster of the century.

— 16. He asked why I had left so early.

— 17. "When do we leave for the party?" asked Helen.

— 18. "To tell the truth," Paul said "I never thought he could do it."

— 19. "Why should I listen" demanded Helen, "since you never do what I tell you anyway."

— 20. "Come early," he suggested, "Alan will be here."

The Hyphen

WITH NUMBERS

The hyphen is used with compound numbers from twenty-one to ninety-nine, when such numbers are spelled out.

twenty-seven   sixty-six
eighty-five   thirty-two

The hyphen is used to separate the numerator from the denominator in fractions that are spelled out.

One-seventh   eight-fourteenths

The hyphen is used between the words in certain compound nouns.

brother-in-law   mayor-elect
author-teacher

WITH PREFIXES

Usually no hyphen is used when such prefixes as anti-, ex-, extra-, mid-, non-, pre-, post-, trans-, ultra-, *and* un- *are added to complete words.*

antislavery   midnight
preseason   extraordinary
nonviolent   transcontinental

There are, however, four exceptions to this general rule:

1. The word to which the prefix is added is a proper (capitalized) noun or adjective.
    all-American   pro-Canadian
    ex-President Clinton

2. The word that is formed when the prefix is added must be distinguished from a homonym.
    re-cover (recover) un-ionized (unionized).

3. The prefix is added to more than one word.
    non-steel-producing nations
    (Note that the original term is "steel-producing nations.")

4. The prefix causes confusion because the same vowels are placed next to each other.
    pre-engineered   anti-inflammatory

But: cooperation coauthors reentry

(These words are familiar because of long-established usage; the hyphen will probably be dropped from many other similar words in the future, for the same reason.)

Note: The prefix *self-* is always followed by a hyphen.

self-control   self-centered

WITH COMPOUND MODIFIERS

A hyphen is used to join two or more words used as a single adjective preceding a noun.

> dual-purpose cleanser
> tried-and-true leader
> well-qualified applicant

But:

> If the first of the compound modifiers ends in *ly,* then no hyphen is used.

> thoroughly researched paper
> quietly conceived solution

If the compound modifier does not precede the noun, no hyphen is used.

> A cleanser that is all purpose
> An applicant who is well qualified
> A leader called tried and true

FOR SYLLABICATION

The hyphen is used to indicate the division of a word at the end of a line—not at the beginning of the next line. It is usually placed at the end of a syllable, but it is best to consult the dictionary to discover the preferred breakpoints.

EXERCISE 12

In each sentence you will find a word in italics. If you think there should be a hyphen joining it to the word that precedes it, write H in the space provided. If you think that there should be no hyphen, write the letter N. Then write the word as it should appear.

— 1. Two post *graduate* students are assisting in the dean's office.

_____

— 2. It is a never *ending* struggle to make ends meet.

_____

— 3. The total is two *hundred.*

_____

— 4. One out of every *ten* will fail this test.

_____

— 5. He is a self *appointed* leader of the group.

_____

— 6. Is it *all* right for us to leave now?

_____

— 7. This is a definitely *incorrect* entry.

_____

— 8. He is the sixty *third* candidate on the list.

_____

— 9. He claims that he is a self *made* man.

_____

— 10. He is working on an anti *pollution* device.

_____

— 11. He attended the post *season* dinner.

_____

— 12. The spectators were a pro *Austrian* crowd.

_____

— 13. He bemoaned his never *realized* dreams.

_____

— 14. These plans of his were never *realized.*

_____

— 15. Three *fifths* of the produce never went to market.

_____

EXERCISE 13

Write A if the hyphen is used correctly in each of the following. Write B if the hyphen is incorrectly used in each of the following. Then write the word correctly.

— 1. He sold me an all-purpose cream.

_____

— 2. The team consists of all-seniors.

_____

— 3. You will have to apply for re-exemption.

_____

___ 4. He fired all twenty-two of the assistants.

_____

___ 5. This is a pre-trial hearing.

_____

___ 6. This book is by ex-President Bush.

_____

___ 7. It was a cleverly-plotted scheme to cheat the villagers.

_____

___ 8. I ate a piece of the so-called pie.

_____

___ 9. The task is all-completed.

_____

___ 10. He turned out to be a never-to-be trusted salesman.

_____

The Dash

WITH ADDITIONS

The dash is used to set off parenthetical phrases, explanatory insertions, and lists of examples.

The visitors—ambassadors, generals, leaders of business—all had to wait their turn before being introduced to the new government leaders.
The visitors—all of our friends—were treated with the greatest courtesy.

The dash is used to show a sudden break, change, or pause in thought.

Do you—can you—allow unqualified personnel to inspect the final products?
The best of all possible worlds—what a cynical phrase—does not describe what our country is going through today!

CAUTION: *The dash is a mark of emphasis; it must be used sparingly. When it is used within a sentence, it is used in pairs. It is not used after a comma, colon, or semicolon. When used at the end of a sentence, the period replaces the second dash.*

We will take full advantage of this opportunity—if it ever comes.

WITH SUMMARIES

The dash is used before a word or phrase that summarizes what has gone before.

Ability to survive by living off the land, knowledge of the ways of the weather, skill in swimming, boating, fishing—all of these and more are needed assets of the professional guide who leads groups through our mountains.

WITH OMISSIONS

A shorter dash is used to mark the omission of the word to between two words or numbers.

April–September 1865
pages 3–132 inclusive
1901–1933
$5.00–$35.00

Note: If the word from *is used, the word* to *should not be omitted.*

From April *to* September 1865

EXERCISE 14

On the line provided, write the word or words that should be preceded by dashes in each of the following—if dashes are required. If no dash is required, then write No.

___ 1. How could we even consider standing by and allowing millions of others to live in misery and degradation this is my primary concern!

___ 2. My classmates those who were still in the city came to offer me their assistance.

___ 3. My closest friends, Henry, Milton, Arthur, and Stanley, agreed to share in the expense.

___ 4. There were from 3 to 303 others who could have done just as well as I did.

___ 5. Read carefully all of the figures on pages 37 and 39.

___ 6. If the company fails and I truly hope it will not he will lose all of his inheritance.

___ 7. I shall now tell you exactly what happened but that would be the wrong thing to do at this moment!

___ 8. These explorations of the moon, outerspace, planets, and the inner core of the earth must be carried on with greatest efficiency if man is to survive for long.

___ 9. The clock ticked loudly oh ever so loudly as the fatal moment approached.

___ 10. Camping, touring, fishing, hunting these are the major outdoor sports of the rural population.

___ 11. Alan actually so he wants us to believe spoke to the President about the plight of the beaver in our valley.

___ 12. Ben Wunder shall we call him friend or foe introduced the bill at our last meeting.

___ 13. Rob Lowe, a the skilled actor, is a most accomplished painter as well.

___ 14. Just when we least expected it, the end came.

___ 15. He left without saying his farewells to any of us, and he left without taking any of the money we had accumulated it had to be that way!

Parentheses

ENCLOSING FIGURES

Parentheses may be used to enclose figures after a spelled-out number.

Fifteen dollars ($15.00)

Parentheses are used around figures or letters to mark divisions of enumerations, especially those run into the text.

The reasons for this request are (1) the lateness of the delivery, (2) the cost of replacement parts, (3) the need for training our staff, and (4) the apathy of the public.

INSERTED ELEMENTS

Parentheses are used to set off inserted elements that do not affect the structure of this sentence, matter that has not been added for emphasis.

He gave a halting (and somewhat obscure) explanation of the process.

EXERCISE 15

On the line provided, write the word or words that should be preceded by parentheses in each of the following—if parentheses are required. If no parentheses are needed, then write N.

___ 1. We wished them as you would have all the happiness and good fortune possible.

___ 2. Two students probably Martin and Louis will be named the winners of the contest.

___ 3. The owner of the parts-factory, Joe Schwab, will interview the successful candidates.

___ 4. My sister Helen you met her in the school library last week has requested this exchange of supplies.

___ 5. It is believed in some areas at least that the mayor is responsible for this mix-up.

___ 6. This sweater is expensive it is hand knitted but so very practical.

___ 7. We ordered kayaks one-man canoes for the expedition down the Colorado.

___ 8. May we—do we have the right to—question so high an official?

___ 9. Edna refused to assist I don't blame her and let them stew all afternoon.

___ 10. The coat cost six pounds about fifteen dollars and was worth every penny.

PRACTICE TEST 1

> DIRECTIONS: In the following paragraphs, you will find numbers in parentheses. If numbers appear where punctuation marks have been used or omitted correctly, write the letter C next to the same number in the answer column at the right. Where punctuation marks have been used or omitted incorrectly, write the correct punctuation mark next to the same number in the answer column.

It[1]s a strange[2] yet true fact that the first discoverers[3] of gold in California[4]s rich soil weren[5]t looking for it. There was Francisco Lopez[6] who discoved a nugget clinging to the roots of a wild onion he'd plucked[7] there was Baptista Ruelle, who found gold near Los Angeles in 1841[8] and General Vallejo, (whose name is always spelled with two l[9]s) who claimed that as early as 1824 gold had been found in the hills[10] of the Sierras[11]! [12]Many people knew these facts,[13] however, no mad stampede was begun.

[14]The tenacious resistance of the Indians in the Sierras,[15] said General Vallejo, [16]prevented people from searching for gold."[17] Many people feel[18] that California would have been discovered there.

In any event, the Gold Rush had it[19]s beginning when a man named Marshall[20] who was building a sawmill for John Augustus Sutter, picked up a piece of gold. Then the rush started. What a rush it was![21] All types of people came,[22] Puritians from England, noblemen from France, convicts, and reckless adventurers from all over the world. Do you think you would like to have been there?[23] I wonder if that question can be answered?[24] The inhabitants[25] days in the temporary towns were filled with danger and violence. "In the days of the Gold Rush[26] wrote Philip Henna,[27] in[28] California. Through Four Centuries,[29] [30]no coward ever started for California and no weakling ever got there." Steadfastly, grimly[31] those men dug for gold that was part of a 300 mile belt[32] which had been deeply buried for thousands and thousands of years. When geological disturbances deep underground pushed the Sierra Mountains up, this buried treasure was also upheaved. Rough[33] unshaven men dug for it[34] they blasted for it, and at times,[35] they even scratched for it with bare fingers. Creeks[36] beds were scraped clean and fortunes[37] were washed into the panners[38] waiting hands.

1. ___
2. ___
3. ___
4. ___
5. ___
6. ___
7. ___
8. ___
9. ___
10. ___
11. ___
12. ___
13. ___
14. ___
15. ___
16. ___
17. ___
18. ___
19. ___
20. ___
21. ___
22. ___
23. ___
24. ___
25. ___
26. ___
27. ___
28. ___
29. ___
30. ___
31. ___
32. ___
33. ___
34. ___
35. ___
36. ___
37. ___
38. ___

Tough^(39) rough towns grew up in the wilderness wastes^(40) as miners moved in. Often, the names of the towns^(41) were vivid and picturesque. Some of those names were^(42) Hangtown, Flea Town, Mosquito Alley^(43) Drunkards^(44) Bar, and Poker Flat.

Incredible amounts of money were made in amazingly brief times. Four hundred thousand dollars was taken out of Bear Gulch in four days^(45) by a few miners. American Bar surrendered $3,000,000 in gold in a matter of weeks. A single pan yielded $1500. The owner of the hotel spent a couple of hours daily^(46) just digging under his building^(47) and made at least $100 a day. I would like to know if anyone ever heard of making money that easily!

Even today^(48) old prospectors^(49) weary and grizzled, search for gold and it can still be found. In the midst of the depression^(50) unemployed workers prospected in the sawdust of an old '49 saloon and found enough gold dust, probably fallen from the clothes of old time celebrating miners, to make it worth their while.

39. ___

40. ___

41. ___

42. ___

43. ___

44. ___

45. ___

46. ___

47. ___

48. ___

49. ___

50. ___

PRACTICE TEST 2

> DIRECTIONS: Read each of the following carefully and then if the sentence contains an error in punctuation, write A. If the sentence contains no error in punctuation, write B.

___ 1. We saw the game and enjoyed it very much.

___ 2. We saw the game but we did not enjoy the score at the end.

___ 3. I ordered fish and chips.

___ 4. Will you send me some refills some erasers and a blotter?

___ 5. I enjoy bread and butter and pickles and sweet cream.

___ 6. It is his wont to take a walk every morning before breakfast.

___ 7. Before breakfast every morning when the weather is fine, he takes a long walk.

___ 8. It is all part of a days work.

___ 9. Its paw was hurt in the accident.

___ 10. You could do it yourself; however I would not advise you to try.

___ 11. Push both levers at the same time, then it will work.

___ 12. I told him "That the problem was solved."

___ 13. I told him, "The problem is solved!"

___ 14. Because he has not followed directions, the problem became overcomplicated.

___ 15. How could you dare think I would not help.

___ 16. Did you see the firemen's new uniforms?

___ 17. It was called Lady's Day.

___ 18. I ordered neither a new book nor another copy of that old one.

___ 19. Now, is the time for you to see how much you can help him.

___ 20. He spells his name with two i's.

___ 21. He borrowed the children's coats for the play.

___ 22. Did I ever show you my brother-in-law's new car?

___ 23. I ate the piece of cake; moreover, I was the one who paid for it!

___ 24. You shall regret this, henceforth, I shall never come to your assistance.

___ 25. Black and white, left and right and tall and short are three examples of extremes.

___ 26. Into the room as quickly as we could; we rushed to save the rest of our supplies.

___ 27. The picture is an unforgettable one; I shall always see that smile on his face.

___ 28. The teams competed against each other in volleyball, and relays.

___ 29. We kept score and the winner received a prize.

___ 30. I had lost the race; I just couldn't run any faster.

___ 31. Ill never forget the look on her face.

___ 32. Willing to learn the rules Phil listened to our advice.

___ 33. Skating over thin ice is a very dangerous pastime.

___ 34. Smoothly silently we glided over the ice.

___ 35. On the morning of the third day the rescue team finally reached us.

___ 36. Harry Smith, my father's best friend, teaches in one of the nearby towns.

___ 37. No, I just can't see how you could ask me to do that.

___ 38. The scouts, tired and hungry, came into the camp at the end of the long hike.

___ 39. Lake Luzerne a town in the foothills of the Adirondacks, is just south of Lake George.

___ 40. My brother, who is a senior in high school, plans to become an electrical engineer.

___ 41. Wishing to please his parents has been the principal cause of his efforts.

___ 42. Franklin D. Roosevelt a victim of polio could have escaped that disease if he had lived twenty years later.

___ 43. Yes is a word that is rarely used by him.

___ 44. I saw Helen but she failed to see me.

___ 45. His request included the following four handkerchiefs, two pairs of woolen gloves and a copy of the Manual.

___ 46. The basic requirements are: goodwill, willingness to help others, and time to devote to our work.

___ 47. I read the New York "Times" regularly.

___ 48. "Must I follow his advice?" I asked. "I am fully capable of doing it on my own!"

___ 49. How many 9's are there in the answer.

___ 50. Cant I help you now?

PRACTICE TEST 3

> DIRECTIONS: Read each of the following carefully and then, if the sentence contains an error
> In the use of an apostrophe, write A.
> In the use of a period, write B.
> In the use of a comma, write C.
> In the use of quotation marks, write D.
> If the sentence contains no error write E.

__ 1. What he doesnt know should be his chief concern.

__ 2. He has a part-time job selling mens' ties.

__ 3. He is not well-trained; nevertheless he plans to do the work all by himself this time.

__ 4. That he had missed the last bus was no reason for his refusing to attend the meeting.

__ 5. Because he had missed the last bus he did not come to the meeting.

__ 6. Peanut butter and jelly or cream cheese and olives can make the most tempting sandwiches.

__ 7. Samuel Clemens, better known as Mark Twain is my favorite humorist.

__ 8. Listen to the music; let its quiet soothing strains melt away your cares.

__ 9. When he finally arrived it was too late.

__ 10. It was much too late when he finally arrived.

__ 11. Seeing that all of the work had been done I decided to take the afternoon off.

__ 12. Seeing that all of the work was completed was my principal concern.

__ 13. The package, bulky and heavy blocked the entrance to the room.

__ 14. Mr. Edwards, my homeroom teacher is very understanding.

__ 15. Paul, who is my favorite cousin, is a member of the varsity baseball team.

__ 16. Our present needs include a first-baseman's mitt.

__ 17. I wondered whether I could ever be as generous as Milton.

__ 18. "If he solves the problem, I said, he will win the prize!"

__ 19. "Give me one chance!" I pleaded, "I know I can do it."

__ 20. "When," I asked, "will you learn to be more patient!"

__ 21. Who said that this was a man's world!

__ 22. Its really time for his plans to be successful.

__ 23. "Here's to your good health!" he shouted.

__ 24. I know that I shall try but never succeed.

__ 25. I know that I shall try but he will be the successful one.

CAPITALIZATION

Rules

We capitalize words as follows:

Proper names of people and animals.

Marty and *Rose Corbett* went for a walk with their dog *Spotty.*

(Notice that *dog* is not capitalized but that *Spotty* is.)

Days of the week and months of the year.

During the summer, Steve spends *Saturdays* and *Sundays* in the country.

(Note that the names of seasons—summer, etc.—are not capitalized.)

> Every July and August, we close our dress shop and do not reopen until the fall.

Nouns and adjectives referring to religious or political holidays.

> Christmas, Hanukkah, Day of Atonement, Thanksgiving, Election Day

Nouns and adjectives denoting nationality, race, or language.

> France, Filipino, Indian, Hispanic, Scottish, African-American, Oriental

Names of countries states, and cities.

> Germany
> Washington, D. C.
> Indiana
> Des Moines, Iowa
> Tokyo, Japan

Names of regions, but not directions.

> In the Civil War, the South fought the North for four long years.

But:

> We turned off the main road and headed south.
> The prairie starts west of the Mississippi River.

Titles of persons and family titles.

> Professor Allesandro was assisted by Doctor Griffith and Colonel Gold.
> Aunt Jessie came with Grandfather.

But:

> Francis Allesandro is a professor.
> Ian Griffith is a doctor.
> Michael Gold is a colonel.

(Note that the title is not capitalized unless it precedes a person's name.)

First letter of every sentence, title of literature, and line of poetry.

> Recently, I read *Of Mice and Men* by John Steinbeck.

> "Who has seen the wind?"
> Neither I nor you:
> But when the leaves hang trembling,
> The wind is passing through.

The pronoun I, the exclamation O.

Words that refer to the Bible or the Deity.

> God revealed His wishes through the Scriptures.
> The Bible is the most widely read book in the world.

Important words in titles (nouns, pronouns, verbs, adverbs, and adjectives).

> The Old Man and the Sea
> The Truth about Flying Missiles
> My Vacation in the Mountains
> How Green Was My Valley

A few parts of the letter form.

> 3016 East Sixth Street
> Oakland, CA 94618
> June 17, 2001
> Dear Sir:
> Gentlemen:
> To Whom It May Concern:
> Very truly yours, (only the first word)
> Cordially yours, (only the first word)

The first word of a sentence in a direct quotation.

> "How are you?" asked Joe.
> Joe asked, "How are you?"

All parts of a hyphenated proper noun except articles or short prepositions or conjunctions.

> Forty-Second Street

The names of organizations, institutions, and schools.

> The Memphis Chamber of Commerce
> The Smithsonian Institution
> Grover Cleveland High School
> Harvard University

The names of political parties, governmental groups, clubs and societies, corporations, religious groups.

> Republican Party
> the Senate
> Audubon Society
> Sears, Roebuck and Company
> Latter-Day Saints

The names of courses but not of subjects.

> Chemistry I comes before Chemistry II in the study of chemistry.

But:

> Of all the sciences, I enjoyed physics and biology the most.
> In many schools, Mathematics 5 is intermediate algebra while Mathematics 6 is trigonometry.

PRACTICE TEST 4

DIRECTIONS: On the lines provided, rewrite the words that require capitalization.

1. next year, i will study english, math, french, and history.

2. the boy asked, "would you please let me look at your bible?"

3. tomorrow will be new year's day, the first of january.

4. there was a cold spell in the northwest last spring.

5. the jacksons are traveling south for the winter.

6. the best book i ever read is *the call of the wild* by jack london.

7. last Wednesday we visited aunt ann.

8. "don't trust doug," leo warned me. "he's a chronic liar.

9. mildred asked martha to join the young women's christian association.

10. tom laughton and harold o'connor belong to the united automobile workers of america.

11. we celebrated the fourth of july in philadelphia, pennsylvania.

12. the near east is rich in oil deposits.

13. protestants, catholics, and jews work together in the national conference of Christians and jews.

14. there are very few arabs living in south america.

15. rosaline told us that she would be leaving in the morning.

16. rosaline said, "i'll be leaving in the morning."

17. the united states of america needed a new flag when alaska and hawaii were admitted to the union as new states.

18. if professor lewis debates senator garlan, dr. fawcett will serve as moderator.

19. among my friends, larry wants to be a
doctor and roy wants to be a baseball
player.

Standard English Usage

GLOSSARY OF THE BASIC TERMS OF GRAMMAR

This alphabetical list of grammatical terms has been included for your convenience when reviewing the sections on Standard English Usage that follow. Grammatical explanations there have been kept to a minimum. However, if any are not clear to you, checking the definitions of the terms involved can clear up many difficulties.

active verb An active verb is one that shows the subject performing some action. (Contrast this with PASSIVE VERB.)

> The boy *chopped* wood.

adjective An adjective is a word that modifies a noun or pronoun; the adjective changes the meaning of the word it modifies by making it more definite.

> *An old brick Colonial* house.

Each adjective contributes to making the picture of "house" more and more definite.

adverb An adverb is a word that modifies a verb. An adverb usually tells *where, when, how,* or to *what extent* a verb performs its action.

> The girl walked *there. (where)*
> The girl walked *yesterday. (when)*
> The girl walked *slowly. (how)*
> The girl walked *much. (to what extent).*

An adverb can also modify an adjective:

> I am *very* tired,

or another adverb:

> I exercised *too* strenuously.

agreement Agreement refers to use of the singular form of the verb with a singular subject and the plural form of the verb with a plural subject.

> *He goes.* (Singular subject—singular verb form)
> *They go.* (Plural subject—plural verb form)
> *Everyone goes. (A* collective pronoun, *everyone* is considered singular and takes the singular form of the verb.)
> *The class goes.* (The word *class* is a collective noun and takes the singular form of the verb when the individuals are thought of as a group.)

Agreement between pronoun and antecedent refers to the use of the same number, person, and gender for a pronoun as for its antecedent.

> Elaine is president of *her* class.

antecedent An antecedent is a word whose place a pronoun takes. Since it would be awkward to say, "John hurried because John was late," we say,

> John hurried because *he* was late.

The pronoun *he* is used instead of *John.* Therefore we say that *John* is the antecedent of *he.*

apposition A word or phrase is said to be in apposition with another word when it is another way of naming that word.

> The Constitution, *a body of laws,* outlines our system of government.

article The article is a kind of adjective used before most nouns.

> *The* house.
> *A* car.
> *An* automobile.

The three examples are the only articles in English.

auxiliary verb Sometimes called a HELPING VERB, the auxiliary is used with a participial form of another verb. Together, they are called the COMPLETE VERB, and the participial form, which always follows the auxiliary, is called the MAIN VERB. The auxiliary form is usually some form of the verb *to be* or *to have.*

> *I   have   gone*
> *auxiliary   main*

In this connection, it is important to remember that the participial form of a verb (present or past participle) may never be used as the main verb in a clause unless it is preceded by a helping verb.

case   Every noun or pronoun in a sentence is related to some other word in that sentence (as subject, object, or indicator of possession). The CASE of a noun or pronoun is a name for that relationship. In English there are only three cases. For further information, see NOMINATIVE, OBJECTIVE, POSSESSIVE CASE.

clause   A clause is a group of words, related in meaning, containing a subject and verb. When a clause makes a completed statement (or has a complete thought), it is a sentence. A clause may be a sentence in itself or, joined by a connecting word to another clause, may be part of a compound or complex sentence.

> *I went home.* (A clause that makes a completed statement—a sentence)
> *When I went home.* (Not a completed statement—therefore not a sentence. This is usually called a DEPENDENT or SUBORDINATE clause.)
> *I went home, and Mary stayed in school.* (Part of a compound sentence)
> *I went home while Mary stayed in school.* (Part of a complex sentence)

There are three types of DEPENDENT or SUBORDINATE clauses: ADJECTIVE, ADVERBIAL, and NOUN.

adjective clause   An adjective clause modifies a noun or pronoun, and is connected to the main clause by a relative pronoun.

> He is a man *whom I like.* (The clause modifies the noun *man.*)

adverbial clause   An adverbial clause modifies a verb (or an adverb) and is connected to the main clause by a subordinate conjunction (sometimes called a RELATIVE CONJUNCTION or CONJUNCTIVE ADVERB).

> He went *when the sun rose.* (The clause modifies the verb *went* by telling *when* he went.)

noun clause   A noun clause is a clause that serves any function served by a noun.

> *Whoever discovered America* was a fearless navigator.

The subject of the verb *was* is the whole clause.

> I know *who committed the crime.*

The object of the verb is the whole clause.

collective noun (pronoun)   A collective noun is a word for a group of individuals (people, animals, or objects). It may describe the group under circumstances where it acts as a single unit.

> The *flock* of sheep *is* large.

At other times, the individuals may not be acting as a unit.

> The *flock* of sheep *were* wandering in many directions.

compound object   Two or more nouns, joined by a coordinating conjunction, both objects of the same verb, form a compound object.

> He liked *baseball* and *tennis.*

compound sentence   Two or more clauses, joined by a coordinate conjunction, make a compound sentence.

> The satellite will revolve around earth for an indefinite period of time, *and* then it will descend like a flaming meteor.

compound subject   Two or more subjects of the same verb form a compound subject.

> *John* and *Jane* went together.

compound verb   Two or more verbs, joined by a coordinating conjunction, each relating to the same subject, form a compound verb.

> The pitcher *wound up* and *threw!*

complex sentence   A complex sentence consists of two or more clauses joined by one or more subordinating conjunctions or relative pronouns.

> Don't shoot *'til* you see the whites of their eyes.
> Grammar is one subject *that* I may never completely understand.
> Grammar is one subject I may never completely understand.

(The relative pronoun may be omitted when the meaning is clear without it.)

comparison of adjectives In addition to modifying nouns, adjectives also show comparison. There are three degrees of comparison: the adjective itself, which is called the POSITIVE degree, the adjective with the suffix *-er* or the word *more* in front of it called the COMPARATIVE degree, and the adjective with the suffix *-est* or the word *most* in front of it called the SUPERLATIVE degree.

POSITIVE: *tall*   *intelligent*   *good*
COMPARATIVE: *taller*   *more intelligent*   *better*
SUPERLATIVE: *tallest*   *most intelligent*   *best*

comparison of adverbs The adverb, usually spelled the same as the adjective with the suffix *-ly* added to it, has the same three degrees. However, in all cases, it is compared by prefixing it with the words *more* or *most*.

POSITIVE: *quickly*   *happily*
COMPARATIVE: *more quickly*   *more happily*
SUPERLATIVE: *most quickly*   *most happily*

Note: In some contexts, *slow* may be used as adverb: Go *slow* (or *slowly*).

conjugate Conjugation is the process of giving the form of a verb in any tense, indicating the changes that follow the use of each person and number.

SIMPLE PRESENT: *I go. You go. He, she,* or *it goes. We go. You go. They go.*

SIMPLE PAST: *I went. You went. He, she* or *it went. We went. You went. They went.*

conjunction A conjunction is a word that joins. It may join two single words, two phrases, or two clauses.

Juan *and* Maria went. (words)
They traveled through the woods *but* not across the river. (phrases)
Juan didn't find the treasure, *nor* did Maria. (clauses)

coordinating conjunction A coordinating conjunction is one type of conjunction. It is used to join independent clauses or words and phrases. See the examples above, which all illustrate the use of coordinating conjunctions. The six coordinating conjunctions are *and, but, or, nor, so* and *yet.*

copulative verb A copulative verb depicts a state of being, and not an action. The most commonly used copulative verb is *to be* and all its forms. Other verbs such as *seems, feels, appears,* and *smells* are copulative when they are used to express a state of being rather than an action.

He *seems* happy.
Everything *appears* in order.

dangling participle When a participle is used as an adjective, it must always modify a noun. When a participle is used in a sentence without a noun to modify, it is said to be dangling. Walking through the streets, the traffic lights are very confusing. The participle *walking* has no noun to modify. We correct it by inserting a noun or pronoun as in the following sentence:

Walking through the streets, *I* found the traffic lights very, confusing.

demonstrative pronoun A demonstrative pronoun points out a specific noun, and is used somewhat like an adjective. In fact, the two demonstrative pronouns are sometimes called DEMONSTRATIVE ADJECTIVES.

SINGULAR:
this pencil
that pencil
PLURAL:
these pencils
those pencils

direct object A direct object receives the action of the verb:

Kevin *threw* the ball.

gender Some nouns and pronouns refer to males or females. Those referring to males are in the MASCULINE GENDER, while those that refer to females are in the FEMININE GENDER. Those that refer to neither are NEUTER. Those that refer to both are COMMON.

MASCULINE: *Brian*   *rooster*   *he*
FEMININE: *Sarah*   *hen*   *she*
NEUTER: *automobile*
COMMON: *cousin*   *poultry*   *they*

gerund Sometimes called a noun participle, the gerund is a participle used as a noun.

Swimming is fun.

idiom An idiom is an expression that is peculiar to or characteristic of a language.

We *catch a cold, toss our heads, throw an idea out.*

imperative See MOOD.

indicative See MOOD.

indirect object An indirect object receives the benefit of the action described by the verb. It is placed between the verb and the direct object, and is never preceded by a preposition.

He gave *me* the pencil.

Throw *John* a ball.

Bake *her* a cake.

infinitive The infinitive is the form of the verb that is preceded by the word *to,* as in *to dance, to sing, to work.* Although never used as a verb, it may be modified by an adverb: *To think quickly is* an asset. It may also take a subject:

I want *Jerry to go,*

or an object:

I want *to see Jerry.*

The infinitive is usually used as a noun. *To dance* well was her ambition. *(To dance* is subject of the verb *was).*

He wanted *to dance. (To dance* is object of the verb *wanted.)*

Note: The word *to* is sometimes omitted:

He did nothing but *(to) cry.*

interrogative adverb In an interrogative sentence, an adverb that asks the question is an interrogative adverb.

When are you going?

Where are you going?

Why are you going?

interrogative pronoun In some interrogative sentences the word that asks the question is a pronoun. Such a pronoun is an interrogative pronoun.

Who are you?

Whom did I choose?

interrogative sentence An interrogative sentence is one that asks a question. For examples, see INTERROGATIVE ADVERB and INTERROGATIVE PRONOUN above.

interjection An interjection is an exclamation, a word usually expressive of feeling that has no grammatical relationship with the rest of the sentence.

Oww! That hurts!

Alas! Poor Yorick, I knew him well.

intransitive verb An intransitive verb takes no object. Some verbs are naturally intransitive and never take an object.

He *sleeps.*

Others may be transitive or intransitive depending on their use in the sentence.

misplaced modifier A modifier should be as close to the word it modifies as possible. Confusion and sometimes ridiculous sentences result when this rule is broken.

I *only* want the money.

What does this sentence mean? It could signify that only *you* and no other person wants the money. It could signify that you only *want* the money, but don't deserve it. It certainly does not mean that you want the money and nothing else.

I like the jockey on the horse *who smokes a cigar.*

Obviously the modifying clause *who smokes a cigar* should be closer to *jockey,* which it modifies.

modify (modifier) Literally, to modify means to change. A word that modifies changes the meaning of the word that it modifies by changing it from the general to the specific. Usually the more modifiers that are used, the more narrow becomes the meaning of the modified word.

Huge, ramshackle, lonely wooden house.

The modifiers have changed the original idea of house to a specific picture of a definite house.

Modifiers are divided into two classes: ADJECTIVES, which modify nouns or pronouns, and ADVERBS, which modify verbs and adjectives.

mood Mood is the form of a verb that changes according to the manner in which the writer or speaker regards the action. There are three recognized moods in English: INDICATIVE MOOD, SUBJUNCTIVE MOOD, and IMPERATIVE MOOD. The following shows the verb *to be* in its three moods:

INDICATIVE MOOD:

I *am* busy.

Is there a doctor in the house?

The speaker regards his statement or question as a fact.

SUBJUNCTIVE MOOD:

If I were President of *the* United States, I'd declare Benjamin Franklin's birthday a holiday. (But *I'm* not President.)

If you were young again, would you

do things differently? (But you are not young again.)

The speaker regards his statement or question as definitely not true.

IMPERATIVE MOOD:

Be still.

The speaker is issuing a command.

nominative case The nominative is one of the three cases in which nouns or pronouns may be used. A noun or pronoun may be in the nominative case for any of the following reasons: SUBJECT OF THE VERB, APPOSITION WITH THIS SUBJECT, or PREDICATE NOMINATIVE.

noun A noun is a word that names a person, place, or thing. A proper noun names a particular person, place, or thing.

	PERSON	PLACE	THING
COMMON:	*boy*	*park*	*statue*
PROPER:	*Joe*	*Prospect Park*	*Statue of Liberty*

number Nouns or pronouns may be singular or plural. Therefore, nouns or pronouns have number, which indicates whether an object referred to is only one, or is more, of its kind. Although verbs change their form and spelling to agree with singular or plural subjects, they do not actually have "number."

object The object of a verb is the noun or pronoun that receives the verb's action.

John slammed the *ball*. (The noun *ball* receives the action of slamming.)

The object of a preposition is the noun or pronoun that first appears after that preposition.

He went to the *store*. (Object of the preposition is *store*.)

objective case Any noun or pronoun that is an object, either of a preposition or verb, is said to be in the objective case. An indirect object is also in the objective case.

objective complement An objective complement completes the meaning of an object.

They elected him *president*.

They made him *chief assistant*.

parallel construction When two words, phrases, or clauses perform the same grammatical function, they should be in the same form.

He likes *dancing* and *to sing*.

Both *dancing* and *to sing* have the same grammatical function; they are objects of the verb *likes*. Therefore, they should have the same form. They should both be participles:

He likes *dancing* and *singing*.

Or they should both be infinitives:

He likes *to sing* and *dance*.

participle The participle is a form of a verb made by dropping the *to* and adding *-ing* to the infinitive.

INFINITIVE: *to go   to pause*

PARTICIPLE (PRESENT): *going   pausing*

The participle is never used as a verb in a sentence unless it is preceded by a helping verb. The PAST PARTICIPLE is a form of the verb usually made by adding the letters *-ed* to the first person singular of the verb, but sometimes the past participle is irregular in form. The past participle of the regular verb *walk* is *walked*. The past participle of the irregular verb *go* is *gone*. A past participle may never be used as a verb unless it is preceded by a helping verb.

When the past participle is not preceded by a helping verb, it is used as an adjective.

The *broken* vase was mended.

parts of speech The eight parts of speech—NOUN, PRONOUN, ADJECTIVE, VERB, ADVERB, CONJUNCTION, PREPOSITION, INTERJECTION—cover the eight basic functions that words may have in a sentence.

passive verb A passive verb is always preceded by some form of the verb *to be* (*was, is, will be, etc.*) and shows action performed upon, rather that by, the subject.

Andrew *was hurt*. (The subject, Andrew, receives the action.)

person There are three "persons" in English *grammar*. The *word* PERSON as used in grammar is a convenient way of identifying a noun or pronoun. The one who speaks is FIRST PERSON, the one spoken to is SECOND PERSON, and the one spoken about is THIRD PERSON.

SINGULAR:

I go.   (*I* is the speaker; and is in the first person.)

You go. (*You* is the one spoken *to*, and is in the second person.)

He goes. (He is the one spoken about, and is in the third person.)

PLURAL:

We go. (first person)

You go. (second person)

They go. (third person)

personal pronoun The personal pronoun is the word *I,* in all its form. Since the forms vary as the person, number, and case vary, the best way to see it in all its forms is through a chart.

SINGULAR

	Nominative	Objective	Possessive
First Person	*I*	*me*	*mine*
Second Person	*you*	*you*	*yours*
Third Person	*he, she, it*	*him, her, it*	*his, hers, its*

PLURAL

	Nominative	Objective	Possessive
First Person	*we*	*us*	*ours*
Second Person	*you*	*you*	*yours*
Third Person	*they*	*then*	*theirs*

phrase A phrase is a group of connected words without a subject or verb.

He went *to the damp, marshy country* to hunt snakes *for his collection.*

To the damp, marshy country is one prepositional phrase, and *for his collection* is another.

possessive case The possessive is one of the three cases in English grammar. It is used to show ownership and is usually indicated by adding an apostrophe and an *s* to the nominative form.

NOMINATIVE: *ship*

POSSESSIVE: *ship's*

He watched the ship's departure.

predicate The predicate is the main verb of the sentence in its complete form, with all its helping verbs.

He *had been playing.* (*Had been playing* is the predicate.)

predicate adjective A predicate adjective is an adjective that is found in the predicate and that modifies the subject.

It occurs only in sentences with copulative verbs.

He was *late.*

predicate noun A predicate noun, sometimes called a PREDICATE NOMINATIVE, is a noun that follows immediately after a copulative verb. It is usually another way of naming the subject.

George Washington was our first *president.*

preposition A preposition is a word that shows a relationship between two nouns or a noun and a verb. Usually this relationship signifies *direction, distance, nearness, ownership,* or *purpose.*

The chalk *is near* the blackboard.

The bridge *is over* the river.

The *proprietor of* the store called the police.

principal parts The principal parts of a verb are the forms of the verb from which the different tenses are derived.

INFINITIVE:	*to watch*	*to think*	*to see*
PRESENT:	*watch*	*think*	*see*
PRESENT PARTICIPLE:	*watching*	*thinking*	*seeing*
PAST:	*watched*	*thought*	*saw*
PAST PARTICIPLE:	*watched*	*thought*	*seen*

pronoun A pronoun is a word used instead of a noun. We could say:

Susan went to school. Susan was late.

Instead we simplify it by saying:

Susan went to school. *She* was late.

relative pronoun A relative pronoun has a double function. It connects two clauses and also replaces a noun in the subordinate clause.

I know a man *who* is an excellent artist.

Who joins the two clauses and also replaces the noun *man.*

run-on sentence A run-on sentence is a form of sentence error in which two or more clauses are improperly connected, or not connected at all.

The ocean pounded at the shore it hurled mighty waves high on the beach.

This is incorrect because there are two clauses and no connecting word.

sentence A sentence is a group of words that are related in meaning, contain a subject and a verb, and make a completed statement or a completed question.

John went.

All three requirements for a sentence are present: a subject, a verb, and a completed statement.

sentence fragment A sentence fragment (incomplete sentence) is incomplete because it lacks one or more of the three ingredients necessary to a sentence.

John, eager to be certain, carefully approaching the stranger and asking his name.

This is a sentence fragment because it lacks a verb.

simple sentence A simple sentence is a sentence with only one clause.

Patiently waiting in the shadows, the tiger listened for its prey.

Standard English Expressions, word forms, and sentence structures in general use and acceptance are labeled as STANDARD ENGLISH. FORMAL ENGLISH includes those forms used on state occasions and solemn occasions. COLLOQUIAL ENGLISH is the level of everyday speech and writing. NONSTANDARD is the label applied to items in usage not in widespread acceptance. Slang terms and ungrammatical forms are considered nonstandard. The examinations for which you are preparing test your mastery of Standard English.

subordinating conjunction A subordinating conjunction is used to connect a modifying or subordinate clause to a main clause.

He went *when* it rained.

He went *since* I did.

superlative degree See COMPARISON OF ADJECTIVES and COMPARISON OF ADVERBS.

syntax Syntax refers to the grammatical relationships among words in sentences. To give the syntax you must explain how a word is used in a particular sentence. Syntax deals with phrase and clause patterns while MORPHOLOGY, the other major component of grammatical study, concentrates on words.

tense TENSE is a grammatical term used only with verbs. It means time, and refers to the time of action of a verb.

PRESENT: *I go*

PRESENT PROGRESSIVE: *I am going*

PAST: *I went*

FUTURE: *I shall go*

PRESENT PERFECT: *I have gone*

PAST PERFECT: *I had gone*

FUTURE PERFECT: *I shall have gone*

transitive verb See INTRANSITIVE VERB. A transitive verb is one that does or can take an object.

I hit the *ball.*

The action of hitting is transferred directly to the object, *ball.*

Mary opened the *window.*

The action of opening is transferred directly to the object, *window.*

usage Usage describes how words and groups of words are employed to convey meaning. It stresses idioms, language conventions, and the level of acceptability of those conventions.

verb Basically, a verb is a word of action or state of being. It tells what the subject does or is.

The *runner,* carefully holding his strength in reserve and waiting for his rivals to tire, suddenly *sprinted* into the lead.

It is easy to see that *runner* is the subject. What word placed after it will make sense and convey the basic action of the sentence? Obviously, it is *sprinted.*

Standard English is the currently accepted usage in which our laws and regulations are written. It is the level of language used in textbooks, newspaper stories, news broadcasts, and television interviews. Because it prevails in our schools and colleges, students must know how to speak and write it if they are to obtain a formal education.

Your knowledge of Standard English usage is tested in two different ways on entrance examinations: One type of question evaluates your ability to identify standard and nonstandard forms, while the other type tests your ability to change nonstandard forms into standard ones.

This section contains a review of the problem in Standard English usage. A form that may be acceptable or correct in another dialect is labeled as nonstandard or incorrect if it is not acceptable in Standard English usage. The terms *error, correct* and *incorrect* as used in this chapter apply only to Standard English.

After working the Exercises, Practice Tests, and Mastery Exams, be sure to check your results with the Answer Key at the end of the chapter.

SENTENCE SENSE ERRORS

Run-ons

I looked everywhere I just couldn't fnd the missing pin.

ANALYSIS: This is a sentence error since it contains two complete ideas (1. I looked everywhere. 2. I just couldn't find the missing pin.) that are not separated by a period or joined together by a conjunction *(in, and, or, but, nor)*. This is an example of a *run-on sentence.*

METHODS OF CORRECTION:

Separate into two sentences.

I looked everywhere. I just couldn't find the missing pin.

Use a conjunction to join properly.

I looked everywhere, and (or but) I just couldn't find the missing pin.

Subordinate one of the ideas.

Although I looked everywhere, I just couldn't find the missing pin.

Comma Splice

I looked everywhere, I just couldn't find the missing pin.

ANALYSIS: This is still a sentence error since a comma cannot serve to separate two complete ideas. This is a variation of the run-on sentence, which is sometimes called a comma-splice or comma sentence, since a comma is incorrectly used to separate two complete ideas.

METHODS OF CORRECTION: Same as for run-on sentences.

Sentence Fragments (Incomplete Sentences)

In the corner.
Coming to the end of the examination.
Since he would not listen to me.
Who is my very best friend.

ANALYSIS: None of these examples is a complete sentence. The first is a prepositional phrase, the second is a participial phrase, the third is an adverbial clause, and the fourth is a relative clause. As they stand now, they are not sentences because they lack one or more of the following: verb, subject, independent clause, question mark.

These are examples of sentence fragments or incomplete sentences.

METHODS OF CORRECTION: Since these groups of words lack complete meaning, there are two possible methods of correction.

Join the group of words to the preceding or following sentence.

Place the package in the corner near the end of table.

Add a sufficient number of words to complete the meaning of the group.

I was pleased when I saw that we were coming to the end of the examination.

Since he would not listen to me, he continued to make the same fundamental errors.

May I tell you about Henry, who is my very best friend?

EXERCISE 16

In the space provided write A *if the sentence is correct. Write* B *if the sentence is a run-on sentence. Write* C *if the sentence is a comma splice. Write* D *if the sentence is a sentence fragment.*

___ 1. I could never have succeeded without the kind assistance I had received from you.

___ 2. Who would have been able to fore-
see such an ending he is certainly a
genius.

___ 3. I have just read the life story of
John Paul Jones, the great
American naval hero.

___ 4. Seeing that the ending was just a
matter of seconds.

___ 5. Don't tell me the answer, I really
want to see whether I can work the
problem out myself.

___ 6. You stay where you are I will send
for you soon.

___ 7. Couldn't the ending have been a
happier one why did he have to disappoint me so!

___ 8. From one end of the campus to the
other, there was only one name
being mentioned.

___ 9. Whenever he tried to tell that story
to one of his friends.

___ 10. Because of the difficulty, he could
not reach home until very late.

___ 11. You tell him I just can't be that
cruel.

___ 12. I planned to use the fishing rod with
which he had so much luck.

___ 13. If I could just see him for one
moment before he begins to take the
test.

___ 14. A book of fun with puzzles.

___ 15. Whichever one you really want me
to choose.

___ 16. Send the book to him today he has
just finished reading the one I had
lent him.

___ 17. Margie plans to go to college, she
wants to follow in her sister's footsteps.

___ 18. Frances is my favorite aunt, we get
along well for hours at a time.

___ 19. I really wish I knew what I wanted
to be my parents would be very
much relieved.

___ 20. Because I had not left the room all
evening.

___ 21. If you so wish, I will write the note
for you.

___ 22. Could we go over the last measure I
don't think that it had the right
tempo.

___ 23. Arriving on time, we were there to
greet the incoming freshmen.

___ 24. Into the lives of all of us at some
time or another.

___ 25. Between you and me.

*Two of the sentences in each of the following
groups contain no errors. Circle the letters of
the correct sentences.*

26. (A) After the entire incident had died
down. We tried to discover what had
been the cause.
(B) After the entire incident had died
down, we tried to discover. What
had been the cause.
(C) After the entire incident had died
down, we tried to discover what had
been the cause.
(D) Joe Louis. A veteran boxer of many
years' standing with a reputation for
honesty and integrity.
(E) Joe Louis was a veteran boxer of
many years' standing with a reputation for honesty and integrity.

27. (A) We had to do all of the calculations without the aid of the machine since we were uncertain of how to operate it.
    (B) We had to do all of the calculations. Without the aid of the machine since we were uncertain of how to operate it.
    (C) Since we were uncertain of how to operate it, we had to do all of the calculations without the aid of the machine.
    (D) Since we were uncertain of how to operate it. We had to do all of the calculations without the aid of the machine.
    (E) Uncertain of how to operate it. We had to do all of the calculations without the aid of the machine.

28. (A) I should like to meet David Warshauer. A famous American psychologist.
    (B) Coming to the end of the story is always a painful experience for me.
    (C) I should like to tell you the entire story. Because I really respect your opinion.
    (D) How could you do such a thing! I am really annoyed with you!
    (E) If you follow the directions. You will become as confused as I!

29. (A) I had just completed reading one of the best books I have ever read, *Hit and Run* by Duane Decker.
    (B I had just completed reading one of the best books I have ever read. *Hit and Run* by Duane Decker.
    (C) It is a story of a ball player. Who must learn to control his temper.
    (D) He had perfect control of his playing ability, but he just couldn't control his tongue.
    (E) He finally learned a lesson it cost him too much to learn it the hard way.

30. (A) Ken taught me how to swim, he insisted on my learning not to be afraid of the water from the very start.
    (B) I like him very much he is one of the most patient men I have ever met.
    (C) We belonged to a class-group, but he seemed to have time to treat us as individuals at all times.
    (D) When I finally passed the beginner's test, it was one of the proudest moments of my life.
    (E) Everyone should know how to swim, don't you agree with me?

31. (A) Dave has always been afraid to be second best in whatever he does.
    (B) When we were learning how to water-ski. He insisted on receiving as much attention as he felt he needed from the instructor.
    (C) Sometimes Jerry had planned to give him that amount of time, sometimes he hadn't.
    (D) We all sensed that his need did not arise from selfishness it seemed to stem from his intense desire to be first.
    (E) I felt that he would have been one of the best, anyway, without his making such an obvious nuisance of himself.

32. (A) George Pulver. Who had owned a store in our neighborhood. Was a very good friend of our family.
    (B) Because he was so understanding, we often went to him with our problems.
    (D) Regardless of how busy he was in his store. He always seemed to find time to listen to our troubles.
    (D) He was so different from others, he rarely offered definite advice.
    (E) He would ask simple questions that would soon make us realize what the correct solution would be—for us.

33. (A) Margie has always found time to practice playing her guitar. Even during examination season.
    (B) At first she had studied it as a musical instrument. Trying to imitate the great Segovia.
    (C) When she realized that she would never be able to spend all of the time required for real study, she took stock of the situation.
    (D) She enjoyed playing the instrument she enjoyed singing the tunes that she played.
    (E) She soon reached her present compromise, to continue playing the instrument, not for its own sake, but as an accompanying musical instrument for social singing.

34. (A) Joel soon learned an important lesson. One that affected his attitude toward many things.
    (B) He noticed the intensity with which Harold had approached everything he did.
    (C) Harold did not push others out of his way, he only insisted that he himself try his best whenever he did anything.
    (D) Joel soon saw that if Harold became involved in an activity, he would devote all of his attention to it.
    (E) Joel now agrees with Harold, whatever is worth doing at all is worth doing well.

THE DOUBLE NEGATIVE

Typical Nonstandard Form

I don't want no one else to know the combination of the lock

ANALYSIS: Standard English does not allow two negatives to control one negative idea. Only one negative verb, adjective, adverb, pronoun, or conjunction can be used in one sentence to convey a negative idea. The example has a negative adverb (*don't*) and a negative adjective (*no*). One of them must go!

METHOD OF CORRECTION: Eliminate one of the negatives.

I want no one to know … or I don't want anyone to know …

Typical Nonstandard Form

I have hardly no money left in that account.

ANALYSIS: Words like *hardly, scarcely, but a,* and *barely* (when it means hardly) are negative in meaning. Therefore, they cannot be used along with another negative to convey a *negative* idea.

METHOD OF CORRECTION: Eliminate one of the negatives.

I have hardly any money left in that account.

EXERCISE 17

Write A if the sentence is standard. Write B if the sentence is nonstandard.

___ 1. He won't listen to nobody in this matter.

___ 2. I can't hardly see the speck on the horizon anymore.

___ 3. It wasn't the double negative that bothered me.

___ 4. That can't be done no more by any member of our team.

___ 5. I would scarcely call that "No time at all!"

___ 6. We hadn't barely enough money to pay for the train fare.

___ 7. We would never ask nobody to do that type of assisting.

___ 8. Can't you never do the right thing the first time you try!

___ 9. I never want to see you again!

___ 10. Don't you want to see the doctor now?

___ 11. I haven't but a single word to say to you—"Courage!"

___ 12. They don't want nothing to do with him.

___ 13. They don't want nothing for nothing.

___ 14. Nobody in his right mind would accept no money for so valuable an object.

___ 15. I don't want either your compliments nor your favors.

Two of the sentences in each of the following groups contain nonstandard forms. Circle the letters of the standard sentences in each group.

16. (A) Harold doesn't want no one to help him.
    (B) Harold wants no one to help him.
    (C) Harold doesn't want anyone to help him.
    (D) Harold doesn't want help from no one.
    (E) Harold doesn't want help any more from anybody.

17. (A) I could scarcely see the end of the pier.
    (B) I couldn't scarcely see the end of the pier.
    (C) I had barely enough time to make the train.
    (D) I hadn't barely enough time to make the train.
    (E) We wouldn't want to do it either.

18. (A) Either you come with me, or I just won't go.
    (B) We hadn't but a moment to spare.
    (C) We could hardly follow his directions.
    (D) We couldn't hardly follow his directions.
    (E) We had but a moment to spare.

19. (A) I have just learned my lesson, and I won't bother him no longer.
    (B) I have learned my lesson, and I won't bother him ever again.
    (C) Don't forget that this letter doesn't belong to you.
    (D) I won't want to see him neither.
    (E) There is scarcely an ounce of flour left in the bin.

20. (A) We couldn't hardly wait for the reply from the advertiser.
    (B) Who said that we could never find the answer?
    (C) We could hardly wait for the reply from the advertiser.
    (D) I am not going there no more.
    (E) No isn't the politest of replies.

PAST TENSE OR PAST PARTICIPLE

Typical Nonstandard Form

I done whatever was expected of me.

ANALYSIS: In Standard English, the past participle *done* cannot be used by itself as a verb. It needs a helping *(auxiliary)* verb.

METHODS OF CORRECTION:

Add a helping verb.

I have done whatever was expected of me.

Use the past tense instead.

I did whatever was expected of me.

Typical Nonstandard Form

He had never *broke his promise before.*

ANALYSIS: The past tense of the verb cannot be used with a helping verb.

METHODS OF CORRECTION:

Remove the helping verb.

He never broke *his promise before.*

Use the past participle instead of the past tense.

He had *never* broken *his promise before.*

EXERCISE 18

Write A *if the sentence is standard. Write* B *if the sentence contains a nonstandard verb form.*

___ 1. I was so thirsty that I could have drank two quarts of milk then and there.

___ 2. The dog had hurt its paw.

___ 3. I would never chosen that copy of the text to give to the principal.

___ 4. When my term come, I was too nervous to begin.

___ 5. What is done is done and nothing further need be said.

___ 6. The pipe had bursted into three parts.

___ 7. An argument had arose very early in the evening.

___ 8. He had been stricken ill during the third act.

___ 9. You should never have wore so flimsy a jacket on such a cold evening.

___ 10. The case has been thrown out of court.

___ 11. I am glad that you had brung that matter up for discussion.

___ 12. My jacket shrank three inches after the soaking it received in the rain last night.

___ 13. He could never have teached me how to do that without your help.

___ 14. The net had been torn into shreds by the struggling, frantic bird.

___ 15. A cold breeze sprang up during the night to hamper the rescue workers.

___ 16. I wish you had seen his face when I rung the bell at three in the morning.

___ 17. I wish I knew now what I had knew then at the time of the test.

___ 18. He did not feel too well after he had ate fourteen pieces of pizza pie.

___ 19. The river had frozen overnight so we could go skating without any danger of falling in.

___ 20. The fun begun when he tried to disregard our suggestions.

___ 21. The river had slowly rose above its banks.

___ 22. He said that I had brang all of the spare parts with me on the first trip.

___ 23. I could have burst with pride when my experiment was described.

___ 24. I awoke with a terrific headache because I had forgot to open the window the night before.

Some of the sentences in each of the following groups contain standard forms. Circle the letters of the standard sentences only.

25. (A) How could I have knew what he had on his mind?
    (B) How could I have known what he had on his mind?
    (C) You should never have chose that topic to write on.
    (D) The toast was burnt to a crisp.
    (E) You should never have chosen that topic to write on.

26. (A) The news of my success bursted the shell that kept me in isolation.
    (B) He had spoke to me about you.
    (C) I could have sworn that you had told me the formula.
    (D) We had drove all night to reach Lake Luzerne by morning.
    (E) I sprung to my feet in protest.

27. (A) This river can be swam during the spring floods.
    (B) This river can be swum during the spring floods.
    (C) He has stoled all of the jokes that I had planned to tell.
    (D) An unpleasant situation has arose.
    (E) I had done all of the work without complaining to anyone.

28. (A) All that I know is that I run as fast as I could to get the message to the officer in charge.
    (B) The bell has already rung.
    (C) The bell has already rang.
    (D) He had never eaten so much in so little time before.
    (E) He said that I had mistook a suggestion for a command.

29. (A) You could never have wrote so unpleasant a note.
    (B) After he had wrang the mop almost dry, he hung it up in the closet.
    (C) The ship was sank when it hit the iceberg.
    (D) I hope you seen what I had been describing to you.
    (E) The record is really broken.

30. (A) He had took the dishes from this closet.
    (B) He sprang to his feet and shouted with joy when he saw us coming toward his cabin.
    (C) I have swum in colder water than this, but I just can't recall when.
    (D) I never would have beat him if he hadn't been so annoyed with himself.
    (E) The picture was stolen as a foolish prank.

31. (A) He has went to see whether we can join the group this afternoon.
    (B) Overnight he become a world famous pianist.
    (C) Overnight he has became a world famous pianist.
    (D) Overnight he has become a world famous pianist.
    (E) Overnight he could have become a world famous pianist.

32. (A) He drunk deeply from the cup of bitter experience and gained sober wisdom.
    (B) I could have swore that you had been with us during the visit.
    (C) I am glad that you were the one who had brought that matter up.
    (D) I am glad that you were the one who had brung that matter up.
    (E) I am glad you were the one who brought that matter up.

33. (A) Yesterday the sun had shone only for a few minutes.
    (B) I wish I could have wrung his neck before he uttered those words.
    (C) I really seen it with my own eyes.
    (D) I had really saw it with my own eyes.
    (E) I could have told you that I had seen it with my own eyes.

34. (A) I am glad that you have spoke to him about this matter.
    (B) The mill has run this way for over one hundred years.
    (C) The mill run this way for over one hundred years.
    (D) The mill has ran this way for over one hundred years.
    (E) The mill ran this way for over one hundred years.

ERRORS IN AGREEMENT

This area is one in which students make a great many of their errors. Test yourself to see whether you are a master or a novice.

Typical Error

Only one of the onlookers (WAS, WERE) *willing to help us.*

ANALYSIS: A verb agrees with its subject in number. Here the subject is *one*, not *onlookers*. *Onlookers* is the object of the preposition *of*. *One*, the subject, is singular and should be followed by the singular form of the verb, *was*, not the plural form, *were*.

CORRECT ANSWER: Only one of the onlookers *was* willing to help us.

Typical Error

Somebody in the class (IS, ARE) *going with me.*

ANALYSIS: *Someone, everyone, no one, somebody, everybody, nobody,* and *each* are singular and should be followed by the singular form of the verb. *Are* is plural; *is* is singular.

CORRECT ANSWER: Somebody in the class *is* going with me.

Typical Error

Alice with her three friends (WRITE, WRITES) *a weekly column for the school newspaper.*

ANALYSIS: Additional phrases introduced by *with, in addition to, including, as well as,* and *together with* are not part of the subject. The subject is still *Alice,* a singular noun. *Write* is plural; *writes* is singular.

CORRECT ANSWER: Alice with her three friends *writes* a weekly column for the school newspaper.

Typical Error

Neither the pen nor the books (WAS, WERE) *on the desk.*

ANALYSIS: With *neither ... nor, either ...or,* the verb form is determined by the noun (or pronoun) that is closest to the verb. *Books* is plural; *were* is the plural verb form.

CORRECT ANSWER: Neither the pen nor the books *were* on the desk.

Typical Error

He is one of the students who (HAVE, HAS) *been elected to the student body executive committee.*

ANALYSIS: In a relative clause, the noun before the *who, whom, which,* or *that* determines the verb form. In the example, *students* precedes *who. Students* is plural; therefore we must use *have,* which is plural.

CORRECT ANSWER: He is one of the students who *have* been elected to the student body executive committee.

Typical Error

Everyone should use (HIS OR HER, THEIR) *own notebook.*

ANALYSIS: *His or her* is singular; *their* is plural. *His* or *her* should be used to refer to a singular antecedent. *Their* should be used to refer to a plural antecedent. Since *everyone* is singular, *his or her* must be used.

CORRECT ANSWER: Everyone should use *his or her* own notebook.

EXERCISE 19

Write A if the sentence is standard. Write B if the sentence contains a nonstandard verb form.

___ 1. One of the students have my homework.

___ 2. Are any of you going to see the game today?

___ 3. One-fourth of the crew was injured in that game.

___ 4. One-fourth of the members are ready to vote now.

___ 5. Any one of the four is as good as these.

___ 6. A box of oranges were received at the depot early this morning.

___ 7. Neither you nor he is responsible for my errors.

___ 8. Either of the men know the combination to the safe.

___ 9. She is one of the girls who is to speak at the rally.

___ 10. Every one of the solutions were rejected by the judges.

___ 11. Either this group or several of those was the object of his search.

___ 12. Pauline together with her four friends wish to see you immediately.

___ 13. The carton of old magazines were placed in the basement.

___ 14. Everyone except the members of the laboratory squad see this as a major problem.

___ 15. Milton and Jerome without the aid of anyone of their friends has solved the problem within the time limits set by the rules.

___ 16. There is only one set of rules that I ever follow.

___ 17. Here are the set of records that he bought for me.

___ 18. Each of the boys who sell newspapers has to have an identification badge.

___ 19. Why don't someone fix the switch for the electric trains?

___ 20. Why don't he mind his own business!

___ 21. Edna accompanied by Margie and her friend has left for the station.

___ 22. No longer do his incessant cries for assistance bother his calloused guards.

___ 23. Neither the time nor the energy is his at this moment.

___ 24. Each of the contestants have three minutes to work out the puzzle.

___ 25. Are there anyone of the players ready to join me in a practice session?

Some of the sentences in each of the following groups contain no errors. Circle the letters of the correct sentences only.

26. (A) Some of the students see an advantage in not going to the game.
   (B) Someone among the students know how to handle this engine.
   (C) Someone among the students knows how to handle this engine.
   (D) Some of the students sees an advantage in not going to the game.
   (E) Is anyone of the students present now?

27. (A) A group of boys was seen walking toward the gymnasium.
   (B) Some of the boys was seen walking toward the gymnasium.
   (C) A group of boys were seen walking toward the gymansium.
   (D) Some of the boys were seen walking toward the gymnasium.
   (E) Someone among the boys were seen walking toward the gymnasium.

28. (A) Each of you are going to use your own notes.
   (B) Each of them are going to use your notes.
   (C) Each of them is going to use your notes.
   (D Each of you is going to use your own notes.
   (E) Everyone wished to use their own notes.

29. (A) None of my friends do the work in just that way.
   (B) None of my friends carried their skates with them.
   (C) Have there been any lessening of effort on his part?
   (D) None of my friends does the work in just that way.
   (E) Has there been any lessening of effort on his part?

30. (A) One of the spectators who was watching the game knows the answer to our question.
    (B) One of the spectators who were watching the game knows the answer to our question.
    (C) One of the spectators were watching the game know the answer to our question.
    (D) One of the spectators who was watching the game know the answer to our question.
    (E) One of the spectators who was watching.

31. (A) Neither your help nor my assistance are needed by him.
    (B) Was there any of them available for our use at that time?
    (C) Were there any of them available for our use at that time?
    (D) Here lie the remnants of my fondest hopes.
    (E) Here lies the remnants of my fondest hopes.

32. (A) Joel along with his parents enter through those doors every day.
    (B) Joel along with his parents enters through those doors every day.
    (C) He is one of those people who always sees the bright side in everything.
    (D) He is one of those people who always see the bright side in everything.
    (E) Is there anyone among you who can explain this problem to me?

33. (A) Everybody, including the three strangers, knows the path through the woods.
    (B) Everybody, including the three strangers, know the path through the woods.
    (C) Are any of you interested in taking a walk with me?
    (D) Did everyone use their own pen?
    (E) Did everyone use his own pen?

34. (A) A group of trees were destroyed by the storm.
    (B) Jack as well as Lucy were invited to join the group.
    (C) Jack as well as Lucy was invited to join the group.
    (D) Neither your sense of humor nor your cruelty affect me much.
    (E) One of the soldiers left his supplies near our cabin.

35. (A) Everyone of the candidates who applies now is going to be approved.
    (B) A set of carving knives, no matter how sharp they may be, are better than the ability of the user.
    (C) Dave with Phyllis and Lewis is coming toward our house.
    (D) Dave with Phyllis and Lewis are coming toward our house.
    (E) Everyone of the candidates who apply now are going to be approved.

ERRORS IN CASE

Typical Error

Paul and (I, ME) *will attend the conference.*

ANALYSIS: The subject is always in the nominative case, whether it is simple or compound. *Paul* will attend; I will attend.

CORRECT: Paul and *I* will attend the conference.

Typical Error

The cake was baked for Allan and (WE, US).

ANALYSIS: The object of a verb or of a preposition is always in the objective case, whether it is simple or compound. The sentence means: The cake was baked for *Allan;* the cake was baked for us.

CORRECT: The cake was baked for Allan and *us.*

Typical Error

She is a better scholar than (HE, HIM).

ANALYSIS: After *than* or *as,* part of the sentence is often omitted. If we complete the sentence, the correct answer becomes obvious.

CORRECT: She is a better scholar than he *(is).*

Typical Error

It is (HE, HIM).

ANALYSIS: A pronoun that comes after any form of the verb *to be* (except the infinitive) is a predicate nominative and such a form uses the nominative case. (Usage has allowed *It is me* to be accepted as a correct colloquial form parallel to the more formal *It is I.* However, this is the only exception.) *Him* is the object form; *he* is the predicate nominative form; therefore, *he* is correct.

CORRECT: It is *he.*

Typical Error

(WE, US) *seniors will have an award assembly this week.*

ANALYSIS: The pronoun is in apposition to the noun *seniors.* The appositive must be in the same case as the noun it is in apposition with. *Seniors* is in the nominative case; therefore, we must choose *we,* which is the nominative form.

CORRECT: *We* seniors will have an award assembly this week.

Typical Error

She asked Henry and (I, ME) *to attend the meeting.*

ANALYSIS: Both the subject and the object of an infinitive are in the objective case. *Me* is the objective form; therefore it is the correct form. The difficulty arises from the fact that the (I, ME) is part of a compound group. Treat it separately. (She asked Henry to attend the meeting. She asked *me* to attend the meeting.) Treated separately, the correct form becomes obvious.

CORRECT: She asked Henry and *me* to attend the meeting.

Special Note: Errors are frequently made with the objective form of the pronouns that should follow the prepositions *between, like, except,* and *but* (when it means except). Memorize as correct: Between you and me!

EXERCISE 20

Write A *if the sentence is correct. Write* B *if the italicized pronoun should be in the nominative case. Write* C *if the italicized pronoun should be in the objective case.*

___ 1. He left the work for you and *I.*

___ 2. You will have to decide between Paula and *us.*

___ 3. Everyone except *they* had heard the shocking news.

___ 4. Hank and *me* decided to handle these matters in our own way.

___ 5. *Who* did you want to see?

___ 6. You are a better peacemaker than *me.*

___ 7. No one but Morris and *us* had any right to handle the matter on hand.

___ 8. For *whom* did you intend that insult?

___ 9. Her brother really looks like *her.*

___ 10. They requested Addie and *we* to visit the dean's office.

___ 11. It is all over between them and *me.*

___ 12. Is it she *whom* you wanted to see?

___ 13. It was *them* all right.

___ 14. She can write as effectively as *him.*

___ 15. He told the truth to *we* members of the club.

___ 16. *Us* sophomores must not lose our identity.

___ 17. After Edna and *me* had played golf, we went to the conference.

___ 18. It was difficult for Lenny and *we* to find the correct solution.

___ 19. Was it they *who* you wished to see?

___ 20. Between you and *I*, I think there is a much better road than this.

___ 21. Did you want to see Alice or *me?*

___ 22. *Who* in your opinion should be chosen to lead the group?

___ 23. *Us* members of the team must be loyal to the coach.

___ 24. She asked him and *I* to speak to you.

___ 25. Everyone except John and *I* had brought skates to the rink.

Some of the sentences in each of the following groups contain errors. Circle the letters of the incorrect sentences only.

26. (A) Neither Henry nor me could see our way clear to joining them.
    (B) He is by far a more skillful driver than me.
    (C) Mother spoke to Phyllis and I about the coming party.
    (D) We men must learn to handle the ax more skillfully.
    (E) Between you and they, I shall never be able to do my own work

27. (A) Tell me whom I must see.
    (B) Tell me who I must see.
    (C) Everybody but me had been invited.
    (D) Everybody but I had been invited.
    (E) Does this ruling apply to Frank and I?

28. (A) He will never be able to swim as well as I.
    (B) He will never be able to swim as well as me.
    (C) He will never be able to swim as well as us.
    (D) He will never be able to swim as well as we.
    (E) He spoke to her as well as to me.

29. (A) He said that it was she.
    (B) He said that it was her.
    (C) He said that it was I.
    (D) He said that is was me.
    (E) He said that it could have been them.

30. (A) He spoke slowly to us beginners.
    (B) He spoke slowly to we beginners.
    (C) We girls must practice if we ever expect to win the game.
    (D) Us girls must practice if we ever expect to win the game.
    (E) Give us leaders some credit for experience and intelligence.

CORRECT USE OF ADJECTIVES AND ADVERBS

Good *is normally the adjective form, and* **well** *the adverb form, but when applied to health,* **well** *is an adjective.*

> ADJECTIVE: She looks *good* in that dress!
> ADJECTIVE: She looks *well* now that she has recovered.
> ADVERB: The machine runs *well.*

A verb that indicates state of being, not action, is followed by a predicate adjective describing the subject rather than by an adverb, which would describe the action in the verb. Whether the verb indicates action or state of being in a particular sentence depends upon the meaning of the sentence since most of these verbs can be used in both senses. Some of these verbs are

sound	grow	look
seem	smell	become
taste	feel	be

ADVERB: This plant grew quickly. (Quickly tells how the plant grew.)
PREDICATE ADJECTIVE: The room grew quiet. (Quiet describes the room.)

The form **an** *is used instead of* **a** *before a word beginning with a vowel sound.*
   an actress   *an* uncle   *an* honor
But: *a* union man   *a* hotel

Just as **ain't** *has been declared unacceptable, certain adjective forms are wrong because they are classified as errors of illiteracy.*

WRONG:	CORRECT:
kind of a	kind of
this here	this
these here	these
that there	that
those there	those
these kind	this kind (*or* these kinds)
those kind	that kind (*or* those kinds)
these sort	this sort
those sort	that sort
them (as an adjective)	that, those

When two persons or things are being compared, use the **comparative**.
   WRONG: He is the *brightest* of the two brothers.
   CORRECT: He is the *brighter* of the two brothers.

When three persons or things are being compared, use the **superlative**.
   WRONG: Of the three, he is the *slower*.
   CORRECT: Of the three, he is the *slowest*.

Never combine both methods of forming either the comparative or the superlative in a given instance.
   WRONG: She is the *most quietest* girl in the class.
   CORRECT: She is the *quietest* (or the *most quiet*) girl in the class.

Use the word **other** *or* **else** *when a person, place, or thing is compared with the entire group to which it belongs.*
   WRONG: He is more capable than *any* boy in his group.
   (He cannot be more capable than himself; yet he is part of the group!)
   CORRECT: He is more capable than *any other* boy in his group.

Some adverbs have the same form as their corresponding adjectives. Some of these are
   ill   slow   fast   deep   sweet
CORRECT:
Go *slow*.
Drive *slow*.
Take a *slow* train.

Note: Usage has made the following also acceptable.
   Go *slowly*.
   Drive *slowly*.

EXERCISE 21

Write A if the sentence is correct. Write B if the sentence contains an error in the use of an adjective or an adverb.

___ 1. That suit sure fits him well!

___ 2. You will have to do more better than that if you expect to remain on the first team.

___ 3. Do not put them there!

___ 4. This is the kind of a sentence that I enjoy reading.

___ 5. Go slow as you approach the curves, and you will do good.

___ 6. This here is as far as I can go now.

___ 7. He doesn't look so good tonight.

___ 8. Go quick, and get Mr. Hammond here as soon as you can.

___ 9. I always enjoy reading those kind of books.

___ 10. May I have one of those over there?

___ 11. He is the best player on his team, without any doubt.

___ 12. These kinds of records must be handled with additional care.

___ 13. She is more capable than any girl in her clique.

___ 14. She took an onion so that she could have a good cry.

___ 15. It was the most noisiest party that I have ever attended, but I enjoyed it.

___ 16. We found that there boat at the end of the lake.

___ 17. Is this the sort of remark that you should make?

___ 18. The machine now runs very quiet.

___ 19. The flowers smelled so sweet that I could not leave the garden.

___ 20. You did good when you really tried.

___ 21. He showed me a real good copy of the picture.

___ 22. She is most funniest when her audience applauds at the right moments.

___ 23 Give him one of those there reports when he comes in.

___ 24. She is brighter than any of her friends.

___ 25. How could you have put that bottle over there!

Some of the sentences in each of the following groups contain no errors. Circle the letters of the correct sentences only.

26. (A) The VCR operates good now that he has fixed it.
    (B) He sure looks well now that he has recovered from his illness.
    (C) Look sharp and breathe deep if you want to survive the crisis.
    (D) Be quiet when you enter that corridor.
    (E) Walk quiet when you go through that corridor.

27. (A) The torch of freedom burns bright throughout the world.
    (B) He drives so careful that I have full confidence in his ability.
    (C) The torch of freedom burns brightly throughout the world.
    (D) He drives so recklessly that I fear for his life.
    (E) They played well during the rehearsal.

28. (A) Please be prompt for tonight's rehearsal.
    (B) Arrive prompt, and you will leave on time.
    (C) Go direct to my office when you arrive.
    (D) Go directly to my office when you arrive.
    (E) That new suit looks good on him.

29. (A) Them words express my feelings exactly.
    (B) Them words express my exact feelings.
    (C) That there was a foul ball.
    (D) That was a foul ball.
    (E) That there sure was a foul ball.

30. (A) Helen is more capable than anyone in her family.
    (B) Helen is the most capable one in her family.
    (C) Jonathans are the most tastiest of all apples.
    (D) Jonathans are more tasty than any apples.
    (E) It was a argument that I just could not answer.

VERBS OFTEN CONFUSED

accept a verb that means to *take* or *receive*. Please *accept* my apology.

except as a preposition means *other than*. Everyone *except* Dan had done the work. Except as a verb means to *omit* or *exempt*. Paul was *excepted* from the ruling.

borrow you borrow *from*. I *borrowed* a book from the library.

lend you lend *to*. Mary needed money so I had to *lend* a dollar to her.

isn't–ain't *ain't* may be in the dictionary, but society has ruled it an outcast. Eliminate *ain't* from your vocabulary!

don't–doesn't *does* and *doesn't* are the third person singular *(he, she, it, body, one,* etc.) Use *does* in the affirmative and *doesn't (does not)* in the negative. *Do* and *don't* are used with the first and second persons *(I* or *you do)* and the third person plural *(they don't).* When in doubt, substitute *do not* for *don't* and *does not* for *doesn't.*

bring–take *bring* means to carry to the person who is speaking. *Bring* the book to me. *Take* means to carry away from the speaker. *Take* it upstairs to my room.

learn–teach you learn *from* someone and teach *to* someone.

stay–stand *stay* means to remain. *Stand* refers to a physical position, being erect. Memorize this incorrect sentence and you will not make the mistake again: WRONG: When he broke his ankle, he *stood* in bed for three weeks. (How cruel!) CORRECT: When he broke his ankle, he *stayed* in bed for three weeks.

beat–beat meaning to *defeat,* does not change its form whether it is in the present or the past. PRESENT: Today I *beat* him in a game of chess. PAST: Yesterday I beat him in a game of chess. (Bet always means to wager. It never means to defeat.) WRONG: They *bet* us by a score of 8-1. CORRECT: They *beat* us by a score of 8-1.

let–leave *let* means to allow. *Leave* is not a substitute for *let.*

WRONG:	CORRECT:
Leave him go.	Let him go.
Leave it be.	Let it be.
Leave him do it.	Let him do it.

sit–set the only thing that sets itself is either the sun or a hen. Someone sits himself down; someone sets something else down. WRONG: *Set* down on that chair. CORRECT: *Sit* down on that chair.

lie–lay these are by far the most difficult verbs on the list for people who refuse to memorize some simple facts. Here are the facts:
Lie means to *rest* or *recline.*
Lay means to *place* or *put.*

PRESENT: Today I *lie* down. Today I *lay* the package down.
PAST: Yesterday I *lay* down. Yesterday I *laid* the package down.
PAST PARTICIPLE: I have (had) *lain* down. I have (had) *laid* the package down. *Note:* The past *of lie* and the present of *lay* are the same. Otherwise, the forms are completely different.
WRONG:
Lay down for a while
I *laid* down when I had a headache.
I *laid* in bed all morning.
It has *laid* on the table for three hours.
CORRECT:
Lie down for a while.
I *lay* down when I had a headache.
I *lay* in bed all morning.
It has *lain* on the table for three hours.

shall–will in formal usage, shall is used to show future action with I and we.
In informal usage, will is used with all pronouns to show simple future. I (He, She, They, We, You) *will* leave soon.
To express determination, promise, threat, or emphasis, shall is used with all pronouns. I (He, She, They, We, You) *shall* do it!
For examinations, follow formal usage.

should–would *should* follows the rules for *shall,* and *would* follows the rules for *will.*
SIMPLE CONDITION: *I should* like to be able to solve the problem. They *would* prefer to sit with us.
EMOTION EMPHASIZED: We *would* never talk to him in that language. They *should* have listened to her!
To express obligation or duty, *should* is used with all persons. He *should* go there much more often.
To express repeated or customary actions, *would* is used with all persons. I *would* go there every morning.

can–may this is another distinction that belongs in formal usage.
Can implies the ability to do something. He *can* swim across the lake.
May implies permission to do something. *May* I leave as soon as I complete the examination?
In formal usage, *can* and *may* are used interchangeably with *can* being preferred.

EXERCISE 22

Write A *if the sentence is correct. Write* B *if the sentence contains an error in choice of correct verb.*

___ 1. It don't seem right to me.

___ 2. May I lend your assignment pad for a moment?

___ 3. Bring that to me as soon as you have finished painting it.

___ 4. Everyone except Paula had voted for the resolution.

___ 5. I have stood for as much of your nonsense as I can take!

___ 6. He bet us decisively when I challenged him to a race.

___ 7. Let the pillow lay where it has fallen.

___ 8. She set down on the edge of the sofa as she talked to her son.

___ 9. Don't they want to see the end of misery for others?

___ 10. May we borrow a copy of the book from you?

___ 11. The word ain't is not an acceptable one in formal English.

___ 12. Did he learn you to work the outboard motor?

___ 13. I except your challenge, and we shall play this afternoon to see who is the champion of Lakeside Avenue.

___ 14. The theme has laid on her desk for three hours.

___ 15. Bring the valise to his room as soon as you can.

___ 16. Don't he seem overworked to you?

___ 17. Leave me go!

___ 18. Don't bet him that he doesn't know the answer to that riddle.

___ 19. How can you leave him do all of that heavy work without assistance!

___ 20. Do you think that he knows enough to be able to learn me how to drive with safety?

___ 21. The pen was laying on the table all the while we looked for it.

___ 22. Borrow little and gossip less.

___ 23. When he hurt his arm, he stood in the hospital overnight.

___ 24. Just leave it to me.

___ 25. Why don't she try to understand my position in this matter!

Some of the sentences in each of the following contain no errors. Circle the letters of the correct sentences only.

26. (A) May I have a lend of your pen for a moment?
    (B) May I lend your pen for a moment?
    (C) Can I lend your pen for a moment?
    (D) May I borrow your pen for a moment?
    (E) Can I borrow your pen for a moment?

27. (A) The present company excepted, the members of the freshman class must be taught how to respect the rights of others.
    (B) How could you have accepted his offer of assistance!
    (C) How could you refuse to except his offer of assistance!
    (D) Everyone except you had watched the televised program.
    (E) I except the gift in the name of the senior class.

28. (A) It ain't right to let it lie there.
    (B) It isn't right to let it lay there.
    (C) It isn't right to let it lie there.
    (D) It ain't right to let it lay there.
    (E) Let it lay where it has fallen.

29. (A) Set the package on the table.
    (B) I set before the television screen, entranced by the play.
    (C) He bet us in three games of tennis.
    (D) May I learn him how to fix the switch?
    (E) He stood at home for three days, hoping to cure his cold.

30. (A) You can't bring your notes with you into the examination room.
    (B) Shall I bring my camera with me?
    (C) He should have listened to me.
    (D) It doesn't mean that much to me, now.
    (E) In two hours I will have completed my homework.

31. (A) They shall be there on time.
    (B) We would receive a note from her every day.
    (C) You should not have left so early!
    (D) She shall not fail this time!
    (E) How would you have done it?

CONJUNCTIONS AND PREPOSITIONS OFTEN CONFUSED

between–among In formal usage, *between* is used when two (persons, things, ideas, groups) are involved. Divide the profits *between* the two owners. In formal usage, *among* is used when three or more items or people or groups are involved. Divide the profits *among* the four owners.

like–as–as if In formal usage, *like* is a preposition. It is followed by an object. It looks *like* an old battleship. *Like* cannot be used as a conjunction in place of *as* or *as if*.
WRONG: It looks like it is going to rain.
He looks *like* the captain of a battleship should.
CORRECT: It looks *as if* it is going to rain.
He looks *as* the captain of a battleship should.

being–being that–because–since Neither *being* nor *being that* can be used as a substitute for *because*. *Since* is sometimes used and is not wrong, but *because* is preferred.

WRONG: *Being* I didn't feel well, I left early.
Being that he is my friend, I asked him for some advice.
CORRECT: *Because (since)* I didn't feel well, I left early.
Because (since) he is my friend, I asked him for some advice.

write up–write down Since the process of writing goes in one direction, onto the paper, *up* and *down* should not follow the word *write* to show direction.
WRONG: Write *down* the directions.
CORRECT: Write the directions.

Memorize the Following Correct Usages

WRONG:	CORRECT:
leap off of, fall off of	leap off, leap from, fall from, fall off
lose out, win out	lose, win
inside of the, outside of the	inside the, outside the
different than	different from
try and, be sure and	try to, be sure to
to graduate school	to be graduated from or graduate from school
is where, is when	occurs where, occurs when
reason is because…	reason is that …
blame on somebody	blame somebody
place something in something else	place something into something else
come over to my house	come to my house
finish up, divide up, polish up, rest up, dress up	finish, divide, polish, rest, dress
refer back, descend down, ascend up, rise up	refer, descend, ascend, rise
cannot help but	cannot help

EXERCISE 23

Some of the sentences in each of the following groups contain no errors. Circle the letters of the correct sentences only.

1. (A) I plan to write up the entire story of the accident.
   (B) I will have to write up to the very last minute.
   (C) Please come over to my house before dinner time.
   (D) It smells like a cigar should.
   (E) The results are so different from what I had expected.

2. (A) Put the dog in the observation cage.
   (B) May I borrow his pen off him for one moment?
   (C) Being a citizen, he refused to be terrorized by threats of imprisonment without trial or revealed charges.
   (D) I hope to graduate elementary school this June.
   (E) I cannot help but regret that I did not listen to his advice.

3. (A) I plan to finish up all of the work today.
   (B) If you lose your head, you will never be able to win out.
   (C) Please refer to the instructions on the back of the carton.
   (D) I found the missing envelope just outside of the house.
   (E) Being that I had not had lunch, my tension increased.

4. (A) I am so tired I will just have to rest up until the very last moment before the contest.
   (B) Divide the profits up among all the members of the club.
   (C) He spoke up like I thought he would.
   (D) The reason he acts that way is because he hadn't been told the reason for our decision.
   (E) Please try and then you will know whether you can do the work.

5. (A) Don't blame your carelessness on someone else.
   (B) Why don't you try and be cooperative?
   (C) Being that I could do the work rapidly, I was put in charge of the crew.
   (D) It seemed like time would never pass.
   (E) Distribute the booklets among the members of the audience.

6. (A) The book fell off of the chair.
   (B) The most exciting scene was when I forgot how to stop the motor.
   (C) The most exciting scene was where I forgot how to stop the motor.
   (D) We polished up the handle on the front door until it shone.
   (E) The cat leaped off of the chair and onto me when she saw me.

WORDS OFTEN CONFUSED IN MEANING

affect   to influence. *Affect* by a decision.

effect   a result; to produce a result. See the *effect* of watering a plant. The new law will *effect* a change.

angel   a spiritual being. An *angel* of mercy.

angle   a figure formed by two lines coming together in a point. A sharp *angle*.

besides   in addition to. I don't want to see that movie and *besides,* I am too tired to go out.

beside   alongside. Lucy sat *beside* Mel during the performance.

capital   chief city; money; of first quality. Washington is the *capital* of the United States. Business requires *capital*. She paid a high price for *capital* seats.

capitol   chief governmental building. The *Capitol* in Washington has a dome.

costume   dress, apparel. The *costume* of a clown is funny.

custom   usage. The *customs* of teenagers are often strange to adults.

desert   to abandon; a barren region. The bear *deserted* her cubs. The great Sahara *Desert*.

dessert   the last course of a meal. We like pie for *dessert*.

everywheres   unacceptable substitute for everywhere. Look *everywhere* for the lost ring.

fewer   refers specifically to number. *Fewer* books were sold today than yesterday.

less   refers to quantity. She bought a hat for *less* money at a sale.

formerly   at an earlier time; heretofore. She was *formerly* a resident here but she moved away.

formally   in a stately manner. She introduced the man *formally* to her parents.

later   comparative degree of late. Mary arrived *later* than John.

latter   second of two. I prefer the *latter* to the former.

loan   something lent. Repay a *loan*.

lone   single, alone. A *lone* diner in a lunchroom.

miner   one who digs ore from the ground. Work as a coal *miner*.

minor   one under age; of little importance. A five-year-old is a *minor*. A *minor* injury.

moral   ethical meaning. A story with a *moral* teaches good behavior.

morale   state of mind in respect to confidence. High *morale* is necessary for the team.

number   refers to individual units. A large *number* of questions.

amount   refers to quantity. A large *amount* of gold is in Fort Knox.

principal   head of a school; money at interest; most important. Mr. Jones is the *principal* of school No. 2. Banks pay interest on your *principal* which is on deposit. My *principal* reason is that I have not enough money.

principle   rule, truth. We try to live by high *principles*.

reign   to rule. Let wisdom *reign* over us.

rein   strap of a bridle. Hold the horse's *rein*.

rain   shower. Caught in a summer *rain* storm, the boy got wet.

slay   to kill. *Slay* a dragon.

sleigh   sled. Go for a *sleigh* ride during the winter.

stationary   not moving. A *stationary* car is used for display.

stationery   writing material. Personal *stationery* is monogrammed.

weather   atmospheric conditions. Stormy *weather*.

whether   a choice between two alternatives. She did not know *whether* to play or to study.

who, whose, whom   refer to people. A man *whom* I know.

which   refers to animals or things. A house *which I* saw.

EXERCISE 24

Some of the sentences in each of the following groups contain no errors. Circle the letters of the correct sentences only.

1. (A) Let me sit besides you.
   (B) You must show your birth certificate to prove that you are not a minor.
   (C) I am glad that the goldfish-eating costume has become a thing of the past.
   (D) What was his principle argument?
   (E) He has less friends now than ever.

2. (A) You just sleigh me!
   (B) I know you from somewheres else!
   (C) The morale of the wounded soldier was excellent.
   (D) The moral of the wounded soldier was excellent.
   (E) He was formerly in the employ of the government.

3. (A) My favorite desert is the Kalihari.
   (B) He always carries a large amount of singles with him.
   (C) He always carries a large number of singles with him.
   (D) I didn't know weather to believe him after the previous incident.
   (E) How many degrees are there in that acute angel?

4. (A) The effect of the storm was considerable.
   (B) He is the man which I came to see.
   (C) What is the capitol of New York?
   (D) Hold the reins lightly.
   (E) If I were offered yogurt and ice cream, I would choose the latter.

5. (A) The loan star state is a land of bigness.
   (B) When dieting, I skip my second dessert.
   (C) She owes me less money than she thinks.
   (D) He has a small amount of unused three-cent stamps.
   (E) He decided to sit down beside me.

CAUSES OF LACK OF CLARITY

Dangling Participle When the *ing* form of the verb is used as an adjective, there must be a word in the sentence for it to modify logically. If there isn't, then the participle dangles.

DANGLING PARTICIPLE: *Rushing* into the room, the unconscious man lay on the floor. (The word *rushing* as used here refers to the *unconscious man.)*

CORRECT: *Rushing* into the room, we saw the unconscious man lying on the floor. (The word *rushing* as used here refers to *we.)*

Dangling Gerund When the *ing* form of the verb is preceded immediately by *when, after, before,* or *since,* the entire phrase must logically modify some noun in that sentence. If it doesn't, then the entire phrase dangles and the name given to that construction is *dangling gerund phrase.*

DANGLING GERUND: When *swimming* long distances, your breathing must be under constant control.

CORRECT: *When you swim* long distances, you must keep your breathing under constant control.

Dangling Infinitive When an infinitive (the *to* verb form) is used as an adjective, there should be a word in the sentence which indicates the performer of the action. If such a word is too distant or absent, then the infinitive is said to dangle.

DANGLING INFINITIVE: *To do* well on the test, your training must be thorough.

CORRECT: *To do* well on the test, you must be thoroughly trained.

Pronoun with Indefinite Antecedent When a pronoun can refer to two or more possible nouns, the sentence must be rephrased.

INDEFINITE ANTECEDENT: Margie told Edna that she had passed the test.

CORRECT: Margie told Edna that Edna had passed the test.
                   or
Margie said to Edna, "I passed that test."

Impersonal Pronoun In the phrase *In this book, they say, they* is a pronoun without any antecedent and is wrongly used. It is not clear who *they* means.

WITHOUT ANTECEDENT: In the newspaper they say that teenagers are maturing faster these days.

CORRECT: The writer of the newspaper article asserts that teenagers mature faster these days.

Dangling Prepositional Phrase Prepositional phrases must logically modify a word or phrase in the rest of the sentence. Otherwise they are said to dangle.

DANGLING PREPOSITIONAL PHRASE: At the age of seven, his family moved to Brooklyn.

CORRECT: When he was seven, his family moved to Brooklyn.

Possessive Case with the Gerund The *ing* form of a verb used as a noun is called a *gerund.* The gerund, being a noun form, requires the possessive case of a noun or pronoun modifying it.

WRONG: I approve of *him* being chosen moderator.

CORRECT: I approve of *his* being chosen moderator.

Singular Compound Subject When a compound subject is thought of as a unit, then it takes a singular verb.

WRONG: Fish and chips are a favorite New England dish.

CORRECT: Fish and chips is a favorite New England dish.

EXERCISE 25

Some of the sentences in each of the following groups contain no errors. Circle the letters of the correct sentences only.

1. (A) When fishing, care must be taken not to entangle your line.
   (B) Coming to my next point, your attitude is completely wrong.
   (C) Coming to my next point is a tedious process.
   (D) Coming to my next point, he attacked it calmly and with logic.
   (E) To be able to drive a car has been my ambition for years.

2. (A) Paul told us that he would not go with us.
   (B) Phyllis told Edna that she could not go with us.
   (C) Phyllis told Dave that she could not go with us.
   (D) Harold told Jerry that he could not go with us.
   (E) We told them that they could not go with us.

3. (A) To solve the problem correctly, algebra should be used.
   (B) To solve the problem correctly is not an easy task.
   (C) To solve the problem correctly, our knowledge had to be pooled.
   (D) To solve the problem correctly, we used trial and error.
   (E) To solve the problem correctly, the instructor gave us two hints.

4. (A) Peanut butter and jelly are the favorite sandwich ingredients for many.
   (B) Peanut butter and jelly is my favorite sandwich mix.
   (C) On this page, it says that all accidents are preventable.
   (D) I just can't stand his trying to appear better than he really is.
   (E) I just can't stand him trying to appear better than we are.

5. (A) When coming into city traffic, your speed should be reduced.
   (B) After seeing the fire break out, I rushed to send in the alarm.
   (C) At the age of nineteen, he was a virtuoso at the piano.
   (D) At the age of ten, his family moved to Newcomb.
   (E) Before washing the dishes, the sink must be cleaned thoroughly.

OTHER ERRORS IN USAGE

Incorrect Sequence

Misplaced Adverbs Words like *not, only, merely, almost* should be placed almost always before the expressions they modify.
MISPLACED: I lost my *breath almost* when he came toward me.
CLEAR: *I almost lost* my breath when he came toward me.

Misplaced Phrases and Clauses Misplaced phrases and clauses are often the basis of unintentional humor. A phrase or clause should be placed as closely as possible to the word that it modifies in the sentence.
WRONG: Lauren stated that she would definitely arrive on Monday in her first paragraph.
CORRECTED: In her first paragraph Lauren stated that she would definitely arrive on Monday.
WRONG: I spent hours looking for the picture of the collie that had been hanging in the attic. (What was hanging, the picture or the collie?)
CORRECTED: I spent hours looking for the picture that had been hanging in the attic. It was the picture of a collie.

Misplaced Correlatives Pairs of correlatives should be placed directly before the words that they bring into comparison. The most frequently used correlative conjunctions are *either ... or, neither ... nor, both ... and, not only ... but also.*

WRONG: *Either* Mary wants the book *or* the pencil.
CORRECT: Mary wants *either* the book *or* the pencil.

Confusion of Tenses

Present and Past Tenses Confused *Do* not shift from the present to the past tense without having a definite reason for doing so.

WRONG: They *come* into the house and *told* me the news.
CORRECT: They *came* into the house and *told* me the news.

Present Perfect and Past Confused The past tense denotes action completed in the past. The present perfect denotes an action perfected (completed) in the present without specification of exactly when it occurred. The present perfect tense denotes action begun in the past and continued up to or into the present.

PAST: I *took* the examination yesterday.
PRESENT PERFECT: I *have taken* the driving test three times in the past six months.

Past and Perfect Confused Two actions are usually involved in this error. When both actions occurred about the same time in the past, the past tense is used for *both verbs.*

We *saw* him the moment he *arrived.*
The past perfect tense is used to indicate an action that was completed *before* the time of other past action.

We *had* already seen him by the time you *arrived.*

Confusion of Pronouns

Pronoun Mixup When using pronouns like *you, we,* and *one* to refer to people in general, do not shift from one to another.

CONFUSING: If *we* wish to remain at peace, one must not use threatening words.
CORRECT: If *we* wish to remain at peace, we must not use threatening words.

or

If *one* wishes to remain at peace, one must not use threatening words.

Miscellaneous Errors

WRONG:	CORRECT:
not as … as…	not so … as …
If I would have…	If I had …
kind of (meaning somewhat)	somewhat, rather
providing (meaning if)	provided
due to (as a preposition)	because of, since, as
My friends, they do …	My friends do …
without (meaning unless)	unless
most (meaning nearly)	almost
hadn't ought	ought not

EXERCISE 26

Some of the sentences in each of the following groups contain no errors. Circle the letters of the correct sentences only.

1. (A) We lived in that house for the past five years.
   (B) I smiled when he nodded his head merely.
   (C) If you had gone with us, we could have solved the entire problem then and there.
   (D) It was the money on the shelf that I needed to pay for the lesson.
   (E) Either you eat the fish or you leave the table now.

2. (A) Providing you help us, we cannot lose.
   (B) Provided you help us, we cannot lose.
   (C) He was most out of breath by the time he arrived in school.
   (D) You are not so smart as you claim to be.
   (E) You are not as smart as you claim to be.

3. (A) Due to circumstances beyond our control, this performance must be discontinued.
   (B) If you had done your work properly, this would not have happened.
   (C) If you would have done your work properly, this could not have happened.
   (D) I was kind of surprised when they decided to elect me chairman.
   (E) He changed his attitude after I told him our side of the story.

4. (A) He told me I was to leave in the morning in the afternoon.
   (B) If one does his work on time, one will receive a just reward in a clear conscience.
   (C) If you do what your training bids, one can make mistakes.
   (D) After he had seen me, I was able to leave the building.
   (E) After he saw me, I was able to leave the building.

5. (A) Helen not only took my pen but also my copy of the textbook.
   (B) Neither a borrower nor a lender be.
   (C) You can either go to see the museum exhibition or attend the lecture.
   (D) Either you listen to me or to him.
   (E) You cannot both talk about a person and have him as a friend.

6. (A) Paul yelled that he needed us to help him badly.
   (B) The children stared into the store windows with wide eyes.
   (C) We found the door to the attic in the bedroom.
   (D) You did not do so badly as you thought you had.
   (E) I want a copy of the picture of the man that is hanging on the wall.

Mastery Exams

EXAM 1

> DIRECTIONS: Following each group of given sentences is a series of statements, designated as A, B, C, D, E. Some of these statements are truc. Some are false. Circle the letters of the true statements only.

1. Wanting to see the end of the contest.
   He came early, he sat down in the jury box.
   I had hardly any time to see the end results.
   We scarcely never go there any more.
   We hadn't but one moment to spare.
   (A) Two of the sentences contain sentence errors.
   (B) Three of the sentences contain double negatives.
   (C) Only two of the sentences contain no errors.
   (D) One of the sentences is a sentence fragment.
   (E) Two of the examples contain run-on sentences.

2. His answer is different from ours.
   Everyone of the soldiers want to volunteer for this duty.
   Someone in this group left their books in the last room.
   You must cither see Paul or Henry immediately.
   Please try to view this matter calmly.
   (A) Two of the sentences contain sentence errors.
   (B) One of the sentences contains an error in the placement of correlatives.
   (C) Two of the sentences are correct.
   (D) Two of the sentences contain errors in agreement.
   (E) One of the sentences contains an error in case.

3. Wishing to end the quarrel, a note of pleading entered my voice.
   Ham and eggs are the ingredients of my favorite breakfast dish.
   Only I had seen the picture once.
   They bet us by a score of 2-1 in a close game yesterday.
   We lived in Brooklyn for the past six years.

(A) One of the sentences contains a dangling gerund.
(B) Two of the sentences are correct.
(C) One of the sentences contains a misused verb.
(D) Two of the sentences contain errors in tense.
(E) One of the sentences contains a misplaced adverb.

4. Bring the book to my room now, before I reach there.
My father said when I left for school I should take the package with me.
He has less friends now than ever before.
Go slow, please, when rounding the corners of the corridors.
Don't he know how to spell *separate* correctly?

(A) Three of the sentences contain no errors.
(B) One sentence contains a misplaced modifier.
(C) One of the sentences contains an adjective form used instead of the adverb form.
(D) One of the sentences contains a sentence error.
(E) Two of the sentences contain errors in verb forms.

5. I object to him being elected chairman.
Being elected chairman is one of my fondest ambitions.
It tastes like chocolate cake should.
I sure appreciate your cooperation.
I lay in bed all day yesterday with a frightful headache.

(A) One of the sentences contains an error in agreement.
(B) Three of the sentences are correct.
(C) One of the sentences contains an error in case.
(D) Two of the sentences contain wrong verb forms.
(E) One of the sentences contains a misused adjective.

EXAM 2

> DIRECTIONS: One, two, or three of the sentences in each of the following groups may be correct. Circle the letters of the correct ones only.

1. (A) May I borrow your pen off you for a moment?
(B) Due to unforeseen circumstances, I shall be unable to be with you tonight.
(C) He was graduated from college last year.

2. (A) We lived in this house ever since my father had bought it three years ago.
(B) How shall we write up the accident report?
(C) He is the kind of person whom I enjoy being with.

3. (A) He gave me final instructions after I saw you.
(B) Everybody in our class knows his part in the pageant thoroughly.
(C) He hasn't looked good ever since he had that cold three weeks ago.

4. (A) You hadn't ought to have listened to him.
(B) If you had left earlier, this could not have been the result.
(C) The ship sunk into the mud.

5. (A) Put your money back into your pocket.
(B) You may either choose this one or the other.
(C) I came to the end of the road nearly before they saw me.

6. (A) He has scarcely any money left.
(B) If one wants to succeed, you have to try and try again and again.
(C) Polish the stairs up to the first landing only.

7. (A) The purse has laid on the sidewalk for hours.
   (B) This *here* is out of place.
   (C) They could have done without our aid.

8. (A) There was three boats at the dock when I had arrived.
   (B) Pauline together with her three friends was waiting for us.
   (C) He is one of the men who is responsible for the new bridge.

9. (A) Between you and I, he is definitely the stronger candidate.
   (B) It was me whom they had asked for.
   (C) Us fishermen must plan the entire trip.

10. (A) He works faster than her.
    (B) She is brighter than anyone in her entire family.
    (C) The machine certainly runs smoothly now.

11. (A) Give me one of them books to read.
    (B) You will have to decide between Jack and him.
    (C) Drive slowly around the corners.

12. (A) These here answers are the only acceptable ones.
    (B) He is the most quiet boy in the group.
    (C) She is the more intelligent of the two.

13. (A) Can I leave the room now?
    (B) May I leave the room now?
    (C) Just leave me be, please!

14. (A) Wait a moment, I want to go with you.
    (B) In this pamphlet it says that a new system of geometry has just been devised.
    (C) Wishing to solve the problem alone, he went over the evidence again with even greater care than ever before.

15. (A) I did say that the reason is because you had left too early.
    (B) He sometimes acts like a real infant.
    (C) I want to win real bad.

EXAM 3

DIRECTIONS: Circle the letter of the choice that best completes each of the following.

1. I don't know _____ there.
   (A) anybody (B) nobody

2. May I have three of this, _____ notebook.
   (A) kind of a (B) kind of

3. The program had _____ by the time we arrived.
   (A) began (B) begun

4. The record was _____ by the Australian team.
   (A) broke (B) broken

5. The thief had _____ in through the half-opened door.
   (A) sneaked (B) snook

6. The river has _____ over early this year.
   (A) froze (B) frozen

7. I could have _____ it by myself.
   (A) did (B) done

8. We could _____ gone to the store without him.
   (A) 've (B) of

9. _____ my carelessness, we lost the game.
   (A) Due to (B) Because of

10. Between you and _____, I have met this phrase before.
    (A) me (B) I

11. I put the coins _____ my pocket.
    (A) in (B) into

12. The bottle fell _____ the shelf.
    (A) off of (B) from

13. It looks _____ it is going to clear up.
    (A) as if (B) like

14. Distribute the extra copies _____ the students in the other school.
    (A) among (B) between

15. _____ I don't feel well, I should like to be excused early.
(A) Being that (B) Since

16. This is much different _____ mine.
(A) from (B) than

17. Why don't you try _____ understand my position?
(A) and (B) to

18. Neither Philip nor his sisters _____ planning to attend the affair.
(A) was (B) were

19. Neither Paul nor Enid _____ ready to debate the issue now.
(A) are (B) is

20. Why not come _____my house after the performance?
(A) over to (B) to

EXAM 4

DIRECTIONS: Circle the letter of the choice that best completes each of the following.

1. I can't _____ remembering how pleasant the entire evening was.
(A) help but (B) help

2. The best scene in the story _____ when the bridge collapses.
(A) is (B) occurs

3. Be sure _____ go into the exhibition room when you reach the museum.
(A) to (B) and

4. I don't see why you have to _____ me.
(A) blame it on (B) blame

5. Just place the lumber _____ my window.
(A) outside of (B) outside

6. The cat leaped _____ the chair and onto my lap.
(A) off of (B) off

7. There was a _____ star in the sky when I looked up at twilight.
(A) lone (B) loan

8. What will be the _____ of the court decision?
(A) affect (B) effect

9. Everyone except Larry and _____ could swim that distance.
(A) I (B) me

10. Go _____ to your seats.
(A) quick (B) quickly

11. She is definitely the _____ one of the two.
(A) politest (B) politer

12. These _____ of apples make me think of lemons.
(A) kinds (B) kind

13. These flowers smell _____.
(A) sweet (B) sweetly

14. Will you please _____ it to me?
(A) make a loan of (B) lend

15. Did you _____ their invitation?
(A) accept (B) except

16. He _____ in the country for a month during the summer.
(A) stood (B) stayed

17. What shall we have for _____ to end the meal?
(A) desert (B) dessert

18. He gave me _____ cards than he kept for himself.
(A) fewer (B) less

19. I could find it _____ in the house.
(A) nowheres (B) nowhere

20. It was _____ known as Fourth Lake, before its name was changed.
(A) formerly (B) formally

EXAM 5

DIRECTIONS: Circle the letter of the word that best completes each of the following.

1. Bread and butter _____ my favorite filler.
(A) is (B) are

2. Will you please sit _____ me.
(A) besides (B) beside

3. Did you visit the _____ in Albany?
(A) capital (B) capitol

4. Will the horse remain _____ while I try to mount the saddle?
(A) stationery (B) stationary

5. Long may genial humor _____ in our comic strips.
(A) reign (B) rain

6. Let us _____ the dragon of tyranny.
(A) sleigh (B) slay

7. Neither Paul nor Edgar _____ going to leave with us.
(A) is (B) are

8. You will have to do it without assistance from Will or _____.
(A) we (B) us

9. He has tried to learn many of the popular American _____.
(A) costumes (B) customs

10. It was, fortunately, just a _____ accident.
(A) minor (B) miner

11. What is his _____ reason for refusing our offer?
(A) principal (B) principle

12. If you _____ followed instructions, this could not have been.
(A) would have (B) had

13. He is not _____ patient as he thinks he is.
(A) so (B) as

14. _____ you do the work properly, the results will be worthwhile.
(A) Provided (B) Providing

15. He is _____ shy some of the time.
(A) kind of (B) somewhat

16. You _____ to listen to such rumors.
(A) ought not (B) hadn't ought

17. I am _____ exhausted from trying to argue with her.
(A) almost (B) most

18. The motor runs so _____ that you can scarcely hear its hum.
(A) quiet (B) quietly

19. They had _____ across the river early this morning.
(A) swam (B) swum

20. She is one of the girls who _____ being considered for membership.
(A) is (B) are

EXAM 6

DIRECTIONS: In each of the following groups, one of the four sentences contains an error in usage. Circle the letter of the incorrect sentence.

EXAMPLE:

(A) It don't do no good.
(B) Everyone brought his book.
(C) They thought we boys had done it.
(D) Did you expect the winner to be him?

1. (A) The work was more difficult than I had expected.
(B) My assignment was different from what I had expected.
(C) Everybody except she agreed to the plan.
(D) It was too bad the two other boys couldn't come too.

2. (A) He hadn't ought to have done it.
(B) She feels all right now.
(C) None of us is ready.
(D) She wanted to go last week.

3. (A) Why do you like Francine better than me?
   (B) She is taller than I.
   (C) A bushel of potatoes have been picked by the children.
   (D) Is there any chance of this coming in time?

4. (A) There should be no quarreling between her and you.
   (B) The part I liked best was when Lassie opened the stable door.
   (C) If I were president, I'd raise taxes.
   (D) If he was there, why didn't we see him?

5. (A) He took my book, which makes me angry.
   (B) None of them did his homework.
   (C) The reason Allen left was that he was hungry.
   (D) Of the two, Joan is neater.

6. (A) Running around during lunchtime is where you can get hurt.
   (B) He would've helped us, if we had asked.
   (C) If it weren't for Al, where would we be now?
   (D) Why doesn't Anne care for rock music?

7. (A) Frank and Tom were nearly pushed off the train.
   (B) He borrowed the money off me yesterday.
   (C) If it was permissible last week, why isn't it permissible this week?
   (D) Ruth, please take this message to the principal's office.

8. (A) They're going to eat their lunch as soon as they get there.
   (B) Whose is this?
   (C) I'm sure you would of done the same thing in my place.
   (D) Such weather! It's raining again.

9. (A) Why weren't you there when we needed you?
   (B) On your way back, bring home some ice cream.
   (C) More time has passed than I care to remember.
   (D) If it was you, wouldn't you feel bad?

10. (A) If the truth be known, I had forgotten all about the appointment.
    (B) Hugh chose David for his team.
    (C) The boat sank before we could reach it.
    (D) We have bought a large amount of toys for the children.

11. (A) It couldn't have been we who did it.
    (B) The bell has already rung.
    (C) Divide the candy evenly between the five girls.
    (D) Every student is expected to show his loyalty to Madison High School.

12. (A) He was all shaken up in the accident.
    (B) I've eaten more than I should have.
    (C) You should not let him play with fire.
    (D) I'll be glad to bring your shoes to the shoemaker. I'm going past the shoestore.

13. (A) Joan felt bad when her boy friend did not phone her.
    (B) Each one of the golfers had his golf clubs carried by his own caddie.
    (C) A neighborhood with no slums has less cases of juvenile delinquency.
    (D) Because Mr. Lyons is kind but firm, he has fewer problems with his students than any of the other teachers.

14. (A) Why don't you try to improve your batting and fielding?
    (B) Five of we boys have formed a basketball team.
    (C) The person in the snapshot is not he.
    (D) The winners of the contest are she and you.

15. (A) Not having anything to do, the movies seemed the best place for us to spend the evening.
    (B) Louise acts as though she were the teacher.
    (C) Set your things down on the desk, and sit in the first seat.
    (D) Try to finish what you start.

16. (A) Please let me go.
    (B) These papers have lain in the closet for months.
    (C) May I leave the room?
    (D) I could of done it for you more cheaply.

17. (A) As for his attendance, he has been absent fewer times than might have been expected.
    (B) Yesterday when Dad came into the house, I saw that he was angry.
    (C) Paul saw nothing wrong in asking for help.
    (D) We ordered a large number of trucks.

18. (A) I'm mad at you for kicking my dog.
    (B) Did you receive the correct number of articles?
    (C) Senator Douglas was the principal speaker at the conference.
    (D) Only a man of principle should hold the high office of mayor.

19. (A) Mr. Jeffers becomes very angry when anyone contradicts him.
    (B) When I seen *The Gladiator,* I liked the chariot race best.
    (C) He suffered a great setback, due to his inexperience.
    (D) Because of illness, he was unable to attend.

20. (A) You must do as I tell you.
    (B) I saw nothing.
    (C) If Geraldine would have come to the party, Jock would have danced with her.
    (D) Frances is taller than I.

EXAM 7

DIRECTIONS: In each of the following groups, one of the four sentences contains an error in usage. Circle the letter of the incorrect sentence.

EXAMPLE:

(A) It don't do no good.
(B) Everyone brought his book.
(C) They thought we boys had done it.
(D) Did you expect him to be the winner?

1. (A) On New Year's Eve we stood up late to greet the New Year.
   (B) I had rather spend a little more and get better quality.
   (C) When he laid his money on the counter, the agent gave him a ticket.
   (D) When the patient lay on his side, he didn't feel the pain so much.

2. (A) We borrowed it from him.
   (B) Tabby, our cat, lays on the rug near the radiator.
   (C) May I borrow your tennis racket please?
   (D) Since it's late, we'll have to leave now.

3. (A) Nothing could've changed the result.
   (B) You hadn't ought to have done that.
   (C) We had better turn back now.
   (D) Is it all right if we sit on this couch?

4. (A) You better not come late to school.
   (B) She would've arrived earlier, if she had known.
   (C) Are you all ready?
   (D) We've laid fifty miles of pipe through the desert.

5. (A) I knew it to be him as soon as I heard his voice.
   (B) Please teach us how to multiply by eleven.
   (C) If you were I, would you do it?
   (D) To build a fire, only dry wood should be selected.

6. (A) What's the idea of his coming here?
   (B) He is the kind of a person who causes trouble wherever he goes.
   (C) You can expect his friends to raise a storm when they hear his rabble-rousing speeches.
   (D) To make money, you must work hard and faithfully.

7. (A) Eric fell off the ladder.
   (B) Bring the dirty dog out of this house immediately!
   (C) I can scarcely believe your story.
   (D) Uncle George is one of the cleverest bridge players at the club.

8. (A) Africa has risen up to throw off its oppressors.
   (B) The doctor has torn the adhesive tape off.
   (C) He is one of the fastest, if not the fastest, baserunner in baseball.
   (D) Have you written home lately?

9. (A) If only Phil were more careful, we could trust him with the car.
   (B) May I borrow your glove?
   (C) With one person excepted, all those attending had a good time.
   (D) While watching the dull basketball game, my attention wandered.

10. (A) After cleaning the sink, please take the garbage out.
    (B) What kind of person do you think I am?
    (C) It's a matter of his solving his own problems.
    (D) The work having been completed, the laborers picked up their tools and left.

11. (A) Beat it.
    (B) We thought it to be her.
    (C) We have not done anything wrong.
    (D) Ain't I right in believing peace is better than war?

12. (A) There were Arthur and Murray, standing in the rain.
    (B) I should greatly appreciate the loan of your lawn mower.
    (C) They should have been here by now.
    (D) Betty doesn't care for these kind of stockings.

13. (A) I hardly know how to begin.
    (B) All term long there has been many examples of mischief in this class.
    (C) This sort of thing must stop.
    (D) I don't know how to begin.

14. (A) If he had been more prudent, he would not have gotten into this difficulty.
    (B) Neither Mr. Cowan nor his business partners is interested in buying any more property.
    (C) Please bring me back a souvenir from the fair.
    (D) He has not stirred in the past half hour.

15. (A) Either Ben or Jerry are going to be elected.
    (B) Phoebe, as well as all the other girls, is welcome to join our club.
    (C) We should've been home half an hour ago.
    (D) It's quality, not quantity, that counts.

16. (A) Except for him, nobody likes me.
    (B) There is altogether too much confusion here.
    (C) Those kind of people don't think for themselves.
    (D) Please leave. Take your things with you.

17. (A) The irritation on his heel was aggravated by his wearing of sneakers.
    (B) This secret is just for you and me.
    (C) What will be the effects of disarmament?
    (D) That there house is the oldest in the neighborhood.

18. (A) How will disarmament affect the world?
    (B) Spring is here already.
    (C) Some people say Fred Astaire was more graceful than any dancer.
    (D) If they are all ready, we ought to leave.

19. (A) Almost all the books have been borrowed.
    (B) Being that it's Saturday, you may go out tonight.
    (C) They accepted our gift.
    (D) Pat ate most of the grapes.

20. (A) Will you raise their salaries?
    (B) In science, we Americans are spending less time and training fewer students than the Japanese.
    (C) Let us give you a token of our affection.
    (D) Those Globetrotters sure know how to dribble.

Answers to All Exercises, Practice Tests, and Mastery Exams

EXERCISES

EXERCISE 1, p. 262

1. C
2. ours
3. weren't
4. C
5. 2's
6. man's
7. king's
8. mother-in-law's
9. coins'
10. C

EXERCISE 2, p. 263

1. men's
2. C
3. policemen's
4. C
5. officer's
6. anyone's
7. teacher's
8. razor's
9 Phyllis'
10. i's
11. Harriet's
12. It's
13. James' or James's
14. He's
15. Won't
16. You'd
17. worm's
18. trees' or tree's
19. animal's
20. boy's

EXERCISE 3, p. 264

1. C   2. B   3. D

EXERCISE 4, p. 264

1. A   4. B   7. B   10. A   13. A
2. B   5. B   8. B   11. B   14. A
3. A   6. A   9. B   12. B   15. B

EXERCISE 5, p. 266

1. N   4. N   7. C   10. C   13. N
2. C   5. N   8. C   11. C   14. N
3. C   6. C   9. C   12. N   15. C

EXERCISE 6, p. 266

1. B   3. A   5. B   7. A   9. A
2. B   4. B   6. A   8. A   10. A

EXERCISE 7, p. 267

1. 11
2. 7
3. N
4. following
5. N
6. N
7. words
8. Evans
9. N
10. following

EXERCISE 8, p. 268

1. period
2. C
3. !
4. C
5. C
6. C
7. C
8. C
9. C
10. C

EXERCISE 9, p. 268

1. A or C   6. D   11. A or C
2. C or A   7. B   12. D
3. D   8. A   13. A
4. C or A   9. A   14. B
5. A or B   10. B or C   15. A

EXERCISE 10, p. 269

1. Q   4. N   7. Q
2. N   5. Q   8. N
3. N   6. N   9. Q

EXERCISE 11, p. 269

1. D   5. B   9. D   13. A   17. D
2. A   6. D   10. D   14. D   18. B
3. D   7. A   11. A   15. A   19. B
4. D   8. D   12. D   16. D   20. C

EXERCISE 12, p. 271

1. (N) postgraduate
2. (H) never-ending
3. (N) two hundred
4. (N) every ten
5. (H) self-appointed
6. (N) all right
7. (N) definitely incorrect
8. (H) sixty-third
9. (H) self-made
10. (N) antipollution
11. (N) postseason
12. (H) pro-Austrian
13. (H) never-realized dreams
14. (N) never realized
15. (H) three-fifths

EXERCISE 13, p. 271

1. (A) all-purpose
2. (B) all seniors
3. (B) reexemption
4. (A) twenty-two
5. (B) pretrial
6. (A) ex-President
7. (B) cleverly plotted
8. (A) so-called
9. (B) all completed
10. (A) never-to-be trusted

EXERCISE 14, p. 272

1. — this
2. — those — came
3. No
4. No
5. No
6. — and — he
7. — but
8. — of — must
9. — oh — as
10. — these
11. — so — spoke
12. — shall
    — introduced
13. No
14. No
15. — it

EXERCISE 15, p. 273

1. as all
2. probably will
3. N
4. you has
5. in that
6. it but
7. one for
8. N
9. I and
10. about and

EXERCISE 16, p. 287

1. A	6. B	11. B	16. B	21. A
2. B	7. B	12. A	17. C	22. B
3. A	8. A	13. D	18. C	23. A
4. D	9. D	14. D	19. B	24. D
5. C	10. A	15. D	20. D	25. D

26. C, E	29. A, D	32. B, E
27. A, C	30. C, D	33. C, E
28. B, D	31. A, E	34. B, D

EXERCISE 17, p. 290

1. B	6. B	11. B	16. B, C, E
2. B	7. B	12. B	17. A, C, E
3. A	8. B	13. B	18. A, C, E
4. B	9. A	14. B	19. B, C, E
5. A	10. A	15. B	20. B, C, E

EXERCISE 18, p. 292

1. B	6. B	11. B	16. B	21. B
2 A	7. B	12. A	17. B	22. B
3. B	8. A	13. B	18. B	23. A
4. B	9. B	14. A	19. A	24. B
5. A	10. A	15. A	20. B	

25. B, D, E	29. E	32. C, E
26. C	30. B, C, E	33. A, B, E
27. B, E	31. D, E	34. B, E
28. B, D		

EXERCISE 19, p. 294

1. B	6. B	11. B	16. A	21. A
2. A	7. A	12. B	17. B	22. A
3. A	8. B	13. B	18. A	23. A
4. A	9. B	14. B	19. B	24. B
5. A	10. B	15. B	20. B	25. B

26. A, C, E	31. C, D
27. A, D	32. B, D, E
28. C, D	33. A, C, E
29. D, E	34. C, E
30. B	35. C

EXERCISE 20, p. 297

1. C	6. B	11. A	16. B	21. A
2. A	7. A	12. A	17. B	22. A
3. C	8. A	13. B	18. C	23. B
4. B	9. A	14. B	19. C	24. C
5. C	10. C	15. C	20. C	25. C

26. A, B, C, E	29. B, E
27. B, D, E	30. B, D
28. B, C	

EXERCISE 21, p. 299

1. B	6. B	11. A	16. B	21. B
2. B	7. B	12. A	17. A	22. B
3 A	8. B	13. B	18. B	23. B
4 B	9. B	14. A	19. A	24. A
5. B	10. A	15. B	20. B	25. A

26. C, D	29. D
27. C, D, E	30. B
28. A, D, E	

EXERCISE 22, p. 302

1. B	6. B	11. A	16. B	21. B
2. B	7. B	12. B	17. B	22. A
3. A	8. B	13. B	18. A	23. B
4. A	9. A	14. B	19. B	24. A
5. A	10. A	15. B	20. B	25. B

26. D   29. A
27. A, B, D   30. C, D, E
28. C   31. A, B, C, D, E

EXERCISE 23, p. 304

1. B, E   4. E
2. C   5. E
3. C   6. none

EXERCISE 24, p. 305

1. B   4. A, D, E
2. C, E   5. B, C
3. A, C

EXERCISE 25, p. 307

1. C, D, E   4. A, B, D
2. A, C, E   5. B, C
3. B, D

EXERCISE 26, p. 308

1. C   4. D
2. B, D   5. B, C, E
3. B   6. D

PRACTICE TESTS

TEST 1, p. 274

1. '	11. C	21. C	31. ,	41. C
2. C	12. C	22. C	32. C	42. :
3. C	13. ;	23. C	33. ,	43. ,
4. C	14. "	24. .	34. ,	44. 's
5. '	15. "	25. C	35. C	45. C
6. ,	16. "	26. ,"	36. s'	46. ,
7. .T	17. C	27. C	37. C	47. ,
8. ,	18. C	28. "	38. s'	48. ,
9. '	19. C	29. "	39. ,	49. ,
10. C	20. ,	30. "	40. C	50. ,

TEST 2, p. 275

1. B	11. A	21. B	31. A	41. B
2. A	12. A	22. B	32. A	42. A
3. B	13. B	23. B	33. B	43. B
4. A	14. B	24. A	34. A	44. B
5. B	15. A	25. A	35. A	45. A
6. B	16. B	26. A	36. B	46. B
7. A	17. A	27. B	37. B	47. A
8. A	18. B	28. A	38. B	48. B
9. B	19. A	29. A	39. A	49. A
10. A	20. B	30. B	40. B	50. A

TEST 3, p. 277

1. A	6. E	11. C	16. E	21. E
2. A	7. C	12. E	17. E	22. A
3. C	8. C	13. C	18. D	23. E
4. E	9. C	14. C	19. B	24. E
5. C	10. E	15. E	20. E	25. C

TEST 4, p. 279

1. Next, I, English, French.
2. The, Would, Bible.
3. Tomorrow, New Year's Day, First of January.
4. There, Northwest.
5. The Jacksons.
6. The, I, _The Call of the Wild_, Jack London.
7. Last, Wednesday, Aunt Ann.
8. Don't, Doug, Leo, He's.
9. Mildred, Martha, Young Women's Christian Association.
10. Tom Laughton, Harold O'Connor, United Automobile Workers of America.
11. We, Fourth of July, Philadelphia, Pennsylvania.
12. The Near East.
13. Protestants, Catholics, Jews, National Conference of Christians and Jews.
14. There, Arabs, South America.
15. Rosaline.
16. Rosaline, I'll.
17. The United States of America, Alaska, Hawaii, Union.
18. If, Professor Lewis, Senator Garlan, Dr. Fawcett.
19. Among, Larry, Roy.

MASTERY EXAMS

Rating Your Results

On exams with 5 questions:
Superior	5 correct
Average	4 correct
Below Average	3 or fewer correct

On exams with 15 questions:
Superior	14–15 correct
Average	11–13 correct
Below Average	10 or fewer correct

On exams with 20 questions:
Superior	18–20 correct
Average	14–17 correct
Below Average	13 or fewer correct

EXAM 1, p. 309

1. A	4. B, E
2. B, C, D	5. C, E
3. C, E	

EXAM 2, p. 310

1. C	5. A	9. B	13. A, B
2. C	6. A, C	10. C	14. C
3. B	7. B, C	11. B, C	15. B
4. B	8. B	12. B, C	

EXAM 3, p. 311

1. A	5. A	9. B	13. A	17. B
2. B	6. B	10. A	14. A	18. B
3. B	7. B	11. B	15. B	19. B
4. B	8. A	12. B	16. A	20. B

EXAM 4, p. 312

1. B	5. B	9. B	13. A	17. B
2. B	6. B	10. B	14. B	18. A
3. A	7. A	11. B	15. A	19. B
4. B	8. B	12. A	16. B	20. A

EXAM 5, p. 313

1. A	5. A	9. B	13. A	17. A
2. B	6. B	10. A	14. A	18. B
3. B	7. A	11. A	15. B	19. B
4. B	8. B	12. B	16. A	20. B

EXAM 6, p. 313

1. C	5. A	9. D	13. C	17. B
2. A	6. A	10. D	14. B	18. A
3. C	7. B	11. C	15. A	19. B
4. B	8. C	12. D	16. D	20. C

EXAM 7, p. 315

1. A	5. D	9. D	13. B	17. D
2. B	6. B	10. D	14. B	18. C
3. B	7. B	11. D	15. A	19. B
4. A	8. C	12. D	16. C	20. D

DIGEST OF MATHEMATICAL SKILLS

Mathematical Skills

In this chapter, many topics of mathematics are reviewed. Most of the topics are followed by three exercise sets. If you do sufficiently well on the first set of practice exercises, you do not need further practice on that topic. If you do not do well on the first set, use the second set, which is usually longer, to build your skill on that topic. Use the third set of exercises to determine that you have mastered the skill. This approach allows you to review the necessary topics in a reasonable amount of time while building skills where they are needed.

Whole Numbers

Practice—Addition

EXERCISE 1

In addition, the *addends* are the numbers that are added. The *sum* is the answer.

Add the following.

1.	235	2.	109	3.	890	4.	523
	482		537		112		909
	706		628		509		347
	859		140		438		400
	121		216		785		571
	360		935		363		686
	718		147		184		195
	+ 525		+ 423		+ 717		+ 230

5.	641	6.	958	7.	1,369	8.	73
	825		139		275		159
	796		264		2,501		8
	104		382		138		807
	378		195		976		42
	909		617		23		87
	264		820		3,085		291
	+ 540		+ 463		+ 1,603		+ 352

If you got seven or eight of these problems correct, go on to the next section on Subtraction. If you got more than one wrong, use Exercise 2 to build your skill.

EXERCISE 2

Add the following.

1.	325	2.	455	3.	904	4.	628	5.	773
	472		137		357		119		508
	814		904		816		247		379
	352		768		749		583		425
	719		319		998		402		667
	115		250		843		380		321
	247		763		122		955		790
	+ 598		+ 275		+ 640		+ 371		+ 112

6.	403	7.	775	8.	829	9.	3,174	10.	418
	725		804		173		429		211
	170		576		729		738		1,074
	819		132		485		1,902		92
	624		849		540		2,400		724
	137		921		277		93		2,225
	950		687		348		329		258
	+ 528		+ 459		+ 104		+ 1,207		+ 29

Now be sure of your skill. Try Exercise 3.

EXERCISE 3

Add the following.

1.	349	2.	158	3.	414	4.	587
	123		324		752		104
	405		605		395		793
	768		789		470		658
	841		457		867		720
	527		593		903		119
	664		640		288		246
	+ 970		+ 898		+ 176		+ 335

5.	782	6.	124	7.	756	8.	2,073
	596		387		2,897		152
	350		359		592		1,270
	829		931		84		732
	111		855		739		409
	478		129		78		381
	502		770		840		72
	+ 227		+ 258		+ 2,016		+ 1,208

Practice—Subtraction

The *subtrahend* is the number to be subtracted. The *minuend* is the number from which the subtrahend is to be subtracted.

EXERCISE 4

Subtract the following.

1.	85765	2.	56324	3.	90521
	− 43512		− 28473		− 38149

4.	65093	5.	71585	6.	90150
	− 30247		− 38618		− 30072

7.	85214	8.	50638	9.	94003
	− 7847		− 27040		− 37512

10.	82513	11.	74391	12.	80203
	− 4162		− 53618		− 7016

13.	45214	14.	15792	15.	70506
	− 34806		− 13849		− 30507

If you got 13 or more correct, go on to the next section on Multiplication. If you got more than 2 wrong, use Exercise 5 to build your skill.

EXERCISE 5

Subtract the following.

1.	62451	2.	85137	3.	60529
	− 31236		− 23489		− 37158

4.	28507	5.	77293	6.	85917
	− 13759		− 30572		− 7645

7.	40321	8.	59001	9.	94052
	− 37512		− 32694		− 7916

10.	48302	11.	80405	12.	70091
	− 25769		− 32906		− 52304

13.	76051	14.	30000	15.	48256
	− 32592		− 25619		− 3957

16.	80304	17.	92003	18.	46387
	− 1205		− 21798		− 9059

19.	53040	20.	65702	21.	80059
	− 17629		− 3982		− 30078

22.	92011	23.	35712	24.	89053
	− 38562		− 28903		− 6778

25.	56893	26.	40932	27.	68439
	− 30276		− 2569		− 19572

28.	50370	29.	10059	30.	60507
	− 2056		− 2006		− 53079

Now be sure of your skill. Try Exercise 6.

EXERCISE 6

Subtract the following.

1.	43795	2.	35672	3.	82950
	− 12482		− 12895		− 34729

4.	79053	5.	30070	6.	92053
	− 46704		− 21563		− 56427

7.	32470	8.	47304	9.	46300
	− 8956		− 39567		− 32495

10.	10563	11.	58923	12.	80530
	− 7429		− 38759		− 79286

13.	92004	14.	36029	15.	70012
	− 89007		− 9583		− 6904

Practice—Multiplication

When two or more numbers are multiplied the result is called a *product*. The numbers that are multiplied to form a product are *factors*. For example, $6 \times 7 = 42$. In this case, 42 is the product and 6 and 7 are factors. Since the product (42) may also be written as $3 \times 2 \times 7$, the numbers 3 and 2 are also factors of 42. The numbers 3, 2, and 7 are called *prime numbers* because they have no factors except themselves and 1. The numbers 3, 2, and 7 are said to be the *prime factors* of 42.

EXERCISE 7

Multiply the following.

1. 5843	2. 6028	3. 5704	4. 3012
× 7	× 8	× 9	× 6
5. 6824	6. 4850	7. 6057	8. 7850
× 37	× 49	× 82	× 56
9. 3852	10. 4037	11. 7590	12. 2859
× 134	× 208	× 356	× 470

If you got 11 or 12 of these problems correct, go on to the next section on Division. If you got more than one wrong, use Exercise 8 to build your skill.

EXERCISE 8

Multiply the following.

1. 6843	2. 5803	3. 7246	4. 5098
× 5	× 9	× 8	× 7
5. 6008	6. 1207	7. 3850	8. 5205
× 4	× 6	× 3	× 2
9. 5831	10. 7046	11. 5103	12. 6009
× 19	× 94	× 57	× 38
13. 2904	14. 9017	15. 3578	16. 7124
× 63	× 82	× 59	× 98
17. 2853	18. 3715	19. 4029	20. 7108
× 124	× 286	× 617	× 509
21. 9007	22. 3592	23. 2570	24. 6853
× 680	× 847	× 319	× 708

Now be sure of your skill. Try Exercise 9.

EXERCISE 9

Multiply.

1. 6234	2. 5037	3. 2509	4. 2053
× 9	× 6	× 8	× 7
5. 7839	6. 6350	7. 4059	8. 6830
× 29	× 47	× 58	× 72
9. 8512	10. 5069	11. 6380	12. 3157
× 128	× 302	× 274	× 940

Practice—Division

When we divide 35 by 5 the result is 7. In this case 35 is called the *dividend*, 5 is called the *divisor*, and 7 is called the *quotient*.

Sometimes, when we divide one number by another there will be a quotient and a *remainder*.

EXAMPLE: Divide 429 by 17.

$$
\begin{array}{r}
25 \rightarrow \text{quotient} \\
\text{divisor} \rightarrow 17\overline{)429} \rightarrow \text{dividend} \\
\underline{34} \\
89 \\
\underline{85} \\
4 \rightarrow \text{remainder}
\end{array}
$$

In this case, the divisor is 17, the dividend is 429, the quotient is 25, and the remainder is 4. The answer may be written $25\frac{4}{17}$.

EXERCISE 10

Divide the following (express remainders, if any, as the numerators of fractions).

EXAMPLE: $\quad 7\overline{)4853}^{\,693\frac{2}{7}}$

1. $4\overline{)5828}$	2. $7\overline{)6146}$
3. $8\overline{)2464}$	4. $6\overline{)4623}$
5. $24\overline{)8232}$	6. $37\overline{)7411}$
7. $89\overline{)8633}$	8. $29\overline{)9109}$
9. $46\overline{)14352}$	10. $92\overline{)37265}$
11. $63\overline{)42218}$	12. $87\overline{)51595}$
13. $352\overline{)164384}$	14. $740\overline{)176123}$
15. $589\overline{)414690}$	16. $416\overline{)164320}$

If you got 14 or more correct, go on to the Practice Tests that follow. If you got more than two wrong, use Exercise 11 to build your skill.

EXERCISE 11

Divide the following (express remainders, if any, as the numerators of fractions).

1. $6\overline{)3474}$
2. $5\overline{)7320}$
3. $9\overline{)8200}$
4. $7\overline{)1764}$
5. $8\overline{)4635}$
6. $6\overline{)3402}$
7. $4\overline{)3841}$
8. $3\overline{)1168}$
9. $7\overline{)8042}$
10. $9\overline{)4639}$
11. $5\overline{)8424}$
12. $6\overline{)5395}$
13. $4\overline{)6845}$
14. $8\overline{)1047}$
15. $9\overline{)4938}$
16. $7\overline{)2103}$
17. $36\overline{)1728}$
18. $49\overline{)1813}$
19. $23\overline{)2001}$
20. $97\overline{)8051}$
21. $45\overline{)2617}$
22. $19\overline{)5792}$
23. $51\overline{)3550}$
24. $64\overline{)4997}$
25. $37\overline{)6420}$
26. $63\overline{)13049}$
27. $89\overline{)65504}$
28. $71\overline{)57439}$
29. $378\overline{)231336}$
30. $465\overline{)368280}$
31. $729\overline{)609470}$
32. $956\overline{)666373}$
33. $508\overline{)354179}$
34. $297\overline{)180899}$
35. $816\overline{)613632}$
36. $470\overline{)283410}$

Now be sure of your skill. Try Exercise 12.

EXERCISE 12

Divide the following (express remainders, if any, as the numerators of fractions).

1. $6\overline{)3564}$
2. $9\overline{)6039}$
3. $7\overline{)3247}$
4. $8\overline{)9403}$
5. $36\overline{)8892}$
6. $49\overline{)8580}$
7. $27\overline{)2646}$
8. $73\overline{)6397}$
9. $68\overline{)24276}$
10. $97\overline{)39891}$
11. $54\overline{)39937}$
12. $19\overline{)17998}$
13. $464\overline{)148016}$
14. $630\overline{)338397}$
15. $379\overline{)228200}$
16. $532\overline{)247380}$

Before you attempt these Practice Tests, be sure to review Test-Taking Tips on page vii.

PRACTICE TEST 1

DIRECTIONS: Circle the letter that corresponds to the correct answer.

1. 2,919 + 3,151 =

   (A) 607   (B) 670   (C) 6,070   (D) 6,060
   (E) 6,065

2. The sum of 387, 58, and 101 =

   (A) 1,061   (B) 546   (C) 536   (D) 446
   (E) 542

3. The difference between 1,001 and 997 is:

   (A) 104   (B) 14   (C) 41   (D) 40   (E) 4

4. 716 is greater than 409 by:

   (A) 207   (B) 406   (C) 703   (D) 227
   (E) none of these

5. The product of 6 and 268 is:

   (A) 1,608   (B) 1,628   (C) 1,604
   (D) 1,508   E) 274

6. The result of multiplying 17 by 98 is:

   (A) 1,766   (B) 1,666   (C) 1,667
   (D) 1,278   (E) 1,756

7. When 405 is multiplied by 24 the result is:

   (A) 972   (B) 2,430   (C) 9,720
   (D) 9,070   (E) 9,620

8. When 1,748 is divided by 7 the dividend is:

   (A) 1,874   (B) 1,478   (C) 1,778
   (D) 1,758   (E) 1,748

9. When 9,747 is divided by 48 the remainder is:

   (A) 1   (B) 20   (C) 5   (D) 52
   (E) none of these

10. If 62,220 is divided by 204 the result is:

    (A) 325   (B) 305   (C) 345   (D) 35
    (E) none of these

PRACTICE TEST 2

DIRECTIONS: Circle the letter that corresponds to the correct answer.

1. 687 + 313 =

    (A) 1,100 (B) 1,010 (C) 990 (D) 1,000
    (E) none of these

2. The sum of 706, 33, and 111 =

    (A) 850 (B) 1,147 (C) 1,120 (D) 950
    (E) none of these

3. 605 − 97 =

    (A) 58 (B) 518 (C) 608 (D) 508
    (E) none of these

4. If 3,079 is subtracted from 5,903 the result is:

    (A) 2,834 (B) 1,824 (C) 1,823
    (D) 2,924 (E) 2,824

5. The product of 8 and 325 =

    (A) 2,610 (B) 2,605 (C) 1,600
    (D) 2,400 (E) 2,600

6. When 315 is multiplied by 50 the result is:

    (A) 1,575 (B) 15,750 (C) 10,575
    (D) 57,510 (E) 3,069

7. The product of 89 and 47 is:

    (A) 4,283 (B) 3,183 (C) 2,183
    (D) 4,083 (E) none of these

8. If 1,116 is divided by 9 the result is:

    (A) 104 (B) 124 (C) 140 (D) 114
    (E) 122

9. When 3,480 is divided by 57 the remainder is:

    (A) 6 (B) 60 (C) 3 (D) 7 (E) 5

10. If 91,020 is divided by 370 the result is:

    (A) 2,460 (B) 246 (C) 264 (D) 240
    (E) none of these

PRACTICE TEST 3

DIRECTIONS: Circle the letter that corresponds to the correct answer.

1. 1,783 + 517 =

    (A) 2,310 (B) 1,390 (C) 2,300
    (D) 2,290 (E) 2,320

2. The sum of 682, 98, and 350 =

    (A) 1,230 (B) 1,130 (C) 1,030
    (D) 930 (E) 1,040

3. 512 − 309 =

    (A) 213 (B) 113 (C) 103 (D) 203
    (E) none of these

4. When 1,758 is subtracted from 2,063 the result is:

    (A) 1,305 (B) 315 (C) 1,215 (D) 1,315
    (E) 305

5. The product of 6 and 150 =

    (A) 90 (B) 650 (C) 903 (D) 300
    (E) none of these

6. When 246 is multiplied by 65 the product is:

    (A) 15,090 (B) 1,599 (C) 15,990
    (D) 16,090 (E) 15,980

7. The product of 99 and 81 is:

    (A) 8,019 (B) 7,119 (C) 7,019
    (D) 7,919 (E) none of these

8. If 6,040 is divided by 8 the result is:

    (A) 750 (B) 705 (C) 755 (D) 745
    (E) 850

9. When 28,849 is divided by 69 the remainder is:

    (A) 9 (B) 19 (C) 5 (D) 17
    (E) none of these

10. When 156,510 is divided by 235 the result is:

    (A) 650 (B) 616 (C) 665 (D) 666
    (E) 606

Fractions

MEANING OF FRACTIONS

The box below is divided into 5 equal parts.

Using a fraction, we say that $\frac{2}{5}$ of the box is shaded. In the fraction $\frac{2}{5}$, 2 is the *numerator* and 5 is the *denominator*. The denominator, 5, indicates that the box has been divided into 5 equal parts. The numerator, 2, indicates that 2 of these parts have been shaded.

A **proper fraction** is a fraction in which the numerator is less than the denominator. Examples of proper fractions are $\frac{7}{8}$ and $\frac{4}{9}$.

An **improper fraction** is a fraction in which the numerator is equal to, or greater than, the denominator. Examples of improper fractions are $\frac{5}{5}$ and $\frac{7}{3}$.

A **mixed number** is a number such as $4\frac{2}{3}$ or $2\frac{5}{6}$ representing the sum of a whole number and a fraction. The number $4\frac{2}{3}$ means $4 + \frac{2}{3}$.

EXERCISE 13

1. (a) Into how many parts is the circle divided?
(b) What fractional part of the circle is marked with *A*?
(c) What fractional part of the circle is marked with *B*? Write this fraction in two ways.
(d) What fractional part of the circle is marked with *C*?

2. (a) Into how many parts is the box divided?
(b) What fractional part of the box is marked with *B*?
(c) What fractional part of the box is shaded? Write this fraction in two ways.
(d) What fractional part of the box is marked with *X*? Write this fraction in two ways.

3. (a) Mark with *C* the parts that would add up to $\frac{1}{2}$ of the box.
(b) Mark with *D* the parts that would make up $\frac{1}{6}$ of the box.
(c) Write, as a fraction, the part of the box that is left unmarked.

4. A major league team has a squad of 24 men consisting of 10 pitchers, 6 infielders, 5 outfielders, and 3 catchers. Express, as fractions, the part of the squad represented by: (a) pitchers (b) infielders (c) outfielders (d) catchers

5. The Stamp Club at the Benton Junior High School has 36 members. In electing a president of the club, all 36 members cast votes. The final total showed the following:

    John Andrews—20 votes
    Philip Verone—12 votes
    Louis Sellers —4 votes

Express as fractions the part of the total vote obtained by each boy.

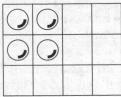

6. Use a mixed number to indicate the number of dozens of golf balls in these boxes.

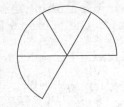

7. Use a mixed number to indicate the number of pies shown above.

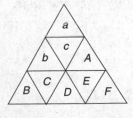

8. Use a mixed number to indicate the number of cups of milk.

9. (a) Into how many parts is the triangle divided?

(b) Express, in two ways, the fractional part of the triangle marked by lower case letters of the alphabet.
(c) Express, in two ways, the fractional part of the triangle marked by upper case letters of the alphabet.
(d) Express, as a fraction, the part of the triangle marked by the letters $B\,C\,D\,E\,F$.

CHANGING THE FORM OF A FRACTION

Reducing Fractions to Lowest Terms

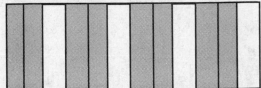

The fact that 8 of the 12 boxes in this diagram are shaded can be represented by the fraction $\frac{8}{12}$.

Also, you can see that two out of every 3 boxes, or $\frac{2}{3}$ of the boxes are shaded. In other words, $\frac{8}{12} = \frac{2}{3}$. This process of writing a fraction with a smaller denominator equivalent to another fraction is called reducing a fraction to lower terms. When the new fraction has the smallest possible denominator, we say that the fraction is *reduced to its lowest terms.* Note that the change from $\frac{8}{12}$ to $\frac{2}{3}$ is performed by dividing both the numerator and denominator of the fraction $\frac{8}{12}$ by 4. This change is based upon the following principle:

THE FUNDAMENTAL PRINCIPLE OF FRACTIONS

The numerator and denominator of a fraction may be multiplied or divided by the same number without changing the value of the fraction.

If n and b are not zero, $\dfrac{a}{b} = \dfrac{a \times n}{b \times n}$

If n and b are not zero, $\dfrac{a}{b} = \dfrac{a \div n}{b \div n}$

Fractions generated by using this principle are called *equivalent fractions.* That is $\frac{12}{20}$ and $\frac{3}{5}$ are equivalent because $\frac{12}{20} = \frac{12 \div 4}{20 \div 4} = \frac{3}{5}$. If the numerator and denominator cannot be divided by any number other than 1, the fraction is said to be *reduced to lowest terms* or *simplified.*

EXAMPLE: Reduce $\frac{15}{25}$ to lowest terms.

SOLUTION: To reduce $\frac{15}{25}$ to lowest terms, we divide both numerator and denominator by 5.

$$\frac{15}{25} = \frac{15 \div 5}{25 \div 5} = \frac{3}{5}$$

EXAMPLE: Reduce $\frac{36}{48}$ to lowest terms.

SOLUTION: We note that 36 and 48 may both be divided by 2, 3, 4, 6, and 12. Since we wish to reduce $\frac{36}{48}$ to lowest terms, we must divide both the numerator and denominator by the largest number that is contained in them evenly. In this case, the largest number is 12.

$$\frac{36}{48} = \frac{36 \div 12}{48 \div 12} = \frac{3}{4}$$

This reduction can also be done in stages:

$$\frac{48}{72} = \frac{6}{9} = \frac{2}{3}$$

Changing from Improper Fractions to Mixed Numbers

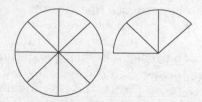

In the diagram, the whole pie is divided into 8 equal portions. The other piece of pie contains 3 additional portions. There is a total of 11 portions or $\frac{11}{8}$ pies. This may also be written as 1 whole pie and $\frac{3}{8}$ of another pie. The amount of pie may thus be written as $\frac{11}{8}$ or $1\frac{3}{8}$, or the improper fraction $\frac{11}{8}$ equals the mixed number $1\frac{3}{8}$. In general, an improper fraction may be changed to a whole or mixed number by dividing the numerator of the improper fraction by its denominator. The quotient is the whole number part of the mixed number and the remainder is the numerator of the fraction part.

EXAMPLE: Change $\frac{19}{7}$ to a mixed number.

SOLUTION: To change $\frac{19}{7}$ to a mixed number we divide 19 by 7, obtaining the result $2\frac{5}{7}$.

EXAMPLE: Change $\frac{40}{12}$ to a mixed number.

SOLUTION: To change $\frac{40}{12}$ to a mixed number, we divide 40 by 12, obtaining the result $3\frac{4}{12}$. If we reduce $\frac{4}{12}$ to $\frac{1}{3}$, the result, $3\frac{4}{12}$, may be written in simplest terms as $3\frac{1}{3}$.

The improper fraction $\frac{40}{12}$ may be simplified first by dividing the numerator and denominator by 4, obtaining $\frac{10}{3}$. Now, if we divide 10 by 3 we obtain the result $3\frac{1}{3}$.

Changing from Mixed Numbers to Improper Fractions

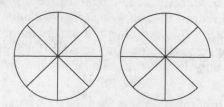

In the diagram, we have 1 whole pie and $\frac{5}{6}$ of another pie. This may be written as $1\frac{5}{6}$

pies. Since there are 11 portions and each portion contains $\frac{1}{6}$ of a pie, we may write the amount of pie as $\frac{11}{6}$ pies. Thus, we see that $1\frac{5}{6} = \frac{11}{6}$.

To change from $1\frac{5}{6}$ to $\frac{11}{6}$, we multiply 1 by 6 and add 5. The result, 11, becomes the numerator of the improper fraction $\frac{11}{6}$.

EXAMPLE: Change $2\frac{4}{9}$ to an improper fraction.

SOLUTION: Multiply 2 by 9 and add 4, obtaining 22. The improper fraction is $\frac{22}{9}$.

EXAMPLE: Change $3\frac{5}{11}$ to an improper fraction.

SOLUTION: Multiply 3 by 11 and add 5, obtaining 38. The improper fraction is $\frac{38}{11}$.

EXERCISE 14

Reduce the following fractions to lowest terms.

1. $\frac{3}{9}$	2. $\frac{4}{10}$	3. $\frac{6}{16}$	4. $\frac{9}{12}$
5. $\frac{12}{20}$	6. $\frac{16}{18}$	7. $\frac{24}{32}$	8. $\frac{8}{14}$
9. $\frac{21}{28}$	10. $\frac{35}{45}$		

Change the following mixed numbers to improper fractions.

11. $1\frac{1}{3}$	12. $2\frac{3}{8}$	13. $3\frac{6}{7}$
14. $4\frac{3}{5}$	15. $5\frac{4}{9}$	16. $7\frac{3}{4}$

Change the following improper fractions to mixed numbers.

17. $\frac{5}{4}$	18. $\frac{7}{3}$	19. $\frac{17}{6}$
20. $\frac{28}{12}$	21. $\frac{31}{9}$	22. $\frac{42}{16}$

If you got 20 or more correct, go on to the next section on Addition of Fractions and Mixed Numbers. If you got more than three wrong, use Exercise 15 to build your skill.

EXERCISE 15

Reduce the following fractions to lowest terms.

1. $\frac{2}{4}$	2. $\frac{8}{10}$	3. $\frac{6}{9}$	4. $\frac{8}{12}$
5. $\frac{3}{6}$	6. $\frac{10}{14}$	7. $\frac{15}{20}$	8. $\frac{20}{24}$
9. $\frac{18}{30}$	10. $\frac{14}{16}$	11. $\frac{22}{32}$	12. $\frac{16}{40}$
13. $\frac{32}{36}$	14. $\frac{16}{28}$	15. $\frac{12}{18}$	16. $\frac{14}{22}$
17. $\frac{12}{27}$	18. $\frac{18}{20}$	19. $\frac{15}{21}$	20. $\frac{25}{35}$

Change the following mixed numbers to improper fractions.

1. $1\frac{3}{4}$ 2. $2\frac{5}{6}$ 3. $3\frac{2}{7}$ 4. $2\frac{4}{5}$

5. $4\frac{2}{9}$ 6. $1\frac{1}{7}$ 7. $2\frac{5}{8}$ 8. $6\frac{1}{3}$

9. $7\frac{5}{6}$ 10. $3\frac{7}{8}$ 11. $4\frac{3}{11}$ 12. $5\frac{7}{12}$

13. $2\frac{7}{9}$ 14. $1\frac{1}{2}$ 15. $6\frac{3}{7}$

Now be sure of your skill. Try Exercise 16.

EXERCISE 16

Reduce the following fractions to lowest terms.

1. $\frac{4}{8}$ 2. $\frac{2}{6}$ 3. $\frac{10}{12}$ 4. $\frac{14}{16}$

5. $\frac{16}{20}$ 6. $\frac{10}{18}$ 7. $\frac{6}{14}$ 8. $\frac{15}{24}$

9. $\frac{28}{32}$ 10. $\frac{25}{35}$

Change the following mixed numbers to improper fractions.

11. $1\frac{1}{4}$ 12. $2\frac{5}{6}$ 13. $3\frac{7}{8}$

14. $2\frac{5}{9}$ 15. $1\frac{5}{6}$ 16. $2\frac{5}{7}$

Change the following improper fractions to mixed numbers.

17. $\frac{19}{6}$ 18. $\frac{9}{4}$ 19. $\frac{11}{9}$

20. $\frac{32}{12}$ 21. $\frac{22}{3}$ 22. $\frac{50}{24}$

ADDITION OF FRACTIONS AND MIXED NUMBERS

In learning to add fractions we make use of the general principle that only like quantities may be combined. For example,

3 eggs + 4 eggs = 7 eggs
5 books + 6 books = 11 books
one-fifth + three-fifths = four-fifths

or

$$\frac{1}{5} + \frac{3}{5} = \frac{4}{5}$$

Thus, we can see that fractions that have the same denominator may be added directly by simply adding the numerators and placing this sum of the numerators over the common denominator.

EXAMPLES:
$$\frac{4}{9} + \frac{3}{9} = \frac{7}{9}$$

$$\frac{2}{7} + \frac{1}{7} = \frac{3}{7}$$

We may not add two fractions with unlike denominators by the same method since we would then be adding two unlike quantities. For example, we may not add the fractions $\frac{1}{2}$ and $\frac{1}{4}$ directly. Before this addition is performed, we must change each of these fractions to an equivalent fraction with the same denominator, as follows:

$$\frac{1}{2} = \frac{2}{4}$$
$$\frac{1}{4} = \frac{1}{4}$$
$$\text{Sum} = \frac{3}{4}$$

The smallest denominator that can be used as a common denominator for combining two or more fractions is called the *least common denominator* (LCD, for short). It is the smallest number that is exactly divisible by the denominators of the given fractions.

To add fractions with unlike denominators, use the Fundamental Principle of Fractions to find their LCD and to change each of the fractions to an equivalent fraction having the LCD as denominator. Then, add the fractions by adding the numerators and writing the sum over the common denominator.

A simple method for finding the LCD is explained in the following examples. You will often be able to find the LCD by inspection.

EXAMPLE: Find the LCD for adding the fractions $\frac{5}{6}$ and $\frac{3}{8}$.

SOLUTION: First, we write the set of multiples of the denominator of the first fraction.

{6, 12, 18, 24, 30, 36, . . .}

Then we write the set of multiples of the denominator of the second fraction.

{8, 16, 24, . . .}

The first multiple that appears in both sets of multiples is the LCD. In this case, the LCD is 24.

EXAMPLE: Find the LCD for adding the fractions $\frac{5}{9}$, $\frac{7}{12}$, and $\frac{3}{4}$.

SOLUTION:
The set of multiples of 9 is:

$$\{9, 18, 27, 36, 45, 54, \ldots\}$$

The set of multiples of 12 is:

$$\{12, 24, 36, 48, 60, \ldots\}$$

The set of multiples of 4 is:

$$\{4, 8, 12, 16, 20, 24, 28, 32, 36, \ldots\}$$

The first multiple that appears in all three sets of multiples is the LCD. In this case, the LCD is 36.

EXAMPLE: $\frac{3}{5} = \frac{6}{10}$.

SOLUTION: We multiply the numerator and denominator of the fraction $\frac{3}{5}$ by 2, obtaining the result $\frac{6}{10}$.

EXAMPLE: $\frac{5}{8} = \frac{?}{16}$.

SOLUTION: In this example, we must write $\frac{5}{8}$ as an equivalent fraction with denominator 16. We must therefore multiply the numerator and denominator of $\frac{5}{8}$ by 2, obtaining

$$\frac{5 \times 2}{8 \times 2} = \frac{10}{16}$$

EXERCISE 17

Change the following fractions to equivalent fractions having the indicated denominators.

1. $\frac{1}{2} = \frac{?}{6}$ 2. $\frac{1}{3} = \frac{?}{12}$ 3. $\frac{3}{4} = \frac{?}{8}$

4. $\frac{2}{5} = \frac{?}{15}$ 5. $\frac{7}{8} = \frac{?}{24}$ 6. $\frac{1}{4} = \frac{?}{16}$

7. $\frac{5}{12} = \frac{?}{36}$ 8. $\frac{3}{5} = \frac{?}{20}$ 9. $\frac{2}{7} = \frac{?}{28}$

10. $\frac{5}{6} = \frac{?}{12}$ 11. $\frac{2}{3} = \frac{?}{24}$ 12. $\frac{5}{9} = \frac{?}{18}$

13. $\frac{7}{9} = \frac{?}{27}$ 14. $\frac{1}{5} = \frac{?}{40}$ 15. $\frac{1}{3} = \frac{?}{15}$

16. $\frac{5}{7} = \frac{?}{21}$ 17. $\frac{7}{12} = \frac{?}{48}$ 18. $\frac{2}{3} = \frac{?}{9}$

19. $\frac{3}{7} = \frac{?}{42}$ 20. $\frac{4}{5} = \frac{?}{30}$

EXAMPLE: Add the fractions $\frac{1}{4}$ and $\frac{3}{8}$.

SOLUTION: The LCD is 8. Therefore, we must write each fraction with denominator 8.

$$\frac{1}{4} = \frac{2}{8}$$
$$\frac{3}{8} = \frac{3}{8}$$
$$\overline{\text{Sum} = \frac{5}{8}}$$

EXAMPLE: Add $\frac{1}{6}$ and $\frac{4}{9}$.

SOLUTION: The LCD is 18. Therefore, we must write each fraction with denominator 18.

$$\frac{1}{6} = \frac{3}{18}$$
$$\frac{4}{9} = \frac{8}{18}$$
$$\overline{\text{Sum} = \frac{11}{18}}$$

EXAMPLE: Add $\frac{7}{8}$ and $\frac{11}{12}$.

SOLUTION: The LCD is 24. Therefore, we must write each fraction with denominator 24.

$$\frac{7}{8} = \frac{21}{24}$$
$$\frac{11}{12} = \frac{22}{24}$$
$$\overline{\text{Sum} = \frac{43}{24} = 1\frac{19}{24}}$$

EXAMPLE: Add $2\frac{5}{12}$ and $3\frac{8}{9}$.

SOLUTION: The LCD is 36. Therefore, we must write each fraction with denominator 36.

$$2\frac{5}{12} = 2\frac{15}{36}$$
$$3\frac{8}{9} = 3\frac{32}{36}$$
$$\overline{\text{Sum} = 5\frac{47}{36} = 5 + 1 + \frac{11}{36} = 6\frac{11}{36}}$$

EXAMPLE: Add $3\frac{2}{3}$, $2\frac{2}{5}$, and $4\frac{5}{6}$.

SOLUTION: The LCD is 30. Therefore, we must write each fraction with denominator 30.

$$3\frac{2}{3} = 3\frac{20}{30}$$
$$2\frac{2}{5} = 2\frac{12}{30}$$
$$4\frac{5}{6} = 4\frac{25}{30}$$
$$\overline{\text{Sum} = 9\frac{57}{30} = 10\frac{27}{30} = 10\frac{9}{10}}$$

EXERCISE 18

Add the following fractions and mixed numbers.

1. $\begin{array}{r} \frac{1}{2} \\ +\frac{1}{4} \\ \hline \end{array}$ 2. $\begin{array}{r} \frac{1}{3} \\ +\frac{1}{2} \\ \hline \end{array}$ 3. $\begin{array}{r} \frac{1}{3} \\ +\frac{1}{4} \\ \hline \end{array}$ 4. $\begin{array}{r} \frac{2}{3} \\ +\frac{1}{6} \\ \hline \end{array}$

5. $\begin{array}{r} \frac{2}{5} \\ +\frac{1}{10} \\ \hline \end{array}$ 6. $\begin{array}{r} \frac{1}{6} \\ +\frac{3}{4} \\ \hline \end{array}$ 7. $\begin{array}{r} \frac{3}{5} \\ +\frac{2}{3} \\ \hline \end{array}$ 8. $\begin{array}{r} \frac{3}{4} \\ +\frac{5}{6} \\ \hline \end{array}$

9. $\begin{array}{r} \frac{3}{8} \\ +\frac{5}{12} \\ \hline \end{array}$ 10. $\begin{array}{r} 1\frac{1}{3} \\ +\frac{1}{6} \\ \hline \end{array}$ 11. $\begin{array}{r} 2\frac{4}{5} \\ +3\frac{8}{15} \\ \hline \end{array}$ 12. $\begin{array}{r} 4\frac{7}{10} \\ +5\frac{5}{6} \\ \hline \end{array}$

13. $2\frac{3}{4}$
    $+3\frac{2}{7}$

14. $\frac{1}{2}$
    $\frac{1}{3}$
    $+\frac{1}{4}$

15. $\frac{2}{5}$
    $\frac{5}{6}$
    $+\frac{1}{3}$

16. $1\frac{1}{2}$
    $2\frac{5}{8}$
    $+3\frac{5}{16}$

37. $\frac{2}{3}$
    $\frac{7}{9}$
    $+\frac{1}{12}$

38. $1\frac{1}{2}$
    $2\frac{1}{4}$
    $+2\frac{1}{3}$

39. $3\frac{1}{5}$
    $6\frac{3}{10}$
    $+4\frac{7}{15}$

40. $2\frac{1}{6}$
    $3\frac{2}{3}$
    $+6\frac{5}{9}$

17. $2\frac{3}{8}$
    $3\frac{2}{3}$
    $+6\frac{5}{12}$

18. $6\frac{7}{10}$
    $\frac{3}{4}$
    $+5\frac{3}{20}$

41. $3\frac{7}{10}$
    $2\frac{5}{6}$
    $+9\frac{1}{4}$

42. $3\frac{5}{8}$
    $2\frac{11}{12}$
    $+8\frac{5}{16}$

If you got 16 or more correct, go on to the next section on Subtraction of Fractions and Mixed Numbers. If you got more than three wriong, use Exercise 19 to build your skill.

EXERCISE 19

Add the following fractions and mixed numbers.

1. $\frac{1}{2}$
   $+\frac{1}{6}$

2. $\frac{1}{4}$
   $+\frac{1}{3}$

3. $\frac{3}{4}$
   $+\frac{1}{6}$

4. $\frac{3}{8}$
   $+\frac{1}{4}$

5. $\frac{5}{6}$
   $+\frac{1}{8}$

6. $\frac{4}{9}$
   $+\frac{1}{3}$

7. $\frac{3}{8}$
   $+\frac{1}{6}$

8. $\frac{1}{12}$
   $+\frac{2}{3}$

9. $\frac{5}{12}$
   $+\frac{2}{9}$

10. $\frac{1}{6}$
    $+\frac{2}{15}$

11. $\frac{7}{8}$
    $+\frac{1}{12}$

12. $\frac{5}{9}$
    $+\frac{1}{6}$

13. $\frac{2}{3}$
    $+\frac{7}{12}$

14. $\frac{2}{9}$
    $+\frac{3}{4}$

15. $\frac{3}{7}$
    $+\frac{1}{2}$

16. $\frac{1}{4}$
    $+\frac{1}{10}$

17. $\frac{7}{8}$
    $+\frac{5}{6}$

18. $\frac{3}{10}$
    $+\frac{5}{6}$

19. $\frac{8}{15}$
    $+\frac{7}{10}$

20. $\frac{3}{8}$
    $+\frac{11}{12}$

21. $2\frac{1}{3}$
    $+\frac{8}{9}$

22. $3\frac{1}{5}$
    $+6\frac{1}{2}$

23. $4\frac{1}{2}$
    $+3\frac{1}{6}$

24. $5\frac{1}{3}$
    $+2\frac{1}{2}$

25. $2\frac{5}{12}$
    $+1\frac{1}{9}$

26. $4\frac{2}{3}$
    $+3\frac{1}{6}$

27. $7\frac{3}{8}$
    $+2\frac{5}{6}$

28. $4\frac{3}{5}$
    $+3\frac{3}{4}$

29. $6\frac{3}{10}$
    $+\frac{1}{2}$

30. $5\frac{3}{7}$
    $+2\frac{1}{2}$

31. $3\frac{4}{5}$
    $+4\frac{1}{3}$

32. $4\frac{7}{9}$
    $+\frac{5}{12}$

33. $\frac{1}{2}$
    $\frac{1}{4}$
    $+\frac{1}{8}$

34. $\frac{1}{3}$
    $\frac{1}{6}$
    $+\frac{4}{9}$

35. $\frac{5}{6}$
    $\frac{7}{12}$
    $+\frac{1}{2}$

36. $\frac{3}{8}$
    $\frac{11}{12}$
    $+\frac{1}{4}$

Now be sure of your skill. Try Exercise 20.

EXERCISE 20

Add the following fractions and mixed numbers.

1. $\frac{1}{2}$
   $+\frac{1}{3}$

2. $\frac{1}{2}$
   $+\frac{1}{8}$

3. $\frac{2}{3}$
   $+\frac{1}{4}$

4. $\frac{5}{8}$
   $+\frac{1}{4}$

5. $\frac{3}{5}$
   $+\frac{3}{10}$

6. $\frac{1}{9}$
   $+\frac{5}{6}$

7. $\frac{3}{4}$
   $+\frac{2}{3}$

8. $\frac{5}{6}$
   $+\frac{1}{2}$

9. $\frac{7}{9}$
   $+\frac{5}{12}$

10. $1\frac{1}{5}$
    $+\frac{7}{10}$

11. $2\frac{2}{3}$
    $+2\frac{11}{12}$

12. $3\frac{1}{4}$
    $+4\frac{6}{7}$

13. $2\frac{3}{10}$
    $+7\frac{5}{6}$

14. $\frac{1}{4}$
    $\frac{1}{6}$
    $+\frac{1}{3}$

15. $\frac{2}{3}$
    $\frac{5}{8}$
    $+\frac{7}{12}$

16. $3\frac{1}{3}$
    $2\frac{3}{4}$
    $+1\frac{5}{6}$

17. $2\frac{7}{9}$
    $3\frac{1}{6}$
    $+4\frac{2}{3}$

18. $3\frac{1}{5}$
    $2\frac{3}{4}$
    $+5\frac{9}{10}$

SUBTRACTION OF FRACTIONS AND MIXED NUMBERS

In subtracting fractions we again make use of the general principle that only like quantities may be combined. For example, when we subtract $\frac{1}{9}$ from $\frac{8}{9}$ we obtain the result $\frac{7}{9}$. If we have unlike quantities, we proceed as in the following example.

EXAMPLE: Subtract $\frac{1}{6}$ from $\frac{5}{9}$.

SOLUTION: We note that the LCD of these two fractions is 18.

$$\frac{5}{9} = \frac{10}{18}$$
$$\frac{1}{6} = \frac{3}{18}$$
$$\text{Difference} = \frac{7}{18}$$

In subtracting one fraction or mixed number from another mixed number it is sometimes necessary to borrow, as is shown in the following examples.

EXAMPLE: From $5\frac{1}{8}$ subtract $\frac{3}{8}$.

SOLUTION: We cannot subtract $\frac{3}{8}$ from $\frac{1}{8}$. Therefore, it is necessary to borrow 1 from 5. Since $1 = \frac{8}{8}$ we may write $5\frac{1}{8}$ as $4 + \frac{8}{8} + \frac{1}{8}$ or $4\frac{9}{8}$. Now, we may subtract $\frac{3}{8}$ from $4\frac{9}{8}$, obtaining the result $4\frac{6}{8}$, or $4\frac{3}{4}$. The work may be arranged as follows.

$$5\frac{1}{8} = 4 + 1 + \frac{1}{8} = 4\frac{9}{8}$$
$$\frac{3}{8} \qquad\qquad \frac{3}{8} \qquad \frac{3}{8}$$
$$\text{Difference} = 4\frac{6}{8} = 4\frac{3}{4}$$

EXAMPLE: Subtract $2\frac{7}{9}$ from $6\frac{5}{12}$.

SOLUTION: The LCD of the two fractions is 36.

$$6\frac{5}{12} = 6\frac{15}{36} = 5 + 1 + \frac{15}{36} = 5\frac{51}{36}$$
$$2\frac{7}{9} = 2\frac{28}{36} = \qquad\quad 2\frac{28}{36} = 2\frac{28}{36}$$
$$\text{Difference} = 3\frac{23}{36}$$

EXERCISE 21

Subtract the following fractions and mixed numbers.

1. $\frac{4}{5}$ $-\frac{1}{5}$
2. $\frac{5}{8}$ $-\frac{1}{8}$
3. $\frac{3}{4}$ $-\frac{1}{3}$
4. $\frac{5}{6}$ $-\frac{2}{9}$

5. $\frac{7}{8}$ $-\frac{5}{6}$
6. $\frac{5}{8}$ $-\frac{5}{12}$
7. 4 $-\frac{1}{6}$
8. $3\frac{1}{2}$ $-1\frac{1}{4}$

9. $5\frac{5}{6}$ $-2\frac{3}{8}$
10. $7\frac{9}{10}$ $-3\frac{1}{4}$
11. $6\frac{1}{4}$ $-\frac{1}{2}$
12. 8 $-2\frac{3}{5}$

13. $7\frac{1}{3}$ $-6\frac{3}{4}$
14. $8\frac{1}{2}$ $-3\frac{2}{3}$
15. $5\frac{2}{9}$ $-4\frac{7}{12}$
16. $9\frac{5}{16}$ $-3\frac{3}{4}$

If you got 15 or 16 of these problems correct, go on to the next section on Comparison of Fractions. If you got more than two wrong, use Exercise 22 to build your skill.

EXERCISE 22

Subtract the following fractions and mixed numbers.

1. $\frac{2}{3}$ $-\frac{1}{3}$
2. $\frac{7}{9}$ $-\frac{2}{9}$
3. $\frac{5}{6}$ $-\frac{1}{6}$
4. $\frac{1}{2}$ $-\frac{1}{4}$

5. $\frac{2}{3}$ $-\frac{1}{6}$
6. $\frac{3}{4}$ $-\frac{1}{8}$
7. $\frac{5}{12}$ $-\frac{1}{3}$
8. $\frac{7}{10}$ $-\frac{2}{5}$

9. $\frac{1}{2}$ $-\frac{1}{3}$
10. $\frac{3}{4}$ $-\frac{1}{6}$
11. $\frac{2}{3}$ $-\frac{2}{9}$
12. $\frac{4}{5}$ $-\frac{2}{3}$

13. $\frac{6}{7}$ $-\frac{1}{2}$
14. $\frac{8}{9}$ $-\frac{5}{12}$
15. 7 $-\frac{1}{3}$
16. $4\frac{3}{5}$ $-2\frac{1}{5}$

17. $9\frac{7}{8}$ $-3\frac{1}{8}$
18. $6\frac{7}{9}$ $-2\frac{1}{9}$
19. $8\frac{3}{4}$ $-2\frac{9}{10}$
20. $6\frac{1}{3}$ $-4\frac{3}{4}$

21. 8 $-\frac{4}{7}$
22. $5\frac{1}{8}$ $-4\frac{1}{2}$
23. $7\frac{1}{3}$ $-6\frac{1}{2}$
24. $5\frac{1}{10}$ $-4\frac{3}{4}$

25. $6\frac{5}{9}$ $-2\frac{5}{6}$
26. $6\frac{5}{8}$ $-5\frac{1}{6}$
27. $4\frac{1}{9}$ $-3\frac{5}{12}$
28. $3\frac{1}{3}$ $-2\frac{4}{7}$

29. $8\frac{1}{4}$ $-6\frac{2}{3}$
30. $5\frac{4}{9}$ $-3\frac{1}{2}$
31. $3\frac{5}{16}$ $-2\frac{3}{4}$
32. $7\frac{2}{3}$ $-5\frac{11}{15}$

33. $6\frac{3}{8}$ $-2\frac{2}{3}$
34. $1\frac{1}{6}$ $-\frac{7}{8}$
35. $7\frac{1}{7}$ $-2\frac{1}{2}$

Now be sure of your skill. Try Exercise 23.

EXERCISE 23

Subtract the following fractions and mixed numbers.

1. $\frac{5}{7}$ $-\frac{1}{7}$
2. $\frac{9}{10}$ $-\frac{3}{10}$
3. $\frac{1}{2}$ $-\frac{1}{3}$
4. $\frac{7}{8}$ $-\frac{1}{4}$

5. $\frac{5}{6}$ $-\frac{1}{3}$
6. $\frac{1}{3}$ $-\frac{1}{4}$
7. $\frac{7}{8}$ $-\frac{5}{12}$
8. 5 $-\frac{1}{8}$

9. $4\frac{1}{2}$ 10. $6\frac{2}{3}$ 11. $7\frac{4}{5}$ 12. $7\frac{1}{8}$

    $-2\frac{1}{8}$ $-2\frac{1}{6}$ $-2\frac{1}{4}$ $-6\frac{1}{4}$

13. 9 14. $3\frac{1}{2}$ 15. $7\frac{1}{12}$ 16. $8\frac{1}{6}$

    $-3\frac{2}{3}$ $-1\frac{4}{7}$ $-6\frac{7}{9}$ $-3\frac{3}{4}$

COMPARISON OF FRACTIONS

Equivalent Fractions

Consider these fractions.

$$\frac{8}{14} \text{ and } \frac{36}{63}$$

Suppose we wish to determine whether these fractions name the same rational number. We could, of course, reduce each fraction to lowest terms and then compare. However, there is a simpler method.

PRINCIPLE OF EQUIVALENCE OF FRACTIONS

If we have two fractions $\frac{a}{b}$ and $\frac{c}{d}$, then $\frac{a}{b} = \frac{c}{d}$ if, and only if, a $\times$ d = b $\times$ c.

EXAMPLE: $\frac{2}{3} = \frac{12}{18}$ because $2 \times 18 = 3 \times 12$.

But $\frac{7}{8} \neq \frac{5}{6}$ because $7 \times 6 \neq 8 \times 5$.

EXERCISE 24

By using the Principle of Equivalence of Fractions, determine which of the following pairs of fractions name the same rational number and which do not name the same rational number.

1. $\frac{3}{5}$ and $\frac{21}{35}$ 9. $\frac{63}{98}$ and $\frac{81}{126}$

2. $\frac{6}{8}$ and $\frac{51}{68}$ 10. $\frac{68}{84}$ and $\frac{153}{189}$

3. $\frac{7}{9}$ and $\frac{21}{35}$ 11. $\frac{27}{66}$ and $\frac{63}{154}$

4. $\frac{29}{37}$ and $\frac{10}{12}$ 12. $\frac{35}{84}$ and $\frac{45}{110}$

5. $\frac{22}{26}$ and $\frac{44}{52}$ 13. $\frac{63}{81}$ and $\frac{91}{127}$

6. $\frac{21}{49}$ and $\frac{24}{55}$ 14. $\frac{49}{105}$ and $\frac{77}{165}$

7. $\frac{25}{45}$ and $\frac{45}{81}$ 15. $\frac{43}{79}$ and $\frac{54}{132}$

8. $\frac{24}{39}$ and $\frac{56}{89}$

Ordering the Fractions

Here is a rule to determine which of two fractions is greater. (The symbol ">" means "is greater than.")

PRINCIPLE OF COMPARISON OF FRACTIONS

If we have two fractions $\frac{a}{b}$ and $\frac{c}{d}$, then $\frac{a}{b} > \frac{c}{d}$ if, and only if, $a \times d > b \times c$.

EXAMPLES:

1. $\frac{3}{4} > \frac{5}{8}$ because $3 \times 8 > 4 \times 5$

2. $\frac{7}{9} > \frac{1}{3}$ because $7 \times 3 > 9 \times 1$

3. $\frac{4}{5} > \frac{2}{9}$ because $4 \times 9 > 5 \times 2$

EXERCISE 25

Use the Principle of Comparison of Fractions to determine which fraction is greater.

1. $\frac{1}{3}$ and $\frac{5}{17}$ 9. $\frac{12}{23}$ and $\frac{8}{17}$

2. $\frac{2}{5}$ and $\frac{4}{9}$ 10. $\frac{16}{25}$ and $\frac{21}{46}$

3. $\frac{3}{7}$ and $\frac{6}{11}$ 11. $\frac{7}{18}$ and $\frac{8}{21}$

4. $\frac{8}{15}$ and $\frac{9}{16}$ 12. $\frac{9}{31}$ and $\frac{6}{23}$

5. $\frac{9}{11}$ and $\frac{5}{6}$ 13. $\frac{16}{27}$ and $\frac{9}{14}$

6. $\frac{5}{13}$ and $\frac{3}{11}$ 14. $\frac{15}{37}$ and $\frac{13}{29}$

7. $\frac{9}{14}$ and $\frac{12}{19}$ 15. $\frac{14}{19}$ and $\frac{27}{37}$

8. $\frac{6}{7}$ and $\frac{8}{9}$

In each case, use the Principle of Comparison of Fractions to arrange each of the following sets of fractions in order from least to greatest. For example, $\frac{1}{3} < \frac{1}{2} < \frac{3}{4}$ (the symbol "<" means "is less than").

16. $\frac{2}{5}, \frac{3}{8}, \frac{3}{4}$ 21. $\frac{6}{7}, \frac{7}{9}, \frac{5}{8}$

17. $\frac{5}{3}, \frac{3}{5}, \frac{11}{20}$ 22. $\frac{8}{11}, \frac{12}{17}, \frac{13}{16}$

18. $\frac{7}{12}, \frac{5}{9}, \frac{5}{6}$ 23. $\frac{11}{21}, \frac{10}{19}, \frac{20}{41}$

19. $\frac{17}{24}, \frac{2}{3}, \frac{5}{8}$ 24. $\frac{8}{18}, \frac{6}{17}, \frac{11}{31}$

20. $\frac{3}{8}, \frac{2}{9}, \frac{4}{11}$ 25. $\frac{7}{23}, \frac{8}{27}, \frac{9}{32}$

Reciprocal Fractions

Before discussing the methods for multiplying and dividing fractions, we will define *reciprocal* fractions. Two numbers are reciprocals of each other if their product is 1. For example, $\frac{2}{5}$ and $\frac{5}{2}$, 7 and $\frac{1}{7}$, and $\frac{8}{3}$ and $\frac{3}{8}$ are pairs of reciprocals. It is clear that every number except 0 has a reciprocal.

If b and d are not zero, $\frac{a}{b} \times \frac{c}{d} = \frac{a \times c}{b \times d}$.

MULTIPLICATION OF FRACTIONS AND MIXED NUMBERS

In multiplying two or more fractions, we multiply the numerators of the fractions to obtain the new numerator, and multiply the denominators of the fractions to obtain the new denominator.

EXAMPLE: Multiply $\frac{2}{5}$ by $\frac{4}{9}$.

SOLUTION: $\frac{2}{5} \times \frac{4}{9} = \frac{2 \times 4}{5 \times 9} = \frac{8}{45}$

Many times the answer must be reduced to lowest terms. This can be done by *cancellation*. Before the multiplication is actually done, divide any numerator and denominator by a common factor. Then multiply what remains. The following examples illustrate cancellation.

EXAMPLE: Multiply $\frac{3}{8}$ by $\frac{4}{9}$.

SOLUTION: Before multiplying the numerators and denominators we may divide the numerator 3 and the denominator 9 by 3. We may also divide the numerator 4 and the denominator 8 by 4. This work may be shown as follows.

$$\overset{1}{\underset{2}{\frac{3}{8}}} \times \overset{5}{\underset{3}{\frac{4}{9}}} = \frac{1 \times 1}{2 \times 3} = \frac{1}{6}$$

EXAMPLE: Multiply $\frac{8}{27}$ by $\frac{15}{16}$.

SOLUTION: $\overset{1}{\underset{9}{\frac{8}{27}}} \times \overset{5}{\underset{2}{\frac{15}{16}}} = \frac{5}{18}$

In multiplying a whole number by a fraction we may regard the whole number as a fraction whose denominator is 1. Then we proceed as we did in multiplying two fractions.

EXAMPLE: Multiply 48 by $\frac{7}{8}$.

SOLUTION: $\overset{6}{\frac{48}{1}} \times \frac{7}{\underset{1}{8}} \times \frac{42}{1} = 42$

EXAMPLE: Multiply 72 by $\frac{5}{28}$.

SOLUTION: $\overset{18}{\frac{72}{1}} \times \frac{5}{\underset{7}{28}} = \frac{5 \times 18}{7} = \frac{90}{7}$ *or* $12\frac{6}{7}$

To multiply (or divide) fractions, all whole numbers or mixed numbers must first be changed to improper fractions.

EXAMPLE: Multiply $3\frac{1}{8}$ by $\frac{4}{5}$.

SOLUTION: $3\frac{1}{8} \times \frac{4}{5}$

Changing $3\frac{1}{8}$ to $\frac{25}{8}$ we have:

$$\overset{5}{\underset{2}{\frac{25}{8}}} \times \overset{1}{\underset{1}{\frac{4}{5}}} = \frac{5}{2} \ \text{or} \ 2\frac{1}{2}$$

EXAMPLE: Multiply $2\frac{2}{3}$ by $2\frac{5}{8}$.

SOLUTION: $2\frac{2}{3} \times 2\frac{5}{8}$

Changing the mixed numbers to improper fractions, we have:

$$\overset{3}{\underset{1}{\frac{8}{3}}} \times \overset{7}{\underset{1}{\frac{21}{8}}} = 7$$

EXAMPLE: Multiply $5\frac{1}{3}$ by $2\frac{7}{10}$.

SOLUTION: $5\frac{1}{3} \times 2\frac{7}{10}$

$$\overset{8}{\underset{1}{\frac{16}{3}}} \times \overset{9}{\underset{5}{\frac{27}{16}}} = \frac{72}{5} \ \text{or} \ 14\frac{2}{5}$$

EXAMPLE: Multiply $\frac{3}{10} \times \frac{8}{9} \times \frac{5}{16}$.

SOLUTION: $\overset{1}{\underset{2}{\frac{3}{10}}} \times \overset{1}{\underset{3}{\frac{8}{9}}} \times \overset{1}{\underset{2}{\frac{5}{16}}} = \frac{1}{12}$

EXAMPLE: Multiply $\frac{6}{7} \times 2\frac{4}{5} \times 1\frac{1}{3}$.

SOLUTION: $\frac{6}{7} \times 2\frac{4}{5} \times 1\frac{1}{3}$

$$\overset{2}{\underset{1}{\frac{6}{7}}} \times \overset{2}{\frac{14}{5}} \times \overset{4}{\underset{1}{\frac{4}{3}}} = \frac{16}{5} = 3\frac{1}{5}$$

EXERCISE 26

Multiply.

1. $\frac{1}{4} \times \frac{3}{5}$ 2. $\frac{1}{2} \times \frac{5}{9}$
3. $\frac{3}{8} \times \frac{2}{7}$ 4. $\frac{2}{3} \times \frac{9}{16}$
5. $\frac{3}{4} \times \frac{8}{15}$ 6. $\frac{9}{10} \times \frac{2}{3}$
7. $\frac{4}{21} \times \frac{7}{8}$ 8. $\frac{5}{8} \times \frac{16}{45}$
9. $10 \times \frac{1}{5}$ 10. $16 \times \frac{3}{4}$
11. $12 \times \frac{7}{9}$ 12. $60 \times \frac{11}{15}$
13. $\frac{3}{8} \times 2$ 14. $\frac{5}{12} \times 16$
15. $18 \times \frac{4}{9}$ 16. $5 \times \frac{2}{3}$
17. $24 \times 2\frac{5}{8}$ 18. $6 \times 7\frac{1}{2}$
19. $3\frac{1}{7} \times \frac{7}{8}$ 20. $6\frac{2}{3} \times \frac{5}{8}$
21. $6\frac{1}{4} \times 1\frac{3}{5}$ 22. $3\frac{3}{4} \times 3\frac{1}{3}$
23. $1\frac{5}{7} \times 2\frac{5}{8}$ 24. $2\frac{2}{3} \times 1\frac{5}{16}$
25. $\frac{2}{3} \times \frac{5}{8} \times \frac{6}{7}$ 26. $\frac{5}{6} \times \frac{3}{4} \times \frac{8}{9}$
27. $4\frac{1}{2} \times 3\frac{1}{9} \times 1\frac{1}{3}$

If you got 24 or more correct, go on to the next section on Division of Fractions and Mixed Numbers. If you got more than 3 wrong, use Exercise 27 to build your skill.

EXERCISE 27

Multiply.

1. $\frac{2}{3} \times \frac{1}{7}$ 2. $\frac{1}{2} \times \frac{3}{5}$
3. $\frac{3}{4} \times \frac{7}{10}$ 4. $\frac{1}{5} \times \frac{3}{4}$
5. $\frac{3}{4} \times \frac{5}{6}$ 6. $\frac{4}{5} \times \frac{1}{2}$
7. $\frac{3}{8} \times \frac{4}{7}$ 8. $\frac{5}{6} \times \frac{9}{10}$
9. $\frac{3}{4} \times \frac{8}{15}$ 10. $\frac{7}{9} \times \frac{3}{14}$
11. $\frac{5}{12} \times \frac{3}{10}$ 12. $\frac{3}{8} \times \frac{5}{6}$
13. $\frac{3}{7} \times \frac{14}{15}$ 14. $\frac{1}{8} \times \frac{4}{9}$
15. $\frac{9}{20} \times \frac{10}{27}$ 16. $\frac{3}{4} \times \frac{6}{7}$
17. $20 \times \frac{2}{5}$ 18. $18 \times \frac{4}{9}$
19. $\frac{1}{3} \times 24$ 20. $\frac{3}{4} \times 16$
21. $18 \times \frac{1}{4}$ 22. $24 \times \frac{3}{8}$
23. $28 \times \frac{5}{6}$ 24. $\frac{7}{10} \times 45$
25. $\frac{7}{24} \times 60$ 26. $\frac{5}{12} \times 40$
27. $\frac{6}{7} \times 4$ 28. $5 \times \frac{5}{6}$

29. $4\frac{1}{2} \times \frac{6}{7}$ 30. $\frac{5}{6} \times 3\frac{3}{5}$
31. $\frac{1}{2} \times 3\frac{1}{3}$ 32. $\frac{5}{12} \times 2\frac{1}{10}$
33. $25 \times 1\frac{1}{5}$ 34. $2\frac{1}{4} \times 18$
35. $5\frac{1}{3} \times 6$ 36. $24 \times 2\frac{5}{8}$
37. $3 \times 7\frac{1}{2}$ 38. $12 \times 5\frac{1}{4}$
39. $3\frac{1}{7} \times 4$ 40. $9 \times 2\frac{5}{6}$
41. $2\frac{1}{4} \times 1\frac{1}{3}$ 42. $3\frac{1}{5} \times 2\frac{5}{8}$
43. $5\frac{5}{6} \times 7\frac{1}{5}$ 44. $2\frac{3}{16} \times 1\frac{3}{5}$
45. $4\frac{5}{7} \times 1\frac{3}{11}$ 46. $\frac{2}{9} \times \frac{3}{5} \times \frac{1}{4}$
47. $8\frac{4}{5} \times 11\frac{1}{4}$ 48. $6\frac{3}{7} \times 4\frac{2}{3}$
49. $3\frac{1}{5} \times 5\frac{1}{6}$ 50. $\frac{5}{6} \times \frac{3}{7} \times \frac{2}{9}$
51. $2\frac{4}{5} \times 3\frac{1}{7} \times \frac{3}{11}$ 52. $6\frac{2}{3} \times 1\frac{3}{5} \times 4\frac{1}{2}$
53. $1\frac{4}{5} \times 2\frac{1}{2} \times 3\frac{1}{3}$ 54. $2\frac{2}{3} \times 1\frac{1}{4} \times 3\frac{1}{5}$

Now be sure of your skill. Try Exercise 28.

EXERCISE 28

Multiply.

1. $\frac{1}{5} \times \frac{2}{3}$ 2. $\frac{5}{7} \times \frac{1}{3}$
3. $\frac{3}{4} \times \frac{2}{5}$ 4. $\frac{5}{8} \times \frac{4}{15}$
5. $\frac{5}{9} \times \frac{3}{10}$ 6. $\frac{7}{16} \times \frac{4}{9}$
7. $\frac{1}{2} \times \frac{6}{11}$ 8. $\frac{3}{10} \times \frac{5}{9}$
9. $15 \times \frac{1}{3}$ 10. $18 \times \frac{5}{6}$
11. $20 \times \frac{3}{8}$ 12. $30 \times \frac{5}{12}$
13. $\frac{5}{6} \times 12$ 14. $\frac{7}{8} \times 24$
15. $28 \times \frac{5}{7}$ 16. $8 \times \frac{2}{3}$
17. $36 \times 1\frac{3}{4}$ 18. $8 \times 3\frac{1}{2}$
19. $\frac{3}{8} \times 2\frac{1}{3}$ 20. $4\frac{2}{5} \times \frac{10}{11}$
21. $3\frac{1}{8} \times 1\frac{1}{3}$ 22. $1\frac{1}{7} \times 5\frac{1}{4}$
23. $4\frac{1}{6} \times 3\frac{5}{8}$ 24. $3\frac{1}{9} \times 2\frac{1}{16}$
25. $\frac{2}{3} \times \frac{4}{5} \times \frac{9}{10}$ 26. $\frac{4}{9} \times \frac{3}{7} \times \frac{5}{8}$
27. $2\frac{2}{5} \times 3\frac{1}{3} \times \frac{3}{4}$ 28. $4\frac{1}{5} \times 1\frac{1}{3} \times 3\frac{4}{7}$

DIVISION OF FRACTIONS AND MIXED NUMBERS

In dividing one fraction by another we invert the divisor and multiply.

EXAMPLE: Divide $\frac{5}{8}$ by $\frac{1}{3}$.

SOLUTION: $\frac{5}{8} \div \frac{1}{3}$

$$\frac{5}{8} \times \frac{3}{1} = \frac{15}{8} \text{ or } 1\frac{7}{8}$$

EXAMPLE: Divide $\frac{8}{9}$ by $\frac{2}{3}$.

SOLUTION: $\frac{8}{9} \div \frac{2}{3}$

$$\frac{\overset{4}{8}}{9} \times \frac{\overset{1}{3}}{\underset{3}{2}} = \frac{4}{3} \text{ or } 1\frac{1}{3}$$

In dividing a fraction, mixed number, or whole number by a mixed number we change mixed numbers and whole numbers into improper fractions and divide.

EXAMPLE: Divide $1\frac{1}{8}$ by $\frac{3}{16}$.

SOLUTION: $1\frac{1}{8} \div \frac{3}{16}$

$\frac{9}{8} \div \frac{3}{16}$

$$\frac{9}{\underset{1}{8}} \times \frac{\overset{2}{16}}{\underset{1}{3}} = 6$$

EXAMPLE: Divide 8 by $3\frac{1}{3}$.

SOLUTION: $8 \div 3\frac{1}{3}$

$8 \div \frac{10}{3}$

$8 \times \frac{3}{10}$

$$\frac{\overset{4}{8}}{1} \times \frac{3}{\underset{5}{10}} = \frac{12}{5} \text{ or } 2\frac{2}{5}$$

EXAMPLE: Divide $2\frac{2}{5}$ by $8\frac{7}{10}$.

SOLUTION: $2\frac{2}{5} \div 8\frac{7}{10}$

$\frac{12}{5} \div \frac{87}{10}$

$$\frac{\overset{4}{12}}{\underset{1}{5}} \times \frac{\overset{2}{10}}{\underset{29}{87}} = \frac{8}{29}$$

EXAMPLE: Divide $3\frac{8}{9}$ by $2\frac{1}{12}$.

SOLUTION: $3\frac{8}{9} \div 2\frac{1}{12}$

$\frac{35}{9} \div \frac{25}{12}$

$$\frac{\overset{7}{35}}{\underset{3}{9}} \times \frac{\overset{4}{12}}{\underset{5}{25}} = \frac{28}{15} \text{ or } 1\frac{13}{15}$$

EXERCISE 29
Divide

1. $\frac{1}{5} \div \frac{1}{3}$ 2. $\frac{3}{4} \div \frac{7}{8}$
3. $\frac{1}{4} \div \frac{2}{3}$ 4. $\frac{11}{12} \div \frac{5}{6}$
5. $\frac{9}{10} \div \frac{3}{5}$ 6. $\frac{2}{7} \div 3$
7. $6 \div \frac{1}{2}$ 8. $8 \div \frac{4}{9}$
9. $12 \div \frac{2}{5}$ 10. $\frac{3}{8} \div 9$
11. $\frac{1}{2} \div 2\frac{1}{4}$ 12. $\frac{3}{10} \div 2\frac{2}{5}$
13. $4\frac{1}{6} \div \frac{2}{3}$ 14. $1\frac{2}{3} \div \frac{5}{6}$
15. $12 \div 6\frac{2}{3}$ 16. $25 \div 3\frac{3}{4}$
17. $3\frac{1}{2} \div 2\frac{1}{3}$ 18. $9\frac{1}{3} \div 1\frac{1}{6}$
19. $5\frac{3}{5} \div 2\frac{1}{10}$ 20. $6\frac{3}{4} \div 2\frac{1}{2}$

If you got 19 or 20 correct, go on to the next section on Complex Fractions. If you got more than two wrong, use Exercise 30 to build your skill.

EXERCISE 30
Divide

1. $\frac{1}{2} \div \frac{1}{3}$ 2. $\frac{2}{5} \div \frac{1}{2}$
3. $\frac{5}{8} \div \frac{3}{4}$ 4. $\frac{2}{3} \div \frac{3}{8}$
5. $\frac{3}{7} \div \frac{9}{14}$ 6. $\frac{5}{12} \div \frac{3}{10}$
7. $\frac{4}{9} \div \frac{1}{3}$ 8. $\frac{2}{5} \div \frac{7}{15}$
9. $\frac{9}{10} \div \frac{3}{4}$ 10. $\frac{7}{12} \div \frac{14}{15}$
11. $\frac{1}{2} \div 2\frac{1}{4}$ 12. $\frac{3}{10} \div 2\frac{2}{5}$
13. $\frac{3}{4} \div 2$ 14. $\frac{6}{7} \div 3$
15. $8 \div \frac{1}{3}$ 16. $12 \div \frac{2}{5}$
17. $20 \div \frac{4}{7}$ 18. $48 \div \frac{8}{9}$
19. $36 \div \frac{9}{11}$ 20. $18 \div \frac{8}{9}$
21. $21 \div \frac{7}{8}$ 22. $\frac{5}{12} \div 10$
23. $\frac{7}{9} \div 14$ 24. $\frac{4}{15} \div 10$
25. $\frac{1}{3} \div 1\frac{1}{6}$ 26. $\frac{7}{8} \div 2\frac{1}{3}$
27. $\frac{9}{10} \div 4\frac{1}{2}$ 28. $\frac{7}{9} \div 5\frac{1}{4}$
29. $3\frac{1}{5} \div \frac{4}{5}$ 30. $3\frac{1}{3} \div \frac{2}{9}$
31. $6\frac{2}{3} \div \frac{5}{6}$ 32. $8\frac{2}{5} \div \frac{3}{10}$
33. $5\frac{1}{4} \div 2\frac{1}{2}$ 34. $3\frac{3}{8} \div 4\frac{1}{2}$
35. $4\frac{1}{8} \div 3\frac{1}{7}$ 36. $8\frac{1}{3} \div 1\frac{1}{9}$
37. $9\frac{3}{4} \div 1\frac{1}{2}$ 38. $2\frac{11}{12} \div 4\frac{1}{6}$
39. $6\frac{1}{4} \div 5\frac{5}{8}$ 40. $7\frac{1}{2} \div 4\frac{1}{6}$

Now be sure of your skill. Try Exercise 31.

EXERCISE 31

Divide

1. $\frac{1}{4} \div \frac{1}{3}$ 2. $\frac{5}{6} \div \frac{2}{3}$

3. $\frac{3}{10} \div \frac{5}{9}$ 4. $\frac{9}{16} \div \frac{3}{4}$

5. $\frac{3}{7} \div \frac{9}{14}$ 6. $\frac{5}{7} \div 2$

7. $9 \div \frac{1}{3}$ 8. $15 \div \frac{5}{9}$

9. $10 \div \frac{4}{7}$ 10. $\frac{7}{8} \div 14$

11. $\frac{1}{3} \div 4\frac{1}{6}$ 12. $\frac{7}{9} \div 4\frac{2}{3}$

13. $4\frac{1}{5} \div \frac{9}{10}$ 14. $7\frac{1}{2} \div \frac{3}{4}$

15. $18 \div 4\frac{1}{2}$ 16. $30 \div 5\frac{1}{4}$

17. $2\frac{1}{2} \div 1\frac{2}{3}$ 18. $8\frac{1}{3} \div 2\frac{1}{2}$

19. $2\frac{5}{8} \div 1\frac{3}{4}$ 20. $11\frac{1}{4} \div 3\frac{3}{5}$

COMPLEX FRACTIONS

Sometimes we are required to simplify fractions.

EXAMPLE: Simplify $\dfrac{\frac{1}{2} + \frac{1}{3}}{\frac{3}{4}}$

SOLUTION: First, we find the LCD of all the fractions within the numerator and the denominator. In this case, the LCD is 12.

Second, we multiply both the numerator and the denominator of the complex fraction by 12. This does not change the value of the fraction.

$$\frac{12\left(\frac{1}{2} + \frac{1}{3}\right)}{12\left(\frac{3}{4}\right)} = \frac{6+4}{9} = \frac{10}{9} \text{ or } 1\frac{1}{9}$$

EXERCISE 32

Simplify the following complex fractions.

1. $\dfrac{\frac{5}{6} + \frac{2}{3}}{\frac{1}{4}}$ 2. $\dfrac{\frac{5}{9} - \frac{1}{12}}{\frac{5}{6}}$

3. $\dfrac{\frac{4}{5} - \frac{3}{10}}{\frac{7}{15}}$ 4. $\dfrac{\frac{5}{6} - \frac{3}{8}}{\frac{7}{12}}$

Review Test-Taking Tips on page vii.

PRACTICE TEST 4

1. The fraction $\frac{36}{54}$ reduced to lowest terms is equal to:

   (A) $\frac{3}{7}$ (B) $\frac{6}{9}$ (C) $\frac{5}{8}$ (D) $\frac{2}{3}$ (E) $\frac{16}{27}$

2. The fraction $\frac{20}{30}$ reduced to lowest terms is equal to:

   (A) $\frac{3}{7}$ (B) $\frac{4}{5}$ (C) $\frac{4}{7}$ (D) $\frac{2}{3}$ (E) $\frac{7}{4}$

3. $\frac{1}{3} + \frac{1}{4} =$

   (A) $\frac{1}{6}$ (B) $\frac{7}{12}$ (C) $\frac{2}{7}$ (D) $\frac{7}{4}$ (E) $\frac{7}{6}$

4. $\frac{5}{6} + \frac{5}{9} =$

   (A) $\frac{2}{3}$ (B) $\frac{5}{54}$ (C) $\frac{25}{54}$ (D) $1\frac{2}{9}$

   (E) none of these

5. $2\frac{6}{7} + \frac{2}{3} =$

   (A) $3\frac{1}{11}$ (B) $2\frac{8}{21}$ (C) $3\frac{11}{21}$ (D) $2\frac{3}{4}$ (E) $2\frac{4}{7}$

6. $\frac{5}{8} + \frac{3}{4} + \frac{5}{6} =$

   (A) $\frac{13}{18}$ (B) $\frac{25}{64}$ (C) $2\frac{5}{12}$ (D) $2\frac{5}{24}$ (E) $\frac{17}{18}$

7. $1\frac{1}{4} + 3\frac{4}{5} + 2\frac{7}{10} =$

   (A) $7\frac{1}{10}$ (B) $7\frac{3}{4}$ (C) $6\frac{3}{5}$ (D) $8\frac{1}{5}$ (E) $6\frac{1}{2}$

8. $\frac{7}{8} - \frac{5}{6} =$

   (A) $\frac{1}{7}$ (B) 1 (C) $\frac{1}{12}$ (D) $\frac{3}{8}$ (E) $\frac{1}{24}$

9. $2\frac{1}{6} - \frac{2}{3} =$

   (A) $\frac{1}{3}$ (B) $1\frac{1}{2}$ (C) $2\frac{1}{9}$ (D) $2\frac{5}{18}$

   (E) none of these

10. $3\frac{3}{8} - 1\frac{7}{12} =$

    (A) $2\frac{1}{12}$ (B) $1\frac{9}{24}$ (C) $1\frac{1}{3}$ (D) $1\frac{19}{24}$ (E) $1\frac{1}{4}$

11. $\frac{9}{10} \times \frac{8}{15} =$

    (A) $\frac{17}{15}$ (B) $\frac{12}{25}$ (C) $1\frac{7}{10}$ (D) $1\frac{2}{15}$ (E) $1\frac{11}{16}$

12. $1\frac{5}{16} \times 4\frac{2}{3} =$

    (A) $4\frac{5}{24}$ (B) $4\frac{1}{8}$ (C) $6\frac{3}{4}$ (D) $6\frac{5}{16}$ (E) $6\frac{1}{8}$

13. $4\frac{1}{2} \times \frac{7}{9} \times \frac{3}{14} =$

    (A) $1\frac{1}{2}$ (B) $\frac{3}{4}$ (C) $4\frac{1}{6}$ (D) $5\frac{1}{7}$

    (E) none of these

14. $2\frac{1}{2} \times 3\frac{3}{4} \times 5\frac{1}{3} =$

    (A) $30\frac{1}{2}$ (B) 25 (C) $30\frac{1}{8}$ (D) 50

    (E) none of these

15. $\frac{2}{3} \div \frac{5}{12} =$

    (A) $\frac{5}{8}$ (B) $\frac{5}{18}$ (C) $1\frac{3}{5}$ (D) $\frac{5}{9}$ (E) $\frac{7}{36}$

16. $6\frac{1}{4} \div 5\frac{5}{12} =$
    (A) $1\frac{5}{12}$ (B) $1\frac{1}{5}$ (C) $1\frac{1}{14}$ (D) $\frac{4}{5}$
    (E) none of these

PRACTICE TEST 5

1. The fraction $\frac{28}{32}$ reduced to lowest terms is equal to:
    (A) $\frac{4}{7}$ (B) $\frac{14}{16}$ (C) $\frac{3}{4}$ (D) $\frac{7}{8}$ (E) $\frac{5}{8}$

2. The fraction $\frac{30}{45}$ reduced to lowest terms is equal to:
    (A) $\frac{3}{5}$ (B) $\frac{2}{3}$ (C) $\frac{5}{7}$ (D) $\frac{4}{5}$ (E) $\frac{3}{4}$

3. $\frac{1}{3} + \frac{1}{5} =$
    (A) $\frac{8}{15}$ (B) $\frac{1}{4}$ (C) $\frac{2}{8}$ (D) $\frac{4}{5}$ (E) $\frac{2}{3}$

4. $\frac{7}{8} + \frac{5}{6} =$
    (A) $\frac{6}{7}$ (B) $1\frac{12}{24}$ (C) $1\frac{19}{24}$ (D) $1\frac{17}{24}$ (E) $1\frac{1}{4}$

5. $2\frac{5}{7} + \frac{1}{2} =$
    (A) $2\frac{3}{14}$ (B) $2\frac{2}{3}$ (C) $3\frac{5}{14}$ (D) $2\frac{5}{9}$
    (E) none of these

6. $\frac{1}{4} + \frac{4}{5} + \frac{7}{10} =$
    (A) $\frac{3}{5}$ (B) $1\frac{1}{2}$ (C) $\frac{11}{20}$ (D) $1\frac{3}{4}$ (E) $1\frac{3}{10}$

7. $1\frac{2}{3} + 2\frac{3}{4} + 1\frac{5}{6} =$
    (A) $4\frac{5}{6}$ (B) $6\frac{1}{4}$ (C) $4\frac{1}{2}$ (D) $6\frac{1}{3}$
    (E) none of these

8. $\frac{11}{12} - \frac{5}{8} =$
    (A) $\frac{7}{24}$ (B) $\frac{6}{4}$ (C) $\frac{1}{2}$ (D) $\frac{5}{16}$ (E) $\frac{6}{10}$

9. $2\frac{5}{7} - \frac{2}{3} =$
    (A) $1\frac{5}{21}$ (B) $2\frac{3}{4}$ (C) $2\frac{1}{21}$ (D) $2\frac{4}{21}$ (E) $2\frac{1}{7}$

10. $3\frac{1}{9} - 1\frac{5}{6} =$
    (A) $1\frac{1}{3}$ (B) $1\frac{7}{18}$ (C) $2\frac{5}{18}$ (D) $2\frac{2}{3}$ (E) $1\frac{5}{18}$

11. $\frac{4}{15} \times \frac{9}{16} =$
    (A) $\frac{3}{10}$ (B) $\frac{6}{10}$ (C) $\frac{3}{20}$ (D) $\frac{13}{60}$ (E) $\frac{7}{30}$

12. $3\frac{3}{4} \times 5\frac{1}{3} =$
    (A) $15\frac{1}{4}$ (B) 16 (C) $15\frac{3}{4}$ (D) 15 (E) 20

13. $2\frac{2}{3} \times \frac{5}{9} \times 3\frac{3}{5} =$
    (A) $6\frac{2}{3}$ (B) $5\frac{1}{3}$ (C) $6\frac{8}{15}$ (D) $4\frac{7}{9}$
    (E) none of these

14. $2\frac{1}{4} \times 3\frac{1}{3} \times 1\frac{1}{5} =$
    (A) 9 (B) $6\frac{1}{2}$ (C) $6\frac{7}{15}$ (D) $7\frac{2}{3}$ (E) $8\frac{1}{2}$

15. $\frac{3}{8} \div \frac{5}{16} =$
    (A) $\frac{5}{6}$ (B) $1\frac{1}{3}$ (C) $\frac{3}{5}$ (D) $1\frac{1}{5}$ (E) $1\frac{3}{8}$

16. $10\frac{2}{3} \div 3\frac{1}{5} =$
    (A) $3\frac{1}{15}$ (B) $3\frac{1}{3}$ (C) $2\frac{2}{15}$ (D) $2\frac{2}{3}$
    (E) none of these

PRACTICE TEST 6

1. The fraction $\frac{24}{42}$ reduced to lowest terms is equal to:
    (A) $\frac{6}{7}$ (B) $\frac{1}{2}$ (C) $\frac{4}{7}$ (D) $\frac{3}{7}$ (E) $1\frac{3}{7}$

2. The fraction $\frac{32}{48}$ reduced to lowest terms is equal to:
    (A) $\frac{2}{3}$ (B) $\frac{3}{4}$ (C) $\frac{4}{6}$ (D) $\frac{6}{16}$ (E) $\frac{5}{6}$

3. $\frac{1}{2} + \frac{1}{3} =$
    (A) $\frac{2}{5}$ (B) $\frac{2}{6}$ (C) $\frac{1}{6}$ (D) $\frac{4}{6}$
    (E) none of these

4. $\frac{4}{5} + \frac{3}{4} =$
    (A) $\frac{7}{20}$ (B) $\frac{7}{9}$ (C) $1\frac{11}{20}$ (D) $1\frac{7}{9}$ (E) $1\frac{17}{20}$

5. $1\frac{5}{6} + \frac{7}{8} =$
    (A) $2\frac{5}{12}$ (B) $2\frac{17}{24}$ (C) $1\frac{23}{24}$ (D) $2\frac{3}{8}$
    (E) none of these

6. $\frac{1}{2} + \frac{1}{6} + \frac{4}{9} =$
    (A) $1\frac{5}{18}$ (B) $2\frac{1}{18}$ (C) $1\frac{4}{9}$ (D) $2\frac{1}{9}$ (E) $1\frac{1}{9}$

7. $2\frac{2}{3} + 3\frac{4}{5} + 1\frac{7}{10} =$
    (A) $6\frac{1}{6}$ (B) $7\frac{17}{30}$ (C) $8\frac{1}{6}$ (D) $6\frac{5}{6}$
    (E) none of these

8. $\frac{8}{9} - \frac{5}{6} =$

(A) $\frac{1}{18}$ (B) $\frac{2}{3}$ (C) $\frac{1}{9}$ (D) $\frac{1}{3}$ (E) $\frac{1}{12}$

9. $2\frac{3}{8} - \frac{1}{2} =$

(A) 2 (B) $1\frac{1}{2}$ (C) $1\frac{3}{4}$ (D) $\frac{1}{3}$

(E) none of these

10. $5\frac{4}{9} - 3\frac{11}{12} =$

(A) $2\frac{38}{72}$ (B) $1\frac{19}{36}$ (C) $2\frac{1}{3}$ (D) $1\frac{1}{3}$ (E) $1\frac{1}{2}$

11. $\frac{3}{8} \times \frac{2}{9} =$

(A) $\frac{1}{2}$ (B) $\frac{2}{3}$ (C) $\frac{3}{4}$ (D) $\frac{1}{6}$

(E) none of these

12. $2\frac{5}{8} \times 3\frac{1}{7} =$

(A) $8\frac{1}{4}$ (B) $6\frac{5}{56}$ (C) $7\frac{1}{2}$ (D) $4\frac{1}{8}$ (E) $6\frac{1}{7}$

13. $7\frac{1}{2} \times \frac{4}{5} \times \frac{2}{3} =$

(A) 8 (B) $2\frac{2}{3}$ (C) 4 (D) $8\frac{4}{15}$ (E) 6

14. $1\frac{5}{6} \times 3\frac{3}{4} \times 1\frac{7}{11} =$

(A) $4\frac{1}{4}$ (B) $10\frac{1}{4}$ (C) $5\frac{3}{8}$ (D) $22\frac{1}{2}$ (E) $11\frac{1}{4}$

15. $\frac{5}{9} \div \frac{2}{3} =$

(A) $\frac{10}{27}$ (B) $1\frac{1}{5}$ (C) $\frac{5}{18}$ (D) $\frac{5}{6}$

(E) none of these

16. $4\frac{1}{6} \div 1\frac{2}{3} =$

(A) $2\frac{1}{2}$ (B) $\frac{2}{5}$ (C) $12\frac{5}{18}$ (D) $2\frac{1}{5}$

(E) none of these

Decimal Fractions

DECIMALS

The place values to the right of the decimal point are:

After the millionths period are billionths, trillonths, quadrillionths, and so on corresponding to the names of the periods of whole numbers. To read such a number, read the digits to the right of the decimal point as if they were a whole number and then name the place value of the right-most digit.

EXAMPLES:

Read 5.0258.
Read: "Five *and* two hundred fifty-eight *ten-thousandths*." The only place where *and* should be read in any number is where the decimal point is located.

Read: 27.120453. (The 3 sits in the millionths' position.)

Read: "Twenty-seven and one hundred twenty thousand four hundred fifty-three millionths."

When the whole number part of the decimal number is zero, the zero is used only for emphasis; it may be deleted. For example, 0.23 may be written merely as .23. Zeros to the right of the right-most nonzero digit may be deleted. Such decimal numbers are equivalent.

$$2.5700 = 2.57$$

COMPARING DECIMAL FRACTIONS

In comparing the sizes of decimal fractions we compare tenths first. If necessary we compare hundredths, thousandths, etc., until the larger value is determined.

EXAMPLE: Which is larger, 0.63 or 0.59?

SOLUTION: Since the first decimal contains 6 tenths and the second decimal contains 5 tenths, the first decimal is larger than the second decimal.

EXAMPLE: Which is larger, 0.137 or 0.45?

SOLUTION: Since the first decimal contains 1 tenth and the second decimal contains 4 tenths, the second decimal is larger than the first decimal.

EXAMPLE: Which is larger, 0.853 or 0.8512?

SOLUTION: The two decimals have the same number of tenths (8) and the same number of hundredths (5). However, the first decimal contains 3 thousandths and the second decimal contains 1 thousandth. Therefore, the first decimal is larger than the second decimal.

ROUNDING OFF DECIMAL FRACTIONS

In writing a decimal fraction to a given number of decimal places, examine the digit in the decimal place that is one place to the right of the decimal required. If this digit is 5 or more, increase the digit to the left by 1. If this digit is less than 5, the digit to the left is not changed. Drop all digits to the right of the required place.

The decimal fraction 0.26, rounded off correctly to the nearest tenth, is 0.3, because 0.26 is closer to 0.3 than it is to 0.2. The decimal fraction 0.762, rounded off correct to the nearest hundredth, is 0.76, because 0.762 is closer to 0.76 than it is to 0.77.

EXAMPLE: Round off 0.83 to the nearest tenth.

SOLUTION: Since 3 is less than 5, 8 is left unchanged and the 3 is dropped. The answer is 0.8.

EXAMPLE: Round off 0.42781 to the nearest hundredth.

SOLUTION: The digit to the right of the hundredths place is 7. Since 7 is more than 5, we increase the 2 to 3 and drop all other digits. The answer is 0.43.

EXERCISE 33

Round off the following decimals as indicated.

1. 0.46 (nearest tenth)
2. 0.307 (nearest hundredth)
3. 0.982 (nearest hundredth)
4. 0.3568 (nearest thousandth)

Arrange each of the following sets of decimal fractions in order of their size, with the largest decimal fraction first.

5. 0.653, 0.67, 0.619
6. 0.712, 0.721, 0.716
7. 0.237, 0.2, 0.218
8. 0.467, 0.4009, 0.4102

If you got 7 or 8 correct, go on to the next section on Addition of Decimals. If you got more than one wrong, use Exercise 34 to build your skill.

EXERCISE 34

Round off the following decimals as indicated.

1. To the nearest tenth
   (a) 0.32   (b) 0.691   (c) 0.052   (d) 0.93
   (e) 0.487   (f) 0.709   (g) 0.85
   (h) 0.4172   (i) 0.9128   (j) 0.63
2. To the nearest hundredth
   (a) 0.163   (b) 0.038   (c) 0.685
   (d) 0.701   (e) 0.854
3. To the nearest thousandth
   (a) 0.6579   (b) 0.4032   (c) 0.8175
   (d) 0.0952   (e) 0.5437

Arrange each of the following sets of decimal fractions in order of their size, with the largest decimal fraction first.

4. 0.309, 0.295, 0.416
5. 0.857, 0.875, 0.902
6. 0.7, 0.605, 0.713
7. 0.489, 0.492, 0.516
8. 0.3, 0.128, 0.41
9. 0.57, 0.712, 0.7
10. 0.914, 0.832, 0.823
11. 0.096, 0.088, 0.123

Now be sure of your skill. Try Exercise 35.

EXERCISE 35

Round off the following decimals as indicated.

1. 0.53 (nearest tenth)
2. 0.209 (nearest hundredth)
3. 0.768 (nearest hundredth)
4. 0.8513 (nearest thousandth)

Arrange each of the following sets of decimal fractions in order of their size, with the largest decimal fraction first.

5. 0.461, 0.47, 0.418
6. 0.385, 0.319, 0.391
7. 0.6, 0.602, 0.59
8. 0.7031, 0.7103, 0.7301

ADDITION OF DECIMALS

The addition of decimal fractions is a much simpler operation than the addition of ordinary fractions since the denominators are 10, 100, 1,000, etc. Arrange the decimals in a column so that the decimal points are aligned. Then add the decimals in the same manner as whole numbers. The decimal point in the answer is in line with the decimal points of the numbers that were added.

EXAMPLES: Add the following.

0.3	4.7	5.73
0.6	3.2	6.04
0.5	0.9	2.59
+ 0.4	+ 1.5	+ 3.60
1.8	10.3	17.96

0.918	28.47
2.403	3.62
0.759	809.03
+ 6.572	+ 37.94
10.652	879.06

EXAMPLE: Add the following:

16.237 + 48.051 + 9.003 + 67.215 + 3.790

SOLUTION: Arrange these numbers, keeping the decimal points in a line.

16.237
48.051
9.003
67.215
+ 3.790
144.296

SUBTRACTION OF DECIMALS

In subtracting decimals, we arrange them in a column, aligning the decimal points. Then we subtract as with whole numbers. The decimal point in the answer appears in the same column as in the numbers that were subtracted.

EXAMPLES: Subtract

0.9	0.63	3.5
− 0.5	− 0.49	− 0.7
0.4	0.14	2.8

48.07	720.72
− 7.68	− 69.58
40.39	651.14

EXAMPLE: Subtract 0.53 from 0.81.

SOLUTION:
0.81
− 0.53
0.28

EXAMPLE: From 4.821 subtract 1.367.

SOLUTION:
4.821
− 1.367
3.454

EXERCISE 36

Add the following.

1. 0.42	2. 6.01	3. 28.3	4. 128.304
0.39	5.29	7.8	7.927
+ 0.75	0.67	65.4	63.518
	+ 3.40	+ 0.2	+ 0.479

5. Add 38.42 + 1.65 + 3.29 + 80.07.
6. Add 5.01 + 7.92 + 63.78 + 40.80.

Subtract

7. 0.83	8. 5.07	9. 34.561	10. 290.103
− 0.49	− 3.48	− 7.483	− 83.561

11. From 2.67 subtract 1.08.
12. Subtract 56.314 from 89.057.

If you got 11 or 12 correct, go on to the next section on Multiplication of Decimals. If you got more than one wrong, use Exercise 37 to build your skill.

EXERCISE 37
Find each sum.

1. 0.53	2. 0.85	3. 6.38
0.29	0.30	5.02
0.48	0.17	0.49
0.65	0.69	3.15
+ 0.34	+ 0.92	+ 4.30

4. 9.12	5. 39.2	6. 50.32
6.73	41.3	67.19
5.28	6.8	8.57
0.09	59.6	32.08
+ 1.25	+ 7.1	+ 9.10

7. 32.95	8. 159.01	9. 459.83
68.17	36.57	60.19
91.24	216.28	203.05
2.39	8.09	75.16
+ 0.46	+ 78.65	+ 2.58

10. 2.069	11. 25.712	12. 3.050
47.135	6.059	2.716
68.926	31.207	85.018
4.007	9.895	16.009
+ 15.298	+ 67.156	+ 07.502

13. 786.14	14. 230.04
95.07	17.98
139.18	169.07
26.49	598.82
+ 18.80	+ 68.75

15. Add 8.1 + 3.7 + 6.5 + 7.9 + 2.4
16. Add 5.3 + 2.5 + 6.9 + 3.8 + 2.7
17. Add 9.52 + 8.76 + 4.37 + 5.09 + 1.06
18. Add 8.75 + 4.69 + 3.06 + 7.27 + 2.58
19. Add 67.34 + 75.08 + 59.17 + 63.92 + 71.47
20. Add 58.51 + 63.47 + 5.94 + 7.83 + 95.82

Subtract.

21. 0.48	22. 0.72	23. 0.51	24. 0.68
− 0.15	− 0.38	− 0.29	− 0.49

25. 4.52	26. 8.14	27. 7.08	28. 5.03
− 1.37	− 3.59	− 3.16	− 2.19

29. 79.91	30. 82.15	31. 63.168
− 43.67	− 45.29	− 15.712

32. 75.065	33. 50.012	34. 841.07
− 38.173	− 18.564	− 68.59

Now be sure of your skill. Try Exercise 38.

EXERCISE 38

Add.

1. 0.38	2. 8.03	3. 57.2	4. 387.207
0.57	7.59	9.7	8.158
+ 0.62	0.72	38.8	59.623
	+ 4.56	+ 00.6	+ 0.385

5. Add 63.79 + 3.48 + 1.67 + 60.06.
6. Add 7.02 + 8.95 + 71.64 + 85.07.

Subtract.

7. 0.62	8. 6.03	9. 68.382	10. 560.208
− 0.38	− 1.59	− 9.597	− 79.472

11. From 3.84 subtract 2.07.
12. Subtract 37.516 from 95.028.

MULTIPLICATION OF DECIMALS

In multiplying decimals, follow the procedure used in multiplying whole numbers. It is not necessary to arrange the numbers so that the decimal points are in a line. The number of decimal places (the places to the right of the decimal point) in the answer is equal to the total of the decimal places in the two numbers that were multiplied.

EXAMPLE: Multiply 75 by 0.8.

SOLUTION:
$$75$$
$$\times\ 0.8 \leftarrow 1 \text{ decimal place}$$
$$60.0 \leftarrow 1 \text{ decimal place}$$

EXAMPLE: Multiply 84 by 0.03.

SOLUTION:
$$84$$
$$\times\ 0.03 \leftarrow 2 \text{ decimal places}$$
$$2.52 \leftarrow 2 \text{ decimal places}$$

EXAMPLE: Multiply 0.27 by 9.

SOLUTION:
$$0.27$$
$$\times\ \ 9$$
$$2.43$$

EXAMPLE: Multiply 65 by 0.87.

SOLUTION:
$$65$$
$$\times\ \ .87$$
$$455$$
$$520$$
$$56.55$$

EXAMPLE: Multiply 3.82 by 5.7.

SOLUTION:
$$3.82 \leftarrow 2 \text{ decimal places}$$
$$\times\ 05.7 \leftarrow 1 \text{ decimal place}$$
$$2674$$
$$1910$$
$$21.774 \leftarrow 3 \text{ decimal places}$$

EXAMPLE: Multiply 68.2 by 0.79.

SOLUTION:
$$68.2$$
$$\times\ 0.79$$
$$6138$$
$$4774$$
$$53.878$$

EXERCISE 39

Multiply.

1.	8 × 0.6	2.	0.9 × 7	3.	37 × 0.4
4.	2.9 × 0.8	5.	67 × 0.03	6.	85 × 0.47
7.	49 × 2.6	8.	6.8 × 79	9.	1.6 × 4.7
10.	0.38 × 59	11.	518 × 0.63	12.	5.07 × 0.682
13.	5.37 × 0.914	14.	6.409 × 0.076	15.	0.0496 × 3.7

If you got 14 or 15 correct, go on to the next section on Division of Decimals. If you got more than one wrong, use Exercise 40 to build your skill.

EXERCISE 40

Multiply.

1.	8 × 0.6	2.	7 × 0.9	3.	0.5 × 7
4.	0.8 × 4	5.	9 × 0.3	6.	0.3 × 7
7.	24 × 0.04	8.	39 × 0.46	9.	67 × 0.34
10.	78 × 0.59	11.	81 × 0.67	12.	59 × 4.5
13.	73 × 6.8	14.	82 × 3.6	15.	43 × 9.7
16.	3.5 × 48	17.	6.7 × 69	18.	2.9 × 53
19.	5.1 × 3.2	20.	6.8 × 8.4	21.	0.19 × 63
22.	0.53 × 0.29	23.	0.77 × 0.48	24.	386 × 0.28
25.	503 × 0.92	26.	890 × 0.25	27.	463 × 0.78
28.	257 × 0.416	29.	409 × 0.324	30.	667 × 0.469

31.	8.07 × 0.624	32.	7.46 × 0.389	33.	8.167 × 0.534
34.	6.809 × 0.247	35.	7.020 × 0.309	36.	0.035 × 7.8
37.	2.035 × 3.9	38.	0.0659 × 4.7		

Now be sure of your skill. Try Exercise 41.

EXERCISE 41

Multiply:

1.	8 × 0.7	2.	0.6 × 9	3.	58 × 0.6
4.	3.9 × 0.7	5.	797 × 0.04	6.	76 × 0.38
7.	43 × 7.9	8.	8.1 × 93	9.	5.6 × 3.7
10.	0.47 × 69	11.	384 × 0.76	12.	608 × 0.483
13.	7.29 × 0.827	14.	9.308 × 0.063	15.	0.0384 × 2.7

DIVISION OF DECIMALS

In dividing a decimal by a whole number, divide as in division of whole numbers, placing the decimal point of the result in line with the decimal point in the dividend.

EXAMPLE: Divide $9\overline{)74.835}$

SOLUTION: Perform the division, placing the decimal point in the result in line with the decimal point in the dividend between 4 and 8.

$$9\overline{)74.835} = 8.315$$

The result is 8.315.

To divide any number by a decimal, first move the decimal point in the divisor to the right as many places as is necessary to make it a whole number. Then move the decimal point in the dividend the same number of places to the right. Divide as in whole number division and place the decimal point in the quotient immediately above the decimal point in the dividend.

EXAMPLE: Divide $0.028 \overline{)3.1407}$, correct to the nearest tenth.

SOLUTION: Make the divisor a whole number by moving the decimal point three places to the right. Also move the decimal point in the dividend three places to the right. The decimal point in the dividend is now between 0 and 7. Proceed with the division as with whole numbers, annexing a zero on the right in the dividend so that we may find the digit in the hundredths place. This will enable us to state the quotient correct to the nearest tenth.

$$
\begin{array}{r}
112.16 \\
0.028 \overline{)3.140.70} \\
28 \\
34 \\
28 \\
60 \\
56 \\
47 \\
28 \\
190 \\
168
\end{array}
$$

The result is 112.2, correct to the nearest tenth.

EXAMPLE: Divide $4.17 \overline{)162.3180}$ finding the quotient correct to the nearest tenth.

SOLUTION: We move the decimal point in both the divisor and the dividend two places to the right. Then we annex a zero on the right to find the digit in the hundredths place. This will enable us to state the quotient correct to the nearest tenth.

$$
\begin{array}{r}
38.92 \\
4.17 \overline{)162.31.80} \\
1251 \\
3721 \\
3336 \\
3858 \\
3753 \\
1050 \\
834
\end{array}
$$

The result is 38.9, correct to the nearest tenth.

EXERCISE 42

Divide. When necessary, round as indicated.

1. $8 \overline{)38.4}$

2. $7 \overline{)45.63}$ (to nearest tenth)

3. $39 \overline{)685.7}$ (to nearest tenth)

4. $56 \overline{)2.057}$ (to nearest hundredth)

5. $0.7 \overline{)58.36}$ (to nearest tenth)

6. $0.6 \overline{)0.2349}$ (to nearest tenth)

7. $0.03 \overline{)5.697}$

8. $0.009 \overline{)3.17862}$

9. $8.7 \overline{)3.0795}$ (to nearest hundredth)

10. $0.36 \overline{)92.052}$

11. $0.59 \overline{)7.0269}$

12. $0.048 \overline{)0.76504}$ (to nearest hundredth)

13. $5.12 \overline{)80.532}$ (to nearest hundredth)

14. $60.7 \overline{)431.052}$ (to nearest tenth)

15. $0.168 \overline{)0.05479}$ (to nearest hundredth)

If you got 14 or 15 correct, go on to the next sections on Multiplication and Division by 10, 100, 1000, etc. If you got more than one wrong, use Exercise 43 to build your skill.

EXERCISE 43

Divide. When necessary, round as indicated.

1. $9 \overline{)32.67}$

2. $6 \overline{)47.16}$

3. $8 \overline{)68.48}$

4. $5 \overline{)30.05}$

5. $7 \overline{)53.78}$ (to nearest tenth)

6. $4 \overline{)28.07}$ (to nearest tenth)

7. $9 \overline{)47.06}$ (to nearest tenth)

8. $67 \overline{)980.7}$ (to nearest tenth)

9. $74 \overline{)80.56}$ (to nearest tenth)

10. $83 \overline{)5.927}$ (to nearest hundredth)

11. $57\overline{)7.604}$ (to nearest hundredth)

12. $19\overline{)5.782}$ (to nearest tenth)

13. $0.9\overline{)47.32}$ (to nearest tenth)

14. $0.7\overline{)85.19}$

15. $0.4\overline{)0.1758}$ (to nearest tenth)

16. $0.8\overline{)0.1609}$ (to nearest tenth)

17. $0.06\overline{)7.236}$

18. $0.07\overline{)8.015}$

19. $0.03\overline{)5.106}$

20. $0.008\overline{)4.10648}$

21. $0.004\overline{)5.6704}$

22. $5.3\overline{)4.1682}$ (to nearest hundredth)

23. $3.9\overline{)5.7106}$ (to nearest hundredth)

24. $0.48\overline{)15.648}$

25. $0.67\overline{)27.336}$

26. $0.91\overline{)64.792}$

27. $0.73\overline{)18.834}$

28. $0.039\overline{)0.65712}$ (to nearest hundredth)

29. $0.017\overline{)0.38706}$ (to nearest hundredth)

30. $3.14\overline{)67.085}$ (to nearest hundredth)

31. $7.08\overline{)91.307}$ (to nearest tenth)

32. $37.6\overline{)582.705}$ (to nearest tenth)

33. $49.3\overline{)609.487}$ (to nearest tenth)

34. $0.234\overline{)0.06789}$ (to nearest hundredth)

35. $0.857\overline{)0.70138}$ (to nearest hundredth)

Now be sure of your skill. Try Exercise 44.

EXERCISE 44

Divide. When necessary, round the quotient to the place indicated.

1. $9\overline{)50.4}$

2. $6\overline{)37.47}$ (to nearest tenth)

3. $47\overline{)593.8}$ (to nearest tenth)

4. $79\overline{)3.068}$ (to nearest hundredth)

5. $0.8\overline{)73.15}$ (to nearest tenth)

6. $0.7\overline{)0.3482}$ (to nearest tenth)

7. $0.04\overline{)6.792}$

8. $0.009\overline{)4.07934}$

9. $7.9\overline{)5.6023}$ (to nearest hundredth)

10. $0.42\overline{)33.012}$

11. $0.67\overline{)3.4103}$

12. $0.052\overline{)18.173}$ (to nearest hundredth)

13. $3.79\overline{)92.036}$ (to nearest hundredth)

14. $58.3\overline{)389.619}$ (to nearest tenth)

15. $236\overline{)68.42}$ (to nearest hundredth)

MULTIPLYING BY 10, 100, 1,000, ETC.

To multiply a number by 10, move the decimal point in the number one place to the right. In some cases, it may be necessary to annex a zero to complete the operation. Similarly, to multiply a number by 100, move the decimal point in the number two places to the right. In some cases, it may be necessary to annex one or two zeros to complete the operation. Similar procedures are followed when multiplying a number by 1,000, 10,000, etc.

EXAMPLES:

Multiply.   **ANSWERS**

(a) 10×3.5—Move the decimal
point 1 place to the right.   35

(b) 10×69—Annex a zero to 69.   690

(c) 100×0.47—Move the decimal
point 2 places to the right.   47

(d) 100×8.72—Move the decimal
point 2 places to the right   872

(e) 10×0.018—Move the decimal
point 1 place to the right.   0.18

(f) 100×0.9—Move the decimal
point 2 places to the right.   90

(g) 100×65.3—Move the decimal
point 2 places to the right.   6,530

(h) $1,000 \times 4.7$—Move the decimal
point 3 places to the right.   4,700

(i) $1,000 \times 0.0019$—Move the decimal
point 3 places to the right.   1.9

(j) 1,000 × 0.056—Move the decimal
point 3 places to the right.   56

(k) 1,000 × 2.78—Move the decimal
point 3 places to the right.   2,780

(l) 1,000 × 8.5—Move the decimal
point 3 places to the right.   8,500

DIVIDING BY 10, 100, 1,000, ETC.

To divide a number by 10, move the decimal
point in the number one place to the left. In
some cases, it may be necessary to insert a
zero between the decimal point and the first
digit on the left, to complete the operation.
Similarly, to divide a number by 100, move
the decimal point in the number two places
to the left. In some cases, it may be necessary
to insert one or two zeros between the decimal
point and the first digit on the left, to complete
the operation. Similar procedures are followed
when dividing a number by 1,000, 10,000, etc.

EXAMPLES:

Divide.   **ANSWERS**

(a) 68 ÷ 10—Move the decimal
point 1 place to the left.   6.8

(b) 759 ÷ 10—Move the decimal
point 1 place to the left.   75.9

(c) 37.5 ÷ 10—Move the decimal
point 1 place to the left.   3.75

(d) 0.47 ÷ 10—Move the decimal
point 1 place to the left and
insert a zero.   0.047

(e) 0.003 ÷ 10—Move the decimal
point 1 place to the left and
insert a zero.   0.0003

(f) 5,670 ÷ 100—Move the decimal
point 2 places to the left.   56.7

(g) 38.5 ÷ 100—Move the decimal
point 2 places to the left.   0.385

(h) 0.24 ÷ 100—Move the decimal
point 2 places to the left and
insert 2 zeros.   0.0024

(i) 4.97 ÷ 100—Move the decimal
point 2 places to the left and
insert a zero.   0.0497

(j) 7,000 ÷ 1,000—Move the decimal
point 3 places to the left.   7

(k) 806 ÷ 1,000—Move the decimal
point 3 places to the left.   0.806

(l) 5.31 ÷ 1,000—Move the decimal
point 3 places to the left and
insert 2 zeros.   0.00531

EXERCISE 45

Perform the following multiplications.

1. 10 × 6.7   2. 10 × 58
3. 10 × 0.05   4. 10 × 736
5. 10 × 0.482   6. 100 × 3.2
7. 100 × 0.725   8. 100 × 356
9. 100 × 0.051   10. 100 × 65.9
11. 1,000 × 0.015   12. 1,000 × 34
13. 1,000 × 2.69   14. 1,000 × 85
15. 1,000 × 3.14

Perform the following divisions.

16. 85 ÷ 10   17. 0.69 ÷ 10
18. 0.043 ÷ 10   19. 68.72 ÷ 10
20. 0.4951 ÷ 10   21. 3,720 ÷ 100
22. 78.4 ÷ 100   23. 3.72 ÷ 100
24. 0.016 ÷ 100   25. 643.7 ÷ 100
26. 9,000 ÷ 1,000   27. 675 ÷ 1,000
28. 4.07 ÷ 1,000   29. 58.62 ÷ 1,000
30. 0.015 ÷ 1,000

If you got 27 or more correct, go on to the
next section on Operations With United
States Money. If you got more than three
wrong, use Exercise 46 to build your skill.

EXERCISE 46

Multiply the following numbers by 10.

1. 3.2   2. 58   3. 7
4. 0.68   5. 57   6. 0.035
7. 2.14   8. 60.5   9. 4.273
10. 285   11. 0.452   12. 2.83
13. 350   14. 6.805   15. 0.0058

Multiply the following numbers by 100.

1. 6.2   2. 351   3. 0.012
4. 750   5. 0.1572   6. 8.531
7. 0.00039   8. 51.32   9. 4
10. 3.79   11. 1,275   12. 0.02
13. 65   14. 3.002   15. 27.1

Multiply the following numbers by 1,000.

1. 25   2. 6.48   3. 583.2
4. 0.0016   5. 9.075   6. 21.7
7. 0.123   8. 0.01534   9. 3.1416
10. 62.5   11. 0.72   12. 0.00035
13. 2.91   14. 0.05   15. 9.126

Divide the following numbers by 10.

1. 58	2. 400	3. 375
4. 0.625	5. 87.5	6. 125
7. 0.46	8. 250	9. 0.02
10. 75	11. 0.0035	12. 8,532
13. 63.7	14. 1.05	15. 5,780

Divide the following numbers by 100.

1. 750	2. 64.5	3. 0.032
4. 8.73	5. 0.0058	6. 297
7. 3,500	8. 0.167	9. 4,850
10. 9.87	11. 0.5036	12. 90.4
13. 8,610	14. 0.53	15. 65.03

Divide the following numbers by 1,000.

1. 5,300	2. 2,070	3. 6.25
4. 0.015	5. 952	6. 3.14
7. 0.67	8. 2.975	9. 75
10. 125	11. 0.025	12. 65.72
13. 8.75	14. 0.0065	15. 0.833

Now be sure of your skill. Try Exercise 47.

EXERCISE 47

Perform the following multiplications.

1. 10×3.5	2. 10×0.69
3. 10×56	4. 10×0.389
5. 10×506	6. 100×0.463
7. 100×5.2	8. 100×0.063
9. 100×875	10. 100×73.4
11. $1,000 \times 58$	12. $1,000 \times 0.018$
13. $1,000 \times 6.2$	14. $1,000 \times 3.87$
15. $1,000 \times 57$	

Perform the following divisions.

16. $97 \div 10$	17. $0.035 \div 10$
18. $0.48 \div 10$	19. $0.6532 \div 10$
20. $52.8 \div 10$	21. $4,680 \div 100$
22. $58.3 \div 100$	23. $6.97 \div 100$
24. $0.018 \div 100$	25. $548.3 \div 100$
26. $315 \div 1,000$	27. $4,000 \div 1,000$
28. $8.73 \div 1,000$	29. $43.78 \div 1,000$
30. $0.026 \div 1,000$	

OPERATIONS WITH UNITED STATES MONEY

United States money, always preceded by a dollar sign ($), is written as a whole number and a two-place decimal, as a two-place decimal either preceded by a zero or not, or as a whole number. Amounts such as $12.96, $5.00, $1.27, $0.48, $.32, and $26 are examples. The operations of addition, subtraction, multiplication, and division with U.S. money follow the methods used with decimals. Note that $.32 = 32¢.

EXERCISE 48

Add.

1. $3.68	2. $0.79
0.49	5.03
15.06	127.45
8.52	69.76
+ 0.58	+ 5.21

3. $580.18	4. $43.62
91.37	120.04
0.84	98.73
602.06	6.96
+ 3.75	+ 9.09

Subtract.

5. $685.47	6. $209.57	7. $500.08
− 26.19	− 143.73	− 379.46

8. $1,467.12
− 708.59

Multiply.

9. $275.08	10. $65.47	11. $8.79
× 9	× 38	× 107

12. $657.08
× 17

Divide.

13. $843.22 \div 7$ 14. $1,290.09 \div 23$
15. $701.04 \div \$0.69$ 16. $2,671.80 \div \$8.76$

If you got 15 or 16 correct, go on to the following Practice Tests. If you got more than one wrong, use Exercise 49 to build your skill.

EXERCISE 49

Add.

1. $4.73	2. $23.89	3. $897.45
18.29	47.21	673.79
143.06	650.04	44.83
0.29	9.15	2.07
+ 6.52	+ 78.46	+ 385.26

4. $2.03
     4.79
  367.85
  412.06
+ 69.98

5. $59.91
  248.05
  374.77
   25.69
+ 87.03

6. $901.11
    8.99
  653.48
    0.98
+   5.04

7. $240.01
  59.89
   3.45
  82.16
+ 302.47

8. $ 85.50
  69.07
 125.48
 304.96
+   2.57

Subtract.

1. $2.07
  – 0.39

2. $6.50
  – 1.68

3. $79.12
 – 42.39

4. $90.01
 – 69.59

5. $432.72
  – 58.87

6. $890.07
– 367.78

7. $1,240.70
 – 589.86

8. $3,282.03
 – 1,569.18

Multiply.

1. $650.03
  ×   7

2. $507.19
  ×   8

3. $84.37
 ×   29

4. $70.09
 ×   36

5. $5.80
 × 205

6. $9.06
× 125

7. $428.45
 ×   78

8. $902.06
 ×   23

Divide the following, finding results to the nearest cent.

1. $930.78 ÷ 9
2. $1,569.50 ÷ 7
3. $3,897.10 ÷ 18
4. $910.78 ÷ 26
5. $95.45 ÷ $0.83
6. $74.48 ÷ $0.76
7. $267.52 ÷ $3.52
8. $1,333.71 ÷ $6.57

Now be sure of your skill. Try Exercise 50.

EXERCISE 50

Add.

1. $4.37
  0.69
 28.43
  7.14
+ 8.48

2. $0.68
   4.07
 249.79
  78.53
+ 0.49

3. $54.69
 837.28
 403.07
  0.65
+ 8.42

4. $180.07
  65.58
   7.92
  94.65
+ 8.01

Subtract.

5. $379.46
 – 39.18

6. $407.62
 – 239.57

7. $700.02
 – 523.39

8. $2,650.14
 – 905.76

Multiply.

9. $587.04
 ×   6

10. $79.48
  ×   47

11. $9.48
 × 209

12. $306.17
 ×   29

Divide. Round to the nearest cent.

13. $694.18 ÷ 9
14. $3,462.05 ÷ 29
15. $119.13 ÷ $0.57
16. $1,412.43 ÷ $5.29

PRACTICE TEST 7

1. The sum of $0.97, $0.68, and $0.04 =

   (A) $2.35 (B) $1.52 (C) $1.62
    (D) $1.69 (E) $1.72

2. The sum of $38.09, $0.57, and $7.44 =

   (A) $56.10 (B) $46.00 (C) $51.23
    (D) $36.10 (E) $46.10

3. When $12.67 is subtracted from $40.05 the result is:

   (A) $28.18 (B) $38.28 (C) $27.28
    (D) $37.18 (E) none of these

4. The difference between $18.79 and $6.98 =

   (A) $12.81 (B) $11.81 (C) $1.81
    (D) $25.77 (E) $12.77

5. When $0.48 is multiplied by 15 the result is:

   (A) $0.72 (B) $6.20 (C) $0.032
    (D) $7.20 (E) $5.40

6. When $19.89 is multiplied by 24 the result is:

   (A) $47.74 (B) $467.36 (C) $477.36
    (D) $377.36 (E) $367.36

7. When $163.45 is divided by 7 the result is:

   (A) $2.35 (B) $2.34 (C) $23.35
    (D) $21.92 (E) $23.15

8. When $88.37 is divided by 29 the result, correct to the nearest cent, is:

(A) $3.05 (B) $3.04 (C) $3.47
(D) $3.46 (E) $3.36

9. When $30.71 is divided by $0.83 the result is:

(A) 3.70 (B) 31 (C) 37 (D) 37.10
(E) none of these

10. When $206.50 is divided by $8.26 the result is:

(A) 2.50 (B) 250 (C) .25 (D) 25 (E) 50

PRACTICE TEST 8

1. The sum of $0.69, $0.47, and $0.05 =

(A) $1.01 (B) $1.10 (C) $1.21
(D) $1.11 (E) $1.20

2. The sum of $46.07, $0.98, and $5.03 =

(A) $51.08 (B) $52.08 (C) $51.98
(D) $52.28 (E) $51.18

3. When $18.08 is subtracted from $30.14 the result is:

(A) $11.06 (B) $12.16 (C) $48.22
(D) $11.16 (E) none of these

4. The difference between $31.25 and $7.98 is:

(A) $23.33 (B) $24.23 (C) $24.27
(D) $23.27 (E) $24.57

5. When $0.36 is multiplied by 35 the result is:

(A) $10.60 (B) $12.60 (C) $2.80
(D) $11.61 (E) $.71

6. When $17.69 is multiplied by 32 the result is:

(A) $566.08 (B) $566.18 (C) $567.08
(D) $565.18 (E) none of these

7. When $153.09 is divided by 9 the result is:

(A) $16.01 (B) $17.21 (C) $10.71
(D) $17.01 (E) $14.01

8. When $101.48 is divided by 37 the result, correct to the nearest cent, is:

(A) $3.72 (B) $2.75 (C) $2.65
(D) $2.74 (E) $2.94

9. When $60.03 is divided by $0.69 the result is:

(A) 0.87 (B) 88 (C) 87 (D) 81 (E) 85

10. When $209.96 is divided by $7.24 the result is:

(A) 0.38 (B) 29. (C) 2.9 (D) 290
(E) 0.31

PRACTICE TEST 9

1. The sum of $0.24, $0.89, and $0.07 is:

(A) $1.10 (B) $13.00 (C) $1.20
(D) $1.11 (E) $1.31

2. The sum of $0.73, $34.05, and $6.89 is:

(A) $40.67 (B) $41.57 (C) $40.57
(D) $40.51 (E) none of these

3. When $10.78 is subtracted from $26.15 the result is:

(A) $15.37 (B) $15.47 (C) $16.37
(D) $16.47 (E) $37.93

4. The difference between $20.62 and $6.57 is:

(A) $13.05 (B) $13.15 (C) $14.05
(D) $13.95 (E) $13.80

5. When $0.48 is multiplied by 75 the result is:

(A) $3.60 (B) $36.00 (C) $36.60
(D) $35.00 (E) $35.60

6. When $19.32 is multiplied by 42 the result is:

(A) $801.44 (B) $810.44 (C) $811.54
(D) $811.44 (E) none of these

7. When $684.32 is divided by 8 the result is:

(A) $86.64 (B) $80.54 (C) $85.54
(D) $86.54 (E) $86.64

8. When $305.37 is divided by 49 the result, correct to the nearest cent, is:

(A) $6.23 (B) $6.24 (C) $6.14
(D) $6.03 (E) none of these

9. When $41.28 is divided by 96 the result is:

(A) 42 (B) $43 (C) $0.43 (D) $42 (E) $47

10. When $111.01 is divided by $6.53 the result is:

(A) 27 (B) 19 (C) 38 (D) 17
(E) none of these

Operations with Fractions, Mixed Numbers, and Decimals

CHANGING FRACTIONS AND MIXED NUMBERS TO DECIMALS

A fraction may be considered as a division of one whole number by another. For example, the fraction $\frac{4}{9}$ indicates that 4 is to be divided by 9. The following examples will indicate the details of this operation.

EXAMPLE: Change $\frac{3}{4}$ to a decimal.

SOLUTION: Divide 3 by 4.

$$4\overline{)3.00} \quad 0.75$$

Thus, $\frac{3}{4} = 0.75$

EXAMPLE: Change $\frac{5}{8}$ to a decimal.

SOLUTION: Divide 5 by 8.

$$8\overline{)5.000} \quad 0.625$$

Thus, $\frac{5}{8} = 0.625$

EXAMPLE: Change $\frac{4}{7}$ to a decimal.

SOLUTION: Divide 4 by 7.

$$7\overline{)4.00} \quad 0.57\tfrac{1}{7}$$

The quotient in this division will be an endlessly repeating decimal. The answer rounded to the nearest hundreth is 0.57.

EXAMPLE: Change $2\frac{5}{6}$ to a decimal, correct to two decimal places.

SOLUTION: Divide 5 by 6.

$$6\overline{)5.00} \quad 0.83\tfrac{2}{6}$$

Thus, $2\frac{5}{6}$

Rounded to the nearest hundredth, $2\frac{5}{6}$ is 2.83.

CHANGING DECIMALS TO FRACTIONS

In changing decimals to fractions it is helpful to remember that a decimal is a fraction whose denominator is 10, 100, 1,000, etc. Thus, to change a decimal to a fraction we write a fraction whose numerator is the given decimal without the decimal point, and whose denominator is 10, 100, 1,000, etc., as indicated by the placement of the decimal point. The fraction thus obtained is then reduced to its lowest terms.

EXAMPLE: Change 0.6 to a fraction.

SOLUTION: $0.6 = \frac{6}{10}$

$\frac{6}{10}$ may be reduced to $\frac{3}{5}$.

EXAMPLE: Change 0.48 to a fraction.

SOLUTION: $0.48 = \frac{48}{100}$

$\frac{48}{100} = \frac{12}{25}$

EXAMPLE: Change 0.015 to a fraction.

SOLUTION: $0.48 = \frac{15}{1,000}$

$\frac{15}{1,000} = \frac{3}{200}$

EXAMPLE: Change $0.663\frac{2}{3}$ to a fraction.

SOLUTION: $0.66\frac{2}{3} = \dfrac{66\frac{2}{3}}{100}$

Consider this as a division of fractions problem.

$$66\tfrac{2}{3} \div 100 = \frac{200}{3} \div \frac{100}{1} = \frac{200}{3} \times \frac{1}{100} = \frac{2}{3}$$

EXAMPLE: Change 3.625 to a mixed number.

SOLUTION: $3.625 = 3\frac{625}{1000} = 3\frac{5}{8}$

The following fractions and their decimal equivalents occur frequently. You are advised to memorize these equivalents.

Fraction	$\frac{1}{2}$	$\frac{1}{3}$	$\frac{2}{3}$	$\frac{1}{4}$	$\frac{3}{4}$	$\frac{1}{5}$
Decimal	0.5	$0.33\frac{1}{3}$	$0.66\frac{2}{3}$	0.25	0.75	0.2

Fraction	$\frac{2}{5}$	$\frac{3}{5}$	$\frac{4}{5}$	$\frac{1}{6}$	$\frac{5}{6}$	$\frac{1}{8}$
Decimal	0.4	0.6	0.8	$0.16\frac{2}{3}$	$0.83\frac{1}{3}$	0.125

Fraction	$\frac{3}{8}$	$\frac{5}{8}$	$\frac{7}{8}$	$\frac{1}{10}$	$\frac{3}{10}$	$\frac{7}{10}$	$\frac{9}{10}$
Decimal	0.375	0.625	0.875	0.1	0.3	0.7	0.9

EXERCISE 51

Express the following fractions or mixed numbers as decimals. Where a remainder occurs, give the decimal correct to two decimal places.

1. $\frac{1}{4}$ 2. $\frac{3}{5}$ 3. $\frac{5}{6}$ 4. $\frac{3}{8}$

5. $\frac{2}{7}$ 6. $\frac{7}{9}$ 7. $2\frac{5}{12}$ 8. $\frac{18}{25}$

9. $\frac{9}{14}$ 10. $\frac{7}{15}$ 11. $\frac{4}{11}$ 12. $3\frac{6}{17}$

Express the following decimals as fractions or mixed numbers.

13. 0.7   14. 0.04   15. 0.45

16. 2.4   17. 0.625   18. 0.245

19. $1.33\frac{1}{3}$ 20. $0.12\frac{1}{2}$ 21. $0.08\frac{1}{3}$

22. 0.008   23. $5.37\frac{1}{2}$ 24. $2.83\frac{1}{3}$

If you got 22 or more correct, go on to the next section on Operations With Fractions and Decimals. If you got more than two wrong, use Exercise 52 to build your skill.

EXERCISE 52

Express the following fractions or mixed numbers as decimals. Where a remainder occurs, give the decimal correct to two decimal places.

1. $\frac{1}{2}$ 2. $\frac{1}{5}$ 3. $\frac{5}{8}$ 4. $\frac{1}{3}$

5. $\frac{1}{6}$ 6. $\frac{3}{7}$ 7. $\frac{2}{9}$ 8. $\frac{7}{10}$

9. $\frac{3}{11}$ 10. $3\frac{1}{8}$ 11. $\frac{9}{20}$ 12. $\frac{4}{15}$

13. $\frac{5}{6}$ 14. $2\frac{1}{12}$ 15. $\frac{3}{4}$ 16. $\frac{3}{14}$

17. $\frac{8}{17}$ 18. $\frac{6}{7}$ 19. $\frac{7}{25}$ 20. $\frac{3}{19}$

Express the following decimals as fractions or mixed numbers.

1. 0.3   2. 0.09   3. 0.11   4. 0.65

5. 3.8   6. 0.275   7. $0.83\frac{1}{3}$ 8. 0.036

9. $2.12\frac{1}{2}$ 10. 0.48   11. $1.33\frac{1}{3}$ 12. 0.375

13. 2.25   14. $2.16\frac{2}{3}$ 15. 3.72   16. 0.625

17. 4.8   18. 2.32   19. $2.66\frac{2}{3}$ 20. 5.85

Now be sure of your skill. Try Exercise 53.

EXERCISE 53

Express the following fractions or mixed numbers as decimals. Where a remainder occurs, give the decimal correct to two decimal places.

1. $\frac{2}{5}$ 2. $\frac{3}{4}$ 3. $\frac{7}{8}$ 4. $\frac{1}{6}$

5. $\frac{5}{9}$ 6. $3\frac{7}{12}$ 7. $\frac{8}{9}$ 8. $\frac{11}{20}$

9. $1\frac{8}{15}$ 10. $\frac{3}{14}$ 11. $2\frac{4}{17}$ 12. $\frac{8}{11}$

Express the following decimals as fractions or mixed numbers.

13. 0.9   14. 0.06   15. 0.85   16. 3.8

17. 0.375   18. 3.485   19. $2.66\frac{2}{3}$ 20. $0.41\frac{2}{3}$

21. 0.018   22. $3.62\frac{1}{2}$ 23. $1.16\frac{2}{3}$ 24. 6.64

OPERATIONS WITH FRACTIONS AND DECIMALS

It is sometimes required to perform operations involving both fractions and decimals. In such cases, we change all quantities either to fractions or to decimals as directed.

EXAMPLE: Add $\frac{1}{4}$ and 0.59. Express the result as a decimal.

SOLUTION:
$$\frac{1}{4} = .25$$
$$0.59 = 0.59$$
$$\frac{1}{4} + 0.59 = 0.84$$

EXAMPLE: From 4.09 subtract $\frac{5}{8}$.

SOLUTION:
$$4.09 = 4.090$$
$$-\frac{5}{8} = 0.625$$
$$4.09 - \frac{5}{8} = 3.465$$

EXAMPLE: Multiply $\frac{4}{9}$ by 0.36. Express the result as a fraction.

SOLUTION: $\frac{4}{9} = \frac{4}{9}$, $0.36 = \frac{36}{100}$

$$\frac{\overset{1}{\cancel{4}}}{\underset{1}{\cancel{9}}} \times \frac{\overset{4}{\cancel{36}}}{\underset{25}{\cancel{100}}} = \frac{4}{25}$$

EXAMPLE: Find $0.83\frac{1}{3}$ of 27.

SOLUTION: Before performing this multiplication it is advisable to change $0.83\frac{1}{3}$ to the fraction $\frac{5}{6}$.

$$\frac{5}{\underset{2}{\cancel{6}}} \times \overset{9}{\cancel{27}} = \frac{45}{2} = 22\frac{1}{2}$$

EXAMPLE: Divide $9.37\frac{1}{2}$ by $\frac{5}{16}$.

SOLUTION: $9.37\frac{1}{2} = 9\frac{3}{8} = \frac{75}{8}$

$$\frac{75}{8} \div \frac{5}{16} = \frac{\overset{15}{\cancel{75}}}{8} \times \frac{\overset{2}{\cancel{16}}}{5} = 30$$

EXAMPLE: Divide $15\frac{3}{4}$ by $4.08\frac{1}{3}$.

SOLUTION: $15\frac{3}{4} = \frac{63}{4}$

$$4.08\frac{1}{3} = 4\frac{1}{12} = \frac{49}{12}$$

$$\frac{63}{4} \div \frac{49}{12} = \frac{\overset{9}{\cancel{63}}}{\underset{1}{\cancel{4}}} \times \frac{\overset{3}{\cancel{12}}}{\underset{7}{\cancel{49}}} = \frac{27}{7} = 3\frac{6}{7}$$

EXERCISE 54

Perform the following operations. Express the results as decimals.

1. Add $\frac{3}{5}$ and 0.46.

2. Add $\frac{7}{8}$ and 0.09.

3. From 3.27 subtract $\frac{3}{4}$.

4. From $8\frac{7}{100}$ subtract 2.59.

5. Multiply $\frac{7}{20}$ by 6.2.

6. Divide $8\frac{1}{5}$ by 2.05.

7. Find $0.16\frac{2}{3}$ of 45.

8. Divide 90 by $2.08\frac{1}{3}$.

Perform the following operations. Express the results as decimals.

9. Add $\frac{5}{12}$ and 0.15.

10. Add $0.83\frac{1}{3}$ and $\frac{4}{9}$.

11. From 6.4 subtract $\frac{1}{2}$.

12. From $5\frac{1}{3}$ subtract $2.16\frac{2}{3}$.

13. Multiply $\frac{8}{15}$ by 0.15.

14. Find $0.37\frac{1}{2}$ of 76.

15. Divide 8 by 0.24.

16. Divide $37\frac{1}{2}$ by $1.12\frac{1}{2}$.

If you got 15 or 16 correct, go on to the following Practice Tests. If you got more than two wrong, use Exercise 55 to build your skill.

EXERCISE 55

Perform the following operations. Express the results as decimals.

1. Add $\frac{1}{2}$ and 0.79.

2. Add $\frac{3}{8}$ and 2.16.

3. Add 5.03 and $\frac{1}{4}$.

4. Add 2.57 and $\frac{3}{5}$.

5. From 6.81 subtract $\frac{1}{8}$.

6. From 3.2 subtract $\frac{9}{20}$.

7. From $7\frac{3}{5}$ subtract 1.09.

8. From $6\frac{3}{8}$ subtract 2.14.

9. Multiply 48 by $0.08\frac{1}{3}$.

10. Multiply 72 by $0.66\frac{2}{3}$.

11. Find $0.33\frac{1}{3}$ of 42.3.

12. Find $0.62\frac{1}{2}$ of 44.

13. Divide 76 by 3.04.

14. Divide 156 by 2.08.

15. Divide 47.5 by $3.16\frac{2}{3}$.

16. Divide 57 by $2.37\frac{1}{2}$.

Perform the following operations. Express the results as fractions.

1. Add $\frac{5}{9}$ and $0.83\frac{1}{3}$.

2. Add $0.62\frac{1}{2}$ and $\frac{7}{12}$.

3. Add $0.33\frac{1}{3}$ and $\frac{2}{5}$.

4. Add $0.58\frac{1}{3}$ and $\frac{11}{15}$.

5. From 9.5 subtract $\frac{3}{4}$.

6. From 4.7 subtract $\frac{2}{5}$.

7. From $9\frac{1}{8}$ subtract $3.37\frac{1}{2}$.

8. From $7\frac{1}{6}$ subtract $4.66\frac{2}{3}$.

9. Multiply $\frac{4}{5}$ by 0.35.

10. Multiply $\frac{6}{7}$ by $0.33\frac{1}{3}$.

11. Multiply $0.16\frac{2}{3}$ by 64.

12. Find 0.45 of 75.

13. Divide 16 by 0.48.

14. Divide 18 by 0.36.

15. Divide 80 by $4.16\frac{2}{3}$.

16. Divide 30 by 1.2.

Now be sure of your skill. Try Exercise 56.

EXERCISE 56

Perform the following operations. Express the results as decimals.

1. Add $\frac{1}{4}$ and 0.38.

2. Add $\frac{3}{8}$ and 0.07.

3. From 6.58 subtract $\frac{3}{5}$.

4. From $7\frac{3}{10}$ subtract 3.46.

5. Multiply $\frac{8}{15}$ by 3.6.

6. Divide $26\frac{4}{5}$ by 3.35.

7. Find $0.83\frac{1}{3}$ of 57.

8. Divide 105 by $0.87\frac{1}{2}$.

Perform the following operations. Express the results as decimals.

9. Add $\frac{3}{4}$ and 0.56.

10. Add $0.37\frac{1}{2}$ and $\frac{7}{12}$.

11. From 7.5 subtract $\frac{1}{6}$.

12. From 7.8 subtract $3.62\frac{1}{2}$.

13. Multiply $\frac{9}{14}$ by 0.35.

14. Find $0.83\frac{1}{3}$ of 40.

15. Divide 36 by 0.15.

16. Divide $24\frac{1}{2}$ by $4.08\frac{1}{3}$.

PRACTICE TEST 10

1. 3.876, correct to the nearest tenth =

   (A) 3.8 (B) 3.88 (C) 3.9 (D) 3.90
   (E) 3.95

2. 2.053, correct to the nearest hundredth =

   (A) 2.15 (B) 2.06 (C) 2.13 (D) 2.03
   (E) none of these

3. Of the following sets of decimals, the set that is ordered, with the largest decimal first, is:

   (A) 0.583, 0.538, 0.835
   (B) 0.538, 0.853, 0.583
   (C) 0.835, 0.583, 0.538
   (D) 0.835, 0.538, 0.583
   (E) 0.538, 0.583, 0.835

4. The sum of 0.32, 0.09, and 0.76 =

   (A) 1.07 (B) 1.27 (C) 1.98 (D) 1.17
   (E) none of these

5. The sum of 8.032, 7.165, and 3.897 =

   (A) 18.994 (B) 19.094 (C) 19.084
   (D) 19.184 (E) 18.184

6. The difference between 8.03 and 5.19 =

   (A) 2.94 (B) 3.84 (C) 3.16 (D) 2.84
   (E) 3.22

7. When 14.803 is subtracted from 207.312 the result is:

   (A) 192.509   (B) 192.519 (C) 193.509
   (D) 182.519 (E) 193.519

8. The product of 0.03 and 8 is:

   (A) 0.024 (B) 24 (C) 2.4 (D) 0.24
   (E) none of these

9. When 60 is multiplied by 0.65 the result is:

   (A) 3.9 (B) 36 (C) 30.9 (D) 30.09
   (E) 39

10. The product of 72 and 0.035 is:

   (A) 5.76 (B) 57.6 (C) 2.52 (D) 25.2
   (E) 2.54

11. When 40.16 is divided by 8 the quotient is:

   (A) 5.2 (B) 5.02 (C) 40.02 (D) 50.2
   (E) 5.22

12. When 0.901 is divided by 0.017 the result is:

   (A) 0.53 (B) .053 (C) 530 (D) 53
   (E) 52.8

13. When 6.852 is divided by 2.7 the quotient, correct to the nearest tenth, is:

    (A) 25.4 (B) 2.5 (C) 2.6 (D) 26.3
    (E) 2.63

14. When 3.75 is multiplied by 1,000 the result is:

    (A) 375,000 (B) 375 (C) 37,500
    (D) 3,750 (E) 37.5

15. When 6.85 is divided by 100 the result is:

    (A) 685 (B) 68.5 (C) 0.0685 (D) 0.685
    (E) 6.85

PRACTICE TEST 11

1. 54.832, correct to the nearest tenth =

    (A) 54.9 (B) 54.83 (C) 54.82 (D) 54.8
    (E) 54.85

2. 6.185, correct to the nearest hundredth =

    (A) 6.18 (B) 6.2 (C) 6.19 (D) 6.16 (E) 6.25

3. Of the following sets of decimals, the one in correct order of their size, with the largest first, is:

    (A) 0.728, 0.827, 0.782
    (B) 0.827, 0.782, 0.728
    (C) 0.827, 0.728, 0.782
    (D) 0.782, 0.827, 0.728
    (E) 0.728, 0.782, 0.827

4. The sum of 0.48, 0.07, and 0.64 =

    (A) 1.09 (B) 2.09 (C) 1.19 (D) 1.21
    (E) none of these

5. The sum of 6.138, 2.009, and 3.715 =

    (A) 11.962 (B) 11.952 (C) 12.862
    (D) 12.962 (E) 11.862

6. The difference between 7.12 and 4.09 =

    (A) 2.03 (B) 3.03 (C) 3.13 (D) 3.3 (E) 2.3

7. When 17.069 is subtracted from 109.347 the result is:

    (A) 102.278 (B) 92.288 (C) 82.278
    (D) 92.278 (E) 91.278

8. The product of 0.07 and 9 is:

    (A) 6.3 (B) 0.063 (C) 0.16 (D) 63
    (E) none of these

9. When 85 is multiplied by 0.24 the result is:

    (A) 204 (B) 240 (C) 20.4 (D) 2400
    (E) 230

10. The product of 120 and 0.065 is:

    (A) 78 (B) 7.8 (C) 7.08 (D) 780
    (E) 78.08

11. When 35.91 is divided by 7 the result is:

    (A) 5.03 (B) 5.11 (C) 5.31 (D) 5.13
    (E) none of these

12. When 0.32048 is divided by 0.0016 the quotient is:

    (A) 20.3 (B) 2.30 (C) 200.3 (D) 230
    (E) 2,300

13. When 10.237 is divided by 3.9 the quotient, correct to the nearest tenth, is:

    (A) 2.4 (B) 2.6 (C) 2.7 (D) 0.27
    (E) 260

14. When 4.869 is multiplied by 100 the result is:

    (A) 4,869 (B) 48.69 (C) 48,690
    (D) 0.4869 (E) 486.9

15. When 73.2 is divided by 1,000 the result is:

    (A) 0.732 (B) 0.0732 (C) 73.2
    (D) 7.32 (E) 730.2

PRACTICE TEST 12

1. 68.708, correct to the nearest tenth =

    (A) 68.8 (B) 68.71 (C) 68.7 (D) 68.88
    (E) 68.08

2. 3.537, correct to the nearest hundredth =

    (A) 3.54 (B) 3.57 (C) 3.58 (D) 3.53
    (E) 3.56

3. Of the following sets of decimals, the set that is ordered, with the largest decimal first, is:

    (A) 0.697, 0.967, 0.769
    (B) 0.967, 0.697, 0.769
    (C) 0.967, 0.769, 0.697
    (D) 0.769, 0.967, 0.697
    (E) 0.697, 0.769, 0.967

4. The sum of 0.87, 0.39, and 0.06 is:

   (A) 1.12 (B) 1.32 (C) 1.02 (D) 2.12
   (E) 0.92

5. The sum of 6.043, 3.918, and 5.307 is:

   (A) 15.258 (B) 14.268 (C) 15.368
   (D) 14.368 (E) none of these

6. The difference between 7.15 and 3.06 is:

   (A) 4.19 (B) 3.09 (C) 3.19 (D) 4.09
   (E) 10.21

7. When 89.17 is subtracted from 340.02 the result is:

   (A) 250.85 (B) 260.85 (C) 250.95
   (D) 260.95 (E) 260.75

8. The product of 0.004 and 9 is:

   (A) 0.36 (B) 3.6 (C) 0.036 (D) 36
   (E) 0.013

9. When 0.92 is multiplied by 85 the result is:

   (A) 77.2 (B) 78.02 (C) 78.12 (D) 78.2
   (E) none of these

10. The product of 650 and 0.042 is:

    (A) 273 (B) 2,730 (C) 27.3 (D) 2.73
    (E) 27,300

11. When 63.09 is divided by 9 the quotient is:

    (A) 7.1 (B) 7.01 (C) 70.01 (D) 70.1
    (E) 7.001

12. When 1.022 is divided by 0.014 the quotient is:

    (A) 0.73 (B) 703 (C) 7.3 (D) 730
    (E) none of these

13. When 69.42 is divided by 4.7 the quotient, correct to the nearest tenth, is:

    (A) 13.8 (B) 14.7 (C) 14.8 (D) 14.0
    (E) 15

14. When 2.64 is multiplied by 1,000 the result is:

    (A) 26.4 (B) 2,640 (C) 264 (D) 26,400
    (E) 2.64

15. When 3.75 is divided by 100 the result is:

    (A) 375 (B) 3,750 (C) 0.375
    (D) 0.0375 (E) 37.5

Percentage

MEANING OF PERCENT

The word *percent* means "hundreths." To change a percent to a decimal, move the decimal point two places to the left and omit the percent sign.

EXAMPLES:
    17% = 0.17   28.3% = 0.283
    6% = 0.06   250% = 2.5

To change a decimal to a percent, just reverse the procedure.

EXAMPLES:
    0.69 = 69%
    0.8333 = 83.33%
    1.53 = 153%

CHANGING DECIMALS TO PERCENTS AND PERCENTS TO DECIMALS

EXAMPLES:
Express the following as percents. **ANSWERS**

1. 18 hundredths	18%
2. 7 hundredths	7%
3. 134 hundredths	134%
4. $\frac{1}{2}$ hundredth	$\frac{1}{2}$%
5. $6\frac{1}{4}$ hundredths	$6\frac{1}{4}$%
6. 0.09	9%
7. 0.63	63%
8. $0.12\frac{1}{2}$	$12\frac{1}{2}$%

9. 3.16 $\frac{2}{3}$ 316 $\frac{2}{3}$%

10. 0.625   62 $\frac{1}{2}$%

                                        or 62.5%

EXAMPLES:

Express the following as decimals.   **ANSWERS**

1. 19%   0.19

2. 6 $\frac{1}{2}$%   0.06 $\frac{1}{2}$ or

                                        0.065

3. 375%   3.75

4. $\frac{1}{2}$%   0.00 $\frac{1}{2}$ or

                                        0.005

5. 150%   1.5

EXERCISE 57

Express the following percents as decimals.

1. 73%	2. 4%	3. 80%
4. 127%	5. 7 $\frac{1}{2}$%	6. 3 $\frac{1}{4}$%
7. 2 $\frac{3}{4}$%	8. 112 $\frac{1}{2}$%	9. 4.3%
10. 0.25%	11. $\frac{1}{2}$%	12. 5.07%

Express the following decimals as percents.

13. 0.48	14. 0.08	15. 0.3
16. 2.07	17. 0.13 $\frac{1}{2}$	18. 3.83 $\frac{1}{3}$
19. 0.025	20. 0.009	21. 6.5
22. 4.08 $\frac{1}{3}$	23. 1.875	24. 0.004

If you got 22 or more correct, go on to the next section on Changing Percents to Fractions. If you got more than three wrong, use Exercise 58 to build your skill.

EXERCISE 58

Express the following percents as decimals.

1. 68%	2. 47%	3. 30%
4. 90%	5. 132%	6. 165%
7. 8 $\frac{1}{2}$%	8. 4 $\frac{1}{2}$%	9. 1 $\frac{1}{4}$%
10. 5 $\frac{1}{4}$%	11. 8 $\frac{3}{4}$%	12. 6 $\frac{3}{4}$%
13. 6.2%	14. 124 $\frac{1}{2}$%	15. 7.8%
16. 144 $\frac{1}{2}$%	17. 0.75%	18. $\frac{1}{5}$%
19. 0.35%	20. 6.4%	21. 7.08%
22. $\frac{1}{4}$%	23. 3.18%	24. 0.3%

Express the following decimals as percents.

25. 0.62	26. 0.38	27. 0.02
28. 0.7	29. 5.09	30. 0.27
31. 3.05	32. 0.08 $\frac{1}{2}$	33. 6.09

34. 0.24 $\frac{1}{2}$	35. 2.37 $\frac{1}{2}$	36. 0.067
37. 7.83 $\frac{1}{3}$	38. 0.089	39. 0.002
40. 7.4	41. 3.04 $\frac{1}{2}$	42. 0.007
43. 3.9	44. 1.125	45. 0.005
46. 8.06 $\frac{2}{3}$	47. 7.8	48. 3.175

Now be sure of your skill. Try Exercise 59.

EXERCISE 59

Express the following percents as decimals.

1. 57%	2. 8%	3. 60%
4. 149%	5. 2 $\frac{1}{2}$%	6. 1 $\frac{1}{4}$%
7. 5 $\frac{3}{4}$%	8. 128 $\frac{1}{2}$%	9. 6.2%
10. 0.5%	11. $\frac{1}{8}$%	12. 3.08%

Express the following decimals as percents.

13. 0.62	14. 0.03	15. 0.8
16. 5.02	17. 0.18 $\frac{1}{2}$	18. 2.17 $\frac{1}{3}$
19. 0.067	20. 0.002	21. 8.2
22. 3.02 $\frac{1}{3}$	23. 2.625	24. 0.009

CHANGING PERCENTS TO FRACTIONS

In changing a percent to a fraction we recall that a percent can be written as a fraction whose denominator is 100. For example, 73% is equal to the fraction $\frac{73}{100}$, and 24% is equal to the fraction $\frac{24}{100}$. The fraction $\frac{24}{100}$ may be reduced to the fraction $\frac{6}{25}$.

Since certain percents appear very frequently, it is best to memorize their fractional equivalents. The following chart contains the most frequently used percents and their equivalents.

$\frac{1}{2}$ = 50%	$\frac{1}{6}$ = 16 $\frac{2}{3}$%	$\frac{1}{10}$ = 10%
$\frac{1}{3}$ = 33 $\frac{1}{3}$%	$\frac{5}{6}$ = 83 $\frac{1}{3}$%	$\frac{3}{10}$ = 30%
$\frac{2}{3}$ = 66 $\frac{2}{3}$%	$\frac{1}{7}$ = 14 $\frac{2}{7}$%	$\frac{7}{10}$ = 70%
$\frac{1}{4}$ = 25%	$\frac{1}{8}$ = 12 $\frac{1}{2}$%	$\frac{9}{10}$ = 90%
$\frac{3}{4}$ = 75%	$\frac{3}{8}$ = 37 $\frac{1}{2}$%	$\frac{1}{12}$ = 8 $\frac{1}{3}$%
$\frac{1}{5}$ = 20%	$\frac{5}{8}$ = 62 $\frac{1}{2}$%	$\frac{1}{16}$ = 6 $\frac{1}{4}$%
$\frac{2}{5}$ = 40%	$\frac{7}{8}$ = 87 $\frac{1}{2}$%	$\frac{1}{20}$ = 5%
$\frac{3}{5}$ = 60%		$\frac{1}{25}$ = 4%
$\frac{4}{5}$ = 80%		$\frac{1}{50}$ = 2%
		$\frac{1}{100}$ = 1%

EXAMPLE: Express 84% as a fraction.

SOLUTION: $84\% = \frac{84}{100}$

$\frac{84}{100}$ may be reduced to $\frac{21}{25}$.

Thus, $84\% = \frac{21}{25}$

EXAMPLE: Express $37\frac{1}{2}\%$ as a fraction.

SOLUTION: We may recall that $37\frac{1}{2}\% = \frac{3}{8}$; or

$$37\frac{1}{2}\% = \frac{37\frac{1}{2}}{100}$$

Do this operation as a division of fractions problem.

$$\frac{37\frac{1}{2}}{100} = 37\frac{1}{2} \div 100 = \frac{75}{2} \div \frac{100}{1} = \frac{75}{2} \times \frac{1}{100} = \frac{\overset{3}{\cancel{75}}}{2} \times \frac{1}{\underset{4}{\cancel{100}}} = \frac{3}{8}$$

EXAMPLE: Express 125% as a mixed number.

SOLUTION: $125\% = \frac{125}{100}$

$\frac{125}{100}$ may be reduced to $\frac{5}{4}$.

Written as a mixed number,

$$\frac{5}{4} = 1\frac{1}{4}$$

CHANGING FRACTIONS TO PERCENTS

To change a fraction to a percent, divide the numerator of the fraction by its denominator, finding the quotient correct to two decimal places. Then write the resulting decimal as a percent.

EXAMPLE: Express $\frac{9}{25}$ as a percent.

SOLUTION: Divide 9 by 25.

$$
\begin{array}{r}
0.36 \\
25\overline{)9.00} \\
7\,5 \\
\overline{1\,50} \\
1\,50 \\
\end{array}
$$

$$\frac{9}{25} = 0.36 = 36\%$$

EXAMPLE: Write $\frac{7}{8}$ as a percent.

SOLUTION: Recall that $\frac{7}{8}$ is equal to $0.87\frac{1}{2}\%$.

$$0.87\frac{1}{2}\% = 87\frac{1}{2}\%$$

Or we may change $\frac{7}{8}$ to $.87\frac{1}{2}$ by dividing 8 into 7.

EXAMPLE: Change $\frac{5}{9}$ to a percent.

SOLUTION:

$$
\begin{array}{r}
0.55\frac{5}{9} \\
9\overline{)5.00}
\end{array}
$$

$$0.55\frac{5}{9} = 55\frac{5}{9}\%$$

EXAMPLE: Change $2\frac{7}{16}$ to a percent.

SOLUTION: Write the mixed number $2\frac{7}{16}$ as the improper fraction $\frac{39}{16}$.

Now divide 39 by 16:

$$
\begin{array}{r}
2.43 \\
16\overline{)39.00} \\
32 \\
\overline{70} \\
64 \\
\overline{60} \\
48 \\
\overline{12}
\end{array}
$$

$$2\frac{7}{16} = 2.43\frac{12}{16} = 2.43\frac{3}{4} = 243\frac{3}{4}\%$$

or 244% to the nearest whole-number percent.

EXAMPLE: Change 3 to a percent.

SOLUTION: $3 = 3.00$

$3.00 = 300\%$

EXERCISE 60

Change the following percents to fractions.

1. 72%   2. $62\frac{1}{2}\%$ 3. 40%

4. 55%   5. 120%   6. 8%

7. $137\frac{1}{2}\%$ 8. $208\frac{1}{3}\%$

Change the following fractions and mixed numbers to percents.

9. $\frac{3}{4}$ 10. $\frac{5}{7}$ 11. $\frac{11}{20}$

12. $\frac{5}{8}$ 13. $1\frac{2}{3}$ 14. $\frac{4}{9}$

15. $2\frac{4}{5}$ 16. $3\frac{1}{6}$

If you got 15 or 16 correct, go on to the next section on Finding a Percent of a Number. If you got more than one wrong, use Exercise 61 to build your skill.

EXERCISE 61

Change the following percents to fractions or mixed numbers.

1. 56%   2. $83\frac{1}{3}\%$ 3. 35%

4. $33\frac{1}{3}\%$ 5. 70%   6. 48%

7. 140%   8. 6%   9. $287\frac{1}{2}\%$

10. $41\frac{2}{3}\%$ 11. $2\frac{1}{2}\%$ 12. 67%

13. 12%   14. 125%   15. $16\frac{2}{3}\%$

16. 220%

Change the following fractions and mixed numbers to percents.

17. $\frac{8}{25}$ 18. $\frac{1}{4}$ 19. $\frac{17}{20}$

20. $\frac{3}{8}$ 21. $\frac{5}{6}$ 22. $\frac{2}{7}$

23. $1\frac{1}{3}$ 24. $\frac{4}{15}$ 25. $1\frac{2}{5}$

26. $\frac{7}{9}$ 27. $3\frac{7}{12}$ 28. $2\frac{4}{11}$

29. $1\frac{3}{5}$ 30. $\frac{2}{3}$ 31. $1\frac{1}{8}$

32. $2\frac{7}{10}$

Now be sure of your skill. Try Exercise 62.

EXERCISE 62

Change the following percents to fractions or mixed numbers.

1. 48%   2. $83\frac{1}{3}\%$ 3. 60%

4. 85%   5. 140%   6. 6%

7. $187\frac{1}{2}\%$ 8. $216\frac{2}{3}\%$

Change the following fractions and mixed numbers to percents.

9. $\frac{4}{5}$ 10. $\frac{8}{9}$ 11. $\frac{3}{8}$

12. $\frac{7}{20}$ 13. $\frac{2}{7}$ 14. $1\frac{1}{3}$

15. $3\frac{3}{5}$ 16. $2\frac{1}{12}$

FINDING A PERCENT OF A NUMBER

To find a percent of a number, change the percent to a fraction or decimal, whichever is more convenient. Then multiply the given number by the fraction or decimal.

EXAMPLE: Find 37% of 84.

SOLUTION: 37%, written as a decimal, is 0.37.

$$\begin{array}{r} 84 \\ \underline{0.37} \\ 5\ 88 \\ \underline{25\ 2\ } \\ 31.08 \end{array}$$

EXAMPLE: Find $62\frac{1}{2}\%$ of 28.

SOLUTION: $62\frac{1}{2}\%$, written as a fraction, is $\frac{5}{8}$.

$$\frac{5}{\underset{2}{8}} \times \frac{\overset{7}{28}}{1} = \frac{35}{2} = 17\frac{1}{2}$$

EXAMPLE: Find $4\frac{1}{2}\%$ of 68.

SOLUTION: $4\frac{1}{2}\%$, written as a decimal, is 0.045.

$$\begin{array}{r} 68 \\ \underline{0.045} \\ 340 \\ \underline{272\ } \\ 3.060 = 3.06 \end{array}$$

EXAMPLE: Find 3.4% of $48.12 to the nearest cent.

SOLUTION: 3.4%, written as a decimal, is 0.034.

$$\begin{array}{r} \$48.12 \\ \underline{0.034} \\ 19248 \\ \underline{14436\ } \\ 1.63608 = \$1.64 \end{array}$$

EXAMPLE: Find $116\frac{2}{3}\%$ of 4.5.

SOLUTION: $116\frac{2}{3}\%$, written as a mixed number, is $1\frac{1}{6}$.

$$1\frac{1}{6} = \frac{7}{6}$$

$$\frac{7}{\underset{2}{6}} \times \frac{\overset{1.5}{4.5}}{1} = \frac{10.5}{2} = 5.25$$

EXERCISE 63

Find the following.

1. 23% of 56   2. 8% of 72

3. 63% of 12.5   4. $3\frac{1}{2}\%$ of 24

5. 118% of 48   6. $37\frac{1}{2}\%$ of 90

7. 2.8% of 140   8. $133\frac{1}{3}\%$ of 153

9. $\frac{3}{4}\%$ of 96   10. 79% of 18.4

11. 200% of 82   12. $4\frac{1}{2}\%$ of $65.38 to the nearest cent

If you got 11 or 12 correct, go on to the next section on Finding What Percent One Number is of Another. If you got more than one wrong, use Exercise 64 to build your skill.

EXERCISE 64

Find the following.

1. 68% of 72
2. 43% of 115
3. 19% of 38.5
4. 27% of 46.8
5. 9% of 137
6. 76% of 114.2
7. 7% of 16.2
8. $5\frac{1}{2}$% of 78
9. $2\frac{1}{2}$% of 48.6
10. 127% of 66
11. 152% of 72
12. $33\frac{1}{3}$% of 112.2
13. $8\frac{1}{3}$% of 64
14. $\frac{3}{4}$% of 170
15. 12.8% of 95
16. $183\frac{1}{3}$% of 108
17. 175% of 84
18. $\frac{1}{2}$% of 628
19. 300% of 29
20. $\frac{1}{5}$% of 58
21. 76% of 14.2
22. $187\frac{1}{2}$% of 240
23. $4\frac{1}{4}$% of 80
24. 35% of 1.28
25. 5% of $37.23 to the nearest cent
26. 9% of $65.48 to the nearest cent
27. $3\frac{1}{2}$% of $87.64 to the nearest cent
28. $2\frac{1}{4}$% of $35.60 to the nearest cent

Now be sure of your skill. Try Exercise 65.

EXERCISE 65

Find the following.

1. 29% of 72
2. 6% of 48
3. 59% of 14.5
4. $4\frac{1}{2}$% of 38
5. 123% of 64
6. $62\frac{1}{2}$% of 76
7. $\frac{3}{4}$% of 160
8. $166\frac{2}{3}$% of 171
9. $\frac{1}{4}$% of 52
10. 83% of 26.4
11. 500% of 43
12. $3\frac{1}{2}$% of $32.74 to the nearest cent

FINDING WHAT PERCENT ONE NUMBER IS OF ANOTHER

To find what percent one number is of another, follow these steps:

1. Make a fraction with the first number as the numerator and the second number as the denominator.

2. Change this fraction to a decimal by dividing the numerator of the fraction by its denominator.

3. Write this decimal as a percent.

EXAMPLE: 48 is what percent of 60?

SOLUTION: $\frac{48}{60} = \frac{4}{5}$

$\frac{4}{5} = 80\%$

EXAMPLE: 17 is what percent of 39?

SOLUTION: $\frac{17}{39}$

$$
\begin{array}{r}
0.43 \\
39\overline{)17.00} \\
15\;6 \\
\hline
1\;40 \\
1\;17 \\
\hline
23
\end{array}
$$

$0.43\frac{23}{39} = 43\frac{23}{39}\%$

EXAMPLE: What percent of 74 is 90?

SOLUTION: $\frac{90}{74} = \frac{45}{37}$

$$
\begin{array}{r}
1.21 \\
37\overline{)45.00} \\
37 \\
\hline
80 \\
74 \\
\hline
60 \\
37 \\
\hline
23
\end{array}
$$

$1.21\frac{23}{37} = 121\frac{23}{37}\%$

FINDING A NUMBER WHEN A PERCENT OF IT IS GIVEN

In this case, we are given part of a number and are required to find the number. The part given may be expressed as a fraction, a decimal, or a percent.

EXAMPLE: One month a man found that he had saved 20% of his income. If he saved $414, what was his monthly income?

SOLUTION: 20% of income = $414

Since 20% = $\frac{1}{5}$, $\frac{1}{5}$ of income = $414

Therefore, total income or

$\frac{5}{5} = 5 \times 414 = \$2,070$

EXAMPLE: At a high school dance, $66\frac{2}{3}\%$ of the students attended. If 156 students attended, how many students were enrolled in the school?

SOLUTION: $66\frac{2}{3}\%$ of the students = 156

Since $66\frac{2}{3}\% = \frac{2}{3}$, $\frac{2}{3}$ of the students = 156

Therefore, $\frac{1}{3}$ of the students = 78

Total number or $\frac{3}{3} = 3 \times 78 = 234$ students.

Note that the same result could have been obtained by dividing 156 by $\frac{2}{3}$.

$$156 \div \frac{2}{3} = 156 \times \frac{3}{2} = 234 \text{ students}$$

EXAMPLE: Mr. Hunter bought a suit in a sale for $63. This was $87\frac{1}{2}\%$ of the original price. What was the original price?

SOLUTION: $87\frac{1}{2}\%$ of the original price = $63

Since $87\frac{1}{2}\% = \frac{7}{8}$, $\frac{7}{8}$ of the original price = $63

Therefore, $\frac{1}{8}$ of the original price = $9

Total number or $\frac{8}{8} = 8 \times \$9 = \$72$

Note that the same result could have been obtained by dividing $63 by $\frac{7}{8}$.

$$\$63 \div \frac{7}{8} = \$63 \times \frac{8}{7} = \$72$$

In general, we may find a number when a percent of it is given by (*a*) changing the percent to a fraction or (*b*) dividing the given number by the fraction.

EXAMPLE: 24% of what number is 30?

SOLUTION: $24\% = \frac{24}{100} = \frac{6}{25}$

$$30 \div \frac{6}{25} = \frac{\overset{5}{\cancel{30}}}{1} \times \frac{25}{6} = 125$$

EXAMPLE: 21 is $83\frac{1}{3}\%$ of what number?

SOLUTION: $83\frac{1}{3}\% = \frac{5}{6}$

$$21 \div \frac{5}{6} = \frac{21}{1} \times \frac{6}{5} = \frac{126}{5} = 25\frac{1}{5}$$

EXERCISE 66

1. 18 is what percent of 24?
2. 28 is what percent of 40?
3. What percent of 32 is 22?
4. What percent of 44 is 36?
5. 54 is what percent of 40?
6. What percent of 53 is 79?
7. 18% of what number is 63?
8. 22.4 is 35% of what number?

9. $62\frac{1}{2}\%$ of what number is 35?
10. $133\frac{1}{3}\%$ of what number is 74?

If you got 18 or more correct, go on the following Practice Tests. If you got more than two wrong, use Exercise 67 to build your skill.

EXERCISE 67

1. 15 is what percent of 75?
2. 17 is what percent of 68?
3. What percent of 98 is 56?
4. What percent of 135 is 81?
5. 19 is what percent of 67?
6. 32 is what percent of 92?
7. 96 is what percent of 78?
8. 65 is what percent of 80?
9. What percent of 96 is 60?
10. 49 is what percent of 40?
11. 69 is what percent of 75?
12. What percent of 42 is 77?
13. 16% of what number is 17?
14. 45% of what number is 17.1?
15. $16\frac{2}{3}\%$ of what number is 17?
16. 98.7 is 47% of what number?
17. 95 is 125% of what number?
18. 64 is $66\frac{2}{3}\%$ of what number?
19. 51 is 68% of what number?
20. 45 is $112\frac{1}{2}\%$ of what number?

Now be sure of your skill. Try Exercise 68.

EXERCISE 68

1. 16 is what percent of 20?
2. 48 is what percent of 80?
3. What percent of 34 is 17?
4. What percent of 56 is 38?
5. 78 is what percent of 60?
6. What percent of 47 is 61?
7. 24% of what number is 84?
8. 37.8 is 45% of what number?
9. $37\frac{1}{2}\%$ of what number is 45?
10. $183\frac{1}{3}\%$ of what number is 132?

PRACTICE TEST 13

1. Find 35% of 250.

2. Write $\frac{3}{8}$ as a percent.

3. 16 is 40% of what number?

4. Write $12\frac{1}{2}\%$ as a fraction reduced to lowest terms.

5. What percent of 24 is 18?

6. Write 5% as a fraction reduced to lowest terms.

7. Find $83\frac{1}{3}\%$ of 384.

8. Write 0.2 as a percent.

9. 63 is $37\frac{1}{2}\%$ of what number?

10. Write 48% as a decimal fraction.

11. Write $\frac{7}{20}$ as a percent.

12. Write 3.4 as a percent.

13. What percent of 72 is 27?

14. What is $\frac{1}{2}\%$ of 40?

15. 60 is what percent of 48?

16. Write 16% as a fraction reduced to lowest terms.

17. Find 120% of 8.

18. Write $\frac{5}{12}$ as a percent.

19. What percent of 48 is 32?

20. Write $87\frac{1}{2}\%$ as a decimal fraction.

21. What percent of 72 is 12?

22. Write 0.245 as a percent.

23. Write $62\frac{1}{2}\%$ as a fraction reduced to lowest terms.

24. 18% of what number is 54?

25. Write 125% as a decimal fraction.

26. Find 6% of 350.

27. What is 4.2% of 85?

28. $2\frac{1}{2}\%$ of what number is 75?

29. Write $\frac{7}{9}$ as a percent.

30. 22.5 is what percent of 15?

31. $16\frac{2}{3}\%$ of what number is 3.2?

32. Find $\frac{3}{5}\%$ of 2,000.

33. 24 is what percent of 30?

34. Find $134\frac{1}{2}\%$ of 80.

35. Write 0.402 as a percent.

36. 28% of what number is 1.4?

37. Write $\frac{7}{200}$ as a percent.

38. Write $15\frac{1}{2}\%$ as a fraction reduced to lowest terms.

39. 42% of what number is 21?

40. Write 1.052 as a percent.

41. Find $112\frac{1}{2}\%$ of 48.

42. Write $\frac{8}{5}$ as a percent.

43. 16 is what percent of 2.5?

44. Write $\frac{17}{32}$ as a percent.

45. Find $42\frac{1}{2}\%$ of 200.

46. 96 is what percent of 72?

47. Write $137\frac{1}{2}\%$ as a fraction reduced to lowest terms.

48. Find 0.3% of 450.

49. $4\frac{1}{2}\%$ of what number is 2.7?

50. Write 0.0035 as a percent.

PRACTICE TEST 14

1. 68%, expressed as a decimal =

   (A) 68 (B) 0.068 (C) 6.8 (D) 0.68 (E) 680

2. $7\frac{1}{2}\%$, expressed as a decimal =

   (A) 750 (B) 0.075 (C) 0.75 (D) $7\frac{1}{2}$ (E) 7.5

3. 125%, expressed as a decimal =

   (A) 1.25 (B) 125 (C) 0.125 (D) 12.5 (E) none of these

4. 0.92, expressed as a percent =

   (A) 0.92% (B) 0.092% (C) 92% (D) 9.2% (E) 920%

5. $0.06\frac{2}{3}$, expressed as a percent =

   (A) $66\frac{2}{3}\%$ (B) 67% (C) $6\frac{2}{3}\%$ (D) $0.06\frac{2}{3}\%$ (E) $.6\frac{2}{3}\%$

6. 0.35%, expressed as a fraction =

   (A) $3\frac{1}{2}$ (B) $\frac{7}{2000}$ (C) $\frac{5}{14}$ (D) $\frac{2}{7}$ (E) none of these

7. $83\frac{1}{3}\%$, expressed as a fraction =

   (A) $\frac{7}{8}$ (B) $\frac{4}{5}$ (C) $\frac{8}{9}$ (D) $\frac{5}{6}$ (E) $\frac{5}{8}$

8. $\frac{3}{5}$, expressed as a percent =

   (A) 30% (B) 75% (C) 6% (D) $\frac{3}{5}\%$ (E) none of these

9. $1\frac{5}{8}$, expressed as a percent =

   (A) $162\frac{1}{2}\%$ (B) $1\frac{5}{8}\%$ (C) $183\frac{1}{3}\%$ (D) 175% (E) $137\frac{1}{2}\%$

10. 12% of 95 =

(A) 114   (B) 10.4   (C) 11.04   (D) 10.14
(E) 11.4

11. $3\frac{1}{2}$% of 218 =

(A) 763   (B) 7.63   (C) 7.53   (D) 8.63
(E) 7.625

12. $116\frac{2}{3}$% of 84 =

(A) 91   (B) 112   (C) 72   (D) 98   (E) 102

13. 48 is what percent of 60?

(A) 125%   (B) 48%   (C) 60%   (D) 75%
(E) none of these

14. What percent of 36 is 48?

(A) 75%   (B) 125%   (C) $133\frac{1}{3}$%
(D) 80%   (E) 130%

15. $87\frac{1}{2}$% of what number is 56?

(A) 49   (B) 64   (C) 35   (D) 63
(E) none of these

16. $133\frac{1}{3}$% of what number is 96?

(A) 72   (B) 128   (C) 144   (D) 120
(E) 160

PRACTICE TEST 15

1. 47%, expressed as a decimal =

(A) 4.7   (B) 0.047   (C) 0.47   (D) 470
(E) 47

2. $3\frac{1}{2}$%, expressed as a decimal =

(A) 3.5   (B) 350   (C) $3\frac{1}{2}$ (D) $1\frac{2}{5}$
(E) none of these

3. 140%, expressed as a decimal =

(A) 140   (B) 1.40   (C) 14.0   (D) $1\frac{2}{5}$
(E) 1.04

4. 0.47, expressed as a percent =

(A) 0.047%   (B) 0.47%   (C) 4.7%
(D) 47%   (E) 470%

5. $0.08\frac{1}{3}$, expressed as a percent =

(A) $83\frac{1}{3}$%   (B) 83%   (C) $8\frac{1}{3}$%
(D) 803%   (E) 0.083%

6. 24%, expressed as a fraction =

(A) $\frac{1}{4}$ (B) $\frac{6}{20}$ (C) $\frac{4}{12}$ (D) $\frac{1}{3}$
(E) none of these

7. $37\frac{1}{2}$%, expressed as a fraction =

(A) $\frac{1}{6}$ (B) $\frac{3}{8}$ (C) $\frac{5}{12}$ (D) $\frac{5}{8}$ (E) $\frac{2}{5}$

8. $\frac{3}{4}$, expressed as a percent =

(A) 80%   (B) 85%   (C) 70%   (D) 75%
(E) 90%

9. $1\frac{5}{6}$%, expressed as a percent =

(A) $183\frac{1}{3}$%   (B) 180%   (C) $187\frac{1}{2}$%
(D) 185%   (E) 18.3%

10. 16% of 75 =

(A) 120   (B) 11   (C) 102   (D) 12
(E) 110

11. $4\frac{1}{2}$% of 148 =

(A) 66   (B) 6.66   (C) 660   (D) 5.66
(E) 5.76

12. $162\frac{1}{2}$% of 96 =

(A) 15.6   (B) 146   (C) 14.6   (D) 156
(E) none of these

13. 32 is what percent of 40?

(A) 75%   (B) 70%   (C) 80%   (D) 125%
(E) 150%

14. What percent of 44 is 55?

(A) 120%   (B) 80%   (C) $36\frac{4}{11}$%
(D) 130%   (E) 125%

15. $66\frac{2}{3}$% of what number is 72?

(A) 48   (B) 108   (C) 90   (D) 96   (E) 102

16. $112\frac{1}{2}$% of what number is 216?

(A) 182.8   (B) 243   (C) 270   (D) 192
(E) 252

PRACTICE TEST 16

1. 81%, expressed as a decimal =

   (A) 0.081 (B) 0.0081 (C) 0.81 (D) 81
   (E) 8.1

2. $6\frac{1}{2}$%, expressed as a decimal =

   (A) 6.5 (B) 0.065 (C) 65 (D) 0.65
   (E) 6.05

3. 105%, expressed as a decimal =

   (A) 1.5 (B) 105 (C) 10.5 (D) 1.50
   (E) 1.05

4. 0.19, expressed as a percent =

   (A) 1.9% (B) 109% (C) 19% (D) 190%
   (E) 0.19 %

5. $0.42\frac{1}{3}$, expressed as a percent =

   (A) $0.42\frac{1}{3}$% (B) $42\frac{1}{3}$% (C) $423\frac{1}{3}$%
   (D) $4.2\frac{1}{3}$% (E) none of these

6. 48%, expressed as a fraction =

   (A) $\frac{48}{50}$ (B) $\frac{12}{20}$ (C) $\frac{3}{8}$ (D) $\frac{12}{25}$ (E) $\frac{12}{18}$

7. $87\frac{1}{2}$%, expressed as a fraction =

   (A) $\frac{8}{9}$ (B) $\frac{5}{6}$ (C) $\frac{7}{8}$ (D) $\frac{3}{4}$ (E) $\frac{5}{8}$

8. $\frac{2}{5}$, expressed as a percent =

   (A) 40% (B) 20% (C) 25% (D) 250%
   (E) none of these

9. $1\frac{2}{3}$, expressed as a percent =

   (A) $133\frac{1}{3}$% (B) 120% (C) 175%
   (D) $166\frac{2}{3}$% (E) $162\frac{1}{2}$%

10. 35% of 78 =

    (A) 26.30 (B) 27.30 (C) 62.40
    (D) 27.34 (E) 27.4

11. $6\frac{1}{2}$% of 132 =

    (A) 85.8 (B) 7.58 (C) 0.858 (D) 14.52
    (E) none of these

12. $183\frac{1}{3}$% of 54 =

    (A) 18 (B) 99 (C) 102 (D) 90
    (E) 104.8

13. 36 is what percent of 96?

    (A) $33\frac{1}{3}$% (B) 35% (C) 40%
    (D) $37\frac{1}{2}$% (E) 42%

14. What percent of 32 is 56?

    (A) 175% (B) $57\frac{1}{7}$% (C) 150%
    (D) 140% (E) none of these

15. $62\frac{1}{2}$% of what number is 40?

    (A) 25 (B) 65 (C) 64 (D) 30 (E) 20

16. 120% of what number is 90?

    (A) 108 (B) 75 (C) 72 (D) 180
    (E) none of these

PRACTICE TEST 17

1. The sum of 3,070, 256, and 4,938 is:

   (A) 8,164 (B) 7,264 (C) 7,164 (D) 8,264
   (E) 8,254

2. When 697 is subtracted from 2,050 the result is:

   (A) 1,453 (B) 1,363 (C) 1,353
   (D) 1,463 (E) 1,443

3. The product of 385 and 79 is:

   (A) 29,415 (B) 29,315 (C) 30,315
   (D) 30,115 (E) 30,415

4. When 3,540 is divided by 6 the result is:

   (A) 59 (B) 590 (C) 509 (D) 599
   (E) none of these

5. When 13,357 is divided by 19 the result is:

   (A) 703 (B) 73 (C) 730 (D) 7,003
   (E) 733

6. The sum of 5.03, 2.79, 6.85 is:

   (A) 13.67 (B) 14.57 (C) 13.57
   (D) 15.67 (E) none of these

7. The difference between 80.13 and 29.87 is:

   (A) 51.26 (B) 50.26 (C) 50.36
   (D) 51.36 (E) 51.26

8. The sum of $\frac{3}{4}$ and $\frac{2}{3}$ is:

   (A) $\frac{5}{7}$ (B) $\frac{5}{12}$ (C) $\frac{1}{2}$ (D) $1\frac{5}{12}$
   (E) none of these

9. The difference between $3\frac{1}{4}$ and $1\frac{2}{5}$ is:

   (A) $2\frac{1}{9}$ (B) $1\frac{17}{20}$ (C) $2\frac{17}{20}$ (D) $1\frac{3}{5}$
   (E) $4\frac{1}{3}$

10. The product of $4\frac{2}{3}$ and $2\frac{1}{7}$ is:

    (A) $6\frac{3}{10}$ (B) $6\frac{17}{21}$ (C) $8\frac{2}{21}$ (D) $9\frac{2}{21}$
    (E) 10

11. When $\frac{2}{3}$ is divided by $\frac{5}{6}$ the result is:

    (A) $\frac{4}{5}$ (B) $\frac{5}{9}$ (C) $\frac{5}{4}$ (D) $\frac{3}{4}$ (E) $\frac{7}{9}$

12. $\frac{1}{3} \times 24 \times 6.03$ is equal to:

    (A) 120.06 (B) 434.16 (C) 49
    (D) 48.24 (E) none of these

13. The product of 36 and $15\frac{1}{2}$ is:

    (A) 540 (B) $540\frac{1}{2}$ (C) 558 (D) 548
    (E) $555\frac{1}{2}$

14. When $42.37 is divided by 17 the result correct to the nearest cent, is:

    (A) $24.90 (B) $2.49 (C) $2.50 (D) $249
    (E) $24.91

15. The product of 3.24 and 2.5 is:

    (A) 8.1 (B) 71 (C) 7.01 (D) 70.1
    (E) none of these

16. When 273.6 is divided by 7.2 the result is:

    (A) 0.38 (B) 3.8 (C) 380 (D) 38
    (E) 37

17. The product of 0.058 and 100 is:

    (A) 58 (B) 0.58 (C) 580 (D) 0.00058
    (E) 5.8

18. 40% written as a fraction reduced to lowest terms is:

    (A) $\frac{1}{2}$ (B) $\frac{40}{100}$ (C) $\frac{2}{5}$ (D) $2\frac{1}{2}$
    (E) none of these

19. $\frac{8}{25}$ written as a percent is:

    (A) 8% (B) 32% (C) 25% (D) 40%
    (E) 48%

20. 76.5 divided by 100 is equal to:

    (A) 7.65 (B) 7,650 (C) 0.0765
    (D) 0.765 (E) 765

21. 0.859 written as a percent is:

    (A) 0.859% (B) 8.59% (C) 85.9%
    (D) 859% (E) none of these

22. $\frac{1}{7}$ divided by 5 is equal to:

    (A) $\frac{5}{7}$ (B) $\frac{7}{5}$ (C) $\frac{6}{7}$ (D) $\frac{1}{35}$ (E) $1\frac{5}{7}$

23. 18% of 45 is equal to:

    (A) 81 (B) 810 (C) 0.63 (D) 8.01
    (E) none of these

24. 12 is what percent of 16?

    (A) 125% (B) 75% (C) 12% (D) 28%
    (E) 200%

25. 48 is 32% of what number?

    (A) 300 (B) 15.34 (C) $\frac{3}{200}$ (D) 150
    (E) 120

26. $3\frac{5}{9}$ divided by $2\frac{2}{3}$ is equal to:

    (A) 12 (B) $1\frac{1}{3}$ (C) $\frac{3}{4}$ (D) $10\frac{2}{3}$
    (E) none of these

PRACTICE TEST 18

1. The sum of 2,857, 406, and 5,793 is:

   (A) 7,956 (B) 8,056 (C) 8,146
   (D) 9,056 (E) 8,046

2. When 859 is subtracted from 3,020 the result is:

   (A) 2,741 (B) 3,241 (C) 2,141
   (D) 2,241 (E) 2,161

3. The product of 496 and 75 is:

   (A) 37,210 (B) 36,200 (C) 36,210
   (D) 5,952 (E) 37,200

4. When 4008 is divided by 8 the result is:

   (A) 51   (B) 501   (C) 510   (D) 500
   (E) 520

5. The sum of 3.89, 2.05, and 7.14 is:

   (A) 12.98   (B) 13.98   (C) 12.08
   (D) 13.08   (E) none of these

6. The difference between 65.03 and 49.18 is:

   (A) 15.95   (B) 16.85   (C) 16.95
   (D) 25.85   (E) none of these

7. When 9,407 is divided by 23 the result is:

   (A) 490   (B) 409   (C) 49   (D) 419
   (E) 4,090

8. The sum of $\frac{5}{8}$ and $\frac{5}{6}$ is:

   (A) $\frac{10}{14}$ (B) $\frac{5}{7}$ (C) $\frac{25}{48}$ (D) $\frac{10}{48}$ (E) $1\frac{11}{24}$

9. The difference between $5\frac{1}{4}$ and $2\frac{2}{3}$ is:

   (A) $3\frac{3}{7}$ (B) $3\frac{1}{12}$ (C) $2\frac{7}{12}$ (D) $3\frac{7}{12}$
   (E) none of these

10. The product of $3\frac{2}{5}$ and $1\frac{1}{4}$ is:

    (A) $3\frac{2}{9}$ (B) $4\frac{1}{4}$ (C) $6\frac{2}{3}$ (D) $3\frac{1}{10}$
    (E) $4\frac{1}{10}$

11. When $\frac{3}{8}$ is divided by $\frac{5}{6}$ the result is:

    (A) $\frac{3}{20}$ (B) $\frac{5}{16}$ (C) $\frac{4}{7}$ (D) $\frac{9}{20}$
    (E) none of these

12. $\frac{3}{4} \times 36 \times 8.12$ is equal to:

    (A) 218.24   (B) 73.08   (C) 219.24
    (D) 119.24   (E) 210.24

13. The product of 57 and $16\frac{1}{3}$ is:

    (A) $912\frac{1}{3}$ (B) $917\frac{1}{3}$ (C) 1,102   (D) 912
    (E) none of these

14. When $58.03 is divided by 19 the result, correct to the nearest cent, is:

    (A) 35   (B) $3.05   (C) $3.06   (D) $3.15
    (E) $3.47

15. The product of 4.85 and 3.6 is:

    (A) 16.46   (B) 17.406   (C) 1.746
    (D) 17.46   (E) 0.1746

16. When 460.2 is divided by 11.8 the result is:

    (A) 309   (B) 390   (C) 39   (D) 3090
    (E) none of these

17. The product of 7.8 and 100 is:

    (A) 78   (B) 780   (C) 7080   (D) 7,800
    (E) 0.078

18. 35% written as a fraction reduced to lowest terms is:

    (A) $\frac{1}{3}$ (B) $\frac{7}{25}$ (C) $\frac{35}{100}$ (D) $\frac{7}{20}$ (E) $\frac{7}{30}$

19. $\frac{3}{7}$ written as a percent is:

    (A) 40%   (B) $42\frac{6}{7}$%   (C) 30%   (D) 21%
    (E) 37%

20. 3.69 divided by 100 is equal to:

    (A) 0.369   (B) 369   (C) 36.9   (D) 0.0369
    (E) none of these

21. 1.57 written as a percent is:

    (A) 1.57%   (B) 0.0157%   (C) 15.7%
    (D) 1,570%   (E) 157%

22. $\frac{2}{3}$ divided by 9 is equal to:

    (A) $\frac{3}{2}$ (B) $\frac{2}{27}$ (C) 6   (D) $13\frac{1}{2}$ (E) $\frac{2}{3}$

23. 27% of 52 is equal to:

    (A) 14.04   (B) 4.78   (C) 15.41
    (D) 15.04   (E) 14.14

24. 24 is what percent of 40?

    (A) 24%   (B) 40%   (C) 60%   (D) 64%
    (E) 10.37

25. 144 is 72% of what number?

    (A) 2   (B) 103.68   (C) 20   (D) 200
    (E) 10.37

26. $7\frac{2}{9}$ divided by $3\frac{1}{3}$ is equal to:

    (A) $2\frac{1}{6}$ (B) $2\frac{2}{3}$ (C) $21\frac{2}{7}$ (D) $4\frac{1}{9}$
    (E) none of these

Common Units of Measure

The following tables of common units of measure should be memorized.

Measures of Length

12 inches	= 1 foot
3 feet	= 1 yard
36 inches	= 1 yard
5,280 feet	= 1 mile
1,760 yards	= 1 mile

Measures of Weight

16 ounces	= 1 pound
2,000 pounds	= 1 ton

Liquid Measures

4 gills	= 1 pint
16 ounces	= 1 pint
2 pints	= 1 quart
4 quarts	= 1 gallon
8 pints	= 1 gallon

Dry Measures

2 pints	= 1 quart
8 quarts	= 1 peck
4 pecks	= 1 bushel
32 quarts	= 1 bushel

Measures of Time

60 seconds	= 1 minute
60 minutes	= 1 hour
24 hours	= 1 day
7 days	= 1 week
30 days	= 1 month (approx.)
12 months	= 1 year

CONVERSION OF UNITS

Each of the relationships above can be expressed as unit fractions to help in conversion from one measurement to another

EXAMPLE: Convert 7 feet to inches.

SOLUTION: Since 12 inches = 1 foot, we can write either unit fraction $\frac{12\ in}{1\ ft}$ or $\frac{1\ ft}{12\ in}$.

Then to convert a measurement such as 7 feet to inches, just multiply by whichever unit fraction cancels the appropriate units. Then multiply by any number that appears on top and divide by any number that appears on the bottom.

$$7\ ft = \frac{7\ ft}{1} \times \frac{12\ in}{1\ ft} = (7 \times 12)in = 84\ in$$

EXAMPLE: Convert 112 ounces to quarts.

SOLUTION: The relationship, 16 ounces = 1 pint can be written $\frac{1\ pt}{16\ oz}$, and the relationship 2 pints = 1 quart can be written $\frac{1\ qt}{2\ pt}$. Therefore,

$$112\ oz = \frac{112\ oz}{1} \times \frac{1\ pt}{16\ oz} \times \frac{1\ qt}{2\ pt} = 3.5\ qt$$

EXAMPLE: Change 5 pounds to ounces.

SOLUTION: 16 ounces = 1 pound

$$\frac{5\ lb}{1} \times \frac{16\ oz}{1\ lb} = 80\ oz$$

EXAMPLE: Change 4 feet to inches.

SOLUTION: 12 inches = 1 foot

$$\frac{4\ ft}{1} \times \frac{12\ in}{1\ ft} = 48\ in$$

EXAMPLE: Find the number of ounces in 9 pints.

SOLUTION: 16 ounces = 1 pint

$$\frac{9\ pt}{1} \times \frac{16\ oz}{1\ pt} = 144\ oz$$

EXAMPLE: Change $3\frac{1}{2}$ hours to minutes.

SOLUTION: 60 minutes = 1 hour

$$\frac{3\frac{1}{2}\ hr}{1} \times \frac{60\ min}{1\ hr} = 210\ min$$

EXAMPLE: Change 66 inches to feet.

SOLUTION: 12 inches = 1 foot

$$\frac{66\ in}{1} \times \frac{1\ ft}{12\ in} = 5\frac{1}{2}\ ft$$

EXAMPLE: Change 124 ounces to pounds.

SOLUTION: 16 ounces = 1 pound

$$\frac{124 \ oz}{1} \times \frac{1 \ lb}{16 \ oz} = 7\frac{3}{4} \ lb$$

EXAMPLE: Change 180 liquid ounces to quarts.

SOLUTION: 32 liquid ounces = 1 quart

$$\frac{180 \ oz}{1} \times \frac{1 \ pt}{16 \ oz} \times \frac{1 \ qt}{2 \ pt} = 5\frac{5}{8} \ qt$$

EXAMPLE: Change 1,470 seconds to minutes.

SOLUTION: 60 seconds = 1 minute

$$\frac{1470 \ sec}{1} \times \frac{1 \ min}{60 \ sec} = 24.5 \ min$$

EXERCISE 69

Make the following changes.

1. 48 ounces to pounds
2. 3 feet to inches
3. 2 hours to minutes
4. 6 quarts to gallons
5. 33 inches to feet
6. 90 seconds to minutes
7. 4 pints to ounces
8. $1\frac{1}{2}$ miles to feet
9. 144 liquid ounces to quarts
10. $2\frac{1}{4}$ pounds to ounces

If you got 9 or 10 correct, go on to the next section on Operations with Units of Measure. If you got more than one wrong, use Exercise 70 to build your skill.

EXERCISE 70

Make the following changes.

1. 64 ounces to pounds
2. 40 ounces to pounds
3. 4 feet to inches
4. $2\frac{1}{2}$ feet to inches
5. 5 hours to minutes
6. $3\frac{1}{4}$ hours to minutes
7. 10 quarts to gallons
8. 14 quarts to gallons
9. 28 inches to feet
10. 21 inches to feet
11. 150 seconds to minutes
12. 100 seconds to minutes
13. 2 pints to ounces
14. 6 pints to ounces
15. $1\frac{1}{8}$ miles to feet

16. $2\frac{1}{4}$ miles to feet
17. 64 liquid ounces to quarts
18. 40 liquid ounces to quarts
19. $3\frac{1}{2}$ pounds to ounces
20. $5\frac{1}{4}$ pounds to ounces

Now be sure of your skill. Try Exercise 71.

EXERCISE 71

Make the following changes.

1. 32 ounces to pounds
2. 5 feet to inches
3. 3 hours to minutes
4. 9 quarts to gallons
5. 39 inches to feet
6. 150 seconds to minutes
7. 3 pints to ounces
8. $1\frac{3}{4}$ miles to feet
9. 112 liquid ounces to quarts
10. $3\frac{3}{4}$ pounds to ounces

OPERATIONS WITH UNITS OF MEASURE

It is sometimes necessary to perform the fundamental operations with common units of measures.

Addition

To add common units of measure, arrange the units in columns, add each column, and simplify the results.

EXAMPLE: Add 3 ft. 5 in., 4 ft. 6 in., and 2 ft. 7 in.

SOLUTION:

$$
\begin{array}{r}
3 \text{ ft. } 5 \text{ in.} \\
4 \text{ ft. } 6 \text{ in.} \\
\underline{2 \text{ ft. } 7 \text{ in.}} \\
9 \text{ ft. } 18 \text{ in.}
\end{array}
$$

Since 12 in. = 1 ft., 9 ft. 18 in. = 9 ft. 12 in. + 6 in. = 10 ft. 6 in.

EXAMPLE: Add 5 hr. 12 min., 3 hr. 47 min., 2 hr. 35 min., and 4 hr. 38 min.

SOLUTION:

$$
\begin{array}{r}
5 \text{ hr. } 12 \text{ min.} \\
3 \text{ hr. } 47 \text{ min.} \\
2 \text{ hr. } 35 \text{ min.} \\
\underline{4 \text{ hr. } 38 \text{ min.}} \\
14 \text{ hr. } 132 \text{ min.} = 16 \text{ hr. } 12 \text{ min.}
\end{array}
$$

Since 60 min. = 1 hr., 14 hr. 132 min. = 14 hr. 120 min. + 12 min. = 16 hr. 12 min.

EXAMPLE: Add 3 lb. 11 oz., 2 lb. 8 oz., and 1 lb. 7 oz.

SOLUTION: 3 lb. 11 oz.
2 lb. 8 oz.
1 lb. 7 oz.
6 lb. 26 oz. = 7 lb. 10 oz.

Since 16 oz. = 1 lb., 6 lb. 26 oz. = 6 lb. 16 oz. + 10 oz. = 7 lb. 10 oz.

Subtraction

To subtract common units of measure, arrange the units in columns, and subtract each column, starting with the smallest unit. It is necessary to borrow if the number in the subtrahend is larger than the number in the minuend.

EXAMPLE: From 30 min. 12 sec. subtract 19 min. 47 sec.

SOLUTION:

30 min. 12 sec. = 29 min. 72 sec.
19 min. 47 sec. = 19 min. 47 sec.
10 min. 25 sec.

EXAMPLE: Subtract 2 gal. 3 qt. from 6 gal. 1 qt.

SOLUTION: 6 gal. 1 qt. = 5 gal. 5 qt.
2 gal. 3 qt. = 2 gal. 3 qt.
3 gal. 2 qt.

EXAMPLE: Subtract 3 yd. 2 ft. 11 in. from 9 yd. 1 ft. 3 in.

SOLUTION:

9 yd. 1 ft. 3 in. = 8 yd. 4 ft. 3 in. = 8 yd. 3 ft. 15 in.
3 yd. 2 ft. 11 in. = 3 yd. 2 ft. 11 in. = 3 yd. 2 ft. 11 in.
5 yd. 1 ft. 4 in.

Multiplication

To multiply common units of measure by a number, multiply each unit by the multiplier and simplify the result.

EXAMPLE: Multiply 3 lb. 9 oz. by 6.

SOLUTION: 3 lb. 9 oz.
6
18 lb. 54 oz. = 21 lb. 6 oz.

Since 16 oz. = 1 lb., 18 lb. 54 oz. = 21 lb. 6 oz.

EXAMPLE: Multiply 8 min. 29 sec. by 9.

SOLUTION: 8 min. 29 sec.
9
72 min. 261 sec.
= 1 hr. 16 min. 21 sec.

Since 60 min. = 1 hr., and 60 sec. = 1 min., 72 min. 261 sec. = 1 hr. 12 min. + 4 min. 21 sec. = 1 hr. 16 min. 21 sec.

Division

To divide common units of measure by a number divide each unit by the divisor, starting with the largest unit. If a remainder is obtained in dividing, convert the remainder to the next smaller unit and add the result to the given number of smaller units. Continue the division.

EXAMPLE: Divide 8 ft. 6 in. by 3.

SOLUTION:

$$\begin{array}{r} 2 \text{ ft. } 10 \text{ in.} \\ 3\overline{)8 \text{ ft. } 6 \text{ in.}} \\ \underline{6 \text{ ft.}} \\ 2 \text{ ft. } 6 \text{ in.} = 30 \text{ in.} \\ \underline{30 \text{ in.}} \end{array}$$

The result is 2 ft. 10 in.

EXAMPLE: Divide 7 lb. 8 oz. by 4.

SOLUTION:

$$\begin{array}{r} 1 \text{ lb. } 14 \text{ oz.} \\ 4\overline{)7 \text{ lb. } 8 \text{ oz.}} \\ \underline{4 \text{ lb.}} \\ 3 \text{ lb. } 8 \text{ oz.} = 56 \text{ oz.} \\ \underline{56 \text{ oz.}} \end{array}$$

The result is 1 lb. 14 oz.

EXERCISE 72

1. Add 4 ft. 2 in., 3 ft. 7 in., and 8 ft. 5 in.
2. Add 6 hr. 28 min., 4 hr. 15 min., and 2 hr. 49 min.
3. Add 1 lb. 12 oz., 3 lb. 7 oz., and 5 lb. 5 oz.
4. Add 4 gal. 2 qt., and 2 gal. 3 qt.
5. Multiply 4 lb. 5 oz. by 7.
6. Multiply 5 min. 17 sec. by 8.
7. Multiply 4 yd. 2 ft. by 9.
8. From 6 lb. 15 oz. subtract 2 lb. 8 oz.
9. From 3 hr. 14 min. subtract 1 hr. 45 min.
10. From 2 gal. 1 qt. subtract 3 qt.

11. Divide 3 hr. 36 min. by 4.
12. Divide 15 lb. 8 oz. by 8.

If you got 9 or 10 correct, go on to the following Practice Tests. If you got more than one wrong, use Exercise 73 to build your skill.

EXERCISE 73

1. Add 3 hr. 8 min., 2 hr. 37 min., and 1 hr. 43 min.
2. Add 1 lb. 3 oz., 2 lb. 9 oz., and 5 lb. 11 oz.
3. Add 4 gal. 1 qt., 2 gal. 3 qt., and 3 gal. 2 qt.
4. Add 4 min. 8 sec., 3 min. 49 sec., and 5 min. 31 sec.
5. Add 2 ft. 5 in., 3 ft. 9 in., and 2 ft. 7 in.
6. Add 2 lb. 7 oz., 8 lb. 4 oz., and 3 lb. 11 oz.
7. Multiply 3 min. 43 sec. by 7.
8. Multiply 2 lb. 7 oz. by 5.
9. Multiply 2 hr. 34 sec. by 4.
10. Multiply 1 gal. 3 qt. by 9.
11. From 5 lb. 11 oz. subtract 2 lb. 3 oz.
12. From 3 hr. 14 min. subtract 1 hr. 37 min.
13. From 3 gal. 1 qt. subtract 1 gal. 2 qt.
14. From 17 min. 12 sec. subtract 5 min. 48 sec.
15. From 8 lb. 1 oz. subtract 3 lb. 8 oz.
16. Divide 8 hr. 56 min. by 4.
17. Divide 6 lb. 2 oz. by 7.
18. Divide 7 gal. 2 qt. by 3.
19. Divide 16 ft. 3 in. by 5.
20. Divide 10 yd. 2 ft. by 4.

Now be sure of your skill. Try Exercise 74.

EXERCISE 74

1. Add 3 ft. 4 in., 5 ft. 11 in., and 2 ft. 7 in.
2. Add 5 hr. 38 min., 7 hr. 25 min., and 1 hr. 57 min.
3. Add 2 lb. 4 oz., 3 lb. 5 oz., and 4 lb. 6 oz.
4. Add 1 gal. 3 qt. and 4 gal. 2 qt.
5. Multiply 6 lb. 8 oz. by 9.
6. Multiply 8 min. 37 sec. by 7.
7. Multiply 3 yd. 1 ft. by 8.
8. From 4 lb. 14 oz. subtract 1 lb. 10 oz.
9. From 4 hr. 12 min. subtract 1 hr. 53 min.
10. From 5 gal. 2 qt. subtract 1 gal. 3 qt.
11. Divide 2 hr. 39 min. by 3.
12. Divide 7 lb. 14 oz. by 9.

Time

Some examinations require you to find the time required to complete a job or the number of days between two calendar dates.

EXAMPLE: A carpenter started a job a 9:15 A.M. and completed it at 4:45 P.M. If she took 45 minutes for lunch, how many hours did it take the carpenter to complete the job?

SOLUTION: From 9:15 A.M. to 12:00 (noon) is 2 hours and 45 minutes, or $2\frac{3}{4}$ hours. From noon to 4:45 P.M. is 4 hours and 45 minutes, or $4\frac{3}{4}$ hours.

$$2\frac{3}{4} + 4\frac{3}{4} = 6\frac{6}{4} \text{ hours, or } 7\frac{1}{2} \text{ hours}$$

If we subtract the lunch time of $\frac{3}{4}$ hour, we have

$$7\frac{1}{2} - \frac{3}{4} = 6\frac{3}{4} \text{ hours}$$

It took the carpenter $6\frac{3}{4}$ hours to complete the job.

EXAMPLE: A man went on a business trip. He left on the morning of April 29 and returned home on the afternoon of May 16. How many nights was he away from home?

SOLUTION: He was away on the nights of April 29 and 30 as well as 15 nights in May. Thus, he spent 17 nights away from home.

EXERCISE 75

1. A boy borrowed a library book on September 26. The book had to be returned within two weeks. By what date did the book have to be returned?
2. A train running between Cedarville and Mountainville left Cedarville at 8:47 A.M. and reached Mountainville at 10:12 A.M. How many minutes did the trip take?
3. A plane leaves Miami at 4:35 P.M. and arrives at Boston at 7:05 P.M. How many hours did the trip take?
4. A cargo vessel left home port on August 25 and returned on December 7 of the same year. How many weeks was the boat away?
5. A movie showing starts at 8:50 P.M. and lasts 2 hours and 45 minutes. At what time is the showing over?

PRACTICE TEST 19

1. The number of feet in 18 in. is:

   (A) $\frac{2}{3}$ (B) 2 (C) 3 (D) $1\frac{1}{2}$ (E) $1\frac{1}{3}$

2. The number of pounds in 24 oz. is:

   (A) 2 (B) 3 (C) $\frac{2}{3}$ (D) $\frac{3}{4}$
   (E) none of these

3. The number of pints in a gallon is:

   (A) 4 (B) 8 (C) 2 (D) 16 (E) 10

4. The number of hours in 45 min. is:

   (A) $\frac{2}{3}$ (B) $1\frac{1}{2}$ (C) $\frac{5}{9}$ (D) $\frac{3}{4}$ (E) $\frac{5}{8}$

5. The number of ounces in $2\frac{1}{2}$ lb. is:

   (A) 50 (B) 40 (C) 24 (D) 32 (E) 38

6. The sum of 3 ft. 9 in. and 6 ft. 8 in. is:

   (A) 9 ft. 7 in. (B) 10 ft. 7 in.
   (C) 10 ft. 5 in. (D) 9 ft. 5 in.
   (E) none of these

7. The number of ounces in a 2 gal. jug is:

   (A) 256 (B) 128 (C) 32 (D) 64 (E) 250

8. When 2 hr. 57 min. is multiplied by 5 the result is:

   (A) 13 hr. 15 min. (B) 10 hr. 35 min.
   (C) 14 hr. 45 min. (D) 11 hr. 15 min.
   (E) none of these

9. The number of feet in 4 yd. 2 ft. is:

   (A) 6 (B) 14 (C) 8 (D) $4\frac{1}{2}$ (E) 12

10. When 3 lb. 8 oz. is subtracted from 5 lb. 1 oz. the result is:

    (A) 2 lb. 9 oz. (B) 1 lb. 11 oz.
    (C) 7 lb. 9 oz. (D) 2 lb. 7 oz.
    (E) none of these

11. The number of pounds in 76 oz. is:

    (A) $4\frac{1}{2}$ (B) $4\frac{2}{3}$ (C) $4\frac{3}{4}$ (D) $4\frac{1}{4}$
    (E) none of these

12. When 8 yd. 4 ft. is divided by 4 the result is:

    (A) 21 yd. (B) 21 ft. (C) 2 yd.
    (D) 2 yd. 1 ft. (E) 3 yd.

13. The sum of 1 hr. 14 min., 3 hr. 59 min., and 2 hr. 37 min. is:

    (A) 6 hr. 10 min. (B) 7 hr. 50 min.
    (C) 7 hr. 10 min. (D) 6 hr. 50 min.
    (E) none of these

14. The number of yards in 7 ft. 6 in. is:

    (A) 2 (B) $2\frac{1}{4}$ (C) $2\frac{2}{3}$ (D) $2\frac{1}{2}$
    (E) none of these

15. When 5 lb. 7 oz. is multiplied by 7 the result is:

    (A) 39 lb. (B) 35 lb. 7 oz.
    (C) 38 lb. 1 oz. (D) 37 lb. 1 oz.
    (E) 40 lb.

16. When 3 hr. 48 min. is subtracted from 6 hr. 20 min. the result is:

    (A) 3 hr. 28 min. (B) 2 hr. 32 min.
    (C) 10 hr. 2 min. (D) 3 hr. 32 min.
    (E) none of these

17. The number of minutes in $1\frac{1}{4}$ hr. is:

    (A) 45 (B) 75 (C) 62 (D) 125 (E) 80

18. The sum of 2 lb. 5 oz., 3 lb. 7 oz., and 6 lb. 11 oz. is:

    (A) 12 lb. 7 oz. (B) 12 lb. 11 oz.
    (C) 12 lb. 2 oz. (D) 13 lb. 2 oz.
    (E) none of these

19. The number of yards in $1\frac{1}{4}$ miles is:

    (A) 6,600 (B) 1,200 (C) 1,500
    (D) 2,200 (E) 2,000

20. When 6 hr. 30 min. is divided by 5 the result is:

    (A) 1 hr. 6 min. (B) 1 hr. 26 min.
    (C) 1 hr. 18 min. (D) 1 hr. 16 min.
    (E) none of these

PRACTICE TEST 20

1. The number of hours in 100 minutes is:

   (A) 1 (B) $1\frac{3}{4}$ (C) $1\frac{1}{2}$ (D) $1\frac{2}{3}$
   (E) none of these

2. The number of gallons in 50 pints is:

   (A) $12\frac{1}{2}$ (B) $6\frac{1}{4}$ (C) $12\frac{1}{4}$ (D) $6\frac{1}{2}$
   (E) none of these

3. The number of ounces in $3\frac{1}{4}$ pounds is:

   (A) 50   (B) 48   (C) 34   (D) 36
   (E) none of these

4. The number of feet in 30 inches is:

   (A) $2\frac{1}{4}$ (B) $1\frac{7}{8}$ (C) $2\frac{1}{2}$ (D) 3
   (E) none of these

5. The number of minutes in 140 seconds is:

   (A) $2\frac{1}{2}$ (B) $2\frac{1}{3}$ (C) $2\frac{1}{4}$ (D) $2\frac{2}{3}$
   (E) none of these

6. The number of pounds in 72 ounces is:

   (A) $7\frac{1}{5}$ (B) $4\frac{1}{4}$ (C) $4\frac{1}{3}$ (D) $4\frac{1}{2}$
   (E) none of these

7. The sum of 5 ft. 9 in. and 2 ft. 6 in. is:

   (A) 8 ft. 5 in.   (B) 8 ft. 3 in.
   (C) 9 ft. 3 in.   (D) 9 ft. 1 in.
   (E) none of these

8. When 2 lb. 11 oz. is multiplied by 8 the result is:

   (A) $20\frac{1}{2}$ lb.   (B) $20\frac{1}{4}$ lb.   (C) $21\frac{1}{2}$ lb.
   (D) $24\frac{1}{2}$ lb.   (E) none of these

9. The number of inches in $3\frac{1}{4}$ feet is:

   (A) 40   (B) 39   (C) $38\frac{1}{2}$ (D) $36\frac{1}{3}$
   (E) none of these

10. When 2 hr. 52 min. is subtracted from 5 hr. 10 min. the result is:

    (A) 3 hr. 58 min.   (B) 2 hr. 58 min.
    (C) 3 hr. 18 min.   (D) 2 hr. 18 min.
    (E) none of these

11. The number of quarts in 2 gal. 1 pt. is:

    (A) 9   (B) 5   (C) $2\frac{1}{2}$ (D) $4\frac{1}{2}$
    (E) none of these

12. When 6 lb. 12 oz. is divided by 3 the result is:

    (A) $2\frac{1}{2}$ lb.   (B) $2\frac{1}{3}$ lb.   (C) $2\frac{1}{4}$ lb.
    (D) $2\frac{2}{3}$ lb.   (E) none of these

13. The sum of 2 hr. 18 min., 3 hr. 43 min., and 1 hr. 19 min. is:

    (A) 6 hr. 20 min.   (B) 6 hr. 48 min.
    (C) 7 hr. 40 min.   (D) 7 hr. 20 min.
    (E) none of these

14. The number of feet in 3 yd. 8 in. is:

    (A) $9\frac{2}{3}$ (B) 11   (C) $6\frac{1}{2}$ (D) $9\frac{3}{4}$
    (E) none of these

15. When 3 lb. 9 oz. is multiplied by 6 the result is:

    (A) $21\frac{1}{2}$ (B) $23\frac{1}{3}$ (C) $19\frac{1}{3}$ (D) $21\frac{3}{8}$
    (E) none of these

16. When 5 ft. 8 in. is subtracted from 9 ft. 3 in. the result is:

    (A) 4 ft. 3 in.   (B) 3 ft. 7 in.
    (C) 3 ft. 5 in.   (D) 4 ft. 5 in.
    (E) none of these

17. The number of seconds in $3\frac{1}{4}$ minutes is:

    (A) 325   (B) 225   (C) 315   (D) 195
    (E) none of these

18. The sum of 3 lb. 9 oz., 2 lb. 6 oz., and 4 lb. 11 oz. is:

    (A) 10 lb. 8 oz.   (B) 9 lb. 10 oz.
    (C) 10 lb. 6 oz.   (D) 10 lb. 9 oz.
    (E) none of these

19. The number of yards in $2\frac{1}{5}$ miles is:

    (A) 2,250   (B) 3,960   (C) 3,872
    (D) 2,500   (E) none of these

20. When 7 hr. 30 min. is divided by 6 the result is:

    (A) 1 hr. 22 min.   (B) 1 hr. 15 min.
    (C) 1 hr. 5 min.   (D) 1 hr. 20 min.
    (E) none of these

The Metric System

The metric system is the system of measurement that is used in most European countries, and is also used extensively in scientific laboratories and in industry. The great advantage in using the metric system is that its units are related by powers of 10 and thus it resembles the decimal system.

The basic unit of **length** in the metric system is the *meter*. The meter is a bit larger than the yard.

1 meter = 39.37 inches approximately.

The *millimeter,* which is equal to $\frac{1}{1,000}$ of a meter, is often used in science to measure very small distances. 1 millimeter is approximately 0.04 inch. The *centimeter* is $\frac{1}{100}$ of a meter and is approximately 0.4 inch. The centimeter is useful in measuring short distances. The *kilometer* is used to measure long distances. The kilometer is approximately equal to $\frac{5}{8}$ of a mile. To sum up:

> 1 meter $\approx$ 39.37 inches
> 1 centimeter $\approx$ 0.4 inch
> 1 kilometer $\approx$ $\frac{5}{8}$ mile

The basic unit of **mass** in the metric system is the *gram*. The *milligram* is equal to $\frac{1}{1,000}$ of a gram and is often used in prescribing medicines. Since the gram is very small, the unit used most often in practical situations is the *kilogram*.

> 1 kilogram = 1,000 grams exerts a force due to gravity approximately 2.2 pounds

The basic unit of **liquid measure** in the metric system is the *liter*.

> 1 liter $\approx$ 1.1 quarts

EXAMPLE: The cost of a kilogram of butter is $3.20. What is the cost of 700 grams of butter?

SOLUTION:
$$1 \text{ kilogram } = 1,000 \text{ grams}$$
$$700 \text{ grams } = \frac{700}{1000} \text{ kilograms}$$
$$= \frac{7}{10} \text{ kilogram}$$
$$\frac{7}{10} \times \$3.20 = \$2.24$$

EXAMPLE: A city posts a speed limit of 48 kilometers per hour. What is the approximate speed in miles per hour?

SOLUTION: Since 1 kilometer $\approx$ $\frac{5}{8}$ of a mile, 48 kilometers per hour is

$$\frac{5}{8} \times 48 \approx 30 \text{ miles per hour.}$$

PRACTICE TEST 21

DIRECTIONS: Solve each of the following problems and then circle the letter that corresponds to the right answer.

1. Five kilograms exerts approximately how many pounds due to gravity?

   (A) 3 (B) 10 (C) 11 (D) 15 (E) 12

2. The distance between two cities in Europe is 96 kilometers. The approximate distance in miles is:

   (A) 50 (B) 48 (C) 156 (D) 90 (E) 60

3. A gallon of milk is approximately how many liters?

   (A) .5 (B) 4.4 (C) 2.5 (D) 3.6 (E) 4

4. One hundred centimeters is approximately equal to:

   (A) a quarter of a mile
    (B) a little more than a yard
     (C) a foot (D) 4 inches
      (E) 400 inches

5. If a man is 2 meters tall, his height in feet is approximately:

   (A) 6 (B) 5 (C) $6\frac{1}{2}$ (D) 7 (E) $5\frac{1}{2}$

6. Approximately how many grams exerts 1 pound of force due to gravity?

   (A) 450 (B) 150 (C) 1,000 (D) 500
   (E) 200

7. A motorist in Europe fills his tank with 50 liters of gasoline. About how many gallons is this?

   (A) 12 (B) $13\frac{3}{4}$ (C) 15 (D) 10 (E) 8

8. A plane in Italy flies at the rate of 600 kilometers per hour. About how fast is this, in miles per hour?

   (A) 300 (B) 500 (C) 250 (D) 450
   (E) 375

9. A woman's mass is 52 kilograms. In pounds, this corresponds to:

   (A) 110 (B) 108 (C) 114 (D) 120
   (E) 125

10. The distance along the right field foul line in a baseball field is marked 108 meters in length. In feet, this is about:

    (A) 354 (B) 300 (C) 420 (D) 320
    (E) 375

11. One millimeter is equal to:

    (A) 10 centimeters (B) $\frac{1}{100}$ of a meter
    (C) $\frac{1}{10}$ of a centimeter
    (D) $\frac{1}{100}$ of a kilometer
    (E) $\frac{1}{1,000}$ of a kilometer

12. One milligram is equal to:

    (A) $\frac{1}{10}$ of a kilogram (B) 10 grams
    (C) $\frac{1}{10}$ of a gram (D) $\frac{1}{1,000}$ of a gram
    (E) $\frac{1}{100}$ of a kilogram

Ratio and Proportion

RATIO

When two quantities are compared by dividing one quantity by the other the comparison is called a *ratio*. A ratio may be expressed as a fraction or by the use of the symbol ":" (colon).

EXAMPLES:
Express the following as ratios:

1. $5.00 to $6.00   1. $\frac{5}{6}$ or 5:6
2. 3 hours to 7 hours   2. $\frac{3}{7}$ or 3:7
3. 4 ft. to 12 ft.   3. $\frac{4}{12} = \frac{1}{3}$ or 1:3
4. 9 lb. to 15 lb.   4. $\frac{9}{15} = \frac{3}{5}$ or 3:5

EXAMPLE: Express as a ratio 10 in. to 2 ft.

SOLUTION: Since the quantities must be expressed *in the same units of measure* we change 2 ft. to 24 in. The ratio is 10:24. Since a ratio is a fraction we may divide both 10 and 24 by the common factor 2 to obtain the result 5:12.

EXAMPLE: Express as a ratio 3 lb. to 9 oz.

SOLUTION: Before writing the ratio, we change 3 lb. to 48 oz. The ratio is 48:9. This may be reduced to 16:3.

EXAMPLE: Express as a ratio 3 days to 8 hours.

SOLUTION: Before writing the ratio, we change 3 days to 72 hours. The ratio is 72:8. This may be reduced to 9:1.

EXAMPLE: Express as a ratio $\frac{3}{8}$ to $\frac{15}{16}$.

SOLUTION:

$$\frac{3}{8} : \frac{15}{16} = \frac{3}{8} \div \frac{15}{16} = \frac{\overset{1}{\cancel{3}}}{\underset{1}{\cancel{8}}} \times \frac{\overset{2}{\cancel{16}}}{\underset{5}{\cancel{15}}}$$

This result may be written as 2:5.

EXAMPLE: Wilson High School defeated Lincoln High School at football by a score of 27 points to 18 points. What is the ratio of the number of points scored by Wilson High to the number of points scored by Lincoln High School?

SOLUTION:

$$\frac{\text{number of points scored by Wilson H.S.}}{\text{number of points scored by Lincoln H.S.}} = \frac{27}{18}$$

This result may be reduced to $\frac{3}{2}$ by dividing the numerator and denominator of the fraction $\frac{27}{18}$ by 9.

The result may be written as 3:2 or $\frac{3}{2}$.

PRACTICE TEST 22

1. The ratio of 7 to 9 is:

    (A) 9:7 (B) $\frac{9}{7}$ (C) 7:9 (D) $\frac{2}{9}$
    (E) none of these

2. The ratio of 12 to 16 is:

    (A) 2:3 (B) 3:4 (C) 4:3 (D) 3:2
    (E) 1 and $\frac{1}{3}$

3. The ratio 1:3 is equal to:

    (A) 3:12 (B) 9:3 (C) 6:12 (D) 3:1
    (E) 5:15

4. The ratio of 3.2 to 2.4 is:

    (A) 3:2 (B) 2:3 (C) 3:4 (D) 4:3
    (E) 2:1

5. The ratio of $\frac{5}{6}$ to $\frac{5}{12}$ is:

    (A) 25:72 (B) 72:25 (C) 1:2 (D) 2:1
    (E) none of these

6. The ratio of 4 yards to 2 feet is:

    (A) 4:2 (B) 2:1 (C) 1:6 (D) 1:4
    (E) none of these

7. The ratio of 20 minutes to $2\frac{1}{2}$ hours is:

    (A) 8:1 (B) 2:15 (C) 4:1 (D) 1:4
    (E) 1:7

8. A man had 12 dress shirts and 3 sport shirts. The ratio of sport shirts to dress shirts is:

    (A) 1:4 (B) 1:5 (C) 4:1 (D) 4:5
    (E) 5:4

9. A football team scored 12 points in the first half and 28 points in the second half. The ratio of the number of points scored in the first half to the total number of points is:

    (A) 3:7 (B) 7:3 (C) 7:10 (D) 3:10
    (E) 10:7

10. On a test, a pupil did 24 problems correctly and 6 problems incorrectly. The ratio of incorrect problems to correct problems is:

    (A) 4:1 (B) 1:5 (C) 1:4 (D) 5:1
    (E) none of these

PRACTICE TEST 23

1. The ratio of 15 to 2 is:

    (A) 15:17 (B) 15:2 (C) 2:15 (D) 13:2
    (E) none of these

2. The ratio 16:36 is equal to:

    (A) 4:9 (B) 4:5 (C) 9:4 (D) 5:4
    (E) 4:13

3. The ratio 1:7 is equal to:

    (A) 1:8 (B) 6:1 (C) 1:6 (D) 3:21
    (E) 28:1

4. The ratio of 4.8 to 4 is:

    (A) 12:1 (B) 3:10 (C) 1:12 (D) 2:1
    (E) 6:5

5. The ratio of $\frac{3}{8}$ to $\frac{5}{4}$ is:

    (A) 15:32 (B) 3:10 (C) 10:3 (D) 32:15
    (E) none of these

6. The ratio of 1 lb. to 6 oz. is:

    (A) 1:6 (B) 6:1 (C) 3:8 (D) 4:1
    (E) 8:3

7. The ratio of 10 in. to $1\frac{1}{2}$ ft. is:

    (A) 20:3 (B) 3:20 (C) 5:9 (D) 1:2
    (E) 10:1

8. Bill caught 9 fish and Henry caught 15 fish. The ratio of the number of fish caught by Bill to the number of fish caught by Henry is:

    (A) 3:8 (B) 3:5 (C) 8:3 (D) 2:3
    (E) none of these

9. A class has 18 boys and 12 girls. The ratio of the number of the girls to the number of boys is:

    (A) 3:2 (B) 2:5 (C) 5:2 (D) 3:4
    (E) none of these

10. A man bought a shirt for $22.50 and a tie for $12.50. The ratio of the cost of the tie to the total amount spent is:

    (A) 5:9 (B) 9:14 (C) 5:14 (D) 14:9
    (E) 1:3

PROPORTION

Let us consider the ratios 3:5 and 12:20. If we write these ratios in fraction form, we have $\frac{3}{5}$ and $\frac{12}{20}$. Now if we apply the Principle of Equivalency of Fractions, we have $3 \times 20 = 5 \times 12$. Thus, the fractions $\frac{3}{5}$ and $\frac{12}{20}$ are equivalent. We can also say that the ratios 3:5 and 12:20 are equivalent.

Thus, we may write 3:5 = 12:20. This statement is called a proportion.

DEFINITION

A *proportion* is a statement that two ratios are equivalent.

EXAMPLES: (a) 1:2 = 4:8
(b) 5:6 = 15:18
(c) $\frac{3}{8} = \frac{9}{24}$

Extremes and Means

In a proportion, the first and fourth numbers are called the *extremes* and the second and third numbers are called the *means*. In example (a) above, 1 and 8 are the extremes and 2 and 4 are the means. In example (b) above, 5 and 18 are the extremes and 6 and 15 are the means. In example (c) above, 3 and 24 are the extremes and 8 and 9 are the means. Thus, if we have a proportion $a{:}b = c{:}d$, then

$$\overbrace{a{:}b = c{:}d}$$
extremes
means

Let us consider the following true proportions.

Proportion	Product of Means	Product of Extremes
2:3 = 4:6	$3 \times 4 = 12$	$2 \times 6 = 12$
3:7 = 9:21	$7 \times 9 = 63$	$3 \times 21 = 63$
4:3 = 12:9	$3 \times 12 = 36$	$4 \times 9 = 36$
10:16 = 5:8	$16 \times 5 = 80$	$10 \times 8 = 80$

Do you notice that, in a true proportion, the product of the means is equal to the product of the extremes? This principle will not hold in a proportion that is not true. This leads us to the following principle:

PRINCIPLE OF PROPORTIONS

In a proportion, the product of the means is equal to the product of the extremes.

EXERCISE 76

Use the Principle of Proportions to determine which of the following are true proportions.

1. 5:7 = 15:21
2. 9:4 = 17:10
3. 6:11 = 12:24
4. 18:12 = 51:34
5. 1.4:3.5 = 4.6:11.5
6. 56:32 = 49:28
7. 63:81 = 77:99
8. 14.5:29 = 8.7:17.4
9. 64:28 = 96:40
10. 58:74 = 174:222

It is often necessary to find the fourth member of a proportion when three members are known. Consider the proportion 3:4 = 6:y. In this proportion, we know that the first three terms are 3, 4, and 6. We do not know the fourth term, which we have called y. If we use the Principle of Proportions we know that $3 \times y = 4 \times 6$, or $3y = 24$. You can see that if 3 times y is equal to 24, then y must be equal to 8. Now, let us replace y in the original proportion to obtain 3:4 = 6:8, a true proportion.

EXAMPLE: What number should replace n to make the following a true proportion?

$$5{:}6 = n{:}12$$

According to the Principle of Proportions

$$6 \times n = 5 \times 12$$
$$6n = 60$$
$$n = \frac{60}{6}$$
$$n = 10$$

EXAMPLE: What number should replace n to make the following a true proportion?

$$7{:}n = 9{:}20$$

According to the Principle of Proportions

$$9 \times n = 7 \times 20$$
$$9n = 140$$
$$n = \frac{140}{9}$$
$$n = 15\frac{5}{9}$$

EXERCISE 77

In each of the following, what number should replace n *to make each a true proportion?*

1. $n{:}5 = 6{:}10$
2. $n{:}4 = 12{:}8$
3. $3{:}n = 9{:}36$
4. $5{:}8 = 35{:}n$
5. $6{:}14 = n{:}7$
6. $17{:}n = 6{:}8$
7. $9{:}15 = 12{:}n$
8. $7{:}n = 11{:}18$
9. $12{:}28 = n{:}14$
10. $15{:}35 = 4{:}n$

Proportions are often useful in solving certain types of problems.

EXAMPLE: If 12 sport shirts cost $54, how much will 15 sport shirts cost at the same rate?

The ratio $\frac{54}{12}$ or 54:12 tells us how much each sport shirt costs. If we let n represent the cost of 15 sport shirts, then the ratio $n/15$ or $n{:}15$ also tells us how much each sport shirt costs. Since these ratios are equal we have

$$54{:}12 = n{:}15$$

According to the Principle of Proportions, we have

$$12 \times n = 54 \times 15$$
$$12n = 810$$
$$n = \frac{810}{12}$$
$$n = 67\tfrac{1}{2}$$

Thus, the 15 sport shirts cost $67.50.

EXERCISE 78

1. If a dealer buys 24 pairs of shoes for $300, how much does he pay for a shipment of 36 pairs of shoes at the same rate?
2. If a carpenter's helper earns $704 for 8 days of work how much does he earn for 11 days of work at the same rate of pay?
3. If ballpoint pens sell for 3 for 65 cents how many pens may be bought for $9.75?
4. A motorist paid $11.88 for 8 gallons of gasoline. How much would she pay for 14 gallons of gasoline at the same rate?
5. A school pays $116.80 for a set of 32 textbooks. How much did the school pay for a set of 47 textbooks at the same rate?
6. A major league baseball player gets 81 hits in 96 games. How many hits will this baseball player get in 160 games if he continues to hit at the same rate?
7. A motorist uses 34 gallons of gasoline in traveling 629 miles. On another trip, he uses 42 gallons of gasoline at the same rate of use. How many miles did the second trip cover?
8. At a special sale, 392 TV sets were sold during the first $3\tfrac{1}{2}$ hours. How many sets were sold during the first $5\tfrac{1}{2}$ hours at the same rate?

Scales and Scale Drawing

Before a building is constructed, a plan is drawn on paper. On this plan each measurement in the building is reduced in size. For example, the length of a 30-foot hallway might be represented by a line 2 inches long. On the other hand, it is sometimes necessary to enlarge the drawing of an object. For example, in a dictionary the drawing of an ant might be 5 times the size of an ant. This process is called drawing to scale. The reduced or enlarged drawing is called a *scale drawing*.

A scale used on a drawing may be indicated in several ways.

EXAMPLES:

(a) $1'' = 5'$
means that every inch on the drawing represents 5 feet in actual size.
(b) $\frac{1}{20}$ means that every measurement on the drawing is equal to $\frac{1}{20}$ of the actual size.
(c) $1{:}15$ means that every measurement on the drawing is equal to $\frac{1}{15}$ of the actual size.

EXAMPLE: Using a scale of $\frac{1}{4}$ in. = 1 ft., how long is a line representing a distance of 16 ft.?

SOLUTION: Establish a proportion:

$$\frac{\frac{1}{4}\ in}{1\ ft} = \frac{n\ in}{16\ ft}$$

Cross multiply:

$$1 \times n = \frac{1}{4} \times 16 = 4$$

So a line 4 inches long represents a length of 16 feet.

EXAMPLE: On a scale drawing $\frac{1}{8}'' = 60$ miles. What is the distance represented by a line $2\frac{1}{4}''$ long?

SOLUTION: Establish a proportion:

$$\frac{\frac{1}{8}\ in}{60\ mi} = \frac{2\frac{1}{4}\ in}{n\ mi}$$

Cross multiply:

$$\frac{1}{8} \times n = 2\frac{1}{4} \times 60$$

$$\frac{1}{8} \times n = 135$$

$$n = 1080$$

So a line $2\frac{1}{4}$ inches long represents a length of 1080 miles.

PRACTICE TEST 24

1. The scale of miles on a certain map is 1 inch = 40 miles. The distance between two cities that are $3\frac{1}{4}$ inches apart on the map is:

   (A) 120 miles   (B) $12\frac{4}{13}$ miles
   (C) 130 miles   (D) 170 miles
   (E) none of these

2. A map is drawn to a scale of 12 miles = 1 inch. The distance represented by $5\frac{3}{4}$ inches is:

   (A) 60 miles   (B) 68 miles
   (C) $2\frac{2}{23}$ miles   (D) 69 miles
   (E) none of these

3. On a certain house plan a line 5 inches long represents 20 feet. The number of inches representing 30 feet is:

   (A) 4   (B) $7\frac{1}{2}$ (C) 6   (D) $3\frac{1}{3}$
   (E) none of these

4. The picture of a moth in a dictionary is drawn to the scale 1:6. If the length of the moth in the picture is $\frac{3}{8}''$ the actual length of the moth in inches is:

   (A) $2''$ (B) $2\frac{1}{8}''$ (C) $1\frac{7}{8}''$ (D) $2\frac{1}{2}''$
   (E) none of these

5. The dimensions of a living room are 14' by 22'. In drawing this room to scale the scale $\frac{1}{16}$ is used. The length of the room on the scale drawing is:

   (A) $1\frac{3}{8}''$ (B) $1\frac{1}{4}''$ (C) $\frac{5}{8}''$ (D) $1\frac{7}{8}''$
   (E) none of these

6. The scale used on a map is 1 inch = 9 feet. This scale expressed as a ratio is:

   (A) 1:9   (B) 1:27   (C) 1:108   (D) 12:1
   (E) none of these

7. The ratio used in making the scale drawing of a machine part is 1:24. The length of the part is 6 feet. The number of inches required to show this length is:

   (A) 4   (B) 6   (C) $2\frac{1}{2}$ (D) 3
   (E) none of these

8. In printing the picture of a gnat the scale $\frac{32}{5}$ is used. If the picture is $\frac{1}{4}''$ long the actual length of the gnat is:

   (A) $1\frac{3}{5}''$ (B) $\frac{5}{128}''$ (C) $6\frac{2}{5}''$ (D) $\frac{1}{24}''$
   (E) none of these

9. The scale used on a drawing is 1:15. This scale may be expressed as:

   (A) $1'' = 15$ feet   (B) 1 ft. = 54 miles
   (C) $\frac{1}{2}'' = 25$ miles   (D) $\frac{1}{4}'' = 6$ miles
   (E) none of these

10. Two cities are 216 miles apart. The distance between them on the map is $4\frac{1}{2}$ inches. The scale used on this map is:

    (A) $1'' = 48$ miles   (B) $1'' = 54$ miles
    (C) $\frac{1}{2}'' = 25$ miles   (D) $\frac{1}{4}'' = 6$ miles
    (E) none of these

PRACTICE TEST 25

1. The scale of miles on a certain map is 1 inch = 36 miles. The distance between two cities that are $2\frac{3}{4}$ inches apart on the map is:

   (A) 100 miles (B) 96 miles (C) 99 miles
   (D) 98 miles   (E) none of these

2. A map is drawn to a scale of 32 miles = 1 inch. The distance represented by $6\frac{5}{8}$ inches is:

   (A) 202 miles   (B) 180 miles
   (C) 192 miles   (D) 212 miles
   (E) none of these

3. On a blueprint a line 4 inches long represents 32 feet. The number of inches representing 80 feet is:

(A) $6\frac{1}{2}$ (B) 8   (C) 12   (D) 16
(E) none of these

4. The picture of a bookcase in a catalogue is drawn to the scale 1:18. If the length of the bookcase in the picture is $1\frac{1}{2}''$, the actual length of the bookcase is:

(A) 2 ft.   (B) $2\frac{1}{4}$ ft.   (C) 20 in.
(D) 30 in.   (E) none of these

5. The dimensions of a garage are 20′ × 30′. In drawing this garage to scale the scale $\frac{1}{24}$ is used. The length of the garage on the scale drawing is:

(A) $1\frac{1}{6}'$ (B) $1\frac{1}{8}'$ (C) $1\frac{1}{2}'$ (D) $1\frac{1}{4}'$
(E) none of these

6. The scale used on a map is 1 inch = 8 feet. This scale expressed as a ratio is:

(A) 1:96   (B) 1:8   (C) 1:32   (D) 1:12
(E) none of these

7. The ratio used in making the scale drawing of a steel beam is 1:36. The length of the beam is 15 feet. The number of inches required to show this length is:

(A) 36   (B) 10   (C) 5   (D) 8
(E) none of these

8. In enlarging a picture the scale used is $\frac{8}{3}$. If the original picture is 9″ long, the length of the enlargement is:

(A) $1\frac{1}{2}'$ (B) 2′   (C) 3′   (D) 8′
(E) none of these

9. The scale used on a blueprint is 1:48. This scale may be expressed as:

(A) 1″ = 48 ft.   (B) 1 ft. = 4 ft.
(C) 1″ = 16″   (D) 1″ = 4 ft.
(E) none of these

10. Two cities are 420 miles apart. The distance between them on a map is $1\frac{3}{4}$ inches. The scale used on this map is:

(A) 1″ = 735 miles   (B) 1″ = 250 miles
(C) 1″ = 240 miles   (D) 1″ = 300 miles
(E) none of these

Answers to All Exercises and Practice Tests

EXERCISES

EXERCISE 1

1. 4,006   3. 3,998   5. 4,457   7. 9,970
2. 3,135   4. 3,861   6. 3,838   8. 1,819

EXERCISE 2

1. 3,642   5. 3,975   8. 3,485
2. 3,871   6. 4,356   9. 10,272
3. 5,429   7. 5,203   10. 5,031
4. 3,685

EXERCISE 3

1. 4,647   3. 4,265   5. 3,875   7. 7,702
2. 4,464   4. 3,562   6. 3,813   8. 6,297

EXERCISE 4

1. 42,253   6. 60,078   11. 20,773
2. 27,851   7. 77,367   12. 73,187
3. 52,372   8. 23,598   13. 10,408
4. 34,846   9. 56,491   14. 1,943
5. 32,967   10. 78,351   15. 39,999

EXERCISE 5

1. 31,215   11. 47,499   21. 49,981
2. 61,648   12. 17,787   22. 53,449
3. 23,371   13. 43,459   23. 6,809
4. 14,748   14. 4,381   24. 82,275
5. 46,721   15. 44,299   25. 26,617
6. 78,272   16. 79,099   26. 38,363
7. 2,809   17. 70,205   27. 48,867
8. 26,307   18. 37,328   28. 48,314
9. 86,136   19. 35,411   29. 8,053
10. 22,533   20. 61,720   30. 7,428

EXERCISE 6

1. 31,313   6. 35,626   11. 20,164
2. 22,777   7. 23,514   12. 1,244
3. 48,221   8. 7,737   13. 2,997
4. 32,349   9. 13,805   14. 26,446
5. 8,507   10. 3,134   15. 63,108

EXERCISE 7

1. 40,901   5. 252,488   9. 516,168
2. 48,224   6. 237,650   10. 839,696
3. 51,336   7. 496,674   11. 2,702,040
4. 18,072   8. 439,600   12. 1,343,730

EXERCISE 8

1. 34,215   9. 110,789   17. 353,772
2. 52,227   10. 662,324   18. 1,062,490
3. 57,968   11. 290,871   19. 2,485,893
4. 35,686   12. 228,342   20. 3,617,972
5. 24,032   13. 182,952   21. 6,124,760
6. 7,242   14. 739,394   22. 3,042,424
7. 11,550   15. 211,102   23. 819,830
8. 10,410   16. 698,152   24. 4,851,924

EXERCISE 9

1. 56,106   5. 227,331   9. 1,089,536
2. 30,222   6. 298,450   10. 1,530,838
3. 20,072   7. 235,422   11. 1,748,120
4. 14,371   8. 491,760   12. 2,967,580

EXERCISE 10

1. 1,457   5. 343   9. 312   13. 467
2. 878   6. 200R11   10. 405R5   14. 238R3
3. 308   7. 97   11. 670R8   15. 704R34
4. 770R3   8. $314\frac{3}{29}$ 12. $593\frac{4}{87}$ 16. 395

EXERCISE 11

1. 579   13. 1,711R1   25. 173R19
2. 1,464   14. 130R7   26. 207R8
3. 911R1   15. 548R6   27. 736
4. 252   16. 300R3   28. 809
5. 579R3   17. 48   29. 612
6. 567   18. 37   30. 792
7. 960R1   19. 87   31. 836R26
8. 389R1   20. 83   32. 697R41
9. 1,148R6   21. 58R7   33. 697R103
10. 515R4   22. 304R16   34. 609R26
11. 1,684R4   23. 69R31   35. 752
12. 899R1   24. 78R5   36. 603

EXERCISE 12

1. 594
2. 671
3. 463R6
4. 1,175R3
5. 247
6. 175R5
7. 98
8. 87R46
9. 357
10. 411R24
11. 739R31
12. 947R5
13. 319
14. 537R87
15. 602R42
16. 465

EXERCISE 13

1. a. 8　　b. $\frac{3}{8}$　　c. $\frac{2}{8}, \frac{1}{4}$　　d. $\frac{1}{8}$
2. a. 12　　b. $\frac{1}{12}$　　c. $\frac{3}{12}, \frac{1}{4}$　　d. $\frac{4}{12}, \frac{1}{3}$
3. c. $\frac{1}{3}$
4. a. $\frac{5}{12}$　　b. $\frac{1}{4}$　　c. $\frac{5}{24}$　　d. $\frac{1}{8}$
5. John Andrews— $\frac{5}{9}$
　 Philip Verone— $\frac{1}{3}$
　 Louis Sellers— $\frac{1}{9}$
6. $1\frac{1}{3}$
7. $1\frac{2}{3}$
8. $2\frac{1}{4}$
9. a. 9　　b. $\frac{3}{9}, \frac{1}{3}$　　c. $\frac{6}{9}, \frac{2}{3}$　　d. $\frac{5}{9}$

EXERCISE 14

1. $\frac{1}{3}$
2. $\frac{2}{5}$
3. $\frac{3}{8}$
4. $\frac{3}{4}$
5. $\frac{3}{5}$
6. $\frac{8}{9}$
7. $\frac{3}{4}$
8. $\frac{4}{7}$
9. $\frac{3}{4}$
10. $\frac{7}{9}$
11. $\frac{4}{3}$
12. $\frac{19}{8}$
13. $\frac{27}{7}$
14. $\frac{23}{5}$
15. $\frac{49}{9}$
16. $\frac{31}{4}$
17. $1\frac{1}{4}$
18. $2\frac{1}{3}$
19. $2\frac{5}{6}$
20. $2\frac{1}{3}$
21. $3\frac{4}{9}$
22. $2\frac{5}{8}$

EXERCISE 15

1. $\frac{1}{2}$
2. $\frac{4}{5}$
3. $\frac{2}{3}$
4. $\frac{2}{3}$
5. $\frac{1}{2}$
6. $\frac{5}{7}$
7. $\frac{3}{4}$
8. $\frac{5}{6}$
9. $\frac{3}{5}$
10. $\frac{7}{8}$
11. $\frac{11}{16}$
12. $\frac{2}{5}$
13. $\frac{8}{9}$
14. $\frac{4}{7}$
15. $\frac{2}{3}$
16. $\frac{7}{11}$
17. $\frac{4}{9}$
18. $\frac{9}{10}$
19. $\frac{5}{7}$
20. $\frac{5}{7}$

1. $\frac{7}{4}$
2. $\frac{17}{6}$
3. $\frac{23}{7}$
4. $\frac{14}{5}$
5. $\frac{38}{9}$
6. $\frac{8}{7}$
7. $\frac{21}{8}$
8. $\frac{19}{3}$
9. $\frac{47}{6}$
10. $\frac{31}{8}$
11. $\frac{47}{11}$
12. $\frac{67}{12}$
13. $\frac{25}{9}$
14. $\frac{3}{2}$
15. $\frac{45}{7}$

EXERCISE 16

1. $\frac{1}{2}$
2. $\frac{1}{3}$
3. $\frac{5}{6}$
4. $\frac{7}{8}$
5. $\frac{4}{5}$
6. $\frac{5}{9}$
7. $\frac{3}{7}$
8. $\frac{5}{8}$
9. $\frac{7}{8}$
10. $\frac{5}{7}$
11. $\frac{5}{4}$
12. $\frac{17}{6}$
13. $\frac{31}{8}$
14. $\frac{23}{9}$
15. $\frac{11}{6}$
16. $\frac{19}{7}$
17. $3\frac{1}{6}$
18. $2\frac{1}{4}$
19. $1\frac{2}{9}$
20. $2\frac{2}{3}$
21. $7\frac{1}{3}$
22. $2\frac{1}{12}$

EXERCISE 17

1. $\frac{3}{6}$
2. $\frac{4}{12}$
3. $\frac{6}{8}$
4. $\frac{6}{15}$
5. $\frac{21}{24}$
6. $\frac{4}{16}$
7. $\frac{15}{36}$
8. $\frac{12}{20}$
9. $\frac{8}{28}$
10. $\frac{10}{12}$
11. $\frac{16}{24}$
12. $\frac{10}{18}$
13. $\frac{21}{27}$
14. $\frac{8}{40}$
15. $\frac{5}{15}$
16. $\frac{15}{21}$
17. $\frac{28}{48}$.
18. $\frac{6}{9}$
19. $\frac{18}{42}$
20. $\frac{24}{30}$

EXERCISE 18

1. $\frac{3}{4}$
2. $\frac{5}{6}$
3. $\frac{7}{12}$
4. $\frac{5}{6}$
5. $\frac{1}{2}$
6. $\frac{11}{12}$
7. $1\frac{4}{15}$
8. $1\frac{7}{12}$
9. $\frac{19}{24}$
10. $1\frac{1}{2}$
11. $6\frac{1}{3}$
12. $10\frac{8}{15}$
13. $6\frac{1}{28}$
14. $1\frac{1}{12}$
15. $4\frac{17}{30}$
16. $7\frac{7}{16}$
17. $12\frac{11}{24}$
18. $12\frac{3}{5}$

EXERCISE 19

1. $\frac{2}{3}$
2. $\frac{7}{12}$
3. $\frac{11}{12}$
4. $\frac{5}{8}$
5. $\frac{23}{24}$
6. $\frac{7}{9}$
7. $\frac{13}{24}$
8. $\frac{3}{4}$
9. $\frac{23}{36}$
10. $\frac{3}{10}$
11. $\frac{23}{24}$
12. $\frac{13}{18}$
13. $1\frac{1}{4}$
14. $\frac{35}{36}$
15. $\frac{13}{14}$
16. $\frac{7}{20}$
17. $1\frac{17}{24}$
18. $1\frac{2}{15}$
19. $1\frac{7}{30}$
20. $1\frac{7}{24}$
21. $3\frac{2}{9}$
22. $9\frac{7}{10}$
23. $7\frac{2}{3}$
24. $7\frac{5}{6}$
25. $3\frac{19}{36}$
26. $10\frac{1}{9}$
27. $10\frac{5}{24}$
28. $8\frac{7}{20}$
29. $6\frac{4}{5}$
30. $7\frac{13}{14}$
31. $8\frac{2}{15}$
32. $8\frac{7}{36}$
33. $\frac{7}{8}$
34. $\frac{17}{18}$
35. $1\frac{11}{12}$
36. $1\frac{13}{24}$
37. $1\frac{19}{36}$
38. $6\frac{1}{12}$
39. $13\frac{29}{30}$
40. $12\frac{7}{18}$
41. $15\frac{47}{60}$
42. $14\frac{41}{48}$

EXERCISE 20

1. $\frac{5}{6}$ 6. $\frac{17}{18}$ 11. $5\frac{7}{12}$ 16. $7\frac{11}{12}$

2. $\frac{5}{8}$ 7. $1\frac{5}{12}$ 12. $8\frac{3}{28}$ 17. $10\frac{11}{18}$

3. $\frac{11}{12}$ 8. $1\frac{1}{3}$ 13. $10\frac{2}{15}$ 18. $11\frac{17}{20}$

4. $\frac{7}{8}$ 9. $1\frac{7}{36}$ 14. $\frac{3}{4}$

5. $\frac{9}{10}$ 10. $1\frac{9}{10}$ 15. $1\frac{7}{8}$

EXERCISE 21

1. $\frac{3}{5}$ 5. $\frac{1}{24}$ 9. $3\frac{11}{24}$ 13. $\frac{7}{12}$

2. $\frac{1}{2}$ 6. $\frac{5}{24}$ 10. $4\frac{13}{20}$ 14. $4\frac{5}{6}$

3. $\frac{5}{12}$ 7. $3\frac{5}{6}$ 11. $5\frac{3}{4}$ 15. $\frac{23}{36}$

4. $\frac{11}{18}$ 8. $2\frac{1}{4}$ 12. $5\frac{2}{5}$ 16. $5\frac{9}{16}$

EXERCISE 22

1. $\frac{1}{3}$ 10. $\frac{7}{12}$ 19. $5\frac{17}{20}$ 28. $\frac{16}{21}$

2. $\frac{5}{9}$ 11. $\frac{4}{9}$ 20. $1\frac{7}{12}$ 29. $1\frac{7}{12}$

3. $\frac{2}{3}$ 12. $\frac{2}{15}$ 21. $7\frac{3}{7}$ 30. $1\frac{17}{18}$

4. $\frac{1}{4}$ 13. $\frac{5}{14}$ 22. $\frac{5}{8}$ 31. $\frac{9}{16}$

5. $\frac{1}{2}$ 14. $\frac{17}{36}$ 23. $\frac{5}{6}$ 32. $1\frac{14}{15}$

6. $\frac{5}{8}$ 15. $6\frac{2}{3}$ 24. $\frac{7}{20}$ 33. $3\frac{17}{24}$

7. $\frac{1}{12}$ 16. $2\frac{2}{5}$ 25. $3\frac{13}{18}$ 34. $\frac{7}{24}$

8. $\frac{3}{10}$ 17. $6\frac{3}{4}$ 26. $1\frac{11}{24}$ 35. $4\frac{9}{14}$

9. $\frac{1}{6}$ 18. $4\frac{2}{3}$ 27. $\frac{25}{36}$

EXERCISE 23

1. $\frac{4}{7}$ 5. $\frac{1}{2}$ 9. $2\frac{3}{8}$ 13. $5\frac{1}{3}$

2. $\frac{3}{5}$ 6. $\frac{1}{12}$ 10. $4\frac{1}{2}$ 14. $1\frac{13}{14}$

3. $\frac{1}{6}$ 7. $\frac{11}{24}$ 11. $5\frac{11}{20}$ 15. $\frac{11}{36}$

4. $\frac{5}{8}$ 8. $4\frac{7}{8}$ 12. $\frac{7}{8}$ 16. $4\frac{5}{12}$

EXERCISE 24

1. Equal   6. Unequal   11. Equal
2. Equal   7. Equal   12. Unequal
3. Unequal   8. Unequal   13. Unequal
4. Unequal   9. Equal   14. Equal
5. Equal   10. Equal   15. Unequal

EXERCISE 25

1. $\frac{1}{3}$ larger   14. $\frac{13}{29}$ larger

2. $\frac{4}{9}$ larger   15. $\frac{14}{19}$ larger

3. $\frac{6}{11}$ larger   16. $\frac{3}{8} < \frac{2}{5} < \frac{3}{4}$

4. $\frac{9}{16}$ larger   17. $\frac{11}{20} < \frac{3}{5} < \frac{5}{8}$

5. $\frac{5}{6}$ larger   18. $\frac{5}{9} < \frac{7}{12} < \frac{5}{6}$

6. $\frac{5}{13}$ larger   19. $\frac{5}{8} < \frac{2}{3} < \frac{17}{24}$

7. $\frac{9}{14}$ larger   20. $\frac{2}{9} < \frac{4}{11} < \frac{3}{8}$

8. $\frac{8}{9}$ larger   21. $\frac{5}{8} < \frac{7}{9} < \frac{6}{7}$

9. $\frac{12}{23}$ larger   22. $\frac{12}{17} < \frac{8}{11} < \frac{13}{16}$

10. $\frac{16}{25}$ larger   23. $\frac{20}{41} < \frac{11}{21} < \frac{10}{19}$

11. $\frac{7}{18}$ larger   24. $\frac{6}{17} < \frac{11}{31} < \frac{8}{19}$

12. $\frac{9}{31}$ larger   25. $\frac{9}{32} < \frac{8}{27} < \frac{7}{23}$

13. $\frac{9}{14}$ larger

EXERCISE 26

1. $\frac{3}{20}$ 8. $\frac{2}{9}$ 15. 8   22. $12\frac{1}{2}$

2. $\frac{5}{18}$ 9. 2   16. $3\frac{1}{3}$ 23. $4\frac{1}{2}$

3. $\frac{3}{28}$ 10. 12   17. 63   24. $3\frac{1}{2}$

4. $\frac{3}{8}$ 11. $9\frac{1}{3}$ 18. 45   25. $\frac{5}{14}$

5. $\frac{2}{5}$ 12. 44   19. $2\frac{3}{4}$ 26. $\frac{5}{9}$

6. $\frac{3}{5}$ 13. $\frac{3}{4}$ 20. $4\frac{1}{6}$ 27. $18\frac{2}{3}$

7. $\frac{1}{6}$ 14. $6\frac{2}{3}$ 21. 10

EXERCISE 27

1. $\frac{2}{21}$ 15. $\frac{1}{6}$ 29. $3\frac{6}{7}$ 42. $8\frac{2}{5}$

2. $\frac{3}{10}$ 16. $\frac{9}{14}$ 30. 3   43. 42

3. $\frac{21}{40}$ 17. 8   31. $1\frac{2}{3}$ 44. $3\frac{1}{2}$

4. $\frac{3}{20}$ 18. 8   32. $\frac{7}{8}$ 45. 6

5. $\frac{5}{8}$ 19. 8   33. 30   46. $\frac{1}{30}$

6. $\frac{2}{5}$ 20. 12   34. $40\frac{1}{2}$ 47. 99

7. $\frac{3}{14}$ 21. $4\frac{1}{2}$ 35. 32   48. 30

8. $\frac{3}{4}$ 22. 9   36. 63   49. $16\frac{8}{15}$

9. $\frac{2}{5}$ 23. $23\frac{1}{3}$ 37. $22\frac{1}{2}$ 50. $\frac{5}{63}$

10. $\frac{1}{6}$ 24. $31\frac{1}{2}$ 38. 63   51. $2\frac{2}{8}$

11. $\frac{1}{8}$ 25. $17\frac{1}{2}$ 39. $12\frac{4}{7}$ 52. 48

12. $\frac{5}{16}$ 26. $16\frac{2}{3}$ 40. $25\frac{1}{2}$ 53. 15

13. $\frac{2}{5}$ 27. $3\frac{3}{7}$ 41. 3   54. $10\frac{2}{3}$

14. $\frac{1}{18}$ 28. $4\frac{1}{6}$

EXERCISE 28

1. $\frac{2}{15}$ 8. $\frac{1}{6}$ 15. 20   22. 6
2. $\frac{5}{21}$ 9. 5   16. $5\frac{1}{3}$ 23. $15\frac{5}{48}$
3. $\frac{3}{10}$ 10. 15   17. 63   24. $6\frac{5}{12}$
4. $\frac{1}{6}$ 11. $7\frac{1}{2}$ 18. 28   25. $\frac{12}{25}$
5. $\frac{1}{6}$ 12. $12\frac{1}{2}$ 19. $\frac{7}{8}$ 26. $\frac{5}{42}$
6. $\frac{7}{36}$ 13. 10   20. 4   27. 6
7. $\frac{3}{11}$ 14. 21   21. $4\frac{1}{6}$ 28. 20

EXERCISE 29

1. $\frac{3}{5}$ 6. $\frac{2}{21}$ 11. $\frac{2}{9}$ 16. $6\frac{2}{3}$
2. $\frac{6}{7}$ 7. 12   12. $\frac{1}{8}$ 17. $1\frac{1}{2}$
3. $\frac{3}{8}$ 8. 18   13. $6\frac{1}{4}$ 18. 8
4. $1\frac{1}{10}$ 9. 30   14. 2   19. $2\frac{2}{3}$
5. $1\frac{1}{2}$ 10. $\frac{1}{24}$ 15. $1\frac{4}{5}$ 20. $2\frac{7}{10}$

EXERCISE 30

1. $1\frac{1}{2}$ 11. $1\frac{2}{9}$ 21. 24   31. 8
2. $\frac{4}{5}$ 12. $\frac{1}{8}$ 22. $\frac{1}{24}$ 32. 28
3. $\frac{5}{6}$ 13. $\frac{3}{8}$ 23. $\frac{1}{18}$ 33. $2\frac{1}{10}$
4. $1\frac{7}{9}$ 14. $\frac{2}{7}$ 24. $\frac{2}{75}$ 34. $\frac{3}{4}$
5. $\frac{2}{3}$ 15. 24   25. $\frac{2}{7}$ 35. $1\frac{5}{16}$
6. $1\frac{7}{18}$ 16. 30   26. $\frac{3}{8}$ 36. $7\frac{1}{2}$
7. $1\frac{1}{3}$ 17. 35   27. $\frac{1}{5}$ 37. $6\frac{1}{2}$
8. $\frac{6}{7}$ 18. 54   28. $\frac{4}{27}$ 38. $\frac{7}{10}$
9. $1\frac{1}{5}$ 19. 44   29. 4   39. $1\frac{1}{9}$
10. $\frac{5}{8}$ 20. $20\frac{1}{4}$ 30. 15   40. $1\frac{4}{5}$

EXERCISE 31

1. $\frac{3}{4}$ 6. $\frac{5}{14}$ 11. $\frac{2}{25}$ 16. $5\frac{5}{7}$
2. $1\frac{1}{4}$ 7. 27   12. $\frac{1}{6}$ 17. $1\frac{1}{2}$
3. $\frac{27}{50}$ 8. 27   13. $4\frac{2}{3}$ 18. $3\frac{1}{3}$
4. $\frac{3}{4}$ 9. $17\frac{1}{2}$ 14. 10   19. $1\frac{1}{2}$
5. $\frac{2}{3}$ 10. $\frac{1}{16}$ 15. 4   20. $3\frac{1}{8}$

EXERCISE 32

1. 6   2. $\frac{17}{30}$ 3. $1\frac{1}{14}$ 4. $\frac{11}{14}$

EXERCISE 33

1. 0.5   5. 0.67, 0.653, 0.619
2. 0.31   6. 0.721, 0.716, 0.712
3. 0.98   7. 0.237, 0.218, 0.2
4. 0.357   8. 0.467, 0.4102, 0.4009

EXERCISE 34

1. (a) 0.3 (b) 0.7 (c) 0.1 (d) 0.9 (e) 0.5
   (f) 0.7 (g) 0.9 (h) 0.4 (i) 0.9 (j) 0.6
2. (a) 0.16 (b) 0.04 (c) 0.69 (d) 0.70
   (e) 0.85
3. (a) 0.658 (b) 0.403 (c) 0.818 (d) 0.095
   (e) 0.544
4. 0.416, 0.309, 0.295
5. 0.902, 0.875, 0.857
6. 0.713, 0.7, 0.605
7. 0.516, 0.492, 0.489
8. 0.41, 0.3, 0.128
9. 0.712, 0.7, 0.57
10. 0.914, 0.832, 0.823
11. 0.123, 0.096, 0.088

EXERCISE 35

1. 0.5   5. 0.47, 0.461, 0.418
2. 0.21   6. 0.391, 0.385, 0.319
3. 0.77   7. 0.602, 0.6, 0.59
4. 0.851   8. 0.7301, 0.7103, 0.7031

EXERCISE 36

1. 1.56   5. 123.43   9. 27.078
2. 15.37   6. 117.51   10. 206.542
3. 101.7   7. 0.34   11. 1.59
4. 200.228   8. 1.59   12. 32.743

EXERCISE 37

1. 2.29   13. 1,065.68   24. 0.19
2. 2.93   14. 1,084.66   25. 3.15
3. 19.34   15. 28.6   26. 4.55
4. 22.47   16. 21.2   27. 3.92
5. 154   17. 28.8   28. 2.84
6. 167.26   18. 26.35   29. 36.24
7. 195.21   19. 336.98   30. 36.86
8. 498.6   20. 231.57   31. 47.456
9. 800.81   21. 0.33   32. 36.892
10. 137.435   22. 0.34   33. 31.448
11. 140.029   23. 0.22   34. 772.48
12. 114.295

EXERCISE 38

1. 1.57	5. 129	9. 58.785
2. 20.9	6. 172.68	10. 480.736
3. 106.3	7. 0.24	11. 1.77
4. 455.373	8. 4.44	12. 57.512

EXERCISE 39

1. 4.8	6. 39.95	11. 326.34
2. 6.3	7. 127.4	12. 3.45774
3. 14.8	8. 537.2	13. 4.90818
4. 2.32	9. 7.52	14. 0.487084
5. 2.01	10. 22.42	15. 0.18352

EXERCISE 40

1. 4.8	14. 295.2	27. 361.14
2. 6.3	15. 417.1	28. 106.912
3. 3.5	16. 168	29. 132.516
4. 3.2	17. 462.3	30. 312.823
5. 2.7	18. 153.7	31. 5.03568
6. 2.1	19. 16.32	32. 2.90194
7. 0.96	20. 57.12	33. 4.361178
8. 17.94	21. 11.97	34. 1.681823
9. 22.78	22. 0.1537	35. 2.16918
10. 46.02	23. 0.3696	36. 0.273
11. 54.27	24. 108.08	37. 7.9365
12. 265.5	25. 462.76	38. 0.30973
13. 496.4	26. 222.5	

EXERCISE 41

1. 5.6	6. 28.88	11. 291.84
2. 5.4	7. 339.7	12. 293.664
3. 34.8	8. 753.3	13. 6.02883
4. 2.73	9. 20.72	14. 0.586404
5. 31.88	10. 32.43	15. 0.10368

EXERCISE 42

1. 4.8	6. 0.4	11. 11.91
2. 6.5	7. 189.9	12. 15.94
3. 17.6	8. 353.18	13. 15.73
4. 0.04	9. 0.35	14. 7.1
5. 83.4	10. 255.7	15. 0.33

EXERCISE 43

1. 3.63	13. 52.6	25. 40.8
2. 7.86	14. 121.7	26. 71.2
3. 8.56	15. 0.4	27. 25.8
4. 6.01	16. 0.2	28. 16.85
5. 7.7	17. 120.6	29. 22.77
6. 7	18. 114.5	30. 21.36
7. 5.2	19. 170.2	31. 12.9
8. 14.6	20. 513.31	32. 15.5
9. 1.1	21. 1417.6	33. 12.4
10. 0.07	22. 0.79	34. 0.29
11. 0.13	23. 1.46	35. 0.82
12. 0.30	24. 32.6	

EXERCISE 44

1. 5.6	6. 0.5	11. 5.09
2. 6.2	7. 169.8	12. 349.48
3. 12.6	8. 453.26	13. 24.28
4. 0.04	9. 0.71	14. 6.7
5. 91.4	10. 78.6	15. 0.29

EXERCISE 45

1. 67	11. 15	21. 37.2
2. 580	12. 34,000	22. 0.784
3. 0.5	13. 2,690	23. 0.0372
4. 7,360	14. 85,000	24. 0.00016
5. 4.82	15. 3,140	25. 6.437
6. 320	16. 8.5	26. 9
7. 72.5	17. 0.069	27. 0.675
8. 35,600	18. 0.0043	28. 0.00407
9. 5.1	19. 6.872	29. 0.05862
10. 6,590	20. 0.04951	30. 0.000015

EXERCISE 46

1. 32	6. 0.35	11. 4.52
2. 580	7. 21.4	12. 28.3
3. 70	8. 605	13. 3,500
4. 6.8	9. 42.73	14. 68.05
5. 570	10. 2,850	15. 0.058

1. 620	6. 853.1	11. 127,500
2. 35,100	7. 0.039	12. 2
3. 1.2	8. 5.132	13. 6,500
4. 75,000	9. 400	14. 300.2
5. 15.72	10. 379	15. 2,710

1. 25,000
2. 6,480
3. 583,200
4. 1.6
5. 9.075
6. 21,700
7. 123
8. 15.34
9. 3,141.6
10. 62,500
11. 720
12. 0.35
13. 2,910
14. 50
15. 9,126

1. 5.8
2. 40
3. 37.5
4. 0.0625
5. 8.75
6. 12.5
7. 0.046
8. 25
9. 0.002
10. 7.5
11. 0.00035
12. 853.2
13. 6.37
14. 0.105
15. 578

1. 7.5
2. 0.645
3. 0.00032
4. 0.0873
5. 0.000058
6. 2.97
7. 35
8. 0.00167
9. 48.5
10. 0.0987
11. 0.005036
12. 0.904
13. 86.1
14. 0.0053
15. 0.6503

1. 5.3
2. 2.07
3. 0.00625
4. 0.000015
5. 0.952
6. 0.00314
7. 0.00067
8. 0.002975
9. 0.075
10. 0.125
11. 0.000025
12. 0.06572
13. 0.00875
14. 0.0000065
15. 0.000833

EXERCISE 47

1. 35
2. 6.9
3. 560
4. 3.89
5. 5,060
6. 46.3
7. 520
8. 6.3
9. 87,500
10. 7,340
11. 58,000
12. 18
13. 6,200
14. 3,870
15. 57,000
16. 9.7
17. 0.0035
18. 0.048
19. 0.06532
20. 5.28
21. 46.8
22. 0.583
23. 0.0697
24. 0.00018
25. 5.483
26. 0.315
27. 4
28. 0.00873
29. 0.04378
30. 0.000026

EXERCISE 48

1. $28.33
2. $208.24
3. $1,278.20
4. $278.44
5. $659.28
6. $65.84
7. $120.62
8. $758.53
9. $2,475.72
10. $2,487.86
11. $940.53
12. $11,170.36
13. $120.46
14. $56.09
15. $1,016
16. $305

EXERCISE 49

1. $172.89
2. $808.75
3. $2,003.40
4. $856.71
5. $795.45
6. $1,569.60
7. $687.98
8. $587.58

1. $1.68
2. $4.82
3. $36.73
4. $20.42
5. $373.85
6. $522.29
7. $650.84
8. $1,712.85

1. $4,550.21
2. $4,057.52
3. $2,446.73
4. $2,523.24
5. $1,189
6. $1,132.50
7. $33,419.10
8. $20,747.38

1. $103.42
2. $224.21
3. $216.51
4. $35.03
5. $115
6. $98
7. $76
8. $203

EXERCISE 50

1. $49.11
2. $333.56
3. $1,304.11
4. $356.23
5. $340.28
6. $168.05
7. $176.63
8. $1,744.38
9. $3,522.24
10. $3,735.56
11. $1,981.32
12. $8,878.93
13. $77.13
14. $119.38
15. $209
16. $267

EXERCISE 51

1. 0.25
2. 0.6
3. 0.83
4. 0.38
5. 0.29
6. 0.78
7. 2.42
8. 0.72
9. 0.64
10. 0.47
11. 0.36
12. 3.35
13. $\frac{7}{10}$
14. $\frac{1}{25}$
15. $\frac{9}{20}$
16. $2\frac{2}{5}$
17. $\frac{5}{8}$
18. $\frac{49}{200}$
19. $1\frac{1}{3}$
20. $\frac{1}{8}$
21. $\frac{1}{12}$
22. $\frac{1}{125}$
23. $5\frac{3}{8}$
24. $2\frac{5}{6}$

EXERCISE 52

1. 0.5
2. 0.2
3. 0.63
4. 0.33
5. 0.17
6. 0.43
7. 0.22
8. 0.7
9. 0.27
10. 3.13
11. 0.45
12. 0.27
13. 0.83
14. 2.08
15. 0.75
16. 0.21
17. 0.47
18. 0.86
19. 0.28
20. 0.16

1. $\frac{3}{10}$
2. $\frac{9}{100}$
3. $\frac{11}{100}$
4. $\frac{13}{20}$
5. $3\frac{4}{5}$
6. $\frac{11}{40}$
7. $\frac{5}{6}$
8. $\frac{9}{250}$
9. $2\frac{1}{8}$
10. $\frac{12}{25}$
11. $1\frac{1}{3}$
12. $\frac{3}{8}$
13. $2\frac{1}{4}$
14. $2\frac{1}{6}$
15. $3\frac{18}{25}$
16. $\frac{5}{8}$
17. $4\frac{4}{5}$
18. $2\frac{8}{25}$
19. $2\frac{2}{3}$
20. $5\frac{17}{20}$

EXERCISE 53

1. 0.4
2. 0.75
3. 0.88
4. 0.17
5. 0.56
6. 3.58
7. 0.89
8. 0.55
9. 1.53
10. 0.21
11. 2.24
12. 0.73
13. $\frac{9}{10}$
14. $\frac{3}{50}$
15. $\frac{17}{20}$
16. $3\frac{4}{5}$
17. $\frac{3}{8}$
18. $3\frac{97}{200}$
19. $2\frac{2}{3}$
20. $\frac{5}{12}$
21. $\frac{9}{500}$
22. $3\frac{5}{8}$
23. $1\frac{1}{6}$
24. $6\frac{16}{25}$

EXERCISE 54

1. 1.06
2. 0.965
3. 2.52
4. 5.48
5. 2.17
6. 4
7. 7.5
8. 43.2
9. $\frac{17}{30}$
10. $1\frac{5}{18}$
11. $5\frac{9}{10}$
12. $3\frac{1}{6}$
13. $\frac{2}{25}$
14. $28\frac{1}{2}$
15. $33\frac{1}{3}$
16. $33\frac{1}{3}$

EXERCISE 55

1. 1.29
2. 2.54
3. 5.28
4. 3.17
5. 6.69
6. 2.75
7. 6.51
8. 4.24
9. 4
10. 48
11. 14.1
12. $27\frac{1}{2}$
13. 25
14. 75
15. 15
16. 24

1. $1\frac{7}{16}$
2. $1\frac{5}{24}$
3. $\frac{11}{15}$
4. $1\frac{19}{60}$
5. $8\frac{3}{4}$
6. $4\frac{3}{10}$
7. $5\frac{3}{4}$
8. $2\frac{1}{2}$
9. $\frac{7}{25}$
10. $\frac{2}{7}$
11. $10\frac{2}{3}$
12. $33\frac{3}{4}$
13. $33\frac{1}{3}$
14. 50
15. $19\frac{1}{5}$
16. 25

EXERCISE 56

1. 0.63
2. 0.45
3. 5.98
4. 3.84
5. $1\frac{23}{25}$
6. 8
7. $47\frac{1}{2}$
8. 120
9. 1.31
10. $\frac{23}{24}$
11. $7\frac{1}{3}$
12. $4\frac{7}{40}$
13. $\frac{9}{40}$
14. $33\frac{1}{3}$
15. 240
16. 6

EXERCISE 57

1. 0.73
2. 0.04
3. 0.8
4. 1.27
5. 0.075
6. 0.0325
7. 0.0275
8. 1.125
9. 0.043
10. 0.0025
11. 0.005
12. 0.0507
13. 48%
14. 8%
15. 30%
16. 207%
17. $13\frac{1}{2}\%$
18. $383\frac{1}{3}\%$
19. 2.5%
20. 0.9%
21. 650%
22. $408\frac{1}{3}\%$
23. $187\frac{1}{2}\%$
24. 0.4%

EXERCISE 58

1. 0.68
2. 0.47
3. 0.3
4. 0.9
5. 1.32
6. 1.65
7. 0.085
8. 0.045
9. 0.0125
10. 0.0525
11. 0.0875
12. 0.0675
13. 0.062
14. 1.245
15. 0.078
16. 1.445
17. 0.0075
18. 0.005
19. 0.0035
20. 0.064
21. 0.0708
22. 0.0025
23. 0.0318
24. 0.003
25. 62%
26. 38%
27. 2%
28. 70%
29. 509%
30. 27%
31. 305%
32. $8\frac{1}{2}\%$
33. 609%
34. $24\frac{1}{2}\%$
35. $237\frac{1}{2}\%$
36. 6.7%
37. $783\frac{1}{3}\%$
38. 8.9%
39. 0.2%
40. 740%
41. $304\frac{1}{2}\%$
42. 0.7%
43. 390%
44. $112\frac{1}{2}\%$
45. 0.5%
46. $806\frac{2}{3}\%$
47. 780%
48. $317\frac{1}{2}\%$

EXERCISE 59

1. 0.57
2. 0.08
3. 0.6
4. 1.49
5. 0.025
6. 0.0125
7. 0.0575
8. 1.285
9. 0.062
10. 0.005
11. 0.0125
12. 0.0308
13. 62%
14. 3%
15. 80%
16. 502%
17. $18\frac{1}{2}\%$
18. $217\frac{1}{3}\%$
19. 6.7%
20. 0.2%
21. 820%
22. $302\frac{1}{3}\%$
23. 262.5%
24. 0.9%

EXERCISE 60

1. $\frac{18}{25}$
2. $\frac{5}{8}$
3. $\frac{2}{5}$
4. $\frac{11}{20}$
5. $1\frac{1}{5}$
6. $\frac{2}{25}$
7. $1\frac{3}{8}$
8. $2\frac{1}{12}$
9. 75%
10. $71\frac{3}{7}\%$
11. 55%
12. $62\frac{1}{2}\%$
13. $166\frac{2}{3}\%$
14. $44\frac{4}{9}\%$
15. 280%
16. $316\frac{2}{3}\%$

EXERCISE 61

1. $\frac{14}{25}$
2. $\frac{5}{6}$
3. $\frac{7}{20}$
4. $\frac{1}{3}$
5. $\frac{7}{20}$
6. $\frac{12}{25}$
7. $1\frac{2}{5}$
8. $\frac{3}{50}$
9. $2\frac{7}{8}$
10. $\frac{5}{12}$
11. $\frac{1}{40}$
12. $\frac{67}{100}$
13. $\frac{3}{25}$
14. $1\frac{1}{4}$
15. $\frac{1}{6}$
16. $2\frac{1}{5}$
17. 32%
18. 25%
19. 85%
20. $37\frac{1}{2}\%$
21. $83\frac{1}{3}\%$
22. $28\frac{4}{7}\%$
23. $133\frac{1}{3}\%$
24. $26\frac{2}{3}\%$
25. 140%
26. $77\frac{7}{9}\%$
27. $358\frac{1}{3}\%$
28. $236\frac{4}{11}\%$
29. 160%
30. $66\frac{2}{3}\%$
31. $112\frac{1}{2}\%$
32. 270%

EXERCISE 62

1. $\frac{12}{25}$
2. $\frac{5}{6}$
3. $\frac{3}{5}$
4. $\frac{17}{20}$
5. $\frac{7}{5}$
6. $\frac{3}{50}$
7. $1\frac{7}{8}$
8. $2\frac{1}{6}$
9. 80%
10. $88\frac{8}{9}\%$
11. $37\frac{1}{2}\%$
12. 35%
13. $28\frac{4}{7}\%$
14. $133\frac{1}{3}\%$
15. 360%
16. $208\frac{1}{3}\%$

EXERCISE 63

1. 12.88
2. 5.76
3. 7.875
4. 0.84
5. 56.64
6. 33.75
7. 3.92
8. 204
9. 0.72
10. 14.536
11. 164
12. $2.94

EXERCISE 64

1. 48.96
2. 49.45
3. 7.315
4. 12.636
5. 12.33
6. 86.792
7. 1.134
8. 4.29
9. 1.215
10. 83.82
11. 109.44
12. 37.4
13. 5.33
14. 1.275
15. 12.16
16. 198
17. 147
18. 3.14
19. 87
20. 0.116
21. 10.792
22. 450
23. 3.4
24. 0.448
25. $1.86
26. $5.89
27. $3.07
28. $0.80

EXERCISE 65

1. 20.88
2. 2.88
3. 8.555
4. 1.71
5. 78.72
6. 47.5
7. 1.2
8. 285
9. 0.13
10. 21.912
11. 215
12. $1.15

EXERCISE 66

1. 75%
2. 70%
3. $68\frac{3}{4}\%$
4. $81\frac{9}{11}\%$
5. 135%
6. $149\frac{3}{53}\%$
7. 350
8. 64
9. 56
10. 55.5

EXERCISE 67

1. 20%
2. 25%
3. $57\frac{1}{7}\%$
4. 60%
5. $28\frac{24}{67}\%$
6. $34\frac{18}{23}\%$
7. $123\frac{1}{13}\%$
8. $81\frac{1}{4}\%$
9. $62\frac{1}{2}\%$
10. $122\frac{1}{2}\%$
11. 92%
12. $183\frac{1}{3}\%$
13. 106.25
14. 38
15. 102
16. 210
17. 76
18. 96
19. 75
20. 40

EXERCISE 68

1. 80%
2. 60%
3. 50%
4. $67\frac{6}{7}\%$
5. 130%
6. $129\frac{37}{47}\%$
7. 350
8. 84
9. 120
10. 72

EXERCISE 69

1. 3 lb.	5. $2\frac{3}{4}$ ft.	8. 7,920 ft.
2. 36 in.	6. $1\frac{1}{2}$ min.	9. $4\frac{1}{2}$ qt.
3. 120 min.	7. 64 oz.	10. 36 oz.
4. $1\frac{1}{2}$ gal.		

EXERCISE 70

1. 4 lb.	8. $3\frac{1}{2}$ gal.	15. 5,940 ft.
2. $2\frac{1}{2}$ lb.	9. $2\frac{1}{3}$ ft.	16. 11,880 ft.
3. 48 in.	10. $1\frac{3}{4}$ ft.	17. 2 qt.
4. 30 in.	11. $2\frac{1}{2}$ min.	18. $1\frac{1}{4}$ qt.
5. 300 min.	12. $1\frac{2}{3}$ min.	19. 56 oz.
6. 195 min.	13. 32 oz.	20. 84 oz.
7. $2\frac{1}{2}$ gal.	14. 96 oz.	

EXERCISE 71

1. 2 lb.	5. $3\frac{1}{4}$ ft.	8. 9,240 ft.
2. 60 in.	6. $2\frac{1}{2}$ min.	9. $3\frac{1}{2}$ qt.
3. 18 min.	7. 48 oz.	10. 60 oz.
4. $2\frac{1}{4}$ gal.		

EXERCISE 72

1. 16 feet 2 inches
2. 13 hours 32 minutes
3. 10 pounds 8 ounces
4. 7 gallons 1 quart
5. 30 pounds 3 ounces
6. 42 minutes 16 seconds
7. 42 yards
8. 4 pounds 7 ounces
9. 1 hour 29 minutes
10. 1 gallon 2 quarts
11. 54 minutes
12. 1 pound 15 ounces

EXERCISE 73

1. 7 hours 28 minutes
2. 9 pounds 7 ounces
3. 10 gallons 2 quarts
4. 13 minutes 28 seconds
5. 8 feet 9 inches
6. 14 pounds 6 ounces
7. 26 minutes 1 second
8. 12 pounds 3 ounces
9. 10 hours 16 minutes

10. 15 gallons 3 quarts
11. 3 pounds 8 ounces
12. 1 hour 37 minutes
13. 1 gallon 3 quarts
14. 11 minutes 24 seconds
15. 4 pounds 9 ounces
16. 2 hours 14 minutes
17. 14 ounces
18. 2 gallons 2 quarts
19. 3 feet 3 inches
20. 2 yards 2 feet

EXERCISE 74

1. 11 feet 10 inches
2. 15 hours
3. 9 pounds 15 ounces
4. 6 gallons 1 quart
5. 58 pounds 8 ounces
6. 1 hour 19 seconds
7. 26 yards 2 feet
8. 3 pounds 4 ounces
9. 2 hours 19 minutes
10. 3 gallons 3 quarts
11. 53 minutes
12. 14 ounces

EXERCISE 75

1. October 10	4. 15 weeks
2. 1 hr. 25 min.	5. 11:35 P.M.
3. 2 hr. 30 min.	

EXERCISE 76

1. True	5. True	8. True
2. False	6. True	9. False
3. False	7. True	10. True
4. True		

EXERCISE 77

1. 3	5. 3	8. $11\frac{5}{11}$
2. 6	6. $22\frac{2}{3}$	9. 6
3. 12	7. 20	10. $9\frac{1}{3}$
4. 56		

EXERCISE 78

1. $450	4. $20.79	7. 777 miles
2. $968	5. $171.55	8. 616 sets
3. 45	6. 135	

PRACTICE TESTS

TEST 1

1. C	3. E	5. A	7. C	9. E
2. B	4. E	6. B	8. E	10. B

TEST 2

1. D	3. D	5. E	7. E	9. C
2. A	4. E	6. B	8. B	10. B

TEST 3

1. C	3. D	5. E	7. A	9. E
2. B	4. E	6. C	8. C	10. D

TEST 4

1. D	5. C	9. B	13. B
2. D	6. D	10. D	14. D
3. B	7. B	11. B	15. C
4. E	8. E	12. E	16. E

TEST 5

1. D	5. E	9. C	13. B
2. B	6. D	10. E	14. A
3. A	7. B	11. C	15. D
4. D	8. A	12. E	16. B

TEST 6

1. C	5. B	9. E	13. C
2. A	6. E	10. B	14. E
3. E	7. C	11. E	15. D
4. C	8. A	12. A	16. A

TEST 7

1. D	3. E	5. D	7. C	9. C
2. E	4. B	6. C	8. A	10. D

TEST 8

1. C	3. E	5. B	7. D	9. C
2. B	4. D	6. A	8. D	10. B

TEST 9

1. C	3. A	5. B	7. C	9. C
2. E	4. C	6. D	8. A	10. D

TEST 10

1. C	4. D	7. A	10. C	13. B
2. E	5. B	8. D	11. B	14. D
3. C	6. D	9. E	12. D	15. C

TEST 11

1. D	6. B	11. D
2. C	7. D	12. C
3. B	8. E	13. B
4. C	9. C	14. E
5. E	10. B	15. B

TEST 12

1. C	6. D	11. B
2. A	7. A	12. E
3. C	8. C	13. C
4. B	9. D	14. B
5. E	10. C	15. D

TEST 13

1. 87.5	18. $41\frac{2}{3}\%$	35. 40.2%
2. $37\frac{1}{2}\%$	19 $66\frac{2}{3}\%$	36. 5
3. 40	20. 0.875	37. $3\frac{1}{2}\%$
4. $\frac{1}{8}$	21. $16\frac{2}{3}\%$	38. $\frac{31}{200}$
5. 75%	22. $24\frac{1}{2}\%$	39. 50
6. $\frac{1}{20}$	23. $\frac{5}{8}$	40. 105.2%
7. 320	24. 300	41. 54
8. 20%	25. 1.25	42. 160%
9. 168	26. 21	43. 640%
10. 0.48	27. 3.57	44. $53\frac{1}{8}\%$
11. 35%	28. 3,000	45. 85
12. 340%	29. $77\frac{7}{9}\%$	46. $133\frac{1}{3}\%$
13. $37\frac{1}{2}\%$	30. 150%	47. $1\frac{3}{8}$
14. 0.2	31. 19.2	48. 1.35
15. 125%	32. 12	49. 60
16. $\frac{4}{25}$	33. 80%	50. 0.35%
17. 9.6	34. 107.6	

TEST 14

1. D	5. C	9. A	13. E
2. B	6. B	10. E	14. C
3. A	7. D	11. B	15. B
4. C	8. E	12. D	16. A

TEST 15

1. C	5. C	9. A	13. C
2. E	6. E	10. D	14. E
3. B	7. B	11. B	15. B
4. D	8. D	12. D	16. D

TEST 16

1. C	5. B	9. D	13. D
2. B	6. D	10. B	14. A
3. E	7. C	11. E	15. C
4. C	8. A	12. B	16. B

TEST 17

1. D	7. B	12. D	17. E	22. D
2. C	8. D	13. C	18. C	23. E
3. E	9. B	14. B	19. B	24. B
4. B	10. E	15. A	20. D	25. D
5. A	11. A	16. D	21. C	26. B
6. E				

TEST 18

1. D	7. B	12. C	17. B	22. B
2. E	8. E	13. E	18. D	23. A
3. E	9. C	14. B	19. B	24. C
4. B	10. B	15. D	20. D	25. D
5. D	11. D	16. C	21. E	26. A
6. E				

TEST 19

1. D	6. C	11. C	16. B
2. E	7. A	12. D	17. B
3. B	8. C	13. B	18. A
4. D	9. B	14. D	19. D
5. B	10. E	15. C	20. C

TEST 20

1. D	6. D	11. E	16. B
2. B	7. B	12. C	17. D
3. E	8. C	13. D	18. E
4. C	9. B	14. A	19. C
5. B	10. D	15. D	20. B

TEST 21

1. C	4. B	7. B	10. A
2. E	5. C	8. E	11. C
3. D	6. A	9. C	12. D

TEST 22

1. C	3. E	5. D	7. B	9. D
2. B	4. D	6. E	8. A	10. C

TEST 23

1. B	3. D	5. B	7. C	9. E
2. A	4. E	6. E	8. B	10. C

TEST 24

1. C	3. B	5. A	7. D	9. E
2. D	4. E	6. C	8. B	10. A

TEST 25

1. C	3. E	5. D	7. C	9. D
2. D	4. B	6. A	8. B	10. C

Application of Basic Mathematical Skills

Verbal Problems

THE BASICS

In solving verbal problems the student must:

1. Read the problem carefully.

2. Determine which facts are given.

3. Determine what must be found.

4. Decide upon a plan that will yield a solution.

5. Solve the problem.

6. Answer the question.

Using Addition

EXAMPLE: A fully loaded coal truck dumped 1,500 pounds of coal at house A and 2,530 pounds at house B. It then had 2,470 pounds left. If the truck when empty weighed 7,200 pounds, what was the weight of the truck when fully loaded?

SOLUTION: The weight of the fully loaded truck consisted of the weight when empty plus the weight of all the coal that was in the truck. We therefore add all the given weights.

$$
\begin{array}{r}
1,500 \\
2,530 \\
2,470 \\
\underline{7,200} \\
13,700
\end{array}
$$

The weight of the truck fully loaded was 13,700 pounds.

PRACTICE TEST 1

1. A pole is made by glueing together pieces of wood measuring $6\frac{3}{4}$ inches, $19\frac{5}{6}$ inches, and $28\frac{2}{3}$ inches respectively. Find the length of the pole.

2. A man's bank balance reads $128.72 after a $23.38 withdrawal. Find the amount he had in the beginning.

3. The weight of chemical A is 6.29 grams more than that of chemical B. If chemical B weighs 17.3 grams, chemical A weighs how many grams?

4. The tax receipts of a certain city for 5 years were as follows: In 1987, $7,426,725.23; in 1988, $17,384,725.68; in 1989, $11,889,979; in 1990, $23,299,864.92; and in 1991, $17,642,746.71. What was the total tax collection over the 5 years?

5. A tank holds $17\frac{3}{5}$ gallons after losing $36\frac{2}{3}$ gallons, $4\frac{5}{6}$ gallons, and $27\frac{7}{12}$ gallons in 3 consecutive days. If at the beginning the tank was $20\frac{3}{4}$ gallons short of capacity, what is the capacity of the tank?

6. The usual price of an electric stapler is $49.75. One store sells the stapler for $4.35 above the usual price, while a second store sells it at a discount of $7.95. What is the difference in the prices set by the two stores?

Using Subtraction

EXAMPLE: Osna's bank deposits exceed Peggy's by $3,679. If Osna has $10,000 in the bank, how much does Peggy have?

SOLUTION: Peggy has less in the bank than Osna. We must therefore subtract from Osna's sum to find Peggy's.

$$
\begin{array}{r}
\$10,000 \\
-\ \underline{3,679} \\
\$\ 6,321
\end{array}
$$

Peggy has $6,321 on deposit.

PRACTICE TEST 2

1. Peg goes to the store and buys $1.84 worth of apples. How much change will she get from a five-dollar bill?

2. At the start of the trip Mr. Prest's speedometer read 23,214.3 miles. If the reading was exactly 25,000 miles at his destination, how many miles did he travel?

3. How much less does Bob earn than Bill, if Bill's salary is $62 and Bob's is $55.80?

4. How many more feet longer is a pipe that is $13\frac{5}{8}$ feet in length than one that is 6 feet 11 inches?

5. A truck that weighs 6,248 pounds when empty now weighs 13,440 pounds. What is the weight of its contents?

6. Last year Nancy weighed $37\frac{5}{8}$ pounds. This year she weighs 42.7 pounds. How much did she gain?

7. A radio lists for $37 but is sold for $29.98. What is the discount?

8. The population of New York City in a certain year was 7,892,463 and that of Los Angeles was 1,974,564. How much larger was New York's population?

9. The weight of chemical A is 6.29 grams more than that of chemical B. If chemical A weighs 17.3 grams, chemical B weighs how many grams?

Using Multiplication

EXAMPLE: A manuscript averages 36 words to a line and 24 lines to a page. There are 100 pages to the manuscript. If only $\frac{7}{8}$ of the words can be incorporated into a book, how many words will there be in the book?

SOLUTION: One line has 36 words. To find the words in 24 of these lines (one page), we multiply 24 by 36. Now that we have the words for one page, we multiply by 100 to find the words on all the printed pages.

Since only $\frac{7}{8}$ of the words are to be included in the book, we multiply the result by $\frac{7}{8}$.

$$\frac{36}{1} \times \frac{\overset{3}{24}}{1} \times \frac{100}{1} \times \frac{7}{8} = 75,600$$

The book will contain 75,600 words.

PRACTICE TEST 3

1. Stan earns $8.80 per hour for an 8-hour day's work. How much does he earn in a 5-day week?

2. Each battalion has 250 soldiers. A regiment consists of 12 battalions. A division has 10 regiments. How many soldiers are there in a division?

3. Each of Mrs. Bernstein's 4 boys averages $15.60 a week by delivering papers. How much do the 4 boys earn each week?

4. A boy cuts up a stick so that he has 16 pieces each $2\frac{3}{4}$ inches long. What was the original length of the stick if there was no waste in cutting?

5. May's rainfall was 0.52 inch. In June the rainfall was 0.13 as much. How much rain, in inches, fell in June?

6. Last year the city's revenue from taxes was $4,723,213. This year the revenue is 0.78 as much. What is the revenue this year?

7. What is the weight of 320 jars if each weighs 3 pounds 2 ounces?

8. How many feet of cloth are needed to manufacture 48 shirts if each shirt requires $2\frac{1}{3}$ yards of the cloth?

9. How far does Judy travel in $2\frac{3}{4}$ hours if she travels at the rate of $5\frac{1}{2}$ miles per hour?

10. A cricket chirps 15 times a minute. How many chirps will it give forth in 2 hours?

11. A car averages 16.8 miles per gallon and uses 265 gallons traveling cross-country. What was the distance the car traveled?

12. A map scale reads 1 inch = 200 miles. How many miles are represented by a line 44 inches long?

Using Division

EXAMPLE: A school has 3,698 children. If there are 86 classrooms in the school, what is the average number of students in each classroom?

SOLUTION: To find the number of students in one classroom, we divide the number of children in the school by the number of classrooms.

$$
\begin{array}{r}
43 \\
86\overline{)3,698} \\
344 \\
\hline
258 \\
\underline{258}
\end{array}
$$

There is an average of 43 students per classroom.

EXAMPLE: A vat holds 695 gallons. If the contents are used to fill flasks each of which has the capacity of $2\frac{1}{2}$ gallons, how many flasks can be filled?

SOLUTION: Each flask holds $2\frac{1}{2}$ gallons. To find how many "$2\frac{1}{2}$ gallons" are contained in 695 gallons, we divide 695 by $2\frac{1}{2}$.

$$695 \div 2\frac{1}{2} = 695 \div \frac{5}{2} = \frac{\overset{139}{695}}{1} \times \frac{2}{5} = 278$$

The number of flasks that can be filled is 278.

PRACTICE TEST 4

1. Phyllis's mother has 6 pounds of candy to divide evenly among her 8 children. This is an average of how many pounds per child?

2. Mr. O'Neill's fence is 425 feet long. How many yards long is it?

3. How many school rooms are needed for 595 children, if each room can hold 35 children?

4. How many $\frac{3}{8}$-inch strips of cloth can a tailor cut out of a piece of cloth 48 inches long?

5. If notebooks cost $15.00 a dozen, what is the price for one?

6. Each bolt weighs 0.14 gram. How many bolts are there in a batch that weighs 50.4 grams?

7. In $2\frac{3}{4}$ hours Steve traveled $1\frac{1}{2}$ miles. What was his rate in miles per hour?

8. Mrs. Colson bought a TV set for $\frac{4}{5}$ of its original value. If she paid $80 for the set, what did it cost originally?

9. Evelyn buys 24 pounds of chocolate and packs it into $\frac{3}{4}$-pound packages. How many packages can she make?

10. Light travels 186,000 miles a second. How long, to the nearest hundredth of a second, will it take a ray of light to travel from the earth to the moon if the approximate distance between them is 242,000 miles?

Using Mixed Operations

EXAMPLE: A plane started a flight at 7:30 A.M. and arrived at its destination at 11:45 A.M. The distance covered was 612 miles. What was the average rate of speed of the plane?

SOLUTION: In order to find the average rate of speed we must divide the distance covered by the time spent. The distance covered is 612 miles. The time spent may be found by subtracting 7:30 from 11:45.

$$
\begin{array}{r}
11:45 \\
7:30 \\
\end{array}
$$

Time spent =   4:15 or $4\frac{1}{4}$ hours

$$612 \div 4\frac{1}{4} = 612 \div \frac{17}{4} = \overset{36}{612} \times \frac{4}{17} = 144$$

The average rate of speed was 144 miles per hour.

EXAMPLE: A gas station operator's gasoline sales for one week were as follows: Monday, 255 gallons; Tuesday, 280 gallons; Wednesday, 235 gallons; Thursday, 375 gallons; Friday, 370 gallons; Saturday, 465 gallons; Sunday, 690 gallons. He paid $117 for 100 gallons of the gasoline and sold it at 6 gallons for $9.15. What was his profit for the week?

SOLUTION: The number of gallons sold may be found by adding: 255 + 280 + 235 + 375 + 370 + 465 + 690 = 2,670 gallons. The cost of $117 per 100 gallons may be regarded as $1.17 per gallon.

If we multiply 2,670 by $1.17, we obtain $3,123.90, the total cost.

To find the selling price we can calculate the number of 6-gallon units in 2,670 gallons by dividing 2,670 by 6. The result is 445.

Since each 6-gallon unit was sold for $9.15, the total selling price is $9.15 × 445 = $4,071.75.

$$\begin{aligned} \text{Profit} &= \text{Selling price} - \text{Cost} \\ &= \$4,071.75 \quad - \$3,123.90 \\ &= \$947.85 \end{aligned}$$

EXAMPLE: A man worked as follows during a week: Monday, 8 hr. 45 min.; Tuesday, 9 hr.; Wednesday, 8 hr. 50 min.; Thursday, 9 hr. 35 min.; Friday, 9 hr. 40 min.; Saturday, 5 hr. 40 min. He earned $8.80 an hour for each of the first 40 hours and $13.20 for each additional hour over 40 hours that he worked. What were his total earnings for the week?

SOLUTION: Total time the man worked may be obtained as follows:

8 hr.	45 min.
9 hr.	
8 hr.	50 min.
9 hr.	35 min.
9 hr.	40 min.
5 hr.	40 min.
48 hr.	210 min.

$$= 48 \text{ hr.} + 180 \text{ min.} + 30 \text{ min.}$$
$$= 51 \text{ hr. } 30 \text{ min.} = 51\tfrac{1}{2} \text{ hr.}$$

At $8.80 for 40 hr., earnings = $352.00
At $13.20 for 11½ hr., earnings = $151.80
Total earnings = $503.80

EXAMPLE: A farmer had some chickens to sell. On August 15 they weighed 240 pounds and could have been sold at $0.42 a pound. He kept them until October 1 and fed them at a cost of $18. He then sold them, a total weight of 265 pounds, at $0.48 a pound. How much did he gain or lose by keeping them?

SOLUTION: On August 15, he could have sold 240 pounds of chicken at $0.42 a pound for a total of $100.80.

On October 1, he sold 265 pounds of chicken at $0.48 a pound for a total of $127.20. From this must be deducted expenses of $18, leaving $109.20.

By keeping the chickens until October 1 he gained $109.20 − $100.80 = $8.40.

EXAMPLE: A boy's club with a membership of 22 decides to go camping for one week. The estimated expenses are as follows: transportation $115, rent for the camp $132, food $295, incidentals $74. The boys have $88 in the treasury and vote to raise the balance necessary by taxing each member an equal amount.
  (a) What will their total expenses be?
  (b) How much must be raised by taxing the members?
  (c) How much must each member be taxed?

SOLUTION:
  (a) The expenses may be found by adding:
      $115 + $132 + $295 + $74 = $616.
  (b) The amount needed by taxing the members is $616 − $88 = $528.
  (c) To find the tax per member we must divide the total tax of $528 by 22. The result is $24.

EXAMPLE: During December and January, Bill, Tom, and Dick shoveled snow from the sidewalks in front of several stores. They agreed to divide their pay according to the number of hours each worked. Bill worked 6 hours. Tom worked 15 hours, and Dick worked 9 hours. They received $135 for their work. How much did each boy receive?

SOLUTION: Since Bill contributed 6 parts, Tom 15 parts, and Dick 9 parts the total number of parts into which the money was to be divided was 30.

Bill's share $= \frac{6}{30} = \frac{1}{5}$

Tom's share $= \frac{15}{30} = \frac{1}{2}$

Dick's share $= \frac{9}{30} = \frac{3}{10}$

Bill received $\frac{1}{5} \times \$135 = \$27$

Tom received $\frac{1}{2} \times \$135 = \$67.50$

Dick received $\frac{3}{10} \times \$135 = \$40.50$

EXAMPLE: The list price of a radio is $90, with a discount of $\frac{1}{10}$ for cash. The same radio can also be purchased on the installment plan for a down payment of $10 and payments of $7.50 a month for one year. How much more does the radio cost when purchased on the installment plan than when cash is paid?

SOLUTION: We must compare price for cash with price on the installment plan.

$$
\begin{aligned}
\text{Price for cash} &= \$90 \text{ less discount} \\
\text{Discount} &= \tfrac{1}{10} \text{ of } \$90 = \$9 \\
\text{Price for cash} &= \$90 - \$9 = \$81 \\
\text{Price on the} & \\
\text{installment plan} &= \$10 + 12 \times \$7.50 \\
&= \$10 + \$90 \\
&= \$100
\end{aligned}
$$

The difference in price is $100 − $81, or $19 more on the installment plan.

PRACTICE TEST 5

1. Twenty gallons of a liquid weigh 400 lb. What is the weight of 1 quart?

2. A. man spends $88 for gas and oil in making a trip. He used 10 quarts of oil at $1.50 per quart. If gasoline was $1.46 a gallon and he averaged 18 miles to the gallon, how many miles did he travel?

3. John bought 240 pens at $3 a dozen, spent $16 on advertising, and sold the pens at 75 cents each. What was his profit?

4. Linda has 26 feet of ribbon. She uses $2\frac{1}{3}$ feet for each of 4 dresses and decides to make 10 hair ornaments, using an equal amount of ribbon for each. How many inches of ribbon are used for each ornament?

5. Barry buys a used car for $2,500. He pays $\frac{1}{5}$ down and the remainder is to be paid monthly for 3 years. What is the monthly payment?

6. Bill is paid $8.00 an hour for a 40-hour week. For every hour over 40 hours, he is paid at a rate that is $1\frac{1}{2}$ times his usual rate. One week he worked 48 hours and the next week 36 hours. What did he earn in the 2 weeks?

7. Jack bought 4 oz. of butter at $1.92 a pound, 12 cans of juice at $0.25 per can, and 8 oranges at $1.26 a dozen. How much did he spend?

8. Lenore gets a monthly check of $1,250 and Millie a weekly check of $980. What is the difference in their yearly earnings?

9. From an 18-pound cut of meat, Mr. Rand cuts off steaks weighing 1 pound 15 ounces, $3\frac{1}{8}$ pounds, and $4\frac{1}{2}$ pounds. He divides up the rest into 9-ounce patties, and sells them at 3 for $3.12. How much does he receive for the patties?

10. Joan worked from 7:20 A.M. to 4:05 P.M. What is her salary if she is paid $5.60 an hour?

11. A carton contains 5 pounds of cookies. If each cookie weighs $\frac{5}{8}$ of an ounce, how many cookies are in the box?

12. A mountain climber ascends 264 feet in 45 minutes. What is her rate in miles per hour?

13. A truckowner pays $120 for the first 100 gallons of gasoline, $1.12 a gallon for the next 300 gallons, and $1.08 a gallon for any additional purchase of gasoline. What is his bill for 700 gallons of gasoline?

14. A man buys 3,400 boxes at $12.50 a hundred and sells them at a profit of 6 cents each. What does he receive for the boxes?

15. Paul Allen lost $\frac{2}{3}$ of his money and has $12 left. How much did he have?

16. Sue's dad opened a bank account for her, depositing $25.00 a month for the first year. He promised to increase the deposit by $\frac{1}{5}$ each year. After three increases, what was the monthly deposit?

17. A man buys 48 quarts of cider at $1.20 a quart and sells it in $\frac{1}{2}$-pint jars at 40 cents a jar. What was his profit?

18. Ronnie sold his bicycle for $35. He had spent $10 on repairs and $4 for a new horn. If he suffered a $6 loss on the sale, what was the original cost of the bicycle?

19. Miriam bought 64 pounds of popcorn. She kept $\frac{1}{4}$ for her family, gave $\frac{1}{8}$ of the remainder to her club, and distributed the rest equally among 8 friends. How many ounces did each friend get?

20. Henry hired a painter and agreed to pay him $26.00 an hour. He supplied him with $1\frac{1}{2}$ gallons of paint that cost $5.70 a quart and 2 quarts of paint thinner that sold for $2.20 a quart. The painter started at 8 A.M. and finished at 4:30 P.M. What was the cost of painting the room?

Percentage Problems

Finding a percent of a number—Type I

EXAMPLE: From a group of 1,200 students $12\frac{1}{2}\%$ took a scholarship examination. Of those who took the test 20% qualified for the semifinals. How many qualified for the semifinals?

SOLUTION: The 1,200 students constitute the whole. To find $12\frac{1}{2}\%$ or $\frac{1}{8}$ of the whole we must take $\frac{1}{8}$ of 1,200; $\frac{1}{8} \times 1,200$ is 150 students. The 150 students represent the whole group who took the test. Of these 150 students, 20% or $\frac{1}{5}$ qualified for the semifinals. Therefore $\frac{1}{5}$ of 150, or 30 students, qualified.

PRACTICE TEST 6

1. Forty percent of the people in a certain class of 35 students are girls. How many girls are in the class?

2. Nina saves $37\frac{1}{2}\%$ of her weekly salary of $520. How much does she spend?

3. Reggie bought 32 pairs of slacks at $25 each and sold them at an increase of 25%. What did he receive for the slacks?

4. The population of a town increased $16\frac{2}{3}\%$ in 1990 and 10% in 1991. If the population at the beginning of 1990 was 30,000, what was its population at the end of 1991?

5. A vat contains 360 gallons of water. Of this, 10% is removed from the vat. Alcohol is then added equal to 10% of the amount of water left in the vat. How many gallons of solution are now in the vat?

6. Mr. Gardner has $30,000 on deposit and receives $9\frac{3}{4}\%$ interest annually. What annual interest does he receive the first year?

7. An iceberg weighs 450,000 pounds. If it loses 0.2% of its weight in a day, what is its new weight at the end of the day?

8. Travelers' checks have a service charge of $\frac{3}{4}\%$. If Leon buys $3,000 worth of checks, what is the service charge?

Finding what percent one number is of another—Type II

EXAMPLE: Karen's weight went up from 60 to 70 pounds in a year. What was the percent of increase?

SOLUTION: In finding the percent of increase, we compare the amount of increase to the original whole and change the resulting fraction to a percent. In this case the amount of increase was 70 – 60, or 10 pounds.

$$\text{Percent of increase} = \frac{\text{Amount of increase}}{\text{Original whole}}$$

$$= \frac{10}{60} = \frac{1}{6} = 16\frac{2}{3}\%$$

The percent of increase was $16\frac{2}{3}\%$.

EXAMPLE: A football team won 26 games in 1996, 34 games in 1997, and 36 games in 1998. What percent of the games did it win in 1998?

SOLUTION: We are asked to compare the number of games won in 1990 to all the games.

Percent of games won in 1990

$$= \frac{\text{Number of games won in 1990}}{\text{Total number of games}}$$

$$= \frac{36}{96} = \frac{3}{8} = 37\frac{1}{2}\%$$

The team won $37\frac{1}{2}\%$ of its games in 1990.

PRACTICE TEST 7

1. Bertha bought 2 apples, 6 pears, and 10 bananas. What percent of the fruit were the pears?

2. The population of a town increased from 560 to 630 people. What was the percent of increase?

3. Mr. Richardson won 36 out of the 108 games he played. What percent of the games did he lose?

4. Ross catches 4 fish and his son catches 12 fish. The son's catch was what percent of his father's?

5. In a test Louise has 64 examples correct and 8 wrong. What percent did she have wrong?

6. A bank paid Mr. Sporn $132 interest on deposits that amounted to $2,400. At what rate of interest was Mr. Sporn being paid?

7. Adele buys a scarf that usually sells for $10.50 at a sale price of $7. What percent was the price reduced?

8. In 1996 Sid weighed 120 pounds. In 1997 his gain in weight was $16\frac{2}{3}\%$. In 1998 he weighed 150 pounds. The increase in his weight from 1997 to 1998 is what percent of his 1996 weight?

9. Paula's salary was raised from $600 to $1,800 in the course of 5 years. What was the percent of increase in salary?

10. Of the 480 children in a school, 180 were absent in a flu epidemic. What percent of the children attended?

Finding the whole if the percent of it is given—Type III

EXAMPLE: Cynthia buys an encyclopedia at an 18% discount and saves $54. What did she pay for the encyclopedia?

SOLUTION: The saving of $54 is the part and represents 18% of the whole or original price. To find the whole we divide the part by the rate.

$$\$54 \div 18\% = 54 \div \frac{18}{100} = \frac{\overset{3}{\cancel{54}}}{1} \times \frac{100}{\underset{1}{\cancel{18}}} = \$300$$

The original price was $300. Since Cynthia saved $54, she paid $300 − 54, or $216.

EXAMPLE: Central Tire Corporation raised the price of heavy-duty truck tires by $16\frac{2}{3}\%$. If the present price is $168, what was the original price?

SOLUTION: The original price (the whole) was increased by $16\frac{2}{3}\%$, or $\frac{1}{6}$ of itself. The price of $168, which is the new price, therefore represents $\frac{6}{6} + \frac{1}{6}$, or $\frac{7}{6}$, of the original price. To find the original whole we divide the $168 by the fraction of the whole that the $168 represents.

$$168 \div \frac{7}{6} = \frac{168}{1} \times \frac{6}{7} = 144$$

The original price of the tire was $144.

PRACTICE TEST 8

1. Twenty-three percent of a town's population owns cars. If the number of cars owned is 5,290, what is the population of the town?

2. Mr. Hall saved $15 by buying a tool at a 10% discount. What did the tool list for?

3. A salesman earned $750 in making sales that paid him a $7\frac{1}{2}\%$ commission. What was the value of his sales?

4. The population of a city dipped $\frac{1}{2}\%$ last year. If the decrease amounted to 2,453 people, what was the population of the town after the decrease?

5. The Continental Office Supply found that a markup of $37\frac{1}{2}\%$ on a desk resulted in making a $48 profit. What was the original cost of the desk?

6. Martin had 14 examples wrong on a test. His score was 72% correct. How many examples were there on the test?

7. A bank pays Sally $6\frac{1}{4}\%$ interest yearly. If the yearly interest payment she receives amounts to $50, how much does she have on deposit?

8. Roy found that after receiving a 25% discount he had to pay $72 for a tape recorder. How much was the discount?

9. Vicki traveled 90 miles and found she had completed $83\frac{1}{3}\%$ of her trip. How many miles did she still have to go?

10. Gladys paid $25.48 for a tablecloth. If the price included a 4% sales tax, what was the price of the cloth itself?

Special Topics in Percent

PROFIT AND LOSS

A merchant's *profit* or loss represents the difference between the *total (gross)* cost and the *selling price* of the goods sold. The gross cost includes the first cost of the merchandise plus the overhead. The *overhead* is the expenses of doing business, such as rent, light, salaries, taxes, insurance. If the selling price is less than the total cost, then of course the merchant suffers a loss. The difference between the original cost of the goods and the selling price is known as the *markup*. It equals the overhead expenses plus the profit. The relationship in the case of profit can be shown as follows:

First cost + Overhead + Profit = Selling price

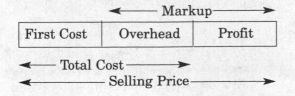

EXAMPLE: Eve buys a bicycle for $11. She spends $6 for repairs and $2 to ship it. If she sells the bicycle for $26, what profit does she make?

SOLUTION: The total cost of the article was $11 + $6 + $2 = $19. The profit Eve made was $26 − $19 or $7.

EXAMPLE: A table costs Mr. Lustig $90. The operating expense is 20% of the cost of the table. He wishes to make a profit of $33\frac{1}{3}\%$ of the first cost. At what price should the table sell?

SOLUTION: Mr. Lustig's overhead expenses are 20% of $90 or $18. His profit is to be $33\frac{1}{3}\%$ or $\frac{1}{3}$ of $90 or $30. The selling price must be $90 + $18 + $30, or $138.

EXAMPLE: Carol buys a tape recorder for $120. After spending $30 for repairs she sells it at a price that is $16\frac{2}{3}\%$ more than what she paid for it. What was the profit or loss on the transaction?

SOLUTION: Carol's total cost was $120 + $30 or $150. The price increase equals $16\frac{2}{3}\%$ of $120, which equals $\frac{1}{6} \times$ $120, or $20. The selling price was, therefore, $120 + $20 or $140. Since the selling price was less than the total cost, Carol suffered a loss of $150 − $140, or $10.

EXAMPLE: If an article costs $12 and sells for $18, what is the percent of profit?

SOLUTION: If just the cost is given we assume that either there are no operating expenses or they are included in the cost. This is a type II percentage problem. Unless otherwise stated, any increase or decrease is based on the original whole. Thus,

$$\text{Percent profit} = \frac{\text{Amount of profit}}{\text{Cost}}$$

$$= \frac{18-12}{12} = \frac{6}{12} = \frac{1}{2} = 50\%$$

EXAMPLE: Barry Metal Products pays $12,000 for raw materials. Its manufacturing expenses are 200% of the cost of these materials. If the amount received for the sale of the finished products is $50,000, what percent of the total cost is the profit?

SOLUTION:

Manufacturing expenses
$$= 200\% \times \$12,000$$
$$= 2(\$12,000) = \$24,000$$
The total cost is $12,000 + $24,000
$$= \$36,000$$
The profit is $50,000 − $36,000
$$= \$14,000$$

The percentage of profit

$$= \frac{14,000}{36,000} = \frac{7}{18}$$

$$\frac{7}{18} = \frac{7}{18} \times 100\% = 38\frac{8}{9}\%$$

EXAMPLE: The Recco Gift Shop wishes to make a 30% profit on the cost of its merchandise. If the profit amounts to $600, what does the merchandise cost?

SOLUTION: This is a type III problem in which the part and the percent that the part represents are known.

$$\text{Cost} = \text{Profit} \div \text{Rate of profit}$$

$$= \$600 \div 30\% = \$600 \div \frac{3}{10}$$

$$= \$600 \times \frac{10}{3} = \$2,000$$

The cost of the merchandise is $2,000.

EXAMPLE: Jesse's toy store sells a doll for $8.00 which represents a profit of 15% of the cost. If the average overhead is 5% of the cost, what profit does Jesse make on the doll?

SOLUTION: The markup is 15% + 5% or 20% of the cost. Since the cost is the base and represents 100%, the selling price is 100% + 20% or 120% of the cost. This is a type III problem. When we wish to find the original whole, in this case the cost, we divide the part by the rate.

$$\text{Cost} = \$8 \div 120\% = \$8 \div \frac{120}{100}$$

$$= \$8 \times \frac{5}{6} = \frac{20}{3} = \$6.66\frac{2}{3}$$

The cost to the nearest cent is $6.67.
The profit is $8.00 − $6.67 = $1.33.

PRACTICE TEST 9

1. What is the selling price of a radio that costs $30 and has a markup of $8\frac{1}{3}\%$?

2. During a blizzard a tire dealer sold a pair of skid chains that cost him $7.50 at a price that netted him a 350% profit. What did the pair of chains sell for?

3. A variety store listed the cost of the goods sold as $50,000, its operating overhead as 20% of the cost, and the value of its sales as $75,000. What percent of the total cost was the profit?

4. A hotel suffered a loss of $45,000 during a season. If the rate of loss was $37\frac{1}{2}\%$ of the gross receipts, what was the value of these receipts?

5. Mr. Lippman bought a dryer for $160 and sold it for $240. If the overhead expenses were 20% of the selling price, what was the rate of profit on the selling price?

6. A music shop sold twenty-five $50 radios at a profit of 8% and six $30 radios at a loss of 15%. How much was the profit or loss on the combined transaction?

7. Mrs. Gold buys a stock of $300 worth of vegetables, which she sells at a 30% markup. If $75 worth of the vegetables spoils and cannot be sold, does Mrs. Gold make a profit or a loss? How much?

8. Alice bought 20 baseball cards at a cost of $1.00 each. She is now willing to sell the whole lot for a total of $12. What will be Alice's percent of loss?

9. The Joneses bought a house 3 years ago for which they paid $65,000. They spent $5,000 repairing it, $1,000 on insurance premiums, and $8,000 in taxes, heat, and light. In order to make a final profit of 5% of his outlay, for how much must Mr. Jones sell his house?

10. After selling twelve books for $180, Bill finds that he has made a profit on them amounting to 25% of the cost and incurred expenses amounting to 10% of the cost. How much did Bill pay for the books?

TAXATION

In order to pay for the government services we must pay taxes. In most communities the greatest source of government income is real estate taxes. Each building and plot of ground is given an assessed valuation. The total assessed valuation is used to fix the tax rate for a community. Let us suppose that a town has a budget of $75,000 for a certain year and the assessed valuation of the taxable property in the town is $1,875,000. The tax rate is computed as follows:

$$\text{Tax rate} = \frac{\text{Amount of money needed}}{\text{Assessed valuation}}$$

In the above case

$$\text{Tax rate} = \frac{\$75,000}{\$1,875,000} = 0.04$$

Thus the tax rate for this community is 4%.

The rate is stated in several ways, such as the following:

4% of the assessed value
$4 on each $100 of assessed value
$40 on each $1,000 of assessed value
$0.04 on each $1 of each assessed value
40 mills on each $1 of assessed value (A mill is equal to $\frac{1}{10}$ of 1 cent.)

EXAMPLE: It is necessary to raise $55,648 by tax in a village with an assessed valuation of $3,478,000. What will be the tax rate per $1,000?

SOLUTION:

$$\text{Tax rate} = \frac{\text{Amount of money needed}}{\text{Assessed valuation}}$$

$$= \frac{\$55,648}{\$3,478,000}$$

$$
\begin{array}{r}
0.016 \\
3,478,000)\overline{55,648.000} \\
\underline{34\ 780\ 00} \\
20\ 868\ 000 \\
\underline{20\ 868\ 000}
\end{array}
$$

The tax rate is 1.6%, or $0.016 per $1, or $16 per $1,000.

EXAMPLE: In the same village a man owns a home with an assessed valuation of $42,500. How much village tax will he pay?

SOLUTION: For each $1,000 of assessed valuation the tax is $16. The assessed valuation of this home is $42.5 thousand. Therefore, the tax is

$$
\begin{array}{r}
\$42.50 \\
\times\ \ \ 16 \\
\hline
255\ 00 \\
425\ 0 \\
\hline
\$680.00
\end{array}
$$

Some communities have other taxes, such as sales taxes, to bring in additional revenue. A sales tax is computed as a percent of the selling price of an article.

COMMISSION

Some salespeople receive salary in the form of a *commission* based on the value of the goods sold. The commission is usually computed by taking an agreed upon percent of sales. Sometimes, the salesperson deducts the commission from the money received and turns the balance over to the employer. The money turned over to the employer is called the *net proceeds*.

EXAMPLE: A farmer shipped 2,650 bushels of apples to market. His agent sold the apples at $8.40 per bushel and deducted $4\frac{1}{2}\%$ commission. What were the net proceeds?

SOLUTION: The total sales were
$$\$8.40 \times 2,660 = \$22,260.00$$
The commission was $4\frac{1}{2}$ of $22,260
$$= \underline{1,001.70}$$
The net proceeds were $\qquad$ \$21,258.30

EXAMPLE: A book salesman receives a commission of 7% on sales. If his commission amounted to $168 on an order, what was the amount of the order?

SOLUTION: 7% of the order was $168.

To find the size of the order we divide the part ($168) by the rate.

$$\frac{\$168}{7\%} = \frac{168}{0.07}$$

$$0.07.\overline{)168.00.}\,\,2400.$$

The amount of the order was $2,400.

EXAMPLE: In buying a jacket, a man pays a sales tax of 3%. If his tax amounted to $1.95, what was the cost of the jacket?

SOLUTION: $1.95 represents 3% of the cost of the jacket. To find the total cost we divide the part by the rate.

$$\$1.95 \div 3\% = \frac{1.95}{0.03} = \frac{195}{3} = \$65$$

The jacket cost $65.

EXAMPLE: A real estate agent sold a house for $85,000 and received a commission of $3,825. What was her rate of commission?

SOLUTION: To find the rate of commission we divide the commission received by the selling price of the house.

$$\frac{\$3,825}{\$85,000}$$

$$85,000\overline{)3,825.000}\,\,0.045$$
$$\underline{3\,400\,00}$$
$$425\,000$$
$$\underline{425\,000}$$

The rate of commission was $4\frac{1}{2}\%$.

DISCOUNT

During sales, articles are usually marked down in price. Sometimes, a buyer will save money by buying for cash. Whenever an article is sold for less than its regular price it is sold at a *discount*. The original price is called the *marked price* or *list price*. The percent of the marked price that is deducted is called the *rate of discount*. Thus,

Discount = List price × Rate of discount
Sale price = List price − Discount

EXAMPLE: At a clearance sale, the Fashion Shop sold a $69.50 raincoat at a discount of 15%. What was the sale price of the raincoat?

SOLUTION: In order to obtain the discount we find 15% of $69.50.

$$\begin{array}{r} \$69.50 \\ \times\ \ 0.15 \\ \hline 34750 \\ \underline{6950} \\ \$10.4250 \end{array} = \$10.43 \text{ to the nearest cent}$$

The sale price is obtained by subtracting the discount from the list price.

$$\begin{array}{r} \$69.50 \\ -\ 10.43 \\ \hline \$59.07 \end{array} = \text{Sale price of the coat}$$

EXAMPLE: A chair was priced at $47.50. During a sale the chair sold for $38.00. What was the rate of discount on the chair?

SOLUTION: The discount on the chair was $47.50 − $38.00 = $9.50.

The rate of discount = $\dfrac{\text{Discount}}{\text{List Price}} = \dfrac{\$9.50}{\$47.50}$.

$$
\begin{array}{r}
0.2 \\
47.50\overline{\smash{)}9.50.0} \\
9.50\ 0
\end{array}
$$

The rate of discount was 0.2, or 20%.

EXAMPLE: On a furniture order, a merchant received a discount of $115 for cash. This represented $2\frac{1}{2}\%$ of the purchase price. What was the purchase price?

SOLUTION: $115 represents $2\frac{1}{2}\%$.
To find the purchase price we divide the part ($115) by the rate ($2\frac{1}{2}\%$).

$$\frac{\$115}{2\frac{1}{2}\%} = \frac{115}{0.025}$$

$$
\begin{array}{r}
4600. \\
0.025\overline{\smash{)}115.000.} \\
100 \\
15\ 0 \\
15\ 0
\end{array}
$$

The purchase price was $4,600.

EXAMPLE: A school wishes to buy baseball equipment that is listed at $600. A.M. Smith Co. quotes discounts of 15% and 10%. C.A. Jones Co. quotes a single discount of 25%. Which offer is better and by how much?

SOLUTION:
A.M. Smith Co. offer

$$
\begin{array}{r}
\$600 \quad \text{(list price)} \\
\times\ \ 0.15 \\
\hline
\$90.00 \quad \text{(first discount)}
\end{array}
$$

$$
\begin{array}{r}
\$510 \quad \text{(price after discount)} \\
\times\ \ 0.10 \\
\hline
\$51 \quad \text{(second discount)}
\end{array}
$$

$$
\begin{array}{r}
\$510 \\
-\ \ 51 \quad \text{(second discount)} \\
\hline
\$459 \quad \text{(net price)}
\end{array}
$$

C.A. Jones Co. offer:

$$
\begin{array}{r}
\$600 \quad \text{(list price)} \\
0.25 \\
\hline
3000 \\
1200 \\
\hline
\$150.00 \quad \text{(discount)}
\end{array}
$$

$$
\begin{array}{r}
\$600.00 \quad \text{(list price)} \\
-\ 150.00 \\
\hline
\$450 \quad \text{(net price)}
\end{array}
$$

The C.A. Jones offer is better by $9.

INTEREST

Business people sometimes need money to buy new equipment or stock. The business person usually borrows this money from a bank. The bank charges the business person interest for the use of the money borrowed. Thus, at the end of the period for which the loan was made, the borrower repays the original amount borrowed, or principal, plus the interest charged. For example, Mr. Barry borrows $6,000 from the National Bank for a period of 3 years. He agrees to pay interest at the rate of 14% annually. In this case,

$$
\begin{aligned}
\$6,000 &= \text{Principal} \\
14\% &= \text{Rate of interest} \\
3 \text{ years} &= \text{Time}
\end{aligned}
$$

The rule for finding the interest is

$$\text{Interest} = \text{Principal} \times \text{Rate} \times \text{Time}$$

The interest on Mr. Barry's loan is computed as follows:

$$
\begin{aligned}
\text{Interest} &= \text{Principal} \times \text{Rate} \times \text{Time} \\
\text{Interest} &= \$6,000 \times 14\% \times 3 \\
&= \$6,000 \times \tfrac{14}{100} \times 3 \\
&= \$2,520
\end{aligned}
$$

At the end of 3 years Mr. Barry will repay the bank the principal ($6,000) plus the interest ($2,520). The sum of the principal and the interest is called the *amount*.

EXAMPLE: Find the interest on $2,500 for 2 years at 12%.

SOLUTION:

$$
\begin{aligned}
\text{Interest} &= \text{Principal} \times \text{Rate} \times \text{Time} \\
&= \$2,500 \times \tfrac{12}{100} \times 2 = \$600
\end{aligned}
$$

EXAMPLE: Find the interest on $3,125 for 4 years at $12\frac{1}{2}\%$.

SOLUTION:

$$\text{Interest} = \text{Principal} \times \text{Rate} \times \text{Time}$$
$$= \$3,125 \times \tfrac{1}{8} \times 4 = \$1,562.50$$

NOTE: $12\dfrac{1}{2}\% = \dfrac{12\frac{1}{2}}{100} = \dfrac{25}{200} = \dfrac{1}{8}$

EXAMPLE: Find the interest on $82.50 for 1 year and 3 months at 6%.

SOLUTION:

$$\text{Interest} = \text{Principal} \times \text{Rate} \times \text{Time}$$
$$= \$82.50 \times \tfrac{6}{100} \times \tfrac{5}{4}$$
$$= \$6.19 \text{ to the nearest cent}$$

NOTE: 1 year and 3 months =
$$1 + \tfrac{3}{12} = 1\tfrac{1}{4} = \tfrac{5}{4} \text{ years}$$

EXAMPLE: Mr. Crane borrowed $875 to buy a car. The money was borrowed for a period of 2 years and 4 months at 15% interest. What amount did Mr. Crane pay back?

SOLUTION:

$$\text{Interest} = \text{Principal} \times \text{Rate} \times \text{Time}$$
$$= \$875 \times \tfrac{15}{100} \times \tfrac{7}{3} = \$306.25$$
$$\text{Amount} = \text{Principal} + \text{Interest}$$
$$= \$875 + \$306.25 = \$1,181.25$$

Mr. Crane paid back $1,181.25.

EXAMPLE: Mrs. James placed $120 in a bank. At the end of the year Mrs. James received $7.80 in interest. What rate of interest did the bank pay Mrs. James?

SOLUTION: To find the rate of interest we divide the interest ($7.80) by the principal ($120).

$$\frac{\$7.80}{\$120} \qquad 120 \overline{)7.800} \;\; 0.065$$
$$\underline{7.200}$$
$$600$$
$$\underline{600}$$

The rate of interest paid by the bank was $6\frac{1}{2}\%$.

EXAMPLE: Mr. Sloan paid $2,520 in interest on a mortgage loan. If the interest rate was $10\frac{1}{2}\%$, what was the amount of the mortgage loan?

SOLUTION: $2,520 is equal to $10\frac{1}{2}\%$ of the amount of the loan. To find the amount of the loan we divide the part ($2,520) by the rate.

$$\frac{\$2,520}{10\frac{1}{2}\%} = \frac{2,520}{0.105}$$

$$0.105.\overline{)2520.000.} \;\; 24\,000.$$
$$\underline{210}$$
$$420$$
$$\underline{420}$$

The amount of the loan was $24,000.

PRACTICE TEST 10

1. The budget for a certain town requires a tax collection of $58,940. The assessed valuation of taxable property in the town is $1,684,000. What is the tax rate?

2. A real estate agent receives a commission of $2\frac{1}{2}\%$ on the sales price of a lot. Find the agent's commission on a lot that sold for $16,250.

3. An agent sold a shipment of 72 radio sets at $23.48 per set. His commission was $92.98. What was his rate of commission?

4. Mrs. Ames bought a chair at a discount of 18%. If the amount of the discount was $75.60, what was the cost of the chair?

5. Mr. Albert bought some merchandise for his business for $8,125. To do this he paid $2,500 in cash and borrowed the balance from his bank for one year at 16% annual interest. What was the actual cost of the merchandise?

6. An agent sold a shipment of 38 dozen golf balls at $14.70 per dozen. What was the agent's commission at $5\frac{1}{2}\%$?

7. The cost of a used car was $2,884.00. This included a sales tax of 3%. Find the cost of the car without the tax.

8. A lot is assessed for $11,500. The real estate tax on the lot is $287.50. What is the tax rate?

9. Money is borrowed for one year at $12\frac{1}{2}\%$ interest. If the interest payment was $850, what was the size of the loan?

10. A salesman sold 42 dozen shorts at $22.50 per dozen. What was the salesman's commission at the rate of $4\frac{1}{2}\%$?

11. By receiving a discount of 15% a buyer saved $28.44 on a table. What was the price of the table before the discount was taken off?

12. A farmer shipped 196 dozen eggs to market. His agent sold the eggs at $0.82 per dozen and charged the farmer 6% of the selling price for his services. How much did the farmer receive?

13. A hat was priced at $10.80. During a sale, the hat sold for $9.18. What was the rate of discount on the hat?

14. A man's tax on his home is $1,952. The tax rate is $3.20 per $100 of assessed value. What is the assessed value of the home?

15. Mr. Fisher deposited $3,210 in his bank for a period of 8 months at $5\frac{1}{2}\%$ annual interest. What amount did Mr. Fisher withdraw at the end of the 8 months?

16. The sales tax on a table was $2.70. If the tax rate was 2% what was the cost of the table?

17. Mr. Leonard bought a shipment of goods for $7,250. He paid $3,000 in cash and agreed to pay the balance in 9 months with interest at $12\frac{1}{2}\%$. What was the total cost of the shipment?

18. A coat was priced at $68.50. At a sale, the coat sold for $54.80. What was the rate of discount on the coat?

19. A real estate agent collected $4,250 in rents. She gave the owner $3,910 and retained the balance as commission. What was her rate of commission?

20. A refrigerator was marked down in price from $249.50 to $199.60 during a sale. What was the rate of discount?

PRACTICE TEST 11

1. Of 480 students in a high school, 180 were in the ninth year. What percent of the students in the school were in the ninth year?

2. A car dealer made 35% of his annual car sales during the months of April and May. If he sold 133 cars during these months, how many cars did he sell during the year?

3. A boy had to save $12.40 to buy a new shirt. What percent of the needed amount had he saved when he had $7.75?

4. A clothing store made sales of $8,560 during a certain month. If $3\frac{1}{2}\%$ of the sales amount was profit, how much profit did the store earn during this month?

5. During the year 1988 a certain type of TV set sold for $368. This was $133\frac{1}{3}\%$ of the price of the same type of TV set in 1998. What was the price of this set in 1998?

6. The Rivera family planned to save 14% of its income. If the total annual income is $55,500, how much do they plan to save each month?

7. In a certain election district 684 voters cast their ballots. This was 60% of the total number of voters in the district. How many voters were in the district?

8. Mr. Denning bought a jacket for $67.50 and a tie for $12.50. If a sales tax of 3% was added to the price of his purchase, what was his total bill?

9. The Blue Sox baseball team won 40 games of 48 games played. The Green Sox won 27 games of 45 games played. Which team won the greater percentage of games? By what percent?

10. A car is insured for $12,000 or 80% of its actual value. What is its actual value?

11. On a snowy day, 85% of the pupils of Wilson High School were present. If 527 pupils were present, how many pupils were enrolled at the school?

12. An oil tank contains 580 gallons. When 87 gallons of oil have been used, what percent of the 580 gallons are left in the tank?

13. Of 580 students in a high school graduating class 45% are planning to go to college. How many of the graduates are planning to go to college?

14. Mr. Albert sold his car for $6,240. This was 65% of the original cost. What was the original cost of Mr. Albert's car?

15. A theater has 1,450 seats. If 42% of these seats are balcony seats, how many balcony seats does the theater have?

16. A motorist planned a trip covering 920 miles. After he had traveled 598 miles, what percent of the mileage planned had he covered?

17. A department store placed 980 overcoats on sale for one week. On Monday 298 overcoats were sold, on Tuesday 312 overcoats were sold, and on Wednesday 223 overcoats were sold. What percent of the 980 overcoats were left unsold?

18. The value of a new car decreases 35% in the first year. If a car costs $9,800, how much would it be worth at the end of the first year?

19. When Mrs. Rogers had paid $374 for her sofa she had paid 68% of the total cost. What was the total cost of the sofa?

20. A homeowner figured that 62% of his expenses were taxes. If his tax bill was $775, what was the total expense of running his house?

21. A machine part manufacturer found that $2\frac{1}{2}$% of the parts made in his factory were defective. If 12 parts were defective, how many parts were made in the factory?

22. A class library contained 325 books. Of these, 36% were history books. How many history books did the class library contain?

23. A TV dealer received a shipment of TV sets that cost him $192 per set. At what price did he sell each of these sets if he made a profit of $12\frac{1}{2}$%?

24. The total admissions in a movie house were 1,550 during one week. If 527 attended the movie house on Saturday, what percent of the total admissions for the week occurred on Saturday?

25. A sporting goods store sells its goods so that the profit is 12% of its sales. What must be the amount of sales if the profit is to be $42,000?

26. A man keeps $2,800 in a savings bank for 1 year at 5% interest compounded semiannually. How much does the man get when he withdraws his money?

27. A manufacturer wishes to make a profit of $1.80 on an article. If this profit is to be 15% of the wholesale price of the article, what is the wholesale price of the article?

28. A woman bought a dress at a discount of $16\frac{2}{3}$%. If the woman paid $32.50, what was the original price of the dress?

29. The price of heating oil was raised from $1.40 to $1.47 per gallon. What was the percent of increase?

30. Cement used for concrete contains 64% lime. How many pounds of lime are there in 650 pounds of cement?

31. A lot is assessed at $15,800 and the tax is $711. What is the tax rate?

32. When 100 new students enrolled in a certain high school its enrollment was increased by 8%. What was the original enrollment of the high school?

33. Ms. Polanski has a $5,000 bond on which she receives annual interest of $450. What rate of interest does the bond pay?

34. A man bought a car for $12,800. He paid 40% down and arranged to pay the balance in 24 equal monthly installments. How much was each installment?

35. On an electricity bill of $40.80, Mrs. Miller pays only $38.76 because she pays before a certain date. What percent discount is Mrs. Miller allowed?

36. On a family income of $29,600 the Burton family saved $8\frac{1}{2}$% one year. How much did the Burton family spend that year?

37. By hiring 45 new employees a department store increased its help by 18% during the Christmas season. How many employees did the store have before the increase?

38. In a high school enrollment of 1,580 students, 1,501 joined the student organization. What percent of the students joined the student organization?

39. A camera usually sells for $68. Because it was slightly damaged it sold for $59.50. What was the rate of discount?

40. Last year, a man earned $19,200. This year, his salary was increased to $20,736. What was the percent of increase?

41. One year, a star baseball player got 220 hits. If 45% of these hits were for extra bases, how many extra base hits did the player get?

42. In a certain high school, $62\frac{1}{2}$% of the students are taking science courses. If 650 students are in science classes in this school, what is the total enrollment of the school?

43. A salesman of machinery sold 148 machines at $79.50 each. If he received a commission of $7\frac{1}{2}$%, how much was his commission?

44. A manufacturer decided to spend 18% of her expense budget for advertising. If she spent $2,700 for advertising, what was her total expense budget?

45. A dealer sold 112 cars during the month of May and 96 cars during the month of June. What was the percent of decrease?

46. At an evening performance 85% of the seats in a movie house were occupied. If 731 people attended this performance what was the seating capacity of the movie house?

47. A bookstore sold 762 books at $3.95 each. If the dealer makes a profit of 40% on each sale, what is his total profit on the sale of the books?

48. In a high school graduating class of 125 students, 35 students received athletic awards. What percent of the graduating class received athletic awards?

49. Mr. Rodriguez bought a jacket at $69.50, a tie at $15.50, and a raincoat at $72.35. If he received a discount of $12\frac{1}{2}$% on each of these items, what was his bill?

50. A merchant sold articles of clothing at 140% of what he paid for them. What did he pay for an article that he sold for $84?

Averages

To find the average of several numbers, we find the sum of the numbers and divide this sum by the number of addends.

EXAMPLE: A boys marks on 6 tests where 90, 85, 82, 68, 84, and 77. What was the average of the boy's marks?

SOLUTION:

$$
\begin{array}{r}
90 \\
85 \\
82 \\
68 \\
84 \\
77 \\
\hline
486
\end{array}
\qquad
6\overline{)486}^{\,81}
$$

The boy's average was 81.

EXAMPLE: A traveling salesman clocked his daily mileages for 7 days as follows:
    327, 462, 184, 217, 92, 149, 198.
Find the average daily mileage to the nearest mile.

SOLUTION:

$$
\begin{array}{r}
327 \\
462 \\
184 \\
217 \\
92 \\
149 \\
198 \\
\hline
1629
\end{array}
\qquad 1629 \div 7 = 232\tfrac{5}{7}
$$

$232\tfrac{5}{7} = 233$ miles to the nearest mile.

The average daily mileage was 233.

EXAMPLE: In a small company, 9 workers each received $72 per day and 6 workers each received $82 per day. What was the average daily wage per worker?

SOLUTION: The total amount of wages was

$$
\begin{array}{r}
9 \times \$72 = \quad \$\ 648 \\
6 \times \$82 = \quad \underline{492} \\
\$1140
\end{array}
$$

Since there were 15 workers we divide $1140 by 15.

$$
\begin{array}{r}
76 \\
15\overline{)1140} \\
\underline{105} \\
90 \\
\underline{90}
\end{array}
$$

The average daily wage was $76 per worker.

EXAMPLE: The Roosevelt High School football team played a schedule of 7 games. The total attendance for the 7 games was 9,443. Find the average attendance per game.

SOLUTION:

$$
7\overline{)9{,}443}^{\,1{,}349}
$$

The average attendance was 1,349.

PRACTICE TEST 12

1. Find the average of 49, 15, 9, 75.

2. A student received the following grades in a series of tests: 78, 85, 92, 65, 71, and 83. What was her average on these tests?

3. A student's budget showed that he spent the following amounts over a period of several weeks: $3.01, $2.89, $4.17, $1.67, $3.96, and $2.06. What was his average expenditure per week over this period of time, to the nearest cent?

4. The Star Theater had an attendance of 5,803 for 7 performances. What was the average attendance per performance?

5. A boy had an average of 84% on 4 tests. He received a mark of 94% on a fifth test. What was his average for the five tests?

6. A garage attendant made the following sales of gasoline: $23.70, $30.80, $39.20, $28.90, $34.70, and $29.50. What was his average sale, to the nearest cent?

7. After 6 games a man's average bowling score was 186. After 3 other games his average score was 201. What was his average score for all 9 games?

8. On a basketball team, the heights of the players are 6'6", 5'7", 6'2", 5'11", and 6'3". What is the average of these heights?

9. A TV set dealer made the following number of sales daily during the holiday season: 87, 67, 38, 47, 79, 82, 99, and 101. What was the average daily number of sales?

10. The average of 5 numbers is 37. What must a sixth number be if the average of the six numbers is to be 46?

ONE HUNDRED VERBAL PROBLEMS

1. Mrs. Abbate wishes to make a dozen towels. If each towel is to be $\frac{3}{4}$ yard long, how many yards of material should Mrs. Abbate buy?

2. On a trip, Mr. Moore drove at an average speed of 42 miles per hour. If the trip took $3\frac{1}{2}$ hours, how far did Mr. Moore drive?

3. Mr. Evans paid $10.60 each for 72 shirts. He sold the shirts for $14.20 each. What was his total profit on the shipment?

4. A plumber had a piece of pipe 5 feet long. He used 2 pieces, each $1\frac{3}{4}$ feet long. How big a piece of pipe was left?

5. Jose spent 6 hours in school. Each school period is $\frac{3}{4}$ hour long. How many periods did Jose spend in school?

6. Mr. Abrams earns $480 per week. He saves 5% of his earnings. How much does Mr. Abrams spend in a year?

7. Anne earns $2.50 per hour for babysitting. At the end of a month she had earned $95.00. How many hours did Anne work?

8. The telephone bills for a family for five months were $25.83, $26.02, $27.34, $26.56, and $25.54. What was the average telephone bill per month?

9. On a map $\frac{1}{8}$ of an inch stands for 24 miles. On this map two cities are $2\frac{1}{4}$ inches apart. What is the actual distance between the cities?

10. A 5-gallon can of motor oil costs $28.00. What is the cost of 1 quart of the oil?

11. A department store placed 144 suits on sale. By the end of the day 108 suits had been sold. What percent of the suits were sold on the day?

12. Mr. Foote placed a cement walk along the side of his house. The walk is 18 inches wide and 32 feet long. What was the cost of the walk at $2.10 a square foot?

13. A car will travel 17.4 miles on a gallon of gas. How many gallons of gas will be needed for a trip of 435 miles?

14. Mrs. Santos buys $3\frac{1}{2}$ pounds of beef at $2.68 per pound and $8\frac{1}{4}$ pounds of turkey at $0.96 per pound. How much did Mrs. Santos spend?

15. The rainfall for three months in a certain city was 4.87 inches, 6.08 inches, and 5.49 inches. What was the average rainfall for the three months?

16. A home was valued at $73,500. It was insured for 80% of its value at a premium of $0.40 per $100. Find the yearly premium.

17. A woman buys 2 pounds of butter at $1.85 per pound and 3 pounds of cheese at $2.15 per pound. She gives the clerk as $20 bill. How much does she receive in change?

18. A traveling salesman drives his car 30,000 miles a year. His car travels 16 miles to the gallon of gas. How many gallons of gas does he use in a year?

19. What will it cost to send a 15-word telegram, if the first 10 words cost 85 cents and each additional word costs 7 cents?

20. A basketball team won 10 of its first 20 games. It then won its next 5 games. What fractional part of its total number of games did it win?

21. At 20 miles per hour, how long does it take to travel 1 mile?

22. In the shop, a boy was given a board 16 feet long and was asked to cut it into pieces, each $1\frac{1}{2}$ feet long. How many full pieces did he get?

23. If 4 oranges cost 66 cents, what will one dozen cost, at the same rate?

24. On a test taken by 96 pupils, $\frac{1}{8}$ of the pupils failed. How many pupils passed?

25. If a space of 18 inches is allowed for each person, how many persons can be seated in a row of bleacher seats 90 feet long?

26. If John can save $0.25 per day, how many days will it take him to save $9.50?

27. If a discount of 16% is allowed on a work shirt that ordinarily sells for $8.50, what is the sales price?

28. Meghan makes a profit of $4\frac{1}{2}$ cents on each paper that she sells. How much profit will she make on 60 papers?

29. A bunch of bananas weighs 3 pounds and 8 ounces. What is the cost of the bananas at $0.60 per pound?

30. A worker receives $7.20 per hour. What is his pay for $42\frac{1}{2}$ hours of work?

31. By paying $10 cash and the balance at $3 per week, how long would it take to pay for a used bicycle costing $64?

32. During the past season, a basketball team won 18 games and lost 7 games. What percent of the games did the team win?

33. A concrete floor 3 inches thick is to be laid in a cellar 30 feet by 24 feet. How many cubic feet of concrete are needed?

34. A babysitter worked from 8:30 P.M. to 11:00 P.M. At the rate of $2.10 per hour, how much did she earn?

35. If there are 7 frankfurters to the pound, how many pounds of frankfurters are needed for a picnic to supply 19 pupils with 2 frankfurters each?

36. An army is organized as follows:

    250 soldiers in a company
      4 companies in a battalion
      3 battalions in a regiment

    How many soldiers are there in a regiment?

37. A homeowner uses 5,015 gallons of oil during the heating season. How much does she spend for oil, if she pays $1.46 per gallon?

38. What must be the length of a box that is 4 feet wide and 3 feet deep, if it has a volume of 96 cubic feet?

39. A saleswoman received $40 per day, plus a commission of 2% on all sales over $300 per week. What was her salary for a 5-day week during which her sales amounted to $1,260?

40. A high school has 480 pupils of whom 80% attend a school concert. If each pupil paid $1.05 for a ticket, find the total receipts.

41. A notebook listed at $2 is sold to the school at a discount of 25%. What is the selling price?

42. A data-entry clerk spends $86 per week for food. This is 20% of his weekly income. What is the weekly income?

43. Mr. Smith owns a lot valued at $12,000. It is assessed at 80% of its value. How much tax does he pay if the tax rate is $1\frac{1}{2}$% of the assessed value?

44. Mr. Adamski's daily pay was $84. He received an increase of $6.30. What is the percent of increase?

45. If 5 ounces of cheese cost $0.85, what is the cost of 24 ounces at the same rate?

46. What will be the cost of 50 feet of hose at 0.55\frac{1}{2}$ per foot?

47. If $\frac{1}{4}$ inch represents 5 yards, how many inches long must a scale drawing be to show a football field 100 yards long?

48. If, on the average, 1 potato out of every 50 in a bin spoils, what percent of the potatoes spoil?

49. A certain grade in a school contains 96 pupils. If there are 40 boys, what is the ratio of boys to girls in this grade?

50. A man borrowed $65 from the bank for one year. He paid $7.80 in interest. What rate of interest was charged by the bank?

51. A merchant paid $40 for 5 dozen notebooks and sold them for $1.25 each. What was her profit?

52. How many stakes $5\frac{1}{2}$ feet long can be cut from 10 lengths of lumber each 12 feet long?

53. If a boy walks 6 miles in 2 hours, how far will he walk in 5 hours, at the same rate?

54. How many square yards of carpeting are needed to cover a floor 18 feet long by 12 feet wide?

55. If a mixture of water and alcohol contains 20% alcohol, what percent of the mixture is water?

56. At the rate of 360 miles per hour, how far would an airplane travel in 1 hour and 20 minutes?

57. A page in an average newspaper has 8 columns of print. Each column consists of 160 lines and each line averages 6 words. Find the average number of words on a full page.

58. A boy spends 45% of his allowance for lunches and 10% for carfare. What percent of his allowance does he have left?

59. At the rate of $0.80 per $100, how much does it cost to insure a car against fire and theft for $1,650?

60. A dealer purchased tee shirts at $2.40 each and sold them for $4.25 each. His overhead was $0.60 per shirt. How much money did he make on each shirt?

61. How much money would you have if you had 2 quarters, 3 dimes, 7 nickels, and 14 pennies?

62. An agent sold 250 boxes of apples at $6.50 each. He charged a commission of 5%. What was his commission?

63. A concrete sidewalk 3 feet wide, 18 feet long, and 4 inches thick contains how many cubic feet of concrete?

64. A boy scores an average of 6 out of every 10 shots. At the same rate, how many scoring shots should he make out of l00 attempts?

65. A baseball team lost 4 games, which were 20% of the total number of games played. How many games did the team play?

66. Maria's class purchased 10 boxes of candy for $43.20. If each box contained 24 candies, what was the cost of each candy?

67. How much profit does a grocer make if he buys a case of beans containing 24 cans for $7.50 and sells it for $0.42 per can?

68. Ms. Delilio borrowed $1,200 from a bank for 90 days at 12% annual interest. How much interest did she pay?

69. If a dress factory uses $3\frac{1}{8}$ yards of cloth to make a dress, how many yards will it take to make 12 dresses?

70. The sales tax in a certain city is 2%. A man buys a camera and pays a sales tax of $3.20. What was the cost of the camera, exclusive of the sales tax?

71. John's father bought 2 turkeys. One weighed $12\frac{1}{2}$ pounds and the other $13\frac{3}{4}$ pounds. How much did they weigh together?

72. A man pays a water bill of $6.75 every three months. How much does he pay in a year?

73. If a car travels 357 miles and uses 21 gallons of gas, how many miles does it average per gallon of gas?

74. Mary receives $2.00 weekly as an allowance. If she saves $0.70 of it, what percent does she save?

75. In six tests Joshua had scores of 80, 90, 100, 70, 90, and 80. What was his average score?

76. If a boy makes 16 free throws out of 20 tries, what percent of his throws are made?

77. A plane traveled 510 miles in $1\frac{1}{2}$ hours. What was the average rate of speed of the plane?

78. Mrs. Jones buys a refrigerator. She pays $230 down and $16.50 a month for 18 months. What was the cost of the refrigerator?

79. A boy spent one third of his money for a tennis racket and one fifth of his money for balls. What fractional part of his money did he spend?

80. By Thursday a family had spent $148, which was 80% of its weekly budget. How much was the budget?

81. Mr. White's farm is mortgaged for $52,000. At a rate of 8% what is the first year's annual interest charge for the mortgage?

82. If 30 inches of leather will make one belt, how many feet of leather would be needed to make 12 belts?

83. Of 75 dozen eggs sold by a dealer, 60 dozen were white eggs. What percent of the eggs sold were white eggs?

84. At a sale, all clothing was marked down 15%. Beth Steinfeld bought a blouse for $10.95 and a scarf for $8.85. What was the discount on her purchase?

85. A certain airplane uses 28.6 gallons of fuel per hour of flight. How many hours can the plane fly if its tank contains 214.5 gallons of fuel?

86. A plumber has a 12-foot length of pipe. From this length he cuts two pieces, each measuring $3\frac{1}{4}$ feet in length. How many feet of pipe remain?

87. A fuel oil bill for 350 gallons amounted to $518. What was the price per gallon of oil?

88. Mr. Frank spent $\frac{3}{8}$ of his savings for a new refrigerator. If the refrigerator cost $540, what were Mr. Frank's savings?

89. A school librarian can buy books at a 20% discount from the list price. One month she spent $72 for books. What was the list price value of the books?

90. At a sale, a furniture dealer sold a sofa for $144. The sofa cost the dealer $150. What was his percent of loss?

91. How many sheets of copper each 0.024 inches thick will make a pile 7.2 inches high?

92. Mr. Downs bought a camera for $56. This was 80% of the list price. What was the list price?

93. Ms. Rojas's yearly income is $23,400 a year. If she decides to save 10% of her yearly income, how much must she save each month?

94. A gallon of paint will cover 420 square feet. How many gallons of paint are needed to paint a porch 45 feet long and 14 feet wide?

95. At a special sale counter, notebooks were sold for $0.98 each. If the cash register at this counter showed sales of $109.76, how many notebooks were sold?

96. The mileage meter on Mr. Sanford's car read 5,684.9 at the start of the month, and 6,512.3 at the end of the month. How many miles did Mr. Sanford drive during the month?

97. Mrs. Frost bought a roast weighing $4\frac{1}{2}$ pounds. If she serves the roast to 6 people, what fraction of a pound of meat per person will the roast provide?

98. On a trip, Mrs. Ahmed drove 188 miles in 4 hours. On the return trip, she took a different route and traveled 197 miles in $4\frac{1}{4}$ hours. What was the average rate of speed for the trip?

99. At an election for class president, the winning candidate received 91 votes. This was 65% of the total vote cast. How many votes were cast?

100. Of 76 pupils in a certain grade, 57 passed a test. What percent of the pupils passed the test?

Mastery Exams

EXAM 1

1. A cab driver uses 18 gallons of gas in driving 264.6 miles. The average number of miles per gallon of gas used is:
   (A) 15.2 (B) 16.7 (C) 14.7 (D) 12.9
   (E) 14.9

2. Mr. Allan gave the clerk a $5 bill to pay for two dozen pencils at $0.59 per dozen. The amount of change he received was:
   (A) $4.41 (B) $4.51 (C) $3.92 (D) $3.82
   (E) $3.85

3. A new paperback sells for $2.48. The cost of a class set of 30 at a discount of 25% is:
   (A) $62.00 (B) $56.55 (C) $55.80
   (D) $74.40 (E) $52.00

4. Ms. Shapiro borrowed $500 for 3 months at 15% annual interest. The amount she paid back at the end of 3 months was:
   (A) $518.75 (B) $520.50 (C) $512.25
   (D) $518.25 (E) $95.25

5. A grocer bought one dozen key rings for $3.48. He sold the key rings for $0.37 each. His profit was:
   (A) $1.08 (B) $4.44 (C) $3.11 (D) $0.60
   (E) none of these

6. A school district with an assessed valuation of $2,480,500 has a tax rate of $12 per $1,000. The amount raised by taxes was:
   (A) $2,976.60 (B) $2,976.06 (C) $29,760
   (D) $29,766 (E) none of these

7. A boy earned $5.50 per hour for time worked up to 40 hours and $1\frac{1}{2}$ as much for all time worked over 40 hours. The amount of money he earned during one week when he worked 52 hours was:
   (A) $253 (B) $249.60 (C) $319
   (D) $324 (E) $195.40

8. A plane started on a flight at 9:30 A.M. and arrived at its destination at 1:45 P.M. The plane used 51 gallons of gas. The number of gallons used per hour was:
   (A) 216.25 (B) 12 (C) 12.75 (D) 204
   (E) none of these

9. A boy traveled 17 miles on his bicycle in 2 hours. At the same rate the time it will take him to travel 42.5 miles is:
   (A) $2\frac{1}{2}$ hours (B) 3 hours (C) $4\frac{1}{2}$ hours
   (D) 5 hours (E) none of these

10. A man bought a house for $75,000. He had it painted and paid the painter $162 per day for 5 days. He also paid a carpenter $174 a day for 3 days of work. Additional expenses amounted to $1,392. He then sold the house for $87,500. His profit was:
    (A) $10,995 (B) $9,796 (C) $9,662
    (D) $10,128 (E) none of these

11. A tank is 22 inches long, 14 inches wide, and 12 inches high. If 1 gallon contains 231 cubic inches the number of gallons the tank will hold is:
    (A) 8 (B) 10 (C) 12 (D) 15
    (E) none of these

12. A man borrowed $650 from the bank for one year. He paid $94.25 in interest. The rate of interest charged by the bank was:
    (A) 14% (B) $14\frac{1}{2}$% (C) $15\frac{1}{2}$% (D) 12%
    (E) none of these

13. A man bought a set of furniture listed at $2,350. He received a discount of 5% and then paid a 3% sales tax on the selling price. The sales tax was:
    (A) $2,232.60 (B) $70.50 (C) $66.98
    (D) $68.39 (E) $72.40

14. A farmer shipped 2,000 bushels of potatoes to a commission merchant. The farmer paid $480 for freight and $140 for trucking. The potatoes were sold for $8.90 a bushel by the merchant, who charged 4% commission. The farmer's net return was:
    (A) $16,468 (B) $17,088 (C) $17,708
    (D) 19,132 (E) none of these

15. A farmer insured her stock of goods for $27,000 at a rate of $1.85 per $100. The cost of the insurance was:
    (A) $4,996 (B) $9.95 (C) $499.50
    (D) $409.50 (E) $501

16. Henry won first place in the shot-put with a heave of 37 feet 1 inch. John won second place with a heave of 35 feet 9 inches. Henry defeated John by:
    (A) 2 feet 2 inches (B) 1 foot 2 inches
    (C) 1 foot 4 inches (D) 2 feet 4 inches
    (E) none of these

17. If $\frac{1}{4}$ inch represents 5 yards, the number of inches needed to show a football field 100 yards long is:
    (A) 4 inches (B) 5 inches (C) 20 inches
    (D) 5 inches (E) 6 inches

18. The dimensions of a living room are 18 ft. by 15 ft. by 8 ft. If air weighs 0.08 lb. per cu. ft., the weight of the air in this room is:
    (A) 2,160 lb. (B) 216 lb. (C) 172.8 lb.
    (D) 17.28 lb. (E) 175 lb.

19. A radiator contains 8 gallons of water and 3 gallons of alcohol. The percent of alcohol in the radiator is:
    (A) $27\frac{3}{11}$% (B) $37\frac{1}{2}$% (C) $72\frac{8}{11}$%
    (D) 30% (E) 29%

20. A grocer paid $31 for 200 lb. of cabbage and sold it at the rate of 2 lb. for $0.39. His profit was:
    (A) $47.00 (B) $16.00 (C) $39.00
    (D) $8.00 (E) none of these

EXAM 2

1. The price of eggs decreased from $0.65 per dozen to $0.59 per dozen. The decrease per egg was:
(A) $0.06 (B) $0.02 (C) $0.01 (D) $0.005 (E) $0.03

2. A train was scheduled to arrive at 2:35 P.M. but was 40 minutes late. The train arrived at:
(A) 1:50 P.M. (B) 3:15 P.M. (C) 3:05 P.M. (D) 1:45 P.M. (E) 4:00 P.M.

3. If rock salt sells for $7.20 per hundred pounds, the cost of 750 pounds is:
(A) $49.00 (B) $49.50 (C) $52.00 (D) $54.00 (E) $56.00

4. At the rate of 360 miles per hour, the number of miles a plane will travel in 20 minutes is:
(A) 72 miles (B) 240 miles (C) 180 miles (D) 144 miles (E) none of these

5. A man receives a salary of $3,150 per month. During the year he spends $4,800 for rent, $8,200 for food, $3,750 for clothing, and $7,500 for other expenses. The amount he saves in one year is:
(A) $24,250 (B) $12,550 (C) $13,550 (D) $14,500 (E) $14,000

6. A motorist left New York City at 9:40 A.M. and arrived at his destination at 1:00 P.M. If he traveled at an average speed of 42 miles per hour the total distance he covered was:
(A) 150 miles (B) 140 miles (C) 126 miles (D) 168 miles (E) none of these

7. Ms. Talento bought some household furnishings. She paid 40% down and agreed to pay the balance in 12 equal installments of $10 each. The total cost of the furnishings was:
(A) $240 (B) $250 (C) $160 (D) $300 (E) none of these

8. At the rate of 2 bushels of seed per acre, the number of bushels of seed required to plant 28 acres is:
(A) 75 (B) 10 (C) 56 (D) 73 (E) 70

9. In a recent basketball game one team made 21 successful shots and missed 66. The percent of successful shots was approximately:
(A) 33% (B) 24% (C) 25% (D) 32% (E) 30%

10. The cost of 8 pounds of cabbage at 3 pounds for $0.65 is:
(A) $1.30 (B) $5.20 (C) $1.08 (D) $1.73 (E) $1.75

11. A homeowner bought 1,500 gallons of heating oil at $1.47 a gallon. The total cost was:
(A) $220.50 (B) $2,205.00 (C) $2,105.00 (D) $1,205.00 (E) $2,200.00

12. A salesman worked on a weekly salary of $180.00. To this was added a commission of 5% on all sales over $500. If his sales for one week were $750, his total salary for the week was:
(A) $217.50 (B) $205.00 (C) $212.50 (D) $192.50 (E) $210.00

13. A dealer has 12 pounds of peanuts. The number of 4-ounce bags she can fill is:
(A) 48 (B) 30 (C) 36 (D) 60 (E) none of these

14. The number of cubic feet of concrete contained in a sidewalk 3 ft. wide, 18 ft. long, and 4 in. thick is:
(A) 54 (B) 162 (C) 216 (D) 27 (E) none of these

15. At the start of a 1,565 mile trip there were 17 gallons of gasoline in the tank. During the trip 89 gallons of gasoline were bought. At the end of the trip 5 gallons of gasoline were left in the tank. The number of miles, to the nearest tenth, that the car averaged per gallon of gasoline, was:
(A) 16.4 (B) 15.5 (C) 17.1 (D) 16.5 (E) 16.1

16. At the rate of $0.72 for the first 10 minutes and $0.09 for each additional minute the cost of a 15-minute phone call is:
    (A) $1.35 (B) $1.27 (C) $1.07 (D) $1.17
    (E) none of these

17. A young man earns $1,350 a month. He pays $\frac{1}{5}$ of this amount for rent, $\frac{1}{3}$ of this amount for food, and $\frac{1}{6}$ for other household expenses. The amount of money he has left is:
    (A) $40.50 (B) $94.50 (C) $945
    (D) $480 (E) none of these

18. A man bought a lot for $1,200 and sold it for $1,500. His percent of gain based on the selling price was:
    (A) 25% (B) 80% (C) 75% (D) 20%
    (E) 22%

19. A room in a public building is to have a floor area of 770 square feet. If its length is 35 feet, then its width is:
    (A) 350 ft. (B) 44 ft. (C) 22 ft. (D) 20 ft.
    (E) none of these

20. Jerry's class purchased 10 boxes of candy for $43.20. If each box contained 24 candy bars the cost of each was:
    (A) $0.08 (B) $0.15 (C) $0.06 (D) $0.18
    (E) $0.12

EXAM 3

1. A salesman receives a salary of $20,900 per year and 2% commission on his sales. During the past year his sales amounted to $125,000. His average weekly salary was:
    (A) $420 (B) $450 (C) $400 (D) $459.50
    (E) $475

2. Mr. Thomas borrowed $1,200 from a bank for 90 days at $12\frac{1}{2}$% annual interest. The interest he paid was:
    (A) $37 (B) $60 (C) $42 (D) $37.50
    (E) $37.40

3. The cost of 36 pencils at the rate of 2 pencils for $0.37 is:
    (A) $13.32 (B) $6.96 (C) $6.66
    (D) $8.64 (E) none of these

4. A dealer sold 13 quart containers and 11 pint containers of ice cream in one day. The number of gallons of ice cream he sold was:
    (A) 6 (B) $4\frac{5}{8}$ (C) $5\frac{1}{8}$ (D) 5 (E) 6

5. In a school cafeteria hamburgers were sold at 65 cents each. During the week, 60 pounds of meat were sold that averaged 12 hamburgers to the pound. The value of the hamburgers sold was:
    (A) $486 (B) $720 (C) $780 (D) $568
    (E) none of these

6. A plane left Atlanta at 11:30 A.M. and flew to an airport near Boston. The plane was due at Boston 3:15 P.M. The plane arrived 25 minutes late. The time of the trip was:
    (A) 3 hr. 42 min. (B) 4 hr. 20 min.
    (C) 4 hr. 10 min. (D) 3 hr. 50 min.
    (E) none of these

7. The number of hours and minutes it will take a boy to ride his bicycle a distance of 10 miles at the rate of 6 miles per hour is:
    (A) 1 hr. 45 min. (B) 1 hr. 40 min.
    (C) 1 hr. 4 min. (D) 1 hr. 24 min.
    (E) none of these

8. Ms. Sanchez drove 198 miles in 5 hours and 30 minutes. Her average rate of speed per hour was:
    (A) 38 (B) 40 (C) 35 (D) 42
    (E) none of these

9. If a man pays a water bill of $6.75 every three months, the amount he pays in a year is:
    (A) $27 (B) $24.70 (C) $25.25
    (D) $26.50 (E) $25.00

10. A watermelon weighs 4 pounds 6 ounces. The cost of the watermelon at $0.40 per pound is:
    (A) $1.80 (B) $1.84 (C) $1.75 (D) $1.92
    (E) none of these

11. The ratio of 1 pint to 4 gallons is:
    (A) 1:4 (B) 1:32 (C) 1:16 (D) 1:8
    (E) 1:40

12. At $15 per square yard, the cost of a rug that is 18 feet long and 10 feet wide is:
(A) $900 (B) $1,200 (C) $600 (D) $300 (E) $400

13. On a plane trip, baggage over 40 pounds is charged at the rate per pound of 1% of the one-way fare. The charge for a bag weighing 52 pounds on a trip where the one-way fare is $98 is:
(A) $11.76 (B) $4.90 (C) $25.48 (D) $5.88 (E) $8.72

14. When Mr. Green bought a used car he made a down payment of $825. This was 30% of the total cost. The total cost was:
(A) $2,475 (B) $2,750 (C) $3,200 (D) $2,650 (E) none of these

15. Mr. Kelly allows 6% of his sales dollar for profit and 69% of his sales dollar for cost. The percent of his sales dollar he allows for other expenses is:
(A) 31% (B) 94% (C) 75% (D) 63% (E) none of these

16. One year a businesswoman made a profit of $15,000. The next year the profit was increased by 11% and the following year was decreased by 5%. The profit during the last year was:
(A) $15,750 (B) $15,850 (C) $17,250 (D) $15,675 (E) none of these

17. Mrs. Dana can buy a coat for $187.50 cash or for $25 down and $15 per month for 12 months. The charge for buying on the installment plan is:
(A) $12.50 (B) $17.50 (C) $22.50 (D) $27.50 (E) $18.50

18. After saving his allowance each week for nine weeks, Billy bought a jacket for $48.50. He found that he had $5.50 left. The amount of Billy's allowance each week was:
(A) $4.83 (B) $5.50 (C) $5.75 (D) $6.00 (E) none of these

19. A swimming pool 75 ft. long and 30 ft. wide is filled to an average depth of 6 ft. If $7\frac{1}{2}$ gal. of water occupy 1 cu ft., the number of gallons of water the pool contains is:
(A) 101,250 (B) 300 (C) $18\frac{3}{4}$ (D) 150 (E) none of these

20. Mr. Wang bought $800 worth of travelers' checks. The service charge was $\frac{3}{4}$ of 1% of the value of the checks. The service charge was:
(A) $5.00 (B) $4.00 (C) $3.00 (D) $8.00 (E) none of these

EXAM 4

1. Mr. Hall bought a car for $12,000. He made a down payment for $4,440 and agreed to pay the balance at the rate of $70 per month. The car was completely paid for in:
(A) 8 yr. (B) 10 yr. (C) 7 yr. 6 mo. (D) 9 yr. (E) none of these

2. Mr. Stanley received a check for $240. This was the interest for 1 year at 6% on money he had lent to Mr. Stein. The amount he had lent to Mr. Stein was:
(A) $5,000 (B) $1,440 (C) $2,400 (D) $400 (E) none of these

3. At a school play 248 student tickets were sold at $0.75 each. If the total receipts were $250 the number of adult tickets sold at $1 each was:
(A) 2 (B) 68 (C) 64 (D) 76 (E) 80

4. Mr. Roll can insure his household silver for $10,500 at $0.32 for $100 for 1 year. A 3-year policy costs $2\frac{1}{2}$ times as much. By buying a 3-year policy instead of three 1-year policies, Mr. Roll saves:
(A) $33.60 (B) $16.80 (C) $25.00 (D) $1.60 E) none of these

5. A train covers 24 miles in 36 minutes. Its rate of speed in miles per hour is:
(A) 60 (B) 45 (C) 48 (D) 40 (E) 38

6. In one state, the income tax law provides for a tax of 1% on the first $1,000 of taxable income and 2% on the second $1,000 of taxable income. Mr. Cable has a taxable income of $1,850. His income tax is:
   (A) $37 (B) $27 (C) $17 (D) $27.75
   (E) $28.50

7. The cost of a ticket to a school concert is $0.90. This includes a tax of 20% on the actual price of the ticket. The tax is:
   (A) $0.20 (B) $0.10 (C) $0.12 (D) $0.15
   (E) $0.18

8. Ballpoint pens sell for 2 for $0.33. A box of pens containing 72 pens sells for:
   (A) $11.88 (B) $23.76 (C) $11.52
   (D) $12.48 (E) none of these

9. The cost of cementing a walk 8 feet wide and 24 feet long at $14.40 a square yard is:
   (A) $31.20 (B) $2,764.80 (C) $307.20
   (D) $921.60 (E) none of these

10. Taxi fare is $1.20 for the first $\frac{1}{4}$ mile and $0.10 for each additional $\frac{1}{8}$ mile. A man pays a fare of $3.00. The number of miles he has traveled is:
    (A) 2 miles (B) $2\frac{1}{4}$ miles (C) $1\frac{3}{4}$ miles
    (D) $2\frac{1}{2}$ miles (E) 3 miles

11. If a TV set is bought on the installment plan there is a down payment of $25 and 12 monthly payments of $15 each. The same set may be bought for cash at 12% less than the installment price. The amount saved by making a cash payment is:
    (A) $20 (B) $21.60 (C) $24.00
    (D) $24.60 (E) $22

12. One state has a tax of $0.04 on each gallon of gasoline sold. One month the tax amounted to $50,013.68. The number of gallons of gasoline sold during the month was:
    (A) 125,342 (B) 1,250,342 (C) 1,205,042
    (D) 1,253,042 (E) 1,023,796

13. A rectangular box is to have a volume of 66 cubic feet. If its length is 8´3˝ and its width is 4´ then its height must be:
    (A) 1 ft. (B) 2 ft. 6 in. (C) 2 ft.
    (D) 2 ft. 3 in. (E) 3 ft.

14. The scale on a map is $\frac{3}{4}$ inch equals 24 miles. The actual distance between 2 cities that are $5\frac{1}{4}$ inches apart on this map is:
    (A) 126 mi. (B) $31\frac{1}{2}$ mi. (C) 63 mi.
    (D) 168 mi. (E) 170 mi.

15. A major league baseball team has won 24 games and lost 20 games. Out of the next 16 games the team wins 12 games. The percentage of games it has won is:
    (A) 60% (B) 36% (C) 50% (D) 75%
    (E) 55%

16. One year an automobile sales agency sells 3,200 cars. The following year sales are increased by 5%. The year after that sales decreased 15%. The number of cars sold that third year was:
    (A) 3,360 (B) 2,880 (C) 2,740 (D) 2,856
    (E) 2,800

17. A man buys furniture that has a list price of $255. He is allowed a discount of 12% but must pay a sales tax of 3% on the cost. The amount he actually pays is:
    (A) $217.67 (B) $231.13 (C) $224.40
    (D) $232.50 (E) none of these

18. A school has 510 students. They are to be divided into 18 classes so that, as far as possible, each class has the same number of students. After the students have been divided:
    (A) all classes have exactly the same number of students
    (B) 12 of the classes are smaller than the other 6
    (C) each class has over 30 students
    (D) one class is larger than all the others
    (E) none of these

19. A man traveled to his country home, a distance of 150 miles, and then back. His average rate of speed going was 50 miles an hour and his average return speed was 30 miles an hour. His average rate of speed for the entire trip was:
    (A) 40 miles per hour
    (B) 42 miles per hour
    (C) $37\frac{1}{2}$ miles per hour
    (D) 35 miles per hour
    (E) 30 miles per hour

20. A garden is 18 feet 3 inches long and 10 feet 8 inches wide. The amount of fencing needed to enclose the garden is:
    (A) 36 feet 11 inches
    (B) 47 feet 2 inches
    (C) 39 feet 7 inches
    (D) 57 feet 10 inches
    (E) none of these

EXAM 5

1. A strip of molding is 20 inches long. Five pieces each $3\frac{1}{2}$ inches long are cut from the strip. The amount of molding remaining is:
   (A) 3 inches (B) $3\frac{1}{2}$ inches
   (C) $2\frac{1}{2}$ inches (D) 2 inches
   (E) none of these

2. A man's income is $14,904 a year. He pays $138 a month for rent. The part of this income spent for rent per year is:
   (A) $\frac{1}{54}$ (B) $\frac{1}{9}$ (C) $\frac{1}{12}$ (D) $\frac{2}{9}$ (E) $\frac{1}{11}$

3. A pantry contains 6 shelves each 42 inches long. The shelves are to be relined with fresh paper. The paper is sold in 1 yard rolls. The number of 1 yard rolls needed is:
   (A) 6 (B) 7 (C) 3 (D) 5 (E) 9

4. A machine is bought for $4,125. It loses 20% of its value each year. The value of the machine at the end of 2 years is:
   (A) $2640 (B) $2475 (C) $3300
   (D) $825 (E) $2500

5. Bill gets up at 7:15 A.M. every morning. The time he must get to sleep if he is to get $9\frac{1}{2}$ hours of sleep is:
   (A) 10:15 P.M. (B) 10:45 P.M.
   (C) 9:45 P.M. (D) 11:00 P.M.
   (E) none of these

6. Round-trip fare between two cities is $68.40 plus 15% tax. At the same rate, one-way fare is:
   (A) $34.20 (B) $78.66 (C) $73.53
   (D) $53.40 (E) none of these

7. Ms. Sun bought a 145-acre farm at $76 an acre. Her down payment was 25% of the cost. The down payment was:
   (A) $11,020 (B) $10,120 (C) $2,755
   (D) $2,900 (E) none of these

8. Betty admired a blouse that was marked at $12.80. She figured that she could make the blouse herself for 35% less than the marked price. The cost of making the blouse was:
   (A) $4.48 (B) $8.32 (C) $21.12
   (D) $10.58 (E) $8.40

9. Mr. Adams harvested 936 bushels of wheat from 52 acres. If the pattern continues, the number of bushels of wheat harvested from 79 acres is:
   (A) 1,015 (B) 1,264 (C) 1,186 (D) 1,422
   (E) 1,500

10. Mr. Stavropoulos owns a cottage worth $68,500. He insured it for 80% of its value at $0.42 per $100. His premium was:
    (A) $2,301 (B) $287.70 (C) $230.16
    (D) $240 (E) none of these

11. Mr. Bates bought a television set for $148. He paid $30 down and the balance in 15 equal payments of $8.50 each. The amount of the carrying charge was:
    (A) $20.50 (B) $9.50 (C) $2.00
    (D) $7.50 (E) $9.00

12. The distance between Seattle and Denver is 1,020 miles. Mr. Riley travels between the two cities by car at an average rate of 45 miles per hour. Mr. Moto made the same trip by plane at the average rate of 306 miles per hour. The number of hours Mr. Moto saved by using the plane was:
(A) $19\frac{1}{3}$ (B) $28\frac{1}{3}$ (C) 24 (D) 20 (E) 30

13. Mr. Corbin is a salesman. He gets a 5% commission on all sales between $100 and $500 and a 10% commission on all sales above $500. His commission on sales of $783 was:
(A) $53.30 (B) $98.30 (C) $48.30 (D) $102.45 (E) $49.00

14. Of the students who tried out for the baseball team, $\frac{1}{8}$ tried out as catchers, $\frac{1}{3}$ as infielders, and $\frac{1}{4}$ as outfielders. The fraction of the students who tried out as pitchers was:
(A) $\frac{2}{3}$ (B) $\frac{5}{8}$ (C) $\frac{7}{8}$ (D) $\frac{7}{24}$ (E) $\frac{7}{25}$

15. John wishes to make a picture frame 2´3″ long and 1´8″ wide. The amount of molding John will need is:
(A) 3´11″ (B) 7´10″ (C) 8´2″ (D) 8´6″ (E) 8´

16. In a foul shooting contest Mario sank 11 out of 16 tries, Plato sank 10 out of 15 tries, Fred sank 15 out of 20 tries, Sam sank 9 out of 17 tries, and Karen sank 15 out of 21 tries. The winner was:
(A) John (B) Bill (C) Fred (D) Sam (E) Karen

17. A dozen golf balls were priced at $7.20. The tax was 15% of the selling price. The cost of each golf ball was:
(A) $0.65 (B) $0.69 (C) $0.72 (D) $0.80 (E) $0.75

18. At the rate of 50 miles per hour a car can travel 14.6 miles for each gallon of gas used. On a trip Mr. Hanson used 12.5 gallons of gas traveling at a speed of 50 miles per hour. The number of miles covered during the trip was:
(A) 62.5 (B) 100 (C) 1,250 (D) 365 (E) none of these

19. For a local talent show, orchestra seats sell for $8.50 and balcony seats sell for $4.50. The box office took in $2,616. If 128 balcony seats were sold, then the number of orchestra seats sold was:
(A) 256 (B) 240 (C) 320 (D) 280 (E) 350

20. On a camping vacation trip of 12 days the Otis family spent $579.84. If $63.48 was spent for automobile expenses then the daily expenses for other items were:
(A) $516.36 (B) $42.93 (C) $48.32 (D) $43.03 (E) none of these

EXAM 6

1. A gallon of a certain kind of paint will cover 224 square feet of surface. In painting two walls, one 36´ by 8´ and the other 24´ by 9´, the number of gallons of paint used is:
(A) 3 (B) $2\frac{1}{2}$ (C) $4\frac{1}{4}$ (D) $2\frac{1}{4}$ (E) $2\frac{1}{2}$

2. At a television station 46% of the workers are employed in the technical department, 23% in the program department, and the rest in other departments. The percent of the workers employed in other departments is:
(A) 21% (B) 41% (C) 31% (D) 69% (E) 32%

3. Mrs. Roberts needs material for four curtains. Each curtain requires 3 yards 1 foot of material. At $3 per yard the cost for material is:
(A) $37 (B) $40 (C) $45 (D) $80 (E) $42

4. Morad finds he can walk a mile in 12 minutes 15 seconds. The time it would take him to walk 8 miles is:
(A) 1 hr. 38 min. (B) 2 hr. 4 min.
(C) 1 hr. 36 min. (D) 1 hr. 30 min.
(E) none of these

5. A kitchen floor is 9 feet long and 6 feet wide. The number of yards of molding needed to hold the linoleum around the outside edge is:
(A) 30 (B) 15 (C) 21 (D) 5
(E) none of these

6. The weights of the members of the backfield of the Adams High School are 184 lb., 178 lb., 191 lb., and 167 lb. Bill Walters weighs 183 lb. Bill's weight is:
(A) 5 lb. above the average of the backfield
(B) 2 lb. below the average of the backfield
(C) 3 lb. above the average of the backfield
(D) equal to the average weight of the backfield
(E) none of these

7. The basketball team of Martin Luther King High School won 12 of its first 15 games. It then won its next 3 games. Its winning percentage was then:
(A) 80% (B) 75% (C) 60% (D) $83\frac{1}{3}$%
(E) 78%

8. Bob got 34 questions right on a test and received a mark of 85%. The number of questions on the test was:
(A) 38 (B) 40 (C) 29 (D) 50 (E) 45

9. Mr. Baker earns $448 a week. He spends 86% of this amount for expenses. The amount he saves in a year of 52 weeks is:
(A) $3,361.18 (B) $1,792.48 (C) $3,136
(D) $3,261.44 (E) none of these

10. In a high school there are 768 pupils. Of these, $\frac{3}{8}$ are girls. If $\frac{5}{6}$ of the girls are below the senior class, the number of senior girls is:
(A) 44 (B) 56 (C) 59 (D) 39
(E) none of these

11. A car is driven at the rate of 30 miles per hour. The distance the car covers in 1 minute is:
(A) $\frac{1}{4}$ mile (B) 2 miles (C) $\frac{1}{2}$ mile
(D) 4 miles (E) 5 miles

12. Mrs. Smiros went on a trip of 780 miles. The first day she covered 297 miles and the second day 379 miles. The part of the trip left was:
(A) $\frac{1}{3}$ (B) $\frac{2}{15}$ (C) $\frac{1}{7}$ (D) $\frac{1}{9}$ (E) $\frac{1}{10}$

13. A package of books weighs 48 pounds. The packing case weighs 3 pounds. If each book weighs $1\frac{1}{4}$ pounds the number of books is:
(A) 40 (B) 44 (C) 32 (D) 36 (E) 40

14. Mr. Sherman earns $7.20 per hour. On Monday he works $8\frac{1}{2}$ hours, Tuesday $7\frac{3}{4}$ hours, Wednesday $7\frac{1}{2}$ hours, Thursday 7 hours, and Friday $7\frac{3}{4}$ hours. His earnings for the week are:
(A) $273.60 (B) $277.20 (C) $280.80
(D) $278.00 (E) none of these

15. Mrs. Simon has a piece of cloth 15 yards long. From this cloth she cuts towels 27 inches long. The number of towels she obtains is:
(A) 12 (B) 16 (C) 18 (D) 20 (E) 25

16. Mr. Barry works on an 8% commission basis. One week his pay was $336. His sales amounted to:
(A) $420 (B) $4,200 (C) $2,688
(D) $2,736 (E) none of these

17. The distance from Los Angeles to Denver is 810 miles. If the scale on the map is 1″ = 180 miles, the distance between these cities on the map is:
(A) $3\frac{1}{2}$″ (B) $5\frac{1}{4}$″ (C) $4\frac{1}{2}$″ (D) $3\frac{1}{4}$″
(E) 4″

18. A store received a shipment of 3 dozen shirts that cost $162. If the shirts are to be sold at a profit of 40%, each shirt must be marked at:
(A) $4.90 (B) $5.20 C) $6.30 (D) $6.00
(E) $6.50

19. A town has a population of 153,000. There are 50,490 telephones in the town. The number of telephones per 100 of population is:
    (A) 50.49 (B) 33 (C) 5.04 (D) 0.504
    (E) 35

20. Mr. Seto borrowed some money from a bank at 15% interest. At the end of the year he made a payment of $517.50 to cover the entire capital plus interest. The amount he had borrowed from the bank was:
    (A) $480 (B) $500 (C) $456.80 (D) $450
    (E) none of these

EXAM 7

1. A bus traveled 156 miles in 3 hours and 15 minutes. The distance the bus traveled in 5 hours and 40 minutes at the same rate of speed was:
   (A) 250 miles (B) 264 miles
      (C) 280 miles (D) 260 miles
         (E) none of these

2. A dealer bought a used car for $270. She spent $50 in repairs and then sold the car for $400. The percent of profit she made on her investment was:
   (A) 29% (B) $33\frac{1}{2}$% (C) 25% (D) 30%
      (E) none of these

3. A man bought a house for $76,000. He made a down payment of $26,000 and agreed to pay $2,500 each year with interest of 14% on the unpaid balance. His payment at the end of the second year was:
   (A) $6,650 (B) $8,150 (C) $7,500
      (D) $9,150 (E) none of these

4. Mr. Fry was paid partly on a commission basis. His commission earnings for 4 weeks were $120, $132, $108, and $116. In order to have an average commission salary of $125 for the 5 weeks his commission earnings for the fifth week must be:
   (A) $137 (B) $149 (C) $151 (D) $119
      (E) $150

5. A ball team won 15 games and lost 22 games. It plays 13 more games and wins 12 of them. The percent of games won is now:
   (A) 27% (B) 80% (C) 92% (D) 66%
      (E) none of these

6. A homeowner buys 450 gallons of oil at $1.49 per gallon and 350 gallons of oil at $1.51 per gallon. His total cost is:
   (A) $670.50 (B) $528.50 (C) $1,199.00
      (D) $764.00 (E) none of these

7. A woman bought a steak weighing 5 pounds 6 ounces at $3.20 per pound and oranges weighing 3 pounds 4 ounces at $0.68 per pound. The amount she received in change from a $20 bill was:
   (A) $1.58 (B) $19.41 (C) $2.43
      (D) $0.59 (E) $0.49

8. Mr. Stone and Mr. Alvin grow potatoes on their farms. Mr. Stone has 168 acres and averages 127.4 bushels to the acre. Mr. Alvin has 149 acres and averages 130.7 bushels to the acre. Together the number of bushels of potatoes grown is:
   (A) 39,877 (B) 40,877.5 (C) 41,877.5
      (D) 1,928.9 (E) none of these

9. Mr. Saul bought a used car for $9,600. Over a 5-year period he paid $289.60 per year for insurance, $948 for repairs, $5,048 for gas, and $690 for other expenses. If he drove 60,000 miles and then sold the car for $3,200 his driving cost per mile was:
   (A) less than $0.20 (B) about $0.24
      (C) between $0.26 and $0.27
         (D) about $0.30 (E) none of these

10. Ms. Russo spent $\frac{2}{3}$ of her income for rent and food and saved $\frac{1}{2}$ of the remainder. The part of her income saved was:
    (A) $\frac{1}{3}$ (B) $\frac{1}{5}$ (C) $\frac{1}{6}$ (D) $\frac{1}{4}$ (E) $\frac{1}{8}$

11. In driving between 2 cities Mr. Bayne drove a distance of 180 miles. The trip took 5 hours including a one-half hour stop for food. The average driving speed on the trip was:
    (A) 36 mph (B) 40 mph (C) 45 mph
       (D) 38 mph (E) 42 mph

12. A city has a 3% sales tax. A motorist buys 8 gallons of gas at $1.289 cents per gallon plus tax. His total cost is:
    (A) $10.62 (B) $10.60 (C) $10.31 (D) $10.00 (E) $10.75

13. A state's budget for a certain year is $78,500,000. Of this amount 28.7% is spent for education. The amount spent for education is:
    (A) $2,252,950 (B) $225,295 (C) $22,529,500 (D) $32,419,500 (E) none of these

14. There are 630 pupils in a high school. If 20% of the pupils are seniors the number who are not seniors is:
    (A) 126 (B) 630 (C) 315 (D) 404 (E) none of these

15. The weight of a certain type of copper wire is 12.8 lb. per 1,000 ft. The weight of 375 ft. of this wire is:
    (A) 4,800 lb. (B) 480 lb. (C) 4.8 lb. (D) 48 lb. (E) 5.2 lb.

16. Joe is 5´4˝ tall and his father is 6´ tall. The ratio of Joe's height to his father's height is:
    (A) 9:8 (B) 9:10 (C) 10:9 (D) 8:9 (E) 8:7

17. The thickness of one sheet of a certain type of sheet aluminum is 0.03 inch. The number of sheets in a pile 6 inches high is:
    (A) 20 (B) 200 (C) 180 (D) 2,000 (E) 250

18. A movie house shows 5 continuous performances over a period of 12 hours. The length of each showing is:
    (A) 2 hr. and 20 min.
    (B) 2 hr. and 40 min.
    (C) 2 hr. and 30 min.
    (D) 2 hr. and 24 min.
    (E) none of these

19. A plane has a fuel tank that holds 5,250 gallons of gas. With a full tank, the plane can cover 4,200 miles. The number of miles the plane can cover for each gallon of gas is:
    (A) 1.25 (B) 0.8 (C) 12 (D) 8 (E) 1.2

20. One gallon of water is equal to 231 cubic inches. The number of gallons needed to fill a tank 22˝ by 9˝ by 7˝ is:
    (A) 5 (B) 7 (C) 9 (D) 6 (E) 8

EXAM 8

1. A student's college education costs $8,500 per year. He saves $1,200 while working during the summer. His father agrees to pay $\frac{1}{2}$ of his expenses. The amount the student still needs is:
   (A) $4,250 (B) $3,650 (C) $3,050 (D) $2,450 (E) none of these

2. Mr. Gage buys furniture valued at $975. He makes a down payment of $260 and agrees to pay the balance in installments of $25 each. The number of installments he pays is:
   (A) 29 (B) 39 (C) 17 (D) 32 (E) 35

3. A certain type of plane uses 4.75 gallons of gas per hour while cruising. If a pilot has 22.8 gallons of gas he can cruise for:
   (A) 4 hours and 8 minutes
   (B) 4 hours and 24 minutes
   (C) 4 hours and 48 minutes
   (D) 4 hours and 40 minutes
   (E) none of these

4. In a high school, $\frac{1}{3}$ of the students are freshmen and $\frac{1}{6}$ of the students are seniors. There are equal numbers of sophomores and juniors. The fraction representing the part of the students who are juniors is:
   (A) $\frac{1}{5}$ (B) $\frac{1}{3}$ (C) $\frac{1}{2}$ (D) $\frac{3}{8}$ (E) none of these

5. In a certain state, a taxpayer is permitted a deduction of $2,500. On the balance of his income he pays 2% on his first $1,000, 3% on the next $2,000, and 5% on the rest of his income. His tax on an income of $16,700 is:
   (A) $740 (B) $680 (C) $640 (D) $720 (E) $800

6. Mr. Van Dyke sells two cars costing $12,000 and $7,600. On the first sale he makes a profit of 8% and on the second he suffers a loss of 10%. The result is:
   (A) a loss of $200 (B) a loss of 2%
   (C) a gain of 2% (D) a gain of $200
   (E) none of these

7. A city has a budget of $6,480,000. It marks 8.45% for public welfare. The amount available for public welfare is:
   (A) $534,320 (B) $547,560 (C) $54,432
   (D) $533,320 (E) none of these

8. Mr. Paul insures his house for $90,000 at $0.38 per $100. The amount he can save by taking a policy for 5 years for a total premium of $1,580 is:
   (A) $30 (B) $230 (C) $150 (D) $130
   (E) $200

9. A dealer buys a shipment of 60 radios for a total of $2,280. If he wishes to make a profit of 30% on the shipment, the sale price of each radio should be:
   (A) $38 (B) $31.80 (C) $49.40
   (D) $34.20 (E) $35.00

10. The Martin Fruit Co. charges 7% commission for selling fruit. The commission for selling 516 crates of oranges at $16.30 per crate is:
    (A) $5,887.56 (B) $58.88 (E) $608.36
    (D) $588.76 (E) $600.00

11. A dealer sold an overcoat for $96. This was at a profit of $33\frac{1}{3}$% of the cost. The cost of the overcoat was:
    (A) $64 (B) $72 (C) $128 (D) $68
    (E) $84

12. A steel bar which is 17 feet long weighs 52.53 pounds. A similar bar 19 feet long weighs:
    (A) 55.91 pounds (B) 56.81 pounds
    (C) 58.71 pounds (D) 60.61 pounds
    (E) none of these

13. Ms. Choung had $1,200. She bought a desk for $158.98, and spent half of what she had left for a sofa. The amount she had left was:
    (A) $1,041.02 (B) $520.01 (C) $520.51
    (D) $679.29 (E) $600

14. A mechanic started working on a car at 10:45 A.M. and finished the job at 12:15 P.M. If the charge for labor is $17.50 per hour, the labor charge for this job was:
    (A) $35.00 (B) $26.25 (C) $25.00
    (D) $33.75 (E) $28.00

15. A boy answered 12 questions on a test correctly and received a rating of 80%. The number of questions on the test was:
    (A) 20 (B) 16 (C) 18 (D) 25
    (E) none of these

16. Bob weighed 96 pounds last year and now weighs 112 pounds. His gain in weight is:
    (A) $16\frac{2}{3}$% (B) 16% (C) 12% (D) $10\frac{1}{2}$%
    (E) none of these

17. A woman bought curtain material 25 yards long. Each curtain takes $5\frac{1}{2}$ yards. After she has made as many curtains as she has material for, the amount of material left is:
    (A) $2\frac{1}{4}$ yards (B) 3 yards (C) 4 yards
    (D) $2\frac{1}{2}$ yards (E) 5 yards

18. A school has 8 classes of 32 pupils and 7 classes of 33 pupils. The school has room for 520 pupils. The number of additional pupils the school can admit is:
    (A) 13 (B) 15 (C) 33 (D) 47 (E) 35

19. Mr. Moran drove his car 2,254 miles one month. His insurance on the car was $61.27 per month. The cost of insurance per mile was approximately:
    (A) $0.29 (B) $0.35\frac{1}{3}$ (C) $0.36
    (D) $0.32\frac{1}{2}$ (E) none of these

20. Mr. Lopez priced ties selling for $4.50 per tie. During a sale the ties were reduced in price by 20%. The number of ties Mr. Lopez bought for $18.00 during the sale was:
    (A) 4 (B) 6 (C) 5 (D) 8 (E) 9

Answers to All Practice Tests, Verbal Problems, and Mastery Exams

PRACTICE TESTS

TEST 1

1. $55\frac{1}{4}$ in.
2. $152.10
3. 23.59 g.
4. $77,644,041.54
5. $107\frac{13}{30}$ gal.
6. $12.30

TEST 2

1. $3.16
2. 1,782.7 mi.
3. $6.20
4. $6\frac{17}{24}$ ft.
5. 7,192 lb.
6. 5.075 or $5\frac{3}{40}$ lb.
7. $7.02
8. 5,917,899
9. 11.01 g.

TEST 3

1. $352
2. 30,000
3. $62.40
4. 44 in.
5. 0.0676 in.
6. $3,684,106
7. 1,000 lb.
8. 336 ft.
9. $15\frac{1}{8}$ mi.
10. 1800
11. 4452 mi.
12. 950 mi.

TEST 4

1. $\frac{3}{4}$ lb.
2. $141\frac{2}{3}$ yd.
3. 17
4. 128
5. $1.25
6. 360
7. $\frac{6}{11}$ m.p.h.
8. $100
9. 32
10. 1.30 sec.

TEST 5

1. 5 lb.
2. 900 mi.
3. $104
4. 20 in.
5. $55.56
6. $704
7. $4.32
8. $3240
9. $15.60
10. $49
11. 128
12. $\frac{1}{15}$ or 0.067 m.p.h.
13. $780
14. $629
15. $36
16. $43.20
17. $19.20
18. $27
19. 84 oz.
20. $233.95

TEST 6

1. 14
2. $325
3. $1,000
4. 38,500
5. 356.4 gal.
6. $2,925
7. 449,100 lb.
8. $22.50

TEST 7

1. $33\frac{1}{3}$%
2. $12\frac{1}{2}$%
3. $66\frac{2}{3}$%
4. 300%
5. $11\frac{1}{9}$%
6. $5\frac{1}{2}$%
7. $33\frac{1}{3}$%
8. $83\frac{1}{3}$%
9. 200%
10. $62\frac{1}{2}$%

TEST 8

1. 23,000
2. $150
3. $10,000
4. 490,600
5. $128
6. 50
7. $800
8. $24
9. 18 mi.
10. $24.50

TEST 9

1. $32.50
2. $33.75
3. 25%
4. $120,000
5. $13\frac{1}{3}$%
6. $73 profit
7. $7.50 loss
8. 8.40%
9. $82,950
10. $144

TEST 10

1. $3\frac{1}{2}$%
2. $406.25
3. $5\frac{1}{2}$%
4. $420
5. $9,025
6. $30.72
7. $2,800
8. $2\frac{1}{2}$%
9. $6,800
10. $42.53
11. $189.60
12. $151.08
13. 15%
14. $61,000
15. $3,327.70
16. $135
17. $7,648.44
18. 20%
19. 8%
20. 20%

TEST 11

1. $37\frac{1}{2}$%
2. 380
3. $62\frac{1}{2}$%
4. $299.60
5. $276
6. $647.50
7. 1,140
8. $82.40
9. The Blue Sox by $23\frac{1}{3}$%
10. $15,000
11. 620
12. 85%
13. 261
14. $9,600
15. 609
16. 65%
17. 15%
18. $6,370
19. $560
20. $1,250
21. 480
22. 117
23. $216
24. 34%
25. $350,000
26. $2,941.75
27. 12
28. $39
29. 5%
30. 416
31. $4\frac{1}{2}$%
32. 1,250
33. 9%
34. $320
35. 5%
36. $27,084
37. 250
38. 95%
39. $12\frac{1}{2}$%
40. 8%
41. 99
42. 1,040
43. $882.45
44. $15,000
45. $14\frac{2}{7}$%
46. 860
47. $1,203.96
48. 28%
49. $138.21
50. $60

TEST 12

1. 37
2. 79
3. $2.96
4. 829
5. 86%

6. $31.13
7. 191
8. 6′ 1″
9. 75
10. 91

ONE HUNDRED VERBAL PROBLEMS

Rating Your Results

Superior	90–100 correct
Average	70–89 correct
Below Average	69 or fewer correct

1. 9 yards
2. 147 miles
3. $259.20
4. $1\frac{1}{2}$ feet
5. 8
6. $23,712
7. 38 hours
8. $26.26
9. 432 miles
10. $1.40
11. 75%
12. $100.80
13. 25 gallons
14. $17.30
15. 5.48 inches
16. $235.20
17. $9.85
18. 1,875 gallons
19. $1.20
20. $\frac{3}{5}$
21. 3 minutes
22. 10
23. $1.98
24. 84
25. 60
26. 38
27. $7.14
28. $2.70
29. $2.10

30. $306
31. 18 weeks
32. 72%
33. 180 cubic feet
34. $5.25
35. $5\frac{3}{7}$ pounds
36. 3,000
37. $7,321.90
38. 8 feet
39. $219.20
40. $403.20
41. $1.50
42. $430
43. $144
44. $7\frac{1}{2}$%
45. $4.08
46. $27.75
47. 5 inches
48. 2%
49. 5:7
50. 12%
51. $35
52. 20
53. 15 miles
54. 24 square yards
55. 80%
56. 480 miles
57. 7,680
58. 45%

59. $13.20
60. $1.25
61. $1.29
62. $81.25
63. 18 cubic feet
64. 60
65. 20
66. $0.18
67. $2.58
68. $36
69. $37\frac{1}{2}$ yards
70. $160
71. $26\frac{1}{4}$ pounds
72. $27
73. 17 miles
74. 35%
75. 85
76. 80%
77. 340 miles per hour
78. $527
79. $\frac{8}{15}$

80. $185
81. $4,160
82. 30 feet
83. 80%
84. $2.97
85. $7\frac{1}{2}$ hours
86. $5\frac{1}{2}$ feet
87. $1.48
88. $1,440
89. $90
90. 4%
91. 300
92. $70
93. $195
94. $1\frac{1}{2}$ gallons
95. 112
96. 827.4 miles
97. $\frac{3}{4}$ pound
98. 44 miles per hour
99. 140
100. 75%

MASTERY EXAMS

Rating Your Results

Superior	18–20 correct
Average	14–17 correct
Below Average	13 or fewer correct

EXAM 1

1. C	5. E	9. D	13. C	17. B
2. D	6. D	10. E	14. A	18. C
3. C	7. C	11. E	15. C	19. A
4. A	8. B	12. B	16. C	20. D

EXAM 2

1. D	5. C	9. B	13. A	17. E
2. B	6. B	10. D	14. E	18. D
3. D	7. A	11. B	15. B	19. C
4. E	8. C	12. D	16. D	20. D

EXAM 3

1. B	5. E	9. A	13. A	17. B
2. D	6. C	10. C	14. B	18. D
3. C	7. B	11. B	15. E	19. A
4. B	8. E	12. A	16. E	20. E

EXAM 4

1. D	5. D	9. D	13. C	17. B
2. E	6. B	10. D	14. D	18. B
3. C	7. D	11. D	15. A	19. C
4. B	8. A	12. B	16. D	20. D

EXAM 5

1. C	5. C	9. D	13. C	17. B
2. B	6. E	10. E	14. D	18. E
3. B	7. C	11. B	15. B	19. B
4. A	8. B	12. A	16. C	20. D

EXAM 6

1. D	5. E	9. D	13. D	17. C
2. C	6. C	10. E	14. B	18. C
3. B	7. D	11. C	15. D	19. B
4. A	8. B	12. B	16. B	20. D

EXAM 7

1. E	5. E	9. B	13. C	17. B
2. C	6. C	10. C	14. E	18. D
3. D	7. D	11. B	15. C	19. A
4. B	8. B	12. A	16. D	20. D

EXAM 8

1. C	5. C	9. C	13. C	17. B
2. A	6. D	10. D	14. B	18. C
3. C	7. B	11. B	15. E	19. D
4. E	8. D	12. C	16. A	20. C

Algebra

CHAPTER 9

Representing Numbers by Letters

We know that we can find the average of three numbers by finding the sum of the numbers and dividing this sum by 3. This idea may be expressed by the following formula:

$$N = \frac{x + y + z}{3}$$

In this formula

N represents the average
x represents the first number
y represents the second number
z represents the third number

Letters used to represent numbers in this manner are called *variables*.

The advantage in writing this formula is that it tells us how to find the average of any three numbers.

The product of two numbers may be expressed by using the × symbol or the raised dot. For example, the product of 4 and 7 may be written as 4×7, or as $4 \cdot 7$. If n represents a number in algebra we may express the product of 5 and n as $5 \times n$, or as $5 \cdot n$, or simply as $5n$. Similarly, $9y$ means "9 times y" and ab means "a times b."

The operations of addition, subtraction, and division are expressed by using the same symbols as used in arithmetic. For example,

$x + y$ means "the sum of x and y"
$a - b$ means "the difference between a and b"
$c \div d$, or $\frac{c}{d}$, means "c divided by d"

In order to learn how to use algebra in solving problems, we must learn how to translate ordinary language into algebraic language.

EXAMPLE: A man has x dollars in the bank. He deposits 100 dollars more. How many dollars does he have in the bank after the deposit?

SOLUTION: $x + \$100$

EXAMPLE: A dealer has b television sets in stock. During a sale the dealer sells y of these sets. How many sets does she have left?

SOLUTION: $b - y$

EXAMPLE: A movie theater has z rows with 28 seats in each row. How many seats does the movie theater have?

SOLUTION: The theater has z times 28 seats, or 28 times z seats. This may be expressed as $28 \times z$, or $28 \cdot z$, or $28z$. The expression "$28z$" is preferred.

EXAMPLE: If 7 apples cost y cents, what is the cost of a apples?

SOLUTION: The cost of one apple is $\frac{y}{7}$ cents. The cost of a apples is $a \times \frac{y}{7}$, or $\frac{ay}{7}$ cents.

EXAMPLE: Express the product of the number $c + 5$ and the number k.

SOLUTION: In order to express this product, we must regard $c + 5$ as one number. To do this, we use parentheses. The result is $k(c + 5)$.

PRACTICE TEST 1

DIRECTIONS: Solve each of the following problems, and then circle the letter that corresponds to the right answer.

1. A man bought a shirt for x dollars and a tie for $6. The total cost for the two items is:
(A) $6x$ (B) $x - 6$ (C) $x \div 6$ (D) $x + 6$
(E) $6 - x$

2. A motorist drives between two cities that are 120 miles apart. After he has covered y miles the remaining distance is:
(A) $120 + y$ (B) $120 - y$ (C) $y - 120$
(D) $120y$ (E) $120 \div y$

3. A woman buys b pounds of apples at 59 cents per pound. The cost of the apples is:
(A) $b + 59¢$ (B) $59¢ - b$ (C) $b - 59¢$
(D) $59¢ \div b$ (E) $59¢b$

4. A girl has $5.00. She buys 4 notebooks at c cents each. The amount she receives in change is:
(A) $5.00 - 4c$ (B) $5.00 + 4c$
(C) $4c - 5.00 (D) $4c \cdot 5.00
(E) $5.00 \div 4c$

5. A Boy Scout troop hikes z miles in 4 hours. The number of miles per hour covered by the troop is:
(A) $4z$ (B) $z + 4$ (C) $z \div 4$ (D) $4 \div z$
(E) $z - 4$

6. Luigi is x years old. His father is 30 years older. The age of Luigi's father is:
(A) $30 - x$ (B) $30 \div x$ (C) $30x$ (D) $x + 30$
(E) $x - 30$

7. If 10 pencils cost y cents, what is the cost of x pencils?
(A) $10xy$ (B) $xy \div 10$ (C) $x + y + 10$
(D) $10x \div y$ (E) $10y \div x$

8. Mr. Burns deposited n dollars in a bank and received 7% interest per year. His interest for one year was:
(A) $7n$ (B) $0.7n$ (C) $7 + n$ (D) $n - 7$
(E) $0.07n$

9. If y dozen eggs cost x cents, how many dozen eggs can be bought for k cents?
(A) $\frac{xk}{y}$ (B) $\frac{ky}{x}$ (C) $\frac{xy}{k}$ (D) $\frac{y}{kx}$ (E) $\frac{x}{ky}$

10. A train travels b miles in 8 hours. What is the average rate of speed of the train?
(A) $8b$ (B) $b + 8$ (C) $b \div 8$ (D) $8 \div b$
(E) $b - 8$

Exponents and Evaluating Algebraic Expressions

When we multiply the number 9 by itself we may express the multiplication by the expression 9×9, or by the expression 9^2. In this case, the 2 is called an *exponent* and 9 is called the *base*. In the same way, $5 \times 5 \times 5 \times 5$ may be expressed as 5^4. The expression b^3 means $b \times b \times b$.

EXAMPLES: a^5 means $a \times a \times a \times a \times a$
$2c^3$ means $2 \times c \times c \times c$

It is necessary to be able to find the numerical value of an algebraic expression when we know the numerical value of each letter of the expression. When an expression has several operations, it is necessary to follow the proper order of operations.

ORDER OF OPERATIONS RULES

1. Do all operations inside grouping symbols first. Grouping symbols include parentheses ( ), brackets [ ], braces { }, and a bar as in $\sqrt{9 + 16}$ or $\frac{3 + 5}{8}$.

2. Do all roots and exponents in order from left to right.

3. Do all multiplications and divisions in order from left to right. This rule does *not* say do all multiplications and then do all divisions—do them as they appear in order from left to right.

4. Do all additions and subtractions in order from left to right. This also does not say do

additions before subtractions—do them as they appear in order from left to right.

EXAMPLE: Find the value of $3a + b - 2c$ when $a = 5$, $b = 3$, and $c = 1$.

$$3a + b - 2c = 3 \cdot 5 + 3 - 2 \cdot 1$$
$$= 15 + 3 - 2$$
$$= 16$$

EXAMPLE: Find the value of $5x^2 - 2y^3 + z$ when $x = 4$, $y = 3$, and $z = 7$.

$$5x^2 - 2y^3 + z = 5 \cdot 4 \cdot 4 - 2 \cdot 3 \cdot 3 \cdot 3 + 7$$
$$= 80 - 54 + 7$$
$$= 33$$

EXAMPLE: Find the value of $6(4y^3 - 3x^2)$ when $x = 5$ and $y = 3$.

$$6(4y^3 - 3x^2) = 6(4 \cdot 3^3 - 3 \cdot 5^2)$$
$$= 6(108 - 75)$$
$$= 6(\pm 33)$$
$$= \pm 198$$

PRACTICE TEST 2

DIRECTIONS: Solve each of the following problems, then circle the letter that corresponds to the right answer.

In the following examples $x = 6$, $y = 5$, $z = 4$, $a = 3$, and $b = 1$.

1. The value of $2x^2 + 2y - 7a$ is:
   (A) 133 (B) 175 (C) 39 (D) 61 (E) 51

2. The value of $x^3 - 2z^2 + b$ is:
   (A) 183 (B) 185 (C) 249 (D) –13 (E) 153

3. The value of $2xa^2b^3$ is:
   (A) 111 (B) 180 (C) 1,296 (D) 105 (E) 108

4. The value of $a(b + x^2)$ is:
   (A) 111 (B) 108 (C) 39 (D) 101 (E) 105

5. The value of $12y^2 \div b^2x$ is:
   (A) 12 (B) 50 (C) 2 (D) 25 (E) $5\frac{5}{6}$

6. The value of $abx^2 - 2y$ is:
   (A) 29 (B) 30 (C) 98 (D) 101 (E) 118

7. The value of $xy^2 + 2yz^2 - 4ab$ is:
   (A) 1,048 (B) 250 (C) 322 (D) 300 (E) 298

8. The value of $z(a + b)^2$ is:
   (A) 12 (B) 32 (C) 144 (D) 64 (E) 20

9. The value of $2b(x - a)^2$ is:
   (A) 18 (B) 12 (C) 162 (D) 27 (E) 36

10. The value of $x^2y^2 - az^3$ is:
    (A) 608 (B) 708 (C) 852 (D) 7 (E) 800

Formulas

In our work in geometry we use formulas such as

$$P = 2l + 2w$$

to find the perimeter of a rectangle and

$$A = \tfrac{1}{2}bh$$

to find the area of a triangle. Formulas are used frequently in science, in engineering, and in business. In this section, we will work with several different types of formulas.

EXAMPLE: The formula $E = IR$ (Ohm's law) is used in electricity. Find the value of E when $I = 5$ and $R = 28$.

SOLUTION:
$$E = IR$$
$$E = 5 \times 28 = 140$$

EXAMPLE: The formula $C = \frac{5}{9}(F - 32)$ is used to convert Fahrenheit temperature readings to Celsius temperature readings. Find the Celsius reading when the Fahrenheit reading is 68°.

SOLUTION:
$$C = \tfrac{5}{9}(F - 32)$$
$$C = \tfrac{5}{9}(68 - 32)$$
$$C = \tfrac{5}{9}(36) = 20$$

PRACTICE TEST 3

DIRECTIONS: Solve each of the following problems, then circle the letter that corresponds to the right answer.

1. The formula $A = \frac{a+b+c+d}{4}$ is used to find the average of four numbers $a, b, c,$ and d. The average of 68, 73, 47, and 84 is:
(A) $65\frac{1}{2}$ (B) 68 (C) 47 (D) 71 (E) 69

2. The formula $D = 16t^2$ is used to find the distance, in feet, of a freely falling body where t represents the number of seconds during which the body falls. The number of feet covered by a freely falling body in 9 seconds is:
(A) 144 (B) 288 (C) 2,304 (D) 400 (E) 1,296

3. The formula $C = 35 + 5(n - 3)$ is used to find the cost of borrowing a book from a circulating library where n represents the number of days during which the book is borrowed. The cost, in cents, of borrowing a book for 12 days is:
(A) 70 (B) 80 (C) 90 (D) 95 (E) 85

4. The formula $S = 5,000 + 20(n - 100)$ is used to find the yearly salary of a machine salesman where n represents the number of machines sold. If the salesman sold 678 machines during a certain year, his salary for that year was:
(A) \$5,678 (B) \$17,500 (C) \$16,560 (D) \$17,000 (E) \$17,800

5. The formula for finding the area of an open rectangular box with a square base is $A = b^2 + 4bh$. If $b = 8$ ft. and $h = 6$ ft., the area of the box, in square feet, is:
(A) 256 (B) 246 (C) 204 (D) 208 (E) 212

6. The recommended weight of an adult man is given by the formula $W = \frac{11}{2}(h - 60) + 100$ where W = weight in pounds and h = height in inches. If a man is 72 inches tall, his weight, in pounds, should be:
(A) 232 (B) 178 (C) 192 (D) 166 (E) 160

Solving Equations

The ability to solve equations enables us to solve many different types of problems.

An *equation* is a statement that two quantities are equal.

Consider the equation

$$2x + 5 = 11$$

This equation tells us that $2x + 5$ and 11 name the same number. Since this is the case, the value of x must be 3, since $2 \cdot 3 + 5 = 11$. And 3 is the only number that balances the equation. The number 3, which represents x and balances or satisfies the equation, is called the solution of the equation.

PRACTICE TEST 4

DIRECTIONS: Solve each of the following problems, then circle the letter that corresponds to the right answer.

Select the letter that represents a solution of the given equation.

1. $x + 3 = 7$
(A) 10 (B) 5 (C) 4 (D) 7 (E) –10

2. $x - 2 = 8$
(A) 6 (B) 4 (C) –6 (D) –10 (E) 10

3. $2x + 1 = 11$
(A) 6 (B) 5 (C) 4 (D) –5 (E) 3

4. $3x - 2 = 4$
(A) $1\frac{1}{2}$ (B) $1\frac{1}{3}$ (C) 2 (D) 3 (E) –1

5. $\frac{x}{2} + 1 = 5$
(A) 8 (B) 2 (C) 3 (D) 5 (E) 7

6. $\frac{x}{3} - 2 = 2$
(A) 0 (B) 1 (C) 4 (D) 12 (E) 6

7. $3x + 1 = 19$
(A) 5 (B) 6 (C) $6\frac{2}{3}$ (D) 3 (E) 2

8. $5x - 4 = 11$
(A) 5 (B) 15 (C) 2 (D) $1\frac{2}{5}$ (E) 3

9. $x^2 + 2x = 3$
(A) 2 (B) –2 (C) 1 (D) 3 (E) 4

10. $y^2 - y - 6 = 0$
(A) 3 (B) –3 (C) 4 (D) 2 (E) 1

11. $x^2 = 5x$
(A) 3 (B) 5 (C) 1 (D) 4 (E) 2

12. $y^2 + 3y - 10 = 0$
(A) 5 (B) 4 (C) 0 (D) 2 (E) 1

We will now consider systematic methods of solving equations.

Consider the equation $x + 1 = 6$. This tells us that when a certain number is added to 1, the result is 6. It is clear that the unknown number is 5, since $5 + 1 = 6$. Thus, $x = 5$. To go from $x + 1$ to x we subtract 1 from $x + 1$, or $x + 1 - 1 = x$. Since $x + 1$ and 6 name the same number, we must subtract the same number from $x + 1$ and from 6 to obtain equal results. We write this process as follows:

$$x + 1 = 6$$
$$x + 1 - 1 = 6 - 1$$
$$x = 5$$

Consider the equation $x - 3 = 1$. In order to obtain x on the left side of the equation, we add 3 to $x - 3$. Since $x - 3$ and 1 name the same number, we must add 3 to both $x - 3$ and 1 to obtain equal results.

$$x - 3 = 1$$
$$x - 3 + 3 = 1 + 3$$
$$x = 4$$

Consider the equation $3x = 12$. In order to obtain x on the left side of the equation, we must divide $3x$ by 3. Since $3x$ and 12 name the same number, we divide both $3x$ and 12 by 3 and we obtain equal results.

$$3x = 12$$
$$\tfrac{1}{3}(3x) = \tfrac{1}{3}(12)$$
$$x = 4$$

Consider the equation $\frac{y}{4} = 5$. In order to obtain y on the left side of the equation, we

must multiply $\frac{y}{4}$ or $\frac{1}{4}y$ by 4. Since $\frac{y}{4}$ and 5 represent the same number, we multiply both $\frac{y}{4}$ and 5 by 4 and we obtain equal results.

$$\frac{y}{4} = 5$$

$$\frac{4 \times y}{4} = 4 \times 5$$

$$y = 20$$

The results of this discussion may be summarized as follows:

To Find the Solution to an Equation

1. Subtract where there is a sum. For example:
$$x + 1 = 6$$
$$x + 1 - 1 = 6 - 1$$
$$x = 5$$

2. Add when there is a difference. For example:
$$x - 3 = 1$$
$$x - 3 + 3 = 1 + 3$$
$$x = 4$$

3. Divide when there is a product. For example:
$$3x = 12$$
$$\frac{3x}{3} = \frac{12}{3}$$
$$x = 4$$

4. Multiply when there is a quotient. For example:
$$\frac{x}{4} = 5$$
$$4\left(\frac{x}{4}\right) = 4(5)$$
$$x = 20$$

PRACTICE TEST 5

DIRECTIONS: Solve the following equations.

1. $x + 2 = 5$ $x =$ _____

2. $x - 2 = 3$ $x =$ _____

3. $3x = 15$ $x =$ _____

4. $\frac{x}{2} = 7$ $x =$ _____

5. $x - 6 = 3$ $x =$ _____

6. $x + 4 = 7$ $x =$ _____

7. $2x = 8$ $x = \_\_\_\_\_$

8. $\frac{x}{3} = 5$ $x = \_\_\_\_\_$

9. $4x = 20$ $x = \_\_\_\_\_$

10. $x - 2 = 7$ $x = \_\_\_\_\_$

11. $x + 7 = 9$ $x = \_\_\_\_\_$

12. $2x = 16$ $x = \_\_\_\_\_$

13. $x - 7 = 1$ $x = \_\_\_\_\_$

14. $\frac{x}{4} = 5$ $x = \_\_\_\_\_$

15. $5x = 10$ $x = \_\_\_\_\_$

16. $x - 2 = 2$ $x = \_\_\_\_\_$

17. $x + 7 = 10$ $x = \_\_\_\_\_$

18. $7x = 35$ $x = \_\_\_\_\_$

19. $x - 8 = 2$ $x = \_\_\_\_\_$

20. $x + 9 = 9$ $x = \_\_\_\_\_$

To solve some equations it is sometimes necessary to combine similar terms. Terms that have the exact same variable factors are called similar (or like) terms, and they can be combined by adding or subtracting the numerical factors of the similar terms.

EXAMPLES:
$$3x + 5x = (3 + 5)x = 8x$$
$$4y - y = (4 - 1)y = 3y$$

In solving some problems it is useful to be able to find the solutions of more difficult equations.

EXAMPLE: Solve the equation $3x + 4x = 35$. Since $3x + 4x = 7x$, we have

$$7x = 35$$
$$x = \frac{35}{7}$$
$$x = 5$$

EXAMPLE: Solve the equation $\frac{3}{4}x = 12$. In order to obtain x on the left side of the equation, we must multiply $\frac{3}{4}x$ by $\frac{4}{3}$. Since $\frac{3}{4}x$ and 12 name the same number, we multiply both $\frac{3}{4}x$ and 12 by $\frac{4}{3}$ to obtain equal results.

$$\frac{4}{3} \cdot \frac{3}{4}x = \frac{4}{3} \cdot 12$$
$$x = 16$$

EXAMPLE: Solve the equation $3x + 2 = 20$.

$$3x + 2 = 20$$
$$3x + 2 - 2 = 20 - 2$$
$$3x = 18$$
$$\frac{3x}{3} = \frac{18}{3}$$
$$x = 6$$

EXAMPLE: Solve the equation $\frac{2}{3}x - 4 = 6$.

$$\frac{2}{3}x - 4 = 6$$
$$\frac{2}{3}x - 4 + 4 = 6 + 4$$
$$\frac{2}{3}x = 10$$
$$\frac{3}{2} \cdot \frac{2}{3}x = \frac{3}{2} \cdot 10$$
$$x = 15$$

PRACTICE TEST 6

DIRECTIONS: Solve the following equations.

1. $3x + 4x = 14$ $x = \_\_\_\_\_$

2. $x + 5x = 30$ $x = \_\_\_\_\_$

3. $4x + 1 = 25$ $x = \_\_\_\_\_$

4. $3x - 4 = 14$ $x = \_\_\_\_\_$

5. $\frac{x}{3} + 2 = 7$ $x = \_\_\_\_\_$

6. $7x - 3x = 32$ $x = \_\_\_\_\_$

7. $2x + 5 = 7$ $x = \_\_\_\_\_$

8. $\frac{3}{5}x + 2 = 8$ $x = \_\_\_\_\_$

9. $3x + 4x + 2 = 16$ $x = \_\_\_\_\_$

10. $2x - 5 = 1$ $x = \_\_\_\_\_$

11. $5x + 1 = 31$ $x = \_\_\_\_\_$

12. $\frac{2}{3}x - 4 = 8$ $x = \_\_\_\_\_$

13. $3x - 7 = 2$ $x = \_\_\_\_\_$

14. $6x - x = 25$ $x = \_\_\_\_\_$

15. $2x + x + 3 = 15$ $x = \_\_\_\_\_$

16. $\frac{4}{3}x - 2 = 6$ $x = \_\_\_\_\_$

17. $7x - 5 = 9$ $x = \_\_\_\_\_$

18. $x + 3x - 1 = 11$ $x = \_\_\_\_\_$

19. $5x + 7 = 22$ $x = \_\_\_\_\_$

20. $4x - 5 = 11$ $x = \_\_\_\_\_$

Solving Problems by the Use of Equations

Since we now know how to solve equations, we may solve a great variety of problems. Consider the following:

EXAMPLE: During a football game 45 points were scored. If the winning team scored 9 points more than the losing team, how many points did each team score?

SOLUTION: Let x = the number of points scored by the losing team.

And $x + 9$ = the number of points scored by the winning team.

Since the total number of points scored was 45, we have

$$x + (x + 9) = 45$$
$$2x + 9 = 45$$
$$2x + 9 - 9 = 45 - 9$$
$$2x = 36$$
$$x = \frac{36}{2} = 18$$
$$x + 9 = 18 + 9 = 27$$

Thus, the losing team scored 18 points and the winning team scored 27 points.

EXAMPLE: Two cars leave Washington, DC traveling in opposite directions. The faster car travels at an average speed of 40 miles per hour and the slower car travels at the rate of 30 miles per hour. In how many hours will the cars be 630 miles apart?

SOLUTION: Let x = the number of hours it takes the cars to be 630 miles apart.

Then $40x$ = the number of miles covered by the faster car.

And $30x$ = the number of miles covered by the slower car. At this point, it is helpful to collect our information in a box.

Rate	$\times$	Time	=	Distance
40	$\times$	x	=	$40x$
30	$\times$	x	=	$30x$

According to the conditions of this problem, the distance covered by the faster car plus the distance covered by the slower car = 630 miles. Thus, we have the equation

$$40x + 30x = 630$$
$$70x = 630$$
$$x = 630 \div 70 = 9$$

It will take 9 hours of driving before the cars are 630 miles apart.

EXAMPLE: Green, Adams, and Burns were the three top scorers in a basketball game. Green scored twice as many points as Adams, and Burns scored 7 points more than Adams. Together the three men scored 75 points. How many points did each man score?

SOLUTION: Let x = the number of points scored by Adams.

And $2x$ = the number of points scored by Green.

And $x + 7$ = the number of points scored by Burns.

Since the total scored by the three men was 75 points, we have

$$x + 2x + x + 7 = 75$$
$$4x + 7 = 75$$
$$4x + 7 - 7 = 75 - 7$$
$$4x = 68$$
$$x = \frac{68}{4} = 17$$
$$2x = 2 \times 17 = 34$$
$$x + 7 = 17 + 7 = 24$$

Thus, Adams scored 17 points, Green scored 34 points, and Burns scored 24 points.

EXAMPLE: The ratio of two numbers is 5:3. If 7 is added to the larger number and 1 is added to the smaller number, the numbers are in the ratio of 2:1. Find the two original numbers.

SOLUTION: Let $5x$ = the larger number.

And $3x$ = the smaller number.

After 7 is added to the larger number and 1 is added to the smaller number, the resulting numbers are $(5x + 7)$ and $(3x + 1)$.

According to the conditions of the problem, the resulting numbers are in the ratio 2:1. This gives us the equation

$$(5x + 7) : (3x + 1) = 2:1$$

In this proportion, if we set the product of the means equal to the product of the extremes we have

$$2(3x + 1) = (5x + 7)$$
$$6x + 2 = 5x + 7$$
$$6x - 5x + 2 = 5x - 5x + 7$$
$$x + 3 = 7$$
$$x + 2 - 2 = 7 - 2$$
$$x = 5$$

The larger number = $5x = 5 \cdot 5 = 25$.
The smaller number = $3x = 3 \cdot 5 = 15$.

Thus, the original numbers are 25 and 15.

EXAMPLE: Mr. Barnes has $25,000 to invest. He plans to invest part of his money at 6% yearly interest and the rest at 7% yearly interest. If his total yearly income from both investments is $1,600, how much did he invest at each rate?

SOLUTION: Let x = the amount invested at 6%.
  Then $25,000 - x$ = the amount invested at 7%.
  The sum of the two incomes is $1,600 yearly.
  Thus, we have the equation

$$.06x + .07\,(25,000 - x) = \$1,600$$

If we multiply both sides of this equation by 100, we have

$$6x + 7\,(250,000 - x) = 160,000$$
$$6x + 1,750,000 - 7x = 160,000$$
$$-x = -1,590,000$$
$$x = 1,590,000$$
$$25,000 - x = 10,000$$

Thus, Mr. Barnes invested $15,000 at 6% and $10,000 at 7%.

EXAMPLE: The difference between $\frac{1}{3}$ of a number and $\frac{1}{8}$ of the same number is 15. Find the number.

SOLUTION: Let x = the number.
  Then $\frac{1}{3}x$, or $\frac{x}{3}$, = $\frac{1}{3}$ of the number.
  And $\frac{1}{8}x$, or $\frac{x}{8}$, = $\frac{1}{8}$ of the number.
  According to the conditions of the problem, the difference between $\frac{1}{3}$ of the number and $\frac{1}{8}$ of the number is 15. This gives the equation

$$\frac{x}{3} - \frac{x}{8} = 15$$

If we multiply all members of the equation by 24 we will obtain the following equation, which does not contain fractions:

$$8x - 3x = 360$$
$$5x = 360$$
$$x = \tfrac{360}{5} = 72$$

Thus, the number is 72.

PRACTICE TEST 7

DIRECTIONS: Solve the following problems.

1. The measure of one angle of a triangle is 6 degrees greater than the measure of a second angle of the triangle. And the measure of the third angle of the triangle is equal to the sum of the measures of the first two angles. Find the measures of the three angles of the triangle.

2. Find four consecutive odd numbers such that the difference between three times the fourth and the first exceeds the third by 31.

3. A man invests $20,000 to yield $1,280 interest annually. If part of his investment pays 6% annually and the rest of his investment pays 7% annually, how much does he invest at each rate?

4. Five less than seven times a certain number is 58. Find the number.

5. A plumber wishes to cut a piece of pipe 32 inches long into two parts so that the smaller part is 4 inches less than three times the larger part. What are the lengths of the two parts of the pipe?

6. A mechanic earns $5 more per hour than his helper. On a six-hour job the two men earn a total of $114. How much does each earn per hour?

7. The sum of two numbers is 26. If the larger number is 2 less than three times the smaller number, what is the smaller number?

8. The perimeter of a triangle is 44 inches. If one side is 5 inches longer than the smallest side and the largest side is 1 inch less than twice the smallest side, how many inches are there in the smallest side?

9. The sum of $\frac{1}{2}$ a certain number and $\frac{1}{3}$ of the same number is 30. Find the number.

10. The ratio of John's money to Fred's money is 8:3. If John gives Fred $6, John will have twice as much money as Fred. How much money does John have before he gives Fred money?

11. Two motorists start at the same time to drive toward each other from cities that are 360 miles apart. If the first motorist averages 48 miles per hour and the second motorist averages 42 miles per hour, in how many hours will they meet?

12. If 19 is subtracted from 4 times a number, the result is 73. Find the number.

13. Two planes start from the same airport at the same time and travel in opposite directions. If the first plane travels at an average speed of 240 miles per hour and the second plane travels at an average speed of 320 miles per hour, in how many hours will the planes be 1,400 miles apart?

14. The difference between $\frac{1}{2}$ of a number and $\frac{1}{5}$ of the same number is 24. Find the number.

15. The ratio of two numbers is 7:4. If 8 is added to the larger number and 4 is subtracted from the smaller number, the ratio of the numbers is 5:2. Find the two original numbers.

16. A man died and left his estate of $125,000 to his wife, his daughter, and his son. If the wife received twice as much as his son, and his daughter received $5,000 more than his son, how much did the man leave to his son?

17. The length of a room, rectangular in shape, is 8 feet greater than its width. If the perimeter of the room is 64 feet, what are the dimensions of the room?

18. A professional baseball player makes 168 hits over a season. Of these, the number of singles is 5 less than three times the number of extra base hits. How many extra base hits did the player make?

19. Two motorists start toward each other from cities 400 miles apart at 1 P.M. If one motorist travels at an average rate of 42 miles per hour and the other motorist travels at an average rate of 38 miles per hour, at what time will the cars meet?

20. If 5 more than a certain number is tripled, the result is 72. What is the number?

21. Two numbers are in the ratio of 5:7. If 12 is added to each number the ratio is 4:5. What are the original two numbers?

Solving Inequalities

An *inequality* is a statement that two quantities are unequal. For example, 7 > 3 and 2 < 6. (Recall that the symbol > means "is greater than," and < means "is less than.")

Consider the inequality

$$3x + 5 > 17$$

This inequality tells us that $3x + 5$ represents a number that is greater than 17. To solve this inequality we must find the value or values of x such that the expression "$3x + 5$" has a value greater than 17. Before we develop systematic methods of solving inequalities, we will use trial methods.

If $x = 1$, then $3x + 5 = 3 \cdot 1 + 5 = 8$
If $x = 2$, then $3x + 5 = 3 \cdot 2 + 5 = 11$
If $x = 3$, then $3x + 5 = 3 \cdot 3 + 5 = 14$
If $x = 4$, then $3x + 5 = 3 \cdot 4 + 5 = 17$
If $x = 5$, then $3x + 5 = 3 \cdot 5 + 5 = 20$

Thus, 5 is a solution of the inequality $3x + 5 > 17$. Also, we can see that when $x > 4$ the inequality is satisfied. For example, $x = 4.1$, $x = 6$, and $x = 7.03$. The inequality has an infinite number of solutions and all these solutions are numbers greater than 4. We may express this result by saying that the solution of the inequality is $x > 4$.

PRACTICE TEST 8

> DIRECTIONS: In each case, select the letter that is a solution of the given inequality.

1. $x + 1 > 3$
   (A) 0 (B) 1 (C) 2 (D) 5 (E) –2

2. $x + 2 < 5$
   (A) 3 (B) 2 (C) 4 (D) 5 (E) 7

3. $2x + 1 > 6$
   (A) 2 (B) $2\frac{1}{2}$ (C) 3 (D) –2 (E) 1

4. $3x - 1 < 7$
   (A) 3 (B) 4 (C) $3\frac{1}{2}$ (D) 5 (E) 2

5. $5x + 3 > 18$
   (A) 3 (B) 2 (C) $3\frac{1}{2}$ (D) 0 (E) 1

6. $2x - 1 < 3$
   (A) 0 (B) 2 (C) 3 (D) 5 (E) 6

We are now ready to consider systematic methods of solving inequalities.

The rules for generating equivalent inequalities are similar to those for solving equations.

The following rules are stated using < (less than) but they could be stated using any of the symbols > (greater than), ≤ (less than or equal), or ≥ (greater than or equal).

1. If $A < B$, then $A + C < B + C$. Adding (or subtracting) the same number to both sides of an inequality generates an equivalent inequality.

EXAMPLE: Solve $x - 4 < 5$.

$$x - 4 < 5$$
$$x - 4 + 4 < 5 + 4$$
$$x < 9$$

2. If $A < B$, then:
   a. $AC < BC$, if C is a positive number.
   b. $AC > BC$, if C is a negative number.

This rule that you can multiply (or divide) both sides of an inequality by the same positive number maintaining the same direction of the inequality. But if you multiply (or divide) both sides of an incquality by a negative number, you must reverse the direction of the inequality.

EXAMPLES: Solve $3x > 15$.

$$3x > 15$$
$$\frac{3x}{3} > \frac{15}{3}$$
$$x > 5$$

Solve $1 - 2x \le 7$.

$$1 - 2x \le 7$$
$$1 - 2x - 1 \le 7 - 1$$
$$-2x \le 6$$
$$\frac{-2x}{-2} \ge \frac{6}{-2}$$
$$x \ge -3$$

Consider the inequality

$$x - 3 < 5$$

In order to solve this inequality, we must add 3 to both numbers. In general, if we add the same quantity to both members of an inequality, we do not change the direction of the inequality. Thus, we have

$$x - 3 + 3 < 5 + 3$$

or

$$x < 8$$

Consider the inequality

$$3x < 12$$

In order to obtain x on the left side of the inequality, we must divide $3x$ by 3. We must also divide the right side of the inequality by 3 in order to maintain the balance of the inequality. In general, we may divide both members of an inequality by the same *positive* number without changing the direction of the inequality. Thus, we have

$$\frac{3x}{3} < \frac{12}{3}$$

or

$$x < 4$$

EXAMPLE: Solve the inequality $x + 5 > 7$.

$$x + 5 > 7$$
$$x + 5 - 5 > 7 - 5$$
$$x > 2$$

EXAMPLE: Solve the inequality $x - 1 < 5$.

$$x - 1 < 5$$
$$x - 1 + 1 < 5 + 1$$
$$x < 6$$

EXAMPLE: Solve the inequality $5x > 15$.

$$5x > 15$$
$$\frac{5x}{5} > \frac{15}{5}$$
$$x > 3$$

EXAMPLE: Solve $2 - 5x > 12$.

$$2 - 5x > 12$$
$$2 - 5x - 2 > 12 - 2$$
$$-5x > 10$$
$$\frac{-5x}{-5} < \frac{10}{-5}$$
$$x < -2$$

PRACTICE TEST 9

DIRECTIONS: Solve the following inequalities.

1. $x + 4 > 7$ $x > $ _____
2. $x - 2 > 4$ $x > $ _____
3. $x + 1 < 10$ $x < $ _____
4. $x - 3 < 6$ $x < $ _____
5. $2x < 8$ $x < $ _____
6. $3x > 18$ $x > $ _____
7. $x - 5 > 1$ $x > $ _____
8. $x + 4 < 7$ $x < $ _____
9. $3x + 5 > 23$ $x > $ _____
10. $\frac{x}{3} + 1 \leq 4$ $x \leq $ _____

In solving inequalities involving two operations, it is generally desirable to add or subtract before dividing. The following examples show how this is done.

EXAMPLE: Solve the inequality

$$2y + 1 > 9$$
$$2y + 1 - 1 > 9 - 1$$
$$2y > 8$$
$$\frac{2y}{2} > \frac{8}{2}$$
$$y > 4$$

EXAMPLE:

$$3y - 2 < 4$$
$$3y - 2 + 2 < 4 + 2$$
$$3y < 6$$
$$\frac{3y}{3} < \frac{6}{3}$$
$$y < 2$$

PRACTICE TEST 10

DIRECTIONS: Solve the following inequalities.

1. $2x + 3 > 11$ $x > $ _____

2. $3y - 1 > 14$ $y > $ _____

3. $4y + 1 > 29$ $y > $ _____

4. $2x - 5 < 9$ $x > $ _____

5. $3x + 7 < 13$ $x < $ _____

6. $5y - 2 > 28$ $y > $ _____

7. $6x + 1 > 25$ $x > $ _____

8. $4y - 5 < 23$ $y < $ _____

9. $4 - 2y < 10$ $y < $ _____

10. $\frac{1}{2}x - 3 > 2$ $x > $ _____

Answers to All Practice Tests

TEST 1

1. **D**	3. **E**	5. **C**	7. **B**	9. **B**
2. **B**	4. **A**	6. **D**	8. **E**	10. **C**

TEST 2

1. **D**	3. **E**	5. **B**	7. **E**	9. **A**
2. **B**	4. **A**	6. **C**	8. **D**	10. **B**

TEST 3

1. **B**	3. **B**	4. **C**	5. **A**	6. **D**
2. **E**				

TEST 4

1. **C**	4. **C**	7. **B**	9. **C**	11. **B**
2. **E**	5. **A**	8. **E**	10. **A**	12. **D**
3. **B**	6. **D**			

TEST 5

1. 3	6. 3	11. 2	16. 4
2. 5	7. 4	12. 8	17. 3
3. 5	8. 15	13. 8	18. 5
4. 14	9. 5	14. 20	19. 10
5. 9	10. 9	15. 2	20. 0

TEST 6

1. 2	6. 8	11. 6	16. 6
2. 5	7. 1	12. 18	17. 2
3. 6	8. 10	13. 3	18. 3
4. 6	9. 2	14. 5	19. 3
5. 15	10. 3	15. 4	20. 4

TEST 7

1. 42, 48, and 90
2. 17, 19, 21, 23
3. $12,000 at 6% and $8,000 at 7%

4. 9
5. 9 inches, 23 inches
6. $12 per hour for mechanic
   $7 per hour for helper
7. 7
8. 10 inches
9. 36
10. $72
11. 4
12. 23
13. $2\frac{1}{2}$ hours
14. 80
15. 42, 24
16. $30,000
17. 12 feet by 20 feet
18. 43
19. 6 P.M.
20. 19
21. 20, 28

TEST 8

1. **D**	3. **C**	5. **C**
2. **B**	4. **E**	6. **A**

TEST 9

1. $x > 3$	5. $x < 4$	9. $x > 6$
2. $x > 6$	6. $x > 6$	10. $x \leq 9$
3. $x < 9$	7. $x > 6$	
4. $x < 9$	8. $x < 3$	

TEST 10

1. $x > 4$	5. $x < 2$	9. $y > -3$
2. $y > 5$	6. $y > 6$	10. $x > 10$
3. $y > 7$	7. $x > 4$	
4. $x < 7$	8. $y < 7$	

Numbers and Number Systems

If you are using this book to prepare for a specific examination, make certain that the material in this chapter is included in the test items *before* you begin studying this section.

Sets

The idea of a set is basic in modern mathematics. In much of our ordinary speaking and writing we talk about collections of objects. For example, we talk about a *set* of checkers, a *deck* of cards, a *circle* of friends, and a *team* of basketball players.

A *set* is a collection of objects. Each item of a set is called an *element* or a *member* of the set. In defining a set, we must make clear which objects are members of the set and which objects are not members of the set. For convenience, we use braces { } to enclose the members of a set. Thus, we may describe a set in words or by the use of braces. A set may have one or more members, or a set may have no members. A set that has no members is called an *empty* set. Either of two symbols may be used to designate an empty set: Ø or { }.

EXAMPLE: A = {Monday, Tuesday, Wednesday, Thursday, Friday, Saturday, Sunday}

A is the set consisting of the names of the days of the week.

EXAMPLE: B = {July 4}

B is the set consisting of the names of the legal United States holidays in the month of July.

EXAMPLE: C = { }

C is the set of the names of women presidents of the United States (an empty set).

EXERCISE 1

1. *Write the following sets by listing their members enclosed in braces.*
   (a) The set of names of months of the year beginning with the letter J.
   (b) The set of the names of the members of your family.
   (c) The set consisting of the names of the first three letters of the English alphabet.
   (d) The set of the names of professional football players who are women.
   (e) The set consisting of the names of the days of the week when you do not attend school.
   (f) The set consisting of the name of the first president of the United States.

2. *Describe each of the following sets in words:*
   (a) {x, y, z}
   (b) {1¢, 5¢, 10¢, 25¢, 50¢}
   (c) {New York, Chicago, Los Angeles}
   (d) {2, 4, 6, 8, 10}
   (e) {right forward, left forward, center, right guard, left guard}

440

The *union* of two sets, A and B, is the set consisting of all members of A together with all members of B. The symbol used to designate union is ∪.

EXAMPLE: $A = \{1, 3, 5, 7\}$
$B = \{2, 4, 5, 6, 7\}$
$A \cup B = \{1, 2, 3, 4, 5, 6, 7\}$

The *intersection* of two sets, A and B, is a set containing the members that are in both set A and set B. The symbol used to designate the intersection is ∩.

EXAMPLE: $A = \{a, b, c, e, f, o\}$
$B = \{a, e, i, o, u\}$
$A \cap B = \{a, e, o\}$
$A \cup B = \{a, b, c, e, f, i, i, o, u\}$

EXERCISE 2

1. *Write the union of the following pairs of sets:*
   (a) $C = \{5, 10, 15, 20\}$,
   $D = \{10, 20, 30, 35\}$
   (b) $F = \{John, Bill, Mary\}$,
   $G = \{John, Fred, Nancy\}$
   (c) $K = \{June, July, August, September\}$,
   $L = \{June, October, December\}$

   (d) $P = \{$the set of names of days of the week beginning with T$\}$
   $Q = \{$the set of names of days of the week beginning with S$\}$

2. *Write the intersection of the following pairs of sets:*
   (a) $B = \{2, 4, 6, 8, 10\}$,
   $E = \{4, 8, 12, 16\}$
   (b) $F = \{Frank, Edna, Sally, Don\}$,
   $G = \{Ben, Sally, Don, Stella\}$
   (c) $H = \{Monday, Wednesday, Friday\}$,
   $R = \{Tuesday, Wednesday, Sunday\}$
   (d) $K = \{$the set of even numbers$\}$,
   $L = \{$the set of odd numbers$\}$

3. *If $A = \{1, 2, 3, 4\}$ and $B = \{2, 4, 6, 8\}$, write the set that is obtained by performing the following operations:*
   (a) $A \cup B$
   (b) $A \cap B$

4. *If $X = \{a, b, c\}$ and $Y = \{d, e\}$, write the set that is obtained by performing the following operations:*
   (a) $X \cup Y$
   (b) $X \cap Y$

Numeration

It is clear that the number 7 may be written in many different ways.

EXAMPLE: $8 - 1$, VII, $\frac{14}{2}$, $4 + 3$, $\sqrt{49}$
The number 7 is an idea that we have in our minds. The symbols that we put on paper to designate 7 are called numerals. Thus,
$$8 - 1, \text{VII}, 4 + 3, \text{ and } \sqrt{49}$$
are numerals. Numerals are names for numbers. And numbers may have many different names just as people may have more than one name. For example, John Smith may be known to some of his friends as Johnnie, to other friends as Smittie, to his baseball coach as Lefty, and to his father as Sonny.

READING AND WRITING NUMBERS

MILLIONS	HUNDRED THOUSANDS	TEN THOUSANDS	THOUSANDS	HUNDREDS	TENS	UNITS	TENTHS	HUNDREDTHS	THOUSANDTHS
1,	3	5	8,	7	0	2.	4	6	9

The number at the bottom is read as one million three hundred fifty-eight thousand seven hundred two *and* four hundred sixty-nine thousandths. Note that the decimal point is indicated by the use of the word *and*.

Note that the positions of the various digits determine the values the digits possess. This may be seen if we write the number 1,358,702.469 as follows:

$$\begin{array}{r} 1,000,000.000 \\ + 300,000.000 \\ + 50,000.000 \\ + 8,000.000 \\ + 700.000 \\ + 00.000 \\ + 2.000 \\ + .400 \\ + .060 \\ + .009 \end{array}$$

For example, we see that 3 represents 300,000 and that 7 represents 700. This is due to the positions of the 3 and the 7 in writing the number. The zero between the 7 and the 2 is merely a place holder and indicates that the number is written with no tens.

EXAMPLE: Which of the following numbers has 5 in the hundreds place and 9 in the tenths place?
(A) 3,516.29 (B) 5,317.94 (C) 6,501.92
(D) 3,519.32

SOLUTION: The answer is (C).

EXAMPLE: Precisely how many tens does the number 5,469 have?

SOLUTION: We may find the precise number of tens by dividing the number 5,469 by 10. The result is 546.9.

EXERCISE 3

Use numerals to write the following numbers:

1. Five thousand sixty and four hundredths

2. Six million four hundred fifty thousand nine hundred and six tenths

3. Two hundred seventy thousand five hundred ninety three

4. Forty million seven hundred sixteen thousand two hundred eighty-four and nineteen thousandths

EXPONENTS AND EXPANDED FORM

Consider the number 537. In this case, the 5 represents 500, the 3 represents 30, and the 7 represents 7. Thus, the number 537 may be written by using the following numerals:

$$537 = (5 \times 100) + (3 \times 10) + 7$$
$$\text{or} \quad 537 = (5 \times 10 \times 10) + (3 \times 10) + 7$$

When numbers are written in this form they are said to be written in *expanded form.*

EXAMPLE: Write 6,942 in expanded form.

$6,942 = (6 \times 1000) + (9 \times 100) + (4 \times 10) + 2$
or $(6 \times 10 \times 10 \times 10) + (9 \times 10 \times 10)$
$$+ (4 \times 10) + 2$$

EXAMPLE: Write 3,050 in expanded form.

$3,050 = (3 \times 1000) + (0 \times 100) + (5 \times 10) + 0$
or $(3 \times 10 \times 10 \times 10) + (0 \times 10 \times 10)$
$$+ (5 \times 10) + 0$$

Notice that there is a zero in the hundreds place. However, we do not leave this place blank as it would be just as confusing as writing 3,050 as 3 5.

EXERCISE 4

Write each of the following in expanded form, as shown in the preceding examples:

1. 28	6. 193	11. 35,729
2. 17	7. 2,486	12. 12,063
3. 40	8. 7,031	13. 70,519
4. 359	9. 1,908	14. 93,702
5. 406	10. 6,007	15. 10,046

In the examples given you have noticed that it was necessary to write numerals such as $10 \times 10 \times 10$, or $10 \times 10 \times 10 \times 10$. There is a shorter way of writing such numerals. $10 \times 10 \times 10$ may be written as 10^3. The small, raised "3" written to the right of 10 is called an *exponent* and indicates the number of times 10 is to be used as a factor.

An *exponent* is defined as follows:
For whole numbers n,

$$a^n = \underbrace{a \cdot a \cdot a \cdots\cdots a}_{n \text{ factors of } a}.$$

In the expression a^n, a is called the base and n is an exponent. When n is greater than 1, the exponent indicates the number of factors of the base that are multiplied.

$$a^1 = a$$
$$a^0 = 1$$

EXAMPLES: $2^4 = 2 \cdot 2 \cdot 2 \cdot 2 = 16$
$3^0 = 1$

Factor is defined as follows:

If a, b, and c are whole numbers, then b is a factor of c if $a \times b = c$, and a *is* also a factor of c.

EXAMPLE: Write 9^5 in expanded form.

$$9^5 = 9 \times 9 \times 9 \times 9 \times 9$$

EXAMPLE: Write $7 \times 7 \times 7 \times 7 \times 7$ by using exponents.

$$7 \times 7 \times 7 \times 7 \times 7 = 7^5$$

EXAMPLE: Write 4,689 in expanded form using exponents.

$4,689 = (4 \times 10 \times 10 \times 10) + (6 \times 10 \times 10)$
$\quad + (8 \times 10) + 9$
$\quad = (4 \times 10^3) + (6 \times 10^2) + (8 \times 10) + 9$

Notice that when 10 is taken once as a factor, we do not use the exponent 1. Thus, $80 = 8 \times 10$, not 8×10^1. It is not incorrect to write 80 as 8×10^1, but the number is not customarily written that way.

EXERCISE 5

1. *Write in expanded form:*
   (a) 3^4 (b) 5^3 (c) 2^5 (d) 10^4

2. *Use exponents to write each of the following:*
   (a) $9 \times 9 \times 9 \times 9$
   (b) $4 \times 4 \times 4$
   (c) $6 \times 6 \times 6 \times 6 \times 6$
   (d) 7×7
   (e) $10 \times 10 \times 10 \times 10 \times 10$
   (f) $3 \times 3 \times 3 \times 3 \times 3 \times 3$

3. *Use exponents to write each of the following in expanded form:*
   (a) 359   (e) 5,307   (i) 90,350
   (b) 7,648   (f) 75,123   (j) 15,026
   (c) 3,052   (g) 890   (k) 43,100
   (d) 704   (h) 6,080   (l) 70,051

The Set of Natural Numbers and the Set of Whole Numbers

The set of numbers {1, 2, 3, 4, 5, ...} is composed of the numbers that are used in counting. This set is called the set of natural numbers or, more simply, the set of *counting numbers*. The set {0, 1, 2, 3, 4, 5, ...} is called the set of *whole numbers*.

It is often helpful to associate sets of numbers with points on a line called the *number line*. This is done as follows: We draw a line, take a point on this line, and label some point 0. Then we take another point to the right of this point and label it 1. We use the distance between 0 and 1 as a unit and mark off other counting numbers on it as follows:

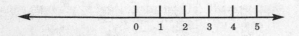

FACTORS AND PRIMES

As we saw in the preceding section, when two numbers are multiplied to form a product each of the numbers is called a *factor* of that product. Thus, 3 and 5 are factors of 15. We say that 8 is a factor of 32, or that 32 is *divisible* by 8.

A *prime number* is any counting number other than 1 that is divisible only by itself and 1. For example, the numbers 2, 3, 5, 7, and 11 are the five smallest prime numbers. A *composite number* is a counting number that can be expressed as the product of two smaller counting numbers other than 1. For example, 6 is a composite number because $6 = 3 \times 2$. A *multiple* of a counting number is the product of that number and a counting number.

EXAMPLE: 4, 8, 12, 16, 20, 24, 28, and 32 are multiples of 4.

Every composite number can be written as a product of prime numbers. The process of determining the prime factors of a given composite number is called *factoring*. The result is the prime factorization of the composite number.

EXAMPLES:

$$12 = 2 \cdot 2 \cdot 3$$
$$80 = 2 \cdot 2 \cdot 2 \cdot 2 \cdot 5$$
$$98 = 2 \cdot 7 \cdot 7$$

One convenient way of determining the prime factorization of a number is to use a factor tree. Name any two factors of the number and write them at the ends of branches below the number. Keep factoring each composite number at the ends of the branches until the numbers at the ends of the branches are all prime. The numbers at the ends of the branches constitute the prime factorization.

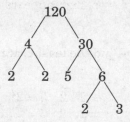

The prime factorization of 120 is $2 \cdot 2 \cdot 2 \cdot 3 \cdot 5$.

EXAMPLE: Write the prime factorization of 150.

$$150 = 2 \times 3 \times 5 \times 5$$

EXERCISE 6

1. *Write all the prime numbers greater than 10 and less than 20.*

2. *Which of the following numbers are prime and which are composite?*
   (a) 23 (b) 25 (c) 37 (d) 31 (e) 36
   (f) 51 (g) 53 (h) 61

3. *Name the four smallest multiples of the following counting numbers:*
   (a) 3 (b) 5 (c) 7 (d) 9

4. *Tell whether each of the following is true or false:*
   (a) 21 is a multiple of 7.
   (b) 2 is the only even prime number.
   (c) 3 is a factor of 10.
   (d) 20 is divisible by 5.
   (e) 3 and 4 are both factors of 12.
   (f) 6 is a prime factor of 42.

5. *Write the prime factorizations of the following numbers:*
   (a) 30 (b) 63 (c) 132 (d) 280 (e) 350

DIVISIBILITY

A number is *divisible by 2* if it is an even number. In other words, a number is divisible by 2 if the digit in the one's place is 0, 2, 4, 6, or 8.

EXAMPLE: The numbers 48, 76, 580, and 394 are divisible by 2.

A number is *divisible by 3* if the sum of its digits is divisible by 3.

EXAMPLE: 71,259 is divisible by 3 because 7 + 1 + 2 + 5 + 9 = 24, and 24 is divisible by 3.

A number is *divisible by 4* if the number formed by the last two digits on the right is divisible by 4.

EXAMPLE: 30,428 is divisible by 4 because 28 is divisible by 4.

A number is *divisible by 5* if the last digit on the right is either 5 or 0.

EXAMPLE: 795 is divisible by 5 because the last digit on the right in 795 is 5.

A number is *divisible by 6* if it is an even number and if the sum of its digits is divisible by 3.

EXAMPLE: 25,794 is divisible by 6 because 25,794 is an even number, and it is divisible by 3 because 2 + 5 + 7 + 9 + 4 = 27, which is divisible by 3.

A number is *divisible by 8* if the number formed by the last three digits on the right is divisible by 8.

EXAMPLE: 75,312 is divisible by 8 because 312 is divisible by 8.

A number is *divisible by 9* if the sum of its digits is divisible by 9.

EXAMPLE: 205,731 is divisible by 9 because 2 + 0 + 5 + 7 + 3 + 1 = 18, which is divisible by 9.

A number is *divisible by 10* if the digit in the one's place is 0.

EXAMPLE: 569,280 is divisible by 10 because the number in the one's place is 0.

EXERCISE 7

1. *Find the smallest prime factor of each of the following:*
   (a) 79,048   (b) 16,251   (c) 32,485
   (d) 1,337   (e) 649   (f) 1,343
   (g) 1,659   (h) 2,231

2. *Let X = {2, 3, 4, 5, 6, 8, 9, 10}. By which members of set X is each of the following numbers divisible?*
   (a) 6,480   (b) 1,756   (c) 5,432
   (d) 2,415   (e) 10,344   (f) 6,513
   (g) 7,002   (h) 4,618

3. *In each of the following, replace □ by a digit that will make the resulting number divisible by the number in the parentheses.*
   (a) 41 □ (2)   (g) □ (9)
   (b) 32 □ (3)   (h) 6, □ 12 (3)
   (c) 6, 7 □ 2 (4)   (i) 7, □ 12 (4)
   (d) 4, 05 □ (5)   (j) 6, 5 □ 0 (8)
   (e) 8, □ 12 (6)   (k) 1, 23 □ (9)
   (f) 4, 3 □ 6 (8)   (l) 9, 21 □ (6)

GREATEST COMMON FACTOR

The *greatest common factor* of two counting numbers is the greatest counting number that is a factor of each of them.

EXAMPLE: 8 is the greatest common factor of 24 and 32.

In order to find the greatest common factor of two counting numbers, we write each number as the product of its prime factors. Then we select the smallest power of each prime factor that appears in each set of prime factors. The product of these prime factors is the greatest common factor of the two numbers.

EXAMPLE: Find the greatest common factor of 60 and 90.

$$60 = 2 \cdot 2 \cdot 5 \cdot 3 = 2^2 \cdot 5 \cdot 3$$
$$90 = 2 \cdot 3 \cdot 3 \cdot 5 = 2 \cdot 3^2 \cdot 5$$

The greatest common factor of 60 and 90 is $2 \cdot 3 \cdot 5 = 30$.

LEAST COMMON MULTIPLE

The *least common multiple* of two counting numbers is the smallest counting number that is a multiple of each of them.

EXAMPLE: 24 is the least common multiple of 6 and 8.

In order to find the least common multiple of two counting numbers, we write each number as the product of its prime factors. Then we find the product of all of the prime factors, with each prime factor raised to the highest power that appears in any of the factors.

EXAMPLE: Find the least common multiple of 12 and 18.

$$12 = 2 \cdot 2 \cdot 3 = 2^2 \cdot 3$$
$$18 = 2 \cdot 3 \cdot 3 = 2 \cdot 3^2$$

The least common multiple of 12 and 18 is $2^2 \cdot 3^2 = 4 \cdot 9 = 36$.

EXERCISE 8

1. *Find the greatest common factor of each of the following pairs of numbers:*
   (a) 8, 12   (e) 49, 70   (i) 12, 30
   (b) 16, 24   (f) 72, 120   (j) 68, 170
   (c) 15, 20   (g) 36, 84   (k) 35, 49
   (d) 32, 48   (h) 96, 132   (l) 81, 108

2. *Find the least common multiple of each of the following pairs of numbers:*
   (a) 6, 8   (e) 4, 5   (i) 12, 16
   (b) 9, 12   (f) 14, 21   (j) 20, 25
   (c) 15, 20   (g) 8, 10   (k) 18, 32
   (d) 7, 14   (h) 10, 15   (l) 30, 40

THE SET OF INTEGERS

In locating the set of whole numbers on the number line, we did not consider points to the left of 0. Such points are located and shown on the number line below.

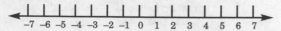

The numbers located on the number line to the left of zero are called *negative integers*. Negative integers are used to indicate temperatures below zero, to indicate a loss in business as opposed to a profit, etc. The set {..., –4, –3, –2, –1, 0, 1, 2, 3, 4, ...} is called the *set of integers*.

Addition of Integers

We may learn how to add integers by using the number line.

EXAMPLE: Find the sum of 2 + 3.

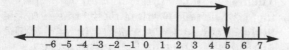

Locate 2 on the number line and then move 3 units to the right. We will interpret a move to the right as positive and a move to the left as negative. The result is 2 + 3 = 5.

EXAMPLE: Find the sum of 3 + (–5)

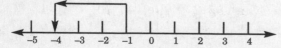

Locate 3 on the number line and then move 5 units to the left. The result is 3 + (–5) = –2.

EXAMPLE: Find the sum of –1 + (–3)

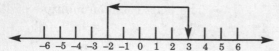

Locate –1 on the number line and then move 3 units to the left. The result is –1 + (–3) = –4.

EXAMPLE: Find the sum of –2 + 6.

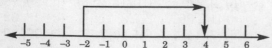

Locate –2 on the number line and then move 6 units to the right. The result is –2 + 6 = 4.

Signed Numbers

The opposite (or additive inverse) of any number is the number located the same distance from 0 on the number line in the opposite direction.

EXAMPLE: Write in symbols, "the opposite of negative seven." –(–7)

The opposite of negative seven is positive seven. –(–7) = +7 = 7

The absolute value of any number is the distance that the number is from 0 on the number line. Remember that distance is positive. The absolute value of –3 is written |–3|.

EXAMPLES: |3| = 3
|–5| = 5
|0| = 0

Addition
1. If two numbers have the same sign, add their absolute values and attach the common sign to the result.

EXAMPLES: 5 + 7 = 12
–3 + (–8) = –11

2. If two numbers have opposite signs, subtract their absolute values, the smaller from the larger, and attach the sign of the number with the larger absolute value to the result.

EXAMPLES: –9 + 3 = –6
–8 + 13 = 5
15 + (–25) = –10

EXERCISE 9

1. *Find the following sums. You may use the number line to help you.*
    (a) 1 + 4   (f) –2 + (–5)
    (b) 1 + (–4)   (g) 6 + (–4)
    (c) 2 + (–3)   (h) –1 + 4
    (d) 3 + (–5)   (i) –2 + (–3)
    (e) –3 + 5   (j) 5 + (–3)

2. *Represent the following quantities by using positive or negative integers.*
   (a) A loss of 3 pounds in weight.
   (b) A gain of 3 yards in football.
   (c) A bank deposit of $20.
   (d) A bank withdrawal of $20.
   (e) Ten degrees below zero.

Subtraction of Integers

Every positive integer may be paired with a negative integer and every negative integer may be paired with a positive integer as shown below. We say that

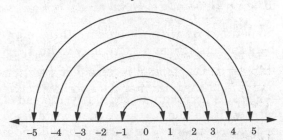

$$-5 \quad -4 \quad -3 \quad -2 \quad -1 \quad 0 \quad 1 \quad 2 \quad 3 \quad 4 \quad 5$$

1 and –1 are opposites, 2 and –2 are opposites, 3 and –3 are opposites, etc.

In order to subtract integer b from integer a, we add a to the opposite of b.

$$a - b = a + (-b)$$

EXAMPLE: Subtract –5 from 7.
$$7 - (-5) = 7 + 5 = 12$$

EXAMPLE: Subtract –2 from –6.
$$-6 - (-2) = -6 + 2 = -4$$

EXAMPLE: Subtract 3 from –4.
$$-4 - 3 = -4 + (-3) = -7$$

EXERCISE 10

Perform the following subtractions:

1. $3 - 5$	6. $10 - 2$
2. $9 - 3$	7. $-3 - 7$
3. $-1 - 4$	8. $6 - 9$
4. $6 - (-2)$	9. $7 - (-4)$
5. $-8 - 2$	10. $-8 - (-3)$

Multiplication of Integers

To multiply two numbers, multiply their absolute values and attach a sign to the result according to the following rule:

1. If the two numbers have the same sign, the result is positive.
2. If the two numbers have opposite signs, the result is negative.

EXAMPLE:
$$5 \times 9 = 45$$
$$-5 \times (-9) = 45$$
$$5 \times (-9) = -45$$
$$-5 \times 9 = -45$$

EXERCISE 11

Find the following products:

1. $6 \cdot (-3)$	6. $-4 \cdot 3$
2. $2 \cdot 7$	7 $(-7) \cdot (-5)$
3. $-4 \cdot 5$	8. $0 \cdot (-6)$
4. $-2 \cdot (-8)$	9. $4 \cdot (-8)$
5. $1 \cdot (-5)$	10. $(-3) \cdot (-7)$

Division of Integers

To divide two numbers, divide their absolute values and attach a sign to the result according to the rule for multiplication.

EXAMPLE:
$$15 \div 5 = 3$$
$$-15 \div (-5) = 3$$
$$15 \div (-5) = -3$$
$$-15 \div 5 = -3$$

EXERCISE 12

Perform the indicated operations:

1. $6 + (-4)$
2. $(-3) + (-5)$
3. $8 + (-2)$
4. $-5 - 9$
5. $8 - (-2)$
6. $6 \times (-2)$
7. $-4 \times (-7)$
8. $-8 \div -2$
9. $-12 \div 4$
10. $18 \div -6$

Symbols of Inequality

In working with numbers, we often wish to indicate that one number is greater than another or that one number is less than another. For this purpose, as you have learned, we use the following symbols:

> means "is greater than"
< means "is less than"

EXAMPLE: 5 > 3 means "5 is greater than 3."
2 < 7 means "2 is less than 7."

EXERCISE 13

Use one of the symbols >, =, < in the place of the □ to make each of the following statements true.

1. 5 + 7 □ 5 + 4
2. 9 − 6 □ 2 + 8
3. 3 × (6 + 5) □ (3 × 6) + (3 × 5)
4. 7 × (5 + 1) □ (7 × 5) × 1
5. 5 + (8 + 3) □ (8 + 3) − 5
6. 8 × 9 □ 8 × (6 + 3)
7. 17 − 1 □ 6 + (9 + 3)
8. 6 × (8 × 3) □ 17 + 2 × (5 + 9)
9. 25 − 3 × (6 + 1) □ 2 + 7
10. 15 + (3 + 9) □ (4 × 6) + 3

EXAMPLE: If set A = {1, 2, 3, 4, 5}, *write the set of natural numbers contained in set A that can be used to replace n to make the statement true.*

1. $n + 2 > 5$

We note that when n is replaced by 4 or 5 of set A, then the statement becomes true. Thus, the correct result is {4, 5}.

2. $7 + n < 11$

We note that when n is replaced by 1, 2, or 3 of set A then the statement becomes true. Thus, the correct result is {1, 2, 3}.

EXERCISE 14

In each case, select the set of numbers from set A = {1, 2, 3, 4, 5, 6} that will make the statement true.

1. $n + 1 > 4$
2. $n − 1 > 3$

3. $n + 5 = 7$
4. $2 + n < 5$
5. $6 − n > 3$
6. $2 \times n < 8$
7. $3 + n < 4 + 5$
8. $7 < 2 \times n$
9. $5 + (3 + 7) = (5 + n) + 7$
10. $(6 \times 4) \times 3 < (6 \times 4) \times n$

Sometimes we wish to compare three numbers such as 4, 5, and 7. We may write 4 < 5 and 5 < 7. However, this is frequently written as 4 < 5 < 7, which means "4 is less than 5 and 5 is less than 7." Similarly, instead of writing 7 > 5 and 5 > 4, we may write 7 > 5 > 4, which means "7 is greater than 5 and 5 is greater than 4." In each case we note that 5 is between 4 and 7.

EXERCISE 15

1. *Use symbols to write each of the following:*
   (a) 6 is greater than 3 and 3 is greater than 2.
   (b) 4 is less than 5 and 5 is less than 9.
   (c) 1 is less than 8 and 8 is less than 11.
   (d) 9 is greater than 7 and 7 is greater than 3.
   (e) 5 is between 4 and 8.
   (f) 6 is between 3 and 12.

2. *State each of the following in words:*
   (a) 7 > 6 > 1
   (b) 4 < 12 < 15
   (c) 14 > 10 > 3
   (d) 5 < 16 < 20

3. *In each case, select the set of numbers from set B = {5, 6, 7, 8, 9, 10} that will make the statement true.*
   (a) $4 < n < 7$
   (b) $9 > n > 6$
   (c) $6 < n < 9$
   (d) $8 > n > 5$

ORDER IN THE SET OF INTEGERS

We have seen that the set of integers may be represented on the number line with the set of negative integers represented to the left of 0 and the set of positive integers represented to the right of 0. We observe that of two integers represented on the number line, the integer to the right is greater than the integer to the left. For example, $8 > 5$, $0 < 3$, $4 > -6$, and $-1 > -5$.

EXERCISE 16

Copy the two integers and insert the correct symbol (> or <):

EXAMPLE: $-7 < 3$

1.	2	5	6.	0	−4
2.	8	4	7.	7	−9
3.	6	−2	8.	−2	−5
4.	−5	−9	9.	−3	0
5.	−1	3	10.	−6	1

Consider the compound sentence:

$$5 > 0 > -4$$

This sentence states that $5 > 0$ *and* $0 > -4$.

EXAMPLE: In the following sentence, replace n by the set of integers that satisfy the sentence

$$-3 < n < 2$$

This sentence states that -3 is less than n and n is less than 2.

The integers that are less than 2 are 1, 0, −1, −2, −3, −4, …. The integers that satisfy the above compound sentence are greater than −3. Thus, the set of integers that satisfy the compound set is

$$\{1, 0 -1, -2\}$$

EXERCISE 17

Write the set of integers that satisfy the sentence:

1. $4 > n > 0$
2. $3 > n > -3$
3. $-2 > n > -5$
4. $2 < n < 7$
5. $-1 < n < 3$
6. $-5 < n < 1$

The Set of Rational Numbers

A *rational number* is a number that can be expressed by a fraction which is the quotient of two integers, with the exception that division by zero is not permissible.

EXAMPLE: $\frac{2}{3}, -\frac{9}{5}, \frac{4}{1}$, and 3.2 are rational numbers.

Note that all integers are rational numbers since they can be expressed as fractions that are quotients of two integers.

EXAMPLE: 7 can be expressed as $\frac{7}{1}$, and −3 can be expressed as $-\frac{3}{1}$.

On the number line below, there are located some rational numbers that are not integers.

Operations with rational numbers are discussed in Chapter 8, "Mathematical Skills."

The Set of Real Numbers

Some rational numbers can be expressed as terminating decimals.

EXAMPLE: $\frac{1}{2} = 0.5$ $\frac{2}{5} = 0.4$

            $\frac{3}{4} = 0.75$ $\frac{7}{8} = 0.875$

Some rational numbers can be expressed as repeating decimals. By repeating decimals we mean decimals that have a repeating block of digits.

EXAMPLE: $\frac{1}{3} = 0.333\ldots$ This may be written as $0.\overline{3}$. The bar indicates that the "3" is repeated infinitely.

$$\frac{5}{6} = 0.8\overline{3} \quad \frac{5}{9} = 0.\overline{5} \quad \frac{3}{11} = 0.\overline{27}$$

All rational numbers may be expressed either as terminating decimals or as repeating decimals.

An *irrational number* is a number whose decimal representation is neither a terminating decimal nor a repeating decimal.

EXAMPLE: $\sqrt{2} = 1.4142135\ldots$ This decimal representation is not terminating; it will never come to an end. Nor is this decimal representation repeating; there is no block of digits that is repeating.

$\sqrt{5} = 2.23606\ldots$ Similarly, this decimal representation is neither a terminating decimal nor a repeating decimal.

All such *radicals* represent irrational numbers.

$\sqrt{7}$ is irrational

$\sqrt{8}$ is irrational

but $\sqrt{9}$ is rational because $\sqrt{9} = 3$.

$\pi = 3.141592654\ldots$ is an irrational number.

The set of *real numbers* is composed of the set of rational numbers and the set of irrational numbers. Thus, the set of real numbers includes the set of counting numbers, the set of integers, the set of rational numbers and the set of irrational numbers.

EXERCISE 18

1. *Identify each of the following real numbers as rational or irrational:*
   (a) 7   (d) $\sqrt{4}$ (g) $\sqrt{16}$
   (b) $\sqrt{6}$ (e) $\sqrt{10}$ (h) -5
   (c) $-2\frac{1}{2}$ (f) -3.7 (i) $\sqrt{8}$

2. *The numbers in the first column of the following chart are members of one or more of the sets of numbers given. Copy the chart in your notebook and complete it by placing a check in the box that applies. The first number is checked as a sample.*

NUMBER	COUNTING NUMBER	INTEGER	RATIONAL NUMBER	IRRATIONAL NUMBER	REAL NUMBER
-6		✔	✔		✔
$\sqrt{7}$					
$3\frac{1}{2}$					
0					
$-2\frac{1}{4}$					
0.37					
$\sqrt{3}$					
$-0.\overline{12}$					
-19					
$\sqrt{25}$					

LAWS OF OPERATION FOR REAL NUMBERS

You know from experience that $3 + 4 = 4 + 3$ and $7 + 9 = 9 + 7$. In fact, the order in which two real numbers are added makes no difference as far as the results are concerned. Mathematicians call this principle the *commutative law for addition of real numbers*. We state this law formally as follows:

Commutative Law for Addition of Real Numbers

If a and b represent real numbers, then

$$a + b = b + a.$$

Similarly, the order of multiplication may be changed without affecting the result.

Commutative Law for Multiplication of Real Numbers

If a and b represent real numbers, then

$$a \times b = b \times a.$$

It is also true that if three numbers are to be added, the result doesn't change by altering the grouping.

$$(4 + 7) + 5 = 11 + 5 = 16$$
$$4 + (7 + 5) = 4 + 12 = 16$$

This is known as:

Associative Law for Addition of Real Numbers

If a, b, and c represent real numbers, then

$$(a + b) + c = a + (b + c).$$

Regrouping does not affect the result of multiplication either. So we have:

Associative Law for Multiplication of Real Numbers

If a, b, and c represent real numbers, then

$$(a \times b) \times c = a \times (b \times c).$$

A man bought 3 solid ties at $12 each and 6 striped ties at $12 each. In computing the total bill, the clerk proceeded as follows:

3 solid ties at $12 each = 3×12 = $36
6 striped ties at $12 each = 6×12 = $\underline{\$72}$
Total =$108

Of course, he could have computed the bill more simply as follows:

(6 + 3) ties at $12 each
$$= \$12 \times (6 + 3) = \$12 \times 9 = \$108$$

This example illustrates the fact that

$$12 \times (6 + 3) = 12 \times 6 + 12 \times 3$$

Mathematicians call the principle described above the *distributive law for multiplication with respect to addition*. We shall simply call it the *distributive law*. We state this law formally as follows:

Distributive Law

If a, b, and c are any real numbers, then

$$a \times (b + c) = a \times b + a \times c.$$

EXERCISE 19

In each case, identify the law illustrated.

1. $5 + 3 = 3 + 5$
2. $(6 \times 7) \times 4 = 6 \times (7 \times 4)$
3. $9 \times (3 + 5) = 9 \times 3 + 9 \times 5$
4. $8 \times 2 = 2 \times 8$
5. $(4 + 7) + 1 = 4 + (7 + 1)$
6. $5 \times (6 + 3) = 5 \times 6 + 5 \times 3$
7. $7 + 3 = 3 + 7$
8. $(5 + 3) + 6 = 5 + (3 + 6)$
9. $1 \times 12 = 12 \times 1$
10. $6 \times (5 + 9) = 6 \times 5 + 6 \times 9$
11. $(7 \times 4) \times 2 = 7 \times (4 \times 2)$
12. $(3 + 12) + 4 = 3 + (12 + 4)$
13. $9 + 5 = 5 + 9$
14. $3 \times (1 + 5) = 3 \times 1 + 3 \times 5$
15. $(6 \times 5) \times 4 = 6 \times (5 \times 4)$
16. $8 \times 7 = 7 \times 8$
17. $(12 + 3) + 2 = 12 + (3 + 2)$
18. $7 \times (5 + 4) = 7 \times 5 + 7 \times 4$
19. $(3 + 5) + 9 = 3 + (5 + 9)$
20. $2 + 15 = 15 + 2$
21. $6 \times (12 + 8) = 6 \times 12 + 6 \times 8$
22. $(2 \times 8) \times 5 = 2 \times (8 \times 5)$
23. $19 \times 3 = 3 \times 19$
24. $(1 + 2) + 7 = 1 + (2 + 7)$
25. $9 + 3 = 3 + 9$

Answers to All Exercises

EXERCISE 1

1. (a) {January, June, July}
   (b) {This will vary.}
   (c) {a,b,c}
   (d) Ø or { }
   (e) {Saturday, Sunday}
   (f) {Washington}

2. (a) The set consisting of the names of the last three letters of the English alphabet.
   (b) The set consisting of the names of the coins in the U.S. money system.
   (c) The set consisting of the names of three American cities.
   (d) The set consisting of the names of the first five even numbers.
   (e) The set consisting of the names of the positions on a basketball court.

EXERCISE 2

1. (a) {5, 10, 15, 20, 30, 35}
   (b) {John, Bill, Mary, Fred, Nancy}
   (c) {June, July, August, September, October, December}
   (d) {Tuesday, Thursday, Saturday, Sunday}

2. (a) {4, 8}
   (b) {Sally, Don}
   (c) {Wednesday}
   (d) The empty set, { }.

3. (a) {1, 2, 3, 4, 6, 8}
   (b) {2, 4}

4. (a) {a, b, c, d, e}
   (b) The empty set, { }

EXERCISE 3

1. 5,060.04
2. 6,450,900.6
3. 270,593
4. 40,716,284.019

EXERCISE 4

1. $(2 \times 10) + 8$
2. $(1 \times 10) + 7$
3. 4×10
4. $(3 \times 100) + (5 \times 10) + 9$
5. $(4 \times 100) + (0 \times 10) + 6$
6. $(1 \times 100) + (9 \times 10) + 3$
7. $(2 \times 1,000) + (4 \times 100) + (8 \times 10) + 6$
8. $(7 \times 1,000) + (0 \times 100) + (3 \times 10) + 1$
9. $(1 \times 1,000) + (9 \times 100) + (0 \times 10) + 8$
10. $(6 \times 1,000) + (0 \times 100) + (0 \times 10) + 7$
11. $(3 \times 10,000) + (5 \times 1000) + (7 \times 100) + (2 \times 10) + 9$
12. $(1 \times 10,000) + (2 \times 1,000) + (0 \times 100) + (6 \times 10) + 3$
13. $(7 \times 10,000) + (0 \times 1,000) + (5 \times 100) + (1 \times 10) + 9$
14. $(9 \times 10,000) + (3 \times 1,000) + (7 \times 100) + (0 \times 10) + 2$
15. $(1 \times 10,000) + (0 \times 1,000) + (0 \times 100) + (4 \times 10) + 6$

EXERCISE 5

1. (a) $3 \times 3 \times 3 \times 3$
   (b) $5 \times 5 \times 5$
   (c) $2 \times 2 \times 2 \times 2 \times 2$
   (d) $10 \times 10 \times 10 \times 10$

2. (a) 9^4 (b) 4^3 (c) 6^5
   (d) 7^2 (e) 10^5 (f) 3^6

3. (a) $(3 \times 10^2) + (5 \times 10) + 9$
   (b) $(7 \times 10^3) + (6 \times 10^2) + (4 \times 10) + 8$
   (c) $(3 \times 10^3) + (0 \times 10^2) + (5 \times 10) + 2$
   (d) $(7 \times 10^2) + (0 \times 10) + 4$
   (e) $(5 \times 10^3) + (3 \times 10^2) + (0 \times 10) + 7$
   (f) $(7 \times 10^4) + (5 \times 10^3) + (1 \times 10^2) + (2 \times 10) + 3$
   (g) $(8 \times 10^2) + (9 \times 10)$
   (h) $(6 \times 10^3) + (0 \times 10^2) + (8 \times 10)$
   (i) $(9 \times 10^4) + (0 \times 10^3) + (3 \times 10^2) + (5 \times 10)$
   (j) $(1 \times 10^4) + (5 \times 10^3) + (0 \times 10^2) + (2 \times 10) + 6$
   (k) $(4 \times 10^4) + (3 \times 10^3) + (1 \times 10^2) + (0 \times 10)$
   (l) $(7 \times 10^4) + (0 \times 10^3) + (0 \times 10^2) + (5 \times 10) + 1$

EXERCISE 6

1. 11, 13, 17, 19

2. (a) Prime (e) Composite
   (b) Composite (f) Composite
   (c) Prime (g) Prime
   (d) Prime (h) Prime

3. (a) 3, 6, 9, 12 (c) 7, 14, 21, 28
   (b) 5, 10, 15, 20 (d) 9, 18, 27, 36

4. (a) True (d) True
   (b) True (e) True
   (c) False (f) False

5. (a) $2 \times 3 \times 5$
   (b) $3 \times 3 \times 7$
   (c) $2 \times 2 \times 3 \times 11$
   (d) $2 \times 2 \times 2 \times 5 \times 7$
   (e) $5 \times 5 \times 2 \times 7$

EXERCISE 7

1. (a) 2 (e) 11
   (b) 3 (f) 17
   (c) 5 (g) 3
   (d) 7 (h) 23

2. (a) {2, 3, 4, 5, 6, 8, 9} (e) {2, 3, 4, 6, 8}
   (b) {2, 4} (f) {3}
   (c) {2, 4, 8} (g) {2, 3, 6, 9}
   (d) {3, 5} (h) {2}

3. (a) 0, 2, 4, 6, or 8 (g) 3
   (b) 1, 4, or 7 (h) 0, 3, 6, or 9
   (c) 1, 3, 5, 7, or 9 (i) any digit
   (d) 0, or 5 (j) 2, or 6
   (e) 1, 4, or 7 (k) 3
   (f) 3, or 7 (l) 0, or 6

EXERCISE 8

1. (a) 4 (e) 7 (i) 6
   (b) 8 (f) 24 (j) 34
   (c) 5 (g) 12 (k) 7
   (d) 16 (h) 12 (l) 27

2. (a) 24 (e) 20 (i) 48
   (b) 36 (f) 42 (j) 100
   (c) 60 (g) 40 (k) 288
   (d) 14 (h) 30 (l) 120

EXERCISE 9

1. (a) 5 (f) −7
   (b) −3 (g) 2
   (c) −1 (h) 3
   (d) −2 (i) −5
   (e) 2 (j) 2

2. (a) −3 (c) $20
   (b) 3 (d) −$20 (e) −10

EXERCISE 10

1. −2 6. 8
2. 6 7. −10
3. −5 8. −3
4. 8 9. 11
5. −10 10. −5

EXERCISE 11

1 −18 6. −12
2. 14 7. 35
3. −20 8. 0
4. 16 9. −32
5. −5 10. 21

EXERCISE 12

1. 2 6. −12
2. −8 7. 28
3. 6 8. 4
4. −14 9. −3
5. 10 10. −3

EXERCISE 13

1. > 6. =
2. < 7. <
3. = 8. <
4. > 9. >
5. > 10. =

EXERCISE 14

1. {4, 5 ,6} 6. {1, 2, 3}
2. {5, 6} 7. {1, 2, 3, 4, 5}
3. {2} 8. (1, 2, 3}
4. {1, 2} 9. {3}
5. {1, 2} 10. {4, 5, 6}

EXERCISE 15

1. (a) 6 > 3 > 2
   (b) 4 < 5 < 9
   (c) 1 < 8 < 11
   (d) 9 > 7 > 3
   (e) 4 < 5 < 8 or 8 > 5 > 4
   (f) 3 < 6 < 12 or 12 > 6 > 3

2. (a) 7 is greater than 6 and 6 is greater than 1.
   (b) 4 is less than 12 and 12 is less than 15.
   (c) 14 is greater than 10 and 10 is greater than 3.
   (d) 5 is less than 16 and 16 is less than 20.

3. (a) {5, 6}   (c) {7, 8}
   (b) {8, 7}   (d) {7, 6}

EXERCISE 16

1. 2 < 5   6. 0 > –4
2. 8 > 4   7. 7 > –9
3. 6 > –2   8. –2 > –5
4. –5 > –9   9. –3 < 0
5. –1 < 3   10. –6 < 1

EXERCISE 17

1. {3, 2, 1}
2. {2, 1, 0, –1, –2}
3. {–3, –4}
4. {3, 4, 5, 6}
5. {0, 1, 2}
6. {–4, –3, –2, –1, 0}

EXERCISE 18

1. (a) rational   (f) rational
   (b) irrational   (g) rational
   (c) rational   (h) rational
   (d) rational   (i) irrational
   (e) irrational

NUMBER	COUNTING NUMBER	INTEGER	RATIONAL NUMBER	IRRATIONAL NUMBER	REAL NUMBER
–6		✔	✔		✔
$\sqrt{7}$				✔	✔
$3\frac{1}{2}$			✔		✔
0		✔	✔		✔
$-2\frac{1}{4}$			✔		✔
0.37			✔		✔
$\sqrt{3}$				✔	✔
$-0.\overline{12}$			✔		✔
–19			✔		✔
$\sqrt{25}$	✔	✔	✔		✔

EXERCISE 19

1. The commutative law for addition
2. The associative law for multiplication
3. The distributive law
4. The commutative law for multiplication
5. The associative law for addition
6. The distributive law
7. The commutative law for addition
8. The associative law for addition
9. The commutative law for multiplication
10. The distributive law
11. The associative law for multiplication
12. The associative law for addition
13. The commutative law for addition
14. The distributive law
15. The associative law for multiplication
16. The commutative law for multiplication
17. The associative law for addition
18. The distributive law
19. The associative law for addition
20. The commutative law for addition
21. The distributive law
22. The associative law for multiplication
23. The commutative law for multiplication
24. The associative law for addition
25. The commutative law for addition

CHAPTER

11

Reading Tables, Maps, and Graphs

Tables

Tables are used to present numerical facts and relationships. Often it is easier to pick out needed information by looking at a table than by reading through written material. Thus, the ability to read tables quickly and accurately is a very useful skill.

PRACTICE TEST 1

DIRECTIONS: Base your answers to the following questions on the table below.

NUMBER OF CARS SOLD

	JAN.	FEB.	MARCH	APRIL	MAY	JUNE
ADAMS	5	6	8	15	18	25
SANCHEZ	8	7	10	12	19	28
GOTTLIEB	3	9	12	14	12	20
JAWORSKI	4	5	11	9	15	19
LUM	7	4	6	10	11	17

The Star Auto Sales Company employs five salespersons. Their sales record for the first six months of the year is shown in the table above. The numbers represent the number of cars sold.

1. The most cars were sold by the five salespersons during the month of
   (A) March (B) May (C) June
   (D) January (E) April

2. The salesperson with the least number of sales for the six-month period was
   (A) Jaworski (B) Gottlieb (C) Sanchez
   (D) Adams (E) Lum

3. The total number of cars sold by salesperson Sanchez for the six-month period was
   (A) 84 (B) 80 (C) 27 (D) 82 (E) 78

4. The difference between the number of cars sold in March and the number of cars sold in February was
   (A) 14 (B) 15 (C) 12 (D) 16 (E) 10

5. If the average car sold for about $12,000 the approximate value of the cars sold in April was
   (A) $600,000 (B) $720,000
   (C) $6,000,000 (D) $7,200,000
   (E) $72,000

455

PRACTICE TEST 2

> DIRECTIONS: Base your answers to the following questions on the table below.

JULY

MON.	TUES.	WED.	THURS.	FRI.	SAT.	SUN.
	1 32	2 29	3 31	4 40	5 46	6 38
7 27	8 34	9 30	10 24	11 39	12 45	13 41
14 23	15 31	16 28	17 26	18 38	19 49	20 39
21 26	22 35	23 27	24 25	25 43	26 47	27 42
28 29	29 27	30 34	31 29			

Ms. Rossi owns the Roadside Motel, which has 50 units. She wishes to keep a handy record of the number of units occupied. To do this she uses a calendar and writes the number of units occupied in a small box in the upper right-hand corner of each date. The following questions are based on the occupancy rate for July.

1. On which day of the week did the Roadside Motel have the best rate of occupancy?
   (A) Wednesday (B) Friday
   (C) Saturday (D) Monday
   (E) Sunday

2. The total number of units occupied during the week of July 14 through July 20 was
   (A) 23 (B) 240 (C) 239 (D) 244 (E) 234

3. The average occupancy rate throughout the month for Thursday was
   (A) 27 (B) 31 (C) 29 (D) 28 (E) 25

4. On how many days during the month were less than one half of the units occupied?
   (A) 4 (B) 5 (C) 0 (D) 2 (E) 3

5. Ms. Rossi regards a 90% occupancy rate as excellent. On how many dates during the month did the Roadside Motel have a 90% or better rate of occupancy?
   (A) 5 (B) 4 (C) 6 (D) 1 (E) 3

Maps

Maps are used to show direction, size, and location and to measure distances between various points. The *scale* on a map tells you how great a distance is represented by each unit on the map. Thus, if the scale on a map says "1 inch = 20 miles," this means that one inch on the map represents a distance of 20 miles.

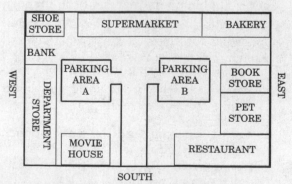

MIDWAY SHOPPING CENTER

PRACTICE TEST 3

DIRECTIONS: Base your answers to the following questions on the accompanying sketch of the Midway Shopping Center.

1. The store with the largest floor area in the Midway Shopping Center is the
   (A) Supermarket
   (B) Bakery
   (C) Movie House
   (D) Department Store
   (E) Shoe Store

2. In walking from the Movie House to the Restaurant the direction is
   (A) north (B) west (C) east (D) south
     (E) northeast

3. Of the following the one nearest Parking Area A is the
   (A) Restaurant (B) Bakery
     (C) Movie House (D) Supermarket
       (E) Book Store

4. The direction from the Shoe Store to the Pet Shop is
   (A) south (B) east (C) southwest
     (D) southeast (E) northeast

5. A shopper plans to park in Parking Area A, shop, and then return to his car. Of the following, which should he follow if he wishes to walk the least distance?
   (A) Book Store, Shoe Store, Bank, Bakery
   (B) Bakery, Bank, Book Store, Shoe Store
   (C) Shoe Store, Book Store, Bank, Bakery
   (D) Book Store, Bank, Bakery, Shoe Store
   (E) Bank, Shoe Store, Bakery, Book Store

PRACTICE TEST 4

DIRECTIONS: Base your answers to the following questions on the accompanying sketch of part of a road map.

1. It is necessary to cross a bridge over the Rapid River in traveling from
   (A) Rand to Elton
   (B) Vernon to Benton
   (C) Dover to Holden
   (D) Benton to Dover
   (E) Vernon to Rand

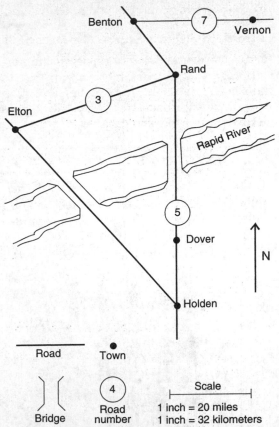

2. In traveling from Benton to Vernon the direction to take is
   (A) west (B) east (C) north
     (D) southeast (E) south

3. The distance from Rand to Dover, is approximately
   (A) 20 miles (B) 30 miles (C) 25 miles
     (D) 50 miles (E) 40 miles

4. Traveling from Vernon to Dover, a motorist takes
   (A) Route 7 and then Route 3
   (B) Route 5 and then Route 7
   (C) Route 7 and then Route 5
   (D) Route 2 and then Route 7
   (E) Route 3 and then Route 5

5. In driving from Holden to Elton a motorist travels
   (A) northwest (B) northeast (C) west
     (D) southeast (E) north

6. The distance from Benton to Vernon, in kilometers, is
   (A) 32 (B) 48 (C) 40 (D) 36 (E) 56

Pictographs

Pictures are often used to represent numerical facts. Pictures are more interesting to the reader and attract his or her attention more readily. Consider the following two picture graphs, or pictographs.

PRACTICE TEST 5

> DIRECTIONS: Base your answers to the following questions on the pictograph below, which shows the growth in population of the town of Springfield.

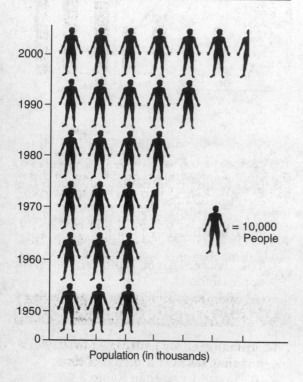

Population (in thousands)

1. If the population of Springfield was 30,000 in 1960, how many people are represented by each symbol in the pictograph?
   (A) 5,000 (B) 20,000 (C) 10,000
   (D) 15,500 (E) 50,000

2. The population of Springfield in 2000 was about
   (A) 30,000 (B) 65,000 (C) 52,000
   (D) 60,000 (E) 39,000

3. The largest population increase for a 10-year period occurred during
   (A) 1960–1970 (B) 2000–2010
   (C) 1970–1980 (D) 1990–2000
   (E) 1980–1990

4. The increase in population in Springfield between 1960 and 2000 was about
   (A) 38,000 (B) 45,000 (C) 48,000
   (D) 50,000 (E) 35,000

5. The Springfield Town Planning Council predicted that the population will reach 80,000 by the year 2020. How many symbols would be needed on the pictograph to represent 80,000 population?
   (A) 10 (B) 20 (C) 16 (D) 12 (E) 8

PRACTICE TEST 6

> DIRECTIONS: Base your answers to the following questions on the pictograph below, which shows the number of feet required to stop a car, at various speeds, after applying the brakes.

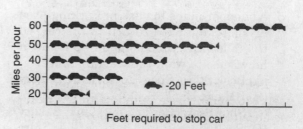

Feet required to stop car

1. A motorist traveling at 30 miles per hour requires 80 feet to stop her car after applying the brakes. Therefore, each car in the pictograph represents how many feet?
   (A) 10 (B) 15 (C) 20 (D) 40 (E) 25

2. If a motorist is traveling at 50 miles per hour, about how many feet are required to stop his car after applying the brakes?
   (A) 180 (B) 160 (C) 200 (D) 195
   (E) 185

3. How many more feet are needed to stop a car traveling at 50 miles per hour than a car going 40 miles per hour?
(A) 80 (B) 60 (C) 40 (D) 45 (E) 75

4. A motorist is traveling at the rate of 60 miles per hour. He sees a stop sign in the distance. About how many feet in advance must he apply the brake in order to stop at the stop sign?
(A) 100 (B) 150 (C) 200 (D) 250
(E) 300

Graphs

Graphs are also used to present numerical facts in visual form. Graphs enable a person to make comparisons and see relationships at a glance. In this section, we will consider three types of graphs: (a) bar graphs, (b) line graphs, (c) circle graphs.

BAR GRAPHS

Bar graphs are frequently used to make it easy to compare quantities.

EXAMPLE: Average attendance by days of the week at the Squire Movie Theater is given below:

Monday—2,407	Thursday—4,612
Tuesday—3,042	Friday—7,045
Wednesday—5,892	Saturday—9,812
	Sunday—8,286

Before trying to draw a bar graph it is useful to round these numbers to the nearest hundred admissions, as follows:

Monday—2,400	Thursday—4,600
Tuesday—3,000	Friday—7,000
Wednesday—5,900	Saturday—9,800
	Sunday—8,300

Next, we must decide upon a scale. In this case, it would be reasonable to let each box on the graph paper represent 1,000 admissions. Thus, Monday's admissions (2,400) would be represented by a height of 2.4 boxes, Tuesday's admissions (3,000) by 3 boxes, Wednesday's admissions (5,900) by almost six boxes, etc. The completed graph is shown in the next column.

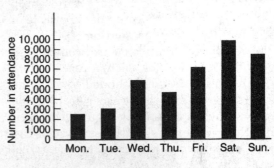

Graph 1

Notice that the scale selected must enable one to fit the graph on paper. Also, the scale selected must enable one to draw box heights so that it is easy to make comparisons at a glance. For example, on Graph 1 it would not be helpful if one box height were to represent 5,000 admissions. In that case, all box heights would be less than two units.

LINE GRAPHS

Line graphs are frequently used to show numerical changes over a period of time.

EXAMPLE: The Adams Motor Company sells automobiles. The number of cars sold during the first eight months of a certain year are shown in the table below:

January—203	May—679
February—316	June—548
March—461	July—412
April—537	August—362

Before drawing the graph it will be helpful to round these numbers to the nearest 50 cars, as shown on the next page:

January—200   May—700
February—300   June—550
March—450   July—400
April—550   August—350

Next, we must decide upon a scale. In this case, it is reasonable to let each interval on the *y*-axis (that is, the vertical axis on the left) represent 50 cars. Thus, January sales (200) are represented by 4 intervals, February sales (300) are represented by 6 intervals, March sales (450) are represented by 9 intervals, etc. We could use the scale of each box height representing 100 sales. However, we get a much clearer comparison by using 50 sales for each interval. Note that the graph is not intended to give the exact sales figures, but rather to give the reader a means of making a quick comparison. If the reader wishes the exact sales figures, he or she must refer to the table. Graph 2 is shown below.

MONTHLY SALES OF ADAMS MOTOR CO.

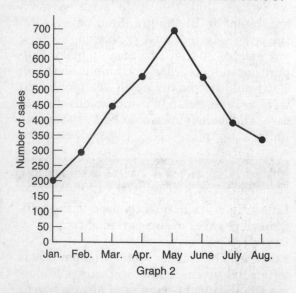

Graph 2

CIRCLE GRAPHS

Circle graphs are used when a whole quantity is divided into parts and we wish to make a comparison among the parts. In representing the parts we use the properties of a circle. Since the measure of a whole revolution is 360°, $\frac{1}{4}$ of a revolution is $\frac{1}{4}$ of 360° or 90°.

EXAMPLE: A city employs 6,000 workers distributed as follows:

Teachers—2,000   Sanitation—600
Police—1,000   Clerks—800
Firefighters—500   Miscellaneous—1,100

Draw a circle graph representing these figures.

GRAPH OF DISTRIBUTION
OF CITY WORKERS

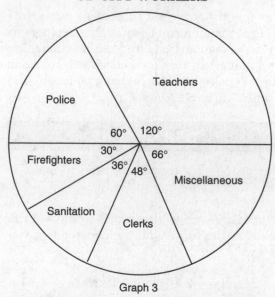

Graph 3

The sector of the circle representing the number of teachers is $\frac{2000}{6000} = \frac{1}{3}$. And $\frac{1}{3}$ of 360° = 120°. Thus the sector of the circle representing the number of teachers has an angle of 120° at the center.

The sector of the circle representing the number of police is $\frac{1000}{6000} = \frac{1}{6}$. And $\frac{1}{6}$ of 360° = 60°. Thus, the sector of the circle representing the number of police has an angle of 60° at the center.

The sector of the circle representing the number of firefighters is $\frac{500}{6000} = \frac{1}{12}$. And $\frac{1}{12}$ of 360° = 30°. Thus, the sector of the circle representing the number of firefighters has an angle of 30° at the center.

The sector of the circle representing the number of sanitation workers is $\frac{600}{6000} = \frac{1}{10}$. And $\frac{1}{10}$ of 360° = 36°. Thus, the sector of the circle representing the number of sanitation workers has an angle of 36° at the center.

The sector of the circle representing the number of clerks is $\frac{800}{6000} = \frac{2}{15}$. And $\frac{2}{15}$ of $360° = 48°$. Thus, the sector of the circle representing the number of clerks has an angle of 48° at the center.

The sector of the circle representing the number of miscellaneous workers is $\frac{1100}{6000} = \frac{11}{60}$. And $\frac{11}{60}$ of $360° = 66°$. Thus, the sector of the circle representing the number of miscellaneous workers has an angle of 66° at the center.

PRACTICE TEST 7

DIRECTIONS: Answer each of the following questions.

1. On a bar graph, the scale is 1 box = 600 people. The number of boxes needed to represent 2,000 people is
   (A) $2\frac{1}{2}$ (B) 3 (C) $3\frac{1}{2}$ (D) $3\frac{1}{3}$ (E) $3\frac{2}{3}$

2. On a bar graph it is necessary to represent the following: $850; $712; $1,548; $438; $903; $679. The best scale to use is 1 box =
   (A) $2,000 (B) $10 (C) $200 (D) $1,000 (E) $25

Answer questions 3–7 based on bar graph 4, which represents the number of traffic violations reported by the Traffic Division of the police department of a large city.

GRAPHS OF NUMBER OF TRAFFIC VIOLATIONS

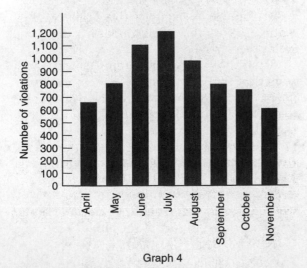

Graph 4

3. The scale on this graph is 1 box = _____ traffic violations.
   (A) 1,200 (B) 100 (C) 500 (D) 200 (E) 400

4. The number of traffic violations reported during the month of April was about
   (A) 600 (B) 700 (C) 650 (D) 550 (E) 575

5. The greatest number of violations occurred during the month of
   (A) May (B) November (C) June (D) August (E) July

6. The number of traffic violations reported during the month of August was about
   (A) 975 (B) 900 (C) 950 (D) 1,000 (E) 850

7. The month during which there were twice the number of traffic violations reported in November was
   (A) April (B) August (C) June (D) July (E) May

8. On a line graph, three intervals represent the number 750. The scale on this graph is 1 interval = _____.
   (A) 200 (B) 300 (C) 350 (D) 100 (E) 250

9. On a line graph it is necessary to represent the numbers 87, 102, 53, 75, 68, 119. The best scale to use is 1 interval =
   (A) 10 (B) 40 (C) 50 (D) 120 (E) 100

Answer questions 10–14 based on line graph 5, which represents the number of tolls collected on the Cross Island Bridge during a certain week.

GRAPH OF NUMBER OF TOLLS COLLECTED ON CROSS ISLAND BRIDGE

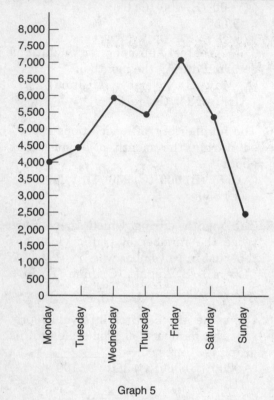

Graph 5

10. The scale on this graph is 1 interval = _____.
    (A) 1,000 (B) 2,000 (C) 1,500
    (D) 500 (E) 700

11. The day on which the lowest number of tolls was collected was
    (A) Monday (B) Sunday (C) Friday
    (D) Tuesday (E) Saturday

12. The number of tolls collected on Friday was about
    (A) 7,500 (B) 7,000 (C) 6,500 (D) 6,000
    (E) 8,000

13. The increase in the number of tolls collected between Tuesday and Wednesday was about
    (A) 1,000 (B) 2,500 (C) 2,000 (D) 1,500
    (E) 500

14. The difference between the number of tolls collected on Saturday and the number of tolls collected on Sunday was about
    (A) 2,500 (B) 2,000 (C) 3,000 (D) 3,500
    (E) 1,500

15. On a circle graph the angle at the center of a sector representing the fraction $\frac{10}{50}$ is
    (A) 72° (B) 20° (C) 50° (D) 10° (E) 100°

16. If an angle at the center of the sector of a circle graph measures 45° it represents the fraction
    (A) $\frac{1}{6}$ (B) $\frac{1}{9}$ (C) $\frac{9}{100}$ (D) $\frac{1}{4}$ (E) $\frac{1}{8}$

Answer questions 17–20 based on circle graph 6, which represents the number of dollars for various items in the monthly budget of the Green family. The Green family has a monthly income of $1,800.

GRAPH OF MONTHLY BUDGET OF THE GREEN FAMILY

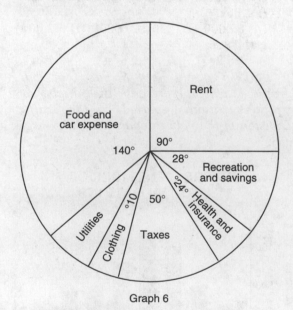

Graph 6

17. The monthly amount spent for rent is
    (A) $400 (B) $425 (C) $500 (D) $450
    (E) $350

18. The sector representing clothing expense is what part of the circle?
    (A) $\frac{1}{10}$ (B) $\frac{1}{20}$ (C) $\frac{1}{36}$ (D) $\frac{1}{15}$ (E) $\frac{1}{25}$

19. One month the Green family spent $200 on the family car for repairs and gas. The amount left in the budget for food this month was
(A) $700 (B) $500 (C) $450 (D) $600 (E) $650

20. The monthly cost of taxes for the Green family was
(A) $200 (B) $50 (C) $150 (D) $300 (E) $250

Answers to All Practice Tests

TEST 1

1. **C**   2. **E**   3. **A**   4. **D**   5. **B**

TEST 2

1. **C**   2. **E**   3. **A**   4. **D**   5. **B**

TEST 3

1. **D**   2. **C**   3. **D**   4. **D**   5. **E**

TEST 4

1. **D**   3. **E**   4. **C**   5. **A**   6. **B**
2. **B**

TEST 5

1. **C**   2. **B**   3. **D**   4. **A**   5. **E**

TEST 6

1. **C**   2. **E**   3. **B**   4. **D**

TEST 7

1. **D**	5. **E**	9. **A**	13. **D**	17. **D**
2. **C**	6. **A**	10. **D**	14. **C**	18. **C**
3. **B**	7. **D**	11. **B**	15. **A**	19. **B**
4. **C**	8. **E**	12. **A**	16. **E**	20. **E**

Geometry

CHAPTER 12

The Basics

POINTS, LINES, RAYS

Geometry is the study of lines, angles, surfaces, and solids. A *point* in geometry is suggested by a dot on a piece of paper, first base on a baseball field, or a star in the sky. A *line* in geometry is a set of points. A line is suggested by an edge of this page, a sideline in football, or a telephone wire stretched between two poles. A line in geometry is always thought of as a straight line and extends infinitely in both directions. For this reason a line is often shown with two arrows, as below. A line is named by naming two points on it with a double arrow above the names of the points. For

example, $\overleftrightarrow{AB}$ is a line containing both points A and B.

Parallel lines are lines in the same plane (flat surface) that never meet regardless of how far they are extended. $\overleftrightarrow{CD}$ is parallel to $\overleftrightarrow{EF}$. This may be written as $\overleftrightarrow{CD} \parallel \overleftrightarrow{EF}$.

Perpendicular lines are lines that meet at right angles (from square corners). $\overleftrightarrow{TV}$ is perpendicular to $\overleftrightarrow{RS}$. This may be written as $\overleftrightarrow{TV} \perp \overleftrightarrow{RS}$.

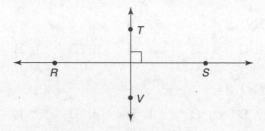

A *line segment* $\overline{AB}$ is a set of points of a line consisting of the points A and B and all the points between them.

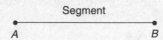

The points A and B are called the *endpoints* of the segment.

The length of $\overline{AB}$ is denoted by AB.

The figure below is a *ray*. A *ray* consists of

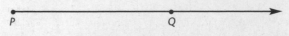

one endpoint and all the points on a line on one side of the endpoint.

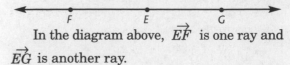

In the diagram above, $\overrightarrow{EF}$ is one ray and $\overrightarrow{EG}$ is another ray.

ANGLES

An *angle* is the union of two rays that have the same endpoint. The two rays are called the *sides* of the angle and their common endpoint is called the *vertex*. An angle is named by naming a point on one side, the vertex, and then a point on the other side. Where there is no ambiguity, an angle may be named by naming only its vertex.

EXAMPLE: In the diagram (right) the sides of the angle are $\vec{CA}$ and $\vec{CB}$, the vertex is C and the angle is named $\angle ACB$, or $\angle BCA$, or simply $\angle C$.

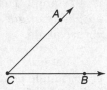

An angle is measured in degrees. An *acute* angle is an angle whose measure is less than 90°. A *right* angle is an angle whose measure is 90°. An *obtuse* angle is an angle whose measure is greater than 90° and less than 180°. A *straight* angle is an angle whose measure is 180°.

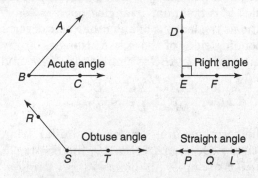

Complementary angles are two angles whose sum is 90°.

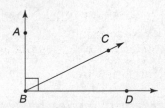

Thus in the diagram, $\angle ABC$ is complementary to $\angle CBD$.

Supplementary angles are two angles whose sum is 180°.

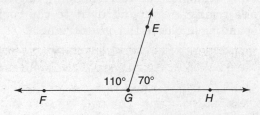

Thus, in the figure, $\angle EGF$ is supplementary to $\angle HGE$.

Two angles are said to be *congruent* if they have the same measure.

Thus, in the figure, $\angle CED$ is congruent to $\angle AFG$.

This may be written as $\angle CED \cong \angle AFG$.

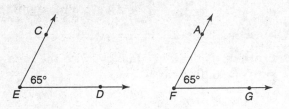

Vertical angles are pairs of opposite angles formed by two intersecting lines. Thus, in the figure, $\angle DAB$ and $\angle EAC$ are a pair of vertical angles. And $\angle BAC$ and $\angle EAD$ are another pair of vertical angles. Vertical angles are congruent.

Thus, in the figure, $\angle DAB \cong \angle EAC$, and $\angle BAC \cong \angle EAD$.

The sum of the measures (abbreviated as "m") of the angles around a point in a plane is 360°.

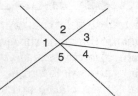

EXAMPLE: $m\angle 1 + m\angle 2 + m\angle 3 + m\angle 4 + m\angle 5 = 360°$.

The sum of the measures of the angles around a point in a plane on one side of a straight line is 180°.

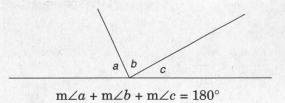

$$m\angle a + m\angle b + m\angle c = 180°$$

EXAMPLE: If $m\angle 1 = 140°$ and $m\angle 2 = m\angle 3$, find $m\angle 2$.

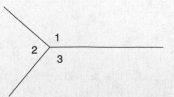

$$m\angle 1 + m\angle 2 + m\angle 3 = 360°$$
$$m\angle 1 = 140°$$
$$m\angle 2 + m\angle 3 = 360 - 140 = 220°$$

Since $m\angle 2 = m\angle 3$, $m\angle 2 = \frac{1}{2}(220) = 110°$

EXAMPLE: If $m\angle 5$ is equal to twice the measure of $\angle 6$, find $m\angle 5$.

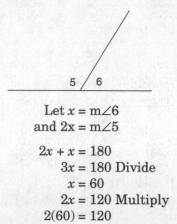

Let $x = m\angle 6$
and $2x = m\angle 5$

$$2x + x = 180$$
$$3x = 180 \quad \text{Divide}$$
$$x = 60$$
$$2x = 120 \quad \text{Multiply}$$
$$2(60) = 120$$

Thus, $m\angle 5 = 120°$.

TRIANGLES

A *triangle* is the union of three line segments that join three points called vertices (plural of vertex) that are not in a straight line. A triangle can be named by three capital letters placed at its vertices.

Triangles can be classified according to their *sides*. Thus, a *scalene triangle* is a triangle in which no two sides are congruent (equal). An *isosceles triangle* has two congruent sides. The base angles, opposite the congruent sides, are also congruent. An *equilateral triangle* has three congruent sides.

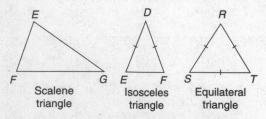

Triangles can also be classified according to their *angles*. An *acute triangle* is a triangle that has three acute angles. A *right triangle*

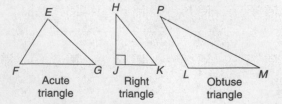

is a triangle that has one right angle. An *obtuse triangle* is a triangle that has one obtuse angle.

The sum of the measures of the angles of a triangle is 180°. Thus, if the measure of one angle of a triangle is 30°, and the measure of a second angle of the triangle is 80°, then the measure of the third angle is $180 - (30 + 80)$, or $180 - 110$, or 70°.

Similar triangles are triangles that have the same shape but not necessarily the same size. The lengths of a pair of corresponding sides of two similar triangles have the same ratio as the lengths of any other pair of corresponding sides of those two triangles. In the figure below $\triangle ABC$ is similar to $\triangle DEF$, and

$$\frac{AB}{DE} = \frac{AC}{DF} = \frac{BC}{EF}.$$

The corresponding angles of similar triangles are equal: $m\angle A = m\angle D$, $m\angle B = m\angle E$, $m\angle C = m\angle F$.

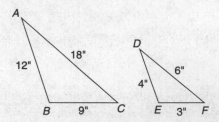

Congruent triangles have the same shape and the same size and can be made to coincide exactly. In the figure below, $\triangle ABC$ is congruent to $\triangle DEF$. Note that the corresponding sides of one triangle are congruent to the corresponding sides of the other triangle. The corresponding angles of one triangle are congruent to the corresponding angles of the other triangle.

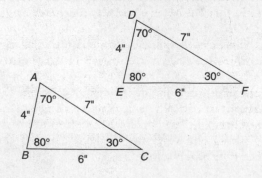

OTHER POLYGONS

A *polygon* is composed of a set of line segments in the same plane, each of which meets exactly two other line segments, one at each endpoint.

A *quadrilateral* is a polygon containing four segments as sides. A *trapezoid* is a quadrilateral with only one pair of sides parallel. Here the bases $\overline{AB}$ and $\overline{CD}$ are parallel. A *parallelogram* is a quadrilateral with two pairs of sides parallel. Here side $\overline{AB}$ is parallel to side $\overline{CD}$, and side $\overline{AD}$ is parallel to side $\overline{CB}$. A *rectangle* is a quadrilateral with four right angles. A *rhombus* is a quadrilateral with all sides congruent. A *square* is a quadrilateral with all sides congruent and all right angles. A *hexagon* is a polygon of six sides.

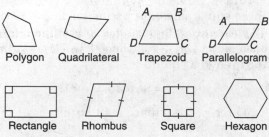

Polygon   Quadrilateral   Trapezoid   Parallelogram

Rectangle   Rhombus   Square   Hexagon

CIRCLES

A *circle* is the set of all points in a plane that are a given fixed distance from a fixed point called the *center*. Any segment from the center to a point on the circle is called a *radius*. Any segment connecting two points on the circle is called a *chord*. A chord that contains the center is called a *diameter*. The length of the diameter is twice that of the radius. An angle formed by two radii is a *central angle* ($\angle BOR$). The length of the circle is known as the *circumference*. The ratio of the circumference to the diameter is a constant and is known as π (pi). The value of π is approximately $3\frac{1}{7}$ or $\frac{22}{7}$ or 3.14. Since the circumference (C) is π times as big as the diameter *(d),* we can find the circumference by using the formula $C = \pi d$. Thus if the diameter of a circle is 14,

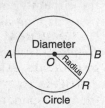

$$C = \pi d = \frac{22}{\underset{1}{7}} \times \frac{\overset{2}{14}}{1} = 44$$

PRACTICE TEST 1

DIRECTIONS: Answer the following questions.

1. If m∠1 is equal to four times the measure of ∠2, m∠1 is:

   (A) 36°   (B) 48°   (C) 154°   (D) 144°

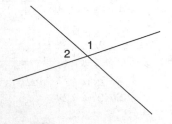

2. If m∠3 = 90° and m∠4 = m∠5, m∠4 is:

   (A) 90°   (B) 45°   (C) 50°   (D) 135°

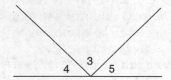

3. If m∠1 = m∠2 and m∠1 = 140°, m∠3 is:

   (A) 80°   (B) 90°   (C) 120°   (D) 100°

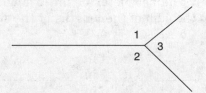

4. If m∠5 is equal to twice the measure of ∠4, m∠6 is:

   (A) 120°   (B) 100°   (C) 60°   (D) 90°

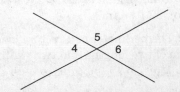

Perimeter, Area, and Volume

PERIMETER

The *perimeter* is the distance around a plane figure. The following formulas will prove helpful in determining perimeters.

Triangle: $P = a + b + c$

Equilateral triangle: $P = 3s$

Rectangle: $P = 2l + 2w$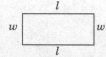

Square: $P = 4s$

Regular or equilateral hexagon: $P = 6s$

Circle: $C = \pi d$ or $C = 2\pi r$

EXAMPLE: Find the perimeter of a triangle whose sides are 3 ft. 4 in., 4 ft. 7 in., and 5 ft. 6 in.

SOLUTION: The perimeter of the triangle is equal to the sum of the lengths of the sides or $P = a + b + c$.

$$
\begin{aligned}
&3 \text{ ft.} \quad 4 \text{ in.} \\
&4 \text{ ft.} \quad 7 \text{ in.} \\
\underline{&5 \text{ ft.} \quad 6 \text{ in.}} \\
&12 \text{ ft. } 17 \text{ in.}
\end{aligned}
$$

The perimeter of the triangle is 13 ft. 5 in.

EXAMPLE: How many feet of fencing are required to enclose a rectangular yard that is 37 ft. by 22 ft. 6 in.?

SOLUTION: The perimeter of a rectangle is equal to the sum of two lengths and two widths.

$$P = 2l + 2w = 2 \times 37 + 2 \times 22\tfrac{1}{2}$$
$$= 74 + 45 = 119$$

The perimeter of the rectangle, and therefore the amount of fencing required, is 119 feet.

EXAMPLE: The perimeter of a rectangle is 82 ft. If the width of the rectangle is 17 ft., find the length.

SOLUTION: If we subtract two widths of the rectangle from the perimeter we will find the value of two lengths: $82 - 34 = 48$. Since the two equal lengths add up to 48 feet, the value of one length is 24 feet.

EXAMPLE: The side of an equilateral triangle is 12 cm. Find the area of a square whose perimeter is equal to that of the triangle.

SOLUTION: Since an equilateral triangle has three equal sides, its perimeter is 3×12 or 36 cm. Since a square has four equal sides, each side is $36 \div 4$ or 9 cm. The formula for the area of a square is

$$A = s^2 = 9^2 = 9 \times 9 = 81.$$

The area of the square is 81 sq. cm.

EXAMPLE: How much rope is needed to put along the edge of a circular pool that has a radius of 21 feet?

SOLUTION: The length of a circle is known as the circumference. The circumference is π times as long as the diameter, or $C = \pi d$ or $C = 2\pi r$. Use $\frac{22}{7}$ as the value of π.

$$C = 2\pi r = 2 \times \frac{22}{7} \times \overset{3}{\underset{1}{21}} = 132$$

The length of the rope is 132 feet.

EXAMPLE: A circle has a circumference of 78.5 feet. Find the length of the diameter. (Let $\pi = 3.14$.)

SOLUTION: Since $C = \pi \times d$, then $d = C \div \pi$.

$$d = 78.5 \div 3.14$$

$$
\begin{array}{r}
25. \\
3.14\,)\overline{78.50.} \\
62\ 8 \\
\overline{15\ 70} \\
15\ 70
\end{array}
$$

The diameter is 25 feet in length.

AREA

The area of a plane figure is the number of square units that the figure contains. For example, the unit of measure used in measuring the area of the rectangle at the right is the square inch. A square inch is a square whose length is 1 inch and whose width is 1 inch. Since a square inch is contained in the rectangle 8 times, we say that the area of the rectangle is 8 square inches. It can be seen that the area of a rectangle is obtained by multiplying the number of units in its length by the number of units in its width. In converting units of area recall that 144 sq. in. = 1 sq. ft. and 9 sq. ft. = 1 sq. yd. The following formulas are useful in finding areas.

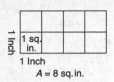

Rectangle: $A = lw$

Parallelogram: $A = bh$

Square: $A = s^2$

Triangle: $A = \frac{1}{2} bh$

Trapezoid:
$A = \frac{1}{2}h (b_1 + b_2)$

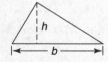

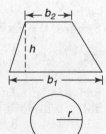

Circle: $A = \pi r^2$

EXAMPLE: A rectangular living room is 22 ft. long and 12 ft. 6 in. wide. How many square feet of carpet are needed to cover the floor of the living room?

SOLUTION: The area of the floor of the living room is found by obtaining the product of the number of units in the length and the number of units in the width.

$$22 \times 12\tfrac{1}{2}$$

$$
\begin{array}{r}
22 \\
\times\ 12\tfrac{1}{2} \\
\hline
11 \\
44 \\
22 \\
\hline
275
\end{array}
$$

275 square feet of carpet are needed.

EXAMPLE: The area of a rectangular room is 207 square feet. If the length of the room is 18 feet, find the width of the room.

SOLUTION: The width of the room is obtained by dividing the area of the room by its length.

$$
\begin{array}{r}
11\tfrac{9}{18} \\
18\overline{)207} \\
18 \\
\hline
27 \\
18 \\
\hline
9
\end{array}
$$

The width of the room is $11\tfrac{9}{18}$ ft. = $11\tfrac{1}{2}$ ft. or 11 ft. 6 in.

EXAMPLE: A tile measures 6 inches by 6 inches. How many such tiles are needed to cover a floor 15 feet long and 12 feet wide?

SOLUTION: The floor area is obtained by multiplying the number of units in its length by the number of units in its width.

$$\text{Area} = 15 \times 12 = 180 \text{ sq. ft.}$$

Each tile has an area of 6 in. by 6 in. or 36 sq. in. Since 144 sq. in. is 1 sq. ft., then 3 sq. in. is $\frac{36}{144}$ or $\frac{1}{4}$ of a square foot. The number of tiles needed is $180 \div \frac{1}{4}$, or 180×4, or 720 tiles.

EXAMPLE: Find the area of a triangle whose base is 8 ft. 4 in. and whose altitude is 9 ft.

SOLUTION: The area of the triangle is equal to one-half the product of its base and altitude.

$$\text{Base} \times \text{Altitude} = 8 \text{ ft. } 4 \text{ in.} \times 9 \text{ ft.}$$
$$= 8\tfrac{1}{3} \times 9 = 75 \text{ sq. ft.}$$

One-half of this product is $37\tfrac{1}{2}$ square feet.

EXAMPLE: A triangular-shaped cloth sail has a base of 10 meters and a height of 6 meters. If the cloth cost $4 a square meter, find the cost of the sail.

SOLUTION: The formula for the area of a triangle is $A = \frac{1}{2}bh$.

$A = \frac{1}{2}bh = \frac{1}{2} \times 10 \times 6 = 30$ square meters.

Since each square meter costs $4, the cost of 30 square meters is 30×4, or $120.

EXAMPLE: Find the surface area of a box that measures 6 cm by 4 cm by 3 cm.

SOLUTION: The box has six rectangular surfaces. The bottom and top surfaces each have an area of 6 cm × 4 cm or 24 sq cm. The surfaces to the right and left each have an area of 3 cm × 4 cm or 12 sq. cm. The front and back rectangles each have an area of 6 cm. × 3 cm or 18 sq. cm.

$$2 \times 24 + 2 \times 12 + 2 \times 18 = 48 + 24 + 36$$
$$= 108 \text{ sq. cm}$$

The total surface is therefore equal to 108 square centimeters.

EXAMPLE: Find the area of a circular garden whose diameter is 20 feet.

SOLUTION: The formula for the area of a circle is $A = \pi r^2$. Since the diameter is 20 feet, the radius is 10 feet. Since 7 does not divide evenly into 10, it is best to select 3.14 as the value of π.

$$A = \pi r^2 = 3.14 \times 10 \times 10 = 314$$

The area of the garden is 314 square feet.

EXAMPLE: The circumference of a circle is 88 inches. Find its area. (Let $\pi = \frac{22}{7}$.)

SOLUTION: The circumference of a circle is π times as long as its diameter. To find the diameter we divide the circumference by π.

$$d = C \div \pi = 88 \div \frac{22}{7} = \overset{4}{88} \times \frac{7}{\underset{1}{22}} = 28$$

Since the diameter is 28, the radius is 14 inches.

$$A = \pi r^2 = \frac{22}{\underset{1}{7}} \times \overset{2}{14} \times 14 = 616$$

The area of the circle is 616 square inches.

VOLUME

The dimensions of a solid are the length, the width, and the height. The volume of a solid is the measure of the quantity of space that the solid occupies. The unit of measure of volume is the *cubic unit*. The cubic inch is a cube whose length, width, and height each measure 1 inch. The following formulas for determining volumes of solids will prove helpful:

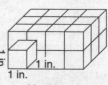

V = 24 cu. in.

Rectangular solid (prism): $V = lwh$

Cube: $V = e^3$

Circular cylinder: $V = \pi r^2 h$

Circular cone: $V = \frac{1}{3}\pi r^2 h$

Sphere: $V = \frac{4}{3}\pi r^3$

EXAMPLE: Find the volume of a rectangular solid whose length is 2 ft. 3 in., whose width is 1 ft. 6 in., and whose height is 8 in.

SOLUTION: The volume of the rectangular solid is obtained by multiplying the number of units in its length by the number of units in its width by the number of units in its height.

Since 2 ft. 3 in. = $2\frac{1}{4}$ ft., 1 ft. 6 in. = $1\frac{1}{2}$ ft., and 8 in. = $\frac{2}{3}$ ft.,

Volume $= 2\frac{1}{4} \times 1\frac{1}{2} \times \frac{2}{3} = \frac{9}{4} \times \frac{3}{2} \times \frac{2}{3} = \frac{9}{4}$

The volume of the rectangular solid is $2\frac{1}{4}$ cubic feet.

EXAMPLE: A candy box is 2.5 inches high, 8 inches long, and 5.4 inches wide. How many cubic inches does the box contain?

SOLUTION: The volume is obtained by multiplying the number of units in the length by the number of units in the width by the number of units in the height.

Volume $= 8 \times 5.4 \times 2.5 = 108$

The candy box contains 108 cubic inches.

EXAMPLE: An excavation for a building is 48 ft. 3 in. long, 24 ft. wide, and 12 ft. deep. How many cubic feet of earth must be removed?

SOLUTION:

Volume $= 48\frac{1}{4} \times 24 \times 12$

Volume $= \frac{193}{4} \times 24 \times 12 = 13,896$

13,896 cubic feet must be removed.

EXAMPLE: A cubical tank in a ship's hold measures 30 feet on an edge. How many gallons of oil can be poured into it ($7\frac{1}{2}$ gal. = 1 cu. ft.)?

SOLUTION: The formula for the volume of a cube is $V = e^3$.

$V = e^3 = 30^3 = 30 \times 30 \times 30 = 27,000$ cu. ft.

Since each cubic foot contains $7\frac{1}{2}$ gallons, the total number of gallons is $27,000 \times 7\frac{1}{2}$.

$$\frac{\overset{13,500}{\cancel{27,000}}}{1} \times \frac{15}{\underset{1}{\cancel{2}}} = 202,500$$

The tank will hold 202,500 gallons of oil.

EXAMPLE: Find the volume of a circular cylindrical tank that has a diameter of 20 feet and a height of 14 feet.

SOLUTION: The formula to find the volume of a circular cylinder is $V = \pi r^2 h$. Here the radius is 10 feet and the height is 14 feet. In this example it is best to use $\frac{22}{7}$ as the value of π since 7 divides evenly into 14.

$$V = \pi r^2 h = \frac{22}{\underset{1}{\cancel{7}}} \times \frac{10}{1} \times \frac{10}{1} \times \frac{\overset{2}{\cancel{14}}}{1} = 4,400$$

The volume of the cylinder is 4,400 cu. ft.

EXAMPLE: Find the volume of a circular cone-shaped pile of sand if its base has a diameter of 20 ft. and its height is 5 ft. 3 in.

SOLUTION: The formula for finding the volume of a circular cone is $V = \frac{1}{3}\pi r^2 h$. The radius is $\frac{1}{2}$ of 20 or 10 ft. The height is $5\frac{1}{4}$ ft.

$$V = \frac{1}{3}\pi r^2 h = \frac{1}{3} \times \frac{22}{7} \times 10 \times 10 \times \frac{21}{4} = 550$$

The volume of the sand pile is 550 cubic feet.

PRACTICE TEST 2

1. The sides of a triangle are 4′2″, 5′9″, and 3′8″. The perimeter of the triangle is:

   (A) 12′9″ (B) 13′9″ (C) 12′3″ (D) 13′7″ (E) 12′7″

2. The perimeter of a triangle is 20′. Two sides of the triangle are 6′8″ and 5′10″. The third side of the triangle is:

   (A) 9′6″ (B) 7′6″ (C) 12′6″ (D) 32′6″ (E) none of these

3. The length and width of a rectangle are 18′8″ and 7′6″. The perimeter of the rectangle is:

   (A) 52′4″ (B) 26′2″ (C) 50′8″ (D) 37′4″ (E) 15′

4. A room is 19′9″ long and 14′8″ wide. A strip of molding is fitted around the ceiling of the room. The length of molding used is:

   (A) 66′ (B) 54′2″ (C) 68′10″ (D) 69′4″ (E) 34′5″

5. The perimeter of a rectangle is 45′6″. The width of the rectangle is 8′6″. The length of the rectangle is:

   (A) 18′6″ (B) 108′ (C) 37′ (D) 74′ (E) 14′3″

PRACTICE TEST 3

1. The sides of a triangle are 6′3″ 3′8″ and 4′7″. The perimeter of the triangle is:

   (A) 13′8″ (B) 15′ (C) 14′8″ (D) 14′6″
   (E) 72′

2. The perimeter of a triangle is 31′2″. Two sides of the triangle are 12′3″ and 10′6″. The other side of the triangle is:

   (A) 53′11″ (B) 9′3″ (C) 10′6″ (D) 8′5″
   (E) 10′3″

3. A rectangle is 6′6″ long and 3′4″ wide. The area of the rectangle is:

   (A) $21\frac{2}{3}$ sq. ft. (B) 26 sq. ft.
   (C) 20 sq. ft. (D) $18\frac{2}{3}$ sq ft.
   (E) $18\frac{1}{3}$ sq. ft.

4. The base of a triangle is 15′9″. Its altitude is 5′4″ wide. The area of the triangle is:

   (A) 76 sq. ft. (B) 48 sq. ft. (C) 75 sq. ft.
   (D) 84 sq. ft. (E) 42 sq. ft.

5. The area of a rectangle is 110 square feet. The length of the rectangle is 15′. The width of the rectangle is:

   (A) 7′ (B) 7′3″ (C) 7′4″ (C) 22′
   (E) 7′6″

6. A rectangular solid has a length of 9′6″, a width of 8′, and a height of 3′3″. The volume of the rectangular solid is:

   (A) 216 cu. ft. (B) 221 cu. ft.
   (C) $20\frac{3}{8}$ cu ft. (D) $226\frac{1}{4}$ cu. ft.
   (E) 247 cu. ft.

7. A drawer is 11.3 inches long, 4.4 inches wide, and 2.5 inches high. The volume of the drawer is:

   (A) 121 cubic inches
   (B) 124 cubic inches
   (C) 113 cubic inches
   (D) 124.3 cubic inches
   (E) 226 cubic inches

8. The volume of a rectangular solid is 156 cubic inches. The length of the solid is 6.5 inches and its width is 5 inches. The height of the solid is:

   (A) 4.8 inches (B) 5 inches
   (C) 5.2 inches (D) 10.2 inches
   (E) 2.8 inches

PRACTICE TEST 4

1. A right isosceles triangle has one angle of:

   (A) 60° (B) 30° (C) 45° (D) 75°
   (E) none of these

2. An obtuse triangle always has:

   (A) only one acute angle
   (B) three obtuse angles
   (C) two obtuse angles
   (D) two acute angles
   (E) equal sides

3. Two angles of a triangle are 20° and 40°. The third angle contains:

   (A) 120° (B) 60° (C) 30° (D) 40°
   (E) 100°

4. Two sides of a right triangle are always:

   (A) equal (B) perpendicular
   (C) oblique (D) vertical
   (E) horizontal

5. Triangles whose corresponding sides are equal in length are said to be:

   (A) congruent (B) equal
   (C) isosceles (D) almost alike
   (E) equilateral

6. A circle has a diameter of 42. Its circumference is (let $\pi = \frac{22}{7}$):

   (A) 264 (B) 1386 (C) 132 (D) 441
   (E) none of these

7. The area of a circle whose diameter is 20 is (let $\pi = 3.14$):

   (A) 1256 (B) 314 (C) 400 (D) 62.8
   (E) none of these

8. The volume of a circular cylinder whose diameter is 10 inches and whose height is 7 feet is (let $\pi = \frac{22}{7}$):

   (A) 2200 cu. in. (B) 550 cu. ft.
   (C) 6600 cu. ft. (D) 66,000 cu. in
   (E) none of these

9. A wire in the shape of a rectangle is twisted into the shape of a square. If the rectangle measures 10 inches by 6 inches, the area of the square is:

   (A) 32 sq. in. (B) 60 sq. in.
   (C) 225 sq. in. (D) 16 sq in.
   (E) 64 sq. in.

10. A cube 6 feet on an edge is filled with water. The water is poured into a container that is the shape of a rectangular solid. If the base measures 12 feet by 3 feet, to what height will the water rise?

    (A) 12 ft. (B) 1 ft. (C) 3 ft. (D) 6 ft.
    (E) 8 ft.

11. The diameter of the base of a circular cone is 3´6˝ and the altitude is 5´. The volume of the cone, in cubic feet, is (let $\pi = \frac{22}{7}$):

    (A) 770 (B) 38.5 (C) 110 (D) $16\frac{1}{24}$
    (E) none of these

12. A machine part is in the form of a semicircle with radius of $5\frac{1}{4}˝$. The area of the machine part, in square inches, is (let $\pi = \frac{22}{7}$):

    (A) $16\frac{1}{8}$ (B) $32\frac{3}{4}$ (C) $43\frac{5}{16}$ (D) $86\frac{2}{7}$
    (E) 33

PRACTICE TEST 5

1. The supplement of an acute angle is:

   (A) a right angle (B) an acute angle
   (C) an obtuse angle (D) a reflex angle
   (E) none of these

2. Two angles of a triangle are 68° and 75°. The value of the third angle is:

   (A) 57° (B) 37° (C) 47° (D) 143°
   (E) none of these

3. The length of a rectangle is 8 feet and its width is 7 feet. The length of a side of a square that has the same perimeter as the rectangle is:

   (A) $3\frac{3}{4}$ feet (B) 4 feet (C) 7 feet
   (D) $7\frac{1}{2}$ feet (E) 8 feet

4. The sum of an angle and its complement is:

   (A) an obtuse angle (B) a right angle
   (C) 135° (D) 180° (E) none of these

5. A vertex angle of an isosceles triangle is 52°. The value of each of the base angles is:

   (A) 52° (B) 62° (C) 60° (D) 64°
   (E) none of these

6. A circular cylindrical jar has a base diameter of 21 inches and a height of 14 inches. When it is half full of water, the volume of water contained in the jar is (let $\pi = \frac{22}{7}$):

   (A) 4,851 cu. in. (B) 462 cu. in.
   (C) 924 cu. in. (D) $2,425\frac{1}{2}$ cu. in.
   (E) none of these

7. If each side of a cube is doubled, the volume of the cube is multiplied by:

   (A) 8 (B) 4 (C) 2 (D) $1\frac{1}{2}$
   (E) none of these

8. The perimeter of a rectangle is 28 inches. If its length is 8 inches then its width is:

   (A) 20 inches (B) 12 inches (C) 4 inches
   (D) 6 inches (E) none of these

9. The difference between the supplement of an angle and its complement is:

   (A) an acute angle (B) an obtuse angle
   (C) a right angle (D) a reflex angle
   (E) none of these

10. One of the equal angles of an isosceles triangle is 48°. The value of the vertex angle is

    (A) 84° (B) 48° (C) 104° (D) 4°
    (E) none of these

11. An oil tank in the form of a rectangular solid has a length of 15 feet and a width of 8 feet. If 300 cubic feet of oil are poured into the tank, what will be the height of the oil in the tank?

(A) 2 feet   (B) $2\frac{1}{2}$ feet   (C) 3 feet
(D) $13\frac{1}{23}$ feet   (E) 20 feet

12. The acute angles of a right triangle are:

(A) complementary
(B) supplementary
(C) 45° each
(D) each greater than 45°
(E) each less than 45°

Indirect Measurement

In measuring such distances as the height of an airplane or the distance across a lake it is not practical to use a ruler or a tape measure. Such measurements are made indirectly, as will be shown in this section.

In making measurements indirectly it is useful to know a property of right triangles called the *Pythagorean Theorem*.

PYTHAGOREAN THEOREM AND SQUARE ROOT

The Pythagorean Theorem states that in a right triangle the square of the length of the hypotenuse is equal to the sum of the squares of the lengths of the legs.

In the diagram, $c^2 = a^2 + b^2$.

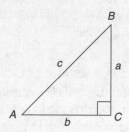

EXAMPLE: A boat travels 30 miles east and then 40 miles north. How many miles is the boat from its starting point?

SOLUTION:

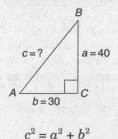

$$c^2 = a^2 + b^2$$

In this case, $a = 40$, $b = 30$, and the value of c must be determined. We have

$$c^2 = (40)^2 + (30)^2$$
$$c^2 = 1{,}600 + 900 = 2{,}500$$

The equation $c^2 = 2{,}500$ asks the question, What number multiplied by itself is equal to 2,500? The number that replaces c, to make the equation $c^2 = 2{,}500$ true, is 50.

The number 50 is called the *square root* of 2,500 since $50 \times 50 = 2{,}500$. We may write $\sqrt{2{,}500} = 50$.

Thus, the boat in this example is 50 miles from its starting point.

In this section, we will develop a systematic method for finding the square root of a number.

We may find the square root of a number by trial. For example, $\sqrt{9} = 3$, $\sqrt{36} = 6$, $\sqrt{81} = 9$. However, trial methods are not always satisfactory. Consider the following examples.

EXAMPLE: Find $\sqrt{289}$.

SOLUTION: We first estimate the answer. Suppose we estimate that the answer is 15. We next divide 15 into 289.

$$\begin{array}{r} 19 \\ 15\overline{)289} \\ 15 \\ \hline 139 \\ 135 \\ \hline \end{array}$$

If 15 were the correct answer we would have obtained a quotient of 15. Since we did not, we get the average of the divisor (15) and the quotient (19).

$$\frac{15 + 19}{2} = \frac{34}{2} = 17$$

Now, we use 17 as a divisor.

$$\begin{array}{r} 17 \\ 17\overline{)289} \\ 17 \\ \hline 119 \\ \underline{119} \end{array}$$

Since the divisor and the quotient are identical, we have found the square root of the number.

Thus, $\sqrt{289} = 17$.

Consider $\sqrt{69}$. Since $8^2 = 64$ and $9^2 = 81$, $\sqrt{69}$ must have a value between 8 and 9. Actually, $\sqrt{69}$ cannot be written precisely in fractional or decimal form. A real number that cannot be written precisely in fractional or decimal form is called an *irrational number*. We may write the square root of an irrational number as a decimal to the nearest thousandth, etc.

EXAMPLE: Find $\sqrt{69}$ to the nearest tenth.

SOLUTION: Our first estimate is 8.2. Therefore we divide 69 by 8.2.

$$\begin{array}{r} 8.4 \\ 8.2\overline{)690.0} \\ \underline{656} \\ 340 \\ \underline{328} \end{array}$$

Next, we average the divisor (8.2) and the quotient (8.4).

$$\frac{8.2 + 8.4}{2} = \frac{16.6}{2} = 8.3$$

Next, we divide 69 by 8.3.

$$\begin{array}{r} 8.3 \\ 8.3\overline{)690.0} \\ \underline{664} \\ 260 \\ \underline{249} \end{array}$$

Since the divisor and the quotient are identical, we have $\sqrt{69} = 8.3$ to the nearest tenth.

PRACTICE TEST 6

1. Find the square roots of the following numbers.

   (A) $\sqrt{1,600}$ (B) $\sqrt{256}$ (C) $\sqrt{324}$ (D) $\sqrt{225}$
   (E) $\sqrt{729}$ (F) $\sqrt{1,024}$

2. Find the square root of each of the following correct to the nearest tenth.

   (A) $\sqrt{45}$ (B) $\sqrt{89}$ (C) $\sqrt{130}$ (D) $\sqrt{162}$
   (E) $\sqrt{116}$ (F) $\sqrt{243}$

EXAMPLE: A ladder is extended to a length of 17 feet and leaned against a wall. If the base of the ladder is 8 feet from the wall, how high up the wall does the ladder reach?

SOLUTION:

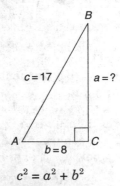

$$c^2 = a^2 + b^2$$

In this case, $b = 8$, $c = 17$, and the value of a must be found.

$$\begin{aligned} (17)^2 &= a^2 + (8)^2 \\ 289 &= a^2 + 64 \\ 289 - 64 &= a^2 + 64 - 64 \\ 225 &= a^2 \\ a &= \sqrt{225} \\ a &= 15 \end{aligned}$$

The ladder reaches a point on the wall 15 feet above the ground.

PRACTICE TEST 7

DIRECTIONS: Solve the following problems and write your answers on the lines provided.

1. A scout troop hikes 5 miles due west and then 12 miles due north. How many miles is the troop from its starting point?

2. A backyard is 20 feet long and 15 feet wide. What is the length of a diagonal path that cuts across the yard?

3. A pole is 24 feet high. A wire is stretched from the top of the pole to a point on the ground 7 feet from the base of the pole. What is the length of the wire?

4. A ladder 15 feet in length leans against the side of a building. If the base of the ladder is 9 feet from the building, how high up the building does the ladder reach?

5. A side of a packing box measures 24 inches in length and 18 inches in width. A piece of supporting tape is stretched diagonally across the side of the box. What is the length of this piece of tape?

Congruence and Similarity

Two plane geometric figures are said to be congruent if they have exactly the same size and the same shape. If two plane geometric figures are congruent, one can be fitted precisely on top of the other. As you have learned, the symbol ≅ is used to express congruence. Triangle *ABC* and triangle *RST* are congruent. If we use the congruence symbol this is expressed as

$$\triangle ABC \cong \triangle RST$$

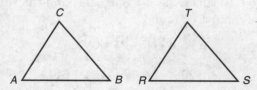

Since $\triangle ABC \cong \triangle RST$, the corresponding sides of these two triangles are equal in length; that is,

$$AB = RS, BC = ST, \text{ and } AC = RT.$$

Congruent triangles can be used to measure distances indirectly.

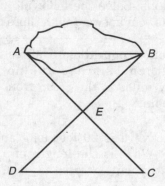

EXAMPLE: To find the distance *AB* across a pond we locate a convenient point, *E*. Then we draw a line, $\overleftrightarrow{AE}$ and extend this line to a point *C* so that *AE = EC*. Similarly, we draw a line, $\overleftrightarrow{BE}$, and extend this line to point *D* so that *BE = ED*. It can be proved that $\triangle ABE \cong \triangle CDE$. Since *DC* and *AB* are corresponding sides of congruent triangles, *DC = AB*. When we measure the length of *DC* on dry land, we are indirectly measuring the length of *AB*. If *DC* = 150 feet, *AB* = 150 feet.

Two geometric figures are said to be similar if they have the same shape. Since similar figures have the same shape, the measures of their corresponding angles are equal and the lengths of their corresponding sides are in proportion. The symbol for similarity is ~. In the diagram, $\triangle ABC$ and $\triangle PQR$ are similar, or $\triangle ABC \sim \triangle PQR$.

Since the lengths of corresponding sides of similar triangles are in proportion, we have

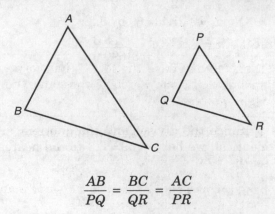

$$\frac{AB}{PQ} = \frac{BC}{QR} = \frac{AC}{PR}$$

We may use similar triangles to measure distances indirectly.

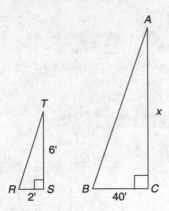

EXAMPLE: To find the height of the building (*AC*) we drive a stake (*TS*) into the ground. We then measure the height of the stake (*TS* = 6´), the length of its shadow (*RS* = 2´) and the length of the shadow of the building (*BC* = 40´). It can be proved that $\triangle ABC \sim \triangle TSR$. Therefore, the lengths of the corresponding sides of the two triangles are in proportion; that is,

$$\frac{AC}{TS} = \frac{BC}{RS}$$

or

$$\frac{x}{6} = \frac{40}{2}$$
$$2x = 6(40) = 240$$
$$x = 120$$

Thus, the height of the building is 120 feet.

PRACTICE TEST 8

> DIRECTIONS: Circle the letter that corresponds to the one you have chosen as the right answer.

1. An example of congruent figures is

   (A) a square and a rectangle
   (B) any two pages of this book
   (C) a man and a picture of the same man
   (D) any two drinking glasses
   (E) any two music records

2. An example of similar figures is

   (A) any two triangles
   (B) any two rectangles
   (C) a wall and a picture on the wall
   (D) a TV picture on a 12-inch screen and the same TV picture on a 9-inch screen
   (E) a circle and a cylinder

3. If $\triangle EDC \cong \triangle PQR$, the value of $x =$

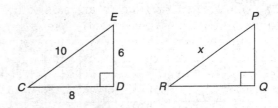

   (A) 6   (B) 8   (C) 10   (D) 7   (E) 9

4. If $\triangle STV \sim \triangle WZB$, then $WB =$

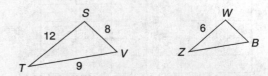

   (A) 6   (B) $4\frac{1}{2}$ (C) 5   (D) 7   (E) 4

5. At noon the shadow of a flagpole is 19 feet. At the same time the shadow of a wall 12 feet high is 4 feet. The height of the flagpole, in feet, is

   (A) 38   (B) $6\frac{1}{2}$ (C) 57   (D) 76   (E) 32

Coordinate Geometry

The diagram below represents a plan of the center of a town. To the right of North-South Street the streets are numbered 1, 2, 3, 4, etc. Similarly, the avenues above East-West Avenue are numbered 1, 2, 3, 4, etc. The avenues below East-West Avenue are numbered –1, –2, –3, –4, etc., and the streets to the left of North-South Street are numbered –1, –2, –3, –4, etc.

point *D*. The first number of a number pair associated with a point is called the *abscissa* and the second number is called the *ordinate*. For the number pair (–4, –2), –4 is the abscissa and –2 is the ordinate. These numbers, taken together, are called the *coordinates* of the point.

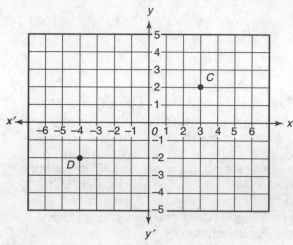

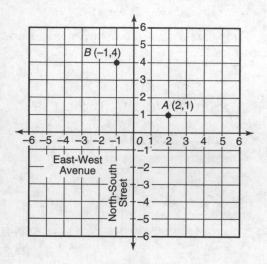

Point *A*, the point where 2nd Street and 1st Avenue meet, is named (2, 1) if we agree that, in the number pair (2, 1) the first number represents the street number and the second number represents the avenue number. Similarly, point *B* represents the point where –1 Street and 4th Avenue meet, or (–1, 4).

We have seen that we can associate points on the number line with real numbers. However, the number line is insufficient if we wish to locate points in the plane that are above or below the number line. To locate points in the plane that are not on the number line we draw two perpendicular number lines. These perpendicular number lines are called the *x*-axis and the *y*-axis, as shown in the diagram. The point where the *x*-axis and the *y*-axis meet is called the *origin,* and the number pair associated with the origin is (0, 0). Using this plan we associate the number pair (3, 2) with the point *C* and the number pair (–4, –2) with the

PRACTICE TEST 9

DIRECTIONS: Answer questions 1–6 based on the diagram below.

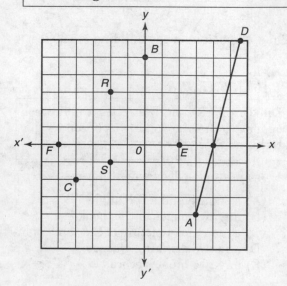

1. The coordinates of point *A* are

(A) (–4, 3) (B) (4, 3) (C) (3, 4)
  (D) (3, –4) (E) (–4, –3)

2. The coordinates of point B are

   (A) $(5, 0)$ (B) $(5, -5)$ (C) $(0, 5)$
   (D) $(5, 5)$ (E) $(0, -5)$

3. The coordinates of point C are

   (A) $(4, -2)$ (B) $(-4, 2)$ (C) $(4, 2)$
   (D) $(-2, 4)$ (E) $(-4, -2)$

4. The coordinates of the point where $\overline{AD}$ crosses the x-axis are

   (A) $(0,4)$ (B) $(4,0)$ (C) $(3,-4)$ (D) $(5,3)$
   (E) $(0,0)$

5. The distance between points E and F, in graph units, is

   (A) 7   (B) 3   (C) -3 (D) 8   (E) -1

6. The distance between points R and S, in graph units, is

   (A) 2   (B) 3   (C) 4   (D) 5   (E) 6

We may use the Pythagorean Theorem to find the distance between any two points whose coordinates are given.

EXAMPLE: Find the distance between point A $(1, 2)$ and point B $(7, 10)$.

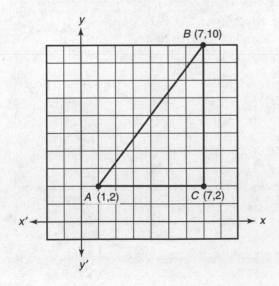

SOLUTION: If we draw $\overline{AC}$ parallel to the x-axis and $\overline{BC}$ parallel to the y-axis, we note that the coordinates of point C are $(7,2)$. Since $\triangle ACB$ is a right triangle with hypotenuse AB, we have, by the Pythagorean Theorem,

$$(AB)^2 = (AC)^2 + (BC)^2$$

By counting we find that $AC = 6$ and $BC = 8$. Thus,

$$(AB)^2 = 6^2 + 8^2$$
$$(AB)^2 = 36 + 64 = 100$$
$$AB = \sqrt{100} = 10$$

Thus, the distance between point A and point B is 10.

PRACTICE TEST 10

DIRECTIONS: Answer the following questions.

1. The distance between A $(1, 1)$ and B $(4, 5)$ is

   (A) 3   (B) 4   (C) 5   (D) 6   (E) 2

2. The distance between C $(3, 2)$ and D $(9, 10)$ is

   (A) 5   (B) 10   (C) 8   (D) 6   (E) 9

3. The distance between E $(0, 0)$ and F $(-3, -4)$ is

   (A) 5   (B) -5 (C) 10   (D) 7   (E) 6

4. The distance between R $(-1, -2)$ and S $(2, 2)$ is

   (A) 3   (B) 4   (C) 10   (D) 6   (E) 5

5. The distance between T $(-4, -3)$ and S $(1, 9)$ is

   (A) 12   (B) 13   (C) 10   (D) 8   (E) 6

Answers to All Practice Tests

TEST 1

1. **D**   2. **B**   3. **A**   4. **C**

TEST 2

1. **D**   2. **B**   3. **A**   4. **C**   5. **E**

TEST 3

1. **D**   2. **D**   3. **A**   4. **E**
5. **C**   6. **E**   7. **D**   8. **A**

TEST 4

1. **C**   2. **D**   3. **A**   4. **B**
5. **A**   6. **C**   7. **B**   8. **B**
9. **E**   10. **D**   11. **D**   12. **C**

TEST 5

1. **C**   2. **B**   3. **D**   4. **B**
5. **D**   6. **D**   7. **A**   8. **D**
9. **C**   10. **A**   11. **B**   12. **C**

TEST 6

1. (A) 40   (C) 18   (E) 27
   (B) 16   (D) 15   (F) 32

2. (A) 6.7   (C) 11.4   (E) 10.8
   (B) 9.4   (D) 12.7   (F) 15.6

TEST 7

1. 13 miles   3. 25 feet   5. 30 inches
2. 25 feet   4. 12 feet

TEST 8

1. **B**   2. **D**   3. **C**   4. **E**   5. **C**

TEST 9

1. **D**   3. **E**   4. **B**   5. **A**   6. **C**
2. **C**

TEST 10

1. **C**   2. **B**   3. **A**   4. **E**   5. **B**

Memory and Reasoning Skills

CHAPTER 13

Memory

The Memory Test on the Coop examination measures a skill fundamental to success in school and life, the ability to remember: to learn, to retain what you have learned, and then to recall what you have learned. The test requires you to learn the definitions of 20 obscure words in a limited time, and then to recall them after an interval of about 25 minutes. It does not test your ability to reason or your skill in comprehending what you have read.

The candidates who score highest are those who quickly associate each new word with something that will help them remember its meaning:

1. They associate the word with a familiar one: A *woad* is a kind of plant: *weed, wheat, wood.*

2. They associate the word with a mental picture absurd or otherwise:
   A *wadget* is a bundle: a grandfather figure staggering under a load of *wads* of paper tied together precariously.

PRACTICE TEST 1

In order to simulate actual test conditions, proceed as follows:

1. Spend 12 minutes in memorizing words and definitions.

2. Do other practice tests, not on memory, for 25 minutes.

3. Spend 8 minutes in doing Part Two.

Part One

DIRECTIONS: Memorize the following group of 20 words and their definitions.

Words and Definitions

1. **Vegete means alive and flourishing.**
2. **A bantling is a brat.**
3. **Harageous means rough and bold.**
4. **A fefnicute is a hypocrite.**
5. **A yapok is a type of opossum.**
6. **Vetust means ancient.**
7. **Ettle means to plan.**
8. **Inficete means without a sense of humor.**
9. **Edulcorate means to sweeten or purify.**
10. **A warmouth is a kind of sunfish.**
11. **Macilent means thin.**
12. **Gledge means to squint.**
13. **Viduous means widowed.**
14. **A frescade is a cool or shady place.**
15. **A dolus is a fraud.**
16. **Halotic means easy to catch.**
17. **Fogram means old fashioned.**
18. **Gausie means large and jolly.**
19. **A gapo is a type of rain forest.**
20. **Frist means to delay.**

Now spend the next 25 minutes on other practice tests. Do not refer to the above words and definitions again.

Part Two

DIRECTIONS: Circle the letter of the word that means the same as the underlined phrase.

1. Which word means <u>ancient</u>?

   (A) gausie (B) vetust (C) vegete
   (D) macilent (E) inficete

2. Which word means <u>to delay</u>?

   (F) ettle (G) dolus (H) gledge
   (J) frist (K) edulcorate

3. Which word means <u>a kind of sunfish</u>?

   (A) bantling (B) yapok (C) frescade
   (D) fefnicute (E) warmouth

4. Which word means <u>alive and flourishing</u>?

   (F) viduous (G) vegete (H) harageous
   (J) vetust (K) fogram

5. Which word means <u>a fraud</u>?

   (A) dolus (B) gledge (C) frescade
   (D) gapo (E) fefnicute

6. Which word means <u>rough and bold</u>?

   (F) viduous (G) gausie (H) halotic
   (J) macilent (K) harageous

7. Which word means <u>to sweeten or purify</u>?

   (A) ettle (B) edulcoriate (C) halotic
   (D) frist (E) fogram

8. Which word means <u>without a sense of humor</u>?

   (F) harageous (G) vegete (H) inficete
   (J) viduous (K) frist

9. Which word means <u>to squint</u>?

   (A) frist (B) dolus (C) yapok
   (D) ettle (E) gledge

10. Which word means <u>a type of rain forest</u>?

    (F) warmouth (G) fefnicute
    (H) bantling (J) gapo (K) yapok

11. Which word means <u>large and jolly</u>?

    (A) vidous (B) vegete (C) bantling
    (D) gausie (E) macilent

12. Which word means <u>old fashioned</u>?

    (F) fogram (G) vetust (H) harageous
    (J) dolus (K) frescade

13. Which word means <u>easy to catch</u>?

    (A) edulcorate (B) gledge (C) gausie
    (D) halotic (E) inficete

14. Which word means <u>a cool or shady place</u>?

    (F) bantling (G) frescade (H) gapo
    (J) vetust (K) gledge

15. Which word means <u>thin</u>?

    (A) macilent (B) warmouth
    (C) viduous (D) edulcorate
    (E) gausie

16. Which word means <u>a type of opossum</u>?

    (F) yapok (G) bantling (H) warmouth
    (J) dolus (K) gapo

17. Which word means <u>to plan</u>?

    (A) gledge (B) frist (C) yapok
    (D) ettle (E) edulcorate

18. Which word means <u>widowed</u>?

    (F) harageous (G) ettle (H) inficete
    (J) viduous (K) malicent

19. Which word means <u>a hypocrite</u>?

    (A) fogram (B) fefnicute (C) halotic
    (D) frescade (E) hapok

20. Which word means <u>a brat</u>?

    (F) vetust (G) halotic (H) bantling
    (J) vegete (K) harageous

PRACTICE TEST 2

In order to simulate actual test conditions, proceed as follows:

1. Spend 12 minutes in memorizing words and definitions.

2. Do other practice tests, other than on memory for 25 minutes.

3. Spend 8 minutes in doing Part Two.

Part One

> DIRECTIONS: Memorize the following group of 20 words and their definitions.

Words and Definitions

1. **A buccala is a double chin.**
2. **Mingy means stingy and mean.**
3. **Dolent means sad.**
4. **A yaffle is a type of woodpecker.**
5. **Exuviate means to shed.**
6. **A thalian is a comedian.**
7. **Docity is the ability to understand quickly.**
8. **A trillibub is a trifle.**
9. **Xerotic means dry.**
10. **Macrobian means long lived.**
11. **Tardigrade means sluggish.**
12. **Fritinancy means the buzzing of an insect.**
13. **A girasol is a type of artichoke.**
14. **Scride means to crawl on all fours.**
15. **Thanitoid means deadly.**
16. **Jojoba is a type of tree.**
17. **Quaddle means to make faces.**
18. **Lancinate means to tear.**
19. **Maracolous means living by the sea.**
20. **Brabble is to quarrel over nothing.**

Now spend the next 25 minutes on other practice tests. Do not refer to the above words and definitions again.

Part Two

> DIRECTIONS: Circle the letter of the word that means the same as the underlined phrase.

1. Which word means <u>to shed</u>?

   (A) lanciate (B) exuviate (C) trillibub (D) scride (E) quaddle

2. Which word means <u>living by the sea</u>?

   (F) tardigrade (G) thanatoid (H) mingy (J) quaddle (K) maracolous

3. Which word means <u>a type of tree</u>?

   (A) girasol (B) brabble (C) jojoba (D) buccala (E) docity

4. Which word means <u>dry</u>?

   (F) thalian (G) maracolous (H) dolent (J) xerotic (K) macrobian

5. Which word means <u>sluggish</u>?

   (A) mingy (B) lancinate (C) scride (D) macrobian (E) tardigrade

6. Which word means <u>a double chin</u>?

   (F) yaffle (G) quaddle (H) buccala (J) girasol (K) fritinancy

7. Which word means <u>stingy and mean</u>?

   (A) dolent (B) thanatoid (C) trillibub (D) mingy (E) thalian

8. Which word means <u>the buzzing of an insect</u>?

   (F) yaffle (G) marcolous (H) xerotic (J) fritinancy (K) docity

9. Which word means <u>sad</u>?

   (A) mingy (B) lancinate (C) dolent (D) macrobian (E) buccala

10. Which word means <u>a type of woodpecker</u>?

    (F) dolent (G) yaffle (H) thalian (J) fritinancy (K) jojoba

11. Which word means <u>deadly</u>?

    (A) tardigate (B) mingy (C) xerotic (D) scride (E) thanatoid

12. Which word means <u>to tear</u>?

    (F) brabble (G) lancinate (H) exuviate (J) jojoba (K) trillibub

13. Which word means <u>a comedian</u>?

    (A) brabble (B) girasol (C) thalian (D) fritinancy (E) tardigrade

14. Which word means <u>to make faces</u>?

    (F) buccala (G) exuviate (H) yaffle (J) scride (K) quaddle

15. Which word means <u>the ability to understand quickly</u>?

    (A) docity (B) buccala (C) tardigrade
    (D) girasol (E) frabble

16. Which word means <u>to quarrel over nothing</u>?

    (F) brabble (G) dolent (H) lancinate
    (J) quaddle (K) yaffle

17. Which word means <u>a trifle</u>?

    (A) macrobian (B) jojoba (C) trillibub
    (D) docity (E) buccala

18. Which word means <u>to crawl on all fours</u>?

    (F) exuviate (G) fritinancy (H) scride
    (J) quaddle (K) dolent

19. Which word means <u>long lived</u>?

    (A) maracolous (B) trillibub
    (C) mingy (D) thanatoid
    (E) macrobian

20. Which word means <u>a type of artichoke</u>?

    (F) fritinancy (G) docity (H) girasol
    (J) thalian (K) buccala

Seeing Number Relationships

Mathematical reasoning involves the ability to see relationships between quantities and to use these relationships in arriving at useful conclusions. The following examples will indicate how problems in mathematical reasoning may be analyzed and solved.

EXAMPLE: If $\frac{4}{9}$ of a number is 20, find the value of $\frac{3}{5}$ of the number.

SOLUTION: If $\frac{4}{9}$ of the number is 20, then $\frac{1}{9}$ of the number is equal to 20 divided by 4, or 5.

If $\frac{1}{9}$ of the number is 5, then $\frac{9}{9}$ or the whole number is equal to 5×9, or 45.

If the number is 45, then $\frac{3}{5}$ of the number is equal to $\frac{3}{5} \times 45 = 27$.

EXAMPLE: How many thirds are there in $\frac{5}{12}$?

SOLUTION: To find the number of thirds in $\frac{5}{12}$ we must divide $\frac{5}{12}$ by $\frac{1}{3}$.

$$\frac{5}{12} \div \frac{1}{3} = \frac{5}{12} \times \frac{3}{1} = \frac{5}{4}$$

There are $\frac{5}{4}$ or $1\frac{1}{4}$ thirds in $\frac{5}{12}$.

EXAMPLE: 18 is 24% of what number?

SOLUTION: 24%, or 24 of the number = 18 Then 0.01 of the number = $\frac{18}{24}$ and the number is equal to

$$\frac{18}{24} \times 100 = \frac{1800}{24}$$

The number is 75.

EXAMPLE: If 3 times a number is $4\frac{1}{8}$ what is the number?

SOLUTION: If 3 times a number is equal to $4\frac{1}{8}$ then the number may be found by dividing $4\frac{1}{8}$ by 3.

$$4\frac{1}{8} = \frac{33}{8}, \frac{33}{8} \div 3 = \frac{\overset{11}{\cancel{33}}}{9} \times \frac{1}{\underset{1}{\cancel{3}}} = \frac{11}{8}$$

The number is $\frac{11}{8}$ or $1\frac{3}{8}$.

PRACTICE TEST 3

DIRECTIONS: Answer the following questions.

1. A number that is closer to 73 than it is 49 is

   (A) 55 (B) 61 (C) 63 (D) 59 (E) 50

2. When 28 is subtracted from the sum of 17 and 36 the result is

   (A) 11 (B) 8 (C) 9 (D) 53
   (E) none of these

3. The product of 8 and 49 is

   (A) less than 100 (B) greater than 400
   (C) an odd number (D) less than 400
   (E) greater than 500

4. Of the fractions $\frac{3}{7}$, $\frac{1}{2}$, $\frac{5}{8}$, $\frac{7}{12}$ and $\frac{4}{9}$ the largest one is

   (A) $\frac{7}{12}$ (B) $\frac{5}{8}$ (C) $\frac{4}{9}$ (D) $\frac{1}{2}$ (E) $\frac{3}{7}$

5. If $\frac{3}{4}$ a number is 12, the number is

    (A) 9   (B) 8   (C) 16   (D) 15   (E) 14

6. The number in which the digit 3 represents the value 300 is

    (A) 5,413   (B) 3,514   (C) 5,134
    (D) 5,314   (E) 3,752

7. When 8,406 is divided by 7 the remainder is

    (A) 0   (B) 1   (C) 2   (D) 1,200
    (E) none of these

8. If 3 times a number is $5\frac{1}{4}$ the number is

    (A) $1\frac{3}{4}$ (B) $2\frac{1}{4}$ (C) $8\frac{1}{4}$ (D) $16\frac{3}{4}$
    (E) $\frac{4}{7}$

9. 5% means

    (A) 5   (B) $\frac{1}{5}$ (C) 500   (D) 0.05   (E) 0.5

10. When the sum of $\frac{1}{4}$ and $\frac{1}{6}$ is subtracted from 1 the result is

    (A) $\frac{5}{12}$ (B) $\frac{7}{12}$ (C) $\frac{4}{5}$ (D) $\frac{2}{10}$ (E) $\frac{1}{2}$

11. The number 59 means

    (A) $5 + 9$ (B) 5×9 (C) 9×10
    (D) $5 \times 10 + 9$ (E) none of these

12. The number that is equal to $\frac{1}{2}$ of $\frac{3}{5}$ is

    (A) $\frac{3}{7}$ (B) $\frac{2}{5}$ (C) $\frac{4}{7}$ (D) $\frac{3}{10}$ (E) $\frac{6}{5}$

13. When 5.17 is multiplied by 65 the result is closest to

    (A) 325   (B) 335   (C) 336   (D) 3,360
    (E) 3,365

14. 16 is 25% of

    (A) 4   (B) 64   (C) 20   (D) 640
    (E) none of these

15. The ratio of one hour to one minute is

    (A) 1:60   (B) 1:1   (C) 30:1   (D) 60:1
    (E) 1:30

16. The fraction that is equal to $\frac{5}{6}$ is

    (A) $\frac{5}{11}$ (B) $\frac{10}{12}$ (C) $\frac{6}{5}$ (D) $\frac{2}{12}$
    (E) none of these

17. The number of days from May 5 to June 15 is

    (A) 41   (B) 20   (C) 21   (D) 30   (E) 45

18. To discover how much bigger one number is than another we

    (A) add   (B) divide   (C) subtract
    (D) multiply   (E) none of these

19. In the number 562.38 the digit 2 is in

    (A) the tens place   (B) the tenths place
    (C) the hundreds place
    (D) the ones place
    (E) the hundredths place

20. When the sum of $\frac{1}{3}$, $\frac{1}{4}$, and $\frac{1}{6}$ is subtracted from 1 the result is

    (A) $\frac{10}{13}$ (B) $\frac{1}{2}$ (C) $\frac{3}{13}$ (D) $\frac{1}{4}$
    (E) none of these

PRACTICE TEST 4

DIRECTIONS: Answer the following questions.

1. $\frac{5}{8}$ of 18 exceeds 11 by

    (A) 7   (B) 5   (C) 26   (D) $\frac{1}{4}$ (E) 2

2. The percent that $\frac{1}{5}$ is of $\frac{1}{2}$ is

    (A) 250%   (B) 10%   (C) 40%   (D) 20%
    (E) 30%

3. 4 hundredths written as a decimal is

    (A) 400   (B) 0.04   (C) 14   (D) 40.0
    (E) none of these

4. The exact number of hundreds in 3,250 is

    (A) 300   (B) 325   (C) 3,250   (D) 3.25
    (E) none of these

5. If $\frac{1}{3}$ of a number is 24, then twice the number is

    (A) 8   (B) 144   (C) 16   (D) 48   (E) 148

6. 0.7 written as a percent is

    (A) 7   (B) 7%   (C) 0.07%   (D) 70%
    (E) 700%

7. The number of tens in a thousand is

   (A) 3 (B) 100 (C) 10 (D) 1,000
   (E) 990

8. In a short-cut method of multiplying 84 by 25, we annex 2 zeros and

   (A) divide by 25 (B) multiply by 4
   (C) divide by 4 (D) add 25
   (E) none of these

9. If 5 times a number is 135 then $\frac{1}{3}$ of the number is

   (A) 45 (B) 9 (C) 27 (D) 225 (E) 6

10. In the number 5,367, if the number in the thousands place is changed to 9, the number becomes

    (A) 5,967 (B) 5,369 (C) 5,397
    (D) 9,367 (E) 5,900

11. 8 is 40% of

    (A) $3\frac{1}{5}$ (B) 12 (C) 16 (D) 18
    (E) none of these

12. The sum of $\frac{1}{3}$ and $\frac{5}{12}$ is greater than $\frac{1}{6}$ by

    (A) $\frac{11}{12}$ (B) $\frac{1}{12}$ (C) $\frac{7}{12}$ (D) $\frac{7}{30}$
    (E) none of these

13. In numerals, the number one thousand three is written as

    (A) 1,030 (B) 1,003 (C) 1,300
    (D) 3,100 (E) 3,001

14. When the quotient of 16 ÷ 2 is added to 7 the result is

    (A) 25 (B) 39 (C) 30 (D) 15 (E) $7\frac{1}{8}$

15. The number that has 8 in the tenths place is

    (A) 485.2 (B) 348.03 (C) 162.85
    (D) 91.08 (E) none of these

16. The next number in the series 4, 9, 14, 19, 24 is

    (A) 25 (B) 29 (C) 28 (D) 27 (E) 30

17. When a number is increased by 25% of itself the result is 30. The number is

    (A) 36 (B) 28 (C) 25 (D) 32
    (E) none of these

18. To find what part one number is of another we

    (A) multiply (B) subtract (C) divide
    (D) add (E) none of these

19. The number that is equivalent to $\frac{32}{40}$ is

    (A) $\frac{9}{10}$ (B) $\frac{3}{4}$ (C) $\frac{4}{5}$ (D) $\frac{3}{5}$ (E) 0.7

20. To change $\frac{4}{7}$ to a decimal we

    (A) add 4 and 7 (B) divide 7 by 4
    (C) multiply 4 by 7 (D) divide 4 by 7
    (E) subtract 4 from 7

PRACTICE TEST 5

> DIRECTIONS: Answer the following questions.

1. The next number in the series 1, 2, 4, 7, 11, 16 is

   (A) 18 (B) 19 (C) 22 (D) 25 (E) 15

2. $83\frac{1}{3}\%$ of a certain number is 30. The number is

   (A) 25 (B) $18\frac{3}{4}$ (C) 48 (D) 36 (E) 34

3. Pencils cost 2 for $0.15. The number of pencils that can be bought for $1.20 is

   (A) 30 (B) 16 (C) 1 dozen (D) 8
   (E) 15

4. When 45 is divided by 1.23 the result will be closest to

   (A) 3.7 (B) 37 (C) 0.38 (D) 380
   (E) 3.8

5. The sum 8, 7, and 9 divided by their product is equal to

   (A) 21 (B) 24 (C) 504 (D) $\frac{5}{3}$
   (E) none of these

6. The average of the numbers 12, 15, and 18 is equal to

   (A) their sum
   (B) their common difference
   (C) the middle number
   (D) their quotient
   (E) their sum divided by their common difference

7. The pecent that $\frac{1}{12}$ is of $\frac{1}{3}$ is

   (A) 25% (B) 75% (C) 36% (D) 400%
   (E) 20%

8. 8% of a number is equal to

   (A) $\frac{1}{8}$ of the number
      (B) 0.8 of the number
         (C) 4% of twice the number
            (D) one-half of twice the number
               (E) none of these

9. In order to find out how many inches there are in 5 feet 3 inches we

   (A) first multiply then divide
      (B) first multiply then add
         (C) first divide than add
            (D) first divide then subtract
               (E) none of these

10. A boy's marks on three tests were 75%, 78%, and 82%. In order to raise his average to 80% his mark on a fourth test must be

    (A) 81 (B) 76 (C) 80 (D) 82
    (E) none of these

11. If 3 times a number is 48 then $\frac{1}{4}$ of the same number is

    (A) 16 (B) 4 (C) 12 (D) 30 (E) 5

12. The smallest number into which the numbers 2, 3, 5, and 7 can be divided without leaving a remainder is

    (A) 6 (B) 420 (C) 280 (D) 210
    (E) 180

13. When half of a number is added to the number the result is 24. The number is

    (A) 12 (B) 15 (C) 16 (D) 24
    (E) 20

14. Of the following numbers, the one that has 0 in the tens place is

    (A) 4,307 (B) 3,270 (C) 650 (D) 4,070
    (E) 780

15. The ratio of 1 pound to 6 ounces is

    (A) 1:6 (B) 6:1 (C) 3:8 (D) 8:3
    (E) 5:3

16. 2% is equal to

    (A) 200 (B) 2 (C) 0.2 (D) 2.0
    (E) none of these

17. The smallest of the fractions $\frac{2}{7}, \frac{1}{3}, \frac{3}{10}, \frac{4}{9}$, and $\frac{2}{5}$ is

    (A) $\frac{2}{5}$ (B) $\frac{3}{10}$ (C) $\frac{1}{3}$ (D) $\frac{4}{9}$ (E) $\frac{2}{7}$

18. If 8 books of the same thickness standing on a shelf occupy 1 foot then the thickness of each book is

    (A) $\frac{2}{3}''$ (B) $1''$ (C) $1\frac{1}{2}''$ (D) $1\frac{1}{3}''$
    (E) none of these

19. The number of eighths in $87\frac{1}{2}$% is

    (A) 1 (B) 3 (C) 8 (D) 7 (E) 6

20. It takes a man 15 days to do a job. The part of the job that he can do in 5 days is

    (A) $\frac{1}{5}$ (B) $\frac{1}{3}$ (C) $\frac{1}{15}$ (D) 3.5 (E) $\frac{1}{4}$

PRACTICE TEST 6

DIRECTIONS: Answer the following questions.

1. The number of halves in $\frac{1}{5}$ is

   (A) $\frac{1}{2}$ (B) $\frac{1}{10}$ (C) $\frac{1}{5}$ (D) $\frac{2}{5}$ (E) $\frac{3}{10}$

2. When a number is divided by 7 the quotient is 4 and the remainder is 3. The number is

   (A) 14 (B) 31 (C) 28 (D) 25 (E) 19

3. It takes Mr. Blane 2 hours and 40 minutes to complete half a job. The time he will take to complete the whole job is

   (A) 4 hours and 20 minutes
      (B) 3 hours and 30 minutes
         (C) 5 hours and 10 minutes
            (D) 5 hours and 20 minutes
               (E) none of these

4. When the fractions $\frac{2}{3}, \frac{3}{4}, \frac{5}{8}$, and $\frac{5}{7}$ are arranged in order of size, with the largest one first, the order is

(A) $\frac{5}{8}, \frac{5}{7}, \frac{3}{4}, \frac{2}{3}$ (B) $\frac{5}{7}, \frac{3}{4}, \frac{2}{3}, \frac{5}{8}$

(C) $\frac{3}{4}, \frac{5}{7}, \frac{2}{3}, \frac{5}{8}$ (D) $\frac{2}{3}, \frac{5}{7}, \frac{3}{4}, \frac{5}{8}$

(E) $\frac{3}{4}, \frac{5}{8}, \frac{5}{7}, \frac{2}{3}$

5. When 1 is divided by a fraction whose value is less than 1 the result is

(A) 1   (B) less than 1   (C) less than $\frac{1}{2}$
(D) less than $\frac{2}{3}$ (E) greater than 1

6. The next number in the series 2, 5, 11, 23, 47 is

(A) 95   (B) 71   (C) 59   (D) 53   (E) 101

7. 6% of 100 is what percent of 150?

(A) 5%   (B) 6%   (C) 4%   (D) 8%
(E) 3%

8. When a certain fraction is added to $\frac{1}{4}$ the result is $\frac{5}{6}$. The fraction that is added is

(A) $\frac{1}{6}$ (B) $\frac{1}{2}$ (C) $\frac{2}{3}$ (D) $\frac{7}{12}$ (E) $\frac{5}{12}$

9. The average of two fractions is $\frac{3}{10}$. One of the fractions is $\frac{1}{2}$. The other fraction is

(A) $\frac{1}{2}$ (B) $\frac{1}{10}$ (C) $\frac{7}{10}$ (D) $\frac{4}{5}$ (E) $\frac{1}{20}$

10. The number in which the tens digit is greater than the units digit is

(A) 155   (B) 237   (C) 859   (D) 275
(E) 336

11. On a test 90% of the members of a class had passing grades. Of these, 10% had minimum passing grades. The percent of the class that had minimum passing grades was

(A) 10%   (B) 1%   (C) 90%   (D) 80%
(E) none of these

12. The product of the numbers 15 and 3.4 exceeds their sum by

(A) 27.4   (B) 32.6   (C) 69.4   (D) 65
(E) 30.6

13. The precise number of tens in the number 486 is

(A) 400   (B) 480   (C) 86   (D) 48.6
(E) 4,860

14. Of the boys reporting for a high school baseball team, $\frac{1}{3}$ were trying out for the outfield and $\frac{4}{7}$ were trying out for the infield. Those not trying out for either infield or outfield were

(A) more than half of those trying out
(B) exactly half of those trying out
(C) less than 10% of those trying out
(D) more than $\frac{1}{3}$ of those trying out
(E) none of these

15. 0.003 written as a percent is

(A) 3%   (B) 30%   (C) 0.003%   (D) 0.03%
(E) none of these

16. The number which when divided by 7 leaves the largest remainder is

(A) 615   (B) 305   (C) 714   (D) 1,001
(E) 701

17. If $\frac{1}{3}$ of a number is added to $\frac{5}{6}$ of a number the result is

(A) greater than 1
(B) less than 1
(C) greater than the number
(D) less than the number
(E) none of these

18. We may multiply a number by $12\frac{1}{2}$ by annexing two zeros to the number and dividing the result by

(A) 6   (B) 10   (C) 12   (D) 8   (E) 5

19. A football team gains 18 yards on one play, loses 3 yards on the next play, and loses 6 yards on a third play. The result is that the team has a

(A) net loss of 11 yards
(B) net gain of 9 yards
(C) net gain of 29 yards
(D) net gain of 23 yards
(E) none of these

20. One-half the difference between 97 and 46 is

    (A) less than 25   (B) greater than 72
    (C) 51   (D) greater than 25   (E) 100

PRACTICE TEST 7

DIRECTIONS: Answer the following questions.

1. 205 students are to be assigned to 7 classes so that, as far as possible the classes are of the same size. The result will be that

    (A) two of the classes will be larger than the others
    (B) all classes will be exactly the same size
    (C) one class will be smaller than all the others
    (D) no class will be larger than 28
    (E) none of these

2. A man invested $\frac{3}{5}$ of his money in bonds and $\frac{3}{10}$ of his money in stocks. He kept the balance of his money in a savings account. The part of his money in the savings account was

    (A) $\frac{9}{10}$ (B) $\frac{4}{5}$ (C) $\frac{3}{5}$ (D) $\frac{1}{10}$ (E) $\frac{1}{15}$

3. The next number in the series 2, 6, 18, 54 is

    (A) 57   (B) 108   (C) 162   (D) 72
    (E) 168

4. 3.12 written as a percent is

    (A) 312%   (B) 3.12%   (C) 31.2%
    (D) 0.0312%   (E) none of these

5. In an election $\frac{5}{8}$ of the votes went to candidate A. Candidate B received $\frac{2}{3}$ of the remaining votes. The part of the votes received by candidate B was

    (A) $\frac{5}{12}$ (B) $\frac{1}{24}$ (C) $\frac{1}{12}$ (D) $\frac{4}{11}$
    (E) none of these

6. When a number is added to $\frac{1}{3}$ of itself the result is 60. The number is

    (A) 80   (B) 45   (C) 40   (D) $60\frac{1}{3}$
    (E) 50

7. Of its broadcast time a radio station spends $\frac{1}{2}$ on music and $\frac{1}{5}$ on news and lectures. The percent of its time spent on other features is

    (A) 20%   (B) 70%   (C) 40%   (D) 30%
    (E) 36%

8. The ratio between the sum of the numbers 18 and 12 and their difference is

    (A) 3:2   (B) $\frac{2}{3}$ (C) 6:1   (D) 1:6
    (E) none of these

9. The number in which the hundreds digit exceeds the units digit by 4 is

    (A) 123   (B) 501   (C) 236   (D) 515
    (E) 620

10. A school has 7 classes with an average size of 31 students and 4 classes with an average size of 34 students. The average size of all classes is

    (A) less than 31   (B) greater than 33
    (C) greater than 34
    (D) greater than 32   (E) none of these

11. $66\frac{2}{3}\%$ of a number exceeds $16\frac{2}{3}\%$ of the same number by

    (A) $\frac{1}{3}$ of the number
    (B) $\frac{2}{3}$ of the number
    (C) $\frac{1}{2}$ of the number
    (D) $\frac{1}{4}$ of the number
    (E) $\frac{2}{5}$ of the number

12. Of the following statements the one that is correct is:

    (A) When an even number is divided by an odd number there is no remainder.
    (B) When an odd number is divided by an even number there is no remainder.
    (C) When an even number is multiplied by 3 the result is an odd number.
    (D) When an odd number is multiplied by 2 the result is an even number.
    (E) When an even number is subtracted from an even number the result is an odd number.

13. A lecture hall is $\frac{1}{2}$ full. After 20 people in the audience leave, the lecture hall is $\frac{1}{3}$ full. The seating capacity of the hall is

    (A) 60 (B) 120 (C) 90 (D) 80 (E) 96

14. 8% of a number is 72. The number is

    (A) 5.76 (B) 57.6 (C) 90 (D) 900
    (E) 960

15. The number of halves in $\frac{4}{9}$ is

    (A) $\frac{2}{9}$ (B) $\frac{1}{9}$ (C) $\frac{9}{8}$ (D) 9
    (E) none of these

16. A mixture contains 12 gallons of water and 3 gallons of acid. If 6 more gallons of water is added, the part of the mixture that is acid is

    (A) $\frac{1}{6}$ (B) $\frac{1}{7}$ (C) $\frac{2}{3}$ (D) $\frac{4}{7}$ (E) $\frac{1}{8}$

17. $\frac{1}{5}$ of a number is 2 less than 12. The number is

    (A) 10 (B) 5 (C) 40 (D) 50 (E) 45

18. The precise number of tens in 305 is

    (A) 0 (B) 3 (C) 30.5 (D) 305
    (E) none of these

19. Among the numbers 2.11, $2\frac{1}{10}$, 2.057, $1\frac{9}{100}$, and 1.92 the number closest to 2 is

    (A) 2.11 (B) $2\frac{1}{10}$ (C) 2.057
    (D) $1\frac{9}{100}$ (E) 1.92

20. The sum of two numbers is 51. One number exceeds twice the other number by 9. The numbers are

    (A) 42 and 9 (B) 24 and 33
    (C) 33 and 18 (D) 37 and 14
    (E) none of these

PRACTICE TEST 8

DIRECTIONS: Answer the following questions.

1. The next number in the series 9, 3, 1, $\frac{1}{3}$ is

    (A) $\frac{1}{4}$ (B) $\frac{1}{6}$ (C) $\frac{1}{12}$ (D) $\frac{1}{5}$
    (E) none of these

2. $\frac{2}{3}$ of one half of 48 is

    (A) 32 (B) 16 (C) 8 (D) 24 (E) 30

3. The number that when multiplied by 2.8 yields 34.16 is

    (A) 36.96 (B) 95.648 (C) 122
    (D) 12.2 (E) 12.4

4. If the numerator of a fraction is doubled and its denominator is halved

    (A) the value of the fraction is multiplied by 4
    (B) the value of the fraction remains unchanged
    (C) the value of the fraction is divided by 2
    (D) the value of the fraction is decreased
    (E) none of these

5. A building contractor uses 12 men to complete a job in 15 days. Had the contractor used 10 men the job would have been completed in

    (A) 22 days   (B) 10 days   (C) 18 days
    (D) 12 days   (E) 20 days

6. A cafeteria served milk in pint-bottle portions. One day the cafeteria served 18 gallons and 2 quarts of milk. The number of portions served was

    (A) 20 portions   (B) 148 portions
    (C) 74 portions (D) 76 portions
    (E) none of these

7. 6.8% written as a decimal is

    (A) 0.68 (B) 0.0068 (C) 0.680
    (D) 0.068 (E) 0.6080

8. If $\frac{1}{3}$ of a number is 6 more than $\frac{1}{4}$ of the number, the number is

    (A) $6\frac{1}{4}$ (B) 72 (C) 24 (D) 48 (E) $6\frac{7}{12}$

9. The average of 5 consecutive whole numbers is

    (A) the sum of the first and last number
    (B) twice the first number
    (C) the difference between the last and the first number
    (D) the second number
    (E) the third number

10. A basketball team has won 18 games and lost 12 games. The number of games it must win in succession to have a winning percentage of 75% is

    (A) 18 (B) 12 (C) 6 (D) 9 (E) 20

11. The fraction that when divided by $\frac{1}{2}$ yields $\frac{3}{7}$ is

    (A) $\frac{1}{3}$ (B) $\frac{2}{21}$ (C) $\frac{7}{6}$ (D) $\frac{3}{14}$ (E) $\frac{1}{5}$

12. 3.05 written as a percent is

    (A) 3.5% (B) 3.05% (C) 305%
    (D) 0.0305% (E) 3.005%

13. When a number is added to twice itself the result is 64 more than the number. The number is

    (A) 96 (B) 64 (C) 48 (D) 32 (E) 36

14. A baseball pitcher has won 12 games and lost 5 games. The percent of the games he has won is

    (A) $57\frac{1}{2}\%$ (B) $58\frac{1}{3}\%$ (C) 60% (D) 75%
    (E) none of these

15. A family spends $\frac{1}{3}$ of its income for food and $\frac{1}{5}$ of its income for rent. The part of its income left for other expenses is

    (A) $\frac{3}{4}$ (B) $\frac{8}{15}$ (C) $\frac{7}{15}$ (D) $\frac{1}{4}$ (E) $\frac{5}{12}$

16. When a number is added to $\frac{1}{3}$ of itself the result is 72. The number is

    (A) 60 (B) 54 (C) 65 (D) 90 (E) 64

17. The number in which the sum of the digits exceeds the tens digit by 15 is

    (A) 932 (B) 846 (C) 689 (D) 767
    (E) 585

Using Diagrams to Solve Verbal Problems in Logic

The questions in logical thinking on high school entrance exams range in difficulty somewhere between the problems encountered in everyday living and elementary exercises in formal logic.

APPLYING LOGIC IN REACHING SOLUTIONS TO EVERYDAY PROBLEMS

As logical as we attempt to be in real life, we often allow extraneous factors to interfere with our thinking.

PRACTICE TEST 9

> DIRECTIONS: For each of the following, write, in the space provided:
> _logical_ if the conclusion is valid;
> _illogical_ if the reasoning is faulty.

_____ 1. Since Milton has played in every game this season, he must be the best player on the team.

_____ 2. All dogs are mammals. Caesar is a dog. Therefore, Caesar is a mammal.

_____ 3. Interstate 95 is always overcrowded. I drive on it four times a week, and every time the traffic is bumper to bumper.

_____ 4. Now that I caught you red-handed, lying to me right to my face, I will never trust you again.

_____ 5. None of the members of our squad ever misbehaves at a game. Allen is not a member of our group. He therefore never behaves properly at a game.

_____ 6. Paula has not learned how to swim. Only students who can pass the swimming test are eligible for graduation. Therefore, Paula is not a graduate.

_____ 7. Do you love your pet dog? Would you want her to be cut up alive in a scientific experiment? Vote to outlaw the use of animals in scientific research.

_____ 8. When I came to Henry's apartment, I saw the newspaper in front of his door. It is Henry's habit to pick up the newspaper when he returns from work. Therefore, Henry has not yet come home.

_____ 9. All acids are corrosive. Therefore, some corrosives are acids.

_____ 10. No cud-chewing animals are meat-eaters. All lions are meat eaters. Therefore, no lions are cud-chewing animals.

DIAGRAMMING EXAM QUESTIONS INVOLVING TWO OR THREE ITEMS

Diagramming quickly reveals relationships. For words like *larger, smaller, taller, greater, brighter,* and similar comparisons, draw a rectangle for each person or item:

Helen is taller than Louise. Ethel is taller than Helen. Louise is shorter than Ethel.

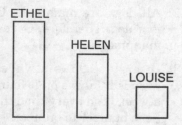

For *all* or *some*, where groups are included or excluded, use a circle for each group: draw separate circles or smaller circles within a larger circle, as the question indicates.

All acids are corrosives. Therefore, some corrosives are acids.

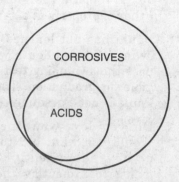

PRACTICE TEST 10

> DIRECTIONS: Use a diagram to help you understand each of the following. Then, in the space provided, write True, False, or Uncertain.

_____ 1. Grammarians are scholars. Grammarians are teachers. Therefore, teachers are scholars.

_____ 2. An interest in logic makes for easy learning. George has an interest in logic. George will learn logic easily.

_____ 3. Every *B* is *A*. Some *C*'s are not *A*. Therefore, some *C*'s are not *B*.

_____ 4. All countries on the Equator are hot. Ecuador is on the Equator. Therefore, Ecuador is hot.

_____ 5. National income rose for the year. The population did not increase. Therefore, per capita income must have risen.

_____ 6. Birds build nests. Eldrites build nests. Therefore, eldrites must be birds.

_____ 7. Henry has scored more goals than Adam. Adam has scored more goals than Bob. Therefore, Henry has scored fewer goals than Bob.

_____ 8. Milton is 3 pounds lighter than Arthur. Stan is 6 pounds heavier than Arthur. Therefore, Milton is 3 pounds lighter than Stan.

_____ 9. Cautious people are seldom embarrassed. Some mathematicians are cautious. Therefore, mathematicians seldom become embarrassed.

_____ 10. Some humanists are nihilists. Some nihilists are anarchists. Therefore, some anarchists are not humanists.

USING VENN DIAGRAMS TO SOLVE PROBLEMS

Venn diagrams are used to solve problems in which there are many items. These diagrams arrange the given information in circles to clarify the relationships among the items.

Let *A* = the set of members of the History Club. As you learned in Chapter 11, we may enclose the names of the members of the club in braces, as follows:

A = {Bill, Fred, Amy, Lois, Nicole, Jack, Rosita, Beth, Henry, Angelo}

and let *B* = the set of members of the Science Club. We may also enclose the names of the members of this club in braces, as follows.

B = {Mary, Paula, John, Lois, Yong, Andrew, Edna, Grace, Angelo, Ben, Charles, Jack}

Also, we may represent these sets in circles:

History   **Science**

Bill
Fred
Amy
Lois
Nicole
Jack
Rosita
Beth
Henry
Angelo

Mary
Paula
John
Lois
Yong
Andrew
Edna
Grace
Angelo
Ben
Charles
Jack

If we examine sets *A* and *B* we notice that Lois, Angelo, and Jack are members of both sets *A* and *B*. Therefore, it is logical to arrange our circles as follows:

History   **Science**

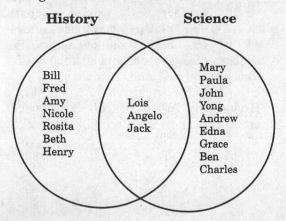

Bill
Fred
Amy
Nicole
Rosita
Beth
Henry

Lois
Angelo
Jack

Mary
Paula
John
Yong
Andrew
Edna
Grace
Ben
Charles

The intersection of two sets *A* and *B* consists of the members common to both *A* and *B*. As you know, the symbol for intersection is ∩. Thus, in this case, *A* ∩ *B* = {Lois, Angelo, Jack}.

We may have three intersection sets. Let *C* = the sets of members of the debating team.

C = {Ed, Ella, Angelo, Tony, Lois}

We may now represent these three sets by circles, as follows:

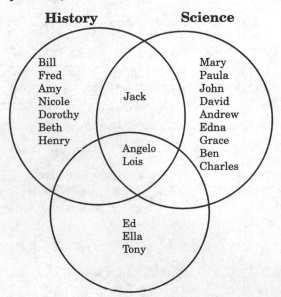

History   **Science**

Bill
Fred
Amy
Nicole
Dorothy
Beth
Henry

Jack

Mary
Paula
John
David
Andrew
Edna
Grace
Ben
Charles

Angelo
Lois

Ed
Ella
Tony

Debating Team

Venn diagrams may be used to solve problems.

EXAMPLE: At Madison High School, enrollments in foreign language were as follows

French   148   French and Spanish 18
Spanish: 96   French and German: 12
German: 67   Spanish and German: 8
   French, Spanish and German: 5

How many individual students were studying foreign languages?

SOLUTION: In this problem, we have the intersection of three sets, those studying French, those studying Spanish, and those studying German.

First, we place 5 in the space that represents the intersection of the three sets. The intersection of the French and Spanish sets has 18 members. Therefore, we place

13 (18 − 5) in the space above the 5. The intersection of the French and German sets has 12 members. Therefore, we place 7 in the space to the left of 5. The intersection of the Spanish and German sets has 8 members. Therefore, we place 3 in the space to the right of 5.

There are 148 students in French classes. Since we have already placed 5 + 13 + 7 = 25 in the French circle, we place 148 − 25 = 123 in the rest of the circle.

There are 96 students in Spanish classes. Since we have already placed 5 + 13 + 3 in the Spanish circle, we place 96 − 21 = 75 in the rest of the circle.

There are 67 students in German classes. Since we have already placed 5 + 7 + 3 = 15 in the German circle, we place 67 − 15 = 52 in the rest of the circle.

French   **Spanish**

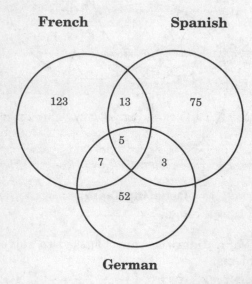

German

To obtain the total individual enrollment, we add *all* the numbers on the Venn diagram:

123 + 13 + 5 + 7 + 3 + 75 + 52 = 278

There are 278 individual students enrolled in foreign language classes.

PRACTICE TEST 11

DIRECTIONS: Use Venn diagrams to answer the following questions.

1. At the Fashion Shop there is a sale on sport coats. The colors of the sale items are as follows.

Gray:	48	Gray and blue:	20
Blue:	56	Gray and green:	12
Green:	32	Blue and green:	8

Gray, blue, and green: 5

How many coats are on sale?

2. At Springfield High School three popular sports are baseball, track, and football. The numbers of students on the squads are shown below:

Baseball:	32	Baseball and track:	10
Track:	26	aseball and football:	18
Football:	45	Track and football:	11

Baseball, track, and football: 7

How many individual students are engaged in these sports?

3. The State Senate has three major committees, legal, budget, and education. The numbers of members of the Senate active on these committees are given below.

Legal:	38	Legal and Budget:	24
Budget:	46	Legal and Education:	16
Education:	22	Budget and Education:	12

Legal, Budget, and Education: 8

How many individual senators work on the committees?

4. At a certain college the enrollments in three major sciences are as follows:

Biology	102	Biology and physics:	28
Physics	48	Biology and chemistry:	35
Chemistry:	65	Physics and chemistry:	25

Biology, physics, and chemistry: 15

How many individual students are enrolled in these sciences?

Seeing Relationships in Sequences and Pictured Analogies, and Verbal Reasoning

The preceding sections have discussed relationships involving numbers, that is, relationships that are clearly mathematical. Three parts of the Cooperative Admissions Test include questions that deal with other types of relationships; such as those in sequences, pictured analogies, or reasoning that does not involve numbers.

EXAMPLE 1 (Sequence): Make the choice that will continue the pattern or sequence.

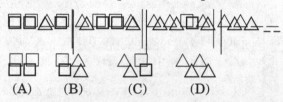

(A)   (B)   (C)   (D)

SOLUTION: There is one triangle in the first section, two in the second, and three in the third. To continue the sequence, the fourth section should have four triangles.

Choice **D** is correct.

EXAMPLE 2 (Analogy): In each case select the picture that will fit the empty box so that the two lower pictures are related in the same way as the two upper pictures.

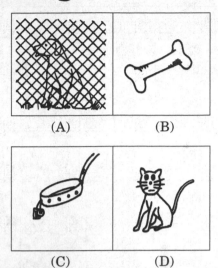

(A)   (B)

(C)   (D)

SOLUTION: A rabbit likes to eat carrots, and a dog likes to chew on bones.

Choice **B** is correct.

EXAMPLE 3 (Verbal Reasoning): The three words in the top row are related in a certain way. The words below the line should be related in the same way. Select the missing word so that the three words in the bottom row will be related in the same way as the words in the top row.

farmer	plow	wheat
carpenter	hammer	

(A) tractor (B) reap (C) house (D) nails

SOLUTION: The top row consists of a worker, something he uses in his work, and the product of his work. Similarly, a carpenter uses a hammer to build a house (**C**).

The test that follows provides practice on the types of questions that appear on the Cooperative Admissions Test.

PRACTICE TEST 12—SEQUENCES, ANALOGIES, AND VERBAL REASONING

Part I—Sequences

DIRECTIONS: In each case, make the choice that will continue the pattern or sequence.

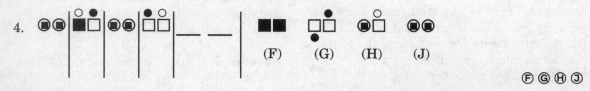

7. 3   15   75 | 4   20   100 | 6   30   __ | 60   120   150   200
                                                     (A) (B)   (C)   (D)
                                                      Ⓐ   Ⓑ   Ⓒ   Ⓓ

8. 7   18   12 | 10   21   15 | 16   __   21 | 27   29   28   25
                                                      (F) (G) (H) (J)
                                                       Ⓕ Ⓖ Ⓗ Ⓙ

9. 2   8   32 | 6   24   96 | 7   28   __ | 84   96   112   120
                                                  (A) (B)   (C)   (D)
                                                   Ⓐ   Ⓑ   Ⓒ   Ⓓ

10. 9   18   35 | 12   24   41 | 15   30   __ | 40   46   45   47
                                                   (F)   (G)   (H)   (J)

$\text{\textcircled{F}}$ $\text{\textcircled{G}}$ $\text{\textcircled{H}}$ $\text{\textcircled{J}}$

11. 2   12   36 | 3   18   54 | 4   24   __ | 70   72   75   78
                                                   (A)   (B)   (C)   (D)

$\text{\textcircled{A}}$ $\text{\textcircled{B}}$ $\text{\textcircled{C}}$ $\text{\textcircled{D}}$

12. 15   12   18 | 20   17   23 | 25   __   28 | 24   25   22   20
                                                   (F)   (G)   (H)   (J)

$\text{\textcircled{F}}$ $\text{\textcircled{G}}$ $\text{\textcircled{H}}$ $\text{\textcircled{J}}$

13. $A_1B_2C_1$ $A_2B_3C_2$ __ $A_4B_5C_4$ | $A_1B_2C_3$ $A_3B_4C_3$ $A_3B_4C_4$ $A_6B_4C_5$
                                                     (A)   (B)   (C)   (D)

$\text{\textcircled{A}}$ $\text{\textcircled{B}}$ $\text{\textcircled{C}}$ $\text{\textcircled{D}}$

14. $X_5Y_4Z_2$ $X_4Y_3Z_3$ __ $X_2Y_1Z_5$ | $X_3Y_2Z_4$ $X_3Y_3Z_4$ $X_3Y_1Z_3$ $X_4Y_2Z_4$
                                                     (F)   (G)   (H)   (J)

$\text{\textcircled{F}}$ $\text{\textcircled{G}}$ $\text{\textcircled{H}}$ $\text{\textcircled{J}}$

15. $R_8Y_7Z_4$ $R_6Y_5Z_4$ __ $R_2Y_1Z_4$ | $R_6Y_3Z_4$ $R_4Y_4Z_3$ $R_4Y_3Z_4$ $R_3Y_4Z_3$
                                                     (A)   (B)   (C)   (D)

$\text{\textcircled{A}}$ $\text{\textcircled{B}}$ $\text{\textcircled{C}}$ $\text{\textcircled{D}}$

16. $A_3B_2C_4$ $A_5B_4C_6$ __ $A_9B_8C_{10}$ | $A_7B_5C_8$ $A_7B_6C_8$ $A_9B_7C_8$ $A_7B_5C_6$
                                                     (F)   (G)   (H)   (J)

$\text{\textcircled{F}}$ $\text{\textcircled{G}}$ $\text{\textcircled{H}}$ $\text{\textcircled{J}}$

17. AEC   ECB   __   BDF | EBD   CBA   BDG   CBD
                                (A)   (B)   (C)   (D)

$\text{\textcircled{A}}$ $\text{\textcircled{B}}$ $\text{\textcircled{C}}$ $\text{\textcircled{D}}$

18. RST   STV   __   VWX | TVW   TVX   VTW   WXY
                                (F)   (G)   (H)   (J)

$\text{\textcircled{F}}$ $\text{\textcircled{G}}$ $\text{\textcircled{H}}$ $\text{\textcircled{J}}$

19. BDG   GDA   __   CDE | ADB   ADC   AGC   BCG
                                (A)   (B)   (C)   (D)

$\text{\textcircled{A}}$ $\text{\textcircled{B}}$ $\text{\textcircled{C}}$ $\text{\textcircled{D}}$

20. STV   VTS   __   XYZ | TSV   YZX   ZYX   XZY
                                (F)   (G)   (H)   (J)

$\text{\textcircled{F}}$ $\text{\textcircled{G}}$ $\text{\textcircled{H}}$ $\text{\textcircled{J}}$

Part 2—Analogies

DIRECTIONS: In each case, select the picture that will fit the empty box so that the two lower pictures are related in the same way as the two upper pictures.

1.

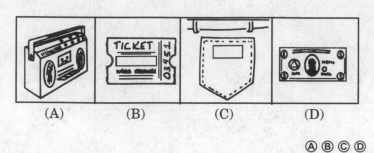

(A)   (B)   (C)   (D)

Ⓐ Ⓑ Ⓒ Ⓓ

2.

(F)   (G)   (H)   (J)

Ⓕ Ⓖ Ⓗ Ⓙ

3.

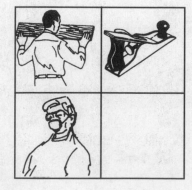

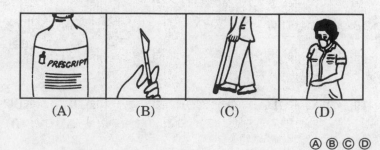

(A)   (B)   (C)   (D)

Ⓐ Ⓑ Ⓒ Ⓓ

4.

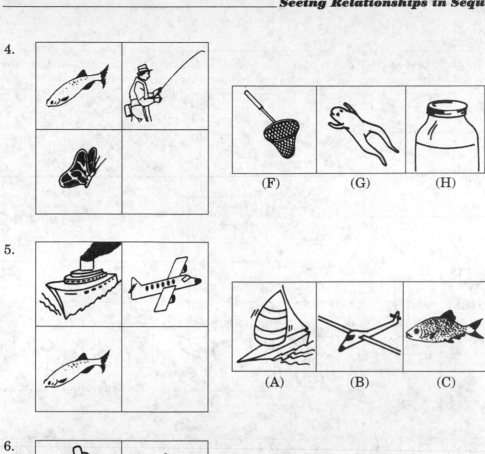

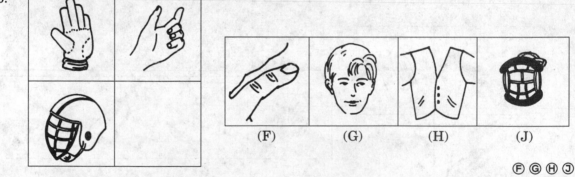

(F)　　　(G)　　　(H)　　　(J)

Ⓕ Ⓖ Ⓗ Ⓙ

5.

(A)　　　(B)　　　(C)　　　(D)

Ⓐ Ⓑ Ⓒ Ⓓ

6.

(F)　　　(G)　　　(H)　　　(J)

Ⓕ Ⓖ Ⓗ Ⓙ

7.

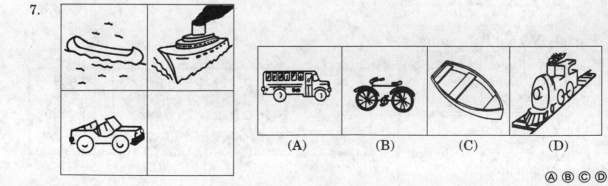

(A)　　　(B)　　　(C)　　　(D)

Ⓐ Ⓑ Ⓒ Ⓓ

8.

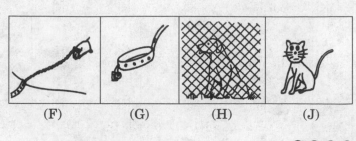

(F)   (G)   (H)   (J)

Ⓕ Ⓖ Ⓗ Ⓙ

9.

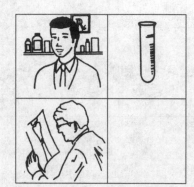

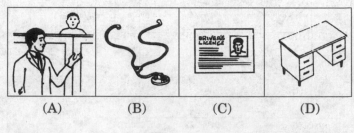

(A)   (B)   (C)   (D)

Ⓐ Ⓑ Ⓒ Ⓓ

10.

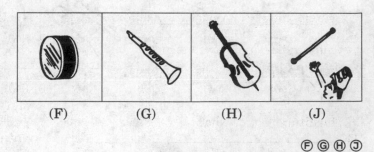

(F)   (G)   (H)   (J)

Ⓕ Ⓖ Ⓗ Ⓙ

Part 3—Verbal Reasoning

DIRECTIONS: For numbers 1–7, select the word that names a necessary part of the word underlined.

1. baseball team

   (A) score card (B) dugout (C) players
   (D) lineup

2. bus

   (F) stops (G) radio (H) passengers
   (J) brakes

3. school

   (A) auditorium (B) blackboards
   (C) books (D) pupils

4. television set

   (F) talk shows (G) screen
   (H) remote control (J) cabinet

5. house

   (A) walls (B) cellar (C) patio
   (D) porch

6. <u>library</u>

   (F) games (G) story hour (H) readers
   (J) books

7. <u>concert</u>

   (A) audience (B) conductor (C) music
   (D) applause

DIRECTIONS: For numbers 8–14, the three words in the top row are related in a certain way. The words below the line should be related in the same way. In each case, select the missing word so that the three words in the bottom row will be related in the same way as the words in the top row.

8.
publication	newspaper	magazine
building	house	

   (F) floor (G) store (H) brick (J) roof

9.
meat	steak	lamb
fish	salmon	

   (A) fins (B) scales (C) liver
   (D) flounder

10.
entertainment	theater	stadium
information	dictionary	

   (F) telephone (G) atlas (H) movies
   (J) novel

11.
furniture	chair	table
meals	lunch	

   (A) sofa (B) lamp (C) dinner
   (D) drawer

12.
drink	soda	milk
dessert	ice cream	

   (F) bread (G) spinach (H) pie
   (J) water

13.
exercise	gymnasium	pool
recreation	television	

   (A) movies (B) track (C) conversation
   (D) sleep

14.
shape	circle	triangle
measurement	circumference	

   (F) arc (G) isosceles (H) perimeter
   (J) altitude

DIRECTIONS: For questions 15–19, select the statement that is true according to the facts given in the paragraph.

---

15. Don King is a sports reporter for the _Journal_. He specializes in covering baseball and football because he played on his college teams in these sports. Don is a popular figure at baseball and football games because he is a keen student of both games.

    (A) Don King is interested only in sports.
    (B) Don King thinks that college sports are inferior to professional sports.
    (C) Don King was an outstanding athlete at college.
    (D) Don King reports baseball and football games for the _Journal_.

16. Edna Brown lives in a New England state. She feels sad when summer fades and autumn begins. But she finds that autumn has its own types of attractions. The trees slowly turn color, and what was once all green becomes eyecatching reds, yellows, browns, and many shades of other colors. The air gradually turns crisp and chilly with the promise of snow and cold.

    (F) Edna Brown enjoys only two seasons, summer and fall.
    (G) During the fall the outdoors in New England are ablaze with bright colors.
    (H) Edna Brown does not like snow and cold.
    (J) Trees are strong and healthy in the summer.

17. Bill Conrad finds travel pleasurable and educational. During a recent trip to France Bill began to understand why the French are renowned for the quality of their food and wines. Bill also developed great respect for the accomplishments of the French in painting, sculpture, and architecture.

    (A) Bill Conrad admires every aspect of the French way of life.
    (B) Bill Conrad considers French painters the greatest in the world.
    (C) Bill Conrad not only enjoys traveling but finds that he learns a great deal on his trips.
    (D) Bill Conrad finds the French language difficult to learn.

18. When David was a senior in high school, he attended a series of meetings on choosing a career. He particularly remembers the meeting on the medical profession. Not only must a doctor have great capacity to study and learn, but he must also have unusual qualities of self-sacrifice and dedication. A doctor must also remain cool and undisturbed under emergency conditions.

    (F) David learned that a doctor must study hard, be dedicated, and have great self-control under critical conditions.
    (G) David learned that a doctor may expect great financial rewards.
    (H) David attended only the career meeting on medicine.
    (J) David learned that a doctor must become a specialist in order to be successful.

19. Jim Chase is on a diet to lose weight. His doctor has advised him to limit his food intake to less than 1,800 calories per day. Jim must choose his food very carefully in order to keep within his limit of 1,800 calories. He learned that a slice of bread yields 100 calories and a glass of milk yields 150 calories.

    (A) Jim should avoid eating bread and drinking milk.
    (B) Jim will lose weight if he consumes no more them 1,800 calories per day.
    (C) Jim does not like to diet.
    (D) Jim can lose weight by strenuous exercise.

20. The following words are translated from an artificial language:

    plader means flatiron

    plaked means flatland

    derbal means ironware

    Which of the words below means flatware?

    (F) plaked
    (G) derked
    (H) plabal
    (J) balked

21. The following words are translated from an artificial language:

    barlac means infield

    perlac means outfield

    perkal means outhouse

    Which of the words below means fieldhouse?

    (A) barber
    (B) lackal
    (C) barkal
    (D) inkal

22. The following words are translated from an artificial language:

    munkel means baseline

    kelbre means lineup

    brepra means upland

    Which of the words below means landbase?

    (F) munbre
    (G) kelpra
    (H) breman
    (J) pramun

Answers to All Practice Tests

TEST 1

1. B	5. A	9. E	13. D	17. D
2. J	6. K	10. J	14. G	18. J
3. E	7. B	11. D	15. A	19. B
4. G	8. H	12. F	16. F	20. H

TEST 2

1. B	5. E	9. C	13. C	17. C
2. K	6. H	10. G	14. K	18. H
3. C	7. D	11. E	15. A	19. E
4. J	8. J	12. G	16. F	20. H

TEST 3

1. C	5. C	9. D	13. C	17. A
2. E	6. D	10. B	14. B	18. C
3. D	7. E	11. D	15. D	19. D
4. B	8. A	12. D	16. B	20. D

TEST 4

1. D	5. B	9. B	13. B	17. E
2. C	6. D	10. D	14. D	18. C
3. B	7. B	11. E	15. C	19. C
4. E	8. C	12. C	16. B	20. D

TEST 5

1. C	5. E	9. B	13. C	17. E
2. D	6. C	10. E	14. A	18. C
3. B	7. A	11. B	15. D	19. D
4. B	8. C	12. D	16. E	20. B

TEST 6

1. D	5. E	9. B	13. D	17. C
2. B	6. A	10. D	14. C	18. D
3. D	7. C	11. E	15. E	19. B
4. C	8. D	12. B	16. A	20. D

TEST 7

1. A	5. E	9. B	13. B	17. D
2. D	6. B	10. D	14. D	18. C
3. C	7. D	11. C	15. E	19. C
4. A	8. E	12. D	16. B	20. D

TEST 8

1. E	5. C	9. E	13. D	17. C
2. B	6. B	10. A	14. E	
3. D	7. D	11. D	15. C	
4. A	8. B	12. C	16. B	

TEST 9

1. Illogical	5. Illogical	9. Logical
2. Logical	6. Logical	10. Logical
3. Illogical	7. Illogical	
4. Illogical	8. Logical	

TEST 10

1. False	5. True	9. False
2. Uncertain	6. Uncertain	10. Uncertain
3. True	7. False	
4. True	8. False	

TEST 11

1. 101	2. 71	3. 62	4. 142

TEST 12

PART 1—SEQUENCES

1. D	5. A	9. C	13. B	17. D
2. G	6. H	10. J	14. F	18. F
3. B	7. C	11. B	15. C	19. B
4. J	8. F	12. H	16. G	20. H

PART 2—ANALOGIES

1. C	3. B	5. D	7. A	9. B
2. J	4. F	6. G	8. H	10. H

PART 3—VERBAL REASONING

1. C	6. J	11. C	16. F	21. B
2. J	7. C	12. H	17. C	22. J
3. D	8. G	13. A	18. F	
4. G	9. D	14. H	19. B	
5. A	10. G	15. D	20. H	

PRACTICE CATHOLIC HIGH SCHOOL ENTRANCE EXAMINATIONS

Answer Sheet
Practice Cooperative Admissions
Examination 1

TEST 1   SEQUENCES

1. Ⓐ Ⓑ Ⓒ Ⓓ	5. Ⓐ Ⓑ Ⓒ Ⓓ	9. Ⓐ Ⓑ Ⓒ Ⓓ	13. Ⓐ Ⓑ Ⓒ Ⓓ	17. Ⓐ Ⓑ Ⓒ Ⓓ
2. Ⓕ Ⓖ Ⓗ Ⓙ	6. Ⓕ Ⓖ Ⓗ Ⓙ	10. Ⓕ Ⓖ Ⓗ Ⓙ	14. Ⓕ Ⓖ Ⓗ Ⓙ	18. Ⓕ Ⓖ Ⓗ Ⓙ
3. Ⓐ Ⓑ Ⓒ Ⓓ	7. Ⓐ Ⓑ Ⓒ Ⓓ	11. Ⓐ Ⓑ Ⓒ Ⓓ	15. Ⓐ Ⓑ Ⓒ Ⓓ	19. Ⓐ Ⓑ Ⓒ Ⓓ
4. Ⓕ Ⓖ Ⓗ Ⓙ	8. Ⓕ Ⓖ Ⓗ Ⓙ	12. Ⓕ Ⓖ Ⓗ Ⓙ	16. Ⓕ Ⓖ Ⓗ Ⓙ	20. Ⓕ Ⓖ Ⓗ Ⓙ

TEST 2   ANALOGIES

1. Ⓐ Ⓑ Ⓒ Ⓓ	5. Ⓐ Ⓑ Ⓒ Ⓓ	9. Ⓐ Ⓑ Ⓒ Ⓓ	13. Ⓐ Ⓑ Ⓒ Ⓓ	17. Ⓐ Ⓑ Ⓒ Ⓓ
2. Ⓕ Ⓖ Ⓗ Ⓙ	6. Ⓕ Ⓖ Ⓗ Ⓙ	10. Ⓕ Ⓖ Ⓗ Ⓙ	14. Ⓕ Ⓖ Ⓗ Ⓙ	18. Ⓕ Ⓖ Ⓗ Ⓙ
3. Ⓐ Ⓑ Ⓒ Ⓓ	7. Ⓐ Ⓑ Ⓒ Ⓓ	11. Ⓐ Ⓑ Ⓒ Ⓓ	15. Ⓐ Ⓑ Ⓒ Ⓓ	19. Ⓐ Ⓑ Ⓒ Ⓓ
4. Ⓕ Ⓖ Ⓗ Ⓙ	8. Ⓕ Ⓖ Ⓗ Ⓙ	12. Ⓕ Ⓖ Ⓗ Ⓙ	16. Ⓕ Ⓖ Ⓗ Ⓙ	20. Ⓕ Ⓖ Ⓗ Ⓙ

TEST 3   MEMORY

1. Ⓐ Ⓑ Ⓒ Ⓓ Ⓔ	6. Ⓕ Ⓖ Ⓗ Ⓙ Ⓚ	11. Ⓐ Ⓑ Ⓒ Ⓓ Ⓔ	16. Ⓕ Ⓖ Ⓗ Ⓙ Ⓚ
2. Ⓕ Ⓖ Ⓗ Ⓙ Ⓚ	7. Ⓐ Ⓑ Ⓒ Ⓓ Ⓔ	12. Ⓕ Ⓖ Ⓗ Ⓙ Ⓚ	17. Ⓐ Ⓑ Ⓒ Ⓓ Ⓔ
3. Ⓐ Ⓑ Ⓒ Ⓓ Ⓔ	8. Ⓕ Ⓖ Ⓗ Ⓙ Ⓚ	13. Ⓐ Ⓑ Ⓒ Ⓓ Ⓔ	18. Ⓕ Ⓖ Ⓗ Ⓙ Ⓚ
4. Ⓕ Ⓖ Ⓗ Ⓙ Ⓚ	9. Ⓐ Ⓑ Ⓒ Ⓓ Ⓔ	14. Ⓕ Ⓖ Ⓗ Ⓙ Ⓚ	19. Ⓐ Ⓑ Ⓒ Ⓓ Ⓔ
5. Ⓐ Ⓑ Ⓒ Ⓓ Ⓔ	10. Ⓕ Ⓖ Ⓗ Ⓙ Ⓚ	15. Ⓐ Ⓑ Ⓒ Ⓓ Ⓔ	20. Ⓕ Ⓖ Ⓗ Ⓙ Ⓚ

TEST 4   VERBAL REASONING

1. Ⓐ Ⓑ Ⓒ Ⓓ	5. Ⓐ Ⓑ Ⓒ Ⓓ	9. Ⓐ Ⓑ Ⓒ Ⓓ	13. Ⓐ Ⓑ Ⓒ Ⓓ	17. Ⓐ Ⓑ Ⓒ Ⓓ
2. Ⓕ Ⓖ Ⓗ Ⓙ	6. Ⓕ Ⓖ Ⓗ Ⓙ	10. Ⓕ Ⓖ Ⓗ Ⓙ	14. Ⓕ Ⓖ Ⓗ Ⓙ	18. Ⓕ Ⓖ Ⓗ Ⓙ
3. Ⓐ Ⓑ Ⓒ Ⓓ	7. Ⓐ Ⓑ Ⓒ Ⓓ	11. Ⓐ Ⓑ Ⓒ Ⓓ	15. Ⓐ Ⓑ Ⓒ Ⓓ	19. Ⓐ Ⓑ Ⓒ Ⓓ
4. Ⓕ Ⓖ Ⓗ Ⓙ	8. Ⓕ Ⓖ Ⓗ Ⓙ	12. Ⓕ Ⓖ Ⓗ Ⓙ	16. Ⓕ Ⓖ Ⓗ Ⓙ	20. Ⓕ Ⓖ Ⓗ Ⓙ

TEST 5   READING VOCABULARY

1. Ⓐ Ⓑ Ⓒ Ⓓ	9. Ⓕ Ⓖ Ⓗ Ⓙ	17. Ⓕ Ⓖ Ⓗ Ⓙ	25. Ⓕ Ⓖ Ⓗ Ⓙ	33. Ⓕ Ⓖ Ⓗ Ⓙ
2. Ⓕ Ⓖ Ⓗ Ⓙ	10. Ⓐ Ⓑ Ⓒ Ⓓ	18. Ⓐ Ⓑ Ⓒ Ⓓ	26. Ⓐ Ⓑ Ⓒ Ⓓ	34. Ⓐ Ⓑ Ⓒ Ⓓ
3. Ⓐ Ⓑ Ⓒ Ⓓ	11. Ⓕ Ⓖ Ⓗ Ⓙ	19. Ⓕ Ⓖ Ⓗ Ⓙ	27. Ⓕ Ⓖ Ⓗ Ⓙ	35. Ⓕ Ⓖ Ⓗ Ⓙ
4. Ⓕ Ⓖ Ⓗ Ⓙ	12. Ⓐ Ⓑ Ⓒ Ⓓ	20. Ⓐ Ⓑ Ⓒ Ⓓ	28. Ⓐ Ⓑ Ⓒ Ⓓ	36. Ⓐ Ⓑ Ⓒ Ⓓ
5. Ⓕ Ⓖ Ⓗ Ⓙ	13. Ⓕ Ⓖ Ⓗ Ⓙ	21. Ⓕ Ⓖ Ⓗ Ⓙ	29. Ⓕ Ⓖ Ⓗ Ⓙ	37. Ⓕ Ⓖ Ⓗ Ⓙ
6. Ⓐ Ⓑ Ⓒ Ⓓ	14. Ⓐ Ⓑ Ⓒ Ⓓ	22. Ⓐ Ⓑ Ⓒ Ⓓ	30. Ⓐ Ⓑ Ⓒ Ⓓ	38. Ⓐ Ⓑ Ⓒ Ⓓ
7. Ⓕ Ⓖ Ⓗ Ⓙ	15. Ⓕ Ⓖ Ⓗ Ⓙ	23. Ⓕ Ⓖ Ⓗ Ⓙ	31. Ⓕ Ⓖ Ⓗ Ⓙ	39. Ⓕ Ⓖ Ⓗ Ⓙ
8. Ⓐ Ⓑ Ⓒ Ⓓ	16. Ⓐ Ⓑ Ⓒ Ⓓ	24. Ⓐ Ⓑ Ⓒ Ⓓ	32. Ⓐ Ⓑ Ⓒ Ⓓ	40. Ⓐ Ⓑ Ⓒ Ⓓ

TEST 6   READING COMPREHENSION

1. F G H J
2. A B C D
3. F G H J
4. A B C D
5. F G H J
6. A B C D
7. F G H J
8. A B C D
9. F G H J
10. A B C D
11. F G H J
12. A B C D
13. F G H J
14. A B C D
15. F G H J
16. A B C D
17. F G H J
18. A B C D
19. F G H J
20. A B C D
21. F G H J
22. A B C D
23. F G H J
24. A B C D
25. F G H J
26. A B C D
27. F G H J
28. A B C D
29. F G H J
30. A B C D
31. F G H J
32. A B C D
33. F G H J
34. A B C D

TEST 7   MATHEMATICS COMPUTATION

1. F G H J K
2. A B C D E
3. F G H J K
4. A B C D E
5. F G H J K
6. A B C D E
7. F G H J K
8. A B C D E
9. F G H J K
10. A B C D E
11. F G H J K
12. A B C D E
13. F G H J K
14. A B C D E
15. F G H J K
16. A B C D E
17. F G H J K
18. A B C D E
19. F H J K K
20. A B C D E
21. F H J K K
22. A B C D E
23. F G H J K
24. A B C D E
25. F G H J K
26. A B C D E
27. F G H J K
28. A B C D E
29. F G H J K
30. A B C D E

TEST 8   MATHEMATICS CONCEPTS AND APPLICATIONS

1. A B C D
2. F G H J
3. A B C D
4. F G H J
5. A B C D
6. F G H J
7. A B C D
8. F G H J
9. A B C D
10. F G H J
11. A B C D
12. F G H J
13. A B C D
14. F G H J
15. A B C D
16. F G H J
17. A B C D
18. F G H J
19. A B C D
20. F G H J
21. A B C D
22. F G H J
23. A B C D
24. F G H J
25. A B C D
26. F G H J
27. A B C D
28. F G H J
29. A B C D
30. F G H J
31. A B C D
32. F G H J
33. A B C D
34. F G H J
35. A B C D

TEST 9   LANGUAGE MECHANICS

1. A B C D E
2. F G H J K
3. A B C D E
4. F G H J K
5. A B C D E
6. F G H J K
7. A B C D E
8. F G H J K
9. A B C D E
10. F G H J K
11. A B C D E
12. F G H J K
13. A B C D E
14. F G H J K
15. A B C D E
16. F G H J K
17. A B C D E
18. F G H J K
19. A B C D E
20. F G H J K

TEST 10   LANGUAGE EXPRESSION

1. A B C D
2. F G H J
3. A B C D
4. F G H J
5. A B C D
6. F G H J
7. A B C D
8. F G H J
9. A B C D
10. F G H J
11. A B C D
12. F G H J
13. A B C D
14. F G H J
15. A B C D
16. F G H J
17. A B C D
18. F G H J
19. A B C D
20. F G H J
21. A B C D
22. F G H J
23. A B C D
24. F G H J
25. A B C D
26. F G H J
27. A B C D
28. F G H J
29. A B C D
30. F G H J
31. A B C D
32. F G H J

Cooperative (Coop) Admissions Examination

Overview

Total Time

Approximately 4 hours.

Type of Questions

The questions are multiple choice, with answers blackened on a machine-scored Answer Sheet.

Pacing

Don't spend too much time on any one question. Take a guess and go on, but put a star next to any question that requires too much thought and come back to it—if time permits—at the end. In many sections of the exam, the questions are arranged so that they progress from easy to difficult. It is therefore better to take the questions in the order they appear than to jump ahead.

Guessing

The examination directions suggest that you answer all questions. When you hit a difficult question, eliminate as many of the choices as you can, and then select the answer you think is most likely to be correct. Do not go back to that question. If you cannot eliminate any of the choices, take a guess.

Exam Content

New forms of the exam are prepared each year. Time limits given below and on the practice tests are guidelines rather than strict timings. Usually the content breaks down as follows:

Test 1: Sequences
20 nonverbal analogy questions: numbers, letters, figures; 12 minutes

Test 2: Analogies
20 picture analogy questions; 7 minutes

Test 3: Memory
20 questions that test memory; 12 minutes for study, 8 minutes to answer

Test 4: Verbal Reasoning
20 questions on reasoning logically and seeing relationships, on drawing conclusions from given information; 12 minutes

Test 5: Reading Vocabulary
40 questions on words in context; 18 minutes

Test 6: Reading Comprehension
34 questions that measure ability to comprehend reading passages; 32 minutes

Test 7: Mathematics Computation
30 questions to measure operations of addition, subtraction, multiplication, and division with whole numbers, decimals, fraction, and integers; 25 minutes

Test 8: Mathematics Concepts and Applications
35 questions on problem solving, geometry, measurement, number sentences, number theory; 27 minutes

Test 9: Language Mechanics
20 questions on capitalization and punctuation; 10 minutes

Test 10: Language Expression
32 questions on usage and sentence structure; 25 minutes

Practice Cooperative Admissions Examination 1

TEST 1   SEQUENCES

Number of questions: 20   *Time limit: 12 minutes*

> DIRECTIONS: For numbers 1 through 20 make the choice that will continue the pattern or sequence and blacken the appropriate circle on the Answer Sheet.

1. ○□□□ | □○□□ | □□□○ | □□ __   ○○   □□   □○   ○□
                                   (A)   (B)   (C)   (D)

2. ▲△ | ▲▲ | ■□ | ■ __   △   ■   □   ▲
                           (F) (G) (H) (J)

3. ♂ ♀ | ♀ ♂ | ⊡ ⊡ | ←△ __   ⊘   ←□→   △   △→
                                 (A)   (B)   (C)   (D)

4. ○□ | ■○□ | □● | ○ __   ■   □   ■   □
                            (F) (G) (H) (J)

5. △○ | △△ | △○ | ▲▲ | △ __   △   ▲   ●   ○
                                  (A) (B) (C) (D)

6. □ ꝺ | bd | △ __ | △   △   △   ⋈
                      (F) (G) (H) (J)

7. 3   12   48 | 4   16   64 | 6   24   __   48   72   84   96
                                              (A) (B) (C) (D)

8. 7   14   4 | 8   16   6 | 15   30   __   40   20   45   35
                                             (F) (G) (H) (J)

9. 3   7   15 | 4   9   19 | 5 __ 23 | 15   9   11   17
                                                (A)   (B)   (C)   (D)

10. 76 72 67 | 63 58 52 | 45 37 __ | 28   31   32   29
                                                (F)   (G)   (H)   (J)

11. 4   5   16 | 7   8   49 | 9   10 __ | 60   64   81   89
                                                (A)   (B)   (C)   (D)

12. 2   4   10 | 3   7   19 | 4   10 __ | 28   26   25   24
                                                (F)   (G)   (H)   (J)

13. 3   4   6 | 7   8   10 | 11 12 __ | 13   14   10   15
                                                (A)   (B)   (C)   (D)

14. 17 10 5 | 29 22 11 | 35 28 __ | 12   15   22   14
                                                (F)   (G)   (H)   (J)

15. AB_1C_1 AB_1C_2 AB_2C_2 __ AB_3C_3 AB_1C_3 AB_2C_3 AB_3C_2 $A_1B_1C_1$
                                                       (A)   (B)   (C)   (D)

16. $R_6S_1T_5$ $R_5S_2T_4$ $R_4S_3T_3$ __ $R_2S_5T_1$ $R_4S_3T_2$ $R_3S_2T_3$ $R_4S_2T_3$ $R_3S_4T_2$

                                                            (F)   (G)   (H)   (J)

17. BAL   ALD   LDC   __   CFG   LCF   DCF   DFB   DFG
                                     (A)   (B)   (C)   (D)

18. ACE   BDF   CEG   DFH   __   EFK   DGH   FHL   EGI
                                     (F)   (G)   (H)   (J)

19. ACD   DCE   ECF   __   GCH   FCG   ECG   GEH   EFG
                                     (A)   (B)   (C)   (D)

20. ARB   BSC   CTD   DUE   __   BEJ   EVF   DFL   HPZ
                                     (F)   (G)   (H)   (J)

TEST 2   ANALOGIES

Number of questions: 20   *Time limit: 7 minutes*

DIRECTIONS: For numbers 1 through 20, select the picture that will fit in the empty box so that the two lower pictures are related in the same way as the two upper pictures.

1.

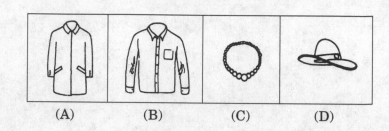

(A)   (B)   (C)   (D)

2.

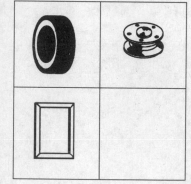

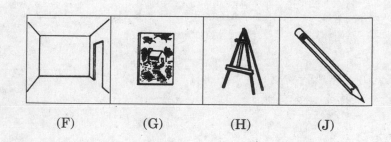

(F)   (G)   (H)   (J)

3.

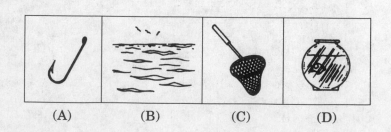

(A)   (B)   (C)   (D)

4.

 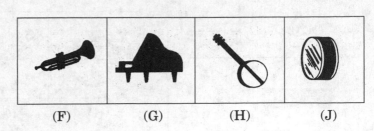

(F)   (G)   (H)   (J)

5.

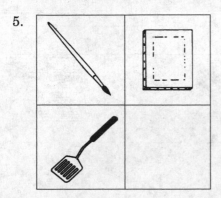 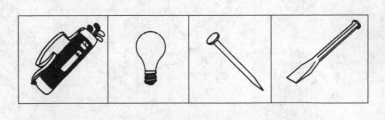

(A)   (B)   (C)   (D)

6.

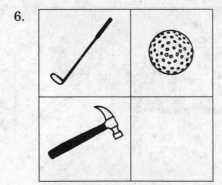 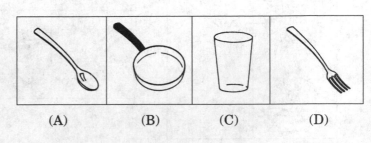

7.

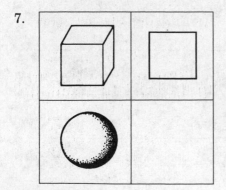 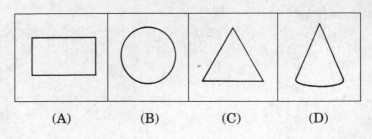

(A)   (B)   (C)   (D)

8.

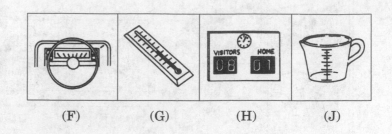

(F)   (G)   (H)   (J)

9.

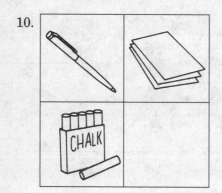

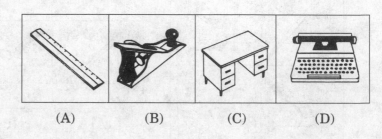

(A)   (B)   (C)   (D)

10.

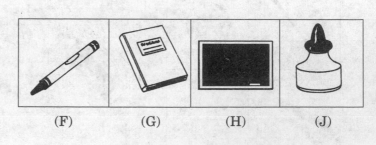

(F)   (G)   (H)   (J)

11.

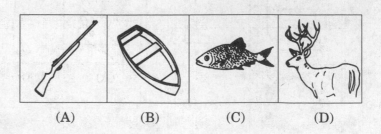

(A)   (B)   (C)   (D)

12.

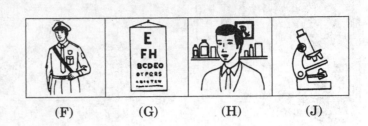

(F)   (G)   (H)   (J)

13.

(A)   (B)   (C)   (D)

14.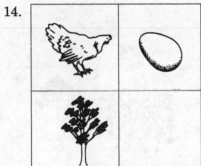

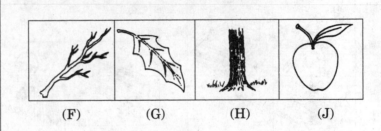

(F)   (G)   (H)   (J)

15.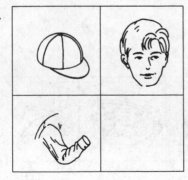

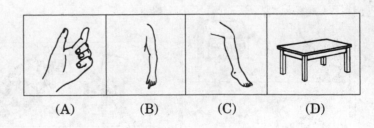

(A)   (B)   (C)   (D)

16.

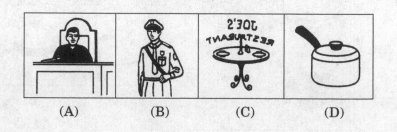

(F)   (G)   (H)   (J)

17.

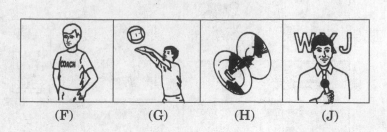

(A)   (B)   (C)   (D)

18.

(F)   (G)   (H)   (J)

19.

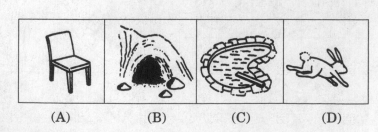

(A)   (B)   (C)   (D)

20.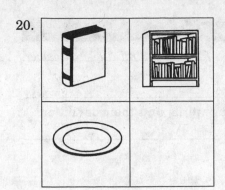
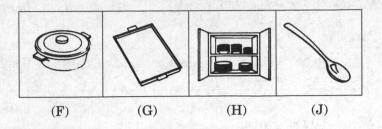

(F)　　　(G)　　　(H)　　　(J)

TEST 3   MEMORY

Number of questions: 20   *Time limit: 12 minutes for study, 8 minutes to answer*

Part One

DIRECTIONS: While someone reads aloud to you the following words and their definitions, read them silently to yourself.

Words and Definitions

1 An impofo is a kind of antelope.
2 Circurate means to tame.
3 Roborant means strengthening.
4 An ereptation is a creeping forth.
5 Guttle means to eat piggishly.
6 A nene is a type of goose.
7 Flagitate means to plead.
8 Heimal means wintry.
9 Abaction means cattle stealing.
10 A tautog is a kind of fish.
11 Absterge means to wipe clean.
12 Queme means pleasant.
13 A sarwan is a camel driver.
14 Ecdemic means of foreign origin.
15 A brool is a low roar.
16 Callidity means shrewdness and cunning.
17 Mussitation means grumbling.
18 Bovaristic means conceited.
19 A cumshaw is a tip.
20 Elute means to wash out.

After studying the words and definitions for 12 minutes, cover them and proceed to Tests 4 and 5.

TEST 4   VERBAL REASONING

Number of questions: 20   *Time limit: 12 minutes*

DIRECTIONS: For numbers 1 through 7, select the word that names a necessary part of the word underlined.

1. aquarium

   (A) tree
   (B) guppies
   (C) water
   (D) building

2. lunch

   (F) table
   (G) food
   (H) restaurant
   (J) sandwich

3. helicopter

   (A) pilot
   (B) passengers
   (C) hangar
   (D) blades

4. cello

   (F) string
   (G) musician
   (H) orchestra
   (J) baton

5. music

   (A) band
   (B) violin
   (C) sound
   (D) drum

6. textile

   (F) skirt
   (G) lining
   (H) leather
   (J) thread

7. parade

   (A) band
   (B) marchers
   (C) spectators
   (D) leader

DIRECTIONS: For numbers 8 through 12, the three words in the top row are related in a certain way. The words below the line are related in the same way. In each case, select the missing word so that the three words in the bottom row will be related in the same way as the words in the top row.

8.

sport	soccer	baseball
athlete	forward	_____

   (F) umpire
   (G) catcher
   (H) coach
   (J) mitt

9.

clothing	hat	coat
person	man	_____

   (A) scarf
   (B) foot
   (C) button
   (D) child

10.

furniture	chair	sofa
entertainment	game	_____

   (F) movie
   (G) stadium
   (H) seat
   (J) stage

11.

dinner	meat	dessert
breakfast	juice	_____

   (A) food
   (B) chicken
   (C) cereal
   (D) lemon

12.

building	floor	walls
kitchen	refrigerator	_____

   (F) typewriter
   (G) oven
   (H) file
   (J) piano

DIRECTIONS: For numbers 13 through 14, select the correct answer.

13. The following words are translated from an artificial language:

    <u>walamiz</u> means anywhere
    <u>shermiz</u> means anybody
    <u>thowala</u> means somewhere

    Which of the words below means <u>somebody</u>?

    (A) sheramat
    (B) thosher
    (C) walatho
    (D) tholacat

14. The following words are translated from an artificial language:

    <u>ebalfull</u> means driveway
    <u>milfull</u> means walkway
    <u>ebalsap</u> means driveshaft

    Which of the words below means <u>shaftway</u>?

    (F) ebalmil
    (G) ebaltho
    (H) sapfull
    (J) fulldor

DIRECTIONS: For numbers 15 through 20, select the statement that is true according to the facts given in the paragraph.

15. Jim and Ruth like to stay out late. One night they went dancing and arrived home after midnight. They had spent an enjoyable evening.

    (A) Jim and Ruth come home after midnight every night.
    (B) Jim and Ruth do not like their home.
    (C) Jim and Ruth enjoy dancing.
    (D) Jim and Ruth enjoy every evening.

16. The United States imports oil and steel but exports wheat and corn as well as other agricultural products. The United States has important trade relations with western European nations as well as with Japan. The American government encourages business firms to export and discourages imports.

    (F) American business firms do not trade with the Russians.
    (G) The American government does not permit imports.
    (H) Western European nations like to trade with American companies.
    (J) The American government prefers exporting over importing.

17. Dan Taylor is a good athlete at Lincoln High School. In the fall he plays varsity football. In the winter he plays varsity basketball and in the spring he plays varsity baseball. Dan is also an honor student and hopes to win an athletic scholarship to college.

    (A) Dan Taylor plays on every varsity team at Lincoln High School.
    (B) Dan Taylor spends so much time on the athletic field that he does not have enough time to study.
    (C) Dan Taylor plays only on varsity teams.
    (D) Dan Taylor is a good athlete and a fine student.

18. A new shopping center was opened on the outskirts of the town of Parkesville last month. Among the food stores in the shopping center are a bake shop, a produce market, a meat shop, and a fish store. There are also an apparel shop, a hardware store, and an appliance shop. When the stores are very busy it is difficult to find a parking space.

    (F) Most stores of the town of Parkesville have moved to the shopping center.
    (G) One cannot buy a suit of clothing at the shopping center.
    (H) It is always difficult to find parking space at the shopping center.
    (J) The shopping center is outside of the town center.

19. Juan Morales enjoys travel and sightseeing. He often flies to distant places, rents a car, and visits places of special interest. Juan prefers to plan his own trips instead of going on organized tours.

   (A) Juan travels only by automobile.
   (B) Juan uses the automobile to help him to visit places of interest.
   (C) Juan takes organized tours to save time and expense.
   (D) Juan dislikes flying but he will use a plane if necessary.

20. Teresa and Frank Christiano enjoy bowling and dancing. They bowl every Tuesday evening and go dancing every Thursday evening. They also find time to attend concerts and the theater and to visit with friends.

   (F) Teresa and Frank Christiano keep themselves too busy to enjoy life.
   (G) Teresa and Frank Christiano go to the theater more often than they attend concerts.
   (H) Teresa and Frank Christiano visit with friends infrequently.
   (J) Teresa and Frank Christiano never attend the theater on Tuesday evening.

TEST 5   READING VOCABULARY

Number of questions: 40   *Time limit: 15 minutes*

DIRECTIONS: For numbers 1 through 10 select the word that means the same, or nearly the same, as the word underlined.

1. <u>confuse</u> her audience

   (F) amuse
   (G) anger
   (H) bewilder
   (J) educate

2. <u>insufficient</u> preparation

   (A) backbreaking
   (B) careless
   (C) unending
   (D) inadequate

3. a <u>defective</u> part

   (F) faulty
   (G) main
   (H) missing
   (J) vital

4. <u>humdrum</u> activities

   (A) daily
   (B) sports
   (C) quiet
   (D) dull

5. avoid <u>blunders</u>

   (F) troubles
   (G) mistakes
   (H) illnesses
   (J) dangers

6. <u>arouse</u> the public

   (A) praise
   (B) control
   (C) condemn
   (D) stir

7. <u>prior</u> events

   (F) earlier
   (G) significant
   (H) recent
   (J) historical

8. <u>demolish</u> her umbrella

   (A) destroy
   (B) purchase
   (C) mislay
   (D) identify

9. sign the <u>accord</u>

   (F) complaint
   (G) completion
   (H) agreement
   (J) petition

10. <u>amend</u> a statement

    (A) deny
    (B) change
    (C) make
    (D) record

DIRECTIONS: For numbers 11 through 20 select the word that means the opposite of the underlined word.

11. have a <u>hazy</u> idea

    (F) confused
    (G) logical
    (H) definite
    (J) clever

12. <u>obstruct</u> the path

    (A) define
    (B) unblock
    (C) label
    (D) cross

13. in an <u>orderly</u> manner

    (F) unsystematic
    (G) understandable
    (H) unconscious
    (J) underhanded

14. have a feeling of <u>relief</u>

    (A) awe
    (B) disrespect
    (C) anxiety
    (D) joy

15. to <u>dawdle</u> on the way home

   (F) discover
   (G) hasten
   (H) notice
   (J) accompany

16. make a <u>glaring</u> error

   (A) fortunate
   (B) subtle
   (C) fatal
   (D) childish

17. an autograph of the <u>celebrity</u>

   (F) daredevil
   (G) veteran
   (H) ballplayer
   (J) unknown

18. to <u>curtail</u> the trip

   (A) relive
   (B) finance
   (C) describe
   (D) prolong

19. to <u>refresh</u> the travelers

   (F) inform
   (G) weary
   (H) conceal
   (J) mislead

20. to <u>hoist</u> the flag

   (A) disrespect
   (B) carry
   (C) lower
   (D) fold

DIRECTIONS: For numbers 21 through 30 select the word that best fits into the blank.

21. By spending as little as possible, the _____ old woman was able to live on her Social Security allowance.

   (F) lovely
   (G) lonely
   (H) cheerful
   (J) thrifty

22. Evelyn becomes _____ every time she visits the beloved scenes of her childhood.

   (A) sarcastic
   (B) lazy
   (C) robust
   (D) sentimental

23. His _____ consent to our visit was given so rudely that we did not go.

   (F) grudging
   (G) enthusiastic
   (H) gracious
   (J) unexpressed

24. The _____ youngster was afraid to ask for a second helping of pie.

   (A) handsome
   (B) happy
   (C) versatile
   (D) timid

25. Making the facts known is the only _____ for these vicious rumors.

   (F) reward
   (G) reason
   (H) antidote
   (J) detection

26. Despite his weakened condition, Alan _____ training for the 26-mile marathon.

   (A) resisted
   (B) rejected
   (C) postponed
   (D) continued

27. It is the unexpected or sudden twists in life that try a person's _____ .

   (F) fortune
   (G) livelihood
   (H) age
   (J) mettle

28. Phyllis is so good natured that she never finds daily household chores _____ .

   (A) useful
   (B) tedious
   (C) quieting
   (D) controllable

29. Distrust can quickly _____ a friend-ship.

    (F) impair
    (G) strengthen
    (H) outstrip
    (J) create

30. Some people speak in words or phrases but my _____ aunt speaks in para-graphs.

    (A) stubborn
    (B) placid
    (C) loquacious
    (D) flexible

DIRECTIONS: For numbers 31 through 40 select the word whose meaning is the same as *both* of the words or phrases underlined.

---

31. touch lightly and eat grass

    (F) scamper
    (G) graze
    (H) tap
    (J) munch

32. equal and nobleman

    (A) peer
    (B) knight
    (C) relative
    (D) grandee

33. a cup and to attack

    (F) bluster
    (G) mug
    (H) tankard
    (J) assault

34. path and part of a book

    (A) chapter
    (B) channel
    (C) partition
    (D) passage

35. breathe in and influence

    (F) inhale
    (G) inspire
    (H) affect
    (J) vaporize

36. courage and sand

    (A) grit
    (B) stamina
    (C) gravel
    (D) dash

37. border and to hold back

    (F) rim
    (G) delay
    (H) train
    (J) curb

38. seed and dent

    (A) burrow
    (B) pit
    (C) pollen
    (D) hint

39. light up and make clear

    (F) intensify
    (G) declare
    (H) decode
    (J) illuminate

40. thirsty and burned

    (A) withered
    (B) browned
    (C) parched
    (D) scarred

Before continuing on to Test 6, now that 25 minutes have passed, complete Part Two of Test 3.

TEST 3   MEMORY

Part Two

DIRECTIONS: For numbers 1 through 20 select the word that means the same as the underlined phrase.

1. Which word means a type of goose?

   (A) brool
   (B) cumshaw
   (C) impofo
   (D) nene
   (E) abaction

2. Which word means wintry?

   (F) queme
   (G) heimal
   (H) bovaristic
   (J) roborant
   (K) ecdemic

3. Which means a low roar?

   (A) ereptation
   (B) tautag
   (C) callidity
   (D) sarwan
   (E) brool

4. Which word means to wipe clean?

   (F) absterge
   (G) circurate
   (H) guttle
   (J) elute
   (K) flagitate

5. Which word means a camel driver?

   (A) sarwan
   (B) mussitation
   (C) cumshaw
   (D) brool
   (E) ereptation

6. Which word means to eat piggishly?

   (F) circurate
   (G) elute
   (H) flagitate
   (J) brool
   (K) guttle

7. Which word means conceited?

   (A) cumshaw
   (B) queme
   (C) heimal
   (D) roborant
   (E) bovaristic

8. Which word means a type of antelope?

   (F) abaction
   (G) impofo
   (H) nene
   (J) tautog
   (K) mussitation

9. Which word means of foreign origin?

   (A) roborant
   (B) queme
   (C) ecdemic
   (D) bovaristic
   (E) sarwan

10. Which word means to wash out?

    (F) absterge
    (G) flagitate
    (H) elute
    (J) guttle
    (K) circurate

11. Which word means grumbling?

    (A) nene
    (B) mussitation
    (C) sarwan
    (D) ecdemic
    (E) callidity

12. Which word means to plead?

    (F) guttle
    (G) circurate
    (H) flagitate
    (J) cumshaw
    (K) brool

13. Which word means a creeping forth?

    (A) callidity
    (B) sarwan
    (C) abaction
    (D) impofo
    (E) ereptation

14. Which word means <u>strengthening</u>?

   (F) heimal
   (G) roborant
   (H) ecdemic
   (J) guttle
   (K) queme

15. Which word means <u>a kind of fish</u>?

   (A) mussitation
   (B) nene
   (C) flagitate
   (D) tautog
   (E) callidity

16. Which word means <u>a tip</u>?

   (F) callidity
   (G) ereptation
   (H) impofo
   (J) cumshaw
   (K) tautog

17. Which word means <u>cattle stealing</u>?

   (A) abaction
   (B) queme
   (C) roborant
   (D) absterge
   (E) bovaristic

18. Which word means <u>to tame</u>?

   (F) ecdemic
   (G) absterge
   (H) sarwan
   (J) circurate
   (K) elute

19. Which word means <u>shrewdness and cunning</u>?

   (A) ecdemic
   (B) tautog
   (C) nene
   (D) brool
   (E) callidity

20. Which word means <u>pleasant</u>?

   (F) heimal
   (G) bovaristic
   (H) elute
   (J) queme
   (K) mussitation

TEST 6   READING COMPREHENSION

Number of questions: 34   *Time limit: 32 minutes*

DIRECTIONS: For numbers 1 through 34 read each selection below and answer the questions that follow it. Choose your answer based on the selection.

The pieces of the puzzle suddenly fit together! Lucy now saw clearly, all too clearly, how carefully Jeff had plotted our destruction. With superhuman patience, he had moved from step to step until he had involved all of us. None would escape from the unjust fate he had planned. It was only a matter of minutes before the net would close in on us. We wouldn't even have an opportunity to plead our innocence. Lucy's initial feelings of panic and anger gave way to an inner calm. There was no escape. Nor was there any feeling of satisfaction in the realization that Jeff would not be there to enjoy the fruits of his evil deeds!

1. In the next few minutes

   (F) Lucy will escape.
   (G) Lucy's companions will be punished.
   (H) Jeff will die.
   (J) everyone involved will be dead.

2. The reader is *not* told

   (A) how successful Jeff was.
   (B) why Jeff planned as he did.
   (C) how Lucy felt.
   (D) how Jeff had worked out his scheme.

3. Lucy's calm resulted from

   (F) knowing Jeff's punishment.
   (G) her patience.
   (H) knowing that nothing could save her.
   (J) creating the puzzle.

4. The action described in the selection could *not* be part of

   (A) a detective story.
   (B) a TV soap opera.
   (C) a situation comedy.
   (D) a tale of adventure.

We must face up to the fact that as a society we have never decided the real purpose of our prisons and reform schools. By and large they are mainly holding pens where offenders are kept for a specified amount of time. Little or nothing is done to help them to become productive citizens when they are released. The prisons and reform schools have become training laboratories for crime. Too often the offenders come out of these institutions more angry, more brutalized, more committed to a life of crime than when they went in. The question is not whether the convicted criminals deserve the punishment given them. We agree that we should have some way of punishing lawbreakers, but prisons and reform schools are wrong! They only make a bad thing much much worse. We have to rethink and reshape our institutional machinery for punishing crime. Once the offenders have paid for their misdeeds they must be led to turn away from crime and reach for a normal, productive human life.

5. The failure of our prison system is shown most clearly by the fact that

   (F) prisoners escape frequently.
   (G) prison terms are too long.
   (H) criminals remain criminals after being released from prison.
   (J) society is afraid of the criminal element among us.

6. The author is opposed to

   (A) the use of prisons as schools for crime.
   (B) punishing evil-doers for their deeds.
   (C) the abolition of reform schools.
   (D) the pardoning of prisoners.

7. The term *holding pens* compare people to

   (F) prisoners.
   (G) cattle.
   (H) cells.
   (J) writing instruments.

8. In the selection, the author

   (A) shows the bad effects of crime.
   (B) reveals the criminal mentality.
   (C) presents facts to prove the claims of prisoners.
   (D) asks for a major reform in the prison system.

There are approximately 6,000 tribes in Africa today. The people of each tribe speak the same language and have the same customs and traditions. They are expected to protect each other from unfriendly outsiders. They have an elected or hereditary chief who may be assisted by a tribal council. When the colonial powers divided Africa, they disregarded tribal groupings. Boundaries drawn to suit the convenience of the Europeans were usually retained when the new nations of Africa were established after World War II. Some tribes were split among several nations. Some smaller tribes gained control over segments of much larger groups. It was impossible to reestablish national states on single tribes or even related tribes. The problem which faces African leaders today is how to combine tribalism with nationalism. Long-standing tribal traditions must blend with the needs of the entire nation. Tribalism and nationalism should be used to reinforce each other rather than to pull in different directions.

9. The boundaries of modern African countries

   (F) follow geographical features like rivers and mountains.
   (G) are based on tribal relationships.
   (H) were reset by the United Nations.
   (J) were made by non-Africans.

10. Tribalism is based on

   (A) democratic selection.
   (B) rules and regulations made in the past.
   (C) European explorations.
   (D) national laws and regulations.

11. Tribalism and nationalism come in conflict when

   (F) there is too much poverty in a country.
   (G) laws are based on tribal custom and national needs.
   (H) members of a tribe are ruled by an outsider.
   (J) national leaders disregard tribal customs.

12. A major task for present-day leaders of African countries is to

   (A) establish national customs and traditions.
   (B) establish tribal customs.
   (C) reset boundaries.
   (D) identify tribes.

Shooting stars neither shoot nor are they stars. The earth is continuously bombarded by fragments of matter that is being pulled into our upper atmosphere by gravity. These particles enter our atmosphere at speeds of from 10 to 20 miles a second. As they speed through the layers of air their surfaces are heated by friction until the particles glow as thin streaks. These streaks are the thin streams that earthlings see for brief moments in the night sky. Most of these "shooting stars" burn up completely and disappear before they can become visible to us. However, if you are patient, on a clear moonless night away from the glow of a city you could see five or ten faint shooting stars an hour. When the particle is larger, it can cause a brilliant flare. It is then called a *fireball*. Fireballs are much less frequent than are shooting stars. Even less frequent are the large particles that do not burn up completely but reach the earth. They are called *meteorites*. Local science museums usually contain samples of these recovered space travellers.

13. Shooting stars enter the earth's atmosphere

(F) on cloudless nights only.
(G) on moonlit nights only.
(H) day and night.
(J) invisibly.

14. Shooting stars become visible

(A) when they slow down.
(B) as they gather speed.
(C) when they are about to land.
(D) only when they travel through the air around the earth.

15. As they approach the surface of the earth, fireballs travel at least

(F) 10 miles an hour.
(G) 36,000 miles an hour.
(H) 600 miles an hour.
(J) 720 miles an hour.

16. Shooting stars disappear because

(A) they travel too fast.
(B) they reach the surface of the earth.
(C) they burn up.
(D) they avoid the pull of gravity.

17. The daily number of shooting stars

(F) varies greatly from day to day.
(G) averages about the same each day.
(H) cannot be determined
(J) is too great to be counted.

About 2,000 years ago the Hohokam migrated to the desert lands of southwestern Arizona. Our research has not revealed where they came from or why they left their former lands. By the time they arrived in Arizona, they had already established a distinctive culture pattern. Their first homes were of the single-unit type with walls of brush, poles, and mud. The hot, dry air soon turned the mud into a clay that bound the parts together. Grouped in walled villages, the Hohokam spread widely over the dry valleys. They were called the *Canal Builders* because of the complicated series of irrigation ditches they built to sustain their major occupation, farming. What eventually became of the Hohokam is not known. The Pueblo people from the north did overrun their towns. The Pueblos built their many-storied dwellings of adobe along-side the one-story houses of the Hohokam. What is seen today are ruins of a compound surrounded by a wall with no opening and entered by a ladder. Nothing else remains. Did the Hohokam intermarry with the Pueblos or were they completely wiped out by their successors? Only ruins and fragments of pottery remain as evidence that the Hohokam had ever inhabited our continent.

18. The Hohokam came to the Southwest

    (A) just after Columbus reached the Americas.
    (B) at the same time as the Pueblos.
    (C) during the Ice Age.
    (D) long before the Europeans explored the area.

19. We know about the Hohokam from

    (F) the written records they left.
    (G) the stories told by the Pueblos.
    (H) what is left of their homes.
    (J) what their descendants tell us.

20. The Hohokam were able to settle successfully because

    (A) they brought cattle with them.
    (B) they were fierce fighters.
    (C) they conquered their neighbors.
    (D) they solved the water problem.

21. When the Pueblos came in contact with the Hohokam

    (F) they took over the Hohokam land.
    (G) they turned the Hohokam into slaves.
    (H) they were beaten off by the Hohokam.
    (J) they destroyed the Hohokam villages.

Until 1930, the basic visual study of cells had to depend on the light microscope. However, that microscope has a severe limitation. The objects under study must be larger than one half of a wavelength of visible light so that the wave will not pass around it. The very small size of most structures in cells made them invisible before the invention of the electron microscope. This instrument uses beams of electrons rather than light waves. It provides magnifications of 100,000 times or more, 100 times more powerful than the best optical microscope. The powerful magnets of the electron microscope bend a stream of electrons, directing it onto a screen, where an image is produced and recorded. However, because of the action of the electron stream, only dead materials can be studied with these microscopes. The electron microscope has revealed some previously unknown parts of the cell and has altered scientists' views of other structures within these units of living organisms.

22. One type of microscope is called a *light microscope* because

    (A) it is easy to move from place to place.
    (B) it is painted white.
    (C) it involves the use of light waves.
    (D) the structures studied are easily placed on slides.

23. An advantage of the light microscope over the electron microscope is that

    (F) it can be used to study living tissue.
    (G) it has greater magnification.
    (H) it has fewer limitations.
    (J) it can be used to study cell structures.

24. The electron microscope has been in use

    (A) since the time of Galileo.
    (B) for more than 200 years.
    (C) for about 70 years.
    (D) for about 120 years.

25. The electron microscope allows us to see objects

    (F) 100 times larger than they are.
    (G) that are invisible.
    (H) that are larger than the electrons.
    (J) that move about slowly.

26. The object viewed through an electron microscope

    (A) is seen as a reflected image.
    (B) is viewed directly.
    (C) can move freely.
    (D) must be studied quickly.

The sales tax is a direct tax which is added to each purchase at a set rate. It is the consumer who has to pay since it is usually applied to retail sales only. Since this "pennies-tax" was first put into use by West Virginia in 1921, it has been adopted by most states and many cities and other local governments. Some people find the tax objectionable because it is not based on the ability to pay and therefore weighs most heavily on the lower income groups. Those who favor its use argue that it brings in large sums that are fairly simple to administer. They also say that it requires some contribution for public services from nearly everyone in the community. Such a tax, they claim, does not overburden any one group. By exempting purchases of food, drugs, and other necessities for the typical low-income families, officials can minimize the regressive feature of the tax.

27. The author of this selection

    (F) favors the sales tax.
    (G) is opposed to the sales tax.
    (H) gives the facts on both sides.
    (J) wants the sales tax abolished as soon as possible.

28. A major objection to the sales tax is that

    (A) it is too easily collected.
    (B) it brings in an unestimated amount of money.
    (C) it leads to graft and evasion.
    (D) those least able pay as much as those who are wealthy.

29. The sales tax is collected by

    (F) the consumers.
    (G) manufacturers.
    (H) sellers.
    (J) government officials.

30. The sales tax was unknown

    (A) during World War I.
    (B) 25 years ago.
    (C) 50 years ago.
    (D) outside large cities.

The first light of dawn began to spread through the starless gloom that surrounded the ill-fated crew. Hope had long vanished from their minds. The only thing they knew for certain was that they were marooned on an unidentied planet in an uncharted star system. Mel still didn't know why things had gone so wrong! From take-off until *it* happened, their craft had functioned perfectly and had not deviated a fraction of a degree from the prescribed course. Suddenly, all semblance of plan and order disappeared. Every instrument ceased to function. The crew could only guess where they were heading as the ship travelled at an ever-increasing rate of speed. Mercifully, they all lost consciousness. When they came to, they discovered that they had landed without injury to the craft or to themselves. The darkness that surrounded them was impenetrable. Mel held a hasty conference with the crew. They agreed to wait for dawn—if it came—before opening the hatch and exploring where they had landed. Then after what seemed like endless hours, the surrounding blackness began to turn to gray.

31. The crew involved in this selection is

    (F) on board an ocean-going ship.
    (G) traveling across America in a jet plane.
    (H) on a voyage through outerspace.
    (J) army officers on a secret mission.

32. They feel hopeless because

    (A) they have a limited supply of food.
    (B) they have landed in enemy territory.
    (C) they are surrounded by unknowns.
    (D) their ship is disabled.

33. The crew will soon learn

    (F) why they went off their course.
    (G) the damage done to their ship.
    (H) how far they have traveled.
    (J) what the landing site looks like.

34. The leader of the group

    (A) tells the crew what fears he has.
    (B) runs the group democratically.
    (C) tries to establish radio contact
    (D) orders the crew to battle stations.

TEST 7   MATHEMATICS COMPUTATION

Number of questions: 30   *Time limit: 25 minutes*

DIRECTIONS: For numbers 1 through 30, select the correct answer to each problem.

EXAMPLE: $17\overline{)6834}$
(A) 42
(B) 420
(C) 402
(D) 400
(E) None of these

Ⓐ Ⓑ ● Ⓓ Ⓔ

Choice C is correct.

1.   1296
       706
    $+\ 478$

(F) 2,470
(G) 2,380
(H) 2,480
(J) 1,380
(K) None of these

2.   10134
    $-\ 9256$

(A) 1,878
(B) 10,878
(C) 1,868
(D) 868
(E) None of these

3.   6504
    $\times\ 925$

(F) 6,016,210
(G) 5,916,200
(H) 5,016,200
(J) 6,016,200
(K) None of these

4. $356\overline{)176257}$

(A) $495\frac{47}{356}$
(B) $495\frac{37}{356}$
(C) $495\frac{17}{356}$
(D) $493\frac{47}{356}$
(E) None of these

5. $\frac{5}{12} + \frac{7}{8} =$

(F) $1\frac{7}{48}$
(G) $1\frac{9}{24}$
(H) $\frac{12}{20}$
(J) $1\frac{7}{24}$
(K) None of these

6. $7\frac{1}{9} - 2\frac{5}{6} =$

(A) $5\frac{5}{18}$
(B) $4\frac{5}{18}$
(C) $4\frac{7}{18}$
(D) $5\frac{7}{18}$
(E) None of these

7. $2\frac{1}{3} \times 2\frac{4}{7} =$

(F) 6
(G) $4\frac{4}{21}$
(H) $5\frac{4}{21}$
(J) $6\frac{1}{10}$
(K) None of these

8. $5\frac{1}{4} \div 3\frac{3}{8} =$

(A) 1
(B) $1\frac{5}{9}$
(C) $1\frac{2}{3}$
(D) $2\frac{5}{9}$
(E) None of these

9. $47 \times 0.065 =$

(F) 3.055
(G) 3.55
(H) 0.3055
(J) 3.155
(K) None of these

10. $0.76 + 3.04 + 6.2 =$

(A) 9
(B) 9.10
(C) 10.01
(D) 10.10
(E) None of these

11. $2.028 \div 0.6 =$

(F) 33.8
(G) 3.38
(H) 3.308
(J) 3.038
(K) None of these

12.   8 m 34 cm
    $-\ 5$ m 65 cm

(A) 3 m 69 cm
(B) 2 m 39 cm
(C) 2 m 69 cm
(D) 3 m 31 cm
(E) None of these

13. $(-3)(-4)(-5) =$

(F) −12
(G) 60
(H) −35
(J) −60
(K) None of these

14. 3 yd. 2 ft. × 4 =
(A) 13 yd.
(B) 14 yd. 2 ft.
(C) 39 ft.
(D) 14 yd.
(E) None of these

15. $\frac{5}{6} + \left(-\frac{1}{3}\right) =$
(F) $\frac{1}{2}$
(G) $-\frac{1}{2}$
(H) $\frac{4}{3}$
(J) $-\frac{5}{2}$
(K) None of these

16. −7 + (−3)
(A) 10
(B) 21
(C) −10
(D) −21
(E) None of these

17. −9 × (−2)
(F) 18
(G) −18
(H) 11
(J) −11
(K) None of these

18. 8 + (−5)
(A) −3
(B) 3
(C) 13
(D) −13
(E) None of these

19. −6 × 4
(F) −2
(G) −10
(H) −24
(J) 24
(K) None of these

20. −12 ÷ (−3)
(A) 4
(B) −4
(C) 9
(D) 36
(E) None of these

21. 7.39 − 0.8 =
(F) 7.59
(G) 7.31
(H) 6.31
(J) 7.49
(K) None of these

22. (−3)(−5)(4) =
(A) 12
(B) −12
(C) 60
(D) −60
(E) None of these

23. $2\frac{4}{7} + 6\frac{3}{7} =$
(F) $8\frac{1}{7}$
(G) $9\frac{1}{7}$
(H) 8
(J) 9
(K) None of these

24. 3.54 ÷ 0.006 =
(A) 590
(B) 59
(C) 5,900
(D) 583
(E) None of these

25. $\left(5 - \frac{1}{3}\right) ÷ 7$
(F) $\frac{5}{9}$
(G) $\frac{13}{7}$
(H) $1\frac{2}{7}$
(J) $\frac{2}{3}$
(K) None of these

26. $0.25 + \frac{3}{8} - \frac{1}{2} =$
(A) $\frac{1}{4}$
(B) $\frac{1}{2}$
(C) $\frac{5}{8}$
(D) $\frac{3}{8}$
(E) None of these

27. 207 × 30 =
(F) 6,021
(G) 621
(H) 6,210
(J) 62,100
(K) None of these

28. $8 - 2\frac{4}{9} =$
(A) $5\frac{5}{9}$
(B) $6\frac{5}{9}$
(C) $6\frac{1}{3}$
(D) $5\frac{2}{3}$
(E) None of these

29. 0.9 ÷ 0.003 =
(F) 3,000
(G) 3
(H) 30
(J) 300
(K) None of these

30. $6 ÷ 1\frac{1}{3} =$
(A) 8
(B) 4
(C) 9
(D) $2\frac{1}{4}$
(E) None of these

TEST 8   MATHEMATICS CONCEPTS AND APPLICATIONS

Number of questions: 35   *Time limit: 27 minutes*

DIRECTIONS: For numbers 1 through 35, select the correct answer in each case.

1. A plane travels at a speed of 480 miles per hour. How many miles does the plane cover in 40 minutes?

   (A) 360
   (B) 320
   (C) 300
   (D) 350

2. $7^2 \times 7^3 =$

   (F) $7 \times 7 \times 7 \times 7 \times 7 \times 7$
   (G) 57
   (H) 7^5
   (J) 75

3. In the number 6,453 what is the value of the 4?

   (A) 4
   (B) 40
   (C) 4,000
   (D) 400

4. At XYZ College the enrollment consisted of 35% freshmen, 25% sophomores, 20% juniors, and the rest seniors. What fractional part of the enrollment consisted of seniors?

   (F) $\frac{1}{4}$

   (G) $\frac{1}{5}$

   (H) $\frac{1}{6}$

   (J) $\frac{3}{8}$

5. Which of the following sets of numbers may replace the box to make the sentence below true?

   $8 > \square > 5$

   (A) 6, 7
   (B) 6, 7, 8
   (C) 5, 6, 7
   (D) 5, 6, 7, 8

6. At a sale, a radio dealer sells 48 radio sets. This is $\frac{3}{4}$ of the sets on sale. How many sets are on sale?

   (F) 36
   (G) 72
   (H) 54
   (J) 64

7. What are the prime factors of 105?

   (A) 3, 7
   (B) 5, 7
   (C) 5, 21
   (D) 3, 5, 7

8. An auditorium contains 750 seats. When the auditorium is $\frac{5}{6}$ full, how many seats are unoccupied?

   (F) 625
   (G) 125
   (H) 120
   (J) $\frac{1}{6}$

9. On the number line below, the letters represent integers with the origin at O.

   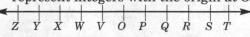

   $2Q + Z =$

   (A) V
   (B) P
   (C) X
   (D) R

10. A cafeteria serves tomato juice in 6-ounce cups. How many servings of tomato juice can be obtained from 9 gallons of tomato juice?

    (F) 182
    (G) 200
    (H) 96
    (J) 192

11. Which of the following represents $\{2, 4, 6, 8, 9\} \cap \{3, 6, 9, 12\}$?

    (A) {2, 3, 4, 6, 8, 9, 12}
    (B) {6}
    (C) {6, 8, 9}
    (D) {6, 9}

12. The difference between two numbers is 6. If one-half of the larger number is 18, find the smaller number.

(F) 3
(G) 30
(H) 42
(J) 9

13. At noon the shadow of a flagpole is 18 feet. At the same time, the shadow of a man 6 feet tall is 4 feet. The height of the flagpole, in feet, is

(A) 10
(B) 27
(C) 18
(D) 15

14. Which of the following is an example of the Associative Property of Addition?

(F) $a + b = b + a$
(G) $a(b + c) = ab + ac$
(H) $(a + b) + c = a + (b + c)$
(J) $a + (b + c) = a + b + ac$

15. The number 1 million may be expressed as

(A) 10^5
(B) 10^6
(C) 10^4
(D) 10^7

16. One kilometer is approximately equal to $\frac{5}{8}$ of 1 mile. If a hiker walks 10 miles, approximately how many kilometers does he walk?

(F) 16
(G) $6\frac{1}{4}$
(H) 6
(J) 12

17. In which case are the numbers arranged in order of value with the largest one first?

(F) $60\%, \frac{2}{3}, 0.69$

(G) $0.75, \frac{4}{5}, 39\%$

(H) $85\%, \frac{5}{6}, 0.78$

(J) $0.09, \frac{1}{8}, 0.21$

18. $\{a, b, c, d, e\} \cup \{a, d, f, g\} =$

(F) $\{a, d\}$
(G) $\{a, b, c, d, f\}$
(H) $\{a, b, d, g\}$
(J) $\{a, b, c, d, e, f, g\}$

19. Which replacement for □ will make the following statement true?

□ $+ 2 < 7$

(A) 5
(B) 6
(C) 4
(D) 7

20. If a pencil costs x cents, then the cost of 5 pencils, in cents, is

(F) $5 + x$
(G) $x - 5$
(H) $x \div 5$
(J) $5x$

21. A dealer bought a table for $60 and sold it at an increase of 35%. What was the selling price of the table?

(A) $95
(B) $71
(C) $75
(D) $81

22. The product of a nonzero real number and its reciprocal is

(F) 0
(G) 1
(H) the number itself
(J) any nonzero number

23. A packing case in the form of a rectangular solid measures 4 feet long, 3 feet wide, and 5 feet high. A manufacturer packs machine parts in boxes measuring 1 foot long, 1 foot wide, and 1 foot high. How many machine part boxes will fit into one packing case?

(A) 12
(B) 20
(C) 60
(D) 15

24. If $3x - 5 = 16$, then the value of x^2 is

    (F) 7
    (G) 14
    (H) 49
    (J) 28

25. If $2x + 1 < 7$, then x may be

    (A) 3
    (B) –1
    (C) 4
    (D) 5

26. Which of the following is equal in value to $65 \times (71 \times 89)$? (Do not multiply or add.)

    (F) $65 \times (71 + 89)$
    (G) $65 + (71 \times 89)$
    (H) $(65 \times 89) \times 71$
    (J) $65 + (71 + 89)$

27. Which of the following fractions has a value between $\frac{3}{7}$ and $\frac{5}{9}$?

    (A) $\frac{2}{3}$

    (B) $\frac{1}{6}$

    (C) $\frac{7}{8}$

    (D) $\frac{6}{11}$

28. If $\triangle ABC \sim \triangle DEF$, then $DF = ?$

    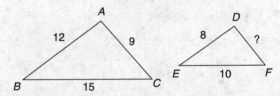

    (F) 6
    (G) 5
    (H) $7\frac{1}{2}$
    (J) $6\frac{1}{2}$

29. A bicycle rider travels 6 miles due north and then 8 miles due east. How many miles is he from his starting point?

    (A) 14
    (B) 10
    (C) 12
    (D) 11

30. The coordinates of point E are

    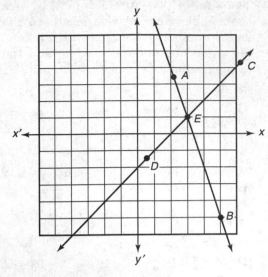

    (F) (3, 1)
    (G) (1, 3)
    (H) (3, 0)
    (J) (1, 2)

31. The diagram below shows how many students in a class at Lincoln High School watch various types of TV programs. How many students watch news and/or sports but not westerns?

    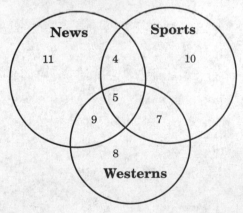

    (A) 25
    (B) 21
    (C) 30
    (D) 38

32. Consider the following problem:
    The sum of two numbers is 23. Twice the smaller number is 5 less than the larger number. Which one of the following equations may be used to find the smaller number?

    (F) $2x = x - 23 - 5$
    (G) $2(23 - x) = x + 5$
    (H) $2(23 - x) = 5 - x$
    (J) $2x = 23 - x - 5$

33. Which of the following sentences is true?

    (A) $4 < -6$
    (B) $-7 > -2$
    (C) $-5 < -2$
    (D) $-4 > 1$

34. 1 gram = 1,000 milligrams
    1 kilogram = 1,000 grams
    The number of milligrams contained in 1 kilogram is

    (F) 1,000
    (G) 100,000
    (H) 10,000
    (J) 1,000,000

35. A square and a triangle have the same area. A side of the square measures 12 inches. If the base of the triangle measures 18 inches, how many inches does the altitude of the triangle measure?

    (A) 12
    (B) 16
    (C) 20
    (D) 15

TEST 9   LANGUAGE MECHANICS

Number of questions: 20   *Time limit: 10 minutes*

DIRECTIONS: For numbers 1 through 5 determine which part of the sentence, if any, has a word that requires a capital letter.

1. Last summer | Paula's aunt | bought a dog | called wiggler.   None
   (A)   (B)   (C)   (D)   (E)

2. Dr. Pipitone | is a professor | at the college | in our town.   None
   (F)   (G)   (H)   (J)   (K)

3. My grandparents | left the north | to live | in a southern city.   None
   (A)   (B)   (C)   (D)   (E)

4. Our president | signed the treaty | between Canada | and our country. None
   (F)   (G)   (H)   (J)   (K)

5. Our next reading | in American literature | is the novel | *On the Street.* None
   (A)   (B)   (C)   (D)   (E)

DIRECTIONS: For numbers 6 through 15 determine which punctuation mark, if any, is required in the sentence.

6. The elephant extended its trunk toward us.
   (F) ,   (G) ;   (H) '   (J) !   (K) None

7. After she had left for school we quickly prepared lunch.
   (A) ,   (B) .   (C) ;   (D) :   (E) None

8. Dear Sir
   (F) .   (G) ;   (H) :   (J) —   (K) None

9. It was selected packed, tied, and shipped this morning.
   (A) ?   (B) .   (C) ,   (D) ;   (E) None

10. The babys toys were scattered over the new porch floor.
   (F) ,   (G) ;   (H) —   (J) '   (K) None

11. I never did it before however, I am most willing to try.

    (A) :   (B) ,   (C) ;   (D) .   (E) None

12. Adam is certain that it was yours that they wanted.

    (F) ,   (G) ;   (H) :   (J) '   (K) None

13. If she does come, what shall I say to her

    (A) "…"   (B) ?   (C) ,   (D) .   (E) None

14. Dorothy please give it to me right now.

    (F) :   (G) .   (H) ,   (J) ?   (K) None

15. Ben told us the news when he saw us entering the school.

    (A) ,   (B) ;   (C) '   (D) "…"   (E) None

DIRECTIONS: For numbers 16 through 20 read the passage and note the underlined, numbered parts. Select the answer that shows the best capitalization and punctuation for each part.

Believe me this was no nightmare! I couldn't believe my eyes the massive creature came
              16   17

closer and closer waving its long arms. I screamed "Won't someone please help me please
            18   19   20

help me!"

16. (F) me; this
    (G) me, this
    (H) me! this
    (J) me, This
    (K) Best as is

17. (A) eyes. The
    (B) eyes' the
    (C) eyes, the
    (D) eyes: the
    (E) Best as is

18. (F) closer waving it's
    (G) closer, waving its'
    (H) closer, waving its
    (J) closer. Waving it's
    (K) Best as is

19. (A) screamed won't
    (B) screamed. "Won't
    (C) screamed, "Won't
    (D) screamed! "Won't
    (E) Best as is

20. (F) me—please
    (G) me, Please
    (H) me! Please
    (J) me: please
    (K) Best as is

TEST 10   LANGUAGE EXPRESSION

Number of questions: 32   *Time limit: 25 minutes*

DIRECTIONS: For numbers 1 through 8, choose the word that best completes the sentence.

1. The replacement part did not fit snugly _____ the mechanic had measured incorrectly.

   (A) , and
   (B) , but
   (C) ; however,
   (D) because

2. Money buys a dog, _____ it doesn't buy the wag of its tail.

   (F) but
   (G) since
   (H) and
   (J) while

3. You begin to cut your wisdom teeth for the first time _____ you bite off more than you can chew.

   (A) if
   (B) when
   (C) because
   (D) although

4. Of the two she is by far the _____ .

   (F) quicker
   (G) quickest
   (H) most quick
   (J) more quicker

5. She always _____ what she is told to do

   (A) did
   (B) done
   (C) does
   (D) do

6. We spoke to _____ students who were interested in the project.

   (F) them
   (G) those
   (H) those there
   (J) them there

7. It is _____ turn now.

   (A) there
   (B) they're
   (C) their
   (D) theyre

8. Paul and _____ work well together.

   (F) myself
   (G) me
   (H) I
   (J) me myself

DIRECTIONS: For numbers 9 through 12 choose the sentence that is correctly written.

9. (A) I agree completely, we could never have done the work without their help.
   (B) I agree that we could not have done the work without their help.
   (C) When we agreed completely that we could not have done the work without their help.
   (D) Having agreed completely that we could not have done the work without their help.

10. (F) Smiling contentedly, he sat wordless, he did not enter the argument.
    (G) He sat wordless and smiled contentedly, he did not enter the argument.
    (H) Not entering the argument, he sat wordless and smiled contentedly.
    (J) Sitting wordless and smiling contentedly because he had not entered the argument.

11. (A) While waiting for the results, Alfred watched a news program and hoped that the telephone would ring.
    (B) Alfred was watching a news program while waiting for the results, he hoped that the phone would ring.
    (C) Hoping that the telephone would ring while he was waiting for the results and watching a news program.

(D) When he was waiting for the results, Alfred watched a news program he hoped that the telephone would ring.

12. (F) Being able to go for that walk now because the wind has died down.
    (G) The wind has died down we can go for that walk now.
    (H) Since the wind has died down, we can go for that walk now.
    (J) Now we can go for that walk, the wind has died down.

DIRECTIONS: For numbers 13 through 17, choose the sentence that is most clearly written.

13. (A) Having spent months in careful preparation, the test proved fairly easy.
    (B) As a result of having spent months in careful preparation, the test proved fairly easy.
    (C) The test proved fairly easy having spent months in careful preparation.
    (D) Having spent months in careful preparation, he found the test fairly easy.

14. (F) Lucy told Susanna that she had won the prize.
    (G) Susanna was told by Lucy that she had won the prize.
    (H) Lucy told Susanna, "You have won the prize!"
    (J) Lucy told Susanna that the prize had been won by her.

15. (A) Adam's favorite pastimes are riding his bicycle and to play computer games.
    (B) Adam's favorite pastimes are riding his bicycle and playing computer games.
    (C) To ride his bicycle and playing computer games are Adam's favorite pastimes.
    (D) The favorite pastimes that Adam has are to ride his bicycle and playing computer games.

16. (F) When three years of age, her parents registered her in the local nursery school.
    (G) At the age of three, her parents registered her in the local nursery school.
    (H) On reaching the age of three, her parents registered her in the local nursery school.
    (J) When she was three, her parents registered her in the local nursery school.

17. (A) We agreed to meet in the evening that morning.
    (B) Ruth said that she would leave on Thursday in her note.
    (C) Turning the cassette player on, we could hear only a loud, continuous buzz.
    (D) After several hours of intensive work, the completed project was ready for the display case.

DIRECTIONS: For numbers 18 through 20, choose the sentence that uses verbs correctly.

18. (F) When the hero finally accepted the villain's challenge, the audience cheers.
    (G) If you had been there, the outcome would have been different!
    (H) Edna will write the note if you wanted her to.
    (J) She has left long before I arrived.

19. (A) When we pressed the button, the alarm goes off.
    (B) If I was in your place, I would apologize right now!
    (C) Having missed the first act, I was unable to follow the action in the play.
    (D) I told them what to say before they made their first offer.

20. (F) We left after the curtain had risen for the last act.
    (G) When he hears my voice, he ran into the store.
    (H) If you came earlier, this would never have happened!
    (J) The bully smirked when he sees how puny our champion was.

DIRECTIONS: For numbers 21 through 24, read the underlined sentences. Then choose the sentence that best combines these sentences into one.

---

21. I walked down the country road.
    I saw three horses.
    They were standing under a huge elm tree.

    (A) I walked down the country road, and I saw three horses, and they were standing under a huge elm tree.
    (B) While walking down the country road, three horses were standing under a huge elm tree.
    (C) While they were standing under a huge elm tree, I walked down the country road and saw three horses.
    (D) When I walked down the country road, I saw three horses standing under a huge elm tree.

22. The bombed-out portion of the cathedral still stands.
    It is being preserved deliberately as a reminder and a symbol.

    (F) The bomb-out portion of the cathedral still stands, a reminder and a symbol which is being preserved deliberately.
    (G) The bombed-out portion of the cathedral still stands, and it is being preserved deliberately as a reminder and a symbol.
    (H) The bombed-out portion of the cathedral, which still stands, is being preserved deliberately as a reminder and a symbol.
    (J) Still standing, the cathedral which had been bombed stands as a reminder and a symbol which is being preserved deliberately.

23. Our car needs a thorough clean-up and polishing.
    It had been the vehicle of choice for our annual family picnic.

    (A) Since it needs a thorough clean-up and polishing, the car has been the vehicle of choice for our annual family picnic.
    (B) Needing a thorough clean-up and polishing, our car has been the vehicle of choice for our annual family picnic.
    (C) Having been the vehicle of choice for our annual family picnic, our car now needs a thorough clean-up and polishing.
    (D) Our car had been the vehicle of choice for our annual family picnic, and it now needs a thorough clean-up and polishing.

24. We bought a small television set.
    Ralph made a shelf for it.
    We plan to use it in the kitchen.

    (F) Ralph made a shelf in the kitchen for the small television set we had bought.
    (G) We bought a small television set, and Ralph made a shelf for it since we plan to use it in the kitchen.
    (H) We plan to use in the kitchen the small television set which we had bought, and Ralph made a shelf for it.
    (J) The small television set we had bought to use in the kitchen needed a shelf, and so Ralph made it.

25. We had to cut our vacation short.
    The car developed engine trouble.
    We spent all our money on the repair.

    (A) Having spent all our money to repair the car when it developed engine trouble, we had to cut our vacation short.
    (B) We had to cut our vacation short when the car developed engine trouble, and we had to spend all our money for the repair.
    (C) The car having developed engine trouble, we spent all of our money on the repair, and thus had to cut our vacation short.

(D) The car developed engine trouble, and we had to spend all our money to repair it, and so we had to cut our vacation short.

DIRECTIONS: For numbers 26 through 28 choose the topic sentence that best fits the paragraph.

---

26. _____ They seemed to be so unreasonable in their demands. She decided that the best thing to do was to run away. As she walked the streets, she realized that her so-called solution would destroy all her hopes and plans. She turned around and retraced her steps.

(F) She left without saying good-bye to her parents.
(G) She had had a serious disagreement with her parents.
(H) It was always easy to discuss problems with her parents.
(J) It was always her policy to let her parents know exactly how she felt.

27. _____ Regardless of how old they are, the buildings of Tibet do not seem to decay. Grains can be stored there for more than half a century without spoiling. Butter and dry raw meat keep for twice that length of time. Despite its dry climate, however, Tibet is the source of all the major rivers of Asia.

(A) There are many fascinating physical features to be found in this thriving country.
(B) Many modern customs and ancient religions have their origin in this fascinating country.
(C) This ancient country is the gateway to the highest peaks in the world.
(D) Beause this ancient country has an average altitude of 15,000 feet, its climate is very dry.

28. _____ During the first 3 weeks, the young worker grooms the queen and her eggs. She cleans out the hive and guards against intruders. She willingly will give up her life to protect the colony. Only after this training period is she allowed to leave the hive and search for nectar and pollen.

(F) The honeybee makes good use of its ability to sting.
(G) Danger is part of the every day life of the honeybee.
(H) Honeybees carry on several occupations.
(J) The honeybee's life is not one of all work and no play.

DIRECTIONS: For numbers 29 through 32 select the pair of sentences that best develops the topic sentence.

---

29. The sun's surface is a violent place.

(A) In ancient times the sun was worshipped as divine. Modern scientists portray it as a moderate-sized variable star.
(B) Solar flares can have a devastating impact on our planet. They can cause radio blackouts and disrupt satellite signals.
(C) Vast explosions take place. Solar flares as powerful as 10 million one-megaton H-bombs erupt often.
(D) Scientists used to assume that the sun's radiance was unwavering. This is not true today.

30. The city of beauty and history, Venice is a metropolis of waterways.

(F) It has a population of over 95,000. It is interlaced with 2,300 alleys.
(G) It remains a pedestrian waterway. Small arched bridges lead the walker over the passing traffic.
(H) Tourists come to see the shops on the Rialto Bridge. In the evening they stroll through Piazza San Marco.
(J) Its main street is the 200-foot-wide Grand Canal. Venice has over 28 miles of winding canals.

31. Accent the positive and think of ways in which that dreaded divebomber, the lowly mosquito, benefits human beings.

    (A) They serve as a source of protein for fish and birds. When feeding on plant nectar, they pollinate wild-flowers.
    (B) Mosquitoes, given a choice, prefer to dine on some other animals. They are known to dig into horses and cows rather than into us.
    (C) Females lay more than 400 eggs at a time. They reproduce several times during their lifetime.
    (D) Male mosquitoes do not bite for blood. They do not, as do the females, transmit disease to human beings.

32. As Mayor of San Antonio, Henry Cisneros stressed business expansion as the solution to unemployment and slums.

    (F) He was the first Hispanic to be elected mayor of a large city. He is a natural politician.
    (G) He is superbly well organized. He is an energetic list-maker.
    (H) He was born in 1947. His father's family had been in this country for several generations.
    (J) He persuaded large concerns to establish factories in his city. He thus brought new jobs to the depressed western side of town

Answers to Practice Cooperative Admissions Examination 1

TEST 1   SEQUENCES

1. C	5. D	9. C	13. B	17. B
2. G	6. H	10. F	14. J	18. J
3. D	7. D	11. C	15. B	19. A
4. F	8. G	12. F	16. J	20. G

Rating Your Results

Superior	17–20 correct
Average	13–16 correct
Below Average	12 or fewer correct

Material to Review: Chapter 13

TEST 2   ANALOGIES

1. C	5. B	9. D	13. B	17. C
2. G	6. H	10. H	14. J	18. D
3. D	7. B	11. A	15. B	19. G
4. F	8. F	12. H	16. F	20. C

Rating Your Results

Superior	17–20 correct
Average	13–16 correct
Below Average	12 or fewer correct

Material to Review: Chapter 13

TEST 3   MEMORY

1. D	5. A	9. C	13. E	17. A
2. G	6. K	10. H	14. G	18. J
3. E	7. E	11. B	15. D	19. E
4. F	8. G	12. H	16. J	20. J

Rating Your Results

Superior	17–20 correct
Average	12–16 correct
Below Average	11 or fewer correct

Material to Review: Chapter 13

TEST 4   VERBAL REASONING

1. C	5. C	9. D	13. B	17. D
2. G	6. J	10. F	14. H	18. J
3. D	7. B	11. C	15. C	19. B
4. F	8. G	12. G	16. J	20. J

Rating Your Results

Superior	17–20 correct
Average	13–16 correct
Below Average	12 or fewer correct

Material to Review: Chapter 4

TEST 5   READING VOCABULARY

1. H	9. H	17. J	25. H	33. G
2. D	10. B	18. D	26. D	34. D
3. F	11. H	19. G	27. J	35. G
4. D	12. B	20. C	28. B	36. A
5. G	13. F	21. J	29. F	37. J
6. D	14. C	22. D	30. C	38. B
7. F	15. G	23. F	31. G	39. J
8. A	16. B	24. D	32. A	40. C

Rating Your Results

Superior	27-40 correct
Average	23-26 correct
Below Average	22 or fewer correct

Material to Review: Chapter 4

TEST 6   READING COMPREHENSION

1. J	8. D	15. G	22. C	29. H
2. B	9. J	16. C	23. F	30. A
3. H	10. B	17. H	24. C	31. H
4. C	11. J	18. D	25. H	32. C
5. H	12. A	19. H	26. A	33. J
6. A	13. H	20. D	27. H	34. B
7. G	14. D	21. F	28. D	

Rating Your Results

Superior	32–34 correct
Average	27–31 correct
Below Average	30 or fewer correct

Material to Review: Chapter 5

TEST 7   MATHEMATICS COMPUTATION

1. H	7. F	13. J	19. H	25. J
2. E	8. B	14. B	20. A	26. E
3. J	9. F	15. F	21. K	27. H
4. B	10. E	16. C	22. C	28. A
5. J	11. G	17. F	23. J	29. J
6. B	12. C	18. B	24. A	30. E

Rating Your Results

Superior	27–30 correct
Average	20–25 correct
Below Average	19 or fewer correct

Material to Review: Chapters 7–12

TEST 8   MATHEMATICS CONCEPTS AND APPLICATIONS

1. B	8. G	15. B	22. G	29. B
2. H	9. A	16. F	23. C	30. F
3. D	10. J	17. C	24. H	31. A
4. G	11. D	18. J	25. B	32. J
5. A	12. G	19. C	26. H	33. C
6. J	13. B	20. J	27. D	34. J
7. D	14. H	21. D	28. F	35. B

Rating Your Results

Superior	32–35 correct
Average	24–31 correct
Below Average	23 or fewer correct

Material to Review: Chapters 7–12

TEST 9   LANGUAGE MECHANICS

1. D	5. B	9. C	13. B	17. A
2. K	6. K	10. J	14. H	18. H
3. B	7. A	11. C	15. E	19. C
4. F	8. H	12. K	16. G	20. H

Rating Your Results

Superior	18–20 correct
Average	15–17 correct
Below Average	14 or fewer correct

Material to Review: Chapter 6

TEST 10   LANGUAGE EXPRESSION

1. D	8. H	15. B	21. D	27. D
2. F	9. B	16. J	22. H	28. H
3. B	10. H	17. C	23. C	29. C
4. F	11. A	18. G	24. F	30. J
5. C	12. H	19. C	25. A	31. A
6. G	13. D	20. F	26. G	32. J
7. C	14. H			

Rating Your Results

Superior	30–32 correct
Average	26–29 correct
Below Average	25 or fewer correct

Material to Review: Chapter 6

Answer Explanations

TEST 1 SEQUENCES

1. **(C)** As we go from left to right the position of one circle is moved one place to the right. In the fourth section, the one circle appears in the last place to the right.

2. **(G)** In this case, the pattern consists of a darkened figure followed by a light figure of the same type, and this is followed by two darkened figures of the same type. Therefore, the fourth section has two darkened figures.

3. **(D)** In each section, the arrows point in opposite directions.

4. **(F)** Each section has a circle followed by a rectangle. Atop each circle is a small rectangle, either light or darkened. The pattern atop the rectangles is light circle, light circle, dark circle, dark circle.

5. **(D)** The sections may be described as triangle-ellipse, triangle-triangle, triangle-ellipse, triangle-triangle, and triangle-ellipse. No ellipse is darkened.

6. **(H)** In each section, a single, small darkened circle is attached above each figure.

7. **(D)** In each section, the first number is multiplied by 4 to obtain the second number and the second number is multiplied by 4 to obtain the third number.

8. **(G)** In each section, the first number is doubled to obtain the second number and the second number is reduced by 10 to obtain the third number.

9. **(C)** Note the pattern as shown below:
$$3 + 4 = 7, \qquad 7 + 8 = 15$$
$$4 + 5 = 9, \qquad 9 + 10 = 19$$
$$5 + 6 = 11, \qquad 11 + 12 = 23$$

10. **(F)** Note the pattern as shown below:
$$76 - 72 = 4, \qquad 72 - 67 = 5$$
$$63 - 58 = 5, \qquad 58 - 52 = 6$$
$$45 - 37 = 8, \qquad 37 - 28 = 9$$

11. **(C)** In each section, the number is 1 greater than the first number and the third number is the square of the first number.

12. **(F)** Note the pattern as shown below:
$$2 + 2 = 4, \qquad 4 + 6 = 10$$
$$3 + 4 = 7, \qquad 7 + 12 = 19$$
$$4 + 6 = 10, \qquad 10 + 18 = 28$$

13. **(B)** In each group, the difference between the first two numbers is 1 and the difference between the second and third numbers is 2.

14. **(J)** In each section, the second number is 7 less than the first number and the third number is one-half the second number.

15. **(B)** Note the pattern as shown below (A is omitted since it remains the same throughout).
$$B_1C_1 \quad B_2C_2 \quad B_3C_3$$
$$B_1C_2 \quad B_2C_3$$

16. **(J)** As we move from left to right the subscript R is reduced by 1, the subscript of S is increased by 1, and the subscript of T is reduced by 1.

17. **(B)** In each case, the last two letters are the first two letters of the next group of three letters.

18. **(J)** In each case, as we move from left to right, the first letters are arranged alphabetically, the second letters are arranged alphabetically and the third letters are arranged alphabetically, as follows:
First letters—A, B, C, D, ...
Second letters—C, D, E, F, ...
Third letters—E, F, G, H, ...

19. **(A)** In each case, as we move from left to right, the last two letters of each group are the first two letters of the next group, but in reverse order. Thus, the letters FC must begin the missing group.

20. **(G)** Note the pattern of the first and third letter of each group: A, B, C, D, ... Also note the pattern of the second letters of each group: R, S, T, U, ...

TEST 2 ANALOGIES

1. **(C)** A tie is worn with a shirt and a necklace is worn with a dress.

2. (**G**) An automobile tire fits around a wheel and a picture frame fits around a painting.

3. (**D**) A kennel is a dog's home and a fish bowl is a fish's home.

4. (**F**) A cello and a violin are stringed instruments and a tuba and a trumpet are brass instruments.

5. (**B**) A brush is used on a canvas and a spatula is used on a frying pan.

6. (**H**) A golf club is used to hit a golf ball and a hammer is used to strike a nail.

7. (**B**) A square can be thought of as a picture of a cube in two dimensions, and a circle can be thought of as a picture of a sphere in two dimensions.

8. (**F**) A clock is frequently fastened to a wall and an odometer is usually part of a car instrument panel.

9. (**D**) A carpenter uses a saw and a writer uses a typewriter.

10. (**H**) A pen is used to write on paper and chalk is used to write on a blackboard.

11. (**A**) A fisherman uses a line and a hunter uses a rifle.

12. (**H**) A stethoscope is used by a medical doctor and a pestle is used by a pharmacist.

13. (**B**) A cookie is a small baked dessert and a pie is a large baked dessert. A hamburger is a small meat portion and a sirloin steak is a large meat portion.

14. (**J**) An egg is the product of a chicken and an apple is the product of a tree.

15. (**B**) A hat is worn on the head and a sleeve is worn on the arm.

16. (**F**) An orchestra is led by a conductor and a team is led by a coach.

17. (**C**) A lawyer does his work in court and at waitress does her work at a restaurant table.

18. (**J**) A boxer spends his time in the ring and a bird spends its time in a cage.

19. (**B**) A man lives in a house and a bear lives in a cave.

20. (**H**) A book is kept in a book case and a dish is kept in a dish closet.

TEST 3 MEMORY

Here are some suggested associations and mental pictures.

1. (**D**) Nene can be associated with the grunting sounds a goose makes when it is feeding.

2. (**G**) We need heat (heimal) in winter.

3. (**E**) Brool sounds like a low roar.

4. (**F**) A de*tergent* (ab*sterge*) is an aid to wiping clean.

5. (**A**) Sarwan sounds exotic enough to associate with an exotic beast of burden, the camel.

6. (**K**) Guttle can be associated with guzzle.

7. (**E**) Bova*ristic* can be associated (rhymed) with ego*tistic*.

8. (**G**) Impofo can be associated with impala, a relative of the antelope.

9. (**C**) Ecdemic can be broken down into *ec* (outside) and *dem* (people), that is, foreign people.

10. (**H**) In the word *elute,* the prefix *e* comes from *ex,* meaning out.

11. (**B**) Mussitation can be associated with the fuss a grumbler makes over almost everything.

12. (**H**) Flagitate can be associated with the white flag that signals surrender and a plea for mercy.

13. (**E**) *Erept*ation can be associated with a creeping *rep*tile.

14. (**G**) Robust (the result of strengthening) can be associated with robarant.

15. (**D**) When you say the word *tautog,* picture a fish darting and changing direction in the water.

16. (**J**) Here's a mnemonic to use for cumshaw: "*Come show* me the tip you were given."

17. **(A)** Here's a mnemonic to use for abaction: "There's a lot of *action* when cattle are stolen."

18. **(J)** *Circ*u*rate* can be associated with *circus,* where tame animals perform.

19. **(E)** To show shrewdness and cunning, a person must be callous (hard); associate callidity with callous.

20. **(J)** When you say the word *queme,* form a mental picture of yourself enjoying a pleasant experience.

TEST 4 VERBAL REASONING

1. **(C)** Water is a necessary part of an aquarium.

2. **(G)** Food of some kind (it need not be a sandwich) is a necessary part of lunch.

3. **(D)** Blades are necessary parts of a helicopter.

4. **(F)** Strings are necessary parts of a cello.

5. **(C)** Sound is a necessary part of music.

6. **(J)** Thread is a necessary part of textiles.

7. **(B)** Marchers are necessary to a parade.

8. **(G)** Soccer and baseball are kinds of sports. A forward and a catcher are kinds of athletes.

9. **(D)** A hat and a coat are kinds of clothing. A man and a child are kinds of persons.

10. **(F)** A chair and a sofa are kinds of furniture. A game and a movie are kinds of entertainment.

11. **(C)** Meat and dessert are kinds of dinner food. Cereal and juice are kinds of breakfast foocl.

12. **(G)** A floor and walls are essential for a building. A refrigerator and an oven are needed in a kitchen.

13. **(B)** *walamiz* means anywhere
     shermiz means anybody
Therefore, *miz* must mean "any" since *miz* is common to both foreign words and *any* is common to both English words.

Also, *wala* means "where" and *sher* means "body." Since *thowala* means "somewhere" and *wala* means "where," *tho* must mean "some." Thus, *somebody* is represented by *thosher.*

14. **(H)** *ebalfull* means driveway
     milfull means walkway
Therefore, *full* must mean "way" since *full* is common to both foreign words and *way* is common to both English words.
Also, *ebal* means "drive" and *mil* means "walk." Since *ebalsap* means "driveshaft" and *ebal* means "drive," *sap* must mean "shaft." Thus, *shaftway* is represented by *sapfull.*

15. **(C)** There is no evidence that Jim and Ruth enjoy every evening, go out every night, or do not like their home.

16. **(J)** No specific information is given as to what countries the United States trades with, apart from Japan and Western Europe. There is no indication of the feelings of other countries. The last sentence supports choice J.

17. **(D)** Choices A, B, and C are not supported by facts given in passage. Dan Taylor must be a fine student if he is an honor student. Since he plays on three varsity teams, he is a good athlete.

18. **(J)** The passage does not support choice F. Choice G is inaccurate; a suit could be bought at the apparel store. Choice H may or may not be true; the last sentence refers only to peak shopping periods.

19. **(B)** Choice A is untrue: "He often flies"; C is untrue: "Juan prefers to plan his own trips"; D may or may not be true. According to the paragraph, Juan "rents a car and visits places of interest" (choice B).

20. **(J)** Choice F is wrong; the passage makes it clear that Teresa and Frank enjoy life. Nothing in the passage supports choice G. The last sentence suggests that they find time for their friends, rather than visiting "infrequently" (choice H). Finally, "They bowl every Tuesday evening" directly supports choice J.

TEST 5 READING VOCABULARY

1.–10. There is only one synonym for each given word.

11.–20. There is only one antonym for each given word.

21. (**J**) A person who spends "as little as possible" is *thrifty*.

22. (**D**) The clue "beloved scenes of childhood" leads to *sentimental*.

23. (**F**) "Consent … rudely" leads to *grudging*.

24. (**D**) A youngster who is "afraid to ask" is likely to be *timid*.

25. (**H**) "Vicious rumors" need an *antidote,* a remedy.

26. (**D**) "Despite'" leads to *continued*.

27. (**J**) "Unexpected or sudden twists" try one's *mettle,* that is, staying quality.

28. (**B**) A good-natured person accepts even *tedious* (boring) tasks.

29. (**F**) "Distrust" is likely to *impair* (damage) a friendship.

30. (**C**) A person who "speaks in paragraphs" is *loquacious* (talkative).

31.–40. In each case there is only one word that means the same as the two given words or phrases.

TEST 6 READING COMPREHENSION

1. (**J**) "Jeff had plotted our destruction" and "None would escape . . ." indicate that all will die.

2. (**B**) Nowhere in the passage is Jeff's motive revealed.

3. (**H**) The key is in the sentence "There was no escape."

4. (**C**) There is no humor reflected in the passage. It could be part of a mystery story, adventure story, or soap opera.

5. (**H**) The fourth and fifth sentences reveal the answer.

6. (**A**) The author states that "prisons and reform schools have become training laboratories for crimes."

7. (**G**) A holding pen is used to contain cattle or sheep.

8. (**D**) "We have to rethink … punishing crime." Big changes are called for.

9. (**J**) See line 5: "Boundaries drawn to suit the convenience of Europeans.…"

10. (**B**) The reference to "customs and traditions" implies the answer.

11. (**J**) Conflict is indicated in "The problem...is how to combine tribalism and nationalism."

12. (**A**) The answer can be inferred from "Tribalism and nationalism should... reinforce each other."

13. (**H**) We are told the earth is continuously being bombarded.

14. (**D**) As shooting stars speed through the earth's atmosphere, friction causes the particles to glow, so that they are visible.

15. (**G**) "… speeds from 10 to 20 miles a second" equals $10 \times 60 \times 60 = 36,000$ mph.

16. (**C**) "Most of these...burn up completely and disappear.…"

17. (**H**) The passage gives no specific clues about the daily number.

18. (**D**) Two thousand years ago Columbus (choice A) wasn't even born. The Pueblos (choice B) came later. The air was hot and dry; therefore, it was not during the Ice Age (choice C) that the Hohokam came.

19. (**H**) See the last sentence: "Only ruins and fragments of pottery remain as evidence …"

20. (**D**) The Hohokam were known as *Canal Builders*; thus we can infer that they solved the water problem by building irrigation ditches.

21. (**F**) We are told (line 9) that the Pueblo overran the Hohokam.

22. (**C**) In line 3, "a wavelength of visible light" is mentioned.

23. (**F**) Lines 9 and 10 state that electron microscopes can be used only with *dead* tissue.

24. **(C)** Until 1930, only the light microscope was in use.

25. **(H)** Electron microscopes provide magnification of 100,000 times or more.

26. **(A)** Line 8 tells us that an image is produced on a screen.

27. **(H)** The author gives the views of both opponents and advocates of the sales tax.

28. **(D)** According to lines 5 and 6, the sales tax "weighs most heavily on the lower income groups."

29. **(H)** Line 1 states that the tax is added when the article is sold.

30. **(A)** World War I ended in 1918; the first sales tax appeared in West Virginia in 1921.

31. **(H)** They are marooned on an unknown planet in "an uncharted system."

32. **(C)** The ship has landed in "an uncharted star system"; the crew will explore their surroundings at dawn.

33. **(J)** The last sentence tells that it was getting lighter, and the crew would be able to see their surroundings.

34. **(B)** The reference to the "hasty conference with the crew" implies a democratic attitude on Mel's part.

TEST 8 MATHEMATICS CONCEPTS AND APPLICATIONS

1. **(B)** 40 minutes = $\frac{40}{60}$, or $\frac{2}{3}$ of an hour
   $\frac{2}{3} \times 480 = 320$

2. **(H)** $7^2 = 7 \times 7$, $7^3 = 7 \times 7 \times 7$
   $7^2 \times 7^3 = 7 \times 7 \times 7 \times 7 \times 7 = 7^5$

3. **(D)** $6,453 = 6,000 + 400 + 50 + 3$
   The 4 represents 400.

4. **(G)** The entire enrollment is represented by 100%.
   $35\% + 25\% + 20\% = 80\%$
   $100\% - 80\% = 20$; the seniors are 20% = $\frac{1}{5}$

5. **(A)** The sentence $8 > \square > 5$ states that the numbers that may be placed in $\square$ are less than 8 and greater than 5. The

number 7 is less than 8 and greater than 5. Also, the number 6 is less than 8 and greater than 5. Thus, the members 7 and 6 may replace $\square$.

6. **(J)** $\frac{3}{4}$ of the sets on sale = 48 sets
   $\frac{1}{4}$ of the sets on sale = $48 \div 3 = 16$ sets
   $\frac{4}{4}$, or all the sets on sale = $16 \times 4 = 64$ sets.

7. **(D)** 3, 5, and 7 are factors of 105. Also 3, 5, and 7 are prime numbers.

8. **(G)** $750 \times \frac{5}{6} = 125 \times 5 = 625$ seats were occupied.
   $750 - 625 = 125$ seats were unoccupied.

9. **(A)** Q represents 2 and Z represents –5.
   $2Q + Z = 2(2) - 5 = 4 - 5 = -1$
   –1 is represented by V.

10. **(J)** 1 quart = 32 fluid ounces
    4 quarts = 1 gallon = $4 \times 32 = 128$ fluid ounces
    $9 \times 128 = 1,152$ ounces, $1,152 \div 6 = 192$

11. **(D)** The symbol $\cap$ represents intersection. The intersection of two sets consists of all elements that are members of both sets. Only the elements 6 and 9 are members of both sets.

12. **(G)** If one-half the larger number is 18, then the larger number is $2 \times 18 = 36$. The smaller number is 6 less than the larger number, or $36 - 6 = 30$.

13. **(B)** Since the triangles are similar the lengths of corresponding sides are in proportion.

$$\frac{x}{6} = \frac{18}{4}$$
$$4x = 108$$
$$x = 27$$

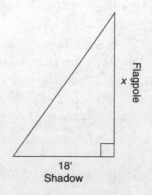

14. **(H)** The Associative Property of Addition states that it does not matter how the terms are grouped (or associated) in performing addition. Thus, first grouping $(a + b)$ and then adding c will give the same result as adding a to the grouping of $(b + c)$. Therefore, $(a + b) + c = a + (b + c)$.

15. **(B)** 1 million = 1,000,000
$10^1 = 10$, $10^2 = 100$, $10^3 = 1,000$, $10^4 = 10,000$, $10^5 = 100,000$, $10^6 = 1,000,000$.

16. **(F)** Let m = the number of miles and k = the number of kilometers. Since each kilometer is approximately equal to $\frac{5}{8}$ of a mile, the number of miles covered is equal approximately to $\frac{5}{8}$ of the number of kilometers, or

$$m = \tfrac{5}{8}k$$
$$8m = 5k$$
$$k = \tfrac{8}{5}m$$

If $m = 10$, we have $k = \frac{8}{5} \times 10 = 16$

17. **(C)** If we write all numbers as decimals we can make comparisons readily:
A. 0.60, 0.66 $\frac{2}{3}$, 0.69—largest one is not first.
B. 0.75, 0.80, 0.39—largest one is not first.
C. 0.85, 0.83 $\frac{1}{3}$, 0.78—arranged in order of value with the largest one first.
D. 0.09, 0.125, 0.21—largest one is not first.

18. **(J)** The symbol $\cup$ is used to designate the union of sets. The union of two sets consists of the elements in the first set plus the elements in the second set.

19. **(C)** $\square + 2 < 7$
The sum of the two numbers on the left side of the inequality must be less than 7. If we replace $\square$ by 4 we have $4 + 2 < 7$, a correct sentence.

20. **(J)** In order to obtain the cost we must multiply the number of pencils bought by the cost of each pencil, obtaining $5x$.

21. **(D)** 35% of 60 = $0.35 \times 60 = 21.0$
Selling price = cost + profit = $60 + 21$ = $81.

22. **(G)** By definition, the product of two reciprocal nonzero real numbers is 1.

23. **(C)** The volume of the packing case = $4 \times 3 \times 5 = 60$ cubic feet. The volume of each box = $1 \times 1 \times 1 = 1$ cubic foot. Therefore, 60 boxes will fit into the packing case.

24. **(H)** $3x - 5 = 16$
$$3x = 16 + 5 = 21$$
$$x = 7$$
$$x^2 = x \cdot x = 7 \cdot 7 = 49$$

25. **(B)** $2x + 1 < 7$
$$2x < 7 - 1$$
$$2x < 6$$
$$x < 3$$
Of the choices given, only -1 is less than 3.

26. **(H)** $65 \times (71 \times 89) = 65 \times (89 \times 71)$—Commutative Property of Multiplication
$65 \times (89 \times 71) = (65 \times 89) \times 71$—Associated Property of Multiplication

27. **(D)** $\frac{39}{7} = 0.42\frac{6}{7}$, $\frac{5}{9} = 0.55\frac{5}{9}$, $\frac{6}{11} = 0.54\frac{6}{11}$

28. **(F)** Since the triangles are similar, the lengths of the corresponding sides are in proportion.

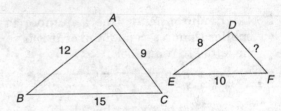

$$\frac{DF}{9} = \frac{10}{15}$$
$$15 \times DF = 10 \times 9 = 90$$
$$DF = 90 \div 15 = 6$$

29. **(B)** We use the Pythagorean Theorem,

$$x^2 = 8^2 + 6^2$$
$$x^2 = 64 + 36$$
$$x^2 = 100$$
$$x = \sqrt{100} = 10$$

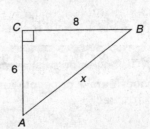

30. **(F)** Point *E* is 3 units to the right of the *y*-axis and 1 unit above the *x*-axis. The coordinates of point *E* are (3, 1).

31. **(A)** 11 students watch only the news, 10 students watch only the sports, and 4 students watch news and sports: 11 + 10 + 4 = 25 students watch news and sports but not westerns.

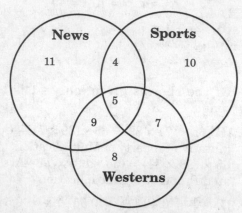

32. **(J)** Let *x* = the smaller number and 23 − *x* = the larger number. Twice small number = larger number − 5: 2*x* = 23 − *x* − 5

33. **(C)** On the number line a number is smaller than a second number if it is to the left of that number.

$$-8\ -7\ -6\ -5\ -4\ -3\ -2\ -1\ \ 0\ \ 1\ \ 2\ \ 3\ \ 4\ \ 5\ \ 6\ \ 7\ \ 8$$

We see that −5 is to the left of −2, or −5 < −2.

34. **(J)** 1 kilogram = 1,000 grams
1 gram = 1,000 milligrams
1,000 grams = 1,000 × 1,000 milligrams = 1,000,000 milligrams

35. **(B)** Area of the square = 12 × 12 = 144 square inches.
Therefore, area of the triangle = 144 square inches.
Area of a triangle = $\frac{1}{2}$ × base × altitude
144 = $\frac{1}{2}$(18) × altitude
144 = 9 × altitude
Altitude = 144 ÷ 9 = 16 inches

TEST 9   LANGUAGE MECHANICS

1. **(D)** Proper names of people and animals are capitalized.

2. **(K)** Titles are not capitalized unless they precede a person's name. The word *college* is not capitalized unless it is preceded by a specific name.

3. **(B)** Names of regions, such as the North, are capitalized.

4. **(F)** A title that refers to a specific person of high rank is capitalized.

5. **(B)** A proper adjective is capitalized.

6. **(K)** The possessive pronoun *its* is an exception to the possessive rule and requires no apostrophe; *it's* means *it is*.

7. **(A)** An introductory clause is set of by a comma.

8. **(H)** Salutation requires a comma or a colon.

9. **(C)** Words in series are set of by commas.

10. **(J)** An apostrophe is needed to show that the *toys* belong to the *baby*.

11. **(C)** A semicolon precedes *however* when it joins two ideas.

12. **(K)** The pronoun *yours* shows possession without an apostrophe.

13. **(B)** The question mark is terminal punctuation for a question.

14. **(H)** An introductory noun in direct address is set off by a comma.

15. **(E)** An adverbial clause at the end of a sentence is *not* set off by a comma.

16. **(G)** An introductory incidental remark is set off by a comma.

17. **(A)** Two complete ideas are punctuated as separate sentences.

18. **(H)** The possessive form is *its*. A participial phrase requires an introductory comma.

19. **(C)** A comma is used to separate a direct statement from the rest of the sentence.

20. **(H)** Complete ideas must be punctuated as separate sentences.

TEST 10 LANGUAGE EXPRESSION

1. (**D**) The causal relationship requires *because*.

2. (**F**) Contrast is expressed by *but*.

3. (**B**) The time relationship is developed by *when*.

4. (**F**) When two persons or things are compared, the correct form is *quicker*.

5. (**C**) The present *does* agrees with the tense of the second verb, *is told*.

6. (**G**) The proper adjective form is *those*. *Them* is a pronoun.

7. (**C**) The possessive form is *their*.

8. (**H**) The subject form of the first-person pronoun is *I*.

9. (**B**) Choice F is a run-on sentence; H and J are sentence fragments.

10. (**H**) Choices A and B are run-on sentences; D is a sentence fragment.

11. (**A**) Choices G and J are run-on sentences; H is a sentence fragment.

12. (**H**) Choice A is a sentence fragment; B and D are run-on sentences.

13. (**D**) *Having spent* cannot modify *test*. In choice J an appropriate subject, *we,* is provided.

14. (**H**) The identity of *she* or, in choice D, *her* must be clarified.

15. (**B**) *Riding* and *playing* provide parallel construction.

16. (**J**) The daughter, not the parents, was three years old.

17. (**C**) Choice F has evening and morning too close together; G has Ruth leaving in a note; J has the project working intensively. Choice H is correct and clear; *we* did the *turning*.

18. (**G**) In choice B, past tenses are used correctly for a condition contrary to fact.

19. (**C**) Both *having missed* and *was* are past tenses.

20. (**F**) The past perfect *had risen* is used correctly for an action that preceded another past action, *left*.

21. (**D**) This choice shows the correct action sequence (*walked, saw*) and subordination of less important elements; *I saw three horses* is the main idea.

22. (**H**) This choice is correct because of proper subordination of the less important idea, *which still stands*.

23. (**C**) Choice H is correct because it shows the correct relationship of the two ideas.

24. (**F**) is correct because of word economy, proper sequence of actions, and correct relationship of ideas.

25. (**A**) is correct because of word economy, proper sequence of actions and correct relationship of ideas.

26. (**G**) All of the actions that follow—the decision, the walking, the realization, the turning back—result from the disagreement with her parents.

27. (**D**) All of the facts mentioned are results of the dry climate mentioned in choice J.

28. (**H**) The paragraph describes the several occupations of the workers and the queen.

29. (**C**) The key word is *violent*.

30. (**J**) The key word is *waterways*.

31. (**A**) Feeding fish and birds and pollinating flowers benefit human beings.

32. (**J**) Bringing in new factories means business expansion.

Answer Sheet
Practice Cooperative Admissions Examination 2

TEST 1   SEQUENCES

1. Ⓐ Ⓑ Ⓒ Ⓓ	5. Ⓐ Ⓑ Ⓒ Ⓓ	9. Ⓐ Ⓑ Ⓒ Ⓓ	13. Ⓐ Ⓑ Ⓒ Ⓓ	17. Ⓐ Ⓑ Ⓒ Ⓓ
2. Ⓕ Ⓖ Ⓗ Ⓙ	6. Ⓕ Ⓖ Ⓗ Ⓙ	10. Ⓕ Ⓖ Ⓗ Ⓙ	14. Ⓕ Ⓖ Ⓗ Ⓙ	18. Ⓕ Ⓖ Ⓗ Ⓙ
3. Ⓐ Ⓑ Ⓒ Ⓓ	7. Ⓐ Ⓑ Ⓒ Ⓓ	11. Ⓐ Ⓑ Ⓒ Ⓓ	15. Ⓐ Ⓑ Ⓒ Ⓓ	19. Ⓐ Ⓑ Ⓒ Ⓓ
4. Ⓕ Ⓖ Ⓗ Ⓙ	8. Ⓕ Ⓖ Ⓗ Ⓙ	12. Ⓕ Ⓖ Ⓗ Ⓙ	16. Ⓕ Ⓖ Ⓗ Ⓙ	20. Ⓕ Ⓖ Ⓗ Ⓙ

TEST 2   ANALOGIES

1. Ⓐ Ⓑ Ⓒ Ⓓ	5. Ⓐ Ⓑ Ⓒ Ⓓ	9. Ⓐ Ⓑ Ⓒ Ⓓ	13. Ⓐ Ⓑ Ⓒ Ⓓ	17. Ⓐ Ⓑ Ⓒ Ⓓ
2. Ⓕ Ⓖ Ⓗ Ⓙ	6. Ⓕ Ⓖ Ⓗ Ⓙ	10. Ⓕ Ⓖ Ⓗ Ⓙ	14. Ⓕ Ⓖ Ⓗ Ⓙ	18. Ⓕ Ⓖ Ⓗ Ⓙ
3. Ⓐ Ⓑ Ⓒ Ⓓ	7. Ⓐ Ⓑ Ⓒ Ⓓ	11. Ⓐ Ⓑ Ⓒ Ⓓ	15. Ⓐ Ⓑ Ⓒ Ⓓ	19. Ⓐ Ⓑ Ⓒ Ⓓ
4. Ⓕ Ⓖ Ⓗ Ⓙ	8. Ⓕ Ⓖ Ⓗ Ⓙ	12. Ⓕ Ⓖ Ⓗ Ⓙ	16. Ⓕ Ⓖ Ⓗ Ⓙ	20. Ⓕ Ⓖ Ⓗ Ⓙ

TEST 3   MEMORY

1. Ⓐ Ⓑ Ⓒ Ⓓ Ⓔ	6. Ⓕ Ⓖ Ⓗ Ⓙ Ⓚ	11. Ⓐ Ⓑ Ⓒ Ⓓ Ⓔ	16. Ⓕ Ⓖ Ⓗ Ⓙ Ⓚ
2. Ⓕ Ⓖ Ⓗ Ⓙ Ⓚ	7. Ⓐ Ⓑ Ⓒ Ⓓ Ⓔ	12. Ⓕ Ⓖ Ⓗ Ⓙ Ⓚ	17. Ⓐ Ⓑ Ⓒ Ⓓ Ⓔ
3. Ⓐ Ⓑ Ⓒ Ⓓ Ⓔ	8. Ⓕ Ⓖ Ⓗ Ⓙ Ⓚ	13. Ⓐ Ⓑ Ⓒ Ⓓ Ⓔ	18. Ⓕ Ⓖ Ⓗ Ⓙ Ⓚ
4. Ⓕ Ⓖ Ⓗ Ⓙ Ⓚ	9. Ⓐ Ⓑ Ⓒ Ⓓ Ⓔ	14. Ⓕ Ⓖ Ⓗ Ⓙ Ⓚ	19. Ⓐ Ⓑ Ⓒ Ⓓ Ⓔ
5. Ⓐ Ⓑ Ⓒ Ⓓ Ⓔ	10. Ⓕ Ⓖ Ⓗ Ⓙ Ⓚ	15. Ⓐ Ⓑ Ⓒ Ⓓ Ⓔ	20. Ⓕ Ⓖ Ⓗ Ⓙ Ⓚ

TEST 4   VERBAL REASONING

1. Ⓐ Ⓑ Ⓒ Ⓓ	5. Ⓐ Ⓑ Ⓒ Ⓓ	9. Ⓐ Ⓑ Ⓒ Ⓓ	13. Ⓐ Ⓑ Ⓒ Ⓓ	17. Ⓐ Ⓑ Ⓒ Ⓓ
2. Ⓕ Ⓖ Ⓗ Ⓙ	6. Ⓕ Ⓖ Ⓗ Ⓙ	10. Ⓕ Ⓖ Ⓗ Ⓙ	14. Ⓕ Ⓖ Ⓗ Ⓙ	18. Ⓕ Ⓖ Ⓗ Ⓙ
3. Ⓐ Ⓑ Ⓒ Ⓓ	7. Ⓐ Ⓑ Ⓒ Ⓓ	11. Ⓐ Ⓑ Ⓒ Ⓓ	15. Ⓐ Ⓑ Ⓒ Ⓓ	19. Ⓐ Ⓑ Ⓒ Ⓓ
4. Ⓕ Ⓖ Ⓗ Ⓙ	8. Ⓕ Ⓖ Ⓗ Ⓙ	12. Ⓕ Ⓖ Ⓗ Ⓙ	16. Ⓕ Ⓖ Ⓗ Ⓙ	20. Ⓕ Ⓖ Ⓗ Ⓙ

TEST 5   READING VOCABULARY

1. Ⓕ Ⓖ Ⓗ Ⓙ	9. Ⓕ Ⓖ Ⓗ Ⓙ	17. Ⓕ Ⓖ Ⓗ Ⓙ	25. Ⓕ Ⓖ Ⓗ Ⓙ	33. Ⓕ Ⓖ Ⓗ Ⓙ
2. Ⓐ Ⓑ Ⓒ Ⓓ	10. Ⓐ Ⓑ Ⓒ Ⓓ	18. Ⓐ Ⓑ Ⓒ Ⓓ	26. Ⓐ Ⓑ Ⓒ Ⓓ	34. Ⓐ Ⓑ Ⓒ Ⓓ
3. Ⓕ Ⓖ Ⓗ Ⓙ	11. Ⓕ Ⓖ Ⓗ Ⓙ	19. Ⓕ Ⓖ Ⓗ Ⓙ	27. Ⓕ Ⓖ Ⓗ Ⓙ	35. Ⓕ Ⓖ Ⓗ Ⓙ
4. Ⓐ Ⓑ Ⓒ Ⓓ	12. Ⓐ Ⓑ Ⓒ Ⓓ	20. Ⓐ Ⓑ Ⓒ Ⓓ	28. Ⓐ Ⓑ Ⓒ Ⓓ	36. Ⓐ Ⓑ Ⓒ Ⓓ
5. Ⓕ Ⓖ Ⓗ Ⓙ	13. Ⓕ Ⓖ Ⓗ Ⓙ	21. Ⓕ Ⓖ Ⓗ Ⓙ	29. Ⓕ Ⓖ Ⓗ Ⓙ	37. Ⓕ Ⓖ Ⓗ Ⓙ
6. Ⓐ Ⓑ Ⓒ Ⓓ	14. Ⓐ Ⓑ Ⓒ Ⓓ	22. Ⓐ Ⓑ Ⓒ Ⓓ	30. Ⓐ Ⓑ Ⓒ Ⓓ	38. Ⓐ Ⓑ Ⓒ Ⓓ
7. Ⓕ Ⓖ Ⓗ Ⓙ	15. Ⓕ Ⓖ Ⓗ Ⓙ	23. Ⓕ Ⓖ Ⓗ Ⓙ	31. Ⓕ Ⓖ Ⓗ Ⓙ	39. Ⓕ Ⓖ Ⓗ Ⓙ
8. Ⓐ Ⓑ Ⓒ Ⓓ	16. Ⓐ Ⓑ Ⓒ Ⓓ	24. Ⓐ Ⓑ Ⓒ Ⓓ	32. Ⓐ Ⓑ Ⓒ Ⓓ	40. Ⓐ Ⓑ Ⓒ Ⓓ

TEST 6   READING COMPREHENSION

1. Ⓐ Ⓑ Ⓒ Ⓓ	8. Ⓕ Ⓖ Ⓗ Ⓙ	15. Ⓐ Ⓑ Ⓒ Ⓓ	22. Ⓕ Ⓖ Ⓗ Ⓙ	29. Ⓐ Ⓑ Ⓒ Ⓓ
2. Ⓕ Ⓖ Ⓗ Ⓙ	9. Ⓐ Ⓑ Ⓒ Ⓓ	16. Ⓕ Ⓖ Ⓗ Ⓙ	23. Ⓐ Ⓑ Ⓒ Ⓓ	30. Ⓕ Ⓖ Ⓗ Ⓙ
3. Ⓐ Ⓑ Ⓒ Ⓓ	10. Ⓕ Ⓖ Ⓗ Ⓙ	17. Ⓐ Ⓑ Ⓒ Ⓓ	24. Ⓕ Ⓖ Ⓗ Ⓙ	31. Ⓐ Ⓑ Ⓒ Ⓓ
4. Ⓕ Ⓖ Ⓗ Ⓙ	11. Ⓐ Ⓑ Ⓒ Ⓓ	18. Ⓕ Ⓖ Ⓗ Ⓙ	25. Ⓐ Ⓑ Ⓒ Ⓓ	32. Ⓕ Ⓖ Ⓗ Ⓙ
5. Ⓐ Ⓑ Ⓒ Ⓓ	12. Ⓕ Ⓖ Ⓗ Ⓙ	19. Ⓐ Ⓑ Ⓒ Ⓓ	26. Ⓕ Ⓖ Ⓗ Ⓙ	33. Ⓐ Ⓑ Ⓒ Ⓓ
6. Ⓕ Ⓖ Ⓗ Ⓙ	13. Ⓐ Ⓑ Ⓒ Ⓓ	20. Ⓕ Ⓖ Ⓗ Ⓙ	27. Ⓐ Ⓑ Ⓒ Ⓓ	34. Ⓕ Ⓖ Ⓗ Ⓙ
7. Ⓐ Ⓑ Ⓒ Ⓓ	14. Ⓕ Ⓖ Ⓗ Ⓙ	21. Ⓐ Ⓑ Ⓒ Ⓓ	28. Ⓕ Ⓖ Ⓗ Ⓙ	

TEST 7   MATHEMATICS COMPUTATION

1. Ⓕ Ⓖ Ⓗ Ⓙ Ⓚ	9. Ⓕ Ⓖ Ⓗ Ⓙ Ⓚ	17. Ⓕ Ⓖ Ⓗ Ⓙ Ⓚ	24. Ⓐ Ⓑ Ⓒ Ⓓ Ⓔ
2. Ⓐ Ⓑ Ⓒ Ⓓ Ⓔ	10. Ⓐ Ⓑ Ⓒ Ⓓ Ⓔ	18. Ⓐ Ⓑ Ⓒ Ⓓ Ⓔ	25. Ⓕ Ⓖ Ⓗ Ⓙ Ⓚ
3. Ⓕ Ⓖ Ⓗ Ⓙ Ⓚ	11. Ⓕ Ⓖ Ⓗ Ⓙ Ⓚ	19. Ⓕ Ⓗ Ⓙ Ⓚ Ⓚ	26. Ⓐ Ⓑ Ⓒ Ⓓ Ⓔ
4. Ⓐ Ⓑ Ⓒ Ⓓ Ⓔ	12. Ⓐ Ⓑ Ⓒ Ⓓ Ⓔ	20. Ⓐ Ⓑ Ⓒ Ⓓ Ⓔ	27. Ⓕ Ⓖ Ⓗ Ⓙ Ⓚ
5. Ⓕ Ⓖ Ⓗ Ⓙ Ⓚ	13. Ⓕ Ⓖ Ⓗ Ⓙ Ⓚ	21. Ⓕ Ⓗ Ⓙ Ⓚ Ⓚ	28. Ⓐ Ⓑ Ⓒ Ⓓ Ⓔ
6. Ⓐ Ⓑ Ⓒ Ⓓ Ⓔ	14. Ⓐ Ⓑ Ⓒ Ⓓ Ⓔ	22. Ⓐ Ⓑ Ⓒ Ⓓ Ⓔ	29. Ⓕ Ⓖ Ⓗ Ⓙ Ⓚ
7. Ⓕ Ⓖ Ⓗ Ⓙ Ⓚ	15. Ⓕ Ⓖ Ⓗ Ⓙ Ⓚ	23. Ⓕ Ⓖ Ⓗ Ⓙ Ⓚ	30. Ⓐ Ⓑ Ⓒ Ⓓ Ⓔ
8. Ⓐ Ⓑ Ⓒ Ⓓ Ⓔ	16. Ⓐ Ⓑ Ⓒ Ⓓ Ⓔ		

TEST 8   MATHEMATICS CONCEPTS AND APPLICATIONS

1. Ⓐ Ⓑ Ⓒ Ⓓ	8. Ⓕ Ⓖ Ⓗ Ⓙ	15. Ⓐ Ⓑ Ⓒ Ⓓ	22. Ⓕ Ⓖ Ⓗ Ⓙ	29. Ⓐ Ⓑ Ⓒ Ⓓ
2. Ⓕ Ⓖ Ⓗ Ⓙ	9. Ⓐ Ⓑ Ⓒ Ⓓ	16. Ⓕ Ⓖ Ⓗ Ⓙ	23. Ⓐ Ⓑ Ⓒ Ⓓ	30. Ⓕ Ⓖ Ⓗ Ⓙ
3. Ⓐ Ⓑ Ⓒ Ⓓ	10. Ⓕ Ⓖ Ⓗ Ⓙ	17. Ⓐ Ⓑ Ⓒ Ⓓ	24. Ⓕ Ⓖ Ⓗ Ⓙ	31. Ⓐ Ⓑ Ⓒ Ⓓ
4. Ⓕ Ⓖ Ⓗ Ⓙ	11. Ⓐ Ⓑ Ⓒ Ⓓ	18. Ⓕ Ⓖ Ⓗ Ⓙ	25. Ⓐ Ⓑ Ⓒ Ⓓ	32. Ⓕ Ⓖ Ⓗ Ⓙ
5. Ⓐ Ⓑ Ⓒ Ⓓ	12. Ⓕ Ⓖ Ⓗ Ⓙ	19. Ⓐ Ⓑ Ⓒ Ⓓ	26. Ⓕ Ⓖ Ⓗ Ⓙ	33. Ⓐ Ⓑ Ⓒ Ⓓ
6. Ⓕ Ⓖ Ⓗ Ⓙ	13. Ⓐ Ⓑ Ⓒ Ⓓ	20. Ⓕ Ⓖ Ⓗ Ⓙ	27. Ⓐ Ⓑ Ⓒ Ⓓ	34. Ⓕ Ⓖ Ⓗ Ⓙ
7. Ⓐ Ⓑ Ⓒ Ⓓ	14. Ⓕ Ⓖ Ⓗ Ⓙ	21. Ⓐ Ⓑ Ⓒ Ⓓ	28. Ⓕ Ⓖ Ⓗ Ⓙ	35. Ⓐ Ⓑ Ⓒ Ⓓ

TEST 9   LANGUAGE MECHANICS

1. Ⓐ Ⓑ Ⓒ Ⓓ Ⓔ	5. Ⓐ Ⓑ Ⓒ Ⓓ Ⓔ	9. Ⓐ Ⓑ Ⓒ Ⓓ Ⓔ	13. Ⓐ Ⓑ Ⓒ Ⓓ Ⓔ	17. Ⓐ Ⓑ Ⓒ Ⓓ Ⓔ
2. Ⓕ Ⓖ Ⓗ Ⓙ Ⓚ	6. Ⓕ Ⓖ Ⓗ Ⓙ Ⓚ	10. Ⓕ Ⓖ Ⓗ Ⓙ Ⓚ	14. Ⓕ Ⓖ Ⓗ Ⓙ Ⓚ	18. Ⓕ Ⓖ Ⓗ Ⓙ Ⓚ
3. Ⓐ Ⓑ Ⓒ Ⓓ Ⓔ	7. Ⓐ Ⓑ Ⓒ Ⓓ Ⓔ	11. Ⓐ Ⓑ Ⓒ Ⓓ Ⓔ	15. Ⓐ Ⓑ Ⓒ Ⓓ Ⓔ	19. Ⓐ Ⓑ Ⓒ Ⓓ Ⓔ
4. Ⓕ Ⓖ Ⓗ Ⓙ Ⓚ	8. Ⓕ Ⓖ Ⓗ Ⓙ Ⓚ	12. Ⓕ Ⓖ Ⓗ Ⓙ Ⓚ	16. Ⓕ Ⓖ Ⓗ Ⓙ Ⓚ	20. Ⓕ Ⓖ Ⓗ Ⓙ Ⓚ

TEST 10   LANGUAGE EXPRESSION

1. Ⓐ Ⓑ Ⓒ Ⓓ	8. Ⓕ Ⓖ Ⓗ Ⓙ	15. Ⓐ Ⓑ Ⓒ Ⓓ	21. Ⓐ Ⓑ Ⓒ Ⓓ	27. Ⓐ Ⓑ Ⓒ Ⓓ
2. Ⓕ Ⓖ Ⓗ Ⓙ	9. Ⓐ Ⓑ Ⓒ Ⓓ	16. Ⓕ Ⓖ Ⓗ Ⓙ	22. Ⓕ Ⓖ Ⓗ Ⓙ	28. Ⓕ Ⓖ Ⓗ Ⓙ
3. Ⓐ Ⓑ Ⓒ Ⓓ	10. Ⓕ Ⓖ Ⓗ Ⓙ	17. Ⓐ Ⓑ Ⓒ Ⓓ	23. Ⓐ Ⓑ Ⓒ Ⓓ	29. Ⓐ Ⓑ Ⓒ Ⓓ
4. Ⓕ Ⓖ Ⓗ Ⓙ	11. Ⓐ Ⓑ Ⓒ Ⓓ	18. Ⓕ Ⓖ Ⓗ Ⓙ	24. Ⓕ Ⓖ Ⓗ Ⓙ	30. Ⓕ Ⓖ Ⓗ Ⓙ
5. Ⓐ Ⓑ Ⓒ Ⓓ	12. Ⓕ Ⓖ Ⓗ Ⓙ	19. Ⓐ Ⓑ Ⓒ Ⓓ	25. Ⓐ Ⓑ Ⓒ Ⓓ	31. Ⓐ Ⓑ Ⓒ Ⓓ
6. Ⓕ Ⓖ Ⓗ Ⓙ	13. Ⓐ Ⓑ Ⓒ Ⓓ	20. Ⓕ Ⓖ Ⓗ Ⓙ	26. Ⓕ Ⓖ Ⓗ Ⓙ	32. Ⓕ Ⓖ Ⓗ Ⓙ
7. Ⓐ Ⓑ Ⓒ Ⓓ	14. Ⓕ Ⓖ Ⓗ Ⓙ			

Practice Cooperative Admissions Examination 2

TEST 1   SEQUENCES

Number of questions: 20   *Time limit: 12 minutes*

DIRECTIONS: For numbers 1 through 20 make the choice that will continue the pattern or sequence and blacken the appropriate circle on the Answer Sheet.

1.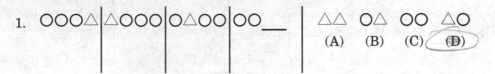

2.

3.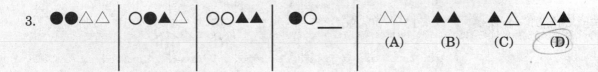

4.

5.

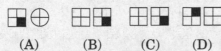

6.

7.   5   15   45 | 8   24   72 | 12   36   __ | 72   108   144   180
                                                (A)   (B)   (C)   (D)

8. 8   16   10 | 10   20   14 | 12   24   __ |
    16   17   18   20
    (F)   (G)   (H)   (J)

9. 6   11   19 | 7   12   20 | 8   13   __ |
    19   21   23   25
    (A)   (B)   (C)   (D)

10. 7   17   28 | 8   20   33 | 9   23   __ |
    32   34   37   38
    (F)   (G)   (H)   (J)

11. 5   6   36 | 6   7   49 | 7   8   __ |
    64   66   70   81
    (A)   (B)   (C)   (D)

12. 7   9   14 | 8   10   15 | 9   11   __ |
    20   45   16   40
    (F)   (G)   (H)   (J)

13. 10   11   9 | 15   16   14 | 20   21   __ |
    16   17   18   19
    (A)   (B)   (C)   (D)

14. 20   16   8 | 24   20   10 | 30   26   __ |
    12   15   14   13
    (F)   (G)   (H)   (J)

15. A_1BC_1 A_1BC_2 A_1BC_5 ___ A_1BC_3
    $A_1B_1C_1$ $A_2B_2C_2$ A_1BC_4 A_1BC_3
    (A)   (B)   (C)   (D)

16. $R_7S_5T_1$ $R_6S_4T_2$ $R_5S_3T_3$ ___ $R_3S_1T_5$
    R_4ST_1 $R_4S_2T_4$ $R_2S_3T_3$ $R_4S_4T_3$
    (F)   (G)   (H)   (J)

17. BAL   LAC   CAD   ___   EAF
    ADF   DAE   AFD   EDF
    (A)   (B)   (C)   (D)

18. BCA   CDB   DEC   EFD   ___
    FGE   CBA   DCF   EGC
    (F)   (G)   (H)   (J)

19. ABD   BCE   CDF   ___   EFH
    DGF   DEG   CDG   DFG
    (A)   (B)   (C)   (D)

20. REV   SDU   TCT   UBS   ___
    STU   RVE   VAR   VRA
    (F)   (G)   (H)   (J)

TEST 2   ANALOGIES

Number of questions: 20   *Time limit: 7 minutes*

DIRECTIONS: For numbers 1 through 20, select the picture that will fit in the empty box so that the two lower pictures are related in the same way as the two upper pictures.

1.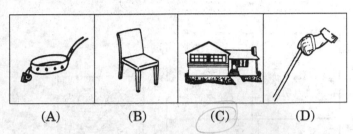

(A)   (B)   (C)   (D)

2.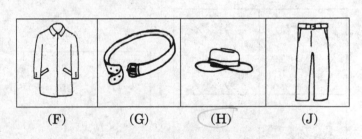

(F)   (G)   (H)   (J)

3.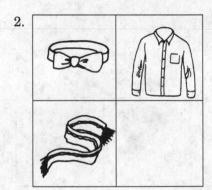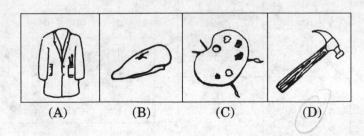

(A)   (B)   (C)   (D)

4.

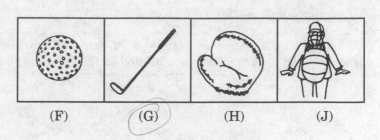

(F)　(G)　(H)　(J)

5.

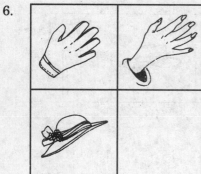

(A)　(B)　(C)　(D)

6.

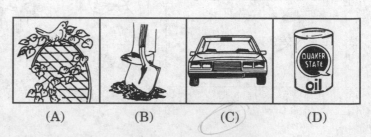

(F)　(G)　(H)　(J)

7.

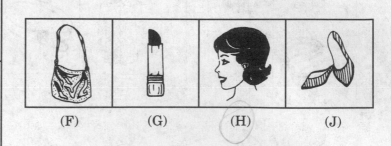

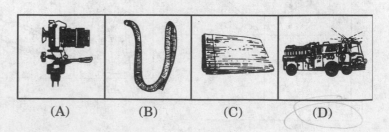

(A)　(B)　(C)　(D)

8.

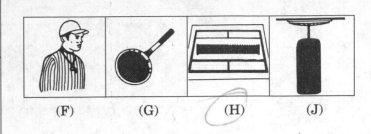

(F) (G) (H) (J)

9.

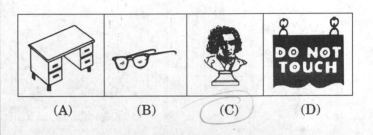

(A) (B) (C) (D)

10.

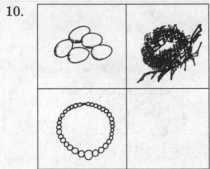

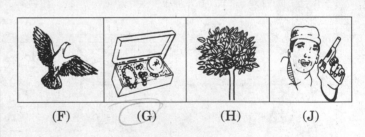

(F) (G) (H) (J)

11.

(A) (B) (C) (D)

12.

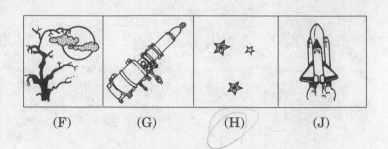

(F)   (G)   (H)   (J)

13.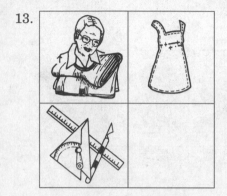

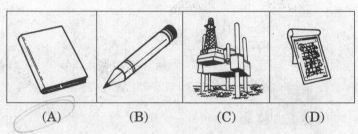

(A)   (B)   (C)   (D)

14.

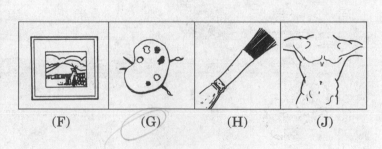

(F)   (G)   (H)   (J)

15.

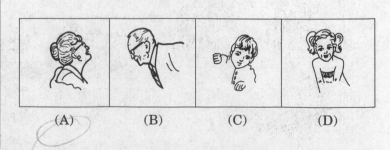

(A)   (B)   (C)   (D)

16.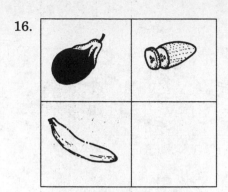

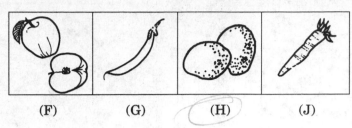

(F) (G) (H) (J)

17.

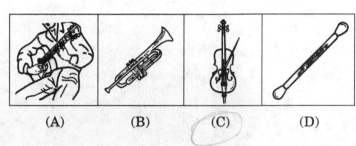

(A) (B) (C) (D)

18.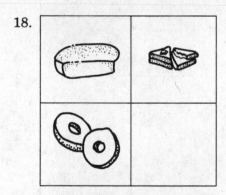

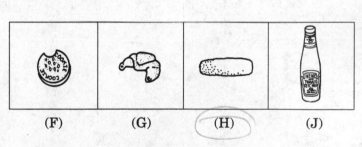

(F) (G) (H) (J)

19.

(A) (B) (C) (D)

20.
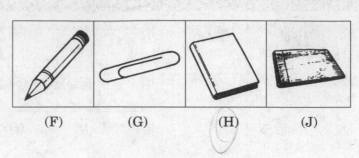

(F)   (G)   (H)   (J)

TEST 3   MEMORY

Number of questions: 20   *Time limit: 12 minutes for study, 8 minutes to answer*

Part One

> DIRECTIONS: While someone reads aloud to you the following words and their definitions, read them silently to yourself.

Words and Definitions

1 A saran is a type of violin.
2 Fashious means troublesome.
3 Decollation is the act of beheading.
4 Frambold means quarrelsome.
5 Euripize means to fluctuate.
6 Hilding means a cowardly person.
7 Globben means to worry.
8 A brockie is a person with a dirty face.
9 Footle means to waste time.
10 Macrology means a long, tiresome talk.
11 An adda is a type of lizard.
12 Eximious means excellent.
13 Desecate means to cut off.
14 Meracious means unspoiled.
15 A sackbutt means a type of trombone.
16 Vitipend means to belittle.
17 Fatiferous means deadly.
18 A saulie is a hired mourner.
19 A grilse is a young salmon.
20 Macrotous means having big ears.

After studying the words and definitions for 12 minutes, cover them and proceed to Tests 4 and 5. Part Two of Test 3 follows Tests 4 and 5.

TEST 4 VERBAL REASONING

Number of questions: 20   *Time limit: 12 minutes*

DIRECTIONS: For numbers 1 through 7, select the word that names a necessary part of the word underlined.

1. automobile

   (A) driver
   (B) computer
   (C) engine
   (D) tire

2. dinner

   (F) waiter
   (G) napkin
   (H) food
   (J) wine

3. bravery

   (A) fear
   (B) recklessness
   (C) neutrality
   (D) courage

4. airplane

   (F) steward
   (G) pilot
   (H) landing gear
   (J) propeller

5. piano

   (A) music
   (B) keys
   (C) virtuoso
   (D) stool

6. clock

   (F) hands
   (G) radio
   (H) chimes
   (J) winder

7. microscope

   (A) scientist
   (B) lens
   (C) case
   (D) base

DIRECTIONS: For numbers 8 through 12, the three words in the top row are related in a certain way. The words below the line are related in the same way. In each case, select the missing word so that the three words in the bottom row will be related in the same way as the words in the top row.

8.

science	biology	physics
art	painting	_____

   (F) geology
   (G) sculpture
   (H) chemistry
   (J) portrait

9.

metal	lead	copper
gem	diamond	_____

   (A) sapphire
   (B) aluminum
   (C) bracelet
   (D) jeweler

10.

color	red	blue
building	courthouse	_____

   (F) business
   (G) food
   (H) clothing
   (J) schoolhouse

11.

lunch	soup	sandwich
dinner	salad	_____

   (A) spoon
   (B) dressing
   (C) entree
   (D) cup

12.

living room	sofa	table
kitchen	refrigerator	_____

   (F) coffee
   (G) microwave
   (H) cereal
   (J) bread

DIRECTIONS: For numbers 13 through 14, select the correct answer.

13. The following words are translated from an artificial language:
    <u>lebdom</u> means downtown
    <u>rabdom</u> means uptown
    <u>lebtur</u> means downstream
    Which of the words below means <u>upstream</u>?

    (A) lebrab
    (B) turdom
    (C) rabtur
    (D) rabdom

14. The following words are translated from an artificial language:
    <u>pracul</u> means skyway
    <u>sulcul</u> means byway
    <u>sulmur</u> means bypath
    Which of the words below means <u>pathway</u>?

    (F) prabcor
    (G) murcul
    (H) sulpra
    (J) borsul

DIRECTIONS: For numbers 15 through 20, select the statement that is true according to the facts given in the paragraph.

15. Frank Gorman is in his freshman year at State College. He enjoys the campus coed social life. He finds the combination of lecture and laboratory work in his science course especially satisfying.

    (A) Frank likes his science course because of the practical work in the laboratory.
    (B) Frank has a busy social life on the campus.
    (C) Frank is happy with both his social life on campus and his science course.
    (D) Frank expects to do well in his college work.

16. John Chase is a manager of a fast food restaurant. He is kept busy with a variety of problems, some of which require immediate attention. One day a number of his workers were absent and he was short of help. Another day his electrical equipment failed, and he was frantic until repairs were made. Nevertheless, John finds that he can meet the challenges reasonably well.

    (F) John Chase is a man with many skills.
    (G) John Chase is a perfectionist.
    (H) John Chase enjoys solving problems.
    (J) John Chase solves his problems with a reasonable degree of success.

17. Doris Martin is a lover of classical music. Although her skill is not on a professional level, she enjoys playing the cello with amateur groups. Her favorite composers are Beethoven and Mozart. Since she lives in New York City, she has many opportunities to attend excellent concerts.

    (A) Doris Martin would rather attend concerts than spend time playing the cello.
    (B) Doris Martin has the skill to be a professional musician.
    (C) Doris Martin plays the cello with amateur groups but would rather perform professionally.
    (D) Doris Martin finds pleasure in the works of most classical composers, but Beethoven and Mozart are her favorites.

18. Ella Burns is a retired businesswoman. Since her health is robust, she seeks activity. In response to an appeal, she has volunteered to help slower students in the local elementary school.

    (F) Ella Burns's good health gives her the impetus to volunteer to help young people.
    (G) Ella Burns likes to change her life style frequently.
    (H) Ella Burns enjoys being with young people.
    (J) The local elementary school is conveniently located for Ella Burns.

19. Since early childhood, Ben Davis has been fascinated by books. This was reinforced when he majored in English literature at college. When he was offered a job as a book salesman, he gladly accepted. Now he spends most of his working time visiting book stores and schools, where he sells textbooks.

(A) Ben Davis visits book stores and schools on social calls.
(B) Ben Davis has always enjoyed reading books.
(C) Most of Ben Davis's book sales are on English literature.
(D) Ben Davis was offered a job as a book salesman because he loves books.

20. When Jane Fenton accepted a job in a travel agency, she thought that the work involved few complications. However, she soon learned that her impression was contrary to the facts. For example, booking an airplane flight involved many different rate schedules, each with its own set of conditions. To find the most suitable booking for a traveler demanded knowledge and judgment of a superior order.

(F) Jane Fenton was looking for an easy job.
(G) Booking an airplane flight is a complex task if the traveler is to be served properly.
(H) Airplane rates on flights between large cities are fixed by law.
(J) Jane Fenton was overwhelmed by the difficulties of her job.

TEST 5   READING VOCABULARY

Number of questions: 40   *Time limit: 15 minutes*

DIRECTIONS: For numbers 1 through 10, select the word that means the same, or nearly the same, as the word underlined.

1. liberate the prisoners

   (F) clothe
   (G) sentence
   (H) execute
   (J) free

2. her eventual reward

   (A) unearned
   (B) rich
   (C) ultimate
   (D) anticipated

3. indispensable advice

   (F) unrequested
   (G) necessary
   (H) useless
   (J) professional

4. obligatory training

   (A) occasional
   (B) planned
   (C) carefree
   (D) required

5. an ancient adage

   (F) house
   (G) proverb
   (H) prophet
   (J) custom

6. a bogus count

   (A) counterfeit
   (B) powerful
   (C) contemporary
   (D) shrewd

7. with minimum effort

   (F) least
   (G) swift
   (H) unplanned
   (J) unexpected

8. alleviate the pain

   (A) locate
   (B) cause
   (C) acknowledge
   (D) soothe

9. laud their efforts

   (F) evaluate
   (G) praise
   (H) criticize
   (J) imitate

10. a prolific writer

    (A) popular
    (B) struggling
    (C) unknown
    (D) productive

DIRECTIONS: For numbers 11 through 20, select the word that means the opposite, or nearly the opposite, of the word underlined.

11. downhearted because of the rejection

    (F) faint
    (G) unfortunate
    (H) relieved
    (J) encouraged

12. an erroneous conclusion

    (A) excellent
    (B) accurate
    (C) advantageous
    (D) unforeseen

13. an ill-tempered neighbor

    (F) amiable
    (G) illustrious
    (H) anxious
    (J) unusual

14. to intimate that all is not well

    (A) decide
    (B) guess
    (C) proclaim
    (D) regret

15. <u>lambasted</u> for his actions

    (F) praised
    (G) discharged
    (H) ridiculed
    (J) compensated

16. a <u>level-headed</u> leader

    (A) sympathetic
    (B) cautious
    (C) enthusiastic
    (D) thoughtless

17. to <u>loathe</u> modern art

    (F) analyze
    (G) study
    (H) reject
    (J) admire

18. a statement filled with <u>malice</u>

    (A) goodwill
    (B) discord
    (C) untruths
    (D) information

19. appear to be <u>nonchalant</u>

    (F) healthy
    (G) informed
    (H) reliable
    (J) concerned

20. to <u>obliterate</u> the impression

    (A) analyze
    (B) create
    (C) describe
    (D) resent

DIRECTIONS: For numbers 21 through 30, select the word that best fits into the blank.

21. The managers were _____ by the public response to the company's successful sales campaign.

    (F) petrified
    (G) recognized
    (H) gratified
    (J) amused

22. The efforts of the rescue team were _____ by the lack of equipment.

    (A) accelerated
    (B) hampered
    (C) resolved
    (D) facilitated

23. Early settlers were _____ by wandering bands of cruel outlaws.

    (F) harassed
    (G) protected
    (H) supervised
    (J) comforted

24. The dense hedge of thorns and barbed wire formed a(n) _____ barrier around the ranch house.

    (A) attractive
    (B) impenetrable
    (C) colorful
    (D) fragile

25. Only a _____ could be sent to the office for a pair of paper stretchers.

    (F) technician
    (G) researcher
    (H) consumer
    (J) novice

26. During the fire drill, the well-trained students left the building in a(n) _____ fashion.

    (A) orderly
    (B) rowdyish
    (C) amateurish
    (D) cordial

27. In the long run, the will of the majority must _____ in a democracy.

    (F) vanish
    (G) falter
    (H) prevail
    (J) recede

28. The _____ spring weather brought thousands of vacationers to the national parks.

    (A) cold
    (B) variable
    (C) humid
    (D) balmy

29. The children tried to _____ their loving grandparents into taking them to the fairgrounds.

    (F) enforce
    (G) cajole
    (H) coerce
    (J) overpower

30. Our form of government is a monument that will _____ the memory of our founding generation.

    (A) perpetuate
    (B) erase
    (C) consolidate
    (D) alter

DIRECTIONS: For numbers 31 through 40, select the word whose meaning is the same as *both* of the words or phrases underlined.

---

31. air current and rough sketch

    (F) outline
    (G) design
    (H) abstract
    (J) draft

32. command and offer a price

    (A) blunder
    (B) charge
    (C) bid
    (D) instruct

33. rage and harden

    (F) humor
    (G) temper
    (H) anger
    (J) storm

34. frank and cliff

    (A) forward
    (B) crag
    (C) bluff
    (D) forthright

35. strainer and weed out

    (F) screen
    (G) shelter
    (H) cover
    (J) veil

36. send off and message

    (A) discharge
    (B) relay
    (C) launch
    (D) dispatch

37. plan and stick out

    (F) project
    (G) design
    (H) propose
    (J) discharge

38. handcuff and moderation

    (A) shackle
    (B) poise
    (C) restraint
    (D) prudence

39. withdrawal and refuge

    (F) confinement
    (G) retirement
    (H) sanctuary
    (J) retreat

40. basic items and fasteners

    (A) features
    (B) staples
    (C) fundamentals
    (D) resources

Before continuing on to Test 6, now that 25 minutes have passed, complete Part Two of Test 3.

TEST 3 MEMORY

Part Two

> DIRECTIONS: For numbers 1 through 20, select the word that means the same as the underlined phrase.

1. Which word means <u>a person with a dirty face</u>?

   (A) grilse
   (B) sackbutt
   (C) saran
   (D) brockie
   (E) adda

2. Which word means <u>having big ears</u>?

   (F) eximious
   (G) macrotous
   (H) fatiferous
   (J) fashious
   (K) frambold

3. Which word means <u>to waste time</u>?

   (A) desecate
   (B) globben
   (C) vitipend
   (D) euripize
   (E) footle

4. Which word means <u>a hired mourner</u>?

   (F) decollation
   (G) saulie
   (H) macrology
   (J) footle
   (K) adda

5. Which word means <u>troublesome</u>?

   (A) fashious
   (B) meracious
   (C) fatiferous
   (D) frambold
   (E) saran

6. Which word means <u>to belittle</u>?

   (F) sackbutt
   (G) globben
   (H) euripize
   (J) desecate
   (K) vitipend

7. Which word means <u>a type of violin</u>?

   (A) hilding
   (B) saran
   (C) grilse
   (D) frambold
   (E) decollation

8. Which word means <u>deadly</u>?

   (F) fashious
   (G) eximious
   (H) meracious
   (J) fatiferous
   (K) macrotous

9. Which word means <u>the act of beheading</u>?

   (A) adda
   (B) hilding
   (C) decollation
   (D) macrology
   (E) footle

10. Which word means <u>unspoiled</u>?

    (F) fetiferous
    (G) eximious
    (H) meracious
    (J) fashious
    (K) brockie

11. Which word means <u>to fluctuate</u>?

    (A) vitipend
    (B) saran
    (C) footle
    (D) euripize
    (E) desecate

12. Which word means <u>a young salmon</u>?

    (F) decollation
    (G) grilse
    (H) adda
    (J) saulie
    (K) sackbutt

13. Which word means <u>quarrelsome</u>?

   (A) fatiferous
   (B) fashious
   (C) macrotous
   (D) brockie
   (E) frambold

14. Which word means <u>a type of lizard</u>?

   (F) globbe
   (G) footle
   (H) adda
   (J) saran
   (K) grilse

15. Which word means <u>a long, tiresome talk</u>?

   (A) meracious
   (B) vitipend
   (C) frambold
   (D) macrology
   (E) brockie

16. Which word means <u>excellent</u>?

   (F) meracious
   (G) saulie
   (H) macrotous
   (J) eximious
   (K) vitipend

17. Which word means <u>a cowardly person</u>?

   (A) decoration
   (B) brockie
   (C) hilding
   (D) grilse
   (E) macrology

18. Which word means <u>to worry</u>?

   (F) saulie
   (G) footle
   (H) macrotous
   (J) euripize
   (K) globben

19. Which word means <u>to cut off</u>?

   (A) globben
   (B) macrology
   (C) desecate
   (D) vitipend
   (E) saulie

20. Which word means <u>a type of trombone</u>?

   (F) saran
   (G) eximious
   (H) sackbutt
   (J) euripize
   (K) hilding

TEST 6   READING COMPREHENSION

Number of questions: 34   *Time limit: 32 minutes*

DIRECTIONS: For numbers 1 through 34, read each selection below and answer the questions that follow it. Choose your answer based on the selection.

Have you ever wondered how the various school and professional teams got their names? Some have taken on the symbol of the city or state they are in. Others just inherited a calling card, and it has stuck. One of the most far-fetched origins is that of the Los Angeles Dodgers.

Those of us with long memories can recall when the Dodgers were not out of California, but were natives of one of New York City's five boroughs, Brooklyn, with a home in Ebbet's Field. In the early twenties, the team was often called the Brooklyn Robins. The name was related, not to birds, but to the name of their longtime manager Wilbert Robinson.

In the decades before the transfer west, for various reasons easy to figure out, the team was affectionately referred to as Dem Bums. However, the name that stuck and was carried over to Los Angeles goes back to the days before busses were the common carriers. Trolleys preceded the busses and dominated the streets of Brooklyn for many years. So numerous were the trolleys that all Brooklyn residents were labeled trolley dodgers. The label was shortened and applied to the ball team. Since Brooklynites are not ones to bear a grudge for very long, they have never sued to have the team or the name returned to the place of origin.

1. What was the author's main purpose in writing this passage?

   (A) to criticize the method of giving nicknames to athletic teams
   (B) to test the memory of the readers
   (C) to improve the names given to teams
   (D) to point out the origin of a particular name

2. Why was the team given the name of Dodgers?

   (F) The players were known for their skill in running bases.
   (G) Pedestrians had to be wary in crossing the streets.
   (H) The owners of the team lived in Brooklyn.
   (J) The team was very popular in Brooklyn.

3. Why did the team first have the name of Robins?

   (A) The players wore orange and dark brown uniforms.
   (B) The team was named after the owner.
   (C) The team's emblem was a robin, sewed on the back of the uniforms.
   (D) The name was associated with the manager of the team.

4. What finally happened to the Brooklyn team?

   (F) It was moved to the minor leagues.
   (G) The owner moved it to another city.
   (H) It was disbanded.
   (J) The ball field was converted into a housing project.

The small park between the two high-rise project houses had its usual occupants. Over in the corner, under the trees, were older men playing chess. In the restricted area were little children on the swings, while their mothers stood chatting in clusters nearby. Some one, as usual, was boom-boxing soft-rock ballads.

Ellen walked slowly to her bench. She took her sandwich out of the wrapping and began to chew small bites.

When she reached the chess players, she told them that she felt good today. She would play six boards simultaneously. The players instantly agreed and set up the boards. A large group of spectators gathered to watch the contest. With a curt nod, Ellen signaled the beginning of the match. As a handicap, she allowed the other players to choose white and have the first move. When they were ready, she walked quickly from board to board, making her moves without breaking her stride. The results were as always; she had no difficulty in checkmating all six opponents, despite the fact that one of them was the state champion.

Just as she finished the games, the DJ announced that his record player had jammed. The audience of school kids began to chant derisively, and the DJ looked at Ellen for help. She walked up to the mike and began to sing, making up the lyrics as she went along. The melody was Mozart; the patter was sung in Madonna style, blending and soaring in contrasts, but miraculously harmonious. Thunderous applause followed her last note.

Ellen had saved the day! She wished her mother didn't have to work Saturdays. Then the two of them could go places together. She looked toward the groups of mothers, chatting casually, close to the playing children. Someday, she too would be a grown-up and have friends.

5. How old do you think Ellen is?

   (A) 2–4 years old
   (B) 5–6 years old
   (C) 7–10 years old
   (D) 12–15 years old

6. What purpose did the author have in telling this story?

   (F) to make us sympathetic with the elderly who go to neighborhood parks for recreation
   (G) to show how attractive miniature parks are
   (H) to have us reform society
   (J) to give us an insight into a child's loneliness

7. Where did most of the action in the story take place?

   (A) in an apartment in a public housing project
   (B) on a park bench
   (C) in a school yard
   (D) in a library

8. What do we learn about Ellen?

   (F) She is an excellent chess player.
   (G) She plays a musical instrument.
   (H) She seldom goes to the park.
   (J) She is trying to cope with loneliness.

9. Why did Ellen's mother send her to the park?

   (A) The mother wanted to be free of her for awhile.
   (B) Ellen would be out of doors in a fairly safe place.
   (C) Ellen had begged her mother to let her go.
   (D) Ellen could learn to play with others.

Settlement houses were established at the end of the nineteenth century to help solve the social and industrial problems brought about by the changing structure of society. The masses of immigrants and the farmers turned factory workers had moved into the decaying centers of the cities, where the available jobs were. Once there, too many found themselves locked into low-paying positions with no chance of advancement. The resultant poverty led inevitably to a rapid increase in the crime rate. Society seemed to be creating a new, undesirable class doomed never to rise out of the slums.

Founded in 1889, Hull House on Chicago's West Side was the most successful of the settlement houses. Under the guidance of Jane Addams, it became the community center for all of Chicago. All age groups flocked there for its recreational activities; they joined athletic teams, took courses in art, music, the dance, and the theater, and developed interests and talents. Teachers and counselors were able to instill hope, ambition, and socially approved goals into the thousands who came.

On another level, Hull House was a training school for workers in social service techniques. As a result, it had the personnel to serve as a rehabilitation center for the troubled, the handicapped, and the unemployed.

10. According to this selection, why were settlement houses established?

(F) to rid cities of slums
(G) to provide employment
(H) to raise the standard of living
(J) to reduce the number of crimes

11. Why did so many people move into the slums?

(A) They could get jobs nearby.
(B) The schools were better there.
(C) They wanted to live near their relatives.
(D) Prices of food and shelter were lower there.

12. Why did Hull House have so many recreational activities?

(F) They taught the participants wage-earning skills.
(G) They kept the children busy.
(H) They brought the people into Hull House.
(J) They helped time to pass quickly.

13. Which of the following was a basic belief to the success of Hull House?

(A) Concentrate your efforts on helping the gifted.
(B) It is not what you know, but whom you know, that will get you ahead.
(C) Given motivation, all people will better themselves.
(D) Little can be done to help those locked into poverty.

Great leaders set patterns of action to be copied by generations to come. Unfortunately, with the passage of time, the lessons that should be taught and the model to be followed by succeeding generations are lost in the mythology of history.

A prime example of a victim of this process is the Revolutionary leader and first President of the United States. The surviving story of the cherry tree and the young Washington does not foster the realization of his true genius.

Some recent evaluations stress that, when Washington was chosen as Commander-in-Chief of the Continental Army to fight for independence from British rule, he had never handled an army larger than a modern division. They conclude that his inexperience was the reason why he was defeated again and again by the larger British forces. Such revelations unaccompanied by more constructive information rob Washington of his deserved stature.

Here are some other facts that should be also told. When Washington took over his command, he became the rallying center of the war effort. Through the hours of darkest gloom, he guided his troops with unflagging patriotism, calm wisdom, and moral courage. His faith in the rightness of the cause never faltered. With patient vigilance, he taught the age-old lesson that what counts is not how many battles are lost, but who wins the last battle. And we are ever grateful that he was the one who won it. Rather than as a father figure, he must be seen for the virtues that led his tattered battalions to victory.

Washington became first in war, first in peace, and first in the hearts of his countrymen for qualities of leadership that are just as important today as they were in our War of Independence: faith in his cause, knowledge of how to use his limited forces, concern for the welfare of his troops, and courage to persevere until the goal is achieved.

14. What was the author's main purpose in writing this selection?

(F) He wants to prove that Washington was responsible for winning the Revolution.
(G) He wants to encourage people to follow Washington's example of leadership.
(H) He wants to rebuke people who draw attention to Washington's failures.
(J) He wants to show that Washington's qualities are not needed any more.

15. What attitude does the author want people to have toward the story of young Washington and the cutting down of the cherry tree?

(A) People may accept it or reject it, but they should remember stories more typical of Washington's leadership qualities.
(B) People should accept the story as true because it reveals Washington's true character.
(C) People should reject the story as untrue because the incident may never have happened.
(D) People should not try to draw a moral from it.

16. From which period in Washington's life does the author draw examples to prove his leaderhip traits?

(F) Washington's career as a surveyor
(G) Washington's Revolutionary War service
(H) Washington's years as President
(J) Washington's entire life

17. As Commander-in-Chief what was Washington's greatest asset?

(A) He was a skilled Indian fighter.
(B) He trained his troops well.
(C) His men believed in his ability to lead them to eventual victory.
(D) The Continental Congress supported him.

18. Which of the following was not one of Washington's qualities?

(F) Patriotism
(G) Concern for his troops
(H) Stubbornness
(J) Perseverance

At present humankind has achieved supremacy over all other species inhabiting this planet called Earth; we are at the head of the food chain. However, we must be mindful of the dinosaurs, which too once ruled supreme but are now extinct.

Which species now on Earth could overtake and replace us? At least two members of the insect world, the ants and the mosquitoes, have been suggested as our potential successors. Of the two, the one that appears less likely to succeed is the mosquito. Or is it?

As carriers of disease-causing germs, mosquitoes have been responsible for more human deaths than any other living species. The bite of a mosquito has caused the death from malaria of hundreds of millions of people. About 200 million people are suffering from the disease now, and some 100 million new cases occur each year. In addition to malaria, mosquitoes transmit more than 100 viral diseases to human beings and animals. Of these, dengue and encephalitis are major health threats, and yellow fever still takes severe human tolls in Africa. Each year filariasis, a nematode worm infection, infects millions of people in the tropics and, in severe cases, causes a type of leprosy. The amazing thing is that the germs mosquitoes carry do not attack the insects themselves.

If the predictions of global warming in the coming decades prove true, we may be creating a worldwide opportunity for mosquitoes. If the warming is accompanied by precipitations, new hordes of hungry, blood-loving mosquitoes could be unleashed in both temperate and arctic zones of the world. Given this gloomy assessment, who can say that the mosquito is not one of our more serious rivals?

19. Why did the author bring dinosaurs into this article dealing with mosquitoes?

(A) He wanted to warn us that what the mosquitoes had done to the dinosaurs, they could do to humankind.
(B) He wanted to warn us that what had happened to the dinosaurs could happen to us.
(C) He wanted to show what happens to species that are our enemies.
(D) He wanted to explain how to extend the food chain.

20. What is the mosquitoes' most formidable advantage?

(F) They do not catch the diseases they transmit.
(G) They can survive in cold, dry climates.
(H) Their lifespan is briefer than that of a human being.
(J) They can alight on human skin without being felt.

21. Which disease carried by the mosquito causes the most deaths?

(A) filariasis
(B) yellow fever
(C) malaria
(D) dengue

22. Why would global warming increase the dangers from mosquitoes?

(F) It would make the mosquitoes hungrier.
(G) It would make disease-causing germs even more deadly.
(H) It would decrease the areas in which humankind could live.
(J) It would increase the areas and the time in which mosquitoes could reproduce.

Meteorology, the science that deals with weather and weather prediction, has made many advances in recent years. However, it has not grown so accurate that it can lay to rest many of the old superstitions. One of the most enduring beliefs involves the rather large and very hairy caterpillar affectionately called the woolly bear.

Unlike other caterpillars, the woolly bear hibernates, but it does so by degrees. When the first frosty nights of winter come, it seeks shelter in a stable, a woodshed, or a pile of brush or stones. During a warm spell, it emerges to bask in the sun. When the temperature lowers again, it goes back to its chosen shelter. As the cold weather settles in earnest, it becomes a fuzzy little knot of ice, apparently frozen to the core. Comes spring, it thaws, wakens, and goes in search of its favorite food, the plaintain leaf. Eventually it weaves itself into its pupa stage and later emerges as a tiger moth.

Because of its furry coat, striped brown and white, and perhaps because of its hibernation, the woolly bear has joined mythology as a weather prophet. Those who examine it for predictions compare the width of its stripes. A narrow brown stripe, the saying goes, means a mild winter. But like so many other prophets, woolly bears in quantity do not stand up well to sharp scrutiny. One says yes; another says no. Yet regularly, during winter thaws, newsmakers sagely report the predictions of the woolly bear.

23. What was the author's purpose in writing this selection?

    (A) He wanted to prove that meteorology is more accurate in predictions than is the woolly bear.
    (B) He wanted to alert his readers about a dangerous superstition.
    (C) He wanted to prove the reliability of the woolly bear as a weather predictor.
    (D) He wanted to treat semihumorously a topic that people would find interesting.

24. Why does the woolly bear come out of hibernation?

    (F) The weather has become colder.
    (G) The weather has turned warm.
    (H) It has become hungry.
    (J) The cold has settled in for the winter.

25. What would a wide brown stripe on the back of the woolly bear signify?

    (A) Winter has come.
    (B) The coming winter will be milder than usual.
    (C) The coming winter will be colder than usual.
    (D) There will be much snow this coming winter.

26. How did the author most likely test the accuracy of woolly bear predictions?

    (F) He checked the weather data in the *Farmer's Almanac.*
    (G) He measured the stripes on more than one woolly bear.
    (H) He kept a record of temperatures all winter.
    (J) He asked the reporters to check their facts.

In the nineteenth century the gradual disappearance of the carrier pigeon was not realized as an omen of things to come. In the twentieth century we have taken in stride the impoverishment of our soils, the destruction of the ozone layer, the disappearance of many animal and plant species, and on and on.

In the last few years the list has grown longer, with the pollution of the waterways and the endless slaughter of organisms living in the oceans of the entire globe. At the same time our human population has been multiplying at an alarming rate, leading to further consumption of natural resources and plunging millions more of our species into poverty and hunger.

The time has come to recognize that, when humankind changes living conditions on Earth, the effect is not local but global. The destruction of a rain forest in South America affects the quality of life everywhere else. We must revalue our relationships with living and nonliving components of Earth before they ... and we ... reach extinction. We must realize that we are only one part of a not too vast ecosystem. The beauty of Earth and the awe that nature inspires in us must be central in our management of the life resources on Earth.

27. What was the author's main purpose in writing this passage?

   (A) He wants us to realize that humankind is on a path of self-destruction.
   (B) He wants us to feel sorry for species that are no longer living on Earth.
   (C) He wants us to see how beautiful nature is.
   (D) He wants us to be thankful for the gifts nature gives us.

28. How does the author try to convince the reader of the truth in his reasoning?

   (F) He shows us what life on Earth will be like if we continue to rearrange nature.
   (G) He shows us what life on Earth was like before humankind began to make changes.
   (H) He gives lists of recent examples of our destructive force.
   (J) He mentions many of the species that have vanished from Earth.

29. Why does the author believe that we should protect other species?

   (A) They were here before us.
   (B) They will destroy us if we don't.
   (C) We need them for food.
   (D) They are part of the natural wonder and beauty of Earth.

30. Which of the following assumptions underlies all of the author's arguments?

   (F) We are unwilling to change our ways.
   (G) We could create in our ecosystem a balance that would avoid massive harm to other species.
   (H) We are not powerful enough to affect the life structure on Earth.
   (J) The Earth is indestructible.

The Social Security Acts enacted by Congress in 1933 were an answer to an important question: To what extent is the government responsible for the well being of the disadvantaged, the unemployed, the aged, and the disabled? Before 1933, matters dealing with such security had been left to the states. Some states had enacted effective legislation for unemployment insurance and old-age pensions. However, with so many millions unemployed and so little tax revenue coming in, it was now clear that the states singly were unable to handle this financial burden. The Great Depression had given the problem national dimensions.

Those opposed to Social Security denounced the program as creeping socialism. They claimed that the federal government was taking over the duties of the state. Moreover, they felt that such legislation encouraged people to be idle and to let the government support them.

Those who favored the acts countered by saying that the program, financed by contributions from workers and employers, was self-sustaining. It was like an insurance policy, with all assuming the obligation to assist the unfortunate in time of need.

The final evaluation of the Social Security Administration has yet to be made. Through the years, Social Security has been broadened to include many more people and to increase benefits.

31. Which of the following adjectives describes the tone of this article?

   (A) argumentative
   (B) factual
   (C) persuasive
   (D) biased

32. Why did the federal government take over social security administration?

   (F) The state systems had become corrupt.
   (G) There was too much money involved for the states to handle.
   (H) The voters wanted the change.
   (J) The states lacked sufficient resources.

33. Which of the following was a major
    argument against social security legis-
    lation?

    (A) Working people do not have to pay
        for the benefits they will later
        receive.
    (B) The people who receive the benefits
        do not deserve them.
    (C) The states should handle social
        security without federal interfer-
        ence.
    (D) The program is too costly.

34. What of the following is a major advan-
    tage of our Social Security system?

    (F) Costs can be controlled easily.
    (G) The payments are not charitable
        handouts.
    (H) It has been in effect for more than
        50 years.
    (J) It has not required any changes
        through the years.

TEST 7   MATHEMATICS COMPUTATION

Number of questions: 30   *Time limit: 25 minutes*

DIRECTIONS: For numbers 1 through 30, select the correct answer to each problem.

EXAMPLE: $23\overline{)7498}$
(A) 316
(B) 306
(C) 346
(D) 326
(E) None of these

Ⓐ Ⓑ Ⓒ ● Ⓔ

Choice D is correct.

1.
3,605
2,540
2,095
+ 4,005

(F) 11,245
(G) 12,245
(H) 12,255
(J) 10,245
(K) None of these

2.
10,257
− 9,378

(A) 879
(B) 1,079
(C) 1,879
(D) 897
(E) None of these

3.
3206
× 715

(F) 2,292,290
(G) 292,290
(H) 2,192,290
(J) 2,092,920
(K) None of these

4. $27\overline{)21770}$

(A) $86\frac{8}{27}$
(B) 8060
(C) $860\frac{8}{27}$
(D) $806\frac{8}{27}$
(E) None of these

5. $\frac{5}{6} + \frac{4}{9} =$

(F) $\frac{17}{18}$
(G) $\frac{29}{36}$
(H) $1\frac{5}{18}$
(J) $1\frac{23}{48}$
(K) None of these

6. $6\frac{1}{4} - 2\frac{5}{6} =$

(A) $3\frac{1}{12}$
(B) $2\frac{11}{12}$
(C) $3\frac{7}{12}$
(D) $3\frac{5}{24}$
(E) None of these

7. $4\frac{2}{3} \times 2\frac{4}{7} =$

(F) 26
(G) 12
(H) $\frac{1}{2}$
(J) 62
(K) None of these

8. $6\frac{2}{3} \div 2\frac{11}{12} =$

(A) $2\frac{1}{7}$
(B) $2\frac{2}{7}$
(C) $1\frac{1}{7}$
(D) $2\frac{5}{7}$
(E) None of these

9. $29 \times 0.035 =$

(F) 1.015
(G) 0.1015
(H) 101.5
(J) 1.105
(K) None of these

10. $0.69 + 2.07 + 7.30 =$

(A) 2.06
(B) 10.16
(C) 10.06
(D) 1.006
(E) None of these

11. $90.56 \div 0.8 =$

(F) 11.32
(G) 0.1132
(H) 113.2
(J) 113.02
(K) None of these

12.
7 m 29 cm
− 2 m 43 cm

(A) 6 m 86 cm
(B) 9 m 72 cm
(C) 5 m 86 cm
(D) 4 m 86 cm
(E) None of these

13. $(-5)(-2)(-6) =$

(F) −13
(G) −60
(H) −42
(J) 60
(K) None of these

14.   3 ft. 5 in. × 6 =   (A) 20 ft. 6 in.
                              (B) 18 ft. 10 in.
                              (C) 19 ft. 10 in.
                              (D) 20 ft. 4 in.
                              (E) None of these

15. $\frac{5}{6} + \left(-\frac{4}{9}\right) =$ (F) $\frac{11}{18}$
                              (G) $\frac{5}{18}$
                              (H) $\frac{7}{36}$
                              (J) $\frac{11}{36}$
                              (K) None of these

16. $-8 + (-4) =$ (A) −12
                              (B) 32
                              (C) −4
                              (D) +4
                              (E) None of these

17. $(-6) \times (-4) =$ (F) 10
                              (G) −10
                              (H) −24
                              (J) 24
                              (K) None of these

18. $7 + (-2) =$ (A) 9
                              (B) −9
                              (C) 5
                              (D) −5
                              (E) None of these

19. $-7 \times 5 =$ (F) −12
                              (G) −35
                              (H) 35
                              (J) 12
                              (K) None of these

20. $-15 + (-4) =$ (A) 19
                              (B) 60
                              (C) −60
                              (D) −19
                              (E) None of these

21. $6.05 - 2.78 =$ (F) −3.27
                              (G) 3.27
                              (H) −8.83
                              (J) 8.83
                              (K) None of these

22. $(-2)(3)(-6) =$ (A) −36
                              (B) −11
                              (C) 11
                              (D) 36
                              (E) None of these

23. $3\frac{5}{9} + 4\frac{2}{9} =$ (F) $7\frac{7}{9}$
                              (G) $12\frac{7}{9}$
                              (H) $7\frac{1}{3}$
                              (J) $1\frac{7}{9}$
                              (K) None of these

24. $4.79 + 2.304 =$ (A) 6.094
                              (B) 7.194
                              (C) 7.094
                              (D) 8.094
                              (E) None of these

25. $\left(4 - \frac{2}{5}\right) \div 6 =$ (F) $\frac{3}{5}$
                              (G) $\frac{5}{3}$
                              (H) $\frac{9}{20}$
                              (J) $1\frac{2}{3}$
                              (K) None of these

26. $0.48 + \frac{3}{5} - \frac{7}{10} =$ (A) 1.38
                              (B) 0.28
                              (C) −0.38
                              (D) 0.38
                              (E) None of these

27. $0.504 \times 60 =$ (F) 3.024
                              (G) 0.3024
                              (H) 0.03024
                              (J) 30.24
                              (K) None of these

28. $6 - 4\frac{3}{8} =$ (A) $2\frac{5}{8}$
                              (B) $1\frac{5}{8}$
                              (C) $1\frac{1}{2}$
                              (D) $1\frac{1}{8}$
                              (E) None of these

29. $0.8 \div 0.002 =$ (F) 4
                              (G) 400
                              (H) 40
                              (J) 0.04
                              (K) None of these

30. $12 \div 1\frac{1}{5} =$ (A) 7
                              (B) 10
                              (C) $14\frac{2}{5}$
                              (D) 12
                              (E) None of these

TEST 8   MATHEMATICS CONCEPTS AND APPLICATIONS

Number of questions: 35   *Time limit: 27 minutes*

> DIRECTIONS: For numbers 1 through 35, select the correct answer in each case.

1. In the number 98,103, what is the value of the 8?

   (A) 80
   (B) 80,000
   (C) 800
   (D) 8,000

2. A concert hall has 24 rows of seats with 32 seats in each row. At a certain concert 75% of the seats were occupied. At $12 per seat, how much money was collected at this concert?

   (F) $768
   (G) $6,912
   (H) $9,216
   (J) $1,536

3. $a^6 \div a^2 =$

   (A) $a \times a \times a$
   (B) $a \times a$
   (C) $a \times a \times a \times a$
   (D) a

4. At a sale of TV sets, a dealer sold $\frac{2}{3}$ of the sets on sale. If she sold 64 sets, how many sets were put on sale?

   (F) 96
   (G) 32
   (H) 128
   (J) 100

5. On the number line below, the letters represent integers with the origin at *O*. Then $2E + T =$

   F E D C B A O P Q R S T U V W

   (A) 10
   (B) 0
   (C) −5
   (D) 5

6. A chicken weighs 2 pounds 10 ounces. At $0.72 per pound, the cost of the chicken is

   (F) $1.53
   (G) $1.50
   (H) $1.89
   (J) $1.76

7. A solution of the inequality $4 > \square > -2$ is

   (A) 5
   (B) −5
   (C) −1
   (D) 7

8. 10^7 is equal to

   (F) 1 million
   (G) 100 thousand
   (H) 10 million
   (J) 100 million

9. A dealer bought a chair for $90 and sold it at a gain of 45%. What was the selling price of the chair?

   (A) $130.50
   (B) $1305
   (C) $140.50
   (D) $145

10. A shirt costs *x* dollars, and a tie costs *y* dollars. The cost of 1 shirt and 2 ties is

    (F) $2xy$
    (G) $2x + y$
    (H) $x + y$
    (J) $x + 2y$

11. $\{a, c, e, f, g\} \cap \{c, f, h, j, k\} =$

    (A) $\{c, f\}$
    (B) $\{a, c, f\}$
    (C) $\{f, g, h\}$
    (D) $\{a, f, j\}$

12. The sum of two numbers is 100. If one-half of the larger number is 30, what is one-fifth of the smaller number?

    (F) 12
    (G) 15
    (H) 8
    (J) 9

13. If $3y - 1 = 11$, then the value of $y^2 + y =$

    (A) 16
    (B) $3\frac{1}{3}$
    (C) 15
    (D) 20

14. Which of the following sentences is *false*?

    (F) $5 > -3$
    (G) $-2 > -1$
    (H) $0 > -4$
    (J) $-6 > -7$

15. A storage room is 14 feet long, 9 feet wide, and 8 feet high. How many cubic feet of storage space does the room contain?

    (A) 31
    (B) 108
    (C) 1,008
    (D) 410

16. The diagram below shows how many students study the sciences of physics, biology, and chemistry at Adams High School. How many students study both physics and biology?

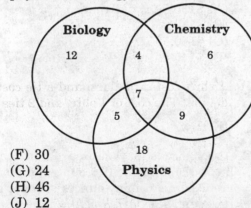

    (F) 30
    (G) 24
    (H) 46
    (J) 12

17. A troop of scouts hikes 6 miles due north and then 8 miles due east. How many miles is the troop from its starting point?

    (A) 10
    (B) 12
    (C) 14
    (D) 16

18. Which of the following sentences is correct?

    (F) $\frac{4}{5} > \frac{3}{4} > \frac{7}{9}$
    (H) $\frac{7}{9} > \frac{4}{5} > \frac{3}{4}$
    (G) $\frac{4}{5} > \frac{7}{9} > \frac{3}{4}$
    (J) $\frac{7}{9} > \frac{3}{4} > \frac{4}{5}$

19. If $x + y = 6$
    and $x - y = 2$,
    then $y =$

    (A) 8
    (B) 5
    (C) 4
    (D) 2

20. At noon the shadow of a building is 24 feet. At the same time the shadow of a flagpole 8 feet tall is 6 feet. The height of the building, in feet, is

    (F) 30
    (G) 36
    (H) 32
    (J) 28

21. The ratio of John's money to Bill's money is 5:3. If John gives Bill $5 they will have equal amounts. Which of the following equations may be used to find out how much money John has?

    (A) $5x = 3x + 5$
    (B) $5x - 5 = 3x$
    (C) $5x + 5 = 3x - 5$
    (D) $5x - 5 = 3x + 5$

22. A reasonable estimate of weight of a bag of apples is

    (F) 10 milligrams
    (G) 2 kilograms
    (H) 10 kilometers
    (J) 10 grams

23. Which of the following sets of numbers may replace the box to make the following sentence true: $4 > \square > 0$?

    (A) 1, –2
    (B) 2, 3, 4
    (C) –2, 3
    (D) –1, 2, 3

24. In △*ABC*, *AB* = *AC*. If the measure of ∠*A* is 64°, then the measure of ∠*B* is

(F) 64°
(G) 60°
(H) 58°
(J) 50°

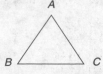

25. The coordinates of the point where the line $\overline{AB}$ crosses the *x*-axis are

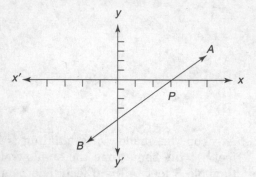

(A) (0, 3)
(B) (0, –4)
(C) (3, 0)
(D) (–3, 4)

26. Two cars start from the same town and travel in opposite directions. The faster car travels at an average speed of 50 miles per hour, and the slower car travels at an average speed of 40 miles per hour. In how many hours will the two cars be 360 miles apart?

(F) 4

(G) 5

(H) $3\frac{1}{2}$

(J) $4\frac{1}{2}$

27. On a certain map the scale is 1 inch = 40 miles. The towns of Chester and Holden are 220 miles apart. Their distance on the map, in inches, is

(A) 4
(B) 5
(C) 6
(H) $5\frac{1}{2}$

28. A man borrowed $8,000 and agreed to pay interest at the rate of $10\frac{1}{2}$% annually. If he repaid the loan after 9 months, how much interest did he have to pay?

(F) $600
(G) $630
(H) $680
(J) $800

29. The ticketed price of a coat was $81. If this price represented a discount of 25%, what was the original price of the coat?

(A) $59.75
(B) $101.25
(C) $98.00
(D) $108.00

30. In the diagram, *AB* = *AC* and the measure of ∠*ACD* = 112°. The measure of ∠*A* =

(F) 68°
(G) 44°
(H) 70°
(J) 65°

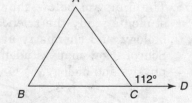

31. If *x* + 2 = *y* – 3, then

(A) *x* exceeds *y* by 5
(B) *x* is greater than *y*
(C) *y* exceeds *x* by 5
(D) *x* = *y*

32. A recipe calls for 9 ounces of butter and 3 ounces of sugar. If 6 ounces of butter are used, how many ounces of sugar are needed?

(F) 2

(G) $2\frac{1}{2}$

(H) $2\frac{3}{4}$

(J) $3\frac{1}{2}$

33. A man earns $10.50 per hour. If he works 7 hours and 20 minutes, he earns

    (A) $75
    (B) $77
    (C) $76.50
    (D) $77.20

34. A family spends 25% of its monthly budget for rent. In drawing a circle graph of the family's budget, the measure of the angle at the center that represents rent expense is

    (F) 90°
    (G) 100°
    (H) 80°
    (J) 75°

35. The circumference of a circle is 24π inches. What is the area, in square inches, of the circle?

    (A) 12π
    (B) 96π
    (C) 144π
    (D) 120π

TEST 9   LANGUAGE MECHANICS

Number of questions: 20   *Time limit: 10 minutes*

> DIRECTIONS: For numbers 1 through 5 determine which part of the sentence, if any, has a word that requires a capital letter.

1. My favorite uncle | will visit | the Lincoln Memorial | this fall. | None
   (A)   (B)   (C)   (D)   (E)

2. During the great depression | my grandfather | worked for two semesters
   (F)   (G)   (H)

   in a small southern university. | None
   (J)   (K)

3. Our family spends | New Year's eve | in northern Texas
   (A)   (B)   (C)

   with our Spanish-speaking relatives. | None
   (D)   (E)

4. Visiting kings | and prime ministers | often visit the white house
   (F)   (G)   (H)

   when they are in our country. | None
   (J)   (K)

5. When my sister | attended high school | in the big city
   (A)   (B)   (C)

   she studied biology and chemistry. | None
   (D)   (E)

> DIRECTIONS: For numbers 6 through 15 determine which punctuation mark, if any, is required in the sentence.

6. All I can say is that theres nothing left for us.

   (F) ,   (G) ;   (H) '   (J) !   (K) None

7. When the package arrives see that I get it.

   (A) ,   (B) .   (C) ;   (D) :   (E) None

8. Dear Ms. Robinson

   (F) .   (G) ;   (H) :   (J) —   (K) None

9. My kindergarten teacher Mrs. Abbott, lives there.

   (A) ,   (B) ;   (C) —   (D) '   (E) None

10. Nevertheless I regret having to take that step.

   (F) ;   (G) ,   (H) :   (J) .   (K) None

11. Whatever is theirs must remain where it is.

   (A) ,   (B) :   (C) '   (D) ;   (E) None

12. "Lucy do not forget the meeting this afternoon."

   (F) :   (G) ,   (H) .   (J) ?   (K) None

13. The fur has lost its sheen by this time.

   (A) ,   (B) '   (C) !   (D) ;   (E) None

14. He said that todays the last day of the fair.

   (F) ,   (G) "..."   (H) :   (J) '   (K) None

15. I am not infantile careless, greedy, and selfish!

   (A) .   (B) '   (C) :   (D) ,   (E) None

DIRECTIONS: For numbers 16 through 20 read the passage and note the underlined, numbered parts. Select the answer that shows the best capitalization and punctuation for each part.

The agora, a public square or market <u>place was</u> found in every ancient Greek city. "It
16

began as the site of public <u>assembly said</u> a well-known <u>anthropologist it</u> was used increasingly
17   18

for political and commercial purposes." The most famous agora is the <u>Athenian situated</u>
19

<u>northwest of the acropolis</u>.
20

16. (F) place; was
   (G) place. Was
   (H) place, was
   (J) place: was
   (K) Best as is

17. (A) assembly;" said
   (B) assembly" said
   (C) assembly," said
   (D) assembly", said
   (K) Best as is

18. (F) anthropologist, "it
   (G) anthropologist. "It
   (H) anthropologist; "it
   (J) anthropologist: "it
   (K) Best as is

19. (A) Athenian, situated
   (B) Athenian. Situated
   (C) athenian situated
   (D) athenian. Situated
   (K) Best as is

20. (F) North West of the acropolis
   (G) Northwest of the Acropolis,
   (H) Northwest of the acropolis
   (J) northwest of the Acropolis
   (K) Best as is

TEST 10   LANGUAGE EXPRESSION

Number of questions: 32   *Time limit: 25 minutes*

DIRECTIONS: For numbers 1 through 7, choose the word that best completes the sentence.

1. The danger of the past was that people became slaves. _____, the danger of the future is that people may become robots.

   (A) Nevertheless
   (B) However
   (C) Besides
   (D) Therefore

2. Be pleasant until ten o'clock in the morning. _____ the rest of the day will take care of itself.

   (F) Because
   (G) Even though
   (H) And then
   (J) But

3. Human action can be modified to some extent, _____ human nature cannot be changed.

   (A) considering
   (B) so
   (C) but
   (D) or

4. She is definitely the _____ of the two sisters.

   (F) most prettiest
   (G) more prettier
   (H) prettier
   (J) prettiest

5. They had _____ in the operatta that night.

   (A) sang
   (B) sing
   (C) singed
   (D) sung

6. She had never _____ that horse before.

   (F) rode
   (G) rided
   (H) ridden
   (J) ride

7. She never could have _____ up with us.

   (A) catch
   (B) catched
   (C) caught
   (D) caughted

DIRECTIONS: For numbers 8 through 10 choose the sentence that is correctly written.

8. (F) Susanna rushed into the room she told us the good news.
   (G) Susanna, after rushing into the room with the good news.
   (H) Susanna rushed into the room to tell us the good news.
   (J) When Susanna rushed into the room with the good news.

9. (A) The motor was repaired, we began our journey.
   (B) After the motor was repaired, and we began our journey.
   (C) The motor was repaired, and we began our journey.
   (D) The motor having been repaired and we beginning our journey.

10. (F) The storm struck suddenly all the lights went out.
    (G) When the storm struck suddenly and the lights went out.
    (H) The storm striking suddenly and the lights going out.
    (J) The sudden storm caused all the lights to go out.

DIRECTIONS: For numbers 11 through 16, choose the sentence that is most clearly written.

11. (A) Coming into the room, the sudden quiet alarmed us.
    (B) When coming into the room, the sudden quiet alarmed us.
    (C) The sudden quiet set off an alarm coming into the room.
    (D) Coming into the room, we were alarmed by the sudden quiet.

12. (F) At the age of five, Jerry's parents moved the family to Brooklyn.
    (G) When Jerry was five, his parents moved the family to Brooklyn.
    (H) When five years old, Jerry's parents moved the family to Brooklyn.
    (J) On reaching the age of five, Jerry's parents moved the family to Brooklyn.

13. (A) When trying to solve the problem quickly, a diagram must be drawn.
    (B) In order to solve the problem quickly, a diagram must be drawn.
    (C) Solving the problem quickly, a diagram must be drawn.
    (D) To solve the problem quickly, you must draw a diagram.

14. (F) We decided to have lunch at one in the morning.
    (G) Alice said she would arrive on Thursday in her last letter.
    (H) The dictator threatened to punish those who opposed him with good reasons.
    (J) Within an hour the planes were assembled and ready for battle.

15. (A) Elated by our success, broad smiles covered our faces.
    (B) Having caught me in an unintentional error, his red pencil slashed across the typewritten page.
    (C) To escape from the crowd, the emergency exit was used.
    (D) Accepting his invitation was the biggest mistake I ever made.

16. (F) When on duty, the regulation uniform must be worn.
    (G) When on duty, they require that regulation uniforms be worn.
    (H) All officers must wear regulation uniforms when on duty.
    (J) Regulation uniforms must be worn when on duty.

DIRECTIONS: For numbers 17 through 20, choose the sentence that uses verbs correctly.

17. (A) Just as she enters the room, they voted on the issue.
    (B) We moved to Florida before my father lost his job.
    (C) Minutes after the accident happened, the rescue squad was on the scene.
    (D) Phyllis will testify if the case went to trial.

18. (F) All of my friends are invited when we had the birthday party.
    (G) After I planted the seeds, I waited impatiently for them to produce fruit.
    (H) My uncle says that you can do anything if you tried hard enough.
    (J) Had I listened to you, I would never have encountered this problem

19. (A) Just as she is about to talk, he walked away.
    (B) If I were you, I would leave now!
    (C) When I saw them coming, I am rushing into the store.
    (D) I go right up to the desk and asked them for my ticket.

20. (F) On Monday we will take the test, and not everyone had planned for it.
    (G) Promotion came but once a year, and yet I always worry about it.
    (H) Having entered the class two weeks late, she expected monumental difficulties.
    (J) Magellan proved that the world was round.

DIRECTIONS: For numbers 21 through 24, read the underlined sentences. Then choose the sentence that best combines these sentences into one.

21. Edna needed some charts for the report. Edna asked the librarian for help.

(A) Edna needed some charts for the report, and Edna asked the librarian for help.
(B) Needing some charts for her report, the librarian was asked for help by Edna.
(C) When Edna needed some charts for her report, Edna asked the librarian for help.
(D) When she needed some charts for her report, Edna asked the librarian for help.

22. Jonas Salk is a true hero. He worked unselfishly. He worked for the betterment of humanity.

(F) Jonas Salk is a true hero, and he worked unselfishly, and he worked for the betterment of humanity
(G) Jonas Salk is a true hero who worked unselfishly, and he worked for the betterment of humanity.
(H) Jonas Salk, a true hero, worked unselfishly for the betterment of humanity.
(J) Working unselfishly, Jonas Salk is a true hero, and he worked for the betterment of humanity.

23. The nineteenth century had physical frontiers. Today we have political, social, and scientific frontiers.

(A) Today we have political, social, and scientific frontiers, and the nineteenth century had physical frontiers.

(B) While the frontiers of the nineteenth century were all physical, the frontiers of today are political, social, and scientific.
(C) When we have political, social, and scientific frontiers today, the nineteenth century had physical frontiers.
(D) The nineteenth century had physical frontiers, and we today have political, social, and scientific frontiers.

24. There is no victory in war. The winner loses, and the loser loses. We must realize this.

(F) We must realize that there is no victory in war and that the winner loses and the loser loses.
(G) That there is no victory in war and that the winner loses and the loser loses is something we must recognize.
(H) We must realize that there is no victory in war since both the winner and loser are losers.
(J) We must realize that there is no victory in war since the winner loses and the loser loses.

25. The little girl was lost in the woods. She wandered off from home on Sunday.

(A) Wandering away from home on Sunday, the little girl was lost in the woods.
(B) The little girl who was lost in the woods had wandered away from home on Sunday.
(C) She wandered away from home on Sunday, and the little girl was lost in the woods.
(D) The girl wandered away from home on Sunday, and she was lost in the woods.

DIRECTIONS: For numbers 26 and 27 choose the topic sentence that best fits the paragraph.

26. _____ The young children flock to the sandy beach to play under the protection of the life guard. The older groups meet in the tree-shaded areas. The many visitors swim, paddle canoes, or sail across the lake. The adventurous explore the fishing grounds upstream.

(F) Ours is a large lake.
(G) On a hot summer's day the lake attracts varied groups.
(H) Being on a lake during the summer can be fun.
(J) Laking on a summer's day has its drawbacks.

27. _____ Two-way traffic invites impatient drivers to attempt unsafe passing of slower cars. The hum of the tires and frequently the lack of interesting scenery can induce driver sleepiness. The long, straight stretches encourage driving at unsafe high speeds.

(A) Driving on an interstate highway develops specialized driving skills.
(B) There are joys and dangers in driving on interstate highways.
(C) Serious hazards face drivers on interstate highways.
(D) Driving on interstate highways has its challenges and rewards.

DIRECTIONS: For numbers 28 and 29 choose the pair of sentences that best develop the topic sentence.

28. Nature's means of seed dispersal are many and varied.

(F) Coconuts can float many miles before the seed is landed on a distant shore. In the tumbleweeds, the whole plant breaks off from the roots when it stops growing.
(G) Many seeds have wings that can cause them to be carried by the wind. For a large group of others, birds serve as the means of transportation.

(H) Birds are tempted by the pleasantly flavored fruit surrounding the seeds. A large percentage of these seeds are destroyed.
(J) Nature is wise. Millions of seeds are produced so that a small number can grow and produce the next generation.

29. Peace in our time must rest upon the success or failure of the United Nations.

(A) History had proved that peace cannot be maintained by a combination of victorious powers. The rift between the Western nations and the Soviet Union widened through the years.
(B) The hopes of the people of the world created the United Nations. Too long have they endured the horrors of war.
(C) The balance of power arrangement has inevitably led to an arms race. Our former policy of isolation is outworn.
(D) By using economic power Japan succeeded in doing what the military power had failed to do. Military alliances have invariably fallen apart.

DIRECTIONS: For numbers 30 through 32, read the paragraph. Choose the sentence that does *not* belong in the paragraph.

30. 1. John Quincy Adams ranks among the ablest of our secretaries of state. 2. He kept open the lines of communication with the most powerful nations of Europe. 3. He was a major spokesman for the antislavery cause. 4. He forced Spain to cede Florida to the United States.

(F) Sentence 1
(G) Sentence 2
(H) Sentence 3
(J) Sentence 4

31. 1. Policing is one of the chief functions of government. 2. Without it, the individual would be without protection for his personal liberties. 3. Foreign governments could not deal with a government lacking this function. 4. Anarchy is the type of social structure in which there are no government controls.

(A) Sentence 1
(B) Sentence 2
(C) Sentence 3
(D) Sentence 4

32. 1. Each succeeding generation must be taught to recoil at the horror that was unleashed by the forces of Nazism 2. Six million Jews were not their only victims. 3. By 1933 the Nazis had formed the largest single political party in Germany. 4. Many millions more from Russia, Poland, France, and England were slaughtered like cattle and their bodies were burned in ovens.

(F) Sentence 1
(G) Sentence 2
(H) Sentence 3
(J) Sentence 4

Answers to Practice Cooperative Admissions Examination 2

TEST 1   SEQUENCES

1. D	5. B	9. B	13. D	17. B
2. G	6. J	10. J	14. J	18. F
3. D	7. B	11. A	15. C	19. B
4. J	8. H	12. H	16. G	20. H

Rating Your Results

Superior	17–20 correct
Average	13–16 correct
Below Average	12 or fewer correct

Material to Review: Chapter 13

TEST 2   ANALOGIES

1. C	5. C	9. C	13. D	17. C
2. F	6. H	10. G	14. F	18. H
3. D	7. B	11. B	15. D	19. A
4. G	8. H	12. F	16. F	20. J

Rating Your Results

Superior	17–20 correct
Average	13–16 correct
Below Average	12 or fewer correct

Material to Review: Chapter 13

TEST 3   MEMORY

1. D	5. A	9. C	13. E	17. C
2. G	6. K	10. H	14. H	18. K
3. E	7. B	11. D	15. D	19. C
4. G	8. J	12. G	16. J	20. H

Rating Your Results

Superior	16–20 correct
Average	12–15 correct
Below Average	11 or fewer correct

Material to Review: Chapter 13

TEST 4   VERBAL REASONING

1. C	5. B	9. A	13. C	17. D
2. H	6. F	10. J	14. G	18. F
3. D	7. B	11. C	15. C	19. B
4. H	8. G	12. G	16. J	20. G

Rating Your Results

Superior	17–20 correct
Average	13–16 correct
Below Average	12 or fewer correct

Material to Review: Chapter 4

TEST 5   READING VOCABULARY

1. J	9. G	17. J	25. J	33. G
2. C	10. D	18. A	26. A	34. C
3. G	11. J	19. J	27. H	35. F
4. D	12. B	20. B	28. D	36. D
5. G	13. F	21. H	29. G	37. F
6. A	14. C	22. B	30. A	38. C
7. F	15. F	23. F	31. J	39. J
8. D	16. D	24. B	32. C	40. B

Rating Your Results

Superior	27–40 correct
Average	23–26 correct
Below Average	22 or fewer correct

Material to Review: Chapter 4

TEST 6   READING COMPREHENSION

1. D	8. J	15. A	22. J	29. D
2. G	9. B	16. G	23. D	30. G
3. D	10. J	17. C	24. G	31. B
4. G	11. A	18. H	25. C	32. J
5. C	12. H	19. B	26. G	33. C
6. J	13. C	20. F	27. A	34. G
7. B	14. G	21. C	28. H	

Rating Your Results

Superior	31–34 correct
Average	26–30 correct
Below Average	29 or fewer correct

Material to Review: Chapter 5

TEST 7 MATHEMATICS COMPUTATION

1. G	7. G	13. G	19. G	25. F
2. A	8. B	14. A	20. D	26. D
3. F	9. F	15. K	21. G	27. J
4. D	10. C	16. A	22. D	28. B
5. H	11. H	17. J	23. F	29. G
6. E	12. D	18. C	24. C	30. B

Rating Your Results

Superior	26–30 correct
Average	20–25 correct
Below Average	19 or fewer correct

Material to Review: Chapters 7–12

TEST 8 MATHEMATICS CONCEPTS AND APPLICATIONS

1. D	8. H	15. C	22. G	29. D
2. G	9. A	16. J	23. D	30. G
3. C	10. J	17. A	24. H	31. C
4. F	11. A	18. H	25. C	32. F
5. C	12. H	19. D	26. F	33. B
6. H	13. D	20. H	27. D	34. F
7. C	14. G	21. D	28. G	35. C

Rating Your Results

Superior	32–35 correct
Average	24–31 correct
Below Average	23 or fewer correct

Material to Review: Chapters 7–12

TEST 9 LANGUAGE MECHANICS

1. C	5. E	9. A	13. E	17. C
2. F	6. H	10. G	14. J	18. G
3. B	7. A	11. E	15. D	19. A
4. H	8. H	12. G	16. H	20. J

Rating Your Results

Superior	18–20 correct
Average	15–17 correct
Below Average	14 or fewer correct

Material to Review: Chapter 6

TEST 10 LANGUAGE EXPRESSION

1. B	8. H	15. D	21. D	27. C
2. H	9. C	16. H	22. H	28. G
3. C	10. J	17. C	23. B	29. C
4. H	11. D	18. J	24. H	30. H
5. D	12. G	19. B	25. B	31. D
6. H	13. D	20. H	26. G	32. H
7. C	14. J			

Rating Your Results

Superior	29–32 correct
Average	25–28 correct
Below Average	24 or fewer correct

Material to Review: Chapter 6

Answer Explanations

TEST 1   SEQUENCES

1. (**D**) As we go from left to right, the position of the triangle (△) goes from fourth place to first place to second place. In the third panel the position of the triangle is the third place, followed by a circle.

2. (**G**) As we go from left to right, the position of the square (□) goes from first place to second place to third place. In the fourth panel the position of the square is the fourth place, preceded by a triangle.

3. (**D**) Each panel has two circles and two triangles. In the first panel the first two figures are shaded. In the second panel figures two and three are shaded. In the third panel figures three and four are shaded. In the fourth panel figures four and one are shaded.

4. (**J**) As we go from left to right, the shading appears in the first figure, then the second figure, and then the third figure. In the fourth panel, the shading should appear in the fourth figure. In each case, only the square figure is shaded.

5. (**B**) In each panel, the figures are the same except for shading. In the first panel, the shading appears in the upper left. In the second panel, the shading appears in the upper right. In the third panel, the shading appears in the lower left. In the fourth panel, the shading should appear in the lower right.

6. (**J**) Notice the pattern shown below:

   first panel: circle—square—triangle
   second panel: triangle—circle—square
   third panel: square—triangle—circle

   Since there are only three figures, we start the pattern again in the fourth panel with circle—square—triangle.

7. (**B**) In each panel, the second number is obtained by multiplying the first number by 3, and the third number is obtained by multiplying the second number by 3.

8. (**H**) In each panel, the second number is obtained by multiplying the first number by 2. The third number in the panel is obtained by subtracting 6 from the second number.

9. (**B**) The first number in each panel is obtained by adding 1 to the first number in the preceding panel (e.g., 6 + 1 = 7). The second number in each panel is obtained by adding 1 to the second number in the preceding panel. The third number in each panel is obtained by adding 1 to the third number in the preceding panel.

10. (**J**) The first number in each panel is obtained by adding 1 to the first number in the preceding panel (e.g. 7 + 1 = 8). The second number in each panel is obtained by adding 3 to the second number in the preceding panel. The third number in each panel is obtained by adding 5 to the third number in the preceding panel.

11. (**A**) The first number in each panel is obtained by adding 1 to the first number in the preceding panel (e.g., 5 + 1 = 6). The second number in each panel is obtained by adding 1 to the first number in the same panel. The third number in each panel is obtained by squaring the second number in the same panel.

12. (**H**) The first number in each panel is obtained by adding 1 to the first number in the preceding panel (e.g., 7 + 1 = 8). The second number in each panel is obtained by adding 2 to the preceding number in the same panel. The third number in each panel is obtained by adding 5 to the second number in the same panel.

13. (**D**) The first number in each panel is obtained by adding 5 to the first number in the preceding panel. The second number in each panel is obtained by adding 1 to the first number in the same panel. The third number in each panel is obtained by subtracting 2 from the second number in the same panel.

14. **(J)** The first number in each panel is obtained by adding 4, 6, 8, etc., in order to the first number in the preceding panel. The second number in each panel is obtained by subtracting 4 from the first number in the same panel. The third number in each panel is obtained by taking one-half of the second number in the same panel.

15. **(C)** In this case the pattern involves the subscripts only. The pattern is 1, 1, then 1, 2, then 1, 3, then 1, 4, and finally 1, 5.

16. **(G)** Here the subscript pattern is 7, 5, 1 then 6, 4, 2, then 5, 3, 3, then 4, 2, 4, and finally 3, 1, 5. In each case, in going from left to right, the first two numbers are each decreased by 1 and the third number is increased by 1.

17. **(B)** The first two letters of each word are obtained from the last two letters of the preceding word in reverse. The last letter is obtained by following the order in the alphabet; that is, C, D, E, etc.

18. **(F)** The first two letters of each word are obtained by following the alphabetic pattern BC, CD, DE, EF. The third letter also follows the alphabet: BCA, CDB etc.

19. **(B)** The first two letters of each word follow the alphabetic pattern AB, BC, CD, etc. The third letter of each word also follows the alphabet, starting with D; thus, we have D, E, F, G, H.

20. **(H)** The first letter of each word follows the alphabet, beginning with R; thus, we have R, S, T, U, V. The second letter of each word follows the alphabet in reverse, beginning with E; thus, we have E, D, C, B, A. The third letter in each word also follows the alphabet in reverse, beginning with V; thus, we have V, U, T, S, R.

TEST 2   ANALOGIES

1. **(C)** A dog lives in a kennel, and a man lives in a house.

2. **(F)** A bow tie is worn with a shirt, and a muffler is worn with a coat.

3. **(D)** A painter uses a brush, and a carpenter uses a hammer.

4. **(G)** A baseball player uses a bat, and a golfer uses a golf club.

5. **(C)** A gardener works with flowers, and an auto mechanic works with cars.

6. **(H)** Gloves are worn on the hands, and a hat is worn on the head.

7. **(B)** A secretary uses a typewriter, and a fireman uses a hose.

8. **(H)** A boxer fights in a ring, and a tennis player plays in a court.

9. **(C)** A library holds books, and a museum holds statues.

10. **(G)** Eggs are contained in a nest, and jewelry is contained in a jewel box.

11. **(B)** Scouts live in tents, and bears live in caves.

12. **(F)** The Earth revolves around the Sun; the Moon revolves around the Earth.

13. **(D)** A seamstress is guided by a pattern; an architect depends on a blueprint;.

14. **(F)** A sculptor works on a statue; an artist works on a painting.

15. **(D)** A father is to a son as a mother is to a daughter.

16. **(F)** An eggplant and a cucumber are both vegetables; a banana and an apple are both fruits.

17. **(C)** Cymbals and drums are both percussion instruments; violins and cellos are both string instruments.

18. **(H)** Bread makes a sandwich; a roll holds a hamburger.

19. **(A)** A lawyer addresses a jury; a preacher addresses a congregation.

20. **(J)** Chalk is used to write on a chalk board. A pen is used to write on a pad.

TEST 3   MEMORY

Here are some suggested associations and mental pictures.

1. **(D)** Picture a broken mirror reflecting the dirty face of a child.

2. (**G**) Picture *Mac Rat,* a rodent with out-size ears.

3. (**E**) Picture a big foot standing motionless (wasting time).

4. (**G**) Associate saulie with *sad liar.*

5. (**A**) Associate to be *fashion*able (*fashious*) can be troublesome because of the cost.

6. (**K**) Associate *viti*pend with *viti*ae, meaning to weaken.

7. (**B**) Picture a violin wrapped in Saran-wrap.

8. (**J**) Associate *fatal* with *fati*ferous.

9. (**C**) Associate de*coll*ation with the idea of cutting a head off at the *coll*ar (neck).

10. (**H**) *Mer*acius means full of *mer*it (unspoiled).

11. (**D**) Associate eu*rip*ize with a ship *rip*ped away from its anchor, so that it swings to and fro (fluctuates).

12. (**G**) A grilled grilse should make a delicious fish (salmon) dish.

13. (**E**) Picture a person who is bold (fram-*bold*) enough to express contrary opinions and get into quarrels.

14. (**H**) A lizard can quickly regrow a missing tail; in other words, it can adda tail!

15. (**D**) Associate *macro* with a *long* strand of *mac*aroni; picture yourself falling asleep during a *long,* boring speech.

16. (**J**) Associate the *ex* in *ex*imious with the *ex* in *ex*cellent.

17. (**C**) A cowardly person is likely to run away from any threat and go into hi(l)ding.

18. (**K**) Picture yourself filled with worry as you face a big test. Coming toward you is Superman, who says reassuringly, "Don't globben! I'm here to help you!"

19. (**C**) Associate de*sec*ate with *sec*tion; picture yourself cutting out a section of an apple pie.

20. (**H**) Sack comes from the Latin word meaning to pull, and butt from the word meaning to push. Sackbutt should give you a mental picture of the push and pull that produces trombone music.

TEST 4   VERBAL REASONING

1. (**C**) An engine is a necessary part of an automobile.

2. (**H**) Food is a necessary part of a dinner.

3. (**D**) One who is brave must have courage.

4. (**H**) Landing gear is a necessary part of an airplane.

5. (**B**) Keys are a necessary part of a piano.

6. (**F**) Hands are a necessary part of a clock.

7. (**B**) A lens is a necessary part of a microscope.

8. (**G**) Biology and physics are sciences. Sculpture and painting are types of art.

9. (**A**) Lead and copper are metals. Diamonds and sapphires are gems.

10. (**J**) Red and blue are colors. Courthouses and schoolhouses are buildings.

11. (**C**) Soup and a sandwich are served for lunch. Salad and an entree are served for dinner.

12. (**G**) A sofa and a table belong in a living room. A refrigerator and a microwave belong in a kitchen.

13. (**C**) The syllable *dom* occurs in both *leb-dom* and *rabdom.* The words *downtown* and *uptown* contain the common syllable *town.* Therefore, *dom* mean "town." Also, *leb* means "down," and *rab* means "up." Since *lebtor* means "downstream" and *leb* means "down," *tur* must mean "stream." Thus, *rabtur* means "upstream."

14. (**G**) The syllable *cul* occurs in both *pra-cul* and *sulcul.* The words *skyway* and *byway* contain the common syllable *way.* Therefore, *cul* means "way." Also, *pra* means "sky," and *sul* means "by." Since *sulmur* means "bypath" and *sul* means "by," *mur* must mean "path." Thus, *murcul* means "pathway."

15. (**C**) According to the paragraph, Frank is happy with both his social life on campus and his science course.

16. (**J**) According to the last sentence, John Chase solves his problems, not all of which he enjoys, with a reasonable degree of success.

17. (**D**) According to the paragraph, Doris Martin finds pleasure in the works of most classical composers, but Beethoven and Mozart are her favorites.

18. (**F**) According to the paragraph, Ella Burns's good health makes her want to remain active, and therefore she has volunteered to help young people.

19. (**B**) According to the paragraph, Ben Davis has always enjoyed reading books.

20. (**G**) According to the paragraph, booking an airplane flight is a complex task involving many factors, all of which must be weighed if the traveler is to be served properly.

TEST 5   READING VOCABULARY

1.–10. There is only one synonym for each given word.

11.–20. There is only one antonym for each given word.

21. (**H**) A *successful sales campaign* leads to *gratified* managers

22. (**B**) *Lack of equipment* justifies *hampered*.

23. (**F**) *Bands of cruel outlaws* points toward *harassed* settlers.

24. (**B**) *Dense hedge of thorns* and *barbed wire* would be *impenetrable*.

25. (**J**) A *pair of paper stretchers* would fool only a *novice*.

26. (**A**) *Well-trained students* would leave in an *orderly fashion*.

27. (**H**) The key phrase is *in a democracy*, where the *will of the majority* must ultimately *prevail*.

28. (**D**) *Thousands of vacationers* will be lured outdoors by *balmy* weather.

29. (**G**) *Loving grandparents* points toward *cajole*.

30. (**A**) The function of a *monument* is to keep alive, to *perpetuate*.

31.–40. In each case, there is only one word that means the same as the two given words or phrases.

TEST 6   READING COMPREHENSION

1. (**D**) After the author has reviewed the Brooklyn background of the Los Angeles Dodgers, he concludes with a humorous tribute to Brooklynite forbearance.

2. (**G**) The people crossing the streets had to avoid being run over by one of the many trolleys.

3. (**D**) They were called Robins in honor of manager Wilbert Robinson.

4. (**G**) Sentence 4 states "... recall when the Dodgers were not out of California, but were natives of ... Brooklyn."

5. (**C**) A child 2–4 years old (choice A) or even 5–6 years old (B) would not be sent alone to the park. A 12- to 15-year-old (D) would not be sitting passively on a bench. A youngster aged 7–10, however, could daydream this way while sitting on a park bench; C is therefore correct.

6. (**J**) By exposing Ellen's daydreams to us, the story leads us to realize her feelings.

7. (**B**) The action had to occur on a park bench as Ellen sat there daydreaming. See the first and second paragraphs of the story.

8. (**J**) Since Ellen was sitting alone with her reveries, we can understand that she used daydreams to compensate for her loneliness.

9. (**B**) We can conclude that, since there were so many people in the park, Ellen's mother thought that it was safe for her to be there alone. All of the other choices are pure guesses.

10. (**J**) The workers could not eliminate poverty, but they could keep the slum dwellers happily busy and out of crime's way.

11. (**A**) The people moved into the "centers of cities, where the available jobs were."

12. (**H**) The recreational activities brought not only children but also adults into the settlement buildings.

13. (**C**) The social workers could not "instill hope, ambition, and socially approved goals" if the people did not want to better themselves when given a chance to do so.

14. (**G**) The author stresses in the first sentence that great leaders should serve as models to generations that follow.

15. (**A**) If leaders are to serve as models, what is told about them should point positively in that direction. The cherry tree story, true or untrue, is of no real importance.

16. (**G**) Most of the selection deals with the time Washington was Commander-in-Chief of the army.

17. (**C**) The key statement is "he became larger than life, the rallying center of the war effort."

18. (**H**) Nowhere is there any implication that Washington refused to bend or adjust.

19. (**B**) The author tells us directly about the "dinosaurs that too once ruled supreme but are now extinct."

20. (**F**) Since they are capable of injecting deadly germs from their bodies into ours without the germs harming them, we can infer that they do not catch the diseases.

21. (**C**) The article specifically cites millions of deaths from malaria. We can infer that the other diseases, although deadly, do not take as great a toll.

22. (**J**) Since global warming will change many areas from cold to warm, we can deduce that there would be many more mosquitoes since they thrive on warmth.

23. (**D**) The woolly bear is not of earth-shaking significance. The tart last sentence can be interpreted as humor.

24. (**G**) This answer is substantiated by the statement in the selection "During a warm spell, it emerges to bask in the sun."

25. (**C**) Given the reverse statement in the third paragraph, we can deduce that a wide brown stripe means a cold winter.

26. (**G**) We can deduce that, since he says one woolly bear's stripes do not match those of another, he must be reporting from first-hand observations.

27. (**A**) This choice paraphrases "We must revalue our relationships...before...we ... reach extinction."

28. (**H**) After listing many examples, the author finally resorts to "and on and on..."

29. (**D**) This conclusion can be deduced from "...we are only one part of a not too vast ecosystem."

30. (**G**) The author's underlying assumption is that, if we change our ways, we can create a balance on Earth that will not benefit us at the expense of other species.

31. (**B**) The author does not argue or try to persuade us to accept a particular point of view. He tries to be impartial by presenting both sides of an issue. He lists provable facts.

32. (**J**) This answer is substantiated by the following quotation from the selection: "...it was now clear that the states singly were unable to handle this financial burden."

33. (**C**) This answer is based on the statement: "They [opponents] claimed that the federal government was taking over the duties of the states."

34. (**G**) This can be deduced from the fact that both employer and worker contribute to the Social Security fund.

TEST 8 MATHEMATICS CONCEPTS AND APPLICATIONS

1. **(D)** The number 8 represents 8,000. If we write the last 4 digits of the given number as 8,103, we can see this more clearly.

2. **(G)** The number of seats in the hall is $24 \times 32 = 768$.
$768 \times 75\% = 768 \times \frac{3}{4} = 576$
$576 \times \$12 = \$6,912$

3. **(C)** $a^6 = a \times a \times a \times a \times a \times a$
$a^2 = a \times a$

When we divide, we drop out the first two sets of a's, leaving $a \times a \times a \times a = a^4$.

4. **(F)** Let x = the number of sets on sale. Then $\frac{2}{3} x = 64$

Multiplying both sides of the equation by $\frac{3}{2}$ we have
$$x = \frac{3}{2} \times 64 = 96$$

5. **(C)** On the number line, E represents -5 and T represents $+5$.

F E D C B A O P Q R S T U V W

$2E + T = 2(-5) + 5 = -10 + 5 = -5$

6. **(H)** 16 ounces = 1 pound

10 ounces $= \frac{10}{16} = \frac{5}{8}$ pound

Thus, the chicken weighs $2\frac{5}{8}$ or $\frac{21}{8}$ pounds.

$\frac{21}{8} \times 0.72 = \$1.89$

7. **(C)** The required solution is less than 4 and greater than -2. Of the numbers given, only -1 meets these requirements.

8. **(H)** 10^7 is equal to 1 followed by 7 zeros. $10^7 = 10,000,000$, or 10 million

9. **(A)** $45\% = 0.45$
$0.45 \times 90 = \$40.5$ gain
$\$90 + \$40.5 = \$130.50$, selling price

10. **(J)** Cost of 1 shirt = x dollars
Cost of 1 tie = y dollars
Cost of 2 ties = $2y$ dollars
Cost of 1 shirt + cost of 2 ties = $x + 2y$

11. **(A)** The symbol $\cap$ means intersection. The intersection of two sets consists of the elements of the sets that are common to both sets. In this case, the elements c and f appear in both sets. Thus, $\{a, c, e, f g\} \cap \{c, f, h, j, k\} = \{c, f\}$

12. **(H)** One-half the larger number is 30. Therefore, the larger number is 2×30, or 60. The smaller number is $100 - 60 = 40$.

One fifth of $40 = \frac{1}{5} \times 40 = 8$

13. **(D)** $3y - 1 = 11$
$3y = 11 + 1 = 12$
$y = 4$
$y^2 = 4 \times 4 = 16$
$y^2 + y = 16 + 4 = 20$

14. **(G)** $5 > -3$. This is true because a positive number is greater than a negative number.

$-2 > -1$. This is false since -2 is to the left of -1 on the number line.

Thus, $-2 < -1$.

15. **(C)** To obtain the volume of a box-shaped figure, we multiply the length by the width by the height; that is, we use the formula
$V = l \times w \times h$
In this, case, $l = 14$, $w = 9$, and $h = 8$.
$V = 14 \times 9 \times 8 = 1,008$ cubic feet.

16. **(J)** If we examine the diagram, we see that numbers 5 and 7 appear in both the biology circle and the physics circle. Thus, $5 + 7 = 12$ students take both biology and physics.

17. **(A)** Let x = the number of miles that the troop is from its starting point.

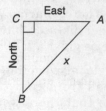

In $\triangle ABC$ we use the Pythagorean Theorem:
$x^2 = 6^2 + 8^2$
$x^2 = 36 + 64 = 100$
$x = 10$

18. (**H**) We can solve this problem readily by converting each fraction to a decimal:

$\frac{4}{5} = 0.80, \frac{3}{4} = 0.75, \frac{7}{9} = 0.78$

Thus, of the three fractions, $\frac{4}{5}$ is the largest, $\frac{7}{9}$ is second in size, and $\frac{3}{4}$ is the smallest.

Thus, $\frac{4}{5} > \frac{7}{9} > \frac{3}{4}$.

19. (**D**) If we add the two given equations, we have $2x = 8$, or $x = 4$.
In the equation $x + y = 6$, if $x = 4$ we have $4 + y = 6$ and $y = 6 - 4$, or 2.

20. (**H**) At noon the two triangles are similar, and the ratio of the building to its shadow is the same as the ratio of the flagpole to its shadow.

Building and shadow

Flagpole and shadow

This gives us the proportion

$\frac{x}{24} = \frac{8}{6}$

$6x = 8 \times 24 = 192$

$x = 192 \div 6 = 32$

The building is 32 feet tall.

21. (**D**) Let $5x$ = John's money.
And $3x$ = Bill's money
$5x - 5$ = John's money after giving $5 to Bill
$3x + 5$ = Bill's money after receiving $5 from John
$5x - 5 = 3x + 5$ is the required equation.

22. (**G**) 1 kilogram = 1,000 grams

= approximately $2\frac{1}{4}$ pounds

2 kilograms = approximately $2\left(2\frac{1}{4}\right)$

= $4\frac{1}{2}$ pounds, which could be the weight of a bag of apples.

23. (**D**) The numbers 1, 2, 3 are both less than 4 and greater than 0.

24. (**H**) Since $AB = AC$, the measure of $\angle B$ is equal to the measure of $\angle C$.

The measure of $\angle B$ + the measure of $\angle C$ + the measure of $\angle A = 180°$.
Let x = the measure of both $\angle B$ and $\angle C$
Then $x + x + 64 = 180$
$2x = 180 - 64 - 116$
$x = 58$
Thus, the measure of $\angle B = 58°$.

25. (**C**) Line $\overleftrightarrow{AB}$ cuts the x-axis at point P. The coordinates of point P are (3, 0).

26. (**F**) Let x = the number of hours each car travels. We can collect all our information in the chart below.

	Rate	× Time	= Distance
First car	50	x	$50x$
Second car	40	x	$40x$

We know that the sum of the two distances is 360 miles. This gives us the following equation:
$50x + 40x = 360$
$90x = 360$
$x = 4$

27. (**D**) 1 inch = 40 miles
If we divide 40 miles into 220 miles, we will obtain the number of inches on the map: $220 \div 40 = 5\frac{1}{2}$

28. (**G**) To find the interest we use this formula:

Interest = Principal × Rate × Time

In this case,

Principal = $8,000
Rate = $10\frac{1}{2}\% = \frac{21}{200}$
Time = 9 months = $\frac{9}{12}$ of a year
Interest = $8,000 \times \frac{21}{200} \times \frac{9}{12}$

$\overset{40}{8,000} \times \frac{21}{\underset{1}{200}} \times \frac{\overset{93}{9}}{\underset{4}{12}} = \frac{2520}{4} = \$630$

29. **(D)** Let x = the original price of the coat.
    Then $0.75x = 81$
    $$x = \frac{81}{0.75} = \$108.00$$

30. **(G)** Since the measure of $\angle ACD = 112°$,
    the measure of $\angle ACB = 180 - 112 = 68°$.
    Since $AB = AC$, the measure of $\angle ACB =$
    the measure of $\angle ABC = 68°$.

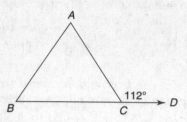

Measure of $\angle A$ + measure of $\angle ACB$ + measure $\angle ABC = 180°$.

Therefore, measure of $\angle A + 68° + 68° = 180°$.

Measure of $\angle A = 180° - 68° - 68° = 44°$

31. **(C)** $x + 2 = y - 3$
    $y - x = 2 + 3$
    $y - x = 5$
    Since $y - x = 5$, y is 5 greater than x, or y exceeds x by 5.

32. **(F)** The recipe calls for 9 ounces of butter, and 6 ounces of butter were used, that is, $\frac{6}{9}$, or $\frac{2}{3}$, of the amount of butter called for.

    Therefore, $\frac{2}{3}$ of the amount of sugar called for should be used.
    $\frac{2}{3} \times 3 = 2$ ounces of sugar

33. **(B)** 20 minutes = $\frac{20}{60}$, or $\frac{1}{3}$, of an hour.
    The man worked $7\frac{1}{3}$, or $\frac{22}{3}$, hours.
    $\frac{22}{3} \times 10.50 = \$77$

34. **(F)** The sum of the measures of the angles at the center of a circle graph is $360°$. In this case we need an angle that indicates 25%, or $\frac{1}{4}$, of $360°$.
    $\frac{1}{4}$ of $360° = 90°$

35. **(C)** We use the formula for the circumference of a circle:
    $C = 2\pi r$
    In this case, $24\pi = 2\pi r$, and $r = 12$.
    To find the area of the circle we use this formula:
    $A = \pi r^2$
    $A = \pi \times 12 \times 12 = 144\pi$

TEST 9   LANGUAGE MECHANICS

1. **(C)** The full name of a famous place is capitalized: *Lincoln Memorial.*

2. **(F)** The name of a well-known period of time is capitalized: *Great Depression.*

3. **(B)** The full name of a holiday is capitalized: *New Year's Eve.*

4. **(H)** The name of a famous building is capitalized: *White House.*

5. **(E)** Names of specific schools, cities, and school subjects that include proper adjectives (French literature) are capitalized. None of the words in this sentence meet this qualification.

6. **(H)** *There's* is a contraction of *there is,* and the apostrophe takes the place of the omitted letter.

7. **(A)** An introductory adverbial clause is followed by a comma: *When ... arrives, ...*

8. **(H)** A colon is used after the salutation of a business letter.

9. **(A)** An appositive is preceded and followed by commas: *My...teacher, Mrs. Abbott, ...*

10. **(G)** An introductory adverb is followed by a comma: *Nevertheless, I...*

11. **(E)** The possessive pronoun *theirs* requires no apostrophe.

12. **(G)** An introductory noun in direct address is followed by a comma: *"Lucy, do ...."*

13. **(E)** The possessive pronoun *its* requires no apostrophe.

14. **(J)** *Today's* is a contraction of *today is.* The apostrophe replaces the missing letter.

15. **(D)** A comma is required when *and* is omitted between the items in a series: *infantile, careless, ...*

16. **(H)** An appositive is separated by commas: *agora, a public square ... place, was ....*

17. (**C**) The comma is always inside the quotation marks at the end of a quotation:...*assembly," said....*

18. (**G**) Sentences are separated by a period, and the first letter of the second sentence is capitalized:...*anthropologist. "It....*

19. (**A**) Adjectives derived from proper nouns are capitalized: *Athenian* from *Athens.* A concluding participial phrase is introduced by a comma:...*Athenian, situated....*

20. (**J**) Points of the compass are not capitalized: *northwest.* Names of specific geographical sites are capitalized: *Acropolis.*

TEST 10 LANGUAGE EXPRESSION

1. (**B**) The connective *however* shows the contrast between the two ideas.

2. (**H**) The connective *and then* shows the time sequence.

3. (**C**) The connective *but* shows the contrast between the two ideas.

4. (**H**) The comparative form, *prettier,* is required when only two persons or things are compared.

5. (**D**) The past participle, *sung,* is required after the helping verb *had.*

6. (**H**) The past participle, *ridden,* is required after the helping verb *had.*

7. (**C**) The past participle, *caught,* is required after the helping verbs *could have.*

8. (**H**) Choice F is a run-on sentence; G and J are sentence fragments; H is a correct sentence.

9. (**C**) Choice A is a run-on sentence. B and D are sentence fragments; C is a correct sentence.

10. (**J**) Choice F is a run-on sentence; G and H are sentence fragments; J is a correct sentence.

11. (**D**) Choice D is the only sentence in which the participial phrase *Coming . . . room* is followed immediately by the word it modifies, *we.*

12. (**G**) This is the only sentence that makes clear who was 5 years old at the time of the move.

13. (**D**) This is the only sentence that makes clear who is to solve the problem. Here the introductory infinitive phrase is followed immediately by *you,* who will draw the diagram.

14. (**J**) This is the only sentence that does not have a misplaced prepositional phrase.

15. (**D**) This is the only sentence that does not contain a dangling participle (*Elated, Having caught*) or a dangling infinitive (*To escape*).

16. (**H**) This is the only sentence that explains who must wear uniforms on duty.

17. (**C**) Choice A mixes present (*enters*) and past (*voted*); D mixes future (*will testify*) and past (*went*). Choice B should have had *had moved* for action preceding another past action (*lost*); in C these two past tenses are used correctly.

18. (**J**) Choices F and H mix past and present tenses illogically. Since the planting came first, *had planted* is required in G. Choice J uses the subjunctive contrary to fact correctly.

19. (**B**) Choice B uses the present subjunctive contrary to fact correctly. The other three sentences mix past and present tenses incorrectly.

20. (**H**) In F the verb should be *has planned* since the present should follow the future *will take;* G mixes past and present incorrectly; J requires the present verb *is* to express an unchanging truth. Choice H uses correctly the parallel tenses *having entered* and *expected.*

21. (**D**) Choices A and C repeat *Edna* unnecessarily; B changes, the meaning; D avoids repetition and the weak *and* connection.

22. (**H**) This is the only sentence avoiding the weak *and.* It expresses all three ideas concisely and clear.

23. (**B**) This choice subordinates one of the ideas through the use of *while* and repeats *frontiers* for emphasis.

24. **(H)** This choice subordinates one idea through the use of *since* and expresses all the ideas concisely.

25. **(B)** This choice clarifies by the use of the subordinating *who* and the past and past perfect tenses of the verbs.

26. **(G)** The paragraph lists the varied groups that are attracted to the lake.

27. **(C)** The paragraph deals only with the serious hazards confronting drivers on highways.

28. **(G)** This is the only choice with two sentences dealing with nature's methods of seed dispersal.

29. **(C)** This is the only choice with two sentences indicating that people must look to the United Nations as a peace keeping mechanism.

30. **(H)** Adams's antislavery position is not related to his performance as secretary of state.

31. **(D)** In this paragraph, anarchy is not related to policing.

32. **(H)** Sentence 3 does not tie in with Nazism and cruelty.

Answer Sheet
Practice High School Placement Test 1

SUBTEST 1 VERBAL SKILLS

1. Ⓐ Ⓑ Ⓒ Ⓓ	13. Ⓐ Ⓑ Ⓒ Ⓓ	25. Ⓐ Ⓑ Ⓒ Ⓓ	37. Ⓐ Ⓑ Ⓒ Ⓓ	49. Ⓐ Ⓑ Ⓒ Ⓓ
2. Ⓐ Ⓑ Ⓒ Ⓓ	14. Ⓐ Ⓑ Ⓒ Ⓓ	26. Ⓐ Ⓑ Ⓒ Ⓓ	38. Ⓐ Ⓑ Ⓒ Ⓓ	50. Ⓐ Ⓑ Ⓒ Ⓓ
3. Ⓐ Ⓑ Ⓒ Ⓓ	15. Ⓐ Ⓑ Ⓒ Ⓓ	27. Ⓐ Ⓑ Ⓒ Ⓓ	39. Ⓐ Ⓑ Ⓒ Ⓓ	51. Ⓐ Ⓑ Ⓒ Ⓓ
4. Ⓐ Ⓑ Ⓒ Ⓓ	16. Ⓐ Ⓑ Ⓒ Ⓓ	28. Ⓐ Ⓑ Ⓒ Ⓓ	40. Ⓐ Ⓑ Ⓒ Ⓓ	52. Ⓐ Ⓑ Ⓒ Ⓓ
5. Ⓐ Ⓑ Ⓒ Ⓓ	17. Ⓐ Ⓑ Ⓒ Ⓓ	29. Ⓐ Ⓑ Ⓒ Ⓓ	41. Ⓐ Ⓑ Ⓒ Ⓓ	53. Ⓐ Ⓑ Ⓒ Ⓓ
6. Ⓐ Ⓑ Ⓒ Ⓓ	18. Ⓐ Ⓑ Ⓒ Ⓓ	30. Ⓐ Ⓑ Ⓒ Ⓓ	42. Ⓐ Ⓑ Ⓒ Ⓓ	54. Ⓐ Ⓑ Ⓒ Ⓓ
7. Ⓐ Ⓑ Ⓒ Ⓓ	19. Ⓐ Ⓑ Ⓒ Ⓓ	31. Ⓐ Ⓑ Ⓒ Ⓓ	43. Ⓐ Ⓑ Ⓒ Ⓓ	55. Ⓐ Ⓑ Ⓒ Ⓓ
8. Ⓐ Ⓑ Ⓒ Ⓓ	20. Ⓐ Ⓑ Ⓒ Ⓓ	32. Ⓐ Ⓑ Ⓒ Ⓓ	44. Ⓐ Ⓑ Ⓒ Ⓓ	56. Ⓐ Ⓑ Ⓒ Ⓓ
9. Ⓐ Ⓑ Ⓒ Ⓓ	21. Ⓐ Ⓑ Ⓒ Ⓓ	33. Ⓐ Ⓑ Ⓒ Ⓓ	45. Ⓐ Ⓑ Ⓒ Ⓓ	57. Ⓐ Ⓑ Ⓒ Ⓓ
10. Ⓐ Ⓑ Ⓒ Ⓓ	22. Ⓐ Ⓑ Ⓒ Ⓓ	34. Ⓐ Ⓑ Ⓒ Ⓓ	46. Ⓐ Ⓑ Ⓒ Ⓓ	58. Ⓐ Ⓑ Ⓒ Ⓓ
11. Ⓐ Ⓑ Ⓒ Ⓓ	23. Ⓐ Ⓑ Ⓒ Ⓓ	35. Ⓐ Ⓑ Ⓒ Ⓓ	47. Ⓐ Ⓑ Ⓒ Ⓓ	59. Ⓐ Ⓑ Ⓒ Ⓓ
12. Ⓐ Ⓑ Ⓒ Ⓓ	24. Ⓐ Ⓑ Ⓒ Ⓓ	36. Ⓐ Ⓑ Ⓒ Ⓓ	48. Ⓐ Ⓑ Ⓒ Ⓓ	60. Ⓐ Ⓑ Ⓒ Ⓓ

SUBTEST 2 QUANTITATIVE SKILLS

61. Ⓐ Ⓑ Ⓒ Ⓓ	72. Ⓐ Ⓑ Ⓒ Ⓓ	83. Ⓐ Ⓑ Ⓒ Ⓓ	93. Ⓐ Ⓑ Ⓒ Ⓓ	103. Ⓐ Ⓑ Ⓒ Ⓓ
62. Ⓐ Ⓑ Ⓒ Ⓓ	73. Ⓐ Ⓑ Ⓒ Ⓓ	84. Ⓐ Ⓑ Ⓒ Ⓓ	94. Ⓐ Ⓑ Ⓒ Ⓓ	104. Ⓐ Ⓑ Ⓒ Ⓓ
63. Ⓐ Ⓑ Ⓒ Ⓓ	74. Ⓐ Ⓑ Ⓒ Ⓓ	85. Ⓐ Ⓑ Ⓒ Ⓓ	95. Ⓐ Ⓑ Ⓒ Ⓓ	105. Ⓐ Ⓑ Ⓒ Ⓓ
64. Ⓐ Ⓑ Ⓒ Ⓓ	75. Ⓐ Ⓑ Ⓒ Ⓓ	86. Ⓐ Ⓑ Ⓒ Ⓓ	96. Ⓐ Ⓑ Ⓒ Ⓓ	106. Ⓐ Ⓑ Ⓒ Ⓓ
65. Ⓐ Ⓑ Ⓒ Ⓓ	76. Ⓐ Ⓑ Ⓒ Ⓓ	87. Ⓐ Ⓑ Ⓒ Ⓓ	97. Ⓐ Ⓑ Ⓒ Ⓓ	107. Ⓐ Ⓑ Ⓒ Ⓓ
66. Ⓐ Ⓑ Ⓒ Ⓓ	77. Ⓐ Ⓑ Ⓒ Ⓓ	88. Ⓐ Ⓑ Ⓒ Ⓓ	98. Ⓐ Ⓑ Ⓒ Ⓓ	108. Ⓐ Ⓑ Ⓒ Ⓓ
67. Ⓐ Ⓑ Ⓒ Ⓓ	78. Ⓐ Ⓑ Ⓒ Ⓓ	89. Ⓐ Ⓑ Ⓒ Ⓓ	99. Ⓐ Ⓑ Ⓒ Ⓓ	109. Ⓐ Ⓑ Ⓒ Ⓓ
68. Ⓐ Ⓑ Ⓒ Ⓓ	79. Ⓐ Ⓑ Ⓒ Ⓓ	90. Ⓐ Ⓑ Ⓒ Ⓓ	100. Ⓐ Ⓑ Ⓒ Ⓓ	110. Ⓐ Ⓑ Ⓒ Ⓓ
69. Ⓐ Ⓑ Ⓒ Ⓓ	80. Ⓐ Ⓑ Ⓒ Ⓓ	91. Ⓐ Ⓑ Ⓒ Ⓓ	101. Ⓐ Ⓑ Ⓒ Ⓓ	111. Ⓐ Ⓑ Ⓒ Ⓓ
70. Ⓐ Ⓑ Ⓒ Ⓓ	81. Ⓐ Ⓑ Ⓒ Ⓓ	92. Ⓐ Ⓑ Ⓒ Ⓓ	102. Ⓐ Ⓑ Ⓒ Ⓓ	112. Ⓐ Ⓑ Ⓒ Ⓓ
71. Ⓐ Ⓑ Ⓒ Ⓓ	82. Ⓐ Ⓑ Ⓒ Ⓓ			

SUBTEST 3 READING

113. Ⓐ Ⓑ Ⓒ Ⓓ	126. Ⓐ Ⓑ Ⓒ Ⓓ	139. Ⓐ Ⓑ Ⓒ Ⓓ	151. Ⓐ Ⓑ Ⓒ Ⓓ	163. Ⓐ Ⓑ Ⓒ Ⓓ
114. Ⓐ Ⓑ Ⓒ Ⓓ	127. Ⓐ Ⓑ Ⓒ Ⓓ	140. Ⓐ Ⓑ Ⓒ Ⓓ	152. Ⓐ Ⓑ Ⓒ Ⓓ	164. Ⓐ Ⓑ Ⓒ Ⓓ
115. Ⓐ Ⓑ Ⓒ Ⓓ	128. Ⓐ Ⓑ Ⓒ Ⓓ	141. Ⓐ Ⓑ Ⓒ Ⓓ	153. Ⓐ Ⓑ Ⓒ Ⓓ	165. Ⓐ Ⓑ Ⓒ Ⓓ
116. Ⓐ Ⓑ Ⓒ Ⓓ	129. Ⓐ Ⓑ Ⓒ Ⓓ	142. Ⓐ Ⓑ Ⓒ Ⓓ	154. Ⓐ Ⓑ Ⓒ Ⓓ	166. Ⓐ Ⓑ Ⓒ Ⓓ
117. Ⓐ Ⓑ Ⓒ Ⓓ	130. Ⓐ Ⓑ Ⓒ Ⓓ	143. Ⓐ Ⓑ Ⓒ Ⓓ	155. Ⓐ Ⓑ Ⓒ Ⓓ	167. Ⓐ Ⓑ Ⓒ Ⓓ
118. Ⓐ Ⓑ Ⓒ Ⓓ	131. Ⓐ Ⓑ Ⓒ Ⓓ	144. Ⓐ Ⓑ Ⓒ Ⓓ	156. Ⓐ Ⓑ Ⓒ Ⓓ	168. Ⓐ Ⓑ Ⓒ Ⓓ
119. Ⓐ Ⓑ Ⓒ Ⓓ	132. Ⓐ Ⓑ Ⓒ Ⓓ	145. Ⓐ Ⓑ Ⓒ Ⓓ	157. Ⓐ Ⓑ Ⓒ Ⓓ	169. Ⓐ Ⓑ Ⓒ Ⓓ
120. Ⓐ Ⓑ Ⓒ Ⓓ	133. Ⓐ Ⓑ Ⓒ Ⓓ	146. Ⓐ Ⓑ Ⓒ Ⓓ	158. Ⓐ Ⓑ Ⓒ Ⓓ	170. Ⓐ Ⓑ Ⓒ Ⓓ
121. Ⓐ Ⓑ Ⓒ Ⓓ	134. Ⓐ Ⓑ Ⓒ Ⓓ	147. Ⓐ Ⓑ Ⓒ Ⓓ	159. Ⓐ Ⓑ Ⓒ Ⓓ	171. Ⓐ Ⓑ Ⓒ Ⓓ
122. Ⓐ Ⓑ Ⓒ Ⓓ	135. Ⓐ Ⓑ Ⓒ Ⓓ	148. Ⓐ Ⓑ Ⓒ Ⓓ	160. Ⓐ Ⓑ Ⓒ Ⓓ	172. Ⓐ Ⓑ Ⓒ Ⓓ
123. Ⓐ Ⓑ Ⓒ Ⓓ	136. Ⓐ Ⓑ Ⓒ Ⓓ	149. Ⓐ Ⓑ Ⓒ Ⓓ	161. Ⓐ Ⓑ Ⓒ Ⓓ	173. Ⓐ Ⓑ Ⓒ Ⓓ
124. Ⓐ Ⓑ Ⓒ Ⓓ	137. Ⓐ Ⓑ Ⓒ Ⓓ	150. Ⓐ Ⓑ Ⓒ Ⓓ	162. Ⓐ Ⓑ Ⓒ Ⓓ	174. Ⓐ Ⓑ Ⓒ Ⓓ
125. Ⓐ Ⓑ Ⓒ Ⓓ	138. Ⓐ Ⓑ Ⓒ Ⓓ			

SUBTEST 4   MATHEMATICS

175. Ⓐ Ⓑ Ⓒ Ⓓ	188. Ⓐ Ⓑ Ⓒ Ⓓ	201. Ⓐ Ⓑ Ⓒ Ⓓ	214. Ⓐ Ⓑ Ⓒ Ⓓ	227. Ⓐ Ⓑ Ⓒ Ⓓ
176. Ⓐ Ⓑ Ⓒ Ⓓ	189. Ⓐ Ⓑ Ⓒ Ⓓ	202. Ⓐ Ⓑ Ⓒ Ⓓ	215. Ⓐ Ⓑ Ⓒ Ⓓ	228. Ⓐ Ⓑ Ⓒ Ⓓ
177. Ⓐ Ⓑ Ⓒ Ⓓ	190. Ⓐ Ⓑ Ⓒ Ⓓ	203. Ⓐ Ⓑ Ⓒ Ⓓ	216. Ⓐ Ⓑ Ⓒ Ⓓ	229. Ⓐ Ⓑ Ⓒ Ⓓ
178. Ⓐ Ⓑ Ⓒ Ⓓ	191. Ⓐ Ⓑ Ⓒ Ⓓ	204. Ⓐ Ⓑ Ⓒ Ⓓ	217. Ⓐ Ⓑ Ⓒ Ⓓ	230. Ⓐ Ⓑ Ⓒ Ⓓ
179. Ⓐ Ⓑ Ⓒ Ⓓ	192. Ⓐ Ⓑ Ⓒ Ⓓ	205. Ⓐ Ⓑ Ⓒ Ⓓ	218. Ⓐ Ⓑ Ⓒ Ⓓ	231. Ⓐ Ⓑ Ⓒ Ⓓ
180. Ⓐ Ⓑ Ⓒ Ⓓ	193. Ⓐ Ⓑ Ⓒ Ⓓ	206. Ⓐ Ⓑ Ⓒ Ⓓ	219. Ⓐ Ⓑ Ⓒ Ⓓ	232. Ⓐ Ⓑ Ⓒ Ⓓ
181. Ⓐ Ⓑ Ⓒ Ⓓ	194. Ⓐ Ⓑ Ⓒ Ⓓ	207. Ⓐ Ⓑ Ⓒ Ⓓ	220. Ⓐ Ⓑ Ⓒ Ⓓ	233. Ⓐ Ⓑ Ⓒ Ⓓ
182. Ⓐ Ⓑ Ⓒ Ⓓ	195. Ⓐ Ⓑ Ⓒ Ⓓ	208. Ⓐ Ⓑ Ⓒ Ⓓ	221. Ⓐ Ⓑ Ⓒ Ⓓ	234. Ⓐ Ⓑ Ⓒ Ⓓ
183. Ⓐ Ⓑ Ⓒ Ⓓ	196. Ⓐ Ⓑ Ⓒ Ⓓ	209. Ⓐ Ⓑ Ⓒ Ⓓ	222. Ⓐ Ⓑ Ⓒ Ⓓ	235. Ⓐ Ⓑ Ⓒ Ⓓ
184. Ⓐ Ⓑ Ⓒ Ⓓ	197. Ⓐ Ⓑ Ⓒ Ⓓ	210. Ⓐ Ⓑ Ⓒ Ⓓ	223. Ⓐ Ⓑ Ⓒ Ⓓ	236. Ⓐ Ⓑ Ⓒ Ⓓ
185. Ⓐ Ⓑ Ⓒ Ⓓ	198. Ⓐ Ⓑ Ⓒ Ⓓ	211. Ⓐ Ⓑ Ⓒ Ⓓ	224. Ⓐ Ⓑ Ⓒ Ⓓ	237. Ⓐ Ⓑ Ⓒ Ⓓ
186. Ⓐ Ⓑ Ⓒ Ⓓ	199. Ⓐ Ⓑ Ⓒ Ⓓ	212. Ⓐ Ⓑ Ⓒ Ⓓ	225. Ⓐ Ⓑ Ⓒ Ⓓ	238. Ⓐ Ⓑ Ⓒ Ⓓ
187. Ⓐ Ⓑ Ⓒ Ⓓ	200. Ⓐ Ⓑ Ⓒ Ⓓ	213. Ⓐ Ⓑ Ⓒ Ⓓ	226. Ⓐ Ⓑ Ⓒ Ⓓ	

SUBTEST 5   LANGUAGE

239. Ⓐ Ⓑ Ⓒ Ⓓ	251. Ⓐ Ⓑ Ⓒ Ⓓ	263. Ⓐ Ⓑ Ⓒ Ⓓ	275. Ⓐ Ⓑ Ⓒ Ⓓ	287. Ⓐ Ⓑ Ⓒ Ⓓ
240. Ⓐ Ⓑ Ⓒ Ⓓ	252. Ⓐ Ⓑ Ⓒ Ⓓ	264. Ⓐ Ⓑ Ⓒ Ⓓ	276. Ⓐ Ⓑ Ⓒ Ⓓ	288. Ⓐ Ⓑ Ⓒ Ⓓ
241. Ⓐ Ⓑ Ⓒ Ⓓ	253. Ⓐ Ⓑ Ⓒ Ⓓ	265. Ⓐ Ⓑ Ⓒ Ⓓ	277. Ⓐ Ⓑ Ⓒ Ⓓ	289. Ⓐ Ⓑ Ⓒ Ⓓ
242. Ⓐ Ⓑ Ⓒ Ⓓ	254. Ⓐ Ⓑ Ⓒ Ⓓ	266. Ⓐ Ⓑ Ⓒ Ⓓ	278. Ⓐ Ⓑ Ⓒ Ⓓ	290. Ⓐ Ⓑ Ⓒ Ⓓ
243. Ⓐ Ⓑ Ⓒ Ⓓ	255. Ⓐ Ⓑ Ⓒ Ⓓ	267. Ⓐ Ⓑ Ⓒ Ⓓ	279. Ⓐ Ⓑ Ⓒ Ⓓ	291. Ⓐ Ⓑ Ⓒ Ⓓ
244. Ⓐ Ⓑ Ⓒ Ⓓ	256. Ⓐ Ⓑ Ⓒ Ⓓ	268. Ⓐ Ⓑ Ⓒ Ⓓ	280. Ⓐ Ⓑ Ⓒ Ⓓ	292. Ⓐ Ⓑ Ⓒ Ⓓ
245. Ⓐ Ⓑ Ⓒ Ⓓ	257. Ⓐ Ⓑ Ⓒ Ⓓ	269. Ⓐ Ⓑ Ⓒ Ⓓ	281. Ⓐ Ⓑ Ⓒ Ⓓ	293. Ⓐ Ⓑ Ⓒ Ⓓ
246. Ⓐ Ⓑ Ⓒ Ⓓ	258. Ⓐ Ⓑ Ⓒ Ⓓ	270. Ⓐ Ⓑ Ⓒ Ⓓ	282. Ⓐ Ⓑ Ⓒ Ⓓ	294. Ⓐ Ⓑ Ⓒ Ⓓ
247. Ⓐ Ⓑ Ⓒ Ⓓ	259. Ⓐ Ⓑ Ⓒ Ⓓ	271. Ⓐ Ⓑ Ⓒ Ⓓ	283. Ⓐ Ⓑ Ⓒ Ⓓ	295. Ⓐ Ⓑ Ⓒ Ⓓ
248. Ⓐ Ⓑ Ⓒ Ⓓ	260. Ⓐ Ⓑ Ⓒ Ⓓ	272. Ⓐ Ⓑ Ⓒ Ⓓ	284. Ⓐ Ⓑ Ⓒ Ⓓ	296. Ⓐ Ⓑ Ⓒ Ⓓ
249. Ⓐ Ⓑ Ⓒ Ⓓ	261. Ⓐ Ⓑ Ⓒ Ⓓ	273. Ⓐ Ⓑ Ⓒ Ⓓ	285. Ⓐ Ⓑ Ⓒ Ⓓ	297. Ⓐ Ⓑ Ⓒ Ⓓ
250. Ⓐ Ⓑ Ⓒ Ⓓ	262. Ⓐ Ⓑ Ⓒ Ⓓ	274. Ⓐ Ⓑ Ⓒ Ⓓ	286. Ⓐ Ⓑ Ⓒ Ⓓ	298. Ⓐ Ⓑ Ⓒ Ⓓ

High School Placement Test (HSPT)

Overview

Total Time

Approximately $2\frac{1}{2}$ hours for a total of 298 questions.

Type of Questions

The questions are multiple choice, with answers blackened on a machine-scored Answer Sheet.

Pacing

You are not expected to complete all items. You are expected to work as fast as possible while maintaining accuracy. The general rule is this: Do not linger over questions you find too difficult. Take a guess and go on. If you finish a section early, you will be allowed to go back over the questions in that section only. You will not be allowed to proceed to the next section until the signal to do so is given.

Guessing

The examination directions suggest that you answer all questions. When you hit a difficult question, eliminate as many choices as you can and then select the answer you think is most likely to be correct. Do *not* go back to that question. If you cannot eliminate any of the choices, take a guess.

Exam Content

New forms of the exam are prepared each year. The time limits given below and on the practice tests that follow are guidelines rather than strict timing. Usually the content breaks down as follows:

Subtest 1: Verbal Skills—*60 questions, 16 minutes*
    Verbal Analogies—*10 questions*
    Synonyms—*15 questions*
    Logic—*10 questions*
    Verbal Classification—*16 questions*
    Antonyms—*9 questions*

Subtest 2: Quantitative Skills—*52 questions, 30 minutes*
    Number Series—*18 questions*
    Geometric Comparisons—*9 questions*
    Nongeometric Comparisons—*8 questions*
    Number Manipulations—*17 questions*

Subtest 3: Reading—*62 questions, 25 minutes*
    Comprehension—*40 questions*
    Vocabulary—*22 questions*

Subtest 4: Mathematics—*64 questions, 45 minutes*
    Concepts—*24 questions*
    Problem Solving—*40 questions*

Subtest 5: Language—*60 questions, 25 minutes*
    Punctuation, Capitalization, and Usage—*40 questions*
    Spelling—*10 questions*
    Composition—*10 questions*

Practice High School Placement Test 1

SUBTEST 1   VERBAL SKILLS

Number of questions: 60   *Time limit: 16 minutes*

> DIRECTIONS: Select the correct answer and blacken the appropriate circle on the Answer Sheet.

1. Susanna is taller than Ellen. Ellen is taller than Sarah. Susanna is taller than Sarah. If the first two statements are true, the third is
   (A) true.
   (B) false.
   (C) uncertain.

2. Which word does <u>not</u> belong with the others?
   (A) total
   (B) whole
   (C) entire
   (D) partial

3. Aimless is the <u>opposite</u> of
   (A) purposeful.
   (B) exaggerated.
   (C) unfortunate.
   (D) expansive.

4. Wallet is to money as tank is to
   (A) warfare.
   (B) swimmer.
   (C) gasoline.
   (D) metal.

5. If Eileen is not in Boston, she is in Chicago. If she is not in Chicago, she is in New Orleans. If she is not in New Orleans, she must be in Boston. If the first two statements are true, the third is
   (A) true.
   (B) false.
   (C) uncertain.

6. Adolescent means most nearly
   (A) citizen.
   (B) child.
   (C) teenager.
   (D) adult.

7. Which word does <u>not</u> belong with the others?
   (A) peace.
   (B) quiet.
   (C) commotion.
   (D) serenity.

8. Henry has scored more goals than Adam. Adam has scored more goals than Bob. Henry has scored fewer goals than Bob. If the first two statements are true, the third is
   (A) true.
   (B) false.
   (C) uncertain.

9. Cry is to pain as growl is to
   (A) lion.
   (B) annoyance.
   (C) pleasure.
   (D) roar.

10. Fantasy means the <u>opposite</u> of
    (A) fairy tale.
    (B) show business.
    (C) extravaganza.
    (D) actuality.

11. Corrupt means most nearly
    (A) regulate.
    (B) degrade.
    (C) imprison.
    (D) police.

12. Entreat means most nearly
    (A) beg.
    (B) entertain.
    (C) deny.
    (D) control.

13. Which word does <u>not</u> belong with the others?
    (A) wares
    (B) shop
    (C) goods
    (D) merchandise

14. Builder is to blueprint as trucker is to
    (A) depositor.
    (B) truck stop.
    (C) cargo.
    (D) map.

15. Eternal means most nearly
    (A) ancient.
    (B) perpetual.
    (C) heavenly
    (D) artistic.

16. Which word does <u>not</u> belong with the others?
    (A) warehouse
    (B) depot
    (C) factory
    (D) storeroom

17. Farina is more expensive than rice but less than oatmeal. Corn is more expensive than rice but less than squash. Of all the foods mentioned, rice is the least expensive. If the first two statements are true, the third is
    (A) true.
    (B) false.
    (C) uncertain.

18. Mediocre is the <u>opposite</u> of
    (A) unconcerned.
    (B) unreasonable.
    (C) intentional.
    (D) superlative.

19. Pliers is to hold as scissors is to
    (A) reconstruct.
    (B) sever.
    (C) mesh.
    (D) mutilate.

20. Marauder means most nearly
    (A) raider.
    (B) visitor.
    (C) murderer.
    (D) official.

21. Essential means the <u>opposite</u> of
    (A) unforeseen.
    (B) unnecessary.
    (C) orderly.
    (D) bland.

22. Banish means most nearly
    (A) disappoint.
    (B) cleanse.
    (C) exile.
    (D) refuse.

23. Pacific means the <u>opposite</u> of
    (A) isolated.
    (B) enlarged.
    (C) ocean.
    (D) quarrelsome.

24. Which word does <u>not</u> belong with the others?
    (A) replenish
    (B) renovate
    (C) resupply
    (D) refill

25. Shack is to chateau as pit is to
    (A) canyon.
    (B) seed.
    (C) fruit.
    (D) shell.

26. Cordial means most nearly
    (A) polite.
    (B) friendly.
    (C) correct.
    (D) hasty.

27. Personnel means most nearly
    (A) population.
    (B) consumer.
    (C) staff.
    (D) supervisor.

28. Which word does <u>not</u> belong with the others?
    (A) conversation
    (B) utterance
    (C) vocabulary
    (D) oration

29. Some A is B. No C is A. No C is B. If the first two statements are true, the third is
    (A) true.
    (B) false.
    (C) uncertain.

30. Town A is larger than Town B. Town B is smaller than Town C. Town A is larger than Town C. If the first two statements are true, the third is
    (A) true.
    (B) false.
    (C) uncertain.

31. Seamy means the <u>opposite</u> of
    (A) wholesome.
    (B) clever.
    (C) tricky.
    (D) contented.

32. Which word does <u>not</u> belong with the others?
    (A) toupee
    (B) pate
    (C) hairpiece
    (D) wig

33. Prevalent means most nearly
    (A) isolated.
    (B) fortunate.
    (C) dangerous.
    (D) widespread.

34. Compliment is to slur as limelight is to
    (A) actor.
    (B) obscurity.
    (C) witticism.
    (D) illumination.

35. All cold-blooded animals are not mammals. All frogs are cold-blooded animals. All frogs are not mammals. If the first two statements are true, the third is
    (A) true.
    (B) false.
    (C) uncertain.

36. Which word does <u>not</u> belong with the others?
    (A) volume
    (B) tome
    (C) vault
    (D) book

37. Aloof means most nearly
    (A) captive.
    (B) lonely.
    (C) noisy.
    (D) standoffish.

38. Which word does <u>not</u> belong with the others?
    (A) box
    (B) vial
    (C) filter
    (D) carton

39. Alpha is more attractive than Beta. Gamma is more attractive than Delta. Alpha is more attractive than Delta. If the first two statements are true, the third is
    (A) true.
    (B) false.
    (C) uncertain.

40. Composed is to agitated as erratic is to
    (A) consistent.
    (B) concentrated.
    (C) creative.
    (D) disastrous.

41. Fashionable means the <u>opposite</u> of
    (A) expensive.
    (B) dowdy.
    (C) sparse.
    (D) tense.

42. Which word does <u>not</u> belong with the others?
    (A) mortal
    (B) celestial
    (C) heavenly
    (D) divine

43. Meander means most nearly
    (A) rush.
    (B) wind.
    (C) encompass.
    (D) encircle.

44. Infamous means most nearly
    (A) notorious.
    (B) willful.
    (C) popular.
    (D) unknown.

45. Coward is to valor as pessimist is to
    (A) loyalty.
    (B) hope.
    (C) concern.
    (D) generosity.

46. Which word does <u>not</u> belong with the others?
    (A) desperado
    (B) deputy
    (C) brigand
    (D) swindler

47. Supple means most nearly
    (A) lithe.
    (B) muscular.
    (C) weak.
    (D) scant.

48. Which word does not belong with the others?
    (A) ancestors
    (B) offspring
    (C) forefathers
    (D) parents

49. Prima donnas are unpredictable. Marie is not a prima donna. Marie is predictable. If the first two statements are true, the third is
    (A) true.
    (B) false.
    (C) uncertain.

50. Weave is to story as unravel is to
    (A) thread.
    (B) mystery.
    (C) food.
    (D) folly.

51. Modesty means the opposite of
    (A) fashion.
    (B) cowardice.
    (C) vanity.
    (D) timidity.

52. Sepulcher means most nearly
    (A) ghost.
    (B) tunnel.
    (C) roadway.
    (D) tomb.

53. Reminisce means most nearly
    (A) remain.
    (B) disregard.
    (C) narrate.
    (D) recall.

54. Which word does not belong with the others?
    (A) den
    (B) garage
    (C) playroom
    (D) kitchen

55. Which word does not belong with the others?
    (A) heart
    (B) core
    (C) artery
    (D) kernel

56. Observer is to sight as auditor is to
    (A) referral.
    (B) figure.
    (C) scene.
    (D) hearing.

57. Which word does not belong with the others?
    (A) intent
    (B) eager
    (C) indifferent
    (D) earnest

58. Confirm means the opposite of
    (A) celebrate.
    (B) scold.
    (C) commune.
    (D) disprove.

59. Milton is brighter than Arthur. Stanley is brighter than Milton. Stanley is not as bright as Arthur. If the first two statements are true, the third is
    (A) true.
    (B) false.
    (C) uncertain.

60. Which word does not belong with the others?
    (A) wages
    (B) profit
    (C) salary
    (D) pay

SUBTEST 2 QUANTITATIVE SKILLS

Number of questions: 52　　　　　　　　　　　　　*Time limit: 30 minutes*

DIRECTIONS: Choose the answer you think is best for each problem.

SAMPLES:

1. Select the number that should come next in the following series: 2, 5, 8, 11, _____.
    (A) 15 (B) 17 (C) 14 (D) 13

    The correct answer is 14, choice (C).

2. O is the center of the circle. The measure of $\angle AOB = 60°$.

    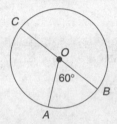

    (A) The area of sector $OAB = \frac{1}{5}$ of the area of the circle.
    (B) $OA > OB$.
    (C) $\overarc{AB} = \frac{1}{6}$ of the circumference of the circle.
    (D) Sector OAB is greater in area than sector OAC.

    The correct answer is (C).

3. If $\frac{3}{4}$ of a number is 12, then 50% of the number is
    (A) 10 (B) 15 (C) 16 (D) 8

    The corect answer is 8, choice (D).

4. Examine (X), (Y), and (Z), and select the correct answer.

    (X) $15 \div 3 + 1$
    (Y) $(12 - 4) - 3$
    (Z) $7 + \frac{1}{3}(15)$

    (A) Y is greater than X.
    (B) $X + Y$ is less than Z.
    (C) Y is greater than Z.
    (D) X is greater than Z.

    The correct answer is (B).

61. If three times a number is $6\frac{3}{4}$, then half the number is
    (A) $1\frac{1}{8}$ (B) $2\frac{1}{4}$ (C) $2\frac{1}{2}$ (D) 6

62. What is the next number in the following series: 1, 5, 9, 13, _____ ?
    (A) 15 (B) 16 (C) 17 (D) 20

63. If in the diagram $a = b = c$, which of the following is correct?

    (A) $a + b = c$
    (B) $a + c > b + c$
    (C) $a + b = b + c$
    (D) $a > b + c$

64. Look at the series 72, 66, 60, _____, 48, 42. What number should fill the blank?
    (A) 58 (B) 56 (C) 55 (D) 54

65. What number subtracted from 50 is 2 more than the product of 6 and 7?
    (A) 5 (B) 6 (C) 7 (D) 8

66. In the diagram below, O is the center of the circle and the measure of each central angle is 60°

Which of the following is true?
(A) $b > a + c$
(B) $d > a$
(C) $f = e$
(D) $a + b + c + d =$ half the circle

67. Examine (X), (Y), and (Z), and choose the correct answer.
(X) $\frac{3}{8}$
(Y) 35%
(Z) 0.4

(A) Of there three numbers given (Y) is the greatest.
(B) $\frac{3}{8} > 35\%$
(C) $0.4 < 35\%$
(D) $0.4 - 35\% = \frac{3}{8}$

68. Look at the series 4, 9, 16, 25, ____. What number should come next?
(A) 30 (B) 35 (C) 36 (D) 40

69. At a track and field meet, each first place counted 5 points, each second place counted 3 points, and each third place counted 1 point.

Team X scored 5 firsts, 7 seconds, and 3 thirds.
Team Y scored 4 firsts, 8 seconds, and 2 thirds.
Team Z scored 8 firsts, 3 seconds, and 4 thirds.

Which of the following is correct?
(A) The number of points scored by team Y exceeded the number of points scored by team X.
(B) The order in which the three teams scored can be expressed as X > Y > Z.
(C) The number of points scored by team Z exceeded the number of points scored by either team X or team Y.
(D) Team X and team Y scored the same number of points.

70. Look at (X), (Y), and (Z) below, and select the correct answer.
(X) $15 - (8 + 1)$
(Y) $(9 - 6) - 2$
(Z) $7 - (5 - 2)$

(A) $X - Y = Z$
(B) $X > Y > Z$
(C) $Y > Z$
(D) $X > Z$

71. In the figure, $\overline{RS} \perp \overline{SV}$, and $\overline{ST} \perp \overline{RV}$.

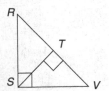

Which of the following is correct?
(A) $RS > RV$
(B) $SV > ST$
(C) $RS + SV = RV$
(D) $RT > RS$

72. Examine (X), (Y), and (Z) and find the correct answer.

(X) 40% of 50
(Y) 50% of 20
(Z) 20% of 80

(A) $2Y = X$
(B) $X + Y = Z$
(C) $X + Z = Y$
(D) $Z + Y = X$

73. Look at the following series, and find the next number: 4, 9, 14, 19, ____.
(A) 25 (B) 20 (C) 24 (D) 23

74. If $\frac{3}{8}$ of a number is 2 less than 14, the number is
(A) 32 (B) 40 (C) 96 (D) 50

75. What fraction of the figure below is shaded?

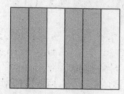

(A) $\frac{1}{3}$ (B) $\frac{2}{5}$ (C) $\frac{2}{3}$ (D) $\frac{3}{4}$

76. If $\frac{1}{4}$ of a number is 1 more than $\frac{1}{5}$ of the same number, find the number.
(A) 20 (B) 30 (C) 40 (D) 48

77. The number of halves in $\frac{5}{8}$ is
(A) $\frac{4}{5}$ (B) $1\frac{1}{4}$ (C) $2\frac{1}{2}$ (D) $2\frac{1}{4}$

78. A lecture hall has 20 rows with 9 seats in row. The hall is to be remodeled to have the same number of total seats but fewer rows. How many rows may the remodeled hall have?
(A) 17 (B) 19 (C) 16 (D) 12

79. In a shortcut method of multiplying 96 by 25, we annex two zeros to 96 and divide the result by
(A) 25 (B) 4 (C) 100 (D) 20

80. Select the number that should come next in the series 64, 32, 16, 8, ___.
(A) 10 (B) 12 (C) 4 (D) 5

81. In $\triangle ABC$, $AB = AC$. Which of the following is true?

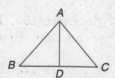

(A) $AB = AD$
(B) $DC > AC$
(C) $AB > AD$
(D) $AD > AB + BD$

82. What fraction divided by $\frac{1}{2}$ is equal to $\frac{3}{7}$?
(A) $\frac{6}{7}$ (B) $\frac{3}{14}$ (C) $\frac{1}{3}$ (D) $\frac{8}{7}$

83. What is the next number in the following series: 1, 2, 4, 7, ___?
(A) 12 (B) 14 (C) 15 (D) 11

84. The circle below is divided into 6 equal sectors. What part of the circle is shaded?

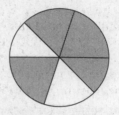

(A) $\frac{1}{2}$ (B) $\frac{3}{4}$ (C) $\frac{1}{3}$ (D) $\frac{2}{3}$

85. *ABCD* is a rectangle.

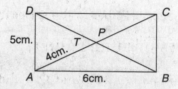

Which of the following is true?
(A) The perimeter of *ABCD* is 15.
(B) The area of *ABCD* is 30 square centimeters.
(C) The area of $\triangle DPA$ is 20 square centimeters.
(D) The perimeter of each triangle in the figure is 14 centimeters.

86. Which one of the following is correct?
(A) $\frac{2}{5} > \frac{1}{3} > \frac{3}{8}$
(B) $\frac{3}{8} > \frac{1}{3} > \frac{2}{5}$
(C) $\frac{1}{3} > \frac{3}{8} > \frac{2}{5}$
(D) $\frac{2}{5} > \frac{3}{8} > \frac{1}{3}$

87. What is the next number in the series 6, 9, 8, 11, 10, 13, 12, ___?
(A) 15 (B) 14 (C) 16 (D) 18

88. By how much does the average of 49 + 29 + 38 + 56 exceed 40?
(A) 5 (B) 4 (C) 12 (D) 3

89. If $x = 3^4$, $y = 5 \cdot 2^3$, and $z = 6 \cdot 4^2$, which of the following is true?
    (A) $x > z$
    (B) $z > x + y$
    (C) $x + y > z$
    (D) $x + y + z < 200$

90. Look at the series 5, 9, 17, 33, 65, ___. What number should come next?
    (A) 120 (B) 129 (C) 130 (D) 135

91. When a number is increased by 40% of itself the result is 28. What is the number?
    (A) 18 (B) 15 (C) 20 (D) 280

92. $5^3 \div 5 + 15 =$
    (A) 40 (B) 50 (C) 65 (D) 25

93. The next number in the series 0, 1, 3, 7, 15, ___ is
    (A) 29 (B) 31 (C) 16 (D) 17

94. Examine (X), (Y), and (Z), and select the correct answer.

    (X) $7 \times 5 - 4$
    (Y) $37 - 4 \times 5$
    (Z) $8 + 6 - 3$

    (A) $Z = X + Y$
    (B) $Z + Y > X$
    (C) $X = 2Y$
    (D) $X > Y > Z$

95. The number of fifths in 40 is
    (A) 8 (B) 200 (C) 48 (D) 20

96. In $\triangle ABC$, R is the midpoint of $\overline{AB}$, S is midpoint of $\overline{BC}$, and T is the midpoint of $\overline{AC}$.

    What part of $\triangle ABC$ is the shaded portion?
    (A) $\frac{1}{3}$ (B) $\frac{1}{4}$ (C) $\frac{3}{8}$ (D) $\frac{1}{6}$

97. What is the next number in the series 15, 11, 7, 3, ___?
    (A) 1 (B) −1 (C) −2 (D) 2

98. When a number is divided by 7, the quotient is 5 and the remainder is 1. What is the number?
    (A) 30 (B) 35 (C) 34 (D) 36

99. Examine (X), (Y), and (Z), and select the correct answer.
    (X) $(5 + 3)^2$
    (Y) $2^3 + 3^2$
    (Z) $17 - 2 \times 6$

    (A) $Y + Z > X$
    (B) $Y^2 > X$
    (C) $Z > Y$
    (D) $X > Y^2$

100. What is the next number in the series 5, 8, 11, 14, ___?
    (A) 17 (B) 19 (C) 20 (D) 16

101. The sum of $\frac{1}{3}$ and $\frac{5}{12}$ is greater than $\frac{1}{2}$ by
    (A) $\frac{1}{4}$ (B) $\frac{1}{6}$ (C) $\frac{1}{8}$ (D) $\frac{1}{10}$

102. Sixty-two and one-half percent of a number is 40. What is the reciprocal of the number?
    (A) 64 (B) $\frac{1}{64}$ (C) 32 (D) 50

103. What is the next number in the series 1, 5, 2, 10, 3, 15, 4, ___?
    (A) 5 (B) 18 (C) 6 (D) 20

104. Look at the series 150, 165 __, 195, 210. What number should fill the blank?
    (A) 200 (B) 205 (C) 175 (D) 180

105. Twenty-four percent of a town's population owns cars. If the number of cars owned is 6,000, what is the population of the town?
    (A) 10,000 (B) 24,000 (C) 25,000 (D) 40,000

106. The smallest number into which the numbers 2, 3, 5, and 7 can be divided without leaving a remainder is
    (A) 60 (B) 90 (C) 200 (D) 210

107. Consider (X), (Y), and (Z).

    (X) $4\frac{1}{2}$ %

    (Y) $4\frac{1}{2}$

    (Z) 0.45

    Which of the following is correct?
    (A) $X > Y$
    (B) $Y > Z$
    (C) $X > Z$
    (D) $X > Y > Z$

108. Look at the series 38, 37, 39, 38, 40, __.
    What number should come next?
    (A) 39 (B) 41 (C) 38 (D) 42

109. What number should come next in the series 5, 11, 6, 13, 7, 15, ___?
    (A) 17 (B) 9 (C) 16 (D) 8

110. Look at the series 64, 35, 32, 29, 16, __.
    What number should come next?
    (A) 23 (B) 25 (C) 24 (D) 15

111. In the series 5, 9, 17, 33, ____, what number should come next?
    (A) 60 (B) 62 (C) 64 (D) 65

112. Select the number that should come next in the following series: 1, 7, 19, 43, ____.
    (A) 76 (B) 86 (C) 91 (D) 100

SUBTEST 3   READING

Number of questions: 62   *Time limit: 25 minutes*

A. Comprehension—40 questions

DIRECTIONS: This subtest presents short reading passages, each one followed by a series of questions. Base your answer choices on the information in the selection.

On February 3, 1943, the U.S. troop carrier *Dorchester* was transporting American soldiers to England. They were among the first of our <u>inductees</u> to be sent for active duty against the forces of Hitler. The *Dorchester* was torpedoed by a German submarine off the coast of Greenland. On the ship were four chaplains representing four religious faiths—Roman Catholic, Jewish, Methodist, and the Reformed Church.

The situation on board ship was soon hopeless, and the captain ordered that the ship be abandoned. The chaplains helped the men search for life jackets and launch lifeboats. When there were no more life jackets to be found, each chaplain gave away his own.

As the *Dorchester* began to slide under the water, the four chaplains linked arms, braced themselves against the deck, and prayed until the seas <u>engulfed</u> them.

Among the memorials to these men is the Chapel of the Four Chaplains, an interfaith place of prayer located on the campus of Temple University in Philadelphia.

113. The incident described in this passage took place during
     (A) the Civil War.
     (B) World War I.
     (C) World War II.
     (D) the Korean War.

114. The *Dorchester* was
     (A) an oil tanker.
     (B) a freighter.
     (C) a pleasure cruiser.
     (D) a military-transport ship.

115. The best title for this selection would be
     (A) "Deadly Torpedoes."
     (B) "Wartime Heroism."
     (C) "Cruelty of the Sea."
     (D) "Forgotten Men."

116. The word <u>inductees</u>, as underlined and used in this passage, means soldiers who
     (A) had enlisted.
     (B) had been wounded.
     (C) had been drafted.
     (D) were prisoners of war.

117. Which of the following definitions of <u>chaplain</u> fits its use in this selection?
     (A) a religious leader in charge of a chapel
     (B) a religious leader attached to the military
     (C) an assistant to a bishop
     (D) a religious leader attached to an institution

118. The chaplains sacrificed their lives because
     (A) they wanted to show how brave they were
     (B) they wanted to enable others to survive.
     (C) they were ordered to.
     (D) they no longer had any reason to live.

119. The word <u>engulfed</u>, as underlined and used in this passage, means most nearly
     (A) submerged.
     (B) battered.
     (C) tossed.
     (D) separated.

120. We can infer that the shortage of life jackets was the result of
     (A) theft before the ship sailed.
     (B) destruction caused by the torpedoes.
     (C) poor training of the soldiers.
     (D) lack of supplies.

Neatness in and of itself will not <u>assure</u> success. Students who hand in a neat paper but reveal that they have not mastered the material will fail with a mark similar to that received by the producer of a sloppy and <u>inadequate</u> paper. Teachers and parents know through experience, however, that the orderly person is usually the efficient person. Students who carefully write their assignments as given and use assignment books will not waste time fussing through pockets or notebooks for a missing assignment. The neat person will not forget to do homework because of an overlooked assignment. Moreover, the neat person soon experiences the personal satisfaction that comes from handling details in an orderly fashion.

121. The best title for this selection would be
(A) "Neatness and Parental Wishes."
(B) "Mastery of Material."
(C) "Teachers, Parents, and Students."
(D) "Advantages of Neatness."

122. The word <u>assure</u>, as underlined and used in this passage, means most nearly
(A) affect.
(B) lessen.
(C) increase.
(D) guarantee.

123. Neatness eventually results in
(A) higher grades.
(B) increased popularity.
(C) happier parents.
(D) a sense of personal satisfaction.

124. Which of the following is emphasized in the selection as an advantage of neatness?
(A) Neatness is next to godliness.
(B) Neat examination papers are more accurate.
(C) Neatness is a time saver.
(D) Neat people are more energetic.

125. This passage most likely was planned for inclusion in
(A) a social studies textbook.
(B) a handbook for pupils entering high school.
(C) an encyclopedia.
(D) a news item in a local paper.

126. Which of the following definitions of <u>inadequate</u> best fits its use in this selection?
(A) incapable
(B) failing
(C) substandard
(D) unqualified

<u>Organisms</u> can be classified in many ways. The modern system is an outgrowth of the one developed in the eighteenth century by a Swedish scientist, Carolus Linnaeus. Linnaeus divided organisms into groups based on similarities of body structure. Today, scientists consider not only structure but also such characteristics as chemical makeup and the way in which the organism develops. Every organism belongs in one of the several kingdoms; the kingdom is the largest possible classification group. Each kingdom is separated into two or more major divisions; and each of these divisions is subdivided into smaller groups. In descending size order, the main groups are kingdom, phylum (plural: phyla), class, order, family, genus (plural: genera), species. The smallest of these groups, the species, contains only closely related organisms.

Every scientific name consists of the genus and the species of the organism. The tiger, for example, belongs to the genus *Felis* and the species *tigris*. The tiger's scientific name is, therefore, *Felis tigris*.

127. Which of the following definitions of <u>organisms</u> best fits its use in this selection?
(A) complex structures
(B) organizations
(C) individual parts of the body
(D) living things

128. The phrase that best expresses the main idea or subject of this selection is
(A) a system for action
(B) the tiger family
(C) important groups
(D) a systematic classification

129. The minimum number of phyla in any one kingdom
    (A) is one.
    (B) is two.
    (C) is three.
    (D) can be infinite.

130. Which of the following is most likely true of Linnaeus?
    (A) He was born in England.
    (B) He spent much of his time in forests.
    (C) His writings were printed on printing presses.
    (D) He was alive at the time of the American Civil War.

131. Which of the following is true of a species?
    (A) It is limited to one individual organism.
    (B) It may consist of millions of loosely related individuals.
    (C) It can exist in only one area.
    (D) It consists of a group of closely related organisms.

132. Which of the following is true of organisms?
    (A) Each one can belong to two kingdoms.
    (B) They all have the same first name.
    (C) Each one has a two-part scientific name.
    (D) Modern scientists classify them on the basis of size.

133. Linnaeus' system of classification was based on
    (A) height and weight.
    (B) shape.
    (C) appearance
    (D) physical structure.

134. Within any one kingdom
    (A) the class is larger than the phylum.
    (B) the order is smaller than the class.
    (C) the genus is smaller than the species.
    (D) all orders are in the same family.

In its earliest sense, the word bachelor meant "novice," one at the entering level. In the Middle Ages, a bachelor was a squire, a trainee who, if he was successful, would become a knight. The bachelor of arts degree means that the recipient has achieved the right to do graduate work at the university. In our society, a bachelor is a single male old enough to be eligible for marriage. The term does not include widowers or divorced men.

The origin of bachelor is unknown. Some linguists trace the word back to the Latin *baccalaris,* meaning "keeper of cows," but this view is not widely accepted.

135. The best title for this selection would be
    (A) "Early Origins."
    (B) "The Meaning of Bachelor."
    (C) "Middle Age Bachelors."
    (D) "Bachelor—An Interesting Word."

136. The word novice, as underlined and used in this passage, means most nearly
    (A) an awkward person.
    (B) a champion.
    (C) an expert.
    (D) a beginner.

137. In the twelfth century a young man lost the title of bachelor when he
    (A) married.
    (B) became a squire.
    (C) graduated from a university.
    (D) became a knight.

138. In its long history, the term bachelor has not been used to identify
    (A) a college graduate.
    (B) a man whose wife has died.
    (C) a medieval squire.
    (D) an unmarried man in his twenties.

139. Comparing the two paragraphs, we can say that
    (A) the first contains more facts about the word *bachelor* than the second.
    (B) the first deals with the origin of the word *bachelor*.
    (C) the first includes more opinions than the second.
    (D) the second presents more facts than the first.

140. The word <u>recipient</u>, as underlined and used in this passage, means most nearly
    (A) receiver.
    (B) donor.
    (C) bearer.
    (D) deliverer.

We must stop measuring our standards of life by automobiles, production drives, and dollars of income. No standard of living is high when jobs become drudgery and hours dreary, when young men and women cannot afford a family, when children are walled off by brick from sod and sky.

 We must measure education less by the amount of knowledge it lodges in youthful minds than by the wisdom for living it instills. The amassment of knowledge is of negative worth when it places business above family in the value systems of men and career women, and when it instructs us in the technology of modern weaponry without teaching us the human values to control these forces.

141. The best title for this selection would be
    (A) "Industrial Technology."
    (B) "Standards of Living Today and Yesterday."
    (C) "Need for New Social Ideals."
    (D) "The Negative Value of Knowledge."

142. The word <u>drudgery</u>, as underlined and used in this selection, means most nearly
    (A) dull, wearying work.
    (B) dangerous work.
    (C) highly competitive work.
    (D) low-paying work.

143. The author implies that the most important aim of education is
    (A) vocational efficiency.
    (B) satisfactory personal relationships.
    (C) extensive information.
    (D) scientific skill.

144. The author attempts to persuade the reader
    (A) using logical arguments.
    (B) giving specific examples.
    (C) appealing to the reader's sense of fairness.
    (D) presenting judgments and generalizations.

145. Children are "walled off by brick" when they
    (A) are being mistreated.
    (B) live in urban housing developments.
    (C) do not do their school work.
    (D) visit relatives living on farms.

146. Something is "of negative worth" when it is
    (A) misunderstood.
    (B) opposed to popular beliefs.
    (C) based on incorrect beliefs.
    (D) harmful rather than beneficial.

147. We can infer that this selection was intended to be part of a
    (A) speech to the Chamber of Commerce.
    (B) sermon.
    (C) textbook chapter.
    (D) lecture in a class on economics.

We must never forget that war is all-consuming. There are no victors, only victims. And with the passage of years and the fiendish improvements in weaponry, the horrors multiply beyond the limits of our imagination to grasp. Each new generation must learn that there are no movie heroes or romance in war, only victims, victims.

 Let's take a stark example. France was a victor in World War I. Now, this was before the age of fleets of bombers and the threat of total wipeout by nuclear explosion, before civilian populations became fair game for unmanned rockets and poison gases. Nevertheless, out of a total population of 39 million, 1.5 million were killed, several millions more were wounded, and many of these were left badly maimed or crippled. Scarcely a family escaped without at least one member killed or wounded. France lost virtually an entire generation of men, those in the age range of twenty to forty. In northeastern France, in the heart of her industrial area, war destruction was total. Every one of the 3000 factories, iron foundries, and mines was damaged or destroyed.

148. The main idea of this passage is that
(A) France won World War I.
(B) the French suffered greater casualties than any other nation in World War I.
(C) French industry never recovered from the damage inflicted on it in World War I.
(D) all participants, even the victors, are consumed by the horrors of war.

149. Which of the following definitions of stark fits its use in this selection?
(A) harsh
(B) absolute
(C) rigid
(D) wholly

150. The writer hopes to reach the readers by
(A) being humorous
(B) describing gory details
(C) using an emotional style
(D) listing facts

151. Why did the author choose an example from World War I?
(A) The casualties were greater then than in most recent wars.
(B) She wanted the readers to question why wars are still being fought more than 75 years later.
(C) She did not want to upset sensitive readers by citing more recent statistics.
(D) She wanted the passage to be scholarly in tone.

152. Which of the following is an example of the use of irony?
(A) "… only victims, victims."
(B) "France was a victor in World War I."
(C) "Let's take a stark example."
(D) "France lost virtually an entire generation of men."

B. Vocabulary—22 questions

DIRECTIONS: Choose the word that means the same or most nearly the same as the underlined word.

153. adapting to the new regulations
(A) confining
(B) limiting
(C) objecting
(D) adjusting

154. reach an accord
(A) arrangement
(B) agreement
(C) alliance
(D) alternative

155. wear a garland
(A) helmet
(B) frown
(C) wreath
(D) mask

156. to loathe their attitude
(A) hate
(B) respect
(C) disregard
(D) resent

157. ladened with responsibility
(A) burdened
(B) constructed
(C) concerned
(D) honored

158. a legitimate excuse
(A) wild
(B) customary
(C) justified
(D) laughable

159. take every precaution
(A) opportunity
(B) risk
(C) advantage
(D) safeguard

160. a <u>quack</u> doctor
     (A) sham
     (B) medical
     (C) famous
     (D) competent

161. remain <u>steadfast</u> friends
     (A) childhood
     (B) distant
     (C) firm
     (D) trustful

162. to <u>abominate</u> war
     (A) seek
     (B) hate
     (C) declare
     (D) talk

163. to <u>berate</u> the offenders
     (A) ridicule
     (B) identify
     (C) applaud
     (D) scold

164. to <u>embezzle</u> funds
     (A) steal
     (B) invest
     (C) expend
     (D) waste

165. the <u>incessant</u> chatter
     (A) unexpected
     (B) constant
     (C) annoying
     (D) audible

166. the <u>prodigious</u> pile
     (A) colorful
     (B) sparkling
     (C) huge
     (D) amazing

167. the <u>ruthless</u> pirates
     (A) drunken
     (B) swaggering
     (C) pitiless
     (D) colorful

168. to remain a <u>novice</u>
     (A) candidate
     (B) teacher
     (C) scholar
     (D) beginner

169. increase their <u>longevity</u>
     (A) duration
     (B) enjoyment
     (C) possessions
     (D) grasp

170. the captain's <u>cronies</u>
     (A) crew
     (B) relatives
     (C) superiors
     (D) pals

171. the <u>wrath</u> of the gods
     (A) gift
     (B) pride
     (C) power
     (D) anger

172. arrested as a <u>vagrant</u>
     (A) thief
     (B) tramp
     (C) swindler
     (D) kidnapper

173. an <u>unabridged</u> dictionary
     (A) unshortened
     (B) unauthorized
     (C) unusual
     (D) authoritative

174. a <u>tedious</u> task
     (A) brief
     (B) stupendous
     (C) tiresome
     (D) welcome

SUBTEST 4 MATHEMATICS

Number of questions: 64   *Time limit: 45 minutes*

A. Concepts—24 questions

> DIRECTIONS: Choose the answer you think is best for each problem.

175. If $x + 5 = 17$, then $x =$
(A) 22 (B) 16 (C) 12 (D) 10

176. $AB = AC$. The measure of $\angle A$ is 80°. The measure of $\angle B =$

(A) 100° (B) 50° (C) 60° (D) 76°

177. The exact number of hundreds in 4,870 is
(A) 487 (B) 4.87 (C) 48.7 (D) 0.4870

178. The number $(4 \times 10^3) + (2 \times 10^2) + (5 \times 10) + (9 \times 1) =$
(A) 42.59 (B) 4,259 (C) 4.259
   (D) 0.04259

179. The circumference of the circle shown below is

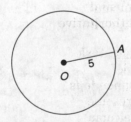

(A) 25π (B) 5π (C) 2.5π (D) 10π

180. Two numbers are in the ratio 3:2. The sum of the two numbers is 20. What is the larger number?
(A) 4 (B) 8 (C) 10 (D) 12

181. A man has 5 white shirts and 3 blue shirts in his closet. If he selects a shirt at random, what is the probability that his choice will be a white shirt?
(A) $\frac{3}{5}$ (B) $\frac{5}{8}$ (C) $\frac{5}{3}$ (D) $\frac{3}{8}$

182. Written as a base 10 numeral, the number 32(five) is
(A) 320 (B) 23 (C) 12 (D) 17

183. Which of the following is true?
(A) $a(b + c) = ab + c$
(B) $(a + b) + c = a + bc$
(C) $(a + b) + c = ab + ac$
(D) $a(b + c) = ab + ac$

184. If a tie costs x dollars, how many dollars do 4 ties cost?
(A) $4 + x$ (B) $x - 4$ (C) $4x$ (D) $\frac{x}{4}$

185. If the measure of $\angle AOB = 80°$, what fractional part of the circle shown below is shaded?

(A) $\frac{4}{5}$
(B) $\frac{2}{9}$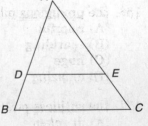
(C) $\frac{1}{3}$
(D) $\frac{1}{5}$

186. If, in the diagram, $\triangle ADE$ is similar to $\triangle ABC$, which of the following proportions is true?

(A) $\frac{AD}{AB} = \frac{AC}{EC}$
(B) $\frac{DE}{BC} = \frac{AD}{DB}$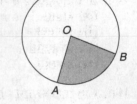
(C) $\frac{AD}{AB} = \frac{DE}{BC}$
(D) $\frac{AC}{AE} = \frac{AD}{DB}$

187. A number that satisfies the inequality $2 > x > -2$ is
(A) 0 (B) 5 (C) –3 (D) 7

188. Which of the following fractions has a value between $\frac{2}{7}$ and $\frac{5}{9}$?
(A) $\frac{7}{10}$ (B) $\frac{1}{6}$ (C) $\frac{1}{3}$ (D) $\frac{5}{8}$

189. $(-3)^4 + (-2)^3 =$
(A) 89 (B) –73 (C) –89 (D) 73

190. The measure of each acute angle of an isosceles right triangle is
(A) 60° (B) 30° (C) 45° (D) 90°

191. A cafeteria serves tomato juice in 6-ounce cups. How many servings may be obtained from 3 gallons of tomato juice?
(A) 64 (B) 96 (C) 120 (D) 32

192. At ABC college the enrollment consisted of 30% freshmen, 28% sophomores, 22% juniors, and the rest seniors. What fractional part of the enrollment consisted of seniors?
(A) $\frac{3}{8}$ (B) $\frac{1}{6}$ (C) $\frac{1}{5}$ (D) $\frac{1}{4}$

193. In which of the following are the numbers arranged in order of value with the largest first?
(A) 60%, $\frac{2}{3}$, 0.57
(B) 0.7, $\frac{4}{5}$, 37%
(C) 85%, $\frac{5}{6}$, 0.72
(D) 0.07, $\frac{1}{8}$, 0.19

194. One month a man saved 20% of his income. If he saved $820, what was his monthly income?
(A) $4,000 (B) $3,280 (C) $4,100
(D) $41,000

195. The number 186,000 written in scientific notation is
(A) 186×10^3
(B) 1860×10^2
(C) 1.86×10^5
(D) 18.6×10^4

196. On a fishing trip, Hector caught 3 more fish than Mario. Together the two boys caught 15 fish. How many fish did Hector catch?
(A) 6 (B) 10 (C) 9 (D) 8

197. After the price of a table was raised 20%, its price was $180. What was the price before the increase?
(A) $160 (B) $150 (C) $175 (D) $190

198. The scale used on a map is 1 inch = 15 feet. Expressed as a ratio, this scale is
(A) 1:90 (B) 1:60 (C) 1:100 (D) 1:180

B. Problem Solving—40 questions

199. Find the difference between $7\frac{1}{3}$ and $2\frac{1}{2}$.
(A) $4\frac{1}{6}$ (B) $3\frac{5}{6}$ (C) $4\frac{5}{6}$ (D) $4\frac{1}{2}$

200. Simplify: $-3 + 5 + (-7) + (-9)$.
(A) -12 (B) -14 (C) -24 (D) -22

201. Solve the following equation:
$6 + 4x = x + 21$.
(A) 5 (B) $6\frac{3}{4}$ (C) 4 (D) 3

202. Mrs. Barnes paid $100.70 for a dress. This included a 6% sales tax. What was the cost of the dress without the tax?
(A) $98.06 (B) $5.70 (C) $89.30
(D) $95.00

203. Find the product: $2\frac{2}{3} \times 1\frac{1}{4} \times 3\frac{1}{5}$.
(A) 10 (B) $10\frac{1}{3}$ (C) $10\frac{2}{3}$ (D) $5\frac{1}{3}$

204. If $y = 4x^3$, the value of y when $x = \frac{1}{2}$ is
(A) $\frac{1}{2}$ (B) $\frac{1}{4}$ (C) $\frac{1}{8}$ (D) 2

205. At a concert 387 tickets were sold at $12 each. In addition, 68 senior-citizen tickets were sold at half the regular price. How much money was collected?
(A) $5,152 (B) $5,052 (C) $5,002
(D) $4,998

206. After driving 140 miles, a motorist found that he had covered 35% of his planned mileage for the day. How many miles did he plan to travel that day?
(A) 450 (B) 420 (C) 400 (D) 510

207. Which of the following is closest in value to 8?
    (A) $(2.8)^2$
    (B) $2\frac{1}{2} + 4\frac{2}{3}$
    (C) $7 \times \frac{4}{3}$
    (D) $6 \div \frac{2}{3}$

208. *ABCD* is a rectangle in which *DC* = 8 cm and *AC* = 10 cm. What is the area, in square centimeters, of the rectangle?
    (A) 80 (B) 18 (C) 60 (D) 48

209. If the sum of two numbers is *x* and one of the numbers is 8, then three times the other number is
    (A) $3x$ (B) $3(8 - x)$ (C) $3(x - 8)$
    (D) $3(x + 8)$

210. A ladder is extended to a length of 15 feet and leaned against a wall. If the base of the ladder is 9 feet from the wall, how high up the wall does the ladder reach?
    (A) 10 feet (B) 18 feet (C) 16 feet
    (D) 12 feet

211. A chicken weighs 3 pounds 6 ounces. What is the cost of the chicken at $0.72 per pound?
    (A) $2.43 (B) $2.50 (C) $2.76 (D) $2.95

212. An agent sold a shipment of 56 dozen golf balls at $15.20 per dozen. What was the agent's commission at 6%?
    (A) $510.70 (B) $5,107.20 (C) $517
    (D) $51.07

213. A home was assessed at $98,000. If the tax rate was $3\frac{1}{2}$% the tax was
    (A) $3,500 (B) $3,430 (C) $3,403
    (D) $3,043

214. If 5 sport shirts cost $92.50, how much will 7 sport shirts cost at the same price?
    (A) $119.50 (B) $109.50 (C) $12.95
    (D) $129.50

215. Add in base 5:
    $132_{(five)}$
    $43_{(five)}$

    (A) $23_{(five)}$ (B) $203_{(five)}$ (C) $230_{(five)}$
    (D) $302_{(five)}$

216. If *x* is an integer and $0 > x > -2$, what is the value of *x*?
    (A) –3 (B) 0 (C) 1 (D) –1

217. A lecture hall is $\frac{2}{3}$ full. After 20 people leave, the lecture hall is $\frac{1}{2}$ full. What is the seating capacity of the hall?
    (A) 100 (B) 80 (C) 120 (D) 150

218. If $8x - 5 = 3x + 7$, the value of *x* is
    (A) 2.4 (B) $\frac{12}{11}$ (C) .4 (D) 1.4

219. Mr. Martin earns $42,000 per year. He saves 8% of his salary. How much does Mr. Martin save per month?
    (A) $3,360 (B) $275 (C) $280 (D) $300

220. Find the value of $2x^2 + 3y - 5$ if $x = \frac{1}{2}$ and $y = 2$.
    (A) 9 (B) 1.5 (C) 2.5 (D) 3

221. Solve: 834×28.
    (A) 23,532 (B) 23,432 (C) 23,352
    (D) 23,252

222. The formula $S = 16t^2$ is used to find the distance, in feet, covered by a freely falling body, where *t* represents the number of seconds during which the body falls. The number of feet covered by a freely falling body in 8 seconds is
    (A) 1,024 (B) 256 (C) 128 (D) 1,280

223. If $x + 2 = y + 5$, then
    (A) $y > x$
    (B) $x = y$
    (C) $y = x + 2$
    (D) $x > y$

224. A major league baseball player gets 86 hits in 100 games played. How many hits will he get in 150 games if he continues to hit at the same rate?
    (A) 130 (B) 129 (C) 140 (D) 132

225. If $2x - 3 > 5$, then x^2 must be
    (A) equal to 16
    (B) greater than 16
    (C) less than 16
    (D) greater than 20

226. The measures of the two acute angles of a right triangle are in the ratio of 3:2. The measure of the larger acute angle is
(A) 36° (B) 18° (C) 54° (D) 60°

227. Solve for x: $2.4x + 3.7 = 4.3$.
(A) 0.25 (B) 4 (C) 12 (D) 6

228. The sum of $3\frac{1}{2}$ and $4\frac{5}{6}$ is 10 less than x. The value of x is
(A) $8\frac{1}{3}$ (B) $17\frac{1}{3}$ (C) $17\frac{2}{3}$ (D) $18\frac{1}{3}$

229. If $\sqrt{x-2} = 7$, then $x =$
(A) 9 (B) 5 (C) 49 (D) 51

230. If $5 > x > 2$ and x is an even-number integer, then $x =$
(A) 3 (B) 5 (C) 4 (D) 10

231. If $\frac{1}{4}x = 20$, find the value of $\frac{3}{8}x$.
(A) 3 (B) 60 (C) $\frac{15}{8}$ (D) 120

232. At noon the temperature reading was 4° above zero. By midnight the temperature had fallen 12°. The temperature reading at midnight was
(A) 8° (B) 16° (C) –8° (D) 10°

233. Sally has twice as much money as Jessie. If Sally gives Jessie $5, the two girls will have equal amounts of money. How much money does Sally have?
(A) $20 (B) $15 (C) $18 (D) $25

234. Mr. Barry borrowed a sum of money at 8% simple interest for a period of 6 months. If he paid $340 in interest, how much did Mr. Barry borrow?
(A) $6,800 (B) $7,000 (C) $8,500 (D) $9,000

235. What is the area of the figure shown in the diagram?

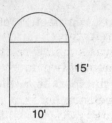

(A) $150 + 12\frac{1}{2}\pi$ square feet
(B) $150 + 25\pi$ square feet
(C) $150 + 5\pi$ square feet
(D) $25 + \frac{25}{2}\pi$ square feet

236. The ratio of $\frac{7}{8}$ to $\frac{3}{4}$ is
(A) $\frac{6}{7}$ (B) $\frac{7}{5}$ (C) $\frac{7}{6}$ (D) $\frac{7}{12}$

237. A carpenter earns $8 an hour more than his helper. The two men together earn $256 for an 8-hour working day. How much per hour does the carpenter earn?
(A) $12 (B) $15 (C) $18 (D) $20

238. If $\frac{5}{8}x = 20$, what is the value of x^2?
(A) 32 (B) 1,024 (C) 40 (D) 1,600

SUBTEST 5 LANGUAGE

Number of questions: 60   *Time limit: 25 minutes*

DIRECTIONS: In questions 239–278, look for errors in punctuation, capitalization, or usage. If there is no error, then blacken D on the Answer Sheet.

239. (A) More time has passed than I care to remember.
     (B) It was a massacre; they bet us by a score of 43–1.
     (C) In the Civil War the North fought the South for four long and bitter years.
     (D) No mistakes

240. (A) Everyone's to blame for this error.
     (B) Why don't you let her learn you how to work the new spray gun?
     (C) He should've listened to us the first time!
     (D) No mistakes

241. (A) I really enjoy Autumn best of all the seasons.
     (B) When we laid our money on the counter, the agent handed us our tickets.
     (C) Africa had risen up to throw off its oppressors.
     (D) No mistakes

242. (A) If they are all ready, we ought to leave.
     (B) "Joseph, come here this very instant!
     (C) Almost all of the books are now on loan.
     (D) No mistakes

243. (A) What will be the effects of this new decree?
     (B) Except for him, nobody seems to like me.
     (C) We plan to turn North at the corner.
     (D) No mistakes

244. (A) We ordered a new supply of personal stationery.
     (B) They refused to accept any money from me.
     (C) Whatever is our's is your's.
     (D) No mistakes

245. (A) Neither the books nor the pen were on the table.
     (B) I always prefer the latter to the former.
     (C) They had swum across the river early this morning.
     (D) No mistakes

246. (A) He is definitely the politer of the two.
     (B) She asked why I had left so early.
     (C) They borrowed the book from the library yesterday.
     (D) No mistakes

247. (A) A crate of oranges is on the platform now.
     (B) They were leaving when I called to them.
     (C) Their's nothing more that I can say.
     (D) No mistakes

248. (A) "I never said that I would go," Helen replied.
     (B) The rock slide is west of the Hudson River
     (C) They won't allow us to go there no more.
     (D) No mistakes

249. (A) Aunt Edna is coming with Grandfather.
     (B) All he could say was that what is done is done.
     (C) Nevertheless the vote must take place tonight.
     (D) No mistakes

250. (A) Does he attend Corlears Junior High School?
     (B) I said that I could never leave them.
     (C) Frank Lesseo is a professor at City University.
     (D) No mistakes

251. (A) She had never broke a promise before.
     (B) A flock of geese was on the golf course.
     (C) Because he was working too quickly, he soon made a fatal error.
     (D) No mistakes

252. (A) I thought I heard a woman's voice.
   (B) She is one of the students who attended the meeting.
   (C) It wasn't hardly worth the effort.
   (D) No mistakes

253. (A) The office will not be open on Veterans day.
   (B) She is a far better player than he.
   (C) "When will the next bus arrive?" asked the visitor.
   (D) No mistakes

254. (A) They asked Paula and I to handle the refreshments.
   (B) I saw the game and enjoyed it very much.
   (C) Between you and me, there is little that we can do.
   (D) No mistakes

255. (A) How sweet these flowers smell!
   (B) A story with a morale teaches good behavior.
   (C) Let the arrow lie just where it has fallen.
   (D) No mistakes

256. (A) She set down in the rocker and began to talk to us.
   (B) The results are so different from what I had expected.
   (C) The enthusiastic audience asked a number of questions.
   (D) No mistakes

257. (A) Don't the motor sound uneven to you?
   (B) Not one of the scouts plans to miss the event.
   (C) I heartily approve of her being chosen resident.
   (D) No mistakes

258. (A) I began dieting by skipping my third dessert.
   (B) We stood up late to see the fireworks.
   (C) Doesn't she want to see justice done?
   (D) No mistakes

259. (A) The plant fell off the window ledge.
   (B) Because of the accident, he arrived late.
   (C) Us seniors must support this worthwhile cause.
   (D) No mistakes

260. (A) It just wouldn't do any good at this time.
   (B) What is the capitol of Florida?
   (C) They insisted that we girls had done it.
   (D) No mistakes

261. (A) The jacket has shrunk, so it no longer fits me.
   (B) Everybody except him agreed to the plan.
   (C) The crowd was nowheres near the anticipated size.
   (D) No mistakes

262. (A) They will all come over my house after the game.
   (B) I wish I could have shaken some sense into her.
   (C) Will you lend me your copy of the book?
   (D) No mistakes

263. (A) They decided to leave without George and her.
   (B) She is faster than any other girl in her class.
   (C) Being that he was there, we asked him to join us.
   (D) No mistakes

264. (A) She is the kind of person I enjoy being with.
   (B) They will have to leave her go at the end of the week.
   (C) Have you wound the old-fashioned clock?
   (D) No mistakes

265. (A) It is never too late to admit your fault.
   (B) It was that there loose bolt that caused the power failure..
   (C) I had completely forgotten about them.
   (D) No mistakes

266. (A) The party was planned for Jonathan and us.
     (B) The motor runs well now that it has been adjusted.
     (C) Let her lay where she fell asleep.
     (D) No mistakes

267. (A) It is he who should be punished!
     (B) Margie as well as Alice were invited.
     (C) Here lie the remnants of my shattered hopes.
     (D) No mistakes

268. (A) Elton sent this candy as a gift for you and I.
     (B) I have tolerated as much of your nonsense as I can take!
     (C) We have lived in Lucerne for the past five years.
     (D) No mistakes

269. (A) You should have spoke up sooner.
     (B) Jack as well as his three sisters was waiting for us.
     (C) This error has cost me more than you can imagine!
     (D) No mistakes

270. (A) Drive slowly when you are in a congested area.
     (B) The pipe had burst early this morning.
     (C) When you bow, one should not have a broad smile on your face.
     (D) No mistakes

271. (A) You will have to get along without Evelyn and me.
     (B) I sure appreciate your helping me.
     (C) All of the students except me will be there.
     (D) No mistakes

272. (A) She has less money now than ever before.
     (B) One of the workers left a car near our cabin.
     (C) She is the kind of a person who enjoys puns.
     (D) No mistakes

273. (A) Their reactions were different from yours.
     (B) We hadn't but seven cents between us.
     (C) Go slow, especially when rounding sharp corners.
     (D) No mistakes

274. (A) Bea shouted that she needed us to help her badly.
     (B) Tonight President Bush will address both houses of Congress.
     (C) He is the more intelligent of the two.
     (D) No mistakes

275. (A) We had to borrow the money off them.
     (B) In dire need of help, I pulled the emergency cord.
     (C) Neither Sarah nor Adam could solve the puzzles.
     (D) No mistakes

276. (A) Between Helen and me stood the angry bear.
     (B) What is your principal reason for rejecting our offer?
     (C) Everyone in the classrooms want to see the play.
     (D) No mistakes

277. (A) She graduated from college this spring.
     (B) When in Rome do as the Romans do.
     (C) You ought not to have said that.
     (D) No mistakes

278. (A) Caroline please put a stamp on this letter.
     (B) If I had been there, he never would have said that.
     (C) I couldn't have done better myself.
     (D) No mistakes

DIRECTIONS: For questions 279–288, look only for spelling errors. If there is no misspelling, blacken D on the Answer Sheet.

279. (A) What arrangements have been made for the trip?
(B) Did you help her write her acceptance speech?
(C) These folders must be seperated from the others.
(D) No mistakes

280. (A) The project has been permanently postponed.
(B) The soup was particuliary tasty today.
(C) You must put your request in writing.
(D) No mistakes

281. (A) You will never acomplish all that!
(B) I hope it becomes an annual school event.
(C) Where are the books they recommended to us?
(D) No mistakes

282. (A) Don't tell me that you too are afraid of lightning!
(B) She hopes to win an atheletic scholarhip.
(C) How much preparation will it require?
(D) No mistakes

283. (A) Time was the real villian in this unfortunate mess.
(B) I really think that their demands are outrageous.
(C) I have to finish my laboratory experiments today.
(D) No mistakes

284. (A) You are being unnecessarily harsh in demanding this.
(B) I plan to look it up in the reference library.
(C) We cannot disregard their wishes indefinitly!
(D) No mistakes

285. (A) He has the temperament of a road hog!
(B) What is the preferred pronunciation of *tomato*?
(C) This exceeds all of my wildest expectations.
(D) No mistakes

286. (A) How could this turn of events have benefited us?
(B) Her lisp was hardly noticeable.
(C) I accidentaly spilled some of the solution.
(D) No mistakes

287. (A) Who will chair the meeting in her absence?
(B) I offer no apology for my actions!
(C) Could you tell me where the guidence office is?
(D) No mistakes

288. (A) The strain is beginning to have an effect on her.
(B) The play was practically over when she arrived.
(C) These kinds of outbursts will occur simultaniously
(D) No mistakes

DIRECTIONS: For questions 289–298, look for errors in composition. Follow the directions for each question.

289. Choose the word that is a clear connective to complete the given sentence.

The storm had turned the road into a muddy, treacherous pond; _____ we had to inch forward toward the distant hospital.
(A) moreover,
(B) consequently,
(C) for example,
(D) none of these

290. Choose the word that is a clear connective to complete the given sentence.

We knew that the hardest part of the trail lay directly ahead; _____ we rested for ten minutes to renew our strength.
(A) indeed,
(B) moreover,
(C) accordingly,
(D) none of these

291. Choose the words that best complete the following sentence.

The company will test _____
(A) a new drug aimed at preventing asthma attacks later this year.
(B) a new drug aimed later this year at preventing asthma attacks.
(C) later this year a new drug aimed at preventing asthma attacks.
(D) a new drug aimed at preventing later this year asthma attacks.

292. Which choice most clearly expresses the intended meaning?
(A) The suburbs of the city looked drab and overcrowded after traveling for hours.
(B) Traveling for hours, the suburbs looked drab and overcrowded.
(C) When we finally arrived after traveling for hours, the suburbs looked drab and overcrowded.
(D) After traveling for hours, the suburbs of the city looked drab and overcrowded.

293. Which choice most clearly expresses the intended meaning?
(A) In their potluck suppers the women included their husbands and children.
(B) The women included their husbands and children among those who shared the potluck suppers.
(C) The potluck suppers of the women included their husbands and children.
(D) The women included their husbands and children in their potluck suppers.

294. Which of the following pairs of sentences fits best under this topic sentence?

"Alum, also called potassium alum, is a colorless mixed salt having several commercial uses."
(A) Alum resembles aluminum in spelling. However, it is a completely different type of substance.
(B) Alum is usually sold as a powder. It can be bought in a chemical supply house.
(C) The basic ingredient used in flameproofing textiles is alum. The original styptic pencil used to stop bleeding from small cuts caused by shaving is usually made entirely of alum.
(D) Baking powder includes alum among its ingredients. It gives off carbon dioxide to cause cakes and bread to rise.

295. Which of the following pairs of sentences fits best under this topic sentence?

"Alvin Ailey is best known for his works expressing the black heritage."
(A) His works incorporate techniques of modern dance, ballet, and African tribal dances. The music he used stresses modern jazz rather than the European traditional classics.
(B) He believed in the power of dance to reveal our inner feelings. He developed a new language in body movements and gestures.
(C) He organized the American Dance Theater. It was the first predominantly black troupe to perform at the Metropolitan Opera House.
(D) His respect for humanity was fundamental. He devised a method for teaching ballet to the visually handicapped.

296. Which of the following sentences best creates an element of suspense?
    (A) The people in this romantic tale lived many years ago in a deep valley nestled among high mountains.
    (B) "If I do not locate the missing deed by 12 o'clock, we shall be ruined!"
    (C) As a direct result of this investigation, fear no longer dominates our lives.
    (D) "If any one is to suffer for this deed, I am the one, since I alone planned every step of the way!"

297. Which sentence does not belong in the paragraph below?

    (1) An offer of friendship can often lead to disastrous results. (2) The Algonquins befriended the French settlers who moved into their territory, present-day Quebec Province, and formed an alliance with them. (3) The French used the name Algonquins to identify all the Indians in that area. (4) Because of their alliance with the French, the Algonquins went to war with the Iroquois, who defeated them and destroyed them as a nation.
    (A) sentence 1
    (B) sentence 2
    (C) sentence 3
    (D) sentence 4

298. Where should the sentence "The oral literature of Africa has a rich variety of forms" be placed in the following paragraph?

    (1) Proverbs and riddles convey the accepted codes of conduct. (2) Folktales dominate the realm of fiction. (3) Myths and legends explain the origins of social organization.
    (A) before sentence 1
    (B) before sentence 2
    (C) before sentence 3
    (D) after sentence 3

Answers to Practice High School Placement Test 1

SUBTEST 1 VERBAL SKILLS

1. A	13. B	25. A	37. D	49. C
2. D	14. D	26. B	38. C	50. B
3. A	15. B	27. C	39. C	51. C
4. C	16. C	28. C	40. A	52. D
5. C	17. A	29. C	41. B	53. D
6. C	18. D	30. C	42. A	54. B
7. C	19. B	31. A	43. B	55. C
8. B	20. A	32. B	44. A	56. D
9. B	21. B	33. D	45. B	57. C
10. D	22. C	34. B	46. B	58. D
11. B	23. D	35. A	47. A	59. B
12. A	24. B	36. C	48. B	60. B

Rating Your Results

Superior	53–60 correct
Average	47–52 correct
Below Average	46 or fewer correct

Material to Review: Chapter 4

SUBTEST 3 READING

A. Reading—Comprehension

113. C	121. D	129. B	137. D	145. B
114. D	122. D	130. C	138. B	146. D
115. B	123. D	131. D	139. A	147. B
116. C	124. C	132. C	140. A	148. D
117. B	125. B	133. D	141. C	149. A
118. B	126. B	134. B	142. A	150. D
119. A	127. D	135. D	143. B	151. A
120. B	128. D	136. D	144. D	152. B

Rating Your Results

Superior	34–40 correct
Average	27–33 correct
Below Average	26 or fewer correct

Material to Review: Chapter 5

SUBTEST 2 QUANTITATIVE SKILLS

61. A	72. A	83. D	93. B	103. D
62. C	73. C	84. D	94. D	104. D
63. C	74. A	85. B	95. B	105. C
64. D	75. C	86. D	96. B	106. D
65. B	76. A	87. A	97. B	107. B
66. C	77. B	88. D	98. D	108. A
67. B	78. D	89. C	99. B	109. D
68. C	79. B	90. B	100. A	110. A
69. C	80. C	91. C	101. A	111. D
70. D	81. C	92. A	102. B	112. C
71. B	82. B			

Rating Your Results

Superior	47–52 correct
Average	40–46 correct
Below Average	39 or fewer correct

Material to Review: Chapter 13

B. Reading—Vocabulary

153. D	158. C	163. D	167. C	171. D
154. B	159. D	164. A	168. D	172. B
155. C	160. A	165. B	169. A	173. A
156. A	161. C	166. C	170. D	174. C
157. A	162. B			

Rating Your Results

Superior	20–22 correct
Average	16–19 correct
Below Average	15 or fewer correct

Material to Review: Chapter 4

SUBTEST 4   MATHEMATICS

A. Mathematics—Concepts

175. C	180. D	185. B	190. C	195. C
176. B	181. B	186. C	191. A	196. C
177. C	182. D	187. A	192. C	197. B
178. B	183. D	188. C	193. C	198. D
179. D	184. C	189. D	194. C	

Rating Your Results	
Superior	21–24 correct
Average	16–20 correct
Below Average	15 or fewer correct

Material to Review: Chapters 7–12

B. Mathematics—Problem Solving

199. C	207. A	215. C	223. D	231. A
200. B	208. D	216. D	224. B	232. C
201. A	209. C	217. C	225. B	233. A
202. D	210. D	218. A	226. C	234. C
203. C	211. A	219. C	227. A	235. A
204. A	212. D	220. B	228. D	236. C
205. B	213. B	221. C	229. D	237. D
206. C	214. D	222. A	230. C	238. B

Rating Your Results	
Superior	35–40 correct
Average	28–34 correct
Below Average	27 or fewer correct

Material to Review: Chapters 7–12

SUBTEST 5   LANGUAGE

239 B	251. A	263. C	275. A	287. C
240 B	252. C	264. B	276. C	288. C
241. A	253. A	265. B	277. D	289. B
242. B	254. A	266. C	278. A	290. C
243. C	255. B	267. B	279. C	291. C
244. C	256. A	268. A	280. B	292. C
245. A	257. A	269. A	281. A	293. B
246. D	258. B	270. C	282. B	294. C
247. C	259. C	271. B	283. A	295. A
248. C	260. B	272. C	284. C	296. B
249. C	261. C	273. B	285. D	297. C
250. D	262. A	274. A	286. C	298. A

Rating Your Results	
Superior	54–60 correct
Average	46–53 correct
Below Average	45 or fewer correct

Material to Review: Chapter 6

Answer Explanations

SUBTEST 1   VERBAL SKILLS

1. (**A**) In terms of descending height, the sequence is Susanna, Ellen, Sarah.

2. (**D**) *Partial* means less than all.

3. (**A**) *Aimless* means without purpose.

4. (**C**) A wallet (hopefully) contains money; a tank holds *gasoline*.

5. (**C**) We are not told where Eileen would be if she was not in New Orleans.

6. (**C**) Only *teenager* fits the definition of *adolescent*.

7. (**C**) *Commotion*, unlike the other choices, denotes upheaval.

8. (**B**) The progression downward is Henry, Adam, Bob. Therefore, Henry is the highest scorer.

9. (**B**) A cry is a response to pain; a growl is a response to *annoyance*.

10. (**D**) Fantasy is unreal, the opposite of what is *actual*.

11. (**B**) Only *degrade* fits the definition of *corrupt*.

12. (**A**) Only *beg* fits the definition of *entreat*.

13. (**B**) A *shop* is a place where one can buy; the other choices denote the contents of a ahop.

14. (**D**) Blueprints and *maps* give directions for action.

15. (**B**) Only *perpetual* fits the definition of *eternal.*

16. (**C**) A *factory* is where things are made; the other choices denote places where they are stored.

17. (**A**) There are two comparisons with rice as the lowest priced food in each group.

18. (**D**) Mediocre means ordinary; *superlative* means the best, or almost the best.

19. (**B**) Pliers are used to hold; scissors to *sever.*

20. (**A**) Only *raider* fits the definition of *marauder.*

21. (**B**) *Essential* means necessary.

22. (**C**) Only *exile* fits the definition of *banish.*

23. (**D**) Pacific people avoid *quarrels.*

24. (**B**) *Renovate* means to change, not add to.

25. (**A**) This is a small-is-to-large analogy.

26. (**B**) Only *friendly* fits the definition of *cordial.*

27. (**C**) Only *staff* fits the definition of *personnel.*

28. (**C**) *Vocabulary* refers to words; the other choices refer to the oral expression of thoughts.

29. (**C**) The key word is *some.* We do not know whether C is part of the B not related to A.

30. (**C**) We have no indication of the size relationship between A and C.

31. (**A**) *Seamy* means sordid, that is, unwholesome.

32. (**B**) The *pate* is where the other three choices are worn.

33. (**D**) Only *widespread* fits the definition of *prevalent.*

34. (**B**) *Compliment* and *slur,* and *limelight* and *obscurity,* are opposites by definition.

35. (**A**) The second sentence excludes frogs from the mammal category.

36. (**C**) A vault, unlike the other choices, is not printed material.

37. (**D**) Only *standoffish* fits the definition of *aloof.*

38. (**C**) A *filter,* unlike the other choices, is not a container.

39. (**C**) There is no comparison of Alpha to Delta.

40. (**A**) *Composed* and *agitated,* and *erratic* and *consistent,* are opposites by definition.

41. (**B**) *Fashionable* clothing is the opposite of *dowdy.*

42. (**A**) What is *mortal* is linked to earth, not heaven.

43. (**B**) Only *wind* fits the definition of *meander.*

44. (**A**) *Infamous* and *notorious* both mean well-known in a negative sense.

45. (**B**) A coward lacks valor; a pessimist, *hope.*

46. (**B**) A *deputy* is an assistant or substitute; the others are lawbreakers.

47. (**A**) Only *lithe* fits the definition of *supple.*

48. (**B**) *Offspring,* unlike the other choices, do not precede.

49. (**C**) Not all people who are not prima donnas are predictable.

50. (**B**) In this analogy, *weave* and *unravel* are used as synonyms for *tell.*

51. (**C**) People who are *vain* are immodest.

52. (**D**) Only *tomb* fits the definition of *sepulcher.*

53. (**D**) Only *recall* fits the definition of *reminisce.*

54. (**B**) A *garage,* unlike the other choices, is not a room within a house.

55. **(C)** An *artery,* unlike the other choices, is not a central part.

56. **(D)** An observer sees; an auditor *hears.*

57. **(C)** *Indifferent,* unlike the other choices, means lacking interest.

58. **(D)** To confirm is to prove; *disprove* is the opposite of *prove.*

59. **(B)** In terms of descending brightness, the sequence is Stanley, Milton, Arthur. Therefore, the third statement is false.

60. **(B)** *Profit,* unlike the other choices, is unearned income.

SUBTEST 2   QUANTITATIVE SKILLS

61. **(A)** Let x = the number

$$3x = 6\tfrac{3}{4} = \tfrac{27}{4}$$

$$x = \tfrac{27}{4} \div 3 = \tfrac{9}{4}$$

Half the number = $\tfrac{1}{2} \times \tfrac{9}{4} = \tfrac{9}{8}$ or $1\tfrac{1}{8}$.

62. **(C)** As we move from left to right, each number in the series is increased by 4. In this case, $13 + 4 = 17$.

63. **(C)** $a = \tfrac{1}{3}$ of the figure

$b = \tfrac{1}{3}$ of the figure

$c = \tfrac{1}{3}$ of the figure

$a + b = \tfrac{2}{3}$ of the figure

$b + c = \tfrac{2}{3}$ of the figure

Thus, $a + b = b + c$

64. **(D)** As we move from left to right, each number of the series is decreased by 6. In this case, $60 - 6 = 54$.

65. **(B)** The product of 6 and 7 is $6 \times 7 = 42$. The product plus $2 = 42 + 2 = 44$. $50 - 44 = 6$.

66. **(C)** Since the measure of each central angle is 60°, all the sectors are equal. The correct choice is $f = e$.

67. **(B)** It is helpful to write the three numbers as decimals:

$\tfrac{3}{8} = 0.375$, $35\% = 0.35$, 0.4.

Since $\tfrac{3}{8} > 35\%$ $(0.375 > 0.35)$, choice **(B)** is correct.

68. **(C)** As we move from left to right, we note that each number is the square of the next integer: $2^2 = 4$, $3^2 = 9$, $4^2 = 16$, $5^2 = 25$, $6^2 = 36$.

69. **(C)** Team X scored 49 points.

Team Y scored 46 points.

Team Z scored 53 points.

Team Z scored more points than either Team X or Team Y.

70. **(D)** $X = 15 - 9 = 6$

$Y = 3 - 2 = 1$

$Z = 7 - 3 = 4$

$X > Z$ because $X = 6$ and $Z = 4$.

71. **(B)** In $\triangle STV$, SV is the largest side because it is opposite the largest angle ($\angle STV$).

Therefore, $SV > ST$.

72. **(A)** $X = 40\%$ of $50 = 0.4 \times 50 = 20$

$Y = 50\%$ of $20 = \tfrac{1}{2} \times 20 = 10$

$Z = 20\%$ of $80 = \tfrac{1}{5}$ of $80 = 16$

The correct choice is **(A)** because $2Y = 20$ and $X = 20$.

73. **(C)** As we move from left to right in the series, we add 5 to each number to reach the next number. In this case, $19 + 5 = 24$.

74. **(A)** 2 less than $14 = 14 - 2 = 12$.

Let x = the number.

$$\tfrac{3}{8}x = 12$$

$$3x = 12 \times 8 = 96$$

$$x = 96 \div 3 = 32$$

75. **(C)** Of each 3 boxes, 2 are shaded.

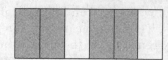

Therefore, $\tfrac{2}{3}$ of the figure is shaded.

76. (**A**) Let x = the number.
$$\tfrac{1}{4}x = \tfrac{1}{5}x + 1$$
$$\tfrac{x}{4} = \tfrac{x}{5} + 1$$

If we multiply both sides of the equation by 20, we have
$$5x = 4x + 20$$
$$5x - 4x = 20$$
$$x = 20$$

77. (**B**) $\tfrac{5}{8} \div \tfrac{1}{2} = \tfrac{5}{8} \times 2 = \tfrac{10}{8}$, or $\tfrac{5}{4}$, or $1\tfrac{1}{4}$

78. (**D**) The hall has $20 \times 9 = 180$ seats. In order to have the same number of seats in each row, 180 must be a multiple of the number of rows. Of the choices given, 180 is a multiple of 12 only. Thus, the lecture hall must have 12 rows.

79. (**B**) When we annex two zeros, we are really multiplying by 100. Then when we divide by 4, we are completing the task of multiplying by $\tfrac{100}{4}$, or by 25.

80. (**C**) Each successive number in the series is obtained by dividing the preceding number by 2. In this case, $8 \div 2 = 4$.

81. (**C**) Since $AB = AC$, $\angle B = \angle C$.
$$\angle 1 > \angle C.$$

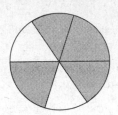

Therefore $\angle 1 > \angle B$ and $AB > AD$.

82. (**B**) Let x = the unknown fraction.
$$x \div \tfrac{1}{2} = \tfrac{3}{7}$$
$$x \cdot 2 = \tfrac{3}{7}$$
$$2x = \tfrac{3}{7}$$
$$x = \tfrac{3}{7} \div 2$$
$$x = \tfrac{3}{7} \times \tfrac{1}{2} = \tfrac{3}{14}$$

83. (**D**) As we move from left to right in the series, we note that in going from 1 to 2 we increase by 1. In going from 2 to 4, we increase by 2. In going from 4 to 7, we increase by 3. In going from 7 to the next number, we should increase by 4, obtaining 11.

84. (**D**) The circle is divided into 6 equal sectors. Four of these sectors are shaded.

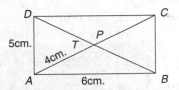

Thus, $\tfrac{4}{6}$, or $\tfrac{2}{3}$, of the circle is shaded.

85. (**B**) The area of rectangle $ABCD$ is equal to the product of its length and width, or $A = lw$.

In this case, $l = 6$ cm and $w = 5$ cm.

Area = 6 cm $\times$ 5 cm = 30 square centimeters.

86. (**D**) We can best determine relative sizes by writing each fraction as a decimal:
$$\tfrac{2}{5} = 0.40, \quad \tfrac{1}{3} = 0.33, \quad \tfrac{3}{8} = 0.375$$

Since $0.40 > 0.375 > 0.33$, we have $\tfrac{2}{5} > \tfrac{3}{8} > \tfrac{1}{3}$ as the correct choice.

87. (**A**) As we move from left to right in the series, we note that the odd-numbered terms are even numbers in succession:

6, ____, 8, ____, 10, ____, 12, ____,

The even-numbered terms are odd numbers in succession:

____, 9, ____, 11, ____, 13, ____.

The next odd number is 15.

88. (**D**) The average of $49 + 29 + 38 + 56 = 172 \div 4$. $172 \div 4 = 43$ and $43 - 40 = 3$.

89. (**C**) $x = 3^4 = 81$
$$y = 5 \cdot 2^3 = 5 \cdot 8 = 40$$
$$z = 6 \cdot 4^2 = 6 \cdot 16 = 96$$
$x + y > z$ because $81 + 40 > 96$.

90. **(B)** In moving from left to right in the series, we note that each successive term is obtained by doubling the preceding term and then subtracting 1. In this case, we have $2(65) - 1$, or $130 - 1 = 129$.

91. **(C)** Let x = the number.
$$x + 0.4x = 28$$
$$1.4x = 28$$
$$x = \frac{28}{1.4} = \frac{280}{14} = 20$$

92. **(A)** $5^3 = 5 \cdot 5 \cdot 5 = 125$
$125 \div 5 = 25$
$25 + 15 = 40$

93. **(B)** In going from left to right in the series, we note that each successive number is obtained by doubling the preceding number and adding 1. In this case, we have $2(15) + 1 = 31$.

94. **(D)** We first find the values of X, Y, and Z.
$X = 7 \times 5 - 4 = 31$
$Y = 37 - 4 \times 5 = 37 - 20 = 17$
$Z = 8 + 6 \div 3 = 8 + 2 = 10$
We see that $X > Y > Z$.

95. **(B)** $40 \div \frac{1}{5} = 40 \times 5 = 200$.

96. **(B)** Since R, S, and T are midpoints, $\triangle ABC$ is divided into four equivalent triangles, of which one is shaded.

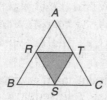

Therefore, $\frac{1}{4}$ of $\triangle ABC$ is shaded.

97. **(B)** In going from left to right in the series, we note that each term is obtained by subtracting 4 from the preceding term. In this case, we have $3 - 4 = -1$.

98. **(D)** Let x = the number.
$$\frac{x}{7} = 5 + \frac{1}{7}$$
$$x = 5 \cdot 7 + 1$$
$$x = 35 + 1 = 36$$

99. **(B)** $X = (5 + 3)^2 = 8^2 = 64$
$Y = 2^3 + 3^2 = 8 + 9 = 17$
$Z = 17 - 12 = 5$

We note that $Y^2 = 17^2 = 289$, and $X = 64$.
Therefore, $Y^2 > X$.

100. **(A)** In going from left to right in the series, we note that each term is obtained from the preceding term by adding 3. In this case, we have $14 + 3 = 17$.

101. **(A)** $\frac{1}{3} + \frac{5}{12} = \frac{4}{12} + \frac{5}{12} = \frac{9}{12}$

$\frac{1}{2} = \frac{6}{12}$

$\frac{9}{12} - \frac{6}{12} = \frac{3}{12} = \frac{1}{4}$

102. **(B)** $62\frac{1}{2}\% = \frac{5}{8}$
Let x = the number.
$$\frac{5}{8}x = 40$$
$$5x = 320$$
$$x = 64$$
The reciprocal of 64 is $\frac{1}{64}$.

103. **(D)** In moving from left to right in the series, we note that the odd-numbered terms follow the counting numbers: 1, 2, 3, 4. Each even-numbered term is 5 times the preceding number: 5, 10, 15. In this case, the even-numbered term following 4 is $4 \times 5 = 20$.

104. **(D)** In moving from left to right in the series, we note that there is a difference of 15 between successive terms. In this case, the missing number is $165 + 15 = 180$.

105. **(C)** Let x = the town's population.
$$0.24x = 6,000$$
$$24x = 600,000$$
$$x = 600,000 \div 24$$
$$x = 25,000$$

106. **(D)** Since 2, 3, 5, and 7 are prime numbers, the least common multiple for these numbers is the product $2 \times 3 \times 5 \times 7 = 210$.

107. **(B)** We write the numbers as decimals:
$X = 0.045$, $Y = 45$, $Z = 0.45$

Since $Y > Z$, the correct choice is (B).

108. **(A)** As we move from left to right in the series, we see that first there is a drop of 1 and then a rise of 2. In this case, we need a drop of 1: $40 - 1 = 39$.

109. (**D**) If we take this series apart, we can see the pattern:

5, _____, 6, _____, 7, _____
11, _____, 13, _____, 15, _____

In effect, we have two series. The correct number to follow 15 is 8 (7 + 1).

110. (**A**) If we take this series apart, we have this pattern:

64, _____, 32, _____, 16, _____,
_____, 35, _____, 29, _____,

The next number in the lower series is 23 (29 − 6).

111. (**D**) In moving from left to right in the series, we note that each term is 1 less than twice the preceding term. In this case, we have (2 × 33) − 1 = 65.

112. (**C**) In moving from left to right in the series, we note the following pattern:

7 − 1 = 6, 19 − 7 = 12, 43 − 19 = 24.

The next difference should be 48. Therefore, the next number is 43 + 48 = 91.

SUBTEST 3   READING

A. Comprehension

113. (**C**) Note "… active duty against the forces of Hitler."

114. (**D**) Note "the U.S. troop carrier *Dorchester.*"

115. (**B**) The selection describes the heroic sacrifice of the four chaplains.

116. (**C**) Dictionary definition of *inductees*.

117. (**B**) The four chaplains were religious leaders on a troop ship.

118. (**B**) They gave away their life jackets.

119. (**A**) Dictionary definition of *engulfed*.

120. (**B**) The men had to search for life jackets in the chaos caused by the torpedoes. There is no mention of theft, poor training, or lack of supplies.

121. (**D**) Choices (B) and (C) are too general. Choice (A) omits teacher and pupils. Choice (D) summarizes the selection.

122. (**D**) Dictionary definition of *assure*.

123. (**D**) The second sentence rules out (A). There is no mention of popularity (B) or of happier parents (C). Choice (D) is supported by the last sentence.

124. (**C**) "Students … will not waste time fussing …."

125. (**B**) The tone and content of the selection are appropriate for a handbook for entering pupils.

126. (**B**) Dictionary definition of *inadequate*.

127. (**D**) The example of the tiger eliminates choices (A), (B), and (C).

128. (**D**) The system described is not for action, eliminating (A). Choice (B) includes only an example; (C) is too general. Choice (D) accurately summarizes the subject matter.

129. (**B**) Since a phylum is a subdivision of a kingdom, it must consist of a minimum of 2 items; otherwise it would be undifferentiable from the kingdom.

130. (**C**) He lived in the eighteenth century, almost 400 years after printing was invented but more than 200 years before word processing.

131. (**D**) The essential fact about a species is the close relationship about members. There may be only a few or millions of such individuals.

132. (**C**) "Every scientific name consists of the genus and the species of the organism."

133. (**D**) "Linnaeus divided organisms into groups based on similarities of body structure."

134. (**B**) A category such as a class must equal the total found in its subdivisions: order, family, genus, species.

135. (**D**) Choice (A) is too broad; (B) is not clear; (C) is too limited. Choice (D) summarizes the content.

136. (**D**) Dictionary definition of *novice*.

137. (**D**) Note "… if he [a bachelor] was successful, [he] would become a knight."

138. (**B**) "The term does not include widowers …"

139. (**A**) The first paragraph contains more facts, as opposed to opinions, than the second. It deals with the meanings of the word, not its origin.

140. (**A**) Dictionary definition of *recipient*.

141. (**C**) Choices (A) and (D) are far too narrow; (B) is wrong because only today's standards are being questioned. The author is pleading for new social ideals; therefore, (C) is correct.

142. (**A**) Dictionary definition of *drudgery*.

143. (**B**) "We must measure education … by the wisdom for living it instills."

144. (**D**) The message is conveyed by means of implied "Thou shoulds" and evaluative comments.

145. (**B**) Choice (B) is the only one that implies bricks.

146. (**D**) "The amassment of knowledge is of negative worth when it places business above family …."

147. (**B**) The writer is too dogmatic for (A), (C), or (D) to be the correct choice.

148. (**D**) Choices (A), (B), and (C) deal with the use of France as an example to support the central idea, which is expressed in (D).

149. (**A**) Dictionary definition of *stark*.

150. (**D**) Choice (A) is wrong because no humor is intended; (B) is wrong because no bloody scenes are described. Although the example of France may stir high emotions (C), the author's main method of development was to state one fact after another; (D) is therefore correct.

151. (**B**) This answer must be inferred since the author stresses the fact that the devastation she describes was due to a less than recent war. Note "We must never forget," "the passage of years," "Each new generation."

152. (**B**) Since irony means saying one thing and meaning the opposite, there is rich irony in calling France a victor in World War I.

B. Vocabulary

Questions 153–174: see page 637 for answers. Please check a standard dictionary for definitions of vocabulary words that are not understood.

SUBTEST 4   MATHEMATICS

A. Concepts

175. (**C**)
$$x + 5 = 17$$
$$x = 17 - 5$$
$$x = 12$$

176. (**B**) Measure of $\angle A$ + measure of $\angle B$ + measure of $\angle C = 180°$.

That is, m $\angle A$ + m $\angle B$ + m $\angle C = 180°$.
   Measure of $\angle A = 80°$
$80 + $ m $\angle B + $ m $\angle C = 180°$
   m $\angle B + $ m $\angle C = 180° - 80° = 100°$
Since $AB = AC$, m $\angle B = $ m $\angle C$.
Therefore, m $\angle B = 50°$.

177. (**C**) To find the exact number of hundreds in 4,870, we must divide 4,870 by 100.
$4,870 \div 100 = 48.7$

178. (**B**)
$$4 \times 10^3 = 4 \times 1,000 = 4,000$$
$$2 \times 10^2 = 2 \times 100 = 200$$
$$5 \times 10 = 50$$
$$9 \times 1 = 9$$

Thus $(4 \times 10^3) + (2 \times 10^2) + (5 \times 10) + (9 + 1) = 4,259$.

179. (**D**) The circumference of a circle is found by using the formula $C = 2\pi r$.
In this case, $r = 5$.
Thus, $C = 2 \cdot \pi \cdot (5) = 10\pi$.

180. (**D**) Let $3x =$ the larger number.
And $2x$ = the smaller number
$3x + 2x = 20$
$5x = 20$
$x = 4$
$3x = 3(4) = 12$

181. (**B**) The man has $5 + 3 = 8$ shirts in the closet. Of the 8 possible choices, 5 would be white shirts. The probability of selecting a white shirt is $\frac{5}{8}$.

182. (**D**) $32_{(five)} = 3 \times 5 + 2 = 15 + 2 = 17$

183. (**D**) According to the distributive property, the true statement is $a(b + c) = ab + ac$.

184. (**C**) To find the cost of 4 ties, we must multiply the cost of 1 tie by 4. This gives us $4 \cdot x = 4x$.

185. (**B**) The sector OAB (which is shaded) is

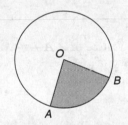

$\frac{80}{360}$, or $\frac{4}{9}$, of the circle.

186. (**C**) Since $\triangle ABC$ and $\triangle ADE$ are similar, their corresponding sides are in proportion.

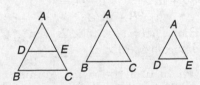

If we separate the two triangles, we can see the proportion readily:

$\frac{AD}{AB} = \frac{DE}{BC}$

187. (**A**) The inequality $2 > x > -2$ tells us that x is less than 2 and greater than -2. Of the choices given, only 0 is less than 2 and greater than -2.

188. (**C**) To make comparisons more readily we convert the fractions to decimals:
$\frac{2}{7} = 0.29$ and $\frac{5}{9} = 0.56$.
Since $\frac{1}{3} = 0.33$, $\frac{1}{3}$ has a value between $\frac{2}{7}$ and $\frac{5}{9}$.

189. (**D**) $(-3)^4 = (-3)(-3)(-3)(-3) = 81$
$(-2)^3 = (-2)(-2)(-2) = -8$
$81 - 8 = 73$

190. (**C**) In an isosceles right triangle one angle measures 90° and two sides are equal in length.

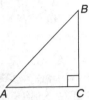

Since $AC = BC$, m $\angle A =$ m $\angle B$
m $\angle A +$ m $\angle B +$ m $\angle C = 180°$
m $\angle A +$ m $\angle B = 180° -$ m $\angle C$
$= 180° - 90° = 90°$
Since m $\angle A =$ m $\angle B$, m $\angle$ A and m $\angle$ B $= 45°$ each.

191. (**A**) 1 quart = 32 fluid ounces
1 gallon = 4 quarts
$= 4 \times 32 = 128$ fluid ounces
3 gallons $= 3 \times 128 = 384$ fl. oz.
$384 \div 6 = 64$ servings

192. (**C**) $30 + 28 + 22 = 80\%$ of enrollment consisted of nonseniors. Therefore, 100 $- 80 = 20\%$ consisted of seniors.
$20\% = \frac{1}{5}$

193. (**C**) To compare these numbers, we change all percentages and fractions to decimals.

(A) 0.6, 0.67, 0.57—not arranged as called for
(B) 0.7, 0.80, 0.37—not arranged as called for
(C) 0.85, 0.83, 0.72—arranged as called for

194. (**C**) $20\% = \frac{1}{5}$

$\frac{1}{5}$ of the man's income = \$820

$\frac{5}{5}$ (his whole income) $= 5 \times 820 = $4,100$

195. **(C)** In scientific notation, a number is expressed as the product of a number between 1 and 10 and a power of 10:

$$186,000 = 1.86 \times 10^5$$

Note that the decimal point was moved 5 places to the left in going from 186,000 to 1.86. In order to compensate, we must then multiply 1.86 by 10^5.

196. **(C)** Let x = number of fish caught by Mario and

$x + 3$ = number of fish caught by Hector

$$
\begin{aligned}
x + x + 3 &= 15 \\
2x + 3 &= 15 \\
2x &= 15 - 3 = 12 \\
x &= 6 \\
x + 3 &= 6 + 3 = 9
\end{aligned}
$$

197. **(B)** $20\% = \frac{1}{5}$

The problem tells us that the new price was 20%, or $\frac{1}{5}$, greater than the old price.

In other words, the new price is $\frac{6}{5}$ of the old price.

Let x = the old price

Then $\frac{6}{5}x = 180$, the new price

$$
\begin{aligned}
6x &= 5(180) = 900 \\
x &= 900 \div 6 = 150
\end{aligned}
$$

198. **(D)** 1 inch = 15 feet

1 foot = 12 inches

1 inch = $15 \times (12) = 180$

The ratio is 1:180.

B. Problem Solving

199. **(C)** $7\frac{1}{3} = \frac{22}{3}$, $2\frac{1}{2} = \frac{5}{2}$

$$\frac{22}{3} - \frac{5}{2} = \frac{44}{6} - \frac{15}{6} = \frac{29}{6}$$

$$\frac{29}{6} = 4\frac{5}{6}$$

200. **(B)** $(-3) + (-7) + (-9) = -19$
$5 + (-19) = -14$

201. **(A)** $6 + 4x = x + 21$

$$
\begin{aligned}
4x - x &= 21 - 6 \\
3x &= 15 \\
x &= \frac{15}{3} = 5
\end{aligned}
$$

202. **(D)** Let x = cost of dress without tax.

$$1.06x = \$100.70$$

If we multiply both sides of the equation by 100, we have

$$
\begin{aligned}
106x &= 10070 \\
x &= \tfrac{10070}{106} \\
x &= \$95
\end{aligned}
$$

203. **(C)** $2\frac{2}{3} = \frac{8}{3}$, $1\frac{1}{4} = \frac{5}{4}$, $3\frac{1}{5} = \frac{16}{5}$

$$\frac{8}{3} \times \frac{5}{4} \times \frac{16}{5} = \frac{32}{3}, \quad \text{or} \quad 10\frac{2}{3}$$

204. **(A)** $Y = 4x^3$

$Y = 4 \cdot \frac{1}{2} \cdot \frac{1}{2} \cdot \frac{1}{2} = \frac{4}{8}$

$\frac{4}{8} = \frac{1}{2}$

205. **(B)** $387 \times 12 = \$4,644$

$68 \times 6 = \$408$

$4,644 + 408 = \$5,052$

206. **(C)** Let x = planned mileage.

$$
\begin{aligned}
0.35x &= 140 \\
35x &= 14,000 \\
x &= 14,000 \div 35 = 400 \text{ miles}
\end{aligned}
$$

207. **(A)** $(2.8)^2 = 7.84$

$2\frac{1}{2} + 4\frac{2}{3} = 7\frac{1}{6}$,

$7 \times \frac{4}{3} = 9\frac{1}{3}$

$6 \div \frac{2}{3} = 9$

Comparing these results, we see that $(2.8)^2$ is closest to 8.

208. **(D)** $\triangle ADC$ is a right triangle.

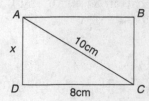

If we use the Pythagorean Theorem, we have

$$
\begin{aligned}
x^2 + 8^2 &= 10^2 \\
x^2 + 64 &= 100 \\
x^2 &= 100 - 64 = 36 \\
x &= 6
\end{aligned}
$$

The area of the rectangle = $AD \times DC = 6 \times 8 = 48$ square centimeters

209. **(C)** If the sum of the two numbers is x and one of the numbers is 8, then the other number is $x - 8$. Three times the other number is $3(x - 8)$.

210. **(D)** ABC is a right triangle, and we use the Pythagorean Theorem to obtain the equation

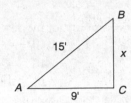

$$x^2 + 9^2 = 15^2$$
$$x^2 + 81 = 255$$
$$x^2 = 225 - 81 = 144$$
$$x = \sqrt{144} = 12 \text{ feet}$$

211. **(A)** 3 pounds 6 ounces = $3\frac{6}{16}$, or $3\frac{3}{8}$, pounds
$3\frac{3}{8} = \frac{27}{8}$
$\frac{27}{8} \times 0.72 = \$2.43$

212. **(D)** $56 \times 15.20 = \$851.80$
6% of $851.80 = 0.06 \times 851.80 = \$51.07$

213. **(B)** $98,000 \times 0.035 = \$3,430$

214. **(D)** We set up this proportion:
$\frac{7}{92.50} = \frac{7}{x}$ (x is the cost of 7 shirts)
$5x = 7(92.50) = 647.50$
$x = 647.50 \div 5 = \$129.50$

215. **(C)** 132
$\underline{+ \ 43}$

When we add 2 and 3, we obtain 5. The 5 is written as one 5 and 0 unit. Thus we have

   1
132
$\underline{+ \ 43}$
   0

The 5 column now has eight 5's, which are written as five 5's and three 5's.

   1
132
$\underline{\ \ 43}$
  30

The five 5's are now carried over to the 5's column, and we have

132
 43
$\underline{\ \ 1}$
230(five)

216. **(D)** The given inequality, $0 > x > -2$, tells us that x is greater than -2 and less than zero. Since x is an integer, it must be -1.

217. **(C)** Let x = seating capacity of the hall. Then $\frac{2}{3}x - 20 = \frac{1}{2}x$
If we multiply both sides of the equation by 6, we have
$4x - 120 = 3x$
$4x - 3x = 120$
$x = 120$

218. **(A)** $8x - 5 = 3x + 7$
$8x - 3x = 7 + 5$
$5x = 12$
$x = 2.4$

219. **(C)** 8% of $42,000 = 3,360$
$3,360 \div 12 = \$280$

220. **(B)** $2x^2 + 3y - 5$
$= 2(\frac{1}{2})(\frac{1}{2}) + 3(2) - 5$
$= \frac{1}{2} + 6 - 5 = 1\frac{1}{2}$ or 1.5

221. **(C)** 834
$\underline{\times \ \ 28}$
6672
$\underline{1668}$
23,352

222. **(A)** $S = 16t^2$
$t = 8$
$S = 16 \times 8 \times 8 = 1,024$ feet

223. **(D)** We may write the given equation, $x + 2 = y + 5$, as $x - y = 5 - 2$, or $x - y = 3$. This tells us that x is 3 more than y, or $x > y$.

224. **(B)** Let x = number of hits in 150 games. We set up the proportion
$\frac{86}{100} = \frac{x}{150}$
$100x = 86 \times 150 = 12,900$
$x = 12,900 \div 100 = 129$

225. (**B**) $2x - 3 > 5$
$$2x > 5 + 3$$
$$2x > 8$$
$$x > 4$$
If $x > 4$, then $x^2 > 16$.

226. (**C**) Since the measures of the two acute angles are in the ratio 3:2, we let
$3x$ = measure of the larger acute angle
and $2x$ = measure of the smaller acute angle
$$3x + 2x = 90$$
$$5x = 90$$
$$x = 18$$
$$3x = 3(18) = 54°$$

227. (**A**) We multiply both sides of the given equation, $2.4x + 3.7 = 4.3$, by 10 to obtain
$$24x + 37 = 43$$
$$24x = 43 - 37$$
$$24x = 6$$
$$x = \frac{6}{24} = \frac{1}{4} = 0.25$$

228. (**D**) $3\frac{1}{2} = \frac{7}{2}$, $4\frac{5}{6} = \frac{29}{6}$

$$\frac{7}{2} + \frac{29}{6} = \frac{21}{6} + \frac{29}{6} = \frac{50}{6}$$

$$\frac{50}{6} = \frac{25}{3}$$

According to the problem, $\frac{25}{3}$ is 10 less than x.
$$\frac{25}{3} = x - 10$$
$$25 = 3x - 30$$
$$25 + 30 = 3x$$
$$3x = 55$$
$$x = 18\frac{1}{3}$$

229. (**D**) If we square both sides of the given equation, $\sqrt{x - 2} = 7$, we have
$$x - 2 = 7^2$$
$$x - 2 = 49$$
$$x = 49 + 2 = 51$$

230. (**C**) Since in the given inequality, $5 > x > 2$, x is an integer, x must be either 4 or 3. Since x is an even number, x must be 4.

231. (**A**) $\frac{1}{4}x = 20$

We multiply both sides of this equation by 4 to obtain
$x = 20 \times 4 = 80$
The value of $\frac{3}{8}x = \frac{3}{8} \times 80 = 30$.

232. (**C**) The temperature reading at midnight was $4 - 12 = -8°$.

233. (**A**) Let $2x$ = Sally's money.
And x = Jessie's money
Then $2x - 5 = x + 5$
$$2x - x = 5 + 5$$
$$x = 10$$
$$2x = \$20$$

234. (**C**) Let x = amount of money borrowed.
Then $x \cdot \frac{8}{100} \cdot \frac{1}{2} = 340$
$$\frac{4x}{100} = 340$$
$$4x = 340 \times 100 = 34,000$$
$$x = \$8,500$$

235. (**A**) To find the area of the figure, we first find the area of the rectangle and then add to this area the area of the semicircle.

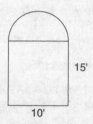

Area of rectangle = 10×15
= 150 square feet
The radius of the semicircle is 5 feet. We use the formula $A = \pi r^2$ to find the area of the circle:
Area of circle = $\pi r^2 =$ or $\times 5 \times 5 = 25\pi$
Then we divide by 2 to find the area of the semicircle:
Area of semicircle = $\frac{25\pi}{2}$
Total area = $150 + \frac{25\pi}{2}$,
or $150 + 12\frac{1}{2}\pi$ square feet

236. (**C**) $\frac{7}{8} : \frac{3}{4} = \frac{7}{8} \div \frac{3}{4} = \frac{7}{8} \times \frac{4}{3} = \frac{7}{6}$

237. (**D**) Let x = helper's hourly wage.
And $x + 8$ = carpenter's hourly wage
$$8x + 8(x + 8) = 256$$
$$8x + 8x + 64 = 256$$
$$16x = 256 - 64 = 192$$
$$x = 12$$
$$x + 8 = 12 + 8 = \$20$$

238. (**B**) $\frac{5}{8}x = 20$
$$5x = 20 \times 8 = 160$$
$$x = 160 \div 5 = 32$$
$$x^2 = (32)^2 = 1,024$$

SUBTEST 5 LANGUAGE

239. **(B)** *Beat* is to defeat; *bet* is to wager: They *beat* …

240. **(B)** You *teach* to and *learn* from: …let her *teach you* …

241. **(A)** The names of the seasons are not capitalized: …enjoy *autumn* best…

242. **(B)** Quotation marks are used at the beginning and the end of a quotation: "… this very instant!"

243. **(C)** Points of the compass are not capitalized: plan to turn *north* …

244. **(C)** Possessive pronouns do not require apostrophes: Whatever is *ours* is *yours.*

245. **(A)** In *neither … nor* constructions the verb agrees with the second subject: … the pen *was* …

246. **(D)** No mistakes

247. **(C)** *Theirs* = possessive pronoun; *there's* = there is: *There's* nothing more …

248. **(C)** *Won't* + *no* = double negative: … *won't … allow … any more* …

249. **(C)** A comma is required after an introductory adverb: *Nevertheless,* … The indirect quotation in (B) does not require quotation marks.

250. **(D)** No mistakes. The indirect quotation in (B) does not require quotation marks.

251. **(A)** The past participle *broken,* not the past tense *broke,* is required after the helping verb *have:* She had never *broken* …

252. **(C)** *Wasn't* + *hardly* = double negative: *was hardly* worth …

253. **(A)** Both words are capitalized in the name of a holiday: *Veterans Day.*

254. **(A)** The object of a verb is in the objective case: They asked … *me.*

255. **(B)** *Moral* = lesson; *morale* = feeling: A story with a *moral* teaches …

256. **(A)** *Set* = place, put; *sit* = occupy a seat: She *sat* down …

257. **(A)** The third-person-singular verb form is *doesn't: Doesn't* the motor …

258. **(B)** *Stood* = past of *stand; stayed* = remained: We *stayed* up late …

259. **(C)** If we omit *seniors,* we readily see that *we,* the subject form, is required: *We* seniors must …

260. **(B)** *Capitol* = building; *capital* = main city: What is the *capital* of Florida?

261. **(C)** *Nowhere,* not *nowheres,* is the accepted form: The crowd was *nowhere* near …

262. **(A)** Come *to,* not *over,* is the accepted idiom: … all *come to my* house …

263. **(C)** *Being that* is not an accepted synonym for *since* or *because: Since (Because)* he was there …

264. **(B)** *Leave* = depart; *let* = permit: *let* her go …

265. **(B)** *That* means the one there; a second *there* is not needed: It was that loose bolt …

266. **(C)** *Lie* = recline; *lay* = past tense of *put:* Let her *lie* …

267. **(B)** The only subject is *Margie; Alice* is object of *as well as:* Margie … *was* invited.

268. **(A)** The objective form *me* is required after the preposition *for:* … a gift *for* … *me.*

269. **(A)** The past participle *spoken* is required with the helping verbs *should have:* should have *spoken* …

270. **(C)** Consistency requires *you … you … your* or *one … one … one's.*

271. **(B)** The adverb *surely* is required to modify the verb *appreciate:* I *surely* appreciate …

272. **(C)** The idiom is *kind of,* not *kind of a:* the *kind of* person …

273. **(B)** Since *but* is negative, *not (n't)* is not required: *had but* seven cents …

274. **(A)** *Badly* is badly placed: logically, it modifies *needed*, not help: ... she *badly needed* us to ...

275. **(A)** The idiom is *to borrow from*: ... *borrow* the money *from* them.

276. **(C)** The singular subject *everyone* requires a singular verb: *Everyone ... wants ...*

277. **(D)** No mistakes

278. **(A)** A noun in direct address should be followed by a comma: *Caroline,* ...

279. **(C)** separated

280. **(B)** particularly

281. **(A)** accomplish

282. **(B)** athletic

283. **(A)** villain

284. **(C)** indefinitely

285. **(D)** No mistakes

286. **(C)** accidentally *or* accidently

287. **(C)** guidance

288. **(C)** simultaneously

289. **(B)** The connective must convey the idea of "as a result"; therefore *consequently* is correct.

290. **(C)** The connective must convey the idea of "given the described situation": therefore, *accordingly* is correct.

291. **(C)** *later this year* must be placed close to *will test,* the verb that this phrase modifies.

292. **(C)** *After traveling for hours* requires a noun or pronoun that it modifies in the sentence. Choices (B) and (C) are wrong because the suburbs had not been traveling.

293. **(B)** The meaning of *included* must be made clear. The other choices suggest cannibalism.

294. **(C)** Both sentences must relate to comercial uses of alum. Only choice (C) meets this criterion.

295. **(A)** *African tribal dances* and *modern jazz* are part of the black heritage.

296. **(B)** The suspense is based on the race against the clock.

297. **(C)** The paragraph deals basically with the Algonquins, not the French, and the results of an alliance formed in friendship.

298. **(A)** The given sentence should be the topic sentence. The other three sentences give examples of the varieties of form mentioned in this sentences.

Answer Sheet
Practice High School Placement Test 2

SUBTEST 1 VERBAL SKILLS

1. Ⓐ Ⓑ Ⓒ Ⓓ   13. Ⓐ Ⓑ Ⓒ Ⓓ   25. Ⓐ Ⓑ Ⓒ Ⓓ   37. Ⓐ Ⓑ Ⓒ Ⓓ   49. Ⓐ Ⓑ Ⓒ Ⓓ
2. Ⓐ Ⓑ Ⓒ Ⓓ   14. Ⓐ Ⓑ Ⓒ Ⓓ   26. Ⓐ Ⓑ Ⓒ Ⓓ   38. Ⓐ Ⓑ Ⓒ Ⓓ   50. Ⓐ Ⓑ Ⓒ Ⓓ
3. Ⓐ Ⓑ Ⓒ Ⓓ   15. Ⓐ Ⓑ Ⓒ Ⓓ   27. Ⓐ Ⓑ Ⓒ Ⓓ   39. Ⓐ Ⓑ Ⓒ Ⓓ   51. Ⓐ Ⓑ Ⓒ Ⓓ
4. Ⓐ Ⓑ Ⓒ Ⓓ   16. Ⓐ Ⓑ Ⓒ Ⓓ   28. Ⓐ Ⓑ Ⓒ Ⓓ   40. Ⓐ Ⓑ Ⓒ Ⓓ   52. Ⓐ Ⓑ Ⓒ Ⓓ
5. Ⓐ Ⓑ Ⓒ Ⓓ   17. Ⓐ Ⓑ Ⓒ Ⓓ   29. Ⓐ Ⓑ Ⓒ Ⓓ   41. Ⓐ Ⓑ Ⓒ Ⓓ   53. Ⓐ Ⓑ Ⓒ Ⓓ
6. Ⓐ Ⓑ Ⓒ Ⓓ   18. Ⓐ Ⓑ Ⓒ Ⓓ   30. Ⓐ Ⓑ Ⓒ Ⓓ   42. Ⓐ Ⓑ Ⓒ Ⓓ   54. Ⓐ Ⓑ Ⓒ Ⓓ
7. Ⓐ Ⓑ Ⓒ Ⓓ   19. Ⓐ Ⓑ Ⓒ Ⓓ   31. Ⓐ Ⓑ Ⓒ Ⓓ   43. Ⓐ Ⓑ Ⓒ Ⓓ   55. Ⓐ Ⓑ Ⓒ Ⓓ
8. Ⓐ Ⓑ Ⓒ Ⓓ   20. Ⓐ Ⓑ Ⓒ Ⓓ   32. Ⓐ Ⓑ Ⓒ Ⓓ   44. Ⓐ Ⓑ Ⓒ Ⓓ   56. Ⓐ Ⓑ Ⓒ Ⓓ
9. Ⓐ Ⓑ Ⓒ Ⓓ   21. Ⓐ Ⓑ Ⓒ Ⓓ   33. Ⓐ Ⓑ Ⓒ Ⓓ   45. Ⓐ Ⓑ Ⓒ Ⓓ   57. Ⓐ Ⓑ Ⓒ Ⓓ
10. Ⓐ Ⓑ Ⓒ Ⓓ   22. Ⓐ Ⓑ Ⓒ Ⓓ   34. Ⓐ Ⓑ Ⓒ Ⓓ   46. Ⓐ Ⓑ Ⓒ Ⓓ   58. Ⓐ Ⓑ Ⓒ Ⓓ
11. Ⓐ Ⓑ Ⓒ Ⓓ   23. Ⓐ Ⓑ Ⓒ Ⓓ   35. Ⓐ Ⓑ Ⓒ Ⓓ   47. Ⓐ Ⓑ Ⓒ Ⓓ   59. Ⓐ Ⓑ Ⓒ Ⓓ
12. Ⓐ Ⓑ Ⓒ Ⓓ   24. Ⓐ Ⓑ Ⓒ Ⓓ   36. Ⓐ Ⓑ Ⓒ Ⓓ   48. Ⓐ Ⓑ Ⓒ Ⓓ   60. Ⓐ Ⓑ Ⓒ Ⓓ

SUBTEST 2 QUANTITATIVE SKILLS

61. Ⓐ Ⓑ Ⓒ Ⓓ   72. Ⓐ Ⓑ Ⓒ Ⓓ   83. Ⓐ Ⓑ Ⓒ Ⓓ   93. Ⓐ Ⓑ Ⓒ Ⓓ   103. Ⓐ Ⓑ Ⓒ Ⓓ
62. Ⓐ Ⓑ Ⓒ Ⓓ   73. Ⓐ Ⓑ Ⓒ Ⓓ   84. Ⓐ Ⓑ Ⓒ Ⓓ   94. Ⓐ Ⓑ Ⓒ Ⓓ   104. Ⓐ Ⓑ Ⓒ Ⓓ
63. Ⓐ Ⓑ Ⓒ Ⓓ   74. Ⓐ Ⓑ Ⓒ Ⓓ   85. Ⓐ Ⓑ Ⓒ Ⓓ   95. Ⓐ Ⓑ Ⓒ Ⓓ   105. Ⓐ Ⓑ Ⓒ Ⓓ
64. Ⓐ Ⓑ Ⓒ Ⓓ   75. Ⓐ Ⓑ Ⓒ Ⓓ   86. Ⓐ Ⓑ Ⓒ Ⓓ   96. Ⓐ Ⓑ Ⓒ Ⓓ   106. Ⓐ Ⓑ Ⓒ Ⓓ
65. Ⓐ Ⓑ Ⓒ Ⓓ   76. Ⓐ Ⓑ Ⓒ Ⓓ   87. Ⓐ Ⓑ Ⓒ Ⓓ   97. Ⓐ Ⓑ Ⓒ Ⓓ   107. Ⓐ Ⓑ Ⓒ Ⓓ
66. Ⓐ Ⓑ Ⓒ Ⓓ   77. Ⓐ Ⓑ Ⓒ Ⓓ   88. Ⓐ Ⓑ Ⓒ Ⓓ   98. Ⓐ Ⓑ Ⓒ Ⓓ   108. Ⓐ Ⓑ Ⓒ Ⓓ
67. Ⓐ Ⓑ Ⓒ Ⓓ   78. Ⓐ Ⓑ Ⓒ Ⓓ   89. Ⓐ Ⓑ Ⓒ Ⓓ   99. Ⓐ Ⓑ Ⓒ Ⓓ   109. Ⓐ Ⓑ Ⓒ Ⓓ
68. Ⓐ Ⓑ Ⓒ Ⓓ   79. Ⓐ Ⓑ Ⓒ Ⓓ   90. Ⓐ Ⓑ Ⓒ Ⓓ   100. Ⓐ Ⓑ Ⓒ Ⓓ   110. Ⓐ Ⓑ Ⓒ Ⓓ
69. Ⓐ Ⓑ Ⓒ Ⓓ   80. Ⓐ Ⓑ Ⓒ Ⓓ   91. Ⓐ Ⓑ Ⓒ Ⓓ   101. Ⓐ Ⓑ Ⓒ Ⓓ   111. Ⓐ Ⓑ Ⓒ Ⓓ
70. Ⓐ Ⓑ Ⓒ Ⓓ   81. Ⓐ Ⓑ Ⓒ Ⓓ   92. Ⓐ Ⓑ Ⓒ Ⓓ   102. Ⓐ Ⓑ Ⓒ Ⓓ   112. Ⓐ Ⓑ Ⓒ Ⓓ
71. Ⓐ Ⓑ Ⓒ Ⓓ   82. Ⓐ Ⓑ Ⓒ Ⓓ

SUBTEST 3 READING

113. Ⓐ Ⓑ Ⓒ Ⓓ   126. Ⓐ Ⓑ Ⓒ Ⓓ   139. Ⓐ Ⓑ Ⓒ Ⓓ   151. Ⓐ Ⓑ Ⓒ Ⓓ   163. Ⓐ Ⓑ Ⓒ Ⓓ
114. Ⓐ Ⓑ Ⓒ Ⓓ   127. Ⓐ Ⓑ Ⓒ Ⓓ   140. Ⓐ Ⓑ Ⓒ Ⓓ   152. Ⓐ Ⓑ Ⓒ Ⓓ   164. Ⓐ Ⓑ Ⓒ Ⓓ
115. Ⓐ Ⓑ Ⓒ Ⓓ   128. Ⓐ Ⓑ Ⓒ Ⓓ   141. Ⓐ Ⓑ Ⓒ Ⓓ   153. Ⓐ Ⓑ Ⓒ Ⓓ   165. Ⓐ Ⓑ Ⓒ Ⓓ
116. Ⓐ Ⓑ Ⓒ Ⓓ   129. Ⓐ Ⓑ Ⓒ Ⓓ   142. Ⓐ Ⓑ Ⓒ Ⓓ   154. Ⓐ Ⓑ Ⓒ Ⓓ   166. Ⓐ Ⓑ Ⓒ Ⓓ
117. Ⓐ Ⓑ Ⓒ Ⓓ   130. Ⓐ Ⓑ Ⓒ Ⓓ   143. Ⓐ Ⓑ Ⓒ Ⓓ   155. Ⓐ Ⓑ Ⓒ Ⓓ   167. Ⓐ Ⓑ Ⓒ Ⓓ
118. Ⓐ Ⓑ Ⓒ Ⓓ   131. Ⓐ Ⓑ Ⓒ Ⓓ   144. Ⓐ Ⓑ Ⓒ Ⓓ   156. Ⓐ Ⓑ Ⓒ Ⓓ   168. Ⓐ Ⓑ Ⓒ Ⓓ
119. Ⓐ Ⓑ Ⓒ Ⓓ   132. Ⓐ Ⓑ Ⓒ Ⓓ   145. Ⓐ Ⓑ Ⓒ Ⓓ   157. Ⓐ Ⓑ Ⓒ Ⓓ   169. Ⓐ Ⓑ Ⓒ Ⓓ
120. Ⓐ Ⓑ Ⓒ Ⓓ   133. Ⓐ Ⓑ Ⓒ Ⓓ   146. Ⓐ Ⓑ Ⓒ Ⓓ   158. Ⓐ Ⓑ Ⓒ Ⓓ   170. Ⓐ Ⓑ Ⓒ Ⓓ
121. Ⓐ Ⓑ Ⓒ Ⓓ   134. Ⓐ Ⓑ Ⓒ Ⓓ   147. Ⓐ Ⓑ Ⓒ Ⓓ   159. Ⓐ Ⓑ Ⓒ Ⓓ   171. Ⓐ Ⓑ Ⓒ Ⓓ
122. Ⓐ Ⓑ Ⓒ Ⓓ   135. Ⓐ Ⓑ Ⓒ Ⓓ   148. Ⓐ Ⓑ Ⓒ Ⓓ   160. Ⓐ Ⓑ Ⓒ Ⓓ   172. Ⓐ Ⓑ Ⓒ Ⓓ
123. Ⓐ Ⓑ Ⓒ Ⓓ   136. Ⓐ Ⓑ Ⓒ Ⓓ   149. Ⓐ Ⓑ Ⓒ Ⓓ   161. Ⓐ Ⓑ Ⓒ Ⓓ   173. Ⓐ Ⓑ Ⓒ Ⓓ
124. Ⓐ Ⓑ Ⓒ Ⓓ   137. Ⓐ Ⓑ Ⓒ Ⓓ   150. Ⓐ Ⓑ Ⓒ Ⓓ   162. Ⓐ Ⓑ Ⓒ Ⓓ   174. Ⓐ Ⓑ Ⓒ Ⓓ
125. Ⓐ Ⓑ Ⓒ Ⓓ   138. Ⓐ Ⓑ Ⓒ Ⓓ

SUBTEST 4   MATHEMATICS

175. Ⓐ Ⓑ Ⓒ Ⓓ 188. Ⓐ Ⓑ Ⓒ Ⓓ 201. Ⓐ Ⓑ Ⓒ Ⓓ 214. Ⓐ Ⓑ Ⓒ Ⓓ 227. Ⓐ Ⓑ Ⓒ Ⓓ
176. Ⓐ Ⓑ Ⓒ Ⓓ 189. Ⓐ Ⓑ Ⓒ Ⓓ 202. Ⓐ Ⓑ Ⓒ Ⓓ 215. Ⓐ Ⓑ Ⓒ Ⓓ 228. Ⓐ Ⓑ Ⓒ Ⓓ
177. Ⓐ Ⓑ Ⓒ Ⓓ 190. Ⓐ Ⓑ Ⓒ Ⓓ 203. Ⓐ Ⓑ Ⓒ Ⓓ 216. Ⓐ Ⓑ Ⓒ Ⓓ 229. Ⓐ Ⓑ Ⓒ Ⓓ
178. Ⓐ Ⓑ Ⓒ Ⓓ 191. Ⓐ Ⓑ Ⓒ Ⓓ 204. Ⓐ Ⓑ Ⓒ Ⓓ 217. Ⓐ Ⓑ Ⓒ Ⓓ 230. Ⓐ Ⓑ Ⓒ Ⓓ
179. Ⓐ Ⓑ Ⓒ Ⓓ 192. Ⓐ Ⓑ Ⓒ Ⓓ 205. Ⓐ Ⓑ Ⓒ Ⓓ 218. Ⓐ Ⓑ Ⓒ Ⓓ 231. Ⓐ Ⓑ Ⓒ Ⓓ
180. Ⓐ Ⓑ Ⓒ Ⓓ 193. Ⓐ Ⓑ Ⓒ Ⓓ 206. Ⓐ Ⓑ Ⓒ Ⓓ 219. Ⓐ Ⓑ Ⓒ Ⓓ 232. Ⓐ Ⓑ Ⓒ Ⓓ
181. Ⓐ Ⓑ Ⓒ Ⓓ 194. Ⓐ Ⓑ Ⓒ Ⓓ 207. Ⓐ Ⓑ Ⓒ Ⓓ 220. Ⓐ Ⓑ Ⓒ Ⓓ 233. Ⓐ Ⓑ Ⓒ Ⓓ
182. Ⓐ Ⓑ Ⓒ Ⓓ 195. Ⓐ Ⓑ Ⓒ Ⓓ 208. Ⓐ Ⓑ Ⓒ Ⓓ 221. Ⓐ Ⓑ Ⓒ Ⓓ 234. Ⓐ Ⓑ Ⓒ Ⓓ
183. Ⓐ Ⓑ Ⓒ Ⓓ 196. Ⓐ Ⓑ Ⓒ Ⓓ 209. Ⓐ Ⓑ Ⓒ Ⓓ 222. Ⓐ Ⓑ Ⓒ Ⓓ 235. Ⓐ Ⓑ Ⓒ Ⓓ
184. Ⓐ Ⓑ Ⓒ Ⓓ 197. Ⓐ Ⓑ Ⓒ Ⓓ 210. Ⓐ Ⓑ Ⓒ Ⓓ 223. Ⓐ Ⓑ Ⓒ Ⓓ 236. Ⓐ Ⓑ Ⓒ Ⓓ
185. Ⓐ Ⓑ Ⓒ Ⓓ 198. Ⓐ Ⓑ Ⓒ Ⓓ 211. Ⓐ Ⓑ Ⓒ Ⓓ 224. Ⓐ Ⓑ Ⓒ Ⓓ 237. Ⓐ Ⓑ Ⓒ Ⓓ
186. Ⓐ Ⓑ Ⓒ Ⓓ 199. Ⓐ Ⓑ Ⓒ Ⓓ 212. Ⓐ Ⓑ Ⓒ Ⓓ 225. Ⓐ Ⓑ Ⓒ Ⓓ 238. Ⓐ Ⓑ Ⓒ Ⓓ
187. Ⓐ Ⓑ Ⓒ Ⓓ 200. Ⓐ Ⓑ Ⓒ Ⓓ 213. Ⓐ Ⓑ Ⓒ Ⓓ 226. Ⓐ Ⓑ Ⓒ Ⓓ

SUBTEST 5   LANGUAGE

239. Ⓐ Ⓑ Ⓒ Ⓓ 251. Ⓐ Ⓑ Ⓒ Ⓓ 263. Ⓐ Ⓑ Ⓒ Ⓓ 275. Ⓐ Ⓑ Ⓒ Ⓓ 287. Ⓐ Ⓑ Ⓒ Ⓓ
240. Ⓐ Ⓑ Ⓒ Ⓓ 252. Ⓐ Ⓑ Ⓒ Ⓓ 264. Ⓐ Ⓑ Ⓒ Ⓓ 276. Ⓐ Ⓑ Ⓒ Ⓓ 288. Ⓐ Ⓑ Ⓒ Ⓓ
241. Ⓐ Ⓑ Ⓒ Ⓓ 253. Ⓐ Ⓑ Ⓒ Ⓓ 265. Ⓐ Ⓑ Ⓒ Ⓓ 277. Ⓐ Ⓑ Ⓒ Ⓓ 289. Ⓐ Ⓑ Ⓒ Ⓓ
242. Ⓐ Ⓑ Ⓒ Ⓓ 254. Ⓐ Ⓑ Ⓒ Ⓓ 266. Ⓐ Ⓑ Ⓒ Ⓓ 278. Ⓐ Ⓑ Ⓒ Ⓓ 290. Ⓐ Ⓑ Ⓒ Ⓓ
243. Ⓐ Ⓑ Ⓒ Ⓓ 255. Ⓐ Ⓑ Ⓒ Ⓓ 267. Ⓐ Ⓑ Ⓒ Ⓓ 279. Ⓐ Ⓑ Ⓒ Ⓓ 291. Ⓐ Ⓑ Ⓒ Ⓓ
244. Ⓐ Ⓑ Ⓒ Ⓓ 256. Ⓐ Ⓑ Ⓒ Ⓓ 268. Ⓐ Ⓑ Ⓒ Ⓓ 280. Ⓐ Ⓑ Ⓒ Ⓓ 292. Ⓐ Ⓑ Ⓒ Ⓓ
245. Ⓐ Ⓑ Ⓒ Ⓓ 257. Ⓐ Ⓑ Ⓒ Ⓓ 269. Ⓐ Ⓑ Ⓒ Ⓓ 281. Ⓐ Ⓑ Ⓒ Ⓓ 293. Ⓐ Ⓑ Ⓒ Ⓓ
246. Ⓐ Ⓑ Ⓒ Ⓓ 258. Ⓐ Ⓑ Ⓒ Ⓓ 270. Ⓐ Ⓑ Ⓒ Ⓓ 282. Ⓐ Ⓑ Ⓒ Ⓓ 294. Ⓐ Ⓑ Ⓒ Ⓓ
247. Ⓐ Ⓑ Ⓒ Ⓓ 259. Ⓐ Ⓑ Ⓒ Ⓓ 271. Ⓐ Ⓑ Ⓒ Ⓓ 283. Ⓐ Ⓑ Ⓒ Ⓓ 295. Ⓐ Ⓑ Ⓒ Ⓓ
248. Ⓐ Ⓑ Ⓒ Ⓓ 260. Ⓐ Ⓑ Ⓒ Ⓓ 272. Ⓐ Ⓑ Ⓒ Ⓓ 284. Ⓐ Ⓑ Ⓒ Ⓓ 296. Ⓐ Ⓑ Ⓒ Ⓓ
249. Ⓐ Ⓑ Ⓒ Ⓓ 261. Ⓐ Ⓑ Ⓒ Ⓓ 273. Ⓐ Ⓑ Ⓒ Ⓓ 285. Ⓐ Ⓑ Ⓒ Ⓓ 297. Ⓐ Ⓑ Ⓒ Ⓓ
250. Ⓐ Ⓑ Ⓒ Ⓓ 262. Ⓐ Ⓑ Ⓒ Ⓓ 274. Ⓐ Ⓑ Ⓒ Ⓓ 286. Ⓐ Ⓑ Ⓒ Ⓓ 298. Ⓐ Ⓑ Ⓒ Ⓓ

Practice High School Placement Test 2

SUBTEST 1 VERBAL SKILLS

Number of questions: 60   *Time limit: 16 minutes*

> DIRECTIONS: Select the correct answer and blacken the appropriate circle on the Answer Sheet.

1. Futile means most nearly
   (A) confined.
   (B) thievish.
   (C) useless.
   (D) catastrophic.

2. Momentous means the opposite of
   (A) humorous.
   (B) fleeting.
   (C) illogical.
   (D) trivial.

3. Which word does not belong with the others?
   (A) morsel
   (B) chunk
   (C) repast
   (D) tidbit

4. Sarah weighs more than Fran. Irene weighs more than Sarah. Irene weighs less than Fran. If the first two statements are true, the third is
   (A) true.
   (B) false.
   (C) uncertain.

5. Watch is to second as calendar is to
   (A) day.
   (B) week.
   (C) month.
   (D) year.

6. Docile means most nearly
   (A) obedient.
   (B) bright.
   (C) slow.
   (D) educated.

7. Which word does not belong with the others?
   (A) exasperate
   (B) captivate
   (C) irritate
   (D) annoy

8. Learned means the opposite of
   (A) illiterate.
   (B) clever.
   (C) competent.
   (D) logical.

9. Deluge means most nearly
   (A) protest.
   (B) resign.
   (C) conquer.
   (D) flood.

10. Which word does not belong with the others?
    (A) hobby
    (B) calling
    (C) occupation
    (D) vocation

11. Freighter is to pier as jet plane is to
    (A) radar.
    (B) destinations.
    (C) terminal.
    (D) runway.

12. Mel reads faster than Larry. Adam reads faster than Irving but slower than Mel. Irving is the slowest reader. If the first two statements are true, then the third is
    (A) true.
    (B) false.
    (C) uncertain.

13. Comply means most nearly
    (A) confer.
    (B) describe.
    (C) obey.
    (D) dignify.

14. Which word does not belong with the others?
    (A) parka
    (B) overcoat
    (C) straitjacket
    (D) topcoat

15. Solace means most nearly
    (A) protection.
    (B) comfort.
    (C) reward.
    (D) shelter.

16. Stately means the opposite of
    (A) diplomatic.
    (B) immoral.
    (C) confident.
    (D) unimpressive.

17. Which word does not belong with the others?
    (A) stoneware
    (B) china
    (C) porcelain
    (D) silverware

18. Felonious means most nearly
    (A) cooperative.
    (B) unprovoked.
    (C) profitable.
    (D) criminal.

19. Workbook is to exercises as cookbook is to
    (A) ingredients.
    (B) illustrations.
    (C) recipes.
    (D) diet.

20. Every judge is just. None of my cousins is just. None of my cousins is a judge. If the first two statements are true, the third is
    (A) true.
    (B) false.
    (C) uncertain.

21. Which word does not belong with the others?
    (A) rout
    (B) departure
    (C) withdrawal
    (D) advance

22. Galleon means most nearly
    (A) ship.
    (B) measurement.
    (C) weapon.
    (D) warrior.

23. Stubborn is to yielding as wavering is to
    (A) peaceful.
    (B) decisive.
    (C) hopeful.
    (D) disobedient.

24. Cache means most nearly
    (A) reward.
    (B) warn.
    (C) wager.
    (D) hide.

25. Fertile means the opposite of
    (A) profitable.
    (B) muddy.
    (C) unused.
    (D) barren.

26. Which word does not belong with the others?
    (A) planet
    (B) promontory
    (C) galaxy
    (D) asteroid

27. Sand is to grain as water is to
    (A) thirst.
    (B) reservoir.
    (C) drop.
    (D) stream.

28. Every A is B. Some C is A. Some C is B. If the first two statements are true, the third is
    (A) true.
    (B) false.
    (C) uncertain.

29. Which word does not belong with the others?
    (A) frigid
    (B) tropical
    (C) sultry
    (D) humid

30. Acme means most nearly
    (A) summit.
    (B) detour.
    (C) route.
    (D) expert.

31. Thermometer is to heat as sundial is to
    (A) pressure.
    (B) time.
    (C) weather.
    (D) direction.

32. Many crimes are committed in the name of liberty. Murder is a crime. Some murders are committed in the name of liberty. If the first two statements are true, the third is
    (A) true.
    (B) false.
    (C) uncertain.

33. Which word does not belong with the others?
    (A) stapler
    (B) vise
    (C) drill
    (D) clamp

34. Variable means most nearly
    (A) tactful.
    (B) inferior.
    (C) changeable.
    (D) complaining.

35. Antiquated means the opposite of
    (A) artificial.
    (B) original.
    (C) foreign.
    (D) modish.

36. Paul is a better player than Harold but a weaker player than Henry. Phil is a better player than Henry but a weaker player than Arthur. Harold is the weakest player. If the first two statements are true, the third is
    (A) true.
    (B) false.
    (C) uncertain.

37. Which word does not belong with the others?
    (A) tripod
    (B) biped
    (C) quadruped
    (D) pedigree

38. Formless is to shape as senseless is to
    (A) territory.
    (B) truthfulness.
    (C) conscience.
    (D) purpose.

39. Relinquish means most nearly
    (A) resent.
    (B) donate.
    (C) destroy.
    (D) abandon.

40. Which word does not belong with the others?
    (A) altitude
    (B) diameter
    (C) angle
    (D) hypotenuse

41. Antagonist means the opposite of
    (A) leader.
    (B) offspring.
    (C) ally.
    (D) spouse.

42. Which word does not belong with the others?
    (A) plump
    (B) obese
    (C) paunchy
    (D) lanky

43. Dejected means the opposite of
    (A) companionable.
    (B) elated.
    (C) flexible.
    (D) unfortunate.

44. Sylvia is older than Elsie. Elsie is younger than Margie. Margie is older than Sylvia. If the first two statements are true, the third is
    (A) true.
    (B) false.
    (C) uncertain.

45. Donation is to charitable as criticism is to
    (A) sharp.
    (B) opposed.
    (C) judgmental.
    (D) sensitive.

46. Which word does not belong with the others?
    (A) nylon
    (B) wool
    (C) rayon
    (D) Dacron

47. Hostile means most nearly
    (A) talkative.
    (B) defensive.
    (C) unfriendly.
    (D) hospitable.

48. City X has more taxis than City Y. City Y has fewer taxis than City Z. City X has more taxis than City Z. If the first two statements are true, the third is
    (A) true.
    (B) false.
    (C) uncertain.

49. Which word does not belong with the others?
    (A) story
    (B) poll
    (C) novel
    (D) tale

50. Eagle is to aerie as fox is to
    (A) den.
    (B) prey.
    (C) pup.
    (D) nest.

51. Admonish means most nearly
    (A) heed.
    (B) scald.
    (C) encourage.
    (D) warn.

52. Which word does not belong with the others?
    (A) manager
    (B) headliner
    (C) director
    (D) coordinator

53. Adequate means most nearly
    (A) scant.
    (B) sufficient.
    (C) poor.
    (D) excellent.

54. Indiscreet means the opposite of
    (A) loud.
    (B) teasing.
    (C) prudent.
    (D) offensive.

55. Which word does not belong with the others?
    (A) rhyme
    (B) sketch
    (C) stanza
    (D) rhythm

56. Every A is B. Every A is C. Every C is B. If the first two statements are true, the third is
    (A) true.
    (B) false.
    (C) uncertain.

57. Play is to director as office is to
    (A) worker.
    (B) teacher
    (C) writer.
    (D) manager.

58. Fruitless means the opposite of
    (A) effective.
    (B) prosperous.
    (C) prominent.
    (D) pleasing.

59. Disburse means most nearly
    (A) scatter.
    (B) scold.
    (C) spend.
    (D) refer.

60. All quinks are four-legged galens. No flying galens have four legs. No quinks can fly. If the first two statements are true, the third is
    (A) true.
    (B) false.
    (C) uncertain.

SUBTEST 2   QUANTITATIVE SKILLS

Number of questions: 52   *Time limit: 30 minutes*

DIRECTIONS: Choose the answer you think is best for each problem.

SAMPLES:

1. Select the number that should come next in the following series: 4, 14, 24, 34, __.
   (A) 38 (B) 35 (C) 44 (D) 50

   The correct answer is 44, choice (C).

2. The measure of $\angle B = 45°$.

   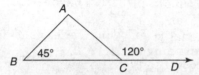

   The measure of $\angle ACD = 120°$.
   The measure of $\angle A =$
   (A) 45° (B) 75° (C) 60° (D) 80°

   The correct answer is 75°, choice (B).

3. If $\frac{5}{8}$ of a number is 15, then 40% of the number is
   (A) 24 (B) $9\frac{1}{2}$ (C) 12 (D) 9.6

   The correct answer is 9.6, choice (D).

4. Examine (X), (Y), and (Z), and select the correct answer.

   (X) $20 + 18 \div 3$
   (Y) $(16 - 6) - 5$
   (Z) $12 + \frac{2}{3}(9)$

   (A) X is greater than $Y + Z$.
   (B) Z is greater than X.
   (C) $Y + Z$ is greater than X.
   (D) Y is greater than X.

   The correct answer is (A).

---

61. If twice a number is 96, then $\frac{2}{3}$ of the number is
    (A) $10\frac{2}{3}$ (B) 32 (C) 72 (D) 64

62. Select the next number in the following series: 10, 14, 18, 22, __.
    (A) 24 (B) 25 (C) 26 (D) 30

63. If, in the diagram below, $a = b = c$, select the correct answer.

    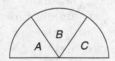

    (A) $a + b = c$
    (B) $a + b = b + c$
    (C) $a + c = b$
    (D) $b = a + c$

64. Look at the series 64, 59, 54, __, 44, 39. What number should fill the blank?
    (A) 50 (B) 51 (C) 48 (D) 49

65. Look at (X), (Y), and (Z), and select the correct answer.

    (X) $\frac{3}{5}$
    (Y) 55%
    (Z) 0.65

    (A) Of the three numbers given, (Y) is the greatest.
    (B) $Y > X$
    (C) $Z > X$
    (D) $Z > X + Y$

66. The number that is 8 less than 50 is the product of 6 and what other number?
    (A) 5 (B) 7 (C) 8 (D) 12

67. If O is the center of the circle below and the measure of $\angle 1 = 80°$, then the measure of $\angle 3$ is

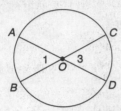

   (A) 80° (B) 100° (C) 90° (D) 95°

68. Mr. Stern has a class of 25 science students. On a test the results were as follows:

(1) Three A's
(2) Nine B's
(3) Eight C's
(4) Five D's

Which of the following is correct?
(A) More than 50% of the class had marks of A or B.
(B) 32% of the class had marks of C.
(C) More than $\frac{1}{5}$ of the class had marks of D.
(D) Less than 10% of the class had marks of A.

69. Look at the series 2, 7, 22, 67, __. What number should come next?
(A) 200 (B) 201 (C) 205 (D) 202

70. Look at (X), (Y), and (Z), and select the correct answer.

(X) $20 - 12 \div 3$
(Y) $(10 - 7) - 4$
(Z) $6 - (9 - 3)$

(A) $X + Y = Z$
(B) $Z > Y$
(C) $Z > X$
(D) $X + Y + Z = 17$

71. What is the next number in the following series: 3, 6, 11, 18, __?
(A) 25 (B) 24 (C) 29 (D) 27

72. If $ABCD$ is a parallelogram and $\overline{DE} \perp \overline{AB}$, select the correct statement.

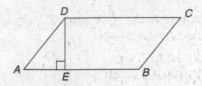

(A) $CB > DE$
(B) $AE = EB$
(C) $CB = AB$
(D) $AE > AD$

73. Which number is divisible by 9?
(A) 3,241 (B) 5,702 (C) 6,039 (D) 7,112

74. Look at the following series, and find the next number: 27, 9, 3, 1, $\frac{1}{3}$, __.
(A) $\frac{1}{6}$ (B) $\frac{1}{9}$ (C) $\frac{1}{12}$ (D) $\frac{1}{15}$

75. If $62\frac{1}{2}\%$ of a number is 10 less than 50, the number is
(A) 320 (B) 32 (C) 64 (D) 640

76. If $\frac{1}{3}$ of a number exceeds $\frac{1}{4}$ of the number by 20, the number is
(A) 24 (B) 240 (C) 48 (D) 120

77. The number of thirds in 30 is
(A) 33 (B) 45 (C) 60 (D) 90

78. Look at the following series, and find the next number: 2, 8, 3, 9, 4, 10, __.
(A) 5 (B) 7 (C) 12 (D) 14

79. A school has 96 classes with 25 students in each class. How many classes will be needed if the same number of students are divided into classes with 24 students in each class?
(A) 98 (B) 95 (C) 100 (D) 106

80. The sum of 40% of a number and 25% of the same number is 39. What is the number?
(A) 30 (B) 40 (C) 60 (D) 90

81. Select the number that should come next in this series: 270, 90, 30, 10, __.
(A) $3\frac{1}{3}$ (B) 3 (C) $\frac{1}{9}$ (D) $\frac{1}{27}$

82. In adding the fractions $\frac{1}{2}$, $\frac{5}{6}$, and $\frac{7}{8}$, the least common denominator is
(A) 16 (B) 12 (C) 24 (D) 48

83. Examine (X), (Y), and (Z), and select the correct answer.

   (X) $108 \div 3 \div 2$
   (Y) $(20 \times 3) - 40$
   (Z) $19 + (5 - 6)$

   (A) $X = Z$
   (B) $Y = X + 6$
   (C) $X > Y$
   (D) $Y = 2Z$

84. Select the next number in the following series: $\frac{1}{2}$, $\frac{1}{4}$, $\frac{1}{8}$, $\frac{1}{16}$, ___.
(A) 32 (B) $\frac{1}{20}$ (C) $\frac{1}{24}$ (D) $\frac{1}{32}$

85. Which of the following is correct?
(A) $\frac{4}{9} > \frac{5}{7} > \frac{2}{3}$
(B) $\frac{5}{7} > \frac{2}{3} > \frac{4}{9}$
(C) $\frac{2}{3} > \frac{4}{9} > \frac{5}{7}$
(D) $\frac{2}{3} > \frac{5}{7} > \frac{4}{9}$

86. O is the center of the circle shown below, and the measure of $\angle O$ is $45°$. The sector OAB is what fractional part of the circle?

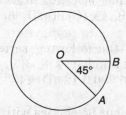

   (A) $\frac{1}{5}$ (B) $\frac{1}{4}$ (C) $\frac{1}{7}$ (D) $\frac{1}{8}$

87. What is the next number in the following series: 3, 8, 15, 24, ___?
(A) 37 (B) 35 (C) 32 (D) 31

88. $ABCD$ is a rectangle. $BD = 15$, and $AB = 12$. The perimeter of $ABCD$ is

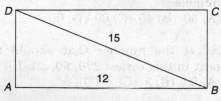

(A) 42 (B) 45 (C) 54 (D) 60

89. The average of 47, 36, 28, and 25 is
(A) less than 36 and greater than 28
(B) greater than 36
(C) greater than the average of 47 and 25
(D) less than 28

90. If $x = 2^5 - 1$, $y = 3^3 + 5$, and $z = 2 \times 4^2$, then
(A) $x = y$
(B) $y = z$
(C) $x = z$
(D) $x + y = z$

91. When a number is decreased by 20% of itself, the result is 96. The number is
(A) 24 (B) 240 (C) 120 (D) 96

92. The next number in the series 3, 5, 9, 17, ___ is
(A) 30 (B) 33 (C) 35 (D) 36

93. Examine (X), (Y), and (Z), and select the correct answer.

   (X) $15 - (6 \div 2)$
   (Y) $18 - (8 - 2)$
   (Z) $10 + (7 - 3)$

   (A) $Z = X + Y$
   (B) $Z = 2Y$
   (C) $X = Y$
   (D) $X = Y + Z$

94. A number that is divisible by 2 and 3 is also divisible by
(A) 9 (B) 8 (C) 12 (D) 6

95. Look at the series 3, 7, 11, ___, 19, 23, 27. What number should fill the blank in the middle of the series?
(A) 17 (B) 25 (C) 15 (D) 21

96. $\frac{2}{3}$ of what number is equal to the product of 12 and 9?
(A) $31\frac{1}{2}$ (B) 72 (C) 96 (D) 162

97. If $\overline{DE}$ is parallel to $\overline{BC}$, which of the following is true?

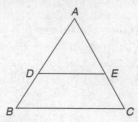

(A) $\frac{AD}{DB} = \frac{DE}{BC}$

(B) $AE = EC$

(C) $\triangle ADE \sim ABC$

(D) $DE = \frac{1}{2}BC$

98. In the series 50, 55, 54, 59, 58, __, __, what numbers should come next?
(A) 64, 65 (B) 63, 62 (C) 61, 60
 (D) 63, 64

99. Examine (X), (Y), and (Z), and select the correct answer.

(X) $3 - (8 - 4)$
(Y) $7 - (10 - 1)$
(Z) $(10 \div 2) - 3$

(A) $X + Y + Z = 12$
(B) $Y = 2X$
(C) $X + Y > Z$
(D) $Y > X + Z$

100. Look at the following series: 60, 54, 65, 59, 70, 64, __. What number should come next?
(A) 75 (B) 72 (C) 78 (D) 80

101. What number should come next in the following series: 15, 11, 7, 3, __?
(A) 1 (B) –2 (C) –1 (D) –3

102. In the diagram below, O is the center of both circles, and $OA = 5$, $OB = 7$.

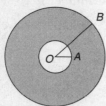

The area of the shaded region, in square units, is
(A) 24π (B) 45π (C) 50π (D) 20π

103. What number should come next in the following series: 27, 9, 3, 1, __?
(A) 1 (B) $\frac{1}{9}$ (C) $\frac{1}{3}$ (D) $\frac{1}{6}$

104. Examine (X), (Y), and (Z), and find the correct answer.

(X) $2 \cdot 2^3$
(Y) $(15 \div 3) - 1$
(Z) $(4 - 7) + 10$

(A) $Y^2 = X$
(B) $Y = Z + X$
(C) $X = Y + Z$
(D) $Y - X = 2Z$

105. Find the area of the following figure, which consists of a triangle atop a rectangle:

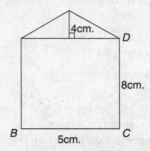

(A) 50 square centimeters
(B) 44 square centimeters
(C) 64 square centimeters
(D) 80 square centimeters

106. Find the next number in the following series: –5, –2, 1, 4, __.
(A) 6 (B) –1 (C) –3 (D) 7

107. What number added to three times itself is 12 less than 52?
(A) 10 (B) 9 (C) 12 (D) 15

108. Find the next term in the following series: 100, 20, 4, $\frac{4}{5}$, __.
(A) $\frac{4}{10}$ (B) $\frac{4}{25}$ (C) $\frac{4}{100}$ (D) $\frac{4}{125}$

109. *ABCD* is a square, and *O* is the center of the circle inscribed in the square.

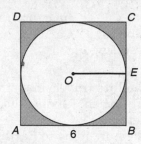

If *AB* = 6, find the area of the shaded portion.
(A) 36 – 36π
(B) 36 – 9π
(C) 12 – 9π
(D) 144 – 36π

110. Find the next term in the following series: –17, –12, –7, –2, __.
(A) 2 (B) 0 (C) 3 (D) 4

111. Which pair of numbers are prime factors of 924?
(A) 11 and 6
(B) 12 and 7
(C) 11 and 7
(D) 7 and 6

112. What number divided by 6 exceeds 7 by $\frac{1}{3}$?
(A) 40 (B) 42 (C) 44 (D) 39

SUBTEST 3   READING

Number of questions: 62   *Time limit: 25 minutes*

A. Comprehension—40 questions

DIRECTIONS: This subtest presents short reading passages, each one followed by a series of questions. Base your answer choices on the information in the selection.

A satellite is launched into space by a series of rockets that <u>impel</u> it outward away from the Earth and toward its planned orbit. At first it travels in a straight line, like a bullet out of a gun. The effect of gravity, however, is to pull it toward the center of the Earth. The <u>net</u> effect of the outward and downward motions reaches a state of balance that allows the satellite to remain in orbit. As the satellite continues in orbit, however, it is slowed down by air friction. As it slows down, the gravitational pull becomes stronger. The satellite then orbits in an increasingly smaller circle until it eventually drops to the Earth.

113. The main idea or subject of this selection is
 (A) how satellites are constructed.
 (B) how satellites return to Earth.
 (C) how the speed of satellites is controlled.
 (D) how satellites travel in space.

114. The word <u>net</u>, as underlined and used in this passage, means most nearly
 (A) temporary.
 (B) single.
 (C) final.
 (D) least.

115. Throughout its journey, the satellite
 (A) maintains a constant speed.
 (B) maintains the same orbit.
 (C) resists the pull of gravity.
 (D) travels in a straight line.

116. As the orbit grows smaller, the satellite travels
 (A) faster.
 (B) slower.
 (C) at a constant speed.
 (D) becomes more difficult to manage.

117. The satellite travels in a straight line
 (A) only when leaving the launching pad.
 (B) when dropping to Earth.
 (C) when in orbit.
 (D) when slowing down.

118. When in a state of balance, the satellite travels
 (A) straight out into space.
 (B) in a circle around the Earth.
 (C) away from the Earth.
 (D) toward the center of the Earth.

119. The word <u>impel</u>, as underlined and used in this passage, means most nearly
 (A) pull.
 (B) push.
 (C) deliver.
 (D) carry.

120. Which one of the following is true?
 (A) The rockets provide a gravitational force.
 (B) Satellites have a life expectancy.
 (C) Satellites create their own power.
 (D) Satellites depend on rockets and gravity for direction.

The study of the origins of words can lead us into many unexpected <u>byways</u>. The lapwing is a <u>crested</u> European plover. This is a bird known for its slow, irregular flight and shrill wailing cry. Also known as a pewit in English, the lapwing in German is a *kiebitz*. Lapwings gather in flocks in fields and pastures. In German their shrill cry is called a *kiebit*. Where does this lead? An offensive, noisy onlooker at cards in German is named, after the bird, a *kiebitsen*. The word passed from German into Yiddish and thence into American English as *kibitzer*, an onlooker who offers unwanted advice or comment.

121. The best title for this selection would be
    (A) "From German into English."
    (B) "The Origin of *Kiebit*."
    (C) "Birds and Words."
    (D) "An Interesting Word Origin."

122. The word byways, as underlined and used in this passage, means most nearly
    (A) familiar avenues.
    (B) major passageways.
    (C) customary paths.
    (D) infrequently used paths.

123. Which one of the following is not another name for the crested European plover?
    (A) pewit
    (B) lapwing
    (C) kiebit
    (D) kiebitz

124. The name *lapwing* most likely resulted from the bird's
    (A) shrill, wailing cry.
    (B) slow, irregular flight.
    (C) habit of gathering in flocks.
    (D) tendency to inhabit fields and pastures.

125. The word crested, as underlined and used in this passage, means most nearly having a
    (A) bald spot.
    (B) showy tuft.
    (C) bright streak.
    (D) colored top.

126. A kibitzer is known for
    (A) skill in playing a game.
    (B) being a heavy winner.
    (C) betting on a game.
    (D) interfering in a game.

127. The author of this passage most likely is a
    (A) bird-watcher.
    (B) card player.
    (C) German scholar.
    (D) language specialist.

Carbon has two crystalline forms—diamonds and graphite. Diamonds, by weight, are among the most costly substances we have. Graphite when mixed with clay is the inexpensive so-called lead of pencils. Under the tremendous pressure near the center of the Earth, carbon turns into diamonds. The diamonds are stable if they remain where they are formed. If, however, they travel slowly toward the outer layers of the Earth, with the decrease in pressure they quickly change into graphite. Only if they pass through the areas of lesser pressure at tremendous speeds and then cool suddenly, will they remain diamonds. As a result, when diamonds in countless quantities shoot through the Earth's crust, very many of them turn into graphite or disappear into the air as carbon dioxide. The particles that remain as diamonds on the Earth's surface are relatively unstable. Given a modest boost in heat, they quickly turn dark gray or black and become soft globs of graphite.

128. The word stable, as underlined and used in this passage, means most nearly
    (A) unchanging.
    (B) invisible.
    (C) valuable.
    (D) passive.

129. The best title for this selection would be
    (A) "Two Forms of Crystal."
    (B) "Carbon for Lead Pencils."
    (C) "Perishable Beauty."
    (D) "Graphite and Carbon."

130. Diamonds may turn to graphite when they are subjected to
    (A) tremendous speed.
    (B) a rapid increase of moderate pressure.
    (C) a decrease in temperature.
    (D) a moderate increase in temperature.

131. We can infer from this article that diamonds are so expensive because
    (A) they are rare.
    (B) they may change to graphite.
    (C) so much pressure is required to change carbon into diamond crystals.
    (D) they develop slowly.

132. The word <u>modest</u>, as underlined and used in this passage, means most nearly
    (A) unassuming.
    (B) moderate.
    (C) shy.
    (D) unobtrusive.

133. We can infer from this passage that
    (A) diamonds do not exist near the Earth's core.
    (B) diamonds are plentiful near the Earth's surface.
    (C) many diamonds change into graphite at the Earth's core.
    (D) graphite and diamonds are always found together.

134. The word <u>relatively</u>, as underlined and used in this passage, means most nearly
    (A) frequently.
    (B) rarely.
    (C) completely.
    (D) somewhat.

No other country has ever come closer to fulfilling humanity's dream of being the hope of the human race. Although Americans are better off than their <u>contemporaries</u> living overseas, they are worse off than they should be. Our achievements and technology are impressive, but our social and cultural achievements have left millions in <u>darkness</u> and want. We have squandered a great part of what we might have used. We have not conserved the bounty of nature. Physical science and manufacturing machinery seem to have outrun social science and political machinery in meeting our needs. The task ahead for us is monumental. Yet it cannot be ignored. To inquire, to challenge, to protest, to eliminate the bad and hold fast to that which is good—these goals have always been native to the American character. Millions of voices in patient yet earnest unison join in chanting, "We shall overcome!"

135. The author suggests that the task facing Americans is
    (A) easy.
    (B) impossible.
    (C) meaningless.
    (D) challenging.

136. The author's attitude toward America's ability to inspire hope and to preserve what is good is best described as
    (A) hopeless.
    (B) passive.
    (C) optimistic.
    (D) sarcastic.

137. The word <u>contemporaries</u>, as underlined and used in this passage, means
    (A) ancestors.
    (B) allies.
    (C) enemies.
    (D) persons living at the same time.

138. Which area of American achievement is <u>not</u> mentioned in the passage?
    (A) cultural development
    (B) nuclear weaponry
    (C) technological skills
    (D) energy conservation

139. The word <u>darkness</u>, as underlined and used in this passage, means most nearly
    (A) lack of fire.
    (B) ignorance.
    (C) lack of electricity.
    (D) poverty.

140. In this selection the author's main purpose is to
    (A) inform.
    (B) arouse.
    (C) amuse.
    (D) anger.

141. To overcome the problems with which we are faced, we must be willing to
    (A) accept the inevitable.
    (B) change our thinking.
    (C) change everything we have done in the past.
    (D) increase our production of weapons.

The greatest asset Ronald Reagan brought to the election process and to the presidency was his personality. Not since Eisenhower had a President enjoyed such general popularity as did Reagan. But that popularity was, like that of Harry Truman and even of Eisenhower himself, not so much a tribute to accomplishments as to character and personality. Reagan's simplicity, <u>affability</u>, humor, and mastery of the television medium won him almost limitless popular affection. Unemployment and the deficit might mount, but the general public did not seem to mind too much as long as they perceived the President as a man who spoke their language. What Ronald Reagan could do better than almost anyone else was to present himself as a good man who could make Americans feel good about their country. Where William Jennings Bryan had gloried in the title "The Great Commoner," Reagan was to become "The Great Communicator": as with Bryan, it was the rhetoric and the eloquence, not the substance of the communication, that proved most significant.

142. All men mentioned in this selection were
 (A) presidents of the United States.
 (B) skilled masters of television.
 (C) known for their senses of humor.
 (D) popular political leaders.

143. The best title for this passage would be
 (A) "Reagan's Major Weakness."
 (B) "Reagan's Achievements."
 (C) "Reagan's Popularity."
 (D) "Popular Presidents."

144. The word affability, as underlined and used in this passage, means
 (A) determination.
 (B) calmness.
 (C) friendliness
 (D) intellectual brilliance.

145. An asset not attributed to Reagan in this selection is
 (A) sense of humor.
 (B) a simple, down-to-earth vocabulary.
 (C) an effective television presence.
 (D) political idealism.

146. The key to Reagan's success as president was
 (A) his far-reaching plans.
 (B) his handling of foreign affairs.
 (C) the loyalty of his staff.
 (D) his ability to read his lines well.

147. The author's attitude toward Reagan is
 (A) evaluative.
 (B) sympathetic.
 (C) bitter.
 (D) amused.

Some sponges are freshwater animals, but most live in salt water. They consist of a body wall surrounding a saclike central cavity that is open at the upper end. Unlike most animals, sponges do not move around; they grow attached to rocks or other objects in the water. They feed on tiny food particles obtained from the water that flows continuously through the pores into the central cavity and out through the open end of the sponge. When sponges are exposed to sun and air, their cells die and decay, leaving behind the tough, saclike tunnel. These remains, sold as "natural sponges," were formerly used for cleaning and bathing. Today most household sponges are made of synthetic material such as nylon.

148. The main purpose of this passage is to
 (A) entertain.
 (B) convince.
 (C) caution.
 (D) inform.

149. The word saclike, as underlined and used in this passage, implies that the central cavity resembles a
 (A) tire tube.
 (B) pouch.
 (C) balloon.
 (D) copper penny.

150. Which of the following is not true of sponges?
 (A) They can live in oceans.
 (B) They hunt about in search of food.
 (C) They die when exposed to sun.
 (D) Some sponges are manufactured.

151. The natural enemy of sponges is
 (A) fresh water.
 (B) fishing boats.
 (C) small fish.
 (D) the sun.

152. The flow of water through the central cavity
 (A) enables the sponge to breathe.
 (B) provides locomotion.
 (C) protects the living cells.
 (D) carries away waste products.

B. Vocabulary—22 questions

DIRECTIONS: Choose the word that means the same or most nearly the same as the underlined word.

153. the boisterous cheerleaders
(A) enthusiastic
(B) noisy
(C) active
(D) attractive

154. an acute observation
(A) humorous
(B) keen
(C) sarcastic
(D) inaccurate

155. the band of brigands
(A) sophomores
(B) politicians
(C) kidnappers
(D) robbers

156. a colossal success
(A) financial
(B) artistic
(C) gigantic
(D) political

157. gratified by the results
(A) enriched
(B) astonished
(C) enraged
(D) pleased

158. her habitual shyness
(A) adolescent
(B) overwhelming
(C) unexpected
(D) customary

159. the illicit transaction
(A) unusual
(B) unlawful
(C) unhurried
(D) unprofitable

160. a short intermission
(A) speech
(B) campaign
(C) celebration
(D) pause

161. keep a memento
(A) souvenir
(B) record
(C) model
(D) timetable

162. a lucrative business
(A) seasonal
(B) distasteful
(C) profitable
(D) complicated

163. a brusque tone
(A) sarcastic
(B) gruff
(C) timid
(D) encouraging

164. the demise of a hero
(A) deeds
(B) modesty
(C) sensitivity
(D) death

165. her coy smile
(A) shy
(B) bright
(C) ready
(D) rare

166. to garner a fistful
(A) discard
(B) gather
(C) bestow
(D) examine

167. check the data
(A) facts
(B) sources
(C) time
(D) credentials

168. to curb his temper
(A) fear
(B) ignore
(C) imitate
(D) restrain

169. advantageous to our side
(A) favorable
(B) dangerous
(C) awkward
(D) valueless

170. to <u>beseech</u> them
    (A) beg
    (B) encourage
    (C) require
    (D) ignore

171. the <u>animated</u> discussion
    (A) amusing
    (B) bitter
    (C) lively
    (D) hilarious

172. pledge our <u>allegiance</u>
    (A) wealth
    (B) lives
    (C) homes
    (D) loyalty

173. a <u>capacious</u> trunk
    (A) shabby
    (B) heavy
    (C) fragile
    (D) roomy

174. to <u>defame</u> an innocent person
    (A) clear
    (B) defend
    (C) slander
    (D) imprison

SUBTEST 4   MATHEMATICS

Number of questions: 64   *Time limit: 45 minutes*

A. Concepts—24 questions

DIRECTIONS: Choose the answer you think is best for each problem.

175. $(3 \times 10^3) + (5 \times 10^2) + (7 \times 10) + (6 \times 1) =$
(A) 3,571 (B) 3,576 (C) 3,567 (D) 3,071

176. The exact number of thousands in 5,879 is
(A) 5 (B) 5.9 (C) 58.79 (D) 5.879

177. If the measure of each base angle of an isosceles triangle is 65°, the measure of the third angle of the triangle is
(A) 70° (B) 80° (C) 50° (D) 60°

178. Two numbers are in the ratio 4:3. Their difference is 6. The larger number is
(A) 24 (B) 16 (C) 32 (D) 28

179. *ABCD* is a rectangle. *AC* = 10 feet, and *BC* = 6 feet.

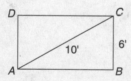

The perimeter of *ABCD* is
(A) 32 feet
(B) 36 feet
(C) 40 feet
(D) 28 feet

180. Written as a base-10 numeral, the number $111_{(two)}$ is
(A) 9 (B) 7 (C) 6 (D) 5

181. If $x - 3 = 5$, then $x^2 =$
(A) 25 (B) 4 (C) 64 (D) 9

182. Which of the following is true?
(A) $3 > -2 > 0$
(B) $0 > -2 > 3$
(C) $-2 > 0 > -3$
(D) $3 > 0 > -2$

183. Which of the following is *not* true?
(A) $a + b = b + a$
(B) $a - b = b - a$
(C) $a \times b = b \times a$
(D) $a(b + c) = ab + ac$

184. In the figure below, $\triangle ADE$ is similar to $\triangle ABC$.

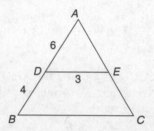

If $AD = 6$, $DB = 4$, and $DE = 3$, then $BC =$
(A) 2 (B) $5\frac{1}{2}$ (C) 5 (D) 8

185. A woman has x dollars in her purse. She buys 3 pounds of meat at y dollars per pound. The number of dollars the woman has left after the meat purchase is
(A) $x - y$
(B) $3(x - y)$
(C) $x - y - 3$
(D) $x - 3y$

186. O is the center of the circle shown below.

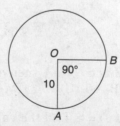

The measure of $\angle AOB = 90°$. Find the area of sector OAB if $OA = 10$.
(A) 100π square units
(B) $8,100\pi$ square units
(C) 20π square units
(D) 25π square units

187. $(-5)^3 + (-2)^4 =$
(A) −125 (B) 11 (C) −109 (D) 141

188. A family spends 24% of its income for rent, 35% for food, and 29% for other expenses. The rest of its income is saved. What percent of the family income is saved?
(A) 10% (B) 12% (C) 15% (D) 14%

189. The ratios of the measures of the acute angles of a right triangle is 5:1. What is the measure of the larger acute angle?
(A) 15° (B) 75° (C) 80° (D) 85°

190. $3.2 \times 10^{-5} =$
(A) 0.000032 (B) 0.00032 (C) 0.0032
(D) 0.032000

191. In which of the following are the numbers arranged in order of value with the smallest one first?
(A) 40%, $\frac{1}{3}$, 0.37
(B) 0.37, $\frac{1}{3}$, 40%
(C) 0.37, 40%, $\frac{1}{3}$
(D) $\frac{1}{3}$, 0.37, 40%

192. A jacket and a pair of slacks cost $102. If the jacket costs $22 more than the slacks, how much did the jacket cost?
(A) $22 (B) $40 (C) $62 (D) $64

193. At ABC State University 28% of the enrollment were freshmen. If there were 560 students in the freshman class, how many students were there in the entire enrollment?
(A) 200 (B) 1,120 (C) 2,000 (D) 2,400

194. The scale used on a road map is 1 inch = 50 miles. How many miles apart are two cities that are $7\frac{1}{2}$ inches apart on the map?
(A) 350 (B) 375 (C) 425 (D) 500

195. In a class that has 19 boys and 16 girls, a student is called upon to read aloud. What is the probability that the student called upon is a girl?
(A) $\frac{16}{19}$ (B) $\frac{19}{16}$ (C) $\frac{16}{35}$ (D) $\frac{19}{35}$

196. The prime factorization of 42 is
(A) 6·7 (B) 3·14 (C) 2·21 (D) 3·2·7

197. If $x - y = 3$, which one of the following is true?
(A) $x > y$
(B) $y > x$
(C) $x = y - 3$
(D) $x + y = 3$

198. Which of the following is true?
(A) $9 > \sqrt{76} > 8$
(B) $8 > \sqrt{76} > 7$
(C) $10 > \sqrt{76} > 9$
(D) $11 > \sqrt{76} > 10$

B. Problem Solving—40 questions

199. If $a = -2$ and $b = -3$, then $a^2 b + b^2 a =$
(A) −6 (B) +6 (C) +30 (D) −30

200. If $5(2x - 3) = 4$, find the value of x.
(A) 19 (B) 1.9 (C) 9 (D) 18

201. Mr. Bond bought a suit for $240 and paid an additional $14.40 in sales tax. What was the rate of the sales tax?
(A) 5% (B) 6% (C) $5\frac{1}{2}$% (D) $6\frac{1}{2}$%

202. Fred has $4 less than twice what Bill has. If Fred has $36, how much does Bill have?
(A) $24 (B) $18 (C) $25 (D) $20

203. Frank Russo had marks of 75, 80, and 70 on three tests. What was his mark on a fourth test if his average on the four tests was 80?
(A) 90 (B) 95 (C) 80 (D) 85

204. The ratio of $\frac{4}{9}$ to $\frac{7}{15}$ is
    (A) 20 to 63
    (B) 9 to 16
    (C) 20 to 21
    (D) 8 to 21

205. Mr. Stone has $150 consisting of $5 bills and $10 bills. If he has as many $5 bills as $10 bills, how many $5 bills does he have?
    (A) 10 (B) 20 (C) 15 (D) 5

206. After driving 3 hours at an average rate of 48 miles per hour, a motorist found that she had completed 36% of her trip. How many miles in all did she plan to cover?
    (A) 400 (B) 500 (C) 450 (D) 475

207. If the perimeter of a rectangle is 30 feet and its width is 6 feet, then its area, in square feet, is
    (A) 50 (B) 54 (C) 48 (D) 60

208. The sum of two numbers is y, and one of the numbers is 7. Three times the other number is
    (A) 21 (B) $3y$ (C) $3y - 7$ (D) $3(y - 7)$

209. By what digit can □ be replaced so that 43□ is divisible by 9?
    (A) 5 (B) 0 (C) 7 (D) 2

210. Find the product: $3\frac{1}{5} \times 4\frac{2}{3} \times 1\frac{1}{4}$.
    (A) $18\frac{2}{3}$ (B) 19 (C) $\frac{35}{12}$ (D) $17\frac{1}{3}$

211. At a movie showing, 426 tickets were sold at $5.00 each. In addition, 84 tickets were sold to senior citizens at half the regular price. The total amount of money that was collected was
    (A) $2,130 (B) $2,340 (C) $2,240 (D) 1,920

212. What is the volume, in cubic centimeters, of a cube whose edge measures 6 cm?
    (A) 36 (B) 180 (C) 216 (D) 192

213. $1011_{(\text{two})} =$
    (A) 9 (B) 10 (C) 11 (D) 12

214. Solve for x: $3.5x + 2.7 = 0.6$.
    (A) 0.6 (B) 2.1 (C) −1.6 (D) −0.6

215. Kevin earns $43.20 for 8 hours of work. How much will he earn for 14 hours of work at the same rate of pay?
    (A) $75.60 (B) $74.50 (C) $70.60 (D) $80.00

216. In the isosceles triangle shown below, $AB = AC$.

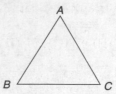

    If the measure of $\angle A$ is 64°, what is the measure of $\angle B$?
    (A) 60° (B) 58° (C) 116° (D) 29°

217. If $3x - 1 < 17$, then x^2 must be
    (A) equal to 36
    (B) less than 36
    (C) greater than 36
    (D) greater than 18

218. The difference between $5\frac{1}{2}$ and $3\frac{1}{4}$ is 6 less than x. The value of x is
    (A) $8\frac{1}{2}$ (B) $8\frac{3}{4}$ (C) $-3\frac{3}{4}$ (D) $8\frac{1}{4}$

219. The prime factors of 140 are
    (A) 4, 5, and 7
    (B) 5 and 7
    (C) 4 and 7
    (D) 2, 5, and 7

220. At 6:00 A.M. the temperature was −12°. At noon the temperature was +2°. Which of the following is true?
    (A) Between 6:00 A.M. and noon the temperature rose 10°.
    (B) Between 6:00 A.M. and noon the temperature rose 14°.
    (C) Between 6:00 A.M. and noon the temperature dropped 10°.
    (D) Between 6:00 A.M. and noon the temperature dropped 14°.

221. O is the center of the circle shown below.

    The measure of $\angle BOA = 90°$, and $OA = 6$. The area of sector $AOB =$
    (A) 36π (B) 6π (C) 9π (D) 8π

222. Mr. Lopez borrowed $850 from a bank at 12% simple interest for a period of 9 months. What was the total repayment Mr. Lopez made to the bank at the end of 9 months?
(A) $926.50 (B) $76.50 (C) $898.50 (D) $916.50

223. By what number must $\frac{2}{3}$ be multiplied to yield a result of $\frac{4}{5}$?
(A) 1.2 (B) $\frac{8}{15}$ (C) 2.4 (D) 0.8

224. A football squad consisted of 25 linemen and 12 backfield men. If one player is chosen at random, what is the probability that the choice will be a backfield man?
(A) $\frac{12}{25}$ (B) $\frac{25}{37}$ (C) $\frac{12}{37}$ (D) $\frac{25}{12}$

225. If $x\%$ of 80 is 16, what is the value of x?
(A) 25 (B) 40 (C) 20 (D) 64

226. If $7x - 5 = 3x + 9$, what is the value of x?
(A) 4.5 (B) 5.2 (C) 3 (D) 3.5

227. A home is assessed at $80,000. If the tax rate is $3.46 per $100, how much is the tax?
(A) $276.80 (B) $2,768 (C) $27,680 (D) $2,678

228. The product of 12 and 7 exceeds x by $\frac{2}{3}$ of 15. Then $x =$
(A) 74 (B) 84 (C) 94 (D) 70

229. The closest number to $\sqrt{30}$ is
(A) 6 (B) $5\frac{1}{3}$ (C) 5.07 (D) 6.5

230. A dealer buys 24 pairs of slacks for $400. How much does he pay for a shipment of 36 pairs of slacks at the same rate?
(A) $600 (B) $540 (C) $480 (D) $640

231. In a school with 502 students, 20 classes are formed. If the classes are equal in size, as far as possible, how many classes are larger than the others?
(A) 2 (B) 1 (C) 3 (D) 5

232. The number 1 million may be expressed as
(A) 10^4 (B) 10^5 (C) 10^6 (D) 10^7

233. One-third of the seats in an auditorium are unoccupied. If 600 seats are occupied, how many seats does the auditorium have?
(A) 900 (B) 750 (C) 800 (D) 850

234. A restaurant serves orange juice in 6-ounce cups. How many servings of orange juice may be obtained from 12 gallons of orange juice?
(A) 250 (B) 256 (C) 128 (D) 150

235. Which of the following is an example of the Associative Property of Addition?
(A) $x + y = y + x$
(B) $x(y + z) = xy + xz$
(C) $(x + y) + z = x + (y + z)$
(D) $x + (y + z) = x + y + xz$

236. The difference between two numbers is 12. If one-half the larger number is 10, find the smaller number
(A) 8 (B) 10 (C) 12 (D) 16

237. Which of the following sentences is true?
(A) $3 < -7$
(B) $-6 > -4$
(C) $-4 < -2$
(D) $-4 > 0$

238. A square and a triangle have equal areas. A side of the square measures 20 inches. If the base of the triangle measures 25 inches, how many inches does the altitude of the triangle measure?
(A) 20 (B) 24 (C) 32 (D) 36

SUBTEST 5   LANGUAGE

Number of questions: 60   *Time limit: 25 minutes*

DIRECTIONS: In questions 239–278, look for errors in punctuation, capitalization, or usage. If there is no error, then blacken D on the Answer Sheet.

---

239. (A) He scarcely never goes there any more.
   (B) She lay in bed all day with a splitting headache.
   (C) The wind is coming from the west.
   (D) No mistakes

240. (A) One of the sentences contains no errors.
   (B) The costumes of teenagers are often strange to adults.
   (C) Don't she know the correct answer?
   (D) No mistakes

241. (A) Sarah introduced us to her Uncle Mel.
   (B) We lived there several years ago.
   (C) Theres nothing we can do about it.
   (D) No mistakes

242. (A) "Come at two," Paul advised. "I will wait for you."
   (B) I'll loan you the money one more time.
   (C) They beat us decisively when we challenged them to a race.
   (D) No mistakes

243. (A) I'll teach you how to drive in three lessons!
   (B) Its time to make the telephone call.
   (C) I let the chips lay just where they had fallen.
   (D) No mistakes

244. (A) Bring the pamphlet to my office immediately.
   (B) She has less friends than she thinks she has.
   (C) Are there many avoidable accidents at this corner?
   (D) No mistakes

245. (A) American presidents and British prime ministers are chosen by completely different processes.
   (B) When you say that, you had better smile, stranger!
   (C) There were Lucy and Gladys waiting for me at the door.
   (D) No mistakes

246. (A) Either Alice or Reggie is going to be elected.
   (B) Those kind of apples are my favorite fruit.
   (C) Fortunately, they sustained only minor injuries.
   (D) No mistakes

247. (A) This bit of gossip is only for you and me.
   (B) The chef prepared a french favorite for us.
   (C) Well, what did you expect!
   (D) No mistakes

248. (A) Have you forgotten all your moral principles?
   (B) Were ready to join you now.
   (C) Between you and me, she should not have gone there.
   (D) No mistakes

249. (A) Every one of the roots curls away from the stem.
   (B) If I had listened to you, this could never have happened.
   (C) We wondered who would be our new principle.
   (D) No mistakes

250. (A) Someone in this group left her books in the last room.
   (B) Strawberries and cream are my favorite dessert.
   (C) "What do you want me to do?" asked Adam.
   (D) No mistakes

251. (A) The ring must be somewhere in this room.
   (B) He will graduate from High School this fall.
   (C) That suit surely fits him well.
   (D) No mistakes

252. (A) She peeled a onion so that she could have a good cry.
   (B) How many degrees are there in a straight angle?
   (C) She is brighter than any of her friends.
   (D) No mistakes

253. (A) I plan to borrow Henrys' coat for the trip.
   (B) They have lived in Yonkers for the past few years.
   (C) He drives so recklessly that I fear for his life.
   (D) No mistakes

254. (A) They're not the ones I ordered.
   (B) She said that Helen could not join us.
   (C) Who shall I say called?
   (D) No mistakes

255. (A) You will have to choose between Alice and me.
   (B) "Now is the time for action," Jack exclaimed. "Let's do the job right this time!"
   (C) How can you leave her do all that work by herself!
   (D) No mistakes

256. (A) Everyone except George and her came to the game.
   (B) I sat beside Margie all during the performance.
   (C) They set in the car so long that they developed leg cramps.
   (D) No mistakes

257. (A) This rumor must be laid to rest.
   (B) She should of left on the earlier train.
   (C) Everybody in our class has read that story.
   (D) No mistakes

258. (A) If I were you I would take the offer.
   (B) Stan told Arthur it was time for him to leave.
   (C) "In all honesty," Jerry said, "I never wanted it!"
   (D) No mistakes

259. (A) Please bring the letter to him immediately.
   (B) You have to listen to either him or me.
   (C) She is the type of person who is well liked by all.
   (D) No mistakes

260. (A) In the early morning hours, she left for the city.
   (B) I should have stood at home and not come here.
   (C) To be chosen class humorist is my present ambition.
   (D) No mistakes

261. (A) Our guidance counselor, Mrs. Shaw will be a member of the committee.
   (B) I object to his being elected class president.
   (C) Paula acts as though she were the teacher.
   (D) No mistakes

262. (A) I tried to contact them but had no success.
   (B) My brother, he plans to become a surgeon.
   (C) The winners were Alex and she.
   (D) No mistakes

263. (A) We were almost pushed off of the train.
   (B) Let it lie just where I put it.
   (C) Divide the candy evenly among them.
   (D) No mistakes

264. (A) She is one of the girls who are to speak at the rally.
   (B) They plan to arrive early Saturday Evening.
   (C) The vice president will address the nation at noon.
   (D) No mistakes

265. (A) Go quickly and get the doctor here as soon as you can.
 (B) Why not ask her to write the letter herself?
 (C) I had ran into him only yesterday.
 (D) No mistakes

266. (A) She spoke as well as you and I.
 (B) Neither the note nor the coins were on the desk.
 (C) If you need my help, do not hesitate to call on me.
 (D) No mistakes

267. (A) I was in the room before the late bell rung.
 (B) He could hardly see the sign during the rain.
 (C) The cloud, dark and threatening, hung over the town.
 (D) No mistakes

268. (A) The picture is on the shelf next to our family Bible.
 (B) One cannot talk out of turn if you wish to stay here.
 (C) Are there any facts that are not clear to you?
 (D) No mistakes

269. (A) Is a hoe-down a type of square dance?
 (B) His answers were completely different from ours.
 (C) Is there any questions that have not been answered?
 (D) No mistakes

270. (A) The inheritance was divided equally among the relatives.
 (B) We hadn't but one moment to spare.
 (C) They live in the southeastern part of the city.
 (D) No mistakes

271. (A) Every one of the tools that were missing was found in his locker.
 (B) The message was for Louise and them.
 (C) I want a copy of the picture of the child that is hanging over the fireplace.
 (D) No mistakes

272. (A) I could have sworn that he had been here.
 (B) Jon along with his four friends are here to see you.
 (C) He is the brighter of the two applicants.
 (D) No mistakes

273. (A) She is most funniest when the audience is with her.
 (B) Why don't you try to be cooperative?
 (C) Going to the party as a loner is not my idea of fun.
 (D) No mistakes

274. (A) The number of questions the interviewer asked was staggering.
 (B) Alice said that "she didn't believe his story."
 (C) Having a free afternoon, we wandered through the shops in the new mall.
 (D) No mistakes

275. (A) We hadn't done anything wrong.
 (B) Alice is taller than Irene and me.
 (C) Our neighborhood has fewer mail boxes than yours.
 (D) No mistakes

276. (A) Hilda felt bad when we did not include her.
 (B) What was her principal reason for refusing to go?
 (C) Why did you ask whether you could borrow my coat.
 (D) No mistakes

277. (A) Before they could stop her, she blurted out the truth.
 (B) I warned him, "Don't play games with me!"
 (C) All of us except Hal and me have free passes.
 (D) No mistakes

278. (A) Willerts, who is a professional politician, will lead the delegation.
 (B) She demanded to know why I had not done it.
 (C) I most lost my breath by the time I reached the top of the hill.
 (D) No mistakes

DIRECTIONS: For questions 279–288, look only for spelling errors. If there is no misspelling, blacken D on the Answer Sheet.

279. (A) It is a great privilege to be here.
   (B) Repitition will strengthen your responses.
   (C) Park the car parallel to the curb.
   (D) No mistakes

280. (A) Who will be chairman of the committee?
   (B) With perserverance, you will succeed.
   (C) It really is none of your business!
   (D) No mistakes

281. (A) I found it comparatively simple.
   (B) Why did she have a mischievous smile?
   (C) I can continue this indefinitly.
   (D) No mistakes

282. (A) Will both displays appear simultaneously?
   (B) The results could be disasterous!
   (C) The marriage will take place in June.
   (D) No mistakes

283. (A) The beginning is the most difficult part.
   (B) Don't let his conscience be your guide.
   (C) We go there only very occassionally.
   (D) No mistakes

284. (A) They will not be disatisfied this time.
   (B) Their comments were most appropriate.
   (C) You will be besieged by creditors.
   (D) No mistakes

285. (A) They are willing to deny its very existance.
   (B) Now is the time for action, not criticism!
   (C) Her performance was most extraordinary.
   (D) No mistakes

286. (A) What is your preference is the matter?
   (B) This escapade must end in tradgedy!
   (C) You will find the experience most exhilarating.
   (D) No mistakes

287. (A) The attendance figures are very encouraging.
   (B) You are requested to leave peaceably.
   (C) He finally conceded to our modest request.
   (D) No mistakes

288. (A) Is there any free time on your calendar?
   (B) She finds getting accustomed to change difficult.
   (C) These results will not embarass her.
   (D) No mistakes

DIRECTIONS: For questions 289–298, look for errors in composition. Follow the directions for each question.

289. Choose the word that is a clear connective to complete the given sentence.

The committee had voted unanimously in favor of the motion; _____ we had no choice but to comply.
   (A) in addition,
   (B) therefore,
   (C) however,
   (D) nevertheless,

290. Choose the word that is a clear connective to complete the given sentence.

They really wanted to join us; _____ there was no reason why we should refuse their request.
   (A) for example,
   (B) however,
   (C) nevertheless,
   (D) moreover,

291. Choose the words that best complete the sentence.

    To succeed in school, _____
    (A) basic study habits must be mastered.
    (B) mastery of basic studied habits must be achieved.
    (C) students must master basic study habits.
    (D) students must plan for success. Basic study habits must be mastered.

292. Which of the following most clearly expresses the intended idea?
    (A) Walking along the quiet street, the houses looked old and comfortable.
    (B) Eve walked along the quiet street, and the houses looked old and comfortable.
    (C) After walking along the quiet street, the houses look old and comfortable.
    (D) As we walked along the quiet street, the houses looked old and comfortable.

293. Which of the following most clearly expresses the intended idea?
    (A) When in company, your manners are always on display.
    (B) When you are in company, your manners are always on display.
    (C) Your manners, when in company, are always on display.
    (D) Your manners are always on display, when in company.

294. Which of the following pairs of sentences fits best under the topic sentence. "Primitive people lived in bondage to nature"?
    (A) They did nothing to interfere with natural processes. They moved away when the environment could not support them.
    (B) The members of the group worked cooperatively. They shared and shared alike.
    (C) Nature could be severe at times. People looked to the gods for explanations of natural phenomena.
    (D) The food gatherers could do little more than forage for berries, fruits, and edible animals. When these food sources were scarce, starvation took a heavy toll.

295. Which of the following pairs of sentences fits best under the topic sentence. "Down's syndrome is a congenital disorder that afflicts approximately one in 650 births"?
    (A) Proof is now at hand that it is typically neither hereditary nor environmental. Rare is the family that does not have a member afflicted by it.
    (B) Parents of children with the disorder share a common fear. They fear what will happen if these children outlive their parents.
    (C) For many years it was described erroneously as a hereditary disease. It was considered the result of some unknown defect of the germ plasma.
    (D) People with the disorder may think and react more slowly than others. However, we must always remember that they have the same feelings that we do.

296. Which of the following sentences would be <u>least</u> appropriate in an encyclopedia article on film director Ingmar Bergman?
    (A) Films as an art form achieved their highest peak to date under the direction of Sweden's Ingmar Bergman.
    (B) He gave visible form to the inner conflicts of human beings.
    (C) He rejected the theatrical tradition that had dominated filmmaking.
    (D) I am positive that you will find his films mature and absorbing.

297. Which sentence does not belong in the paragraph below?

(1) I look forward to the time when I can retire. (2) They who have been gifted with the love of retirement possess, as it were, another sense. (3) I shall then do all the reading I have missed for the past three years. (4) I shall seek a cabin somewhere and let others worry about budgets.

(A) sentence 1
(B) sentence 2
(C) sentence 3
(D) sentence 4

298. Where should the sentence "These recordings preserve the utterances of living creatures on sea and land throughout the world" be placed in the following paragraph?

(1) The growing sense that many species of wildlife are vanishing has helped to expand a different type of library. (2) Instead of books, it stores for posterity recordings on tape. (3) The largest, Cornell's Library of Natural Sounds, holds over 65,000 recordings.

(A) before sentence 1
(B) before sentence 2
(C) before sentence 3
(D) after sentence 3

Answers to Practice High School Placement Test 2

SUBTEST 1   VERBAL SKILLS

1. C	13. C	25. D	37. D	49. B
2. D	14. C	26. B	38. D	50. A
3. C	15. B	27. C	39. D	51. D
4. B	16. D	28. A	40. B	52. B
5. A	17. D	29. A	41. C	53. B
6. A	18. D	30. A	42. D	54. C
7. B	19. C	31. B	43. B	55. B
8. A	20. A	32. A	44. C	56. A
9. D	21. D	33. C	45. C	57. D
10. A	22. A	34. C	46. B	58. A
11. C	23. B	35. D	47. C	59. C
12. C	24. D	36. A	48. C	60. A

Rating Your Results

Superior	54–60 correct
Average	47–53 correct
Below Average	46 or fewer correct

Material to Review: Chapter 4

SUBTEST 2   QUANTITATIVE SKILLS

61. B	72. A	83. A	93. C	103. C
62. C	73. C	84. D	94. D	104. A
63. B	74. B	85. B	95. C	105. A
64. D	75. C	86. D	96. D	106. D
65. C	76. B	87. B	97. C	107. A
66. B	77. D	88. A	98. B	108. B
67. A	78. A	89. A	99. B	109. B
68. B	79. C	90. B	100. A	110. C
69. D	80. C	91. C	101. C	111. C
70. B	81. A	92. B	102. A	112. C
71. D	82. C			

Rating Your Results

Superior	47–52 correct
Average	40–46 correct
Below Average	37 or fewer correct

Material to Review: Chapter 13

SUBTEST 3   READING

A.   Reading—Comprehension

113. D	121. D	129. C	137. D	145. D
114. C	122. D	130. D	138. B	146. D
115. C	123. C	131. A	139. B	147. A
116. B	124. B	132. B	140. B	148. D
117. A	125. B	133. B	141. B	149. B
118. B	126. D	134. D	142. D	150. B
119. B	127. D	135. D	143. C	151. D
120. B	128. A	136. C	144. C	152. D

Rating Your Results

Superior	34–40 correct
Average	28–34 correct
Below Average	27 or fewer correct

Material to Review: Chapter 5

B.   Reading—Vocabulary

153. B	158. D	163. B	167. A	171. C
154. B	159. B	164. D	168. D	172. D
155. D	160. D	165. A	169. A	173. D
156. C	161. A	166. B	170. A	174. C
157. D	162. C			

Rating Your Results

Superior	19–22 correct
Average	15–18 correct
Below Average	14 or fewer correct

Material to Review: Chapter 4

SUBTEST 4   MATHEMATICS

A.   Mathematics—Concepts

175. **B**	180. **B**	185. **D**	190. **A**	195. **C**
176. **D**	181. **C**	186. **D**	191. **D**	196. **D**
177. **C**	182. **D**	187. **C**	192. **C**	197. **A**
178. **A**	183. **B**	188. **B**	193. **C**	198. **A**
179. **D**	184. **C**	189. **B**	194. **B**	

Rating Your Results

Superior	21–24 correct
Average	16–20 correct
Below Average	15 or fewer correct

Material to Review: Chapters 7–12

B.   Mathematics—Problem Solving

199. **D**	207. **B**	215. **A**	223. **A**	231. **A**
200. **B**	208. **D**	216. **B**	224. **C**	232. **C**
201. **B**	209. **D**	217. **B**	225. **C**	233. **A**
202. **D**	210. **A**	218. **D**	226. **D**	234. **B**
203. **B**	211. **B**	219. **D**	227. **B**	235. **C**
204. **C**	212. **C**	220. **B**	228. **A**	236. **A**
205. **A**	213. **C**	221. **C**	229. **D**	237. **C**
206. **A**	214. **D**	222. **A**	230. **A**	238. **C**

Rating Your Results

Superior	35–40 correct
Average	26–34 correct
Below Average	25 or fewer correct

Material to Review: Chapters 7–12

SUBTEST 5   LANGUAGE

239. **A**	251. **B**	263. **A**	275. **B**	287. **D**
240. **C**	252. **A**	264. **B**	276. **C**	288. **C**
241. **C**	253. **A**	265. **C**	277. **D**	289. **B**
242. **B**	254. **D**	266. **D**	278. **C**	290. **D**
243. **B**	255. **C**	267. **A**	279. **B**	291. **C**
244. **B**	256. **C**	268. **B**	280. **B**	292. **D**
245. **A**	257. **B**	269. **C**	281. **C**	293. **B**
246. **B**	258. **B**	270. **B**	282. **B**	294. **D**
247. **B**	259. **A**	271. **C**	283. **C**	295. **C**
248. **B**	260. **B**	272. **B**	284. **A**	296. **D**
249. **C**	261. **A**	273. **A**	285. **A**	297. **B**
250. **B**	262. **B**	274. **B**	286. **B**	298. **C**

Rating Your Results

Superior	54–60 correct
Average	46–53 correct
Below Average	45 or fewer correct

Material to Review: Chapter 6

Answer Explanations

SUBTEST 1   VERBAL SKILLS

1. (**C**) Only *useless* fits the definition of *futile*.

2. (**D**) *Momentous* means of great importance; *trivial* means insignificant.

3. (**C**) A *repast* is a full meal; the others are parts.

4. (**B**) In terms of descending weight, the sequence is Irene, Sarah, Fran.

5. (**A**) In each case the smallest units, second and day, are being compared.

6. (**A**) Only *obedient* fits the definition of *docile*.

7. (**B**) *Captivate* means to please, enchant.

8. (**A**) A learned person must be skilled in reading; an illiterate person lacks reading ability.

9. (**D**) Only *flood* fits the definition of *deluge*.

10. (**A**) A hobby, unlike the other choices, is not a means of livelihood.

11. (**C**) Supply, storage, and service occurs at the pier and the terminal.

12. (**C**) No data are given that enable us to compare Irving and Larry.

13. (**C**) Only *obey* fits the definition of *comply*.

14. (**C**) A straitjacket, unlike the other choices, is used for restraint.

15. (**B**) Only *comfort* fits the definition of *solace*.

16. (**D**) To be stately is to be impressive.

17. (**D**) Silverware, unlike the other choices, is made of metal.

18. (**D**) Only *criminal* fits the definition of *felonious*.

19. (**C**) Exercises and recipes are the basic material contained in the two types of book.

20. (**A**) If every judge is just, no unjust person can be a judge.

21. (**D**) *Advance* is the only choice that denotes forward movement.

22. (**A**) Only *ship* fits the definition of *galleon*.

23. (**B**) Stubborn is opposite of *yielding; wavering* of *decisive*.

24. (**D**) Only *hide* fits the definition of *cache*.

25. (**D**) Fertile means lush; *barren* means desolate.

26. (**B**) A promontory, unlike the other choices, is a land feature.

27. (**C**) Grain and drop are the smallest units of sand and water, respectively.

28. (**A**) Since A equals B, wherever is A, including some C, is B.

29. (**A**) Frigid is cold; the others relate to higher temperatures.

30. (**A**) Only *summit* fits the definition of acme.

31. (**B**) A thermometer measures heat; a sundial measures time.

32. (**A**) The word *some* gives validity to the conclusion.

33. (**C**) A drill cannot be used to join items.

34. (**C**) Only *changeable* fits the definition of *variable*.

35. (**D**) Modish means in the present; antiquated means in the far past.

36. (**A**) Henry is the bridge between the two best players, Arthur and Phil, and the two weakest, Paul and Harold.

37. (**D**) A pedigree is a record of ancestry; unlike the other choices, it has no legs.

38. (**D**) Formless is without definite shape; senseless is without definite purpose.

39. (**D**) Only *abandon* fits the definition of *relinquish*.

40. (**B**) *Diameter,* unlike the other choices, is not associated with a triangle.

41. (**C**) An antagonist opposes; an ally supports.

42. (**D**) A lanky person is tall and thin; the other choices describe someone who is overweight.

43. (**B**) Dejected means low-spirited; elated means joyful.

44. (**C**) We cannot tell who is older, Margie or Sylvia. All we know is that both are older than Elsie.

45. (**C**) A person is being charitable when giving a donation; a person is being judgmental when giving criticism.

46. (**B**) Wool is a natural fabric; the others are synthetic.

47. (**C**) Only *unfriendly* fits the definition of *hostile*.

48. (**C**) We have no basis for rating City X and City Z. All we know is that both these cities have more taxis than City Y.

49. (**B**) A poll records opinions; the other choices are forms of fiction.

50. (**A**) An eagle raises its young in an aerie; a fox uses a den.

51. (**D**) Only *scold* fits the definition of *admonish*.

52. **(B)** A headliner is a solitary performer, not one who plans for others.

53. **(B)** Only *sufficient* fits the definition of *adequate*.

54. **(C)** *Indiscreet* means rash, reckless, imprudent.

55. **(B)** Unlike the other choices, *sketch* is not a term descriptive of poetry.

56. **(A)** Since A = B = C, all C must equal B.

57. **(D)** A director is in charge of a play, a manager of an office.

58. **(A)** *Fruitless* means ineffective, useless. A helpful phrase to remember is "a fruitless effort."

59. **(C)** Only *spend* fits the definition of *disburse*.

60. **(A)** Whatever is true of four-legged galens is true of quinks. Since no four-legged galens can fly, no quinks can fly.

SUBTEST 2   QUANTITATIVE SKILLS

61. **(B)** Let x = the number.

    Then $2x = 96$

    $x = 96 \div 2 = 48$

    $\frac{2}{3}$ of $48 = \frac{2}{3} \times 48 = 32$

62. **(C)** In moving from left to right, we see that each number is 4 more than the preceding number. Thus, the next number is $22 + 4 = 26$.

63. **(B)** If $a = b = c$, then $a + b$ is equal to $\frac{2}{3}$ of the figure. Likewise, $b + c$ is equal to $\frac{2}{3}$ of the figure. Thus $a + b = b + c$.

64. **(D)** In moving from left to right, we note that each number is 5 less than the preceding number. Thus, $54 - 5 = 49$.

65. **(C)** When X is written as a decimal, we have $\frac{3}{5} = 0.60$. Thus, X is 0.60, and Z is 0.65. Therefore $Z > X$.

66. **(B)** The number that is less than 50 is $50 - 8 = 42$, and 42 is the product of 6 and 7. The correct answer is 7.

67. **(A)** The measure of $\angle 1 = 80°$. The measure of $\angle X = 180° - 80° = 100°$.

    The measure of $\angle 3 = 180° -$ the measure of $\angle X$.

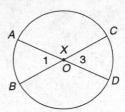

    Thus, the measure of $\angle 3 = 180° - 100° = 80°$.

68. **(B)** The class had a register of $3 + 9 + 8 + 5 = 25$ students. Of these 25 students, 8 had marks of C.

    $\frac{8}{25} = \frac{32}{100} = 32\%$

    The correct choice is (B).

69. **(D)** As we move from left to right, we note that each term is equal to three times the preceding term + 1.

    Thus, $7 = 3 \times 2 + 1$, $22 = 3 \times 7 + 1$, $67 = 3 \times 22 + 1$, $202 = 3 \times 67 + 1$.

70. **(B)** $x = 20 - 4 = 16$

    $y = 3 - 4 = -1$

    $z = 6 - 6 = 0$

    We take the choices in turn until we find one that is true.

    (A) $x + y = z$: $16 - 1 = 0$, not true.

    (B) $z > y$: $0 > -1$, true.

    The correct choice is (B).

71. **(D)** As we move from left to right, we note that each successive term is higher in value by a number that increases by 2:

    $3 + \underline{3} = 6$

    $6 + \underline{5} = 11$

    $11 + \underline{7} = 18$

    The next number is $18 + \underline{9} = 27$.

72. **(A)** Since *ABCD* is a parallelogram, $CB = AD$.

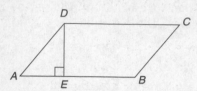

In $\triangle AED$, $AD > DE$: In a triangle, the larger side lies opposite the larger angle.

Therefore $CB > DE$.

73. **(C)** $9\overline{)6,039} = 671$

Therefore, 6,039 is divisible by 9.

Alternative Method. A number is divisible by 9 if the sum of the digits of the number is divisible by 9. In this case, the sum of the digits is $6 + 0 + 3 + 9 = 18$. Since 18 is divisible by 9, the number 6,039 is divisible by 9.

74. **(B)** As we move from left to right, we observe that each number is obtained by taking $\frac{1}{3}$ of the preceding number:

$9 = \frac{1}{3}$ of 27, $3 = \frac{1}{3}$ of 9, $1 = \frac{1}{3}$ of 3,

$\frac{1}{3} = \frac{1}{3}$ of 1, $\frac{1}{9} = \frac{1}{3}$ of $\frac{1}{3}$

Alternative Method. The same result can be obtained by dividing each number by 3 to obtain the next number.

$27 \div 3 = 9, ..., \frac{1}{3} \div 3 = \frac{1}{9}$.

75. **(C)** Let x = the unknown number.

10 less than $50 = 40$

$62\frac{1}{2}\% = \frac{5}{8}$

$\frac{5}{8}x = 40$

$x = 40 \div \frac{5}{8} = 40 \times \frac{8}{5} = 64$

76. **(B)** Let x = the number.

$\frac{1}{3}x - \frac{1}{4}x = 20$

If we multiply both sides of the equation by 12, we have

$4x - 3x = 240$

$x = 240$

77. **(D)** $30 \div \frac{1}{3} = 30 \times 3 = 90$

78. **(A)** This series may be broken up into two series as follows:

2, 3, 4, __

8, 9, 10, __

The next number, 5, is in the top series.

79. **(C)** The school as $96 \times 25 = 2,400$ students. If these 2,400 students are divided into classes with 24 students in each class, $2400 \div 24 = 100$ classes will be needed.

80. **(C)** Let x = the number.

$40\% + 25\% = 65\%$, $65\% = \frac{65}{100} = 0.65$

$x = \frac{39}{0.65} = \frac{3900}{65} = 60$

81. **(A)** As we move from left to right in the series, we note that each number is equal to $\frac{1}{3}$ of the preceding number:

$90 = \frac{1}{3}$ of 270, $30 = \frac{1}{3}$ of 90, $10 = \frac{1}{3}$ of

30, $\frac{10}{3}$, or $3\frac{1}{3} = \frac{1}{3}$ of 10

Alternative Method. The same result can be obtained by dividing each number by 3 to obtain the next number.

$270 \div 3 = 90, ..., 10 \div 3 = 3\frac{1}{3}$.

82. **(C)** To determine the least common denominator, we write the multiples of the denominators. The first number that appears in all three sets of multiples is the least common denominator.

Multiples of 2: 2, 4, 6, 8, 10, 12, 14, 16, 18, 20, 22, 24, ...

Multiples of 6: 6, 12, 18, 24, ...

Multiples of 8: 8, 16, 24

Since 24 is the first number that appears in all three sets of multiples, it is the least common denominator.

83. **(A)** $x = 108 \div 3 \div 2 = 36 \div 2 = 18$

$y = (20 \cdot 3) - 40 = 60 - 40 = 20$

$z = 19 + (-1) = 18$

Since $x = 18$ and $z = 18$, $x = z$ and choice (A) is correct.

84. (**D**) As we move from left to right in the series, we note that each term is equal to $\frac{1}{2}$ of the preceding term:

$$\frac{1}{4}=\frac{1}{2}\times\frac{1}{2}, \quad \frac{1}{8}=\frac{1}{2}\times\frac{1}{4}, \quad \frac{1}{16}=\frac{1}{2}\times\frac{1}{8},$$
$$\frac{1}{32}=\frac{1}{2}\times\frac{1}{16}.$$

85. (**B**) We can make comparisons more readily if we convert the fractions into decimals:

$$\frac{4}{9}=0.44, \quad \frac{5}{7}=0.71, \quad \frac{2}{3}=0.67$$

We see that $\frac{5}{7}$ is the largest fraction, $\frac{2}{3}$ is the next to largest, and $\frac{4}{9}$ is the smallest.

Thus, the order $\frac{5}{7} > \frac{2}{3} > \frac{4}{9}$ is correct.

86. (**D**) The sum of the measures of the angles around a point in a plane = 360°.

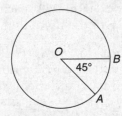

$$\frac{45}{360} = \frac{1}{8}$$

The sector $OAB = \frac{1}{8}$ of the circle.

87. (**B**) As we move from left to right in the series, we note that the difference between each two successive numbers increases by 2: $8 - 3 = 5$, $15 - 8 = 7$, $24 - 15 = 9$, $35 - 24 = 11$.

88. (**A**) In right traingle *DAB* we have

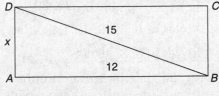

$$x^2 + (12)^2 = (15)^2$$
$$x^2 + 144 = 225$$
$$x^2 = 225 - 144$$
$$x^2 = 81$$
$$x = 9$$

The perimeter of *ABCD* = 9 + 12 + 9 + 12 = 42.

89. (**A**) To find the average of the four numbers, we divide their sum by 4:

$$47 + 36 + 28 + 25 = 136$$
$$136 \div 4 = 34$$

90. (**B**) $x = 2^5 - 1 = 32 - 1 = 31$
$y = 3^3 + 5 = 27 + 5 = 32$
$z = 2 \times 4^2 = 2 \times 16 = 32$

Since $y = z$, the correct choice is (B).

91. (**C**) Let x = the number.
$$20\% = \frac{1}{5}$$
$$x - \frac{1}{5}x = 96$$
$$\frac{4}{5}x = 96$$
$$x = 96 \div \frac{4}{5}$$
$$x = 96 \times \frac{5}{4}$$
$$x = 120$$

92. (**B**) As we move from left to right in the series, we note that each successive term is greater by an increasing power of 2:
$5 = 3 + 2$, $9 = 5 + 2^2$, $17 = 9 + 2^3$, $33 = 17 + 2^4$

93. (**C**) (*X*) $15 - (6 \div 2) = 15 - 3 = 12$
(*Y*) $18 - (8 - 2) = 18 - 6 = 12$
(*Z*) $10 + (7 - 3) = 10 + 4 = 14$
Since $X = Y$, the correct choice is (C).

94. (**D**) A number that is divisible by both 3 and 2 must be a multiple of both 3 and 2. Therefore, this number must be a multiple of 6. A number that is a multiple of 6 is divisible by 6.

95. (**C**) As me move from left to right in the series, we note that each successive number of the series is obtained by adding 4 to the preceding number. Thus we have $11 + 4 = 15$.

96. (**D**) Let x = the number.
$$\frac{2}{3}x = 12 \cdot 9$$
$$\frac{2}{3}x = 108$$
$$x = 108 \div \frac{2}{3}$$
$$x = 108 \times \frac{3}{2} = 162$$

97. **(C)** If $\overline{DE}$ is parallel to $\overline{BC}$, then $\triangle ADE$ is similar to $\triangle ABC$ since two pairs of corresponding angles have equal measures.

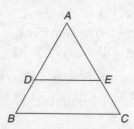

Thus, (C) is the correct choice.

98. **(B)** As we move from left to right in the series, we note that the second term is 5 more than the first term and the third term is 1 less than the second term. Again, the fourth term is 5 more than the third term and the fifth term is 1 less than the fourth term. The sixth term must be 5 more than the fifth term ($58 + 5 = 63$), and the sixth term must be 1 less than the fifth term ($63 - 1 = 62$).

99. **(B)** $X = 3 - 4 = -1$
$Y = 7 - 9 = -2$
$Z = 5 - 3 = 2$

The correct choice is (B) since $Y(-2) = 2(-1)$.

100. **(A)** This series may be broken up into two series as follows:

60, 65, 70, __

54, 59, 64, __

In each case, the next number in the series is obtained by adding 5 to the preceding number. In this case, the next number in the first series is needed: $70 + 5 = 75$.

101. **(C)** In this series each number is obtained by subtracting 4 from the preceding number. In this case, we have $3 - 4 = -1$.

102. **(A)** The area of the larger circle is $7 \times 7 \times \pi = 49\pi$.

The area of the smaller circle is $5 \times 5 \times \pi = 25\pi$.

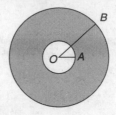

The area of the shaded region is $49\pi - 25\pi = 24\pi$.

103. **(C)** In moving from left to right in the series, we note that each term is obtained by taking $\frac{1}{3}$ of the preceding term. For example,

$9 = \frac{1}{3}$ of 27, $3 = \frac{1}{3}$ of 9, $1 = \frac{1}{3}$ of 3, and

$\frac{1}{3} = \frac{1}{3}$ of 1.

Alternative Method. The same result can be obtained by dividing each number by 3 to obtain the next number.

$27 \div 3 = 9, \ldots, 1 \div 3 = \frac{1}{3}$.

104. **(A)** $X = 2 \cdot 2^3 = 2 \times 8 = 16$
$Y = (15 \div 3) - 1 = 5 - 1 = 4$
$Z = (4 - 7) + 10 = -3 + 10 = 7$
Since $Y = 4$ and $X = 16$, $Y^2 = X$, and the correct choice is (A).

105. **(A)** Area of rectangle $ABCD = 8 \times 5 = 40$ square centimeters

Area of $\triangle AED = \frac{1}{2}(4)(5) = 10$ square centimeters

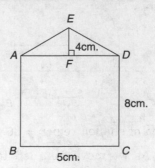

Area of figure = $40 + 10 = 50$ square centimeters.

106. (**D**) As we move from left to right in the series, we note that each term is obtained by adding 3 to the preceding term:

$$-2 = -5 + 3, \ 1 = -2 + 3, \ 4 = 1 + 3, \ 7 = 4 + 3$$

107. (**A**) Let x = the number.

Then $x + 3x = 52 - 12$

$$4x = 40$$

$$x = 10$$

108. (**B**) As we move from left to right in the series, we note that each term is obtained by taking $\frac{1}{5}$ of the preceding term:

$$20 = \tfrac{1}{5} \text{ of } 100, \ 4 = \tfrac{1}{5} \text{ of } 20, \ \tfrac{4}{5} = \tfrac{1}{5} \text{ of } 4,$$

$$\tfrac{4}{25} = \tfrac{1}{5} \text{ of } \tfrac{4}{5}$$

Alternative Method. The same result can be obtained by dividing each number by 5 to obtain the next number:

$$100 \div 5 = 20, \ \ldots, \ \tfrac{4}{5} \div 5 = \tfrac{4}{25}.$$

109. (**B**) Since $AB = 6$, the area of square $ABCD$ is $6 \times 6 = 36$.

Since $AB = 6$, $OE = 3$.

The area of circle $O = 3 \times 3 \times \pi = 9\pi$.

The area of the shaded region is equal to the area of the square minus the area of the circle.

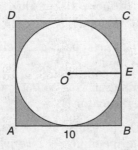

Area of shaded region = $36 - 9\pi$.

110. (**C**) As we move from left to right, we note that each term in the series is 5 more than the preceding term:
$$-12 = -17 + 5, \ -7 = -12 + 5,$$
$$-2 = -7 + 5, \ 3 = -2 + 5$$

111. (**C**) $924 = 2 \times 2 \times 3 \times 7 \times 11$

2, 3, 7, and 11 includes all the prime factors of 924. Of the choices given, only 11 and 7 are a pair of prime factors of 924.

112. (**C**) Let x = the number.

Then, $\frac{x}{6} = 7 + \frac{1}{3}$

If we multiply both sides of this equation by 6, we have

$$x = 42 + 2$$

$$x = 44$$

SUBTEST 3 READING

A. Comprehension

113. (**D**) No mention is made of (A) or (B). Although speed is mentioned, speed control is not discussed, eliminating (C). Choice (D) wins by elimination and its pertinence to satellites and space.

114. (**C**) The second and third sentences describe two different motions of the satellite. In the fourth sentence the meaning "final" is suggested for *net* by the words "effect of the outward and downward motion reaches a state of balance ..."

115. (**C**) The entire selection stresses the effect of gravity.

116. (**B**) The closer the satellite gets to Earth, the greater the air friction. The greater the air friction, the slower the satellite goes.

117. (**A**) "At first it travels in a straight line..."

118. (**B**) "It is this state of balance that allows it [the satellite] to remain in orbit." An orbit is a circular path.

119. (**B**) Note "... rockets that impel it *outward* away from Earth."

120. (**B**) "The satellite then orbits ... until it eventually drops to the Earth."

121. (**D**) The entire paragraph leads up to the origin of the word *kibitzer*.

122. (**D**) The sentence "Where does this lead?" in the middle of the paragraph suggests a digression—here, from a bird to an unwelcome onlooker. In other words, we are leaving "familiar avenues," "major passageways," and "customary paths"— choices (A), (B), and (C)—to follow "infrequently used paths" —choice (D).

123. (**C**) A kiebit is the shrill cry of the bird, not the bird itself.

124. (**B**) The name *lapwing* suggests a relationship to the bird's method of flight, rather than its cry or its flocking habits.

125. (**B**) Tuft, a bunch of hair standing up, resembles a crest.

126. (**D**) Note: "*kibitzer*, an onlooker who offers unwanted advice or comment."

127. (**D**) "The study of the origins of words can lead us into many unexpected byways." The bird-watcher, cardplayer, and German scholar are only incidental to the passage.

128. (**A**) "The diamonds are stable if they remain where they are formed." The entire selection deals with their ability to become graphite, that is, to change, under other conditions.

129. (**C**) The entire selection discusses how easily diamond, a costly gem, turns into smudgy graphite.

130. (**D**) "Given a modest boost in heat, they quickly...become soft globs of graphite."

131. (**A**) We can infer that diamonds are rare from the fact that "very many" turn to graphite at the Earth's surface.

132. (**B**) Although the other choices are possible meanings of *modest*, they do not make sense in this scientific context.

133. (**B**) Note: "...when diamonds in countless quantities shoot through the Earth's crust ..."

134. (**D**) The next sentence tells us that "Given a modest boost in heat, they [diamonds] quickly turn ..."

135. (**D**) The author points out the huge task facing Americans, thereby eliminating choices (A) and (C). Choice (B) is contradicted by the last sentence.

136. (**C**) The last sentence sums up the author's attitude. He is aware of the huge task confronting Americans but is confident that they will succeed in meeting the challenge.

137. (**D**) Contemporaries are people living at the same time. Since the passage deals with conditions today, they are the people of the present.

138. (**B**) Nuclear weaponry is not mentioned in the passage.

139. (**B**) Figuratively, *darkness* means lacking the light of knowledge.

140. (**B**) The author's aim is to arouse his readers to work for change.

141. (**B**) In order to overcome, people must be willing to change.

142. (**D**) The one thing that the selection establishes as common for the four men was their popularity.

143. (**C**) The selection analyzes the reasons for Reagan's popularity.

144. (**C**) This choice fits in with "simplicity" and "humor" as qualities that would win affection.

145. (**D**) Reagan's political beliefs are not mentioned.

146. (**D**) "Reagan was to become the 'Great Communicator'."

147. (**A**) The passage as a whole evaluates the source of power of a president.

148. (**D**) The author is informing the reader about sponges. Nothing suggests that his purpose is to entertain (A), convince (B), or caution (C).

149. (**B**) A pouch is the only item having the oval shape implied by *saclike*.

150. (**B**) Note: "...sponges do not move around; ..."

151. (**D**) "when sponges are exposed to sun and air, their cells die..."

152. (**D**) Since the flow of water through the pores into the central cavity and out through the open end of the sponge brings food, by inference the same flow must carry away waste products.

B. Vocabulary

Questions 153–174: see page 678 for answers. Please check a standard dictionary for definitions of vocabulary words that are not understood.

SUBTEST 4 MATHEMATICS

A. Concepts

175. (**B**) $3 \times 10^3 = 3,000$
$5 \times 10^2 = 500$
$7 \times 10 = 70$
$6 \times 1 = 6$

The sum is $3,000 + 500 + 70 + 6 = 3,576$.

176. (**D**) $5,879 \div 1,000 = 5.789$

177. (**C**) The measure of $\angle A$ + the measure of $\angle B$ + the measure of $\angle C = 180°$.

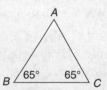

The measure of $\angle A + 65 + 65 = 180$.
The measure of $\angle A = 180 - 65 - 65 = 50°$.

178. (**A**) Let $4x$ = the larger number,
and $3x$ = the smaller number.
$4x - 3x = 6$
$x = 6$
$4x = 4(6) = 24$

179. (**D**) In $\triangle ABC$, $x^2 + 6^2 = 10^2$

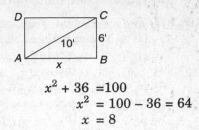

$x^2 + 36 = 100$
$x^2 = 100 - 36 = 64$
$x = 8$

The perimeter of $ABCD = 8 + 6 + 8 + 6 = 28$ feet.

180. (**B**) $111_{(two)} = 1 + 2(1) + 4(1) = 1 + 2 + 4 = 7$

181. (**C**) The given equation is
$x - 3 = 5$
$x = 5 + 3 = 8$
$x^2 = 8 \times 8 = 64$

182. (**D**) Since $3 > 0$ and $0 > -2$, sentence $3 > 0 > -2$, which is choice (D), is true.

183. (**B**) The expression $a - b = b - a$ is not true. For example, if $a = 10$ and $b = 5$, we have $10 - 5 = 5 - 10$, or $5 = -5$.

184. (**C**) We separate the two triangles to make the explanation clearer.

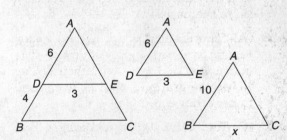

Since $\triangle ADE$ are similar to $\triangle ABC$, the measures of corresponding sides are in proportion. Therefore,

$\frac{AD}{AB} = \frac{DE}{BC}$

$\frac{6}{10} = \frac{3}{x}$

$6x = 30$

$x = 5$

185. **(D)** The cost of the meat is $3y$ dollars. The number of dollars left is $x - 3y$.

186. **(D)** The area of the circle $= \pi r^2$.

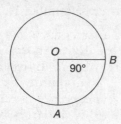

In this case, the area of the circle $= 10 \times 10 \times \pi$.

Area of circle $= 100\pi$

The sector $OAB = \frac{1}{4}$ of the circle, since $\frac{90}{360} = \frac{1}{4}$.

$\frac{1}{4}(100\pi) = 25$ square units

187. **(C)** $(-5)^3 = (-5) \times (-5) \times (-5) = -125$
$(-2)^4 = (-2) \times (-2) \times (-2) \times (-2) = 16$
$-125 + 16 = -109$

188. **(B)** $24\% + 35\% + 29\% + = 88\%$
Entire family income $= 100\%$
$100\% - 88\% = 12\%$ saved

189. **(B)** Let $x =$ the measure of the smaller angle,
and $5x =$ the measure of the larger angle.
Then $x + 5x = 90°$
$6x = 90°$
$x = 15°$
$5x = 5(15) = 75°$

190. **(A)** The given expression is 3.2×10^{-5}.

Each negative power of 10 represents 1 move of the decimal point to the left. Thus, 10^{-5} represents 5 moves of the decimal point to the left.

This move gives us .000032, or 0.000032.

191. **(D)** Comparison is more convenient if we write all of the numbers as decimals, correct to 2 decimal places. Then we have

$40\% = 0.40$, $\frac{1}{3} = 0.33$, and 0.37.

We see that the correct order is $\frac{1}{3}$, 0.37, 40%.

192. **(C)** Let $x =$ cost of slacks,
and $x + 22 =$ cost of jacket.
Then $x + x + 22 = 102$
$2x + 22 = 102$
$2x = 102 - 22 = 80$
$x = 40$
$x + 22 = 62$

The jacket cost $62.

193. **(C)** Let $x =$ the total enrollment.
Then $0.28x = 560$
$x = \frac{560}{0.28} = 2,000$

The total enrollment was 2,000 students.

194. **(B)** 1 inch on the map $= 50$ miles
$7\frac{1}{2}$ inches $= 50 \times 7\frac{1}{2}$, $50 \times \frac{15}{2} = 375$
The cities are 375 miles apart.

195. **(C)** There are $19 + 16 = 35$ students in the class. Thus, there are 35 possible ways in which a student may be called upon. Of these 35 ways there are 16 ways in which a girl may be called upon. Thus, the probability of a girl being called upon is $\frac{16}{35}$.

196. **(D)** 3, 2, and 7 are prime numbers.
$3 \times 2 \times 7 = 42$
Thus, the prime factorization of 42 is $3 \times 2 \times 7$.

197. **(A)** The given equation, $x - y = 3$, tells us that, if we subtract y from x, the result is 3. In other words, x is 3 more than y. Thus, $x > y$.

198. **(A)** $\sqrt{76} = 8.7$, correct to the nearest tenth. Thus, $\sqrt{76}$ is between 8 and 9, and the correct choice is (A).

B. Problem Solving

199. **(D)** $a^2b = (-2)(-2)(-3) = -12$
$b^2a = (-3)(-3)(-2) = -18$
$(-12) + (-18) = -30$

200. **(B)** $5(2x - 3) = 4$
$10x - 15 = 4$
$10x = 4 + 15 = 19$
$x = 1.9$

201. **(B)**   Let x = sales tax rate.
$$\frac{x}{100}(240) = 14.40$$
$$240x = 1440$$
$$x = \frac{1440}{240} = 6\%$$

202. **(D)**   Let x = Bill's money.
Then $2x - 4$ = Fred's money
$$2x - 4 = 36$$
$$2x = 36 + 4 = 40$$
$$x = 20$$
Bill has $20.

203. **(B)** Let x = Frank's mark on the fourth test.

$$\frac{75 + 80 + 70 + x}{4} = 80$$
$$75 + 80 + 70 + x = 4(80) = 320$$
$$225 + x = 320$$
$$x = 320 - 225 = 95$$

Frank's mark on the fourth test was 95.

204. **(C)** $\frac{4}{9} : \frac{7}{15} = \frac{4}{9} \div \frac{7}{15} = \frac{4}{9} \times \frac{15}{7}$

$\frac{4}{9} \times \frac{15}{7} = \frac{20}{21}$, or 20 to 21

205. **(A)**   Let x = the number of $5 bills,
and x = the number of $10 bills.
$5x$ = the value of the $5 bills
$10x$ = the value of the $10 bills
$$5x + 10x = 150$$
$$15x = 150$$
$$x = 10$$
Mr. Stone has ten $5 bills.

206. **(A)** $3 \times 48 = 144$ miles completed, 36% of trip

Let x = total mileage to be covered
Then $0.36x = 144$
$$36x = 14,400$$
$$x = \frac{14,400}{36} = 400$$

207. **(B)** Let x = length of the rectangle.

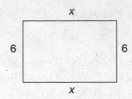

$$x + 6 + x + 6 = 30$$
$$2x + 12 = 30$$
$$2x = 30 - 12 = 18$$
$$x = 9$$
Area = $9 \times 6 = 54$ square feet

208. **(D)** If the sum of two numbers is y and one number is 7, the other number is obtained by subtracting 7 from y. Thus, the other number is $y - 7$, and 3 times the other number is $3(y - 7)$.

209. **(D)** A number is divisible by 9 if the sum of its digits is divisible by 9. Therefore, $43\square$ is divisible by 9 if $4 + 3 + \square$ is divisible by 9. Of the choices given, only 2 is correct, since $4 + 3 + 2$ (9) is divisible by 9.

210. **(A)** The given expression is

$$3\frac{1}{5} \times 4\frac{2}{3} \times 1\frac{1}{4}$$

$$3\frac{1}{5} = \frac{16}{5}, 4\frac{2}{3} = \frac{14}{3}, 1\frac{1}{4} = \frac{5}{4}$$

$$\frac{16}{5} \times \frac{14}{3} \times \frac{5}{4} = \frac{56}{3} = 18\frac{2}{3}$$

211. **(B)** $426 \times 5 = \$2,130$ collected for regular tickets
$84 \times 2.5 = \$210$ collected for half-price tickets
$2,130 + 210 = \$2,340$ total collection

212. **(C)** The length, the width, and the height of a cube are equal. In this case, each of the three dimensions is 6 centimeters.

Volume = $6 \times 6 \times 6 = 216$ cubic centimeters.

213. **(C)** $1011_{(two)} = 1 + (2 \times 1) + (4 \times 0) + (8 \times 1) = 1 + 2 + 0 + 8 = 11$

214. **(D)** If we multiply both sides of the given equation, $3.5x + 2.7 = 0.6$, by 10, we obtain $35x + 27 = 6$

$$35x + 27 = 6$$
$$35x = 6 - 27 = -21$$
$$x = -\frac{21}{35} = -\frac{3}{5}$$
$$-\frac{3}{5} = -0.6$$

215. **(A)** Let x = the amount earned for 14 hours of work. We set up this proportion:

$$\frac{8}{43.20} = \frac{14}{x}$$

$$8x = 14(43.20) = 604.8$$

$$x = \frac{604.8}{8} = \$75.60$$

216. **(B)** $m\angle A + m\angle B + m\angle C = 180°$
$$64 + m\angle B + m\angle C = 180$$
$$m\angle B + m\angle C = 180 - 64$$
$$= 116$$

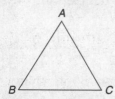

Since $m\angle B = m\angle C$, $m\angle B = \frac{1}{2}(116) = 58°$

217. **(B)** The given inequality is
$3x - 1 < 17$
$$3x < 17 + 1$$
$$3x < 18$$
$$x < 6$$
$$x^2 < 36$$

218. **(D)** We set up the equation
$5\frac{1}{2} - 3\frac{1}{4} = x - 6$
$$2\frac{1}{4} = x - 6$$
$$x = 6 + 2\frac{1}{4} = 8\frac{1}{4}$$

219. **(D)** 2 is a divisor of 140.
5 is a divisor of 140.
4 is a divisor of 140.
2, 5, and 7 are prime numbers.
140 has no other prime-number divisors.

220. **(B)** Between 6:00 A.M. and noon the temperature rose from $-12°$ to $+2°$. From $-12°$ to $0°$ represents a rise of $12°$. From $0°$ to $2°$ represents a rise of $2°$.
$$12° + 2° = 14° \text{ rise}$$

221. **(C)** Since the measure of $\angle BOA = 90°$, sector AOB is $\frac{90}{360} = \frac{1}{4}$ of the area of the circle.

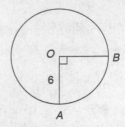

The area of the circle $= \pi r^2 = \pi \times 6 \times 6 = 36\pi$

The area of sector $AOB = \frac{1}{4}$ of $36\pi = 9\pi$

222. **(A)** To find the interest on the loan, we set up the equation

Interest $= 805 \times \frac{9}{12} \times \frac{12}{100}$

Interest $= \$76.50$

Mr. Lopez must pay $850 + 76.50 = \$926.50$

223. **(A)** Let x = the number to be found.

Then $\frac{2}{3}x = \frac{4}{5}$

$$x = \frac{4}{5} \div \frac{2}{3}$$

$$x = \frac{4}{5} \times \frac{3}{2} = \frac{6}{5}, \text{ and } \frac{6}{5} = 1.2$$

224. **(C)** There is a total of $25 + 12 = 37$ players on the squad. The choice of a backfield man can be made in 12 ways. Thus, of the 37 possible choices 12 will be backfield men. The probability of the choice of a backfield man is $\frac{12}{37}$.

225. **(C)** We can express $x\%$ as a fraction:
$$x\% = \frac{x}{100}$$
$$\frac{x}{100}(80) = 16$$
$$\frac{8x}{10} = 16$$
$$8x = 16 \times 10 = 160$$
$$x = 20$$

226. **(D)** $7x - 5 = 3x + 9$
$$7x - 3x = 9 + 5$$
$$4x = 14$$
$$x = \frac{14}{4}$$
$$x = \frac{7}{2}, \text{ or } 3.5$$

227. **(B)** There are 800 hundreds in 80,000. Each $100 carries a tax of $3.46. To find the total tax we multiply 800 by $3.46:

$$800 \times 3.46 = \$2,768$$

228. **(A)**
$$12 \times 7 = 84$$
$$\tfrac{2}{3} \text{ of } 15 = 10$$
$$84 = x + 10$$
$$x = 84 - 10 = 74$$

229. **(D)** $\sqrt{30} = 5.5$, to the nearest tenth.

230. **(A)** Let x = the cost of a shipment of 36 pairs of slacks. We set up the proportion

$$\frac{36}{x} = \frac{24}{400}$$
$$\frac{36}{x} = \frac{6}{100}$$
$$6x = 3,600$$
$$x = \$600$$

231. **(A)** We divide 502 by 20:

```
      25
20)502
     40
    102
    100
      2
```

Thus, we have 20 classes with 25 students each, but 2 students are left. Two of the classes must have 26 students each.

232. **(C)**
$$10^1 = 10 \qquad 10^4 = 10,000$$
$$10^2 = 100 \qquad 10^5 = 100,000$$
$$10^3 = 1,000 \qquad 10^6 = 1,000,000$$

233. **(A)** If $\tfrac{1}{3}$ of the seats are unoccupied, then $\tfrac{2}{3}$ are occupied.

Let x = the number of seats in the auditorium.

Then $\tfrac{2}{3}x = 600$
$$x = 600 \div \tfrac{2}{3}$$
$$x = 600 \times \tfrac{3}{2} = 900$$

234. **(B)** 12 gallons = $12 \times 4 = 48$ quarts

Each quart has 32 fluid ounces. Thus, the restaurant as $48 \times 32 = 1,536$ fluid ounces of orange juice.

$$1,535 \div 6 = 256 \text{ servings}$$

235. **(C)** $(x + y) + z = x + (y + z)$ is an example of the Associative Property of Addition.

236. **(A)** Since one-half the larger number is 10, then the larger number is $2 \times 10 = 20$.

If the difference between the numbers is 12, the smaller number is $20 - 12 = 8$.

237. **(C)** The sentence $-4 < -2$ is true. If we look at the number line, we see that -4 is to the left of -2.

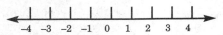

238. **(C)** The area of the square = $(20)^2 = 400$ square inches

The area of the triangle = $\tfrac{1}{2}(25)x = \frac{25x}{2}$.

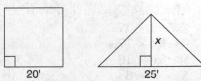

Since the areas are equal, we have

$$\frac{25x}{2} = 400$$
$$25x = 800$$
$$x = 800 \div 25 = 32$$

SUBTEST 5   LANGUAGE

239. **(A)** *Scarcely* + *never* = double negative. *Ever*, nor *never*, must follow *scarcely*: He *scarcely ever* goes...

240. **(C)** The third-person-singular form *doesn't* is needed with *she*: *Doesn't* she know...

241. **(C)** An apostrophe is required in a contraction where the letter has been omitted: *There is = There's: There's* nothing...

242. **(B)** *Loan* is a noun; *lend* is a verb: I'll *lend* you...

243. **(B)** *Its* shows possession; *it's = it is: It's* time to...

244. **(B)** *Fewer* = number; *amount* = quantity: She has *fewer* friends...

245. **(A)** Titles of high officials are capitalized: American *Presidents* and British *Prime Ministers*...

246. **(B)** Since the noun *kind* is singular, it should be preceded by the singular adjective *that,* not the plural *those: That* kind of apple...

247. **(B)** Adjectives derived from the names of countries are capitalized:...a *French* favorite ...

248. **(B)** *Were* = plural verb form; *we're* = *we are: We're* ready...

249. **(C)** *Principle* = rule, *principal* = head person: our new *principal.*

250. **(B)** Since the words *strawberries and cream* denote a unit, a single dessert, a singular verb is needed: strawberries and cream *is*...

251. **(B)** Only the names of specific high schools (*Martin Luther King High School*) are capitalized: graduated from *high school.*

252. **(A)** Before a word beginning with a vowel sound, *an* rather than *a* is used:...peeled *an* onion.

253. **(A)** The possessive singular is formed by adding an apostrophe and *s* to the noun: *Henry's* coat...

254. **(D)** No mistakes

255. **(C)** *Leave* = depart; *let* = allow:...*let* her do...

256. **(C)** *Sat* = occupied a seat; *set* = placed: They *sat*...

257. **(B)** The correct form is *should have* or *should've: She should have (should've)* left ...

258. **(B)** Sentence is not clear—time for whom to leave? We need to repeat the name: Stan told Arthur it was time for *Arthur* [or *Stan*] to leave.

259. **(A)** *Bring* = carry to speaker; *take* = carry elsewhere: Please *take* the leter to him...

260. **(B)** *Stayed* = remained; *stood* = was on one's feet: I should have *stayed* at home...

261. **(A)** An appositive in the middle of a sentence is set off by two commas: Our guidance counselor, *Mrs. Shaw,*...

262. **(B)** The pronoun *he* is redundant (unnecessary): My *brother plans* to become...

263. **(A)** The second preposition is unnecessary:...pushed *off* the train.

264. **(B)** Since *evening* is not part of the name of a holiday, it should not be capitalized:...early Saturday *even-ing.* (But note *New Year's Eve.*)

265. **(C)** The past tense of *run* is *ran;* a past tense does not require a helping verb: I had *run*...

266. **(D)** No mistakes

267. **(A)** *Rung* is the past participle of *ring;* here the past tense *rang* is re-quired: before the late bell *rang.*

268. **(B)** In this sentence, consistency requires that one follow *One* or *You* precede *you: One*...if *one*...or *You* ... if *you* ...

269. **(C)** The subject of the sentence, the plural noun *questions,* must be followed by a plural verb: *Are* there any *questions*...

270. **(B)** *Hadn't* + *but* = double negative. Since *but* is negative, *not ('nt)* is unnecessary: We *had but* one moment...

271. **(C)** There is a misplaced modifier—the picture, not the child, is hanging: I want a copy of the picture of the child. The *picture is hanging* over the fireplace.

272. **(B)** The subject is *Jon,* not *friends,* so a singular verb is needed: Jon, along with his four friends, *is* here...

273. **(A)** The superlative of *funny* is *funniest;* most is not needed: She is the *funniest*...

274. (**B**) Quotation marks are used to set off a direct quotation, but not an indirect quotation introduced by *that:* Alice said *that she* didn't believe his *story.*

275. (**B**) To see the correct form, complete the sentence:...than Irene and *I are tall.*

276. (**C**) A question must be followed by a question mark:...borrow my *coat?*

277. (**D**) No mistakes

278. (**C**) *Most,* meaning to be greatest degree, cannot be used as a substitute for *almost* (nearly): I *almost* lost my breath...

279. (**B**) repetition

280. (**B**) perseverance

281. (**C**) indefinitely

282. (**B**) disastrous

283. (**C**) occasionally

284. (**A**) dissatisfied

285. (**A**) existence

286. (**B**) tragedy

287. (**D**) No mistakes

288. (**C**) embarrass

289. (**B**) The connective must convey the idea of "as a result"; *therefore* is the correct answer.

290. (**D**) The connective must convey the idea of "in addition": *moreover* is the correct answer.

291. (**C**) A word (*students*) must be added to indicate who is *to succeed.* Choice (D) is repetitious; (B) and (C) supply the wrong subjects. Therefore (C) is the answer.

292. (**D**) *We,* not the houses, did the walking. Choice (B) is less precise than (D); it does not show the time relationship.

293. (**B**) A word (*you*) is needed to explain who is in company.

294. (**D**) This is the only pair of sentences that supports the concept of bondage.

295. (**C**) This is the only choice that continues to address the cause (*congenital disorder*) of Down's syndrome.

296. (**D**) An encyclopedia article would not contain a personal remark (*I, you*).

297. (**B**) Sentence 2 does not relate to the topic sentence, "I look forward to the time when I can *retire.*"

298. (**C**) The given sentence explains the recordings mentioned in sentence 2.